WE KNOW MONEY

DOESN

ON TR

At Triple Disc, we u
independent musicia
high quality CD rep
budget. That's why
replicated CDs star

TRIPLE ... LICATION

EXPEC

Just don't PAY more.

CD BABY

FREE ONLINE
DISTRIBUTION
WITH CD BABY,
THE WORLD'S
LEADING SOURCE
FOR INDEPENDENT
MUSIC.

PROMO CDS

FOR YOUR PRESS KIT
AND RADIO PROMOTION.
$0.75 EACH
IN TYVEK SLEEVES WITH
REPLICATION ORDER.

POSTERS

PROMOTE YOUR GIGS
AND NEW CDs WITH
TRIPLE DISC'S 11" x 17"
FULL COLOR POSTERS.
100 POSTERS $99

FREE BARCODE

AND SOUNDSCAN
REGISTRATION WITH
EVERY PROJECT,
REGARDLESS OF
QUANTITY.
$750 VALUE!

GRAPHIC DESIGN

EYE-CATCHING, PROFESSIONAL
DESIGN. LOOK AS GOOD AS
YOU SOUND! $75 PER HOUR.

ENHANCED CDS & CD TEXT

TAKE YOUR CD TO THE NEXT LEVEL.
SCREENSAVERS, SLIDESHOWS,
WEBLINKS, AND MORE.
STARTING FROM $75.

TOP SPINE STICKERS

STORES LOVE 'EM!
GIVE YOUR CD
THAT MAJOR LABEL LOOK.
JUST $.06 A PIECE.

Triple Disc
media design and duplication

1-800-414-7564
www.tripledisc.com

What people are saying about The Indie Bible...

"All the artists I work with personally are required to have a copy."
- **Tim Sweeney, author of "Tim Sweeney's Guide To Releasing Independent Records"**

"My press kit is full of positive press from around the WORLD because of The Indie Bible."
- **Terry Christopher, Award Winning Singer/Songwriter**

"The Indie Bible is a MUST HAVE for any Indie artist!"
- **Madalyn Sklar, founder of GoGirlsMusic.com**

" I would have never imagined it being so full of information. No wonder there is some much talk about the Indie Bible!"
- **Lyric, Recording Artist**

"I bought the Indie Bible and am still overwhelmed by it!"
- **Michael Grady, The Strange Angels**

"I've been in publicity for years and I still find myself using your resource daily. I don't think another book could possibly save us as much time as yours. Thanks so much again!"
- **Jessika Brunè, Unite PR**

"It's great! The articles alone are worth the price."
- **Beau Wadsworth, Recording Artist**

"This book is stuffed FULL of amazing tips and articles!"
- **Naomi DeBruyn, Linear Reflections**

Just got the Indie Bible...AWESOME!!"
- **Dax Wadley, The Soul Elephant**

WHAT IS THE INDIE BIBLE?

The Indie Bible is a valuable promotional tool for Independent Musicians and Songwriters that lists:

- 4000 publications that will REVIEW your music!
- 3200 radio stations that will PLAY your songs!
- 675 services that will help you to SELL your music!
- 200 sites where you can upload your band's MP3s!
- ...and 53 articles that will IGNITE your music career!

ALL styles of music are covered!

Pop, Rock, Hip Hop, Folk, Blues, Jazz, Punk, oi, Hardcore, ALL Metals, Indie Rock, Electronic, Experimental, Dance, World Music, Soul, R&B, Women in Music, Christian, Country, Rap, Roots, Bluegrass, Reggae, Ska, Rockabilly, Ambient, emo, Gothic, Industrial, Progressive Rock, Alternative, Americana, Garage, House, Trip Hop, Celtic, EBM, Sacred, Gospel, Space Rock, Noise, Alt Country, Children's Music and New Age.

The Indie Bible also provides you with **53** amazing articles that will help your career to move in a positive direction!

Articles Include

- **How to Submit Your Music for Review**
- **How to Get Radio Airplay**
- **Getting Your Music into Film**
- **How to Market Your Music**
- **Why You Need an Entertainment Lawyer**
- **Band and Press Kit Essentials**
- **How Royalties Work**
- **How to Copyright Your Music**

and MANY more!

HOW TO USE THIS BOOK

Thank you for purchasing the Indie Bible. This directory is sorted in the following way

- the *type* of SERVICE *(publication, radio station, online vendor etc.)*
- within each service, listings are sorted by *GENRE* of music.
- within each genre, the resources are then sorted by *GEOGRAPHIC LOCATION*.

It's set up this way so that you can quickly find a specific service in a specific area for a specific style of music. *ie: finding a Hip Hop Publication in England that will review your CD.*

When using The Indie Bible, it is very important to keep in mind:

1. If a publication welcomes MANY genres, and non of them are "extreme", that publication would be listed in the *Mainstream* section. Resources in the *Mainstream* section welcome a *variety* of styles, but usually nothing too radical. Common genres in this section are Pop, Rock, Indie Rock etc.

2. There is a large amount of genre overflow from section to section. For instance, if you are in a "Punk" band, you will not only find sites that will review your music in the *Punk* section, but you will also find a number of sites that welcome your style of music in the *Metal* and *Goth* sections. The sites are listed in each section based on the *PRIMARY* musical style that each site lists as their preference. For instance, if a publication states that they welcome Folk, Blues and Jazz music, that publication would be listed in the *Folk Music* section, because "Folk" was the first genre mentioned.

3. Now where do you place a listing for an online zine that reviews the music of Christian Women Hip Hop Artists that live in the Chicago area? Should it be listed in the

    a) Christian Music section?
    b) Hip Hop section?
    c) Women in Music section?
    d) Local Music section for Chicago?

    The answer is "d", the *Local Music* section. I'm using this example to point out that the *Local Music* section <u>overrides</u> all other characteristics of any given resource. If it is a resource of any genre that provides a service for a *specific area*, then that resource is listed in the *Local Music* section (ie: a resource for Montana country bands.). I have arranged it this was so that you can turn to the listings in your area to find out what kind of help is available for you locally. Please make sure to check out the "Local Music" section for your area. I think you will be surprised how many resources there are in your community that are willing to help you take the next step in your career.

4. The majority of the stations listed in the "Mainstream Radio" area of Section Two are College or University stations that have a weekly show catering to EVERY style of music, both mild and extreme (Country, Pop, Hip Hop, Death Metal, Goth…etc), so make sure you CHECK THEM ALL.

THE ARTICLES

Before you start contacting the various resources listed in the Indie Bible, I suggest that you read the articles in SECTION 6 to better understand how to submit your music for review, radio airplay etc. These articles are written by industry professionals who have a *wealth* of experience. They know what works, what doesn't work – and why. Reading the articles in Section 6 will save you an ENORMOUS amount of time and money, and will help your career to move in a positive direction right from the start. In other words, you won't have to make the same mistakes that I and many others have made while trying to survive in the music business. Please take the time to read these articles….you will be glad that you did!

THE ISSUE OF SENDING MASS E-MAILS

As computer technology rolls along, one thing that is apparent is that a major side effect of this advancement is the overwhelming amount of SPAM that people are confronted with every day.

For those of you that don't know what SPAM is, it is simply an unsolicited e-mail – an e-mail sent to you in an attempt to sell you a product that you didn't ask for any information on in the first place. Rarely is it anything useful. It's usually a scam of some sort (ie: porn sites, penis enlargement products, some dude with $15,000,000 that he wants to put into your bank account, online pharmacies selling discount drugs etc.). And, as the SPAM increases, people get more and more angry having to wade through it all EVERY day.

Many people that have purchased the Indie Bible in the past have chose to send out mass e-mails to the various music reviewers, radio stations etc., rather than taking the time to contact them one by one. What this means is that many of the services listed in the Indie Bible are being bombarded by artists that are from outside of their genre. For this reason, many have asked to have their e-mail address removed from the resource (and in some cases, they have asked that their service be removed completely).

For example, what if you are the editor of a magazine that supports *female Folk Singers* and you keep getting mass e-mails from guys in *Metal* and *Punk* bands. Eventually you are going to have to put a stop to it. It's understandably aggravating.

All I'm suggesting is that you take the time to *research* the various sites listed in the book *before* you contact them. Once you know a bit about the service, THEN send a personal e-mail in order to make your initial contact.

Note that there are **53** articles in this edition. You will not find, in any of these **53** articles, an author saying that a good way to make initial contact is by sending out mass e-mailings. They all say the same thing, which is "take the time to do some research, and THEN contact the various services". The recipient of your e-mail will respect it, and most often will get back to you quickly. On the other hand, your mass mailing is an insult to him/her, and in most cases, your e-mail will be deleted immediately.

Take the time to make your e-mails *personal*. It will pay off for you in a big way in the end!

FINAL NOTES...

Please contact me with information on any broken links, outdated sites or mistakes of any kind. They will be addressed right away. Also, feel free to send your comments and suggestions to me. ALL suggestions will be taken into consideration. Thanks to your input, the Indie Bible continues to grow with each new edition.

As was the case with the last two editions, the artwork for the 5th Edition cover was done by famous poster artist Bob Masse (www.bmasse.com). Thanks to Jane Taylor for helping to put this together. I would like to give special thanks to Barb Lougheed for her incredible help down the stretch. I couldn't have published this edition without her help and support.

I hope by utilizing the many contacts found in this book that you make some solid progress with your career. If you feel that you made a worthwhile investment by purchasing the Indie Bible, please tell your friends about it.

Good luck with your music!

David Wimble

David Wimble
Editor, The Indie Bible
www.indiebible.com
Phone: 613-596-4996
indiebible@rogers.com

Table of Contents

Section One:
Reviewers of Independent Music 1

Mainstream
(publications that will review a variety of genres – but nothing too extreme) 1

   North America 1
   South America 14
   Europe 14
   Australia - New Zealand 21
   Asia 21

Blues 21
Children's Music 22
Christian Music 22
Classical Music 23
Country Music 27
Dance Music 29
Experimental Music 31
Folk/Celtic Music 35
Gothic 37
Hip Hop 40
Jazz 44
Latin Music 46
Metal 47
New Age Music 54
Progressive Rock 55
Punk 56
Reggae 62
Women in Music 63
World Music 66

"Regional" Publications and Resources 66

   United States 66
   Canada 132
   Europe 145
   Australia/New Zealand 154
   Africa 157
   Asia 157

Section Two:
Radio Stations that are Willing to Play Independent Music 158

Radio Promoters 158

Stations that Play a Variety of Genres 159

   North America 159
   Internet 172
   Europe 177
   Australia – New Zealand 180

Children's Music Radio 181
Christian Radio 182
Classical Music Radio 184

   North America 184
   Europe 187

Country Radio 187
Dance Radio 191
Experimental Radio 193
Gothic Radio 195
Hip Hop Radio 197
Jazz/Blues/Folk Radio 199

   North America 199
   Europe 209
   Australia 209

Latin Radio 209
Metal Radio 210
New Age Radio 212
Progressive Rock Radio 214
Punk Radio 214
Reggae Radio 215
Women in Music - Radio 216

   North America 216
   Europe 220
   Australia 220

World Music Radio 221

Radio Shows that Spotlight Local Musicians 221

   United States 221
   Canada 229
   Europe 232
   Australia 232

Section Three:
Services that Will Help You to Sell Your Music 234

Promotional Services 234

Mainstream Vendors 239

   North America 239
   Europe 246
   Australia 248

Specialty Vendors & Labels 248

   Blues 248
   Children's Music 248
   Christian Music 249
   Classical 250
   Country 252
   Dance Music 252
   Experimental 252
   Film/Television Music 252
   Folk/Celtic 254
   Gothic 255
   Hip Hop 256
   Jazz 257
   Latin Music 257
   Metal 258
   New Age Music 259
   Punk 259
   Women in Music 260
   World Music 261

Section Four:
Sites that Will Allow You to Upload Your Music and Video Files 262

All Styles 262

   North America 262
   Europe 265
   Australia/New Zealand 266

Specialty Sites 266

Section Five:
Helpful Resources for Musicians and Songwriters! 270

Resources for All Styles of Music 270

Specialty Sites 280

Section Six:

53 Helpful Articles 290

radio airplay

GETTING RADIO AIRPLAY by Lord Litter, host of Lord Litter's Radio Show..................290

RADIO AIRPLAY - TIPS FOR SUCCESS by Geneva World, GirlMedea......................291

RADIO AIRPLAY 101 - COMMERCIAL AIRPLAY MYTHS by Bryan Farrish, Bryan Farrish Radio Promotion 291

HOW RETAIL AND RADIO WORK TOGETHER by Bryan Farrish, Bryan Farrish Radio Promotion 292

INDEPENDENT RADIO PROMOTER CHECKLIST by Bryan Farrish, Bryan Farrish Radio Promotion 292

getting your music reviewed

HOW TO SUBMIT MUSIC FOR REVIEW by Jodi Krangle, The Muse's Muse 293

WHAT A REVIEWER WANTS FROM AN ARTIST by Keith Hannaleck, Independent Music Reviewer........................295

GOOD REVIEWS BUT NO SALES? 5 POSSIBLE REASONS WHY by Marco Mahler...............................296

technical

CREATING REAL AUDIO FILES by Lynn Carey Saylor, GuitarGirls.com 296

POSTING REAL AUDIO FILES ON YOUR WEBSITE by Lynn Carey Saylor, GuitarGirls.com 297

STREAMING YOUR MP3 FILES by Luke Sales, GlassWing Media 297

legal

HOW TO COPYRIGHT YOUR MUSIC by Nancy Falkow , Ask Nancy........................298

ENTERTAINMENT INDUSTRY LAWYERS: WHO, WHAT, WHEN, WHERE AND HOW MUCH?! by Wallace Collins, Entertainment Lawyer 298

ROYALTIES IN THE MUSIC BUSINESS by Joyce Sydnee Dollinger, Entertainment Lawyer 301

ARTIST-MANAGEMENT CONTRACTS by Richard P. Dieguez, Entertainment Lawyer 302

HOW TO TRADEMARK YOUR BAND NAME by Derek Sivers, CEO of CD Baby .304

TRADEMARKING YOUR LOGO by Vivek J. Tiwary and Gary L. Kaplan, StarPolish.com.....................................304

THE WRITTEN AGREEMENT AMONGST BAND MEMBERS by John Tormey III, Entertainment Lawyer 305

marketing and promotion

THE 10 RULES OF SUCCESSFUL INDEPENDENT MUSICIANS by Nyree Belleville, author of "Booking, Promoting & Marketing Your Music" 306

ALERT THE MEDIA! - PUBLICIZING YOUR CAREER by Publicist Teresa Conboy 308

HOW TO BE YOUR OWN PUBLICIST by Ariel Hyatt, Ariel Publicity 310

PREPARING FOR DISTRIBUTION by Daylle Deanna Schwartz, author of "The Real Deal" 312

MUSIC MARKETING STRATEGIES by Derek Sivers, CEO CD Baby....................312

HOW TO GET INTO THE COLLEGE MARKET IN 4 STEPS by Derek Sivers, CEO of CD Baby 315

THE IMPORTANCE OF TEST MARKETING by Derek Sivers, CEO of CD Baby 315

BUILD CAREER AWARENESS BY INCREASING YOUR INTERNET PRESENCE by Bobby Borg, author of "The Musician's Handbook". 316

25 THINGS TO REMEMBER ABOUT RECORD DISTRIBUTION by Christopher Knab, author of "Music Is Your Business". ...317

DESIGNING YOUR CD COVER by Valerie Michele Hoskins, President of The Pursuit Studio......................317

SUCCEEDING WITHOUT A LABEL by Bernard Baur, Music Connection Magazine ..319

INDIE POWER: A BUSINESS-BUILDING GUIDE FOR RECORD LABELS, MUSIC PRODUCTION HOUSES AND MERCHANT MUSICIANS by Peter Spellman, author of The Self-Promoting Musician........321

WHY AND WHEN IS CONSIGNMENT BETTER THAN DISTRIBUTION? by Tim Sweeney, Tim Sweeney & Associates 322

GETTING YOUR MUSIC INTO FILM by Scooter Johnson, Musician/Actor 323

tools

WHAT ARE PERFORMANCE RIGHTS ORGANIZATIONS? (ASCAP, BMI, SESAC...) by Jer Olsen, CEO MusicBootCamp.com..........................324

BAND AND PRESS KIT ESSENTIALS by Richard V. Tuttell, author of "Good Press: An Insider's Guide to Publicizing Business and Community News" 324

SO, WHAT'S THE SCOOP WITH ELECTRONIC PRESS KITS? by Panos Panay, CEO Sonic Bids 325

WHY MAILING LISTS ARE SO IMPORTANT by Vivek J. Tiwary, StarPolish.com 326

DATABASE TIPS by Derek Sivers, CEO of CD Baby 327

LEARN THE IMPORTANT SKILLS by Derek Sivers, CEO of CD Baby 327

HOW TO MAKE THE MOST OUT OF A MUSIC CONFERENCE by Valerie DeLaCruz, Musician/Songwriter 328

WHAT IS A BUSINESS PLAN AND WHY DO YOU NEED ONE by John Stiernberg author of "Succeeding In Music: A Business Handbook for Performers, Songwriters, Agents, Managers, and Promoters". 329

WEBSITE BASICS FOR THE SINGER/SONGWRITER by Valerie DeLaCruz 330

BUILDING A MUSIC WEBSITE THAT SELLS: PROMOTE YOUR CD, NOT YOURSELF by Mihkel Raud, author of "How to Build a Music Website that Sells"...331

CLARIFYING YOUR MUSICAL MISSION STATEMENT by John Stiernberg, President of Stiernberg Consulting................332

the music business

MAKE $$$$ FROM YOUR MUSIC! by Daylle Deanna Schwartz, author of "The Real Deal"...............................333

LOOKING FOR AN AGENT by Jeri Goldstein, author of "How to Be Your Own Booking Agent and Save Thousands of Dollars" 334

10 KEY BUSINESS PRINCIPLES by Diane Rappaport, author of "A Music Business Primer". 334

WHEN TO QUIT YOUR DAY JOB - YOUR RISK ANALYSIS AS A BUSINESS PLANNING TOOL by John Stiernberg, Stiernberg Consulting....................................335

CHOOSING A PRODUCER (an interview with Producer Arty Skye) by Daylle Deanna Schwartz, author of "The Real Deal"............336

motivational articles

STAGE FRIGHT? ME? by Anne Minnery, singer/songwriter 337

DRUNKEN MELODIES by Kate Hart, Joe Records 337

DEALING WITH REJECTION IN THE MUSIC BUSINESS by Suzanne Glass, Indie-Music.com 338

THE PROCESS AND POWER OF PERSISTENCE by Brian Austin Whitney, Founder of the Just Plain Folks Music Organization 338

MAKING A GOOD LIVING AS AN INDEPENDENT ARTIST by Daylle Deanna Schwartz, author of "How to Start and Run Your Own Record Label"..340

SO HOW DO WE MAKE OUR DREAM BECOME REALITY? by Janet Fisher, Director of Goodnight Kiss Music................341

Section One
Reviewers of Independent Music

"As a reviewer I want to give my best because I know each and every artist out there does the same when they record their music."

Keith "MuzikMan" Hannaleck,
Music Reviewer

Mainstream
(publications that will review a variety of genres – but nothing too extreme)

Just to clarify, when I say mainstream, I'm not talking about Perry Como music. Mainstream is any sort of music that isn't too far "out there". That's not to say that publications in this section won't listen to all types of music, but they are more likely to enjoy Rock, Pop, Indie Rock etc. They are less likely to go for the Death Metal, Industrial, Hardcore etc....although some will accept those styles.

North America

United States

1340mag.com
mark1340@aol.com
www.1340mag.com
We do listen to everything we receive and it is considered for coverage. Independent artists are welcome to submit and will be treated as equals with the label artists.

2 Walls Webzine
Michael Walls mwalls@2walls.com
www.2walls.com
Commentary for the socially misguided - music reviews, book reviews, social commentary, rants and blogs.

30music.com
staff@30music.com
www.30music.com
Please keep in mind that we do our best to review everything that we receive, but due to limitations and time constraints it's sometimes not possible for our staff to get to every release. We typically do not review compilations, re-releases, anything by Audioslave, discs containing fewer than three tracks, or split releases with fewer than two tracks by each artist.

75 or Less
75orLess@slatch.com
www.75orless.com
Album reviews in 75 words or less. We'll review pretty much anything. You can take a look at past reviews and get a pretty good idea of what sort of review we specialize in. Just don't send us any tapes.

actionmanMAGAZINE
info@actionmanMAGAZINE.com
www.actionmanmagazine.com
Want to send us music to review? Want to review music for us? Get in touch.

AfterFX MAgazine
James noah1996@hotmail.com
Published since 1993, distributed world wide and free in the Philly area.. We are always looking for new music for review, as well as submissions from writers, artists, poets etc.

Agouti Music
info@agoutimusic.com
www.agoutimusic.com
A comprehensive resource for independent music. We listen to ALL submissions.

Aiding & Abetting
jworley@cent.com
www.cent.com/abetting
Reviews, web links, label contact info, release dates and other useful information.

alt.culture.guide
reverendk@mondogordo.com
www.mondogordo.com
We place an editorial emphasis on indie artists and labels and try to promote their efforts at every chance.

Altar Native
Omar Perez omar@altarnative.com
www.altarnative.com
We review indie music and also feature bands in our Local Native section, which covers the local music scenes of various areas around the United States.

Alternate Music Press *(AMP)*
www.alternatemusicpress.com
Covers acoustic, ambient, bluegrass, blues, Celtic, classical, electronic, folk, jazz, fusion etc. and features streaming audio, hundreds of reviews, interviews, articles, daily music news and a lot more.

Alternative Addiction
Webmaster@alternativeaddiction.com
www.alternativeaddiction.com
You have found your internet source for the best new Alternative/Modern rock. Everything you need to feed your Alternative Addiction is here!

Alternative Press
editorial@altpress.com
www.altpress.com
News, reviews, new releases etc.

American Songwriter
info@americansongwriter.com
www.americansongwriter.com
Reporting on the craft and business of songwriting. Includes interviews, writing tips, industry news, reviews, lyric contest and more.

Amplifier
amplifier@twomp.com
www.amplifiermagazine.com
A bi-monthly, internationally distributed publication devoted primarily to the pop, melodic rock and roots rock musical genres. Amplifier has become a recognized source of all that's melodic and rocks.

Artists Studio Magazine
Editor submissions@artists-studio.org
www.artists-studio.org
Arts & Music magazine; includes features, reviews, new releases and interviews.

Audiophile Audition
info@audaud.com
www.audaud.com
The Web Magazine for Audio, Music, & Home Theater.

Auralgasms.com
Scott Zumberg szumberg@auralgasms.com
www.auralgasms.com
The web's best portal for discovery and discussion of under-appreciated artists. Reviews, sound samples, bios, discographies, tour dates and links.

Aversion.com
info@aversion.com
www.aversion.com
If you would like us to consider your band for inclusion in our index, please send a press kit including an audio sample of your band to our address on the contact page.

Babysue
lmnop@babysue.com
www.babysue.com
We review anything, anyone, anywhere and any place we feel like reviewing. We welcome recordings (and everything else) from major labels and independent labels, as well as individual artists and bands.

BANDRADIO
suggest@bandradio.com
www.bandradio.com
Each week we'll post 5 new reviews of songs in the MP3 format. Demos are also reviewed for Band of the Week honors.

BANDOPPLER Magazine
treble@bandoppler.com
www.bandoppler.com
Published 4 times a year. Send in your CD for review.

Bangsheet
editor@bangsheet.com
www.geocities.com/SunsetStrip/Studio/2040
Devoted to quality rock and roll writing. Not your typical fare in that we provide more interesting analysis and interviews than most because we believe that the way you write about music ought to be as interesting as the music itself.

Basement Life Online Magazine
Mike Conklin Mike@basement-life.com
www.basement-life.com
Read about, listen to and buy the best new records.

Bassics
bassicsrg@aol.com
www.bassics.com
Each issue includes a companion CD that features tracks from the featured artists, as well as a number of music transcriptions. We like to say, "Read It, Hear it, Play it." All styles of music are covered.

BB Gun Magazine
bbgunmagazine@aol.com
www.bbgun.org
An annual alternative literary digest featuring interviews with independent musicians, artists, photographers, filmmakers, actors and writers.

Beautiful Decay
bd@beautifuldecay.com
www.beautifuldecay.com
We want to review your band in one of our future issues.

BettaWreckonize
the_dogg@bettawreckonize.com
www.bettawreckonize.com
If you are interested in having your CD reviewed, contact us to get our mailing address.

Beyond The Scene
www.beyondthescene.8m.com
We are dedicated to bands as our primary focus when adding things to this Zine. We feel that focusing on the band itself is most important since they are the primary reason for our being.

Big Orange Crayon
nick@bigorangecrayon.com
www.bigorangecrayon.com
An indie pop/rock zine run by a kid named Nick.

Big Takeover
jrabid@bigtakeover.com
www.bigtakeover.com
It's an unbelievably huge publication that checks in at over 270 pages. The monster-sized music review section sustains itself across 100 pages. It's packed with bands you've never heard of.

Billboard
bjeckell@billboard.com
www.billboard.com

blah3.com
editor@blah3.com
www.blah3.com
If your band has released a CD or cassette and you need press, we can help you out! Blah3.com is always looking for new music to review and we'll take every submission into consideration for a feature review.

blue coupe
editor@bluecoupe.com
www.bluecoupe.com
All of the CDs we review and the artists we interview are chosen because one of our writers or editors had a strong interest in the subject or the person. We approach all of this with a very real passion. We're certainly open to interviewing you about your music.

Blue Tint Magazine
Mike@bluetintmagazine.com
bluetintmagazine.com
I have drawn an affinity for the struggling artists trying to make more than a niche for themselves in a market that is decidedly against them. So you will see more local bands and artists that we feel are worth checking out.

bofosoco
chris chris@bofosoco.com
www.bofosoco.com
A multimedia e-zine that publishes the works of independent artists.

Bornbackwards.com
adam@bornbackwards.com
www.bornbackwards.com
We'll review just about anything. All submissions must be commercially available. Also, please send all albums with complete artwork (doesn't matter if the artwork is only a plastic sleeve but we want the total package that someone would be purchasing).

Brokenstar.com
brokenstarpro@hotmail.com
www.brokenstar.com
What we want to do is support labels and bands that we like through promotion. Anything you would like to send us would gladly be reviewed.

Brutarian
www.brutarian.com
Music, interviews, comics, reviews. Updated every week!

The Buchtelite
buchtel@uakron.edu
www.uakron.edu/buchtelite
U. Akron student newspaper. The Buchtelite circulates 15k copies 2 times a week. We traditionally cover a lot of indie/underground music.

Buddyhead
travis@buddyhead.com
www.buddyhead.com
We offer you more than something you can see on a screen. We have realized that it can't even be defined at this point in the game, not even by its perplexed, yet delighted creators. It has now become its own living, breathing, manipulative being. We are the Doctor Frankensteins of the 21st century.

Burning Angel
CHUMMY@Burningangel.net
www.burningangel.com
Contains extensive musical content. We encourage you all to keep an eye out for the new independent releases. Labels, if you want your newest releases to be ripped apart here, send us some free shit.

Burst Music
Jeanne jeanjean13@hotmail.com
www.burstmusic.net
We cover (review/interview) all bands, signed and unsigned.

Buzzgrinder
www.buzzgrinder.com
A music related mess of opinion and panic. We write about new albums, old news, broken hearts and Top 40 floozies.

Buzzine.com
www.buzzine.com
Online Entertainment magazine with exclusive interviews, concert reviews and pictures and up-to-date news.

Catascopic
lisa@catascopic.com
www.catascopic.com
An irregularly published forum for independent and underground music designed to get the word out on obscure, evasive and talented artists from many genres.

CD Reviews.com
feedback@cdreviews.com
www.cdreviews.com
If you are an artist, send us a promo pack.

CD Shakedown
www.cdshakedown.com
Weekly reviews of new music releases, mostly pop, rock, alternative and singer/songwriter.

CDSmash
CDsmash@clnk.com
cdsmash.com
We want to help in promoting artists and labels with Interviews, News and Reviews. Tell us what you want and we'll be more than happy to help.

Circle Magazine
circlemag@aol.com
www.circlemagazine.com
We welcome all onto our pages - both on paper and online. We work to make this a place where artists can share, learn, grow and find something to connect with.

CMJ New Music Report
www.cmj.com
Both signed and unsigned artists are encouraged to submit their releases. All styles of music are welcome!

Concert Direct
webmaster@concertdirect.com
www.concertdirect.com
Reviews of your favorite bands performing lives. Read the reviews and submit your own!

concertlivewire.com
philb@concertlivewire.com
www.concertlivewire.com
Center stage for today's music scene. With up to the minute original concert reviews and award winning photographs that capture the soul of each artist. Brutally honest CD reviews from the latest artists. Cut-to-the-bone artist interviews.

concertreview.com
robby@concertreview.com
www.concertreview.com
We would like every artist to be represented in the pages of the site, so we encourage fans to voice their support for the artist by submitting reviews for local artists. Local artists will be grouped together by city or geographic area.

Cosmik Debris Magazine
editors@cosmik.com
www.cosmik.com
Hundreds of reviews of every kind of music and a spoken word CD to boot!

The Creative Line Great Songs Chart and Reviews
Kathi info@artistshelpingartists.org
www.TheCreativeLine.us
www.ArtistsHelpingArtists.org
A grassroots arts and music oriented magazine that is geared to songwriters, fine artists, poets, musicians, actors, writers etc. as well as general art and music lovers. Send your CDs for review,

Creem Magazine
creemmedia.com
BoyHowdy@CreemMagazine.com
We're back to show kids around the world that it's okay again to pick up guitars and make some fucking noise. It wasn't rock 'n' roll for sissies then and you can bet your ass it won't be now.

critically hip music-reviewer.com
rlewis@music-reviewer.com
www.music-reviewer.com
Lots of interviews and reviews each issue. All genres of music are welcome!

Crud Music
info@2-4-7-music.com
www.2-4-7-music.com
Everything submitted by legitimate rock and indie sources will be reviewed and scheduled for inclusion on an ASAP basis.

Culture Shocker!

Yolanda Best cultureshocker@hotmail.com
groups.yahoo.com/group/cultureshocker
Online newsletter that reviews and promotes artist of all types for free. International subscriber base.

The Cutting Edge

tkscutedge@aol.com
www.thecutting-edge.net
Rock's finest web magazine!

cyclops

monster8@ro.com
home.hiwaay.net/~monster8
Here at Cyclops, we cover that evil monster that is rock and roll. We have music news, reviews and anything else we deem cool.

Dagger Zine

daggerboy@prodigy.net
www.indiepages.com/dagger
Comes out roughly 2-3 times a year. It is usually between 80-110 pages and has interviews with bands, article on bands, reviews of cds (hundreds of them), 7"singles and other zines too.

The Daily Vault

webmaster@dailyvault.com
www.dailyvault.com
Loads of CD reviews.

Dead Flowers

Shake6677@aol.com
members.aol.com/Shake6677/DeadFlowers.html
Returned to continue our obsessive excavations of music, culture and other tangents concerning rock'n'roll, its ancestors and offshoots, in all their many varieties.

Deadwinter

footsteps0@aol.com
members.aol.com/Footsteps0

Deep Water Acres

Kmm104@psu.edu
www.dwacres.com
Reviews, interviews, rants, social commentaries, oddball this-and-that's and whatever suits our fancy. We quite like music, especially your more non-obvious varieties of rock, folk, jazz, soul, blues etc.

demo diaries

www.demodiaries.com
A newsletter that critiques several artists each issue.

Demo Universe

www.demouniverse.com
Send your recording and whatever else you care to me. Because of my workload and tendency to procrastinate, it might take up to 6 months for your review to appear. Hey, that's sooner than SPIN will get to it!

demorama

Demorama@visi.com
www.demorama.com
If you are in any way affiliated with a big label, we will not review your material. We accept vinyl, cassettes and CD's. We will also do online reviews. Just send us a link to where your music is at and we'll go get it. We review all genres of music.

De'Pressed Int'l Magazine

depintl@aol.com
depressed-intl.com
The HQ of low-class lit with poetry, music reviews and high heels thrown in for good measure.

Dert!

Dawn Laureen photodol@aol.com
www.dertonline.com
Cover the indie, mainstream and everything in between. You can send hard copy kits to PO 29126 LA CA 90029 or email your music website for review.

Devil in the Woods

www.devilinthewoods.com
Independent thought on Independent music.

Dig This Real

edie@digthisreal.com
www.digthisreal.com
A magazine that concentrates on performers, bands and musicians. We accept unsolicited material for reviews or upcoming features.

Digress Magazine

Annie Knight (Mable) mable@digressonline.com
www.digressonline.com
An indie art and music publication that promotes artists, their work and their creative process.

Drawer B

www.drawerb.com
Unsolicited submissions are indeed encouraged. Please do not email Drawer B asking if we accept submissions. Of course we do!

Dusted Magazine

dusted@dustedmagazine.com
www.dustedmagazine.com
Updated every day. We run new reviews on Mondays and Thursdays, new features on Tuesdays and Fridays and new charts on Wednesdays.

Earpollution

music@earpollution.com
www.earpollution.com
Published monthly, each issue contains rotating columns profiling bands and musical influences, a diverse collection of both live and album reviews. Our writers have a wide range of musical tastes and influences.

The Edge of Insanity

Terri "TC" Cantu tc@theedgeofinsanity.com
www.theedgeofinsanity.com
Online community for promotions, reviews and networking for music, art, film and video.

EIOzine.com

Entertain@EIOzine.com
www.eiozine.com
Subscription based e-zine with news, reviews, interviews etc.

Emergent Music

contact@emergentmusic.com
www.emergentmusic.com
Our goal is to create a new market for undiscovered music where you can connect your fans.

emuse-ic

emuse-ic@emuse-ic.com
www.emuse-ic.com
Features review, interviews and live concert photos from bands and musicians from all genres.

Energy Castle Reviews

Josh Davis chasingcassady@hotmail.com
www.energycastle.com
Experienced reviewer Josh Davis writes the reviews for the EC website. Indie bands are encouraged to send their material to: Josh Davis, 4059 Grand Sark Drive, Salisbury, MD 21804 USA.

Enjoy the Music.com

www.EnjoyTheMusic.com
We do accept submissions, though you should be aware we are critical of not just the music, but also the RECORDING QUALITY. Those submitting music should be advised the sound quality/mixing/mastering had better be up to snuff. Do NOT send us an e-mail!

Epinions.com

www.epinions.com/musc

Erasing Clouds

dvheaton@hotmail.com
www.erasingclouds.com
We are an online magazine, published right here every two to three months, where regular people write about the music, films and other things that they are currently obsessing over.

Euphonic Zine

euphonic@ureach.com
www.euphoniczine.com
Created with one idea in mind... to spread music. Not just the music you hear every day on the radio, but music you might not have heard of. This zine is a collection of pictures, reviews, interviews etc. that pertains to rock music.

Eve's Magazine

Eve Berliner evesmag@aol.com
www.evesmag.com
Writing, Music and the Arts.

Evolving Artist

Derek Tremblay derek.tremblay@evolvingartist.com
www.evolvingartist.com
Features state-of-the-art streaming facilities geared to the success and exposure of musicians worldwide. Artists from independent to major recording labels are interviewed and posted regularly. CD reviews are done regularly of any received compilations.

Fader

newsstand@thefader.com
www.thefader.com

fakejazz

info@fakejazz.com
www.fakejazz.com
If you would like to submit your material for review in our publication, please send it to us. All writers for this publication may also be contacted directly if you wish to submit your material to them personally or discuss something they have written.

Fallenstars Magazine

editor@fallenstars.com
www.fallenstars.com
Features user submitted poetry, photography, book reviews, life, music and more.

Figgle

info@figgle.com
www.figgle.com
We feature album reviews and interviews with artists we think are interesting for one reason or another. We're always anxious to hear new music - or even old music that didn't get its proper audience. We can't promise we'll review it, but we'll definitely give it a listen.

If you know of a local resource that should be listed, please contact indiebible@rogers.com

Firesideometer
comments@firesideometer.com
www.firesideometer.com
There are plenty of bands that are out there killing themselves to make the kind of music that (sadly) only a small percentage of this planet's population will ever hear, much less truly appreciate.

fm Sound
editor@fmsound.org
www.fmsound.org
Twice a month fm sound features tons of new release reviews from the mainstream area, as well as an entire site dedicated to the indie scene.

Flow Online
flowonline@hotmail.com
www.flowonline.com
Want to send me a CD for review? Visit our site for details.

Foundmusic.com
nick@foundmusic.com
www.foundmusic.com
We review shows, bands and new releases weekly in our rant and rave section as well as our message boards and archive it for all genres.

The Free Music Archive
www.free-music.com

Frizzowear.com
Chad Pappas chad@aebn.net
www.frizzowear.com
Funny Pictures, Music Reviews and Photos, Humorous Antic's, Great links!

fufkin.com
dfufkin@fufkin.com
www.fufkin.com
This site was created out of sincere love of good music and all the very good people who really appreciate the music that we will talk about here.

funender.com
www.funender.com
Here you can tell us about your music and listen to the latest creations from Music Artists of all Genres. We will review your songs and give you more plays.

FYD
John Marcher FYDork@yahoo.com
fyd.fuxored.net
Scrappy web-zine dedicated to all genres. We like music that doesn't suck.

Gajoob
info@gajoob.com
www.gajoob.com
A resource for artistic activities — music, film & video, publishing etc. GAJOOB reviews independent music.

Gallery of Sound
nardone@galleryofsound.com
www.galleryofsound.com
Monthly publication reviewing alternative, pop/rock, jazz, blues and rap and hip hop, along with interviews with new musicians. We review titles if we are carrying them in our stores.

Geek America
brent@geekamerica.com
www.geekamerica.com
Geek America is an online zine that focuses on independent media and entertainment. Reviews are up on the 1st and 15th of every month and a new issue launches every other month.

Get Underground
www.getunderground.com
Underground creative community featuring art, articles, poetry, music and reviews biweekly. Submissions welcome.

GhettoBlaster
info@ghettoblastermagazine.com
www.ghettoblastermagazine.com
The most in Pop Culture with News, Interviews, Reviews, MP3's and our very own Photo Gallery.

Girl Talk Magazine
Reverend Dan reverenddan@hotmail.com
www.girltalkmag.com
For those who enjoy the fun of cross dressing! We would like to review your release! We are a bi-monthly publication, accepting all styles of music.

Glorious Noise
jake@gloriousnoise.com
www.gloriousnoise.com
You can send us stuff (cds, stickers, t-shirts, flowers etc.) if you want to. While this doesn't mean we will necessarily write about it, we do promise to give it our undivided attention for a while. Of course, if it changes our lives, we will be sure to let everybody know.

Groovevolt.com

Chauncy Jackson press@groovevolt.com
www.groovevolt.com
Features indie and upcoming artist in our Ubergroove channel, INDIELIFE. Indielife will open our users to a whole new world of indie artist.

Guitar Noise

gnoisereviews@hotmail.com
www.guitarnoise.com
We like to help non-mainstream artists. We want to review your music in a timely and fair manner. It would be best if you first contact us and give us an idea of what it is you would like reviewed and we will make sure it goes to the right person.

Guitar Player Magazine

www.guitarplayer.com

Harmody.Com

marko@harmody.com
www.harmody.com
We like music that you can really 'get into.' Stuff you would sing along to. Each of us has their own particular leanings, but we all agree that nothing beats a good song, put out by a good to great vocalist, with great production quality.

Harp Magazine

scott@harpmagazine.com
www.harpmagazine.com
Combining in-depth features, exclusive photography, insightful artist profiles and dozens of reviews. This is a magazine for people truly passionate about their music – published by people who share that passion.

Hear/Say

mark.watt@hearsay.cc
www.hearsay.cc
A free, music publication that strives to be an original and educated voice for music-loving college students across the US and beyond. Distributed to more than 650 bookstores at college campuses across the United State (circulation 105,000).

Heckler

Lance@heckler.com
www.heckler.com
A snowboarding, skateboarding and music magazine web site. We feature interviews, photos and over 150 music reviews every issue. Heckler has international distribution and comes out eight times a year.

HEET Magazine

staff@heetmag.com
www.heetmag.com
Our goal is simple - to present the best of the best to the record buying public, the music industry and everyone in between. We will always do our best to represent our name and its meaning to the fullest extent possible. HELPING-EXTRA-EXTRAORDINARY-TALENTS.

Here and There

Michael Sullivan bookermps@aol.com
www.thehereandthere.net
We are reviewing anything and everything that comes our way and then posting it with information on how to find those "hard to find cds, that Sam Goody doesn't seem to ever have in stock.

High Times

hteditor@hightimes.com
www.hightimes.com

HitSession.com

www.hitsession.com
Each "HitSession" is recorded so you can listen to the music as the kids are reviewing it. They'll tell you if the music is good or if it sucks. No holding back. We provide all of the links so you can download or buy the music recommended by our young critics.

The Honest Truth

Debra Roque prorockreviewer@hotmail.com
pro_rock_reviewer.tripod.com
New Indie Music e-zine devoted to music reviews and promotion of indie bands/artists.

Hot Pants

clubhotpants@earthlink.net
www.hotpantsla.com
Los Angeles webzine specializing in indie, punk, gothic, garage and experimental music with interviews, reviews etc.

House of Shred

webmaster@houseofshred.com
www.houseofshred.com

HYBRID Magazine

dherrera@hybridmagazine.com
www.hybridmagazine.com
Your best source for indie rock, punk, classic soul, hip-hop, electronica, film and pop culture related content. Fresh music news and reviews daily.

Ice Magazine

info@icemagazine.com
www.icemagazine.com
The CD news authority!

IconoFAN

reviews@antimusic.com
www.iconofan.com
A network of web sites dedicated to fan based entertainment content presented with an iconoclastic flavor.

iHerald.com

editor@Iherald.com
www.iherald.com

ilikemusic.com

Cheryl Rickman cheryl@ilikemusic.com
www.ilikemusic.com/soundstage.html
Unsigned Acts Soundstage (new unsigned talent reviewed), music promotion articles, tips and links galore. For musicians, djs, unsigned talent and music lovers.

ill&alice.com

music@illandalice.com
www.illandalice.com
We will post your poetry, prose, short stories, political opinions and philosophies, paintings, drawings, pictures, show/concert reviews and album reviews with intentions of creating a database of information and a friendly, interactive community.

Impact Press

editor@impactpress.com
www.impactpress.com
If your band or label has a new release, feel free to send it to us for review consideration.

In Music We Trust

alex@inmusicwetrust.com
www.inmusicwetrust.com
A vehicle in which to help expose talented artists to a larger audience. We are also a label, a national publicity company and a zine.

The Independent Mind

submit@mail.independentmind.com
www.independentmind.com
Devoted to writing, music and art created outside of formal industry/business. It is our goal to present our readers with a lot of really great things to read, listen to and look at that they might not otherwise be exposed to, as well as to provide an outlet for independent artists.

Independent Musician Magazine

info@imindie.com
www.imindie.com
We stay on the pulse of the Indie Music Scene and deliver top-notch editorial content that teaches readers what they need to carve out an independent career in the music industry.

The Independent Music Site

webmaster@indiemusicsite.com
www.indiemusicsite.com
We have greatly expanded our reviews section. We now offer cover art on artist reviews, streaming sound clips for reviews and improved Artist and Venue searches.

Independent Songwriter Web-Magazine

Jan Best jan@independentsongwriter.com
www.independentsongwriter.com
Independent music web-publication with CD reviews, internet radio station and much more.

Indie Al's Online Reviews

Alex alex@indieal.com
www.indieal.com
Short and to the point reviews of independent artists/albums. We review all genres.

Indie Artist Station

Maya Sunpongco info@indieartiststation.com
www.indieartiststation.com
We interview musicians and music industry professionals. The interview will be syndicated either as a text-based Q&A or as an audio interview segment published for the Listening Station.

Indie Music Explosion

www.IndieMusicExplosion.com
We are an artist friendly company determined to get the voice of Indie Music heard! Through our events, bookings and promotions... we'll get your music out there!

Indie Journal

ijeditor@strangecloud.com
www.indiejournal.com
Reviews, interviews, internet radio, mp3 site guide, poetry, art and more.

Indie Pages

chris@indiepages.com
www.indiepages.com
We've got info about your favorite indie bands, labels, mail orders and zines, along with sounds and reviews.

Indie Rock Resource

dani@indierockresource.com
www.indierockresource.com
Features, CD reviews, live reviews and more!

IndieFan

www.indiefan.com
A community of independent bands, labels and fans. Many IndieFan contributors are in bands or involved in the indie scene in their regions. A "for us by us" site. We don't care if it ever makes a dime. We just want to bring indie to the masses!

IndieMonkey
Gordon@indiemonkey.com
www.indiemonkey.com
Dedicated purely to minor label and self-released artists. Indie Monkey features interviews, reviews and opinion pieces. Oh and it is owned by a geriatric ex-film star monkey!

Indie-music.com
Suzanne Glass indie@indie-music.com
www.indie-music.com
We have feature reviews. Venue, radio, label, media and resource lists. Original articles by founder Suzanne Glass and guest authors. Exclusive discounts with other music companies. Log on and get your free listing. Then explore the massive information available at your fingertips. The ultimate little black book... all FREE for musicians! It's about the MUSIC!

IndieMusicReview.com
Jeff Leisawitz sales@indiemusicreview.com
www.indiemusicreview.com
We empower indie artists by offering critical reviews of any and every independent CD that is submitted. Guaranteed!

Indiepop.com
editor@indiepop.com
www.indiepop.com
Spotlights, show reviews and record reviews are just a few examples of what this magazine has to offer. Our goal is to promote the indiepop genre and focus on bands and labels that get the least recognition for, what we feel are tremendous and talented achievements.

IndiePro.com
design@indiepro.com
www.indiepro.com
There are two ways to feature your music on Indiepro.com. You can submit your CD for a review to be published on this site, or you can sell your music in our on-line catalog and be featured permanently with all sales processed by us.

Indieville
Matt Shimmer mattshimmer@hotmail.com
www.indieville.com
A webzine dedicated to independent music of all sorts, from indie to experimental and everything thing in between.

indieworkshop
info@indieworkshop.com
www.indieworkshop.com
If you are considering submitting items for review, please e-mail us.

Indulged
andy@indulged.com
www.indulged.com
We advocate open minds toward music and support all genres that are noteworthy. Our goal is to spread the word about the latest musical artists, whether they are unsigned or signed. It's the music that counts; not a fancy label or music video.

Ink 19
julio@ink19.com
www.ink19.com
Monthly alternative magazine. Covers all indie music, reviews 150 CD's per issue, accepts CD's and artist bio's for review.

Ink Blot
jesse@inkblotmagazine.com
www.inkblotmagazine.com
Our aim is to keep you abreast of quality music through insightful features on artists whose work we find deserving of some modicum of respect. We don't like to be pinned down to one genre any more than you do — the only rule is quality and if we like it, we'll cover it.

Inquisitor Zine
info@inquisitor.com
www.inquisitor.com

The Inside Connection
editor@insidecx.com
www.insidecx.com
Today's #1 source for the music industry. We keep you up-to-date on new releases from up and coming independent bands, while playing a sneak preview of their music.

Insiderone.net
contact@neumu.net
www.neumu.net
A new alternative pop culture site.

InterMixx
Noel Ramos MixxMag@InterMixx.com
www.intermixx.com
The nation's first and only "internetwork" for independent musicians and related businesses, as well as fans of indie music. We help Indies market themselves directly to their consumers! Become a part of the fast-growing indie music market, join today!

iPLUGiN
info@iplugin.com
www.iplugin.com
An arts and entertainment network that gives emerging and independent filmmakers, musicians, artists and fashion designers an opportunity to increase their visibility in the International market through a print magazine, an innovative website and artist events.

Issues Magazine
Earl or Loretta editors@issues-mag.com
www.issues-mag.com
General interest ezine that reviews any music that is good enough to play on radio!

Jelly
inbox@jellyroll.com
www.jellyroll.com
Crisp reviews of honest music in the great American tradition.

Junkmedia
ben@junkmedia.org
www.junkmedia.org
It is our goal to provide our readers with diverse, informed and intelligent writing on today's music. We strive to highlight music and musicians who have been overlooked by the mainstream music press.

Keyboard Magazine
keyboard@musicplayer.com
www.keyboardmag.com
Our mission: To inform, educate and inspire musicians. Keyboard strives to be the premier monthly resource for keyboard players, composers, remixers, home studio enthusiasts, desktop musicians and all others who use technology to make music.

Kiss My Heart
info@kissmyheart.com
www.kissmyheart.com
We interview bands and review CDs for our Website, which is updated every 2 weeks. Bands and single artists can email us and ask to be interviewed.

Kludge Magazine
ksm@ekmag.com
www.kludgemagazine.com
We like to feature local and up and coming bands.

Kweevak's Tracks Music Portal
mr_kweevak@yahoo.com
www.kweevak.com
Music promotion, CD reviews, music news, exclusive articles, mp3 links & more!

Lab Productions
albums@labproductions.com
www.labproductions.com
If you would like to have your band reviewed, interviewed or featured, send us your demo! Once your demo is received it will be reviewed by the Lab Productions staff.

Law of Inertia
Info@lawofinertia.com
www.lawofinertia.com
Print magazine. 20 pages of record and zine reviews, great photos of all your favorite bands.

Lefkin Encoded
Floyyd Isaacs lefkin@hotmail.com
www.lefkin.n3.net
Online music magazine for indie artists and mainstream too. Always on the lookout of good bands to review.

light rotation
aj@lightrotation.com
www.lightrotation.com
Honestly, there's nothing like the feeling of getting a new record you're so excited about that you want to tell all your friends. Digitally preserving such love for music is how light rotation aims to keep it real.

Lexicon
guerue@erols.com
www.lexiconmagazine.com
New Wave to Modern Synthpop and everything in between.

Lightword Publishing Company *Mindquest Recommendations*
Bernie P. Nelson mindq@drtx.com
www.lightwordreviews.com/Indie.html
Submit a nonreturnable, uplifting CD to be considered for a free recommendation and mini-review.

LIVE Magazine
Martin Brown Printcreat@aol.com
www.livemagazine.com
We will endeavor to review every CD which we receive at LIVE Magazine.

Luminous Flux Records
webmonkey@fluxnet.com
www.fluxnet.com/submiss.html
We're always interested in hearing new music from new bands. So send in your CD's and Vinyl and we'll review it. Free!

MadcapMusic
info@madcapmusic.com
www.madcapmusic.com
I write about music because I love music. I spend many of my waking hours following bands and listening to records. I inexplicably feel compelled to write down what I think and distribute it to the unsuspecting public.

Magnet
magnetmag@aol.com
www.magnetmagazine.com
Shedding light on the underground, reporting on alternative rock music like no other magazine around. Whether it's topical features, band profiles, record reviews or up-to-the-minute news, MAGNET is written by and for people who are passionate about music, not trends.

Mainstream Magazine
Unsigned@MainstreamMag.com
www.mainstreammag.com
Submit, a brief Biography (about you/your band), a single promo photo, website URL, contact info and a link to download some of your own music (i.e. MP3.com).

manateeBound
info@manateeBound.com
www.manateebound.com
An internet magazine devoted to the coverage of a variety of independent and corporate forms of artistic expression: books, movies, music, video games, zines and so forth.

Masstransfer
editor@masstransfer.net
www.masstransfer.net
Articles, reviews, upcoming releases etc.

Maximum Rock and Roll
www.maximumrockandroll.com

Mean Street Magazine
hello@meanstreet.com
www.meanstreet.com
We cover a wide variety of music but there are several writers, like myself, who only cover the independent music scene.

Mental Contagion
submission@mentalcontagion.com
www.mentalcontagion.com
A magazine for the exhibition and promotion of music, art, literature, philosophy, poetry and film.

Mere Exposure
mereexposure@hotmail.com
www.mereexposure.com
Created to give musicians an outlet to discuss their lives and music with in-depth feature articles, audio interviews, video documentaries and photography combined in a multimedia format.

Milk Magazine
josh@milkmag.com
www.milkmag.com
You'll still be able to read and disagree with record reviews and enjoy the swift styling of your favorite music journalists.

Minor 7th
alan@minor7th.com
www.minor7th.com
Reviewing CDs which prominently feature guitar (especially acoustic): folk, jazz, fingerstyle, blues, new age, world and ambient.

Modern Drummer
mdinfo@moderndrummer.com
www.moderndrummer.com

Modern Fix
extra@modernfix.com
www.modernfix.com
The definitive free music publication. We cover all genres and also feature, art, video games, illustrations, comics, fiction, car culture, skateboarding, news, book reviews, editorials and anything else we think is rad.

ModernRock.com
Support@mail.ModernRock.com
www.modernrock.com
All about the music. Our audience comes back to us because we are the best source of modern rock news, reviews and music.

ModaMag.com
editor@modamag.com
www.modamag.com
We interview well-known award-winning folks, but we also make a lot of room for up and comers.

Moe Magazine
info@moemagazine.com
www.moemagazine.com
Reviews and feature albums.

MP3 Scene
Shauna Skye shaunaskye@hotmail.com
www.fortunecity.com/tinpan/clap/127/mp3scene
Hardcopy zine covering indie music online.

MP3yak.com
www.mp3yak.com
There are lots of other sites doing full-on written reviews. MP3yak.com is different in that we give a simple, "quick and dirty" look at what music we enjoy and links to get to it fast!

MrLee.com
mrlee@mrlee.com
www.mrlee.com
If we've got something good to say about your CD, then it'll at least get a mention in the Journal and likely a write-up in the CD Review section of the site.

Muddle
ron@muddle.com
www.muddle.com
The zine that reads like a friend. Centered around the music that makes us swoon, whether it's punk, hardcore, indie rock, brit pop, whatever. If we dig it, it's in Muddle.

Mundanesounds.com
joseph@mundanesounds.com
www.mundanesounds.com
Soooo, you've got a record that you think I might like, or that you want reviewed. Well, pardner, you've come to the right place! I'm more than willing to listen to anything that you send me unless it's really bad mainstream R&B or Pop. I'm not much of one for overtly mainstream music, period.

The Music Box
John Metzger editor@musicbox-online.com
www.musicbox-online.com
Covers a wide array of music, including blues, jazz, country, bluegrass, folk and the many configurations of rock and roll.. We offer the latest concert and album reviews, the occasional interview and daily music news and tour updates.

Music Connection
Michael Dolan MichaelD@musicconnection.com
www.musicconnection.com
Published every other Thursday since 1977, Music Connection magazine is a bi-weekly music trade publication catering to the music industry, its loyal fans and support services.

Music-Critic.com
requests@music-critic.com
www.music-critic.com
THE source for music reviews!

Music Head
musichead@musichead.org
www.musichead.org
We provide music lovers with accurate and honest information about the artists—from unsigned acts to current stars—making up the realm of today's music. With interviews, features, columns and reviews written by people (music heads!) just like you.

The Music Korner
musccorn@aol.com
members.aol.com/musccorn
A webzine devoted to covering virtually all styles of music.

Music Dish Reviews
editor@musicdish.com
www.musicdish.com
Trade publication showcasing the cutting-edge players and developments in the online music industry.

Music Morsels
Sandy Serge SergeEnt@aol.com
www.serge.org
Free monthly ezine with major and independent CD reviews, unsigned band spotlight and an Industry profile every month along with listings of music industry opportunities for independent musicians. To subscribe, send an email to MusMorsels@aol.com

Music4Guys
webmaster@music4guys.com
www.music4guys.com
A music site that focuses on bands & artists who have (at least) some artistic integrity. Mostly rock, with a good-sized helping of hip-hop.

The Musician's Homepage
digialex@enteract.com
www.themusicianshomepage.com

Musician's Realm
yanno.tom@att.net
www.musiciansrealm.com
Would you like to have your CD reviewed on Musicians Realm? Drop us a line and send us a copy of your CD. We'll assign someone from our staff to review it.

MusicRemedy.com
info@musicremedy.com
www.musicremedy.com
If you are an artist (signed or unsigned) we would like to hear your music so we can review it for our visitors.

MustHear.com
ed@gildred.com
www.musthear.com
Our goal is to wade through the countless volumes of garbage that litter the shelves of online and offline music retailers in order to reveal to you, the listener of taste, musical gems you might otherwise be denied.

MuzikMan's Reviews

muzikman@surfglobal.net
www.musicdish.com/muzikman
Music news, reviews and interviews.

The MysteryKitchen

reviews@mysterykitchen.net
www.mysterykitchen.net
I'm inviting people to send any sort of music or demo recordings my way. I'm not picky. I'll listen to everything, say a little about each one,

Nada Mucho

Matt editor@nadamucho.com
www.nadamucho.com
An entertainment webzine focusing on music, movies, television and more. Our goal is to entertain and educate the MTV generation through witty, vibrant and irreverent writing.

National Noise

Sabrina.Gunaca@nationalnoise.com
www.nationalnoise.com
Tour info and exclusive interviews with the newest faces in music.

Naughty Secretary Club

naughtysecretaryclub@yahoo.com
www.naughtysecretaryclub.com
Online zine featuring music reviews, crafty ideas, fashion tips, contests, interviews, recipes and more!

Negative Pop

negative@negativepop.com
www.negativepop.com
We cater to everything "Geek" in modern day pop culture.

NeoHippy.net

neohippy@neohippy.net
www.neohippy.net
A grassroots promotional site for folk/rock/pop music. This music genre is commonly known as "Adult Alternative" or "Adult Album Alternative" (A3) in America. The goal of this site is to find more avenues for folk/rock/pop artists to get their music heard.

newbeats.com

newbeats@newbeats.com
www.newbeats.com
We cover new and current album releases, as well as featuring artist interviews, show reviews and features on arts related happenings and events.

The Night Guide

info@thenightguide.com
www.thenightguide.com
Dedicated to promoting performing independent artists everywhere. News, reviews, resources and web design services.

The Night Owl

editor@thenightowl.com
www.thenightowl.com
Music reviews covering most styles from rock to jazz.

No Cover

mark@nocover.com
www.nocover.com
The largest free music magazine in California. We distribute 100,000 copies worldwide. Currently, 25% of unsigned bands featured on our cover get signed shortly after.

Norman Famous Rants and Reviews

Norman Famous normanfamous@elvis.com
www.elsob.net/ normanfamous.html
In my continuing efforts to expose the world to good music by deserving musicians, I offer online reviews of independent cd releases along with my customary barbed witticisms and wry social comment.

NowOnTour.com

feedback@nowontour.com
www.NowOnTour.com
We offer tour and show listings for any band, in any city, for any venue, irregardless of size or genre. We also have record reviews of indie bands and major label recording artists, including reviews of demo recordings and reviews of live shows from up-and-coming indie and unsigned artists.

Nude as the News

Tallboy67@aol.com
www.nudeasthenews.com
Focusing on the expansive current state of rock.

Obscurity Unlimited

Bands@dimestoreproductions.com
www.dimestoreproductions.com/Obscurity
We will review your music and post your MP3s. We will work out distribution deals with bands whose recordings are selling well through our site on an individual basis.

ONE WAY Magazine

info@onewaymagazine.com
www.onewaymagazine.com
Our goal is to showcase new music by both established and developing artists to adult eclectic listeners and to promote a music lifestyle.

OpeningBands

Steve Sobel letters@openingbands.com
www.openingbands.com
To get your CD reviewed - mail two copies (so we can have two people review it) and other press info to our mailing address.

Orange Entropy Records

Contact@orangeentropy.com
www.orangeentropy.com
To be frank, there are plenty of review submissions that just don't fit in with what we do here and therefore, we here at OE HQ find little interest in them. All of this in mind, it's probably a good idea to e-mail us before you send us your stuff. The usual turnaround is 4-6 weeks.

Outer Shell

Roy OUTERSHEL@aol.com
members.aol.com/outershel
We have always leaned to helping Indie bands, whom for whatever reason, have been neglected or overlooked, when their talent proves that they should be known and given a chance to be heard. In reviewing artists, we request 2 copies of their release/s, as Outer Shell has 'Reader Give-Aways' of the artists in each issue.

Past and Present Music

Hans J. Eidisgard ane.erlandsen@get2net.dk
www.geocities.com/pastandpresent2001
Each month we review 50+ CD's that are sent to us by some of the most important record-labels as well as independent artists. We review every album, EP, single, demo that we receive and it doesn't matter what kind of music it is - we cover it all.

REVENGE PRODUCTIONS

Let Daylle empower you to help yourself.

Daylle Deanna Schwartz heads **Revenge Productions**. She is well-known for her best-selling books, *Start & Run Your Own Record Label* (Billboard Books). A new, completely revised and expanded edition has just been released. According to Ryan Kuper, founder of Redemption Records

"Daylle Deanna Schwartz has conveniently packaged all you need to know to start your own record label in a very reader-friendly book. What took me over ten years to learn the hard way, has been easily explained by Daylle. If you are thinking of competing in the oftentimes treacherous world of independent record labels, arm yourself with this book!"

Daylle is available to do workshops on starting a record label, getting a record deal and artist development. Her full day seminars in NYC are listed on her website.

Daylle also does phone and in-person consulting for musicians and record labels.

Sign up for Daylle's *News & Resources*, a free newsletter featuring interviews and resources from Daylle's research for her books. Send an email with your name, city/state to **revenge@erols.com** with **subscribe** as the subject.

Pathetic Caverns
cavernsp@pathetic-caverns.com
www.pathetic-caverns.com
*Opinionated and eclectic reviews of music, film and
books.*

Pause & Play
gerry@pauseandplay.com
www.pauseandplay.com
*Weekly pop/rock artist interview column, with vast
archives.*

Pause Record
john@pauserecord.com
www.pauserecord.com
*Provides breaking music and industry news and
reviews as well as exclusive CD reviews in the jam,
jazz, groove, funk, folk and bluegrass genres. Its link
directory features over 15,000 music links for tape
traders, official band sites, recording resources, venue
listings and much more.*

Perfect Sound Forever
perfect@furious.com
furious.com/perfect
*The heralded home of musical underdogs of all styles
of music, full of warped perspectives.*

Performer Magazine
editorial-ne@performermag.com
www.performermag.com
*Want your CD reviewed? Do you have news on your
band? Send your CDs and press releases to the office
in your area for publication.*

Performing Songwriter
editorsps@performingsongwriter.com
www.performingsongwriter.com
*Each issue includes exclusive interviews with
recording artists and producers, columns detailing the
use of equipment in the studio and on the road; record
reviews and new release spotlights.*

Pig Publications
press@pigpublications.com
www.pigpublications.com
*Our goal is to be a respected underground source for
information on lesser known artists and to sell out
effectively while doing so.*

Plug In music
Corinne corinne@pluginmusic.com
www.pluginmusic.com
*Feature band profiles, reviews, interviews, contests
and more. Focusing on up-and-coming musicians.*

Plugged in Music
bands@plugged-in-music.com
www.pluggedinmusic.net
*Submit your band for our consideration. We can do
many things to aid in the promotion. Interviews,
reviews, featured bands and many more. Let us know
what you would like us to do.*

Pop Culture Press
editor@popculturepress.com
www.popculturepress.com
*Pop and the rest of the musical spectrum. Plus a free
CD sampler!*

Pop Shots
daver@popshots.org
popshots.org

POPLIFE
Info@poplife.net
www.poplife.net
*Feature articles, music reviews, music and video
selections. We can sell your band's CD in our
online super store.*

PopMatters
Sarah editor@popmatters.com
www.popmatters.com
*We run approximately 200 CD reviews per month,
plus concert reviews, interviews and artist profiles.*

POPsmear
info@popsmear.com
www.popsmear.com
*We will be updating the site on a regular basis, so you
can feel free to continue to send us your stuff for
review or ridicule.*

PopZine
questions@popzineonline.com
www.popzineonline.com
*Your source for entertainment news. Reviews,
interviews, features and more!*

Prefix Magazine
brandon@prefixmag.com
www.prefixmag.com
*Articles range from the latest hip-hop and rock
sensations to social injustices occurring before our
eyes. We will review CDs and concerts. We also
publish interviews with artists and people we think are
revolutionizing their industry.*

Prick
music@prickmag.net
www.prickmag.net
*Tattoo and piercing lifestyle magazine that features
reviews on regional and national bands worth
hearing.*

Projector Magazine
feedback@projectormag.com
www.projectormag.com
*A grotesque fusion of art, politics and pop culture
multimedia experience.*

Pucknation
pucknation@hotmail.com
www.pucknation.com
*Got a Demo CD or Comic you want us to review?
Send it to us. E-mail us for more details.*

Pulse!
feedback@towerrecords.com
www.towerrecords.com
Tower Records' free in store publication.

Punkt
Greg Mercer editor@punktzine.com
punktzine.com
*An independent online magazine dedicated to
providing quality in all areas of life... and having a
good laugh.*

Purr Magazine
lbeck99703@aol.com
www.purrmag.com
*If you are sending in a CD for review please either
send along any promotional material you have, some
type of history/information on the band or give us the
link to your website if the information can be found
there.*

RAD Cyberzine
jeff@radcyberzine.com
www.radcyberzine.com
*We provide CDs to review, concerts to attend and
photo passes with bands.*

Randomartist.com
info@randomartist.com
www.randomartist.com
*The use of randomartist is free for all musicians and
labels. At least one song must be free for
download/streaming.*

The Rawk
manthon@therawk.com
www.therawk.com
*Real rawk for rawk people. Send items for review or
for rawk radio play.*

Razorcake
webzine.editor@razorcake.com
www.razorcake.com
*Razorcake is here to knock you flat on your butt with
quality, in-depth coverage and to probe deep into the
heart, mind and ass of this beast we call music.*

Renegade Newsletter
geoff@geoffwilbur.com
www.geoffwilbur.com
*Contains interviews and reviews covering signed and
unsigned bands.*

Request Magazine
editors@requestmagazine.com
www.requestmagazine.com
News, reviews, features etc.

Resonance Magazine
info@resonancemag.com
www.resonancemag.com
*Since 1994 Resonance has scraped together the most
innovative artists from all over the music spectrum:
from deep inside the electronic, jazz and hip-hop
underground; to pop, indie rock and the avante garde.*

Reviewed4u.Com
reviews@reviewed4u.com
www.reviewed4u.com

Reviews Unlimited
editor6060@att.net
www.reviewunlimited.com
*Since 1995 we have given readers in both hard copy
and online the best reviews in terms of quality and
variety, in music, books, DVD's, business, games and
technology.*

Reviewstation.com
Samuel Barker samuel@reviewstation.com
www.reviewstation.com
*We cover all kinds of music as well as movies and
other types of entertainment. CD reviews, show
reviews, interviews and more.*

RewiReviews.com
editori@rewireviews.com
www.rewireviews.com
*A site dedicated to reviewing music releases and
concerts. Have a CD you want reviewed, write editor
for a mailing address.*

Rhythm and News
info@rhythmandnews.com
www.rhythmandnews.com
Where unsigned artists and hitmakers meet!

Rikks Revues

Rikk Matheson rikk@rikksrevues.com
rikksrevues.4t.com
A free music revue site. Mainly focusing on independent artists. All genres are accepted.

RisingStarsInc.com

Gypsy Nicole editor@RisingStarsInc.com
RisingStarsInc.com
An online magazine dedicated to showcasing musicians! Aspiring, Independent, Unsigned or Signed.

rivalmag.com

MiamiBranch@RivalMag.com
www.rivalmag.com
A music magazine specifically geared towards teenage fans of many music genres. The site features unsigned bands and bands that are predicted by the staff as being "The Next Big Thing" with interviews, reviews and downloadable MP3's.

The Rock Quarry.net

Devin O'Bryan quarrymaster@devinobryan.com
www.therockquarry.net
American rock reviews along the I-20 strip between Texas and Mississippi!! We bring it!

Rock & Read Magazine

FretTalk@aol.com
www.rocknread.com
Supporting rock bands and musicians of all levels.

Rocket Fuel Online

jonas_7@yahoo.com
www.rocket-fuel.com
In the interest of reviewing more promptly and comprehensively, we will no longer review EPs (except under special circumstances - ask before sending!) or vinyl. Rocket Fuel has never reviewed demos (unsigned acts).

Rocknworld.com *Unsung Heros*

keavin@rocknworld.com
www.rocknworld.com
Mainstream major label music got you bored? Go local as we profile exciting unsigned and indie bands.

Rockpile Magazine

rockpile@rockpile.net
www.rockpile.net
Your source for new music!

Rocktober Magazine

info@roctober.com
www.roctober.com
A music magazine featuring lengthy, well-researched pieces on historically important, unjustly obscure musicians in all genres of popular music.

ROCKZONE.COM

submissions@rockzone.com
www.rockzone.com
We review CDs, cover live shows and do interviews.

RoundSound

maydelott@aol.com
www.roundsound.net
A source for new and recommended music. RoundSound provides CD suggestions covering many types of music linked by their quality and distinguished by their diversity.

Scoot! Quarterly

scoot@scooter.com
www.scooter.com
We do both music and video reviews in each issue.

Scram

scram@bubblegum.net
www.scrammagazine.com
Unpopular culture, beatniks, garage rock, novelty acts and anything offbeat.

The Sentimentalist Magazine

Asthetik@aol.com
www.asthetik.com/sentimentalist
An alternative music and arts magazine published three times a year. The magazine is available throughout the US and Canada. For more information please visit our website.

SHE DIVINE

Héctor Noble Fernández
shedivine@hotmail.com
www.shedivine.com
We accept absolutely any type of music. We especially look for musicians inspired by DEATH, BEAUTY and HEDONISM (no matter the genre). I attempt to make better known any musical release, band or artist; without any type of prejudice concerning the musical style.

Shotgun Reviews

psikotyk@aol.com
www.shotgunreviews.com
Reviews on entertainment, the media and society in general.

The Shred Zone

www.theshredzone.com
A total guitar resource center with CD, demo and product reviews. Free online lessons, interviews and more! Updated weekly!

Signum

www.signumpress.com
We're especially into independently-produced stuff and the idea that you don't have to stay in lock-step with the mega conglomerate pan global corporate mentality to participate in yr cultural world. CDs only; no demos please, but quality full-length self-releases are accepted.

Singer Magazine

greg@singermagazine.com
www.singermagazine.com
Focused solely on educating and inspiring amateur and semi-professional vocal performers and independent recording artists.

Slender

webmaster@slendermusic.com
www.slendermusic.com
A nice place to find out about great music!

SLIPCUE
www.slipcue.com
Focusing on indie pop, Cuban, Brazilian and hick music, with reviews by Joe Sixpack. Joe believes that music criticism is "not brain surgery or rocket science" and offers his reviews only as one person's opinions, free of commercial bias.

Smother.Net
J-Sin editor@smother.net
www.smother.net
We cover music ranging from emo to black metal to drum&bass to lo-fi to hip-hop to reggae. We review EVERYTHING we receive. We also focus on liberal politics to help invigorate the youth of today into interest in the political process.

SongCritic.com
J Atkinson songcritic@attbi.com
www.SongCritic.com
A site where fans can download and listen to your song(s) and then post "reviews" of your tune. Also review other artists.

Songsalive!
losangeles@songsalive.org
www.songsalive.org
A voluntary non-profit organization, dedicated to nurturing, supporting and promoting songwriters worldwide.

Songwriter Universe Song and CD Evaluation
Dale Kawashima SongwrtrUniverse@aol.com
www.songwriteruniverse.com
If we hear a song or artist presentation that we believe is truly exceptional, with outstanding market potential, we will be happy to recommend and refer your music to very high-level, industry professionals. The fee for the three-song evaluation is $50.00 U.S. The fee for the one-song evaluation is $25.00 U.S.

Sonic Switchblade
webmaster@sonicswitchblade.com
www.sonicswitchblade.com
If you would like to be featured on Sonic Switchblade, please send us your CD and some information on your band.

sonicnet.com
feedback@sonicnet.com
www.sonicnet.com
The home for music created by people who are passionate about music. Our mission is to ignite, inspire and nurture the passion for music that fans of all genres share.

Sonicpress.com
esp@sonicpress.com
www.sonicpress.com
We are dedicated to maximum interactivity. This means we want you to participate in any and every way. We like all kinds of music.

The Sound Magazine
Andie Jones andie@soundmag.com
www.soundmag.com
Unique Regional Multimedia Performing and Visual Arts Community, Resource and Publication.

Sound the Sirens
www.soundthesirens.com
We accept all formats except for vinyl (we love vinyl and hope we will be able to support the format soon). If you are going to send us a CDR or home made recording, please make sure that it is properly packaged with appropriate information. Please do not send us MP3 files or links to them. We welcome unsolicited material.

soundsxp
reviews@soundsxp.com
www.soundsxp.com
If you're crazy about indie, punk and electronica then you'll want to check out soundsxp. Have you got a product that you'd like to push? An album or single you'd like reviewed? Get it to us and we'll give it a spin and there's a pretty good chance it'll appear on the site.

Southbound Beat
Ray Carver southboundbeat@yahoo.com
www.southboundbeat.com
Cd Reviews, Interviews, Columns & More. Send 3 CDs for a review.

Space Age Bachelor Pad Magazine
contact@space-age-bachelor.com
www.space-age-bachelor.com

Sparechange Magazine
www.sparechangemagazine.com
All of the reviews on our website are reviewed by our own staff. We review anything and everything we receive from artists, labels, distribution companies etc. We are always excited to receive new material.

SPIN Magazine
spin.com
We promise to bring you the absolute most in infotainment. We've got some pie in the oven with your name on it.

Splendid
gzahora@splendidezine.com
www.splendidezine.com
Our focus is on independently-released material and we review everything we receive. You'll find just about everything here from punk to country, home-recorded CDRs and a whole lot of stuff that resists qualification.

SPONIC
John Wenzel jhnwenzel@yahoo.com
www.sponiczine.com
An indie-rock zine dedicated to non-traditional reviews and interviews of national and local acts.

StarPolish
info@StarPolish.com
www.starpolish.com
We invite artists to submit their music for review by some of the industry's most prominent music reviewers. To get reviewed in our Critic's Corner, you need to be a StarPolish member artist (don't worry — it's free AND easy!) with at least one track uploaded to your profile page.

Starstruck Magazine
admin@starstruck-mag.com
www.starstruck-mag.com
Not only a magazine dedicated to promoting all genres of music and Hollywood on-goings, but also a magazine run, written and edited by teenagers. As an online magazine, we hope to provide you with the latest album reviews, show reviews, stories and fan interaction as much as possible.

Stinkweeds Online
kimber@stinkweeds.com
www.stinkweeds.com
Your source for independent music on the web. With reviews of new music added weekly and release lists updated weekly, you'll stay on top of everything indie.

Stomp and Stammer
mailroom@stompandstammer.com
www.stompandstammer.com
Our website offers selected content from the print edition, including feature articles and interviews, record reviews, music news, columns and concert listings. We cover a wide range of popular and not-so-popular music and some of it we actually admit to liking.

Stomping Ground
info@stompingground.com
www.stompingground.com
Do you have an unsigned band that needs some FREE exposure? If so please fill out the form at our site and get listed in our unsigned band listings. Also be sure and check out how to be featured for FREE and get a FREE web cast concert.

Storyline Records
psuedoburton@aol.com
www.storylinerecords.com
All music that is received by Storyline Records WILL BE REVIEWED!!! Though it may take up to several weeks for a review to be posted, you can get an "instant review" by choosing our $4 promotional package deal.

The Stranger
postmaster@thestranger.com
www.thestranger.com

Stylus Magazine
adam@stylusmagazine.com
www.stylusmagazine.com
Our reviewers are individuals and they don't necessarily feel the same way about each release. That is why we allow each reviewer on the site the chance to write about the reviews of the day that they may not agree with or support.

Suite 101
Adam McKibbin mckibbin@suite101.com
www.suite101.com/welcome.cfm/current_independent_music
Reviewing and interviewing indie music's latest & greatest.

Superstar in Stereo
sis@superstarinstereo.com
www.superstarinstereo.com

Sweetbob.com
Bobby Roberts sweetbob@sweetbob.com
www.sweetbob.com
Send us your press kit for review.

The Synthesis
bill@synthesis.net
www.thesynthesis.com
Our goal is to provide a forum for entertainment, music, community awareness, opinions, change and political involvement.

Taco Truffles
www.tacotruffles.com
We empower artists with the tools and knowledge necessary to create an effective online presence that will enhance their offline success.

Talk Music Future Hits
daily@talkmusic.com
www.talkmusic.com
A web site for the Music Industry Professional. The Home of the Music Business Daily offers much more than just our popular newsletter.

talkbass.com
admin@talkbass.com
www.talkbass.com
Does interviews for bass players with upcoming or new releases.

Tangerine Magazine
Glenn Tillman hollenhouse@aol.com
www.tangerinemagazine.com
Tons of reviews!

TangMonkey.com
jp@tangmonkey.com
www.tangmonkey.com
We listen to alt.folk and indie rock, fuzz-pop and doo-wop, psychedelic, slowcore, twingtwang and twee.

ThirdRoad.com
williamb@thirdroad.com
www.ThirdRoad.com
Everything at ThirdRoad is about promoting the new world of music, the Indie World. Take the time to check out some of these great sites, reviews, artists and bands.

Tiny Mix Tapes
editor@tinymixtapes.com
www.tinymixtapes.com
Please send a jpg along with your music so that we can place a picture on the page. Also, please include a press release. Press photos are annoying, but you can send them so we can laugh at how you look.. E-mail us for details where to send materials.

The Toilet
submit@thetoiletonline.com
www.thetoiletonline.com
We welcome bands from all musical genres to showcase their talent online at our expense. We do NOT require the exclusive right to exhibit your music, so don't worry about us stealing your shit.

Truth In Stuff
jaywightman@hotmail.com
www.truthinstuff.com
A discussion forum for musicians and fans alike. Reviews and MP3s as well!

Turk's Head Review
editor@turksheadreview.com
www.turksheadreview.com
Dedicated to serving up independent reviews, a web log of uncanny perceptions, features worthy of focused attention, wormholes into expressive content and visionary subjects, threads and knots of semantically clustered thoughts.

Twee Kitten
popmusic@tweekitten.com
www.tweekitten.com

the twinstar revolution
miss.em contribute@twinstarrevolution.com
www.twinstarrevolution.com
Independent music journal kicking up a little revolution dust in the faces of sour music critics. Also a fund for bands/musicians.

UmbrellaZine
Lee Hansen editor@umbrellazine.com
www.umbrellazine.com
Arts, Music, Poetry. Publishing, reviews, interviews, music, lyrics, news, tips and resources.

Underdog Online
mail@underdog-online.com
www.underdog-online.com
Global coverage of underground arts and music.

UnEarthed.Com
brian@unearthed.com
www.unearthed.com
The main purpose of UnEarthed.Com is to get the music that we like out there to be heard by the masses.

Uno MAS
jim@unomas.com
www.unomas.com

Unsigned
hund2110@hotmail.com
www.theunsigned.cjb.net
Where great unsigned bands get promoted and reviewed.

Upbeat Online
upbeatmag@aol.com
www.2upbeatmag.com
Humor, concise reviews and cool entertainment news for the discriminating reader.

The Uroc Network
info@uroc.net
uroc.net
Developed to benefit both the fan and musician by providing access to the most up-to date info on emerging music.

usounds
www.usounds.com
Concerts, downloads, interviews, reviews ...

Utter Music
editor@uttermusic.com
www.uttermusic.com
Online Indie Music Magazine featuring reviews, sound clips, videos, MP3's and much more. See what is new in the music industry.

Varla Magazine
Rachel varla@varla.com
www.varla.com
An entertainment magazine, combining women and music of all genres. We cover everything from Punk to Rockabilly, Bluegrass to the Blues. We will review your CDs.

VibeRate
Info@Vibe-Rate.com
www.vibe-rate.com
Send your CDs to VibeRate, 305 West Lemon Street, Lancaster, PA 17603. A press kit would be nice as well, but a short bio on your band will work.

VOCALmag
vocalmag1@aol.com
www.vocalmag.com
We review live shows and tours as well as CD releases from a vocal and performance perspective.

The War Against Silence
twasfeedback@furia.com
www.furia.com

Well Rounded Entertainment
cmorris@well-rounded.com
www.well-rounded.com/music

Whatever
whatever@whatevermagazine.com
www.whatevermagazine.com
Ezine with concert photos and reviews, cartoons and comedic features.

Whispering Wind Magazine
Gene M. Bates, Music Editor gbates@dps.state.la.us
www.whisperingwind.com
We offer Indie Musicians a place to get their music reviewed. Musicians can showcase their works. We also do artist profiles of 'up and coming' artists and groups as well as established indie performers.

Zzaj Productions
Dick Metcalf, aka Rotcod Zzaj rotcod@reachone.com
www.cdstreet.com/cgi-bin/artisthome_db.cgi?81048
home.attbi.com/~rzzaj/
Highly evocative music to stimulate you!

Canada

actionCANCELLED
jeff@actioncancelled.com
www.actioncancelled.com
We feel that it is imperative to display and promote folks that consider what the world is about, whether through visuals or word. ::aC:: will continue to provide this service for as long as it is relevant.

Broken Pencil
editor@brokenpencil.com
www.brokenpencil.com
We cover zines, books, music, film/video and art produced with an indie attitude. Reviews, essays, interviews, original fiction and excerpts from the best of the underground press.

Carte Blanche Magazine
Info@CarteBlancheMagazine.com
www.carteblanchemagazine.com
News, reviews, interviews etc.

Ductape
zach@ductape.org
www.ductape.org
Interviews, reviews, contests, pictures and other fun stuff!

Extreme Online Music Magazine
Roxanne Blanford roxanneb@usa.net
www.extreme-online.com
To qualify for a review you must have a pressed CD, have minimal distribution and a website so readers/labels/writers can get more info on your band. If you only sell your CD at shows then you will not be a review priority. We generally DO NOT review demo material, EPs, or cassettes.

the GATE
editor@thegate.ca
www.thegate.ca
Reviews, interviews etc. Check out our new video feature, The Fixxx - where you can watch our interviews and recent event coverage.

Global Bass
marty@globalbass.com
www.globalbass.com
Features, reviews and interviews of bass players from around the world.

Mohair Sweets
mohairsweets@yahoo.co.uk
www.mohairsweets.mb.ca
An on-line zine and music promotions site featuring record and book reviews of Mod, Soul, R&B;, Roots, Punk, Exotica and Reggae and also features interviews with musicians, authors, record labels and more!

Mote MGZN
motemgzn@moteinteractive.com
www.moregoatthangoose.com
Reviews, interviews, live reviews etc.

Muse's Muse
jodi@musesmuse.com
www.musesmuse.com
Indie reviews, songwriting tips, tools and interactivities.

The PRP
pedro@theprp.com
theprp.com
Located in Canada, England and Brazil in offices cunningly disguised as bedrooms, ThePRP work relentlessly all year round providing news, reviews and uncovering the very latest acts.

Somnie's Cyberspace
Léa Langelier somnie@hotmail.com
www.geocities.com/somnie2001
Band reviews, show reviews, cd reviews, message board: slam/defend bands, free band announcements - all genres - pro indie scene coverage.

Virus Zine
general@viruszine.com
www.viruszine.com
A zine dedicated to indie artists.

South America

Argentina

Rock Under
Andres Medina agencia@ru.com.ar
www.ru.com.ar
The best site in South America for reviews and interviews about indie bands!

Europe

Finland

dagensskiva.com
dagensskiva.com

BAND'S
BEST FRIEND

A PROMOTER
ON THE LOOKOUT
FOR NEW ACTS

CONNECT WITH HIM USING YOUR
SONICBIDS EPK™ (ELECTRONIC PRESS KIT)

- **CREATE** your Sonicbids EPK™ (electronic press kit) complete with MP3s, photos, bio, calendar and press reviews.
- **SAVE** time and money by emailing you EPK™ to live music promoters, radio programmers, and record company execs.
- **SUBMIT** your EPK™ directly to some of the world's biggest festivals, conferences, songwriting competitions, and clubs using the promoter drop box.
- **SHOWCASE** in some of the hottest music conferences and festivals through Sonicbids' exclusive performance slots.
- **QUALIFY** for tour sponsorships and showcase opportunities.
- **CONNECT** with some of the best live promoters in the business- we have 1 for every 3 bands on Sonicbids.

SIGN UP AT
WWW.SONICBIDS.COM

FASTER. BETTER. EASIER. CHEAPER.

Rockmusica
palaute@rockmusica.net
www.rockmusica.net

SOUNDi
www.soundi.fi

France

Actu-net.com
info@actu-net.com
www.actu-net.com
Agenda des concerts en France, Suisse et Allemagne. Chat, forum, reviews, radio, interviews etc.

bubblegum perfume
glamrockgirl@elvis.com
www.bubblegumperfume.ht.st
Fanzine in French about twee pop.

Le CARGo
www.terant.com

Critic Instinct
nwurd@canz.com
www.critic-instinct.com

Culturekiosque
editors@culturekiosque.com
www.culturekiosque.com
The European Guide to Arts, Entertainment and Culture in North America, Europe and worldwide.

Dangerhouse
dangerhouse@free.fr
dangerhouse.free.fr
Comprehensive zine from a record store in France.

Dig It!
digitfanzine@Chez.com
www.chez.com/digitfanzine
Rawk 'n' Roll French fanzine!!!

Inrockuptibles
www.lesinrocks.com
A perfect guide to French cultural life and an extension of a magazine that has existed for more than 15 years. Its vault are full of astonishing and unique interviews with all the great musicians, writers, film directors or actors of the last thirty years.

magnetophone.com
www.magnetophone.com
All genres welcome. Independent, underground, experimental, French pop, English pop, electronic music...

Nova Planet
www.novaplanet.com
Consortium quotidien de culture underground.

Panic
p.paut@free.fr
www.chez.com/panic

POPnews
redacteurs@popnews.com
www.popnews.com
We are one of the major French music webzines. Very keen on discovering new talents we also publish regular compilation CD of our favorite "newcomers".

positiverage
positiverage@hotmail.com
www.positiverage.com

Sans Tambour ni Trompette
info@stnt.org
www.stnt.org
Interactive ezine & radio show from France with news (a lot!), reviews, links, interviews (GORGE TRIO, ARAB ON RADAR)...

sefronia
info@sefronia.com
www.sefronia.com
CD review free e-mail magazine (in French).

Speedvibes
speedvibes@speedvibes.com
www.speedvibes.com
A French web site for anyone who enjoys skate, surf, snowboarding and music. Bands from everywhere are welcome to submit.

zicline.com
zicline@zicline.com
www.zicline.com
Each week all music info from jazz to heavy metal, new CD presentations, games with music gifts, live shows.

Germany

CD-KRITIK.DE
www.cd-kritik.de
Wir beschreiben Ihnen die CDs, aber die Wahl haben Sie. Deshalb benoten wir die CDs auch nicht, weder mit Sternchen noch mit erhobenem oder gesenktem Daumen und schon gar nicht mit Zensuren.

DocRock Show
contact@infomusic.de
www.docrock.de

Discover
andre@discover.de
www.discover.de
CDs, stories, interviews...

Guitars Galore
Mike Korbik mike@twang-tone.de
www.twang-tone.de/gg.html
A flyer zine that appears every two weeks in Berlin and it is a monthly radio show as well.

The Kinda Muzik You Like
redactie@kindamuzik.net
www.kindamuzik.net
Offering free indie/rock/pop/electronica content in order to give alternative and underground music the attention it deserves.

Lodown Online
lodown@lodown.com
www.lodown.de
Reviews of the newest and hottest beats & rhymes & Rock 'n' Roll.

Lord Litter's Reviews
LordLitter@LordLitter.de
www.lordlitter.de
Lord Litter is described as "one of the most important personalities in the underground scene this side of John Peel" - on air, internet and satellite via 6 networks worldwide presents only true indie-underground releases of all styles 'n genres - most successful show.

Plattentests Online
post@plattentests.de
www.plattentests.de

PNG *(Persona Non Grata)*
www.popculture.de

Sound De Verlagsgellschaft
info@sound.de
www.sound.de
Sound.de, a source for good music of all kinds, online since 1995! We offer you daily updates in news, cd-reviews (currently more than 3000 in our archive!) and interviews.

VISIONS.de
info@visions.de
www.visions.de
Musikmagazin seit 1995 im Netz. Musikportal mit News, Archiv, Tourdaten, Community, Mailorder, Platten, umfangreichen Informationen und sehr großer musikalischer Bandbreite. Tägliche Neuigkeiten aus allen Musik-Bereichen.

Whiskey Soda
redaktion@whiskey-soda.de
www.whiskey-soda.de
Tauch ein in die Welt der Alternative Rock Music.

Greece

Avopolis
www.avopolis.gr

Babylon
www.babylon.gr
The biggest music site in Greece. Daily music news, reviews, free MP3s, interviews, special features, music links index and more...

MiC
bar@mic.gr
www.mic.gr
Alternative music magazine.

Italy

altatensione
info@altatensione.it
www.altatensione.it

MusicbOOm
Carlo Crudele musicboom@musicboom.it
www.musicboom.it
Italy's best resource for indie music. Covering all genres with experience, knowledge and sheer passion.

Rockit
materiale@rockit.it
www.rockit.it

Sodapop
sodapop@sodapop.it
www.sodapop.it
News, reviews, demos etc.

Wallace Records
mirko@wallacerecords.com
www.wallacerecords.com

The Netherlands

Music Minded
office@musicminded.nl
www.musicminded.nl

OOR
info@oor.nl
www.oor.nl

think small
thinksmall@thinksmall.nl
www.thinksmall.nl
News, reviews and articles written in Dutch.

Norway

Kongoi Productions
kongoi@kongoi.com
www.kongoi.com
*Online Artists Promotion, Music, Musicians
Management and Publishing Company. Specializing
in African music and poetry.*

Luna Kafe
luna@fuzzlogic.com
www.fuzzlogic.com/lunakafe
*Record reviews, concert reviews, interviews and more.
Written by contributors from around the world.
Covers a variety of styles and genres.*

Nephilius
Joost Hegle joost@serv1.ub.ntnu.no
crash.to/joost
*A webzine for music lovers. It's not about categorizing
music to death. The main idea is to review music
that's interesting, fresh and experimental. Music that
appeals to your feelings.*

Poland

Post Industry
radek.turkiewicz@se.com.pl
www.postindustry.org
*Serwis muzyki electro, EBM, industrial, IDM, noise,
gothic, synthpop itp.*

Russia

Èñòîðèÿ èíäè-ìóçûêè. (Indie music history)
Mitia Berkhin meetee@online.ru
www.evermusica.com
*The review of Joy Division and some great Indie
bands.*

Slovakia

Music Box
music.box.sk

Spain

desorden.net
desorden@desorden.net
www.desorden.net
*Revista online en castellano especializada en música
independiente.*

espacio3
Gustavo Zapico gus@espacio3.com
www.espacio3.com
Moda, arte, música, sexo, libros, cine, mensual...

Incultura
Toño incultura@terra.es
fly.to/incultura
*A Spanish independent music webzine. Updated daily
with interviews, articles, news etc.*

Indy Rock
info@indyrock.es
www.ideal.es/indyrock

Sweden

Allt på ett kort
popoga@algonet.se
www.algonet.se/~popoga

benno
benno@benno.com
www.benno.com

Bomben
bomben.nu
*Features interviews, chronicles, articles and reviews
about hip hop, r'n'b, jazz, indie pop, rock, soul and
anything else, as well as a Swedish club guide.*

Chrome Magazine
chrome_mag@spray.se
come.to/chrome_mag

Ettnollett
webmaster@nordling.com
www.nordling.com/ettnollett
*We have been going for 15 years and we are still
writing about the new fresh pop and rock scene of
Sweden. Enjoy it!*

melodic.net
jta@algonet.se
www.melodic.net
Reviews, interviews and "Artist of the Week".

More than Music
anthem@home.se
www.mtm.musicpage.com
*If you would like your music review, please send your
CD and info to us.*

Passagen
www.passagen.se

Revolver
farid@revolver.nu
www.revolver.nu

United Kingdom

5 Arabs and a Camel
editor@atomtan.co.uk
www.atomtan.co.uk

Alternative Music Links
reviews@alternative-links.co.uk
www.alternative-links.co.uk
*If you wish to contact us regarding possible gig or
album reviews please contact us.*

Aquamarine
kim@blissaquamarine.net
www.blissaquamarine.net
*I don't like to limit myself to just one type of music
and would rather judge music on how it sounds, not
what label it's on or what scene it's from.*

Atomic Duster
nick@copydesign.co.uk
www.atomicduster.com

atomtan.co.uk
editor@atomtan.co.uk
www.atomtan.co.uk
Music and show reviews, videos and more!

Ballroom Favourites
ballroomfavourites@another.com
www.ballroomfavourites.com
Reviews and artist spotlights.

BIRDpages Record Review
info@birdpages.co.uk
www.birdpages.co.uk
*Your online gateway to UK record shops, record
dealers and record collecting plus the latest music
reviews in the Album Leaves Magazine.*

Biting Bullets
geocities.com/dehumanized_uk
*An open minded web site that is designed to get as
many musical genres colliding together as possible.
As long as it rocks us, we'll include it, it is basically
that simple.*

Bleedmusic
admin@bleedmusic.net
www.bleed-music.com
Send press releases and review enquiries.

BonaFideStudio
Deanna info@bonafidestudio.co.uk
www.bonafidestudio.co.uk
*We offer: Reviews, Artist Page, Notice Board, Sound
Tutorial etc. Run by musicians for musicians, we are
different - we really do care. Check us out!*

bumblebeetree
alcwsy@hotmail.com
members.lycos.co.uk/bumblebeetree
A site for new and alternative music.

Busker's Ball
busker@freeuk.com
www.busker.freeuk.com

Careless Talk Costs Lives
info@carelesstalkcostslives.com
www.carelesstalkcostslives.com
An arts magazine that is available nationwide.

CHA CHA CHA
www.chachacha.co.uk

Clean Shaven
ric@badmusic.net
www.badmusic.net

CLUAS
feedback@cluas.com
www.cluas.com
Lending an ear to the Irish music scene.

Comes with a Smile
cwasmatt@yahoo.co.uk
cwas.hinah.com
*Published a few times a year. Each issue includes a
CD.*

Darcy's on the Pull
bsx@kenickie.com
www.kenickie.com/darcy.htm

deliveryman
www.musicworkz.co.uk
*An introduction platform, to bring non-mainstream
music (from anywhere in the world), regardless of
music genre, to a wider audience. Although much of
the site content is aimed predominantly at UK visitors,
I certainly hope that there is something of general
interest to everyone visiting the site.*

Diskant
overlord@diskant.net
www.diskant.net
*A network of websites by independent fanzines, bands
and record labels.*

the dive music magazine
info@thedivemusicmagazine.com
www.thedivemusicmagazine.com
*You guide to the new music scene, featuring the latest
music news, listings, reviews, interviews, photos,
features, radio and more.*

Do Something Pretty
Dosomethingpretty@Hotmail.com
dosomethingpretty.com
One of the main points to this site is to attempt to help build connections between like-minded people whom share a passion for independent music.

Drowned in Sound
sean@drownedinsound.com
www.drownedinsound.com
An all new Music and Arts site which aims to submerse the reader in the cutting edge of contemporary culture. Find out what's new in music, both underground and mainstream.

Eclectic Honey
webmaster@eclectichoney.com
www.eclectichoney.com
If you are in a band and would like to submit a copy of your record to review fill out the form on our website and make sure to include a link to any online sound samples you have or a relevant website.

EMDS Rockzine
emds@listen.to
listen.to/emds
We'll review your demos, releases etc. The stuff you send us won't be returned. E-mail us for further inquiries.

Excellent Online.com
eadmin@odc.net
www.excellentonline.com
The Home for North American fans of UK Music.

fakeDIY
reviews@fakediy.net
www.fakediy.net
We review CDs, demos, MP3s and gigs. Visit our website for details on how to submit.

Fast Cow
Peter Carter p.carter@bathspa.ac.uk
www.fastcow.co.uk
An I!N!D!I!E! music webzine that gives FAIR reviews to any artist. Also runs interviews and misc articles.

The Fly
fly@channelfly.com
www.channelfly.com
An alternative music site featuring webcasts, legal MP3s, features, interviews, competitions and music news.

Freaky Trigger
www.freakytrigger.co.uk
Enjoy! Read! Comment! And remember, comments aren't merely welcome, but encouraged — and if you want to contribute to FT yourself, I'm always willing to hear new ideas.

French Music E-Zine UK
parris@frenchmusicezine.co.uk
www.frenchmusicezine.co.uk
French music in plain English!

Glamage
Glamage@hotmail.com
www.glamage.tk
Get in touch to request reviews, to be interviewed, featured, to submit an article, or just requesting information.

Home and Away
Pete Cole homeandaway86@hotmail.com
move.to/H&Azine
A short & sweet, honest bi-monthly hard & soft copy fanzine that covers studio/live reviews of guitar/punk/pop bands.

The Horse
thehorse@bigfoot.com
www.uk-image.net/horse
An online reviews ezine based in London, covering music and film in particular, but welcoming submissions on any subject. It's funny and deep and intelligent and irreverent.

Hot Press
feedback@hotpress.com
www.hotpress.com
We have consistently rattled the cages of Irish society and broken exciting new ground in contemporary journalism. With an abiding commitment to music at its core, it remains the essential guide to rock, pop, dance and all the best in contemporary music, both nationally and internationally.

IF E-zine
Andy Malt editor@indigoflow.co.uk
www.indigoflow.co.uk
An independent music e-zine. We don't mess around with genres and elitism; we just cover the music we like.

in love with these times in spite of these times
tryhappiness@aol.com
www.ilwtt.org
We welcome anything and everything, whether vinyl or cassette or cd or md. So if you want to send us anything, again just e mail and we'll give you our intimate details.

is this music?
Stuart McHugh editor@isthismusic.com
www.isthismusic.com
A Scottish music monthly. Our aim is to cover the music that you might not see written about elsewhere. That includes acts local to Scotland who can't even get a fair crack of the whip from the local press and also the kinds of acts from around the world that are ignored by the mainstream publications.

Kaboom!
nialldebuitlear@yahoo.ie
www.kaboommusic.cjb.net
Irish alternative music zine.

KlubKat
features@klubkat.com
www.klubkat.com
We promote not only local bands, but local venues and events too. We are based in the UK, but the Internet is of course a global entity - so our services aren't limited by geography!

Leonard's Lair
leonards.lair@ntlworld.com
www.leonardslair.co.uk
I will gladly review your music and will give honest opinions on the recordings sent to me. It would however be useful if you could direct me to any audio samples you have on-line, or at least describe the genre of the music you offer.

Live Club
Justin Coll justin@liveclub.co.uk
www.liveclub.co.uk
British site for new & unsigned bands. Reviews, radio station, live venues listing, live band listings, email & classified adverts.

LOGO Magazine
submissions@logo-magazine.com
www.logo-magazine.com
We are here to let you know what's hot and what's not. We also have strong links with venues, promoters and studios across the country, as well as a network of contacts within the film industry. If you're in a band, we can help you to be seen and heard.

lostharbour.org
sendsomething@lostharbour.org
www.lostharbour.org
If you're from a band or label, contact me and I'll write about whatever you have, unless it's deep house, of course.

Manilla
reviews@manillame.com
www.manillame.com
Free mag which promotes unsigned acts.

musicOMH.com
www.musicomh.com
We hope you enjoy reading our reviews, interviews and other articles - they are written purely because people here want to write them.

music week
ajax@musicweek.com
www.musicweek.com
Music, news, charts, reviews, analysis, features. The UK music industry bible.

Muzik.com
support@muzik.com
www.miuzik.com
Reviewing the works of known artists as well as trying to spot new talents.

New Music Express (NME)
news@nme.com
www.nme.com
The Official UK No 1 music web site. Reviews, interviews, quotes…

No Ripcord
editor@noripcord.co.uk
www.noripcord.co.uk
A free online music fanzine specializing in reviews and features of indie/alternative bands.

Nunuworld
nunununa@nunuworldmusic.co.uk
www.nunuworldmusic.co.uk

Organ Zine
organ@organart.demon.co.uk
www.organart.com
Send in whatever you want to send in (useful hint no 23: make the package exciting, we always open the big ones that are covered in glitter and look like they're full of chocolate, underwear and silver stiletto type bribes first). We have no time for safe average stale music!

pennyblackmusic.com
rich@pennyblackmusic.com
www.pennyblackmusic.com

www.indielinkexchange.com

pH Magazine
pH@phantomfm.com
www.phantomfm.com/ph
Dublin's modern rock magazine!

PHASE9 Entertainment
Nigel M editorial@phase9.net
www.phase9.tv
Independent site for reviews and information on music and movies in the USA and UK - over 3000 pages online.

PLAYLOUDER
site@playlouder.com
www.playlouder.com
Brought to you by a creative community of record labels, artists, journalists and real music fans. You'll find us at the bleeding edge of both technology and culture, bringing you the very best in new music and direct access to the most innovative and groundbreaking artists.

Qwirky Purple
Dammo qwirkypurple@hotmail.com
www.qwirkypurple.co.uk
Qwirky indie/alternative website containing interviews, live reviews, single & album reviews, demos, up-and-coming bands.

Rainsound
mail@rainsound.net
www.rainsound.net
We've been going for almost a decade, mainly focusing on Scottish bands and the 80's legacy. We don't care about being cool or uncool - it's about the love of music, be it great songwriting or interesting sonic qualities.

Red Roses For Me
steve@redrosesforme.co.uk
www.redrosesforme.co.uk

R*E*P*E*A*T Online
rosey@repeatfanzine.co.uk
www.repeatfanzine.co.uk
The 'Repeat' legacy focuses on the underground music scene with zest akimbo.

revolutionsUK.com
john@revolutionsUK.com
www.revolutionsuk.com
A weekly online magazine covering world, blues, soul, folk, reggae and country music. Features news, reviews, interviews, gig guide, airplay and label information.

Robots and Electric Brains
www.geocities.com/SunsetStrip/Backstage/1472
Eclectic zine for music with that extra something special (come.to/robots)

ROCK SOUND
graham.finney@ixopub.co.uk
www.rock-sound.net
Dedicated to bringing you all the best new music from around the world.

Rock's Backpages
barney@rocksbackpages.com
www.rocksbackpages.com
A vast archive of classic. Also news, reviews and interviews of new artists.

rockcity.co.uk
mark@rock-city.co.uk
www.rock-city.co.uk
A regularly updated guide to alternative music gigs and club nights at the Rock City venue in Nottingham, UK. Also includes reviews of both signed and unsigned recorded material and live shows.

Rocked sounds
rockedsounds@hotmail.com
www.rockedsounds.co.uk
We bring you the best news, reviews and everything from the world of indie music.

RockFeedback.com
press@rockfeedback.com
www.rockfeedback.com
In general, we approach bands we want to feature on the site, but if you want to get in contact with us regarding getting press for your band, then please contact us.

Saint Mary Mead Zine
Laura smm@tooshytogetajob.org.uk
www.tooshytogetajob.org.uk
New UK zine covering pop in all its guises, esp in the synth- indie- twee-pop vein. Demos welcome!

Shindig
olivercrumb@yahoo.com
www.geocities.com/shindig_magazine

Saint Mary Mead
smm@tooshytogetajob.org.uk
www.tooshytogetajob.org.uk
A little, indie pop (ish) webzine.

sleazenation.com
www.sleazenation.com
A lively labyrinth that allows visitors to sample our cultural hotbed and communicate with like-minded souls.

Society Review
www.societyreview.com
A lifestyle magazine giving, "everything you need for modern living". Covering a broad range of topics, from fashion, lifestyle, health, arts and interiors, music, technology, gaming and more.

Sorted
editor@sortedmagazine.com
sortedmagazine.com
Ireland's original online music magazine. It features interviews, album, single and concert reviews from a wide variety of bands, as well as the specialist sections BPM (dance music) and Sordid (Gothic/ Industrial).

Spitting Glass Stars
Sarah Kirk-Browne spitting_glass_stars@lineone.net
www.spittingglassstars.co.uk
Long-established fanzine with popular website. Always looking for new music to review - all genres welcome.

State 51 Motion Reviews
intouch@state51.co.uk
www.state51.co.uk
Showcasing the best new music, across all genres. Updated daily.

theStereoEffect
Karen Piper matic@theStereoEffect.com
www.theStereoEffect.com
Reviews and Interviews of the newest and most exciting music in the US and the UK.

Tangents Online
editor@tangents.co.uk
www.tangents.co.uk
The home of Un-Popular Culture on the World Wide Web.

Tastyzine
info@tastyfanzine.org.uk
www.tastyfanzine.org.uk
Recommending the soundtrack for the revolution.

terraform
info@universalsource.co.uk
www.universalsource.co.uk
Bristol, UK based e-zine covering music, the arts and ideas

Too Many DJs
matthew@parkview2.screaming.net
www.toomanydjs.co.uk
Interviews, links, pics, band features, multimedia and many many reviews of the best singles, albums and live gigs.

TweeNet
www.twee.net
To be featured on our main page, you have to send a copy of the record along with a press release to us. We don't guarantee to feature your record on the home page; we have to like it to put it up there.

The Twinstar Revolution
bands@twinstarrevolution.com
www.twinstarrevolution.com
In a band, want to let us know about what you're up to? Contact us.

unbarred
david@unbarred.co.uk
www.unbarred.co.uk
Deals with bands that aren't usually covered by larger publications. It deals with all sorts of styles, from indie, rock, pop and dance; also gigs concerts, records and CDs.

The Universal
mazhar1@juno.com
www.the-universal.com

Unsharp
unsharp@diskant.net
www.diskant.net/unsharp
We make it easy and cheap for bands, labels and fanzines to get their stuff online and to help people to find out about what's happening in their local area and around the world.

unsignedcentral
sales@unsignedcentral.co.uk
www.unsignedcentral.co.uk
Unfortunately we are unable to review MP3s. Why? Because we forget to download them, forget where we put them; forget the names of songs and bands. Plus it could take a good while to dl if this started to happen.

Whisperin & Hollerin
james@whisperinandhollerin.com
www.whisperinandhollerin.com
Music reviews and interviews with an alternative bias - covers a huge range of genres.

The Wiseacre
wiseacre@clara.net
www.wiseacre.clara.net
A music reviews site offering criticism where it's due on the week's new releases in the UK. Just about anything and everything is covered in these pages.

Zeitgeist
info@the-rocker.co.uk
the-rocker.freeservers.com
Reflecting the Underground through music and lifestyle and art.

Australia - New Zealand

Australia

Alternative Melbourne
info@mediasearch.com.au
www.mediasearch.com.au
We are an Australian-based entertainment website that includes news, reviews and feature stories about worldwide music of most musical styles.

The Beam Magazine
warren@highbeammusic.net
www.highbeammusic.com
The FREE magazine features interviews, as well as a stack of reviews and much more. This is a quarterly publication and all reviews and interviews can be found here on this website which is updated with each issue of the magazine.

Blunt Review
emily@bluntreview.com
www.bluntreview.com
We review indie music, indie and studio films, interview musicians and actors. The venue is blunt and honest riddled with a particular style and wit. Come on in for some "Emily-isms."

Buzz Magazine
psutton@r150.aone.net.au
www.buzzmagazine.com.au
A street press in Melbourne Australia. The online site features interviews with Australian and international artists, reviews, columns and information about the Australian Music Industry.

Digi-Scape Productions
digiscape@live.com.au
www.listen.to/digiscape
Virtual Studios. Virtual Reality. Virtually Anything!

Electric Newspaper
aweaver@chariot.net.au
www.theelectricnewspaper.com
News, reviews, interviews...

Gods of Music
nycran@godsofmusic.com
www.godsofmusic.com
Dedicated to providing detailed, constructive and honest reviews for all bands / artists.

Gravity Girl
ac@office.net.au
gravitygirl.shafted.com.au

hEARd
hmag@ozemail.com.au
heard.com.au
Promoting new music & youth culture in general. Covers all genres of music & accepts unsolicited material.

Long Gone Loser
damo@longgoneloser.com
SamanthaFoxIsTheEditor@longgoneloser.com
www.longgoneloser.com
Please send a press kit and all that jive that sounds wanky but all bands do it and we'll give it all a whirl and be in contact with you if we dig it. Feel free to also send anything for review. Please don't send us religious music.

Mediasearch
info@mediasearch.com.au
www.mediasearch.com.au

Rockus
mail@rockus.com.au
www.rockus.com.au
Specializing in the indie, pop, alternative and rock genres. Frequently updated with reviews, features, interviews, news, show dates and much more. We review any material sent to us.

Secrets of Home Theater and High Fidelity
staff@hometheaterhifi.com
www.hometheaterhifi.com
Devoted to the enjoyment of audio and video experiences. The website has music reviews, movie reviews, product reviews, DIY projects and feature articles that explain audio and video technology.

Smelly Donkey
fergusnoodle@aol.com
www.geocities.com/
fergus_noodle
Described as 'oddly amusing without the slightest risk of being overly informative' and sometimes we talk about Australian things too.

Songsalive!
sydney@songsalive.org
www.songsalive.org
A voluntary non-profit organization, dedicated to nurturing, supporting and promoting songwriters worldwide.

Undercover
undercover@undercover.com.au
www.undercover.net.au
Your MUsic Entertainment ZOne. News, reviews, interviews and more!

New Zealand

Start Spyring
Deborah Wai Kapohe deborah@ringtroutcds.com
homepages.paradise.net.nz/spyring
New Zealand based CD Review Site. Interesting in reviewing any Indie Artist.

Asia

India

Gigpad.com
vijay@gigpad.com
www.gigpad.com
Our mission is to bridge gaps. Gaps between musician- musician, musician-industry and musician-audience by using the power of the Internet to enable information exchange, interaction and transactions.

Japan

Asian Rock Rising
e-rock@din.or.jp
www.asianrockrising.org
The place to support Asian rock bands (including some folk and pop bands). Please send your band information bio, news, future plans, contact info etc.

Singapore

BigO
singbigo@signet.com
www.bigo.com.sg
Features more than 150 reviews each issue.

Blues

Blues On Stage
Ray mnblues@aol.com
www.mnblues.com
Send 2 copies of CD along with any promotional material for reviews.

The Blues Revue
info@bluesrevue.com
www.bluesrevue.com
Published 10 times per year and each issue is packed with artist profiles, interviews, album reviews and columns by the most respected writers on today's blues scene.

Blues Bytes
info@bluenight.com
www.bluenight.com/BluesBytes
A monthly blues CD review magazine.

Bluesbuff.com
BluesBuff@bluesbuff.com
www.bluesbuff.com
A site dedicated to the discovery, promotion and sale of CDs of all independent artists that play the blues.

Blues.Net
jim@blues.net
www.blues.net
Send us your CDs for review and national airplay. You can also become our "feature artist".

Blueswax.com
www.blueswax.com
Weekly blues e-zine with reviews, industry news, interviews, gossip and MP3 blues samples.

Delta Snake
www.netmagic.net/~snake
News, reviews, articles etc.

Electric Blues
herm@electricblues.com
www.electricblues.com
Our main focus is evaluating CDs and I will be giving my opinion of many in the coming months.

gottheblues.com
info@gottheblues.com
www.gottheblues.com
Our mission is to help give Blues music the exposure that it deserves. We love the Blues and are giving Blues music a true home on the internet.

Jelly
editor@jellyroll.com
www.jellyroll.com
The very best in blues, jazz, country, soul and rock'n'roll. Entertaining, knowledgeable articles and reviews that honor the great tradition of (mostly) American popular music, especially the stuff you won't easily find on the radio.

Juke Blues Magazine
www.bluesworld.com/JukeBlues.html
This journal is packed with articles, interviews, news reviews, gig guide and lots of great photos of classic American blues heroes, as well as new stars on the scene.

NothinButDaBlues.com
mail@nothinbutdablues.com
www.nothinbutdablues.com
Enjoy viewing favorite and well-known blues artists in the Featured Artist section, or let us introduce you to some great, yet lesser-well-known, blues artists on the Spotlight page.

Canada

Real Blues Magazine
rblues@realbluesmagazine.com
www.realbluesmagazine.com
Guide for the Connoisseur of Blues Music. Blues, Soul, Gospel and Zydeco are much more than just categories or genres of music; they are each and all passionate and eloquent avenues of the expression of human feelings.

Europe

Austria

BluesArtStudio
bluesart@bluesartstudio.at
www.bluesartstudio.at

Belgium

Back to the Roots
backtotheroots.franky@pi.be
www.backtotheroots.be
Is een nederlandstalig magazine voor blues en aanverwante muziekstijlen.

France

BluesRoad
bluesroad.free.fr
Among the artists mentioned here are founders, giants, revivalists and promising rookies.

Sweden

Jefferson Blues Magazine
bhu327c@tninet.se
jeffersonbluesmag.com
The name (now shortened to Jefferson) derives from the legendary Texas blues man Blind Lemon Jefferson. A few years later (1972) the Scandinavian Blues Association (SBA) was founded to administer Jefferson.

United Kingdom

Blueprint
info@bluesinbritain.org
www.blueprint-blues.co.uk
Each month, Blueprint reports on the blues scene, with emphasis on what's happening in the UK. You can read about stars of the blues past and present, the latest CD releases, live blues as it happens.

Blues & Rhythm
tony@bluestb.demon.co.uk
www.bluesworld.com/BnR
Europe's leading English language Blues, R&B and Gospel magazine.

Australia

Mr. Blues Online Haven
radar@radarsbluesandgraphics.com
www.radarsbluesandgraphics.com
Blues related artists can have information online, which can be shared around the world. Both International and Australian Artists may submit CD's for review.

Japan

Tokyo-Blues
Tokyo_Blues_Brothers@yahoo.com
www.tokyo-blues.com
All over the blues scene in Japan like kudzu in Georgia.

Children's Music

Booklist
Sue-Ellen Beauregard sbeaureg@ala.org
www.ala.org/booklist
For more than 90 years, Booklist has been the librarian's leading choice for reviews of the latest books and (more recently) electronic media.

EdutainingKids.com
feedback@edutainingkids.com
www.edutainingkids.com
Dedicated to providing parents with reviews and recommendations of "edutainment" products for children. We strive to produce reviews that are impartial and objective.

Fred Koch Reviews
tellus@bestchildrensmusic.com
www.bestchildrensmusic.com/kochrevs.htm
Fred Koch's children's music review column appears monthly in Chicago Parent magazine.

Guide to Children's Music
feedback@edutainingkids.com
www.edutainingkids.com/music.html
Articles, spotlights, reviews etc.

The John Wood Revue
john@kidzmusic.com
www.kidzmusic.net/index_reviews.htm
A great place to find some of the best children's music.

Christian Music

America's Best Rock
g0d@buffbody.com
www.AmericasBestRock.com
You have a chance on being featured on AmericasBestRock.com!

CatholicMusicNetwork.com
webmaster@catholicmusicnetwork.com
www.catholicmusicnetwork.com
The Premier online source for music by today's top Catholic artists.

CCMplanet
www.ccmplanet.com
Our goal is to stimulate Christian music in a general way and to provide you with all the news and information you need about your favorite artists. We do this by bringing you daily news, artist information, concert information, album reviews and more!

Christian Metal Network
cmn@christianmetal.com
www.christianmetal.com/cmn

Christian Metal Resource
scottmoore@christianmetal.com
www.christianmetal.com/cmr
The encyclopedia of Christian metal.

Christian Pirate Radio
josh@mycpr.com
www.christianpirateradio.com
We pirates grew tired of waiting for someone else to start a local Christian music so we built our own radio station on the Internet, playing your favorite artists.

The Christian Rapper
thechristianrapper@yahoo.com
www.thechristianrapper.com
Please send all materials, even pictures to us and we will try to be a blessing to your group/ministry!

Christian Rockers Online
info@christianrockersonline.com
www.christianrockersonline.com
Reviews, news, featured bands, MP3s...

ChristianActivities.com
Info@christianactivities.com
www.ChristianActivities.com
We do sometimes carry new artist reviews, so you are welcome to contact us - but understand we do not review all, or even most of what we receive.

ChristianBEATS.org
davyg@christianbeats.org
christianbeats.org
News, reviews etc.

Christianity Today
rbreimeier@christianitytoday.com
www.christianitytoday.com
Discover the latest about your favorite Christian music artists through interviews, reviews, news and message boards.

Churchhouse Records
Undra Hill undra@churchhouserecords.com
www.churchhouserecords.com
We have a Bi- Monthly online magazine called the Churchouse Connection. We are willing to do an article on an outstanding independent Christian / Gospel artist.

Club Praize
info@clubpraize.org
www.clubpraize.org
Features Gospel Music and Ministry entertainment news and views on today's most popular independent and celebrity Gospel music artists, current events and issues in the urban Christian entertainment community.

CMCentral.com
WSpencer@CMCentral.com
www.cmcentral.com
Welcome to your source for discovering Christian music. We feature some of today's hottest Christian acts offering loads of information such as biographies, tour dates, links and downloads.

Contemporary Christian Magazine *CCM*
CCMWebEditors@ccmmagazine.com
www.ccmcom.com

Cornerstone Magazine Music
lte@jpusa.org
www.cornerstonemag.com
Reviews, Interviews and more.

Cross Rhythms Magazine
admin@crossrhythms.co.uk
www.crossrhythms.com
Articles and features on all aspects of Contemporary Christian Music Lifestyle teaching with a music emphasis, chart, news, Gig Guide and a HUGE review section that you simply can't afford to miss!

Cross RAWK
InThisDay@AmericasBestRock.com
www.inthisdayzine.com
Yu have a chance on being featured! There is only one requirement... your band has to be Christian Rock (alternative, rapcore, punk etc. is cool)!

Crossrock.com
crossrock@crossrock.com
www.crossrock.com
The Christian Music Revolution to the World!

Ex-Reprobate Webzine
Al Newberry al@ex-reprobate.com
www.ex-reprobate.com
A webzine dedicated to Christianity and Liberty, with an emphasis on the arts.

EXIT Zine
info@exitzine.com
www.exitzine.com
We are dedicated to all the best in the Christian music world and dedicated above all to the inspiration behind that music — Jesus Christ. He is the "who" behind everything we do.

Feed *Canada*
www.feedstop.com
Remember back in the day when you wanted to find Holy Hip-Hop or good Urban Christian Music and the chances of finding anything were slim, nil or WACK? Well look no further, why remain uninformed? FEED the NEED! Feed is your source for the best in Beats, Rhymes & Light.

Godcore.com
jason@godcore.com
www.godcore.com
Designed to help Christian Rock Artists gain worldwide exposure through a chain of like-minded artists and ministries. Each band or artist that joins Godcore.com will profit from the efforts of the chain. Your band will receive more exposure and you will receive additional hits to your website.

Gospel Crib
Kenny G. gospelcrib2001@yahoo.com
gospelcrib.8m.com
In honor of all independent gospel music artists Gospel Crib is showcasing choirs, groups and soloists on this website. I am looking for new independent gospel artists who exhibit style & grace in music and exemplify excellence in their ministry for the Lord. If you are a new independent gospel recording artist and would like to be featured on this website please send an email.

Gospel Music Profiles Magazine
gmpmagazine@aol.com
www.gospelmusicprofiles.com
A quarterly magazine featuring in-depth conversations with national and regional gospel music artists.

Gospel Synergy Magazine
alcarter@gospelsynergy.com
www.gospelsynergy.com
The Premier Gospel Magazine with articles about God's Word - Good News - and Gospel Music.

Gospel Today
gospeltodaymag@aol.com
www.gospeltoday.com
An inspiring magazine with stories about celebrities, sections about new Gospel CDs and record sales charts, columns about health, dating, family issues and other information for the person who enjoys positive information.

Gospel Vibrations
gospelvibrations@aol.com
www.gospelvibrations.cc
Music reviews, where you'll find out what's happening in today's Contemporary Christian Music. All CDs have been reviewed and selected based on their style, musical and lyrical content.

The Gospel Zone
crj_lawn@msn.com
www.thegospelzone.com
Reviews, news, message boards and upcoming events.

GospelCity.com
dareen@corp.gospelcity.com
gospelcity.com
News, reviews, articles, messages boards, radio and more!

GospelFlava.com
info@gospelflava.com
www.gospelflava.com
We share current industry information, profiles and interviews established and new artists and provide an exhaustive list of upcoming new releases. New CD and video Gospel releases are reviewed.

Gospelsite Deutschland *Germany*
webmaster@gospelsite.de
www.gospelsite.de
Our goal is to stimulate Christian music in a general way and to provide you with all the news and information you need about your favorite artists. We do this by bringing you daily news, artist information, concert information, album reviews and more! In German.

gospelticker
editor@gospelticker.com
www.gospelticker.com

GospelWire.com
info@gospelwire.com
www.gospelwire.com
Dedicated to providing news, information and resources related to Black Gospel Music. We feature up to date and important information though our informative weekly newsletter.

G-VIBE
mail@g-vibe.com
www.g-vibe.com
Get all your reviews at G-Vibe.com - from gospel to garage, hip-hop to house it's all happenin' here!

HM Magazine
david@hmmagazine.com
www.hmmag.com
Covering Christian hard music since 1985. Reviews tons of Indie music. Each issue features interviews, news and reviews of your favorite hard music (alternative, hard rock, industrial, metal, punk) artists.

IntenseRadio.com
www.intenseradio.com
We look at the actual people and personalities that shaped the Christian metal sound, instead of just defending the music as a valid vehicle for the Gospel message. We feel this form of music needs to have a web site that specializes in content and media devoted to the style.

Jamsline.com
jamsline@jamsline.com
www.jamsline.com
Weekly single reviews.

Jesusfreakhideout.com
email@jesusfreakhideout.com
www.jesusfreakhideout.com
Note that due to the volume of CDs we receive to review, if you send a CD to us for review, we cannot guarantee it will be reviewed. Please especially consider this in regard to independent releases.

Kay 3 Music
info@kay3music.com
www.kay3music.com
Our mission is to help artists gain support and also provide readers with an understanding of the artist and give a general opinion from a musician/ consumer's perspective. Artists interested in being reviewed should send CD and bio information to the address listed on the contact page.

Light Online
editor@lightonline.org
www.lightonline.org
Online Christian Hip Hop magazine. New, reviews and interviews.

ListenFirst.com
info@listenfirst.com
www.listenfirst.com
Our Indie Showcase is the hottest place for emerging Christian artists. If you are an independent artist and would like more information on joining the Indie Showcase, visit our site.

MINI-MAGazine ZINE
indiepop@evansville.net
www.indiepoprecords.com
Available 4X a year at your local Christian Bookstore! News and reviews.

monastereo.com
webguide@monastereo.com
www.monastereo.com
Please send CDs for music reviews/features, printed matter, photographs and similar items to the address provided on our website.

Music News and Review
info@klove.com
www.klove.com/newspaper

Music Spot
www.undergroundtechniques.com
To help promote and create awareness of those Hip-Hop and R&B artists who seek to glorify God through their work (meaning: artists who live a lifestyle which is holy and pleasing in the eyes of God).

Ncubator
editor@ncubator.com
www.ncubator.com
We will review your Christian music CD, book, or video. The review may be used by you in any form of media: print or electronic.

nuthinbutgospel.com
totalprayze@lycos.com
www.nuthinbutgospel.com
Send your music in for review, or write a review about music that you like.

Onemind Magazine
editor@om95.com
om95.com
ALL press kit materials should be sent to: ONEMIND, PO Box 670885, Houston TX 77267

Opus' Album Reviews
jason@opuszine.com
www.opuszine.com
Most of the reviews you'll find fall into the categories of indie-rock, emo, post-rock, electronica, ambient, underground and the avant-garde. But I'm sure you'll find a few surprises along the way...

The Phantom Tollbooth
feedback@tollbooth.org
www.tollbooth.org
We are an on-line magazine that publishes a wide range of album, concert and movie reviews, interviews, features and resource links. We're always looking for the best in mainstream and underground music.

Power Source Music Magazine
www.ccma.cc
Your Complete Music Resource for Today's Christian Country Music.

PraiseTV.com
editor@praisetv.com
www.praisetv.com
Our new interactive site offers live video, message boards, chatrooms, private messaging, Christian artist profiles, features, reviews and much more!

Rhythm N' Praise Gospel Radio
info@rhythmandpraise.com
www.rhythmandpraise.freeservers.com
As well as broadcasting Hip Hop, Contemporary, Rhythm and Praise and JAZZ, we also do CD reviews.

Servant's Heart
www.servantsheart.net
New releases, reviews, concerts etc.

The Singing News Magazine
danny@singingnews.com
www.singingnews.com
The country's largest Christian music publication. Up to date information on every facet of our industry, including concerts, conventions, banquets, new recordings and the latest chart action.

SoGospelNews.Com
webmaster@sogospelnews.com
sogospelnews.com
Your online source for all things southern gospel related; news, information, Artist Interviews, CD reviews, e-mail Chat and more!

Sphere of Hip Hop
sphereo@sphereofhiphop.com
www.sphereofhiphop.com
A conglomerate of hip-hop artists (well over 250) brought together to form a unified "push" into the masses of people around the world. Featured items: MP3, reviews, charts, email list, articles and more!

talkGospel.com *UK*
enquiries@talkGospel.com
www.talkgospel.com
Our mission is to support the Gospel music scene, particularly British artists. If you are a Gospel music artist and you are interested in reaching the wider community with your music, tell us about yourself, your music and any gigs or concerts you are playing at and we will consider you for our playlist and be able to help promote you.

TrueTunes.com
TrueTunes@TrueTunes.com
www.truetunes.com
There are artists out there who see the world differently than the standard. They see a light and they see things as illuminated by the light. The dream is that these artists can get the exposure they deserve, but often will never find in our secularized, homogenized and sterilized culture.

United by ONE *UK*
info@unitedbyone.co.uk
www.unitedbyone.co.uk
We are a team of Christians based in London, England, who share this vision of standing for unity in the Body of Christ. By this we mean, that we want to break down the cultural and denominational barriers that sometimes exist within the Church.

The Urban Cross Network *Hip-Hopzone.com*
jelani@urbancross.com
www.hiphopzone.com
Hip-Hop from a Christian perspective. Email us and will give you an address and a contact person to send your project to be evaluated.

Urban Music Review
urbanmusic7.tripod.com
Your Source for Urban Christian Music News, Interviews, Reviews, Release Dates and more.

The Urban Web Link
www.urbanweblink.com
Your source for Christian Events in Philadelphia and surrounding areas; plus information, people, music, reviews and resources related to Urban Ministry, Urban Missions, Multiculturism, the Hip Hop Culture & more of the same vein! Check it out now and help spread the word!

UTVortex.com - Music Spot
www.utvortex.com
Our mission is to help promote and create awareness of those Hip-Hop and R&B artists who seek to glorify God through their work and to provide visitors with insight into the music itself through reviews, artist profiles, music clips, articles and many other resources.

The Vagrant Café
vagrant@vagrantcafe.com
www.vagrantcafe.com
We do our best to provide our perspectives on the music we love, the God we serve and the world around us from where we stand. We love indie bands and want to do whatever we can to give the many great Indies out there the exposure they deserve.

Wendy V's Christian/Gospel CD spotlight
wendyv2941@aol.com
www.wendyv.com
Brief reviews of new Southern Gospel/Christian product. E-mail Query first before sending CDs or attachments.

What's the Word Magazine
wtwmagazine@hotmail.com
www.wtwmagazine.com
We will be keeping the truth blazing just for you. New, reviews, interviews, a chat room and message boards.

Classical Music

North America

All Things Strings
webeditor@stringletter.com
www.stringsmagazine.com
The web version of Strings Magazine.

Alternate Music Press *(AMP)*
amp@audiophile.com
www.alternatemusicpress.com/classical.html
An online music archive with a world-wide readership. Since its inception in the spring of 1997, AMP has been visited by nearly six million readers.

andante magazine
info@andante.com
andante.com
News, reviews, concert reviews, essays and more.

Bass World

info@isbworldoffice.com
www.isbworldoffice.com
Serves as a vital link among the members of the international bass-playing community. Regular features include: columns for soloists, orchestra members and jazz bassists; reviews of new recordings and music; and interviews with leading bassists from around the world.

Brass Band World

editor@brassbandworld.com
www.brassbandworld.com
An Independent monthly magazine for bands.

Chamber Music Magazine

info@chamber-music.org
www.chamber-music.org
Published by Chamber Music America. We are eager to keep up with news from CMA members. Send story ideas, new CDs and books, as well as press releases by mail

Classical CD Review

bob@classicalcdreview.com
www.classicalcdreview.com
We review CDs we feel are of particular interest to us and to our readers and make no attempt to offer a comprehensive review of all new releases.

Classicalist.com

info@classicalist.com
www.classicalist.com
Adding your review to Classicalist could not be easier. Simply fill out the form giving as much information as possible. You can even post your e-mail address and a web address for added benefit. Your review should be added automatically.

Classics Today

editors@classicstoday.com
www.classicstoday.com
Each day, a minimum of five (5) feature reviews are selected by the editors to appear on the front page of the site. The "daily five" also are visible and accessible from all individual review pages. The selection of the "daily five" is a matter of editorial discretion.

Culture Kiosque

klassiknet@culturekiosque.com
www.culturekiosque.com/klassik
CD and performance reviews, interviews and feature stories bring you the best in classical music.

Early Music America

info@earlymusic.org
earlymusic.org
News and newsmakers. Artist profiles and interviews. Record reviews. Festivals and workshops. Early music education and controversial issues.

Early Music NEWS

info@earlymusicla.org
www.earlymusicla.org
Features reviews of early music CD recordings and other related topics.

La Folia

editor@lafolia.com
www.lafolia.com
Online review site.

Guitar Review

mail@guitarreview.com
www.guitarreview.com
Classical guitar news, reviews, new recordings etc.

The Horn Call

editor@hornsociety.org
www.hornsociety.org
Each issue includes news and announcements, feature articles, clinics, music and recording reviews, workshop reports, biographical features and advertisements for horn-related products and services.

Independent Reviewer Dr. Karl F. Miller

lyaa071@uts.cc.utexas.edu
I review and broadcast releases on independent labels. My reviews have been published in our local paper, the Austin American Statesman and classical.net. My interest is less familiar repertoire, from late romantic to the present.

International Trombone Association Journal

www.ita-web.org
The ITA Journal has been in production since 1971 with a series of newsletters printed from 1973 to 1980. Published quarterly since 1982, it is edited by Vern Kagarice and includes scholarly articles, trombone news, job announcements and literature and record reviews.

International Trumpet Guild

cdreviews@trumpetguild.org
www.trumpetguild.org
Founded in 1974 to promote communications among trumpet players around the world and to improve the artistic level of performance, teaching and literature associated with the trumpet.

MUSIC & VISION

www.mvdaily.com
A daily music magazine on the internet. It deals principally with music other than jazz and pop, encouraging and educating young writers about serious music.

The New Music Connoisseur

publisher@newmusicon.org
www.newmusicon.org
A newsletter focusing on the work of the composers of our time, with additional coverage of rare and neglected classical music from all national and ethnic sources.

NewMusicBox

Frank J. Oteri frank@amc.net
www.newmusicbox.org
Dedicated to the promulgation of non-commercial music by American composers (so-called classical music, jazz, theatre, experimental and electronic music etc.). We don't "review" per se, but we feature any new CD that includes repertoire by American composers (each with a RealAudio sample).

The Online Trombone Journal

www.trombone.org
Dedicated to the advancement of the trombone, its literature and pedagogy by using the technologies of the Internet to share thoughts, ideas, information and philosophies pertaining to the same.

Opera Base

mike.gibb@operabase.org
www.operabase.com
The most comprehensive online resource for opera, including details of international productions, recordings, libretti and artists.

The Opera Critic

michael@theoperacritic.com
theoperacritic.com
Providing published reviews, articles and news about opera and opera companies worldwide.

La Scena Musicale *Canada*

lucie@scena.org
www.scena.org
We do publish reviews from independent labels on occasion, if we feel the product is worthwhile. Readers will find interviews, profiles and reviews of musicians and the music scene in the perspective of local, national and international interest.

Sequenza21

Jerry jbowles@bellatlantic.net
www.sequenza21.com
We cover contemporary classical music with a particular emphasis on the work of living composers. In addition to news, interviews and featured composers, the site highlights 16-20 new CDs each month as "Editor's Picks".

Strings Magazine

editors.st@stringletter.com
www.stringsmagazine.com
The magazine for all those who love playing the violin, viola, cello, bass or fiddle.

Turok's Choice

tchoice@concentric.net
www.concentric.net/~Tchoice
I do a monthly newsletter reviewing new classical CDs. I am happy to consider anything I am sent for inclusion.

USOperaweb.com

rwb@usoperaweb.com
www.usoperaweb.com
Online magazine devoted to American Opera.

Web Concert Hall

webconcerthall@usa.com
www.webconcerthall.com
For performers we provide a new venue, especially to those performers who have little opportunity to present themselves to a wide enough audience to make their work known and appreciated. Many very able performers enjoy limited if any opportunity to reach a wide or an extremely sophisticated audience, typically because of geography and money.

World Guitarist

Gunnar Eisel geisel@worldguitarist.com
www.worldguitarist.com
Daily News Coverage for the World Classical Guitar Community.

Europe

Czech Republic

Harmonie

info@muzikus.cz
casopisy.muzikus.cz/harmonie
Classical music and jazz magazine.

Finland

Finnish Music Quarterly

ulla.lahdensuo@gramex.fi
www.musicfinland.com/classical/fmq
FMQ contains articles written by music experts from both Finland and abroad. It covers all aspects of the Finnish music scene and keeps track of what happens in Finland.

France

Avant-Scène Opéra
premieres.loges@wanadoo.fr
www.asopera.com
A publication for professionals and large public of music-lovers.

Paris Transatlantic.com
www.paristransatlantic.com
Global Coverage of New, Classical and Avant-Garde Music, Film and Dance: The Paris New Music Review, founded in 1993, was re-structured as an online magazine in 1995: Paris Transatlantic.com. We feature the best of the European, Japanese and American Avant-Garde.

Germany

Crescendo
crescendo@portmedia.de
www.crescendo-online.de
Deutschlands Klassik Magazin

klassik.com
redaktion@klassik.com
www.klassik.com

Klassik-Heute.com
info@klassik-treff.de
www.klassik-heute.com
Musik, Festival, Konzert, Oper, Künstler, CD, Komponist. Das spartenübergreifende Internetportal bietet Informationen aus allen Bereichen der Klassischen Musik.

Musica Sacra
redaktion@musica-sacra-online.de
www.musica-sacra-online.de
Die Zeitschrift für katholische Kirchenmusik.

Online Muzik Magazin
leserbriefe@omm.de
www.omm.de
Das erste deutschsprachige Musikmagazin im Internet.

Oper&Tanz
redaktion@operundtanz.de
www.operundtanz.de

Das Opernglas
Opernglas@compuserve.com
www.opernglas.de

Italy

Audio Review
tommolini@tommolini.com
www.audioreview.it

Hortus Musicus
info@hortusmusicus.com
www.hortusmusicus.com
Italian Early Music magazine.

PromArt
promart@promart.it
www.promart.it
Classical music in Italy. News, reviews and an artist database.

The Netherlands

Het ORGEL
fidom@bart.nl
www.hetorgel.nl
Europe's oldest magazine on Organ Art. ORGEL is a magazine of Dutch origin.

Spain

FILOMUSICA Classical music and Opera
Daniel Mateos filomusica@terra.es
www.filomusica.com
We have a section for reviewing classical music CD's. We review all kinds of classical music, also independent, but not specially independent.

Goldberg
www.goldberg-magazine.com
We review only CD's of early music, that is, the music written before 1750. If there are independent performers who perform early music, it could be interesting for us. We use to review Cds from a very small independent record labels. Our system is: we offer the CD to a critic and if they accept it, we publish the review. They accept in general a wide range of CD's. But, if the review is bad for the CD, we aren't responsible.

Mundo Clasico
redaccion@mundoclasico.com
www.mundoclasico.com
Articles, interviews, reviews and news.

Opera Actual
director@operaactual.es
www.operaactual.es
"Spain's only opera magazine."

Ritmo
correo@ritmo.es
www.ritmo.es
Disfrute del mundo de la música clásica desde Internet. Los aficionados españoles, así como de otros países de habla hispana, tienen ya a su disposición un Portal de música clásica en Internet que se llama RITMO.

Sweden

Musik Dramatik
torbjorn.eriksson@mbox303.swipnet.se
md.partitur.se
Sweden's foremost Opera Magazine!

Sonoloco Record Reviews
loco.nordin@mbox200.swipnet.se
sonoloco.just.nu
Any kind of music may be reviewed, as long as it is original and honest and has its very own artistic integrity. Record labels and artists should feel free to send CDs for reviews. We also welcome CD-Rs, DATs and cassettes of yet unpublished works.

Switzerland

Brass Bulletin
jm@brass-bulletin.com
www.brass-bulletin.ch
Our "Young Artists" section brings you the artists of today.

Cosmopolis Musikarchiv
feedback@cosmopolis.ch
www.cosmopolis.ch/musik.htm
We review music by major labels and independent artists. The German and the English edition are not identical.

HarpEvents Magazine
office@harpa.com
www.harpa.com
News, announcements, CDs and articles. We can also create your own web within the framework of HARPA Web: An ideal place, since thousands of interested people visit our Internet web site every month.

Musik & Theater
musikundtheater@bluewin.ch
www.musikundtheater.ch

United Kingdom

BBC Music Magazine
www.bbc.co.uk/music/classical
www.bbc.co.uk/radio3/classical
The world's best-selling monthly classical music magazine, with a monthly circulation of over 80,000. Each issue contains a mine of invaluable information, including more than 150 CD reviews, interviews, features, news, comment and analysis from our expert writers. You'll also find a comprehensive listing of live concerts and opera and all the music broadcasts on TV and radio.

The Classical Source
editor@classicalsource.com
www.classicalsource.com
Providing news and reviews.

ClassicalLink *MusicWeb*
Len@musicweb.uk.net
www.classicallink.com
MusicWeb is now part of the ClassicAll network. Our partner site within the ClassicAll network is www.ludwigvanWeb.com You will now be able to hear extract from reviews of any of our partner labels.

Horn Magazine
mike@british-horn.org
www.british-horn.org
News, Views, Reviews and the Hornascope, which makes conventional astrology look predictable.

International Record Review
editorial@recordreview.co.uk
www.recordreview.co.uk
Our mission is to review classical compact discs from all over the world irrespective of distribution arrangements. Some of the smaller labels simply don't have the opportunity to secure distribution in the major countries outside their own. Unlike many other classical magazines we actively seek out these CDs for review.

New Classics
webmaster@new-classics.co.uk
www.new-classics.co.uk
Discover the latest classical releases, including our CD of the month.

New Notes
spnm@spnm.org.uk
www.spnm.org.uk/newnotes
The magazine of spnm - promoting new music!

Opera Magazine
editor@operamag.clara.co.uk
www.opera.co.uk
Each issue contains news, letters, interviews or profiles, reviews of performances from around the world and a diary section giving listings for all major opera-houses and forthcoming season programs.

Seen and Heard
furtwangler@btinternet.com
www.musicweb.uk.net/SandH
The Seen & Heard section constitutes the largest live music review site on the World Wide Web and is one of the many jewels in the crown of MusicWeb (UK).

The Strad
Peter Quantrill pquantrill@orpheuspublications.com
www.thestrad.com
We publish reviews each month of concerts in London and New York and of CDs of string music and string musicians. To be considered for review, the disc must be commercially available via a recognized distributor or via a secure ordering service on the net. Full details of price and distribution should be sent with the disc.

The Trombonist
EditBTS@aol.com
www.trombone-society.org.uk
The magazine of the British Trombone Society.

Australia

Opera~Opera
deg@opera-opera.com.au
www.opera-opera.com.au
Australasia's independent monthly newspaper of the musical theatre, established in 1978.

Asia

Japan

CLASSICA
iio@tka.att.ne.jp
www.classicajapan.com
Classical Music News and Links.

Korea

Classical Netizen Club
cnc.or.kr
News, CD reviews, message board and classifieds.

Country Music

This section also contains Americana, bluegrass, roots, alternative country and rockabilly publications.

Publications

United States

3rd COAST MUSIC
John Conquest john@3rdcoastmusic.com
3rdcm.austinamericana.com
Texas-based print monthly. Only indie label and self-released albums reviewed, Hillbilly, Americana, Twang, Rockabilly, Singer-Songwriters. Home of Freeform American Roots radio chart, reported to by over 100 freeform DJs.

alternativecountry.com
www.alternativecountry.com
We review music, list radio stations that play real country music, we include news and information and shortly there will be artist profiles and audio streaming

The Americana Music Guide
guide@americanamusicguide.com
www.americanamusicguide.com
Your gateway to the best in Americana music in Texas and beyond. Featuring a comprehensive guide to Americana Music Web Sites, Mailing Lists/Discussion Groups, Publications, Festivals and Music Events, Internet Radio & Streaming Audio, plus reviews of current CD releases.

Blue Suede News
shakinboss@aol.com
www.bluesuedenews.com
We cover the entire spectrum of American Roots Music, from '50 s Rock'n'Roll styles - Rockabilly and Rhythm & Blues to Country, Folk, Bluegrass, Blues, Cajun & Zydeco, Swing and you-name-it hybrids.

bluegrass now
kumr@umr.edu
www.bluegrassnow.com

The Bluegrass Page
Graylen Cook cgraylen@hotmail.com
groups.msn.com/TheBluegrassPage
Will review cds for indie artists. My core group is dedicated bluegrass fans.

Bluegrass Unlimited
editor@bluegrassmusic.com
www.bluegrassmusic.com
Created in 1966, this publication is dedicated to the furtherance of bluegrass and old-time country musicians, devotees and associates.

BluegrassAmericana.com
info@GoAmericana.com
www.AmericanaConnect.com
We invite performing Bands, Artists, Recording and Distribution Companies to send their music releases (CDs) for review.

Broadcast Texas
Cody Austin caustin@cableone.net
myweb.cableone.net/caustin
Independent Country Music Magazine.

Clink Magazine
music@clinkmagazine.com
www.clinkmagazine.com
Reviews focus on old-time, bluegrass and Americana music.

Country Grapevine
advertising@countrygrapevine.com
www.countrygrapevine.com
A grass roots newspaper about entertaining things to do concerning Country music, dance and fun. We deal primarily with Florida but we have tons of resources for other parts of the world too!

Country Interviews Online
Laura countryinterviews@yahoo.com
www.CountryInterviewsOnline.net
Country music website that reviews & does interviews with major & indie label artists. Please do NOT send MP3s.

Country Line Magazine
tj@countrylinemagazine.com
www.countrylinemagazine.com

Country Music Planet
jerry@countrymusicplanet.com
www.countrymusicplanet.com
Country music featuring independent country music singers and independent country music songwriters!

Country Music Source Magazine
Tim Jones countrymusicsource@yahoo.com
www.geocities.com/countrymusicsource
Dedicated entirely to Independent Country Artists, Songwriters, Labels, Publishers and Fans. We emphasize Traditional Country Music. Everything published in CMS is entirely Independent. It's a great way for any Indie Country Insider or Fan to be seen and heard.

Country Standard Time
countryst@aol.com
countrystandardtime.com
Your Guide To Roadhouse, Roots and Rockabilly.

Country Western Corner
Ed and Barbara King Ekingehk@cs.com
www.wingnut.net/ehk.htm
Any artist or songwriter may send their press package to us and they will have a review for sure (as space allows) and also a possible article in a future issue of the magazine. We cater to Country and Gospel music, but will also accept R&B, Jazz, Pop and Cajun.

Cyber-Country
editor@cyber-country.com
www.cyber-country.com

Flatpicking Guitar
info@flatpick.com
www.flatpick.com
A bi-monthly periodical and companion audio CD, dedicated to presenting all aspects of the art of flat picking the acoustic guitar. Our goal is to help you increase your own skill level and enjoyment of this fine art.

Freight Train Boogie
frater@sonic.net
www.freighttrainboogie.com
Features news and reviews of Roots music with an emphasis on Alt.Country or Americana music, including some Rock, Folk and Blues and everything in between.

Great Lakes Twang
gltwang@hotmail.com
www.geocities.com/Nashville/Stage/9596/gltwang.html
Bands or performers should be from the Great Lakes area (Minnesota, Wisconsin, Illinois, Indiana, Michigan, Ohio, West Pennsylvania, West New York and Southern Ontario). Music must be of the Americana/Roots-Rock/Alt-Country genre.

Grindstone Magazine
grind55@aol.com
www.grindstonemagazine.com
Your Guide To Roadhouse, Roots And Rockabilly.

Honky Tonk Angels
tammy@honkytonkangels.com
www.honkytonkangels.com
I would love to have independent musicians send me their music for review and I would love to put your songs on my jukebox!

iBluegrass
gogden@ibest.net
www.ibluegrass.com
We will accept unsolicited material for review and submission for publication. Please follow the guidelines stated at our website for submitting material to us.

MandoZine

john@mandozine.com
www.mandozine.com
MandoZine is intended as a resource for those who are just starting out, the more advanced players that are always ready to help the beginners and those who don't play, but love the music.

Marq's Texas Music Kitchen

marq@lonestarwebstation.com
www.lonestarwebstation.com
To submit a recording for consideration for review, please mail one copy of the album with a brief cover letter with your name & address, e-mail address and web site URL, if applicable.

Miles of Music *(MOM Zine)*

corrie@milesofmusic.com
www.milesofmusic.com

Miss Lana's Texicana Music Central

lana@misslana.com
www.misslana.com
This website is designed to express my love for Texas and Texicana music. Reviews will be done in the order received and you will be notified by e-mail when their review is posted on the site.

My Kind of Country

marli@mkoc.com
www.mkoc.com
Country music at it's finest from yesterday's legends, to the newest up and coming country singers and songwriters. Featured in Real Audio and video.

No Depression

NoDepress@aol.com
www.nodepression.net
A bimonthly magazine covering alternative-country music (whatever that is). We exist primarily as an actual old-fashioned in-print publication, available at record stores, bookstores and newsstands across the U.S.A. (and beyond) and via mail-order subscriptions.

Old-Time Herald Online

info@oldtimeherald.org
www.oldtimeherald.org
Old-time music shares origins, influences and musical characteristics with roots music across America. Our magazine casts a wide net, highlighting the Southeastern tradition while opening its pages to kindred and comparable traditions and new directions.

Rockabilly Central

rob@rockabilly.net
www.rockabilly.net
The ideal starting point in your search for rockabilly music. We have links to just about every rockabilly band and site out there, along with lots of tour dates; reviews press articles, photos etc.

The Rockabilly Hall of Fame

ww686@victoria.tc.ca
www.rockabillyhall.com
Great rockabilly compilations and individual artists, including Italy's world famous Dimaggio Bros. Label use available to rockabilly performers.

Rockzilla.net

reviews@rockzilla.net
www.rockzilla.net
Our primary focus is Americana music. Even though we are small and our writers are not professional journalists, we take what we do very seriously. Any review posted on the Rockzillaworld site will be fair.

Rootin' Around

kevrave@rootinaround.com
www.rootinaround.com
Ragtag roots music review, surveying the best (and worst) of yesterday and today's country, blues, conjunto, juju, bluegrass, jazz, hokum, old-timey, ska, rockabilly, merengue, surf and kazoo band releases.

Roots Music Report

rmr@rootsmusicreport.com
www.rootsmusicreport.com
We feature weekly music charts, reviews and articles on roots music, its artists and labels. These charts will identify and help develop new recording artists, independent record labels and bring to light the careers of many exceptional but otherwise "unknown" performers.

STARDUST COUNTRY GAZETTE

Colonel Buster Doss cbd@vallnet.com
www.stardustcountrymusic.com
A Country Monthly Magazine dedicated to helping Indie Artists!

TwangCast

wkg@austin78704.com
www.twangcast.com
Articles and reviews on Twang and Americana music from around the country.

Western Beat

billy@westernbeat.com
www.westernbeat.com
A place of musical variety... A place where musical integrity rules, not the bottom line... Where naming the "sound" is irrelevant. It is a place of No Borderlines and -Welcome! You have arrived!

Canada

Fiddler Magazine

fiddlermagazine@ns.sympatico.ca
www.fiddle.com
Current feature articles, regular columns and tunes are summarized. Excerpts of primary features are provided. Should these tantalizing tidbits lead to an insatiable desire for more, subscription information and prices are provided.

Opry North

www.oprynorth.com
Canada's #1 site for everything country, dedicated to providing information and support for the artists and fun for the fans.

Belgium

Roots Town Music Magazine

roots.town@glo.be
members.tripod.com/RootsTown
Het biedt blues, country, soul, cajun, rootsrock, broederlijk naast Zuid-Amerikaanse, Afrikaanse, Aziatische en Europese muziek. Het bevat een breed aanbod van interviews, artikelen, concert- informatie en talrijke recensies van bekende en veelal ook minder bekende releases op kleine, onafhankelijke labels.

France

Country Music France

pierre@countryfr.com
country-music-france.com
French directory about country music, bluegrass, old time, traditional and new country.

Le Cri du Coyote

Jacques Brémond Cricoyote@aol.com
countryfr.com
A 16 year old fanzine, dealing with American "black & white roots music" (country, bluegrass, rock 'n' roll, Cajun, folk, tex-mex, songwriting, whatever you call it, from Alt-country to No Depression or even Americana).

Germany

COUNTRY JUKEBOX

Max W. Achatz achatz@countryjukebox.de
www.countryjukebox.de
I have written about independent country music for years. Country Jukebox is published monthly in Germany's Country Circle magazine as well as on the web.

CountryHome

iwde@iwde.de
www.countryhome.de

Keep it Country

webmaster@countrynet.de
www.countrynet.de
Online Magazine in German and English of the Independent CMA Germany, with CD Reviews, Stories about Singers, Songwriters, Bands etc.

Insurgent Country

settler@mailer.uni-marburg.de
www.insurgentcountry.com

Slovakia

Country Fest

www.countryfest.sk

Svonky

jan.bratinka@bluegrass.sk
www.bluegrass.sk/zvonky

Sweden

Anita Haglund *Country Music Reviewer*

anita-haglund@privat.utfors.se
I write for two magazines, Kountry Korral Magazine and River Post. I also have radio shows from time to time. I'm interested in writing about Bluegrass, Country and Country & Bluegrass gospel music. Are you interested in sending me your music? I might also write an article on you if there is something interesting to write about. My address is: Anita Haglund, Duettvägen 3, 284 37 PERSTORP, Sweden

Switzerland

Bluegrass Europe Magazine

www.bluegrass.de
We know that you have been waiting for this - a magazine dedicated to bringing you closer to what's happening in bluegrass music in Europe, National and international news, concert dates, feature articles and reviews and much more!

United Kingdom

Alan Cackett *Country Music Journalist*

alan@acackett.freeserve.co.uk
www.alancackett.net
Here you will find information about much of what is happening today in Country music, both in the UK and abroad. I will feature show and album reviews, tour information, news, artist information as well as promotional material for artists visiting the UK.

Country Music Gazette
www.mkoc.com/Gazette/gazette.htm
Published bi-monthly, features articles covering the latest news on country music around the world. There are many features on the new artists to hit the scene as well as reviving interest in the legends of country.

Country Music People
info@countrymusicpeople.com
www.countrymusicpeople.com
In depth reviews of latest CDs, videos and books. Star features and interviews. News and tour information. Country Music Questions page. Charts and much more...

Country Music Roundup
editor@cmru.co.uk
www.cmru.co.uk
Now you can read highlights of the magazine online. Of course the best way to ensure you get ALL the news straight away is to SUBSCRIBE. Remember to check back to this site regularly as we add more of the printed magazine each week.

Fiddle On
fiddleon@freenetname.co.uk
www.fiddleon.co.uk
A publication aimed specifically at the UK fiddle player.

House of Plank
hop@beeb.net
hop.members.beeb.net
A FREE monthly magazine that gives an 'alternative' view on bluegrass music.

Maverick
editor@maverick-country.com
www.maverick-country.com
We are breaking the mould of how country music is perceived in the UK. The emphasis is firmly on music - no line dancing, an absence of MOR pap, glitter, belly buttons and other clutter that gets in the way of the music.

Metro Country
ray@metrocountry.co.uk
www.metrocountry.co.uk
Any artist or record company who would like their CDs reviewed on this website and played on Metro Country, please E mail me.

roots-and-branches.com
brumbeat@blueyonder.co.uk
www.roots-and-branches.com
A magazine dedicated to that impossible category, er, roots and branches. A category that happily embraces the obvious - Americana / country, folk, world and blues music. Contact us with news, views, gig dates etc.

Australia

Country Goss
www.countrygoss.com.au

Ice International
Deb Minter minters@spiderweb.com.au
www.minters.spiderweb.com.au
A worldwide network of Entertainers Media and Industry. Artist news, editorials etc.

Japan

Moonshiner
info@bomserv.com
www.bomserv.com/MoonShiner

Dance Music

North America

United States

25
mheumann@earthlink.net
www.hauntedink.com
For each review, I not only provide a complete run-down of the CD, but I provide links to sound samples, fan sites, official sites and online music stores where you can buy the CD.

Alpha-n-Omega Magazine
anomag@aol.com
www.alphabeats.com
Focused on providing a hub for both novice and professional music producers. Our site offers interviews with established producers, news, tips, music reviews and more. We believe the music producer deserves some light in an industry that focuses on the artist.

DJ Times
www.djtimes.com
Considered the "bible of the industry" for the professional DJ. Every month, more mobile and club DJs turn to DJ Times than any other industry publication, making it their primary source for products, technologies, news and information.

djsinbox.com
djsinbox@hotmail.com
djsinbox.com
Please send promotional material for review to: djsinbox.com, 6002 S. Switzer Ave. Tampa, FL. 33611

Freebass
mail@freebass.tv
www.freebass.tv
We provide an outlet for people to find out about music that isn't being written about in the mainstream press or even the majority of electronic dance music magazine.

groovefactory.com
groovemasters@groovefactory.com
www.groovefactory.com
We have a mission to provide our listeners with the best house music on the web via live and pre-recorded shows from the top DJ's and clubs in the world.

housemusic.com
info@housemusic.com
www.housemusic.com
The website for house music on the web. Started by a dj for serious dj's and househeads, DJ Eldon has put together a site for dj charts, record label links and reviews of new music.

Igloo Magazine!
editor@igloomag.com
www.igloomag.com
Your online source for Electronic Music coverage.

Jive Magazine
jewels@jivemagazine.com
www.jivemagazine.com

JungleVoodoo.com
sharee@junglevoodoo.com
www.junglevoodoo.com
An interactive online magazine for drum 'n bass. 12" reviews, album reviews, interviews, DJ booking info and Up 'N' Comin' DJ/Producer/MC profiles.

LiveDJs.com
darin@livedjs.com
www.livedjs.com
Performances live on the internet of electronica music (all genres) turntablism mainly but our studio is wired for bands also. DJs still cannot sell there skills on cd!

Lotus Magazine
thomas@lotusmag.com
www.lotusmag.com
News, reviews, articles etc.

Ministry of Sound
arnie@ministryofsound.com
www.ministryofsound.com

The Official DJ Style Web Site
DJ Style djstyle@djstyle.com
www.djstyle.com
Free Dance Music Reviews specializing in underground progressive house, trance and techno. Can add your own link and post on the WWWBoard.

Pax Acidus
Larry Zoumas sloth@paxacidus.com
www.paxacidus.com
Pax Acidus is a techno literary website dedicated to the underground arts of site and sound.

Progressive Sounds
charnish@progressive-sounds.com
www.progressive-sounds.com
Bringing you the latest in progressive trance, progressive house and progressive breaks.

The Selekta
info@selekta.com
www.selekta.com
As a collective, we are constantly seeking out individuals who can be defined as exceptional for their thoughts, ideas and their contribution to the dance and electronic music communities.

Sonic Curiosity
matt@soniccuriosity.com
www.soniccuriosity.com
The alternative/electronic music review site. Do not expect us to review music from unrelated genres (like rap, C&W, religious, folk and blues).

Synthpopalooza
bobclark@korrnet.org
www.synthpop.fm
An audio resource which promotes and exposes the genre of SYNTHPOP ... The BEST MUSIC IN THE UNIVERSE! It is my aim here to promote and expose new synthpop acts ... revisit the past with synthpop classics and one hit wonders ... and dig up rare and obscure synthpop music no one even knew existed!

synthpop.net
synthpop.net
CD's, demo's, mp3's.... the list is long how artists choose to reach out to the outside world. Reaching their own masses. Of course, we review all this and the more promotion material we get in, the more we review and the more information for you to find here.

URB
rroker@urb.com
www.urb.com

UTRaves.org
element@utrave.org
www.utrave.org
MP3s, events, dance, music, culture, community.

Canada

Klublife Magazine
nicola@klublife.com
www.klublife.com
Up to date music reviews and articles.

Cognition
Andrew cognition@techno.ca
techno.ca/cognition
An online magazine encompassing news, interviews, reviews and commentaries on electronic music, along with RealAudio features.

dub.ca
dubmaster@dub.ca
www.dub.ca
The collective output of the dub.ca staff - musings, thoughts, rants, essays about music, DJing and the surrounding culture.

STiFFY.CA
thenaughtydeejay@hotmail.com
www.stiffy.ca
If you would like your demo hosted on this site, please indicate in the email and we will let you know how to upload it! Send your music for review too!

Tribe Magazine
editor@tribe.ca
www.tribemagazine.com
Canada's leading after dark entertainment magazine. In TRIBE you'll find gossip, news and lots of photographs taken at events. The magazine is music driven but inspired by the people who go out after dark.

Europe

Estonia

Club Arena
clubarena@clubarena.com
www.clubarena.com
Please send your d&b promos (preferably 12") to the address listed on our site. Promos will be reverberated as well as in Circulation news as in our website.

Finland

5HT
www.sci.fi/~phinnweb/5HT
Our purpose is to spread information and educate mainly on Finnish but also international electronic dance, listening and avant-garde music scene, rave and club culture, artists, record labels and underground in their various sub genres, forms and history.

Findance
antti.niemela@findance.com
www.findance.com

Music Mission
music.mission@mission.fi
www.kauhajoki.fi/musicmission

France

Atome
atome@atome.com
www.atome.com
DJ's, labels, producers, promoters, webmasters, ravers, hoovers: send us your charts, promo-copies, demos, news, presents (!)

Speedfonk
speedfonk@speedfonk.net
www.speedfonk.net
Drum and bass jungle.

Germany

Motor
webmaster@motor.de
www.motor.de

Techno Online
info@techno.de
www.techno.de
News, reviews, charts, interviews etc.

Italy

Discoid
discopiu@infotel.it
www.discoid.it
Dedicated to DJs (and Dance Music), with reviews, regular columns, charts and advance news (direct from top DJs and producers in Italy and abroad), as well as the Home Pages of many of them.

THEVibes.net
info@thevibes.net
www.thevibes.net

The Netherlands

After Dark
info@afterdarkmagazine.nl
www.afterdarkmagazine.nl

Xpander
info@xpander.nl
www.xpander.nl
Forward thinking dance music and global clubbing.

Russia

jungle.ru
www.jungle.ru

United Kingdom

Absorb
enquiries@absorb.org
www.absorb.org
Dedicated primarily to electronic music.

Burnitblue.com
jim.byers@burnitblue.com
www.burnitblue.com
We aim to capture the excitement and diversity of dance culture and provide the dance music and clubbing fraternity with an entertaining and highly irreverent resource. To send music to our reviewers, contact me and I will distribute it to the requisite reviewer.

DJmag
www.djmag.com
We have been long revered for our in-depth and up-front coverage of the exciting dance music scene. Unlike most of the other dance music titles DJ magazine is not a watery, 'dumbed down' take on what is going on, but a full strength dose.

Drum n' Bass Arena
www.breakbeat.co.uk
Welcome to the biggest & most up-to-date Drum'n'Bass site on the internet. We aim to bring you all the latest info on everything to do with d'n'b.

Epidemik
webmaster@epidemik.co.uk
www.epidemik.net
See yourself as the next Dr Dre/MJ Cole/Dillinja/Tall Paul/Aitken? Cut a track and now lost in the world of arse-licking? Then let them come to you by promoting yourself!

FLY Magazine
www.fly.co.uk
Our fly review section is one of the most extensive on the web.

Free Radical Sounds
bimble@freeradicalsounds.com
www.freeradicalsounds.com
This much visited UK based e-zine run by DJ's and writers from the UK underground scene, is here to shed light. To shed light on artists and opinions not usually given the space to do so.

gaialive Radio Reviews
www.gaialive.co.uk

Haywire
www.haywire.co.uk
Rather than have a host of different DJs and producers we only work with a selection of artists, those who we feel belong here, who often collaborate on projects and whose music was the true inspiration of this haywire hub.

Hyperdub
steve@hyperdub.com
www.hyperdub.com

jungle kidz
www.basedonbass.com
DnB/Jungle Site Displaying MC Samples, Dubplates, DJ Sets, DnB Reviews/Reports, Pics and Artist Bios! Site based out of SF.

M8 Magazine
jill@m8magazine.com
www.m8magazine.com
The most authoritative dance music and club culture magazine in the UK. The site covers, the latest music reviews, fashion, babes, a lively chatroom and a daily update of all the music news.

Miscreat
tesco@miscreat.com
www.miscreat.com
A site for musicians, bands, clubs, DJs, visual arts, or anything at all music related. The site is mainly geared towards non-commercial dance music, but other types of music are welcome.

mixmag
www.mixmag.net

Muzik Magazine
www.muzik.co.uk
Magazine for all dance and trance music news from around the world.

off its face
neil@offitsface.com
www.offitsface.com
If you are a producer or involved with a record label and would like to have your latest dance music 12" releases reviewed (with a sound clip), please contact Neil.

Overload Media

office@overloadmedia.co.uk
www.overloadmedia.co.uk
Committed to providing free, up-to-date information concerning electronic music and wider-ranging issues.

Rollin

info@rollin.com
www.rollin.com

solidpulse.net

www.solidpulse.net
Drum N Bass, Garage, House, Hip Hop, RnB. Underground radio stations, clubs, interviews, record reviews.

stage4

chris@stage4.co.uk
www.stage4.co.uk
An ezine for the wired artist featuring net DJs, mp3 artists, video and film makers, poets and the best of independent webcasting.

tiptopmusic.com

info@tiptopmusic.com
www.tiptopmusic.com
Our vision was to create a website that was independent from the outset. Our raison d'etre is music: house, deep house, other. Sounds that speak one language regardless of language. Sustenance for the global soul.

Australia

Resident Advisor

paul@residentadvisor.com.au
www.residentadvisor.com.au
We felt there was an opportunity to provide a website that gave free access to unbiased news, interviews, reviews, photos and various other forms of information related to the Australian/Global dance scene and culture.

Spraci

support@spraci.com
spraci.cia.com.au

TransZfusion

Fuzion@tranzfusion.net
www.tranzfusion.net

Experimental Music

Experimental, Electronic, Ambient, Avant Garde, Psychedelic and Noise.

North America

United States

almostcool.org

wabbyboy@almostcool.org
www.almostcool.org
Updated weekly, this long-running site features a huge music review archive of independent and electronic artists.

ambience for the masses

www.sleepbot.com/ambience
Excellent archive of artist profiles and reviews.

aural innovations

jkranitz@aural-innovations.com
aural-innovations.com
Our interpretation of spacerock is intentionally broad and includes psychedelia and related electronic music. Although we cover the great pioneers, we also strive to be a source of recognition for lesser known artists and those who are making tapes or burning CDR's of their work in their homes.

Bullfight Party

info@bullfightparty.org
www.bullfightparty.org
A collective venture dedicated to quixotic multimedia philanthropy.

Chaos Control

bob@chaoscontrol.com
www.chaoscontrol.com

Choler Magazine

music@choler.com
www.choler.com
We would love to hear from you, whether you're a reader, a writer looking for a chance to get some exposure, or an artist looking to be reviewed or profiled.

The Circular Cosmic Spot

hal9000@sdriver.com
www.sdriver.com/spot
Electronic/experimental music reviews and news. The bleeding edge of the outer limits.

Computer Music Journal

mitpress.mit.edu/e-journals/Computer-Music-Journal
A quarterly Journal that covers a wide range of topics related to digital audio signal processing and electro acoustic music.

Cool and Strange Music

coolstrge@aol.com
www.coolandstrange.com
We are proudly the FIRST AND FOREMOST regularly published PRINT magazine devoted to unusual music, comedy records and other oddball forms of music. Each issue of Cool & Strange Music! Chock full of CD reviews.

Danse Assembly Music Network (DAMn!)

DAMnet@aol.com
hometown.aol.com/DAMnet
3x yearly - 5,000 copies 2 colour cover b/w inside pages.

Deconstructing Man

www.deconstructing-man.com
Isn't the purpose of art to elicit a response? I love seeing someone else's expressive work and it inevitably becomes intrinsically tied into my own life upon viewing. And this site is here to comment on that. Not the art, but the response.

disquiet.com

marc@disquiet.com
www.disquiet.com
Reflections on ambient/electronic music and interviews with the people who make it.

DOT:ALT

xvscott3@aol.com
dot-alt.co.uk
The focus is on music and art that sets a challenge to popular culture as it stands. We try to cover music that is progressive, creative and interesting and has thought behind it.

Dream Magazine

geo@gv.net
www.dreamgeo.com
This magazine exists mainly because of music, much of it psychedelic (old and new), experimental, pop, jazz, folk, or somewhere happily beyond classification.

The Electrogarden Network

info@electrogarden.com
www.electrogarden.net
Our mission is to promote the underground electronic music scene by providing our audience with exposure to the artists in that scene, developing an online community of like-minded individuals and combining as much related content as possible into a single Internet entity while serving up such content in the most aesthetic and interactive fashion.

Electro-music.com

admin@electro-music.com
electro-music.com
Dedicated to experimental, electro-acoustic and electronic music and art. Articles, reviews and editorials plus an online store where Independent artists can sell their CDs.

The Electronic Music Network

www.electronicscene.com
You will find several services here - all of which are focused on bringing the music to the people and to acknowledge the people behind the music. The Electronic Music Scene is moving rapidly, we are building an infrastructure which will grow with it and if we have done our jobs correctly... the Scene will come together globally and everyone will be have a great time.

Electronic Musician

www.emusician.com
The #1 magazine for musicians recording and producing music in a home or personal studio. EM supports the musician from the initial musical concept to the final mix down and the live gig.

electronicmusic.com

core@electronicmusic.com
www.electronicmusic.com
Originally conceived in 1995 by electronic music composer Basehart Snitch. We soon attracted a small team of dedicated electronic musicians, technicians and enthusiasts.

Exposé

ptlk@expose.org
www.expose.org
Specializing in the music the record and radio industries stubbornly choose to ignore. Our focus is outside the mainstream, in the progressive and experimental hinterlands where rock meets jazz, classical meets folk, electronic meets avant-garde and so on.

feelingandform.com

David Sharp dsharp@feelingandform.com
www.feelingandform.com
Our primary goal is to provide a platform to get people involved with one another and while our members work on getting connected to each other, we will work at getting their work exposed, getting professionals to see their work and anything else we can do to help perpetuate their goals.

Free City Media

Heidi@FreeCityMedia.Com
www.freecitymedia.com
A magazine about psychedelic music and fresh perspectives - all hyped up with intense low res graphics.

Get Underground
shlomo@underground.net
www.getunderground.com
Our focus is on the personal and experimental. We are interested in writings and arts related more to personal impressions and experimental visions/techniques than to political or social reporting, commentary or art.

Go Ahead, You Review It!
Don Campau campaudj@jps.net
lonelywhistle.tripod.com/GoAheadYouReviewIt
This is a review site dealing with underground music, film and art. You are invited to write and participate. The guidelines are easy: you send me a review of something like a CD or film in a plain e mail. Not an attachment. Simple. Now, I am asking that you write intelligently and provocatively, with a sense of humor and personal insight. Anything goes...let's hear your opinion.

Halana
halana@halana.com
www.halana.com
Dedicated to the discovery and glorification of the adventurous and experimental in music and sound— field recordings and soundscapes; improvisation; modern composition; sound art; site-specific and electroacoustic works; collage and found sound.

Harsh Reality Music
Chris aliensix@bellsouth.net
www.homemademusic.com/artists/harshreality
Trying to bring you the best in experimental electronic music since 1984. Styles to name a few are experimental electronics, space rock, industrial, ambient, avant-garde, power electronics & much more.

Innerviews
feedback@innerviews.org
www.innerviews.org

Leonardo Music Journal
mitpress.mit.edu/Leonardo
Devoted to aesthetic and technical issues in contemporary music and sonic arts. Each thematic volume features artists/writers from around the world, representing a wide range of stylistic viewpoints and includes an audio CD or CD-ROM.

Lunar Magazine
www.lunarmagazine.com
To educate, promote, discuss, inform and unite electronic dance music and the associated culture in the greater Atlanta area and beyond.

Music Ramblings
me@ram.org
www.ram.org/music
Hundreds of album reviews, concert reviews and interviews!

MusicEmissions.com
dscanland@hotmail.com
www.musicemissions.com
A music review site that focuses on non-mainstream music. Sure, every once and a while a semi-mainstream album makes its way in, but overall we do a pretty good job at keeping the music fairly different and independent.

NakedPoetry.com
lovemeadorememakemebreakfast@hotmail.com
www.nakedpoetry.com
If you are an artist or musician who wishes for your work to be reviewed, send us samples and photos by the means listed in our Submission Formats.

NoiseWeb
tspann@charterhouse.net
noiseweb.com

Neumu
contact@neumu.net
neumu.net
Neumu is where you will find the work of artists following their creative vision. You'll find writers taking chances, experimenting with the way they communicate.

new-music.net
info@new-music.net
www.new-music.net
An irregularly published New Music ezine introducing artists and their music which cannot be adequately labeled, categorized or stuffed into any of the established genres fabricated by the Music Industry.

Seven
seven@nezzwerk.com
www.nezzwerk.com/seven
Anything music-related, mostly electronic music, but if something outside of the genre deserves attention - it will be mentioned as well.

SIGNAL to NOISE
Pete Gershon editor@signaltonoisemagazine.org
www.signaltonoisemagazine.org
The journal of improvised and experimental music.

SynGate.net
mail@syngate.net
www.syngate.net
The gate to synthesizer based music.

Synthmuseum.com
info@synthmuseum.com
www.synthmuseum.com
Created out of a need for a centralized, organized and authoritative resource for information about vintage electronic musical instruments. We offer objective and technically accurate information on synthesizers and drum machines manufactured before 1990.

Technotica Times
Times@technotica.com
www.technotica.com
Please note that it is a 'work in progress' and that additional editing of content, including reviews continues to keep it fresh and timely.

(((Thump))) Radio
brian@thump-radio.com
www.thump-radio.com
Dedicated to exposing local talent and artists from around the world.

XLR8R
letters@xlr8r.com
www.xlr8r.com
After much hard work, XLR8R is now over 100 color pages every issue, often comes with a free sampler CD and is internationally distributed.

Zhopka Records
Peter Mezensky peter@zhopkarecords.com
www.zhopkarecords.com
Artists can submit experimental music CDs to be reviewed and sold by our site.

Zu Casa
thedonkey@zucasa.com
www.zucasa.com
An online laboratory for exhibition, performance and promotion of experimental and improvised music.

Canada

earsay
info@earsay.com
www.earsay.com
Gutsy, new, experimental, electronic music.

Feedback Monitor
greg@feedbackmonitor.com
www.stainedproductions.com
A website and radio program dedicated to new sounds in electronic and experimental music. You'll find reviews/interviews of electronic and experimental music/artists.

Incursion Music Review
info@incursion.org
www.incursion.org
Committed to exploring new forms of music and sound art. Anomalous music for curious ears.

musicworks
sound@musicworks.ca
www.musicworks.ca
For more than twenty years, MUSICWORKS has provided readers worldwide with artists' perspectives on the exploration of new and possible music and sound. — sounds as yet unfamiliar to (most of) our ears.

raw42
ian.sims@raw42.com
www.raw42.com
We can provide you with reviews of your music to complement our other free services such as charts, promo cds, technical articles and news, plenty of exposure and our new a&r service.

Shift Magazine
info@shift.com
www.shift.com
We are about the collision between technology and culture. Shift examines the often overlooked human side of technology and how technology, in innumerable ways, changes how we live. It's about the personalities driving this change and the issues confronting this ongoing (r)evolution.

SoundList
soundlst@audiolab.uwaterloo.ca
audiolab.uwaterloo.ca/~soundlst
An e-mail newsletter devoted to announcements of free-improvisation, experimental music and sound art events in the Toronto area.

If you know of a resource that should be listed, please contact
indiebible@rogers.com

Get Avril's CD
"Let Go"

get a **$20 Rebate** on Evolution 100 Series Wireless Systems
See your dealer or go to
www.evolutionmics.com
for details

"I run around a lot on stage and the Sennheiser never cuts out. I'm very happy with it. It rocks!"—A.L.

HOT PERFORMANCES FROM AVRIL LAVIGNE & SENNHEISER **e**volution

Avril Lavignes' Input List:	
Avril Voc	EW565
Bkd Voc	E835
Spare Voc	E835
Bkd Voc	E835
Kick	E602
Snare Bottom	E609
Hi Hat	KM184
Rack	E604
Floor	E604
Floor	E604
OH SR	KM184
OH SL	KM184
Ride	KM184
Bass Mic	E602
Dirt Guitar	E609
Clean Guitar	MD421

"Evolution Wireless is reliable, has great sound with no dropouts, and we never have a problem finding a clean frequency." —Mark LeCorre, FOH Engineer

SENNHEISER

www.sennheiserusa.com
www.evolutionmics.com

Sennheiser Electronic Corporation • 1 Enterprise Drive, Old Lyme, Connecticut 06371 USA • Tel: 860-434-9190 • Fax: 860-434-1759
Mexico: Tel: (525) 639-0956 • Fax: (525) 639-9482 • Canada: Tel: 514-426-3013. Fax: 514-426-3953 • Mfg: Am Labor 1, 30900 Wedemark, Germany

Europe

Austria

monochrom
www.monochrom.at
Medienmogulerie. der verein zur förderung der selektiven rezeptionsforschung im sinne futurologischer belange. staatlich geprüftes rhizom. holpernd herb, erbärmlich fett, drall. unschwer erkennbar, erdgebunden.

Belgium

l'entrepot
tom.wilks@skynet.be
users.skynet.be/entrepot
We are an unconventional music site. The music styles and genres we deal with are unlimited. The goal of this site is to be a resource center for unconventional tunes.

SIDE-LINE
bernard@side-line.com
www.side-line.com

Uzine
www.dma.be/p/ultra
Dealing with music, film, (multi)media, travel and everything else we think is interesting.

France

Spirale
laspirale@laspirale.org
www.laspirale.org

Germany

Auf Abwegen
www.aufabwegen.de
The label, publisher and organizer for experimental music.

de:bug
www.de-bug.de

dense
dense@dense.de
www.dense.de
Founded in order to promote sound visionaries, their products and their live appearances by channeling information about their art, music and concepts to the right spots.

Dominion Club
dominionclub@aol.com
www.dominionclub.de

e-lectric
info@e-lectric.de
www.e-lectric.de
Ein Online-Magazin, das sich mit der Musikrichtung Synthie-Pop beschäftigt. Wir berichten über die altbekannten Bands wie Depeche Mode, Erasure and One, De/Vision, Wolfsheim... ,versuchen aber auch neuen Synthie-Bands ein Forum zu bieten. Solltest Du auch eine Synthie-Pop-CD eingespielt haben, her damit!

Elektrocution
www.elektrocution.de

Lametta Radio
Lametta@gmx.de
www.muenster.org/lametta
Our show features interviews with musicians, presentation and reviews of new albums, label and country specials. We specialize in Alternative, Electronic and Progressive Pop music.

MEMi
info@memi.com
www.memi.com

NMZ
www.nmz.de

reclaim
www.reclaim.de

Recycle Your Ears
info@recycleyourears.com
www.recycleyourears.com
Everything that I get will be reviewed, if it matches the musical direction of Recycle Your Ears. So, please no metal, no mainstream rock or things like that. You would be wasting your time and your money.

re.fleXion
www.re-flexion.de

shift!
info@shift.de
www.shift.de

spex
www.spex.de
News and reviews.

synthetics
micha@synthiepop.de
www.synthiepop.de
BODY and SOUL come together...Wir führen zusammen was zusammen gehört! Im neuen Jahr führt das Laudanum Magazin und das Synthetics Magazin ihre Webseiten zusammen. Synthetics....immer einen Besuch wert!!

Westzeit
info@westzeit.de
www.westzeit.de

Italy

Neural
a.ludovico@neural.it
www.neural.it
An Italian daily updated site on new media art, electronic music and hacktivism, quarterly printed as magazine.

United Kingdom

Compulsion
tonycompulsion@hotmail.com
www.callnetuk.com/home/compulsion
An online version of the alternative culture magazine featuring articles, interviews, news and music.

Computer Music
Ronan.macdonald@futurenet.co.uk
www.computermusic.co.uk
We offer all sorts of music and interactivity as well as advice, reviews of the latest gear and news as it happens.

Future Music
Andy.jones@futurenet.co.uk
futuremusic.co.uk

The Milk Factory
www.themilkfactory.co.uk
Monthly site packed with alternative reviews on electronica, dance and quality pop. Come by and see yourself!

Misfit City
dchinn@btinternet.com
www.collective.co.uk/misfitcity
Eclectic, in-depth music reviews - anything good considered and covered.

The Ptolemaic Terrascope
philmcm@dircon.co.uk
www.terrascope.org
Long-running fanzine renowned for unearthing predominantly psychedelic/folk nuggets.

Rubberneck
rubberneck@btinternet.com
www.btinternet.com/~rubberneck
The longest-running experimental music magazine in Britain specializing in improvised music. CD reviews, book reviews and a video review section devoted to non-mainstream film, including silent film and animation.

The Wire
projects@thewire.co.uk
www.thewire.co.uk
Leading international monthly specializing in electronica, breakbeat, avant rock, free jazz, classical, global and beyond.

Australia/New Zealand

Australia

Ampers & Etcetera
jeremy@pretentious.net
ampersandetc.virtualave.net/ampersand.html
Ambient & microwave & electronica & experimental & lowercase & postclassical & minimal & techno & etcetera

Folk/Celtic Music

Acoustic Guitar Magazine
editors.ag@stringletter.com
www.acguitar.com
Free lessons, giveaways, homegrown CD awards, gear reviews, beginner tips, Guitar Talk discussion forums and the latest from Acoustic Guitar magazine.

acousticmusician.com
DNPyles@acousticmusic.com
www.acousticmusic.com
A gateway to information about folk and acoustic artists, venues, resources and CD reviews. The site contains links to the web sites of over 200 musicians plus the Folk and Acoustic Music Exchange; reviews of over 500 compact disks.

An Honest Tune
info@anhonesttune.com
anhonesttune.com
The Southern Journal of Jam: Documenting the journey through improvisational and roots music and the community that surrounds that music from a distinctly southern point of view.

Celtic Beat
celt56@aol.com
www.mv.com/ipusers/celticbeat
Dedicated to all traditional and progressive Celtic music. Concert and CD Reviews Galore!

The Celtic Cafe
Bernadette Price bernadette@celticcafe.com
www.celticcafe.com
Our mission is to promote "Celtic culture," mostly Irish dance, Celtic music, books etc. Our associated mail lists are large and very international and we love letting folks know about things we hear and like!

Celtic Grove
crange@celticgrove.com
www.celticgrove.com
World's first and finest Celtic radio webcast and e-zine.

Celtic Ways
John Willmott john@celticways.com
celticways.com
We review, present and distribute MP3s of Celtic, Folk, World Fusion and World Tradition music. Free Services.

CelticJigsnReels.com
Bands@CelticJigsnReels.com
www.celticjigsnreels.com
Devoted to the Celtic music scene. We have artist information pages, artist links, interviews, bands of the month and an event calendar.

Ceolas
www.ceolas.org/ceolas.html

Dirty Linen
info@dirtylinen.com
www.DirtyLinen.com
We welcome submission of audio, video and written material that is in some way connected to the wide spectrum of roots music we cover. Please, no demo tapes, 7" singles, CD singles etc. The recording must also be commercially available (even if it's only via mail order and at gigs).

eFolkMusic
artists@efolkMusic.org
www.efolkmusic.org
Our mission is further the understanding, appreciation, preservation and performance of traditional and contemporary folk music from around the world and to support and develop awareness of and interest and involvement in folk music both as cultural history and entertainment.

Folk & Acoustic Music Exchange
dnpyles@acousticmusic.com
www.acousticmusic.com/fame/famehome.htm
When submitting recordings for review, please do not include full press kits, glossy photographs, copies of prior reviews etc. A brief artist's bio may be included with your submission.

folklinks.com
David W. Johnson djohnson@ehc.edu
www.folklinks.com
We provide an informed Web presence for folk and acoustic music performers, presenters, organizations, radio shows, Webcasts, magazines, business services and all friends of folk music.

The Green Man Review
kim@greenmanreview.com
www.greenmanreview.com
Our musical focus, whether CDs or live performances, is folk music in all its aspects, whether it be the Celtic and English traditions or folk rock or world music — even roots music (such as jazz, Cajun, English ceilidh, contradance, bluegrass, old-timey, country and blues).

Kevin's Celtic & Folk Music CD Reviews
celtic-folk@surfnetusa.com
www.surfnetusa.com/celtic-folk
This is a web site devoted to reviewing Celtic music CDs, UK folk music CDs and folk music CDs and making these reviews available to the public.

The Music Matters Review
thefolks@mmreview.com
www.mmreview.com
Reviews of the latest releases from your favorite and many "under discovered" artists!

Rambles
feedback@rambles.net
www.rambles.net
Your best source on the web for folk & traditional music, speculative fiction, folklore, movies & more.

The Review Of Original Music
scotrsim@reviewoforiginalmusic.com
www.reviewoforiginalmusic.com
The focus is to bring listeners and folk artists together through the medium of a periodical and interactive website. We will feature full feature stories on 13 artists in each issue. The magazine also contains a professionally mastered sampler CD.

The Roots Network
www.rootsnetwork.com
Our mission is to further advance the cause of acoustic-related music by educating the unknowing, enlightening the informed and entertaining the readership while remaining perched on the leading edge of modern Internet technology.

Sing Out!
info@singout.org
www.singout.org
A quarterly journal, published since May of 1950, each 200+ page issue includes feature articles and interviews and tons of recording and book reviews.

Europe

Belgium

The Folk Pages
club.euronet.be/claude.calteux

France

Trad Magazine
tradmag@wanadoo.fr
www.tradmagazine.com
Französisches Magazin für Folk und traditionelle Musik.

Germany

Folker!
webmaster@folker.de
www.folker.de
Das deutsche Musikmagazin. Folk, Blues, Cajun...

FolkWorld
editors@folkworld.de
www.folkworld.de
An independent magazine published in the internet only. It is also a forum for its readers - contributions from you (news, reviews etc) are welcome!

The Netherlands

Newfolksounds
abonnee@newfolksounds.nl
www.newfolksounds.nl
Een Nederlands tijdschrift dat één keer in de twee maanden verschijnt. Al bijna vijfentwintig jaar besteedt het blad, aanvankelijk onder de naam "Jan Viool", aandacht aan folk- en wereldmuziek afkomstig uit binnen- en buitenland.

United Kingdom

BBC Folk and Acoustic Page
www.bbc.co.uk/radio2/folk

Folk and Roots
folkandroots@aol.com
www.folkandroots.co.uk
Gigs, reviews, interview featured artists and more.

Folk on Tap
editor@folkontap.co.uk
www.freenetpages.co.uk/hp/trg/SCoFF/fotsend.htm
The Magazine of the Southern Counties Folk Federation containing: features on international, national and local artists, regular columns written by national artists, a comprehensive section of reviews of the latest album releases, reviews and previews of festivals and live gigs.

Folk Roots
froots@frootsmag.com
www.frootsmag.com
The world's leading roots, folk and world music magazine. Our circulation is high for British specialist magazines - around 14,000 (giving a readership of around 40,000), with a full national spread and some 30% going overseas - but our influence is even greater.

Folking.com
folkmaster@folking.com
www.folking.com
A Folk - Roots and Acoustic music development organization created for fans and artists alike. Album reviews, gig reviews, CD of the month, MP3s.

NetRhythms.co.uk
sue@netrhythms.co.uk
www.netrhythms.co.uk
Home to the best roots music. We bring you our favorite Folk, Blues, Americana, World, Alt.Country, Songwriters and more. NetRhythms focuses on distributed CDs or those available from artists' websites.

Tradition Magazine
paul@salmonp56.fsnet.co.uk
www.traditionmagazine.com
The online magazine devoted entirely to world custom and tradition. In this and subsequent issues of this magazine, we'll be peeling back the layers of modern society to reveal some of the ancient traditions lying just beneath the surface.

Traditional Music Maker
Brian Healey tradmusic@btclick.com
www.tradmusic.net
The magazine covers all forms of traditional music from Folk to Country and World Music, supporting unsigned artists with CD reviews, profiles, compilation disc, mail order sales through the magazine and website.

worldmusic.org.uk
reviews@worldmusic.org.uk
www.worldmusic.org.uk
We feature news, CD reviews, features and links for roots based music from around the world. The scope of the site is varied and growing all of the time. Contact us to get your CD reviewed.

Australia

Trad&Now
nti@bigpond.com
www.tradandnow.com
Our mission is to promote, preserve and support the cultural diversity and heritage of all traditional and contemporary folk music and related performance arts such as poetry, dance, storytelling and folklore and to encourage this as part of our everyday lives.

Gothic

Goth, Industrial, EBM, ethereal, synthpop and Darkwave.

North America

United States

13thTrack.com
Reviews@13thTrack.com
www.13thtrack.com
We review any and all Halloween related items.

4 A.M. Publishing
info@gothicsociety.net
www.gothicsociety.net/4AMPublishing
Reviews new music and writes small column on music reviewed. Also responsible for finding music that is to be featured our site, magazine or website.

Beautiful Cruelty Magazine
bcm_submissions@yahoo.com
www.cryfordawn.net/bcm
Our magazine is 90% submission based, which makes it an open forum for everything Gothic, Nu-metal, Industrial, Grave and beyond.

Beyond the Grave
eberhardklauke@hotmail.com
www.beyondthegravemusic.com
Beyond the grave is an Internet label and zine and is dedicated to promoting and provide honest reviews of all type of music.

BiteMe!
Nikki J1Fix@aol.com
www.bitemezine.net
The zine with crunch features reviews, interviews, commentary and crap about punk, rock, dance, metal, Goth and industrial bands we love. We also review demos.

BlueBlood.net
sadistintern@blueblood.net
www.blueblood.net

The Brain
brain@brainwashed.com
www.brainwashed.com
If you're a band or a label and you want your music listened to, turn your attention to The Brain, a weekly webzine compiled by the staff of Brainwashed.

Charlotte Sometimes
charlotte@charlottesometimes.com
www.charlottesometimes.com
Provides visitors with visual, mental and aural stimulation with sections on art, music, fashion and often lively reviews and social commentary.

Dark Culture Magazine
submissions@darkculture.net
www.darkculture.net
An open forum for writers to get their words read. We encourage anyone with a love for the written work or some modicum of talent to submit articles and reviews on topics ranging from art, fashion, music, literature and pop-culture.

Dark Realms Magazine
Music Editor dark@monolithgraphics.com
www.monolithgraphics.com/darkrealms.html
Nationally distributed print magazine covering Goth and industrial music. Visit our website for guidelines to submitting your music.

Dead Angel
monorecs@monotremata.com
www.monotremata.com/dead
E-zine with wide variety of underground music reviews and interviews.

deathrock.com
Mark Splatter ghoul@deathrock.com
www.deathrock.com
I'd like to help out any gloom and doom rock bands that play punk deathrock., horror rock, or Goth rock.

Dragon Flight Mailorder/Magazine
Clint info@dragonflightrec.org
www.dragonflightrec.org
Experimental, Dark Industrial/Ambient, Noise and Doom label, mailorder & Print magazine.

EsoTerra
hecate999@mailexcite.com
www.esoterra.org
Interviews with musicians, writers and artists existing on society's fringes. Also included are articles on bizarre phenomena and occult strangeness.

GotBlack.com
joi@gotblack.com
www.gotblack.com
Gothic community, including over 200 resources, radio, chat, about 50 forums, over 600 profiles, DJ playlists etc.

Gothic Beauty
info@gothicbeauty.com
www.gothicbeauty.com
If you are a Musician or Label that would like a possible CD Review or Featured Interview, please send us your press kit Attention: Constantine.

gothicsociety.net
www.gothicsociety.net
We are looking for reviews for music and print, just about anything you have an interest in actually.

Industrial Az Fuck
worlock@mr-potatohead.com
www.half-asleep.com/industrial
Our goal here is simple: To supply you... the industrial fans, with as much information about Industrial/ EBM, as we can get our hands on.

Industrial Nation
info@industrialnation.com
www.industrialnation.com
Covers all music electronic: Industrial, Gothic, Techno, Trance, Experimental, Electro, Synth-Pop, Ambient, Gabber and everything in between.

Loop
info@loop.Every1.net
welcome.to/Loop
If you are a "DarkWave", "Gothic", "Electro" or "Industrial" band and would like to be a featured artist in a future issue of Loop, you must be prepared to give Loop permission to use images and words from your web site and/or press kit.

Morbid Outlook
morbidoutlook@yahoo.com
www.morbidoutlook.com
*Musicians - we do not do traditional music reviews, however, we do highlight our favorites in our "in rotation" section every month. We do listen to everything we receive; feel free to send your cds and press kits to us! Links to mp3 pages tend to get skipped over (get the hint? *mail your music*!)*

Neo-Barbaric
Carnal H. Coitus chcoitus@hotmail.com
www.fortunecity.com/roswell/spells/49/neobar.htm
Paper & internet zine, DIY, all forms of extreme recording styles, reviews, interviews, cosmic combat comics, all underground, Ads free with submissions. Paper-$1.

Newgrave
contact@newgrave.com
www.newgrave.com
Devoted to the preservation and growth of dark and gothic culture. Newgrave Magazine is 56 glossy pages of extreme death rock fashion, cutting edge music, art, photography, film, video, DVD and concert reviews. Send in you music CD's, vinyl and demo cassettes.

Outburn
octavia@outburn.com
www.outburn.com
The leader of the subversive and post-alternative music revolution that covers many diverse genres. Outburn includes in-depth interviews with popular musicians and established underground favorites.

Propaganda
propazine@aol.com
www.propagandamagazine.net
Chronicle, purveyor of all things dark, gothic, industrial, fetish, erotic and sinful, including poetry, fashion, literature, music reviews, band interviews and other aesthetic pleasures.

Recycle Your Ears
info@recycleyourears.com
www.recycleyourears.com
The goal of this zine is to present new releases or artists to persons listening to this kind of music and to enhance discussion between them.

Ruined Culture
warden.gdn.net/~ruinnation/E-zine
E-zine for the neo-punk sub-culture.

The Sentimentalist
www.asthetik.com/print/Sentimentalist/home.html
Alternative music, art, film and fashion magazine deemed "a must read for the dark aesthete".

The Seventh Circle

sparrow@seventh-circle.com
www.seventh-circle.com
Music artists found featured on the site are those that are able to reach down to the dark recesses of their madness and produce something dark and beautiful.

Sistinas

info@sistinas.com
www.sistinas.com
A monthly experiment in merging the arts in a creative social atmosphere. The entertainment is provided by local painters, poets, filmmakers, musicians, performance artists and everything surrounding and in between.

Sonic Envelope

nastybyte@sonicEnvelope.com
www.sonicenvelope.com
Covers a wide variety of electronic-based music, including the sub-genres of Industrial, Gothic, darkwave, IDM and experimental. With a large international readership, Sonic Envelope continues to be an important force in electronic media since its inception (1994).

StarVox

blu@starvox.net
www.starvox.net
Geared towards the promotion of underground music genres such as darkwave, gothic, ambient, ethereal, industrial, electro, synth pop and dark metal. Bands and Labels wanting to be featured on StarVox can visit our site for details.

Suffering is Hip

kallisti@sepulchritude.com
www.sepulchritude.com

Swag Magazine

sadistintern@blueblood.net
www.swagmag.com
All about everything the successful rock stars, styling club kids and all around artists and cool individuals want and need. Swag is about the rewards you deserve. Swag is about the rewards you will get. Swag is the style guide for the wild life.

theatrumaethereum

theatrum@hotmail.com
www.wnyu.org/theatrumaethereum
We present transcripts of past interviews of people involved in the genre and reviews, written by DJ Carlos, of the music he features on our radio show.

Vampirefreaks.com

jet@vampirefreaks.com
www.vampirefreaks.com

Voidstar Productions

deftlyd@hotmail.com
www.voidstarproductions.com
Our reviews give constructive criticism directly to the artists which the reader can review if they like.

Canada

The Brains Never Stop

www.thebrainsneverstop.cjb.net
email the_brains_never_stop@hotmail.com
Send us your CD for review.

Chaotic Critiques

www.geocities.com/SunsetStrip/Palms/6031
Forty fun-filled pages jam-packed with critical but open-minded reviews and in-depth interviews.

Comatose Rose Magazine

azriel@comatoserose.com
www.comatoserose.com
Interviews, reviews, features and more!

Corridor of Cells

zaraza@corridorofcells.com
zaraza.cjb.net

Rue Morgue

info@rue-morgue.com
www.rue-morgue.com
We review music releases (no demos) of horror related music; soundtracks, Goth, dark electronica, horror themed punk, black metal, dark rock, ambient music and anything else.

The Seventh Circle

sparrow@seventh-circle.com
www.seventh-circle.com
Formed to expose everyone online to music that typically doesn't reach everyone's eyes and ears through traditional means. Music artists found featured on the site are those that are able to reach down to the dark recesses of their madness and produce something dark and beautiful.

Wrapped in Wire Canada

mail@wrappedinwire.com
www.wrappedinwire.com
We support the digital revolution with over 550 music CD reviews, an art gallery, humor, music news and plain old weirdness, grossness, obscurity, sex and it's all free! We accept submissions and demo tapes for review.

Europe

Belgium

Darker than the Bat

Peter-Jan dttb.pjvd@pi.be
www.proservcenter.be/darkerthanthebat
We try to be a help for young and new bands by doing CD reviews, interviews and giving them airplay in the gothic/electro/EBM/industrial/darkwave/ethereal-scene.

De Kagen Kalender

info@kagankalender.com
www.kagankalender.com
Focuses on wave-gothic-electro-industrial, including all the related styles. It has a weekly radio-show, a gig- and party-guide including reviews, a dj-team, parties and a web-site. Each promo is assured to get a review and will be played on the radio-show.

Croatia

Elektronski Zvuk

info@elektronskizvuk.com
www.elektronskizvuk.com
We review electro, industrial, synth pop, trance, idm and other styles of electronic music from bands around the world. Besides e-zine, Elektronski Zvuk is also featured as radio show.

Czech Republic

teenage.cz

ebm@teenage.cz
teenage.cz

heimdallr

Heimdallr@ifrance.com
www.heimdallr.ch
Bands, Labels..., please don't hesitate to send us any news, promotional records, CDs, vinyl, tapes! Any record, demo, received will be reviewed adding discography, contacts and links to your site.

Finland

!DEGENERATE!

fanimal@hotmail.com
www.kaos-kontrol.org
Our editors will be focusing on some specific areas of 'industrial' sounds instead of wasting their energy on material they do not feel enough enthusiastic about or interested in.

Sub-Fennica

subfennica@yahoo.co.uk
move.to/sub-fennica
A Webzine focusing on the Dark Music genres. Band and labels, you are welcome to submit material for review, but write an e-mail first informing what kind of Musickal material is in question.

France

Cynfeirdd

cynfeirdd@free.fr
cynfeirdd.free.fr
We aim to build through time, complete data storage about this dark culture we share and make alive.

Darkface

darkface@multimania.com
www.multimania.com/darkface
Se donne le but de faire connaître le mouvement Electro & goth, faire circuler le maximum d'informations.

DarkSonus.com

admin@darksonus.com
darksonus.com
Covering Industrial, Gothic, Darkwave, EBM. Band of the month feature.

D-Side

dside@free.fr
www.d-side.org
Gothic, Rock Metal, Electro, Industrial, Electronica, Darkwave.

Psychedelic Trance Goa Music Reviews

goatrance.free.fr
Because Goa-Trance came out of New Beat, Gothic, New Wave, Industrial, Electro, Detroit & Psychedelic Rock, it has an unique sound that is more complicated as the most modern Electronic dance music.

Germany

Astan Magazine

astanmagazin@t-online.de
www.astan-magazin.de

Back Again

www.backagain.de
CD-Kritiken und Interviews aus dem Independentbereich.

The Black Gift
office@the-black-gift.de
www.the-black-gift.de

Black Rain
www.blackrain.de

Black Screen
holger@blackscreen.de
www.blackscreen.de
*Willkommen bei BLACK SCREEN, dem
Internetmagazin der Dark Wave Szene im Rhein-
Main-Gebiet.*

The Dark Site
contact@wavegothic.de
www.wavegothic.de
*Schickt einfach euer Material an unsere Anschrift und
gebt uns ein paar Wochen Zeit (wir müssen die CDs
ja auch intern verteilen).*

Der Medienkonverter
www.medienkonverter.de

electric diary
webmaster@electric-diary.de
www.electric-diary.de

e-lectric.de
info@e-lectric.de
www.e-lectric.de
*e-lectric ist ein Online-Magazin, das sich mit der
Musikrichtung Synthie-Pop und der etwas "härteren"
Variante Future-Pop beschäftigt.*

elektrauma
www.elektrauma.de

Equinoxe
www.equinoxe-magazin.de
*Promotes dark music ranging from ambient music to
neofolk and harsh industrial noise.*

FallingLife
UEC0101@failinglife.com
www.failinglife.com
*A gateway to signed/unsigned artists sharing a similar
direction for the underground scene. We'd like to see
a more united underground scene amongst the
industrial and experimental artists that is able to
avoid mediocrity and elitism.*

FAN BASE
info@fan-base.de
www.fan-base.de
*Ezine (Electro, Synthpop, Dark, Gothic, Wave) where
you find over 1000 weekly updated links, news, cd-
reviews, message board.*

Gothic Magazin
info@gothic-magazin.de
www.gothic-magazin.de

Gothic Paradise
www.gothicparadise.de

Gothic World
www.the-gothicworld.de
*Ein unabhängiges, nichtkommerzielles, spontan im
Chat gegründetes Projekt, daß sich mittlerweile zu
einem anerkannten Internetzine entwickelt hat.*

Kato's Net Zine
KatosNetZine@gmx.de
katosnetzine.here.de

Klangwald
www.klangwald.de
*Synth-Pop, Dark-Wave & Gothic: Rezensionen,
Interviews, News & more.*

Nacht Wandler
mail@nacht-wandler.de
www.nacht-wandler.de

Noise Nation
www.noisenation.de

Sinful Gothic
sinfulgothiccs@aol.com
www.sinfulgothic.com
*Got a band? Are you good? I want to promote some
good Goth bands and add a list to my site with
reviews. If you'd like exposure contact me.*

Sonic Seducer
info@sonic-seducer.de
www.sonic-seducer.de

soulsangel
www.soulsangel.de
The dark web-portal. News, releases, downloads etc.

Strobelight Magazine
www.strobelight-magazine.de

TranceForM
www.tranceform.de
*Cd-kritiken, interviews, termine, mp3, galerien,
kolumnen, großes archiv, dark wave, gothic, electro,
futurepop, independent, xover, grunge, core,
alternative rock. E-zine, zeitschrift, forum fuer
entartete kunst musik lebensart kultur.*

Wet-Works
Wetworks@wetworksezine.com
www.wetworksezine.com
*Dedicated to the promotion of electronic music, media
and culture...Interviews, Reviews, Interaction,
Downloads and much much more.*

Yabbas World
www.yabbas.de

Zillo Musikmagazin
www.zillo.de
*Leading German magazine featuring mainly dark
wave, alternative, industrial music.*

Italy

Chain D.L.K.
rivaragl@aries.it
www.chaindlk.com
*Fresh news, weekly reviews, interviews and Real
Audio radio show. We support the real independent
scene reviewing everyone who submits their music.
Just visit us!*

Kronic.it
info@kronic.it
www.kronic.it
Encouraging music addiction since 2002.

Twilight Realm
twilight.rose@libero.it
www.twilightrealmzine.com
*All the individuals, Labels and Bands are encouraged
to keep in touch to make this dark side of the Web
more interesting to the Souls that still need the lymph
of REAL Music to survive!!!*

:twilight zone:
spleenzone@libero.it
www.twilight-zone.it
*Everything about darkambient:industrial:ebm:neofolk
music.*

Ver Sacrum
redazione@versacrum.com
www.versacrum.com
Rivista Gotica di letteratura, cinema, musica e arte.

The Netherlands

Above the Ruins
atr@home.nl
www.abovetheruins.com
*Bands & labels that want to send us promo-copies
should email us for our post address.*

Euphrodita's Empire
Euphrodita@hotmail.com
www.euphrodita.com
*Enter Euphrodita's labyrinth and discover her world
of reviews and interviews.*

Funeral Procession
info@funprox.com
www.funprox.com
*I take gothic in a broad sense, including all 'dark'
music styles, you can call it darkwave, industrial,
electro/EBM, noise, dark techno, dark ambient, neofolk, or whatever you want.*

Gothcore
Ate Hoekstra info@gothcore.nl
come.to/gothcore
Contact us concerning reviews and interviews.

Norway

Musique Machine
info@musiquemachine.com
www.musiquemachine.com
*Reviews, interviews, editorial columns and mp3s.
Beware, eclectic is our middle name and we cover
many genres from Black-Metal to Trip-Hop, Jazz,
Avant-Garde, Industrial, Ambient, Post-Rock, Indie &
everything in between.*

Russia

Deluge
anri@skeptik.net
deluge.narod.ru
*If you want us to review your band, check our website
for the Russian and US contact information.*

Industrial Onego
industrial@onego.ru
industrial.onego.ru
Music Reviews Archive.

Slovakia

Darkroom
arsobscurus@hotmail.com
www.multiweb.cz/darkroom

Spain

drumnnoise
info@drum-n-noise.com
www.drum-n-noise.com
Industrial Music e-zine.

SEKUENCIAS DE CULTO
sdczine@arrakis.es
www.arrakis.es/%7Esdczine
Webzine and radio.

Sonidobscuro
so@sonidobscuro.com
www.sonidobscuro.com

Sweden

Moving Hands
info@movinghands.net
www.movinghands.net
If you have any questions for us, or if you're interested in submitting material, e-mail or write us.

Release
info@releasemagazine.net
www.releasemagazine.net
Contains features, reviews, news, classified ads, tour guide, letters, playlists and more. We print 10 000 copies and have distribution all over Sweden.

Moving Hands Music Magazine
johan.astemark@movinghands.net
www.movinghands.net
Highly acclaimed Swedish mag. We review everything that fits our style (synth, industrial, electronica, electronic, EBM, postpunk, deathrock, alternative etc.)

Switzerland

Sanctuary
spiderb@sanctuary.ch
www.sanctuary.ch
We make a monthly selection of the 10 best releases of CD's. This is in order to promote the musical alternative scene (Dark-Wave, Gothic, Electro, Industrial, German Wave, Dark Folk and so on).

United Kingdom

DJ Martian's
djmartian.blogspot.com
Delivering cultural sound knowledge for the intelligent generation.

Fluxeuropa
rik@fluxeuropa.com
www.fluxeuropa.com
We specialize in 'dark-edged' alternative and avant-garde music: dark folk, neofolk, apocalyptic folk, gothic-industrial, darkwave, dark-ambient and ambient-industrial etc. We also cover some early and traditional music.

MK ULTRA
mkultraman@mkultramag.com
www.mkultramag.com
News, reviews and interviews. Evil and funny. Definitely the darkest rock n' roll publication in the world.

meltdown magazine
editor@meltdownmagazine.com
www.meltdownmagazine.com
The UK's best-selling independent glossy magazine for the uk.gothic.alternative.lifestyle.

The Slaghuis
sam@slaghuis.net
www.slaghuis.net
Gothic, Darkwave, Industrial Reviews & Radio Free Abattoir.

Ukraine

Ukrainian Gothic
stranger@gothic.com.ua
www.gothic.com.ua
The aim is to bring world gothic, dark music and subculture to Ukraine and to support dying national Ukrainian gothic / industrial / independent scene. If you want that we promote you music or label in Ukraine, let us know.

Australia/New Zealand

Australia

Blatant Propaganda
www.blatantpropaganda.com
A record label of progressive-post-industrial-electronica-acid-punk-drum&bass noises; a journal of (anti)propaganda, activism, culture-jamming & music reviews; a bunch of radio shows & more.

Ritual
ritual@ar.com.au
ritual.ar.com.au
We are a gothic/industrial/electro nightclub (disco) in Sydney, Australia. We have a genuine interest in new 'gothic' music and are happy to promote CD releases but we do not have live bands at the club.

Hip Hop

Hip Hop, Rap, Soul and R&B

United States

The 411 Online
storm@the411online.com
www.the411online.com
If albums don't make dollars, then they don't make sense. That's the whole concept behind The 411 Online's rating system. See what kind of earning power your favorite artists have in our reviews section.

allhiphop.com
mail@allhiphop.com
www.allhiphop.com
Articles, audio, reviews, chat, boards etc.

Altrap.com
mail@altrap.com
www.altrap.com
The main factor of altrap.com is to elevate and educate the hip-hop nation with mad precise views on hip-hop. News, reviews, interviews and MP3s.

Backwash
marc@backwashzine.com
backwashzine.com
Music, interviews, plus weird, bizarre, freaky fun stuff.

B-Boys.com
www.b-boys.com
If you are a writer, photographer, artist, poet or whatever and would like to contribute some of your work or pieces to be featured on our site, please Contact us and we will get in touch with you.

BIG BAER Alternative Music Magazine
Jack C. Baer promote@bigbaer.com
www.bigbaer.com
Feature interviews and articles by today's movers & shakers in the music world. We will bring you insights to consider and resources to utilize, whether you are a musician, songwriter, producer or promoter, we will have the features and articles for you.

bringthenoise.com
info@bringthenoise.com
www.bringthenoise.com
Featuring live feeds, artist interviews, reviews and news.

Cellar Noise
CellarNoise902@aol.com
www.cellarnoise.com
Here you will find latest Hiphop News, Reviews, Interviews, Story's, Photography and much more! Lay back and get your read on!

contrabandit
hollabandit@hotmail.com
www.contrabandit.com
Hip-Hop's last hope! Reviews, articles, commentary and critical essays to blueprint your own course of resistance.

DaveyD's Hip Hop Corner
mrdaveyd@aol.com
www.daveyd.com

EarsToTheStreets dot COM
Dre@earstothestreets.com
www.earstothestreets.com
We want to influence your minds with a simple dose of ours. So, I hope you people find to respect our opinions, just like we would yours.

eJams
feedback@ejams.com
www.ejams.com
We are proud to sponsor our brothers and sisters who are trying to make it in the recording business on their own. Let us feature your new CD.

Elemental Magazine
info@elementalmag.com
www.elementalmag.com
True, we never update the site. But we don't care. That's because we run a magazine. We update the magazine every month, without fail, so take your lazy self to the store and buy Elemental Magazine!

The Elements
inquiries@hiphop-elements.com
www.hiphop-elements.com
Your #1 source for Hip Hop related issues.

GlobalHipHop.com
globalhiphop@hotmail.com
www.globalhiphop.com
Reviews, Interviews, Mixshows & home of Regenerated Headpiece, the epitome of dope independent future hiphop.

GuerillaOne.com
webinfo@guerillaone.com
www.guerillaone.com

If you know of a resource that should be listed, please contact
indiebible@rogers.com

Hip Hop Congress

www.hiphopcongress.org

We are an organized, liquid support network of students, artists, activists and many others dedicated to the upliftment of society through Hip Hop art and culture and unified social action. Send in your music for review.

Hip Hop Domain

go.to/hiphopdomain

Hip Hop Infinity

retail@hiphopinfinity.com

www.hiphopinfinity.com

The purpose of HHI is to provide underground hip hop fans with a venue to preview the latest music, read reviews, exchange ideas and buy products that may be unavailable locally or even elsewhere on the net.

HipHop-Directory.com

www.hiphop-directory.com

Would you like to see your material reviewed? All reviews are done free of charge and we strive to publish reviews on every single record we receive. Please only send in your own material or releases from your record label. No MP3s or bootlegs will ever be accepted.

HipHopDX.com

reviews@hiphopdx.com

www.hiphopdx.com

Hip hop news, album reviews, links, release dates etc.

hiphopgateway.com

admin@hiphopgateway.com

www.hiphopgateway.com

Want a chance to get your cd reviewed? Send 2 packaged copies to us at: Hip Hop Gateway, Attn: reviews, 2213 S. 79 West Allis, WI. 53219

HipHopist.com

www.hiphopist.com

Album reviews, hiphop news, free weekly hiphop ezine, large hiphop community and online radio make hiphopist.com the place to be for all hiphopists.

HipHopHotSpot.com

admin@hiphophotspot.com

hiphophotspot.com

We support the growth of hip hop artists world wide through exhausting a network of free resources designed to give artists more promotion, exposure and positive press on a global scale.

HipHopSite.com

mistapizzo@hiphopsite.com

www.hiphopsite.com

Online Magazine featuring 12' reviews, CD's, vinyl and other interesting items related to Hip Hop.

Illtip

contact@theilltip.com

www.theilltip.com

The last real street magazine.

Insomniac

insom@mindspring.com

www.insomniacmagazine.com

A national publication that features the best in pure hip hop. Insomniac supports indie releases.

It's On Tonight

London Moore london@itsontonight.com

www.itsontonight.com

I'll be happy to review any music related to urban culture (hip hop, R&B and Pop).

junglevoodoo.com

sharee@junglevoodoo.com

www.junglevoodoo.com

Although the site is primarily focused on jungle/drum & bass music, there are a lot of other things for you to check out.

Kronic Magazine

mrblaq@kronick.com

www.kronick.com

An attempt to provide true and accessible hip hop coverage from a different perspective.

Manhunt

info@manhunt.com

www.manhunt.com

News, reviews and artist spotlight.

Murder Dog

info@murderdog.com

www.murderdog.com

America's #1 Rap magazine. Read by most, envied by everyone else.

MUSIC2G.com

charlie@music2g.com

www.music2g.com

Contact us if you would like to be featured in our "New Artist" section.

OHHLA

www.ohhla.com

Okay Player

dan@okayplayer.com

www.okayplayer.com

Artists, reviews, insights and much more.

OpenZine

www.openzine.com

We blend the street styles of music to fulfill the open mined urban reader. OpenZine is also an interactive magazine where people can submit articles, graffiti art pictures & many other outlets.

Pass the Mic

www.passthemic.com

Our mission is to create a community for independent hip-hop artists to learn, share, market, promote and interact amongst themselves and with the hip-hop community at large.

Phatmag

Theeditor@phatmag.com

www.phatmag.com

Real news, interviews and reviews by real people for real people. Our intention is to say how it is, either we like it or we don't. If you have an arse, please keep it firmly inside your trousers, we never intend to kiss it.

Planet-hiphop.com

info@planet-hiphop.com

www.planet-hiphop.com

Online community made up of a network of theme based indie hip hop sites and stations and more. The Source of conscious hip hop online. News, reviews, spotlights etc.

Planet Rap Network

webmaster@planetrap.net

www.planetrap.net

We got full albums, singles, breakbeats, pictures, free e-mail, voice chat and a lot more...updated daily.

Pound Magazine

elena@poundmag.com

www.poundmag.com

Rap Scene

rapscene@hotmail.com

www.rapscene.com

Check out our "New Artist Showcase".

Rap Sheet

www.rapsheet.com

The only black owned national hip hop publication and has a monthly newsstand circulation of 100,000.

The Rap Source.com

pr@therapsource.com

www.therapsource.com

Plenty of Reviews. List of New Artists. The source for Rap, Gangster Rap, Hip Hop, Hardcore Rap.

RapAttackLives

nastynes1@aol.com

www.rapattacklives.com

The true voice of Hip Hop!

RapIndustry.Com

info@Rapindustry.com

rapindustry.com

Our goal is to be the premiere source for Hip Hop music - whether it be to listen to the dopest raps or check out the latest hip hop news. Showcase your talent!

Rapmusic.com

www.rapmusic.com

Check out our Underground Artist Section and submit your artist info and/or get on our Radio Show for free.

Rapnetwork.com

urbanminded@aol.com

www.rapnetwork.com

Your source for the hottest rap music on the planet. Exclusive joints, the newest mixtapes, original interviews, videos, news and forums. We update the site daily and add all the hottest mixtapes when they come out.

rapreviews.com

www.rapreviews.com

An independent site dedicated to equal coverage of both mainstream and up-and-coming artists, regardless of what label they are signed to or how large it is. At RapReviews, music comes first!

Raptism.com

webmaster@raptism.com

www.raptism.com

"The System behind Hip Hop"-Reviews, Interviews, News etc.

Rap-Up

info@rap-up.com

www.rap-up.com

News, reviews, interviews etc.

RealRap.net

webmaster@realrap.net

www.realrap.net

Offers reviews of hip-hop albums, listening parties and artist bios.

RNation

info@rnation.com

www.rnation.com

News, reviews, interviews and more!

Shine Magazine

shinemagazine@excite.com

www.planetshine.com

Siccness-Dot-Net

vamps@impalermedia.com
www.siccness.net
The last sanctuary of Gangsta Rap. CD Vendors, Reviews, Interviews etc.

The Source *Unsigned Hype*

www.thesource.com
Each month in our Unsigned Hype section we profile a talented unsigned group or artist. Send top-quality demo tapes with a description of the contents, a color or black-and- white photo and contact info.

Sphere of Hip Hop

Plastic webmaster@sphereofhiphop.com
www.sphereofhiphop.com
Review positive hip hop, like it used to be before all the crap out today.

The SOL of HIPHOP

www.solofhiphop.com
The SOL of HIPHOP Community is here. Login and enjoy the luxuries of the message board and other great features. Take a survey or two and check the reviews.

Soul Strut

411@soulstrut.com
www.soulstrut.com
A webzine emphasizing music & culture involving heavy beats, from genres such as 70s funk, hiphop, jazz, rock and more. There are articles, audio & interviews on site.

spinemagazine

info@spinemagazine.com
www.spinemagazine.com
You'll find in-depth music reviews sitting alongside the latest fashion and surrounded by fresh artwork from the upcoming generation of artists, illustrators and designers.

State of the Union

andthem@hotmail.com
www.stateoftheunion.net
Send us all your music with a bio (if you've got one) and production information.

Stink Zone

regional@stinkzone.com
www.stinkzone.com
Reviews, Funk, Reggae and all kinds of Hip Hop. Focuses in on various local scenes through North America.

Stylus Wars

www.styluswars.com
Every Month Dj P-Sol will be bringing you more and more reviews of different mix tapes. To have your mixtape reviewed send us a copy.

Suckarepellent.com

devi@prodigy.net
www.suckarepellent.com
An e-zine with artist features, articles on politics, Real Audio mixes, fashion and more.

Support Online Hip Hop *(SOHH)*

q@sohh.com
www.sohh.com

Tha Formula.com

info@thaformula.com
www.thaformula.com
Containing exclusive artist interviews, audio, streaming radio station, news and much more.

Thugzone.com

webmaster@thugzone.com
www.thugzone.com
Digital audio, Internet radio, video, news, reviews, e-commerce, exclusive Web events and convergence initiatives.

Trickology

opus@trickology.com
www.trickology.com
Check out our archive of 12' singles and exclusive joints we got our hands on. Find freestyles of all your favorite artist spitting unwritten or so they claim.

underground sound

Noyz319@ugsmag.com
www.ugsmag.com
We post/review submitted hip-hop mp3s & even have a feedback board on each artist's page.

Undergroundhip-hop.net

josh@undergroundhip-hop.net
www.undergroundhip-hop.net
We have one purpose; to spread the word about hip-hop talent that is overlooked when put in a market full of artists backed by wealthy record labels.

Unsigned the Magazine

Kitty Estes kitty@unsignedthemagazine.com
www.unsignedthemagazine.com
Designed to give unsigned artists and labels the maximum exposure and support they endeavor. Assuming a leadership role, our primary objective is to promote unsigned artists and independent labels of all styles with no geographical limits.

Urban Ambiance Journal

info@uajournal.com
www.uajournal.com
Music in the rhythm of life: reviews of independents alongside major-label.

Urban Earth

editor@urbanearth.com
www.urbanearth.com
So you think you got skills? Let us decide. Send your bangin' ass tracks to us. If your shit is really dope (and I mean REALLY dope), you just might get featured in our Time Bombs section.

UrbanJoint.com

www.urbanjoint.com
Devoted to the varied essence of urban talents. We offer a venue to showcase talents, via the growing electronic media. We represent a community of aspiring creative artists of all mediums and talents.

Unsigned the Magazine

info@unsignedthemagazine.com
www.unsignedthemagazine.com
An online music magazine designed to give unsigned artists and labels the maximum exposure and support they endeavor.

The Vinyl Exchange

stef@vinylexchange.com
www.vinylexchange.com
The magazine for vinyl junkies.

WFNK.com

wfnk@wfnk.com
www.wfnk.com
Welcome to Earth's funk supersite!

wildout.com

problemz@yahoo.com
wildout.com
The Streets of the Internet. Keepin' you informed of the real ghettoness.

WireTap

editor@wiretapmag.org
www.alternet.org/wiretapmag
We showcase investigative news articles, personal essays and opinions; artwork and activism resources that challenge stereotypes, inspire creativity, foster dialogue and give young people a voice in the media. The WireTap Web portal provides a new generation of writers, artists and activists a space to network, organize and mobilize.

XXL

xxl@harris-pub.com
www.xxlmag.com
Hip-Hop on a higher level. Features eye candy, street team, articles and more.

Canada

The CyberKrib.com

theichibanson@thecyberkrib.com
www.thecyberkrib.com
If you'd like coverage just e-mail me and we'll get you some coverage on the site. All that we ask, is that you supply us with a demo tape/recorded material, photos and bio information on the artist/group.

JACKHOUSE

www.urbnet.com/Jackhouse
The Urban Entertainment Network: Online Urban Magazine, web development, Digital music delivery and rich media advertising solutions.

Peace Magazine

info@peacemagazine.com
www.peacemagazine.com
Music. Fashion. Athletics. Lifestyle.

ThickOnline.com

reviewteam@thickonline.com
www.thickonline.com
Shedding light on unknown talent. ThickOnline will go out of its way to provide you with exclusive nooz and a review section covering a wide array of music & mediums.

UrbanGOAT.com

webmaster@urbangoat.com
www.urbangoat.com
Our preference for music is for urban based, electronic DJ oriented genres.

urbnet.com

info@urbnet.com
www.urbnet.com
The Urban entertainment network.

viceland.com

wassup@viceland.com
www.viceland.com
We refuse to use our web presence simply to repurpose our magazine content. Rather we've created a community for people who share the same desire for cutting-edge music, culture, fashion and multimedia.

Europe

Belgium

Da Bomb Shop
dabomb_gent@hotmail.com
www.users.skynet.be/bk285261/dabomb
Yes, we will be glad to listen to your music and if we feel it; we will sell it. Send in your own 'mixtapes' etc:

Czech Republic

BBaRák CZ
rawe@bbarak.cz
www.bbarak.cz
Reviews local and international artists.

France

HipHopGame
www.hiphopgame.com
Our goal is to provide Hip-Hop heads with daily information from around the world. We are trying to cover all the aspects of this culture through reviews, interviews, videos and audios.

Just Like HipHop
service-redactionnel@justlikevibes.com
www.justlikehiphop.com
News, reviews, interviews, downloads etc.

LeHiphop.com
redaction@lehiphop.com
www.lehiphop.com
We propose reviewz, interviewz, articlez, MP3 etc. French Staff ready to rock the hip-hop planet !!

Vivonzeureux
vivonzeureux@wanadoo.fr
perso.wanadoo.fr/vivonzeureux
100% optimistic hip-pop fanzine (in French and English)

Germany

0711hiphop.com
redAKTION@0711hiphop.com
www.0711hiphop.com

Backspin
www.backspin.de

Deflok
deflok@hiphopmagazin.com
www.deflok.de

freaknetz.de
webmaster@freaknetz.de
www.freaknetz.de
News, reviews, interviews etc.

Hardcore-HipHop.de
astrid.hilgemann@t-online.de
www.hardcore-hiphop.de
We are looking for: Oldschool-HipHop, Electro, Hardcore-HipHop, Britcore, Jungle, Drum&Bass, Dj-Art and other alternative stuff!

Heftig!
presse@heftig.com
www.heftig.com
Contains reviews, news, release dates, interviews, graff flicks etc.

MK Zwo
webmaster@mkzwo.com
www.mkzwo.com
Magazin für Hip Hop, Dancehall und Raggae.

Punchline
info@punchlinemag.de
www.punchlinemag.de

Rap.de
www.rap.de
HipHop, Deutschrap, blackmusic, vinyl, mixtapes, Music, radio, video, shop, reviews, interviews.

raplounge.de
rio@raplounge.de
www.rap-lounge.de

saargebeat.de
info@saargebeat.de
www.saargebeat.de

Truehead.de
webmaster@truehead.de
www.truehead.de

Wicked
www.wicked.de

The Netherlands

Globaldarkness
info@globaldarkness.com
www.globaldarkness.com
We dig the beats that break: Jungle, Electro-Funk, Hip-Hop & Reggae and we have a morbid fascination for old school stuff in any genre, but there's plenty more madness to explore here.

theBoombap
www.theboombap.nl

Russia

Hip Hop Zone
hiphopinfo.da.ru

Spain

Muevelo Hip Hop
muevelo@cuatrogrados.com
www.cuatrogrados.com/muevelo

Sweden

Boom Bap
abnorm@boom-bap.com
www.boom-bap.com
If you want your shit reviewed by BOOMBAP send your demos to us. MC's, DJ's, Producers, Labels: Send in your promotional material! We'll review as much as possible.

Fat Bankroll
fat-red@fatbankroll.nu
www.fatbankroll.nu
Concentrating on the good things in life. Let it be hiphop, reggae, electronica, punk rock, TV-shows or toys, if we like it - we write about it. The site features reviews, articles, small news features, interviews and RealAudio mixes.

hiphopper.org
tip@hiphopper.org
www.hiphopper.org

Mokka Mekka
www.mokkamekka.com
Lots of reviews, news, articles and interviews and also a crowded forum.

Street Zone
www.streetzone.com

Switzerland

Aight-Genossen
www.aight-genossen.ch
Swiss Hip Hop online.

Cosmic Hip Hop
staff@cosmichiphop.com
www.cosmichiphop.com
The biggest French speaking Webmag exclusively dedicated to Hip-Hop. Updated each week with at least 3 articles, music excerpts and much much more...

Urban Smarts
get@urbansmarts.com
www.urbansmarts.com
Features reviews that are committed, in-depth, sometimes a little wacky and bordering the lengthy too. This site sheds light on independent hip hop artists from all coasts and continents. ...and it's in color!

United Kingdom

Blues and Soul
bluesandsoul_online@hotmail.com
www.bluesandsoul.co.uk
News, reviews, charts, events, clubs and an online shop.

The Dainty Crew
Miss Mention MissMention@daintycrew.com
www.daintycrew.com
Urban music and entertainment website covering Reggae, Dancehall, Soul, R&B, Hip Hop including interviews, reviews, headlines, black history and more.

Down4Whatever
d4w2002@hotmail.com
www.down4whatever.co.uk
Music reviews, charts, special features, audio and more.

Elusive Styles
ideas@elusivestyles.co.uk
www.elusivestyles.co.uk
You can find out about the best current hip hop/beats releases in our review section and monthly chart. Send vinyl/ tapes/ CDs, artwork etc.

Fat Lace Magazine
info@fatlacemagazine.com
www.fatlacemagazine.com
The magazine for aging B-Boys.

hip-hop domain
jake.thomas1@ntlworld.com
go.to/hiphopdomain
If you are part of a record label, Hip-Hop Domain would be happy to review your new releases. Our mailing address can be found at the Contact HHD section. However, please email/phone before sending stuff off.

HipHopist.com
webmaster@hiphopist.com
www.hiphopist.com
Representing all the elements for all the different sides of hiphop. From online radio to daily hiphop news,hiphopist.com is aiming to be the main hiphop website.

Knowledge
editor@knowledgemag.co.uk
www.knowledgemag.co.uk
The magazine for drum & bass, jungle, hip hop, breakbeat and urban culture.

RAGO Magazine
info@wolftown.co.uk
www.wolftown.co.uk
The voice of Wolftown Recordings and the worldwide underground hip-hop & rap movement. It provides interviews, features, news and mixed tape, album, single & video reviews along with live reviews of events, worldwide scene reports and much more.

The Situation
comments@thesituation.co.uk
www.thesituation.co.uk
We intend to inform, educate and entertain all those interested in urban music and popular culture.

spinemagazine.com
theteam@spinemagazine.com
www.spinemagazine.com
We have reviews of the latest hip-hop music, skateboarding, fashion and artwork - and we've had lots of support from the media and everyone involved in the hip-hop scene.

Y2Hiphop.com
www.y2hiphop.com
For the latest news, reviews, audio and the BEST Album Release Date's section on the web, check out our site. You will also find features such as interviews, editorial columns and articles.

Australia

Bombhiphop.com
usa@bombhiphop.com
www.bombhiphop.com

Stealth
info@stealthmag.com
www.stealthmag.com
Australia's premier hip hop magazine Points of interest: the magazine has developed from a basic zine to a full colour publication with a CD-Rom attached.

Jazz

North America

United States

52nd Street
www.52ndstreet.com
The Internet's number one Jazz review site!

All About Jazz
mricci@visionx.com
www.allaboutjazz.com
The premiere jazz & blues magazine/resource on the web.

allJaZZGuiTar
webmaster@alljazzguitar.com
www.alljazzguitar.com
An Educational, Reference and Resource Site for the Jazz Guitar Enthusiast!

The American Rag
don@americanrag.com
www.americanrag.com
Each month our hard copy version serves up over sixty pages of commentary, news, articles of interest and reviews as well as the people, places and festivals defining the excitement of today's Traditional Jazz and Ragtime scene.

Any Swing Goes
doug@anyswinggoes.com
www.anyswinggoes.com
We are a publication that allows Indie CDs for review, primarily in the categories of swing, big band, jump blues and rockabilly.

Atomic Mag
info@atomicmag.com
www.atomicmag.com
The essential guide to retro culture. Specializing in swing music.

Cadence
cadence@cadencebuilding.com
www.cadencebuilding.com
A priceless archive of interviews, oral histories, book reviews and more than 35,000 reviews of improvised music worldwide.

Contemporary Jazz
cjazz@contemporaryjazz.com
www.contemporaryjazz.com
Up to date information about Contemporary Jazz. Site includes the latest news, reviews, interviews and new release listings.

DownBeat.com
jasonk@downbeatjazz.com
www.downbeat.com

Eclectic Earwig Reviews
eermusic@nc.rr.com
www.eer-music.com
Your online source for jazz, jazzrock fusion, progressive rock, electronic, ambient, psych/space rock and more eclectica.

FUSE Online
Dave Dorkin ddorkin1@yahoo.com
www.fusemag.com
Innovative and challenging music performed by the world's greatest musicians. If you would like your music considered for review, send your CD and promo materials to me.

Hittin' the Note
www.hittinthenote.com
Devoted to the Americana sounds of Blues, Rock & Jazz.

Independent Reviewer - Frank Matheis
matheisf@aol.com
www.frankspicks.com
Frank Matheis is host of "Frank's Picks" on WKZE, 98.1 FM, in Sharon Connecticut, beaming his eclectic roots & blues program to the tri-state region. He writes a weekly column as music critic for Taconic Press.

Jazz Guitar Online
bob@jazzguitar.com
www.jazzguitar.com

Jazz Improv
jazz@jazzimprov.com
www.jazzimprov.com
You'll find as many as 100 detailed jazz CD reviews in each issue.

The Jazz Nation
elizabeth@thejazznation.com
www.thejazznation.com
Imagine a nation with infinite diversity that welcomes any and everyone who wishes to participate in a genuine spirit of enthusiasm, love and passion, for that wonderfully broad and defiantly, ever-changing genre of music called jazz.

Jazz Now
jazzinfo@jazznow.com
www.jazznow.com
Covering the hottest up-and-coming stars and giving the latest updates on today's legendary greats and nonmusicians who have promoted and contributed to the Jazz, blues, improvised music and Latin Jazz communities.

Jazz Online Fresh Reviews
jazzonline@jazzonline.com
www.jazzonline.com
We present the music in a manner that is accessible and inviting to the curious newcomer while remaining interesting and useful to the serious fan.

The Jazz Report Magazine Online
www.jazzreport.com
The voice of the artist. Profiles, reviews, news and essays.

Jazz-Sax.Com
ericdano@jazz-sax.com
www.jazz-sax.com
The great thing about Jazz-Sax (besides all the audio clips and PDF files) is how easy it is for everyone to participate. In fact, the site depends on users to spark discussions, conversations and even arguments in their comments. Post your own reviews.

Jazz Times
info@jazztimes.com
www.jazztimes.com
Has continued to evolve into what is widely regarded as the world's leading jazz publication.

Jazz USA
jazzmaster@jazzusa.com
jazzusa.com
Please submit music that you would like reviewed or mentioned in the new releases on CD or DAT tape. Indicate whether you want it mentioned or reviewed. Be careful...reviews get more space but they can go either way!.

Jazzconnect.com
info@jazzconnect.com
www.jazzconnect.com
Your direct connection to Jazz musicians and their music. MP3s, websites, CD store, new releases and artist spotlights.

Jazziz
www.jazziz.com
We have been called "the voice of a new jazz culture; a culture it helped create," and over the past 20 years has grown to become the largest-circulated jazz publication in the world the undisputed authority on jazz music and style.

JazzReview.com
Morrice Blackwell morrice@jazzreview.com
www.jazzreview.com
We strive to promote "all" styles of jazz music to jazz fans around the world. If you would like to submit music for review consideration please send two copies of the following: artist / group bios, press kits, CDs and promotional materials for staff distribution.

iaje The World's Largest Jazz Conference!

Make plans to join over 7,000 attendees from 35 countries as IAJE comes to New York, NY in 2004 and Long Beach, CA in 2005

International Association for Jazz Education
Annual International Conference

January 21-24, 2004
Hilton New York and Towers
Sheraton New York Hotel and Towers
New York, New York USA

January 5-8, 2005
Long Beach Convention Center
Long Beach, California USA

Highlights include:

• **Over 200 Concerts and Workshops**

• **Teacher Training Sessions**

• **Extensive Jazz Industry Track**

• **NPR Live Broadcasts**

• **Jazz Industry Exposition**

• **National Endowment for the Arts American Jazz Masters Awards**

• **IJFO International Jazz Award**

For a detailed brochure, contact:
info@iaje.org • (785) 776-8744
www.iaje.org

The Mississippi Rag
editor@mississippirag.com
www.mississippirag.com
*New and current performers and bands are
highlighted in each issue, with information about
where and when they're playing.*

Mr. Lucky
editor@mrlucky.com
www.mrlucky.com
*Not a "zine", but a musical communiqué celebrating
music of a "jazz-centric" nature. This can be as direct
as Dizzy Gillespie or as offbeat as samba-reggae from
Brazil. Our only criteria are harmony, melody and
rhythm.*

Music Steps
o@musicsteps.com
www.musicsteps.com
*We provide music, history, reviews, radio and festival
information for the jazz music enthusiast.*

Pause Record
www.pauserecord.com
*Dedicated to jam rock, jazz, bluegrass and amateur
recording.*

Red Hot and Cool Jazz
members.aol.com/Jlackritz/jazz
The Jazz Resource for the Net.

Saxophone Journal
David Dempsey DemseyD@wpunj.edu
www.dornpub.com/saxophonejournal.html
*We only publish reviews that are supportive and
positive in nature. Any critical writing is kept at an
absolute professional minimum. If a writer doesn't like
a product, they simply do not review it. Please send
CDs that are retail quality.*

Canada

eJazzNews
news@ejazznews.com
www.ejazznews.com
*Online edition of the magazine features news, profiles,
interviews with many Canadian and international
artists.*

Europe

Belguim

Jazz'halo
info@jazzhalo.be
www.jazzhalo.be
*We aim to promote modern jazz and improvised music
by producing CD's, by publishing a magazine (4
issues a year), by organizing concerts and by
distributing small independent labels (mostly run by
musicians).*

France

Centraljazz
musicien@centraljazz.com
www.centraljazz.com
*Le site français de tous les jazz : cd reviews, real
audio, flash, forum etc...*

Citizen Jazz
redaction@citizenjazz.com
www.citizenjazz.com
*Daily news about jazz in Europe and all over the
world. CD review, articles, interviews. Video, audio
and radio.*

Improjazz
perso.wanadoo.fr/improjazz
Le Magazine du Jazz et des Musiques Improvisées.

Jazz Hot
jazzhot@wanadoo.fr
www.jazzhot.net
*La revue internationale du Jazz depuis 1935. 11 issues
a year + the monthly internet supplement.*

Jazz Magazine
info@jazzmagazine.com
www.jazzmagazine.com
*The second oldest French Jazz magazine (since 1954).
Posting interviews, articles, exhibitions, concert dates,
news reviews etc.*

Germany

JAZZ SPECIAL
jazzspecial@sundance.dk
www.jazzspecial.dk
The world's most widely distributed jazz magazine!

Jazz Thing
redaction@jazzthing.de
www.jazzthing.de
*Die Zeitschrift für weltoffene Musikliebhaber von
heute. Jazz thing versteht Jazz nicht als
ausgrenzenden Stilbegriff, sondern als potentiell
grenzenlosen Spirit der Open-Mindedness.*

jazzlive
jazzlive@aon.at
www.onstage.at/jazzlive
Magazin für zeitgenössische Musik.

Italy

CiaoJazz
marco.valente@ijm.it
www.ciaojazz.com

Poland

ERA JAZZU
Dioni Piatkowski erajazzu@jazz.pl
www.jazz.pl
*If you are interested in our assistance in reaching jazz
market in Poland (from radio and press promotion to
distribution and concerts) as well selling licenses of
yours recordings — could you please send us
samples of CDs, DVD, publications, press-kits,
promo-sets etc.*

Russia

Jazz News
jazz@nestor.minsk.by
home.nestor.minsk.by/jazz
*A monthly magazine on jazz, blues and other genders
of improvisation music.*

Spain

Cuaderno de Jazz
cuadernos@cuadernosdejazz.com
www.cuadernosdejazz.com
*Reflecting the diverse facets of jazz. Articles about
musicians (biographies, analysis of their work,
musical career, interviews).*

Sweden

Jazz Stage
jazzstage@merit.se
www.jazzstage.nu
The Scandinavian Jazz magazine.

United Kingdom

Avant
ttaylor228@aol.com
www.avantmag.com
*Jazz, free improvised music, electronic, experimental,
contemporary classical music and essentially
anything that is genuinely new and challenging.*

Jazz Break
info@jazzbreak.com
www.jazzbreak.com
*Our goal is to contribute, in our own way, to inform a
large international audience about the jazz actuality
in UK, France and anywhere else...*

Jazz UK
jazzuk.cardiff@virgin.net
www.jazzservices.org.uk
*The largest circulation (over 40,000) of any jazz
publication in the UK.*

Jazzwise
admin@jazzwise.com
www.jazzwise.com
*The only magazine devoted to covering the entire
spectrum, from cutting-edge contemporary jazz,
mainstream, fusion and improv to jazz-club crossover
and world-jazz.*

King's Jazz Review
ds.dial.pipex.com/jazzitoria
*A voice for New Orleans, Dixieland and Traditional
jazz in the UK.*

Liquid Jazz
www.liquidjazz.org.uk
*We strive to better promote jazz music. Let us know
what you want and need for your music to flow.*

Australia

Jazz Views
Greg Fisher glfisher@mail.picknowl.com.au
www.ozemail.com.au/~fishergl
*I do review CDs, books & concerts. I also do jazz
presentation on community radio - "Jazz at Six" 5UV
(531 AM)/5MBS (101.5 FM), "Jazz at One" 5MBS
(101.5 FM) and also the "Esoteric Circle" - 2 hours
of contemporary jazz and new music on Three D
Radio (93.7FM).*

Latin Music

La Banda Elástica
www.labandaelastica.com
Latin Alternative Music Magazine.

BoomOnline.com
promotions@boomonline.com
www.boomonline.com
*The community site for Latin rock, pop and
alternative entertainment.*

Brownpride Online
www.brownpride.com
*While Latinos, as a whole begin spreading across the
States and the world, Latinos in hip-hop will continue
to grow. Today, the underground scene is as big as it
has ever been. Good links to latino-artists all over.*

HispanicOnline.com
www.hispaniconline.com
Does reviews and has an artist-of-the-month feature.

LA FACTORÍA DEL RITMO
info@lafactoriadelritmo.com
www.lafactoriadelritmo.com
El primer magazine musical en español vía Internet.
En la red desde Febrero 1995.

Flamenco-world.com
magazine@flamenco-world.com
www.flamenco-world.com
Your one stop shop for anything and everything
Flamenco! The Flamenco-world site offers music
reviews, concert and conference information, links to
Flamenco music and dance classes and much more.

LaMusica.com
info@lamusica.com
www.lamusica.com
News, events, artists and some independent reviews
on this bilingual Latin music and entertainment site.

Latin Beat Magazine
info@latinbeatmagazine.com
www.latinbeatmagazine.com
News, reviews, features etc.

LatinJazzClub.com
news@latinjazzclub.com
www.latinjazzclub.com
A virtual on-line magazine dedicated to the
promotion, education and historical preservation of
Latin Jazz. Submit all Latin Jazz related press
releases, cd reviews, upcoming events and concerts,
new music bios.

LatinO Midwest News
www.latinomidwestnews.com
News, reviews, interviews...

MUSICA SALSA *Germany*
stefanrenz@musicasalsa.de
www.musicasalsa.de
Salsa, tropical and Caribbean music, artists,
orchestras, bands, disc-jockeys, events and Latin-
American culture in Germany, Colombia and more...

Picadillo
bishikawa@picadillo.com
www.picadillo.com
The web home of Latin Music. Here you can listen to
the best music in the world. Start here and follow links
to Latin music sites around the world. And visit our
band pages to meet the people that make this beautiful
music.

PicanteXpress *Canada*
info@picantexpress.com
www.picantexpress.com
Toronto's Latin entertainment magazine.

'LA'Ritmo.com
info@laritmo.com
www.laritmo.com
Straight from Nueva York, 'LA'Ritmo.com acts as a
bridge between the Latin music community and the
Net, featuring interviews of established and up-and-
coming artists, Top Latin charts, music news and
reviews of the latest hits.

Sabor
editor@sabormagazine.com
www.sabormagazine.net
Arts and entertainment magazine.

Salsaholic *Germany*
klaus@salsaholic.de
www.salsaholic.de
This German based site provides information about
salsa, a concert calendar for central Europe, 'gig
contacts' for musicians and promoters in Europe,
dancing workshops, a glossary of Latin music, CD
reviews with RealAudio sound samples and more.

SalsaPower.com
jacira@salsapower.com
www.salsapower.com
There are numerous Salsa related websites on the
internet, but this one is your definitive source for
Casino style Salsa and Rueda de Casino dance, as
well as Cuban music. Reviews, cyber radio links and
more.

Salsaroots.com
rita@salsacrazy.com
www.salsaroots.com
CD Reviews of everything new, old and
sizzling.devotees of Latin music.

Timba.com
mail@timba.com
www.timba.com
A Cuban culture and music website devoted to
bringing cyber surfers the latest in timba music news,
some independent reviews and concert information.

Vista USA
editor@vistausa.com
vistausa.com
For the latest and hottest updates in the world of
"Tropical Music" and more.

Metal

Heavy, Thrash, Grindcore, Death, Black, Doom,
Speed, Progressive, Viking metal, Hard Rock,
modern rock, stoner rock etc.

North America

United States

Abrasive Rock
www.abrasiverock.com
We cover Rock, Metal, Punk, Industrial, Death Metal,
Black Metal, Prog Metal, Stoner Rock, Doom Rock,
Sludge Rock and any other form of 'abrasive' rock.

Absolut Metal
Wolfie@AbsolutMetal.com
www.absolutmetal.com
Reviews, local tour dates/shows and other random
comments from the underground...

Adrenalin Metal Fanzine
Mike Burmeister adrenalinzine@hotmail.com
www.adrenalinfanzine.com
This is a 'zine that promotes bands of the various
metal styles via interviews, reviews, photos, links, ads
and more!

allthingsrock.com
Matt@allthingsrock.com
www.allthingsrock.com
Interviews, news, reviews, articles etc.

antimtv
masterantimtv@hotmail.com
www.antimtv.com
I built this site because of my undying love of metal
and a void that exists when it comes to metal videos
as well as metal coverage in general.

Anvil
www.anvilmagazine.com
The unholy bible of extreme music.

Aphelium
news@aphelium.com
www.aphelium.com
The Internet news channel for extreme music.

Atomic Chaser
TheAtomicChaser@yahoo.com
www.geocities.com/atomicchaser
Everything I wanted to hear in rock and roll music.
Melodic yet possessing a hard metallica edge.

Aural Decimation
Vomified@hotmail.com
www.auraldecimation.com
A metal/grind/underground extreme 'zine with a
dedicated staff fixated on bringing you honest, no-
bullshit reviews, interviews and resources. When you
send your material us you will get an honest,
relatively quick review. Material sent for review will
ALWAYS be reviewed.

Aversion Online
aversionline@holyterror.com
www.aversionline.com
Provides comprehensive coverage and exposure for
all forms of extreme/underground music, including
metal, hardcore/punk, emo/indie rock, experimental
electronic noise and everything in between.

BallBusterHardMUSIC.com
David La Duke BallBusterHard@webtv.net
www.ballbusterhardmusic.com
Without Prejudice, 100% Lead for your Head!! &
then some... SinBad Productions / Ball-Buster Music
Distribution & Recordings: Your International
Underground HARD Disc Connection!

Beyond Webzine
Nicolas Arnaud info@beyondwebzine.com
www.beyondwebzine.com
We review all Rock and Metal material. Signed or
unsigned bands.

Blabbermouth.net
bmouth@bellatlantic.net
www.roadrun.com/blabbermouth.net
All the latest metal news.

Black Cauldron
editor@black-cauldron.com
www.black-cauldron.com
Interested in having your music reviewed by Black
Cauldron? If so send me an email for more
information concerning the location to send material.

Black Metal Reviews
support@evilmusic.com
www.evilmusic.com/reviews
We promote the metal artists whose art is profound
enough that all of us want a copy and ignore trends
and superficial music. Our thought is that if we never
sell anything but what we'd give to a friend, we will
never have regrets - and nor will our customers.

Bludgawd
bludgawd@bludgawd.com
www.bludgawd.com
We collaborate with bands, labels, artists, fans etc...
To bring you up to date info on your favorites as well
as information for bands when they need a studio,
artist, producer, engineer or if they are looking for a
bit of promotional help.

Brutalism
twan@brutalism.com
www.brutalism.com
Interviews, Reviews etc.

Bully Magazine
info@bullymag.com
www.bullymag.com
Biting social and political commentary, sarcastic comedy pieces and in-depth coverage of the music that matters.

Chronicles of Chaos
www.chroniclesofchaos.com
Extreme music webzine. Updated daily!

Crusher Magazine
editatrix@crushermagazine.com
www.crushermagazine.com
We have our finger on the pulse of the ever-changing, ever-growing loud music scene. We reach into the underground as well as play above board with the mainstream.

DBN Magazine
Tim Maher dbn@gsta.net
www.dbnmagazine.com
We cover a wide range of musical genres including but not limited to all types of metal, Goth, hard rock, punk, hardcore, industrial and alternative. We've been around (as a print zine) since 1989 and have no plans to stop now.

Death Metal and Black Metal
prozak@anus.com
www.anus.com/metal
Reviews of metal, grindcore, punk, thrash as evolving history. Contains involved reviews of MP3 samples track lists covers. You can't buy anything - it's non profit.

Death Metal Reviews
www.evilmusic.com

deathgrind.com
jash@deathgrind.com
www.deathgrind.com
You must record your demo/CD/LP/EP whatever with a raw production. Therefore at home or garage with your own recording equipment. Good production is NOT what GoreGrind is all about.

DigitalMetal.com
info@digitalmetal.com
www.digitalmetal.com
Offering daily site updates in categories such as news, reviews and interviews as well as unlimited metal MP3 downloads through our partner E-music.

Dynamic Rock
www.dynamicrock.com
Our "Unknown" section is devoted to bands we have discovered. They have very little press coverage, but in our opinions, kick some ass. As always, we are looking for new bands, so email us if you are in an underground band.

The Edge
edgemag@satx.rr.com
www.theedgemagazine.com
A monthly music magazine that covers Rock, Heavy Metal, Classic Rock and Alternative Rock. THE EDGE supports national and unsigned bands. THE EDGE features in-depth one on one interviews, CD Reviews, show reviews as well as great stories from today's and yesterday's favorite artists.

ElectricBasement.com
rockdevil@electricbasement.com
www.electricbasement.com
This website has been constructed by traditional heavy rock enthusiasts who wish to promote the music they love and in turn enjoy the process of doing so. Promo materials sent that don't fit our SPECIFIC area of coverage will NOT be reviewed. No exceptions!

The End Times
endtimes@email.com
www.fortunecity.com/tinpan/4skins/212
An exhaustive and growing archive of Metal reviews from the more extreme side of the genre.

Euphony Magazine
Euphonymag@aol.com
www.euphonymag.com
We are a rock/metal publication with a print zine that appears 4 times a year. Due to constraints on time, energy and computers, we do NOT review MP3s. If you want us to hear your music, send a CD.

FAC 193
www.fac193.com
Reviews of modern rock music.

Feast of Hate and Fear
info@feastofhateandfear.com
feastofhateandfear.com
Online zine with a tongue planted firmly in every cheek. Dark archives, travelogs, strange articles, music reviews and the Ever-Increasing Interview Project.

FuBARM
anubis@fubarm.com
www.fubarm.com

The Gauntlet
Jason fisher moshpit@thegauntlet.com
www.thegauntlet.com
Huge archive of metal indie musicians, bi-weekly mailing list, reviews, videos and more.

The Grimoire of Exalted Deeds
masterzebub@aol.com
www.thegrimoire.com
A death metal magazine for assholes...written by assholes. The web site is based on the 64 page magazine.

Hammerhead
hamhedzine@aol.com
www.hammerheadzine.com
Over a decade on paper and now infecting the web.

The Hard Rock Society
dans@icnt1.com
www.hardrocksociety.com
A Hard Rock/Heavy Metal site with news, reviews and photos. Home of Riff Radio, a 24 hour streaming metal station with live requests, so submit your material for the playlist! Riff Radio - Metal. The way it should be.

Harvest Moon Music
Dave Knoch tattooz@harvestmoonmusic.com
www.harvestmoonmusic.com
Webzine focused primarily on rock and heavy metal album reviews and band information.

Headbanger's Delight
info@headbangersdelight.com
www.headbangersdelight.com
Bands interested in us reviewing their material let us know. We would be glad to help.

Hellfrost.com
mirrorsaweye@aol.com
www.hellfrost.com
We offer hundreds of mp3's, contacts, interviews and in-depth CD reviews of death, black, thrash, doom, heavy metal, grindcore, industrial, ambient and more!

HitThePit.Com
derek@hitthepit.com
www.hitthepit.com
Unsigned bands can pick any writer from HitThePit.com to review their material. What we suggest doing is reading different writers style and pick the one you like most.

In Depth
ConcertRag@aol.com
www.indepthzine.com
An internet music magazine focusing on the live aspect of new and established talent through interviews, show and album reviews and live pictures.

Infernal Combustion
keith@infernalcombustion.com
www.infernalcombustion.com
A heavy metal website divided into two parts. "Lies" (the 'original' IC, for all y'all old-schoolers) was launched in 1998 as a parody heavy metal webzine. "Truth" was launched in March 2001 as a legitimate source of metal news, album reviews, band interviews and other information.

Inside Metal
Sam Culpin inside_metal@hotmail.com
www.insidemetal.tk
This website is one of your best sources for Heavy Music. With MP3's, Videos, Photos, Reviews, New Releases, Links and more.

Into Obscurity
bane@into-obscurity.com
www.into-obscurity.com
An online zine dedicated to all forms of metal, hardcore, punk, indie, emo and any other forms of underground music.

Inversemusic.com
andrew@inverse-music.com
www.inverse-music.com
News, reviews, interviews etc.

Jen's Metal Page
JensMetalPage@comcast.net
www.jensmetalpage.com
News, reviews, interviews, mp3s etc.

Justin's Heavy Metal Site
justinh@seanet.com
members.tripod.com/~JustinHarvey

lambgoat.com
info@lambgoat.com
www.lambgoat.com
A webzine dedicated to hardcore and metal music. We feature news, reviews, interviews, audio samples, discussion forums and more. The site is updated daily and viewed by thousands of music fans every week

Lamentations of the Flame Princess Weekly
Jim Raggi lotfp@mindspring.com
www.mindspring.com/~raggije
LotFP looks favorably upon ambitious and unique metal bands of most styles. Don't ask me if you can submit anything. Just send the thing if you want review consideration. You're a fucking musician! Be BOLD! CDs only. No tapes or vinyl or DVDs.

Last Labyrinth
rich@lastlabyrinth.com
www.lastlabyrinth.com
We cover True, Thrash, Death and Black Metal bands, ranging from Iron Maiden to Immortal. We have News, Reviews, Interviews, Live Photos and anything else we feel is worth covering.

Maximum Metal
www.maximmetal.com
If you want to be reviewed, interviewed, poked, or prodded, send us your demos, promos, or videos. We will review every promo and demo we receive!!!!!

Live 4 Metal
live4metal666@aol.com
www.live4metal.com
The best of the Metal World. From the major players to the best of the underground.

Loudside
info@loudside.com
www.loudside.com

Maelstrom
Roberto Martinelli roma@maelstrom.nu
www.maelstrom.nu
We hope that this site will serve as a forum for anyone around the world to learn more about metal and other underground forms of music and to talk and correspond with other people.

MegaKungFu.com
brent@megakungfu.com
megakungfu.com
Metal, Punk and Hardcore MKF style.

Metal Core
metalczine@aol.com
www.metalcorefanzine.com
Our webzine has a review section that signed and unsigned bands can send stuff for review. We prefer the heavier side of things.

The Metal Directory
Matt B. webmaster@metal-directory.com
www.metal-directory.com
A comprehensive online resource for extreme music.

The Metal Exiles
robin@internationallonghairs.com
www.metal-exiles.com
Submit your band for our local/unsigned feature.

metal-e-zine.com
www.metal-e-zine.com
Featuring reviews grouped into music and book categories. Extra categories (Artists of the Moment, Interviews and News) cater for background information.

Metal Fanatix
LEGION59@aol.com
www.metalfanatix.com
Bands interested in getting their album reviewed, contact us.

Metal Judgement
info@metaljudgment.com
www.metaljudgment.com
Dedicated to delivering the most in-depth reviews on the world of heavy metal; from new albums and concerts to the classics of yesteryear.

Metal Kung Fu
webmaster@megakungfu.com
www.megakungfu.com

Metal Maniacs
MetalManiacsNews@aol.com
www.metalmaniacs.com
News, reviews etc.

Metal Meltdown
drmetal@metalmeltdown.com
www.metalmeltdown.com
Metal interviews, radio, reviews, news and pictures.

Metal Online Magazine (MoM)
Erik Linneman xoderusx@aol.com
www.metalonmag.com
If you want to contact us in order to submit materials for reviewing, please send an e-mail.

Metal Reviews
contact@metalreviews.com
www.metalreviews.com
Loads of reviews. Updated weekly!

Metal Rules! Magazine
metaljef@yahoo.com
www.metalrulesmagazine.com
Reviews all Heavy Music, signed and unsigned!

Metal Sludge
metalsludge@metal-sludge.com
www.metal-sludge.com
Rock's biggest and most controversial website!

The Metal Update
editor@metalupdate.com
www.metalupdate.com
Providing the most accurate, unbiased, up to date and complete metal news possible. If you, your band, your label, your website, your 'zine or your friends have information that you believe would be of interest to Metal Update readers, please contact us.

MetalGospel.com
skyklad@metalgospel.com
www.MetalGospel.com
While my label might lead some to believe I only listen to traditional Black/Death/Thrash Metal I in fact listen to everything that is clearly Metal with balls.

METALREVIEW.COM
www.metalreview.com
The site that provides you with insightful and focused reviews with the intention to steer you to the finest metal for your dollar. We specialize in Album Reviews, Concert Reviews, Band Interviews and DVD Reviews.

metalunderground.com
metalunderground.com
Run by metal-lovers and we appreciate any promo items and/or merchandise sent to us. We also love discovering new bands and music, so the more underground, the better! Feel free to send promo CDs, demos, stickers, t-shirts etc. We strive to have each CD reviewed by more than one staff member for a balanced opinion.

Midwest Metal Magazine
tom@MidwestMetalMagazine.com
www.midwestmetalmagazine.com
Send Metal music, CD's, Cassette Tapes, Vinyl and contact/photos (if available) to above address. No Mp3 files or any other computer shit.

Modern Music Magazine
wright@modernmusicmagazine.com
www.modernmusicmagazine.com

Mourning the Ancient
sunlessdawn@mourningtheancient.com
www.mourningtheancient.com
Offering unique black and death metal interviews, poetry, dark medieval photography, samples and much more.

Museum of Rock
daryl@psychic-rebel.com
www.psychic-rebel.com
Long live excellent music forever!

Music Extreme
info@musicextreme.com
www.musicextreme.com
Lots of new reviews every month!

Music Mayhem
j@musicmayhem.com
www.musicmayhem.com
Everything from Interviews, to reviews of the new releases, to concert shots.

Neckbreaker Online Metal Reviews
Metalmark55@hotmail.com
clix.to/Metalmark
The reviewer is also the host of a local metal radio show.

Noize Pollution
info@noizepollution.com
noizepollution.com
Every month our beloved metal miester T-Bone will dig up his latest local band for you dirt heads. Want to become a Local spotlight band? Send us your CDs, bio's, live VHS tapes, pictures, website address and contact info.

Nosebleed17
www.nosebleed17.com
The latest news, album reviews, concert reviews, tour dates, interviews and features MANY unsigned bands!

Oddshaped
kevinsnotdead@hotmail.com
www.oddshaped.com
I don't like to post negative reviews. We're about the promotion of hardcore/metal, not shit talking a label and its band.

On Track Magazine
Info@ontrackmagazine.com
www.ontrackmagazine.com
Our mission is to bring the best up-to-date coverage of your favorite hard music bands. We provide interviews with intelligent, innovative questions and topics. We supply concert and CD reviews from a wide range of hard music artists.

Open Up And Say
Wes Royer editor@openupandsay.com
www.openupandsay.com
An online music magazine with reviews, interviews, news and links on anything that is of the rock and metal genres.

Pit Magazine
pitmag@aol.com
www.pitmagazine.com
The Extreme Music Magazine.

PiTRiFF Online
richwithhatred@pitriff.com
www.pitriff.com
News, reviews, radio etc.

Polluteme.com
Clayton White pollutedone@polluteme.com
www.polluteme.com
Your one-stop resource for rock, metal, death, punk, alternative, grunge, hardcore and ska. Our mission is to revolutionize the music industry as it is known today into a more fair production and promotion of musicians based on their talent, dedication and drive.

The Pure Rock Shop
Kara Uhrlen kara@tprs.com
www.tprs.com
If you are in a band or represent a band and would like to have your material reviewed, be featured in our spotlight artist sections and/or contribute items for a Pure Rock Shop contest, please contact us.

Rainbow Flame's Metal Domain
Rainstar2k@hotmail.com
www.geocities.com/SoHo/Studios/2786
We specialize in long, detailed reviews of heavy metal albums from both the past and the present and have had several feature and novelty pages that have made the site somewhat unique.

RevelationZ
mail@revelationz.net
www.revelationz.net
Your Heavy metal and Hard Rock resource.

Revolver
revolvermag@aol.com
www.revolvermag.com
The world's loudest rock magazine!

Rock and a Hard Place Zine
rockhardtorch@hotmail.com
www.rockhardplace.com
CD reviews, independent and imported Rock, Metal and AOR.

Rocknation
info@rocknation.tv
www.rocknation.tv
Hard rock, heavy metal and punk news, reviews and interviews. Demos accepted.

RockNet Webzine
RockNetWebzine@aol.com
www.rocknetwebzine.com
Would you like us to review your CD? Email us!

RockRage.com
info@rockrage.com
www.rockrage.com
We also highlight the independent rock artist with reviews, suggestions and downloadable MP3's.

Rough Edge
rscottb@roughedge.com
www.roughedge.com
Featuring CD and live reviews, news, photos and more.

Satan Stole My Teddybear
ssmt@chedsey.com
www.chedsey.com
Reviews on heavy metal, punk, industrial, progressive, ambient and other music guaranteed to upset your folks. Please do not send cassettes or vinyl for review.

Score! Music Magazine
score@scorerocks.com
www.scorerocks.com
We provide our readers with the best cross section of today's artist's possible, understanding that radio play and record sales, while useful mediums, are poor indicators of greatness.

Screachen Publications
Editor@Screachen.com
www.screachen.com
Hard Rock / Alternative Music Journal featuring: Music News and Press Releases, Interviews and Reviews. The world's largest and most accurate database detailing the true origins behind band/stage names, music related company names etc. / Weird (yet true) Music Stories.

Sea of Tranquility
info@seaoftranquility.org
www.seaoftranquility.org
The Quarterly Journal of Heavy Metal, Progressive Metal and Progressive Rock.

Silent Uproar
p-layer@silentuproar.com
www.silentuproar.com
We cover a wide range of alternative, metal, hardcore, punk, techno and various other kinds of music.

slackerSnation.com
jk@slackersnation.com
www.slackersnation.com
This is not only a website for a few internet dorks to express themselves. Far from it. While the majority of the articles and reviews written and posted on this site are done by a core few, slackerSnation.com is an open forum for ANYONE from ANYWHERE to get their opinions and thoughts heard.

Sleaze Roxx
skid@sleazeroxx.com
www.sleazeroxx.com
Your Hard Rock and Heavy Metal resource.

Sleazegrinder
Ken McIntyre thesleazegrinder@hotmail.com
www.sleazegrinder.com
Wholly dedicated- like a tiger to its prey- to the preservation and ultimate domination of full-tilt, high octane, blistering rock and roll. Reviews? We've got a million of 'em...hell, we've even got our own label. The catch? Oh, you've gotta rock. And we do mean ROCK.

Sociopathic Despair
sociod@hotmail.com
come.to/despair
Covers a variety of styles in heavy metal and hardcore and an array of libertarian/nationalist socio-political issues. Bands, record labels and zines can send items for review.

Soul Killer
neil@soulburn3d.com
www.soulkillerwebzine.com
Dedicated To The Very Best In Death, Grind, Classic, Techno and New Metal.

Soulineyes.com
Maurice Brand maurice@soulineyes.com
www.soulineyes.com
Music webzine that covers bands in the genres of metal/rock/punk/hardcore and other alternative music.

Tartarean Desire Webzine
tartareandesire@yahoo.com
embark.to/tartareandesire
A webzine dedicated to metal and dark music with reviews, interviews etc. Usually updated once a week.

theprp.com
wookubus@theprp.com
www.theprp.com
Our goal is to introduce lesser known acts to a wider audience while also covering the established bands that currently make up the metal scene.

Throat Culture
info@throatculture.net
www.throatculture.net
A quarterly print magazine with national and international distribution. The web zine contains all the content of the print issue in an easy to navigate internet context.

The Tribal Rock Company
matt@thetrc.net
thetrc.net
Your source for hard rock, metal and hardcore.

Ultimate Metal Reviews
info@metal-reviews.com
www.metal-reviews.com
Once an album review is posted, it stays up forever. Because of this, plus the fact that well over 2,000 people visit the page a day, indie bands are getting a good amount of exposure. Because of the rising costs, a $20 processing fee is now required with your CD/promo kit.

Unchain the Underground
al@unchain.com
www.unchain.com
Web site featuring reviews and interviews related to all forms of extreme music. Unchain the underground receives, on the average, 3000 unique visitors a day.

Uranium
smathers@uraniummusic.com
www.uraniummusic.com
Uranium is one of the deadliest metals known to man. Its relative molecular mass is 238 grams and is therefore not only one of the deadliest metals but one of the heaviest. Need I explain any further?

Vibrations of Doom
vibrationsofdoom@hotmail.com
vibrationsofdoom.com
My magazine may not be the best on the planet, but I offer as much for the music (and metal) fan as anyone else!

Violated Rot
byro33@attbi.com
www.violatedrot.com
If you want to be reviewed on this site, Send demos, Promo packs etc. to us.

White Trash Devil
Sick Royale sick@whitetrashdevil.com
www.whitetrashdevil.com
You'll never find a more wretched hive of scum and villainy. We accept CDs, CD-Rs, VHS and DVD. No cassettes or vinyl, please. After you mail your package, please contact Sick Royale and let him know who you are and what you're sending.

wickedland
propheci@wickedland.com
www.wickedland.com

Worm Gear
korgull@chartermi.net
www.crionicmind.org/wormgear

you got rocked
info@yougotrocked.com
www.yougotrocked.com
Bands or labels that want to submit material to be reviewed, get in touch with us.

Canada

Blistering.com
rob@blistering.com
www.blistering.com
Submit your CD's and demo's as we currently review both signed & independent acts.

Brave Words and Bloody Knuckles
bwbk@inforamp.net
www.bravewords.com
BW &BK bangs heads with the finest METAL talent from around the world. BW &BK is 64 (or more!) glossy pages loaded with the most current METAL news, features, columns, reviews and the massive METAL Forecast!

martinpopoff.com
martinp@inforamp.net
www.martinpopoff.com
Reviews Editor and Writer (Hard Reviews), Views Editor and Writer (Hard Views).

Metallian.com
metallian@canada.com
www.metallian.com
A site dedicated to the promotion of all sub-genres of heavy metal. It is designed to act as a metal resource and as a fans' page. Metallian.com welcomes all metal music and news submissions.

Metalpus
thrall6@yahoo.com
www.homestead.com/metalpus/mainpage.html
Dedicated to extreme metal of all kinds, Grindcore, Death Metal, Black Metal, you name it. It includes CD / Demo / 7" reviews, album covers and links to other really cool sites that you should check out.

Midnight Metal
mike@midnightmetal.com
www.midnightmetal.com
If you think you've got a cool band and you'd like me to review, sample or preview your album on air just send it to me by snail mail.

Monster's World of Metal
mwomzine@yahoo.com
www.monstersworldofmetal.com
If you would like to have your cd reviewed, please take note of our new snail mail address (found on our website).

Rooted Edmonton
monica@rootededmonton.com
www.rootededmonton.com
This site is for anyone who loves music. You will not find any mainstream bands though. I am asking you to open your minds & experience the world of original Indie music. Most of the music you will find on this site is Metal, Alterative, Punk, Hardcore or Rock n' Roll.

Stoner Rock Chick
Deanna St.Croix deanna@stonerrockchick.com
www.stonerrockchick.com
This site is dedicated to bring you information about new albums, news, tour dates and events. Bands and Labels, send your CDs for review.

stonerrock.com
dan@stonerrock.com
www.stonerrock.com
If you're disgusted with the pathetic state of popular music, you've come to the right place.

Unrestrained
info@unrestrainedmag.com
www.unrestrainedmag.com
Devoted to the underground and below. Coverage takes form in interviews, record reviews, zine reviews, demo reviews and concert reviews. Whether it be death metal, black metal, thrash metal, grindcore, whatever, it's here.

South America

Brazil

Roadie Crew
metal@roadiecrew.com
www.roadiecrew.com

Valhalla
Eliton Tomasi eliton@valhalla.com.br
www.valhalla.com.br
One of the most important Metal Magazines from South America.

Chile

Metal Kingdom
contacto@metalkingdom.cl
www.metalkingdom.cl
If you have a band and video clips and you want to participate in our program and be reviewed in our site, contact us.

Colombia

himnosrituales
himnosrituales@himnosrituales.com
www.himnosrituales.com

Europe

Austria

Resurrection
webmaster@resurrection.at
www.resurrection.at

Belgium

Abla Zine
www.multimania.com/caddaric

The Dark Towers of Lugburz
rC@lugburz.be
www.dma.be/p/lugburz
A support site for Belgian Black & Death Metal bands.

Deafness
deafness@wanadoo.be
www.deafness.fr.fm
On this website you can find all you want about Metal and our radio show spreading Metal every Saturday between 17:00 and 19:00. Death, Black, Brutal, Grind, Underground, Interviews, Info sequences and so on...

Doom-metal.com
info@doom-metal.com
www.doom-metal.com
Keeping you updated about the latest happenings in the Doom-metal scene. From new releases to news bites about bands. If you are in a band or own an independent record label and wish to submit albums to us we are always welcome to review them.

New Flesh
newflesh@multimania.com
membres.lycos.fr/newflesh
All material send to us will get a fair and honest review by the crewmember that has the closest feeling with your music style. We may also contact you for interviews or other fun stuff.

Denmark

Metalized
metalized@metalized.net
www.metalized.net
The Greatest Metal Magazine in Scandinavia.

mighty music
info@mightymusic.dk
www.mightymusic.dk
We recommend bands, signed as well as unsigned to send material for review.

Finland

meteli.net
tapahtumat@meteli.net
www.meteli.net
Metal in Finland.

France

Decibels
www.metal-extreme.com
Le metal extreme.

Heavy Metal Universe
Ludovic Castelbou
webmaster@heavymetaluniverse.com
www.heavymetaluniverse.com
Send us your promo material for review. Visit our website for the mailing address.

Lords of Winter
lord-of-winter@caramail.com
lordsofwinter.free.fr
Vous trouverez ici de nombreuses chroniques, des mini-sites complets (bio, disco, photos...) sur de nombreux groupes, des news régulières de la scène et plein d'autres choses que nous vous laissons découvrir.

secret-of-steel.com
j.astruc@wanadoo.fr
www.secret-of-steel.com
News, reviews, concert reviews etc.

Germany

Amboss
info@amboss-mag.de
www.amboss-mag.de
Heavy metal and Gothic music magazine.

Ancient Spirit
sascha@ancientspirit.de
www.ancientspirit.de

BARBARIAN WRATH
blackgoat@barbarianwrath.org
www.BarbarianWrath.org
I have gathered strength and force to create a stronghold in the true Underground spirit of the 80s and it is my expressed will to turn back the wheel of time in order to preserve Metal in its pure essence.

Bright Eyes Germany
info@brighteyes.de
www.bright-eyes.de
Updates, Interviews, Reviews, Tour dates, Festival-News und vieles mehr ...

Daredevil
daredevil@tesionmail.de
www.daredevil.de
Hey there Lovers and Makers of Heavy-Rock, if you want your stuff reviewed just send it to us.

Deathgrind
mail@deathgrind.de
www.deathgrind.de

Die Geister, die ich rief
www.geister-bremen.de

echoes-online.de
redaktion@echoes-online.de
www.echoes-online.de

Eternity
redaktion@eternitymagazin.de
eternitymagazin.de
Alle Infos rund um die aktuelle und ältere Ausgaben, sowie, News, Interviews, Specials, Diskussionen, Festivalberichte, Dates...

Guts Fuck Magazine
members.tripod.com/BSBB

Heavy-Metal.de
mail@heavy-metal.de
www.heavy-metal.de

Internet@Metal
michael.schild@metalius.de
www.internet-metal.de
The ballbreaker in the WorldWideWeb! We have a newcomer bands, includes sound files and a lot of pictures as well as reviews of band CD's and videos.

Invader
editorial@invader.de
www.invader.de

Metal District
redaktion@metal-district.de
www.metal-district.de
We review all styles of Metal, do many interviews, have an underground and demo-section and much more!

Metal Inside
torben@metal-inside.de
www.metal-inside.de

The Metal Observer
alex@metal-observer.de
www.metal-observer.com
Principally every release (be it tape, CD, LP or anything like that) is accepted, as long as it can be counted among Hard'n'Heavy, no matter if it is AOR or Power Metal, Gothic Metal or Grindcore, we have (next to) no limits here.

Metal Online
Bounce@metal.de
metal-online.de

Noize Magazine
editorial@noize-magazine.com
www.noize-magazine.de
Mainly concerning the Death/Black and Thrash Metal genre also firing you into the Grindcore and Hardcore dimension. Check out interviews, CD reviews and also the latest news, tour dates and much more from the scene!

Panzer Magazine
info@panzer-magazine.com
www.panzer-magazine.com
The latest news, reviews, interviews, releases, tour dates up to the minute headlines!

Powermetal.de
weihrauch@powermetal.de
www.powermetal.de
A German online metal fan magazine. You can get much information about metal and gothic bands, also reviews about concerts and cds and interviews. Check it out!

Powertrip
axel@powertrip.de
www.powertrip.de
The dark and heavy magazine.

Rock Hard Online
hansi@rockhard.de
www.rockhard.de

Rockbytes
info@rockbytes.de
www.rockbytes.de

The Sacred Metal Page
mkohsiek@t-online.de
www.geocities.com/SunsetStrip/Stage/5007

Silentium Noctis
info@silentium-noctis.de
www.silentium-noctis.de

Snakepit
heinz.konzett@EUnet.at
truemetal.org/snakepit
Around 200 reviews per issue.

Tiefgang
verlosung@tiefgang-online.de
www.tiefgang-online.de
Endlich ist es soweit. Mit der Rubrik "Support the Underground" wollen wir Nachwuchs/Underground Bands, die noch keinen Plattenvertrag haben, die Möglichkeit bieten auf sich aufmerksam zu machen!

The Underground Empire Metal Magazine
Battle Angel ba@underground-empire.de
www.underground-empire.de
Präsentiert Deutschlands führendes metal e-mag..

Underground Society
Undersociety@aol.com
undersociety.free.fr
A french e-zine dedicated to all metal styles!! Bands, labels, zines and others send your promo packages for reviews / interviews / articles to us.

Vampster
kontakt@vampster.com
www.vampster.com
Bands! Labels! Veranstalter! Schickt Daten, Promos, Demos etc. an die obenstehende Adresse. Bei Fragen wendet Ihr Euch bitte an Andrea, andrea@vampster.com, Tel. +49 (7144) 894099.

Voices from the Darkside
www.voicesfromthedarkside.de
The magazine for brutal Death, Thrash and Black Metal!

Vönger
webmaster@voenger.de
www.voenger.de
Deutsche Black Metal Seite mit Reviews, Konzertberichten, Interviews, Merchandise, Fotos, Forum, Links, Terminen und vielem mehr!

Greece

Altars of Metal
www.altarsofmetal.com
German Metal/Rock/Gothic Music Magazine with Reviews, Tour dates etc.

Metal Domination
Webmaster@metaldomination.com
www.metaldomination.com
Send stuff for review (CD's, Demos, 'Zines, MONEY!!!) All stuff will be reviewed or mentioned in the webzine.

Metal Eagle
vrkirik@hotmail.com
www.metaleagle.com
The bands that would like to see their demos/promos reviewed by the editors of METAL E@GLE, should visit our DEMOS section.

Metal Temple
webmaster@metal-temple.com
www.metal-temple.com
Spread the word, the metal religion has its own Temple!

SKYLIGHT
Billy Infantis Byfantis@yahoo.com
www.geocities.com/skylightgr
An on-line zine that covers classic rock/hard rock and also has a partnership with The Dog Zine that is distributed for free all over Greece.

Tombstone.gr
info@tombstone.gr
www.tombstone.gr
By metalheads.....for metalheads.

Italy

Heavy Metal Portal
zoltanthemage@hmportal.it
www.hmportal.it

Malta

Solemn Music
solemusic@hotmail.com
www.solemn.tk
Dedicated to extreme metal music from heavy metal to black metal and ambient. Reviews and interviews.

The Netherlands

Aardschok
mike@aardschok.com
www.aardschok.com
You can send all CD's, demos and bios to: Aardschok bv, PO Box 7, 5690 AA Son, the Netherlands

Lords of Metal
belegost@multiweb.nl
www.lordsofmetal.nl/english
Published 12 times a year with fresh CD reviews, gig reviews and of course new interviews. The other sections will also be updated if need be.

Roadburn
Walter Hoeijmakers walter@roadburn.com
www.roadburn.com
A gut level understanding of the hard rock riffs born in the late 60's that have come to adulthood with today's amazing recording technology. Contribute all your comments, recommendations, CD's, LP's demo's, gifts etc, to us.

ROCKEZINE
info@rockezine.com
www.rockezine.com
Hard rock magazine. Reviews, interviews etc.

Stoned Gods
El Niño elnino999@stonedgods.com
www.stonedgods.com
Heavy-psychedelia and dirty rock'n roll.

Strickle
www.strickle.com
A rock review site and more specific in the general stoner-rock genre. Heavy rock, stonerrock, fuzz, riffrock, southern rock, 70tiz rock, sludge, doomrock, garagerock... you can find it all here. Strickle.com is here to spice up the poor amount of stoner sites in the Benelux area.

Vampire Magazine
Ricardo@vampire-magazine.com
www.vampire-magazine.com
Bands, Labels, Distro, Zines...just send in your stuff for a fair review and a possible interview!

Norway

Demonic Horde
poem_4_the_dead@hotmail.com
www.demonichorde.com
News, reviews, shows etc.

Metal Express Radio Show
info@metalexpress.no
www.metalexpress.no
While you listen to the show make sure you check out the album reviews site that will be updated frequently!

Scream Magazine
scream@scream.no
www.scream.no
Norway's biggest metal magazine!

Poland

Agonia
noxfil@poczta.onet.pl
www.agonia.dagdy.net
We deal with extreme & flamboyant music.

Legion Magazine
legion@nestor.minsk.by
www.nestor.minsk.by/legion

Masterful
olo@masterful.art.pl
www.masterful.art.pl
Dedicated to the most brutal genres of metal music. We mainly deal with Death, Grind, sometimes thrash and black. Just send me info about your band, activity, your web page, link to MP3 files you'd like to see on our page...

Multum In Parvo
marjush@o2.pl
www.mip.av.pl/mip

rockmetal.pl
rockmetal@rockmetal.pl
www.rockmetal.pl
Rock i metal po polsku.

Portugal

Ancient Ceremonies
ancient.cer@netcabo.pt
www.ancientceremonies.com
Ancient Ceremonies magazine is now sold worldwide at TOWER RECORDS stores.

Romania

Arbor |Mundi
dango@as.ro
www.arbormundi.as.ro
Underground e-zine from Romania. Metal, experimental, avant-garde, noise, death, black and many more.

Russia

Extreme Music News
emn@nestor.minsk.by
nestor.minsk.by/emn
We hope that we can help musicians and labels by promoting their releases and distributing any related information for them.

Musica Must Die
musica@mustdie.ru
musica.mustdie.ru
Professional metal magazine. Everything about metal music. Frequently updated reviews, news, interviews with musicians and articles about heavy music.

totalmetal.net
info@totalmetal.net
www.totalmetal.net
Russian's #1 Heavy Metal. Contributions by top Russian music journalists.

Spain

Basa Rock
rafabasa@telepolis.com
www.rafabasa.com

fleshrites.com
info@fleshrites.com
fleshrites.com
Reviews, interviews, promotions.

Heavy Weight
www.truemetal.org/heavyweight

XTREEM MUSIC
info@xtreemmusic.com
www.xtreemmusic.com
Our goal is to become the world's biggest portal devoted to extreme music.

Sweden

Close Up
mail@closeupmagazine.net
www.closeupmagazine.net
A forum for all types of extreme and heavy music!

GL Productions
metalculte@hotmail.com
hem.passagen.se/lillie

Switzerland

Swiss Metal Factory
metal@metalfactory.ch
www.metalfactory.ch
Reviews, interviews, concerts etc.

United Kingdom

Black Velvet
editor@blackvelvetmagazine.com
www.blackvelvetmagazine.com
A glossy, professionally printed 36 paged fanzine/independent magazine based in the UK which features glam, punk, rock, metal and more. It's written with honesty and enthusiasm. We love rock music and we love writing about it.

Justwannarock.com
editor@justwannarock.com
www.justwannarock.com
Got a band? Got a web site for the band? Want to be interviewed? Well we can help. If you want a bit of publicity for your band and to have an interview/gig review conducted then all you have to do is email us and we'll sort something out for you.

Lykos
Sam Wright editor@lykoszine.co.uk
www.lykoszine.co.uk
Website, fanzine and free newsletter combined. Underground and mainstream metal. All styles, from death to heavy. Interviews, reviews, free email etc.

Metal Hammer
daniel.lane@futurenet.co.uk
www.metalhammer.co.uk
If you would like to see your band in the pages of Metal Hammer, send a copy of your latest demo (preferably on CD or CDR), along with a brief biography of your band and a recent photo

Metalville
metalliville@hotmail.com
www.metalliville.com
An Excellent Rock/Metal Webzine featuring Interviews and many reviews.

Planet-Loud
info@planet-loud.com
www.planet-loud.com
The loudest music site on the net!

Powerplay
webmaster@powerplaymagazine.co.uk
www.powerplaymagazine.co.uk
Hard, Heavy, Power, Prog, Progressive, Speed, AOR, FM, Death, Extreme and Black.

ROCK SOUND
darren.taylor@ixopub.co.uk
www.rock-sound.net
The fastest growing monthly music magazine in the UK. We feature all your favourite bands as well as a whole host of up and coming talent.

ROCKREVIEW.co.uk
cbo@rockreview.co.uk
www.rockreview.co.uk
Our aim to provide news and reviews from the world of rock & metal.

Stormbringer
derek@stormbringerwebzine.co.uk
www.stormbringerwebzine.co.uk
*Heavy Metal, Hard Rock, Progressive Rock,
Progressive Metal Webzine featuring latest news, CD
Reviews, Interviews, Tour Information and Demo
Tape Reviews.*

Terrorizer
editorial@terrorizer.com
www.terrorizer.co.uk
*The world's number one magazine for extreme music
of ANY kind. Whether it's Metal, Hardcore or
Industrial, we aim to include it and write about it.*

UK RockNet
info@ukrocknet.com
www.ukrocknet.com
*We promise we will attempt to review all material sent
in.*

Australia/New Zealand

The Buzz
psutton@r150.aone.net.au
www.ozonline.com.au/buzz
CD reviews, interviews and coverage of local artists.

Loud! Online
edjkrusha@nextcentury.com.au
www.geocities.com/SunsetStrip/Stage/4599
*Dedicated to the promotion and exposure of
Australian heavy metal music in all its forms. You'll
find playlists from my radio program; elsewhere
within you'll find CD reviews, demo reviews and an
up to the minute guide to gigs nationwide.*

Metalshop.com
www.Metalshop.com
*Under The Gun has features, ramblings and reviews
from metal's experts. There are regular columns from
Murray Engleheart, Rod Yates and Metalshop's own
Metal Monitor and Gig Guide amongst other regular
contributors.*

metalshtorm
apapworth@yahoo.com
www.metalshtorm.com
*Storming onto the web with the grace and enthusiasm
of a fat alcoholic, METALSHTORM is a webzine
dedicated to promoting the UNDERGROUND, with
an emphasis on DEATH METAL.*

Primal Agony
primalagony@iprimus.com.au
www.primalagony.musicpage.com
*An Aussie site with heaps of Aussie and international
Metal of all metal styles.*

New Age Music

Amazing Sounds
mail@amazings.com
www.amazings.com
*Covers electronic music, Ambient, New Instrumental
Music, World Music, Electroacoustic, New Age and
other alternative genres. In Amazing Sounds you will
find all the ingredients that can be found in
conventional magazines (news, articles, interviews, a
great amount of album reviews…).*

AmbiEntrance
dopdyke@spiderbytes.com
www.ambientrance.org
*Covers ambient, electronic and/or experimental
recordings.*

Awareness Magazine
awarenessmag@earthlink.net
www.awarenessmag.com
*Holistic magazine with an estimated readership of
about 165,000 individuals, distributed mainly in
California. Articles on alternative health treatments,
spiritual issues, self esteem, a variety of regular
columns, book, music and video reviews.*

Changes
comments@changes.org
www.changes.org
*A page whose home was born in the Kosmos. We
believe in the capacity of the human race to evolve.
We have just opened a new CD review page on our
site.*

electronicmusic.com
core@electronicmusic.com
www.electronicmusic.com
*Please send a CD, biography, contact information
and a little about the musical equipment used to us. If
we like what we hear, you'll get your music reviewed.*

EarthLight Magazine
www.earthlight.org
*We do very occasional reviews, usually CD's that are
linked to an issue theme. We would consider
reviewing a CD if it was linked in that way.*

Innerchange
Karen Newton editor@innerchangemag.com
innerchangemag.com
*A forum to share information with others on spiritual
journeys. Our focus includes, but is not limited to,
exploring oneness with the universe, bringing spirit
into the workplace, investigating complementary
healing practices and voicing environmental
concerns.*

Kindred Spirit *UK*
mail@kindredspirit.co.uk
www.kindredspirit.co.uk
The UK's leading guide for body, mind and spirit.

Magical Blend
info@magicalblend.com
www.magicalblend.com
*An entertaining and thoroughly unique look at the
modern spiritual lifestyle. We show you how to get in
touch with the spirituality that exists both within
yourself and in the world at large.*

Music for a New Age
nleacy@cix.compulink.co.uk
www.mfna.org
*If anyone would like me to review their music then
please email me for further details.*

NAPRA Music Reviews
napraexec@napra.com
www.napra.com
*A trade association involved in the creation,
distribution and sale of books and other products that
support spiritual growth, healthy living and positive
social change.*

New Age Retailer
Luanne@newageretailer.com
Ray@NewAgeRetailer.com
www.newageretailer.com
*We are the #1 trade magazine for retailers of New Age
books, music and sidelines. We have two independent
music review columns that run in all 7 issues of the
magazine. Music reviews are complementary.*

New Age Publishing
editor@bodyandsoulmag.com
www.bodyandsoulmag.com
*You'll read about the latest thinking on subjects such
as alternative medicine, spirituality, the mind/body
connection, work, money and the environment. You'll
also find reviews of current books and music.*

New Earth Records
www.newearthrecords.com
*Founded in 1990 in Munich, Germany, New Earth
Records quickly became one of Europe's best selling
new age and world music labels and now is a new
age global powerhouse.*

New Renaissance
newren@ru.org
www.ru.org
*An international quarterly with a holistic and
progressive perspective on ecological, social,
economic, political and cultural issues. An arts in
review section contains reviews of books, recordings,
exhibitions and other cultural events.*

The New Times
editor@newtimes.org
www.newtimes.org
*Dedicated to helping readers live richer, fuller, more
responsible and spiritually fulfilled lives. It's rare that
we run more than one music review per issue. The
types of music we cover include New Age, classical,
world and trance/ ambient/chill.*

Spirit of Change
spiritpub@aol.com
www.spiritofchange.org
*We are the largest, most widely-circulated free holistic
magazine in New England. We welcome independent
music reviews and all music releases.*

Wind and Wire
www.windandwire.com
*You do not need to query for submission. In fact, it's
easier for me if you just send me your CDs. If you
want to be notified upon receipt of your CDs, let me
know in a brief letter in the package. Please not that I
will accept Ambient and New Age Music -
instrumental only!*

Writings by Serge Kozlovsky
S.Kozlovsky@gtp.by
mkmk.com/kozlovsky
*Personal web site of Serge Kozlovsky. There are many
articles, interviews and reviews about new age,
contemporary instrumental, ambient, world and other
genres of music. Sweet and poetic. Visual poetry.*

The Yoga Journal
webmaster@yogajournal.com
www.yogajournal.com

Yoga Magazine *UK*
Laura McCreddie laura@yogamagazine.co.uk
www.yogamagazine.co.uk
*We are willing to listen to anything you send and then
take it from there. Send your CD for review then we'll
see what we can do.*

Progressive Rock

This section includes Progressive Rock, AOR, Jazzrock, Jambands, Melodic rock, Progressive Metal, Spacerock, Krautrock, Psychedelic and Improvisational Rock.

North America

United States

AOR Heaven
Georg.Siegl@aorheaven.com
www.aorheaven.com
We are always looking for new talents in the classic AOR/melodic hard rock vein. If you have a demo tape or demo CD-R please feel free to contact us.

ghostland.com
chad@ghostland.com
ghostland.com
Your source for Progressive Rock on the web!

Ground and Sky
webmaster@progreviews.com
www.progreviews.com
These "reviews", in their finished form, are not simply reviews, but full informational resources, containing cover scans, track listings, sound samples and links to relevant resources such as band or label home pages or fan pages.

Heavy Harmonies
Webmaster@HeavyHarmonies.Com
heavyharmonies.com
This is meant to be an informational resource for people looking for obscure and/or minor-label CD releases. If you wish to have your CD reviewed, visit our site for the address to send your music too (no demos please).

JamBands.com
dean@jambands.com
www.jambands.com
An on-line web zine devoted to improvisational music.

Music Street Journal
MusicStJournal@hotmail.com
www.musicstreetjournal.com
News, reviews, interviews ...

Progression Magazine
Progzine@aol.com
www.progressionmagazine.com
A full-size quarterly magazine devoted to news, reviews, interviews and features covering a wide range of progressive/electronic/avant-garde music artists from around the globe.

ProgressiveWorld.net
Stephanie sollows@progressiveworld.net
www.progressiveworld.net
All items sent for review will be considered. Reviews are usually published within a month of receipt. When sending items (preferably on CD), please include a bio and contact address.

ProgNaut.com
WebMaster@ProgNaut.com
www.prognaut.com
The definitive vessel for Southern California progressive music. Let Ron's ship guide you past the Scylla and Charybdis of pop music dreck to find the true islands of harmonious beauty in the clear waters of artistic depth.

progrock.com
jerryg@progrock.com
www.progrock.com
If you would like to submit your band's CD for review, contact me.

ProgScape.Com
www.progscape.com
Due to popular demand, we have started doing reviews of what's new and hot in the progressive (and related) world. Want your CD to be reviewed? Not a problem! For more info on how to get your CD or DVD reviewed, visit our reviews page!

Relix Magazine
questions@relix.com
www.relix.com
Covering of "jambands" that have filled the void left by the passing of Jerry Garcia, as well as other, non-mainstream, types of music.

Rocksector
mark_apps@yahoo.co.uk
www.rocksector.com
My mission is to indicate quality music featured at MP3.com. I focus on blues rock, progressive metal, melodic hard rock & classic metal - the artists are only featured if they're of worthy quality & hence you've quick access to great music.

Europe

Belgium

Rock Report
info@rockreport.be
www.rockreport.be
It was the lack of coverage in the better known music mags that made us decide to create a new medium, totally dedicated to AOR.

Finland

RockUnited.com
Urban urban@rockunited.com
www.rockunited.com
We intend to give young, fresh, unsigned bands the opportunity to let their voices be heard. We will review demos or independent releases of unsigned bands looking for promotion.

France

Acid Dragon
perso.club-internet.fr/acidrago/ad2.htm
A precious collection of biographies, stories, studies, documents and interviews. Although we have subscribers in France, our readership is mainly from abroad.

Big Bang
calyx@club-internet.fr
perso.club-internet.fr/calyx/bigbang
Une revue française consacrée aux musiques progressives. Centrée sur le rock progressif, elle traite également de new-age, musiques nouvelles et jazz-fusion.

Germany

Babyblaue Prog-Reviews
www.babyblaue-seiten.de
Die Prog-Enzyklopädie der Mailingliste.

Bright Eyes
info@brighteyes.de
www.brighteyes.de
Interviews und Reviews aus der Metal und Hardrock Szene.

Italy

AOR Web Site
Andrea aorwebsite@email.it
www.geocities.com/aorwebsite
The home for AOR, Hard Rock, Prog Rock, major and unsigned artists worldwide, reviews and interviews.

The Netherlands

Axiom of Choice
jur@cs.uu.nl
www.cs.uu.nl/people/jur/progrock.html
A source of subjective and objective information about progressive rock music and related genres. As a rule, music that will fit into the Gibraltar Encyclopedia of Progressive Rock, can and will be reviewed on this site.

The Dutch Progressive Rock Page
dprp@vuurwerk.nl
www.dprp.vuurwerk.nl
One of the leading Internet magazines on progressive rock.

Strutter
gabor.fabian@wxs.nl
www.strutter.8m.com
We are a non-profit fanzine that is only there to promote AOR/Melodic Rock bands that deserve to become known.

Norway

Tarkus
sven@tarkus.org
www.tarkus.org
Our ambition is that Tarkus Magazine shall be a living forum for progressive rock. We think it is of utmost importance that we have a large percentage of original material, such as exclusive interviews and record reviews.

Spain

Prog Visions
webmaster@progvisions.net
www.progvisions.net
Published both in English and Spanish and made by an international group of members. Our objective is to become a center of information that contributes to the knowledge, growth and development of progressive rock.

Sweden

more than music
anthem@home.se
morethanmusic.cjb.net
Reviews, news, interviews, links from genres such as progressive rock, AOR, melodic rock, metal, soul and blues.

United Kingdom

Acid Attack
martyn@acidattackmusic.co.uk
www.acidattackmusic.co.uk
On-line since August 1998 we give reviews and news on mostly independent music.

Mood Swings
nigel@mswings.com
www.mswings.com
If you want to get in touch for any reason (e.g. comments, news, links, interviews, or submission of review material), please feel free to e-mail me.

Progression
info@progression.co.uk
www.progresion.co.uk
World's largest art-rock magazine. Display advertising available. Contact us!

Uzbekistan

ProgressoR
vit_men@mail.ru
www.progressor.net
We're looking for the unknown and underrated Progressive Rock bands all over the world. To have your material fairly and professionally reviewed and added to the ProgressoR database please send your CDs to us.

New Zealand

The HEART of the ROCK
press@heartoftherock.com
www.heartoftherock.com
A news, reviews and interviews based site, revolving around the various sub-genres of melodic rock music. Whether it be AOR (album oriented rock), A/C (adult/contemporary), heavy metal, progressive rock and metal, modern pop or Christian rock, it has a home here at HOTR.

Punk

Punk, Hardcore, Emo, oi, garage, ska

North America

United States

A Day in June
victimofaasha@hotmail.com
www.geekcorerecords.cjb.net
We want to help other DIY bands, so send stuff for review!

Absolute Punk
jason.tate@absolutepunk.net
www.absolutepunk.net
This website is seen by thousands of people each day — and your band can be right there in the middle of it. It's simple — submit your demo, album, ep, to us and we will give it an honest, no shit, review. And we actually like punk (yeah, even pop-punk music) - unlike some sites.

Action Attack Helicopter
kurtmorris@hotmail.com
www.actionattackhelicopter.com
We're an online zine that covers independent emo, hardcore, punk and the like.

The Agro
Ceth Carter demonmaster@earthlink.net
www.theagro.com
An underground hardcore and metal website devoted to exposing bands through interviews, reviews and listing band information and offering cd sales.

American Upstart
rants@americanupstart.com
www.americanupstart.com
Opinions, rants, misconceived facts, power, glory, politics, violence, anti-violence, meat-eaters, love, war, drunk, wasted, more violence, sloppy sex, road stories, war stories, bore stories we got it all from across the globe.

Americore Magazine
larry@americoremagazine.com
www.americoremagazine.com
Punk, Rawk, Metal, Indie, Noise and other related genre smashing cliques. Reviews, interviews, gear, shows, listings, the works. 100% indie/underground/chaos!

American Music Press
ampmagazine.com
Interviews, reviews, columns, articles etc.

Anesthesia
anesthesiazine@hotmail.com
www.anesthesia.8m.com
The Premier Site for Bad Reviews, Meaningless Rants and Horrid Photos.

Annoyance
web@annoyances.com
www.annoyances.com/zine.html
Punkin' up da web with fun and silliness.

Askew Reviews
denis@askewreviews.com
www.askewreviews.com
We cover and promote music and movies not covered by the so called entertainment media.

Bean Soda
aimeebelle@beansoda.com
beansoda.com
Interviews, reviews, artwork etc.

Blank Generation
ShawnAbnoxious@aol.com
www.blankgeneration.com
We review garage, power pop and '77 style punk rock.

Break the Static
tinytizzy@hotmail.com
www.breakthestatic.cjb.net
We are a new music site that promotes underground and unsigned artists. News, pics, bands, CD reviews and more!

bulletproof popemobile
al@bulletproofpopemobile.com
www.bulletproofpopemobile.com
If you want a review, just make sure you write in the subject area of your e-mail what you want (review submission, link trades etc.)

bushmado
dj@bushmado.com
www.bushmado.com
Dedicated to helping underground heavy bands get the exposure they deserve. Will review anything sent and will add your bands music to the web radio. We will also set up an Interview or feature.

Bystander Fanzine
scottj@bystanderfanzine.com
www.bystanderfanzine.com
Covering the hardcore scene.

calamityproject
joe@calamityproject.com
www.calamityproject.com
Hot ass zine containing reviews, interviews, editorials, videos, mp3s, message board, art and more!

Carbon 14
fableslieg@c14.com
www.c14.com
A smorgasbord of art, music, rants, wrestling, porn and other assorted weirdness. And to get the true C14 experience you need to absorb the print edition. This site brings you highlights from the print version of our zine.

centerfuse.net
reviews@centerfuse.net
www.centerfuse.net
Dedicated to the independent music scene. If you want to have your CD/ Tape/ Vinyl release reviewed? Send us an email to find out how!

The Continental Magazine
Sean Berry records@dblcrown.com
www.dblcrown.com
Annual magazine covering surf/instrumental and garage rock n' roll. Each issue comes with a CD sampler.

Cool Beans!
rock@coolbeans.com
www.coolbeans.com
A magazine for the indie, punk, alternative obsessed music fan. We offer interviews with great indie, punk and alternative bands as well as articles about different themes.

Corn 'Zine
dana@cornzine.com
www.cornzine.com
Covering hardcore, punk, ska, indie, emo etc. since 1994.

Culture Bunker
culturebunker@fsmail.net
www.culturebunker.com
Indiscriminate, wholesale, erotic, power-mad killing...

Cut the Tension
donnymutt@fast.net
www.cutthetension.com
This is a 64 page Cut & Paste zine featuring interviews, reviews, stories, opinions, flyer art and a huge photo gallery.

Da' Core
Dacoremag@aol.com
www.da-core.com
A hardcore label and magazine based out of Pittsburgh, PA. Label releases include bands like Endless, No Retreat, Allan, Built Upon Frustration, 4 In Tha Chamber and the Steel City Aggression series.

Deadwinter
footsteps0@aol.com
come.to/deadwinter
Reviews for mostly emo/indie/hardcore type stuff, also poetry, editorials, interviews etc.

Decoy Music Magazine
aaron@decoy-online.com
www.decoymusic.com
Send us your demos for review, drop us a line with links to your songs. We're here to get the word out about bands.

Deep Fry Bonanza
daniel@deepfrybonanza.com
www.dfbpunk.com
If you are from a band or label and would like to submit your work for review (DIY projects are especially encouraged), send everything to the address listed on our website.

Delusions of Adequacy
doa@adequacy.net
www.adequacy.net
We focus on the independent scene, featuring music reviews, interviews, concert reviews and more in the genres of indie rock and pop, emo, hardcore, punk, folk and more.

depressing music
depressed@depressingmusic.com
www.depressingmusic.com
Zines, music, reviews and much more!

Dreemykreem
dreemy@dreemykreem.com
www.dreemykreem.com
If you are interested in a trade or having us review your art projects, (zines, music etc.) send us your material.

Driver's Side Air Bag
info@dsazine.com
www.dsazine.com
Lots of diversity of thought and ideas make this zine a real individualistic and unique freak show.

emotionalpunk.com
andrew@emotionalpunk.com
www.emotionalpunk.com
New, reviews, interviews...

EpiMag.com
jeremy@epimag.com
www.epimag.com
We always welcome anyone's opinions, reviews, interviews... whatever.

Faceless
rachel@facelesszine.com
www.facelesszine.com
CD reviews, interviews with your favorite punk, emo and ska bands, exclusive contests and awesome galleries of photos for you to look at.

Flipout!
stahr_monroe@yahoo.com
www.geocities.com/albanystudent/flipout.html

Friction
melissa@frictionmagazine.com
www.frictionmagazine.com
We are expanding and taking our online magazine more seriously. This means that you will be able to watch shows, download MP3s, read about music, art, extreme sports, film and everything else independent and DIY.

Frigid Ember
paul@frigidember.com
frigidember.com

geekburger.com
geekc0re@hotmail.com
www.geekburger.com
I hope to cover as many bands as possible and continue to attract and entertain viewers. This isn't ever going to be the flashiest website on the internet, but it's like they always say: "It wudn't this classy, but, y'know, nice." It's not supposed to make sense.

GOODMUSICROCKSdotCOM
russ@goodmusicrocks.com
www.goodmusicrocks.com
Anything free is always welcome. Go to the contacts page of the site to send stuff in. If you want an interview, well....we'll contact you if we wanna. Best way to get some exposure is by emailing me with some news about your band.

graynoise.net
jesse@graynoise.net
www.graynoise.net
A proud member of the punk music community.

Hand Carved Magazine
mail@hcmagazine.com
hcmagazine.com
We are always accepting albums to be reviewed and possible contributions from readers.

Hardcore Central *(xmulletx.com)*
Webmaster@xmulletx.com
www.xmulletx.com
Want to know what records to buy? What records to ditch? Missed a show and wanna hear what happened?

hardcoremusic.com
greg@hardcoremusic.com
www.hardcoremusic.com

hardcorewebsite.net
nycore@hardcorewebsite.net
www.hardcorewebsite.net
I only support bands that support our scene, not those that use it to advance and then forget us.

hardtolive.com
info@hardtolive.com
www.hardtolive.com
For info about reviews or interviews please email us.

Head in a Milk Bottle
HIAMB@garagepunk.com
www.lamebasement.com/HIAMB
A zine focusing on garage, punk and primitive rock n' roll.

Heavyweight Sound
blackeye@heavyweightsound.com
www.heavyweightsound.com
Dedicated to spreading the UK garage sound in the US and Canada.

Hectic World
info@hecticworld.com
www.hecticworld.com
A punk and independent music publication from Detroit. Please visit our website or write for more info.

Holy Titclamps/Queer Zine Explosion
www.holytitclamps.com

House of the Rising Punk
www.punkrock.org
The ultimate punk rock directory.

I Dunno
xxslurpeex@aol.com
www.sonic.net/~mpaglia/zine
We are God's gift to the Internet. Bow to us.

The idobi Network
music@idobi.com
www.idobi.com
Alternative rock and punk music news, reviews and interviews.

ihateyour.com
press@ihateyour.com
www.ihateyour.com
Send us your Press kit, along with your latest release. We will promote it! (must resemble punk, hardcore, indie)

in an nutshell
press@in-a-nutshell.net
www.in-a-nutshell.net
Want to get interviewed? Email us and we'll arrange something.

IndieUprising
christian@indieuprising.com
www.indieuprising.com
We are not only a punk/hardcore site. IndieUprising was built for the benefit of the independent artist. It is our goal to supplant mainstream music with a fresh infusion of indie music that is equally worthy.

infopunks.net
www.infopunks.net
News, reviews, interviews.

Inkdrinker.net
john@inkdrinker.net
www.inkdrinker.net
News, reviews, interviews, articles...

InStrife
propheci@instrife.com
www.instrife.com

Intellectos
intellectos@care2.com
www.intellectos.com
From Electro to Pop to Hardcore and more.

Invisible Youth
info@invisibleyouth.com
www.invisibleyouth.com
Not only do we update our site monthly with new reviews, articles and interviews, but we also have contests each month. We also love feedback and will review absolutely anything we are sent.

Joy
Paul Madden info@joynet.tk
www.joynet.tk
A music ezine featuring reviews, interviews and features on the best new and established bands from the indie, post-punk, lo-fi and electro scenes.

Juice
JuiceSSS@aol.com
www.juicemagazine.com
Sounds, surf and skate.

JunkRock.com
garbagemen@junkrock.com
www.junkrock.com
Always around but never popular enough to dominate any charts, Junk is neither Punk, Heavy Metal or Rock 'n Roll, in actual fact a pretty difficult phenomenon to define.

The Lance Monthly
lancerecords@hotmail.com
www.lancerecords.com
The Internet Source for '60s Surf and Garage Band Music.

Last Life Media
greg@lastlifemedia.com
www.lastlifemedia.com
Reviews, tabs, features, downloads...

Lollipop

info@lollipop.com
www.lollipop.com
A music and entertainment magazine published 4 times per year with a circulation of 15,000. We cover all that fiercely alternative music - ya know: punk, hardcore, indie rock, alternapop, ska, techno, heavy/industrial/sludge/noise and multiple combinations therein, as well as comics, 'zines, movies, fiction, rants and raves.

Mtska.com

thejoe@mtska.com
www.mtska.com
Our mission is to bring you, the humble reader, all the latest in ska news, Reviews of the latest CD's and Interviews with those making a name for themselves in the ska world.

Music Spork

aeiou@musicspork.com
www.musicspork.com
The essential guide to new indie rock, garage, electronica, emo and the other consequential music that make the world a better place.

Nacho Cheese and Anarchy

www.nachocheeseandanarchy.50g.com
Music-based standard format of band interviews and CD reviews. Currently growing to feature other points of nonsense and entertainment.

Neo-Zine

chc neo-zine@earthlink.net
www.Neo-Zine.com
A web zine dedicated to DIY, underground and extreme recording styles. Free ad space, reviews, interviews with very deep underground bands and noise artists + art, banners, links and other attractions.

Neu Futur

James McQuiston editor@neufutur.com
www.neufutur.com
News, reviews, interviews. Any band can place their tour dates here by e-mailing the editor.

neus subjex.net

mail@neussubjex.net
www.neussubjex.net
We always love getting free records. Send in vinyl, CDs, cassettes and zines. WE DO NOT REVIEW MP3s!!! The opinions expressed in the reviews are the opinions of the reviewer only and not that of the Neus Subjex, unless it's blatantly fucking obvious that your band sucks profoundly.

New Jersey Hardstyle

www.njhardstyle.cjb.net
Have a demo? Want it reviewed?

The New Scheme

stuart@thenewscheme.com
www.thenewscheme.com
A small, self-published magazine that is predominantly about music. A new issue is released quarterly. Send your music along with any pertinent info and it will be considered for review in the next possible issue.

noreasterzine.com

editor@noreasterzine.com
www.noreasterzine.com
We can't Review it if we don't have it! Send those releases in vinyl or CD format to us (we like demos too!)

Obscene Army

www.obscenearmy.com
Submit your news, reviews, downloads etc.

Oddshaped

kevinsnotdead@hotmail.com
oddshaped.com
We're about the promotion of hardcore/metal, not shit (talking a label and its band). Just because I haven't reviewed it, doesn't mean it's a bad album. We mostly like to keep up to date with releases, although we occasionally like to review older albums.

Off My Jammy

off_my_jammy@hotmail.com
sinkcharmer.com/omj
Showing the ticklish side of indie and punk rock.

Overated Magazine

OveratedMag@aol.com
www.overatedmag.com
An online entertainment magazine specifically geared towards high school & college students. Overated's main focus is on music...Punk Rawk, Metal, Ska, Grunge, Alternative and just plain old Rock and Roll.

Planet Ska

niff007@hotmail.com
www.planetska.com
If you want your stuff reviewed on the site, visit our website for contact details.

On the Rag

webmistress@ontherag.net
www.ontherag.net
Is it your time of the month already? Time for you to find out what the hell is happening in the California punk rock scene and the latest happenings at On The Rag Records and 'Zine?!

pastepunk

jordan@pastepunk.com
www.pastepunk.com
Punk and hardcore webzine devoted to covering some of the most widely talented and original bands currently storming the scene. At the site you'll find tons of reviews, interviews and columns.

Pin-Up Magazine

Margo Tiffen margo@pinupmagazine.net
www.pinupmagazine.net
Feature articles and interviews with authors and musicians from punk to rockabilly, indie, hardcore, ska, reggae and rocknroll. Album, movie, book reviews, fiction, erotic fiction, sex advice, events listings.

Poppunk.com

steve@poppunk.com
www.poppunk.com
Send us your stuff to be reviewed! We accept CD's, 7"s and demo tapes. Be aware, if we don't like something, we won't review it. Why? Because bashing bands or labels isn't our gig baby! So you have nothing to lose.

Pretty Bruises

prettybruises@rivulets.net
www.rivulets.net
Music, zine and book reviews, interviews and personal writing.

Primal Chaos

info@primalchaosonline.com
www.primalchaosonline.com
News, reviews, interviews. Send us your music!

The Probe

www.punkrocksex.com
A free newsprint publication featuring punk rock and sex.

Psychobilly Homepage

www.wreckingpit.com
The easiest way to describe Psychobilly is to say it's a mixture of Rockabilly and Punk.

Punk Fix

punk_fix@yahoo.com
www.punkfix.net
Reviews, articles, interviews and photographs covering the span of punk rock and hardcore history from the 70s to the present.

Punk Magazine

Editor@punkmagazine.com
www.punkmagazine.com
Send all snail mail, promo material, CDs, advertising art, "Letters to PUNK," mash notes and other hard copy to us.

Punk Sucks

Punkass@punksucks.com
www.punksucks.com
Huge punk site with reviews, news and more. Takes submissions from indie artists.

punkbeat.com

info@punkbeat.com
www.punkbeat.com
Mail anything you want us to review (music, videos, books, drawings of armadillos).

punkhardcore.com

ryan@punkhardcore.com
www.punkhardcore.com
We have set out to become the definitive on-line resource for the Punk and Hardcore music scene by providing ... the most up to date news, interviews, CD Reviews and Guitar Tabs.

Punk-it.net

sev@punk-it.net
www.punk-it.net
Interviews, show and CD reviews, columns...

Punkmusic.com

www.punkmusic.com
The punk community center with news, interviews, reviews, links, message boards and more.

punknews.org

www.punknews.org

punkplanet.com

punkplanet@punkplanet.com
www.punkplanet.com
We will make every attempt to include you in our reviews section. Just because we believe in punk rock and we hold independence close to our hearts, it does not mean that you're going to get a good review.

punkrockreviews.com

info@punkrockreviews.com
www.punkrockreviews.com
What we want to do is to describe the material in a way that allows you, our reader, to make an educated decision, on whether this is something you could get your groove on to.

punkROCKS.net
orion@punkrocks.net
www.punkrocks.net
Our extensive CD review library, combined with our show reviews, interviews, up-to-date news and ever-growing band-features section provide people with information on what is available to you.

READ
editor@readmag.com
www.readmag.com
Want to send us something? We review everything!

Recluse
info @reclusezine.com
www.reclusezine.com
We gratefully accept any and all types of media works for review. Movies, books, CD's, zines etc. (We love it all!)

Rock Fiend
www.rockfiend.net
Our focus is on the new rock revolution as well as an interest in the good old fashion business of horror. We guarantee that all submissions will be reviewed.

Rock Rage
rockragezine@yahoo.com
www.rockragezine.com

Rock n Roll Outbreak
peladorecords@hotmail.com
www.peladorecords.com
Browse through this site to view (and buy) the many releases we carry - TKO, Junk, Hostage, Beer City....and many more from the world over.

Rock n Roll Purgatory
www.rocknrollpurgatory.com
We review Rockabilly, Surf, Punk, oi, Swing, Psychobilly and then some...

SChUeLL
mixelpricks@hotmail.com
www.murkta.com
The website has contains text only versions of all the columns, interviews and reviews from the paper version of the zine.

ScrawnyKids.com
Trent girl@scrawnykids.com
www.scrawnykids.com
An independent webzine that is published once a month. The 'zine features all kinds of music including reviews, columns, interviews, photos, news etc. Check us out!

screamo.org
stierch@screamo.org
links.screamo.org
Opening peoples minds, answering people's questions and keeping punk rock thriving in some way.

Sidewinder
Sky skyharbor22@aol.com
www.sidewinderzine.com
Focuses mainly on the independent rock/emo/punk/hardcore scene, as well as movies, books and comics. We also have a few regular columns, as well as editorials, short stories and the like.

Sincere Brutality
james@sincerebrutality.com
www.sincerebrutality.com
Please send CDs only. No cassettes or MP3s.

Ska Au Go-Go
SkaAuGoGo@aol.com
go.to/SkaAuGoGo
We are a free newsprint zine focusing on music and art.

Ska Summit
Ska JoE joe@ocska.com
www.skasummit.com
"Where the ska world meets." Local shows, bands, MP3s and reviews.

Skratch Magazine
scott scott@SkratchMagazine.com
www.SkratchMagazine.com
Covers a wide variety of indie, garage rock, punk, hardcore and emo music. I'm confident you'll move mountains with our 120,000 readership and regional/national distribution. Today, we are proudly the biggest free independent music magazine (of our kind) in the United States.

sleepforever
www.sleepforever.com
News, reviews, message board etc.

Someday Never
somedaypress@yahoo.com
www.somedaynever.com
Devoted to music and opinion. We are really just music fans ourselves, providing honest and thorough coverage of music the way we see it.

Soundnova.com
Corey Evans corey@digitalattak.com
www.Soundnova.com
A fast growing online music e-zine covering mainstream and underground acts in the genres of rock, metal, industrial, punk, electronic and hardcore.

soundriot
kristin@sound-riot.com
www.sound-riot.com
News, reviews, interviews and more!

Stand Up Jack zine
john@standupjackzine.com
www.standupjackzine.com
We're open to all kinds of music. However, what sits best with us are indie/ emo/ punk /ska /alternative /rock /pop-rock. Send us what you have and we'll make our own decisions.

Static Void
www.static-void.net
Send Demo's, CD's etc. for review and/or for consideration by the ultra-corporate board of directors tyrannically dictating the future of media at Static-Void Records.

Njmusicsource
chris@njmusicsource.com
www.njmusicsource.com
A great site for any type of music consisting from ska.punk.emo.hardcore.etc... I can have your review up within two weeks of receiving material.

Ska, Punk and Other Junk
webmaster@skapunkandotherjunk.com
www.skapunkandotherjunk.com

The Skabuster Times
skabustertimes@aol.com
www.skabustertimes.cjb.net
We specialize in SKA interviews and reviews.

Skate the Planet
shows@skatetheplanet.com
www.cthardcore.com
Your information source for worldwide underground metal and hardcore information.

Skratch
ads@skratchmagazine.com
www.skratchmagazine.com
25,000 free copies monthly of punk/hardcore/emo/ skate and misc. garb for all your cerebral desires.

Skyscraper
skyscraperzine@hotmail.com
www.skyscrapermagazine.com
Covers music from indie rock to hardcore to punk to emo to metal to rock.

So Fuckin' What?
spindelsfw@hotmail.com
sfwzine.cjb.net

Some Day Never
joe@somedaynever.com
gotpunkzine@yahoo.com
www.somedaynever.com
Monthly webzine devoted to the punk scene including reviews, opinion and lots more.

StraightEdge.com
sxe@straightedge.com
www.straightedge.com
This is a website devoted to the straightedge lifestyle.

superpunk.com
jason@masshysteria.org
www.superpunk.com
It's about time someone decided to create an online community where fans of punk rock music and extreme sports can get together to discuss and exchange their ideas.

Supertrash
webmaster@supertrash.zzn.com
www.angelfire.com/rock/supertrash
We need more stuff to review! Send us your goods so we can make this bigger and more helpful!

Switch Magazine
switch@switchmagazine.com
switchmagazine.com
We do mostly punk and hip-hop reviews. Contact us about your band.

TESTicle PRESSure
jefe@testicle.com
www.testicle.com
Highly Unpopular Opinions on Music, Art, Sex, Comix, Politix and Anti-Corporate Indie-ness.

TheScout.Net
thekillingmoon@aol.com
www.thescout.net
News and show reviews. Updated Every Day Damn It!!

Three and a Half
info@threeandahalf.com
www.threeandahalf.com
This is not your typical "fanzine" or music zine. While music is surely the backbone of Three and a Half it is not the only focus!

Through These Eyes
Dustin dewaddikt@hotmail.com
www.throughtheseeyes.net
A hardcore music site dedicated to showcasing new bands and keeping the public informed with news, reviews etc.

The Toilet
ralph@thetoiletonline.com
www.thetoiletonline.com
One of the "Greatest Human Accomplishments of 20th Century by Two Guys Named Ralph and Billy".

trakMARX.com - the needle & the damage done
wastebin@trakMARX.com
www.trakmarx.com
We bring you the juice on young upstarts.

truepunk.com
staff@truepunk.com
www.truepunk.com
News, reviews, interviews and a message board. If you are an unsigned band please send us a previous independent full-length or EP and a press kit. We will contact you, if we like what we hear and we'll be pouring our hearts into making your band heard.

Tweed
tweed.cjb.net
Hardcore, politics, philosophy, debates, interviews, reviews, technology, hacking, stories, poems, pictures, reader submissions.

The Underground Band Network
matt@theubn.com
www.theubn.com
Provides resources such as booking and studio time in Michigan. Also does reviews, interviews and posts news. Produces a periodical compilation open for all artists of all genres.

Undevoured
webmaster@undevoured.com
www.undevoured.com
Hardcore, industrial, emo, metal...

Variable to Knife
info@variabletoknife.com
www.variabletoknife.com
News, articles, columns, reviews etc.

xadamx
atom@xadamx.com
www.xadamx.com
A DIY ezine based out of Boston with reviews, interviews and a band of the month.

Canada

Caustic Truths
www.caustictruths.com
A small independent zine which focuses on punk, hardcore, garage and other noizy music.

Flex Your Head
flexyourhead.vancouverhardcore.com
Hardcore and punk online. Reviews, audio samples, photos, program and local scene information, interviews, links and more.

Frantic Ska
mark@franticska.com
www.franticska.com
Want something reviewed? This site gets 500+ unique hits a month. E-mail us for info.

newhardcore.net
www.newhardcore.net

Peanut-Tree.com
trip@peanut-tree.com
www.peanut-tree.com

punkbands.com
webmaster@punkbands.com
www.punkbands.com
Our mission is to be the rendevouz page for punk music lovers. We want to promote punk/ska/oi- bands from all corners of the world.

punkinternational.com
tim@punkinternational.com
www.punkinternational.com
If you want to submit material just send an email to the above address and ask for my mailing address.

Scandalized Human Zine
editor@shzine.com
www.shzine.com
News, gig and CD reviews etc.

World Wide Punk
vic@worldwidepunk.com
www.worldwidepunk.com
Your one-stop directory of punk stuff on the Internet. Thousands of links to bands, record labels, zines, radio shows, reviews and much more can be found here.

YouAsTheDriver.com
a@youasthedriver.com
www.youasthedriver.com
Showcasing new features, album reviews, news etc. (updated weekly).

Mexico

FIxcAT
fixcatmusika@yahoo.com
www.fixcat.net
Comprehensive fan's guide to all aspects of Mexican ska in all of North America.

SkaMty
jrgu86@hotmail.com
www.skamty.cjb.net
Fotos, bandas, letras, download, discos...

South America

Argentina

This is SKA
info@thisisska.com.ar
www.thisisska.com.ar
Comprehensive listing of bands, mp3 files etc.

Europe

Belgium

Boring World
surfwax@hotpop.com
www.boringworld.net
Webzine francophone consacré au punk et au ska avec des tas de chroniques de cds, de concerts, des interviews, des mp3, un forum...

I|AM|NO|HERO
kevin@iamnohero.com
www.iamnohero.com
Articles, interviews, reviews etc.

Mashnote.Magazine
info@mashnote.net
www.mashnote.net
We do not accept copies (ie. cassettes, cd-r's, ...) of your releases unless they are demos or records that are released as a benefit for charity.

Munchkin Music
www.munchkinmusic.be
News, reviews, interviews etc.

Nameless
www.webzinenameless.net

Punk Updates
Hein Terweduwe hein@punkupdates.com
www.punkupdates.com
A site that focuses on keeping a very up to date chronological list of all upcoming and recent punk releases. A good percentage of records are reviewed by the Belgian webmaster. Bands are free to send in stuff for reviewing or to put up links. If provided, mp3's will be posted.

Skanner
www.satchmo.com/skanner
Ska rocksteady reggae.

Denmark

Deadbeat
www.deadbeat.dk
Reviews, interviews and features on all kinds of trash. The leading truck stop on the net for everything rock'n'roll, Punk, surf, trash, garage etc. Also out in print!

Finland

La Bruta
Maddie bamalama@jippii.fi
www.labruta.com
An international rockzine, originating from Finland, concentrating on rock'n'roll-punk-garagerock- powerpop and a few other genres. We are mostly focusing on underground stuff, but also keep an eye on the mainstream level.

France

Kill...What?
kelly@killwhat.com
www.killwhat.com
The most American French fanzine. In French and distributed all over France, Quebec, Switzerland and Belgium.

No Brain No Headache
www.nobrainnoheadache.fr.st

SDZ
sdz.free.fr
Un fanzine rock'n'roll qui sonde l'underground punk, hardcore, noise, garage, surf, stoner...pour en ressortir quelques interviews bien frappées, une bonne dose de news et un chargement de chroniques de disques, démos et lectures souterraines.

skanews.net
skanews.net
ska reggae rocksteady nutty sound dub....

SxU
standup.free.fr
News, reviews (Lp, 7", Demo, CD, newsletter, Zines), shows & scene report. All stuff sent is reviewed!!

Walked in Line Fanzine
Chris Pelle redac@wilrecords.com
www.wilrecords.com
The French underground label: offset Fanzine + CD audio compilation / Webzine with tons of reviews and info concerts / +1500 records /Mailorder...and more!

Wardance
www.wardance.net

Worst
www.multimania.com/worst

Germany

4P Fanzine
www.4p-fanzine.de

Active Detective Journal
actdet@yahoo.com
www.active-detective-journal.de

Allschools Network
www.allschools.de
Network Hardcore eZine.

Back to the Boots
webmaster@bttb.de
www.bttb.de

Broken Violence
battaglia@brokenviolence.de
www.brokenviolence.de
E-Zine für Hardcore, Punk, Indie und Metal.

CORE Ground
holger@coreground.de
www.coreground.de

creative-eclipse.com
mj@creative-eclipse.com
www.creative-eclipse.com
An online publication dedicated to prime forms of music, art and poetry. If you'd like to see your stuff reviewed, get in touch with us.

Daredevil Magazine
daredevil@tesionmail.de
www.daredevil.de
If you are a band/label you may ADD the URLs (links) to as many MP3 files as you'd like- provided you are a copyright owner or licensed party to the song(s).

DerDude Goes SKA.de
nuhr@gmx.de
www.derdude-goes-ska.de
SKA ist nicht einfach eine Musik! SKA ist Lebensphilosophie, multiple Weltanschauung und der musikalische Ausdruck von Fun, aber auch der Beweis dafür, dass Jamaica überall ist und sein kann.

Enough
david@punkrawk.de
www.enoughfanzine.com
A non-profit DIY punk/HC/Ska/Indi E-Zine for the Scene! If you are a band that wants to get an interview or if you have some personal thoughts on ENOUGH just drop me a line via email or snail-mail.

In-Your-Face
info@in-your-face.de
www.in-your-face.de
News, reviews, interviews.

Interpol Times
www.scenepolice.de

it's not just boy's fun
Elena Stöhr elena@notjustboysfun.de
www.notjustboysfun.de

Moloko Plus
www.moloko-plus.de

Noise Engine
webmaster@noiseengine.de
www.noiseengine.de

Online Zine
bogus@onlinezine.de
www.onlinezine.net

Ox Fanzine
www.ox-fanzine.de
Germany's biggest punk rock & hardcore zine

Plastic Bomb
plastic-bomb@punkrawk.com
www.plastic-bomb.de

purerock.de
www.purerock.de
Your alternative rock community. Rock, punk, alternative, metal, ska, indie, hardcore, crossover, grunge and guitar pop.

Route 77
www.route77.de

STILL HOLDING ON
webmaster@stillholdingon.net
www.stillholdingon.net
If you're interested in helping me out, please drop me a line. I'm always looking for dedicated and reliable people that want to add something to the site.

Stupid Over You
mitglied.tripod.de/Stupid

Trust Fanzine
www.trust-zine.de
Our focus has always been somewhere between punk and hardcore, yet trying to avoid the pitfalls of a narrow minded music taste by occasionally listening to something else.

Waste of Mind
wom@wasteofmind.de
www.wasteofmind.de

Italy

Be Nice to Mommy
theguru@benicetomommy.com
www.benicetomommy.com
Fanzine italiana dedicata al Punk-Rock.

Freak Out
freakout@libero.it
www.freakout-online.com
Independent music magazine from Naples, Italy since 1989 - postrock noise, emo, metal...

In Your Eyes
simone@iyezine.com
www.iyezine.com
About what we think and what we feel.

komakino
www.inkoma.com

punk will never die
rbxpunk@pwnd.net
www.pwnd.net
Dedicated to punk bands with news, bios, discos, mp3z and more.

skabadip.com
testi@skabadip.com
www.skabadip.com
Italy's first ska site.

SThINK
sthink@sthink.com
www.sthink.com

The Netherlands

Inside Knowledge
info@insideknowledge.net
www.insideknowledge.net
For our site we review everything we get (including ska, metal, indierock). For our zine we only review hardcore, oi, punk and the sorts.

Opposite
Marco@oppositezine.com
www.oppositezine.com
Started as a zine for the Rotterdam area it evolved to a national zine that focused exclusively on punkrock, ska and hardcore.

Pitfather.com
info@pitfather.com
www.pitfather.com
Hardcore, punk and metal community.

Spain

I wanna
escribe@ipunkrock.com
www.ipunkrock.com
On-line punk-rock'n'roll zine in Spanish with interviews, reviews and articles.

Iron Skies
info@ironskies.com
www.ironskies.com

Sonic Wave
escribe@sonicwavemagazine.com
www.sonicwavemagazine.com
Fanzine en internet sobre punk-rock'n'roll, power-pop, 60s, soul, surf, música negra... con noticias, entrevistas, reseñas de discos y conciertos, una completa Agenda de conciertos, enlaces.

Time Bomb
timebomb@timebombzine.com
www.timebombzine.com

Sweden

Backlash
hem1.passagen.se/backlash

Chaos is King
www.come.to/chaosisking
Only in Swedish. Send us your music for review.

Doomsday Magazine
come.to/doomsdaymag

Happy as Raw Sewage *(HARS)*
contact@happyasrawsewage.com
www.happyasrawsewage.com
We cover the areas around genres like ska, swing, punk, emo and hardcore and have been doing this since 1996.

Iron Skies
info@ironskies.com
www.ironskies.com
Get your music reviewed in the best Spanish online magazine which covers rock, emo, punk, indie ...

No Rule Zine
Dick Sandström norule@telia.com
www.norule.nu
Kick ass punk rock for weirdos and other losers!

Ska Wars
johan@skawars.nu
www.skawars.nu
Comprehensive guide to ska, reggae and rocksteady in Scandanavia.

United Kingdom

Armed with Anger
awa@awarecords.com
www.awarecords.com

Brain Love
www.brainlove.cjb.net

collective
www.collective-zine.co.uk
A UK based music reviews zine covering whatever the heck we feel like within the indie scene. hardcore / emo / punk / indie / post rock / screamo / stoner. And all those combined. ..if such a record exists.

Count Me Out
info@countmeout.tk
www.countmeout.tk
News, Interviews, Reviews...

Dripfed
editor@dripfed.co.uk
www.dripfed.co.uk
This is a full-on orgy of music writing that cares not for genre distinctions, so called 'music press' trends or anything so trivial. Dripfed is about rekindling the spirit of punk fanzines but imbuing it with the design and content of a professional publication.

Fracture
www.seanchai.dircon.co.uk
5,000 circulation free fanzine covering punk, hardcore and the rest.

Hardcore Times
xhardcoretimesx@hotmail.com
www.hardcore-times.com
The site consists of News, Interviews, Reviews, Views, Listings, Photos, Links and more. We also sell hardcore & punk videos here.

He's The Greatest Dancer!
ajopenshaw@openshaw34.freeserve.co.uk
www.maxpages.com/ballroomantics
All the news and reviews of the moment, including information on the upcoming bands of today.

PlanetPunk
webmaster@planetpunk.co.uk
www.planetpunk.co.uk
Due to the huge volume of CDs we receive, we cannot guarantee if or when a band will be featured at PlanetPunk. However, we will shortly be launching a service whereby bands can pay a fee (won't be too much!) to ensure a speedy inclusion on the site.

Real Overdose
tard@realod.com
www.realod.com/realod
Always review a ton o' wax, a heap o' zines and a stack o' shows, got columns and shitlists and news and contacts.

Skinhead World
eds@skinhead-world.com
www.skinhead-world.com
Ska, Skinheads & Scooterists. Info, gig list, reviews & more.

Sonic Dirt
lee@sonicdirt.co.uk
www.sonicdirt.co.uk
Punk news, reviews etc.

State Of Emergency.net
marketing@stateofemergency.net
www.stateofemergency.net
Send promos and any other promotional materials or competition prizes to us.

vanity project
skif@vanityproject.co.uk
www.vanityproject.co.uk
Each issue provides some informative interviews, reviews and articles on new alternative music makers. Not to say we don't like a bit of pop around here, but our passions lie elsewhere.

Yugoslavia

S.C.A.B. zine
Vladimir Gosic vlada@scabzine.com
www.scabzine.com
Punk fanzine from Yugoslavia (in English, distributed Europe-wide, coming out quarterly). Also available as a huge on-line zine that also broadcasts a radio show.

Australia

(noise) Theory
Justin Robertson a_hundred_reasons@hotmail.com
www.noisetheory.net
We cover music from different alternative styles such as punk, heavy rock, hardcore, indie and even some emo stuff. If you are inquiring about where to send a CD/press kit for review or other purposes, drop us an email and we'll get back to you with an address to send it.

These Boots!
Tracey Newman skacrazy@hotmail.com
www.geocities.com/theseboots66
Our aim is promote ska, punk, hardcore, rockabilly and anything in between to our readers. We publish interviews (bands/ labels), reviews (gig, cd and vinyl) and feature articles. If you're not from Australia- we don't care- we want to hear from artists all over the globe.

Thought Control
www.thoughtcontrol.8m.com
Set up to serve the Australian and the wider punk scene

New Zealand

Black Cat
www.black-cat.co.nz
An arts and entertainment site for those looking for a decent film, book, album or feature.

Japan

The Ska Tipz
mail@neoska.com
neoska.com
A site for Japanese ska bands and other ska music.

Reggae

Jammin Reggae
eznoh@niceup.com
niceup.com
The Gateway to Reggae Music on the Internet!

Niceup.com
eznoh@niceup.com
www.niceup.com
The Gateway to Reggae Music on the Internet.

Reggae Report
mpq@reggaereport.com
www.reggaereport.com
Reggae Report has an international following, a collection of awards and accolades and a history of consistency and dependability.

The Reggae Source
www.reggaesource.com
We believe reggae music is as important as jazz, gospel, or any other genre of music. We take reggae music seriously and want to provide you with solid information on this crucial music form.

Reggae Train.com
reggaetrain.com
The largest and most comprehensive reggae music portal on the web. We offer Webcast Radio, ReggaeTrain-TV, interviews, a Festival Guide, Concert Calendar, a Reggae Forum and "Artist of the Week".

Reggae Vibes
info@reggae-vibes.com
www.reggae-vibes.com
In everything we do our main aim is to spread the "Reggae Vibes"...anyway & anywhere!

The Reggae Web
webmaster@reggaeweb.com
www.reggaeweb.com

RudeGal.com
rudegal@rudegal.com
www.rudegal.com
Dancehall Reggae Music - The Internet Resource.

Surforeggae
contato@surforeggae.com.br
www.surforeggae.com.br

Women in Music

Most of the publications in the section review exclusively women's music. However, there are a few that will accept the music of male musicians as well.

United States

3BlackChicks Review
Rose "Bams" Cooper bams@3blackchicks.com
www.3blackchicks.com
I'm interested in submissions from Black artists to start, specifically soul, jazz and gospel artists. I prefer minidisc, CD, or tape submissions (in that order), though I will accept whatever the artist has available to use.

absolutedivas
media@creativereality.com
www.absolutedivas.com
A tribute to women in the music industry.

Amaranth Womyn
amaranthwomyn@yahoo.com
www.AmaranthWomyn.com
Part of the Amaranth Womyn Lesbian Community.

Awakened Woman
Stephanie Hiller editor@awakenedwoman.com
www.awakenedwoman.com
We love to review women's music — especially radical, spiritual, healing, feminist music!

Bamboo Girl
Sabrina Margarita BambooGirl@aol.com
www.bamboogirl.com
I like to review music that is more on the indie/progressive/sometimes hip hoppy end. Mostly the music of women and/or of color, but also all people in general.

The Beltane Papers
submissions@thebeltanepapers.net
www.thebeltanepapers.net
We review the music of independent female artists... but it needs to have some sort of women's spirituality/pagan and/or feminist/woman-empowering, earth-centered POV. That doesn't really narrow down the field much, since much of women's music these days includes a lot of that. So send us something...

The Best Female Musicians
dennis@bestfemalemusicians.com
www.bestfemalemusicians.com
Each month I will post ten or so HOT artists for you to check out. Read reviews of new releases by many of the artists featured on this site.

b-gYrL
bgyrl4life bgyrl4life@b-gyrl.com
www.b-gyrl.com
This all female hip hop network features a search engine, live weekly radio show, a 24/7 hip hop stream, Female MC Week, b-7, b-gYrL stations at mp3.com, an online networking club, a freestyle/spoken word hotline, the Women of MP3.com and a newsletter/mail list.

Bitch
bitch@bitchmagazine.com
www.bitchmagazine.com
Contact for all music coverage is Andi Zeisler and the address is 2765 16th street, San Francisco, CA 94103.

Blue Jean Online
Sherry Handel editors@bluejeanonline.com
www.bluejeanonline.com
Our young women reviewers are looking for more women artists to feature in our Music Review department and our Music Showcase (where we interview women musicians/songwriters)!

BlueBlood.net
Amelia@BlueBlood.net
www.blueblood.net
Original Gothic decadence supporting female musicians and bands.

CandyforBadChildren.Com
editor@candyforbadchildren.com
www.candyforbadchildren.com
Bands, record labels and video/dvd distributors are welcome to send us press kits, promos and screeners for review. Please include your full contact information. If we dig it, chances are we'll review it. We will notify you if we review your submission.

Celestial Voices
submit@loobie.com
www.loobie.com
Dedicated to promoting haunting, atmospheric and ethereal female vocals on the internet. We feature both well-known performers as well as many newly discovered artists who are leading innovators in this field of music and have yet to receive recognition.

Cha Cha Charming
editor@chachacharming.com
www.chachacharming.com
A journalistic tribute to girl-powered pop- past, present and future and from all over the globe. This girl pop web magazine is bursting with interviews, rare photos and comprehensive articles covering female pop stars from Tokyo to Paris.

Collected Sounds
amy@collectedsounds.com
www.collectedsounds.com
A site dedicated to Women in Music. Here you can discover new artists or learn more about the ones you already love.

Concerning Women *Women Rock*
womenrock@concerningwomen.com
www.concerningwomen.com
We feature an artist of the month.

Cool Grrrls
editors@coolgrrrls.com
www.coolgrrrls.com
The worldwide grrrls' guide to all that grooves, featuring show & CD reviews, interviews and more.

Daily Diva
webmaster@dailydiva.com
www.dailydiva.com
Fashion, music, culture and fine women of color. We review Independent music in a section called NAS (New Artists Spotlight).

Dish Magazine – Xpose Yourself
xposeyourself@dishmag.com
www.dishmag.com/xposeyourself
So You Play Music! So You've Got a Web Site! So You've Got a CD! So You're Really GOOD! So Your Songs are great! So Your Band Is Wildly Popular! NOW WHAT? WE'VE GOT THE ANSWER! XposeYourself. Where You and the Recording Industry Collide!

Drummergirl
dginfo@happymazza.com
www.drummergirl.com
Our mission: to give props to drummergirls everywhere and to provide a place to exchange ideas, info and good vibes.

DryerBuzz
www.dryerbuzz.com
Covering entertainment and news conducive to the uniqueness of African American women.

Ectophile's Guide
ectoguide@smoe.org
www.smoe.org/ectoguide
What will we do with your music? Listen to it, we promise. Find an appropriate, sympathetic reviewer. If such a reviewer cannot be found we will return your music to you if possible. Providing we can find the right reviewer for your materials, we will put up a review page.

Elements
Jennifer Sjolin editor@elements-mag.com
www.elements-mag.com
The only teen webzine for the unique female. Do you know how to rock? Elements wants to get young, talented female musicians the publicity they deserve with interviews, reviews and more. Send an email to find out what we can offer you.

Endemoniada
Lucifera999@yahoo.com
www.endemoniada666.com
Dedicated to giving exposure to female bands and artists of the metal, hardcore, punk, industrial, gothic and bizarre genre. We don't exclude bands which are predominantly male. We seek to balance the gender role within our musical scene.

Eve Magazine
eve@evemag.com
www.evemag.com
Bringing Down the Patriarchy One Prom Queen at a Time.

Expository Magazine
Tina Coggins ExpositoryMagazine@herspace.com
www.expositorymagazine.net
Brimming with music, art and poetry.

The Female Musician
Theresa J. Orlando fm@femalemusician.com
www.femalemusician.com
FM's electronic monthly publication offers interviews & cd reviews with commercial and independent artists. Free classifieds for musicians. Offers paid & non paid areas for cd review & interview placement (female artists only).

FEMMUSIC.com
alex@femmusic.com
www.femmusic.com
An international, online, monthly magazine devoted to emerging women in music. FEMMUSIC features interviews, show reviews, CD reviews, show previews, genre based artist directory, artist of the month, demo of the month, website of the month and more

Gilded Serpent
editor@gildedserpent.com
www.gildedserpent.com
Dedicated to providing and nurturing a digital community for Middle Eastern performers and other adventurers. The Gilded Serpent is a creative forum for you to express your burning passions about dance and music.

Girl Musician Online

www.girlmusician.com
Designed with the female singer/ songwriter in mind with an emphasis on the independent recording artist.

Girlfriends Magazine

staff@girlfriendsmag.com
www.girlfriendsmag.com
Each month we print a full page lead review on the month's top album, along with four shorter CD reviews in a half-page column. We review all kinds of music by women, but lean towards lesbian, alternative, cutting edge, independent folk/rock/pop/jazz.

Girlposse

info@girlposse.com
www.girlposse.com
We review Independent artists from time to time. Girlposse.com LLC, Reviews Dept. 476 Welsh Lane, Granville, OH 43023

GirlPunk.Net

jessica@girlpunk.net
www.girlpunk.net
News, reviews, articles, featured bands etc.

Girly Thing

christina@girlything.com
www.girlything.com

Glittergrrrls.com

editors@glittergrrrls.com
www.glittergrrrls.com
The online teen mag for Grrrls that rock! We cover live shows, club gigs, openings and events - complete with klubbing photos; we review CDs and books, plays and film. We feature mp3s and demos by any indie or established band and conduct Q&As with established and up-and-coming artists.

GoGirlsMusic.com

info@gogirlsmusic.com
www.gogirlsmusic.com
THE oldest online community of independent women artists. Started in 1996, the organization is dedicated to promoting women in music. If you are a musician and would like to join our discussion group, send an email to werock@gogirlsmusic.com.

Grrl.com

bonnie@grrl.com
www.grrl.com
And if you'd like to send Grrl.com a CD to possibly be reviewed, go ahead and send it to: Bonnie Burton, Content Dept., Excite, 430 Broadway, Redwood City, CA 94063

grrlyrock.com

grrlyrock@magicstarr.net
www.grrlyrock.com
Overall, this site is a promotional tool for everyone to check out new bands and artists that they may have not heard. Download song samples, view pictures and navigate your way to many other sites and pages that we provide links for, for each individual band/artist.

GuitarGirls.com

Lynn Cary Saylor Lynn@guitargirls.com
www.guitargirls.com
I do music reviews of women artists on a one-on-one basis by email for people who ask. I don't do them for the purpose of posting the review on my site. It's more of a courtesy thing I will do when someone asks me. GuitarGirls.com continues to promote female through its "Featured Artist of the Week" page.

GURLmusic

staff @gURL.com
www.gurl.com

Heartless Bitches International

nataliep@heartless-bitches.com
www.heartless-bitches.com
You ever get tired of those whiners in the newsgroups? Or the guys who hit on you and you politely decline and they keep pestering you and pestering you and pestering you like some obnoxious, festering, pus-filled sore, until you finally have to WHAP them over the head with a VERY LARGE CLUE-BY-FOUR (tm)....?

herspace.com

www.herspace.com
If you are a musician you can submit work and/or a biography of yourself to be featured in the Herspace.com Showcase. Being featured in the Herspace showcase is a great way to get exposure for your work.

Jade Magazine

ellen@jademagazine.com
audrey@jademagazine.com
www.jademagazine.com
We strive to be the voice of English-speaking Asian women around the world by creating a forum to shatter the myths that exist about us. We highlight and showcase the talents and successes of Asian and Asian American women in all arenas.

LadySixString

info@ladysixstring.com
www.ladysixstring.com
Attention female guitarists! If you feel you are a good role model and would like yourself or your band listed free on LadySixString, for consideration, contact us by e-mail.

LOUDITH FAIRE

danise@loudithfaire.com
www.loudithfaire.com
A website for and about the women who SHOULD HAVE toured together. It AIN'T the LILITH FAIR. Whatever comes to mind when you think of that little festival of estrogen . . . well, this website will be the opposite and with BIGGER doses of estrogen.

Making Face - Making Soul

Susana L. Gallardo, webjefa@chicanas.com
chicanas.com
A site by, for and about Chicanas, meaning women of Mexican descent in the United States.

MS. Magazine

webmstress@msmagazine.com
www.msmagazine.com
We do publish music reviews, but not in every issue. The person in charge of music reviews is Ms. AnnMarie Dobosz. She can be contacted at AMDobosz@msmagazine.com or (212) 509-2092 ext. 217.

musical discoveries

rwelliot@hotmail.com
www.musicaldiscoveries.com
Comprehensive reviews of contemporary, progressive and crossover recordings and live performances of music featuring female vocalists.

MusiqQueen.com

queen@musiqqueen.com
www.MusiqQueen.com
A place where women in music rule. It was designed as a way to bring other women in music together to learn the aspect of the Music Business, meet other women, gather resources and more.

pinknoises.com

info@pinknoises.com
www.pinknoises.com
The one-stop web resource on women and electronic music.

Purple Pyjamas

Martine editor@purplepjs.com
www.purplepjs.com
Reviews of some of the most interesting music CD's, musical shows and concerts.

The REnaiSsance Lesbian

theresles@www.com
dreamwater.com/women/theresles
Music of bonds between women.

The Rising of Women in Music

rising@thirdroad.com
www.thirdroad.com/rising
We are a web site, broadcast and list membership for any woman involved in the music business in any way. Our magazine features news, reviews and interviews.

ROCKERCHICK

dahlia@getgalvanized.com
www.rockerchick.com
A site for girls in bands and their supporters, providing a valuable resource for the exchange of information and plain old networking. Featuring reviews of stores and venues, calendar listings of chick bands playing in NYC/Boston/DC, a photo gallery and a monthly zine, Rockerchick aims to serve women left cold by acoustic-folk "women's music."

Rockrgrl

feedback@rockrgrl.com
www.rockrgrl.com
Women playing music is neither "trend" nor "genre" and ROCKRGRL proves this in every bi-monthly print issue. Readers are treated to intelligent interviews with exceptional women of note from Ani to Yoko.

Ruby Slipper

Lulu Brooks lulu@rubyslipper.zzn.com
www.dork.com/rubyslipper
To get your music reviewed all you have to do is email me the above address. The people I've talked to so far are ones that I'm already somewhat familiar with their art/music/whatever, but I'm always up for talking to new people and its a cool forum to get featured on.

Saucy Chicks

Blanch info@saucychicks.com
www.saucychicks.com
Hell yes, we do music reviews of indie artists! For more information, please email our content coordinator Jody Reale at jody@saucychicks.com

She Caribbean

waynem@candw.lc
www.shecaribbean.com
We are only interested in Caribbean labels or artists, especially women.

Sister Divas
sisterdivasorg@yahoo.com
www.sisterdivas.org
Uniting, Entertaining, Educating and Uplifting the African American Woman.

Southwest Women
cheryl@southwestwomen.com
www.southwestwomen.com
Whether you are a woman of the Southwest or you live elsewhere and are like-minded, this site is for you and is full of features, photos, music, art and business listings catering to women or women-owned businesses and much more. We also have our very own Radio show.

sweetcherrie.com
anna@sweetcherrie.com
sweetcherrie.com
Independent artists are welcome to get their music reviewed. I am really interested in promoting independent and lesser known bands. The Rock Divas page is basically for all females involved in music, so independent female artists definitely apply.

technodyke.com
Stacy info@technodyke.com
www.technodyke.com
We've launched a new music section called DykeRock. We're looking for indie, female-fronted bands of all genres. Ideally queer (bi/trans inclusive) and/or with a queer twist.

Venus Magazine
feedback@venuszine.com
www.venuszine.com
Although the focus is on music, you'll also find stories about women's issues, feature stories on women who do it themselves (zines, sites, record labels etc.) and first-person columns that range from silly stuff to really serious stuff.

Voice is Venom
venomous@voiceisvenom.com
www.voiceisvenom.com
More than just a Web Zine, Voice Is Venom is a Bay Area resource network committed to the advancement of women in rock through information, events and visibility. Voice Is Venom review CDs, put on shows, write articles and interviews and help promote bands.

Whispers Online Magazine for Women
whispers@cyberpathway.com
www.cyberpathway.com/whispers
A free subscription based magazine with 8 categories: food, travel, romance, A&E, computing, finance, home and image. It's all about women helping women. We've been trying to expand the A&E section and sending your CDs in will help. We'd love to look at submissions from people who write about the music industry.

withitgirl
www.withitgirl.com
Profiles and affirms girls in sports and lifestyles. withitgirl supports active living that challenges traditional roles. Sponsors events, contests and art exhibitions and supports musicians through our compilation CD series.

Woman's Monthly
womo@womo.com
www.womo.com
Interested folk should write our Managing Editor, Melanie Alston-Akers at editors@womo.com, or 1718 M Street, NW, Suite 198, Washington, DC 20036.

Women in the Arts Magazine
www.nmwa.org/pubs
Devoted to promoting the achievements of women in the visual arts, as well as in music, theater, dance, film and literature. It is published as a benefit to members of the National Museum of Women in the Arts, providing information on NMWA exhibitions, programs and events.

Women in Production
support@womeninproduction.com
www.womeninproduction.com
TOTALLY Dedicated to featuring, reviewing and providing online resources for women in music. The sites are updated weekly with acts from all over the world.

Women of Country
staff@womenofcountry.com
www.womenofcountry.com
The Internet's #1 Guide to Female Country Music. We feature undiscovered musical gems in our Independent Artist Roundup. Are you an artist looking for more exposure? If so simply fill out the form on our site and submit it to us.

Women of MP3.com
asknancynow@hotmail.com
stations.mp3s.com/stations/0/the_women_of_mp3com.html
We are dedicated to promoting the advancement and achievements of women in the music industry. Show your support and visit often!

Women Who Rock
www.Starvox.net
A monthly feature on Starvox.net

Women Who Rock Magazine
Michael Mueller
womenwhorockmag@cherrylane.com
womenwhorockmag.com
We present the best and the brightest of today's up-and-coming stars.

Womanrock.com
brenda@womanrock.com
www.womanrock.com
The emerging voice for critical content and the promotion of women's music on the web. Run by musician and industry veteran, Brenda Kahn, the webzine launched in May of 1999 in conjunction with a live event series.

YELL - Oh Girls!
Vickie YELLOHGIRLS@aol.com
www.yellohgirls.com
We feature reviews of up-and-coming and independent women musicians. If you are in a band you think might be relevant to our audience— mostly Asian American gals between 13 and 25, let me know. I'll either have one of our writers handle the review, or I'll write the article myself.

xsisterhoodx.com
kelly@xsisterhoodx.com
www.xsisterhoodx.com
A site that promotes girls in hardcore and straightedge. It is not a site for girls only. In fact the more male involvement the better! We recognize that there is a division within the scenes. We are making an effort to change that. We're working on creating a solid network of girl friendly sites and scenes.

Canada

Dixie Tucker Magazine
dixie@dixietucker.com
www.dixietucker.com
Features the most intriguing and innovative people making music today. If your band would like to be reviewed by Dixie Tucker Magazine, please send us your press package. You can increase your chances of getting reviewed by having a professional product and sound.

FEMMUSICCanada.com
Alex Teitz alex@femmusic.com
www.FEMMUSICCanada.com
An international online monthly magazine focusing on emerging women in music. FEMMUSIC features interviews, CD reviews, show reviews, show previews, resource links, FEMBooks and feature areas on artists. In its first expansion FEMMUSIC focuses on the musician friendly nation of Canada.

good girl magazine
info@goodgirl.ca
www.goodgirl.ca
A quarterly magazine dedicated to publishing ideas that challenge, critique and break the rules of the status quo. Showcasing young writers and artists of all genders, colours, dimensions, persuasions and abilities.

Herizons
editor@herizons.ca
www.herizons.ca
We publish news articles from Canada, campaign updates, profiles on feminist activists and artists, plenty of book reviews and short snappers on women's accomplishments, called "Nelliegrams".

France

Les Filles du Metal (The Girls of Metal)
webmaster@metalgirls.com
www.metalgirls.fr.st
This website is here for you to discover the "Female Atmospheric Metal" in the form of interviews.

The Netherlands

Metal Maidens
metalmaid@globalxs.nl
www.metalmaidens.com
We are entirely focused on the women in (Heavy) Metal and (Hard) Rock and the most important ladies in the punk rock music. Our magazine includes the latest CDs, seven inches, demo tapes and concert reviews and dates.

Sweden

Darling
red@drrling.se
darling.spray.se

United Kingdom

AMP: IT'S THE TITS!
ed@ampnet.co.uk
www.ampnet.co.uk
An elegant pink pamphlet dedicated to the finer things in life. For chicks and dicks and... just about anybody, really.

Chicks Kick
noz287@yahoo.co.uk
www.chicks-kick.cjb.net
*Mainly dedicated to all girls punk/emo/hardcore,
whatever!! A chance for females to input their ideas in
a place where they are very much welcomed.*

the f-word
mail@thefword.org.uk
www.thefword.org.uk
*Young UK feminism. Includes a section for album
reviews, gig reviews, critiques of lyrics and music
videos (good or bad), or anything else about specific
music - analyzed from a feminist perspective.*

Freewheel Zine
nat@freewheelzine.co.uk
www.freewheelzine.co.uk
*Dedicated to punk, HC and underground pop, with an
emphasis on female and queer bands. We have
interviews, reviews, columns, all of it written by girls
and boys from all around the world!*

Heroine Chick
mail@heroinechick.co.uk
www.philford.org/heroinechick
*Within these pages you'll find comprehensive, up to
date links to yr favourite grrrl bands and those you
haven't discovered yet. Don't forget to get in touch if
yr in a band you want included here, or if you know of
a band we might be interested in!*

grrlsinrock @ planetgrrl
planetgrrl@planetgrrl.com
www.planetgrrl.com
*We try to encourage, support, befriend, teach, respect
and recognise other women and grrls online
regardless of race, religion, political standpoint, age,
orientation, employment status or anything else.
Promote individuality and freedom of expression and
opinion, through new media.*

MissMinx.com
Rockgrrlie@yahoo.co.uk
www.missminx.com
*An alternative music site attempting to bring back the
balance. It's not just a website, it's a mission. A
mission to give female musicians and their fans a
forum for their music and to meet other kick-ass
chicks.*

Tribe8industry
Hazel O' Keefe info@tribe8industry.com
www.tribe8industry.com
*UK based company aimed at female rock and punk
bands, other genres considered.*

Women in Music UK
info@bandwagonstudios.co.uk
www.womeninmusic.org.uk
*A highly influential national membership organisation
that supports, encourages and enables women to
make music. "Women in Music Now" is the lively
magazine received by WiM members six times a year.
Featuring essential features, news and views on all
types of women's music-making.*

Japan

Girly Heaven Music
webmaster@girlyheaven.com
www.girlyheaven.com

World Music

Allafrica.com
allafrica.com/music

Global Rhythm
edit@globalrhythm.net
www.globalrhythm.net
The Music the Movement the Culture.

globalvillageidiot.net
cnicks@globalvillageidiot.net
www.globalvillageidiot.net
*Find the latest news in world music. The freshest
reviews and interviews with artists well-known and
unknown.*

Jewish Entertainment Resources
info@jewishentertainment.net
www.jewishentertainment.net
*We strive to let you know about the wealth and variety
of Jewish music resources available. If you would like
your new release considered for review, please send a
copy to us.*

Klezmer Shack
ari@ivritype.com
www.klezmershack.com
*Klezmer is the music that speaks to me. It's balkans
and blues, ancient Jewish culture and prayer and
history, spirit and jazz all mixed together. Good
klezmer and the music inspired by it, demands that
one dance.*

Musical Traditions
rod@mustrad.org.uk
www.mustrad.org.uk
*The Magazine for Traditional Music throughout the
world.*

New World Buzz
nwbfeedback@hotmail.com
www.newworldbuzz.com
*Provides a showcase to promote the composers,
artists and performers of music genres from all over
the world.*

The Piper & Drummer
editor@piperanddrummer.com
www.piperanddrummer.com
*The magazine is North America's most established
publication devoted solely to piping and drumming.*

"Regional" Publications and Resources

*The resources listed in this section can help you
to gain exposure, whether it be allowing you to
post information about your band, new releases,
upcoming shows, CD reviews etc. Most of the
organizations listed (Folk, Jazz, Blues etc.)
publish a newsletter that will review your CD.
Note that some resources will review music from
outside of their region, but give preference to
local talent.*

North America

United States

communitymusician.com
feedback@communitymusician.com
communitymusician.com
*Conceived by musicians, communitymusician is a
network of Web sites that provide artists with a free
and practical resource.*

Fold the Corners
Chris.Abbott@foldthecorners.com
www.foldthecorners.com
*This site is dedicated to local music, everywhere!
Write reviews, submit some news, add a band, spread
the word. These are your scenes and you can help
build this site with your contribution.*

Great Local Band Exchange
info@golocalrock.com
www.golocalrock.com
*A website where local bands can add themselves and
you can check out local bands in your area!*

Hometown Music
rick@hometownmusic.us
www.hometownmusic.us
*We still have a FREE add your Link and Band's News
section on 11 websites to help promote a band or
music type business.*

Local Band Finder
www.localbandfinder.us
*Linking local bands, promoters, Clubs and recording
companies and other music resources on one site.*

The Local Mix
info@thelocalmix.com
www.thelocalmix.com
*Our online community will be filled with reviews,
MP3's, classifieds, message boards and even TLM
Radio, to help promote local bands and artists and
provide them with global exposure.*

Local Band Network
fitz@localband.net
www.localband.net
*Information about local bands and local music
venues... no matter where "local" is to you.*

Local Music Scenes.com
Jeff Higginbotham jeff@localmusicscenes.com
www.localmusicscenes.com
*Local music support in scenes near you. Grassroots
coverage of your local music market.*

localmusic2.com
vinchawla1@netscape.net
www.localmusic2.com
*Gig listings, message boards, classifieds and general
info covering the music scene in various US cities.*

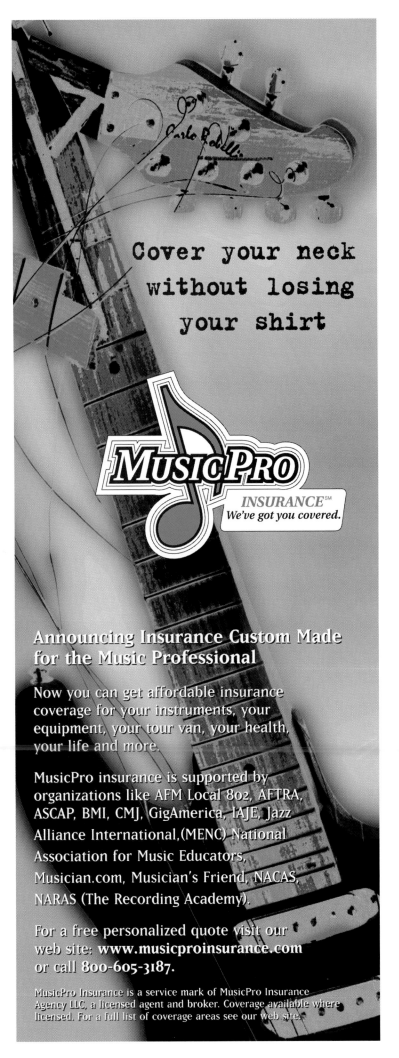

Cover your neck without losing your shirt

MusicPro INSURANCE℠
We've got you covered.

Announcing Insurance Custom Made for the Music Professional

Now you can get affordable insurance coverage for your instruments, your equipment, your tour van, your health, your life and more.

MusicPro insurance is supported by organizations like AFM Local 802, AFTRA, ASCAP, BMI, CMJ, GigAmerica, IAJE, Jazz Alliance International,(MENC) National Association for Music Educators, Musician.com, Musician's Friend, NACAS, NARAS (The Recording Academy).

For a free personalized quote visit our web site: **www.musicproinsurance.com** or call **800-605-3187.**

MusicPro Insurance is a service mark of MusicPro Insurance Agency LLC, a licensed agent and broker. Coverage available where licensed. For a full list of coverage areas see our web site.

Our comfortable facility includes
Spacious Control Room
Live Instrument Room
Iso Booth
Client Lounge

ATL's premier entertainment complex now offering 32 track protools recording, mixing and mastering...photography, graphic design and print...cd duplication and manufacturing, marketing, promotion and distribution

State of the art recording gear
soundcraft 32 channel console
32 track protools
Akai MPC 2000 XL
Roland JV-2080
Emu Proteus 2000
TL Audio & TC Electronics
Tascam & Korg

Other Onsite Amenities
Professional Engineers
Experienced Producers
Graphic Design
Photography
CD Duplication

Plus
Printing
Marketing
Promotion
Distribution

**mindzai multimedia
650 hamilton unit g
atlanta ga 30312
ph# 404.622.1897
www.mindzai.net**

When Good Gigs Go Bad

Have the only organization dedicated to representing the interests of professional musicians behind you. Default Protection, Legal Service, Contracts, Emergency Travel Assistance and more available through the AFM.

Join the only musician's organization that will help you network, find gigs, obtain insurance, get better pay, and take advantage of some serious benefits.

The AFM

To learn more about the American Federation of Musicians of the United States and Canada, visit www.afm.org.

scenepoints.com
webmaster@scenepoints.com
www.scenepoints.com
Covering punk shows in all states.

Alabama

al.com
www.al.com/music
Online presence for the Birmingham News, the Huntsville Times and the Mobile Register. Local music section.

The Alabama Bluegrass Music Association
webmaster@alabamabluegrass.org
www.alabamabluegrass.org
The Objective of the association is to promote bluegrass music in the state of Alabama.

The Alabama Blues Project
Alablues@aol.com
www.alabamablues.org
An organization dedicated to the preservation of blues music as a traditional American art form. Live performances of the blues coupled with projects which educate the younger generation is the way we work towards this goal.

Alabama Blues Society
alablues@aol.com
www.alabamablues.org
Your gateway to a state of the blues.

The Auburn Plainsman
editor@theplainsman.com
www.theplainsman.com

Aumnibus
www.aum.edu/aumnibus
University of Auburn - Montgomery student publication.

Bama Hip Hop
Bamahiphop@mail.com
bamahiphop.homestead.com
We'll list your bio, company profile, concert and festival schedule, release dates, booking contact and upcoming projects for your fans and entertainment industry contacts.

Birmingham Buzz
curtg@bhambuzz.com
screamsophie.net/ezine
Dedicated to covering the local rock music scene in Birmingham. Stop by to find the latest news on all your favorite local bands, get show dates and times, get insider tips from musicians, read reviews on the latest music to come out of Birmingham and the surrounding areas.

The Birmingham Music Guide
birmingham.citysearch.com
Extensive coverage of the local music scene. Post your shows and events.

The Birmingham News
www.bhamnews.com
Daily paper. A&E section published Friday features interviews, reviews and previews.

Birmingham Rocks
webmaster@steelecom.net
www.steelecom.net/bhamrocks
An all-inclusive tool for local artists in the Birmingham Area and the Southeast. If your band, venue, organization, or website is not listed, please let us know.

Black & White
www.bwcitypaper.com
Birmingham's city paper. Events, concerts and live music sections.

The Crimson White
www.cw.ua.edu
University of Alabama newspaper.

fleabomb.com
Stanley sholditch@yahoo.com
www.fleabomb.com
Promotes local bands in Birmingham, AL, as well as any bands that we deem original or worthy that may come through the Birmingham or the Southeast area. We have done interviews with local hip-hop acts and numerous local indie-bands. I would love to help out any talented bands.

The Mobile Music Guide
mobile.citysearch.com
Extensive coverage of the local music scene. Post your shows and events.

The MobileSucks Website
webmaster@mobilesucks.net
www.mobilesucks.net
Covering the punk scene in Mobile. Use this site for the betterment of the Mobile scene and working together we can make Mobile suck less.

The Montgomery Music Scene
www.onlinemontgomery.com/music
Sign up your band. Send us your show dates.

The Toe
ramoore@TheToe.cc
www.thetoe.cc
North Alabama's premiere Music and Nightlife site. Musicians: If you want a profile page set up for you e-mail us. List your gig in our "Local Licks" section.

tuscaloosanews.com
www.tuscaloosanews.com
Daily paper covers seven counties in Alabama. A&E section Thursday and Sunday has interviews, previews and reviews.

Alaska

AK Ink
jennink@hotmail.com
www.geocities.com/akinkzine
Anchorage based punk zine covering local and international bands.

AK This Month
www.alaskathismonth.com
Your Comprehensive Guide to Entertainment in the 49th State - FREE!

Anchorage Daily News
www.adn.com
Alaska's largest newspaper.

The Anchorage Music Guide
anchorage.citysearch.com
Extensive coverage of the local music scene. Post your shows and events.

The Anchorage Press
calendar@anchoragepress.com
www.anchoragepress.com
An Anchorage-wide Art, Entertainment, Recreation and Metro weekly newspaper.

Indie Rock Alaska
design@matthopper.com
www.velvetclub.com
We exist because we love what we do and want to bridge the gap between the public and our work, perhaps even take a stab at making a living at it. Don't hesitate to contact us with any project you might be worrying about.

Juneau Empire
www.juneauempire.com
Daily paper serving the capital city and surrounding communities as the state's third largest newspaper.

Arizona

602 Streets.com
info@602streets.com
www.602streets.com
Arizona Rap and Hip Hop network. Arizona's Matrix of Hustlaz, Grindaz and Game Spittaz.

Arizona Bluegrass Association
lloydand@juno.com
www.azbluegrass.org
Designed to provide you with up-to-date information about news, events, festivals and bluegrass bands in Arizona and the Desert Southwest.

Arizona Bluegrass & Old-Time Musicians Association
www.arizonabluegrass.org
Created for the promotion of Bluegrass, Old-time, Gospel and Traditional instrumental and vocal music.

Arizona Daily Star
www.azstarnet.com
Tucson daily paper. Record reviews for bands touring in Tucson. Weekend entertainment guide on Friday.

Arizona Goth Scene
webmaster@disillude.com
www.tres-gothique.com/AZGoth

Arizona Heads
azheads@azheads.com
www.azheads.com
A place for fans of improvisational music in Arizona. Check out upcoming shows, download music, post messages, view our photo gallery and more.

The Arizona Hip-Hop Network
Ryan "Creepz" Piercey creepz@cox.net
www.ArizonaHipHop.com
Your online/one-stop spot for Arizona Hip-Hop. Album Reviews, Artist Interviews, Monthly Features, A-Zona Radio, Promotion and Networking Forums and much more.

Arizona Irish Music Society
aims@azirishmusic.com
www.azirishmusic.com
News, events, listings etc.

The Arizona Music Club
music@blackdogpromotions.com
www.arizonamusicclub.com
Help Us Spread The Word About The Great Music Of Arizona!

Arizona Music Scene
directory@arizonamusicscene.com
www.ArizonaMusicScene.Com
Comprehensive resource for the music scene in Arizona: business directories, Arizona Band Index, local music news, CD reviews, free promotional tools for bands/artists etc.

The Arizona Republic
www.arizonarepublic.com
Phoenix daily paper. Thursday CD reviews.

ASU Web Devil
seth.scott@asu.edu
www.statepress.com
Arizona State University online publication.

AZ Local Music
www.azlocalmusic.com
Covering the Arizona music scene.

AZ-Raves
galxygrl@getnet.net
www.azraves.org
The paramount information point for dance music in our area since 1996. Use it wisely.

azcentral.com
www.azcentral.com
Post your music and reach thousands of local music fans! If you are an Arizona-based musical artist, we want your music on this site! We get more traffic than any other website in the state, giving you a unique opportunity to reach thousands of local music fans.

AZjazz Magazine
www.arizonajazz.com
From the valley to the borders...we are your source of information about the best Jazz in Arizona and beyond. Check out the latest Jazz news, local action and today's live Jazz.

azNight
admin@aznight.com
www.aznight.com
An Independent Guide to Phoenix. Blues, MP3, music, bars. Gay, lesbian, gothic and rock clubs in the Phoenix, Mesa, Scottsdale area. Local musicians and artists.

AZPunk.com
chris@azpunk.com
www.AZPunk.com
Arizona's #1 source for punk rock!

Bandwidth Rock Magazine
editor@bandwidthrockmagazine.com
www.bandwidthrockmagazine.com
The local Phoenix scene is where bands expose their music to us for the first time. It is our goal to show you bands at all levels, from the beginning to national recording artists.

ClubAZ.com
promo@clubaz.com
www.clubaz.com
Arizona's premier guide to the hottest night clubs, nightlife, parties, events, profiles, links and pictures.

CollectiveUnderground.com
kayn@pluhextreme.com
www.collectiveunderground.com
Dedicated to Arizona's heaviest music.

The Desert Bluegrass Association
reifdoc@aol.com
home.att.net/~fertilepickens
Our goal is to develop and promote Bluegrass music for the diverse audience in the Greater Tucson Area.

hiphopAZ.com
www.hiphopaz.com
Everyone's Hip Hop Highway. E-Zine for info from Arizona.

Human Target Productions
aaron@humantargetproductions.com
humantargetproductions.com
A Phoenix based label who's working hard to get more exposure for local music.

In Your Ear
info@in-your-ear.net
www.in-your-ear.net
A music zine out of Tucson. News, reviews, interviews etc.

Lake Havasu Musician's Network
lnt@npgcable.com
www.lhmn.com
Our purpose is to help all local musicians get together in various settings in order to promote musical growth in Lake Havasu.

LiNK Music
Rachel@linkmusicaz.com
www.linkmusicaz.com
The Musician Directory, Classifieds and Calendar of Events allow for real time access to musicians and musical resources across Arizona.

Live and Local
Chita@KLPX.com
www.liveandlocal.net
A site dedicated to promoting local Tucson music.

Mock Brawn Records
jesus@mockbrawn.com
www.mockbrawn.com
Please post your shows in the local shows area. Purchasing items from Mockbrawn shows your support for local artists working overtime to produce and promote their own music, free from an industry that has turned its back on creativity.

The Phoenix Blues Society
info@phoenixblues.org
www.phoenixblues.org
Our goal is to promote and perpetuate Blues music and is the globally recognized clearinghouse for the Blues.

The Phoenix Early Music Society
info@pems.org
www.pems.org
An organization that brings together everyone with an interest in music of the Medieval, Renaissance and Baroque eras. Whether you are a performer, teacher, critic, or just enjoy listening, we will keep you in touch with the best in local events to stimulate, educate and make early music come "alive."

Phoenix Music
info@phoenixmusic.com
www.phoenixmusic.com
Music Supersite For The Phoenix Metro Area...And Beyond! We have produced the Phoenix Metro area's most extensive music website. Our calendar contains the most complete list of upcoming musical events in the valley.

The Phoenix Music Guide
phoenix.citysearch.com
Extensive coverage of the local music scene. Post your shows and events.

The Phoenix New Times
www.phoenixnewtimes.com
Free weekly alternative paper. Thursday has local reviews.

Prescott Jazz Society
milt@pjazz.org
www.pjazz.org
Presenting, promoting and celebrating jazz performance and education in northern Arizona.

Rock in Phoenix
rockinphoenix@hotmail.com
www.rockinphoenix.org
A Spanish Rock/Punk/Metal website dedicated to the Spanish rock scene here in Phoenix.

RockThis.net
nikki@rockthis.net
www.rockthis.net
A music resource and promotion site for musicians surrounding Bullhead City including venue information for the area.

Southwest Acoustic Music Association
SAMcomment@aol.com
www.inficad.com/~sfma
The Acoustic Scene is the monthly publication of the Southwest Acoustic Music Association. It is an informative and entertaining magazine of articles, events, CD reviews, venue and open mic listings, poetry and more.

The Tucson Guitar Society
info@tucsongs.org
www.tucsongs.org
Dedicated to promoting the art of the classical guitar. We organize classical guitar concerts and recitals in the Tucson area for local, national and international talent.

Tucson Friends of Traditional Music *(TFTM)*
office@tftm.org
www.tftm.org
Dedicated to keeping the traditions of community music and dance alive and growing in Tucson. TFTM sponsors and promotes concerts, dances, workshops and informal music sessions

The Tucson Jazz Society
tjsmail@tucsonjazz.org
www.tucsonjazz.org
The Society boasts over 2,600 members, making it one of the nation's largest. It serves all of southern Arizona with concerts, festivals, media activities and youth programs. The society presents or co-presents about 40 concerts throughout the year.

The Tucson Music Guide
tucson.citysearch.com
Extensive coverage of the local music scene. Post your shows and events.

The Tucson Weekly
www.tucsonweekly.com
Free weekly paper. Indie record reviews. Publish the annual "Tucson Musician's Register".

The Yuma Sun
www.yumasun.com
Yuma daily newspaper.

Zia Record Exchange
www.ziarecords.com
We can set you up with a consignment arrangement.

Arkansas

Arkansas Democrat-Gazette
www.ardemgaz.com
Little Rock daily paper.

Arkansas Jazz Heritage Foundation
ajc@arjazz.org
www.arjazz.org
Sponsors jazz performances by musicians with Arkansas connections and educational clinics for H.S. and college musicians throughout the state.

The Arkansas River Blues Society
comments@arkansasriverblues.org
www.arkansasriverblues.org
Formed to preserve and promote the indigenous musical art form known as the "Blues".

Arkansas Times
arktimes@arktimes.com
www.arktimes.com
Arkansas's Newspaper of Politics and Culture.

Arkansas Traveler
www.uark.edu/~travinfo
The University of Arkansas's student newspaper.

arkansasrockers.com
webmaster@arkansasrockers.com
www.arkansasrockers.com

Delta Boogie
www.deltaboogie.com
Online information about music, art, entertainment and sports in Northeast Arkansas and the Mississippi Delta. Site includes chat, news and reviews.

Fayetteville Free Weekly
ambassador@arkansas.net
www.freeweekly.com
Entertainment weekly. Covers local music.

Followmearound
followmearound@fastmail.fm
clix.to/followmearound
Got a band that wants to be linked up or an upcoming show, well hit it up.

Arkansas Goth/Punk/Industrial E-Group
groups.yahoo.com/group/Arkansas_Goth_Punk_Industrial
A group dedicated to Gothic, Punk and Industrial music in the Arkansas area. Topics include lifestyle, clothing and possible venues and concerts. This is intended to be a clearing house for information about the Goth-punk-industrial scene in Arkansas.

Little Rock Folk Club
len@lrfolkclub.org
www.lrfolkclub.org
Dedicated to preserving the link between the musical traditions of the old and new worlds.

Little Rock Hardcore
adam@littlerockhardcore.com
www.littlerockhardcore.com
Interviews, concert and album reviews, downloads etc.

The Little Rock Music Guide
littlerock.citysearch.com
Extensive coverage of the local music scene. Post your shows and events.

The Morning News of North West Arkansas
www.nwaonline.net
Daily paper. Covers Springdale and North West Arkansas. Has an entertainment calendar.

Nightflying
info@nightflying.com
www.nightflying.com
Free monthly alternative magazine. Live music guide, CD reviews, features and previews.

Northwest Arkansas Times
www.nwarktimes.com
Daily paper. Sometimes interviews gigging bands two weeks before the show. National album reviews and local previews.

California

American Guitar Society
www.csun.edu/%7Eigra/ags
Since 1923 the Society, based at California State University, has presented monthly programs, featuring solo and ensemble performances of music from the Renaissance to the present. We provide an opportunity for you to perform before an appreciative audience.

American River Folk Society
bruce@americanriverfolk.com
www.americanriverfolk.com
Based in Georgetown, our mission is to support the promotion, education and presentation of contemporary, traditional and multi-cultural folk music and folklore in the Mother lode of the California Sierra Gold Country.

Ascensive Marketing Promotions
Ascensive@aol.com
www.ascensive.net
Based in Sacramento, we are successful in exposing new artists by getting the promotional materials into the hands of the music lovers who are most likely going to enjoy the music they receive. The website contains CD Reviews, Interviews and Concert Photography from shows we constantly attends. Refer to the "bands" section for artists who are currently being promoted.

Blackbird World Empire
contact@blackbirdworldempire.com
www.blackbirdworldempire.com
Ventura based resource. Our mission is to promote underground, Do-It-Yourselfers and independent music as an alternative to mainstream radio and television.

Bluegrass West
peterf@silcom.com
www.bluegrasswest.com
We have been presenting music and selected performers in shows throughout the Southern California area for the past thirty-five years.

Butte Folk Music Society
bobharrison@mindspring.com
www.bfms.freeservers.com
Organized to encourage and support traditional and folk music in the North Sacramento Valley through concert venues and other music-related activities with the purpose of providing cultural enrichment and community education.

CA Bands
robert@cabands.com
www.cabands.com
The #1 ranked website to find California bands, concert reviews, live interviews, labels, venues as well as the latest news on bands from all genres of music.

The California Aggie
www.californiaaggie.com
UC Davis Student paper. The Aggie is distributed free on the UC Davis campus and in the Davis community.

The California Bluegrass Association
rcornish@sjcoe.net
www.cbaontheweb.org
Dedicated to the furtherance of Bluegrass, Old Time and Gospel music.

California Hardcore
nick@calihardcore.com
www.calihardcore.com
Here you will find all the latest information on the phattest hardcore bands, zines, record labels, distros and more from the Bay Area and California.

California Lawyers for the Arts
cla@calawyersforthearts.org
www.calawyersforthearts.org
A nonprofit tax-exempt service organization founded in 1974 which provides lawyer referrals, dispute resolution services, educational programs, publications and a resource library to artists of all disciplines and arts organizations.

California Traditional Music Society
info@ctmsfolkmusic.org
www.ctmsfolkmusic.org
Dedicated to the preservation and dissemination of traditional Folk Music, dance and related folk arts of America's diverse cultural heritage by broadening public involvement with Folk Music.

The Carmel Classic Guitar Society
CarmelClassicGuitar@starrsites.com
www.starrsites.com/CarmelClassicGuitar
Promotes the classical guitar through education, recitals and gatherings.

Central Valley Noize
webmaster@centralvalleynoize.com
www.centralvalleynoize.com
This site is dedicated to the central valley metal and hardcore music scene. Do you have a band? Want some help getting your band to the local scene or do just want your cd reviewed? We can help.

CentralCali.com
www.centralcali.com
A site about the Hip Hop scene in Central California, featuring message boards, reviews and news on local events.

Chico News and Reviews
kathyb@newsreview.com
www.newsreview.com/chico
Passionate about providing informative and enlightened coverage of grassroots issues, the News & Review has long been a trusted member of the Chico community. Extensive coverage of the local music scene.

chico underground show info
chicolist@synthesis.net
www.chicolist.com
The basic goal of this organization is to promote the local indie/punk/hardcore scene in the Chico area. Another goal is the promotion of unity in the scene.

Coast Weekly
mail@coastweekly.com
www.coastweekly.com
Our goal is to be the reflective voice of Monterey County by providing lively and comprehensive coverage of the events and issues that shape our community.

The Davis Enterprise
newsroom@davisenterprise.net
www.davisenterprise.com
Daily newspaper. Entertainment section covers local music.

The Downtown Gazette
www.gazettes.com/downtown.html
Long Beach weekly newspaper.

Earwax
info@redflagmedia.com
www.redflagmedia.com
Distributed in over 200 locations throughout the Sacramento area.

East Bay Express
katy.StClair@eastbayexpress.com
www.eastbayexpress.com
Entertainment weekly based in Emeryville. Extensive coverage of local music including reviews and gig listings.

Fresno Area Bands
matt@mcic.net
www.localbands.org
Over 638 Bands from the Central San Joaquin Valley are listed here! By far the largest Local Music information site. News, gigs, downloads etc.

The Fresno Bee
www.fresnobee.com
Central California's leading daily newspaper. It is our mission to serve the San Joaquin Valley as the region's premiere information source.

Fresno City Hardcore
DavidDead@beer.com
www.fresnohardcore.net
If you would like your bands CD/LP/EP/Demo reviewed on the FRESNO CITY HARDCORE page please send us a copy. Make sure to send info on how to order the product.

The Fresno Folklore Society
patwolk@yahoo.com
www.fresnofolklore.org
Founded for the purpose of preserving folk arts, especially traditional music, in California's San Joaquin Valley.

The Fresno Music Guide
fresno.citysearch.com
Extensive coverage of the local music scene. Post your shows and events.

Good Times
events@gdtimes.com
www.gdtimes.com
Santa Cruz County's leading news and entertainment weekly. Extensive coverage of the local music scene.

hollywoodband.com
web1@parkproduction.com
www.hollywoodband.com
Underground news from Hollywood, USA. We provide FREE web services include, RealAudio, RealVideo, show schedule, show reviews, news, CD sales, & more...

HollywoodMusic.com
deanc@hollywoodmusic.com
www.hollywoodmusic.com
A full service entertainment company with a FREE website dedicated to marketing unsigned musicians. Offering MP3, Realaudio, Live video on demand and webcasting. Come see the music!

Hopland Women's Festival
Hopland@AOL.com
www.hoplandwomensfestival.com
When women unite, celebrate and embrace our diversity, we build a stronger, confident and capable community which empowers us all on both our individual and collective paths. Located in beautiful Mendocino County, the Festival provides a safe space for women to come together to learn, laugh and enjoy the serenity of the land.

Humboldt Folklife Society
folk@humboldtfolklife.org
www.humboldtfolklife.org
Working to bring together folk dancers, musicians and music lovers.

HumboldtMusic.com
mike@humboldtmusic.com
www.humboldtmusic.com
A free resource built by and for the local music community. The site provides an extensive and searchable directory of local musicians and music resources, as well as customizable artist web pages which feature downloadable and streaming audio.

HumGuide
info@humguide.com
www.humguide.com
Event calendars, bands, art and more in Humboldt County.

InTune
info@skipsintune.com
www.skipsintune.com
A service to the Northern and Central California music scene. We welcome and encourage your submissions of band photos and bios, gig schedules, club and event calendars and CD releases.

The Jazz Society of Santa Cruz County
editor@santacruzjazz.org
santacruzjazz.org
Dedicated to the promotion of Jazz in and around Santa Cruz. This site contains a Bulletin Board, Musicians Directory Service, news and views of Jazz.

Keeper Magazine
editor@keepermagazine.com
www.keepermagazine.com
California's free metal magazine. Keeper hits the streets the 1st of every month. Keeper features: Band interviews and articles, CD & DVD reviews, Monthly columns, live show reviews, Lifestyle interests, Original artwork & more... Covering the scope of extreme music.

The List
skoepke@stevelist.com
jon.luini.com/thelist
stevelist.com
Southern California funk-punk-thrash-ska upcoming shows of interest.

The Living Tradition
livingtradition@hotmail.com
www.thelivingtradition.org
Working to support and preserve traditional music and dance. The Living Tradition sponsors regular contra dances, folk music concerts and folk music jams in Bellflower and Anaheim, California.

Long Beach Press-Telegram
www.presstelegram.com
Daily paper. Has a local beats section covering the local music scene.

Los Altos Town Crier
www.losaltosonline.com
Weekly publication. Has a music section that covers local music events.

Mach Turtle
jamie@machturtleprods.com
www.machturtleprods.com
Listing of Live Surf Music events in Southern California.

MetroSantaCruz
msc@metcruz.com
www.metcruz.com
Free weekly alternative paper. Indie music reviews.

Modesto Area Musician Association
www.modestoview.com/mama/bands
News, reviews, MP3s etc.

The Modesto Music Guide
modesto.citysearch.com
Extensive coverage of the local music scene. Post your shows and events.

Moshking.com
moshking@moshking.com
www.moshking.com
The best source on the net for information on all Metal and guitar driven Hard Rock concerts, events and local bands in the Southern California area.

MusicKatz
music@musickatz.com
musickatz.com
Resource for Humboldt County. If you or your band have a homepage or are looking for a band or musician, have instruments for sale, or have gig or record info for your band. Hook Up With MusicKatz NOW!

MYLOCALBANDS.com
concerts@mylocalbands.com
www.mylocalbands.com
Add information about your band as well as your MP3s. Interested in playing the next MyLocalBands show? Good, because we want you to play. Email us for more information.

New Times
calendar@newtimesslo.com
www.newtimes-slo.com
San Luis Obispo County's News and Entertainment Weekly.

norcalmusic.com
info@norcalmusic.com
www.norcalmusic.com
Why do we do it? We love the music and we support the music.

NorCalUnderground
stickyicky@norcalunderground.com
www.norcalunderground.com
This site is about underground and independent Hip Hop/Rap from Northern Cali across the world.

North Bay Bohemian
editor@bohemian.com
www.metroactive.com/sonoma
Arts and entertainment weekly. Covers the local music scene.

OC Punk
www.ocpunk.com
A resource for Orange County bands and their fans. We are working on becoming the one stop for all things punk in Orange County - home of the best music in the world! OC leads and everyone else follows.

OC Weekly
letters@ocweekly.com
www.ocweekly.com
Orange County Arts and Entertainment weekly. Lots of local music coverage.

OnStageNow.net
support@onstagenow.net
www.onstagenow.net
See Videos and hear Music of your favorite Local Bands, or take a video tour of the coolest Clubs with live music! Get info and schedules for Bands and Clubs in So. California, find musicians for your band, place ads in our musicians classifieds and much more!

Orange County Bands
admin@ocbands.com
www.ocbands.com
Band listings (all genres) and MP3s.

Orange County Music Awards
Martin Brown Printcreat@aol.com
www.orangecountymusicawards.com
Over 20 categories. Judging by press, TV, radio, bookers. High profile event full of artistic integrity (what a concept!). For full information check visit our website or call 714-624-8729.

The Orion
www.orion-online.net
California State U. Chico's student publication.

Pacific Sun
www.pacificsun.com
North Bay's weekly paper.

Palo Alto Jazz Alliance
jazzbuff@sbcglobal.net
www.jazzbuff.org
The PAJA's "Jazz Buff" newsletter contains CD reviews, articles, listings and other information about the Palo Alto Jazz scene.

Palo Alto Weekly
editor@paweekly.com
www.paloaltoonline.com
Award-winning semi-weekly newspaper. Are you planning an event? Send it to us to include in the calendar!

Pasadena Weekly
Joe Piasecki joep@pasadenaweekly.com
www.pasadenaweekly.com
Greater Pasadena's Alternative News and Entertainment Weekly.

Powerslave.com
submissions@powerslave.com
www.powerslave.com
The Northern California Underground Metal Scene is once again setting the trends in aggressive music. This InfoZine exists to expose these bands and sounds and introduce the world to the next wave of heavy music.

Riverside Jazz Society
ladyjazz@c-zone.net
www.c-zone.net/jazzjoy
Dedicated to the preservation and perpetuation of our country's only original art form - Traditional Jazz. Our goal is not only to provide quality entertainment for the community but to support artists and encourage students through using raffle proceeds toward jazz workshops.

Riverside Press-Enterprise
www.pe.com
Riverside daily paper.

The Rolling Grape
rollinggrapeguy@yahoo.com
www.therollinggrape.com
Music for the No. Cal. Wine Country. Why a Web Site dedicated to the Music Industry in the Wine Country? It's about time, don't you think?

Rose Street Music
rosestreetmusic@yahoo.com
www.rosestreetmusic.com
A Berkeley house concert venue featuring women musicians and songwriters.

Sacramento Bee
www.sacbee.com
Daily paper. Local music is covered in the Entertainment section.

The Sacramento Guitar Society
gregorwilliams@attbi.com
www.sacguitar.org
Established to promote the art of the guitar and its music by providing education and performance opportunities to people of diverse cultures, ages, abilities and economic means.

The Sacramento Music Guide
sacramento.citysearch.com
Extensive coverage of the local music scene. Post your shows and events.

Sacramento News & Review
www.newsreview.com
Free weekly alternative paper. Indie reviews and local artist features.

Sacramento Traditional Jazz Society
www.sacjazz.com
To preserve and promote traditional jazz music.

Sacramento.com
Laura Johnson lljohnson@sacbee.com
www.sacramento.com
Bands from Northern California can submit their gigs in Sacramento and surrounding areas for free to Sacramento.com, the region's best entertainment guide. The site also has a list of Web sites for local bands.

Santa Barbara Choral Society
www.sbchoral.org
The goal of the Santa Barbara Choral Society is to provide qualified singers with an opportunity to study and perform great works of music and to stimulate the community interest in that music.

Santa Barbara Independent
arts@independent.com
www.independent.com
The county's news and entertainment paper.

Santa Barbara Live!
itc@santabarbaralive.com
www.santabarbaralive.com
A magazine about Santa Barbara. Photos, music, interviews, services, information.

Santa Barbara On Stage
www.sbonstage.com
Our mission is simply to provide quality localized content to live music fans in the Santa Barbara area. The goal of this publication is to provide musicians, publicists and promoters an outlet to reach local concert attendees and to support the various venues that cater to your need for live musical entertainment.

Santa Cruz Sentinel
www.santacruzsentinel.com
Entertainment section includes a calendar of music events.

Seven South
webmaster@sevensouth.com
sevensouth.com
Covering the Santa Barbara music scene.

The Seven South Record Shop
recordshop@sevensouth.com
sevensouth.com/recordshop
If you want to sell your recordings through The Seven South Record Shop you must be from the Santa Barbara / Ventura area.

The Shasta Blues Society
jmike@snowcrest.net
www.shastablues.org
We are dedicated to the enhancement and promulgation of the Blues as an American cultural art form.

Showcase for SoCal DJs and Electronic Music Artists
info@djla.com
www.djla.com
Listings for the Southern California dance/electronic music community. Once a member you may submit articles and reviews, add comments, participate in discussions, contribute web links and much more.

singingmonkey.com
contact@singingmonkey.com
www.singingmonkey.com
Your guide to the Santa Barbara music scene.

Skinnie
jimmy@skinniezine.com
www.skinniezine.com
A monthly entertainment and lifestyles magazine based out of Rancho Cucamonga.

Songmakers
g_lynch@pacbell.net
www.songmakers.org
A Southern California organization of singers and musicians devoted to the enjoyment and support of traditional and contemporary folk and other forms of homemade and acoustic music. Keeping Home-Made Music Alive!

Sonoma County Blues Society
scbswebmaster@yahoo.com
www.sonomacountybluessociety.org
Interviews and CD reviews in our monthly newsletter.

Sonoma County Folk Society
nudelman@sonic.net
socofoso.org
Promotes the knowledge and performance of traditional and contemporary folk music.

Sonoma Tunes
webmaster@sonomatunes.com
www.sonomatunes.com
This website is dedicated to live blues in Northern California in general and Sonoma County in particular.

The Southern California Artist's Network
www.artistnet.thecreativeline.us
Info on large artists' gatherings, festivals, conventions, expos etc.

Southern California Early Music Society
info@earlymusicla.org
www.earlymusicla.org
Supports the study, performance and enjoyment of Medieval, Renaissance, Baroque and Classical music. Publishes Early Music News magazine.

Southern California Pure Rock Local Bands
moshking@moshking.com
www.moshking.com
The best source on the net for information on all Metal and guitar driven Hard Rock concerts, night clubs, events and local bands in the Southern California area.

Southern California Songwriters Association
scsa@neonflame.com
www.neonflame.com/scsa
Our goal is to develop and sharpen our songwriting skills and to find ways to expose our music to the music industry as well as our audience.

SouthWest Bluegrass Association
swba@s-w-b-a.com
www.s-w-b-a.com
We promote bluegrass music with a bi-monthly newsletter, information about bluegrass festivals, campouts, weekly bluegrass house jams and school education programs. Members get a FREE web page. Our band pages include information w/streaming audio.

The Switchboard
ladynoir@cox.net
www.socalgoth.com
Southern California Goth directory. Promoters and bands interested in being included on The Switchboard, please contact me.

Top Secret Records
mike@humboldtmusic.com
www.humboldtmusic.com/tsr
Music from the Redwood Coast of California. Owned by the musicians for the express purpose of producing music under the total control of the musicians themselves.

Valley Scene Magazine
mailbox@valleyscenemagazine.com
www.valleyscenemagazine.com
Our goal is to provide the most current and interesting information available to reach our audience and to provide the best entertainment, restaurants, retail, services and more.

Ventura County Music Scene
Thug@venturacountymusicscene.com
www.venturacountymusicscene.com
A listing of bands, venues and music events in and around Ventura County, Ca. Band showcases, news and reviews.

Ventura Reporter
editor@vcreporter.com
www.vcreporter.com
Ventura County's News and Entertainment Weekly. Covers local music with articles and show listings.

VenturaMusicScene.com
venturamusicscene@hotmail.com
www.venturamusicscene.com
The Complete Guide to upcoming music events for Ventura County and Ventura County bands playing out of county gigs.

Westcoast Worldwide
lordmike@westcoastworldwide.com
www.westcoastworldwide.com
Covers west coast punk/hardcore scene. Has a message board, zine (that does CD reviews), gig listings, booking etc.

The Bay Area

ba-newmus
ba-newmus-events@mills.edu
www.mills.edu/LIFE/CCM/ba-newmus.html
Provides discussion and concert information of creative new music in the San Francisco Bay Area. Creators and listeners of contemporary classical, electronic, experimental, free improvisation, interactive and digital media, noise, out-rock, performance art, sound installations etc. are encouraged to subscribe to our lists.

Bay Area Bunch Newsletter
bab_news@yahoo.com
www.geocities.com/SunsetStrip/Venue/9842
A web based newsletter about live acoustic music performed by women singer-songwriters in small venues in the San Francisco Bay area.

Bay Area Improvisers Network
johnlee@bayimproviser.com
www.bayimproviser.com
Created to provide a forum for Creative Musicians in the San Francisco Bay area. At this site, you can find musician's biographical information, upcoming concert info, reviews, links to other sites and more.

The Bay Area Music Guide
bayarea.citysearch.com
Extensive coverage of the local music scene. Post your shows and events.

Bay Area Ska Page
info@bayareaska.com
www.bayareaska.com
Reviews are broken up between albums or demos by a band, compilations and shows. I am always looking for show reviews. If you would like to review a recent ska show, send it to me.

Bay Area Surf, Twang and Reverb Directory
(B.A.S.T.A.R.D.)
bastard@poprecords.com
www.poprecords.com
Listings for Live Surf and Instrumental shows in the San Francisco Bay Area and Northern California.

Bay Area Woman in Creative Music
almag@mills.edu
www.mills.edu/SHOWCASE/F97/MUS16/mus16.homepage.html
If you are a Bay Area woman in creative music and are not listed on our site, please send your name and information. You will be welcomed to the list as it is updated.

Bay Guardian
www.sfbg.com
San Francisco free weekly alternative paper. Local indie music, concert reviews and artist interviews.

BayInsider.com
bayinsider@ktvu.com
www.bayinsider.com
Entertainment zine sponsored by KTVU TV.

Bluegrass by the Bay
deirdre@deirdre-cassandra.com
www.scbs.org/bbb.htm
The monthly publication of the Northern California Bluegrass Society. BBB contains reviews and articles about shows, venues, albums, artists and upcoming bluegrass events as well as the calendar which is reprinted on line.

Dub Beautiful Collective
www.dub-beautiful.org
A production organization in San Francisco that presents live electronic music events. We record all of our shows and stream the best recordings on this station, thanks to the good grace of all the artists. If you are in the San Francisco area or plan to be in the San Francisco area, please contact us if you're interested in playing for an event.

Five Spot
sayhi2@fivespot.com
www.fivespot.com
View information on some of the best independent artists on the San Francisco Bay Area jazz scene today. Find out who they are and where they're playing, hear their music, order their CDs. Check out the "Featured artist of the week".

Flavorpill SF
sf-events@flavorpill.net
sf.flavorpill.net
A publishing company which seeks out the best in arts, music and culture and delivers its findings via email each week. Every event listed on flavorpill is there because it's worthwhile — no money is accepted from venues, promoters, or artists for mentioning events.

Hip Hop Slam
skratchjam@aol.com
www.hiphopslam.com
We are a mixed media company with a record label, radio show, videotape series and website. We give love to all areas of hip hop with an emphasis on the Bay Area and West Coast.

Jazz in Flight
info@jazzinflight.org
www.jazzinflight.org
The perseverance and continuity of Jazz in Flight has significantly impacted the quality of creative musical performance in the Bay Area for many years and continues to do so.

JazzWest.com
mail@jazzwest.com
www.jazzwest.com
The Bay area's online jazz network. Reviews, articles, new releases etc.

Ladyfest Bay Area
info@ladyfestbayarea.org
www.ladyfestbayarea.org
A community-based event organized by volunteers, both women and trans-identified, to showcase, celebrate and encourage the artistic, organizational and political achievements of self-identified women.

Laughing Squid
www.laughingsquid.org
An online resource for underground art and culture of San Francisco and beyond. It also is home to the Squid List: a daily event announcements list, The Tentacle List: a list to find artists & performers and the Tentacle Sessions: a monthly series that features many of the artists featured on the Laughing Squid website and The Squid List.

Metro San Jose
letters@metronews.com
www.metroactive.com/metro

Metroactive
webmaster@metroactive.com
www.metroactive.com
A Northern California meta-site specializing in arts and entertainment information and featuring content from four of the San Francisco Bay Area's leading publications: Metro, Silicon Valley's Weekly Newspaper; Metro Santa Cruz; and the North Bay Bohemian.

North Bay Music
contact@northbaymusic.com
www.northbaymusic.com
An online guide to live music in the San Francisco area.

Northern California Bluegrass Society
admin@scbs.org
www.scbs.org
CDs of area bands are also published in our magazine "Bluegrass by the Bay".

Oakland's Urbanview
staff@urbanview.com
www.urbanview.com
Entertainment available free of charge to Bay Area residents. Now featuring local artists on the cover.

oakland.com *Local Bands Page*
webmaster@oakland.com
www.oakland.com/music/localbands.html
Does your band have a web site? E-mail us to get your band linked here.

On The Tip of My Tongue
ceemoon@yahoo.com
www.tipofmytongue.net
We produce a cable video show in San Francisco that focuses on local Bay area talent.

Outsound
www.outsound.org
A collective of new sonic musicians who among other things are involved in running music performance venues, recording labels and other D.I.Y. endeavors in San Francisco. The mission of Outsound is to raise public awareness of music not otherwise made available by presenting public performance, co-op promotion and education.

RacketNet Loudness Project
webmaster@racket.net
www.racket.net
Sound clips, live dates, reviews and more about the Bay Area's loudest local punk, metal and underground bands.

San Francisco Bay Guardian
tom_tompkins@sfbg.com
www.sfbayguardian.com
Arts and Entertainment weekly. Covers local music in the "Local Live" and "Local Groove" sections.

San Francisco Bay Salsa & Latin Jazz
info@salsasf.com
www.salsasf.com
Your info site for Northern California and beyond.

San Francisco Chronicle
www.sfgate.com
Daily paper. Has an entertainment section and extensive calendar of live music.

San Francisco Classical Guitar Society
mail@sfcgs.org
www.sfcgs.org
Our mission is to promote the awareness, understanding and appreciation of the classical guitar.

San Francisco Classical Voice
Editor@SFCV.org
www.sfcv.org
The Bay Area's website journal of classical music criticism. Published every Tuesday, SFCV features reviews of musical performances in the greater Bay Area. They are written by writers drawn from our group of 70 musicians-composers, performers, musicologists, mostly assigned according their specialties.

The San Francisco Early Music Society
sfems@sfems.org
www.sfems.org
Seeks to create an appreciative and supportive environment for the study and performance of medieval, Renaissance and baroque music by both amateurs and professionals in northern California.

The San Francisco Examiner
www.examiner.com
Daily paper. Local music covered in the Entertainment "Ex Files" section.

The San Francisco Traditional Jazz Foundation
webdesigner@sftradjazz.org
www.sftradjazz.org
Helps foster live, high quality traditional jazz, regionally and worldwide.

sanfranciscohiphop.com
John Harrison click411@aol.com
www.sanfranciscohiphop.com
The San Francisco Bay Area's biggest hiphop/R&B site. Live 10 min interviews, instant full track samples with artist pictures and contact.

San Jose Jazz Society
jazzmaster@sanjosejazz.org
www.sanjosejazz.org
Presents Jazz to the public in a myriad of ways, including: free concerts, festivals, hands-on workshops, clinics, master classes, commissions for new works and education & outreach initiatives.

San Jose Mercury News
www.bayarea.com/mld/mercurynews
Entertainment section covers the local music scene.

The San Jose Music Guide
siliconvalley.citysearch.com
Extensive coverage of the local music scene. Post your shows and events.

Section M
editor@sectionM.com
www.sectionm.com
The magazine of the SF Bay area scene.

SF Bay Hip Hop
info@sfbayhiphop.com
www.sfbayhiphop.com
If you are a Bay Area Hip Hop artist and you would like you or your crew represented here, simply e-mail me with your URL.

SFJAZZ
mailbox@sfjazz.org
www.sfjazz.org
Artistically, SFJAZZ is devoted to jazz at the highest level, with concert performers ranging from acknowledged masters to the newest and most promising talents on the international, national and San Francisco Bay Area scenes.

SF Music Online
webmaster@sfmusiconline.com
www.sfmusiconline.com
Your online source for local music information here in the SF Bay Area.

SF Weekly
feedback@sfweekly.com
www.sfweekly.com
SF Weekly is San Francisco's smartest publication. That's because we take journalism seriously, but not so seriously that we let ourselves be guided by an agenda.

SFBAYou
epapper@msn.com
www.sfbayou.com
The San Francisco Bay Area has one of the most active Cajun and Zydeco music and dance scenes outside of Louisiana. This web site will keep you informed on Bay Area and other events, new CDs and books, Cajun-Zydeco news and other items of interest.

SFBlues.net
Peach@SFBlues.net
www.sfblues.net
Your source of information on San Francisco's Blues Scene.

sfcelticmusic.com
jim@sfcelticmusic.com
www.sfcelticmusic.com
Traditional Celtic Music of Ireland, Scotland, Cape Breton and Brittany in the San Francisco Bay area. A calendar of upcoming events, local resources and CD reviews.

sfgoth.com
www.sfgoth.com
Provided for free to the San Francisco net.goth community for hosting gothic or industrial club pages, concert or event info, or annoying of interest to the SF net.goth community.

sfstation.com
webmaster@sfstation.com
www.sfstation.com
San Francisco's Independent information resource.

SiFt
www.metroactive.com/sfmetro
San Francisco weekly that posts upcoming music events.

Sister SF

sistersf@sistersf.com
www.sistersf.com
Providing a supportive, friendly platform for any female DJ, MC or live performer to enjoy their music where gender is not an issue. We're not raging feminists - we just think it's better to be viewed as a DJ first and then as a woman, when you're behind the decks.

South Bay Folks

www.SouthBayFolks.org
Dedicated to promoting folk music in the greater San Jose, California area. All SBF activities focus on developing the musical talents of the participants and on bringing folk music to a wider audience.

South Bay Guitar Society

sbgs@sbgs.org
www.sbgs.org
Bringing critically acclaimed guitarists to the Bay Area, producing a regular series of concerts and bringing classical guitar to local schools.

Thrasher Magazine

greg@thrashermagazine.com
www.thrashermagazine.com
Covers SF punk and hardcore music scene.

The Transbay Creative Music Calendar

mail@transbaycalendar.org
transbaycalendar.org
A comprehensive concert listing for non-commercial, adventurous new music in the San Francisco Bay Area. We have created this web site to provide a central listing for events covering wide range of modern music, including: experimental, improvised, noise, electronic, free-jazz, outrock, 21st century composition and sonic art.

Underground Productions

info@undergroundproductions.org
www.undergroundproductions.org
The Bay Area's premier networking music site, dedicated to bringing you the best of what this area has to offer. Our goal here at UGP is to ensure the longevity of the Bay Area underground music scene, while getting exposure for bands via networking at the same time.

Walfredo.com

adam@walfredo.com
www.walfredo.com
Walfredo...not to be confused with the sauce. Covering the Bay Area Jam Band scene.

West Coast Songwriters Association

info@ncsasong.org
www.ncsasong.org
Dedicated to Providing the Environment, Opportunities and Tools to Nurture, Educate and Promote Songwriters.

Women in Music - Women Who Rock

info@rock101promotions.com
www.rock101promotions.com/women_who_rock.htm
There are very gifted bands and musicians in the Bay Area that are female driven - but don't get the credit they deserve. ROCK101 is collaborating with several organizations in the Bay Area that support women in the music industry. Creating this community and working within it, will help everybody involved.

Zero Magazine

josh@zeromag.com
www.zeromag.com
San Jose free monthly music magazine. Alternative record reviews, articles and interviews plus local spotlight.

Los Angeles

100 Punks

100punks@100punks.com
www.100punks.com
Distributed in the Los Angeles area. Bands, let us know when you're coming to town and send stuff to review.

Daily Bruin

www.dailybruin.ucla.edu
UCLA student paper. Entertainment section covers local music.

Digital City Los Angeles *Music*

home.digitalcity.com/losangeles
Regional music column and forum. The area contains weekly feature articles plus weekend entertainment highlights, a running music poll and interactive message board.

Flavorpill LA

la-events@flavorpill.net
la.flavorpill.net
A publishing company which seeks out the best in arts, music and culture and delivers its findings via email each week. Every event listed on flavorpill is there because it's worthwhile — no money is accepted from venues, promoters, or artists for mentioning events.

folkWorks

mail@folkworks.org
www.folkworks.org
A newspaper dedicated to promoting Folk Music, Dance, Storytelling and other folk arts in the greater Los Angeles area.

The Hip Hop Show

thehiphopshow@latv.com
www.thehiphopshow.com
Los Angeles TV program documenting the culture of underground hip hop locally and globally. Fridays at 9PM on KJLA LATV. Visit our website for more information on submitting your video.

JesusJams.com

jjid@jesusjams.com
www.jesusjams.com
L.A. area Christian music concerts and events.

KC Productions Los Angeles

Kathy Cook kathyc@kcproductions-notorioustechnology.com
www.kcproductions-notorioustechnology.com
International live music & film/ video production services, included stage & lighting design and tour management. Based in Los Angeles & NYC.

Koala Bear Studios

Kelly McTiernan kelly@kbearstudios.com
www.kbearstudios.com
We promote and feature new local talent from the greater Los Angeles area. Record free if your music has merit!

LA Jambands.com

fred@bobsdogotis.com
www.lajambands.com
Post your band's info. We need your reviews, photos and just plain feedback! Check out a show and send in your review. Maybe your favorite new CD or music DVD.

the L.A. punk scene

lapunk@suburbias.com
www.suburbias.com/la
News, reviews, gig listings etc.

LA Weekly

letters@laweekly.com
www.laweekly.com
Los Angeles arts and entertainment weekly. Local music coverage includes spotlight artists, reviews and gig listings.

Ladyfest Los Angeles

info@ladyfestlosangeles.org
www.ladyfestlosangeles.org
An event which aims to "celebrate, showcase and encourage the artistic, organizational and political talents of women." Designed by women for women, this event will feature various workshops, panel discussions, music, film, visual arts, spoken word, dance and theater.

LALOCALMUSICSCENE.COM

info@lalocalmusicscene.com
www.lalocalmusicscene.com
We have become the singular source in cyberspace for Los Angeles band info, music samples and club dates.

LAmusic.com

dean@lamusic.com
www.lama.com
LAMA exists in the belief that there is a tremendous undercurrent of musical artists with wide potential appeal that currently have little or no access to the airwaves. These artists are excluded from airplay for economic rather than creative reasons.

lamusicians.com

feedback@communitymusician.com
lamusicians.com
Gig calendar and artist listings.

Los Angeles Goes Underground

lagu@attbi.com
lagu.somaweb.org
Dedicated to showcase select Los Angeles based underground, alternative & indie rock bands. We serve as an Internet showcase for select artists from the Greater Los Angeles Area.

Los Angeles Jazz Society

information@lajazzsociety.org
www.lajazzsociety.org
The Jazz Society keeps its members and others informed about its many activities as well as other jazz news through its quarterly newsletter, "Quarter Notes."

The Los Angeles Music Guide

editor_losangeles@citysearch.com
losangeles.citysearch.com
Extensive coverage of the local music scene. Post your shows and events.

Los Angeles-Music-Scene.com

Eric J. Olsen eric@losangeles-music-scene.com
www.losangeles-music-scene.com
A site dedicated to the local music scene in the Los Angeles area, providing band listings, concert listings, reviews, contests and more.

www.indielinkexchange.com

Los Angeles Music Network
info@lamn.com
www.lamn.com
Promotes career advancement, continued education and communication among music industry professionals. We also sponsor industry gatherings, private dinners and seminars.

Los Angeles Music Productions *(LAMP)*
leslie@lamusicproductions.com
www.lamusicproductions.com
LAMP offers access to the music industry's top experts. Whether you're a songwriter, composer, performer, producer, or engineer, LAMP offers the information you need to succeed. LAMP sheds light on the music industry!

Los Angeles & Orange County Gothic-Industrial Network
mary@lagoth.net
www.lagoth.net
If you are in a goth/industrial/deathrock band, are local to LA/OC and would like to be featured on our site, then please visit our site and submit a band form.

The Los Angeles Songwriters' Network
songnet@songnet.org
www.songnet.org
A network of career-minded songwriters, musicians, artists and music industry professionals supporting each other through network events, seminars, showcases and collaboration.

The Los Angeles Swing Times
swing@nocturne.com
www.nocturne.com/swing
Covering all things "Swing" in L.A.

Los Angeles Times
www.latimes.com
Covers local and national music scene.

Los Angeles Women in Music
lawim@lawim.org
www.lawim.org
The goals and activities of this organization are founded on the belief that women and men working together in mutual respect, sharing abilities and expertise, will strengthen the music business and the music that is at its heart.

LosAngeles.com
webmaster@losangeles.com
www.losangeles.com/music
Our insider's look at the L.A. music scene. Does your band have a web site? E-mail us to get your band linked here.

LosAngelesPunk.com
jason@losangelespunk.com
www.losangelespunk.com
Show reviews, news, gigs etc.

musicLA
info@musicla.com
www.musicla.com
Bands, musicians, artists and songwriters living, working and playing in the greater Los Angeles area, as large and diverse a group of creative people found anywhere in the world; including photos, audio and video clips, bios, calendars, tapes and CDs!

New Times Los Angeles
www.newtimesla.com
Alternative weekly with local news coverage, dining guide and event listings. Covers the local music scene.

Pork TarTare
Rebecca Hill rebecca@porktartare.com
www.porktartare.com
A Los Angeles online magazine devoted to the Sounds, Sights, Eats and living of all things not yet discovered. I am the music writer and would love to get CDs / tapes and even records to review.

Rock City News
webmaster@rockcitynews.com
www.rockcitynews.com
Giving you in-depth activity in the Los Angeles area. Covering Local Bands, Clubs and other social gatherings.

ShadowBand
dpm@power.net
www.shadowworld.com
A local music scene magazine and guide, from the South Bay of Los Angeles.

thelamusicscene.com
Seth Schwartz seth@thelamusicscene.com
www.thelamusicscene.com
Los Angeles music scene site featuring artists / bands, clubs, reviews, show dates a discussion forum and more!

TheSceneLA.com
editor@thescenela.com
www.thescenela.com
Articles, reviews, release information...

Totally LA
Editor@TotallyLA.com
www.totallyla.com
Interviews, concert reviews.

Webookbands.com
info@webookbands.com
www.webookbands.com
A booking service dedicated to giving local unsigned talent easy access to 12 or more clubs throughout the Los Angeles area.

WHERE Magazine
art@wherela.com
www.wherela.com
Los Angeles based magazine. List your upcoming events.

San Diego

Accretions
sounds@accretions.com
www.accretions.com
An artist-based label with an ear towards experimental, improvisational and global sounds. We strive to grow a community of artists whose creative works reflect cultural and stylistic diversity.

The Daily Aztec
daztec@mail.sdsu.edu
www.dailyaztec.com
Disseminating the free flow of information to the San Diego State University community.

Klubs.com
DJLatex69@aol.com
www.klubs.com
Home of the best Industrial, EBM, Fetish, Darkwave and Gothic Klubs in San Diego. List bands and new releases.

Local San Diego Music
support@localsdmusic.com
www.localsdmusic.com
Visit our website to check out our many services.

mp3it.com
info@mp3it.com
www.mp3it.com
Alternative and experimental MP3's from San Diego bands.

San Diego CityBEAT
www.sdcitybeat.com
Has "Locals Only" section.

San Diego Early Music Society
SDEMS@sdems.org
www.sdems.org
Founded to showcase the musical treasures of Europe's medieval, Renaissance and Baroque periods.

San Diego Folk Heritage
SDFH@san.rr.com
sdfolkheritage.org
Preserves and promotes acoustic music, storytelling and Contra Dance in greater San Diego. We provide an opportunity for members of the community to see, hear and take part in these activities.

San Diego Goth
staff@sdgoth.org
www.sdgoth.org
The central source for all that is dark electronic in San Diego County. Promoters. If you're looking to advertise your events or promotional products to people in the Gothic/Industrial scene in San Diego, how about sending it to our Announcements mailing list. If you are working on a tour and would like to play in San Diego, let SDGoth help you find a venue!

San Diego Local Metal
raymond@sdmetal.com
www.sdmetal.com
Presenting the best of San Diego's local metal bands.

San Diego Magazine
www.sandiego-online.com
We welcome information on upcoming events in the San Diego area. Submit information in writing at least six weeks before the month in which the event occurs.

San Diego Reader - Music Scene
e-music@sdreader.com
www.sdreader.com/ed/calendar/music.html
San Diego's most complete and accurate listings for Concerts, Clubs and Bands. Also of Note; concert previews, recent music feature and news and gossip (in our "Blurt" section) about the San Diego music community.

The San Diego Songwriter's Guild
sdsongwriters@hotmail.com
www.sdsongwriters.org
Meet publishers, guild members and other people in the music industry. Share information on what works and what doesn't. Trade skills with other musicians. Live showcases – for those that perform, shows at coffeehouses and other events help hone your performing skills.

San Diego Swings
mail@sandiegoswings.com
www.sandiegoswings.com
Your source for Swing and Big Band music in America's finest city.

San Diego Union-Tribune
www.uniontrib.com
Submit a music event or take a look at what's going on in San Diego in our music community database.

SanDiegoPunk.com
joel@sandiegopunk.com
www.sandiegopunk.com
*Our goal is to give our readers in-depth coverage of
the San Diego "punk" community (by punk we mean
pop-punk, hardcore, indie, emo, old-school punk etc).
This coverage includes show listings, pictures,
interviews, places to hang out and buy records and
more.*

sandiegounderground.com
webmaster@sandiegounderground.com
www.sandiegounderground.com
*Send anything you want. Poems, events, pictures,
anything. We need to know what's up around San
Diego, so send us news.*

SDAM.com *(San Diego Area Music)*
Webmaster@SDAM.com
www.sdam.com
*If you are an independent band, we can help you
reach a worldwide audience for your music. We will
stream your audio, post your bios and gigs on our
calendar and sell your CDs and other merchandise in
our online store - all with a minimum of hassle to you.*

sdmetal.org
www.sdmetal.org
San Diego's online realm for metal.

The Trummerflora Collective
rubble@trummerflora.com
www.trummerflora.com
*An independent group of music makers dedicated to
experimental and improvisational music. The
collective embraces the pluralistic nature of creative
music as an important means of artistic expression for
the individual and the community and provides an
atmosphere that nurtures the creative development of
its member artists.*

Colorado

The Black Rose Acoustic Society
feedback@BlackRoseAcoustic.org
www.blackroseacoustic.org
*An organization dedicated to the education,
performance, enjoyment and preservation of all types
of traditional acoustic music in the Black Forest and
Colorado Springs.*

Boulder Weekly
www.boulderweekly.com
*Free weekly alternative paper. CD and concert
reviews, club listings.*

Classical Guitar Society of Northern Colorado
donsimon@coloradoguitar.com
www.coloradoguitar.com
*Brings both classical and acoustic guitar players and
friends together each month in a pleasant cafe
atmosphere, where members can socialize and play
for each other... demonstrating their growing skill
among peers.*

Colorado Arts Net
letters@CoArts.net
www.coloradoarts.net
*My vision for Colorado Arts Net is to make it the
ultimate, the most informative and most exciting tool
any local fan of the arts could possibly encounter.*

Colorado Blues Alliance
cba@colsbluesalliance.org
www.colsbluesalliance.org
*Blues music is an always evolving art form and we
pay homage to both the unknowns and celebrities who
have defined and preserved it.*

The Colorado Bluegrass Music Society
cbms@coloradobluegrass.org
www.coloradobluegrass.org
*To promote and encourage the development,
performance and preservation of bluegrass music in
the community.*

Colorado Blues Society
Holler@COBlues.com
www.coblues.com

Colorado Daily
www.coloradodaily.com
*Boulder daily paper. Entertainment section does
music reviews and bios.*

**Colorado Friends of Cajun/Zydeco Music and
Dance**
webmaster@rockymountainweb.com
www.harbormusic.com/cfcz
*Your guide for the best in Cajun and Zydeco music in
the Front Range area of Colorado.*

Colorado Heavy Metal Homepage
guy@coloradometal.org
www.coloradometal.org
Event listings and newsletter.

Colorado Music Association *(COMA)*
info@coloradomusic.org
www.coloradomusic.org
*Some of our goals are to present music festivals
showcasing and celebrating local talent, possibly in
conjunction with other organizations and to provide
free UPC codes for their independently released
recordings.*

**The Colorado Springs Independent
Newsweekly**
Noel Black nblack@csindy.com
www.csindy.com
*Colorado Springs weekly Arts & Entertainment paper.
Articles and where to find live music in the Colorado
Springs area.*

The Colorado Springs Music Guide
coloradosprings.citysearch.com
*Extensive coverage of the local music scene. Post
your shows and events.*

The Coloradoan
Calendars@coloradoan.com
www.coloradoan.com
*Our mission is to be the market leader in providing
daily news and information in the Fort Collins area.*

ColoradoRock.com
webmaster@coloradorock.com
www.coloradorock.com
Resource site and TV show.

Daily Camera
Editor@thedailycamera.com
www.bouldernews.com

Denver Musicians Association
infodma@aol.com
www.dmamusic.org/dma
*Provides the Rocky Mountain region with the finest
professional classical, symphonic, jazz, rock, country
and commercial musicians throughout Colorado,
south-central Wyoming and eastern Utah. Sell your
music through our store.*

THE DIRT
UNHOLIESTGODDESS@yahoo.com
denver.erebusmusic.com
Colorado's Live Metal Music Network.

Fort Collins Colorado Music Index
cbk@seldomfed.com
www.seldomfed.com/fcmusic.htm
*We list musician's pages, artists, music projects,
venues, stores and more... everything you want to
know about the music business and performing scene
in Fort Collins is right here. We hope this is a helpful
resource for musicians and our community.
Maintained for musicians by musicians.*

Hapi Skratch Entertainment
info@hapiskratch.com
www.hapiskratch.com
*By offering a complete line of services that are
essential to the growth and development of any band
or artist, new or established, Hapi Skratch has
positioned itself as a full service artist development
company for the independent music industry. Based in
Loveland.*

Higher Listening
connection@higherlistening.com
www.higherlistening.com
Your weekly update of Denver's live local music.

JamSpace.net
jamspacenet@attbi.com
www.jamspace.net
Covering Colorado Jam Music.

Kaffeine Buzz
info@kaffeinebuzz.com
www.kaffeinebuzz.com
*An online music and entertainment source for
Colorado and beyond!*

The Local Music Connection
info@localmusicconnection.com
www.localmusicconnection.com
*Created to help support Colorado's incredible music
scene!*

Mesa State Criterion
Kyle Halkett khack19@aol.com
mesastate.edu/crite
Mesa State College student paper.

Reggae Movement
Larry@Reggaemovement.com
www.reggaemovement.com
*An organization dedicated to the spread and
cultivation of Reggae Music throughout the Rocky
Mountain region and beyond.*

RIFF Music Magazine
comments@riffmusicmag.com
www.raven-flight.com
*Dedicated to the music talent of Middle America,
specializing in features that spotlight local unsigned
artists and the clubs they play. Any style of music,
any genre, from country to classical, rock to rap.*

Rock on Colorado!
Tommy@RockOnColorado.com
www.rockoncolorado.com
A Celebration of Colorado's Music Scene!

Rocky Mountain Bullhorn
music@rockymountainbullhorn.com
www.rockymountainbullhorn.com
*Fort Collins weekly Arts & Entertainment paper.
Committed to providing a reliable and high-quality
news and information source for Northern Colorado
that is an independent alternative to the traditional
mainstream press.*

The Rocky Mountain Collegian
online@lamar.colostate.edu
collegian.colostate.edu
Colorado State University's student-run daily newspaper. Local music coverage.

Scene Magazine
editor@scenemagazine.info
www.scenemagazine.info
Ft. Collins arts and music information for the Northern Front Range. Covers local and national acts. Profiles bands and reviews CD's.

Denver

blood.sweat.tears music syndicate
NDEddyMo@netscape.net
www.bloodsweattears.net
Punk zine. News, reviews, band of the month...

CitySearch Denver
denver.citysearch.com
Local gig listings, live reviews, band info.

Creative Music Works
info@creativemusicworks.org
creativemusicworks.org
A Denver organization providing educational and performance opportunities for cutting-edge jazz, mainstream jazz and other contemporary music.

The Denver Music Guide
editor_denver@citysearch.com
denver.citysearch.com
Extensive coverage of the local music scene. Post your shows and events.

Denver Music Scene
denvermusicscene@hotmail.com
www.denvermusicscene.com
Reviews and interviews of local bands.

Denver Post
www.denverpost.com
Album reviews, previews upcoming shows, Friday calendar listings.

DenverBoulderMusic.com
info@denverbouldermusic.com
www.denverbouldermusic.com
The finest site on the web to find the best music in Denver, Boulder and all over Colorado.

DENVERLOCALMUSICSCENE.COM
info@denverlocalmusicscene.com
www.denverlocalmusicscene.com
We have become the singular source in cyberspace for Denver band info, music samples and club dates.

DenverMix.com
submit@denvermix.com
www.denvermix.com
Denver's hippest online entertainment guide. Submit your bands information and website address for free. Be sure to include type of music.

Ladyfest Out West
info@ladyfestoutwest.org
www.ladyfestoutwest.org
Celebrating various forms of expression through visual/performance art, music, discussions and workshops, the festival encourages past, present and future women as well as their allies to fully participate in and contribute to an inclusive and proactive feminist community.

Roamteam Productions
Tommy Anderson tanderson@roamteam.com
roamteam.com
Supports up and coming talent with local monthly music showcases, promotion and a large network for booking in the Denver area and the surrounding ski resort circuit.

Rocky Mountain News
www.rockymountainnews.com
Denver daily paper. Reviews indie releases. Friday calendar.

Swallow Hill Music Association
info@swallowhill.com
www.swallowhill.com
Denver's home for Folk and Acoustic music. Our mission is to preserve and foster folk music and traditional music from around the world. We publish the Swallow Hill Quarterly.

The Underground Network
www.undergroundnet.net
Denver Electronic/Experimental music site. When you sign an account you can submit events, club nights, links, event reviews, CD or dj reviews and much more.

Westword
www.westword.com
Denver free weekly alternative paper. Accepts albums for review and press kits a week before the show. Previews concerts. Normally does a full bio on one local band a week.

Connecticut

Another Octave: Connecticut Women's Chorus
newmember@anotheroctave.org
www.anotheroctave.org
With roots in the lesbian community and open to all women, the chorus performs an eclectic repertoire, including standard concert pieces as well as traditional and contemporary music which reflect women's lives.

Club CT Live Bands
info@clubct.com
www.clubct.com/bands.htm
Is your Band performing in Connecticut? Submit it here. Also a "Band of the Month" feature.

CONNcept
krista@alchemywebdesign.com
www.conncept.com
A Connecticut Music Collective, is a network of bands, musicians, record labels, radio stations, media and venues that exist to support independent music. Post your MP3s!

The Connecticut Blues Society
chilijonesy@aol.com
www.ctblues.org
Promoting a sense of community through our newsletters and special events.

The Connecticut Classical Guitar Society
info@ccgs.org
www.ccgs.org
It is the largest organization of its kind serving the general public and classical guitarists by providing a forum for listening, learning, performing and teaching.

Connecticut Post
www.connpost.com
Bridgeport daily paper. Covers local music.

Connecticut Songwriters Association
Paul4CSA@aol.com
www.ctsongs.com
We have grown to become one of the oldest and best known songwriters associations in the country. Our newsletter is chock full of helpful information, news, events, classified ads, upcoming events and more!

CT Punx
mark@ctpunx.com
www.ctpunx.com
News, reviews, profiles and MP3s. If you are in a Connecticut punk band and you want 1 or 2 mp3s up here, let me know.

CTFolk.com
meth@smoe.org
www.ctfolk.com
Current Info on the Connecticut Folk Music Scene.

Fairfield County Weekly
www.fairfieldweekly.com
Free weekly paper. CD and concert reviews, previews shows, interviews bands.

The Hartford Advocate
www.hartfordadvocate.com
CD reviews. Local Bands and Happenings, updated every Thursday.

The Hartford Courant
www.ctnow.com
Daily paper. Accepts press kit and CD for review if playing in Connecticut. Previews shows and interviews bands.

Hartford Jazz Society
hartjazzsocinc@aol.com
www.hartfordjazzsociety.com
Our goal is to improve Jazz as America's gift to the music world and to foster in each succeeding generation both an appreciation and love for Jazz in all its many forms.

The Hartford Music Guide
hartford.citysearch.com
Extensive coverage of the local music scene. Post your shows and events.

IrieJam.com
www.iriejam.com
Covers the Hartford Reggae scene. Greater Hartford is home to the third largest West Indian community in USA and the fourth largest in North America.

Madrock.com
www.madrock.com
A local music scene site for Hartford, CT and the surrounding area.

New Haven Advocate
jmamis@newhavenadvocate.com
www.newhavenadvocate.com
New Haven's weekly news and entertainment paper. Local Bands and Happenings, updated every Thursday.

The New London Music Guide
newlondon.citysearch.com
Extensive coverage of the local music scene. Post your shows and events.

Soundwaves
editor@swaves.com
www.swaves.com
Southern New England's Entertainment Guide. In-depth Band & Club Info! Links for Bands & the General Public!

The Stage Newspaper
www.stagenewspaper.com
*Eastern Connecticut's Leading FREE Arts &
Entertainment Newspaper. Check out our Local Band
Spotlight.*

Delaware

302 Music
de_302music@yahoo.com
302music.tripod.com
*Promoting original bands & artists in Newark,
Delaware & surrounding areas.*

Big Shout
gtmag@optonline.net
www.goodtimesmag.com/bigshout.html
*Music/Entertainment Magazine of the
Delaware/Philadelphia Area. Hey all Delaware and
Philadelphia Bands you can get your Band's website
address on the Web and in Big Shout Magazine for
the entire Tri-State Area to see... it's FREE. So e-mail
your band name, website and e-mail address to us.*

The Brandywine Friends of Old Time Music
www.brandywinefriends.org
*An organization dedicated to the preservation and
presentation of Traditional American Music.*

Delaware Friends of Folk
www.delfolk.org
*Dedicated to furthering the cause of folk music and
folk musicians in our area.*

Delaware Hardcore
www.delawarehardcore.com
*Covering the Delaware punk scene. News, reviews,
shows etc.*

DelawareOnline
www.delawareonline.com/entertainment
*Concerts, clubs and local nightlife around Delaware
and Philadelphia.*

Delaware Today
editors@delawaretoday.com
www.delawaretoday.com
List your upcoming events.

Diamond State Blues Society
MRBLUZ2@aol.com
www.diamondstateblues.com
*Our goal is to support local artists as well as to bring
national acts to the Diamond State. We're music
lovers intent on fostering an appreciation of the blues.
We will be staging live shows and events towards that
end.*

freedelaware.com
info@freedelaware.com
freedelaware.com
*Delaware's best FREE web site. Included on this web
site is a message board, MP3 service area and search
engine.*

Key of DE
info@keyofde.com
www.keyofde.com
*Delaware's Premiere Source for Entertainment
Information. Be sure to check out the video & audio
clips, we know you'll enjoy them.*

The Newark Post
newpost@dca.net
www.ncbl.com/post
*Newark's daily paper. The staff compiles a calendar of
events, meetings and exhibits each week for
publication in the newspaper.*

The News Journal
www.newsjournal.com
*Wilmington daily paper. Covers local music in the
entertainment section.*

Project Unity
xprojectunityx@hotmail.com
www.projectunity.cjb.net
*We want to do something good for bands and fans
alike. We have a spot for local up coming bands to
play and gain exposure while also giving touring and
out of state bands opportunity to stop here for a show.*

Signalfading
daniel@signalfading.com
www.signalfading.com
*Covering the D.C., Delaware, Maryland, New Jersey,
New York, Ohio, Pennsylvania and Virginia music
scenes. Promotions include "Band of the Month" and
"MP3 of the Week".*

Florida

305
doSys19@hotmail.com
threezerofive.cjb.net
Dedicated to the Florida local scene.

Alligator MP3
online@alligator.org
www.alligator.org
*Your new headquarters for local music. Here you can
not only read about bands in Gainesville, but you can
listen to their music, see their pictures and find out
where they're playing! Sponsored by the University of
Florida's Independent Alligator (student paper).*

aquaunderground.com
aquaunderground2001@yahoo.com
www.aquaunderground.com
*Our mission is to help support Florida's Local Art &
Music. We welcome you to experience some of
Florida's finest Artists, Bands and DJ's. Most talent
never gets any exposure or recognition, until now!!*

Axis Magazine
rwheeler@axismag.com
www.axismag.com
Orlando's arts & entertainment magazine.

baydomain.com
www.baydomain.com
*Our mission is to provide an alternative space where
Tampa talent and unique personalities will be
showcased, creating an interactive community online.*

The Blues Society of Northwest Florida
www.bluessociety.org
*We publish The BluesNews, a monthly newsletter
containing features on musicians, a calendar of
performances in the area of the Florida Panhandle,
reviews, musician listings and concert information.*

Boca Raton News
www.bocanews.com
Posts a calendar of events.

The Broward Folk Club
SNAGYS@prodigy.net
www.browardfolkclub.com
*Our purpose is to promote folk and acoustic music
and to provide a community for people who share a
love for it.*

Brutal Noise
ar@brutalnoise.com
www.brutalnoise.com
*Covering the Florida hard music scene. Reviews,
featured bands etc. The best way to ensure your
demos get the attention they deserve is to forward
them along with bio information and a photograph (if
possible) to our A&R Department.*

Central Florida Future
www.ucffuture.com
University of Central Florida student paper.

City Link
www.clo-sfl.com
*Your link to news, arts and entertainment in Broward
& Palm Beach County.*

The Classical Guitar Society of Tallahassee
tatkinson@ohfc.com
www.istal.com/cgst
*By sharing their experiences, members of the Society,
young and old, have an opportunity to grow as part of
a community through Concerts, Master Classes with
visiting and area artists, Impromptu performances by
members at monthly meetings and by Ensemble
practice and performance.*

Coffee Stain
joe@coffeestain.com
www.coffeestain.com
*The premier Florida music website on the net. Band
news, reviews, interviews, listings etc.*

daytona hardcore
www.DaytonaHardcore.com
*A listing of shows and hardcore, punk, emo and metal
bands from the Daytona/Volusia county area.*

DecadentArtWorks.com
David Goodman
davidgoodman@decadentartworks.com
decadentartworks.com
*An independent South Florida music label dedicated
to pushing the edge of music.*

Explore the Space Coast
cityguide.flatoday.com
*Melbourne based publication. Extensive coverage of
the local music scene.*

Flint Records
Christine frictionfarm@hotmail.com
www.geocities.com/flintrecords
*An independent artist collective, seeks Florida based
musicians and bands to add to its cooperative label
roster.*

Florida Coven
groups.yahoo.com/group/FloridaCoven
*A mailing list dedicated to supporting Gothic/Music
interests in the state of Florida.*

**The Florida East Coast Classical Guitar
Society**
dale31@earthlink.net
home.earthlink.net/~dale31
*Provides an opportunity for members to meet each
other and to gain performance experience in a
supportive environment. We also sponsor a wonderful
array of concerts featuring both promising young
artists just beginning their careers as well as
internationally-acclaimed musicians.*

Florida Freaks
nigma@floridafreaks.com
www.floridafreaks.com
Florida's premier Gothic/Industrial site. Submit your band info and we'll put it online for you.

Florida Harpers and Friends
florida@harper.org
www.florida.harper.org
An organizing force for Florida harpers and friends. (Friends meaning fiddle, whistle, guitar, flute, pipes and drum players).

Florida Music Makers' Directory
ktunes@inklein.com
donnaklein.com/floridamusic.htm
Submit your band's info. Florida residents only, please.

Florida Spins
spins.us/florida
A regional dance music community dedicated to Florida dance music, electronic music, DJ's, artists and community.

Florida State Fiddlers Association
www.nettally.com/fiddler
A group of musicians who hold a yearly convention and fiddle contest, as well as increase communication among fiddlers and other old-time musicians in the State of Florida.

Florida Stuff *Local Bands*
www.floridastuff.com/events
Weekly music & art listings and a resource for local band and musician pages. Miami, Fort Lauderdale, Key West, West Palm Beach and the Florida Keys Local City and County Information.

The Florida Times-Union
www.jacksonville.com
Daily paper. Considers reviews for indie bands playing in the area.

Florida Today
www.floridatoday.com
Melbourne daily paper. Covers local and national acts.

FloridaBackstage.com
info@FloridaBackstage.com
www.floridabackstage.com
An interactive online resource for musicians, bands and artists. A place for them to communicate, collaborate, meet, discuss, showcase and get information essential to furthering their careers.

FloridaLocalMusic.Com
herman@floridalocalmusic.com
www.floridalocalmusic.com
We are proud to bring you one of the finest websites for finding information on our thriving Florida local music scene. Our news section will be updated almost daily.

FloridaMusicians.com
Dennis Walters menacemedia@cfl.rr.com
www.floridamusicians.com
Online resource center and meeting point for Florida-based musicians or musicians traveling through Florida.

Flshows.com
digitalmask@hotmail.com
www.flshows.com
Your guide to all upcoming Florida shows. News, reviews etc.

Folio Weekly
www.folioweekly.com
Jacksonville free weekly alternative paper. Stories about emerging stars and old favorites, plus Northeast Florida's most complete concert calendar.

Folk Music in Orlando
Halsey@CFFolk.com
cffolk.com
All about folk music & related stuff in & around Orlando.

Folking Around Newsletter
cffolk.com/FolkingAround.htm
Covering Central Florida folk events and resources.

For the Florida Punx
admin@fordapunx.com
www.geocities.com/fordapunx
Shows, spotlight artists, reviews and more!

Fordapunx
admin@fordapunx.com
www.fordapunx.com
South Florida Local scene website. Punk , Ska, Hardcore: reviews, pics, show dates, links and much more!

Fort Pierce Jazz Society
www.jazzsociety.org
Discover the hidden treasures of Jazz found on the Treasure Coast of Florida. To the community, the FPJS hopes to be a cultural, educational and entertainment resource.

Friends of Florida Folk
news@foff.org
www.foff.org
Our mission is to identify, protect, preserve, encourage and protect folk arts, crafts, dance and music. To educate the public in folk tradition by encouraging, publicizing, sponsoring and producing newsletters, film, tapes, records, festivals and other events.

The G-Note
rachaels@ufl.edu
gnv.fdt.net/~bsmith
Gainesville's first and only local music source, started in June of 1997.

The Gainesville Band Family Tree
gbft@gainesvillebandfamilytree.com
www.gainesvillebandfamilytree.com
A list of every band that has ever been in Gainesville.

Gainesville Friends of Jazz and Blues
friendsofjazznetwork@gnvfriendsofjazz.org
www.gnvfriendsofjazz.org
Dedicated to the promotion and support of jazz and blues music in Gainesville and surrounding areas, by way of sponsored concerts, education and networking of jazz and blues musicians. Our goal is to increase public interest and participation in these classic musical arts.

The Gainesville Sun
gainesvillesun.com
Daily paper. Scene Magazine, our entertainment guide, covers local music.

GainesvilleBandPage.com
Gristlejaw@Gainesvillebandpage.com
www.geocities.com/gristlejaw
For all the great, hardworking punk bands and all the kind, fun and generous people that this city has seen.

Gorilla Paste
www.gorillapaste.cjb.net
Show listings and reviews of the Florida punk scene.

The Gulf Coast Bluegrass Music Association
gcbma@cox.net
members.cox.net/gcbma
Bringing more bluegrass music to northwest Florida and southern Alabama.

Gulf Jazz Society
raborich@compuserve.com
www.gulfjazzsociety.com
The GJS offers jazz education programs at area schools, sponsors jazz clinics, awards music scholarships and stages jazz festivals and concerts at various venues in Bay County. In addition, musician members of the society perform pro-bono at various charities and benefits.

Hiphopelements
webmaster@hiphopelements.com
www.hiphopelements.com
One of the strongest supporters of the Florida Hip Hop Scene.

The Independent Journal
www.ucfindependent.com
University of Central Florida's student paper.

The Jacksonville Music Guide
jacksonville.citysearch.com
Extensive coverage of the local music scene. Post your shows and events.

Jazz Club of Sarasota
admin@jazzclubsarasota.com
www.jazzclubsarasota.com
It is one of The liveliest, toe-tappingest groups in town, providing loads of great jazz and community programs for Florida's West Coast.

The Jazz Society of Brevard
spacecoastjazz@hotmail.com
www.spacecoastjazzsociety.com
To promote, preserve, educate and enjoy jazz music by bringing together jazz-music lovers and jazz-music makers.

localrocksite.com
localrock@cfl.rr.com
localrocksite.com
Local live music schedules, venues and band bios covering Brevard County. Has a "Featured Artist" section.

Malak Christian Productions
Kenn or Nate Info@malak1.com
www.malak1.com
A music production facility and independent record label featuring CD releases by some of the top independent recording artists and groups. We only sell the best in Gospel, Christian and Inspirational music.

MASSIV
massiv@midfirecords.com
midfi.com/massiv
South Florida Local Music Ezine since 1997.

METAL MASTERS
MetalTV@hotmail.com
www.metalmasters.net
A one hour video/interview show that has been on the air in Florida, every week, since September 1992. We interview the top names in the rock music industry along with up and coming new artists.

MusicPensacola.com
tiger@gulfbreeze.net
www.musicpensacola.com
Pensacola's weekly live entertainment guide. Local artists, concerts, festivals and services.

New Times Broward Palm Beach
www.newtimesbpb.com
Ft. Lauderdale weekly alternative paper. Covers local music scene. Interviews, reviews and previews bands playing the area.

The North Florida Bluegrass Association
info@nfbluegrass.org
www.nfbluegrass.org
Dedicated to the promotion and preservation of Bluegrass music. Our base of operations is in North Florida, but we have members all over the country, including Canada.

The Orlando Music Guide
orlando.citysearch.com
Extensive coverage of the local music scene. Post your shows and events.

Orlando Weekly
www.orlandoweekly.com
Free weekly alternative paper. Covers local music scene, reviews new CD releases.

OrlandoSwing.com
swing-info@orlandoswing.com
www.orlandoswing.com
A swing music enthusiast and dancer supported web site dedicated to brining you the latest swing news and events.

Palm Beach Post
pbonline@pbpost.com
www.palmbeachpost.com
Entertainment section covers local music.

Queen of the Scene
queenscene305@hotmail.com
www.queenofthescene.com
This site has been devoted to supporting south Florida local music since 1996. I hope to provide any info you could possibly need and more.

Rag Magazine
info@ragmagazine.com
www.ragmagazine.com
South Florida's music magazine.

Reality Snap
ken@realitysnap.com
www.realitysnap.com
Committed to promote the Tampa Bay area's music scene.

The Rhythm Foundation
info@rhythmfoundation.com
www.rhythmfoundation.com
We promote multi-cultural exchange through the presentation of live music. We focus on Caribbean, Latin American, Brazilian and African music - those cultures which are of greatest interest to South Florida residents, allowing greater depth of understanding between communities.

Rock Solid Promotions
rocksolidpromo@hotmail.com
www.rocksolidpromotions.com
We work with local, regional and national acts. We create and direct concert events, provide connections for bands, promoters and venues in North Central Florida. We are a full service artist management company.

Sarasota Folk Club
luwinberg@sarafolk.org
www.sarafolk.org
Our mission is to encourage the development of local folk talent and to showcase local and national performers.

The Setup
thesetup@prodigy.net
www.geocities.com/thsetup
Hardcore is a way to have fun, share ideas and learn. The Southeast and especially Florida, had a large number of great bands, zines and show spaces making a name for themselves in a d.i.y. manner.

South Florida Country Music Club
dm1972a@cs.com
www.sfcmc.homestead.com
Dedicated to the promotion and preservation of Country Music and Local Talent!

The Southeast Music Alliance
Joran Oppelt the.gita@verizon.net
www.sma.toosquare.com
Started by a handful of Tampa Bay musicians decided to pool their resources in an attempt to raise awareness of the scene they'd worked so hard to help create. We invite others to join and inspiring others to unify.

SouthernGothic.net
www.southerngothic.net
On-line resource for the gothic community in the Southern United States. Add your news, reviews and gig dates.

The Suncoast Blues Society
info@suncoastblues.org
www.suncoastblues.org
Includes calendar, CD reviews, links to local bands and more.

Tallahassee Democrat
Kati Schardl kschardl@taldem.com
www.tallahassee.com
Daily paper. Covers local music.

tallahasseeshows.com
www.tallahasseeshows.com
This site is dedicated to keeping an accurate and complete listing of all shows in the Tallahassee area. This will include rock, punk, hip-hop, folk and whatever else we can find. If you like live music, we want this to be your one-stop-shop to finding local entertainment.

Tampa Band Page
gristlejaw@radon222.com
www.geocities.com/tampabandpage
Covering the Tampa punk scene.

Tampa Bay Area Upcoming Events List
www.statemedia.com/shows.html

The Tampa Bay Music Guide
tampabay.citysearch.com
Extensive coverage of the local music scene. Post your shows and events.

The Tampa Tribune
Curtis Ross CRoss@tampatrib.com
www.tampatrib.com
Daily paper.

TampaBay Entertainment Guide
webmster@oltb.com
tampabayentertainment.com
Promoting Tampa Bay's Entertainment industry.

Tampazine
www.tampazine.com
A voice for the local musicians of Tampa. If you're in a band, send us your latest release. Whether it is on vinyl, cassette, or CD, we will be happy to review it. Tampazine also has a radio show on the WBUL radio station and we play strictly Florida bands.

Traditional Country Music in Florida
Steve L. Butts cwosteve50@hotmail.com
books.dreambook.com/radiocountry/markbeard.html
Our goal is to promote all "NEW" and existing artists who strive to keep "Traditional Country Music" alive.

Veltrox Local
veltroxlocal@aol.com
www.veltroxlocal.com
Where Florida musicians meet. Updated daily with new ads being posted as they are received. We feature tons of links to music industry related professionals and businesses from everywhere.

The Weekly Planet
scott.harrell@weeklyplanet.com
www.weeklyplanet.com
Tampa free weekly alternative paper. Covers local scene and reviews indie CD releases.

Miami

CityLink Online
www.citylinkonline.com
South Florida's Alternative News Magazine.

CLOSER Magazine
submissions@closermagazine.com
www.closermagazine.com
We're networking for you. Meet the funkiest, funniest, wisest, most talented and outrageous folks from Palm Beach to Miami musicians, DJ's, painters, poets, filmmakers, performers, kids who go bump in the night. Consider it our personal introduction to the people you need to know.

The Folk Club of South Florida
bwtamia@bellsouth.net
members.aol.com/souflafolk
Our mission is to promote the performance, awareness and appreciation of traditional and contemporary folk music and other folk arts and to encourage the development of local folk talent and to showcase local and national folk performers.

GoPBI.com
www.gopbi.com/events/music
Music Guide for the Palm Beaches and South Florida. Local musicians are encouraged to submit their site for a listing. Your site should have original content and clear indications that it is local. Publishing a local address on such a site does not constitute local content.

Miami Herald
www.miami.com
Miami daily paper. Covers local music scene.

The Miami Music Guide
editor_miami@citysearch.com
miami.citysearch.com
Extensive coverage of the local music scene. Post your shows and events.

Miami New Times Online
feedback@miaminewtimes.com
www.miaminewtimes.com
...reputation for compelling stories ignored or overlooked by major media...moves to a Latin beat.

Slammie Productions

Slammiep@aol.com
www.Slammie.com
We are an independent concert promoter presenting club shows in South Florida. What we look for is South Florida bands who are generating a buzz, playing lots of shows (and drawing well), selling lots of CDs, getting press and radio airplay etc. Also, we mainly highlight punk, new metal and hardcore bands.

South Florida's Entertainment News & Views

hsalus@entnews.com
www.entnews.com
Miami's premiere arts & entertainment weekly.

South Florida Jams

ethan@southfloridajams.com
www.southfloridajams.com
Bringing the best live music to South Florida...

South Florida Sun-Sentinel

www.sun-sentinel.com
Entertainment section contains a local events calendar.

South Florida Zydeco Society

soflozydeco@aol.com
www.soflozydeco.com
Formed with the intent to educate and encourage Zydeco music and dance in South Florida.

The Southwest Florida Bluegrass Association

Nina lgooch11@comcast.net
www.southwestfloridabluegrass.org
Preserving, encouraging and promoting traditional bluegrass music and to bring together those persons desiring to preserve, encourage and promote said music.

StreetMiami

www.streetmiami.com
Miami's entertainment and lifestyle weekly. You'll find opinionated editorial and colorful commentary on all of the entertainment and lifestyle options that South Florida has to offer.

TheHoneyComb.com

steve@thehoneycomb.com
thehoneycomb.com
This site is an "underground" resource module for the So-Fla area. We love turning people on to sounds. New and old... stuff that gets us goin'.

Georgia

Athens Folk Music and Dance Society

www.uga.edu/folkdance
Our mission is to promote folk music by providing an opportunity for traditional folk musicians and artists to perform in our area.

The Augusta Chronicle

www.augustachronicle.com
Daily paper. Lists local events.

Augusta Goth

www.angelfire.com/sc2/nocturn
Info on the Goth scene in Augusta, Georgia. This page exists as a beacon and as a means to keep our scene connected.

The Augusta Music Guide

augusta.citysearch.com
Extensive coverage of the local music scene. Post your shows and events.

Connect Savannah

letters@connectsavannah.com
www.connectsavannah.com
Weekly news, arts & entertainment publication. Extensive coverage of local music.

Flagpole

music@flagpole.com
www.flagpole.com
Athens' free weekly Arts and Entertainment magazine. Covers local music scene and bands playing in the area.

The Georgia Music Industry Association

www.gmia.org
The purpose of GMIA is to provide avenues of communication and cooperation between the leaders of the music community, as well as educating the songwriter and performer on all aspects of the music industry.

Georgia Spins

spins.us/georgia
A regional dance music community dedicated to Georgia dance music, electronic music, DJ's, artists and community.

Lokal Loudness

editor@lokalloudness.zzn.com
www.lokalloudness.cjb.net
Covering the Augusta music scene.

The Macon Telegraph

www.macon.com/mld/telegraph
Daily paper. Extensive coverage of local music scene.

The Metropolitan Spirit

www.metrospirit.com
Augusta's Most Popular Newsweekly! Editorial coverage includes the arts, issues, news, entertainment, people, places and events.

Nuçi's Space

www.nuci.org
A resource center for musicians located in Athens.

redandblack.com

webmaster@randb.com
www.redandblack.com
University of Georgia student publication.

Rock Athens

bhay@onlineathens.com
www.onlineathens.com/rockathens
Created by the Athens Banner-Herald. We're here to get the word out about Athens bands. If you're an Athens musician, we can help you get your music heard. Visit our site to upload your MP3s, photos etc.

Savannah Morning News

letted@savannahnow.com
www.savannahnow.com
Daily paper. Diversions section covers local music.

Southeast Performer

sepeditorial@performermag.com
www.performermag.com
Covers the south east US.

Southern Local Area Bands *(SLAB)*

admin@slabmusic.com
www.slabmusic.com
We offer services, awards, annual festivals and opportunities for FREE to 1000+ members who are all local bands from the Southeast United States.

SouthEastern Bluegrass Association

chairman@sebabluegrass.org
www.sebabluegrass.org
To preserve, promote and publicize the music and bluegrass activities and to serve as a source of information through our award-winning newsletter, The SEBA Breakdown.

Technique

entertainment@technique.gatech.edu
cyberbuzz.gatech.edu/nique
Georgia Tech's student newspaper.

Atlanta

The Atlanta Blues Society

absmail@mindspring.com
www.atlantablues.org
Our members are a delightfully diverse group of people—all ages, colors and creeds—who have fun keeping the blues alive.

Atlanta Early Music Alliance

info@atlema.org
www.atlema.org
Our mission is to teach, perform and foster enjoyment and awareness of music created before 1800.

Atlanta Gothic

jfoster@atlantagothic.net
www.atlantagothic.net
Informational page about the Atlanta gothic, industrial, ethereal and darkwave scene.

Atlanta Journal

www.accessatlanta.com
... helping Atlanta residents manage their busy lives by providing online tools and features...

Atlanta Magazine

www.atlantamagazine.com
The premiere monthly lifestyle publication in Georgia, the magazine exudes the glamour, excitement and enviable lifestyle associated with the South's most exciting city. Feel free to list your upcoming events online.

The Atlanta Music Guide

info@atlantamusicguide.com
www.atlantamusicguide.com
Atlanta bands, news, concerts, reviews and store, venues, radio stations, recording studios and rehearsal spaces. Don't forget to visit our online music store while you're here, to pick up the best Atlanta CD's and our pick of the imports.

The Atlanta Music Guide *Citysearch*

gmassey@citysearch.com
atlanta.citysearch.com
Extensive coverage of the local music scene. Post your shows and events.

Atlanta Ska

ksealus@yahoo.com
www.atlantaska.com
All your skankin' needs, from Punk to Pure.

atlantagoth.com

admin@atlantagoth.com
www.atlantagoth.com
Provides information about music, events, club nights, people and other fun stuff in Atlanta. Its meant as a resource for promoters, DJs, club goers, tourists and anyone who might be interested in goth/industrial/synth/ebm/dark/etc/ad nauseum happenings in the Atlanta area.

atlantashows.com
shows@atlantashows.com
www.atlantashows.com
In a band? Would you like to see your band featured at AtlantaShows.com? Drop us a line. e'll tell you how.

atlantashows.org
darian@atlantashows.org
www.atlantashows.org
Listing of Metro Atlanta and surrounding area shows.

Creative Loafing Atlanta
letters.atl@creativeloafing.com
www.atlanta.creativeloafing.com
Free weekly alternative paper. Covers local music scene and reviews CDs of bands playing in the area.

Degenerate Press Earplugs for Atlanta
earplugs@degeneratepress.com
www.degeneratepress.com
The superior, unpaid and ad-free review of the Atlanta music scene! We see every band personally before we post a thing. If you want cutting edge local music news, reviews and such contact us and subscribe to Electric Degeneration, a free semi-weekly e-zine.

Golistenlive.net
www.golistenlive.net
We want to support the stars of tomorrow and the influences of the future. You can use our interactive calendar for shows in the Atlanta area or rate the bands that are members of our site. Review any band and if we like it we'll post it here. This is your chance to let everyone know how good your favorite local band really is.

HOLLA!! Magazine
Info@hollamag.com
www.hollamag.com
Provides insights into the urban music entertainment media. HOLLA!! Is positive print media that influences and impacts the lives of Atlanta's urban contemporaries.

Metro Atlanta Country Music Club
macmc@macmc.net
www.macmc.net
Promotes country, bluegrass and southern gospel music in the Atlanta area. If you would like to submit a news item for the MACMC Monthly Update or Web page, please contact us.

Next Level Promotions
Nicole Oxford nicole@nextlevelpromo.net
www.nextlevelpromo.net
A promotions and booking company that works with independent artists throughout the Southeast. We strive to promote artists and book shows throughout the southeast by constant contact to clubs and other venues or colleges, street team organization, grassroots marketing, gig swap setups and monthly shows.

Noise Zone Magazine
noisezone@hotmail.com
www.geocities.com/SoHo/Bistro/4205
Making new noise from Atlanta and beyond with a whole new attitude!

Stage 96 Local Music Site
www.96rock.com/stage96
Sponsored by 96 Rock. We're dedicated to bringing you the finest in local music, with band bios, concert updates and local news in the Atlanta music market. Send us your CD's, promotional material etc.

Vid's Electric Blues
retroactive1@hotmail.com
vidsutton.electricblues.com
Profiles on Atlanta bands and musicians and where they're playing. Has a "Show Spotlight" page.

Hawaii

808shows.com
evan@imbicycle.com
www.808shows.com
Bands can list their upcoming shows on this site sponsored by Hawaiian Express Records.

Aloha Joe
alohajoe@alohajoe.com
www.alohajoe.com
Will review any music created on the Island.

BuyHawaiianMusic.com
info@buyhawaiianmusic.com
www.buyhawaiianmusic.com
All your favorite Hawaiian CDs and new releases.

Cade's Hawaiian Music Page
simplerhythms@msn.com
cadesmusic.homestead.com
Aloha and welcome to the best source for info on Hawaiian, Local and Reggae music on the web! Here, you will find, Lyrics+Chords, CD reviews, Group info., Upcoming Bands and plenty more.

Hawaii Blues Society
Bluesman@hiblues.org
hiblues.org
Our members are musicians, artists, promoters and people who support the blues.

Hawaiian Express Records
Jason HwnExp@aol.com
members.aol.com/hwnexp
Our goal is to provide as much information as possible about the current, non-traditional, Hawaiian music scene... specializing in punk, ska, metal, reggae and rock in the islands of Hawaii.

The Hawaiian Music Guide
stevo@hawaii-music.com
www.hawaii-music.com
The sole purpose of the guide is to promote Hawaiian Music, the most beautiful music on earth.

Hawaiian Music Island
auntie@mele.com
www.mele.com
The Internet's largest in-stock catalog of Hawaiian music CD titles, with nearly 1,500 titles available for immediate purchase.

Hawaiian Steel Guitar Association
hsga@lava.net
www.hsga.org
Our mission is the promotion and perpetuation of traditional Hawaiian music which includes the unique "signature sound" of Hawaiian steel guitar.

HawaiiEventsOnline.com
www.hawaiieventsonline.com
Includes listings of live shows going on throughout Hawaii.

The Honolulu Music Guide
honolulu.citysearch.com
Extensive coverage of the local music scene. Post your shows and events.

Honolulu Weekly
calendar@honoluluweekly.com
www.honoluluweekly.com
Honolulu's arts & entertainment weekly.

Maui Time Weekly
mauitime@mauitime.com
www.mauitime.com
Maui weekly arts & entertainment paper.

NahenaheNet
keola@nahenahe.net
www.nahenahe.net
Comprehensive collection of Hawaiian music artist sites with breaking news on new releases, gigs and concerts.

Nativemusic.com
info@nativemusic.com
www.nativemusic.com
Whether you miss music from your Island home or seek world rhythms from around the globe, Nativemusic.com can bring you there.

Quad Magazine
info@quadmag.com
www.quadmag.com
Hiphop, house, drumNbase, dub, live music and you! Beaming out of Honolulu and into your brain. Not just media, but a state of mind. Drop us a line and stay connected!

TropicalStormHawaii.com
kilbey@tropicalstormhawaii.com
www.tropicalstormhawaii.com
You can use the Message Board to post messages for other musicians the Song Post utility to post songs for others to download.

Idaho

The Arbiter
www.arbiteronline.com
Boise State University's student newspaper.

Argonaut
www.argonaut.uidaho.edu
University of Idaho's student paper.

Boise Blues Society
greasyregs@mindspring.com
www.boiseblues.org
Our mission is to bring the blues in all its forms to fans of all ages, to promote the blues as an American art form.

The Boise Music Guide
boise.citysearch.com
Extensive coverage of local music. Post your shows and events.

Boise Area WOMEN Musicians!
womensnight@yffn.org
www.yffn.org/women/music.html
Send in your calendar or booking info, phone and other contact info, e-mail and any links we may use.

Idaho Press-Tribune
features@idahopress.com
news.mywebpal.com/partners/347/public
Nampa daily paper.

Idaho State Journal
pressrelease@journalnet.com
www.journalnet.com
Pocatello daily paper.

WINNING SONGS GET RADIO AIRPLAY!
$50,000 TOP PRIZE & MORE!

Chance to Showcase in LA, Nashville, Atlanta, New York, etc.

Industry Professionals Judging!
ENTER TODAY!

*Sponsored by Indie Bible, Tonos.com, Musician.com, Mackie, Guild Guitars, D'Addraio Strings, Music Connection Magazine, LiveWireContacts.com, Singer Magazine, Acoustic Café, GigAmerica.com, Onstage Magazine, Electronic Musician, Superdups, ASN, Sonic Foundry, Steinberg, Bandwear & Audio-Technica

FREE INFO
www.songwriting.net

Call toll free: 1-877-USA-SONG
outside US call: (954) 776-1577

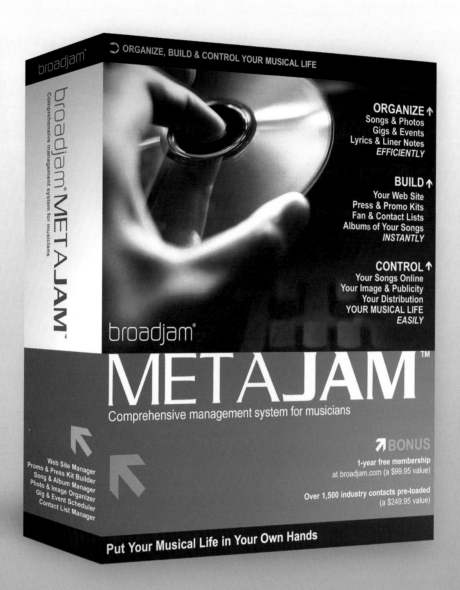

The Idaho Statesman
www.idahostatesman.com
Daily paper. Covers local music shows.

Women's Night
womensnight@yahoo.com
www.yffn.org/women
Art, events and information by women, for women, in Boise. Post information about you or your band.

Zidaho
www.zidaho.com
Everything in Idaho from A to Z. Add your event listing.

Illinois

Admit One
info@sonic-media.com
ntv6.tripod.com/admitone
Peoria's free biweekly A/E newspaper serving the needs of the active lifestyle, while maintaining a focus on newsworthy articles suitable for the entire family.

The Bloomington Music Guide
bloomington.citysearch.com
Extensive coverage of the local music scene. Post your shows and events.

The Blues Blowtorch Society
ralph@bluesblowtorch.com
www.bluesblowtorch.com/society
To enhance the culture of blues music in the Central Illinois area through the promotion of local artists, as well as regional and national talents.

Buzz
buzz@dailyillini.com
illinimedia.com/buzz
The Daily Illini's weekly entertainment magazine. Every Thursday, buzz helps readers gear up for the weekend, with anything and everything that is entertainment in Champaign- Urbana. Film, television, music and theatre reviews, a calendar of events and feature stories on the local entertainment scene.

CarbondaleRocks.com
nightlif@midwest.net
www.carbondalerocks.com
Extensive musician resource that includes the Local Musician Guide and MP3 Library.

The Central Illinois Jazz Society
jazz@flink.com
www.midil.com/cijs.html
The purpose of the organization is to further the appreciation and quality of jazz in Central Illinois. We do this by providing opportunities for jazz artists to play and for jazz lovers to enjoy their favorite music.

Champaign-Urbana Punk Page
cycopunk@hotmail.com
www.geocities.com/c_u_punk/CUpunkscene.html
Show and event listings, band listings etc.

Experimental Sound Studio *(ESS)*
ears@expsoundstudio.org
www.expsoundstudio.org
An organization founded for the production and promotion of innovative approaches to the sonic arts. The mission of ESS is to make audio technology accessible and affordable as well as to encourage the creative process.

findusat309.com
cthornquist@frontiernet.net
findusat309.com
Our goal here is to help expose the local residents to our great Quad City music scene. We currently have about 150 local artists' web pages with one minute RealAudio clips of their music. You will also find interviews & reviews of area bands and local music resources.

Fox Valley Blues Society
Fvbsblues@worldnet.att.net
www.foxvalleyblues.org
All CD's, books, press releases and interviews etc. for the Web site and Blues News should be sent to ATTN: Blues News, FVBS, PO Box 797, Oswego, IL.

Illiana Club of Traditional Jazz
jazzman@tradjazz.org
www.tradjazz.org
Promotes unconditional live concerts of sensational Big Band, Swing, Dixieland and Traditional Jazz in a comfortable and unsurpassed authentic Jazz atmosphere in Illinois and Indiana.

Illinois Local Band Directory
unitedmusician.org
Promote Your Band. Announce Show Dates. Upload your MP3s.

Illinois Times
editor@illinoistimes.com
www.illinoistimes.com
Springfield's arts & entertainment weekly.

Midwest Massacre
midwestmassacre@hotmail.com
midwestmassacre.tripod.com
The new source for Midwest Hip Hop.

Mr.Michael Productions
michael@midwest.net
www.mrmichaelproductions.com
Established to help nurture and promote local talent. Every city is host to a number of artists/bands and the Salem area is no different. I am committed to helping this talent reach the next step by becoming more than a "garage band" that plays for friends or not at all.

News-Gazette
www.news-gazette.com
Champaign daily paper.

Northern Illinois Bluegrass Association
niba@nibaweb.org
www.nibaweb.org
Our purpose is to promote bluegrass music by educating and enhancing public awareness, compiling and providing information and sponsoring bluegrass events.

OpeningBands.com
Steve Sobel steve@openingbands.com
www.openingbands.com
Based in Champaign Illinois, we primarily promote local and regional music, but we receive CD submissions from people all over the world. We are entirely volunteer-run and our site even has caught the attention of major labels with no direct promotion whatsoever.

Pantagraph
Dan Craft dcraft@pantagraph.com
www.pantagraph.com
Bloomington daily paper. Extensive coverage of local music.

Peoria Journal Star
www.pjstar.com
Daily paper.

Peoria Shows
peoriashows@hotmail.com
www.angelfire.com/il2/PeoriaShows
We're not biased to posting shows. As long it's in the Central Illinois area, send it...I'll even post the Alkaline Trio shows...however, we would rarely have to worry about those rock stars lowering themselves to play Peoria.

Round Lake Underground
webmaster@roundlakeug.com
www.roundlakeug.com
Established to help local bands get exposure and spread their music. Every month or so we have a Featured Band. To get your CD reviewed send a promo pack (with demo) to us.

Sonic-Media Group
info@sonic-media.com
www.sonic-media.com
Peoria based Midwest band promotional site. Post your news and gig listings.

Southern Illinois Metal Collective
athjones@yahoo.com
www.simc.org
A coming together of the heavy aggressive bands in the Southern Illinois region to provide a central hub for everyone to make contacts through, set up and promote shows and turn fans of heavy music onto the entire scene at once.

Southern Illinois Music E-Zine
Tad VanDyke ld_manager45@hotmail.com
www.sime-zine.com
Bands submit their news and we post it on our site for the public to know when and where they will be playing. It is a good resource for the public and the bands to get info on their favorite local band. We also have links to bands for fans and bands to visit.

Springfield State Journal-Register
sjr@sj-r.com
www.sj-r.com
Daily paper. Covers local music.

Chicago

180 Entertainment
info@180entertainment.com
www.180entertainment.com
We work hard at being the best there is at what they do and that is to be the number 1 entertainment organization in Chicago. 180 specializes in event coordination and production, performance, DJ's, design, modeling and promotion.

Alternative Echo
alternative_echo@hotmail.com
www.alt-echo.cjb.net
Dedicated to punk bands from Chicago, Milwaukee and Worldwide. News, CD reviews, show reviews etc. Want your show listed? Contact us.

American Gothic Productions
scaryladysarah@aol.com
www.americangothicprod.com
We accept CDs and VHS videotape submissions from bands looking to play live in Chicago or have club play. Send us your recordings for consideration along with promotional materials.

Blackout Chicago
Phil@darklink.org
www.blackoutzine.com
Chicago's electronic music news source. All submissions are more than welcome. All materials will be kept in mind for future radio shows, interviews, spotlights and so forth.

Centerstage Chicago
center@centerstage.net
centerstage.net
The oldest and largest guide to The Windy City's arts & entertainment scene, with hundreds of music performance venues and nearly two thousands musicians and arts. Find and post gigs, announce auditions, buy & sell gear! Sell your music through our online store.

Chicago Cajun Connection
cajunconnx@earthlink.net
home.earthlink.net/~cterra440
Lists local events featuring traditional Cajun and Zydeco music.

The Chicago Classical Guitar Society
chicagocgs@bizland.com
www.chicagoclassicalguitarsociety.org
Serves as a means of communication among guitarists throughout the Midwest. The society publishes a monthly newsletter, Chicago Guitar and sponsors recitals, master classes, evaluated recitals and lectures on topics of interest to classical and flamenco guitarists.

Chicago Flame
www.chicagoflame.com
Independent student newspaper of the U. Illinois @ Chicago.

Chicago Fusion
chicagofusion@attbi.com
www.chicagofusion.com
Chicago's #1 club web site. If you are looking to promote your venue or special event, please contact us.

Chicago Harmony and Truth *(CHaT)*
webmaster@chatmusic.com
www.chatmusic.com
By fostering the general growth of the Chicago music scene, Chicago Harmony and Truth seeks to build on our city's rich musical heritage by creating a stronger, more hospitable business environment: one where more people are exposed to greater opportunities and more talent has the chance to shine.

Chicago Indie Radio
Charles Leet info@livexradio.com
www.chicago-indie.com
Our website promotes all the great independent artists in the Chicagoland area.

Chicago Local Bands
bandinfo@chicagolocalbands.com
www.chicagolocalbands.com
Chicago's Fastest Growing Music Resource!

Chicago Magazine
www.chicagomag.com
Covers local music scene. News, reviews.

Chicago Metromix
metromix@tribune.com
metromix.com

The Chicago Music Guide
chicago.citysearch.com
Extensive coverage of local music. Post your shows and events.

chicago-music-scene.com
eric@chicago-music-scene.com
www.chicago-music-scene.com
A site dedicated to the Chicago local music scene with band listings, reviews, concert listings, downloads and more. All free.

Chicago Open Mics
www.risingstarmusic.com/ommonday.html
List of places to play in the Chicago area. Reviews are posted of each venue.

Chicago Punk & Ska
tony@coppoletta.net
www.cpsw.net
Live shows listings, images, bands, message board and articles.

Chicago Reader
musiclistings@chicagoreader.com
www.chicagoreader.com
Free weekly paper. Chicago's essential music guide.

Chicago-Scene.com
info@Chicago-Scene.Com
www.chicago-scene.com
Chicago's leading online entertainment guide.

Chicago Songwriters Collective
info@chicagosongwriters.com
www.chicagosongwriters.com
Promotes and encourages the art of songwriting, storytelling, composing and lyricists with information and opportunities for performance and networking.

Chicago and Suburbs Musicians
d@andrewlehman.com
www.chicagolandmusicians.com
Paid service that lists Chicago (and area) artists.

Chicago Sun-Times
www.suntimes.com
Daily paper. Highlights artists playing in the area, reviews CDs.

Chicago Tribune
mmcguire@tribune.com
www.chicagotribune.com
Daily paper.

ChicagoAfterhours.com
info@chicagoafterhours.com
www.chicagoafterhours.com
Your resource guide to nightlife in Chicago. We travel near and far to provide information on Chicago's brightest Restaurants, Night Clubs, DJ's, Artists, Bartenders and take Pictures of the people who love them.

ChicagoBandConnection.com
sweetprodesign@aol.com
www.chicagobandconnection.com
The goal is to get as much information in one place as possible and make it easier for the Chicago Area Music Industry to keep in touch. It is also a resource for bands that are just starting or trying to break into the main music scene.

ChicagoFun.org
www.chicagofun.org
Provides a comprehensive and concise guide to Chicago entertainment with a leaning to the offbeat.

ChicagoGigs.com
contact@chicagogigs.com
www.Chicagogigs.com
A unique music community serving the greater Chicago area with comprehensive coverage of both local and national touring acts. A searchable concert database, music-related contests, news, reviews, photo galleries, local artist websites and active musician classifieds are the main features.

ChicagoGroove.com
ramiros@chicagogroove.com
www.chicagogroove.com
Pics and audio sets from local DJs.

Chicagoland Music
Info@chicagolandmusic.net
www.chicagolandmusic.net
Your #1 source for Chicago's metal. If you have an mp3 of a band in the Chicagoland area or you're in a band in the Chicagoland area and want to promote with CLM, visit our site for submission info. Please do not send any MP3s to the above e-mail address.

ChicagoRockabilly.com
amy@rockabilly.net
www.rockabilly.net/chicago
Find out what's rockin' in Chicago. Post your gig.

Citysearch Chicago
CSEvents@citysearch.com
chicago.citysearch.com/section/music

Daisy Glaze Entertainment
info@daisyglaze.com
www.daisyglaze.com
Specializes in artist management and consulting for bands/musicians in the Chicago area and the greater Midwest.

dead ceo
woody@deadceo.com
www.deadceo.com
A distributor of a wide variety of music (free improvisation, contemporary composition, laptop minimalism etc.), focusing on hard-to-find cds, cdrs, vinyl and print by Chicago area artists and labels.

Digital City Chicago *Music*
home.digitalcity.com/chicago
Regional music column and forum. The area contains weekly feature articles plus weekend entertainment highlights, a running music poll and interactive message board.

Gothic Chicago
davidb@gothicchicago.com
www.gothicchicago.com
Since 1996, GothicChicago.com has been your number one resource for all things gothic/industrial in the Chicagoland area.

Hot Local Bands
drumfoo22@yahoo.com
www.hotlocalbands.2ya.com
This website features some of the coolest bands from the Chicagoland area.

Illinois Entertainer
editors@illinoisentertainer.com
www.illinoisentertainer.com
Chicago arts & entertainment weekly. Loads of local music coverage!

Imagine Chicago
info@imaginechicago.com
www.imaginechicago.com
Our goal is to create a new experience for Chicago's club heads. We're here to show we are a unique crew unlike anything ever seen. We bring you the finest DJs and mind blowing sounds. We are here to take the art of clubbing to a higher plane.

Intergrüv Networks
info@intergruv.net
www.intergruv.net
A collective of creative minds and DJs banded together to build events designed at the idea of expanding Chicago's entertainment to the new millennium. The members of this collective have dedicated themselves to building a foundation of keeping the Chicago scene alive.

Jazz Institute of Chicago
Editor@JazzInstituteOfChicago.org
www.JazzInstituteOfChicago.org
We commissioned new works by Chicago musicians, sponsor musician residencies and workshops, collaborate with educational, government and cultural institutions, all in the effort to pursue our goal of preserving and perpetuating the unique American art form that although called by many names is most often known as jazz.

JazzSingers.com *Chicago*
calendar@jazzsingers.com
www.jazzsingers.com/ChicagoScene
A support site for jazz singers, with information on the Chicago scene and a place for singers to list their 'gigs.

JstreetZine.com
jesse@jstreetzine.com
www.jstreetzine.com
Covering the Chicago music scene. We do not support major labels or bands currently under major label representation. Our focus is on unsigned artists and people who bust their asses to get their music heard.

LatinFade.com
ronald@latinfade.com
www.toprockproductions.com
Keeping up to date with the Chicago Scene. Hip-Hop / House / Merengue / Bachata / Salsa / Old Skool / Progressive.

Local 101's CD Reviews
www.q101.com/local101
Radio station Q101 reviews CDs of Chicago artists.

local girls chicago
thelocalgirls007@hotmail.com
www.geocities.com/thelocalgirls
Spreading the love of local music in the Chicago 'burbs. News, gig listings, interviews etc.

Local Shibby
submissions@localshibby.com
www.localshibby.com
Covering the Chicago area punk scene. News, reviews, interviews etc.

Metromix
mmcguire@tribune.com
www.metromix.com
The Chicago Tribune's online entertainment magazine.

Midwest BEAT Magazine
beatboss@aol.com
www.midwestbeat.com
A free monthly entertainment/lifestyles print magazine that is distributed extensively throughout Chicagoland and North West Indiana.

Newcity Chicago
www.newcitychicago.com
The online version of Newcity Magazine - Chicago's free arts & entertainment publication.

noise:chicago
noise@no-nothingrock.com
www.no-nothingrock.com/noise
The beginning of the next evolution of the Chicago Mailing List. Lists every show in the Chicago area.

OS Magazine
info@osmag.com
www.osmag.com
Covering the Chicago dance music scene.

PsyberView
info@chitown.com
www.chitown.com
If you have an MP3, professional cassette, vinyl recording or CD in current release or production, if you have an upcoming or current exhibition or publication of your artwork we encourage you to participate, if you are near Chicago or the neighboring tri-state area.

Red Magazine
www.red-mag.com
Chicago Art, Music and Culture.

Rising Star Music
risingstarmusic@ameritech.net
www.risingstarmusic.com
Our mission is to present quality recording artists to an international audience and to list their music products for purchase.

Suburban NiteLife
bart@nitelife.to
www.nitelife.to
Chicago entertainment magazine.

UnifiedBeats.com
www.unifiedbeats.com
This site is dedicated to support House Music and to give it the recognition it deserves. Our goal is to bring you a variety of mixes heard on the net along with providing exposure for many DJ's. We also feature new sets regularly from guest DJ's along with their biography and pictures.

UR Chicago Magazine
editorial@urchicago.com
www.urchicago.com
Find out about up-and-comers, new releases, local shows and more from Chicago's premier source for the best in music.

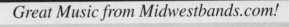
Voiceless Productions
voicelessp@excite.com
www.oneway.com/voiceless
An artist alliance dedicated to revitalizing the Chicago music scene by presenting creative, daring, interesting and entertaining musical events.

Windyhop
www.windyhop.org
Covering the Chicago swing scene.

Indiana

6 String Design
getlisted@6string.net
www.6string.net
Northwest Indiana's #1 musician's resource.

All is Dead
Ryan Kasparian ryan@kolobos.com
www.midwestmetal.org
Based out of Lowell. The leader in local metal and hardcore!

CarpeMidwest
Grunt@CarpeMidwest.com
www.carpemidwest.com
Regional Darkwave, EBM, World, Ambient & Experimental Events.

Central Indiana Folk Music & Mountain Dulcimer Society
dsilk@iupui.edu
www.iupui.edu/%7Ecnl60/dulsoc
Dedicated to the promotion and preservation of American folk music and acoustic instruments.

EvansvilleScene.com
Adam Ferguson webmaster@evansvillescene.com
www.evansvillescene.com
Dedicated to the promotion local talent in Evansville, Indiana and the surrounding cities. Local Music is where it's at!

Flatfun Bloomington Music Calendar
ffun.net/bloo
Listing/Promoting musical events that happen in Bloomington, Indiana. Bands can submit sites, MP3s, photos and other info.

Fort Wayne Journal Gazette
www.fortwayne.com/mld/journalgazette
Daily paper.

Fort Wayne News-Sentinel
www.fortwayne.com/mld/newssentinel
Daily paper.

fortwaynemusic.com
musicmaster@fortwaynemusic.com
www.fortwaynemusic.com
Where is your band? If it isn't listed on our site, then let us know!

Gignet
gignet@indiana.edu
php.indiana.edu/~gignet
Bloomington's local music network.

HoosierTimes.com
www.hoosiertimes.com
Bloomington daily paper. Reviews and profiles bands submit your events to be included in their calendar.

The Indiana Daily Student
arts@idsnews.com
www.idsnews.com
Indiana University's student newspaper.

Indiana SKAlendar
tgatkins@indiana.edu
php.indiana.edu/~tgatkins/ska.html
A collection of upcoming SKA shows throughout the Indiana area. Also links to all of the Indiana ska bands that I currently know of, as well as some other useful ska resources.

The Indianapolis Music Guide
indianapolis.citysearch.com
Extensive coverage of the local music scene. Post your shows and events.

Indianapolis Musicians
info@indymusicians.com
www.indymusicians.com
Dedicated to the enhancement and promotion of the music profession in Indiana.

The Indianapolis Star
www.indystar.com
Daily paper. Local music info.

IndianapolisMusic.net
matt@indianapolismusic.net
indianapolismusic.net
A service to help Indianapolis area musicians and bands (regardless of genre, age, race, religion, or financial status) come together and create a thriving scene. We're working together to help spark more interest in local music.

LafayetteMusicians.com
drumroll@LafayetteMusicians.com
www.lafayettemusicians.com
Lafayette's web site for our local Musicians

lafayettemusic.net
webteam@lafayettemusic.net
lafayettemusic.net
Want to write an article about the music scene, gear, music, your band, or anything else? Send it over. It'll get posted. Pictures are always welcomed too.

Let's Pop
letspop@stateofmind.net
www.stateofmind.net/letspop
Covering the Bloomington music scene.

LiveMusicIndiana.com
kim@livemusicindiana.com
livemusicindiana.com
LMI is unique as it not only represents the finest musicians from all genres of music, but it also touts a full color, 100 page plus comprehensive music and entertainment magazine.

Midwest after Dark
mre@mwafterdark.com
www.mwafterdark.com
Gothic Industrial events for the Indianapolis area.

Midwest BEAT Magazine
tom@midwestbeat.com
www.midwestbeat.com
A 36-40 page monthly entertainment/lifestyles publication that is distributed free of charge the first weekend of each month to hundreds of locations throughout N.W. Indiana and Chicagoland (with a limited amount distributed in Central Illinois and Cleveland, OH).

MidWestBands.com
mwbcontact@MidWestBands.com
www.midwestbands.com
Exists to provide musicians in the Midwest with the opportunity to connect with other musicians and working bands free of charge. It is also a site to showcase their talents and provide a wealth of resources to aid bands and individuals alike.

Missing Link Records
info@missinglinkrecords.com
www.missinglinkrecords.com
We are Central Indiana's best source for new, used and rare vinyl. We support local artists.

The Muncie Music Guide
munciekokomo.citysearch.com
Extensive coverage of the local music scene. Post your shows and events.

Naptown Reggae
the_lioness@naptownreggae.com
www.naptownreggae.com
Covering the Indianapolis Reggae scene.

NIGHTLIFE
nightlif@midwest.net
www.carbondalerocks.com
Carbondale and Southern Illinois's Independent Weekly Alternative.

Noise
KD1noise@aol.com
www.enoise.com
Northern Indiana's source for entertainment!

North West Indiana Rap Online
nwirap@hotmail.com
www.nwirap.cjb.net
The home of Chicago and Gary Hip-Hop. We've got chat, downloads, music, personal e-mail, CDs to buy, links and more.

Northern Indiana Bluegrass Association
nibga@mixi.net
www.ft-wayne.com/bluegrass
Information on bluegrass music in a 200 mile radius of Fort Wayne, Indiana.

NUVO Newsweekly
www.nuvo.net
Indianapolis free weekly alternative paper. Covers local music scene. MP3s of great new music from local artists!

The Observer
www.nd.edu/~observer
The student-run, daily print and online newspaper serving Notre Dame and Saint Mary's.

One Kind Radio
jbowles@onekindradio.com
www.onekindradio.com
Bringing a worldwide audience the best in local and independent music from NW Indiana, Chicago and beyond. CD reviews, band performance dates and locations and more!

punkrocknight.com
greg@punkrocknight.com
www.punkrocknight.com
Resource with reviews, forums, audio, video etc. covering the Indianapolis punk scene.

South Bend Tribune
www.southbendtribune.com
Daily paper.

Whatzup Magazine
whatzup@whatzup.com
www.whatzup.com
Indianapolis based entertainment magazine. Show listings and reviews of local bands.

Iowa

515 Crew/ Iowa Hardcore
Zhoyt@515crew.com
www.515crew.com
Covering the Iowa hardcore scene. News, shows, band listings etc.

Cedar Rapids Gazette
www.gazetteonline.com
Your source for the most complete and up-to-date news, sports and entertainment coverage of Eastern Iowa.

The Central Iowa Blues Society
webmaster@cibs.org
www.cibs.org
Keeping the Blues alive through appreciation and education since 1992.

cityview
www.dmcityview.com
Des Moines alternative newspaper. Want to get your band noticed? Add your info to our local music database. Tell us how you got your name, what type of music you play, where you often play, discographies, web sites and more!

The Daily Iowan
daily-iowan@uiowa.edu
www.dailyiowan.com
University of Iowa's student paper.

The Des Moines Music Guide
desmoines.citysearch.com
Extensive coverage of the local music scene. Post your shows and events.

The Des Moines Register
www.desmoinesregister.com
Daily Arts and Entertainment paper. Covers new music and indie bands.

Iowa City Press-Citizen
online@press-citizen.com
www.press-citizen.com
Daily paper. CD reviews, previews and interviews with bands.

Iowa Hip Hop List
SkylarJohnson@JTrey.com
www.jtrey.com/list.html
The most comprehensive list of Iowa Hip Hop artists and groups.

Iowa HomeGrown Music
bronson@iowahomegrown.com
www.iowahomegrown.com
Our song catalog has grown to represent many great Songwriters and Artists who create music that encompasses a wide variety of musical styling.

Iowa Music Listings
kuni@uni.edu
kuniradio.org/calendars.html
KUNI/KHKE regional calendars of live performances.

Iowa State Daily
www.iowastatedaily.com
Iowa State University's daily paper.

IowaHardcore.com
Zhoyt@515crew.com
www.iowahardcore.com
Please send info on bands (hardcore, punk, ska, emo) in Iowa, email me, keep me updated!!

Jazz Society of Eastern Iowa
JazzKnight@aol.com
www.homestead.com/JazzInEastIowa
Our mission is to promote and support jazz events and education in Eastern Iowa.

The Linn County Blues Society
kbrostad@mcleodusa.net
www.lcbs.org
Dedicated to the preservation, promotion and perpetuation of Blues music in Eastern Iowa.

Lizard Creek Blues Society
bobwood@frontiernet.net
www.lizardcreekblues.org

Midwest Music Review
clubs.yahoo.com/clubs/midwestmonster
If you're a fan, sign up and tell us about the Midwest bands you know. Post news, links, pictures and tour dates here.

Mississippi Valley Blues Society
mvbs@revealed.net
www.mvbs.org
Educating the general public about the native art form of blues related music by performance, enhancing appreciation and understanding.

Quad-City Times
www.qctimes.com
Davenport daily paper. Local and national CD reviews and interviews with bands playing the area.

The River Cities' Reader
info@rcreader.com
www.rcreader.com
Davenport news & entertainment weekly.

Sioux City Journal
www.siouxcityjournal.com
Daily paper.

Kansas

The Kansas Bluegrass Association
sfunk@kansasbluegrass.org
www.kansasbluegrass.org
An organization for the promotion of bluegrass music in Central Kansas.

Kansas Prairie Pickers Association
fidlnjohn@yahoo.com
www.ink.org/public/kppa
A music organization in northeast Kansas interested in the preservation of Bluegrass and Old Time acoustic music.

Lawrence Journal-World
www.ljworld.com
Daily paper. Considers profiling bands playing in the area. "The Mag" entertainment section does CD reviews.

Lawrence.com
Phil pcauthon@ljworld.com
www.lawrence.com
Good coverage of local music scene.

LawrenceHipHop.com
lawrencehiphop@hotmail.com
www.lawrencehiphop.com
Our goal is to unite heads in the Lawrence, Kansas City and surrounding areas.

Lawrencerock.com
www.lawrencerock.com
An independent resource for music and culture in Lawrence. We want to promote not only local music and musicians who come through, but also other cultural events around Lawrence (theater, art, film, poetry readings etc).

The Manhattan Mercury
net@themercury.com
www.themercury.com/music
Contact us if you would like your band showcased.

RockKansas.com
411@rockkansas.com
www.RockKansas.com
The most comprehensive local music resource in Kansas. Band Directory, Calendar, Rk Radio, News, Interviews, Reviews, Columns and Ticket Contests.

Topeka Capital-Journal
www.cjonline.com
Daily paper.

Wichita Kansas Blues Society
ann@wichitablues.org
www.wichitablues.com
An organization dedicated to the preservation, education and the enjoyment of America's musical art form known as the BLUES.

The Wichita Music Guide
wichita.citysearch.com
Extensive coverage of the local music scene. Post your shows and events.

Kentucky

ACE Weekly
jshambhu@aceweekly.com
www.aceweekly.com
Lexington arts & entertainment weekly.

The Amplifier
info@ky.net
amplifier.ky.net
Bowling Green monthly music & entertainment magazine.

Big Rock Bands
info@bigrockbands.com
www.bigrockbands.com
Louisville bands online.

College Heights Herald
www.wkuherald.com
Western Kentucky University's daily student newspaper.

The Courier-Journal
www.courier-journal.com
Louisville daily newspaper.

cre8iv.com
ec@cre8iv.com
www.cre8iv.com
A Christian owned and operated company. Complete Music Artists Services!

Daily News
www.bgdailynews.com
Bowling Green daily paper.

The Kentuckiana Blues Society
membership@kbsblues.org
KBSBlues.org
If your local group has produced a CD and you want it listed here send us the details, or better yet send us a CD.

The Kentucky Friends of Bluegrass Music Club
kfobg@chapel1.com
kyfriends.us
Dedicated to preserving and furthering Bluegrass Music.

KYKernel
www.kykernel.com
The student newspaper at the University of Kentucky.

Lexgoth
in_a_coma_dial_999@yahoo.com
lexgoth.com
On-line community for members of the Lexington gothic scene.

Lexington Herald Leader
www.kentucky.com/mld/heraldleader
Lexington daily paper.

The Lexington Music Guide
lexington.citysearch.com
Extensive coverage of the local music scene. Post your shows and events.

Lexmusic.com
Lexmusic@lexmusic.com
www.lexmusic.com
Venues, bands, Musicians referrals and much more!

Louisville Eccentric Observer
www.louisville.com/leo.html
Free weekly alternative paper. Covers local music scene and national indie scene.

The Louisville Jazz Society
loujazz@bellsouth.net
www.louisvillejazz.org
Seeks to promote Jazz awareness by sponsoring concerts featuring local and national artists, subsidizing Jazz educational programs in schools and universities and assisting any activity related to Jazz.

Louisville Metal
louisvillemetal@yahoo.com
louisvillemetal.cruor.com
Local Metal show info, band pics, message board, as well as regional shows.

Louisville Music Index
louisvilleshows@yahoo.com
www.louisvillemusicindex.org
Pictures, interviews and MP3s. We are only listing for Louisville and the metro area. If your band is in town and playing with a Louisville band we will list that show however.

The Louisville Music Guide
louisville.citysearch.com
Extensive coverage of the local music scene. Post your shows and events.

Louisville Music News
pmm@LouisvilleMusic.com
www.louisvillemusicnews.com
Free monthly music paper. Covers regional music scene.

The Louisville Scene
www.louisvillescene.com
Your Monday-Friday guide to what's going on in Louisville.

undergroundlou.com
www.undergroundlou.com
Providing info on the underground music scene in the Louisville area. This site is dedicated to all the bands who fuck the corporate machine and enjoy staying underground. Support your local music scene!

Louisiana

The Advocate
www.2theadvocate.com
Baton Rouge daily paper. Covers Baton Rouge, Lafayette and New Orleans music scene. Interviews and reviews bands and shows.

The Baton Rouge Music Guide
batonrouge.citysearch.com
Extensive coverage of the local music scene. Post your shows and events.

The Baton Rouge Ultimate Band List
main@brcentral.com
brcentral.com/bands
Fill in our online form with your band's name, a brief description, a contact phone number and if possible, an email address and web page link.

Caffeine Music
caffeinemusic@yahoo.com
www.satchmo.com/caffeinemusic
An independent music publisher, which aims to present the best of contemporary Americana and country songwriting, particularly that which is coming from New Orleans, LA.

Cajun French Music Association
president@cajunfrenchmusic.org
www.cajunfrenchmusic.org
Working to preserve and promote traditional French Cajun music.

Cajunfun.com
info@cajunfun.com
www.cajunfun.com
Acadiana's Premier Entertainment Resource.

Gambit Weekly
response@gambitweekly.com
www.bestofneworleans.com
New Orleans' award winning alternative weekly.

The Gumbo Pages
chuck@gumbopages.com
www.gumbopages.com
Keeping your taste buds, eardrums and funny bone tickled since 1994.

HisMusic.com
info@hismusic.com
www.hismusic.com
Providing Christian coffee house and concert listings for New Orleans and surrounding areas of Louisiana and Mississippi.

InsideNewOrleans.com *Music*
neworleans.cox.net
Got a show? Let us know!

The Lafayette Music Guide
lafayette.citysearch.com
Extensive coverage of the local music scene. Post your shows and events.

lapunx.com
info@lapunx.com
www.lapunx.com
The Louisiana music directory. If you've got news to share, send it our way. Recording an album? Going on tour? See a cool show? Tell us about it. We'll post it for all to know.

Louisiana Folk Roots
info@lafolkroots.org
www.lafolkroots.org
Dedicated to nurturing the unique folkways and cultural resources that are of such legendary abundance in Louisiana.

Louisiana Jukebox
goodemedia@kfbol.com
www.louisianajukebox.com
The state's only live music television show. Post your new CD release on our website.

The Louisiana Music Commission
lmc@louisianamusic.org
www.louisianamusic.org
We're dedicated to promoting and developing our music industry to its fullest potential.

The Louisiana Music Factory
info@louisianamusicfactory.com
www.louisianamusicfactory.com
The one stop site for all of your New Orleans and Louisiana music needs.

Louisiana Songwriters Association
info@lasongwriters.org
www.lasongwriters.org
LSA holds workshops, seminars and provides speakers for our membership to increase each member's understanding of the music industry, the craft of songwriting, demo production and marketing.

MojoNO.com
staff@mojono.com
www.mojono.com
If you are a local Louisiana band, you are entitled to a free band listing and your own personal gig calendar on MojoNO.com!

The Monroe Music Guide
monroe.citysearch.com
Extensive coverage of the local music scene. Post your shows and events.

NeonBridge
kd_hobgood@yahoo.com
www.neonbridge.com
Shreveport/Bossier City's music magazine. We always love hearing from musicians and artists. If you have any information you'd like to submit (i.e. url, address of your home page, upcoming show dates, or songs you want converted to MP3 format for the site) let us know and we will put it online.

The New Orleans Blues Project
contact@bluesproject.com
www.bluesproject.com
Seeks to promote communication, dialogue and understanding between diverse communities through awareness and appreciation of blues and roots music and its related culture and heritage.

New Orleans Jazz Club
info@nojazzclub.com
www.nojazzclub.com
Since 1948, the New Orleans Jazz Club has helped to promote jazz all over the world.

New Orleans Live
jdonley@nola.com
www.nolalive.com/music
News and reviews of local music.

The New Orleans Music Guide
neworleans.citysearch.com
Extensive coverage of the local music scene. Post your shows and events.

The New Orleans Musicians' Clinic
mgegen@lsuhsc.edu
www.wwoz.org/clinic
An innovative not-for-profit occupational medicine and wellness partnership offering comprehensive health care to our community's most precious resource: our musicians.

New Orleans Radio
info@neworleansradio.com
www.neworleansradio.com
We've incorporated your user submitted information into the design of the New Orleans Radio website. So, whether you're a listener, writer, musician, record label, club owner or arts patron, you can promote it here. Use our account set-up selection below to begin your promotional blitz.

New Orleans Times-Picayune
www.nola.com/music
Daily paper. Previews shows and announces local CD releases.

NewOrleansGospel.com
www.neworleansgospel.com
Welcome to New Orleans' premier LIVE Gospel music info source!!!!!!

NewOrleansOnline.com
www.neworleansonline.com/neworleans/music
Extensive coverage of local music.

Offbeat
offbeat@offbeat.com
www.offbeat.com
New Orleans' and Louisiana's music and entertainment magazine. Published every month, OffBeat contains interviews and features on the music and musicians in the nation's most musical city, as well as the city's most comprehensive club listings.

Pershing Well's South Louisiana Music Site
pershing@pershingwells.com
www.pershingwells.com
If you have a band, are a songwriter, write prose, paint or have anything to do with the art of South Louisiana, please contact us to be listed on this site. It's FREE and there is no obligation whatsoever!

The Reveille
editor@lsureveille.com
www.lsureveille.com
Louisiana State University's student daily newspaper.

Satchmo.com
editor@satchmo.com
www.satchmo.com
New Orleans & Louisiana music news, CD reviews, listings etc.

Shreveport City Lights
info@shreveportcitylights.com
www.shreveportcitylights.com
Info on the Louisiana & East Texas music scene. Sign up to be a spotlight band!

ShreveportRocks.com
musician@shreveportrocks.com
www.shreveportrocks.com
Our mission is simple: Make it easy for our local musicians to showcase their talents to the world.

The Silver Machine
info@thesilvermachine.com
www.thesilvermachine.com
Dedicated to the support and promotion of creative endeavor not usually associated with the traditional view of New Orleans. It is our intention to raise global awareness of the abundance and quality of art and music produced here on the "Third Coast."

South Louisiana Bluegrass Association
info@southlouisianabluegrass.org
www.southlouisianabluegrass.org
Our mission is to promote and preserve bluegrass music.

The Times of Acadiana
Arsenio Orteza arsenioort@aol.com
www.timesofacadiana.com
Lafayette's arts & entertainment weekly.

Where y'at Magazine
info@whereyatnola.com
www.whereyatnola.com
New Orleans' monthly entertainment magazine.

Zyde.com
zydecom@aol.com
members.aol.com/zydecom
The Internet Magazine for Louisiana Music.

Maine

Bangor Daily News
www.bangornews.com
Daily paper.

Casco Bay Weekly
cbwpub@maine.rr.com
www.cascobayweekly.com

Dirigo Music Distribution
jdub@dirigomusic.com
www.dirigomusic.com
An independent music distribution system that can help your independent band or label have better distribution with less effort. Dirigo Music Distribution offers music retailers consistent and diverse inventory by serving as a funnel for Maine music and regional independent artists.

Down East
editorial@downeast.com
www.downeast.com
A monthly, full-color magazine celebrating Maine. Post your upcoming events.

East of Nowhere
kevinn@javanet.com
www.mainemusicscene.com
Your guide to Maine music.

Entertainment in Maine Today.com
entertainment.mainetoday.com
Maine music resource including reviews, previews, nightclub listings and the Nightnotes column.

Face Magazine
mail@facemag.com
www.facemag.com
Portland free bi-weekly music magazine. Covers local music scene. Band interviews, CD and concert previews and reviews.

Maine Blues Society
patpepin@msn.com
www.mainebluessociety.org
CD reviews and Artist Spotlights.

Maine Hip Hop
www.mainehiphop.com
Maine's Hip Hop site and message board.

Maine Punx
mainepunx@mainepunx.com
www.mainepunx.com
Our goals are to provide a means of communication for Punks all over Maine, to strengthen our scene through an up to date source of information, to give a place for Maine punk bands to gain exposure from a large audience, possibly a place to buy their records.

The Maine Songwriters Association
Judd@tlmgi.com
www.mesongwriters.com
Dedicated to the support of songwriters and their art. The MSA mission is to encourage, recognize, educate, support and promote developing songwriters.

MaineList.com
www.mainelist.com
Use our online form to submit your Maine-based web site. Your listing will appear on our page within 24 hours.

MaineMusic.com
edc@mainemusic.com
www.mainemusic.com
Enter your own events or your own artist links.

MaineMusic.Org
info@maineperformingarts.org
www.mainemusic.org
Maine's diverse musical heritage is firmly rooted in community life, reflecting the culture, geography and aspirations of its residents.

mainestream.nu
comments@mainestream.nu
www.mainestream.nu
Streaming Independent films & music by Maine artists. Mainestream.nu exists to broaden awareness of Maine filmmakers and musicians regionally and worldwide by publishing their works online and providing a community that develops, promotes and recognizes Maine artists.

Portland Maine Music
anton@portlandmainemusic.com
www.portlandmainemusic.com
This is a site to support original Portland Maine Music and music created in Maine, this region, as well as the rest of the Northeast.

The Portland Music Guide
portlandme.citysearch.com
Extensive coverage of the local music scene. Post your shows and events.

Portland Phoenix
portlandletters@phx.com
www.portlandphoenix.com
Local band coverage including MP3s from locally-based musicians.

Portland Press Herald
www.portland.com
Daily paper.

The Presque Isle Music Guide
presqueisle.citysearch.com
Extensive coverage of the local music scene. Post your shows and events.

Maryland

Baltimore Blues Society
Bob@mojoworkin.com
www.mojoworkin.com
Reviews of new CD releases by national, regional and local artists.

Baltimore City Paper
Bret McCabe bmccabe@citypaper.com
www.citypaper.com
Baltimore's weekly news and entertainment paper. Covers local music.

The Baltimore Classical Guitar Society
president@bcgs.org
www.bcgs.org
An organization dedicated to promoting the art of the classical guitar. Benefits include the organization of classical guitar concerts and recitals in the Baltimore area for local, national and international talent.

The Baltimore Folk Music Society
newsletter@bfms.org
www.bfms.org
Dedicated to teaching, preserving and promoting the music, dance and traditions of the American people.

The Baltimore Music Guide
baltimore.citysearch.com
Extensive coverage of the local music scene. Post your shows and events.

The Baltimore Songwriters Association
iwancio@umbc.edu
www.electrobus.com/bsa
We provide networking and mutual support for musicians and performing singer-songwriters addressing many of their common concerns. We publish a quarterly newsletter complete with interviews with well known songwriters.

The Baltimore Sun
www.sunspot.net
Gig listings. Reviews indie and major CD releases.

BaltimoreBands.com
www.baltimorebands.com
Providing a "Home" for Baltimore and Maryland's finest music makers.

BaltimoreHipHop.com
djkaboom@hotmail.com
www.baltimorehiphop.com
Maryland & Southern Delaware artists!! If you're prepared for an HONEST review, send us a PHOTO, BIO & CD and we'll highlight it on the site.

baltimorejazz.com
webmaster@baltimorejazz.com
baltimorejazz.com
Dedicated to promoting live jazz in Baltimore.

BaltimorePunk.com
webmaster@baltimorepunk.com
www.baltimorepunk.com
This website is for Baltimore Area shows only and for hardcore and punk bands only. This is primarily a shows page. If you're in a band, put on shows, write a zine, or do anything else for the scene, make sure you're listed on our pages.

Bands for Benefit
MikeCatania@bandsforbenefit.com
www.bandsforbenefit.com
An organization ran out of Westminster, Maryland. Our motto is that we hold benefit shows for "those in need". Each event raises money to help fight deadly diseases and any other causes that we feel need attention.

East Coast Bands
keny@eastcoastbands.com
www.eastcoastbands.com
A full service artist management and recording facility. Book an affordable recording session, have the artwork designed, get your duplication done, have some help with grassroots promotion, get your press kit together, we do it all.

Hagerstown Hardcore
Chad nosurrender23@yahoo.com
www.geocities.com/hagerstownhc
Show organizer/promoter for bands wishing to play/be heard in the Hagerstown, MD area and South Central PA. The place for punk, hardcore, metal, emo, indy rock, grind, death, thrash and anything underground.

Jazz Chaser
jazzchaser@comcast.net
www.jazzchaser.com
Covers the Baltimore area (includes VA and DC). We are committed to supporting, preserving and promoting America's original art form, jazz.

The Left Bank Jazz Society
www.leftbankjazz.org
Promotes Jazz through its Sunday evening Concert Series; its critically acclaimed archival CD jazz series and other activities in Baltimore.

The Local Groove
thelocalgroove@hotmail.com
thelocalgroove.com
This is my way of supporting, promoting and showing the love to the great local bands of the MD/DC/VA area and beyond, through a "grass roots, word-of-mouth, in your face" style of promoting by a fan, for the fans - my website - The Local Groove!

Maryland Night Life.com
www.marylandnightlife.com
We are a free, online, entertainment guide for all of Maryland. We have a local music section.

Maryland Spins
spins.us/maryland
A regional dance music community dedicated to Maryland dance music, electronic music, DJ's, artists and community.

MarylandParty.com
WebMaster@MDparty.com
www.mdparty.com
A comprehensive guide to live music in Maryland and surrounding states. Your band must be based in MD, VA, DC, DE, WV, or PA.

Music Monthly
musicmonthly@comcast.net
www.musicmonthly.com
Baltimore monthly music magazine. Register your band! Keep an up to date show schedule and get listed in our Artist's Directory. Submit your material for consideration for review! Send your press kits and CDs to us.

Potomac River Jazz Club
prjcweb@prjc.org
www.prjc.org
Our purpose is to preserve, encourage and promote the playing and appreciation of traditional jazz in the Washington-Baltimore metro area

Swing Baltimore
swingbaltimore@ureach.com
www.swingbaltimore.org
Devoted to the preservation and promotion of swing music.

Massachusetts

angeldustrial.com
info@angeldustrial.com
www.angeldustrial.com
News related to the local New England electro/industrial/noise scene. List your band and any shows coming up. Information is power so get the word out.

Alarm Press
chris@alarmpress.com
www.alarmpress.com
Bi-monthly magazine. Covers Northeast concerts and national and international indie music.

The Cambridge Society for Early Music
info@csem.org
www.csem.org
Our mission is to entertain, enlighten, educate and, in general, promote the rich musical culture of five centuries of Western music occurring up to the early nineteenth century.

capecodmusic.com
www.capecodmusic.com
Cape Cod has a most enviable talent pool. Rock, jazz, blues, classical, country, folk... you name it - and you'll find it here.

Concert and Venue Listings for New England
concertlistings@yahoo.com
www.geocities.com/concertlistings
Listings of concerts and hundreds of venues in MA, CT, NH, ME, RI and VT. Also, listings of hundreds of musicians' web sites.

Country Dance and Song Society
office@cdss.org
www.cdss.org
Celebrating a Living Tradition of English and Anglo-American Folk Dance and Music since 1915.

The East Coast Romper
romperchic@aol.com
www.eastcoastromper.com
A help in the music scene since its inception back in April 1994, starting out as an outlet to help the local/unsigned bands throughout Massachusetts and Rhode Island and beyond.

The Folk Arts Center of New England
fac@facone.org
www.facone.org
Dedicated to promoting traditional dance, music and related folk arts of many cultures.

Imagine News
www.imaginenews.com
Your Source for Media Arts News in the Northeast.

in newsweekly
arts@innewsweekly.com
www.innewsweekly.com
Companion publications to New England's largest Gay and Lesbian news & entertainment weekly.

Link2Rock
Kingkevinis@hotmail.com
www.link2rock.com
Focuses on the Western Mass indie rock scene.

mass musician
massmusician.com
A place where the local music community has a voice, enabling musicians to be seen and heard by their peers.

Massachusetts Spins
spins.us/massachusetts
A regional dance music community dedicated to the Massachusetts dance music, electronic music, DJ's, artists and community.

MassConcerts
MassMediaGirl@aol.com
www.massconcerts.com
Here you will find information about music and entertainment events in the northeast United States, information about specific artists.

Music For Robin
bhockett@music-for-robin.org
www.music-for-robin.org
Concerts, Folk & Celtic resources covering Mass.

The New Bedford Music Guide
newbedford.citysearch.com
Extensive coverage of the local music scene. Post your shows and events.

The New England Blues Society
dukeblues@aol.com
www.newenglandblues.com
We want to create more opportunities for the musicians and let more people know what the blues is all about. We share one common interest — we love the music and we want to support the future of the blues.

The New England Country Music Club
dm1972a@cs.com
www.necmc.homestead.com
Dedicated to the promotion and preservation of Country Music and Local Talent!

New England Entertainment Digest
jacneed@aol.com
www.jacneed.com
An entertainment monthly covering all of New England and New York.

The New England Jazz Alliance
info@nejazz.org
www.nejazz.org
Celebrating and perpetuating the tradition of jazz in New England.

New England's Music Directory
SuggestionBox@BandShack.com
bandshack.com
Listings and MP3 samples of local bands.

New England Traditional Jazz
home.attbi.com/%7Enewenglandtradjazz
Your key to traditional, plus other good jazz in New England.

Not Common
joe@notcommon.net
notcommon.cjb.net
The Massachusetts rock scene, whether it be metal, hardcore, punk, or just rock. This site is dedicated to the local rock scene and has several features to it.

Sin Promotions
Megan sinpromos@comcast.net
www.sinpromos.com
We provide promotion for New England area metal & hardcore bands through many different types of shows, battles, cd compilations, festivals, & MORE. Our site also has infinite resources for these bands.

Skope Magazine
Winifred Chane wchane@skopemagazine.com
www.skopemagazine.com
Taking local music global! All genres of Bands, PR's, Booking agents, clubs and anyone else looking to get in touch with us should submit their press packs.

tonyandpals.com
www.tonyandpals.com
In a Massachusetts band? Visit our site for info on where to send your CD for review. In addition to your CD being reviewed, we will post two of your MP3s for our visitors to sample.

townonline
www.townonline.com/arts
Free weekly paper. CD reviews and concert previews and reviews.

Valley Advocate
www.valleyadvocate.com
Springfield free weekly alternative paper. Local Bands and Happenings, updated every Thursday.

Worcester County Jazz Scene
dricklin@speakeasy.org
www.speakeasy.org/~dricklin/worcjazz
Everything you want to know about Jazz in Worcester County.

Worcester Magazine
editorial@worcestermag.com
www.worcestermag.com
Worcester's arts & entertainment weekly.

The Worcester Music Guide
worcester.citysearch.com
Extensive coverage of the local music scene. Post your shows and events.

Worcester Telegram & Gazette
www.telegram.com
Daily paper.

Wormtown
www.wormtown.org
Info on the Worcester, MA scene. Bands and performers looking to be listed in our Music Makers section should send a short description of themselves along with their web page address to John Voegtlin at j@wormtown.org.

Boston

Barrio Records
Lee Soto info@barriorecords.com
www.barriorecords.com
Boston and New England's Premiere Label, first to represent area talent regionally, nationally and internationally. Also developing new talents everywhere in all genres Salsa, Pop, R&B and others.

Bone Dry Productions
bone@bonedryproductions.com
www.bonedryproductions.com
Deals with bands from around the Boston area.

The Boston Bluegrass Union
info@bbu.org
www.bbu.org
Promoting and supporting the wealth of regional bands.

Boston Blues Society
mcg101@hotmail.com
www.bostonblues.com
A nonprofit organization dedicated to preserving and promoting the Blues.

The Boston Classical Guitar Society
www.bostonguitar.org
Our mission is to bring an awareness of the classical guitar to communities and individuals in the Boston area. A bimonthly newsletter presents music and concert reviews, biographies and informational articles on the guitar and the study of this instrument.

The Boston Globe
www.boston.com
Daily paper. Concert and CD previews and reviews, band interviews.

The Boston Herald
www.bostonherald.com
Daily paper. Covers local scene with previews, reviews and interviews.

Boston Irish Reporter
pstevens@bostonirish.com
www.bostonirish.com
New England's monthly Irish American newspaper.

The Boston Music Guide
editor_boston@citysearch.com
boston.citysearch.com
Extensive coverage of local music. Post your shows and events.

Boston Musicians' Association
info@bostonmusicians.org
www.bostonmusicians.org
You get recording rights protection, low cost instrument and equipment insurance and union privilege legal, loan, travel and mortgage services. Not enough? If you perform a job and your employer does not pay you or your group, the BMA will work on your behalf to secure your wages.

Boston Phoenix
feedback@phx.com
www.bostonphoenix.com
Entertainment magazine covering the New England region.

Boston PUNK!
Bostonpunk@bostonpunk.net
www.bostonpunk.net
You'll find info on the Boston streetpunk/hardcore punk rock scene. Please keep in mind, not every Boston band is represented here, but I try my best to include all the most active ones.

Boston Ska
grant@bostonska.com
www.bostonska.com
Check out exclusive LiveMP3s of Boston and national bands playing in and around Boston.

Boston Society of Mechanics
submit@bsm.us
www.bsm.us
One of the oldest and most enduring websites for Boston industrial bands. News, events, band profiles and other New England electronic music resources.

Boston Songwriters Workshop
www.bostonsongwriters.org
A professional organization of songwriters and composers helping each other develop in the art, craft and business of songwriting and composition.

Boston's Weekly Dig
jbennett@weeklydig.com
www.weeklydig.com
Entertainment section with music news and reviews. Covers local acts.

BostonBands.com
support@bostonbands.com
www.BostonBands.com
It is our pleasure to showcase local talent from the Boston area.

boston.cc.com *(DLC Live)*
service@clearchannel.com
www.dlclive.com
New England's largest producer of live music and other events offers something for concert fans of all musical tastes from today's new artists to the legends of years past.

Boston.com
ae.boston.com
Reviews of local music.

BostonJazzFest.com
Chris Allen centralarteryproject@yahoo.com
bostonjazzfest.com
Dedicated to providing accurate information on improvised music in the metropolitan Boston area. This site features interviews, articles and reviews on Boston area jazz artists. BostonJazzFest.com's online radio station also showcases the area's talent.

bostonlocalmusicscene.com
info@bostonlocalmusicscene.com
www.bostonlocalmusicscene.com
Looking to get your band on bostonlocalmusicscene.com? Here's what we need: 1. For you to sign up. 2. Mail us a CD and pick 3 songs you want us to stream for ya. 3. Include a photo of band or YOU.

BostonNoise.org
submit@bostonnoise.org
bostonnoise.org
Submit your noise act and MP3s to our site. If you have any doubts about whether your band is "noise" or not, read the "What is noise?" section of the FAQ.

the Buzzpan
master@buzzpan.com
www.buzzpan.com
This site is dedicated to supporting the Boston music scene. Reviews of local albums, live shows and a place to find musicians to join your band. If you want to help out with a review of a band send it on down! You can also contact me if you want to do an interview to be posted here.

Exploit Boston!
contact@exploitboston.com
www.exploitboston.com
Metro Boston's Independent Guide to Art, Culture and Entertainment.

The Folk Song Society of Greater Boston
fssgb@fssgb.org
www.fssgb.org
We are dedicated to providing opportunities for everyone to make, enjoy and support this music.

The FolkZone
George@folkzone.com
www.folkzone.com
The place to stay informed about the latest group of singer/songwriters on the Boston Acoustic Music Scene.

gothicboston
webmaster@gothicboston.org
www.gothicboston.org
The public section has resources that are readily available and useful to anyone interested. The private section is specific to the Boston NetGoth 'scene' so to speak. That means you are on, have been on, or are friends with someone on the netgoth mailing list. If you meet that description, e-mail about a login.

Improper Bostonian
music@improper.com
www.improper.com
Boston's arts & entertainment magazine.

Mic Stand
www.micstandonline.com
Our goal is to report to and serve the music lover and the music industry with informative articles and timely reviews featuring the local and national entertainment scenes. We serve our readers all things rock through the spin of our own distinct New England perspective.

MP3.Boston.com
mp3.boston.com
MP3s of local bands.

MP3s @Boston.com
music.boston.com
Welcome to MP3.Boston.com, where you can hear New England's best new music. Discover music from folk to ska that originated in towns from Portland, Maine, to Providence, Rhode Island, saved in the popular audio format MP3.

The Noise
www.thenoise-boston.com
If you're interested in what's going on in the Boston music scene, you've come to the right place. Free issues of The Noise can be picked up in clubs, music stores and other fine establishments throughout the Boston area.

Pig Pile Records
info@pigpilerecords.com
www.pigpilerecords.com
Boston's newest home for Rock, Punk, Pop, Bluegrass and any other damn good music we can find.

Purerockfury.com
deek@purerockfury.com
www.purerockfury.com
Covering the Boston area hard rock/metal scene. Includes a Local Band Spotlight.

SalsaBoston.com
salsaboston.com
Boston's premiere Latin music and dance website.

Michigan

Ann Arbor Classical Guitar Society
society@brianroberts.org
www.society.arborguitar.org
Dedicated to bringing to the community excellent and artistic performances of classical guitar music through hosting concerts, master classes and other events and to help develop a community for people to share their love of music and classical guitar.

Ann Arbor Council for Traditional Music and Dance
stein@pa.msu.edu
thedance.net/~aactmad
Dedicated to the promotion and preservation of folk music and dance.

Ann Arbor Gothic
webmaster@aagothic.com
www.aagothic.com
Post events, news and listings for your band.

The Ark
feedback@a2ark.org
www.a2ark.org
Located in Ann Arbor, we are dedicated to the enrichment of the human spirit through the presentation, preservation and encouragement of folk, roots and ethnic music and related arts.

Between the Lines
www.pridesource.com
Farmington's Gay & Lesbian news & entertainment weekly.

Capital Area Blues Society
www.cabsblues.org
Bringin' the mid-Michigan blues to ya. Every month, reviews of new album releases for your perusal.

Cola.Martini
green_hatch@yahoo.com
colamartini.cjb.net
A site for the promotion of Michigan bands. If anyone wants to suggest I add a certain band then e-mail me and you'll get hooked up phat.

Current Magazine
music@sgipub.com
ecurrent.com
Ann Arbor free monthly Arts and Entertainment magazine. Covers local music scene, news and reviews.

Everything Michigan
www.everythingmichigan.net/ent/index.htm
Post information about your band.

The Flint Folk Music Society
jim@flintfolkmusic.org
www.flintfolkmusic.org
Dedicated to promoting folk music in the Flint and Genesee County area through performances, workshops and services to folk singers and musicians.

The Flint Music Guide
flint.citysearch.com
Extensive coverage of the Flint music scene. Post your shows and events.

Folk Alliance Region Midwest
info@farmfolk.org
www.farmfolk.org
FARM invites you to contribute your talents to this supportive community. Together we promote the growth of Folk music and dance in the Midwest for the good of ourselves, our communities and future generations.

forcedmustache.net
info@forcedmustache.net
www.forcedmustache.net
Punk, Indie, Doom, Experimental, Stoner rock, Metal, IDM, Noise, Turntablism, Garage, WHATEVER. BRING IT! We are here to help YOU build a kick ass northern Michigan Music scene from Cadillac through the U.P. focusing on all-ages, alcohol-free shows.

From the Garage
Sarah noisynerd@yahoo.com
www.fromthegarage.com
This site lists punk, ska, emo, & hardcore bands and shows from all over Michigan.

The Grand Rapids Music Guide
grandrapids.citysearch.com
Extensive coverage of the Grand Rapids music scene.
Post your shows and events.

Grand River Folk Arts Society
grfasbooker@mail.grfolkarts.org
www.grfolkarts.org
Bringing to West Michigan the BEST Folk Music. If
you would like to perform, contact us.

Great Lakes Acoustic Music Association
www.geocities.com/glacoustic
To preserve, perform and promote the traditions of
bluegrass and related forms of acoustic music.

Healthy Scene
www.geocities.com/healthyscene
Dedicated to Southern Michigan's music scene. The
purpose of this site is to unite musicians, promoters,
concertgoers and anyone who loves music. This site is
a tool to spread the word about area shows, discover
and list local bands and communicate with other
Michigan music enthusiasts.

JAM RAG
jamrag@glis.net
jamrag.com
This magazine exists to promote our local community
of independent, creative musicians. Jam Rag strives to
foster a creative environment, draw attention to
talented independent artists in our area and
invigorate our local music economy.

Kalamazoo Valley Blues Association
kvba@kvba.org
www.kvba.org
To promote, educate and preserve the rich history of
blues music as it concerns Kalamazoo and its impact
on American culture and commerce in musical arts
and industry.

K'zoo Folklife Organization
peggy91193@yahoo.com
www.geocities.com/Vienna/Studio/5893
Promotes the presentation and preservation of multi-
cultural, traditional and contemporary folk music,
dance and arts for the education and enrichment of
the greater Kalamazoo community.

Lake Orion Band Site
poserskakid@canada.com
lobands.cjb.net
I'm hoping that this site will help people find out more
information about their local music scene and maybe
bring Lake Orion's bands into a web-ring type thing
for the benefit of all the bands. If you do want your
band listed on here, email me.

The Lansing Music Guide
lansing.citysearch.com
Extensive coverage of the local music scene. Post
your shows and events.

The Lansing State Journal
www.lsj.com
Daily paper. Reviews and music news.

Local-Bands.net
www.local-bands.net
Local bands, events, promotions etc....

The Magazine of Country Music
staff@magazineofcountrymusic.com
www.magazineofcountrymusic.com
A monthly publication based out of Warren since
1979. We feature national and local country music.

Michiana Listings
list@michianalistings.com
www.michianalistings.com
The easiest place to find details on events, concerts
and entertainment in and around the Southern
Michigan-Northern Indiana region. We also provide
Chicago event listings as well.

Michigan Artists
contactus@michiganartists.com
www.michiganartists.com
Support Michigan Artists with postings of history,
bios, pictures and more!

Michigan Bands dot Com
mitch@michiganbands.com
www.michiganbands.com
As a registered user you have some advantages like
posting to forums, submitting news and press releases,
add links to your band page and lots of other features.

The Michigan Daily
www.michigandaily.com
University of Michigan's student newspaper.

Michigan Hardcore
michigan@plusminusrecords.com
www.plusminusrecords.com/michigan
Shows, profiles, reviews etc.

Michigan Music
michiganmusic.webhop.net
List your shows, post your MP3s etc. I also promote
shows on my page and work with band from different
parts of Michigan so they can play shows here.

Michigan Punk
mipunk@punkandjunk.com
www.michigan.punkandjunk.com
I'm always hearing from kids in bands complaining
that they don't know where to play or how to get in.
Well, you have it all laid out for you here. We also
want this site to be the place that out-of-state punk
bands come to, to help plan the Michigan leg of their
tour and research who they may be playing with if
they know before hand.

Michigan Television Network
MichiganTV@hotmail.com
mitvnet.tripod.com/home.html
We are a non-profit organization dedicated to
recognizing local entertainment. Our mission is to
support and encourage the development of television
quality in Michigan and increase public awareness of
Michigan's home grown talent, through such means as
producing broadcast quality television programs
displaying the great wealth of talent in Michigan's
creative community.

The Michigan Times
www.themichigantimes.com
The student voice of the University of Michigan.

Michigan Womyn's Music Festival
www.michfest.com
Spread over 650 private acres, the Festival week
offers 40 performances, hundreds of workshops, a film
festival and the crafts of 150 artisans.

MLive
www.mlive.com
Michigan's home on the net. CD and concert reviews,
music news.

Music Revue
www.musicrevue.com
Grand Rapids monthly alternative paper. Reviews
indie artists. Accepts press kits for review.

Northern Express
info@northernexpress.com
www.northernexpress.com
Covering Northern Michigan. Does features on local
musicians.

Northern Michigan Bands
nmms@michigan.zzn.com
www.northernmichiganmusicscene.com
Any new CD releases, Big events, you would like me
to promote?

Oakland Press
www.theoaklandpress.com
Pontiac daily paper. Reviews CD's and concerts.

Paint Creek Folklore Society
pcfs@paintcreek.rochester.mi.us
www.paintcreek.rochester.mi.us
Our Rochester Hills based society gets together to
share folk and traditional music during monthly
meetings that include a workshop, a song swap and
jam sessions. We also present four house concerts per
year and organize one major concert.

Review Magazine (*The Review*)
www.review-mag.com
Accepts cd and cassette submissions for consideration
for review.

The Saginaw Music Guide
saginaw.citysearch.com
Extensive coverage of the local music scene. Post
your shows and events.

The Southeast Michigan Jazz Association
semja@semja.org
www.semja.org
Stresses jazz education, participates in the
organization of the Montreux Detroit Jazz Festival
and publishes a monthly newsletter, "Update" that is
now regularly posted on the web site along with
archive issues.

The State News
www.statenews.com
Michigan State University's student paper.

TRAVERSE
www.traversemagazine.com
Northern Michigan's Magazine. Does features on
local artists.

Turn Up the Radio
catchingmaybes@turnuptheradio.org
www.turnuptheradio.org
Covering the Flint area punk scene.

West Michigan Blues Society
april4757@attbi.com
www.wmbs.org
News of the Blues in Western Michigan, USA.
Promote blues appreciation by sponsoring concerts,
festivals and community events.

West Michigan Jazz Society
james.l.akins@att.net
www.wmichjazz.org
Promotes numerous events throughout the year and
supports events presented by other arts organizations,
schools and colleges in the West Michigan area. Has
offered mainstream jazz at monthly events and special
programs showcasing local and national jazz
musicians since its inception.

WGRD Local Music Page
grdbrian@yahoo.com
www.wgrd.com/localmusic
The latest news from Western Michigan bands. If you are in a local band and want to submit your news for GRD's local music page, e-mail your information to us.

Wheatland Music Organization
wmo@wheatlandmusic.org
www.wheatlandmusic.org
Our mission is to serve as a resource center for the preservation and presentation of traditional music and arts.

Detroit

Detroit Blues Society
dbsblues@flash.net
home.flash.net/~dbsblues
Our primary goal is to promote a wider appreciation for the blues by the general public and to serve the members of the Society.

Detroit City Prospects
detroitcityprospects@hotmail.com
www.msu.edu/~baileyr4/dcp_main.htm
An Entertainment Company / Record Label that is slowly taking Metro-Detroit by storm. Services include: advertising, bookings, consulting, distribution, graphic design, management, marketing, promotions and more! DCP can also direct aspiring artists / musicians to services that will fit their needs, including: recording, mixing, mastering, everything listed above and more!!

The Detroit Electronica Coalition (DEC)
dec-admin@detroitelectronica.com
www.detroitelectronica.com
An organization with the common goal of promoting the talent, recordings and performances of the area's best electronic acts and to help bring international attention back to the Detroit electronic music scene.

Detroit Free Press
readrep@freepress.com
www.freep.com

Detroit Metro Times
feedback@metrotimes.com
www.metrotimes.com
Free weekly alternative. CD reviews, concert reviews and previews.

The Detroit Music Guide
detroit.citysearch.com
Extensive coverage of the local music scene. Post your shows and events.

Detroit News
www.detnews.com
Daily paper. Music reviews and news.

DetroitCountryMusic.com
larry@detroitcountrymusic.com
www.detroitcountrymusic.com
Designed to fill a void many of us saw in the Detroit Country Music Scene; a venue to locate, promote and showcase the local talent that is in this wonderful city. While most people think of Nashville when they think of Country Music, It's amazing the incredible entertainers we all find in our own backyards.

Detroitmusic.com
www.detroitmusic.com
A free service to the Detroit music community. Please respect it and use it wisely.

Lo-Key Magazine
nobudget@vanglobal.com
www.vanglobal.com
Detroit Hip Hop magazine. Wanna be reviewed? Submit 2 promo copies of your material to us. We can also sell your CD from our online store.

Metro Times
sonic@metrotimes.com
www.metrotimes.com
Interactive guides to Detroit (& beyond). Our comprehensive Night & Day and Metropolis guides work together, creating one giant integrated directory to metro-Detroit's essential people, places and events.

The Motor City Music Foundation
motorcitymusic@hotmail.com
www.detroitmusicawards.com
Our purpose is to honor Detroit area musicians working on a national, regional and local level, to nurture music that is being made in the Detroit metropolitan area and to create a sense of music industry community that cuts across genres and styles.

Nestor in Detroit
hectop@peoplepc.com
www.nestorindetroit.com
This is my own personal web site dedicated to the city of Detroit and its great local music scene.

Online Bands
joe@onlinebands.com
www.onlinebands.com
Visit our site where you will find exciting fresh music from Detroit area bands.

Real Detroit Weekly
www.getrealdetroit.com
Weekly music paper. Covers Detroit and Ann Arbor with CD reviews, concert previews and band interviews.

Minnesota

The Association of Local Musicians
info@associationoflocalmusicians.net
home.attbi.com/~weis0205/ALM.html
Providing a forum in which local musicians, supporters and businesses can meet to network, educate and discuss issues as they pertain to the local music community.

City King Records
Mr.Baker Citykingrecords@msn.com
www.Citykingrecords.com
We are Minnesota's leading Hip Hop Label.

The Groove Garden
groovy612@hotmail.com
www.groove-garden.com
The Groove Garden has grown into a cornerstone of the jazzy groovy Minnesota music scene. It's an amateur snob kind of thing.

KXXR's Loud & Local Page
loudnlocal@93xrocks.com
www.93x.com/loudnlocal.asp
www.93x.com
If you have any news on your band you would like known. Sorry, no "musicians wanted" type stuff. Please write your story in a "news" or press release kind of format. Thanks!

Midwest Movement
info@midwestmovement.com
www.midwestmovement.com
Covering the Midwest punk scene. Reviews, interviews, spotlight bands etc.

The Minnesota Association of Songwriters (MAS)
info@mnsongwriters.org
www.mnsongwriters.org
Our mission is to inspire, educate and promote the art and craft of songwriting. As a resource, the MAS is a connection between the writer, other music oriented organizations and the music industry.

Minnesota Bluegrass and Old-Time Music Association
waltzmn@skypoint.com
www.minnesotabluegrass.org
As a member you'll be invited to participate in bluegrass and old-time music events and celebrations sharing your love and devotion for the music.

The Minnesota Daily
www.mndaily.com
World's largest student produced and managed newspaper.

The Minnesota Music Directory
www.citypages.com/mmd
City Pages Magazine's resource for local musicians.

MusicScene
scott@musicscene.org
www.musicscene.org
Resource for artists local to Minnesota. Submit your band, gig, news etc., Send your Demos and CDs for review.

The MusicScene Network
Conal Garrity gonzo@musicscene.org
www.musicscenenetwork.com
MN's largest independent listing for the Music Industry. All Local. ALL MN! Watch for us in other cities soon.

RiplFX Magazine
info@riplfx.com
music.riplfx.com
Entertainment Mag covering the St Cloud, Fargo/Moorhead region.

Ripsaw News
cdean@ripsawnews.com
www.ripsawnews.com
Duluth news and entertainment weekly.

Springboard for the Arts
info@springboardforthearts.org
www.springboardforthearts.org
Our mission is to provide affordable management information, consulting and training services designed to improve the business competence and confidence of independent artists in the Upper Midwest.

STATIC magazine
Kristi@freeSTATIConline.com
www.freestaticonline.com
Your Standing Source for Arts & Entertainment in Southern Minnesota.

Wendy V's Local Blend
wendyv2941@aol.com
www.wendyv.com
Brief notes on singer/songwriter, folk/acoustic/pop artists from Minnesota. E-mail query first before sending CDs or attachments.

Minneapolis/St. Paul

Acoustic Vision
vizier@acoustic-vision.net
www.acoustic-vision.net
Our list provides information for musicians about Twin Cities and regional venues that offer musical entertainment to the public.

Anonymous Magazine
anonymous_mag@yahoo.com
www.anonymousmag.com
Dedicated to covering local music and culture while providing a forum for a wide range of opinion. It is our goal to establish ourselves in creative communities throughout the Twin Cities as a viable and reliable resource for information, communication and promotion.

Blues on Stage
mnblues@aol.com
www.mnblues.com
Your Guide to the Blues in the Twin Cities & Around the World. If you would like your CD's reviewed please send 2 copies of new releases (or any past releases you would also like reviewed), plus any promotional material.

City Pages
www.citypages.com/mmd
Twin Cities' weekly alternative paper. Online version features the Minnesota Music Directory.

D.U. Nation Underground Hip-Hop
hype@dunation.com
www.dunation.com
Providing you with up-to-date information about upcoming concerts in the Minneapolis/St. Paul Area. As well as what's new with various clubs and acts around town. We also present you with hip hop videos from live concerts, interviews, street ballin', local events and more.

folkrocks.com
bob@folkrocks.com
www.folkrocks.com
This site is intended to be the focus of acoustic music in many genres of contemporary and traditional folk music. I have a particular interest in the musicians of Minnesota and especially those who I've come to know in the Twin Cities area.

The Foundation Magazine
info@first-avenue.com
www.first-avenue.com
Developing Arts & Music Foundation's Minneapolis based publication. DAMF supports a wide range of activities that encourage artistic development and cultural diversity in the local and regional community.

freenoise.org
wrongjohn@freenoise.org
www.freenoise.org
This site exists to provide information on "unusual" music and arts; the word "unusual" being easily replaced by "unconventional," "non-mainstream," "underground," "extreme" or by any one of a dozen other useless labels. Covers Minneapolis and Chicago.

gothling.com
admingoth@gothling.com
www.gothling.com
The Twin Cities premiere Gothic source.

The Independent Music Foundation (IMF)
www.nosmallcompass.com/imf.html
Dedicated to the booking and promotion of independent non-commercial underground music in the Minneapolis-St Paul area. Our goal is to provide a drug, alcohol and violence free alternative to existing music industry venues which have traditionally not supported truly underground music and ideas.

Minneapolis Star Tribune
www.startribune.com
Daily paper. Covers indie releases and shows.

Pulse of the Twin Cities
pulsetc.com
Weekly alternative paper. CD reviews and concert previews. Concentrates mainly on local artists.

The Rake Magazine
hans@rakemag.com
www.rakemag.com
Our main intent is to provide entertaining reading for the Twin Cities, whether that appears in columns, essays, arts criticism, profiles, feature stories or investigative reports.

Skyway
skywaynews@skywaynews.net
www.skywaynews.net
Covers the Twin Cities music scene.

SoundScene.com
info@soundscene.com
www.soundscene.com
Twin Cities concert photography and music news. Featuring great local and national artists. If you are in a band and would like to give us a scoop on what's happening in your world, we would love to hear from you. Please email us your info or fax us a press release.

St. Paul Pioneer Press
www.twincities.com/mld/pioneerpress
Daily paper.

tchardcore.com
nicole@tchardcore.com
www.tchardcore.com
Covering the Twin Cities' hardcore scene.

The Twin Cities Alternative Shows List
sparks@tiny.net
www.visi.com/~sparks
A calendar of upcoming alternative music shows in the Twin Cities area.

Twin Cities Bands
email@twincitiesbands.com
www.twincitiesbands.com
Events, local band listings, message boards and much more!

Twin Cities Jazz Society
tcjs@attbi.com
www.tcjs.org
We sponsor concerts, workshops and education programs in area schools and we have just begun a new scholarship program to help rising young local talent. Most of our effort goes into publishing our monthly award winning Jazz Notes newsletter.

The Twin Cities Music Guide
editor_twincities@citysearch.com
twincities.citysearch.com
Extensive coverage of the local music scene. Post your shows and events.

Twin Cities Music Network
email@tcmusic.net
www.tcmusic.net
A place for musicians to find the resources they need to be as successful as possible. Whether you're looking for information about how to write a grant proposal, or where your next gig will be, TCMN is a great place to start. List performances, band info and sell your CDs online.

Mississippi

Clarion-Ledger
www.clarionledger.com
Jackson daily paper.

The Daily Mississippian
arts@thedmonline.com
www.thedmonline.com
The University of Mississippi's student newspaper.

Dead Man Dancing Promotions
deadman@deadmandancing.com
www.deadmandancing.com
The bare-bones source for the Hattiesburg music scene.

Hattiesburg American
www.hattiesburgamerican.com
Daily paper. Thursday's edition contains an Entertainment Guide, where you can learn about local bands and events.

Lee County Courier
leecourier@netbci.com
www.leecountycourier.com
Tupelo daily paper.

Living Blues Magazine
lblues@olemiss.edu
www.livingblues.com
A bimonthly magazine published by the University of Mississippi. The premiere source on the blues since its founding in 1970.

The Magnolia State Bluegrass Association
ed@tunesource.com
www.geocities.com/magnoliabluegrass
Formed to promote, preserve, produce, publicize and perpetuate Bluegrass music and to provide a fellowship of Bluegrass musicians and fans in the Deep South. Our main area of membership and influence includes Mississippi, Louisiana and Alabama, but the association is open to members residing in all states.

The Mississippi Delta Blues Society
www.mudcat.org/mdbs.cfm
We recognize our obligation to champion blues in the Delta - the land where this art form began.

The Mississippi Link
www.mississippilink.com
Jackson weekly paper.

Mississippi Raves
msraves@msraves.com
www.msraves.com
Local rave information including events calendar, artist profiles, promoter contact data, venue data, pictures and much more.

The Northeast Mississippi Daily Journal
www.djournal.com
Tupelo daily paper.

Planet Weekly
feedback@planetweekly.com
www.planetweekly.com
A weekly newspaper covering the arts, entertainment and public issues in the Jackson Metro area.

The Reflector
www.reflector-online.com
Mississippi State University's student paper.

slawdawg
www.slawdawg.com
Hattiesburg music site focuses on local bands with a metal edge.

Missouri

Becki's Land of Local Music
beckibess@hotmail.com
www.geocities.com/electricpear
Information on local bands in the states of Kansas and Missouri, including the most comprehensive list of local band links you can find, pictures of local bands, lyrics to songs, a fabulous list of upcoming concerts you should attend, plus much much more!

The Blues Society of the Ozarks
bsoeditor@yahoo.com
www.ozarksblues.org
Our goal is to encourage performance of the blues at clubs, at festivals and on radio. CD and live show reviews.

Central Plains Jamband Society
john.bollin@cpjs.org
www.cpjs.org
An organization that promotes the arts, music and spirit of what jamband music has to offer the local, regional and national communities.

The Columbia Daily Tribune
www.columbiatribune.com

Columbia Gothic Community
ErmaZimmerman@earthlink.net
goths.mu.org
Please send me any information you would like added to this site.

The Columbia Missourian
www.digmo.com
Daily paper.

Columbia360.com
submit@columbia360.com
www.columbia360.com
List your band, event, news etc.

Heavy Frequency
heather@heavyfrequency.com
www.heavyfrequency.com
We aim to provide recognition and respect for the talented, promising heavy metal/hardcore bands emerging from the depths of the Midwest underground. The good metal and hardcore acts are not always mainstream label groups.

Lake of the Ozarks Blues Society
www.lotobs.org
Our goal is to raise awareness and appreciation of LIVE Blues music at Lake of the Ozarks.

Maneater
maneater@themaneater.com
www.themaneater.com
The independent student newspaper of the University of Missouri - Columbia.

Misery's Kaos
ErmaZimmerman@earthlink.net
goths.mu.org
The homepage of the Columbia, Missouri Gothic Community.

Missouri Area Bluegrass Committee
bluegrassamerica@starband.net
www.bluegrassamerica.com

MObands.com
www.mobands.com
Our mission is to bring Missouri bands and artists together as one unit, in order to share ideas and opportunities related to the creativity of its members, as well as the growth of their careers.

MOHeads.com
brooks@moheads.com
www.moheads.com
A MO Head is a resident of the state of Missouri who considers him/herself a fan of the jamband genre. Post your news, listings, events etc.

The Pulp
ron@readthepulp.com
www.readthepulp.com
Springfield's alternative entertainment news magazine.

Unsigned Hype: Midwest Promoter
unsignedhype@stlhiphop.com
unsignedhype.stlhiphop.com
Artist promotion and services. Test the market in the Midwest or find hot new Midwest rap & hip hop talent!

Voxmagazine
vox@missouri.edu
www.voxmagazine.com
Columbians weekly guide to area new, arts and entertainment.

Kansas City

91-9 Local Music Network
www.91-9.com/home/localmusic/musicnetwork
www.91-9.com
Are you a Kansas City artist who wants mass exposure? Are you an avid fan who wants to share good music? We encourage everyone to make the most of our servers! Just follow the file submission requirements on our site and upload your music.

Kansas City Blues Society
info@kcbluessociety.com
www.kcbluessociety.com

Kansas City Christian Concerts
kcconcerts@kc.rr.com
webpages.charter.net/kcconcerts
There are many coffeehouses in Kansas City that you might not have known about. Find out where and when on this page.

Kansas City Concert Page
drrnmrsh@birch.net
www.tfs.net/~drrnmrsh/concert.html
Submit your Kansas City Concert.

The Kansas City Guitar Society
KCGuitarSociety@aol.com
www.kansascityguitarsociety.org
Established to foster appreciation and encourage artistry of the classical guitar in the greater Kansas City community.

Kansas City Hardcore
jon@kansascityhardcore.com
www.kansascityhardcore.com
Covering local Core, Indie and Metal Bands. News, reviews, shows etc.

The Kansas City Jazz Ambassadors
info@jazzkc.org
www.jazzkc.org
Dedicated to the development and promotion of this vibrant, historic and uniquely American art form. Publish Jam Magazine. To submit CDs for review, please email us for instructions on how to submit.

Kansas City Magazine
lbennett@abartapub.com
www.kcmag.com

The Kansas City Music Guide
kansascity.citysearch.com
Extensive coverage of the local music scene. Post your shows and events.

The Kansas City Star
www.kansascity.com
Daily paper.

kcconcerts.com
kcconcerts@kcconcerts.com
kcconcerts.com
Local music news and shows.

kcska.com
www.kcska.com
The electronic home of Kansas City's SKA scene.

Pitch Weekly
feedback@pitch.com
www.pitch.com
Kansas City free weekly alternative. Reviews new CDs, focuses on local music scene.

Serious Vanity
dana@seriousvanity.com
www.seriousvanity.com
Reviews for local KC area shows, as well as CDs and mp3s from all over the web.

Songwriters Circle of Kansas City
DavidHakan@kc.rr.com
www.songwriterscircle.org
To support original songwriting and songwriters in the greater Kansas City area. To help each other get noticed. To cooperate to provide more performance venues for original songs. To assist songwriters in their creative and business development.

Too Much Rock
toomuchrock.com
Kansas City based resource. Pictures, CD reviews and reviews of local shows. You want me to review something? Send it my way.

The Zone
danielle@thezone.org
www.thezone.org
Kansas City's source for local music. News, reviews, classifieds etc.

Willow
crosscurrents@kc.rr.com
www.songwriterscircle.org
A Kansas City based, women-operated production company committed to empowering women by creating, producing and sustaining women-centered culture.

St. Louis

The Commonspace
info@thecommonspace.org
www.thecommonspace.org
A progressive, monthly, online magazine dedicated to grassroots civics and culture in the city of St. Louis and its surrounding region.

gtp-inc.com
shaunbrooks@gtp-inc.com
www.gtp-inc.com
Dedicated to the St. Louis music scene.

LameBasement.com
lamebas@lamebasement.com
www.lamebasement.com
Provides unsigned original bands and artists with a place to have their music heard and video clips seen. At this time, this is a FREE service and no guarantees that we will post everything that is sent are implied.

THE metro i
www.themetroi.com
The arts & entertainment authority of St. Louis. Local band coverage and reviews.

Night Times
wordgirl@nighttimes.com
www.nighttimes.com
The premier St. Louis music magazine offering CD reviews, show previews and artist interviews.

playback
Laura Hamlett editor@playbackstl.com
www.playbackstl.com
St. Louis Pop Culture. Want to see your name in print? Send your news, updates and pleas for publicity to us.

Post Mortem Productions
Rose info@rosemortem.com
www.postmortem.us.com
St. Louis based Production Company hosting regular events for gothic and associated genre artists.

Pulse
pulse@stl-pulse.com
www.stl-pulse.com
St. Louis' music source. Downloads, featured artists, events and more!

The Riverfront Times
www.rftstl.com
St. Louis free weekly arts and entertainment paper. Covers local music scene.

Spin City Record, L.L.C.
Clifton Wade III cwade@spincityrecordz.com
www.spincityrecordz.com
An Independent Record Label formed to identify, develop, produce and market musical artist from St. Louis and the middle of the U.S. The genres of music consist of Hip-Hop, Rap, Neo-Soul, Integrated Soul, R&B and Jazz.

The St. Louis Concert Web
Plugthis@stl-music.com
www.stl-music.com
To rave about your favorite concert experience, review the shows at the clubs or rate new CD releases. Bands can also submit a short preview for an upcoming play date in the St. Louis area.

St. Louis Donna Page
o2bkjn@swbell.net
home.swbell.net/o2bkjn
Featuring Cajun and Zydeco and this weeks' music and dance events.

St. Louis Front Page Entertainment Guide
editor@slfp.com
www.slfp.com
A St. Louis Internet-only publication. Post your event.

St. Louis FolkFire Music and Dance
webmaster@folkfire.org
www.folkfire.org
A free resource for and about folk and ethnic groups and events in the U.S and particularly around the central area of St. Louis.

St. Louis Gothic
Skeletal13@hellmail.zzn.com
www.stlouisgothic.com
Your source for St. Louis darkwave events and information!

St. Louis Magazine
www.stlmag.com
Insight into city issues and what's happening in the arts, sports, politics, the media and more.

St. Louis Post Dispatch
www.stltoday.com
Daily paper. Concert previews and reviews, CD reviews.

The St. Louis Music Guide
stlouis.citysearch.com
Extensive coverage of the local music scene. Post your shows and events.

St. Louis Punk Page
jerome@stlpunk.com
www.stlpunk.com
To get your band on our site send us an email letting us know your band name and what you would like your password to be.

STLBlues
stlouisblues@swbell.net
www.stlblues.net
My mission to bring to you the Blues talent that calls St. Louis home. E-mail us a picture and 250 words that describe you and your band. Add any contact and booking info you want and we'll see you get a spot in our Band Info section!

stlhiphop.com
bgyrl4life webmaster@stlhiphop.com
stlhiphop.com
Consists of a 24/7 local hip hop radio station, networking, search engine, crew and dj database, graffiti, calendar, chat, boards, radio stations, dj mixes, live broadcasts, videos, mp3s, a live radio show and a record store.

STLmetal.com
stl_metal@yahoo.com
www.stlmetal.com
Dedicated to the St. Louis, MO and surrounding area metal bands. If you would like to submit your band, ideas, or anything else, feel free to send it in.

stlouis.com *Local Music Page*
webmaster@stlouis.com
www.stlouis.com/music/localbands.html
Does your band have a web site? E-mail us to get your band linked.

STLtoday.com
www.stltoday.com/entertainment
Extensive local music coverage. News, reviews, spotlights etc. Submit your band's info.

Montana

The Billings Gazette
www.billingsgazette.com
Daily paper.

The Bozeman Daily Chronicle
www.gomontana.com
Daily paper. Reviews and concert previews.

The Butte Jazz Society
jazzz@in-tch.com
www.buttejazz.org
A music and cultural education organization dedicated to the preservation and enhancement of the area's rich Jazz heritage through performance, scholarship, education and community partnerships.

End of Transmission
scandabolical@yahoo.com
www.satokomag.com/eot
A small-time, xeroxed publication based in Billings, MT. Features include interviews with local punk bands, artwork, opinion articles and lots of childish toilet humor.

Exponent
exponent.montana.edu
Montana State University's student newspaper.

Hansen Music
pat@hansenmusic.net.
www.hansenmusic.net
Shouldn't your Billings band be here? If you would like to get your band linked on this page, complete with large thumbnail images, a short description of your band and a link to your bands website.

Lively Times
writeus@livelytimes.com
www.livelytimes.com
Montana's most complete arts and entertainment calendar.

Made in Montana Music
labree@midrivers.com
www.midrivers.com/~labree
Our recordings represent all styles and types of music from the old standards to new country and feature some original songs by some excellent local artists.

The Missoulian Daily
www.missoulian.com
Daily paper. CD and concert reviews, interviews and previews.

The Missoula Folklore Society
mtfolk@montanafolk.org
www.montanafolk.org
Dedicated to promoting, preserving, enjoying and sharing the music, dance, arts, crafts and skills of contemporary and traditional cultures and generally having a pretty good time.

The Missoula Independent
www.missoulanews.com
Free weekly alternative paper. CD and concert reviews, interviews and previews.

Montana Kaimin
www.kaimin.org
The University of Montana's student paper.

Montana Punk
brent@mtpunk.com
mtpunk.com
Your guide to punk/underground music and DIY happenings in and about our fair state. Here, you'll find the scoop on activism, bands, radio shows, venues and zines. There's also a state-wide showlist, a discussion board, sound clips, pictures and much, much more.

Nebraska

BluesGroup
blues@bluesgroup.com
www.bluesgroup.com
Official news network of the Omaha Blues Society.

The Daily Nebraskan
www.dailynebraskan.com
University of Nebraska's student paper.

The Gateway
www.unogateway.com
University of Nebraska, Omaha's student paper.

KIBZ Radio's Local Bands Page
luna@kibz.com
www.kibz.com/localbandscalendar.html
Listings of the local bands you can find in and around Lincoln. If you want your band's website or shows listed e-mail us.

Lazy-i(lazyeye)
timmymac29@aol.com
www.timmcmahan.com/lazyeye.htm
Interviews and band profiles, reviews and hype. The focus is on the indie music scene. Although there's a special emphasis on the best original bands in the Omaha area, Lazyeye also offers interviews, stories and reviews about national indie bands.

The Lincoln Journal Star
www.journalstar.com
Daily paper. Interviews, previews and reviews.

Omaha Blues Society
tsedivy@yahoo.com
www.omahablues.com
We are dedicated to promoting blues music in the greater Omaha-Lincoln area.

Omaha World Herald
www.omaha.com
Daily paper. Band interviews, CD and concert previews and reviews.

OMAHAMUSIC.com
webmaster@omahamusic.com
www.omahamusic.com
Official website of the Omaha Musician's Association. Band and event listings.

OmahaSongWriters.com
www.omahasongwriters.com
Created and developed to help promote, encourage and market local area singer-songwriters.

The Reader
lesliep@thereader.com
www.thereader.com
The leader of alternative news in the Omaha, Council Bluffs and Lincoln areas.

SLAM Omaha
bubba@slamomaha.com
www.slamomaha.com
Local music, featured bands, new releases etc.

Someday Never
somedaypress@yahoo.com
www.somedaynever.com
A great Omaha music web site with extensive band list, show calendar and reviews.

Nevada

Las Vegas

BrownBagMag.com
kelly@brownbagmag.com
www.brownbagmag.com
Punk, ska and emo source. News, reviews, interviews with local bands and those playing in Las Vegas.

The Guitar Society of Las Vegas
finegtrplayer@yahoo.com
www.gslv.org
We assist in the promotion, education and appreciation of the acoustic guitar and develop and administer programs to enhance and enrich members' musical experiences.

Jazzlasvegas.com
jazzlasvegas@mediaband.net
www.jazzlasvegas.com
Dedicated to the proliferation and dissemination of music based information with the emphasis on jazz in the Las Vegas area.

Las Vegas City Life
www.lvcitylife.com
Besides featuring hard-hitting news and opinion, CityLife also covers progressive entertainment and culture, which includes an extensive music section with profiles and reviews of musicians, MCs and DJs.

The Las Vegas Jamband Society
www.lvjambandsociety.com
Becoming a member means you will have lots of good times, meet some beautiful people and be a part of a wonderful and sometimes spiritual musical culture we call Jamband.

Las Vegas Jazz Society
www.vegasjazz.org
LVJS publishes Jazz Notes bimonthly, reporting what's happening in Las Vegas jazz. It includes concerts, club dates and special events; reviews of concerts and CDs; musician profiles; and jazz programming on KUNV 91.5-FM.

Las Vegas Local Music
info@lvlocalmusicscene.com
www.lvlocalmusicscene.com
Think of it as the place to be in cyber space where you can read about, sample music and see where your favorite bands appearing next.

Las Vegas Mercury
gschumacher@lasvegasmercury.com
www.lasvegasmercury.com
Weekly publication. Includes local music information.

The Las Vegas Music Guide
lasvegas.citysearch.com
Extensive coverage of the local music scene. Post your shows and events.

Las Vegas Weekly
www.lasvegasweekly.com
Free alternative weekly paper. Covers Las Vegas music scene. Extensive coverage of both local and touring bands.

LasVegasLocalMusic.com
webmaster@lasvegaslocalmusic.com
www.lasvegaslocalmusic.com
Event calendar, band listings, MP3s and more!

LasVegasMusic.us
www.lasvegasmusic.us
Add a link or event. Become a featured artist.

LVLOCALMUSICSCENE.com
info@lvlocalmusicscene.com
www.lvlocalmusicscene.com
The site was created to provide a virtual headquarters for the local music scene, so that Las Vegas musicians and music enthusiasts can find all the information they seek in one place.

Lv Punk: The Las Vegas Punk Scene
Jason@lvpunk.com
www.lvpunk.com

Metal & Rock of Las Vegas
webmaster@darksoul7.com
www.darksoul7.com
Band and show information for the Las Vegas scene.

Neon
www.lvrj.com
Entertainment section of the Las Vegas Review-Journal.

Sin City Sounds
news@SinCitySounds.com
www.sincitysounds.com
If you are in a Las Vegas area band or manage a local venue, be sure to e-mail us your news and events. And if you'd like to invite us to your next show, or send us a CD for review, that's cool too.

sincitymusic.com
sincitymusic@hotmail.com
www.sincitymusic.com
In-depth information on the Las Vegas music scene, both local and national.

Stardoom Labs
shylow@stardoom.com
www.stardoom.com
Las Vegas local artists and bands showcased.

vegas.com
www.vegas.com
Calendar of local music events.

vegashustler.com
info@vegashustler.com
www.vegashustler.com
The brutally honest underground guide to what's worth seeing in Sin City. Has a local music section.

Reno

Reno Blues Society
soulman@renoblues.org
www.renoblues.org

Reno Gazette-Journal
www.rgj.com
Daily paper. Previews concerts and CD's, interviews bands.

Reno Hard Core
Jim jim@twicemusic.com
www.twicemusic.com/rhc.html
Reviews of indie, punk rock, hardcore, metal, emo etc. CD reviews, local area show listing. Will help with booking shows in the Reno NV area.

The Reno Music Guide
reno.citysearch.com
Extensive coverage of the local music scene. Post your shows and events.

Reno News & Review
www.newsreview.com
Reno's news and entertainment weekly.

The Reno Performer
reviews@renoperformer.com
www.renoperformer.com
A meeting place for Entertainers & their audience.

Reno Regional Workshop *NSAI*
doug@nostrebor.net
www.softcom.net/users/nostrebor
A professional trade organization that meets twice a month for the express purpose of empowering songwriters to improve on their craft and career.

RenoPunk.com
jeannejo@hotmail.com
www.renopunk.com
I consider this page to be part of the punk movement but it encompasses any style of music as long as they bear punk ethics. Send demo's CD's LP's 7in's to be reviewed.

New Hampshire

The Alternative News
thealternativenews@comcast.net
www.thealternativenews.com
Our mission is to bring various music communities together by keeping readers aware of and informed about bands, events, clubs/venues and music scenes in various parts of the country; especially in and around New England.

Guide to Portsmouth
portcity@portsmouthnh.com
www.portsmouthnh.com
Post your shows and band info online.

HIPPOPRESS
hippo@hippopress.com
www.hippopress.com
New Hampshire's alternative publication.

Jam Music Magazine
letters@jammusicmagazine.com
www.jammusicmagazine.com
New Hampshire's premier arts and entertainment online resource.

Monadnock Folklore Society
msh4u@monad.net
www.monadnockfolk.org
Providing new venues for performers, offering support to local musicians' projects and providing educational services in the folk arts to the communities of Southern New Hampshire.

New England Rock
info@newenglandrock.com
www.newenglandrock.com
Show listings of your favorite local New England Rock Bands. This site also includes an upcoming events calendar, a musician's classified section, New England Rock Bands web site listings and shows and more. Our newest addition to the website is our "CD reviews section".

The New Hampshire Country Music Association
dondar@prodigy.net
www.nhcma.com
An organization of volunteers dedicated to promoting country music talent throughout the State of New Hampshire.

New Hampshire Women's Music Festival
info@nhwomensmusicfest.org
www.nhwomensmusicfest.org
This festival is a wonderful celebration of the many talented women musicians in New Hampshire.

NH Events
www.nhevents.com
List your shows or events.

NH ROCKS.COM
info@nhrocks.com
www.nhrocks.com
New Hampshire's source for live entertainment.

NHTunes.com
webmaster@nhtunes.com
nhtunes.com
A site all about local New Hampshire music. Our site allows artists to promote themselves or their band absolutely free - list your band, post your MP3 etc.

Peterborough Folk Music Society
dnpyles@acousticmusic.com
www.acousticmusic.com/frames/pfms.htm
Dedicated to bringing the most innovative, entertaining and diverse musicians to the Monadnock Region.

Portsmouth Herald
www.portsmouthherald.com
Daily paper.

The Portlsmouth Music Guide
portsmouth.citysearch.com
Extensive coverage of the local music scene. Post your shows and events.

Showcase Magazine
www4.fosters.com/pages/entertainment/showcase.asp
Dover weekly arts & entertainment magazine. Comes in the Foster's Daily Democrat newspaper.

Spotlight Magazine
spotlight@seacoastonline.com
www.seacoastonline.com/calendar/nightlife.htm
Portsmouth's arts & entertainment magazine.

The Union Leader
www.theunionleader.com
Manchester daily paper. Interviews, previews and reviews bands. Accepts CD's for review.

New Jersey

The Acoustic Musicians Guild
denise_and_son@yahoo.com
www.amg.org
An organization created to promote and preserve the tradition of acoustic music.

Aquarian Weekly
www.theaquarian.com
Covers the area of New York, New Jersey and Connecticut

Atlantic City Jazz Foundation
dorian-g@usa.net
community.nj.com/cc/acjf
Serves as an advocacy to stimulate the exposure, to promote the growth and to foster the inter-generational awareness, appreciation & enjoyment of Jazz Music.

The Atlantic City Music Guide
atlanticcity.citysearch.com
Extensive coverage of the local music scene. Post your shows and events.

Basically-HipHop.Com
maxjeromeo@basically-hiphop.com
www.basically-hiphop.com
We're creating A HipHop Web Site With Content That Represents UnderGround-Mainstream-Old School, Also Promoting Online Up and Coming New Jersey Emcees.

Blow Up Radio
lazlo@blowupradio.com
blowupradio.tripod.com/main.html
Online station that plays the music of New Jersey bands. Also posts news, reviews, downloads and concert listings.

The Bomb Shelter
thebombsheltercollective@yahoo.com
www.punkrockonline.com/shows
Lists punk rock shows in the New Jersey area.

Central NJ Song Circle
info@jerseysongs.com
www.jerseysongs.com
A friendly, casual, in-the-round get-together for testing out new songs, swapping old ones, or just hanging out and picking up pointers.

Chorus and Verse
editor@chorusandverse.com
www.chorusandverse.com
We want to give our readers exposure and insight into the New Jersey scene. Our goal is to present the legendary history, current noise and future buzz to all music fans.

The Composers Guild of New Jersey
wanderso@mail.slc.edu
www.cgnj.org

The Crooked Beat
feedback@crooked-beat.com
www.crooked-beat.com
Band pages and gig listings for NY and NJ bands.

The Folk Project
Secretary@FolkProject.org
www.research.att.com/psa/folkproject
A folk music and dance organization which sponsors or organizes a wide variety of folk music and dance activities in the Northern New Jersey area.

If you know of a resource that should be listed, please contact

indiebible@rogers.com

gardenstatepunk.com
Chrissy indkgeek@aol.com
www.gardenstatepunk.com
Covering the NJ punk scene.

The Hammonton Gazette
Jim Calder jcalder@mail.hammontongazette.com
www.hammontongazette.com
*Our newspaper contains an extensive Entertainment
section including information and reviews for music,
movies, books, shows and other issues within the
industry. I have started writing a column where in
which I review unknown bands and CD's.*

HardcoreNJ.com
xhardcorenjx@aol.com
www.hardcorenj.com
*Created to keep people updated with the NJ
metal/hardcore scene. Band news, shows etc.*

Hoboken Music Scene
www.hobokeni.com
List your band, post your upcoming events.

Home News Tribune
www.thnt.com
New Brunswick daily paper.

The Hudson Current
current@hudsonreporter.com
www.hudsoncurrent.com
*Hoboken weekly news and entertainment paper. Did
you just open a show? Is your band playing
somewhere? Sponsoring an event? Let us know. Send
us your photos and/or information.*

JenAud Music
Jenaud jenaudmusic@yahoo.com
www.geocities.com/jenaudmusic
*Promotions, website design and set-up, photography...
all resources for musicians BY musicians! Located in
central NJ. We work one on one with you to provide
what you need on a free or very low cost budget. We
do this because we love what we do and take pride in
our work.*

Jersey Beat
jim@jerseybeat.com
www.jerseybeat.com
*Our motto: You try to play it, we try to like it. Serving
the DIY community since 1982. Will accept all CDs
(we prefer punk), but local releases (from New Jersey
and NYC-area acts) get the highest priority.*

Jersey Jam
www@jerseyjam.com
www.JerseyJam.com
*If you're an artist, or in a band, you may add your
web site to the list! The JerseyJam staff will
continually visit your web site, listen to your music,
see what you're up to and decide if you should be the
SpotLight Artist of the month!*

Jersey Shore Jazz and Blues Foundation
webmaster@jsjbf.com
www.jsjbf.com
*Formed to preserve, promote and perpetuate Jazz,
Blues and other indigenous music forms here in New
Jersey.*

JERSEYMUSIC.COM
jerseymusic.com
*This site is a place for New Jersey musicians and
music-lovers to connect, share information and get
involved in the Garden State's thriving local music
scene.*

Muziq For Everyone
aclatina@hotmail.com
aclatina.tripod.com
All sorts of information on NJ Bands.

NBGroove.com
WebMaster@NBGroove.com
www.nbgroove.com
*Your guide to New Brunswick nightlife and music
scene. If you would like to have your music calendar
added to our list, please e-mail me.*

New Brunswick Underground
nbu@nbunderground.com
www.nbunderground.com
*Serving Central New Jersey since 1996. We do NOT
guarantee that your music will be reviewed. We DO
guarantee that it will be listened to.*

New Jersey Bands
webmaster@njbands.org
www.njbands.org
*Paid service that posts a variety of information about
New Jersey bands.*

New Jersey Country Music Association
CowboyMC@netzero.net
www.geocities.com/njcma.geo
*Dedicated to "Keep Country Alive" by promoting
Country Music and Dance.*

New Jersey Jazz Society
kate3@casano.com
www.njjs.org
*The Society publishes a monthly magazine, Jersey
Jazz, which contains feature articles, photos, music
calendars, concert reviews and Society information
and is free with membership.*

NewJerseyRocks.com
webmaster@njrocks.com
www.njrocks.com
The best portal to the entire New Jersey Music scene.

Newark Arts Alliance
info@newarkartsalliance.org
www.newarkartsalliance.org
*Dedicated to developing a sense of community in
Newark through the arts, to provoke thought,
stimulate the imagination and celebrate the diversity
of the human spirit.*

Newark Post
www.ncbl.com/post
Daily paper.

The Newark Star-Ledger
www.starledger.com
*Daily paper. Considers submissions of press kit
materials if the band is playing in the Northern New
Jersey area.*

Night & Day
www.ndmag.com
*New Jersey's premiere music magazine. Covers
movies, concerts, local bands, theatre, dining,
celebrity interviews and travel.*

NJ.com *Music*
www.nj.com/music
Events and listings of local music.

NJMUSIC.net
info@njmusic.net
www.njmusic.net
*Your complete guide to the music scene in the Great
State Of New Jersey. Post your band's info.*

Njmusicsource.com
chris@njmusicsource.com
www.njmusicsource.com
*Send us your show information/news, press kits and
anything else.*

Planet Verge
planetverge@journalist.com
www.planetverge.com
*A magazine that interviews both and-and-coming and
established punk/rock bands when they tour in NJ.
We'll advertise your band's website in out next issue!
You'll gain fans from around the world, sell CD's and
get people to your shows!*

PressofAtlanticCity.com
dbergen@pressofac.com
www.pressofatlanticcity.com
Covers local music scene.

The Princeton Folk Music Society
princetonfolk@att.net
www.princetonol.com/groups/pfms
*We have encouraged the growth of folk music in
central New Jersey for over 35 years.*

The Princeton Songwriters
Anne Freeman princetonsongs@aol.com
community.nj.com/cc/princetonsongwriters
*Princeton chapter of the Nashville Songwriters
Association. Formed to provide aspiring songwriters
with educational activities to promote learning the
art, craft and business of songwriting.*

Showcase
info@jerseyarts.com
www.jerseyarts.com
*Your online guide to arts and culture in New Jersey.
The site serves as the online component of the
Discover Jersey Arts initiative - a project designed to
increase the awareness of and participation in the arts
in New Jersey.*

Silly Rabbit Zine
mindtwist697@aol.com
www.sillyrabbit.cjb.net
*Covering the NJ/NY punk scene. Our main goal is to
give the right exposure to the bands we feel deserve it,
because we love it and this is our passion.*

A Social Disease.com
chris@asocialdisease.com
www.asocialdisease.com
*Covering metal, punk, indie, hardcore, rock and hip
hop in New Jersey.*

South Jersey Underground.com
Bob Headley sjunderground@aol.com
www.southjerseyunderground.com
*This site is the source for finding out what's going on
in and around the South Jersey Hardcore, Punk and
Metal scene. I do links, show listings, show/cd
reviews, show booking and I take pictures at shows. I
also do referrals for bands looking to play or clubs
looking for bands.*

SouthJerseyClubs.com
info@southjerseyclubs.com
www.southjerseyclubs.com
*Your online source for local bands and live music
venues in South Jersey and the Philadelphia area. It is
our goal to provide you with up to date information
about the hottest live music clubs and live music
events in the area while providing links and
information on local bands.*

Steppin' Out Magazine
stepoutmag@aol.com
www.steppinoutmagazine.com
North Jersey/NYC music weekly.

TheNJScene.com
mike@thenjscene.com
thenjscene.com
We'd like to connect all of the show-goers in the state and give them a place to read news about their favorite local bands, get the scoop on what shows are happening in the future and more importantly provide a forum for meeting and discussing with similar (but yet oh-so-different) people.

The Traditional MusicLine
info@fiddlingwithwords.com
fiddlingwithwords.com/tradml.htm
The only monthly publication of its kind. A comprehensive calendar for acoustic folk music concerts, dances and festivals. An average of 300 monthly listings covering an approximate 4-hour radius from New York City and Long Island. It's always FREE to list your shows and events.

The Tri-State Jazz Society
harryschmoll2@comcast.net
www.tristatejazz.com
Dedicated to the preservation and presentation of traditional and Dixieland jazz.

Tri-State Hardcore and Punk
webmasterStumpy@tristatepunk.com
www.tristatepunk.com
Our overall goal is to make sure the tri-state area (NJ, NY, CT and PA), is informed about all musical events coming through the area (we know it should actually be called Four-State Punk).

New Mexico

Albuquerque Journal
www.abqjournal.com
Daily paper. Interviews, previews and reviews local scene.

The Albuquerque Music Guide
albuquerque.citysearch.com
Extensive coverage of the local music scene. Post your shows and events.

Albuquerque Tribune
www.abqtrib.com
Daily paper.

Alibi
rockstar@alibi.com
alibi.com
Albuquerque's weekly arts & entertainment paper. Extensive local music coverage.

Daily Lobo
www.dailylobo.com
University of New Mexico's student paper.

The New Mexico Folk Music & Dance Society
folkmads@nmia.com
www.folkmads.org
An organization dedicated to promoting and teaching traditional music and dance.

New Mexico Music Portal
info@nmmusic.com
www.nmmusic.com
Band listings, events, classifieds etc.

NewMexicoEvents.com
calendar@nmevents.com
www.newmexicoevents.com
Tell us what you're doing. If you're a performer, submit your event. All we need are names, places, dates, times, entry prices, age restrictions and any other information that you feel needs to be known.

Santa Fe New Mexican
www.sfnewmexican.com
Daily paper.

Santa Fe Reporter
culture@sfreporter.com
www.sfreporter.com
Weekly news and culture paper. Covers local music scene. Check our website to see how to get your event listed in the Arts & Culture Calendar.

Santa Fe Times
www.santafetimes.com
Daily paper.

Southwest Traditional and Bluegrass Music Association
manasounds@aol.com
www.southwestpickers.org
Providing acoustic music to New Mexico and regional audiences on a yearly basis and promoting the furtherance of acoustic music by providing jams and workshops for all ages.

Taos News
www.taosnews.com
Weekly paper. Spotlights local and regional music, interviews, previews and reviews.

WIMINFEST
wiminfest@hotmail.com
www.wiminfest.org
An annual three day celebration of women's music, comedy and culture in Albuquerque, NM.

New York

A Place for Jazz.
zjazz3@aol.com
timesunion.com/communities/jazz
An organization whose programs include a fall concert series, public workshops, school-based clinics and general support of Jazz and its musicians in the Albany area.

The Albany Music Guide
albany.citysearch.com
Extensive coverage of the local music scene. Post your shows and events.

Albany Goths
Myron Getman baron_army@albanygoths.com
www.albanygoths.com
A Goth resource page, mailing list and calendar for upstate New York. Bands are encouraged to send information for posting.

Albany Times Union
www.timesunion.com
Daily paper. Reviews new CD releases.

AlmostPunk NY
AlmostPunkNY@aol.com
www.geocities.com/almostpunkny
Promoting local punk rock bands in the New York, Jersey and other surrounding areas. We are here to provide you fellow rockers with up to the minute NEWS on these kick ass bands... and... hopefully... help these budding artists get a little more exposure.

The American Music Group
amgorg@pipeline.com
www.pipeline.com/~dengor/amg.html
Fostering collaboration among New York's finest composers and performers of American Jazz. This unique musicians collective gives its members the opportunity to develop and present their art through a series of live performances of commissioned works, original material and classic jazz standards.

Artvoice
editorial@artvoice.com
www.artvoice.com
Buffalo free weekly Arts & Entertainment paper Reviews album releases and profiles new bands.

Bandblast.com
scottjames@rcn.com
www.bandblast.com
Live music resource for Westchester County, New York, Connecticut, New Jersey and Long Island.

Bands of New York State
ableals@juno.com
www.yrbook.com/music
Supporting Upstate NY groups and artists since 1996.

The Blues Society of Western New York
wnyblues@hotmail.com
www.wnyblues.com
Dedicated to unite, educate, promote and inform regarding Blues events, record releases and club scenes.

Buffalo Friends of Folk Music
ddarcy3553@aol.com
bfn.org/~folkmusic
Supports folk music in the Buffalo, NY area through local events including concerts and sing-arounds.

The Buffalo Music Guide
buffalo.citysearch.com
Extensive coverage of the local music scene. Post your shows and events.

Buffalo Music Online
admin@wnymusic.com
www.wnymusic.com
If you have news, or would like to have your event mentioned on this page, please pass it along.

Buffalo News
www.buffalonews.com/entertainment
Daily paper. Covers music news and local music scene.

The Buffalo Shows Listing
buffalo@dangpow.com
www.buffaloshows.org
Covering the Buffalo Punk/Hardcore scene.

BUMlocal
editor@bumrock.com
The Albany Music Scene Online
The first place to go when looking up anything and everything involving the Albany, NY area modern rock music scene.

Capital Region Unofficial Musicians and Bands Site *(CRUMBS)*
feedback@crumbs.net
www.crumbs.net
The ORIGINAL online music resource for the Albany/Schenectady/Troy area of New York State.

Central New York Bluegrass Association
rhayden357@aol.com
www.cnyba.com

Central New York Friends of Folk
LHoyt2000@netscape.net
www.folkus.org/fof
Encouraging and supporting the presentation of folk and acoustic music in this region.

Central New York Music
webmaster@cnymusic.com
www.cnymusic.com
Since 1995, CNY Music has promoted and supported live music in and around Central New York State.

CNY Music and Art . com
thefirstspark@yahoo.com
www.cnymusicandart.com
News, CD reviews, spotlights.

Cornell Daily Sun
www.cornellsun.com
Daily student paper.

Dankfunk
info@dankfunk.com
www.dankfunk.com
A production group comprised of a number of DJs and producers dedicated to bringing back the underground vibe. We are centered in the northeast, mainly in New York and New Jersey.

Democrat and Chronicle
www.rochesterdandc.com
Rochester daily paper.

The East Coast Hardcore Website
nycore@hardcorewebsite.net
www.hardcorewebsite.net
Want your demo or CD reviewed?

emocuse.com
johnnyd@emocuse.com
www.emocuse.com
Syracuse punk.indi.emo.hardcore. News, shows, bands and downloads.

Empyre Lounge
ian@empyrelounge.com
www.empyrelounge.com
We focus on the upstate NY music scene with music clips, interviews, as well as photos of great music events. Check back each week as we will shine our spotlight to center stage and bring you an up-close look at one of the great bands that visit the area.

The Folkus Project
joe@folkus.org
www.folkus.org
Presenting folk and acoustic music in Syracuse and Central New York. Includes artist spotlight.

Freetime Magazine
www.freetime.com
Rochester free bi-weekly arts and entertainment magazine. Covers local and national music with reviews and interviews.

The Genesee Early Music Society
gems@rochester.rr.com
www.gems-earlymusic.org
Fosters interest in and support for early music. Our musicians play authentic instruments and adhere to historically correct performance practices. GEMS also provides performing opportunities for aspiring early-music professionals.

Golden Link
goldenlink@goldenlink.org
www.goldenlink.org
Rochester publication. Include concerts of folk performers, a monthly newsletter, a folk musician's reference service, folk music workshops, an annual weekend folk festival, free weekly Tuesday night sing-arounds and much, much more.

The Hudson Valley Bluegrass Association
bradley@adelphi.edu
www.hvbluegrass.org
Jamboree is the Hudson Valley Bluegrass Association's official quarterly newsletter. It contains news, show schedules, CD reviews etc.

Hudson Valley Folk Guild
HVFOLKS@aol.com
www.hvfg.org
We produce high quality events, encourage amateur folk performers, find and nurture new folk songwriters and produce high quality publications.

In-Music
JohnPatGallagher@aol.com
www.in-nyc.com/in-music
Submit your music info and a couple of MP3s so you can be featured artists on In-Music.

Ithaca Journal
www.theithacajournal.com
Daily paper. Reviews CDs from area musicians, covers touring bands playing the area.

The Ithaca Music Guide
ithaca.citysearch.com
Extensive coverage of the local music scene. Post your shows and events.

Ithaca Times
www.ithacatimes.com
Free weekly alternative paper. Local concert reviews, accepts CD's for review.

Metroland
www.metroland.net
Albany's alternative newsweekly.

More Sugar Entertainment
tom55more@aol.com
www.moresugar.com
We cover Westchester, Putnam and Dutchess counties as well as parts of Fairfield and NYC; featuring club, band and entertainment happenings in the region. More Sugar is published and distributed monthly. There are articles on local talent, concerts in the area and much more.

Music 315
thedude@music315.com
www.music315.com
A site for the Central New York area within the 315 area code. If you're a working band within this area contact us to get your site listed. You can also get your local venue or happening listed.

Music Life Online
MLO4NY@aol.com
www.musiclifeonline.com
New York offers numerous types of bands from Long Island to Upstate New York. This website is here to help guide you and make it easier for both the bands and their fans to be link to one another. All bands mentioned are both from NY and those that have performed in NY from the Tri-state area.

The Music Station
stop@themusicstation.com
www.themusicstation.com/bands
Buffalo's music center and local music scene brought to you by The Music Station. Band links, gig listings and message boards.

Musicians On Call
info@musiciansoncall.org
www.musiciansoncall.org
In bringing both live and recorded music to patients' bedsides we provide a much needed outlet for the many feelings that a hospitalization engenders. The effectiveness of our programs has been reported by patients themselves, family and medical staff who interact with patients on a daily basis. They all have suggested that our music-related programs have helped distract them from the often unpleasant sterile and anonymous hospital atmosphere.

My City Underground
David Anderson danderson@digitalhecht.com
www.mycityunderground.com
A 30 minute showcase of independent short films, music videos, comedy and music. The show airs on the public access in Buffalo and the surrounding region (total population is approx 1 million). We're very interested in airing videos from indie artists. We're also looking for CDs to review and use as background and bumper music.

MyRochester.com
www.myrochester.com
Rochester's ultimate online music guide.

Nadeau Music
nadeaumusic@aol.com
www.nadeaumusic.net
Watertown based company dedicated to promoting local, independent and international Blues and Rock artists and the venues of the US Northeast and Southern Ontario.

New York Power Pop Page
powerpop@att.net
powerpop.home.att.net
This website is dedicated to the musicians on the New York Power Pop Scene, in the quixotic hope that the publicity will encourage the popularity of my favorite musical genre.

The Pulse
www.thepulse.com
City Guide for Utica. Post your gigs.

The Refrigerator
www.therefrigerator.net
Rochester Arts & Entertainment online zine.

The Rochester Music Coalition
rochestermusiccoalition@hotmail.com
rochestermusiccoalition.org
Set up to create a thriving, profitable music community in Rochester NY. We will support and promote the art of music and the musicians who create it regardless of genre.

The Rochester Music Guide
www.rochester.citysearch.com
Extensive coverage of the local music scene. Post your shows and events.

RochesterNightlife.com
www.rochesternightlife.com
Post your show listings.

Scenester
ace@inertskate.com
www.scenesteronline.com
Covering the Albany punk/hardcore scene.

The Syracuse Music Guide
syracuse.citysearch.com
Extensive coverage of the local music scene. Post your shows and events.

Syracuse New Times
newtimes.rway.com
The leading provider of News, Arts and Entertainment information throughout the greater Syracuse area.

Syracuse Post-Standard
www.syracuse.com
Daily paper.

The Syracuse Punk Page
rich@syracusepunk.com
www.syracusepunk.com
Bands, show dates, venues etc.

Syracuse ska scene
danny@dreamscape.com
syracuseska.com
Shows, classifieds, MP3s and more!

syracusebands.com
webmaster@syracusebands.com
www.syracusebands.com
This site is free for all artists and bands in Syracuse, NY and the surrounding areas to promote their gigs, CD's, or whatever else they are up to.

Syracuse.com
www.syracuse.com/music
Post your shows.

Underground Music Television
Rich umtv2002@yahoo.com
umtv.info
A TV show which features local, unsigned and underground artist's music videos. Bands can either submit their own produced videos or work with us to create one. We can do live performance videos or scripted/acted synched music videos to your CD audio

Upstate NY Reggae
rasadam12@hotmail.com
web.syr.edu/~affellem/upstate.html
A centralized source for Reggae related info in the upstate NY region. Please send me info of reggae in the region. Concerts, radio shows, shops, venues, contacts etc.

UpstateRocks.com
king-of-sleep@webtv.net
upstaterocks.com
Source for news and information about Upstate New York's progressive rock and metal scene. The purpose of this site is to give exposure to deserving bands and clubs in the upstate area.

Video City TV
videocitytv@aol.com
www.videocity.tv
The cable show is seen on various stations throughout NY State. To appear on the show, you need to have a video produced by Video City.

Westchester County Weekly
Brita Brundage bbrundage@fairfieldweekly.com
westchesterweekly.com
Local Bands and Happenings. Updated every Thursday.

WestchesterRocks.com
moonshyne@aol.com
www.westchesterrocks.com
Showcasing the local rock musicians of Westchester County, New York and the surrounding area.

Western New York / Southern Ontario Raves
www.wnysor.net
Creating some real unity within the Western New York and Southern Ontario rave scene into more of a community, to promote all upcoming events, dj's and everything else that makes our area one of the best in North America to party in.

Long Island

AURAL FIX
aurali@aol.com
www.auralfix.com
Giving coverage to the independent and local creative scene of the Long Island region.

Digital City Long Island
Music
home.digitalcity.com/longisland
Regional music column and forum. The area contains weekly feature articles plus weekend entertainment highlights, a running music poll and interactive message board.

The Island Ear
www.islandear.com
Bi-weekly arts and entertainment paper. Reviews concerts and profiles and interviews bands.

The Island Songwriter Showcase
mcspeed@aol.com
www.islandsongwriters.org
An organization of songwriters, lyricists, producers, engineers, performers and DJ's with one common goal - to support original music through its workshops and live showcases.

LIconcerts.com
richa@liglobal.com
www.liconcerts.com
Concert Listings for Long Island/Metro New York. Attention all bands, clubs and promoters; add your concerts to our database now - it's FREE!

LIrock.com
richa@liglobal.com
www.lirock.com
Any Long Island bands who would like a review done, contact me. If you are a writer and want to submit a review, please email it to me.

localmetal.com
luke_rosco@hotmail.com
www.angelfire.com/indie/resproj
Our goal is to help out the local heavy music scene in Buffalo.

The Long Island Blues Society
webmaster@pcideasintl.com
www.liblues.org
Band listings, newsletter, events etc.

The Long Island Classical Guitar Society
licgs@licgs.us
www.licgs.us
Provides a forum for students, professional teachers, performers and enthusiasts of the classical guitar. Members will also be invited to a quarterly mixer for a chance to meet your fellow guitar enthusiasts and play your favorite pieces on your guitar.

Long Island Entertainment News
Richard L'Hommedieu publisher@lienews.com
www.lienews.com
We are a FREE Entertainment Newspaper covering the Long Island NY area. We are the home of the largest and most complete music event calendar on the island.

Long Island Hardcore
neil@longislandhardcore.com
www.longislandhardcore.com
If any band wants show dates or info posted about their band E-Mail me. Also, I NEED PHOTOS, show dates or anything you have.

The Long Island Music Coalition
limusiccoalition@hotmail.com
www.limc.org
A conglomeration of musicians, managers, promoters, club owners, music journalists, radio personalities, record labels, A&R reps, recording studios, music retailers and music fans. Its purpose is to promote local original music.

Long Island Punx
Joe@Lipunx.com
77.lipunx.com:6080
Covering the Long Island scene. News, reviews, gig calendar .

Long Island Revolt

media@longislandrevolt.org
www.longislandrevolt.org
Long Island punk site that allows you to post listings and band news.

Long Island Traditional Music Association

litmaweb@optonline.net
www.litma.org
Supporting traditional music on Long Island. We sponsor and participate in more than 20 events each month across 5 locations on Long Island.

LongIsland.com *Nightlife*

feedback@longisland.com
nightlife.longisland.com
Long Island band pages, calendar, interviews, bulletin boards and more.

longislandmusicscene

groups.yahoo.com/group/longislandmusicscene
This is a list to discuss the original music scene on Long Island, NY. All are welcome to join, including musicians, managers, promoters, music journalists, club owners, radio personnel, label people and fans.

longislandmusicscene.com

Paul Cuthbert-Vice paul@longislandmusicscene.com
www.longislandmusicscene.com
Long Island's hometown portal for music and entertainment providing free exposure and resources for musicians and music fans.

The Music Never Stops

Bill Frey Themusicneverstops@wusb.org
community-2.webtv.net/musicnostop/THEMUSICNEVERSTOPS
Info on things happening on Long Island, as well as links to other websites of interest to musicians and music freaks.

NetTowns of Long Island

davekot@yahoo.com
www.nettowns.com/music.htm
Attention: Musicians, Bands us your Name and Info about your Gig. We will post it on our Gig Page for Free.

PopCore

rick@popcore.net
popcore.net
Our members are from the best indie rock bands from the Long Island and NYC area!

Saifimusic

info@saifimusic.com
www.saifimusic.com
All music services for the freelance Long Island New York Tri-state area musician. Created by musicians and producers.

Sick Promotions

www.sickpromotions.com
We are a full service independent street team and promotion company located on Long Island, NY. We can do all of the promotional work for you, so you can do what you do the best, play music. From merchandise, distribution, advertising, web sites and booking we do it all.

TheFreezer.com

mike@thefreezer.com
www.thefreezer.com
News, band and gig listings for Long Island bands.

New York City

Acoustic Live!

riccco@earthlink.net
www.acousticlive.com
Every month, we present the most comprehensive and easy to use list of acoustic performances in the New York Metropolitan area.

Associated Musicians of Greater New York - Local 802

Joseph Eisman jeisman@local802afm.org
www.local802afm.org
Our mission, simply put, is to fight for the interests and well being of the musicians employed in New York's music and entertainment industries.

BANDSHOT.com

erik@bandshot.com
www.bandshot.com
The Home New York City's Best Live Bands.

Big Apple Jazz

gordon@bigapplejazz.com
www.bigapplejazz.com
The complete New York City Jazz Club resource.

The Bronx Underground

Rudenychik@aol.com
www.bronxunderground.com
Our goal is to promote local music in the Bronx. Since the first show in October of 2000, we have organized and promoted DIY shows at the City Island Community Center, Shannon Seaview and most recently, at the Manhem Beach club.

Cari Cole Voice Studios

Cari Cole voice@vocalmag.com
www.vocalmag.com
Specializes in private vocal technique, vocal problems, keeping singers healthy on tour and contemporary styling. Our studio has one of the very finest methodologies available for building, toning, strengthening and repairing voices. Get your voice in the best shape of your career!

The Circle

Richard RPDieguez.com@RPDieguez.com
www.rpdieguez.com
A monthly music industry educational and networking forum. RSVP For The Best Deal In New York City!

Crack the Whip Promotions.com

Mandy@CrackTheWhipPromotions.com
www.CrackTheWhipPromotions.com
We are a NY based rock promotions company sponsoring the hottest signed and unsigned bands!

Digital City New York *Music*

home.digitalcity.com/newyork
Regional music column and forum. The area contains weekly feature articles plus weekend entertainment highlights, a running music poll and interactive message board.

eIndie Records

Jacob Bouchard kickitonetime@hotmail.com
www.eindie.com
Promotion and Distribution for NYC local bands.

Elementary Hip Hop

sjy6@columbia.edu
www.columbia.edu/cu/elementary
Our goal is to promote the knowledge of, the respect for and the love toward hip-hop and what it stands for. We accomplish this goal through various means: we plan concerts, open mics and informative lectures.

Elizabeth Records

info@elizabethrecords.com
www.elizabethrecords.com
Formed to nurture, develop and promote the talents of independent singer/songwriters performing on the thriving New York City folk scene. We aspire to offer burgeoning performers the chance to create major-label quality recordings in a supportive environment.

eXtreme NY

info@extremeNY.com
www.extremeny.com
We're a cooperative of live musicians and composers dedicated to the lover of spectacle, the avant garde and the bizarre. We have a calendar of extreme music and arts events and reviews of events from extreme NY music and arts events.

Flavorpill NYC

events@flavorpill.net
flavorpill.net
A publishing company which seeks out the best in arts, music and culture and delivers its findings via email each week. Every event listed on flavorpill is there because it's worthwhile — no money is accepted from venues, promoters, or artists for mentioning events.

Free Williamsburg

www.freewilliamsburg.com
It is our intent to provide you with cutting edge art, listings and information that is not compromised by our advertisers or by homogenous perspectives.

Good Times Magazine

gtmag@optonline.net
www.goodtimesmag.com
New York's music paper since 1969.

GothamJazz

webmaster@gothamjazz.com
www.gothamjazz.com
We provide up-to-date, accurate and comprehensive information for listeners in search of jazz listings. Through accessible presentation and informed research, GothamJazz.com sheds light on the many lesser-known performers and venues that are often overlooked by other publications.

Greenwich Village Gazette

www.nycny.com
Weekly news & entertainment paper.

Greenwich Village Gazette *Jazz Listings*

www.nycny.com/entertainment/jazz/index.html
The most complete listing of New York City Jazz events on the world wide web or in print.

HelloBrooklyn.com

events@hellobrooklyn.com
www.hellobrooklyn.com
Send your calendar listings by e-mail. Events must take place in Brooklyn, New York. Please include name of event, name of organization, description of event, exact location of event, telephone number, ticket price or "free," date and time of event.

HUGE!

HUGEmassif@aol.com
www.hugemassif.com
A very REAL look into the NYC-based rave scene focusing on party kids themselves.

in-nyc
JohnPatGallagher@aol.com
www.in-nyc.com
*Send info on you or your band so that you can be
featured artists on In-Music and get into the
Backroom. Also send an MP3 or two.*

The Jazz Composers Collective
info@jazzcollective.com
www.jazzcollective.com
*Dedicated to advancing the development and
presentation of music by forward-thinking composers.
We have been working to construct an environment
where participating artists can exercise their ideals of
creating and risking through the exploration of new
music, while building new audiences.*

JazzNewYork – Art Attack
musicmargaret@earthlink.net
www.jazznewyork.org
*The publication for & about liberation musicians in
NYC. Resources for musicians (grants, prizes,
funding, health care, housing, legal rights,
scholarships etc.). Listings of concerts & special
events for music lovers.*

JazzSingers.com
nycscene@jazzsingers.com
www.jazzsingers.com/NewYorkCityScene
*A support site for jazz singers, with information on the
NY scene and a place for singers to list their gigs.*

LADYFEST*EAST
info@ladyfesteast.org
www.ladyfesteast.org
*An annual New York City-based event dedicated to
showcasing, promoting and encouraging the artistic
talents, organizational abilities and political goals of
women. Ladyfest is an all-inclusive, women-run event
and all are welcome to attend.*

LetsGoOutNY.com
info@LetsGoOutNY.com
www.letsgooutny.com
*Our MetroGuide is your one stop for EVERYTHING
in the NYC area!*

LocalbandsNYC.com
max@localbandsnyc.com
www.localbandsnyc.com
*Tell us about your band or your favorite band and we
will list them. This site will give you a one minute
streaming audio sound bite of bands currently playing
NY, a link to the venue where the band is playing and
a link to the band's website.*

Mass Appeal
www.massappealmag.com
*Focuses on urban culture, music, art and fashion;
delivering the goods on what's going on in NY and
abroad. Mass Appeal defines the culture which exists
between contemporary visual and recording artists, as
well as connoisseurs of the metropolitan aesthetic.*

Neatness.com
webmaster@neatness.com
www.neatness.com
*Music resource for the NYC area. Photos, calendar
and more!*

The Neitherland
www.neitherland.com
*Your guide to gothic, industrial, vampyre and fetish
clubs, events, dwellings, cemeteries and lifestyle in
NYC and surrounding states.*

The New York Blues and Jazz Society
info@nybluessociety.org
www.nybluesandjazz.org
*Uniting the Blues and jazz community in the New York
area and giving it a central voice. News, reviews,
listings etc.*

New York Blade
www.nyblade.com
*A weekly newspaper covering the New York and
national Gay communities. Bands and artists can
post events in the Entertainment section.*

New York City Area Bluegrass Music Scene
benfreed@aol.com
banjoben.com
*A calendar and list of all New York City and Metro
area bluegrass music events, bands and related stuff.
Send in your information about upcoming events.*

New York City Art
info@newyorkcityart.com
www.newyorkcityart.com
*New York City's Directory of Fine Artists and
Musicians.*

New York Daily News
www.nydailynews.com
Daily paper.

The New York Industrial Front
DasKreestof@Juno.com
www.geocities.com/SunsetStrip/Studio/4696
*A coalition of NY industrial bands conspiring to
strengthen the NY industrial scene.*

The New York Music Guide
dsiegler@citysearch.com
newyork.citysearch.com
*Extensive coverage of the local music scene. Post
your shows and events.*

New York-Music-Scene.com
Eric J. Olsen eric@newyork-music-scene.com
www.newyork-music-scene.com
*A site dedicated to the local music scene in the New
York City Area. The site provides bands a place to
promote themselves, as well as the opportunity to post
MP3s. There are also reviews, concert listings,
contests, music resources and more.*

New York Musician
info@newyorkmusician.com
www.newyorkmusician.com
*Every month, 7500 copies are distributed, free of
charge, through, music stores, record stores, rehearsal
studios, Pro Audio dealers, recording studios and
other outlets in Manhattan, Brooklyn and Queens.*

New York Pinewoods Folk Music Club
nypinewood@aol.com
www.folkmusicny.org
*Concerts & Events (6/year) plus a monthly newsletter
with listings of folk events around NYC, radio shows,
festivals etc.*

New York Press
www.nypress.com
*New York free weekly arts and entertainment paper.
Reviews CDs and concerts by indie artists.*

Newsday
www.newsday.com
NYC daily paper.

NewYorkCity.com
www.nyc.com
Guide to New York Music & Clubs.

newyorkjazzjams.com
mail@pepenieto.com
www.newyorkjazzjams.com
*Web site devoted to jazz jam sessions in New York.
The site includes an entry form to post jam sessions
and a forum to promote interaction among jam goers.*

Notorious Marketing & Promotion
Liz Koch aka Notorious L.I.Z.
notorious@notoriousradio.com
www.notoriousradio.com
*I promote bands to New Music shows on Commercial
Radio. I get your music heard or at least get you
feedback.*

NY Rock
www.nyrock.com
*If you would like your CD to be reviewed by NY Rock,
see the instructions at the bottom of our CDs reviews
page. Note, we do not accept MP3s, demos, or EPs...
only full-length CDs.*

NY Waste
NYWaste@aol.com
www.newyorkwaste.com
*New York's punk rock newspaper. News, reviews and
attitude.*

NYC Country Music Scene
babswinn@babswinn.com
www.babswinn.com
*NYC's Country/Western Community information
center featuring an appearance schedule highlighting
local bands, a directory of bands, artists, clubs and
shops and excerpts from the local monthly Country
Music Assoc. magazines. We also have an online shop
featuring local C/W CDs.*

NYC Goth
www.nycgoth.com
*We help promote talented artists and artisans who
otherwise might get much less exposure.
Consequently, this site will expand further into the
realms of original content as time goes on; fiction,
artwork and so on.*

NYC Gothic Events
nygothic@razorwire.com
anon.razorwire.com/events
Add your news or upcoming events.

NYC punk
noah@nycpunk.com
www.nycpunk.com
News, reviews, mp3s.

NYC Reggae
rasadam12@hotmail.com
web.syr.edu/~affellem/nycshows.html
*Covering concerts, shows and dances in the NYC
area.*

NYCSKA .org
info@nycska.org
www.nycska.org
Send us your news and events.

NYMusicLife.com
MLO4NY@aol.com
nymusiclife.com
*New York offers numerous types of bands from Long
Island to Upstate New York. This website is here to
help guide you and make it easier for both the bands
and their fans to be link to one another. All bands
mentioned are both from NY and those that have
performed in NY from the Tri-state area.*

PAPERMAG

edit@papermag.com
www.papermag.com
An original daily, New York based pop culture and style digizine. Your guide to urban culture, fashion, society, film, food, fetish, events, people, news and entertainment.

Pin-Up NYC Magazine

comments@pinupnyc.com
www.pinupnyc.com
If you'd like to send us an album or novel for review, please include a press kit or bio and contact information.

pmgotham.com

pmGotham@aol.com
www.pmgotham.com
The only guide to the best of NYC's nightlife alternatives! Covers Goth, Industrial, Gay, Lesbian, Transsexual, Fetish and Deep House events. Visit our site to submit your event.

Rash

editor@rashmagazine.com
www.rashmagazine.com
An online magazine published as frequently as possible. We ~~want to enslave the human race and make them our minions~~ have no ambitions beyond that.

Roulette

info@roulette.org
www.roulette.org
Our purpose is to provide opportunities for innovative composers, musicians and interdisciplinary collaborators to present their work in accessible, appropriate and professional concert productions. The organization is committed to supporting work by young and emerging artists as well as by established innovators.

The Songwriter's Beat

val@valghent.com
songwritersbeat.com
An ever expanding group of singer/songwriters who want an opportunity to perform their newer material in an acoustic setting. We want to create an environment where musicians can share their experiences and ways of recording, releasing, promoting one's own CD.

SoundArt

soundarts@soundart.org
www.soundart.org
New York City's source for information on concerts of contemporary music.

Staten Island Hardcore Punk

cory4president@aol.com
www.sihardcorepunk.com
Send me information about your band. Visit the site for details.

subCreate.com

info@subCreate.com
www.subcreate.com
Covering the New York underground.

Suburban Clash

suburbanclashzine@yahoo.com
suburbanclashzine.cjb.net
A load of information of the Long Island/NYC hardcore scene. News, reviews etc.

theNYmusicscene.com

editor@thenymusicscene.com
www.theNYmusicScene.com
The New York Music Scene is happening all the time; we're just bringing it all to one common place. The site is intended to bring it all a little closer and encourage the support of the bands and clubs we enjoy.

Time Out New York

webmaster@timeoutny.com
www.timeoutny.com
The obsessive guide to impulsive entertainment.

Underground Music Online *(UMO)*

questions@umo.com
www.umo.com
If you are a Musician, Singer, Songwriter or Band Member who plays music part-time or full-time, creates original music or plays the music of your favorite artists, UMO Membership provides a wide array of support, services, promotion and marketing tools.

Unique Profiles

info@uniqueprofiles.com
www.uniqueprofiles.com
We are revolutionizing the way our community communicates by giving you a direct line to an aspect of urban culture ignored by traditional media. We feature MP3s by artists who correctly represent New York.

UNYPunk

jweldin@unypunk.com
unypunk.com
The ultimate New York punk directory. Submit your band info.

Village Voice

www.villagevoice.com
As the nation's first and largest alternative newsweekly, the Voice maintains the same tradition of no-holds barred reporting and criticism it first embraced when it began publishing more than forty years ago.

Volunteer Lawyers for the Arts

Askvla@vlany.org
www.vlany.org
The exclusive provider of pro bono legal services (legal representation for Art Related Issues), mediation services, educational programs and publications and advocacy to the arts community in the greater New York Metropolitan Area.

Webtunes

John Elder tunemaster@webtunes.com
www.webtunes.com
New York City's Premier Music guide. Concert listings for the NYC area with syndication, music clips, video clips, CD sales and much more. PDA channel available.

WOW Cafe

info@wowcafe.org
www.wowcafe.org
A nonprofit theatre space producing work by, about and for women. We showcase plays or performances in any genre; on Fridays we add a late-night cabaret of spoken word, music and skits. WOW invites all women to explore and enjoy the many facets of low-budget theatre.

ZydecoRoad.com

zydecoroad@yahoo.com
www.zydecoroad.com
Covering Zydeco and Cajun music in New York City and on Long Island.

North Carolina

alt.music.chapel-hill guide to the triangle

grady@ibiblio.org
www.ibiblio.org/ch-scene
List your upcoming shows with photos.

Asheville Citizen Times

www.citizen-times.com
Daily paper. Covers local music scene, will review CD's and interview bands if playing in the area.

The Beat Magazine

raabpub@aol.com
www.thebeatmag.com
North Carolina's only local all-music publication.

The Blues Society of the Lower Cape Fear

bluesman@capefearblues.com
www.capefearblues.com
A vibrant, all-inclusive organization that welcomes listeners, musicians and blues enthusiasts from all walks of life.

Breaking Boundaries

thecrew@breakingboundaries.net
www.breakingboundaries.net
Dedicated to the local music scene in North Carolina.

Bull City Hip Hop

bullcityhh@nc.rr.com
home.nc.rr.com/homid
The source for hip hop music, video's, DJ mix tapes, graf pics and news from local independent hip hop artists in Durham, N.C.

Cape Fear Live

www.cflive.com
Wilmington's arts & entertainment magazine.

Carolina Spins

spins.us/Carolina
A regional community dedicated to North Carolina and South Carolina electronic dance music,

carolinamusic.net

band_exposure@markduncan.net
www.carolinamusic.net
Dedicated to musicians in the Carolinas. If you know of a great band that needs exposure, drop us an email.

Central Carolina Songwriters Association

davisshantel@hotmail.com
www.ncneighbors.com/147
An association for songwriters, lyricists, musicians and bands to promote songwriting and music.

Charlotte Chapter NSAI

secondwindmusic@secondwindmusic.com
www.secondwindmusic.com/NSAICLT
An organization dedicated to the support of songwriters.

The Charlotte Folk Society

shsnow@mindspring.com
www.folksociety.org
Dedicated to promoting the ongoing enjoyment and preservation of traditional and contemporary folk music, dance, crafts and lore in the Southern Piedmont, since 1982.

Charlotte Mix
info@charlottemix.com
www.charlottemix.com
The Music Lover's Guide to Charlotte's BEST Bands.

Charlotte Live Music.com
info@charlottelivemusic.com
www.charlottelivemusic.com
The BEST guide for live music, bands, venues, Internet radio show and the local music scene in and around Charlotte!

The Charlotte Music Guide
charlotte.citysearch.com
Extensive coverage of the local music scene. Post your shows and events.

Charlotte Observer
www.charlotte.com
Daily paper. Covers local music scene and touring bands playing in town, band interviews, previews and reviews.

ChillWebCo
mary@mekons.com
www.chapel-hill.nc.us
Covering the greater Chapel Hill/Carrboro metro area. We got yer Local Band links. We got yer Local Clubs, Organizations and Schedules links too.

The Chronicle
www.chronicle.duke.edu
Duke University's student paper.

Contemporary Christian Concerts in North Carolina
ConcertList@barnabas.com
www.barnabas.com/concertList.shtml
Get your concert listed on our site. Send me a note with details.

Creative Loafing Charlotte
charlotte.creativeloafing.com
Free weekly alternative paper. Covers local and national music, interviews, previews and reviews.

The Daily Jolt
unc@dailyjolt.com
unc.dailyjolt.com
University of North Carolina's student publication.

Daily Tarheel
www.dailytarheel.com
University of North Carolina's student paper.

Dalloway Records
Christina Lewis clewis@dallowayrecords.com
www.dallowayrecords.com
An independent record label based in North Carolina. Dalloway is interested in most music genres and endeavors to promulgate excellent independent music at a national level.

Durham Herald-Sun
www.herald-sun.com
Daily paper.

The East Carolinian
www.theeastcarolinian.com
East Carolina University's student paper.

Eastern North Carolina Bluegrass Association
adam1@icomnet.com
www.encbluegrass.freeservers.com
Promoting bluegrass music as clean, wholesome entertainment for the entire family.

Edge Magazine
edgeguy@edgemagazineonline.com
www.edgemagazineonline.com
The only magazine in Eastern NC that doesn't suck!

Encore
encorepub@aol.com
www.encorepub.com
Wilmington's free weekly alternative arts and entertainment paper. Covers local music and touring bands playing in the area with interviews, previews and reviews.

ESP Magazine
www.espmagazine.com
Greensboro free weekly arts and entertainment magazine. Covers local and national music with artist interviews, CD and concert previews and reviews.

Fiddle & Bow Society
www.fiddleandbow.org
Winston-Salem organization dedicated to the promotion and preservation of folk music and dance and their related arts.

gate city noise
gatecitynoise@mindspring.com
www.gatecitynoise.com
Covering the Greensboro music scene.

goTriad.com
www.gotriad.com
Covering arts & entertainment in Greensboro.

Guitartown
webmaster@guitartown.org
www.guitartown.org
A web site featuring news of the thriving North Carolina roots music scene.

Independent Reviewer - Arthur Shuey
webmaster@lovewhip.zzn.com
I review all styles of music for three local entertainment magazines in Wilmington, North Carolina and my own "Word on the Street" e-zine, Blues for American Harmonica Newsmagazine and a dozen or so Blues Societies in the US and Canada. Arthur Shuey, 108 South 13th Street, Wilmington NC 28401

Independent Weekly
Angie Carlson carlson@indyweek.com
indyweek.com
Durham free weekly alternative paper. Interviews bands, previews and reviews CDs and concerts.

Mountain XPress
webmaster@mountainx.com
www.mountainx.com
Weekly independent news, arts & events for Asheville & Western North Carolina.

musicomet
cometriderx@yahoo.com
www.musicomet.com
News, reviews....and great, frequently updated list of live shows happening in the Carolinas.

NC Goth DOT COM
www.ncgoth.com
Information on club, club nights, bands, upcoming shows and other information pertaining to North Carolina. Let me know about upcoming shows, events and anything else you think might be relevant. If it's relevant, I'll put it up on the site.

NC Hip Hop
nchiphop@yahoo.com
www.netweed.com/nchiphop
Linking you to North Carolina hip hop culture and rap music!

NCMusic.com
info@ncmusic.com
www.ncmusic.com
Opinions and reviews about music in North Carolina.

NCSC Buzz
www.ncscbuzz.com
Our goal is become the largest Carolinas music portal on the web.

NCScene.com
webmaster@ncscene.com
www.ncscene.com
Rock, metal, hardcore and more! All Bands & Artists May Submit Music and/or Press Material.

News & Record
www.news-record.com
Greensboro daily paper. Music reviews and artist interviews. Get information about upcoming events every Thursday in the City Life section.

News & Observer
www.newsobserver.com
Raleigh daily paper.

North Carolina Hip Hop
ncadmin@northcarolinahiphop.com
www.northcarolinahiphop.com
We rep the Carolina Blue from Raleigh to Charlotte, ——to —— and all there is in between. Wanna know what pops in North Cacky? Well, you've found it right here. So visit us as often as you can to find out what goes down in your part of town. Ya heard!!

North Carolina Songwriters Co-op
Mike_Germano@Hotmail.com
www.ncsongwriters.org
Dedicated to the support and promotion of songwriters is the state of North Carolina.

North Carolina Underground
webmaster@ncunderground.com
www.quintina.com/ncu
If you are a local artist in the field of hip hop, rap, turntablism, R&B, or production than this site may be able to help you. Connect with others through the message boards, get yourself featured on the site and pick up useful tips on how to make your sound come off better.

Piedmont Blues Preservation Society
info@piedmontblues.org
www.piedmontblues.org
Dedicated to the preservation and presentation of the American Blues tradition through live performances, educational programs and workshops and the documentation of local North Carolina tradition through written, audio and visual media and our own Blues archives.

The Piedmont Guitar Society
jthash@earthlink.net
ncnatural.com/PCGS/guitar.html
Our purpose is to increase understanding and enjoyment of the guitar and similar stringed instruments in Winston-Salem, Greensboro, High Point and surrounding areas. Meetings feature free performances by outstanding local guitarists, students and faculty members.

PRAXIS Magazine
whatup@praxismagazine.net
www.praxismagazine.net
*Covering the Raleigh music scene. North Carolina
and its surrounding areas are crawling with city
culture, amazing talent and a lot of raw energy, but -
until now - there has not been a media channel to
support our scene, what we are all about and our
continued growth. This means exposure for you!*

Queen City Music
info@queencitymusic.com
www.queencitymusic.com
Covering the Charlotte music scene.

The Raleigh-Durham Music Guide
triangle.citysearch.com
*Extensive coverage of the local music scene. Post
your shows and events.*

Raleigh Underground
joey@raleighunderground.com
www.raleighunderground.com
Lists info on Raleigh's underground music scene.

Raleighmusic.com
www.raleighmusic.com
*Our goal is to bring original music in North Carolina
to a bigger audience. That's right, not just Raleigh but
the whole state.*

The Record Exchange
Don Rosenberg drose@trexonline.com
www.trexonline.com
*Vendor that sells independent music / holds in-store
performances. (Located in NC and VA)*

SouthEastern Bluegrass Association
info@sebabluegrass.org
www.sebabluegrass.org
*Serving Alabama, Georgia, North Carolina, South
Carolina and Tennessee since 1984. Dedicated to the
preservation, education and promotion of Bluegrass
Music.*

Technician
technicianonline.com
North Carolina State University's student newspaper.

The Triangle Blues Society
randy@triangleblues.org
www.triangleblues.org
*Dedicated to preserving the Piedmont blues style
traditional to the Triangle area of central North
Carolina including the cities of Raleigh, Durham and
Chapel Hill.*

Up & Coming Magazine
www.upandcomingmag.com
*Fayetteville free bi-weekly arts and entertainment
magazine. Artist interviews, CD and concert reviews.*

The Wilkes Acoustic/Folk Society
kwatts@wilkes.net
www.wilkesfolks.com
*Our objectives include but are not limited to
educating the public in music appreciation and forms
of self-entertainment, sharing of musical ideas,
venues, performing, passing down and preserving this
region's musical heritage for our youth and just plain
fun.*

WilmingtonNCMusic.com
webmaster@wilmingtonncmusic.com
www.wilmingtonncmusic.com
Please send in your CD's and Demo's for review.

Winston-Salem Journal
www.journalnow.com
*Daily paper. Covers music news with previews,
reviews and artist interviews.*

The Winston-Salem Music Guide
winstonsalem.citysearch.com
*Extensive coverage of the local music scene. Post
your shows and events.*

ZSpotlight
webmaster@ZSpotlight.com
www.zspotlight.com
*We are proud to present you with a centralized
website dedicated to providing you with the latest up-
to-date information on who's playing where in the
Triangle. Whatever your musical taste you'll be
certain to find it here.*

North Dakota

Barking Dog Records
coates@barkingdogrecords.com
www.barkingdogrecords.com
*A label founded to identify outstanding artists from
the Upper Midwest and to get their music out to a
broad audience.*

The Bismarck Tribune
www.bismarcktribune.com
*Daily paper. Covers music scene with interviews,
previews and reviews.*

High Plains Reader
hpr@hpr1.com
www.highplainsreader.com
*Fargo free weekly alternative paper. Covers local and
national bands with interviews, previews and reviews.
Sponsors local concerts.*

The Forum
new.in-forum.com
*Fargo daily paper. Covers music scene with
interviews, previews and reviews.*

North Dakota State University Spectrum
Matt Perrine mperrine@ndsuspectrum.com
www.ndsuspectrum.com
Campus publication. Covers local music.

saboingaden.com
www.saboingaden.com
Covering the Fargo music scene.

The Spectrum
www.ndsuspectrum.com
North Dakota State University's student paper.

Ohio

Akron Beacon-Journal
www.ohio.com
Daily paper.

The Athens Musician's Network
amn@frognet.net
www.athensmusician.net
*Covers the local music scene in and around a small
college town called Athens, Ohio. The AMN covers
local bars, venues, contains links to bands and band
web sites and has articles written by local musicians.*

The Black Swamp Blues Society
www.bsbs.net
*Our Mission is to promote and preserve the Blues in
Northwest Ohio and Southeast Michigan, creating
more opportunities for fans to see quality national and
local blues artists.*

The Blues, Jazz & Folk Music Society
bjfm@bjfm.org
www.bjfm.org
*Promoting blues, jazz & folk music in the Mid-Ohio
Valley.*

The Central Ohio Hot Jazz Society
mevans49@columbus.rr.com
gravity.biosci.ohio-state.edu/cohjs
*Dedicated to the preservation and advancement of
traditional jazz as a distinctive American art form.
The Society has been active in the presentation of
traditional jazz concerts by local jazz bands as well as
bands from around the United States and Canada.*

CowTownMusic.com
sixis@columbus.rr.com
www.cowtownmusic.com
*Your online source for Live Entertainment in Central
Ohio. Local music by local bands and where they are
playing.*

Highlands of Ohio
highlands@neo.rr.com
www.highlandsofohio.com
*A Folk and Celtic Music Society. It is our hope to
bring more of the Celtic music and culture to the
North Central part of Ohio and our website is
intended to keep the local community informed of
concerts and other events.*

Kickin' it in Kent
gary22fret@yahoo.com
listen.to/kentmusic
*This site is dedicated to the many great bands from
the Kent area. All the bands (will) have two MP3s up
for download.*

Midwest Invasion
info@midwestinvasion.com
www.midwestinvasion.com
Your #1 source for Midwest Hip Hop.

moonchicken.com
webmaster@moonchicken.com
moonchicken.com
South West Ohio's Guide to Local Music.

Ohio Bands Online
ohiobandsonline@yahoo.com
www.ohiobandsonline.com
A listing of Ohio bands by city and genre.

**The Ohio Hystairical Musick Society
(O.H.M.S.)**
jimi_imij1us@yahoo.com
ohms.nu
*Dedicated to preserving and presenting local music as
we know it. Send in your band and gig info.*

Ohio Local Music
olmgarvin@yahoo.com
olmv2.cjb.net
*Promote all your news on OLM. Get your music
heard, your shows promoted and your CDs sold. Drop
me a line and get your get your material up on our
site!*

Ohio Online Magazine
www.ohioonline.com
*Well, the music scene has exploded!! You wanted
more- here it is!! Feel free to contribute and send us
the goods!!*

Revue Magazine

www.revuemagazine.com

Fairlawn free monthly Music paper. We are committed to bringing you the most comprehensive coverage of concerts, cd reviews and features on the music you care about, both nationally and regionally.

Songwriters and Poets Critique

DMeyers@SongWritersCritique.com
spcmusic.freeyellow.com

A central Ohio based organization, dedicated to the craft of writing songs and poems through critiques, workshops, concerts, demos and more.

Utter Trash

trashmag@uttertrash.net
www.uttertrash.net

Covering the best underground entertainment in Northeast Ohio and beyond.

The Village Buzz

amanda@village-buzz.com
www.village-buzz.com

All the cool with the n/e Ohio music scene.

YoungstownScene.com

shakes@youngstownscene.com
www.youngstownscene.com

Covering the Youngstown punk/hardcore scene.

Cincinnati

Cincinnati Blues

bluesman@cincinnatiblues.com
www.cincinnatiblues.com

Info on local bands, clubs, classifieds, calendar of events and local jams.

Cincinnati CityBeat

Mike Breen mbreen@citybeat.com
www.citybeat.com

Covers news, public issues, arts and entertainment of interest to readers in Greater Cincinnati and Northern Kentucky. You can send Mike a disc to review, or just let him know when you're playing. You never know, you might make Gig of the Week.

Cincinnati Enquirer

Larry Nager lnager@enquirer.com
enquirer.com

Daily paper. Contact Larry for any music related information.

The Cincinnati Music Guide

cincinnati.citysearch.com

Extensive coverage of the local music scene. Post your shows and events.

Cincinnati Music Online

cincymusic.com

An organization providing free promotion of Greater Cincinnati artists and music.

Cincinnati Post

Rick Bird rbird@cincypost.com
www.cincypost.com

Daily paper. Contact Rick for any music related news.

Cincinnati Shows

cincyshows@niceguyrecords.com
www.cincinnatishows.com

Show listings, downloads, links, pictures etc. of Cincinnati bands.

Cincinnatibands.com

www.cincinnati-atlas.com

Music section of Cincinnati-Atlas.com covering everything about local bands.

Cincy Metal

cincymetal@cincymetal.com
www.cincymetal.com

You will never believe this, but hard rock/metal does exist in Cincinnati!! Cincymetal is the one-stop website for all your headbanging needs.

cincymusic.com

Michael DeWees mdewees@cincymusic.com
Tara O'Donnell tara@cincymusic.com
www.cincymusic.com

Submit your press kit, CD, or materials for inclusion on our site.

Greater Cincinnati Blues Society

info@cincyblues.org
www.cincyblues.org

Our goal is to promote and advance the culture and tradition of blues music as an original American art form.

The Greater Cincinnati Guitar Society

gtr2971@fuse.net
www.geocities.com/cinciguitars

Our membership consists of classical and steel-string acoustic players and aficionados.

The Neus Subjex

neussubjex.net

Covering Cincinnati Punk Rock, mostly, though that won't stop us from making things up about people who don't live in the Cincinnati area.

Cleveland

The Brush Border

info@brushborder.com
www.jah-img-jam.com

A place devoted to promoting the work and talents of local artists, musicians and photographers. We provide photo galleries of individual artists' work, musical events and art available for purchase.

ClePunk

Mark.Vocca@ClePunk.com
www.clepunk.com

This site is your refuge, your confessional. A site to shed all your past moments, your stories, your demons. Also a place to share all your current ones. We are definately a family and this is our scrapbook... a living, breathing tale of what the fuck we are... please contribute... for your own good.

Cleveland Composers Guild

jaquick@en.com
my.en.com/~jaquick/ccg.html

Exists to promote the music of composers living in Northeast Ohio, primarily by sponsoring 3-4 concerts of member works each season. Over the past 40 years, the CCG has built an enviable record of supporting new music, with recordings on the CRI, Crystal and Advent labels.

Cleveland Country Magazine

imriz@aol.com
www.cwmusic.com

We are a monthly print magazine serving country music fans in Northeastern Ohio. To get a listing for your band, e-mail us with the band name, phone number and/or website info and we'll list you for FREE!

Cleveland Free Times

www.freetimes.com

Free weekly alternative paper. Covers local and national music scene with CD and concert previews and reviews.

Cleveland Metal

jtk2112@cleveland-metal.com
www.cleveland-metal.com

News, reviews, downloads etc.

Cleveland Metal Connection

submissions@clevmetalconn.org
www.clevmetalconn.org

Support Local Metal or Die! Each month we will randomly select a band to be that month's featured artist.

The Cleveland Music Guide

cleveland.citysearch.com

Extensive coverage of local music. Post your shows and events.

Cleveland Rock Net

www.clevelandrock.net

A web site dedicated to the Cleveland Ohio and surrounding area local Rock scene. This web site will offer local band links, reviews, show listings, MP3 downloads and much more to come.

Cleveland Scene Magazine

www.clevescene.com

Free weekly alternative paper. CD and concert reviews.

Cleveland Ska Scene

skapunk1919@aol.com
www.clevelandskascene.cjb.net

A directory of all local ska bands. If you're a local ska influenced band and I don't have you linked up, contact me and I'll put you on.

Cleveland.com

entertainment@cleveland.com
www.cleveland.com/music

Log on and rock out with your favorite area acts, both past and present, or create a free Web site for your band.

clevelandmp3.com

webmaster@clevelandmp3.com
www.clevelandmp3.com

Our goal is to be Cleveland's best guide for live, local music and entertainment locations. By using the latest MP3 technologies we offer audio previews of local bands to help you choose who you want to see and where they are performing.

ClevelandWeirdness

audio@clevelandweirdness.com
www.clevelandweirdness.com

Highlights different local talent every month in our LOOK AT ME section and brings you mp3s, links and info on bands, musicians and clubs from Cleveland on the Featured Artists page.

darkcleveland.com

events@darkcleveland.com
www.darkcleveland.com

A comprehensive list of dark/electronic recording artists, music and events in the greater-Cleveland + northeast-Ohio area, with a focus on live shows, bands and artists.

Domain Cleveland

Dougless R. Esper dougless@domaincleveland.com
www.domaincleveland.com

A booking and promotions company. We book/promote shows as well as conduct interviews, review live shows, review recorded music, run a message board and mailing list about music, bring in national/regional/local bands of all genres and release compilation cd's as well.

Grandpa Rocker Music Reviews

gramps@grandparocker.com
www.grandparocker.com
Check out bands, CDs, upcoming events, concerts and clubs in the Cleveland area. All music styles are welcome.

Music's Bottom Line

mbleditor@mblzine.net
www.mblzine.net
Cleveland's only all music magazine with a readership of over 30,000 in the Cleveland area and monthly web hits reaching 100,000 per month. We are the only publication that features unsigned bands in every monthly issue.

Undercurrents

music@undercurrents.com
www.undercurrents.com
We connect fans with Cleveland area bands. Our objectives are simple: assist musician's network, improve and succeed by providing showcase opportunities for musicians, music industry exposure and access to the Undercurrents database for links to music business services.

Columbus

Columbus Alive

stephen@columbusalive.com
www.columbusalive.com
Free weekly alternative paper. Covers local indie music with concert previews and reviews.

Columbus Blues Alliance

herbs@columbus.rr.com
www.colsbluesalliance.org
Our intent is to maintain and encourage ties with all forms of this musical genre including both traditional and electric.

The Columbus Dispatch

www.dispatch.com
Daily paper.

The Columbus Guitar Society

info@columbusguitarsociety.org
www.columbusguitarsociety.org
Dedicated to promoting classical guitar education and performance in Central Ohio.

The Columbus Music Guide

columbus.citysearch.com
Extensive coverage of the local music scene. Post your shows and events.

Columbus Folk Music Society

JRSTAATS@aol.com
www.geocities.com/colsfolk
Promoting Folk Music, Dance, Story Telling and other Folk arts.

ColumbusArts.com

tkauffman@gcac.org
www.columbusarts.com
Your most comprehensive resource for Central Ohio culture and arts on the Web.

Columbusmusic.com

info@columbusmusic.com
www.columbusmusic.com
Adding your band to Columbusmusic.com is easy and best of all it's free!

columbusound.com

paul@artclix.com
www.columbusound.com
Central Ohio's #1 Music Directory!

Cringe

webmaster@cringe.com
www.cringe.com
Accepts nearly all submissions from the Columbus area.

Idiot Press

idiotpress@idiotpress.com
www.idiotpress.com
People have compared this pillar of the Columbus music scene to MTV's Tom Green. However, Melvin contends that, unlike Green, he is an "artist" and each action he takes and word he utters is rigorously designed to provoke an exact predetermined reaction.

The Lantern

www.thelantern.com
Ohio State University's student paper.

The Other Paper

www.theotherpaper.com
Columbus free weekly alternative paper. Covers indie music with band interviews, CD and concert previews and reviews.

Dayton

Dayton Band Resource Page

Info@DaytonBands.com
www.daytonbands.com
Dedicated to helping Independent Dayton Local Musicians to become successful in today's Music Industry.

Dayton Local Music Page

daytonlocalmusic@hotmail.com
www.dayton.net/~rwarrick
Add your music and bio.

The Dayton Music Guide

dayton.citysearch.com
Extensive coverage of the local music scene. Post your shows and events.

daytonbands.com

Info@DaytonBands.com
www.daytonbands.com

The Music Lair

webmaster@themusiclair.com
www.themusiclair.com
Our mission is to bring the fans closer to what's happening in the Dayton music scene We will feature articles, interviews, links and much more. We're just getting started so keep checking back to see what we're up to!

NiteOnTheTown.com

webmaster@niteonthetown.com
www.niteonthetown.com
Dedicated to helping people in Dayton go out and have a good time. Includes local music listings.

Toledo

Sin Klub Entertainment

sinklub@sinklub.com
www.sinklub.com
A vehicle in which to release music made by deserving musicians of the Toledo area. The label embodies everything from metal and punk to industrial and rap.

The Toledo Blade

www.toledoblade.com
Daily paper.

The Toledo Jazz Society

toledojazz@toledojazzsociety.org
www.toledojazzsociety.org
We increase the appreciation of Jazz by going into classrooms to introduce children to the excitement and beauty of jazz and by sponsoring live performances.

The Toledo Music Guide

toledo.citysearch.com
Extensive coverage of the local music scene. Post your shows and events.

toledoentertainment.com

toledoentertainment.com
We encourage you to help us stay informed by letting us know about an event you would like to see listed on TEDC.

Toledopunks.com

edit@lactose-intolerant.com
www.toledopunks.com
Local punk rock site with all the contacts, bands and info needed on the Toledo punk scene. Sign up for the weekly email-newsletter that contains shows and much more.

T-townmusic.com

scott-stamp@t-townmusic.com
www.t-townmusic.com
Your source for Northwest Ohio and Southeast Michigan's local music scene.

Oklahoma

BestofTulsa.com *Music*

info@BestofTulsa.com
bestoftulsa.com/html/music.shtml
Listings, spotlights, events etc.

The Collegian

www.utulsa.edu/collegian
University of Tulsa's student paper.

The Daily Oklahoman

www.oklahoman.com
Oklahoma City daily paper. Covers local music scene with band interviews, CD and concert previews and reviews.

Green Country Bluegrass Association

coypollock@aol.com
www.homestead.com/gcba
Promoting Bluegrass in Northeast Oklahoma.

The Minor

rsuradio@yahoo.com
www.theminor.com
Covering the Oklahoma music scene. E-mail us your band's name, URL, hometown and a short description of your sound. It will be posted in no time.

NormanMusicScene.com

pchelp@normanmusicscene.com
www.normanmusicscene.com
Linking local musical artists, events & venues.

NormanNow.com

www.normannow.com
Post your band info and upcoming shows.

OKC Live

info@okclive.com
www.okclive.com
Oklahoma City's Online Entertainment Source.

The Oklahoma Blues Society
www.okblues.org
CD reviews, news, gig listings etc. can be found in our "Backbeat Newsletter".

The Oklahoma City Music Guide
oklahomacity.citysearch.com
Extensive coverage of the local music scene. Post your shows and events.

The Oklahoma City Traditional Music Association
www.octma.org
Learning, teaching and playing acoustic folk music. We offer workshops in a variety of instruments, for beginners through advanced players. Following the workshops are the Play Arounds, where folks of all skill levels take turns entertaining us on a small stage.

Oklahoma Daily
www.oudaily.com
University of Oklahoma's student paper.

The Oklahoma Gazette
www.okgazette.com
Oklahoma City free weekly arts and entertainment paper. Accepts press kits and CD's from local artists for review.

Oklahoma Songwriters & Composers Association (OSCA)
mchardin@itlnet.net
www.oksongwriters.org
We welcome all songwriters, composers and lyricists. Our membership over the years has included all levels of talent; from beginning writers to authors of Number One hit songs.

Omnizine
sbeaumont@omnizine.com
www.omnizine.com
A regional independent music zine featuring album reviews, concert reviews, interviews, editorial articles, label and venue directories for the Omnizine region (Oklahoma, Texas, Arkansas, Missouri, Kansas).

The Oracle
www.oru.edu/oracle
Oral Roberts University's student paper. Does spotlights on local musicians.

Southwest Songwriters Association
music@sirinet.net
www.swsongwriters.com
An important point of contact for musicians looking for bands, or bands looking for musicians.

The Tulsa Folk Music Society
tulsafolkmusic@yahoo.com
members.aol.com/tulsafms
To promote traditional and contemporary folk music in the Tulsa area.

The Tulsa Music Guide
tulsa.citysearch.com
Extensive coverage of the local music scene. Post your shows and events.

Tulsa World
www.tulsaworld.com
Daily paper.

Tulsa Gothic
info@tulsagothic.com
www.tulsagothic.com
Oklahoma bands, send us your info!

TulsaMusicScene.COM
www.tulsamusicscene.com
Tulsa's Lastest Music Information Source!

Urban Tulsa Weekly
www.urbantulsa.com
Free weekly arts and entertainment paper. Covers local music scene.

Oregon

Beyer Sound Productions
Erik Beyer beyersoundprod@hotmail.com
www.beyersp.com
We are here to create an umbrella over the city of Portland OR and impose a new positive working atmosphere between musicians and venues, as well as providing high quality services in Artist Relations, assisting in representation, consulting, booking locally and along the West Coast and handling other important aspects of the industry.

Cascade Blues Association
cbastaff@cascadeblues.org
www.cascadeblues.org
Dedicated to the preservation and promotion of blues and roots music in the Great Northwest.

Creative Music Guild
cmg@creativemusicguild.org
www.creativemusicguild.org
This organization promotes new music that advances the arts of improvisation and composition. The Guild's focus is on jazz-related music that is artistically vital but under-represented in Portland.

Daily Barometer
baro.editor@studentmedia.orst.edu
barometer.orst.edu
Oregon State University's student paper.

Daily Emerald
www.dailyemerald.com
University of Oregon's student paper.

ePuget Magazine
admin@epuget.com
www.epuget.com
An electronic magazine for people living and working on or near the spectacular waters of the Puget Sound. We invite articles from and about both bands and venues.

Eugene Register-Guard
www.registerguard.com
Daily paper.

Eugene Weekly
cal@eugeneweekly.com
www.eugeneweekly.com
Eugene's arts & entertainment publication.

In2une Networks
boyd@indieavenue.com
www.indieavenue.com
The world's largest database of Northwest Musicians, Bands and Venues in the hopes of assisting musicians and venues in the delivery of live music in the Pacific Northwest.

Internet Exploiter
Mark submissions@internet-exploiter.com
www.internet-exploiter.com
An online publication that reviews live shows, cds and interviews indie bands in the Northwest.

Jazz Society of Oregon
csights@teleport.com
www.jsojazzscene.org
To promote jazz musicians, jazz education and jazz appreciation. Jazzscene Magazine serves as the JSO's strong right arm, featuring a monthly calendar of jazz events, jazz happenings on campus, CD reviews, Musician of the Month, news about jazz in the clubs, JSO Bulletin Board and great feature articles.

Kingbanana
kngbanana@aol.com
www.kingbanana.net
Covering the Portland Punk/Hardcore/Metal scene. Shows, reviews, classified, new...

NAIL Distribution
www.naildistribution.com
The premiere distributor of alternative, independent music in the Pacific Northwest. It was founded in 1995 to fulfill a specific need: To effectively place independent music in Northwest stores.

Nexus Underground
steve@nexusunderground.com
www.nexusunderground.com
A Portland based indie distribution center offering free distribution, mp3s and more. Keep your ear to the underground.

NightPiper Productions
Geoff Minor geoff@nightpiper.com
nightpiper.com
Portland based music promotion and booking company featuring information on many local acts, clubs and upcoming events.

The Northeast Oregon Folklore Society
neofls@eoni.com
www.eoni.com/~mlewis/neofs
A somewhat loosely organized group that promotes traditional forms of music and dance in the Grande Ronde Valley of Northeast Oregon.

The Oregon Bluegrass Association
meredith@epud.net
www.oregonbluegrass.org
To promote, encourage, foster and cultivate the preservation, appreciation, understanding, enjoyment, support and performance of bluegrass and related music.

The Early Music Guild of Oregon
dgroves@emgo.org
www.emgo.org
Our mission is to foster communication among Oregon's early musicians, to serve as a virtual bulletin board of news and events, and, in general, to further the cause of early music.

Oregon Live
kcosgrov@oregonlive.com
www.oregonlive.com/music

Oregon Ska Pages
cschatz@efn.org
www.efn.org/~cschatz/ska/ska.shtml
We never did have a big ska scene, but I thought there needed to be a place where people could find information about our scene.

The Oregonian
www.oregonian.com
Portland daily paper.

PDX Bands
info@pdxbands.com
www.pdxbands.com
*What Portland sounds like. Streaming Audio from
Local Artists. Updated frequently.*

pdxindgoth.com
pdxindgoth.com
Covering the Portland Goth scene.

PDXnet
michele@pdxnet.net
www.pdxnet.net
*Portland's Alternative guide to local Arts,
Entertainment, Music, Theater, Bands and more.*

Portland Music Central
Fran Gray fgray@teleport.com
www.portlandmusiccentral.com
Sheet music, tabs, midi files and band reviews.

Portland Folklore Society
mail@portlandfolklore.org
www.portlandfolklore.org
*Dedicated to promoting folk music and arts in the
greater Portland area.*

The Portland Guitar Society
pgs@guitarist.com
www.guitarist.com/pgs
*As well as the benefits we offer, we publish a quarterly
newsletter full of articles, reviews and a calendar of
guitar events.*

Portland Mercury
mercuryeditorial@portlandmercury
www.portlandmercury.com
Portland's arts & entertainment weekly.

The Portland Music Guide
portland.citysearch.com
*Extensive coverage of the local music scene. Post
your shows and events.*

Portland Online MusicNet
www.pomn.com
*We have grown to be one of Portland's most popular
online publications. Please do not submit a CD for
review unless you are from Oregon.*

Portland Songwriters Association
www.pdxsongwriters.org
*Our mission is to develop the songwriting talents of
our members and to support them in their quest to
become great songwriters!*

portlandmusicians.com
tim@portlandmusicians.com
www.portlandmusicians.com
Your online connection to the Portland music scene.

**Pacific Northwest Electro-Acoustic Music
Organization**
board@nweamo.org
www.nweamo.org
*Dedicated to the promotion of music that involves the
creative use of computers and electronics and to
putting electro-acoustic composers and musicians in
the Pacific Northwest in contact with the international
electronic music community.*

Two Louies Magazine
TwoLouie@aol.com
www.twolouiesmagazine.com
*Portland monthly music paper. CD and concert
reviews.*

Willamette Week
mzusman@wweek.com
www.wweek.com
*A weekly calendar of live music in venues throughout
the city.*

Pennsylvania

The Allentown Music Guide
allentown.citysearch.com
*Extensive coverage of the local music scene. Post
your shows and events.*

ArtFortress.com
music@artfortress.com
www.artfortress.com
*If you are a musician or a music lover this is the web
site for you! Our goal is simple, to promote music in a
way that will benefit the musician, club owner and
music lover. All our music services are FREE!*

Arts & Music PA
greeneyedlady@happyhippie.com
www.artsandmusicpa.com
*Guide to the arts, music and local cultures of
Pennsylvania, New York City and the Northeast.*

Berks Tonight
Skip@berkstonight.com
www.berkstonight.com
*The source for what's happening in Reading PA and
Berks County.*

Billtown Blues Association
bbaweb88@suscom.net
www.billtownblues.org
*Dedicated to providing opportunities for area
residents to experience blues music; producing quality
performance opportunities for national, regional and
local artists.*

Black Thorn Entertainment
dimensions@pa.net
blackthornentertainment.com
*Created to assist local and regional talent throughout
Pennsylvania and surrounding areas. We are able to
assist musicians and artists in the realm of
advertising, promotion, web design, photography,
recording, consulting and band representation.*

Bucks County Blues Society
www.bucksnet.com/bcbs
The world's oldest continuously active blues society.

Bucks County Folk Song Society
folkman@comcast.net
www.bucksfolk.org
*Dedicated to furthering the interest and appreciation
of folk music through education, research and
participation; familiarizing the people of southeastern
Pennsylvania with authentic folk art.*

Central PA Friends of Jazz
pajazz@epix.net
www.pajazz.org
*Our vision is to be the leading and premier
organization in Central PA to present, preserve and
promote live jazz by local, regional, national and
international artists for a diverse audience.*

Delta's Blues
www.delta-blues.com
*CDs & links to Pennsylvania's Blues Musicians,
clubs, bars & festivals. Our Blues Calendar lists blues
events in central and northern PA.*

Entertainment In Pennsylvania
Dave Blackledge dave@dblackledge.com
www.PAEntertainment.com
*Site listing musicians, singer-songwriters, bands and
venues in Pennsylvania.*

Fly Magazine
info@flymagazine.net
www.flymagazine.net
*Central PA's most complete guide to entertainment.
Fly Magazine publishes three separate editions
covering Lancaster, York and Harrisburg. Fly
Magazine is always looking for new subjects for our
editorial. If you are in a band please contact our
office.*

Gallery of Sound
galleryofsound.com
*Chain of CD stores that places reviews of local music
online.*

gothicstatecollege.com
www.gothicstatecollege.com
Central Pennsylvania's Gothic/Industrial resource.

The Harrisburg Music Guide
harrisburg.citysearch.com
*Extensive coverage of the local music scene. Post
your shows and events.*

Harrisburg Online
specialk@hbgonline.com
www.hbgonline.com
Central PA's entertainment guide.

Homegrown Bands
webmaster@homegrownbands.net
www.homegrownbands.net
*Central Pennsylvania's Home for Promoting Local
Bands.*

The LAB *(Local Area Bands)*
admin@thelab-pa.com
www.thelab-pa.com
*Supporting, encouraging and enjoying the Local Area
Bands of Pennsylvania and other nearby states.*

The Lancaster Music Guide
lancaster.citysearch.com
*Extensive coverage of the local music scene. Post
your shows and events.*

Lehigh Valley 2Night
webmaster@lehighvalley2night.com
www.lehighvalley2night.com
*From interviews with bands and DJ's to reader polls
on the most entertaining show offer in the valley. Each
week we will spotlight on one specific band or DJ and
we will always let you know where all of your favorite
local bands and DJ's will be.*

Lehigh Valley Blues Network
jcm46@earthlink.net
www.lvbn.org
*Dedicated to the Preservation and Promotion of The
Blues in The Lehigh Valley Area of Pennsylvania.*

Lehigh Valley Folk Music Society
kristbenj@aol.com
www.lvfolkmusicsociety.org
*Dedicated to promoting the appreciation of the old
time American folk music for people of all ages in the
Lehigh Valley of eastern Pennsylvania.*

LVMUSICART.COM
info@lvmusicart.com
www.lvmusicart.com
This purpose of this website is to celebrate the diverse artistic minds of those who perform and/or support the music and arts scene in the Lehigh Valley.

The Morning Call
www.mcall.com
Allentown daily paper covering the Allentown, Bethlehem, Easton and Philadelphia music scenes.

New Zoo Band Review
Joey G. nzbr@hotmail.com
www.hbgonline.com/zoo
Covering the Harrisburg area. Does your band kick ass yet once again for some unmentionable reason does not get the exposure and promotion it deserves? For possible qualification send us your bio, CD, videotape, pictures etc.

The Northeast PA Blues Society
greeneyedlady@happyhippie.com
www.nepablues.org

Out On the Town
www.ootweb.com
Entertainment trade paper, comes out every three weeks. Covers Pennsylvania and New Jersey.

PA Entertainment
dave@dblackledge.com
www.paentertainment.com
A good source for discovering entertainment in Pennsylvania and for getting the word out about what's happening.

PA Rocks
parocks@parocks.com
www.parocks.com
News, reviews, interviews, gig listings etc.

PABands.com
webmaster@pabands.com
www.pabands.com
Sign your band up today. Your band's listing is free forever! All that we ask is that you please link us from your site.

PaMidstate
tom@pamidstate.com
www.pamidstate.com
Your events and entertainment guide to the Midstate Region of Pennsylvania. (The Susquehanna Valley) Events, venues and guides and a forum to complain, comment or question, PaMidstate is your online resource!

The Patriot News
www.patriot-news.com
Harrisburg weekly arts and entertainment paper. Interviews bands, previews and reviews CDs and concerts.

Pennsylvania Hardcore
pa215hxc@voicenet.com
members.tripod.com/~pahxc
PA style hardcore and Philly graffiti.

Pennsylvania Jazz Society
Info@pajazzsociety.org
www.pajazzsociety.org
Dedicated to the preservation, promotion and presentation of traditional and mainstream jazz.

Pennsylvania Musician Magazine
rnoll@pamusician.net
www.pamusician.net
Designed as a guide and marketing tool to further the growth of the entertainment industry in PA.

The Pennsylvania Ska Page
paska@kozlek.com
paska.kozlek.com
This page should accurately cover every aspect of the PA ska scene.

Pennsylvania's Southern Gospel Website
scott@southerngospelpa.com
www.southerngospelpa.com
If you have a Southern Gospel Group or Organization in Pennsylvania or know of one that is not listed on our site, please email the specifics to me.

The Pocono Bluegrass and Folk Society
felixpap@ptd.net
www.poconobluegrass.org
Dedicated to the promotion and preservation of authentic acoustic music.

Pulse Weekly
Michael Faillace Michaelf@pulseweekly.com
www.pulseweekly.com
Covering the arts and entertainment scene in the Lehigh Valley and beyond.

Rock in PA
andy@rockinpa.com
www.rockinpa.com
Features information about up-and-coming Pennsylvania-area bands, concert venues in our area, Central PA club schedules and information and sound clips in our "Featured Local Bands" section.

Seven Mountains Bluegrass Association
www2.epix.net/~7mtns
The purpose of this Association shall be to preserve, promote and enjoy bluegrass music and to bring said music to an ever increasing number of people. Based in Central Pennsylvania.

StateCollegeMusic
info@statecollegemusic.com
www.statecollegemusic.com
For local musicians and bands that perform in and around State College, PA and around Centre County. Here you will hopefully find information that is useful to you and the music community in State College (Happy Valley).

The Susquehanna Folk Music Society
susarts@aol.com
www.sfmsfolk.org
Dedicated to preserving and encouraging the traditional arts in Central Pennsylvania.

The Snapper
www.thesnapper.com
Millersville University's student paper.

Sonicdrift.com
sonic_drift79@yahoo.com
www.sonicdrift.com
Southwestern Pennsylvania's source for local music and more.

Stage Take
Info@StageTake.com
www.stagetake.com
Feel free to list your band, check the top ten, vote for your favorite or browse the classifieds. Supporting Original Music in PA.

The Swarthmore Phoenix
phoenix@swarthmore.edu
www.sccs.swarthmore.edu/org/phoenix
Published every Thursday by students of Swarthmore College, except during examination and vacation periods.

Unsung Hero
www.uhero.com
An innovative music/art magazine showcasing local and regional musicians, artists, & writers/poets. Covers Pennsylvania, Washington DC, Maryland and New York.

WebJHN.com
johng@webjhn.com
webjhn.com
From all-the-way live local MC performances to the hottest parties, Your JHN Hip Hop and R&B Street Team is taking Hip Hop entertainment in Pittsburgh to the next level.

The Weekender
www.timesleader.com
Wilkes-Barre free weekly arts and entertainment paper. Interviews bands and previews concerts.

The Wilkes-Barre Music Guide
wilkesbarre.citysearch.com
Extensive coverage of the local music scene. Post your shows and events.

Philadelphia

The 13th Child
the13thchyld@lycos.com
the13thchild.com
Philadelphia gothic & industrial promotions & productions.

Audiogliphix Magazine
audiogliphix@aol.com
www.audiogliphix.freeservers.com
In 1997 AG made a commitment to Philadelphia's artists, by always featuring local talent on the cover. Audiogliphix Magazine has consistently led Philadelphia's print media in both content and design and will continue to do so.

Break Even
ptb@breakeven.org
www.breakeven.org
An independent non-profit label based in Philadelphia. It is dedicated to providing an outlet for artists to have their art heard and seen, rather than making money. Please support independent artists.

Candelabra
seniors@candelabra.org
www.candelabra.org
Philly-Based Goth/Industrial Scene Mag.

Groove Lingo
trishy@groovelingo.com
www.groovelingo.com
Covering the Philadelphia music scene. News, reviews and interviews.

Ladyfest Philly
info@ladyfestphilly.org
www.ladyfestphilly.org
This event will showcase women's activism through visual arts, music, dance, theater, film, the written word, the spoken word, workshops and panel discussions.

maneo.com

www.maneo.com
Philadelphia's online nightlife guide. Spotlights local bands. Local events guide.

Obzine

www.obzineonline.com
Philadelphia's premiere FREE news publication. Your guide to underground events.

origivation

Origivation@aol.com
www.origivation.com
Philadelphia's only all-original music publication. If sending CDs for review you must include 3 copies for it to be considered for review. No exceptions.

The Philadelphia Ambient Consortium

Aharon Varady aharon@simpletone.com
www.simpletone.com
Are you an artist who feels isolated and friendless in this so-called "City of Brotherly Love"? The Philadelphia Ambient Consortium seeks to remedy this situation by unifying the city's dedicated space, ambient, chill drumnbass, intelligent, improvisational, drone and experimental electronic audiophiles by providing a centralized information resource and the kernel of a community.

Philadelphia City Paper

pat@citypaper.net
citypaper.net
Free weekly alternative paper. Covers all music styles.

The Philadelphia Classical Guitar Society

membership@phillyguitar.com
www.phillyguitar.org
Dedicated to supporting and encouraging classical guitar activities throughout the Delaware Valley.

The Philadelphia Folksong Society

pfs@pfs.org
www.pfs.org
An organization dedicated to furthering folk music in the Greater Philadelphia area and beyond. Members can participate in concerts, workshops, sings and other special events and receive our newsletter nine times per year.

Philadelphia Inquirer

www.philly.com/mld/inquirer
Daily paper.

Philadelphia Music Guide

philadelphia.citysearch.com
Extensive coverage of local music. Post your shows and events.

The Philadelphia Weekly

www.philadelphiaweekly.com
Free weekly alternative paper. Does CD reviews.

Philly at Night

philly@phillyatnight.com
www.phillynightlife.com
Because PhillyAtNight.com offers free listings to every business and artist in the Philadelphia area, the site will remain a completely comprehensive and convenient tool.

Philly Blues

info@phillyblues.com
www.phillyblues.com
The tri-state areas most comprehensive list of blues bands, links to their websites and where you can see them this weekend!!!

Philly Goth

jules@fusion-web.org
www.fusion-web.org/phillygoth
An effort to coordinate and advertise concerts and activities of interest to the Philadelphia area Goths and their associates. Our calendar is primarily for Philadelphia events, but also includes shows in neighboring cities (NYC, DC, Pittsburgh) if they are special events or feature Philly bands or DJs.

Philly Word

www.phillyword.com
The final say in Hip Hop. Covers local music.

PhillyHipHop.com

snow@phillyhiphop.com
www.phillyhiphop.com
Philly area artists!!! If you're prepared for an HONEST review, send us your material on CD along with cover art & a bio and we'll highlight it on the site.

phillyjunglemassive.com

www.phillyjunglemassive.com
Covering the Philadelphia Jungle music scene.

phillymusic.com

theuberdude@yahoo.com
www.phillymusic.com
Feel free to send observations, insults, dirty jokes, questions... whatever floats your boat.

phillytown.com

webmaster@phillytown.com
www.phillytown.com
Everybody likes live music and we here at Phillytown.com are no different. We review the Good, the Bad and the Ugly of local musical talent in Philly. Also, add your events to our local music schedule.

Sharpshooter

brian@sharpshooter.cc
sharpshooter.cc
Covers the Philadelphia area hardcore scene.

tbtmo.com

info@tbtmo.com
www.tbtmo.com
Covering the Philadelphia electronic music scene.

Three Hot Chicks Promotions

Robyn robynm@threehotchicks.com
www.threehotchicks.com
We are a promotions company based out of Philadelphia. Our purpose is to spread the word about local musicians.

Pittsburgh

AcoustiCafe.org

mark@acousticafe.org
www.acousticafe.org
Pittsburgh musician's resource. We strive to promote not only all genres of acoustic music, but all singer-songwriters in general. If you would like to submit music for review or be a part of AcoustiCafe, please me and send two copies of the following: artist / group bios, press kits, CDs and promotional materials for consideration.

Artist Match

email@artistmatch.com
www.artistmatch.com
A free resource for Pittsburgh artists, clubs, agencies, or individuals looking to find the right artist for the right gig. We are looking for good original music; contact us if you have any you would like to have debuted.

pghgoth.com

raphrat@tyranny.com
www.pghgoth.com
There are an amazingly large number of Goth/industrial bands in Pittsburgh for a mid-sized east coast city. Many of the bands listed here have played little or no live shows and have few or no releases, but asked to be listed; however, the majority of them do shows frequently and have recorded material available.

PghLocalMusic.com

info@pghlocalmusic.com
www.pghlocalmusic.com
The Pittsburgh local musicians listed in our directory now have an option for a low-cost, low-risk means of vending their merchandise online via our storefront.

Pittbands.com

bridgeportent@hotmail.com
www.pittbands.com
If you need to send us any sort of package regarding shows, CD reviews or whatever, please visit our website to get our mailing address.

pittgoth.com

darklogik@pittgoth.com
www.pittgoth.com
Pittsburgh Gothic information and listings.

pittpunk.com

www.pittpunk.com
CD and Show Reviews, event calendar and MP3s.

Pittsburgh Artist Match

email@artistmatch.com
www.artistmatch.com
A free resource for local artists, clubs, agencies, or individuals looking to find the right artist for the right gig. We are looking for good original music, contact us if you have any you would like to have debuted.

Pittsburgh Blues Women

jtdavies@bigfoot.com
www.pghblueswomen.com
Who thinks of Pittsburgh when it comes to the blues? Actually, Pittsburgh has some of the most talented female blues artists in the country. If you're a fan of the blues, you definitely want to make sure that you see these women strut their stuff—you will be amazed!

Pittsburgh City Paper

www.pghcitypaper.com
Free weekly arts and entertainment paper.

The Pittsburgh Folk Music Society

calliopePA@aol.com
www.calliopehouse.org
Promotes and preserves traditional and contemporary folk music and its allied arts.

Pittsburgh Jazz Society

info@pittsburghjazz.org
www.pittsburghjazz.org
Dedicated to the promotion, preservation and perpetuation of all jazz.

The Pittsburgh Music Guide

pittsburgh.citysearch.com
Extensive coverage of local music. Post your shows and events.

The Pittsburgh Songwriters Association

psa@trfn.clpgh.org
trfn.clpgh.org/psa
Dedicated to helping its members develop and market their songs.

Pittsburgh Tribune-Review
www.pittsburghlive.com/x/tribune-review
Daily paper.

PittsburghHipHop.com
john@pittsburghhiphop.com
www.pittsburghhiphop.com
Your local Pittsburgh Hip Hop authority.

PittsburghRock.com
manny@PittsburghRock.com
www.pittsburghrock.com
Focused on advancing the presence of the Pittsburgh/Western Pennsylvania Region in the national independent music scene.

The Renaissance and Baroque Society of Pittsburgh
www.rbsp.org
Presents performances of the music of the Middle Ages, Renaissance, Baroque and Early Classical periods and fosters a broader understanding and appreciation of the music, arts and culture of the times.

Ultimate Pittsburgh-Area Band Link Page
yairi@randombrothers.com
www.randombrothers.com/bandlink.htm
Supporting Pittsburgh music. E-mail us if you would like us to link up your band page!

Rhode Island

Lotsofnoise
contact@lotsofnoise.com
www.lotsofnoise.com
Devoted to Providence-area indie shows, leaning towards noise and punk rock.

Providence Arts & Culture
provri@as220.org
www.providenceri.com/as220/music.html
Covering the Providence local music scene.

Providence Attacks!
xbenbarnettx@yahoo.com
www.geocities.com/xbenbarnettx/ProvidenceAttacks
Dedicated to the independent music scene in Providence. Check out bands, labels, businesses and other info sites that promote the various activities here.

The Providence Journal
www.projo.com
Daily paper. Covers local music scene. Accepts CDs for review consideration.

The Providence Music Guide
providence.citysearch.com
Extensive coverage of the local music scene. Post your shows and events.

The Providence Phoenix
www.providencephoenix.com
Free weekly alternative paper. Covers Rhode Island and the South Eastern Massachusetts music scene. CD and concert reviews.

Rhode Island Songwriters Association
RhodySong@aol.com
members.aol.com/rhodysong
Holds monthly critique sessions, as well as open mics.

South Carolina

The Beaufort Gazette
www.beaufortgazette.com
Daily paper in Beaufort, SC. Has an entertainment section.

Charleston City Paper
www.charlestoncitypaper.com
Free weekly arts and entertainment paper. Covers local music scene with artist interviews, CD and concert previews and reviews.

The Charleston Music Guide
charleston.citysearch.com
Extensive coverage of the local music scene. Post your shows and events.

Charleston Post and Courier
www.charleston.net
Daily newspaper.

Charleston Swing!
charlestonswings@aol.com
www.charlestonswing.com
This website is dedicated to swing music and dancing in Charleston, South Carolina. If it's a big band, rockabilly, lounge, western, or a rockin' swing sound—you'll find it here.

CharlestonRocks
shawnte@charlestonrocks.com
www.geocities.com/charlestonrocks
This is a website devoted to local music in the Charleston, SC area (and beyond!). It was started by three cool chicks with a vision of music and happiness everywhere...

Chuck Nice Inc.com
chuckinc@bellsouth.net
www.chuckniceinc.com
South Carolina's #1 entertainment website.

The Columbia Music Guide
columbia.citysearch.com
Extensive coverage of the local music scene. Post your shows and events.

Creative Loafing Greenville
www.cln.com
Free weekly arts and entertainment paper. Interviews artists, previews and reviews concerts and CDs.

Demboy.com
chawledawk@37.com
www.demboy.com
Karolina's Hip Hop Gateway: Demboy.com, dedicated to the Carolina Hip Hop Movement.

Free Times
www.free-times.com
Columbia's free alternative weekly arts and entertainment paper. CD and concert previews and reviews.

The Gamecock
www.dailygamecock.com
University of South Carolina's student paper.

Greenville Chapter NSAI
www.nsaigreenville.com
Meet other writers in the Greenville area, learn about the craft of songwriting and find out how the music business works.

The Greenville Music Guide
greenville.citysearch.com
Extensive coverage of the local music scene. Post your shows and events.

GRITZ
www.gritz.net
Based in Greenville, we review Southern music of all types, as well as blues, classic rock, pop. No metal or rap. Folks can send cds and packages anytime.

Real-Local.com
Neill webmaster@real-local.com
www.real-local.com
24 hour internet broadcast and ezine featuring Charleston SC's thriving music scene.

Rivertown Bluegrass Society
mickey@rivertownbluegrasssociety.com
www.rivertownbluegrasssociety.com
Based in Conway SC. Keeping America's Music alive in the hearts of American's where it was born.

SChiphop.com
reviews@schiphop.com
www.schiphop.com
An online community of the hottest underground and nationally known talent in SC. It is a site where visitors can browse through music produced and written by local talent. Visitors are able to purchase that music.

scunderground.com
www.scunderground.com
Your source for the South Carolina music scene.

South Carolina Bluegrass and Traditional Music Association
expresswebs.com/scbtma
To preserve, promote, publicize and support this unique musical style through concerts, work shops and public educational programs.

SouthCarolinaBands.com
www.southcarolinabands.com
To have your CD considered for review, please submit your CD and information to us.

Southeastern Bluegrass Association of South Carolina
ccalder@sc.rr.com
www.sebga.org
Our mission is to help preserve and further the love of Bluegrass music.

The State
www.thestate.com
Columbia daily paper. Covers local music scene with interviews, previews and reviews.

South Dakota

The Argus Leader
www.argusleader.com
Sioux Falls daily paper. Covers local music scene, reviews CD releases, previews concerts, interviews bands.

Black Hills Music
si@blackhillsbusiness.com
blackhillsmusic.com
Covering all aspects of the Black Hill's music scene. Add yourself, your CD, your radio show, or your open mic at this site.

Mg Studio
Mike kc0ftm@dailypost.com
www.watertownrock.com
A protools studio, located in Watertown, SD. We also help bands book shows about 8 times a year.

Panache Magazine
barb@panachepages.com
www.panachepages.com
Rapid City free bi-weekly alternative arts and entertainment magazine. Covers local scene. Accepts press kits from bands playing in the area.

Rapid City Journal
www.rapidcityjournal.com
Daily paper. Covers local music scene with band interviews, CD and concert previews and reviews.

Sioux Falls Jazz and Blues Society
info@sfjb.org
www.sfjb.org
Our mission is to increase awareness of Jazz and Blues music in the Sioux Falls community, via musical events and education.

South Dakota Friends of Traditional Music
info@fotm.org
www.fotm.org
Dedicated to preserving and promoting traditional music for generations of South Dakotans.

Wipe Your Eyes and Face the Day
Jayson jweihs@hotmail.com
www.wipeyoureyes.com
This site is mainly a report for Sioux Falls punk scene, along with pictures, reviews, shows and other randomness. Interact with the locals on the message board and check it out!

Tennessee

CIA Music
www.ciamusic.com
Supporting Chattanooga Independent Artists since 1998.

The Chattanooga Music Guide
chattanooga.citysearch.com
Extensive coverage of the local music scene. Post your shows and events.

Chattanooga Times Free Press
www.timesfreepress.com
Daily paper.

The Daily Beacon
beacon@utk.edu
dailybeacon.utk.edu
University of Tennessee's student paper.

Down-South.com
DownSouth@Comcast.net
www.down-south.com
We do reviews on current southern Hip Hop albums, both independent and major releases as well as interviews with those artists. Based in Tennessee, we also cover artists from Alabama, Arkansas, Florida, Georgia, Louisiana, Mississippi, North Carolina, S Carolina and Texas.

Enigma Online
www.enigmaonline.com
We support the local Chattanooga music scene. We do not cater to the "folks that live on the mountain" or to local station managers or the corporate establishment. EOL is the real thing - and doesn't cater to the "NORM".

KnoxGothic.com
www.knoxgothic.com
Knoxville and East Tennessee's Gothic Source.

Knoxville Metro Pulse
musiceditor@metropulse.com
www.metropulse.com
Entertainment sections allows local bands to list their info and post their MP3s.

Knoxville Music Directory
www.kmusic.com
Knoxville and East Tennessee's directory of music performers and services.

The Knoxville City Music Guide
knoxville.citysearch.com
Extensive coverage of the local music scene. Post your shows and events.

Knoxville News-Sentinel
www.knoxnews.com
Daily paper.

KnoxShows
Renée renee@knoxshows.com
www.knoxshows.com
Bands, send in your profiles for the bands section and kids, send in your profiles for the people section. As always, if you have any show information, or any links or pictures for the site, please email them to me and I'll put them up.

Memphis Acoustic Music Association
jkitts1662@aol.com
www.mamamusic.org
We sponsor the preservation, proliferation and performance of acoustic music, both American folk and Celtic.

Memphis Area Bluegrass Association
bigpalooka62@aol.com
www.memphis-bluegrass.org
Our newsletter lets you know what is going on around the Mid-South, gives backgrounds of some of our members, reviews of CDs, books and much more.

The Memphis Commercial Appeal
www.gomemphis.com
Daily paper. Covers Tennessee, Arkansas and Mississippi music scenes. Profiles touring bands, reviews CDs.

The Memphis Flyer
www.memphisflyer.com
Free weekly paper. Covers local scene and touring bands playing the area.

The Memphis Mojo
boxcar61@memphismojo.com
www.memphismojo.com
Focusing on local music, where it's played and by whom.

The Memphis Music Guide
memphis.citysearch.com
Extensive coverage of the local music scene. Post your shows and events.

Memphis Songwriters Association
admin@memphissongwriters.com
www.memphissongwriters.org
Our mission is to help the songwriter with composition, lyric & song, to promote Memphis Music and to secure and protect the rights of our members.

MemphisRap.com
webmaster@memphisrap.com
www.MemphisRap.com
We at MemphisRap.com want your submissions and feedback! Artists can submit news, links, demos, audio files and more! It's all on our submission page!

Our Memphis
davidsparks@ourmemphis.net
www.ourmemphis.net
Information about the Memphis punk scene.

Sensored
trey@sensored.com
www.sensored.com
Our mission is to create a progressive media that demonstrates the value the arts in society as well as introducing lesser-known artists and musicians to a large audience that is craving a medium that solely supports the arts.

Southeasthiphop
southeasthiphop@yahoo.com
www.southeasthiphop.com
Based out of Knoxville, covering the South East Hip Hop scene.

Southern Ska
www.southernska.com
Listing of Ska bands in the south-east US.

The Tennessee Country Music Alliance
TCMA2000@aol.com
tennesseecma.org
Formed to provide an opportunity for undiscovered new talent to advance their careers by performing and networking with experienced leaders in the country music industry.

Tennessee Hip Hop.com
Tenn_HipHop@hotmail.com
www.tennesseehiphop.com
We bring you the best in underground hip hop from all over Tennessee. We welcome artists from anywhere in the US to showcase their music as well.

Tennessee Jazz & Blues Society
austinbel@earthlink.net
www.jazzblues.org
For the newsletter, Jazz & Blues News, you can write a letter to the editor, submit news, articles, or creative writing, submit CDs for review, get a live music event listed in the calendar, or advertise your business.

The Tennessee Songwriters Association
AskTSAI@aol.com
www.clubnashville.com/tsai.htm
Dedicated to informing, educating, assisting and representing all songwriters.

Tennessee Spins
spins.us/tennessee
A regional dance music community dedicated to Tennessee dance music, electronic music, DJ's, artists and community.

The Tri-Cities Music Guide
tricities.citysearch.com
Extensive coverage of the local music scene. Post your shows and events.

Nashville

Eyemix Magazine
PO Box 121462, Nashville, TN 37212
PH: 615-320-7379
Covering the Nashville music scene. If you would like to be featured in an upcoming issue, please contact us. Circulation is 5,000 printed and distributed throughout MusicRow and the Nashville area.

Independent Nashville Network
kyle@kissmannconsulting.com
indienews.8m.com
This site features artists and bands of middle TN that are interested in gaining attention in order to proceed or continue toward a career in the music industry.

Middleman Music
kelly@middlemanmusic.com
www.middlemanmusicpresents.com
Nashville's hottest rock scene. Get info on the latest bands and current music in Nashville.

Music City Blues
webmaster@musiccityblues.org
www.musiccityblues.org/Specialevents.htm
The group is actively involved in the middle Tennessee community by presenting musical performances and special programs designed to promote and sustain this music. You can also sell your CD online.

Music Row
news@musicrow.com
www.musicrow.com
Nashville's music industry publication. To list an Upcoming Release on the Music Row CD Release Schedule, please send us an e-mail with the name of the artist, album, label and date. The event must be of relative importance to Nashville's music industry to be listed.

Nashville Gothic
Exile exile313@mac.com
www.nashvillegothic.com
Dedicated to serving the needs of the gothic community in the Nashville and surrounding areas. If you would like to contribute information, photographs, or anything else please email us.

The Nashville Music Guide
nashville.citysearch.com
Extensive coverage of the local music scene. Post your shows and events.

Nashville Scene
editor@nashvillescene.com
www.nashscene.com
Free weekly alternative paper. Free weekly alternative paper. Covers local scene. Considers CDs for review in all styles.

Nashville Songwriter's Association International *(NSAI)*
nsai@NashvilleSongwriters.com
www.nashvillesongwriters.com
The world's largest not-for-profit songwriters trade organization. Established in 1967, our membership of nearly 5,000 spans the United States and 5 other countries. We are dedicated to protecting the rights and serving aspiring and professional songwriters in all genres of music.

NashvilleMusic.us
www.nashvillemusic.us
Add a link or event. Become a featured artist.

NashvilleSongwriter.net
Jerry Work jerry@lavodica.com
NashvilleSongwriter.net
This is a site for songwriters looking to expose their music to the people in Nashville looking for songs.

NashvilleRock.net
info@nashvillerock.net
nashvillerock.net
Nashville's home for the latest LOCAL rock news, reviews and concert information.

Nashvillerockscene.com
bands@nashvillerockscene.com
nashvillerockscene.com
Interviews, CD reviews, gig listings and more!

The Rage
pembry@nashvillerage.com
www.nashvillerage.com
Nashville free arts & entertainment weekly.

The Tennessean
www.tennessean.com
Nashville daily paper. Covers local music scene with band profiles, CD and concert previews and reviews.

Tunesmith
info@tunesmith.net
www.tunesmith.net
We proudly present some of Nashville's best undiscovered songwriting! Hear these songwriters and their demos before they're recorded by your favorite artists! This is what professional songwriting is all about!

Unsigned Nashville Artists
myike@unsignednashvilleartists.com
www.unsignednashvilleartists.com
Get your name out there in the public eye and possibly sell your music as the process!

The Vanderbilt Hustler
www.vanderbilthustler.com
Vanderbilt University's student paper.

Writer/Artist Showcase
mail@writerartist.com
www.writerartist.com
This site consists of information regarding the weekly songwriters shows held each Tuesday and Thursday at the Boardwalk Cafe in Nashville, TN and also regarding the music industry in general. It is also a tool for aspiring songwriters and artists in their effort to achieve success in the music industry.

Texas

The Bay Area Bluegrass Association
www.bayareabluegrass.org
The primary purpose is to preserve, encourage and promote Bluegrass and Bluegrass Gospel music as an American art form throughout the Houston area and beyond.

CD TEX
contact@bgmnetwork.com
www.cd-tex.com
A new online CD store designed specifically for Texas and Americana Music. We're just getting started, so we will be adding new artists and titles daily.

Central Texas Bluegrass Association
ctba@centraltexasbluegrass.org
www.centraltexasbluegrass.org
CTBA Bands! Let us know what you're up to! Got a new CD out? Get it reviewed or listed in our newsletter. Have a big show coming up? Put CTBA to work for you!

corpusmusic.com
corpusmusic.com
The purpose of this site is to help inform the Corpus Christi, Texas area about local music. By providing band information, show dates and even song downloads of local artists, we hope to help draw more attention to the local music scene.

The Daily Texan
entertainment@dailytexanonline.com
www.dailytexanonline.com
University of Texas at Austin student paper.

eguidemag.com
www.eguideonline.net
The entertainment magazine for the eastern Texas region.

The El Paso Music Guide
elpaso.citysearch.com
Extensive coverage of the local music scene. Post your shows and events.

El Paso Scene
www.epscene.com
Free monthly arts and entertainment paper. Concert previews and CD reviews.

The Foghorn
Entertainment_fg@delmar.edu
www.delmar.edu/foghorn
Campus newspaper of Del Mar College in Corpus Christi.

INsite Magazine
mail@insiteaustin.com
www.insiteaustin.com
Include features with local up-in-coming and national touring acts. We also provide the most comprehensive local (Local Tracts) and national (SchoolHouse Rock) CD Reviews.

The Juice
avista@thejuiceonline.com
www.thejuiceonline.com
San Antonio's entertainment magazine.

Ladyfest Texas
info@ladyfesttx.org
www.ladyfesttx.org
Our mission is to provide a forum in which all members of the community can celebrate, showcase and encourage the artistic, organizational and political talents of women.

Lone Star Music
artists@lonestarmusic.com
www.lonestarmusic.com
Your internet guide to Texas music. A huge selection CDs, MP3s, Reviews, Tour Dates, Contests, Prizes and much more. Buy CDs online. Texas tour dates has a comprehensive list of hundreds of tour dates for artists.

LubbockMusic.com
music@lubbockonline.com
www.lubbockmusic.com
MP3s, listings, gigs, resources etc.

Music Scene Magazine
musicscene@webtv.net
community-2.webtv.net/musicscene
Texoma's music and entertainment magazine.

MyTexasMusic.com
LuckyBoyd7@aol.com
www.mytexasmusic.com
If you are interested in selling your CD from our site, please contact us.

San Antonio Blues Society
www.sanantonioblues.com
Our sole purpose is promoting and preserving various styles of blues music. SABS presents quarterly jam sessions and special events featuring the hottest local blues acts.

San Antonio Express-News
www.mysanantonio.com
Daily paper. Covers local scene with artist interviews, CD and concert reviews.

The San Antonio Music Guide
sanantonio.citysearch.com
Extensive coverage of the local music scene. Post your shows and events.

San Antonio Rocks
SanAntonioZine@aol.com
www.sanantoniorocks.fr.st
Serving the greater San Antonio area and beyond! If you have any ideas or creative input, or if you know of a Christian band, venue, artist, or Church link, please send us some e-mail and share the wealth.

San Antonio Weekly Music News
Editor@sambe.org
sambe.org
An online newsletter with all that's going on in the SA music scene.

The Shorthorn
www.theshorthorn.com
University of Texas at Arlington campus paper.

Sounds like Texas
nancy@soundsliketexas.com
soundsliketexas.com
Online CD vendor. The best music in Texas, heard 'round the world. Check our site to find out how to submit your new release material for possible inclusion on Sounds like Texas.

South East Texas Blues Society
bfulbright@setbs.com
www.setbs.com
Dedicated to those who play the blues, enjoy the blues and to those that would like to.

Spring Creek Bluegrass Club *(SCBC)*
bluegrass22@ev1.net
users.ev1.net/~bluegrass22
An organization dedicated to preserving the wonderful tradition of bluegrass music.

State of Texas Gospel Announcers Guild
texgag@worldnet.att.net
www.texasgag.com
Our mission is to increase the penetration of gospel music in cities and towns in America through a greater awareness of and a greater acceptance of, this original contributing art form of Black America to American Music and the world.

Texas Jam - the resource that rocks!
TJ Taylor info@TexasJam.com
www.TexasJam.com
Dedicated to all the hard working musicians from the Lone Star State.

Texas Monthly
www.texasmonthly.com
We continue to be the indispensable authority on the Texas scene, covering music, the arts and cultural events with its insightful recommendations.

Texas Music Express
merch@texasmusicexpress.com
www.texasmusicexpress.com
If you are an artist/singer/songwriter/musician with Texas roots and are interested in marketing your CD's and other merchandise through TME, we would love to talk to you.

Texas Music Magazine
info@txmusic.com
www.txmusic.com
Texas is known for its uniqueness - not just the people but the culture. Most people cannot explain why Texans are the way they are, but they certainly notice a difference. It is in the unrivaled state pride. It is in the rich state history. Call it what you want, there is something special about Texas.

Texas Music Movement
cary@texasmusicmovement.com
www.texasmusicmovement.com
This website is dedicated to the Texas artists and their fans.

Texas Ska
ska@billtanner.net
www.billtanner.net/ska/skatex.html
News, reviews etc.

Texas Ska and Punk
peterchansen@hotmail.com
www.geocities.com/rude_pete
Reviews, interviews and other info from around the Texas scene.

Texas Talent Register
www.governor.state.tx.us/music
Listing of Texas born or based recording artists.

TexasMusicGuide.com
info@texasmusicguide.com
www.texasmusicguide.com
Your one-stop shop for Texas music festivals, events, venues, CD releases and artist links.

TexasReggae.org
TexasReggaeList@earthlink.net
www.texasreggae.org
Covering all things reggae in Texas.

TexasTroubadours.com
webmaster@texastroubadours.com
www.texastroubadours.com
Delivering the latest news of the Texas music scene to the general public. The information about the latest CD releases, concert reviews, artist interviews and CD review archives.

The University Review
review@uts.cc.utexas.edu.
www.utexas.edu/students/review
The University of Texas student paper.

West Texas Country
webmaster@westtexascountry.com
www.westtexascountry.com
Enjoy the spice of the West Texas area through WTC's unique artists and their music.

Women in Jazz
Hartbeat@swbell.net
www.womeninjazz.org
Our purpose is to provide professional development for female jazz vocalists, provide a professional setting in which female jazz artists can share their talents and provide Austin audiences with an opportunity to hear quality vocal jazz.

Austin

Austin 360 *Ultimate Austin Band List*
music@cim.austin360.com
www.austin360.com
List your band, events etc.

Austin American-Statesman
www.austin360.com
Daily paper. Covers local music scene with artist interviews, CD and concert previews and reviews.

Austin Americana
bill@austinamericana.com
www.austinamericana.com
Read reviews of the best in Americana music. Find out about great CDs by local and Americana artists.

The Austin Classical Guitar Society
acgspublications@hotmail.com
www.austinclassicalguitar.org
Serving as an educational and social link between amateur and professional guitarists and the community.

Austin Friends of Traditional Music
erhunt@austin.rr.com
www.main.org/aftm/aftmhome.htm
Dedicated to encouraging the performance, appreciation, preservation and sharing of all genres of traditional / folk / ethnic / international music and dance.

Austin Metal Music
i_amm_ironman@yahoo.com
www.austinmetalmusic.homestead.com
We are committed to bringing you info about the underground heavy metal scene in Austin.

Austin Metro Entertainment
Derrall Frost difrost@austinmetro.com
www.austinmetro.com
An entertainment guide for Austin and Central Texas, listing live music performances, events and on-going activities for all ages.

Austin Music
WebMina@austinlinks.com
www.austinlinks.com/Music
Listing of Austin bands.

The Austin Music Foundation
info@austinmusicfoundation.org
www.austinmusicfoundation.org
Dedicated to the professional development and economic advancement of musicians, the creation and preservation of Austin's unique musical heritage and the development of a strong local music community.

The Austin Music Guide
editor_austin@citysearch.com
austin.citysearch.com
Extensive coverage of the local music scene. Post your shows and events.

austinbands.net
Chris.tom@austinbands.net
www.austinbands.net
Please check out our band list and add your band to it. Also take a look at our calendar with band gigs, CD releases, concerts and more. Submit your bands gig dates and info along with CD releases.

AustinExperience.com
content@austinexperience.com
www.austinexperience.com
Musicians, get the word out! Send your CDs, press packets or anything else you'd like to share. We'll help you spread the word.

AustinGoGo.com
webmaster@austingogo.com
www.austingogo.com
Founded to promote the small and independent businesses and community organizations, including music stores, labels, websites etc. that make Austin, Texas, a great place to live.

austinlive.com
lisa@austinlive.com
www.austinlive.com
News, reviews and band info.

AustinSINGER.com
www.austinsinger.com
It's our goal to provide as much info about the Austin music scene as possible and be a valuable resource in finding all the fun that makes Austin GREAT!

Capitol-City A&E Zine
larue@capitol-city.com
www.capitol-city.com
Music and arts in Austin.

Local Flavor
localflavor@austinmetro.com
www.austinmetro.com/Localflavor
CDs for sale of Austin & Texas Musicians.

MusicAustin
www.musicaustin.com
A catalog of the Austin music scene. Over 250 individual artist pages and hundreds of music clips.

SoundsOfAustin.com
ContactUs@SoundsOfAustin.com
www.soundsofaustin.com
Here, you'll find information about new artists, music from some of Austin's best songwriters and musicians and links to businesses that help make up the music scene in Austin, Texas.

Texas Observer
observer@texasobserver.org
texasobserver.org
Austin news & entertainment weekly.

Dallas/Fort Worth

Dallas Band Connection
jbreeves@jbreevesfamily.com
www.dallasbandconnection.com
Wanna be listed? Email us and we'll see who the next featured band will be.

The Dallas Classic Guitar Society
office@dallasguitar.org
www.dallasguitar.org
Through concerts and outreach efforts, the Guitar Society touches thousands of lives each year.

Dallas Hardcore
sam@dallashardcore.com
www.dallashardcore.com
Our purpose is to promote the scene and help it grow by providing a forum where people from the Dallas/Fort Worth area can exchange information and to introduce people to the scene that wouldn't have otherwise known it existed.

Dallas Morning News
www.dallasnews.com
Daily paper. Covers local music scene with artist profiles and concert previews.

Dallas Music Guide
ccomley@dallasmusicguide.com
www.dallasmusicguide.com
The site is updated weekly with album reviews and our picks of the week's best gigs. Live reviews and interviews are added as they happen.

Dallas Observer
feedback@dallasobserver.com
www.dallasobserver.com
Dallas news & entertainment weekly.

Dallas, Tyler, Shreveport Underground
james@dtsunderground.com
www.dtsunderground.com
All reviews are presented as honest opinions and should be taken with a grain of salt, because one man's trash is another man's treasure.

Dallas Songwriter's Association
info@dallassongwriters.org
www.dallassongwriters.org
We exist to enhance the overall personal growth and professionalism of our members.

dallas.com
www.dallas.com
The Dallas area music scene: clubs, concerts, bars, nightlife and a local band directory.

dallaslocalmusicscene.com
info@dallaslocalmusicscene.com
www.dallaslocalmusicscene.com
We'll set up you band online with MP3s, photos etc. A one time fee of $50 for the initial setup.

dallasmusic
dallasmusic@hotmail.com
www.dallasmusic.com
Our mission is to cover and help promote the local music scene. If you live out of the area and would like a CD review, mail us a promo pack. All entries are listened to.

DallasMusic.us
www.dallasmusic.us
Add a link or event. Become a featured artist.

DFWSCENE.com
info@dfwscene.com
www.dfwscene.com
Covering Dallas/Fort Worth music. We've tried to maintain our site with news, articles and calendar events as best we can. We appreciate your emails, suggestions, criticisms, invitations and updates as to where the best shows are around town. Send us your Demo's or Press Kits.

The Fort Worth Songwriters Association
info@fwsa.com
www.fwsa.com
Dedicated to improving our lyrical and musical work through fellowship, workshops and education.

Fort Worth Star Telegram
www.dfw.com/mld/dfw
Daily paper.

Fort Worth Weekly
www.fwweekly.com
Fort Worth's arts & entertainment weekly.

GuideLive.com
Sunni Thompson jsthompson@dallasnews.com
www.guidelive.com
Extensive coverage of the Dallas/Ft. Worth music scene. Post your shows and events.

Headbanger's Delight
linda@harderbeat.com
www.harderbeat.com
HB magazine (in print and online) is in its 10th year of publication, covering from alternative to harder music. We do national, regional and local (D/FW area bands) as features, live and CD reviews. Also have extremities, alternative, cyberbeat, for musicians only and local buzz columns.

The Sound Magazine
Andie Jones andie@soundmag.com
www.soundmag.com
Unique Dallas multimedia performing and visual arts community, resource and publication. Sections for local and national reviews.

Southwest Blues
swblues@aol.com
www.southwestblues.com
A Dallas based magazine focusing on Blues artists of the southwest. We feature and spot light many recording artists signed with major labels and also some artists that deserve the recognition after years of paying their dues.

Spune Productions
www.spune.com
It is the desire of Spune to promote quality independent artists, rich in integrity, that compose music that is passionate, honest and creative. To truly believe in the artist, not just the music and to simply make you aware of both.

Women Rockin' 4 Women
webmaster@womenrockin4women.org
www.womenrockin4women.org
Dallas based charity. Benefiting shelters for victims of domestic violence. With the support of local artists and businesses, Women Rockin' 4 Women is now more than just a vision. With your help, the foundation can raise more money and donations with each event. Get involved - stop domestic violence.

Houston

The Daily Cougar
dcougar@mail.uh.edu
www.uh.edu/campus/cougar
University of Houston's student paper.

GrooveRevolution
webmaster@grooverevolution.com
www.grooverevolution.com
Houston's online music community.

Guitar Houston
mail@guitarhouston.org
www.guitarhouston.org
*Bringing together people that love classical guitar
and its historical relatives such as the lute. We support
worthy and talented developing artists at the
beginning of their careers through free concerts and
community outreach programs.*

Houston Bands and Clubs "Live"
stuart.lindow@imsicorp.com
www.houstonbandslive.com
www.houstonclubslive.com
*View and hear live music from Houston clubs and
bands.*

Houston Beat
heyhb@houstonbeat.com
www.houstonbeat.com
List your bands, shows and special events.

Houston Bluegrass
willsmith@pdq.net
www.houstonbluegrass.com
*This site is dedicated to all those hardworking
bluegrass people in and around the Houston area.
The clubs, bands and the fans all work together to
promote the growth and advancement of the music
and the family-oriented spirit which is strong within
the bluegrass community.*

The Houston Blues Society
diunna@yahoo.com
www.houstonbluessociety.org
*HBS focuses on five main programs: education,
archives, newsletter and Internet publications, special
events and a monthly jam session.*

Houston Chronicle
www.chron.com
Daily paper.

Houston Folklore & Folk Music Society
www.houstonfolkmusic.org
*Dedicated to the preservation and promotion of
folklore and folk music.*

Houston/Fort Bend Songwriters Association
www.hfbsa.org
*Our mission is to support and encourage the art and
craft of songwriting, to provide professional resources
and educational opportunities to songwriters and to
nurture a positive environment in which songwriters
may fully develop their potential as songwriters,
musicians, performers and artists.*

The Houston Music Guide
editor_houston@citysearch.com
houston.citysearch.com
*Extensive coverage of the local music scene. Post
your shows and events.*

Houston Press
feedback@houstonpress.com
www.houstonpress.com
The city's only major news and entertainment weekly.

The Houston Scene
ragegirl6@aol.com
houstonscene.homestead.com
Covering the Houston hardcore scene.

Houston Women's Festival
hwfestival@earthlink.net
www.hwfestival.org
*The festival is open to all friends of the women's
community and includes a full day of excellent music,
a visual and performing art exhibit and a community
marketplace of vendors. Volunteers are always
welcome.*

houstonbands.net
webmaster@houstonbands.net
www.houstonbands.net
The network for Houston bands on the internet.

Jazz Houston
www.jazzhouston.com
*This regional web site has it all: gig listings, player
profiles, recordings, news and a thriving community
area. The Forum is active and interesting. You may be
surprised to learn that Houston actually has a pretty
cool jazz scene.*

North Star News
Eric Harvey eric.d.harvey@nhmccd.edu
www.northstarnewsonline.com
*The college/community newspaper of North Harris
College, located in Houston, Texas.*

Real Folk Music
www.realfolkmusic.com
*Future releases will feature songwriters from
Houston's pool of exceptionally talented unknowns
and sounds from players who thrive on the cross-
pollination of the musical cultures in this city; a
happy byproduct of Houston's status as a crossroads
for the world energy business.*

Space City Rock
gaijin@spacecityrock.com
www.spacecityrock.com
Covering the Houston music scene.

Utah

Daily Universe
newsnet.byu.edu
Brigham Young University's student paper.

Deseret News
deseretnews.com
Salt Lake City daily paper.

Draztikbeatz.net
www.draztikbeatz.net
*The HipHop/Rap Resource for the Salt Lake City
Area!*

The Rock Salt
staff@therocksalt.com
www.therocksalt.com
Bringing you the rock from the great salt lake.

Intermountain Acoustic Music Association
iamaedit@attbi.com
www.iamaweb.org
*Based out of Salt Lake City. Dedicated to the
preservation, furtherance and spread of acoustic
music, including bluegrass, British isles, folk, old-time
and related musical forms.*

LDS Music World
comments@ldsmusicworld.com
www.ldsmusicworld.com
*Bringing you the best in Latter Day Saints music -
offering news, reviews, features, music downloads,
internet radio - all from a wide variety of LDS artists.*

LDSMusicians.com
feedback@ldsmusicians.com
www.ldsmusicians.com
*We have given a voice and a family to many hopeful
Latter Day Saints musicians across the world and it's
just getting started!*

LDSsongs
feedback@ldsmusicians.com
www.ldsmusicians.com
*A reference site for Latter Day Saints music, including
reviews and information about albums, artists, labels,
dealers and distributors*

Local Salt Lake City
www.localslc.com
*Your spot on the web for entertainment and arts in
Utah. News, reviews, interviews and MP3s.*

Music Utah
info@MusicUtah.com
www.musicutah.com
*Features an event calendar, a venue directory, a band
directory, classifieds and more.*

The Salt Lake City Music Guide
utah.citysearch.com
*Extensive coverage of the local music scene. Post
your shows and events.*

Salt Lake City Weekly
comments@slweekly.com
www.slweekly.com
*Free weekly alternative paper. Covers local music
scene with band interviews, CD and concert previews
and reviews.*

The Salt Lake Tribune
www.sltrib.com
Daily paper.

Salt Lake Under Ground *(SLUG)*
slugmag@slugmag.com
www.slugmag.com
*Salt Lake's oldest non-mainstream magazine reaching
over 25,000 viewers in 3 states. Covers local music
scene with concert and indie CD reviews.*

The Seldom Scene
matt@theseldomscene.com
www.theseldomscene.com
*A collective of friends/bands dedicated to playing,
promoting, watching, coordinating and just being a
part of the music they love.*

SLC Billy Central
slcbillygirl@yahoo.com
www.rockabilly.net/slc
*Rockabilly, swing and country in Salt Lake City. Send
us your show dates and CDs for review.*

UT Punx
nftbd@punks.org
www.angelfire.com/ut/socialoutcast
*Help UT Punx! Send in show dates, pictures, venues
info, links other anything else! the more that people
contribute, the bigger & better this shit-hole will be.*

Utah Area Music
editor@utahareamusic.com
www.utahareamusic.com
*A monthly publication that is uniquely interested in
music created in Utah. We really like the struggling,
unknown bands and solo artists, particularly the ones
that play to all-ages crowds wherever and whenever
they can.*

The Utah Music Guide
editor_utah@citysearch.com
utah.citysearch.com
Extensive coverage of the local music scene. Post your shows and events.

UtahBands.com
info@fungusent.com
www.utahbands.com
The Premiere Web Site for the Band Scene in Utah We are open to all types of music. For added convenience, you can sort the concert listings by band, date, venue, or city—just click the respective heading. UtahBands.com offers a state of the art music posting service for band members to promote their concerts.

utahska.com
ryan@azska.com
www.utahska.com
Covering the Utah ska scene.

Vermont

artvt
artvt@together.net
www.artvt.com
A listing of Vermont musical artists. You can e-mail a .jpeg or .gif file and some info on the artist's background etc.

Big Heavy World
groundzero@bigheavyworld.com
www.bigheavyworld.com
Our MP3 Showcase is an opportunity for Vermont musicians and bands to give away songs promotionally as CD quality downloads. Tracks in the Showcase also have a great chance of being promoted by Creative Labs with their LAVA! 3D music video software. There are also TV opportunities.

Burlington Free Press
www.burlingtonfreepress.com
Daily paper.

Deerfield Valley News
www.dvalnews.com
Southern Vermont's source for entertainment.

Early Music Vermont
www.earlymusicvermont.org
Bringing together singers and players from the Vermont region who share a passion for music, especially early music from the medieval, renaissance and baroque eras.

WEQX Local Music Page
www.weqx.com
Add in your band info and upcoming gigs.

Seven Days
info@sevendaysvt.com
www.sevendaysvt.com
Burlington weekly alternative paper. Covers Vermont music scene. Accepts press kit and CD for review if playing in the area.

The Times Argus
www.timesargus.com
Our paper is over 100 years old and Vermont's largest afternoon newspaper publishing seven days a week.

Vermont Collegian
www.vtliving.com/newspapers/vtcollegian
Burlington biweekly paper.

The Vermont MIDI Project
sandi@vtmidi.org
www.vtmidi.org
A network of over 60 schools across Vermont. An online music mentoring project where students in grades 1-12 submit their music compositions for sharing and critique by professional composers, teachers and other students.

Vermont Music Shop
musicshop@bigheavyworld.net
www.vermontmusicshop.com
We invite all Vermont-based musicians and bands to consign your CDs with us.

Vermont Nightlife & Events
www.vermont.worldweb.com
Enter your upcoming music event in the entertainment calendar.

Virginia

64 Magazine
www.richmond.com/redesign_2001/64mag
Arts, culture and life in Virginia.

Acoustic Charlottesville
SalPal5000@Juno.com
www.geocities.com/acousticcharlottesville
A community organization that promotes local, original music in the Charlottesville, Virginia area. Our goal is to expand the music community of Charlottesville by creating a venue in which acoustic music and authentic expression can be truly enjoyed.

The Bluegrass Connection
pmilano@gotech.com
www.gotech.com
Band, Performer, Festival and other types of Official Home Pages for the Washington DC and central Virginia area.

The Breeze
www.thebreeze.org
James Madison University's student paper.

C-Ville Weekly
music@c-ville.com
www.c-ville.com
Charlottesville free weekly paper. Covers local music scene.

Cavalier Daily
www.cavalierdaily.com
University of Virginia's student newspaper.

The Collegiate Times
www.collegiatetimes.com
Virginia Polytechnic Institute's student paper.

Crossroads Music Festivals
Gary Hunt turtle-guy@worldnet.att.net
Based in Roanoke, Virginia and is the promoter for 2 benefit concerts a year- in May, we do a show for Ronald McDonald House- the world's biggest children's charity... no explanation needed here... In October we do a show for the Music Makers Relief Foundation- a benefit by musicians for an organization that helps musicians.... I may be able to assist in arranging a tour in this area by sending contact numbers and e-mails to local "club sponsors" willing to schedule paid gigs to accommodate bands that agree to perform at one of the 2 annual benefits. There is no charge, or promoter's cut, for this service...

Daily Press
www.dailypress.com
Newport News / Hampton Roads daily paper.

The Daily Progress
www.dailyprogress.com
Charlottesville daily paper. Covers local music scene, previews concerts.

facedownfall
dave@facedownfall.com
www.facedownfall.com
Covering the Virginia (and area) punk/hardcore scene.

Fredericksburg Songwriters' Showcase
showcase@bobgramann.com
www.webliminal.com/songwrite
A forum for a growing community of local and regional songwriters. We offer live monthly showcases by songwriters who perform a wide variety of styles.

HamptonRoads.com
www.hamptonroads.com
News, information, calendars, reviews and more for Hampton Roads, VA.

The Hook
Leah Woody leah@readthehook.com
www.readthehook.com
We are an alternative news weekly and web site that covers local and national acts that play shows in Charlottesville, VA.

Hyperville
www.hyperville.com
Arts & Entertainment Resource for the Charlottesville area.

The James River Blues Society
jamrivblusoc@aol.com
www.geocities.com/sunsetstrip/basement/2101
Dedicated to promoting and preserving blues music in the central and southwest areas of Virginia.

Jason's Accounting and Music-Firm *(JAM)*
JAM@JasonHowell.com
www.jasonhowell.com
Dedicated to serving local musicians and artists. We work with performing musicians, we listen to their music and we go see them perform. We know what it's like to rehearse, play gigs, sell merchandise, travel and try to remember to keep the receipts — we understand.

MEONA
meona@bellatlantic.net
www.meona.net
The word MEONA stands for MUSIC EVENTS OUTDOOR of NOTABLE ACHIEVEMENT. This web site is provided to support the local music scene in the Southeastern Virginia area.

Natchel Blues Network
john.bright@bigfoot.com
www.natchelblues.org
Promoting the blues in southeastern Virginia. Newsletter, reviews, gig listings and a "spotlight artist" feature.

Nine Volt Magazine
webmaster@ninevoltmag.com
www.ninevoltmag.com
Hampton Road's entertainment magazine.

The Norfolk Music Guide
norfolk.citysearch.com
Extensive coverage of the local music scene. Post your shows and events.

NorVaGoth.Net
figurehead@norvagoth.net
www.norvagoth.net
The Norfolk/Tidewater area Goth Industrial guide. If you would like to have your band listed here please contact me.

Punchline
music@punchlinemag.com
www.punchlinemag.com
Richmond free weekly arts and entertainment magazine. Covers local scene. Concert previews, local and national CD reviews.

Reload
webmaster@710.com
www.710.com/reload
This site is dedicated to promoting the local talent of Hampton Roads and Richmond, Virginia.

Richmond Jazz Society
admin@vajazz.org
www.vajazz.org
To promote the advancement of Jazz as an American art form via activities such as performances, lectures, workshops and exhibits.

The Richmond Music Guide
richmond.citysearch.com
Extensive coverage of the local music scene. Post your shows and events.

Richmond Music Journal
rmjournal@mindspring.com
www.mindspring.com/~rmjournal
Monthly magazine. Covering local music in Richmond, Virginia since 1993!

Richmond Times Dispatch
www.timesdispatch.com
Daily paper. Covers local music scene with artist features, CD and concert previews and reviews.

Richmond.com
www.richmond.com
News, reviews, concert dates and local MP3s.

The Roanoke Music Guide
roanoke.citysearch.com
Extensive coverage of the local music scene. Post your shows and events.

The Roanoke Times
www.roanoke.com
Covers Southern Virginia music scene.

SevenZeroThree
info@sevenzerothree.com
www.sevenzerothree.com
A union of musical acts that are working together to build a grassroots base for themselves and other area musicians. We strive to raise awareness of the local media to the quality and variety of music artists that call Northern Virginia home.

Shenandoah Valley Music and Art Network
markbarreres@planetcomm.net
www.shenandoahmusic.com
Its mission is three fold: (1) to heighten public awareness, (2) to bring local musicians together and (3) to bring live music to as many area venues as possible.

Splash Magazine
ur@splashmag.org
www.splashmag.org
Music and Entertainment in Tidewater.

The Tidewater Classical Guitar Society
www.tcgs.cx
Our mission is to provide cultural and educational opportunities to those interested in the classical guitar. Our concert schedule features local performers.

Tidewater Friends of Folk Music
tffm@tffm.org
www.tffm.org
Formed to advance, preserve and promote "traditional" and "contemporary" folk music in Southeast Virginia.

Tidewater Rocks!
edrocker@tidewaterrocks.com
www.tidewaterrocks.com
Your place in Hampton Roads to get the lowdown on our local bands.

Virginia Organization of Composers and Lyricists
info@vocalsongwriter.org
www.vocalsongwriter.org
Dedicated to advancing and promoting the art and craft of songwriting and musical composition. Membership is open to anyone with a serious interest in songwriting, composing, or lyric writing, regardless of style, whether novice or professional.

Virginia Spins
spins.us/virginia
A regional dance music community dedicated to Virginia dance music, electronic music, DJ's, artists and community.

The Virginian-Pilot
www.pilotonline.com
Hampton Roads daily paper.

Washington

AnacortesOnline.com
www.anacortesonline.com
Covers local music.

The Bellingham Independent Music Association
dweiss@bima.com
www.bima.com
An educational charity association of independent musicians and music supporters, in collaborative effort to promote local art in the community.

Blues to Do
info@bluestodo.com
www.bluestodo.com
The most complete source of information about live blues in the Northwest! Send 2 CD's for review consideration. Many of our reviewers are Northwest blues DJ's, musicians and blues fans.

The City Limits
previous@olywa.net
www.olywa.net/previous
We are based in Olympia, Washington where we regularly promote shows and work with local and out of town acts. We are interested in supporting the work of any artist who is willing to create, perform and promote their own work regardless of our personal tastes.

ForceWeb.com
Chris@ForceWeb.com
www.forceweb.com
Puget Sound Live Music.

The Inland Empire Blues Society
ted@bluessociety.ca
www.ieblues.org
We are based in Spokane Washington, but we try to represent Eastern and Central Washington, Northern Idaho, Eastern Oregon, Southern British Columbia and Western Montana.

Inland Northwest Bluegrass Association
www.spokanebluegrass.org
Our mission is to build awareness of bluegrass music in the Inland Northwest, through concerts, jams, festivals and other events.

k records
website@krecs.com
www.kpunk.com
The main focus of K has been artists working in and around Olympia, but has included comrades from across the U.S.A. and as far away as Japan, Scotland, Australia, Canada, Germany and England. Yes, explodes the teenage underground into passionate revolt against the corporate ogre world-wide.

KNW-YR-OWN
info@knw-yr-own.com
www.knw-yr-own.com
A label formed as an outlet for Anacortes, WA area music.

The Local Planet
mspaur@thelocalplanet.com
www.thelocalplanet.com
Spokane arts & entertainment magazine.

Northwest Artist Management
www.nwmusicpro.com
We represent only the finest Northwest artists that you can select with complete confidence, knowing they are as dedicated to creating special memories as you are! We are knowledgeable about all music from the grand Baroque period to the hottest Top 40.

Northwest Dance Music Association
john.england@nwdma.org
www.nwdma.org
The premier record pool covering the Pacific Northwest. DJ's throughout the area rely on us to fulfill their promotional nightclub music needs as well as serving as a key point for the music industry seeking feedback and exposure for nightclubs, radio and mix shows and DJ retail stores throughout the region.

Northwest Folklife
folklife@nwfolklife.org
www.nwfolklife.org
The most visible advocate of the traditional arts in the Northwest region.

Northwest Hardcore
webmaster@nwhardcore.com
www.nwhardcore.com
All about the hardcore scene in the Pacific Northwest.

Northwest Hip-Hop Underground
Kikko koolkatz21@foxinternet.net
206hip-hop.8m.com
Contact me if you want me to review your music. Send me vinyl if you can, but tapes and cds are ok.

Northwest Music Network
info@northwestmusic.net
www.northwestmusic.net
Your Online Guide and Directory To All Things Musical In the Great Northwest!

NWBlues.com
carol@nwblues.com
www.nwblues.com
On this site we are going to introduce you to the talented people of the beautiful Northwest area of the United States; Washington, Oregon, Canada and Idaho and give you the opportunity to purchase their CDs and other merchandise through our online catalog.

NWEXPLOSION.com
chaunceymclean@nwxmusic.com
www.nwexplosion.com
Covering Hip Hop in the Great Pacific Northwest. We got ourselves a strong knit family composed of conscious artists of all kinds.

Old Time Music in Portland
nkm@bubbaguitar.com
www.bubbaguitar.com
Lists old time music gigs and music gatherings in the Portland area.

Olymusic.com
webbies@olymusic.com
www.olymusic.com
Site for Olympia musicians. If you know of a music event which isn't on the calendar, please add it.

The Pacific Northwest Inlander
www.theinlander.com
Spokane weekly that reviews and covers local music.

Spokanebands.com
info@spokanebands.com
www.spokanebands.com
Covering all genres of music in the Inland Northwest. We are dedicated to covering the news, events and anything do to with the local bands here in the Inland Northwest and surrounding areas.

Songwriters of the Northwest Guild
scotth@qualdata.com
www.songnw.com
To provide a supportive environment for Northwest songwriters, to encourage collaboration and to help songwriters define and pursue their artistic goals.

The Spokane Music Guide
spokane.citysearch.com
Extensive coverage of the local music scene. Post your shows and events.

Spokanebands.com
Dan dan@spokanebands.com
www.spokanebands.com
Check out the other Northwest Music Scene! Spokane Bands dot com, events, bands, news, forums, venues and much more.

Tacoma New Music
kim@new-music.org
www.new-music.org
An organization working to create more opportunities for the performance of new chamber music in Tacoma and the Puget Sound area.

Tacoma News Tribune
www.tribnet.com
Daily paper.

The Tentacle
tentacle@tentacle.org
www.tentacle.org
Our purview includes exploratory jazz, free improvisation, new composition, electronic music, sonic exploration, multimedia performance, noise and avant rock. We welcome submissions of performance dates and recording release announcements — Northwest artists only, please.

Three Rivers Folklife Society
mail@3rfs.org
www.owt.com/3r-folkmusic
Dedicated to promoting folk music in the Tri-Cities (Richland, Kennewick and Pasco) in the southeastern corner of Washington.

Victory Music
info@victorymusic.org
www.victorymusic.org
An acoustic music resource founded in 1969 to support local acoustic, jazz, blues and folk music.

Walla Walla Blues Society
wwbs@bmi.net
www.wwbs.org
Dedicated to keeping in touch with our American musical heritage.

The Washington Bluegrass Association
paisely3@attbi.com
www.washingtonbluegrassassociation.org
Our purpose is to promote, encourage, foster and cultivate the preservation and understanding, enjoyment and support of bluegrass and other closely related music.

Washington Blues Society
bluzwork@aol.com
www.wablues.org
News, CD reviews, classifieds etc.

Seattle

Early Music Guild of Seattle
emg@earlymusicguild.org
www.earlymusicguild.org
We continue support of Seattle-based artists through the EMG Concert Assistance Program and the Professional Affiliate Program. The Concert Assistance Program provides artistic fee subsidies and administrative assistance including nonprofit rate mailings and ticket sales.

Earshot Jazz
jazz@earshot.org
www.earshot.org
Formed to support jazz and increase awareness in the community. We publish a monthly newsletter, present creative music and educational programs, assist jazz artists, increase listenership, complement existing services and programs and network with the national and international jazz community.

Giant Radio
bandinfo@giantradio.com
www.giantradio.com
MP3s and videos of Seattle & Northwest Musicians.

Gospel Music Workshop of America Pacific
Northwest Chapter
PacificNWC@aol.com
www.pacificnwchapter.com
Our goal is to strengthen existing and to open new channels of communication between local churches and their Pastors, radio announcers, community choirs and local artists and to provide a forum where they can come together to seal differences and design a positive course for the growth of gospel music in our local area.

Ladyfest Seattle
info@ladyfestseattle.org
www.ladyfestseattle.org
We welcome all women from the community to showcase their talents in music, film, visual arts, dance, business and all other positive forms of creativity. We are excited to educate the community about the women who have inspired us and to inspire those who will carry the torch for future generations.

Minty Magazine
editor@mintymagazine.com
www.mintymagazine.com
Our focus is the electronic music and DJ scene. More than anything we want to educate and inform you about nightlife in Seattle.

seagoth.org
webmaster@seagoth.org
www.seagoth.org
This site belongs to everyone in the online Seattle Gothic scene and it's intended as a showcase for all of their creative endeavors.

Seaspot.com
info@seaspot.com
www.seaspot.com
Covering the entertainment scene in the Seattle area.

Seattle's Best Live Music
ben@seattlelivemusic.net
seattlelivemusic.homestead.com
This is the best resource for upcoming live music events - complete with hyperlinks, bios, previews and reviews to further explore the music and musicians.

Seattle Booking & Entertainment
Tonya Terbrueggen tonya@seattlebooking.com
www.seattlebooking.com
A booking, promotions and management company. We are able to accommodate touring acts of all sizes into various venues.

The Seattle Classic Guitar Society
www.seattleguitar.org
Membership includes periodic performance opportunities. Also a one-year subscription to the Guitar Soundings, the SCGS's newsletter which includes a calendar of upcoming concerts, local news, announcements of events and articles of interest to enthusiasts of the art of the classic guitar.

Seattle Composer's Alliance
questions@seattlecomposers.org
www.seattlecomposers.org
Our mission is to bring Seattle composers together in a non-competitive atmosphere to share ideas, disseminate pertinent information and attract guest speakers of interest to the group.

Keep current with Bible updates
www.indiebible.com/ud

Seattle Drummer
darrellgrey@seattledrummer.com
www.seattledrummer.com
We want to create a strong network of information to help musicians achieve their personal and professional goals.

Seattle Folklore Society
info@seafolklore.org
seafolklore.org
Our purpose is to preserve and foster awareness and appreciation of folk and traditional arts in the Seattle area.

Seattle Gay News
sgn2@sgn.org
www.sgn.org
Post your shows and events.

Seattle Metal Online
www.seattlemetal.com
A complete resource for metal fans and bands alike. We strive to increase the exposure of all metal bands in the area and to kick the entire scene up a few notches. This is a 'band participation' site, bands who are active within the site and its members will benefit from it more than non active bands.

The Seattle Music Guide
seattle.citysearch.com
Extensive coverage of the local music scene. Post your shows and events.

Seattle Music Web
turmoil@hemp.net
www.seattlemusicweb.com
Focusing on Punk Rock and other hard edge music. MP3 files and Real Audio Files.

Seattle Post-Intelligencer
editpage@seattle-pi.com
www.seattle-pi.com
Daily paper. Covers Seattle music scene.

Seattle Times
www.seattletimes.com
Daily paper. Covers local music scene with CD and concert reviews.

Seattle Twang
groups.yahoo.com/group/SeattleTwang
A discussion group that connects you to Seattle's original country, alt-country scene. Features bands, shows, venues, news, CD reviews, MP3 twang-o-meter alerts and anything else that makes up the Northwest's twang-music scene can be found here.

Seattle Weekly
webmaster@seattleweekly.com
www.seattleweekly.com
Free weekly alternative paper. Covers local music scene with artist interviews, CD and concert previews and reviews.

SeattleMusic.net
admin@seattlemusic.net
www.seattlemusic.net
We aim to establish an active forum for a local community interested in fostering local music.

SeattleSounds.com
www.seattlesounds.com
We support Seattle area musicians. Listen to MP3 music files, see photos and read bios on your favorite local bands. SeattleSounds.com is free for bands and free for downloads.

Seattlite.com
www.seattlite.com
Dedicated to the music and bands of Seattle and the surrounding regions. Our goal is to provide music fans with immediate access to music from the many great artists our city has to offer while also keeping you updated on those artists' activities.

Sounds of Seattle
info@soundsofseattle.com
www.soundsofseattle.com
Dedicated to reporting on the music industry in Seattle as it relates to both enthusiasts as well as industry members all over the world. We do CD reviews of local Puget Sound Artists.

The Stranger
calendar@thestranger.com
www.thestranger.com
Seattle free weekly alternative paper. Covers local music with concert previews and CD reviews.

Student Hip Hop Organization of Washington
(The S.H.O.W.)
theshow@u.washington.edu
students.washington.edu/theshow
Dedicated to facilitating youth-oriented music and art experiences in the greater Seattle area.

Tablet
submissions@tabletnewspaper.com
editor@tabletnewspaper.com
www.tabletnewspaper.com
A forum for the exchange of information and opinion as it relates to the community of Seattle and beyond.

Washington DC

Black Hole
webmaster@tmottgogo.com
www.tmottgogo.com
Hip Hop site for Washington artists only.

DC Blues Society
jpdelaney2@yahoo.com
www.dcblues.org
Dedicated to preserving and promoting the blues.

DC Freaks
dcfreaks.com
Washington DC Goth resource.

DC Music Net
Info@dcmusicnet.com
www.dcmusicnet.com
Washington's scene for local talent. Providing a searchable database and direct links to your site, we believe is the best and easiest way to help you promote your band on the internet.

DCGoGo.COM
www.dcgogo.com
Being the #1 Source for Go Go Music in our Nations Capital and a leader in the Go Go Music Industry, DCGOGO.COM receives thousand of unique hits on over 400 pages of resource information regarding the Go Go Music Culture which includes concerts and other musical events.

DCjazz.com
www.dcjazz.com
MP3s, videos, CD store and more!

dcMusicNews
info@dcMusicNews.com
www.dcmusicnews.com
We are excited to present you with one of the top music resource sites for independent musicians in Washington DC, Maryland and Virginia.

DCpages.com Music
dcpages.com/Music
This guide accesses favorite DC artists and the latest music news and resources.

DCShows.net
strangebeer@dcshows.net
www.dcshows.net
Local punk, metal and hardcore shows for the mid-Atlantic.

dcska.com
Michelle dcskagirl@dcska.com
www.dcska.com
Ska site for the DC area and its citizens, reviews, show dates, interviews, multimedia, online store.

Digital City Washington *Music*
home.digitalcity.com/washington
Regional music column and forum. The area contains weekly feature articles of DC/VA/MD artists, plus weekend entertainment highlights, a running music poll and interactive message board.

District of Columbia Spins
spins.us/dc
A regional dance music community dedicated to the DC dance music, electronic music, DJ's, artists and community.

Exotic Fever Records
exoticfever@exoticfever.com
www.exoticfever.com
A brand new approach to releasing independent music/writing/art from our home base of Washington, D.C.

Folklore Society of Greater Washington
Webmaster@fsgw.org
www.fsgw.org
To further the understanding, investigation, appreciation and performance of the traditional folk music and folklore of the American people.

Left Off the Dial
Catherine Nicholas webmaster@leftoffthedial.com
www.leftoffthedial.com
Provides exposure for music, past and present, that tends to get ignored or go under-recognized by radio and mainstream media. We're accepting press kits and CD's for review, particularly from artists from Virginia, North Carolina and Washington, D.C.

Mantis Magazine
submissions@mantismagazine.com
www.mantismagazine.com
Devoted to promoting local artists, photographers and writers. Our mission is to form a network of musicians and artists, managers, promoters and studios. We wish to increase awareness of what DC has to offer.

Metro Music Connection
Nocrap1@bellatlantic.net
www.metromusicconnection.com
A free service to local area bands in the Washington DC, Northern Virginia and Maryland Areas. We are always looking for musical groups that are interested in being our featured band.

On Tap
www.ontaponline.com
Arts & entertainment magazine for the DC area.

Pheer.com
pablo@pheer.com
www.pheer.com
DC, Maryland and Virginia shows listing for punk/hardcore bands. Bands are welcome to post their MP3s.

Psychoburbia
tony@project2501.com
www.psychoburbia.com
The DC Area's longest running dark music weekly!

Rhythmplaza.com
peno@rhythmplaza.com
www.rhythmplaza.com
Your #1 source for hip-hop artists, club listings, videos, go-go music, interviews and events in the Washington, DC area.

The SalsaNews
note@thesalsanews.com
www.thesalsanews.com
Provides the latest information on classes, clubs, concerts and special events regarding the music and dance of salsa in the Washington, DC Community.

The Songwriters' Association of Washington
Membership@saw.org
saw.org
Established to benefit aspiring and professional songwriters by providing an active forum for songwriters and their work.

The Washington Area Lawyers for the Arts
executivedirector@thewala.org
www.thewala.org
Supporting artistic expression and creative innovation by serving the legal needs of Washington, Maryland and Virginia's arts and cultural communities.

Washington Area Music Association (WAMA)
dcmusic@wamadc.com
wamadc.com
Our main goal is to promote Washington DC area music in general and to achieve national recognition of the region as an important center for live and recorded music. WAMA's membership embraces all musical styles.

Washington Area Music eXchange
mail@wamex.org
wamex.org
You will find local bands of every kind, recording studios, labels, plus local music instructors. This is a community service where artists can support each other by trading or selling. Take advantage of our free publicity and list your band. WAMeX serves the District of Columbia, nearby Maryland and Virginia.

Washington City Paper
www.washingtoncitypaper.com
Covers the local music scene and previews upcoming arts and entertainment events.

The Washington Post
www.washingtonpost.com
Considers indie albums for review. Covers local music scene, previews in weekend edition.

washingtonpost.com MP3
mp3@wpni.com
mp3.washingtonpost.com
Self-publishing by and for the Metro region's music community.

West Virginia

304live.com
irunshit@304live.com
www.304live.com
West Virginia Hip Hop artists please send your Vinyl or CD to us. Visit our site for submission details.

The Charleston Gazette
www.wvgazette.com
Daily paper. Covers local music with band interviews and concert previews and reviews.

The Daily Athenaeum
www.da.wvu.edu
West Virginia University's student newspaper.

Dominion Post
www.dominionpost.com
Morgantown daily paper.

Graffiti
editor@grafwv.com
www.grafwv.com
Charleston free monthly alternative paper. Covers local music scene with artist interviews, concert and CD previews and reviews.

The Pocahontas Times
editor@pocahontastimes.com
www.pocahontastimes.com
Marlinton newspaper.

Shepherd College Picket
www.shepherd.edu/pickweb
Student paper.

Thermal Breakdown Entertainment
webmaster@thermalbreakdown.com
www.thermalbreakdown.com
Based in Huntington, WV, we are dedicated to exposing the talent of state, regional and unsigned bands into the national eye.

WV Music Scene
anderson@wvmusicscene.com
wvmusicscene.com
Everything that rocks in West Virginia!

West Virginia Music Center
max@wvmc.com
www.wvmc.com
Information on professional live-performance musical acts working in West Virginia.

Wisconsin

Black Hawk Folk Society
gk500@uniontel.net
www.focol.org/bhfs
Based out of Mount Morris. Promotes local events, newsletter etc.

Bluescds.com
info@bluescds.com
www.bluescds.com
Designed to assist in making mostly independent and generally non-commercial music available to the world through the internet. There is a focus on Midwestern music, particularly from the Milwaukee, Wisconsin area, although we offer CDs from all over the world.

Capital Times
tctnews@madison.com
www.captimes.com
Madison daily paper. Covers mainly the local music scene. Accepts press kit and CD for review.

Cty Murph's Music Page
cty@ctymurph.com
www.ctymurph.com
Listing of Wisconsin bands and show dates.

didn't that hurt?
didntthathurt@yahoo.com
www.didntthathurt.com
Punk show listings in Milwaukee.

FolkLib
henkle@pobox.com
www.folklib.net
Loads of information on Wisconsin folk, bluegrass, Celtic, acoustic and blues artists and resources.

Fond du Lac Features
webmaster@fdlfeatures.com
www.fdlfeatures.com
Fond du Lac's online community. Add your event in the entertainment section.

Fondy Acoustic Music Alliance
fondyacoustic@yahoo.com
www.fondyacoustic.org
Dedicated to providing listening and playing opportunities for fans of acoustic music.

Greater Milwaukee Today
www.gmtoday.com
Timeout entertainment section covers local music and events.

Green Apple Folk Music Society
www.focol.org/grapple
Promotes and encourage folk music, particularly in northeast/east central Wisconsin.

The Green Bay Music Guide
greenbay.citysearch.com
Extensive coverage of the local music scene. Post your shows and events.

The Green Bay News-Chronicle
www.greenbaynewschron.com
Daily paper.

Hexentanz
kyandjoolz@yahoo.com
www.hexentanz.com
This site is an information site for Goth events and gatherings in the Milwaukee and Chicago areas.

Isthmus
Dean Robbins robbins@isthmus.com
www.thedailypage.com
Madison's news & entertainment weekly.

Kenosha Music
Rhianon kenoshamusic@yahoo.com
www.kenoshamusic.cjb.net
Covering the punk/hardcore scene in Kenosha.

Local Music Online
zombie@localm.org
www.localm.org
Devoted to helping the local music scene in Northwestern Wisconsin. We help bands get shows, musicians find bands and much much more.

mad.city.hard.core

Don Smith Don_Smith@FamousMortimer.com
www.MadHC.com
A Madison/Milwaukee, WI area music site focusing on Punk, Metal, Hardcore and Rock. A fully interactive site including a user maintained database of area bands, shows and news Streamable music by local artists. Online discussions and private messaging, videos of live performances and much, much more!

Madison Capital Times

www.madison.com
Daily paper.

Madison Jazz Society

mjs@madisonjazz.com
www.madisonjazz.com
Dedicated to preserving and promoting jazz music.

Madison Music Online

info@netphoria.com
www.madison-online.com/music
We loosely define a Madison band as one whose members live and work in Madison or the nearby suburbs of Middleton, Monona etc. We hope that, by viewing this page, you'll get some idea of what the Madison music scene is like.

MadisonSongwriters.com

madisonsongwriters@hotmail.com
www.madisonsongwriters.com
Our mission is to provide education and networking opportunities within the music business through workshops, song contests, showcases, clinics, seminars and open mics.

MadisonMusicians.Net

admin@madisonmusicians.net
www.madisonmusicians.net
A free web-based network for Madison and surrounding communities. Helping area musicians find each other, buy and sell gear and stay informed of local music events. All styles, ages and levels welcome.

Maximum Ink

Rokker Rokker@maximumink.com
www.maximumink.com
A Wisconsin based music magazine featuring interviews/stories and cd reviews of national/local artists, plus, the most comprehensive, live music calendar for WI and monthly columns. Send in your music for review!

The Milwaukee Gothic Council

seabrite@execpc.com
www.geocities.com/milwaukeegothiccouncil
A cable-access program which is broadcast eight times monthly. Hey, Bands! Send us your music videos to play on the MGC cable show (they've got to be really awful for us NOT to play them, so send 'em in)!!!

Milwaukee-Hardcore.com

milwaukeehardcore@yahoo.com
www.milwaukee-hardcore.com
Covering the Milwaukee punk/hardcore scene.

The Milwaukee Journal Sentinel

www.jsonline.com
Daily paper. Covers local scene with artist features, CD and concert previews and reviews.

The Milwaukee Music Guide

milwaukee.citysearch.com
Extensive coverage of the local music scene. Post your shows and events.

MilwaukeeRocks.com

webmaster@milwaukeerocks.com
www.milwaukeerocks.com
Here to serve the entire Southeastern Wisconsin music community. You'll find all styles of music here at MilwaukeeRocks.com. All listings are completely FREE! Plus, we're adding more and more features all the time.

OnMilwaukee.com

info@staff.onmilwaukee.com
www.onmilwaukee.com
We have the best Milwaukee music guide on the Internet. Add your band to our local music database. Searchable by name and by musical genre.

The Scene

info@valleyscene.com
www.valleyscene.com
Appleton arts & entertainment weekly. We feature stories on local musicians and artists offering a glimpse into the creative process, musicians' backgrounds, their styles and where they can be heard locally.

The Shepherd Express

editor@shepherd-express.com
www.shepherd-express.com
Milwaukee free daily alternative paper. Covers local music scene with concert previews and CD reviews. Our annual Band Guide remains Milwaukee's sourcebook for local music.

Southern Wisconsin Bluegrass Music Association

plansi@merr.com
www.swbmai.org
Our bimonthly newsletter contains timely information about the activities of the Association along with news about bluegrass events and people, including profiles of area bands and reviews of bluegrass concerts, festivals and recordings.

Wild Chirp

aaron@wildchirp.com
wildchirp.com
A free distribution music and culture quarterly with circulation in Chicago, Milwaukee, Madison and Minneapolis.

WISCONLINE

reception@wisconline.com
www.wisconline.com
Submit your music event.

Wisconsin Alliance for Composers

www.wiscomposers.org
Founded to encourage and support the composition and performance of new music by Wisconsin composers.

The Wisconsin Area Music Industry (WAMI)

wamimusic@yahoo.com
www.wisconsinareamusicindustry.com
Promoting the Wisconsin music scene, WAMI provides scholarships to students and emerging artists and offers continuing education for music industry professionals through monthly meetings and semi-annual music seminars.

Wisconsin Musical Groups

regent@execpc.com
www.execpc.com/~regent
Wisconsin's largest music resource! What's your musical group doing? Promote it here!

Wisconsin Punk

notjustforpunx@yahoo.com
www.wiscpunk.org
Shows, mp3s, photographs etc.

Wisconsin State Journal

www.madison.com
Madison daily paper. Covers local music scene with CD and concert reviews and artist features.

WisRocks.com

www.wisrocks.com
Bulletin Board for discussion of Wisconsin music interests.

Wyoming

Jackson Hole Online

info@jacksonholenet.com
www.jacksonholenet.com
Entertainment section covers local music.

The Wyoming Companion

editor@wyomingcompanion.com
www.wyomingcompanion.com
Wyoming's Hometown Magazine & Worldwide Visitor Guide. Covers local music events.

Wyoming Tribune-Eagle

www.wyomingnews.com
Cheyenne daily paper.

Canada

Access Magazine

access@wwonline.com
www.accessmag.com
Music, film, fashion, technology, games, sex, travel, sport, work. Not only are these the components of a well-balanced life, they are also the key ingredients to a successful entertainment lifestyle magazine. Together they equal ACCESS all areas.

The ANR Lounge

www.mincanada.com
One of our amazing free services is the ANR Lounge whereby Canadian recording artists promote their latest CD through e-mail notification to radio stations across the nation. The ANR Lounge is open to all artists, labels, managers, agents, publishers and promoters of Canadian music at no charge.

Association of Canadian Women Composers (ACWC)

lhoffman@is.dal.ca
music.acu.edu/www/iawm/acwc
Promotion of music written by Canadian Women composers and endeavors to help these composers achieve a higher profile in the community.

AtlanticSeabreeze.com

info@AtlanticSeabreeze.com
www.atlanticseabreeze.com
Celtic, East Coast and Country Music in Canada

The Borealis Recording Company

info@borealisrecords.com
www.borealisrecords.com
Our mission is to create an artist-friendly home for Folk and Roots music in Canada. We aim to present all the diverse styles of Canadian-made music under the Folk and Roots umbrella: Celtic, Blues, Singer/songwriters, Political/Topical, Traditional, Bluegrass, World etc.

Canada.com

www.canada.com
The network is made up of 12 major and 39 smaller Canadian city sites that offer Canadians breaking news and information from their communities, their country and their world. Post your event news on canada.com! (check for the contact e-mail for your city).

Canadian Amateur Musicians/ Musiciens Amateurs du Canada (CAMMAC)

national@cammac.ca
www.cammac.ca
Devoted to creating opportunities for musicians of all levels to make music together in a relaxed, non-competitive atmosphere.

Canadian Celtic Music

members.shaw.ca/kimberleyw/canadacelticmusic
The purpose of this page is to spread the word about Canadian Celtic Musicians.

Canadian Copyright Act

webadmin@justice.gc.ca
laws.justice.gc.ca/en/C-42

The Canadian Country Music Association

country@ccma.org
www.ccma.org
As a professional, you share a common goal with the CCMA— the continued development of Canadian country music. Your membership ensures you the opportunity to participate in that growth.

Canadian Electroacoustic Community (CEC)

cec@vax2.concordia.ca
cec.concordia.ca
Draws together like-minded people: those interested and active in electroacoustics and computer music. With membership from all provinces and internationally, the CEC provides a clearly defined network for the flow and exchange of information and ideas.

The Canadian Intellectual Property Office (CIPO)

strategis.gc.ca/sc_mrksv/cipo
Associated with Industry Canada, we are responsible for the administration and processing of the greater part of intellectual property (copyright and trademarks) in Canada.

The Canadian Music Center (CMC)

ds@musiccentre.ca
www.musiccentre.ca
Collecting, distributing and promoting music by Canada's composers. From 20th century conservative classical concert works to wild electroacoustic sound art and improvisational jazz - whatever your taste in Canadian contemporary music - you can find it here.

Canadian-Music.com

info@canadian-music.com
www.canadian-music.com
Our goal at is to create the definitive online resource for Canadian artists and the Canadian Music industry as well as create the ultimate resource for consumers seeking information on Canadian music.

Canadian Music Network

info@canadianmusicnetwork.com
www.canadianmusicnetwork.com
We feature three to four album reviews per week. The reviews are not of a critical nature, but will instead feature information about the album, the style, the tracks and any specialty marketing that the company is doing to back up the release.

Canadian Musician

mail@nor.com
www.canadianmusician.com
Showcases unsigned Canadian acts in showcase section.

Canadian Online Musician's Association (COMA)

coma@cpreal.com
www.coolname.com/coma
A site promoting Canadian music. There are sound samples and bios of hundreds of musicians. We will sell your CD as well.

Canadian Ska/Reggae Events

skacanada@boss-sounds.net
www.geocities.com/soul_stomper
Devoted to both the Ska and Reggae scenes in Canada with a strong emphasis on Canadian (or Canada-based) artists.

The Canadian Society for Traditional Music

cstm@yorku.ca
www.yorku.ca/cstm
We issue two different publications. There is a quarterly bulletin, which contains articles, notices, reviews and commentary on all aspects of Canadian folk music. The annual journal, Canadian Journal for Traditional Music, includes refereed articles pertaining to Canadian and traditional music.

CanadianBands.com

www.canadianbands.com
Heard a great album recently? See a great concert last night? Let us know about it - we welcome your contributions!

CanadianBlues.ca

inquiries@canadianblues.ca
www.canadianblues.ca
We have listings, pictures, sound clips and feature stories on dozens of Canadian blues musicians and bands. Visit the store section to buy CDs from Canadian blues artists.

canEHdian.com

info@canehdian.com
www.canehdian.com
Our objective is to build an extensive, comprehensive resource for Canadian music. We have worked over the past three years in bringing together biographies, reviews and interviews with many of Canada's best musical talents.

CBC Records

cbcrecords@toronto.cbc.ca
www.cbcrecords.cbc.ca
Dedicated to making the music of Canadian performers and composers available to music lovers in Canada and around the world. We deal exclusively with Canadian independent classical musicians.

Chart Magazine

chart@chartattack.com
www.chartattack.com
Each issue contains feature articles on current acts, scene reports from across Canada, Canadian college radio and retail charts, reviews and lots more. Chart is an essential source of entertainment and information for those who need to know about new music.

CM: Canadian Review of Materials

cm@umanitoba.ca
www.umanitoba.ca/cm
We review Canadiana of interest to children and young adults, including publications produced in Canada, or published elsewhere but of special interest or significance to Canada, such as those having a Canadian writer, illustrator or subject.

Composers.ca

office@composers.ca
www.composers.ca
Features information and support for active composers of all genres.

Dave's Records of Guelph (DROG)

dave@drog.com
www.drog.com
Our goal is to bring to the world Canadian music that by its own quality deserves to be heard.

Dig Your Roots

info@digyourroots.ca
www.digyourroots.ca
An exploration of independent talent from the Canadian underground. Its scope is wide ranging and focuses on original forms of music that are currently under-represented in the Canadian music scene.

Down Side Up Network

HipHopBear hiphopbear@shaw.ca
dsunetwork.ca
The mission statement of dsu is to do everything we can to connect Canada's underground or independent hip hop scenes, to bring artists and groups together using an interactive Network.

!*@# Exclaim!

exclaim@exclaim.ca
www.exclaim.ca
In-depth coverage of new music across all genres with special focus on Canadian and cutting-edge artists. A circulation of over 100,000 copies across Canada every month. Exclaim.ca also features reviews, interviews and profiles not found in the print publication.

Festival Distribution

fdi@festival.bc.ca
www.festival.bc.ca
We are an independent Canadian-owned company with sales representatives serving retailers from coast to coast. And we are proud to distribute some of the planet's finest examples of independent music in many different musical genres.

Folk Alliance Canada

info@folkalliancecanada.org
www.folkalliancecanada.org
Official Canadian branch of the North American Folk Music and Dance Alliance. Folk Alliance membership gives you access to all sorts of tools to help you create, perform and market your folk music here and internationally.

www.indielinkexchange.com

Great White Noise.ca
bandsubs@greatwhitenoise.ca
www.greatwhitenoise.ca
Canadian Independent music exposed.

Groove Music Canada
www.groovemusiccanada.com
Pop / R&B Record Label based in Toronto, Canada with National & international distribution.

Groove.ca
fpilato@groove.ca
www.groove.ca
In an attempt to keep you in touch with this ever-changing scene, we are observing and reviewing underground music, artists and music culture on a day-to-day basis. Whether it's House, Garage, Techno, Trance, Hip Hop, or just a night out, Groove.ca has the info you're after.

GuitarsCanada
info@guitarscanada.com
www.guitarscanada.com
We would like to help out any up and coming Canadian Bands. If you are currently touring, have a steady gig or just recording some music, fill out the form below and we will publish a bio and picture of your band.

hiphopcanada.com
elements@hiphopcanada.com
www.hiphopcanada.com
Send artist press-kits, new updates etc. Emcees, Turntablists, Graf artists, B-boys/B-girls etc.

Home County Folk League
www.homecounty.ca
Based in London, we provide year-round events accessible to all, which celebrate, promote and enhance folk-based traditions with an emphasis on Canadian content.

Indie Band Database
jam@canoe.ca
www.canoe.ca/IndieBands
A one-stop forum in which to explore the thriving musical community in this country that remains proudly independent.

Indie Pool
contact@indiepool.com
www.indiepool.com
Since 1996, Indie Pool has dedicated itself to pooling the resources of Canadian independent recording artists, in order to provide an effective and affordable distribution alternative.

jambands.ca
kevo@jambands.ca
www.jambands.ca
Our mission with this web site is to facilitate a bigger and more vibrant Canadian grassroots/jam/groove music scene by bringing together great bands and appreciative fans. We also publish "Scene and Heard" magazine.

Jazz_Can
Swing2jazz@hotmail.com
www.jazzcanada.homestead.com
Canada may not be the largest place in the world but we have produced some of the finest talent around and we should be very proud of them

Jazz Canadiana
bebop@sympatico.ca
www.jazzcanadiana.on.ca
Devoted to people everywhere who enjoy Jazz and the artists who make it happen.

JazzPromo.com
jazz@jazzpromo.com
www.jazzpromo.com/canadajazz.php
Being a Canadian-based company, we take great pride in the quality and talent of our homegrown artists and work hard to showcase their music as much as possible. Check into becoming our "Featured Artist of the Month".

kickinthehead.com
info@kickinthehead.com
www.kickinthehead.com
Created by musicians for musicians who love their music and want control. KickInTheHead.com is a comprehensive, searchable web database that lets artists add and update their own information for free.

Linear Reflections
nai@shaw.ca
www.linearreflections.com
An arts review e-magazine, which deals with ALL genres of music. We would be pleased to give your disc a listen, then write an honest and unbiased review. We are here to provide a showcase for talent, especially Canadian talent of many types and we sincerely hope you enjoy your stay!

LiveTourArtists
darcy@livetourartists.com
www.livetourartists.com
Canada's newest national and international booking agency representing artists in the entertainment business. Though we have to be selective we are always looking for great new talent.

Maple Blues
info@torontobluessociety.com
www.torontobluessociety.com/maple.htm
Toronto Blues Society's magazine. Dedicated to the promotion and preservation of the blues.

MapleMusic
justcurious@maplemusic.com
www.maplemusic.com
We wanted to create a site where Canadian musicians hold centre stage for music lovers around the world. We add new bands every couple of weeks; some will be ones that you know very well and others will be bands that you may not have heard of, but that you will want to get to know. Bands are welcome to sell their CD from our site.

Music By Mail Canada
ck580@freenet.carleton.ca
www.musicbymailcanada.com
This site is primarily dedicated to Canadian sources for music but you will also find a listing of Foreign sources for Canadian music and various other useful information, most relating to ordering music by mail and Canadian Music.

Music Industry Network Canada *The ANR Lounge*
mincanada.com
This FREE service will make sure that music and programming directors see and hear about your latest release. Canadian radio has never been more accessible. All you have to do is register online. You will be able to upload information about your new releases, including sound clips and images.

New Music Canada
mymusic@newmusiccanada.com
www.newmusiccanada.com
Fresh, current, recently recorded music is what you'll find here. Independent bands, underground DJs and just-about-to-be-discovered artists make up the eclectic sound mix on NMC. Send us your new Canadian music MP3s and we put it up on the site for everyone to hear.

Newbands.ca
newbands@newbands.ca
www.newbands.ca
You can post comments, upload your mp3's, vote on other mp3's, post your website address and vote on others. In the very near future your registration will allow you to create your home page right here!

Northern Journey Online
gene@wilburn.ca
www.northernjourney.com
This website celebrates Canadian folk music! For every internationally-known Canadian folk performer, there are dozens of lesser-known artists who are making uncommonly good music. Use this site to discover these artists.

ONYXCanada
wezel@wezel.com
www.wezel.com/onyx
The ONYX team specializes in helping independent musicians with publicity materials, web pages and internet marketing. We also offer these services to any other person needing them. Our motto is: "We kick serious butt..." (and we do).

Penguin Eggs
penguineggs@hotmail.com
www.penguineggs.ab.ca
Canada's Folk, Roots and World music magazine.

Salsa Canada
info@salsacanada.com
www.salsacanada.com
Canada's premier salsa dance site with sections on events, bands and clubs.

The Society of Composers, Authors and Music Publishers of Canada *(SOCAN)*
socan@socan.ca
www.socan.ca
We represent individuals who make their living creating music. As a collective for the performing right of our members – creators and publishers of music – we make sure they get paid for performances of their work.

Songwriters Association of Canada *(SAC)*
sac@songwriters.ca
www.songwriters.ca
The only national arts service organization dedicated exclusively to Canadian composers, lyricists and songwriters.

Sound Bytes
lyricist@afm.org
communication.ca/soundbytes
While all styles of music will be accepted for review, the focus is on music with a roots or traditional component, including folk, blues, jazz, country and their many variants. Artists — especially independent and Canadian — or their distributors are invited to submit new CD releases for review.

Soundwave Magazine
danielotis@soundwavemagazine.com
www.soundwavemagazine.com
*We are looking for innovative Canadian alternative
rock bands to feature in our online indie artist section.
We offer artists free exposure to our growing
readership in Canada and overseas.*

Stamm'ler International
ragna@sympatico.ca
www.stammlerinternational.com
*Services include launching publicity campaigns for
new CD releases, books and movies/DVD's,
coordinating national media itineraries for
international and national artists, organizing release
parties, arranging press conferences, conducting
national press campaigns and more.*

techno.ca
info@techno.ca
techno.ca
*Dance music site. Send your clean CD, CD-ROM,
DAT, cassette or minidisc to us.*

UmbrellaMusic
info@umbrellamusic.com
www.umbrellamusic.com
*Canada music lives here! Check our site every week
for Umbrella's weekly pick.*

Urban Music Association of Canada
info@umac.ca
www.umac.ca
*Dedicated to the domestic and international
promotion, education and development of Canadian
Urban music.*

URBNET.COM
info@urbnet.com
www.urbnet.com
*Covering the Canadian Urban Music Scene. Reviews,
CDs, downloads, Techno, House etc.*

Words & Music
socan@socan.ca
www.socan.ca
*Society of Composers, Authors and Music Publishers
of Canada's (SOCAN) publication. Music news and
bios are done on a few members each month. New
releases are also listed.*

Alberta

**ALBERTA METAL - Where Heavy Music
Lives... Out West**
Christine Garton info@albertametal.net
www.albertametal.net
*An online network for everything you ever wanted to
know about Alberta's independent Metal Scene. A
great resource if your band is looking to set up a
show, get contact information or would just like to
know what is going on in our area. Alberta and other
Canadian metal bands may submit a profile, including
an MP3 soundfile.*

Alberta Music Network
info@albertamusic.net
www.albertamusic.net
*AMN hopes to provide convergence for all Alberta
internet based music content. If we can get local
calendars published regularly in your local papers, if
we can provide hosts and topics for community TV
shows each week, if we can direct radio hosts to
notice your event, then you can be sure our local
music scenes would be greatly enhanced.*

Babe's Music Page
monica@babesmusicpage.com
www.babesmusicpage.com
CD and gig reviews of Calgary and area bands.

The Bricklayer
thebricklayer@canoemail.com
www.sardc.ab.ca/public_brick.htm
*Red Deer College's student publication. Topics
covered include the arts, music, sports, health,
campus news and other activities all across the
campus.*

Calgary Sun
louis.hobson@calgarysun.com
www.calgarysun.com
Daily paper. Covers local music.

CalgaryPlus.ca *Sound Factory*
submit@sl.ca
www.calgaryplus.ca
*The Sound Factory section takes a look at the local
music scene.*

calgarypunk.com
general@calgarypunk.com
www.calgarypunk.com
*Our long term goal is to attract interest and attention
to our local scene and keep it there.*

The Classical Guitar Society of Calgary
www.classicalguitarsocietyofcalgary.freeservers.com
*The Society presents an annual concert series that
features internationally acclaimed guitarists and
outstanding Alberta musicians.*

CowTownRaverZ.com
info@cowtownraverz.com
www.cowtownraverz.com
Covering Calgary's Dance music scene.

Dark Calgary
webmaster@darkcalgary.com
www.darkcalgary.com
*This service is provided as a means for local Goth
artists and organizers to promote their creations and
as a method for the community to stay in touch and
keep up to date on items of note in our area.*

Dark Edmonton
coded@darkedmonton.com
www.darkedmonton.com
Post your Goth music events and band info.

The Edmonton Classical Guitar Society
mail@edmontonclassicalguitarsociety.org
www.edmontonclassicalguitarsociety.org
*Our desire is for members of all playing levels to
gather encouragement and motivation through a
positive and constructive atmosphere and to gain
playing experience through performance before others
with the same interest.*

The Edmonton Jazz Society
info@yardbirdsuite.com
www.yardbirdsuite.com
*Promotes live jazz music in Edmonton. In addition to
presenting performances, the EJS is an active
participant in both musical and educational
communities. From classes with the masters of jazz to
liaisons with college and university departments, EJS
strives to promote jazz awareness.*

Edmonton Journal
www.canada.com/edmonton
Daily paper with local music listings.

Edmonton Sun
www.fyiedmonton.com
Daily paper.

EdmontonPlus.ca
edmontoncontenteditor@sl.ca
www.edmontonplus.ca
*Online arts & entertainment magazine covering the
local music scene.*

FFWD
info@ffwd.greatwest.ca
www.ffwdweekly.com
Calgary's news and entertainment weekly.

Foothills Bluegrass Music Society
fbms@melmusic.com
www.melmusic.com/fbms
*A Society Dedicated to the Promotion and
Performance of Bluegrass Music in Calgary.*

Gothic Calgary
webmaster@darkcalgary.com
www.darkcalgary.com
*Listing events, organizations, bands and businesses of
interest to the local gothic and industrial
communities. This service is provided as a means for
local artists and organizers to promote their creations.*

indecline
www.indecline.net
Covering the Edmonton punk scene.

JUSTaBUNCHoKiDS
mdaines@shaw.ca
www.jbk.ca
*An all age concert collective based out of Calgary.
Our mission is to ensure that information, literature
and scene related materials are available at all jbk
shows, diversify the music and culture at all ages
shows, encourage new people to participate in the
community, maximize the awareness of the community
and provide opportunities for new bands to play.*

Medicine Hat Jazz Society
mhjazz@yahoo.com
www.memlane.com/nonprofit/jazz/society.htm

Megatunes
customer.service@megatunes.com
www.megatunes.com
*An independent music store established in and
retailing music in Calgary. We carry a great selection
of Alternative, Blues, Folk & Roots, Jazz, Pop &
Rock, Punk Rock, Urban & World Music.*

The Red Deer Express
express@reddeer.greatwest.ca
www.reddeerexpress.com
Cover local music.

The Red Deer Scene
pocko7@yahoo.com
go.to/rdscene
*A collective of writing, art, fanzines, recipes, do-it-
yourself info and upcoming events for the red deer
scene and community. to submit your work, ideas or
anything you feel fit, please contact by email.*

SEE Magazine
info@see.greatwest.ca
www.seemagazine.com
*Edmonton's Weekly Source For News, Arts and
Entertainment.*

The Uptown Folk Club
uptownfc@ecn.ab.ca
www.ecn.ab.ca/uptownfc
Based in Edmonton, we provide affordable, quality entertainment and assist local musicians in promoting their talent through the use of various performance formats and media.

British Columbia

Abbotsford Times
editorial@abbotsfordtimes.com
www.abbotsfordtimes.com
Covers local music in the "Showtime!" section.

B.C. Country Music Association
bccountrymusic@telus.net
www.bccountry.com
To promote, foster and encourage the development and public appreciation of and interest in, the British Columbia Country Music community. Includes an "Artist Spotlight".

BC Touring Council
fyi@bctouring.org
www.bctouring.org
Our mission is to serve presenters and touring professional artists in British Columbia. Our goals are to expand touring opportunities, promote audience development and be an advocate for artists and presenters.

BCpunk.com
BCpunk@hotmail.com
www.bcpunk.com
A community site trying to promote the local punk scene in British Columbia.

The British Columbia Folklore Society
info@folklore.bc.ca
www.folklore.bc.ca
To Collect and Preserve the Traditional and Contemporary Folklife and Folklore of the People of British Columbia.

Cdlsle
info@cdisle.com
www.cdisle.com
Island recording artists living in British Columbia, past and present.

Chilliwack Times
editorial@chilliwacktimes.com
www.chilliwacktimes.com
A twice-weekly community newspaper. Has an Arts & Entertainment section called "Showtime!"

The Cowichan Folk Guild
information@folkfest.bc.ca
www.folkfest.bc.ca
Our mandate is to "preserve and promote folk performing arts in Duncan and the Cowichan Valley".

The Early Music Society of the Islands
joy@uvic.ca
web.uvic.ca/hrd/earlymusic
Based in Victoria, the society brings the Islands performers of international reputation. EMSI also sponsors concerts by accomplished local musicians.

Festival Distribution Inc.
fdi@festival.bc.ca
www.festival.bc.ca
We are a company dedicated to marketing independently produced recordings. Our roster includes releases by many independent musicians.

Gothic BC
atratus@gothic.bc.ca
www.gothic.bc.ca
British Columbia's gothic source.

The Hornby Island Blues Society
doucette@mars.ark.com
www.hornby-blues.bc.ca
Our goal is to provide the opportunity for listeners and players of Blues to share their knowledge with others. Our main emphasis is on Canadian blues performers.

Kelowna Capital News
edit@kelownacapnews.com
www.kelownacapnews.com
The Central Okanogan's best-read newspaper. Covers local music.

New Westminster News Leader
publisher@newwestnewsleader.com
www.newwestnewsleader.com

Pacific Music Industry Association (*PMIA*)
info@pmia.org
www.pmia.org
Created to provide information about our industry and professional development for our industry.

Redwire Magazine
info@redwiremag.com
www.redwiremag.com
Supporting Aboriginal music.

Richmond News
editor@richmond-news.com
www.richmond-news.com
Has an arts and leisure guide called "The Beat".

Richmond Review
news@richmondreview.com
www.richmondreview.com
The entertainment section covering local events.

SaltSpringMusic.Com
info@saltspringmusic.com
www.saltspringmusic.com
This site began as a showcase for musicians on Salt Spring Island, internationally renowned for its arts community. Since it was launched in 2001, We have begun to expand to take in other Western Canadian artists.

Sounds of Surrey
soundsofsurrey.com
Dedicated to the music of Surrey BC.

Victoria Jazz Society
vicjazz@pacificcoast.net
www.vicjazz.bc.ca
Committed to presenting the highest quality of Jazz possible to our community.

West Kootenay Bluegrass Site
pickingrinin@shaw.ca
www.westkootenaybluegrass.com
If you have any info or bluegrass events that you would like posted, please send us an e-mail.

Vancouver

Citygigs *Vancouver*
info@citygigs.com
www.citygigs.com
You need to know more than just who's playing when. You need REAL information on ALL the shows that come to town, not just Cher. We offer featured stories, reviews, interviews, concert previews and more!

Coastal Jazz & Blues Society
cjbs@jazzvancouver.com
www.jazzvancouver.com
Contributing vigorously to the development of the jazz scene both locally and nationally since 1985. Our vision encompasses a wide spectrum of jazz, blues, world and improvised music including music and media that are influencing jazz as an art form.

Cosmic Debris
cosmic@cvnet.net
www.cvnet.net/cosmic
A Vancouver Island based entertainment magazine and music industry reference guide, published about 8 times per year. The publisher and most of the writers are active musicians.

The Rogue Folk Club
roguefolk@hotmail.com
www.roguefolk.bc.ca
Vancouver area folk dancing, jam sessions etc.

The Georgia Straight
info@straight.com
www.straight.com
No other city publication knows more about Vancouver than the Georgia Straight. The magazine is an integral part of the active urban West Coast lifestyle with a per issue readership in excess of 369,000.

The Greater Vancouver Alliance for Arts and Culture
info@allianceforarts.com
www.allianceforarts.com
Our mission is to represent and serve the local arts community in Vancouver.

The Nerve Magazine
Bradley C. Damsgaard
editor@thenervemagazine.com
www.thenervemagazine.com
Circulation of 10 000 in Vancouver, Victoria and subscriptions.

North Shore News
editor@nsnews.com
www.nsnews.com
The voice of North and West Vancouver. Covers local music.

North Shore Outlook
newsroom@northshoreoutlook.com
www.northshoreoutlook.com
Vancouver paper. Lifestyles section covers local events.

The Peak
www.peak.sfu.ca
Simon Fraser University's independent student newspaper.

RANCH Productions
Shelley ranchsociety@direct.ca
ranchprod.tripod.com
Our mandate is to promote Vancouver (and Victoria's) strong Roots Music community and to create more media exposure and public awareness of who we all are. We're seeking more info on bands, new discs, live shows etc. - reviews or comments that we can share with the community.

Spawner Records
Kyle Richardson spawner1@yahoo.com
www.spawnerrecords.com
100% independent non profit label run by bands for bands from Vancouver B.C. Canada!

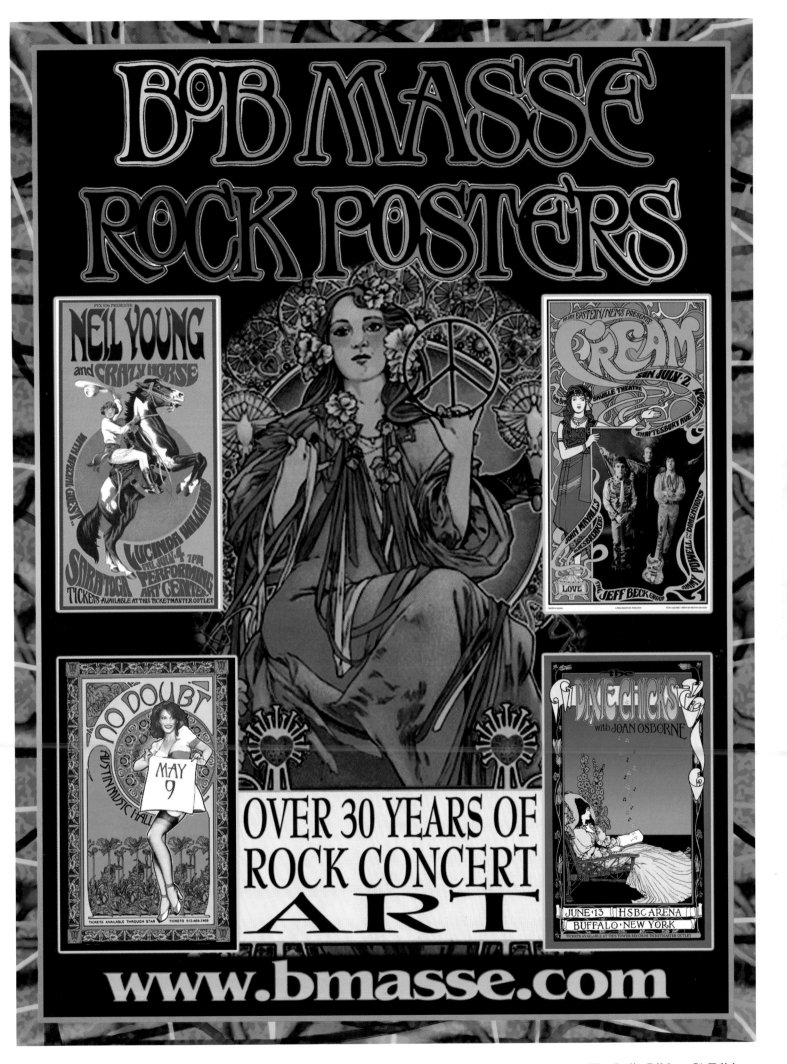

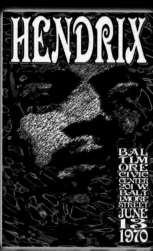

The Ubyssey
www.ubyssey.bc.ca
The official student newspaper of the University of British Columbia.

Vancouver Courier
mmaloney@vancourier.com
www.vancourier.com
Your source for Vancouver news and entertainment. Covers local music.

vancouverJazz.com
www.vancouverjazz.com
Covering the Vancouver Jazz scene. Reviews, news, interviews etc.

Vancouver New Music
info@newmusic.org
www.newmusic.org
Western Canada's major producer of serious contemporary music commissions and premieres new works by Canadian composers; presents leading electroacoustic music, international composers and performers.

VancouverPlus.ca
asktheeditor@sl.ca
www.vancouverplus.ca
Online arts & entertainment magazine covering the local music scene. We encourage you to submit your events. We will review and publish your events for free on our Web site. Visitors have come to rely on as a comprehensive source for all events in Vancouver and the surrounding communities.

Westender
editor@westender.com
www.westender.com
Vancouver's urban voice. Covers local music in the entertainment section.

The Western Front Society
admin@front.bc.ca
www.front.bc.ca
An artist run centre that is dedicated to the production, exhibition and promotion of contemporary electronic/media art.

Manitoba

The Blues Music in Winnipeg
cdreviews@winnipegblues.com
www.winnipegblues.com
If you would like your CD reviewed, please send 1 copy along with promotional material.

Conifera
info@conifera.ca
www.conifera.ca
If you make music of any sort and are looking for a way to get exposure or collaborate with like-minded people, Conifera can help you. We can help you get in the direction you want to go, or as something much more — a network of creative people that will challenge you and help you develop you skills.

Manitoba Audio Recording Industry Association
info@manitobamusic.com
www.manitobamusic.com
We serve anyone involved in or benefiting from the music industry in Manitoba.

Manitoba Blues Society
flkraft@shaw.ca
www.mbblues.mb.ca
Dedicated to promote, foster and support the Blues in Manitoba.

The Musicians Network
mgarbutt@mb.sympatico.ca
www.bytes4u.ca
I'll update the web site every couple of days, so if you are a musician and want to meet other musicians, join a band, form a band, tour, record or jam, email me your profile and I'll add it to the relevant categories.

newWinnipeg
info@newWinnipeg.com
www.newwinnipeg.com
Winnipeg's arts & entertainment magazine.

Stylus Magazine
stylus@uwinnipeg.ca
www.stylusmag.mb.ca
A music magazine published monthly by the University of Winnipeg Students' Association with a circulation of 3,000.

The Winnipeg Classical Guitar Society
wcgs@canada.com
www.fortunecity.com/tinpan/fascination/222
We are committed to promoting the classical guitar in Winnipeg, Manitoba.

Winnipeg Early Music Society
wems@mb.sympatico.ca
www.mts.net/~mhultin/wems.htm
The society gives members the opportunity to play or sing in an ensemble setting. Members have the opportunity to meet other players and are encouraged to form smaller ensembles if they desire.

Winnipeg Free Press
www.winnipegfreepress.com
Daily paper. Local music covered in the Entertainment section.

Winnipeg Music
info@newWinnipeg.com
www.newwinnipeg.com/music
Covering the local music scene.

Winnipeg Sun
www.fyiwinnipeg.com/winsun.shtml
Daily paper. Lots of local music coverage.

winnipegbands.com
shevil_one@hotmail.com
www.winnipegbands.com
Send in any information that you have about your band such as biographies, pictures, mp3s, video and show dates.

Winnipeg-Ska.com
nk@nkmail.com
www.winnipeg-ska.com
This website is an online community for the Winnipeg SKA community. Feel free to sign up and submit some content to the site.

You As The Driver
a@youasthedriver.com
youasthedriver.com
Winnipeg music e-zine. News, reviews, interviews etc.

New Brunswick

Argosy
argosy@mta.ca
argosy.mta.ca
Mount Allison University's Independent Student Journal.

The Brunswickan
www.unb.ca/web/bruns
University of New Brunswick's campus paper.

canadaeast.com
www.canadaeast.com
Local music covered in the entertainment section.

Deleted Scene
ace1@nbnet.nb.ca
www23.brinkster.com/deletedscene
A Fredericton show journal. On this page you will find pictures from the shows, links to the bands' sites and places to download their MP3s.

giraffecycle.com
giraffecycle@hotmail.com
www.giraffecycle.com
A webzine that is dedicated to the Saint John, NB hardcore music scene.

PalsOfOtherPerformers
palsofotherperformers@hotmail.com
www.smythe.nbcc.nb.ca/class2000/campbell/main.html
Fredericton area shows, bands and news. This site is intended to showcase the bands and individuals who make up the independent music scene in the Province of New Brunswick's capital city.

Route 66 Productions
info@route66sj.com
www.route66sj.com
Our mission is to provide positive experiences to the youth of Saint John and to promote indie music and the musicians who labour endlessly while maintaining their artistic integrity.

Saint John Now!
krista@sjnow.com
www.sjnow.com
List your upcoming event.

Newfoundland

Music Industry Association of Newfoundland & Labrador
dparker@nfld.com
www.mia.nf.ca
To create and encourage opportunities which will stimulate growth of the industry.

newfoundlandmusic.com
admin@newfoundlandmusic.com
www.newfoundlandmusic.com
If you are a Newfoundland musician, songwriter or band and have made a CD, cassette or LP please contact us. We offer a great package, so please get in touch!

Nova Scotia

Aliant.net – AtlanticZone *(MediaPipe)*
www.atlanticzone.ca/
A place that provides an entertaining and grass roots window into what's happening within our community via reviews, previews, features and a roll call of events in the MediaPipe calendar.

Cape Breton Music Online
info@cbmusic.com
cbmusic.com
The gateway to Cape Breton music on the Internet.

The Cape Bretoner Magazine
editorial@capebretoner.com
www.capebretoner.com
Keep up to date with the latest Cape Breton releases, performances, movies, exhibits etc.

Castlebay Music
info@castlebaymusic.com
www.castlebaymusic.com
The best in Cape Breton and East Coast music.

cblocals.com
admin@cblocals.com
www.cblocals.com
The very best in the Cape Breton underground culture.

Charlie's Music
charlie@ns.sympatico.ca
www.capebretonisland.com/Music/Charlies
One of the largest selections of recorded music from Atlantic Canada.

The Coast
theguide@thecoast.ns.ca
www.thecoast.ns.ca
Halifax's weekly. Get the info about your event, art show, performance or gig to us. If you have a photo (local bands, this means you) feel free to drop it off.

East Coast Catalogue Company Ltd.
catalogue@eastcoastcatalogue.com
www.eastcoastcatalogue.com
We are a mail order retailer of traditional and unique Atlantic Canadian products.

East Coast Music Online
wendy@eastcoastmusiconline.com
www.eastcoastmusiconline.com
Online Resource for the Canadian East Coast Music Scene. News, reviews and links to music industry related websites. If you have a website or news that should be listed, email us.

Halifax Herald
www.halifaxherald.com
Daily paper.

halifaxlocals.com
halifax@locals.ca
www.halifaxlocals.com
The very best in the Halifax underground culture.

The Inverness Oran
admin@oran.ca
oran.ca
A very popular newspaper published weekly in Inverness County.

JazzEast
general@jazzeast.com
www.jazzeast.com
Presents live jazz concerts and workshops by Atlantic and touring jazz artists, maintains a membership of jazz enthusiasts, publishes a newsletter, JazzEast News, to keep its membership informed about up-coming events and activities and presents the Atlantic Jazz Festival each summer.

The Music Industry Association of Nova Scotia
info@mians.ca
www.mians.ca
To foster, develop and promote the full potential of the music industry in Nova Scotia. Through communication, education, promotion and advocacy.

What's Goin On
wgoweekly@ns.sympatico.ca
www.whatsgoinon.ca
Cape Breton's arts & entertainment magazine.

Ontario

Barrie Folk Society
princess@barriefolk.com
www.barriefolk.com
Striving to build a community that supports artistic talent, style and creative vision.

The Brantford Folk Club
folk@rogers.com
www.brantford.folk.on.ca
Keeping the tradition alive!

The Brock Press
www.brockpress.com
Brock University's campus paper.

BronteSound Project
info@brontesound.ca
www.brontesound.ca
An association of people living in and around the west shore of Lake Ontario in the Oakville Burlington areas. We have an appreciation for the Arts and want to promote the Arts and the artists in our community. We intend this web site become a showcase for artists and a retail outlet to sell their works.

Canada South Blues Society
ThePrez@BluesSociety.ca
www.bluessociety.ca
Helping to keep the blues alive in SW Ontario.

The Charlatan
edstaff@thecharlatan.on.ca
www.thecharlatan.on.ca
Carleton University's independent student newspaper. Covers local music.

Christian Underground Rock In Ontario
(CURIO)
webmaster@curio.org
www.curio.org
An informal organization of Christian band. Our mission is to foster a more connected and interactive Christian music scene in Ontario—to improve band, ministry and industry networking in pursuit of growth and opportunity.

The Cornwall Underground
afi@cogeco.ca
www.geocities.com/cornwallunderground
Serving the punk / ska / emo / metal / hardcore / indie rock music scene in Cornwall since 1999.

The Cuckoo's Nest Folk Club
folk@iandavies.com
www.cuckoosnest.folk.on.ca
Promoting traditional folk music in London.

Frantic Ska
mark@franticska.com
www.skapages.com/franticska
Covering the Southern Ontario ska scene.

The Gazette
www.gazette.uwo.ca
University of Ontario's daily newspaper.

Headwaters Acoustic Music Society
h.a.m.s@sympatico.ca
www.whatson.on.ca/Bands/HAMS.htm
Based in Orangeville, we are an organization committed to supporting Canadian performing artists in the Traditional, Folk and Roots category.

Imprint
imprint.uwaterloo.ca
The University of Waterloo's student paper.

The Journal
RebeccaZamon@hotmail.com
www.queensjournal.ca
Queens University's student paper.

The Kingston Jazz Society
kingstonjazz@hotmail.com
kingstonjazz.com
Dedicated to the preservation and appreciation of jazz music as a distinctive North American art form in the Limestone City.

The Local London Music Scene
webmaster@cleverjoe.com
www.mmpro.on.ca/local

The Madrigal
madrigal@mirror.org
www.mirror.org/madrigal
Our CD selection and web site is the only one of its kind that is based on merit alone. Regardless of artist profile or sales, we neither list, stock, nor recommend mediocre recordings, especially in the standard classical repertoire.

Music and Film in Motion
info@musicandfilminmotion.com
www.musicandfilminmotion.com
Our purpose is to foster and promote the development of the film and music industries in Sudbury and

NorthBeat Productions
northbeat@elitegroup.on.ca
www.elitegroup.on.ca/northbeat
Founded to specifically promote local musical talent in the communities of Northern Huronia.

The Northern Bluegrass Committee
www.northernbluegrass.com

Northern Blues
fred@northernblues.com
www.northernblues.com
Canada's newest blues label, dedicated to bringing you the best in world class blues.

The Ontario Council of Folk Festivals
info@ocff.ca
www.ocff.ca
By joining the OCFF, you join the largest provincial networking organization devoted to our traditional, contemporary and multicultural folk music community and *you* become an integral part of the ever expanding network of folk activities across Canada.

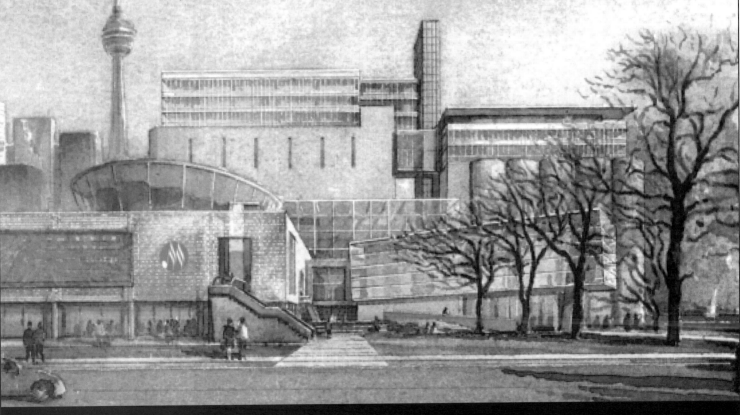

The Ontario Metal Pages
DJDaimon@PunkAss.com
www.ontariometal.net
The Definitive Guide To Metal In Ontario!

Ontariomusic.com
info@ontariomusic.com
www.ontariomusic.com
*Reviews, Sounds, Video, Photographs, Interviews,
Biographies, Show Listings, Site Hosting, Promotions,
Music Store and more for all musical genres.*

The Ontarion
pbialski@uoguelph.ca
www.uoguelph.ca/~ontarion
University of Guelph's campus publication.

OntarioPunk.com
ontariopunk@rogers.com
www.ontariopunk.com
*Interviews, reviews, downloads. Got your own stuff?
Send it to us!*

Orillia Folk Society
cyberfolkie@hotmail.com
www.geocities.com/liveatjives/ofs1.html
*Dedicated to providing a venue for contemporary and
traditional folk music in Orillia, Huronia and the
Near North.*

overhear
webmaster@overhear.com
www.overhear.com
*If you are an Ontario indie artist or band and would
like to have a featured listing on overhear, visit our
site for details.*

Peanut-Tree
trip@peanut-tree.com
www.peanut-tree.com
Covering the North Bay punk scene.

Sault Music Scene.com
saultmusic@Hotmail.com
www.thesaultmusicscene.com
*Created with the purpose of bringing together an
informative look at the local punk music community in
Sault Ste. Marie.*

Steel City Music
alenecouture@steelcitymusic.ca
www.steelcitymusic.ca
*Covering the Hamilton area. If you or your band
would like to be added to the our index, please
contact us with a short summary about your band (i.e.
member names, style, misc. info), a picture or your
band's logo, website address, show dates and
locations, and/or anything else your little hearts
desire!*

Traditions Folk Club
folkclub@acoustictraditions.com
www.acoustictraditions.com/folkclub.html
*Based in Orangeville. In addition to showcasing local
performers, our concert series has been hosting
musicians from other parts of Ontario, Canada and
beyond. If you are a performer or music lover and
would like to become involved, please contact us.*

VIEW Magazine
editor@viewmag.com
www.viewmag.com
Greater Hamilton's weekly alternative.

Wow! Sudbury
www.wowsudbury.com
*Greater Sudbury's entertainment website. Covers
local music.*

Ottawa

allblues4U.com
steam@allblues4u.com
www.allblues4u.com
Covering the Ottawa blues scene

Dark Ottawa
pub36.ezboard.com/bdarkottawa
*An Alternative Guide to Canada's Capital. If you have
or know of an event that you feel should be listed here
then please email me.*

The Fulcrum
arts@thefulcrum.com
www.thefulcrum.com
University of Ottawa's student paper.

Ladyfest Ottawa
ladyfestottawa@bust.com
www.jellyfish.ca/~ladyfest
*If three days of lady-positive workshops, art shows,
dance parties and rock 'n roll sounds good to you
please come and check it all out.*

Modern Drunk
rollergirl@moderndrunk.com
www.moderndrunk.com
Covering the Ottawa music scene.

Nine Planets Hip Hop
info@nineplanetshiphop.com
www.nineplanetshiphop.com
*Based in Ottawa, our vision is to provide the best in
Hip Hop Culture to hungry Canadian Fans looking
for new talent. Our key goal is to become Canada's
first successful independent record label by providing
tailored urban products that will be perceived by the
end user as unique in sound, quality and design.*

Ottawa Blues, Jazz and Swing Guide
bu932@ncf.ca
www.ncf.ca/ottawa-blues-jazz
Ottawa's one-stop blues and jazz event site.

Ottawa Blues Society
blueschicky@yahoo.ca
www.devant.com/OttawaBluesSociety
*This 4 times a year newsletter is packed with
information on the blues and includes CD reviews,
concert reviews and lots of information on the
International, Canadian and the local scene.*

Ottawa Citizen
www.canada.com/ottawa
*Daily paper. Entertainment section covers local music
events.*

The Ottawa Music Association
www.ottawamusic.net
*A FREE membership service that was founded to
open the lines of communication between local artists
and industry professionals. The Ottawa Music
Association hosts free monthly seminars on various
topics covering all aspects of the music industry.*

Ottawa Sun
www.fyiottawa.com/ottsun.shtml
*Daily paper. Cover local music in the entertainment
section.*

**The Ottawa Valley Bluegrass Music
Association**
WebAdmin@ValleyGrass.Ca
www.valleygrass.ca
*Our goal is to promote and publicize bluegrass music
and activities.*

The Ottawa Valley Music Association
www.ovmas.ca
*An association of musicians, recording artists
Technicians, songwriters, story tellers, disc jockeys,
producers and just plain folk who are interested in
producing, playing, developing, promoting and just
listening to music in, of and about the Ottawa Valley.*

Ottawa XPress
info@ottawaxpress.ca
www.ottawaxpress.ca
*Ottawa's weekly news and entertainment voice,
published every Thursday. Extensive coverage of local
music.*

OttawaJazz.com
kgrace@entrenet.com
www.ottawajazz.com
*Use our events calendar to lists upcoming gigs and
special events.*

OttawaPlus.ca
www.ottawaplus.ca
Online Arts & Entertainment guide.

OttawaStart
events@ottawastart.com
ottawastart.com
Add your events for free to our calendar.

punkottawa.com
info@punkottawa.com
www.punkottawa.com
*Covering the Ottawa scene. If you are submitting a
new listing please email us and make sure to include:
band name, website URL, city/neighbourhood, style of
music and email address.*

soundzgood
brad@soundzgood.com
www.soundzgood.com
*An Entertainment Resource in Canada's Capital.
We're looking for bands who want to live on our
page...the best place in Ottawa to sell your CDs. We
offer a RealAudio server and encrypted VISA line.
Anyone in the world will be able to sample your CD
and buy it directly from us, off the net.*

THRUST
John Sekerka whoops@cyberus.ca
thrust_2.tripod.com
*Record companies, publishing houses and cartoon
joints can send review material.*

Women's Voices Festival
artistic_submissions@womensvoices.on.ca
womensvoices.on.ca
*What better way to spend a summer's weekend than at
Canada's one of a kind Outdoor Women's festival.
Women, country air, comedy, arts... sunshine (may the
goddess be good to us!) and most of all... music in the
air.*

Toronto

The Ambient Ping
pingco@dreamstate.to
www.theambientping.com
*Toronto's unique weekly live ambient, chillout and
experimental music performance event. Relax with
other creative spirits every Tuesday night at a laid-
back club featuring the cream of Toronto's ambient
musicians and performers from across the continent.*

ARRAYMUSIC
info@arraymusic.com
www.arraymusic.com
Toronto based organization that exists to provide composers with an environment in which they are free to take risks, challenge themselves and push the traditional boundaries of musical expression.

Citygigs *Toronto*
info@citygigs.com
www.citygigs.com
You need to know more than just who's playing when. You need REAL information on ALL the shows that come to town, not just Cher. We offer featured stories, reviews, interviews, concert previews and more!

Classic Jazz Society of Toronto
www.classicjazztoronto.com
To promote the original form of jazz performed in the early part of the 20th Century. Classic Jazz includes 20's/30's style, traditional, Dixieland and any other form of jazz from the swing era.

Developmental Disorder
punkorezine@excite.com
ddisorder.cjb.net
A Toronto based online and print zine featuring Southern Ontario punk/ska/hardcore/etc. music and everything that come through the area.

eye
Stuart Berman sberman@eye.net
www.eye.net
Toronto's news and entertainment weekly. Local music covered.

The Eyeopener
entertainment@theeyeopener.com
www.theeyeopener.com
Ryerson's largest independent student newspaper.

Flying Cloud Folk Club
flying_cloud_folk@sympatico.ca
www3.sympatico.ca/flying_cloud_folk
Up to date information about the Toronto Folk Music scene.

The Guitar Society of Toronto
eli.kassner@utoronto.ca
www.guitar-toronto.on.ca
Dedicated to promoting the classical guitar. The Society has helped to develop local talent. Student concerts are part of the program every year and students from across Ontario have given performances.

Indie Rage
indierage@hotmail.com
www.geocities.com/indierage
An Indie music guide with contacts, info and everything you need to know about being in an Indie Band. Our main focus is Ontario.

indieMUSICpaper.ca
Christina bio@indiemusicpaper.ca
www.indiemusicpaper.ca
Reviews of indie artist are featured in the paper. Sells 5,000 copies monthly throughout the Toronto area.

Jazz in Toronto
info@jazzintoronto.com
www.jazzintoronto.com
The official guide to jazz in Toronto.

The Music Gallery
staff@musicgallery.org
www.musicgallery.org
We support the creation, performance and production of work in the following broadly defined areas: contemporary concert music, original, experimental or free jazz, ethnocentric music, electroacoustic or electronic music, work involving mixed or experimental media and performance arts.

Nocturnal
phantasm@nocturnalmagazine.net
www.nocturnalmagazine.net
Complete guide to the music and the people that make Toronto the best place to party in the world.

NOW
entertainment@nowtoronto.com
www.nowtoronto.com
Toronto's weekly news and entertainment voice, published every Thursday. Extensive coverage of local music.

SoundList
soundlst@audiolab.uwaterloo.ca
audiolab.uwaterloo.ca/~soundlst
An e-mail newsletter devoted to announcements of free-improvisation, experimental music and sound art events in the Toronto area.

The Spill
info@spillmagazine.com
www.spillmagazine.com
Features local Toronto talent and independent talent from around the world in all genres. We have a news section, concert listings, live reviews, CD reviews as well as interview features and columns.

The Textbook Zine
zine@textbookrecords.com
www.textbookrecords.com
We do one Indie review each month.

to-nite
gary17@to-nite.net
www.to-nite.net
Magazine published every Wednesday. Covers the Toronto music scene.

Toronto Blues Society
info@torontobluessociety.com
www.torontobluessociety.com
Dedicated to the promotion and preservation of the blues.

Toronto Early Music News
temc@interlog.com
www.interlog.com/~temc
Quarterly publication of the Toronto Early Music Centre which contains a calendar of upcoming events, CD reviews, profiles, articles etc.

Toronto Early Music Players Organization
dresher@chass.utoronto.ca
www.chass.utoronto.ca/~dresher/TEMPO
Our members are amateur musicians joined together to nurture and encourage the appreciation of Early Music (music from the Mediæval, Renaissance and Baroque periods).

The Toronto Globe and Mail
Arts@GlobeAndMail.ca
www.theglobeandmail.com
Daily paper. Covers local music.

Toronto-goth.com
reviews@toronto-goth.com
www.toronto-goth.com
A resource for Toronto's gothic/industrial/darkwave scene. Information includes bars, reviews, events, local people, shops, a discussion list and much more.

Toronto Hip Hop Online
torontohiphop@eagleson.com
www.eagleson.com/hiphop/toronto
Attention Toronto artists/DJs/graf artists/bboys/bgirls: Send in a short bio and a photo and get more exposure. You can also send a copy of your work to be reviewed and put up on the site. Email me for more information; put 'Toronto Artists' in the subject line.

ToRonTo HisPaNo.com
info@torontohispano.com
www.torontohispano.com
Covering music and entertainment in the Toronto Hispanic community.

Toronto Industrial Kollective
tik@yip.org
www.industrialkollective.org
The idea behind T.i.K. was to bring together a bunch of like minded people on the quest to eternally expand humanity's stagnant perceptions of industrial music (ie. to help promote the Industrial scene within the Toronto area).

Toronto Star
city@thestar.ca
www.thestar.com
Daily paper. Covers local music.

Toronto Sun
editor@sunpub.com
www.fyitoronto.com/torsun.shtml
Daily paper. Covers local music.

toronto-underground.com
music@toronto-underground.com
www.toronto-underground.com
To list your show or event, please email a text version of your basic press release (bios, pictures etc. are not necessary). PLEASE DO NOT SEND FILE ATTACHMENTS, but links to appropriate web sites are encouraged.

toronto.com
info@toronto.com
www.toronto.com
All you need to know about Toronto. Covers the local music scene.

TorontoJungle.com
music@torontojungle.com
torontojungle.com
Our staff voluntarily document events, review new music and interview the very best in local and international drum and bass talent.

TOsalsa.com
rose@tosalsa.com
www.tosalsa.com
We have interviews and various articles in our Latin music section.

The Varsity
review@thevarsity.ca
www.thevarsity.ca
The University of Toronto's Student Newspaper.

Wavelength
howdy@wavelengthtoronto.com
www.wavelengthtoronto.com
Weekly live music series and monthly zine, dedicated to uncovering underground music from Toronto and beyond.

Prince Edward Island

The Buzz
buzzon@isn.net
www.buzzon.com
A monthly newspaper guide to what's going on in the lively cultural scene of Prince Edward Island.

The East Coast Music Association
ecma@ecma.ca
www.ecma.ca
A regional collaboration of people in the music industry of Atlantic Canada. ECMA fosters, develops, promotes and celebrates its music locally and globally.

Music PEI
lee@isn.net
www.isn.net/musicpei
Promoting Island musicians to the industry.

peilocals.com
pei@locals.ca
www.peilocals.com
The very best in the PEI underground scene.

Quebec

33-MTL POINT COM
vagabbond@33-mtl.com
www.33-mtl.com
Webzine urbaine underground Québécoise.

Bandeapart.fm
www.bandeapart.fm
Magazine internet sur les musiques alternatives francophones. Reportage et portraits de groupes en audio-vidéo, diffusion de concerts, actualités, web radio 24 heures sur 24 etc...

Club Culture
club-culture.com
A site which posts French Canadian MP3s.

FOLQUÉBEC
info@folquebec.com
www.folquebec.com
The primary objective of FOLQUÉBEC is to increase recognition nationally and internationally of the abundance and quality of Québéc's folk music and dance culture. FOLQUÉBEC activities are open to participation by any and all members of the folk music community.

Hour
info@hour.ca
www.hour.ca
Montreal's weekly news and entertainment voice, published every Thursday. Extensive coverage of local music.

Jazz Montreal
webmaster@jazzmontreal.com
www.jazzmontreal.com
Musicians, venues and labels can add or update their information, listings and releases by registering with the site. All are welcome to contribute articles and reviews.

MetalQuebec.com
www.metalquebec.com
Critiques, MP3, Vidéos etc.

Montreal Mirror
Rupert Bottenberg rbottenberg@mtl-mirror.com
www.montrealmirror.com
Weekly arts & entertainment paper. Covers local music.

Montreal-Virtuel.com *x-trem musik*
carcass@sla-m.com
xtremmusik.montreal-virtuel.com
Montréal: ville extrême... La Mecque de la musique underground en Amérique du Nord.

Montrealgroove
info@montrealgroove.com
www.montrealgroove.com
CD Vendor for local Montreal artists.

Montreal Shows
shows@email.com
www.montrealshows.com
Send in info about your upcoming gigs.

MontrealPlus.ca
english.montrealplus.ca
Online arts & entertainment magazine covering the local music scene.

orcasound
orcasound@videotron.ca
www.orcasound.com
Each edition focuses on various aspects of Montreal city life. Our regular Review Features include Films, CDs, Resto / Clubs, Live Music and Orcastyle. Our music critic is on the trail of the hottest musical attractions and recordings. Get our thoughts on the latest CD releases.

Punk-Oueb
punk_oueb@hotmail.com
www.punk-oueb.cjb.net
La Scène Locale Québécoise.

Quebec Hardcore
www.qchc.com
100% dedicated to promoting local bands, labels and other hardcore/punk organizations. All material sent will be listened to and honestly reviewed. Don't ask us to check out your MP3s... we most likely won't.

Quebec Punk Scene
quebecpunk@hotmail.com
www.quebecpunkscene.net
La source #1 de la scène punk Québécoise.

QuebecPlus.ca
www.quebecplus.ca
Online arts & entertainment magazine covering the local music scene.

Rien à Déclarer
nelson@radzine.com
www.radzine.com
Covering the Montreal punk scene.

Rimouski Metal
www.rimouskimetal.net
News, reviews, gig dates etc.

Sang Frais
slug_666@hotmail.com
www.sangfrais.com
Le 'zine métal Québécoise 100% francophone.

Société de Guitare de Montréal
info@guitare-drummond.com
www.sgmontreal.qc.ca
Dedicated to promoting the classical guitar.

SOPREF
info@sopref.org
www.sopref.org
Société pour la promotion de la relève musicale de l'espace francophone.

SubQuebec.com
webmestres@subquebec.com
www.subquebec.com
Covering the hard music scene in Quebec.

Sur Scene
webmaster@surscene.qc.ca
www.surscene.qc.ca
Parlez-vous francais? Quebec music and arts scene.

Thirty Below
thirtybe@qbc.clic.net
www.qbc.clic.net/~thirtybe
Quebec traditional and folk music site.

Trois-Rivières Metal
www.troisrivieresmetal.com
Vous êtes un groupe de la région de la mauricie et vous voulez ajouter votre groupes sur TroisRivieresMetal.com alors contactez-moi.

Trois-Rivières Shows
mail@trshows.cjb.net
trshows.cjb.net
La liste des shows hardcore/punk/emo/ska... de Trois-Rivières et les environs.

TZMagazine.com
tino@tzmagazine.com
www.tzmagazine.com
An Independent artist resource whose purpose is to liven up the Montreal music scene.

Voir
info@voir.ca
www.voir.ca
Arts & Entertainment magazine with editions for Montreal and Quebec City.

What's up Tonight
info@whatsuptonight.com
www.whatsuptonight.com
We've created this site to make sure that no one will ever miss any musical events going on around the city of Montreal.

Zone Francophone
www.francoculture.ca
A site dedicated to francophone culture and arts.

Saskatchewan

The Carillon
ursu.uregina.ca/~carillon
University of Regina's student publication.

QueenCityPunk.com
queencitypunks@hotmail.com
queencitypunk.com
Here you will find everything you need to know and some other stuff you might be interested in about the Regina punk scene (we also welcome metal, hardcore, emo, rock and alternative bands).

saskhiphop.com
www.saskhiphop.com
Promoting the music of Saskatchewan artists.

Saskatchewan Country Music Association
scma@scma.sk.ca
www.scma.sk.ca
Dedicated to the promotion, development and enhancement of all aspects of Saskatchewan Country Music, at local, national and international levels.

The Saskatchewan Recording Industry Association
info@saskrecording.ca
www.saskrecording.ca
Develops and promotes the music and sound recording industries of Saskatchewan through partnering, education, effective communication, community involvement and encouraging fair and equitable compensation.

The Saskatoon Blues Society
saskblues@shaw.ca
members.shaw.ca/saskblues
Promotes, fosters, supports and celebrates Blues music in Saskatoon and throughout Saskatchewan.

Saskatoon Jazz Society
jazzsociety@sk.sympatico.ca
www3.sk.sympatico.ca/sjs

The Sheaf
duke.usask.ca/~ss_sheaf
University of Saskatchewan students' newspaper.

Threeohsix.org
setaside@threeohsix.org
threeohsix.org
A cross-genre underground music webzine and online community focusing specifically on Saskatchewan artists and events. We aim to provide information and support for music enthusiasts as well as bands and promoters alike.

Mexico

Rock Nacional Mx
nollpunk@hotmail.com
www.rocknacionalmx.cjb.net
Punk, hardcore, ska, metal. Fotos - audios - entrevistas - bandas entrevistas - bandas - noticias - tokadas.

RockSka.com
sugerencias@rockska.com
www.rockska.com
Los mejores grupos de Rock y Ska Mexicano, sus demos, discos, letras de canciones y canciones.

South America

BermudaMusic.Com
tony@bermuda.com
www.bermudamusic.com
The World-Wide Source for Bermuda Music!

The Brazilian Sound
thebraziliansound@hotmail.com
www.thebraziliansound.com
A Guide to Brazilian Music, Books, Movies & Culture.

Colombian Metal
juliancarcass@epm.net.co
www.truemetal.org/colombianmetal
Concert dates, downloads, reviews etc.

Rock Under
info@ru.com.ar
www.ru.com.ar
Covering the Argentina independent music scene.

Uniao Brasilera de Compositores *(UBC)*
www.ubc.org.br
Brazilian performing rights association. Active in the field of public performance rights of musical works, defending the copyrightable works of its members, or of those which it administers and represents.

Europe

American Voices
americanvoices@wxs.nl
www.americanvoices.org
Dedicated to the promotion of quality American music. With concert programs reflecting the uniqueness and cultural diversity of the United States, we feature selections from American classical, contemporary, opera, Broadway and jazz repertoire.

euromusic
webmaster@euromusic.com
www.euromusic.com
As long as you are based in a European territory from the Atlantic to Ural, you are welcome to register and create your page on Euromusic and present your activities to the worldwide music community.

The European Bluegrass Music Association
bluegrasseurope@datacomm.ch
www.europe-bma.org
Our goal is to further bluegrass music in Europe and further the exposure of European bluegrass musicians and bands.

European Country Music Association
eurocma@suport.org
www.europeancma.org
Visit the site for DJ reviews, message boards, news, charts etc.

European Free Improvisation Home
p.stubley@shef.ac.uk
www.shef.ac.uk/misc/rec/ps/efi
A comprehensive information resource for all aspects of the type of music known as European free improvisation. Every effort has been made to check the information on this site as far as possible; in most cases the information has been sourced from the musicians themselves.

Europe Jazz Network
ejn@ejn.it
www.ejn.it
Association of promoters, musicians, associations, artistic directors, consultants of music programs in Europe working mainly in the field of jazz and improvised music. E.J.N wants to promote collaboration among the professionals in this field to improve organizational efficiency and programming of concerts and tours and, therefore, the working conditions of musicians, agents, promoters.

geekrock
john@geekrock.co.uk
www.geekrock.com
An online gig guide & music resource covering 600 venues in the UK and Europe.

Live Hip Hop
livehiphop@4elementi.com
www.livehiphop.it
An online calendar dedicated to Hip Hop. Using these pages you'll be able to know what's happening in your town and where to find your favourite flava when you're movin' around Europe.

LiveMusicEurope
info@livemusiceurope.com
livemusiceurope.com
Visit our FREE Classified Resource Center. Musicians Bios, Gig Guides, Record Companies, Agents, Legal aid, Lost friends, suppliers, Equipment new & used and much More.

Riotgrrl Europe
rge.cjb.net
Riot Grrrl is a well known phenomenon in the USA, with a scene where grrrls can find their home. But in Europe, most riot grrrls feel alone. That's why we made this website. We want to establish a riot grrrl network in Europe. Underground-feminist bands, zines, distros, groups, projects etc., contact us!

Rocksie
www.rocksie.de
European Music Network for Women. We are taking measures to help increase the portion of professional female musicians, artists, sound engineers and other experts in public and in the music sectors.

Saucy Trout
saucytrout.com
An independent E-zine, currently Dutch only, about music festivals in Western Europe. All the information about festivals like Lowlands, Pinkpop, Roskilde, Glastonbury and many more can be found.

Austria

austria hardcore dot com
www.austriahardcore.com
d.i.y. hardcore, punk, emo, indie and more.

Belgium

Belgian Metal Underground *(BMU)*
users.pandora.be/bmu
Registered bands are given a chance to perform on stage. We do this on a voluntarily basis. We don't earn a dime doing this and it's just that that seems "suspicious" in our present society. People don't seem to accept the fact that someone makes such an effort just for the fun of it. Well ... we do !

Bluegrass in Belgium
www.bluegrass.be
Created to bring together bluegrass musicians and fans in Belgium. And to let people know what the hell is going on.

Cyprès
info@cypres-records.com
www.cypres-records.com
A Belgian record label featuring producers, orchestras and artists who promote Belgian music. Cyprès's international distribution network presents productions whose innovative and intelligent programming is matched by the highest artistic quality.

deathmetal.be
www.deathmetal.be
Everything you need to know about the Belgian metal scene.

Jazz in Belguim
ldh.jazz@wanadoo.be
www.jazzinbelgium.org
This is the web site of LES LUNDIS D'HORTENSE (the Belgian association of jazz musicians).

Prog-résiste
info@progresiste.com
www.progresiste.com
A "Non Profit Organization" having the aim to promote the musical arts, especially the Progressive Rock in Belgium, french speaking countries and, when and if possible, all around the world!

SKA-ntwerpen
klaas.vantomme@planetinternet.be
www.ska.be
Ska, punk en Oi!

Czech Republic

AllMetal
allmetal@pandora.cz
www.allmetal.cz
Online metal magazine, radio and much more!

BADPOINT.com
badpoint@badpoint.com
www.badpoint.com
Prague publication covering the local music scene.

Folk & Country
redakce@folkcountry.cz
www.folkcountry.cz
A monthly published magazine about folk, country, bluegrass, ethno etc. music – and not only about it. Hot news, events, chapters from history, interviews, reports and reviews.

His Voice
his@vol.cz
www.hisvoice.cz
Portraits, Interviews, Festivals and Reviews of New Czech Contemporary Music CDs.

MP3.cz
www.mp3.cz
The Czech Republic's largest MP3 site.

Denmark

The Copenhagen Music Guide
www.aok.dk/Copenhagen/Visiting_Copenhagen
Extensive coverage of the local music scene. Post your shows and events.

The Danish Folk Council
ffs@folkemusik.dk
www.folkemusik.dk
Serves as information point for the Danish folk scene. Publishes Folk&Musik, featuring articles, reviews, adverts etc.

Danish Metal
martin@danishmetal.dk
www.danishmetal.dk
A dedicated website that serves as a portal for info on Danish heavy metal bands.

Danish Metal Pages
headbanger@danishmetalpages.dk
www.danishmetalpages.dk
News, reviews, interviews and more!

Danish Music Information Center
mic@mic.dk
www.mic.dk
MIC is a state-funded, non-profit organization for providing information about and promoting Danish music at home and abroad.

Dansk Guitar Selskab
mikkel@andersen.mail.dk
www.danskguitarselskab.dk
Dedicated to the classical guitar.

Gritt Records
jay@gritt.dk
gritt.dk
News, reviews, downloads and info on the Alternative music scene in Denmark. Sell your CD from our site.

KODA
www.koda.dk
A Danish society that administers Danish and international copyrights for composers, songwriters and music publishers, when their musical works are performed in public.

Estonia

Eesti Autorite Ühing *(EAÜ)*
eau@eau.org
www.eauthors.ee
The main aim for the society is to represent authors of musical works and authors of works of drama.

Finland

Finnish All Music Media
info@allmusicmedia.com
www.allmusicmedia.com

Finnish Hip Hop Groups
Teemu@hiphopgroups.net
www.hiphopgroups.net
Lots of Finnish artists. The place for all hip hop in Finland.

Finnish Jazz Federation
info@jazzfin.com
www.jazzfin.com

Finnish Punk Guide
webmaster@punkinfinland.net
www.punkinfinland.net
Covering all things punk in Finland!

Jazzrytmit
osku@jazzrytmit.com
www.jazzrytmit.com
All about Finnish jazz!

MusicFinland.com
www.musicfinland.com
The domain for all Finnish music.

Rockdata
latvis@latvis.pp.fi
www.rockdata.net
Covering the Finnish music scene.

Suomihiphop.com
ilkka@suomihiphop.com
www.suomihiphop.com
For everything hip hop in Finland: This is the place: Artists, links and more!

Teosto - Finnish Composers' Copyright Society
teosto@teosto.fi
www.teosto.fi
Established in 1928 to administer the copyright of Finnish creators of music.

France

Confédération Internationale des Sociétés d'Auteurs et Compositeurs *(CISAC)*
cisac@cisac.org
www.cisac.org
Les organismes internationaux représentant les éditeurs de musique, les auteurs, les compositeurs et les producteurs de disque se sont accordés pour développer conjointement un projet d'identifiant unique des contenus numériques de musique.

France Bluegrass Musique Association
FBMA-WebMaster@country-junction-production.com
www.country-junction-production.com/FBMA
Un site pour les amateurs et les professionnels du Bluegrass en France.

French Beatz
frenchbeatz.online.fr
Here you will find only the best French rap MP3z.

Jazz in France
info@erb.com
www.jazzfrance.com
We've got everything you need to know about Jazz in France today.

Mix-Tape
jegeor@mix-tape.com
www.mix-tape.com
Mixtapes de rap francais.

MP3.fr
xavier@musiwave.com
www.mp3.fr
France's largest MP3 site.

mptrois.com
abo@mptrois.com
www.mptrois.com
French MP3 site.

NetGoth.fr
netgothfr@altern.org
netgoth.free.fr
Covers the Goth scene in France.

Societe Des Auteurs Compositeurs Et Editeurs De Musique *(SACEM)*
communication@sacem.fr
www.sacem.fr
An advocate for French performers. SACEM protects all musical works, whether French or foreign, except for works whose copyright protection has expired and have entered the public domain (70 years after the death of the author and the composer).

Xphases
xphases@xphases.com
www.xphases.com
Rap Français Indépendant.

Germany

3AM Magazine
andrew@3ammagazine.com
www.3ammagazine.com
A new issue each month, including a regular section called Musik San Frontieres. Sometimes it's a band interview, sometimes concert or CD reviews. Style-wise, I am pretty flexible (rock, garage, blues, world...) but I am most interested in artists who will be touring in or near Cologne, Germany.

berlin-ska.de
pate@berlin-ska.de
www.berlin-ska.de
Covering the Berlin ska scene.

CrossOver
crossover@ag-musik.de
www.crossover-agm.de
The AGM - network for youth culture.

GEMA
www.gema.de
German performing rights society.

hamburghiphop.de
hamburghiphop@gmx.de
www.hamburghiphop.de
News, reviews, interviews and MP3s.

Innovative Music Corporation
imc_kms@hotmail.com
www.geocities.com/SunsetStrip/Performance/3412
CD Vendor, Vinyl, Real-Audio files and much more! Good source for German Beats.

Ladyfest Hamburg
info@ladyfesthamburg.org
www.ladyfesthamburg.org
A festival to represent female artists. Ladyfest is rooted in the riot grrl movement.

MP3.de
www.mp3.de
Germany's largest MP3 site.

Reggae in Germany
peter@reggaenode.de
www.reggaenode.de
Main language is German but the you will find a short English abstract with each message!

Worst Munich Ska Page
ska69timm@gmx.de
www.2-tone.de
A local SKA, Punk and Oi! homepage, to let you know what's going on in Munich and the rest of the world.

Wrath
www.wrath.de
Goth music site. We feature a weekly up-to-date event guide of Germany, new CD reviews also every week, as well as interviews, concert reviews, small ads, eCards, a download section and many things more...

Greece

Gothic.gr
feedback@gothic.gr
www.gothic.gr
This idea for this site came to us because we thought that if there is an active gothic.gr site then more bands might consider visiting us, by noticing our strong presence and activities.

Hungary

industrial.hu
info@industrial.hu
www.industrial.hu

Iceland

dordingull.com
valli@dordingull.com
www.dordingull.com
Covering the Icelandic metal/hardcore scene.

Italy

All About Jazz
mricci@visionx.com
www.allaboutjazz.com/italy

Angelic North-East Alternative Bands Club
info@angelic.it
www.angelic.it
Interesting Goth-Dark guide to the Italian scene. Band pages, MP3 downloads etc.

GenerazioneX
webmaster@generazionex.com
www.generazionex.com
Music promotion for underground musicians and labels.

hotmc.com
s.lippolis@hotmc.com
news.hotmc.com
News, articles and reviews, mainly on Italian hiphop scene.

Italian Jazz Musicians
marco.valente@ijm.it
www.ijm.it
News, reviews, MP3s and online CD sales.

MP3.it
www.mp3.it
Italy's largest MP3 site.

Music Italiana
Tarrikone@hotmail.com
musicaitaliana.com

Societa Italiana Degli Autori Ed Editori *(SIAE)*
Musica@siae.it
www.siae.it
Performing Rights Association of Italy.

The Netherlands

Dutch Gothic
troy@dutchgothic.org
www.dutchgothic.org
News & information about the musical side from the Dutch gothic scene, as well as new releases. If you are interested in being featured or presented contact me on how and where to send your press packages etc.

Dutch Jazz Musicians
info@renelaanen.com
www.jazzmasters.nl
This web site is dedicated to all 'Jazz Musicians' in the Netherlands and Belgium.

Gun
gunmagazine@hotmail.com
jump.to/gun
Een gratis blad dat bedoeld is voor iedereen die meer wil weten over Utrechtse gitaarpop.

Hip Hop in je Smoel
yid@hiphopinjesmoel.nl
www.hiphopinjesmoel.nl
Good section of Reviews for everything Dutch in Hip Hop.

Holland Rocks
www.hollandrocks.com
Every month music-related news from the Netherlands including CD reviews, interviews and a gig guide among others.

MP3.nl
info@mp3.nl
www.mp3.nl
The site MP3.nl is not a single web site, but a collection of different sites by different people. The heart of the web site is a large database with information about tracks, albums and artists.

MusicFrom.NL
info@musicfrom.nl
www.musicfrom.nl
Netherlands musician's resource. Interviews, news, columns etc.

Urban Legends
mazl@urbanlegends.nl
www.urbanlegends.nl
For everything in Dutch Hip Hop. Local artists etc.

Norway

Beat the Blizzard
blizzard@tiscali.no
www.beattheblizzard.tk
Norwegian metal web 'zine with interviews, reviews, news, message board and more... Small and big labels and bands, signed and unsigned, are welcome to ship CDs for review.

Christiansand Blues Club
www.christiansandbluesclub.com

.no

organisation with the object of
llecting and distributing remuneration
for br.... ng in Norway of phonograms and other
recordings.

MP3.no
info@mp3.no
www.mp3.no
Norway's largest MP3 site. Must register to log in.

Norwegian Music Information Centre
info@mic.no
www.mic.no
Music catalogues, contact addresses, biographies of
Norwegian composers, articles on Norwegian music
and many links.

TONO
tono@tono.no
www.tono.no
Norway's Performing Rights Society. A work of art is
protected by law. We issue licenses for music users,
collect fees from venues and producers and distribute
the money to the right owners.

Poland

Era Jazzu
erajazzu@jazz.pl
www.jazz.pl
Promotes jazz in Poland. We not only present jazz
artists on a regular basis, but also have annual Jazz
festival, publications, CD releases etc.

INDEPENDENT.pl
info@independent.pl
www.independent.pl
Polski portal kulturalny - muzyka, film, teatr,
literatura, plastyka, galerie sztuki, komiksy, vlepki,
tatua¿e, graffiti.

INTERIAL.PL
interia@firma.interia.pl
meloman.interia.pl
Featuring Poland's classical music scene? Daily
classical music news, CD reviews, repertoire lists and
radio and TV listings.

MP3.pl
www.mp3.pl
Poland's largest MP3 site.

Polish Jazz
info@polishjazz.com
www.polishjazz.com
A coalition of musicians, professionals and jazz
enthusiasts. The mission is to promote the work of
Polish jazz artists and jazz professionals.

Post Industry
radek.turkiewicz@se.com.pl
www.postindustry.org
Electro, EBM, industrial, IDM, noise, gothic,
synthpop, foto, mp3...

terra.pl
terra@terra.pl
www.terra.pl
The best of underground music in Poland. Info,
sounds, news, concerts, labels.

Romania

Pendul
Daniel Dorobantu pendul@pendul.ro
www.pendul.ro
Romanian / International news, reviews, information
in the independent and underground fields.

Russia

Industrial Music Digest
Ben sup_ben@hotmail.com
www.postindustrial.org
Dedicated to the world of industrial, postindustrial
and crossover music. English part is devoted to local
Ukrainian postindustrial bands.

Jazz in Russia
moshkow@jazz.ru
www.jazz.ru
The most comprehensive Jazz Web resource in
Russian.

MP3.ru
www.mp3.ru
Russia's largest MP3 site.

Russian Gothic Page
coroner@gothic.ru
www.gothic.ru
An underground project dedicated to promotion of
gothic subculture in Russia. With art, music,
literature, film, pictures, reviews and links.

Spain

Jazz in Spain
www.jazzspain.com
Resources of jazz music in Spain, festivals, clubs,
Records labels, stores, schools, Associations,
Musicians...

Sociedad General de Autores y Editores
(SGAE)
www.sgae.es
Spain's Performing Rights Society.

Sweden

Crossroads Blues Society
kjell.wikstrom@kommun.kalmar.se
crossroads.just.nu
We organize concerts, issue a newsletter,
Bluesbulletinen, four times a year and work in other
various ways to support Blues music.

The Göteborg Music Guide
www.alltomgoteborg.se
Extensive coverage of the local music scene. Post
your shows and events.

LoFidelity
mike@lofidelity.net
www.lofidelity.net
Interviews, MP3s and more. Help support the scene!

The Malmö Music Guide
www.alltommalmo.tv4.se
Extensive coverage of the local music scene. Post
your shows and events.

MP3.nu
info@mp3.nu
www.mp3.nu
Sweden's largest MP3 site.

Nefertiti Jazz Club
info@nefertiti.se
www.nefertiti.se
Association based out of Goteborg, Sweden.

The Stockholm Music Guide
www.alltomstockholm.tv4.se
Extensive coverage of the local music scene. Post
your shows and events.

Svenska Tonsattares Internationella
Musikbyra (STIM)
info@stim.se
www.stim.se
The Swedish Performing Rights Society. The Swedish
link in an international system established to
safeguard the financial rights of composers and
lyricists under copyright law.

swedejazz.se
kansli@swedejazz.se
www.swedejazz.se
An enlightening jazz site from The Swedish Jazz
Federation. Here you will find lists of Swedish jazz
clubs and festivals, the latest news and CD
recommendations.

Swedish Metal
fredrik@swedishmetal.net
www.swedishmetal.net
News, reviews, interviews, downloads etc.

Swedish Music Information Center
per.floberg@stim.se
www.mic.stim.se
Music catalogues, reviews, contact addresses,
biographies of Swedish composers, articles on
Swedish music and many links.

Switzerland

MP3.ch
info@mp3.ch
www.mp3.ch
Switzerland's largest MP3 site.

The SKAlender
celli@skalender.ch
www.skalender.ch
Bands, concert dates, pictures, sounds...

Swiss Bluegrass Music Association
president@bluegrass.ch
www.bluegrass.ch

United Kingdom

All Things Music
webmaster@allthingsmusic.co.uk
www.allthingsmusic.co.uk
This site was started with one aim in mind to provide
a place where Musicians and Entertainers
Professional and Amateur with all levels of ability can
promote themselves FREE of charge.

Americana UK
feedback@americana-uk.com
www.americana-uk.com
UK home for Americana, alt-country and "No
Depression" music. We are committed to bringing you
the best news, reviews, interviews and listings for the
genre within the UK.

The Association of British Orchestras
info@abo.org.uk
www.abo.org.uk
The national body representing the collective interests of professional orchestras throughout the UK.

BandBase Online
enquiries@bandbase.co.uk
bandbase.co.uk
If you are in the entertainments business and looking to broaden your horizons, then add yourself to BandBase. You will get a free account which you can use to use to promote your band, keep an up-to-the-minute "Gig Guide" and even upload a photograph for visitors to see!

Bandcontacts.co.uk
webmaster@bandcontacts.co.uk
www.bandcontacts.co.uk
Part of musicians-web.co.uk. We offer bands a free gig guide and classifieds.

The Bandit A&R Newsletter
John Waterman bandit.42@aweber.com
www.banditnewsletter.com
We have been helping ambitious bands, singers, songwriters and producers for 14 years to target their demo's to Labels, Publishers, Managements and Producers World-wide which are CURRENTLY looking for new acts, songs or masters, in all commercial genres.

The Big-Gig Guide to Live Music
admin@biggig.co.uk
www.big-gig.co.uk
A music events guide, UK festival guide and live music forum section. Use the forums to propagate information and for general comments.

BIGMOUTH
tours@bigmouth.co.uk
www.bigmouth.co.uk
Complete listings of UK tours by both UK and non UK artists, online ticket sales for most UK gigs, links to artists sites, UK festival dates and information, on line purchase of CD's and Videos and much more... Contact us with your band info and tour dates.

Brit Links
news@britlinks.co.uk
www.britlinks.co.uk
We list a large number of Christian bands from all over the UK and Ireland.

British Academy of Composers & Songwriters
info@britishacademy.com
www.britishacademy.com
The largest composer/songwriter membership organisation in the world, representing the interests of over 3,000 UK music writers.

The British Bluegrass Music Association
Chairman@BritishBluegrass.com
www.britishbluegrass.com
We plan to co-ordinate and assist individual efforts to promote bluegrass music in Britain and to provide a means of improving communication.

The British Horn Society
mike@british-horn.org
www.british-horn.org
Dedicated to the art, craft and fun of horn playing. The Society publishes The Horn, organizes festivals and other special horn playing and study events featuring the best international soloists and arranges concessions for members from leading orchestras and retailers.

The British Music Information Centre (BMIC)
info@bmic.co.uk
www.bmic.co.uk
Our resources and activities include a major collection of scores, recordings and information on composers, accessible to the public; publicity and promotion schemes for composers; live events programmes, including The Cutting edge, The Cutting Edge Tour and our concert series at 10 Stratford Place.

British Music Rights
britishmusic@bmr.org
www.bmr.org
A trade organisation promoting the interests of composers, songwriters, music publishers and their collecting societies by raising awareness of copyright and piracy issues like MP3 downloading.

British Musician's Union
info@musiciansunion.org.uk
www.musiciansunion.org.uk
Loads of resources and benefits for members.

The British Trombone Society
webmaster@trombone-society.org.uk
www.trombone-society.org.uk
The BTS commissions new compositions, arranges concerto performances, recitals, workshops, lectures and seminars. Once a year, we usually stage a major festival, held at a different location on each occasion, when a full day of trombone education and entertainment is on offer.

British Underground Rock Band site (BURBs)
Barry@burbs.org.uk
www.burbs.org.uk
Offers promotion, airplay, world sales, reviews and lots more!

BritishHipHop.co.uk
peter@low-life.fsnet.co.uk
www.britishhiphop.co.uk
The groups showcased on our demo page should be relatively unknown Hip Hop acts from the United Kingdom and we hope to be able to aid in their development and exposure. We intend to focus on upcoming artists we think should progress on to better things and those you should check for in the future.

Cajun UK
cajun.uk@ntlworld.com
www.cajunuk.freeserve.co.uk
The objective of this site is to raise awareness of the UK Cajun and Zydeco music and dance scene.

Classical Music UK
editor@classicalmusic.co.uk
www.classicalmusic.co.uk
Add your site to our comprehensive list of classical music sites and add your events to our calendar.

Country Music In Britain
iain@cmib.co.uk
www.cmib.co.uk
Any Artists, Bands, Clubs, Promoters, Agents, Festivals, Events or anything else UK Country Music related who would like to be included on this site please contact me.

The Crate Estate
Ollie ollie@thecrateestate.co.uk.
www.thecrateestate.co.uk
A web site that promotes the largely underrated Hip-Hop scene in the United Kingdom. Acts that submit their material are guaranteed a fair review and a lot of coverage on the site.

falmusic.co.uk
info@falmusic.co.uk
www.falmusic.co.uk
This site is a forum for the many talented musicians and lively venues in the vicinity of Falmouth, UK. The writer and webmaster are into jazz and blues but we're open-minded.

GigHit.com
andy@gighit.com
www.gighit.com
Gighit has been set up as a quick stop guide for musicians and gig-goers all over the country. Enjoy our gig & club listings for Brighton, London and the UK, as well as details for venues, bars, pubs and much more.

Jagged Music
www.jaggedmusic.com
The British underground music website offering musicians and music lovers easy access to new music, information and services. You can browse our roster of artists and listen (free of charge) and order music on-line.

Jazz in Britain
john.r@ision.co.uk
www.jazz-in-britain.com

Jazz Services
admin@jazzservices.org.uk
www.jazzservices.org.uk
We exist to promote and develop jazz in the UK. We offer services in information, education, touring, communications, marketing and publishing. In short, Jazz Services provides a voice for jazz.

Jazz UK
webmaster@jazzuk.com
www.jazzuk.com
If you would like your band, gig, instrument or venue listed on the World Wide Web free of charge, just e-mail us for details.

Live Club
justin@liveclub.net
www.liveclub.co.uk
We are a non profit organization that does many services for new bands, all for free!!

lovealbatross
albatross@lovealbatross.com
www.lovealbatross.com
We provide free promotion for unsigned bands in the UK. Shout as loud as you like, include pics if you've got 'em, tours dates, album covers blah blah...

Mechanical Copyright Protection Society
classicalquery@mcps-prs-alliance.co.uk
www.mcps.co.uk
British organisation which licenses the recording and use of music and oversees the collection of royalties. MCPS generates mechanical royalties by running a number of different licensing schemes. Some of these schemes are more difficult to administer than others and this is reflected in the amount of commission charged and/or the length of time that it takes to distribute royalties.

Musician-Online.com
richard@musician-online.com
www.musician-online.com
A free directory of musicians of all kinds in the UK. All of the services in this site are completely free. Advertise yourself, your band and concerts.

musicians-web.co.uk
feedback@musicians-web.co.uk
www.musicians-web.co.uk
We work on a regional basis; one site per region,
each site reflecting local flavours yet at the same time
co-operating within the context of an umbrella
network, sharing ideas and resources and benefiting
from mutual promotion.

Musicindie
christel@musicindie.com
www.musicindie.org
www.musicindie.org/intro/music_indie
An R&D company set up by AIM to participate in a
series of innovative projects designed to increase the
market share & business potential of the UK
Independent Music Industry. In particular, Musicindie
is addressing changing market needs caused by
industry consolidation.

netgoth.org.uk
www.netgoth.org.uk/music
Post your news and events - and your MP3s.

NMC Recordings
nmc@nmcrec.co.uk
www.nmcrec.co.uk
Independent record label set up to record new music
by British composers.

Performing Arts Media Rights Association
(PAMRA)
office@pamra.org.uk
www.pamra.org.uk
The UK's collecting society for performers, paying out
royalties to qualifying performers for the broadcast of
their recorded performances.

The Performing Right Society
admissions@mcps-prs-alliance.co.uk
www.prs.co.uk
Collects licence fees for the public performance and
broadcast of musical works. It distributes this money
to its members - writers and publishers of music.

Prostar UK
David Priest david@priest01.freeserve.co.uk
www.prostaruk.co.uk
We are an A&R talent scout agency searching for the
stars of tomorrow. We are currently developing an
easy access site so we may provide an audition
platform for unsigned Bands & Artists to showcase
their work to us and the music industry.

Real UK Music
www.realukmusic.co.uk
The UK music portal and resource for events venues
festivals clubs performers concerts studios etc.

SERIOUSLY GROOVY
info@seriouslygroovy.com
www.seriouslygroovy.com
London's top indie music company. For the best and
newest alternative, indie, guitar-techno, rock and
progressive dance records coming out of the UK. We
bring you great music through 5 very different Record
Labels.

Singers U.K.
singers@singers-uk.org
www.singers-uk.net
Our on-line directory has been created to help the
promotion of fellow professional singers on the
internet. The success of Singers U.K. will depend
upon those who wish to join this community and help
to build this site into a U.K. based internet Singers
directory.

Society for the Promotion of New Music
(spnm)
spnm@spnm.org.uk
www.spnm.org.uk
From contemporary, jazz, classical and popular music
to that written for film, dance and other creative
media, spnm is one of the main advocates of new
music in Britain today. Encourages the
understanding, appreciation and development of
music composed by living musicians born or resident
in the UK and of music generally as expressed in any
other medium or form.

swampmusic
chrishall@swampmusic.co.uk
www.swampmusic.demon.co.uk
A comprehensive guide to all things Cajun & Zydeco
in the UK.

The Talent Scout
info@thetalentscout.co.uk
www.thetalentscout.co.uk
A unique service which gives all unsigned bands, solo
artists and songwriters the opportunity to get their
material listened to by A&R Personnel throughout the
music industry - COMPLETELY FREE OF
CHARGE.

tourdates.co.uk
dean@ita1.co.uk
www.tourdates.co.uk
The Very Best Half Arsed Underfunded Music Site On
The Whole Damn Web!!!

UK Gospel
reviews@ukgospel.com
www.ukgospel.com
We carefully select and review some of the best Urban
projects in the country.

The UK Hip Hop Database
peter@low-life.fsnet.co.uk
www.britishhiphop.co.uk
Extensive reviews, wide artist section.

UK Mix
www.ukmix.net
Your guide to the UK music scene starts here.

UKbands.net
support@ukbands.net
www.ukbands.net
THE one-stop music promotion portal for UK artists.
Is your band listed? If not, add your information into
the Artist Database. You can also have links to your
Web site, music and contact details.

UKbase
uk.base@ntlworld.com
www.ukbase.org.uk
My Aim is to have a one stop UK-Ireland Punk band
register with all the info you want to introduce
yourself to the great bands out there, with
comprehensive tour-date and release-date and review
pages.

ukevents.net
Michelle@ukevents.net
www.ukevents.net
Guide to music events in the UK. If you feel that a
particular event is unrepresented on this site, we
would like to hear from you.

UKSounds
info@uksounds.com
www.uksounds.com
Defining the future of music. In the last century we've
seen recorded music progress from wax cylinders to
vinyl discs to cassette tape and finally to CDs. Now
we're progressing things into the new millennium.

ukhh.com
2hip 2hip@ukhh.com
www.ukhh.com
We offer a great chance to gain exposure for all UK
Hip Hop acts.

Unsigned UK
www.unsigneduk.com
The definitive resource for the UK's New and
Established bands / artists, where all downloads is
free!

Vitamin UK
info@vitaminic.co.uk
www.vitaminic.co.uk
MP3s of British artists.

Wiseacre
www.wiseacre.clara.net/music
Music reviews site offering criticism where it's due on
the week's new music in the UK. Just about anything
and everything is covered in these pages, which are
updated every Sunday with reviews of the pick of the
week's new albums and singles.

England

AcoustiCity.co.uk
info@AcoustiCity.co.uk
www.acousticity.co.uk
Home of views, reviews, links & listings for acoustic
based, singer-songwriter & folk music in South East
England.

Birmingham Jazz
paul@diablodesign.co.uk
wavespace.waverider.co.uk/~bhamjazz
Dedicated to providing the best in jazz and
contemporary music.

The BRISTOL Jazz Society
secretary@bristoljazzsoc.co.uk
www.bristoljazzsoc.co.uk
Involved in promoting and supporting jazz throughout
the Bristol area and beyond!

Bristol Live Music
mike@bristollivemusic.co.uk
www.bristollivemusic.co.uk
The ultimate gig guide for Bristol and the surrounding
areas.

Brit-is UK Hip-Hop
members.tripod.com/brit_ish
We aim to bring you the best journalism and extensive
coverage of what's hot in the griminess of the UK
underground scene.

brumrocks.com
oroku_saki@hotmail.com
www.brumrocks.com
Helping live music in and around Birmingham.

Cambridge shire Musicians
dialspace.dial.pipex.com/town/walk/yls17
The site attempts to cater for all musical tastes and
styles.

Choke Magazine
williethedisc@yahoo.co.uk
www.chokecentral.co.uk
Based in Bristol, an ever-expanding group of music fans and musicians began to discuss how best to link the South-West's musical community with like minded people in other parts of the world.

Classical London
sub@classical-london.com
welcome.to/classicallondon
A free monthly international classical music newsletter, distributed by e-mail. Classical London includes CD, DVD and concert reviews, information about competitions and jobs for performers and composers, classical music news, information about classical music on the internet and information about concerts in London.

clubinlondon.co.uk
www.clubinlondon.co.uk
Covers London's dance music scene. News, reviews, spotlights etc.

The Collective
Matt Sealers rococo_band@hotmail.com
www.freewebs.com/musiccollective
We gig together, appear on each other's demos and releases and contribute to each other's compilations and sets. We review each other on various websites and fanzines and ensure that we give each other maximum exposure when approached by outsiders from the industry. Our DJs play our songs and our bands get them slots at their gigs.

Concrete Chaos
info@concretechaos.co.uk
www.concretechaos.co.uk
News, reviews, interviews etc. covering the Buckingham scene. If you want something submitted to the news section, send a short paragraph to Concrete and we'll put it up.

Connect Magazine
www.connect-magazine.co.uk
A Positive Living magazine published in Devon and distributed free across the counties of Devon & Cornwall. If you are involved in a local arts project and want to spread the word, or are looking for free publicity, here on the website and in the magazine, email us now.

Devon Folk Music
devonfolk@devonfolk.f9.co.uk
www.devonfolk.f9.co.uk
Serving the whole of Devon in all aspects of Folk.

The Dorset Blues Society
webmaster@bluesnights.co.uk
www.bluesnights.co.uk
For blues lovers everywhere and particularly for those visiting or living in the Dorchester and Weymouth areas.

East Midlands Folk Pages
mail@richardashe.co.uk
www.emfp.co.uk
Information and CD reviews.

Eerie Powers
andrewk@eeriepowers.co.uk
www.eeriepowers.co.uk
Welcome to Eerie Powers a comprehensive guide to the Doncaster music scene.

English Folk Dance & Song Society
efdss@efdss.org
www.efdss.org
To provide a national service providing support and assistance to anyone who participates or wishes to participate in folk activities.

Essex Folk Association *efn Magazine*
essex_folk_news@hotmail.com
www.pvcw.freeserve.co.uk
A comprehensive diary of folk/roots events for people living within the historic boundaries of the County of Essex. In addition we print articles, record reviews, songs and tunes.

Folk Around Bristol
woolley101@hotmail.com
folkaroundbristol.co.uk
Dedicated to encouraging, developing and coordinating folk activity in the greater Bristol area. We also like to give local and new bands a chance.

Folk London
gerry@grove-cottage.demon.co.uk
www.grove-cottage.demon.co.uk/folklon
Listings magazine for Folk Clubs and events in London and the South-east of England.

Folk Talk
Jim@folktalk.co.uk
www.folktalk.co.uk
The magazine for folk music in Lincolnshire & East Yorkshire.

Folkus
rustyandstu@compuserve.com
www.folkus.co.uk
We work with agents in the world of folk music and dance to obtain the best of the word's artists on tour in the UK, without neglecting our own homegrown artists.

Fresh Sounds
Michael East info@fresh-sounds.co.uk
www.fresh-sounds.co.uk
We run some of the largest showcases in Britain for unsigned bands. Our showcases enable bands to play in front of over 25 labels, both Major and Independent. We can take your unsigned band to the next step.

Gigwise
andy@gigwise.com
www.gigwise.com
Covering the Liverpool music scene. Gigs, reviews, news etc.

GlassWerk Media
editor@glasswerk.co.uk
www.glasswerk.co.uk
The North-West's premier website for unsigned musical artists. We offer CDs of these artists at reduced prices and provide other services such as gig listings, promotions and information for bands to help them get started.

The Insight
listings@theinsight.co.uk
www.theinsight.co.uk
A monthly comprehensive listings magazine for the city of Brighton and Hove. It explores local issues, entertainment and lifestyle via features and interviews.

irLondon
matty@irLondon.co.uk
www.irlondon.co.uk
Online club/gig guide as well as reviews & news.

The London Musicians Collective
lmc@lmcltd.demon.co.uk
www.l-m-c.org.uk
Promotes improvised and experimental music via concerts and an annual festival.

LondonNet *London Music Guide*
ahoy-talkback@londonnet.co.uk
www.londonnet.co.uk
News and reviews of local music.

London Punks
JJ@londonpunks.co.uk
www.londonpunks.co.uk
Gigs, reviews, photos, DIY, political art, demo adverts and more.

Low Life Records
info@lowliferecords.co.uk
www.lowliferecords.co.uk
The place to check for quality British Rap: News, Releases, Biographies, Audio samples and Mail Order etc. Underground Hip Hop from the UK's foremost artists.

Manchester Bands A-Z
info@manchester-bands.co.uk
www.manchester-bands.co.uk
Band listings, news, shows etc.

manchestermusic.co.uk
sovrec@yahoo.co.uk
www.manchestermusic.co.uk
The core resource for information regarding local music and information about bands.

melting vinyl
info@meltingvinyl.co.uk
www.meltingvinyl.co.uk
We welcome tapes or cds from people who wish to play in Brighton. We like Independence; originality; excitement; style; crazed electronica through to messed up garage punk; glamorous pop; bands in the gutter with their heads in the stars; original bribes.

MerseyMusic
reviews@merseymusic.org.uk
www.merseymusic.org.uk
Your #1 FREE resource and contact site for the Merseyside area. We aim to bring you weekly updated information to benefit everyone in the area. Whether you are a band looking to recruit a new member or a venue looking to book an act we hope to eventually become your one-stop-shop!

Midnight Mango
gigs@midnightmango.co.uk
www.midnightmango.co.uk
More than just a typical navel gazing page, Midnight Mango aims to cover all things to do with the interests of like minded people who move in the sea; that is Bridgwater, Somerset. Bands, Gigs, Reviews, Poetry, Photography...

musicmk
ndmweb@hotmail.com
www.musicmk.org.uk
Covering the music scene in Bedfordshire, Buckinghamshire and Hertfordshire

North West Bluegrass News
Editor@NWBN.freeserve.co.uk
www.nwbn.freeserve.co.uk
A non-profit British Bluegrass Magazine, hard copy and free online archive, with quality articles with photos, reviews, tablature etc.

nwdnb.co.uk
asok@nwdnb.co.uk
www.nwdnb.co.uk
Central hub of information for Drum and bass in Liverpool and Manchester.

nwuku.co.uk
info@nwuku.co.uk
www.nwuku.co.uk
Covering the Manchester, Leeds and Liverpool scene.

Peterborough Folk Diary
info@pborofolk.co.uk
www.pborofolk.co.uk
Your guide to music and Folk events in Peterborough and adjoining parts of Cambridgeshire, Lincolnshire, Norfolk and Northamptonshire.

Plymouth Music
plymouthmusic.co.uk
We'll bring you everything you need to know about your local music scene. We have a range of services from online band profiles to new local and national releases. Hopefully there will be something for everyone here.

Probe Magazine
info@probemusic.co.uk
www.probemusic.co.uk
Covering the London music scene. To be reviewed send recorded material, blurb about your band and an image to us.

Punk & Oi in the UK
rebecca@punkoiuk.co.uk
www.punkoiuk.co.uk
Everything, the good, the bad and the down right shite gets reviewed (punk & oi releases naturally get the best reviews) - who am I to say what is punk rock!

Random Consciousness
music@random-consciousness.co.uk
www.random-consciousness.co.uk
East Midlands based webzine. We aim to provide music / book reviews and interviews, with a definite focus on local / unsigned bands!

Rhythm and Booze
chris@rhythm-and-booze.co.uk
www.rhythm-and-booze.co.uk
Covering the Birmingham music scene. Send us info, ideas, comments, gig dates, reviews, scene reports, stuff to sell....basically anything you wanna see on this site.

Rocklands
therocklands@yahoo.com
welcome.to/rocklands
In this bohemian quarter of London Punk City is a wealth all kinds of music, music fans, musicians, DJs, music organisations, festivals, events, counter culture and more venues, theatres etc than just about any part of the city you can name.

Sandman Magazine
info@sandmanmagazine.co.uk
www.sandmanmagazine.co.uk
Sheffield's independent music magazine.

Sit On That
contact@sitonthat.co.uk
www.sitonthat.co.uk
The ultimate guide to unsigned music in the Staffordshire area.

Skippy's Cage
skippy@skippyscage.com
www.skippyscage.com
Showcasing the best bands around London at the moment. Detailed information on the bands including links to photos, discography, live dates and reviews.

South Riding Folk Network
info@folk-network.com
www.folk-network.com
Run by and for folk artists and enthusiasts, we are dedicated to maintaining the strength and vibrancy of the Folk Arts throughout our region and beyond.

South Yorkshire Folk
editor@syfolk.co.uk
www.syfolk.co.uk
News, festivals and CD reviews.

Southern Country
scountry3@aol.com
angelfire.com/sd/scountry
As well as reporting on the live events, we carry album reviews, book reviews, reader's letters, news, features and articles on related subjects. We also sponsor the annual UK Country Radio Awards.

Southwest Gig Guide
info@southwestgigguide.co.uk
www.southwestgigguide.co.uk
Artist listings, gigs and more.

Spire Folk
spirefolk@spirefolk.org.uk
www.spirefolk.org.uk
Folk, Roots and World Music from the heart of England.

Stirrings
www.stirrings.co.uk
Folk, Roots and Acoustic music in South York and beyond.

The Sussex Folk Guide
folk@brighton.co.uk
whatson.brighton.co.uk/folk
Free publication listing folk events in Brighton and Hove.

totallywired
listings@totallywired.co.uk
www.totallywired.co.uk
Covering the Brighton music scene.

Twenty4-Seven
comments@afterdarkmedia.net
www.twenty4-seven.co.uk
The guide to music in the South-West of England. Listings for events, gigs, clubs....

Wiltshire Folk Association
user@wiltsfolka.fsnet.co.uk
www.wiltsfolka.fsnet.co.uk
Folk performers can find both publicity and links with other groups or individuals through the wfa. It is possible to gain advice on aspects of performance.

Ireland

The Association of Irish Composers (AIC)
info@composers.ie
www.composers.ie
The representative body of composers in Ireland (including Northern Ireland). AIC represents the interests of composers in all areas of copyright and seeks to enhance the professional status of its members through promotional activities.

Bluegrass In Ireland
kgill@cit.ie
www.geocities.com/Nashville/8737
Information on Bluegrass Activities in Ireland.

The Chamber
teknique@utvinternet.com
www.teknique.utvinternet.com
Any Cork Heads out there, get in contact whether you're a DJ, EMCEE, Graf Head, BBoy or just a lover of Hip Hop.

CLUSA
webmaster@cluas.com
www.cluas.com
Lending an ear to life & adventure in Ireland.

The Contemporary Music Centre
info@cmc.ie
www.cmc.ie
Documents and promotes contemporary Irish concert music.

Dublin Jazz Society
dublinjazz.com
Dedicated to the promotion of live mainstream jazz in Dublin, featuring top international and Irish jazz musicians on a regular basis.

fastfude
www.fastfude.com
Northern Ireland's music scene.

Folk North West
suggestions@folknorthwest.co.uk
www.folknorthwest.co.uk
The Magazine of the North West Federation of Folk Clubs. Published quarterly, each magazine contains news from the North West Folk Scene as well as reviews of Live Events, CDs & Books.

Folktalk
jim@folktalk.co.uk
www.folktalk.co.uk
Providing information on folk music events within the regions of Lincolnshire and East Yorkshire. News, CD reviews, gig listings.

In Rhythm In Sound (Iris)
chiefeditor@irismagazine.net
www.irismagazine.net
Irish Homegrown Magazine for Irish Homegrown Talent.

Irish Music Magazine
irishmusic@mayo-ireland.ie
mag.irish-music.net
CD reviews, live reviews, articles and more!

Irish Music Network IMN Unsigned
www.irishmusicnetwork.tk
A new service in Ireland for unsigned bands. To see what all the hype is about visit our website.

IrishBeats.com
Ay Cee aycee@irishbeats.com
www.irishbeats.com
MC's, DJ's & Producers: To submit your material please contact me.

Irish Music Rights Organization (IMRO)
info@imro.ie
www.imro.ie
Administers the performing right in copyright music in Ireland on behalf of its members - songwriters, composers and music publishers - and on behalf of the members of the international overseas societies that are affiliated to it. IMRO's function is to collect and distribute royalties arising from the public performance of copyright works.

irishhiphop.com
info@irishhiphop.com
www.irishhiphop.f2s.com
MP3s, DJ Shows, links to UK and Irish shows.

IrishUnsigned.com
Ron Healy ron@IrishUnsigned.com
www.IrishUnsigned.com
Resource for the development and promotion of any unsigned Irish artists, anywhere.

Local Dublin
dublin.local.ie/entertainment
This is the place to visit for all that crucial lifestyle and entertainment information.

Northern Ireland Music Industry Commision (NIMIC)
Tony Talbot tonyt@nimusic.com
www.nimusic.com
Provides news and information for the music industry in Northern Ireland. NIMIC will support artist, bands, technicians and business people working in any music genre at any level. Services include marketing and promotion of the industry through the showcasing of bands nationally and internationally.

Soundweb
info@soundweb.ie
www.soundweb.ie
Since going live in late 2001, our aim has been to provide an attractive, informative and valuable on-line meeting point for aspiring artists, industry professionals and gig-going fans alike.

Studio Loop Records
Gareth Desmond garethd@slr.ie
www.slr.ie
We are a new Irish independent label with four acts on our roster. We deal in recording, publishing and management for the Territories of Ireland and England with distribution arranged through RMG/Chart.

Things You're Missing
info@thingsyouremissing.com
www.thingsyouremissing.com
A group of people scattered around the island of Ireland, all involved with our local independent music scene(s), who are co-operating in order to make the various headaches involved with independent music more easy to deal with.

Thumped
thumped.com
Irish Underground Music. Interviews, reviews, listings, mp3, real audio, real video.

Scotland

Assembly Direct
info@assemblydirect.ednet.co.uk
www.jazzmusic.co.uk
Organisation promoting jazz in Scotland through venues in Aberdeen, Edinburgh, Glasgow & Stirling. Background details on artists, venues, buy tickets on-line, CD shop.

Bluegrass in Scotland
cameron49@aol.com
www.ednet.co.uk/~russell
This website is your best source for up-to-date information on the Scottish bluegrass scene...

Elevation Station
Pat Fagan patfagan2002@yahoo.com
www.elevationstation.net
Dedicated to promoting and supporting the music of unsigned artists and Bands in Scotland.

The Glasgow Songwriter's Homepage
www.glasgowsongwriters.co.uk
For 10 years the organization has provided a platform for singers and songwriters in the Glasgow area.

Jazz in Scotland
admin@jazz-in-scotland.co.uk
www.jazz-in-scotland.co.uk
Our aim is to promote, encourage and unite the Scottish jazz music scene and to provide as much information as possible on Scottish jazz music and jazz music throughout the world to as many people as possible. We cover all styles of jazz music.

Jockrock
Stuart McHugh stuart@vacant.org.uk
www.jockrock.org
Scotland's longest running music site. For all things Caledonian. Reviews, competitions, radio and a very active messageboard.

MusicScotland.com
info@musicscotland.com
www.musicscotland.com
Scottish and Celtic music direct from Scotland with mp3 sounds.

New Music in Scotland (NEMIS)
info@nemis.co.uk
nemis.co.uk
A music network for Scottish artists, labels, music businesses, media, recording studios, venues, radio, creative and professional services within the industry in order to bring together those with a strong interest in the promotion and development of new music in Scotland.

Nightnews
webmaster@nightnews.net
www.nightnews.net
The Edinburgh based, alternative culture and entertainments portal for Scotland. Nightnews has established new links with the new music development scene in Scotland and can put artists or bands in contact with labels and venues.

Rainsound
mail@rainsound.net
www.rainsound.net
Covers Scotland.

The Scottish Bluegrass Association
john.sheldon@scottishbluegrass.com
www.scottishbluegrass.com
Set up to promote and develop Bluegrass music.

The Scottish Music Information Centre
info@smic.dircon.co.uk
www.smic.dircon.co.uk
Featuring composers and songwriters - from the Middle Ages to the present day, published and unpublished. If you are a composer and would like your music represented in the Scottish Music Information Centre, please read the submission guidelines and details of our membership schemes.

skye live!
contact@skyelive.com
www.skyelive.com
We track mainly the gigs of Scottish & Celtic bands wherever they are playing. we also list non-Celtic bands if they are playing in Scotland. If you are in a band playing Celtic music, contact us and we'll list your details & gigs.

Wales

Buzz
editorial@buzzmag.co.uk
www.buzzmag.co.uk
The leading entertainment magazine for 9 years. It is the free monthly 'Entertainments and What's on Guide' for Cardiff & South East Wales, including Newport, Swansea, the Valleys, Gwent and West Glamorgan.

Cardiff Soundscene
info@soundsceneuk.com
www.soundsceneuk.com
A music organisation run by and for young people in the Cardiff area, with the aim of improving the music scene for young bands/musicians in Cardiff by organising events and providing music related services.

Honk - Welsh Music News Online
www.welshmusicfoundation.com/honk
Covering the Welsh music scene. If you are promoting or performing a gig get yourself some FREE publicity in our on-line gig guide and newsletter.

Link2wales
Neil Crud neilcrud@aol.com
www.link2wales.co.uk
An encyclopaedic guide to the alternative scene past & present in Wales & Liverpool, receiving over 1,000 hits per week.

Planet
planet.enquiries@planetmagazine.org.uk
www.planetmagazine.org.uk
A bi-monthly magazine covering the arts, culture and politics in Wales and beyond. Includes features and interviews with contemporary Welsh artists.

South Wales Massive
www.southwalesmassive.com
A punk/hardcore site trying to bring everyone in South Wales together. We list as many gigs as we know about and will profile as many bands as we can, so everyone knows what's happening and who's about. We have a zine aspect to the site, where people are encouraged to contribute interviews, columns, reviews they have.

Welsh Music Foundation
natasha.hale@welshmusicfoundation.com
www.welshmusicfoundation.com
The role of WMF is to ensure that Wales develops a thriving music infrastructure, where local businesses take future Welsh pop music to an international audience.

Women in Tune
info@womenintune.org.uk
www.womenintune.org.uk
Our mission is to advance the education of the public in Wales by the provision of advice and assistance in music making and the performance of musical works by women.

Australia/New Zealand

Australia

Anemic
simon@anemicmagazine.com
www.anemicmagazine.com
Created to get the Australian underground bands some notice. If you send me some stuff I usually review it and sometimes if I like the stuff which is more often than not you might get an interview as well.

Artists helping Artists *(AHA)*
join@ahadirect.com.au
www.ahadirect.com.au
Dedicated to fostering a link of communication from the Venue to the Artist, The Artist to the Client and Artist to Artist, Ensuring a Positive and fulfilling experience for all concerned and to generate more work and a friendlier working environment for all involved.

The Arts Law Centre of Australia
artslaw@artslaw.com.au
www.artslaw.com.au
Arts Law gives preliminary advice and information to artists and arts organisations across all art forms on a wide range of arts related legal and business matters including contracts, copyright, business names and structures, defamation, insurance and employment.

AUSMUSIC
info@ausmusic.org.au
www.ausmusic.org.au
Providing skills and promotional opportunities for the Australian Music Industry.

Aussie Divas
groups.msn.com/aussiedivas
Here you'll be kept up to date with all the latest information, Articles, Lyrics, Biographies, Profiles, CD's Videos, Tour Dates, Photos etc.

The Australasian Mechanical Copyright Owners Society *(AMCOS)*
krug@apra.com.au
www.apra.com.au
Represents virtually all music publishers in Australia and New Zealand and, by way of reciprocal arrangements, the vast majority of the world's composers, writers and music publishers.

The Australasian Performing Right Association Limited *(APRA)*
krug@apra.com.au
www.apra.com.au
The first copyright collecting society set up in Australia, APRA represents 30,000 music writer and publisher members. As part of a world-wide network of similar organisations, APRA also provides local representation for more than 1,000,000 international composers. By arrangement, APRA also administers the rights of AMCOS.

The Australian Christian Artists Network
nationaloffice@acan.org.au
www.acan.org.au
Bringing you Australia's finest Christian artists. MP3 sound samples, the ACAN Gig Guide, classifieds and comprehensive database of Australian Christian Music, Industry Contacts.

The Australian Copyright Council
info@copyright.org.au
www.copyright.org.au

Australian Hip Hop Online
djlucious@hiphop.net.au
hiphop.net.au
Dedicated to Hip Hop culture, with a refreshing Australian perspective. Look out for fresh concert reviews, Hip Hop critiques, real-time chat, Aussie Hip Hop crews, the latest local & international news and a real attempt at taking Hip Hop to another level.

The Australian Music Association
info@australianmusic.asn.au
www.australianmusic.asn.au
An industry association representing and furthering the interests of the music products industry. It exists to pursue goals collectively to enhance the industry's development and prosperity.

Australian Music Foundation Inc.
amf@ausmusic.org.au
www.ausmusic.org.au
Our initial focus is to assist emerging Australian performers, composers and their support networks. To establish a "not-for-profit" foundation for the promotion and expansion of music and music development in Australia.

Australian Music Info
geoff@australianmusic.info
www.australianmusic.info
FREE audio reviews which come with your own page for each review. This is an excellent way to give your CD a bigger boost to a highly targeted audience which you can refer to in your own marketing material offline and link to from your own site.

Australian Music Online *(AMO)*
info@amo.net.au
www.amo.org.au
Designed to promote all new Australian music through a network of local and international content sharing partnerships.

Australian Music Web Site
webmistress@amws.com.au
www.amws.com.au
To make sure that Australian music always had a presence on the web, we started AMWS to be a complete resource for tracking down anything to do with Australian music.

Australian Musician
info@australianmusic.asn.au
www.australianmusic.asn.au
Australia's only A4 glossy publication designed for all musicians. Independent CDs reviewed.

Australian Punk*Hardcore*Ska
ozpunkhc@hotmail.com
surf.to/ozpunkhc
If anyone would like to add something to this site, like any info on bands, suggestions of bands who could appear on the site, photos or gig/cd reviews please email me with the info.

Australian Songwriters Association
secretary@asai.org.au
www.asai.org.au
The ASA mission is to encourage, recognise, educate, support and promote developing Australian songwriters.

The Blurb Magazine
feedback@theblurb.com.au
www.theblurb.com.au
Our "Soundscape" section has a heap of new releases from Australia's emerging talents, plus a spidery new soundtrack and music events.

Bombshell Zine
info@bombshellzine.com
www.bombshellzine.com
News, reviews, MP3s etc.

Buywell.com
sales@buywell.com
www.buywell.com
We specialise in classical music CDs, especially those manufactured or produced in Australia and New Zealand, those featuring composers and artists from these countries or having particular significance to them.

ChaosMusic
info@chaosmusic.com
www.chaosmusic.com
We specialize in the promotion of Australian music to the massive global market. We currently retail more than 400,000 different titles - from unsigned artists and independent local labels to collector's items, back catalogues and new release top charting artists. Your act will be given a unique URL upon request.

Clan Analogue
www.clananalogue.org
Clan aims to allow artists to produce work free of the constraints of the commercial music industry by developing self funded; artist initiated recording and publishing projects. This 'do it yourself' philosophy encourages the direct transmission of the artist's works to the listener without filtering it via label mediation.

Country Music Association of Australia
info@countrymusic.asn.au
www.countrymusic.asn.au
The CMAA was formed in 1992 to represent and promote all aspects of the Australian country music industry.

The Country Music Store
cmstore@countrymusic.com.au
www.countrymusic.com.au
A great online resource for all your Country Music, especially by Australian artists.

Crusty Music.net
crusty@crustymusic.net
www.crustymusic.net
We showcase many great Australian bands, from Metal to Rock. Includes music news, Australian and International, Streams and image gallery.

Indie-CDs
enquiries@indie-cds.com
www.indie-cds.com
We feature only music by independent Australian artists, in the folk, world, roots and new music genres.

Folk Alliance Australia
admin@folkalliance.org.au
www.folkalliance.org.au
I am always happy to review your new (or older) releases - so please send them to the Folk Alliance for review and other useful reference purposes.

Folk Australia
info@mountaintracks.com.au
folk.mountaintracks.com.au/Folk_Australia
A selection of reviews of CDs, books, cassettes etc both traditional and contemporary. Read the reviews or submit a review or product for review.

gothic.net.au
webbastard@gothic.net.au
www.gothic.net.au
We aim to be an online repository for all persuasions of gothic, neo-gothic culture in Australia. Listed are events and clubs for the major cities in Australia.

HUGEmusic.com.au
info@staff.hugemusic.com.au
www.hugemusic.com.au
Reviews on CDs, movies and artists that tell it like it is, not how the bio makes it out to be - written in a way that cuts through the PR hyperbole. HUGEmusic is about interviews and news concerning the artists and performers of today and tomorrow, not flavors of the month and the latest stock market quotes.

In Music & Media
sumo@themusic.com.au
www.themusic.com.au
Australian music news and resource site.

Indie News
Fred E. Gostein indienews@live.com.au
www.indienews.live.com.au
An online column that provides valuable information for indie acts.

Loud! Online
edjkrusha@nextcentury.com.au
www.geocities.com/SunsetStrip/Stage/4599
This website is dedicated to the promotion and exposure of Australian heavy metal music in all its forms.

Middle Eight Music
mem@bigpond.net.au
www.middle8.com
Online CD shop specialising in Australian artists - cabaret, theatre, jazz, pop, rock, folk, Latin, relaxation & meditation, children's music and more.

mono.net
peta@mono.net
www.mono.net
The ultimate resource for Australian music information, encompassing both the recognised and the undiscovered. Featuring hundreds of artists along side their respective noise.

Move Records
move@move.com.au
www.move.com.au
Australia's longest running independent classical label and is proud to support the creative work of Australian composers and performers. It has a large, spacious studio ideal for acoustic music. Unsolicited material is accepted in the classical, jazz, world and new age categories, preferably on CD.

MP3.com.au
info@MP3.com.au
www.mp3.com.au
One of Australia's top music websites, MP3.com.au is a place where music lovers can listen to and download exciting new music for free (both unsigned and commercial artists), talk about all things music in our forum and chatroom and buy music-related products.

New Australian Music Magazine
Norman James McCort amma@netspace.net.au
PO Box 319 Fitzroy, 3065, VIC, Australia

New Music Network
nmn@chilli.net.au
www.newmusicnetwork.com.au
Dedicated to the promotion and performance of Australian new music. The Network is a collection of impressive and passionate contemporary music ensembles and organisations. Based in Sydney, but with its eyes and ears to Australia and the world, the network was formed with the idea of informing audiences about the newest music performances by outstanding Australian artists.

Oz Music Central
ozmusic-central@bigpond.com
www.ozmusic-central.com.au
The paramount Australian music resource. Reviews, featured artists and more!

Oz Music Project
jaz@ozmusicproject.net
www.ozmusicproject.net
We have been dedicated to promoting Australian Music and look forward to doing so in the years beyond.

OzRock.com
webmaster@ozrock.com
www.ozrock.com
Australia's home-grown independent, unsigned and undiscovered artists, bands and music.

Pig Meat
pigmeat@pigmeat.cjb.net
www.pigmeat.cjb.net
We're open to anything you choose to contribute - interviews, reviews, news… Just about anything will be published, just as long as it gets past the pedantic Mr. Poo Chops.

revolve.com.au
dstrahan@revolve.com.au
www.revolve.com.au
Specialising in recordings of Modern Australian Classical Music on CD. Music scores and music kits are also available.

SCALA News
scala@senet.com.au
www.senet.com.au/~scala/newslett.htm
The Newsletter of the Songwriters, Composers And Lyricists Association Inc. Includes any information relevant to original music including news items, interviews, book reviews, reviews of members' CDs and cassettes, articles on songwriting, composing and lyric writing and other items of relevance to our members.

Songwriting Society of Australia
songsoc@ozemail.com.au
members.ozemail.com.au/~songsoc
Established to provide songwriters of Australia with assistance in developing and marketing their skills and offerings to the music industry.

SUBSTRATA
info@substrata.com.au
www.substrata.com.au
Australia's first independent online dance and electronic music store. SUBSTRATA offer secure ordering of CDs and vinyl through techno, house, electronic, hip-hop and experimental sounds. Real audio previews, interviews, news, reviews, charts and a passionate commitment to our homegrown music.

Tamworth Songwriters' Association Inc.
tsa@tpgi.com.au
www.tsaonline.com.au
Representing and promoting the interests of Australasian Country Music Songwriters.

Time Off
timeoff@timeoff.com.au
www.timeoff.com.au
Time Off is Australia's longest-running street paper and the market leader in Queensland. An independently owned and operated publication with an independent philosophy, Time Off covers all genres of music including a dedicated dance music section.

Whammo
help@whammo.com.au
www.whammo.com.au
We sell the biggest and best range of Australian music anywhere on the internet.

New South Wales

3D World Magazine
3d@threedworld.com.au
www.threedworld.com.au
Sydney's largest free circulating street press magazine with 32,000 copies a week. Embracing all walks of life from surfers, skaters, ravers, clubbers, artists, nerds and more, 3D World is the new voice of today's generation.

Bookings Direct
steve@bookingsdirect.com.au
www.bookingsdirect.com.au
Free to use information and booking service for Sydney bands and entertainment

The Canberra Blues Society
www.canberrablues.com
Dedicated to promoting blues music and blues performers in the Canberra region.

The Folk Federation of NSW
www.newsouthfolk.com/ffnsw
Our aim is to present, support and encourage the performance of folk music, folk song, folk dance and spoken word by providing - through its magazine, Cornstalk Gazette an opportunity for artists, audience, groups, clubs and festivals to get together.

I-94 Bar
cregan@optushome.com.au
www.i94bar.com
A virtual Bar and e-zine bringing you Rock Action from Sydney, Australia via the Bowery and the Motor City.

NewSouthFolk Agency
jim@newsouthfolk.com
www.newsouthfolk.com
Providing assistance to touring artists wishing to perform folk and roots music in venues throughout Australia.

Newcastle Music
www.newcastlemusic.net
Covers all of the Newcastle music scene. Bands, albums, downloads, gigs etc.

Newy Punk
punktribe@hotmail.com
www.newypunk.cjb.net
Newcastle's best site for all your local punk/ska/hardcore info, gigs, news etc.

OB(ZINE)
fly.to/obzine
OB(ZINE) is a music zine based in Western Sydney, Aus. We try to promote local unsigned bands by publishing a zine every month with CD reviews, interviews etc.

Sydney Friction
info@sydneyfriction.com
www.sydneyfriction.com
Sydney drum'n'bass resource. If you're a local producer and would like to add some MP3 extracts for others to hear, contact us.

Sydney Gothic
mary@phodis.com
www.sydneygothic.com
Want to add to our Reviews area? If you are involved in a Sydney project or know of a something happening in the scene, please send the details to SYDNEY GOTHIC and we will gladly review it.

The Sydney Music Guide
sydney.citysearch.com.au
Extensive coverage of the local music scene. Post your shows and events.

Sydney Music Web
iangav@tpg.com.au
www.sydneymusicweb.com
Everything you need to know about the Sydney music scene.

Sydneybands.com
contact@sydneybands.com
www.sydneybands.com
If you would like to be listed on this site please send us a logo, bio and your website address if you have one.

Queensland

Blues Association of South East Queensland
baseq@ozblues.zzn.com
baseq.tripod.com
Our aim is to increase the profile of South-East Queensland blues musicians around Australia and the world.

The Brisbane Music Guide
brisbane.citysearch.com.au
Extensive coverage of the local music scene. Post your shows and events.

brispop.com
admin@brispop.com
www.brispop.com
This site is intended as home to our Brispop friends and also a portal to access independent homepages of bands from in and around Brisbane.

Hellbane
hellbane@start.com.au
hellbane.cjb.net
Covering the Brisbane Goth scene.

South Australia

Rip it Up
www.ripitup.com.au
Adelaide's leading street press magazine.

South Australian Music Site *(SAMS)*
www.senet.com.au/~paulhas
This site is dedicated to the incredible wealth and diversity of musical talent in South Australia. This site is a resource for all music lovers, musicians and music industry people alike.

South Australian Blues Society
bluessa@senet.com.au
users.senet.com.au/~bluessa
Promoting the Blues in South Australia.

Victoria

Beat Magazine
music@beat.com.au
www.beat.com.au
A free Melbourne street paper, published weekly, focusing on the music, arts and entertainment industries.

The Early Music Society of Victoria
earlymusicsocietyvic@yahoo.com
home.vicnet.net.au/~emsv
Encourages and promotes the performance and enjoyment of medieval, renaissance and baroque music through a wide range of activities.

GrooveOn.com.au
vinee@grooveon.com.au
www.grooveon.com.au
Australian's urban culture online. Provides the latest news, event and club information on the RnB / HipHop / Latin scene in Melbourne and around Australia

MELBAND
info@melband.com.au
www.melband.com.au
A directory listing of all things music in Melbourne.

The Melbourne Music Guide
melbourne.citysearch.com.au
Extensive coverage of the local music scene. Post your shows and events.

The Melbourne Ska Page
manicmike@netscape.net
www.melbourneska.dhs.org
All about the Melbourne ska scene.

Victorian Folk Music Club
vfmc@bigpond.net.au
users.bigpond.net.au/vfmc
One of the oldest folk music organisations in Australia.

Western Australia

Bubblehead
www.bubbleheadzine.com
Covers the music scene of Perth.

Perthbands.com
feedback@perthbands.com
www.perthbands.com
This site aims to give Perth bands, national and international exposure by showcasing the many talents in the scene.

Western Front
clay@wf.com.au
www.wf.com.au
Dedicated to Western Australia's Metal Music Scene.

Westska- *Western Ska Online*
westska@westska.ii.net
westska.ii.net
All about Western Australian Ska and Ska in general. Gig and CD reviews, downloads, Gig Guides and Show Listings in the area.

XPress Magazine
localmusic@xpressmag.com.au
www.xpressmag.com.au
Australia's largest street press magazine. We offer all sorts of interviews and music industry news for Perth and all over Western Australia.

New Zealand

Bands.co.nz
nzbands@paradise.net.nz
www.bands.co.nz
A site for and about unsigned New Zealand bands. It is regularly updated and features a raft of news, informative articles and band links.

Beatmerchants

beatmerchants@beatmerchants.co.nz
www.beatmerchants.co.nz
Online CD Vendors of Hip Hop, Drum & Bass, House and Reggae.

cdkiwi.com

hq@cdkiwi.com
www.cdkiwi.com
The definitive New Zealand Music On-Line Store.

The Centre for New Zealand Music *(SOUNZ)*

info@sounz.org.nz
www.sounz.org.nz
A music information centre promoting the music of New Zealand through a range of services, projects and activities.

KiwiFolk

mikem@earthlight.co.nz
www.kiwifolk.org.nz
The website for folk and acoustic music in New Zealand.

Mp3.net.nz *Amplifier*

info@mp3.net.nz
www.mp3.net.nz
Wholly New Zealand owned and operated. We are not some large organisation but a collection of people who are supporters of New Zealand Music. We operate with New Zealand artists in a spirit of partnership and our aim is to help spread New Zealand Music around the world.

The New Zealand Blues Society

nzbs@blues.co.nz
www.blues.co.nz
Directories, news and CD reviews.

New Zealand Musician

nzmusician@paradise.net.nz
www.nzmusician.co.nz
The country's only magazine dedicated 100% to Kiwi music. In addition to features on bands and artists, the magazine includes reviews of the latest gear, industry and technique columns, all aimed at helping musicians navigate their way through the local industry to international fame.

NoiZyland

james@noizyland.com
www.noizyland.com
A guide to New Zealand indie rock and pop music (and an increasing amount of electronic and dance music and major label stuff too). We also sell a selection of indie NZ CDs and vinyl releases. If you're a NZ band and want to sell via our site, contact Natalie at: biz@noizyland.com

NZ On Air

info@nzonair.govt.nz
www.nzonair.govt.nz
Our main music mission is to get more New Zealand music played on the radio - especially commercial radio.

NZMusic.com

www.newzealandmusic.com
You got some super interesting news that we haven't reported yet? If so you can now let us know about it.

Obscure

www.obscure.co.nz
Dance music in New Zealand.

Punk As

toomuchrock@antisocial.com
www.punkas.com
New Zealand punk, ska and hardcore. Got any news, rants, columns, stories or rumours? Send them in to us.

Someone Up There Music

some1up@attglobal.net
www.someone.co.nz
We produce and distribute a range of Kiwi Music with an emphasis on Christian singer/songwriters.

Songwriters NZ

songwriters@musicnz.co.nz
www.musicnz.co.nz/sanzsa.html

Tearaway Magazine

editor@tearaway.co.nz
www.tearaway.co.nz
Lifestyle news-magazine for teenagers. Regular features include a big music section covering alternative and mainstream music.

www.hip-hop.co.nz

webmaster@hip-hop.co.nz
www.hip-hop.co.nz
Resource site for New Zealand artists.

Africa

Africa's Gateway

Shane Heusdens heusdens@mweb.co.za
www.AfricasGateway.com
The only site in Africa to give coverage to the best in underground hip hop/rap. The biggest hip hop site in Africa. Established 1997.

Africanhiphop.com

info@africanhiphop.com
www.africanhiphop.com
Serves the goal of unifying everybody who's inspired by hip hop and by the cultures of Africa and of African origins. The info at Africanhiphop.com is provided mostly by the artists themselves.

All About Jazz *South Africa*

mricci@visionx.com
www.allaboutjazz.com/southafrica
Many people outside South Africa have not had a chance to hear this music because of media, marketing and politics... but make no mistake: South African jazz deserves your ear. It's incredibly diverse, articulate and glowingly expressive.

Tha City Unplugged

www.nairobicity.net
Nairobi City hip hop resource. Articles, reviews etc.

kerpunk

www.punk.co.za
Covering the South African punk scene. News, reviews, articles etc.

SeneRap.Com

promotion@senerap.com
www.senegalhiphop.com
We specialize in promoting and advertising talented African crews and artists in the most innovative way to put the Senegalese R&B, Jazz, Rap, HipHop and Reggae music information online on our web pages.

Asia

arab-music.com

webmaster@arab-music.com
arab-music.com

The-Bazement.com

www.The-Bazement.com
Malaysian Hip Hop Radio, reviews, interviews, Malaysian Hip Hop Artists, CDs.

Beatrip

www.beatrip.com
Covering the Japanese pop music scene. News, events, spotlights etc.

Goth in Asia

littlefoot_69@yahoo.com
gothinasia.cjb.net
Shows, forums, MP3s etc.

Hong Kong Jazz Association

hkjawm@hkja.org
www.hkja.org
A non-profit-making Jazz organization based in Hong Kong, aims at promoting Jazz music in the Chinese community.

Malaysian Turntablism Scene

djideaz@skratchboarder.com
turntablism.the-bazement.com
Site exposing the turntablism in Malaysia as well as the hip-hop scenes worldwide.

Mp3.com Japan

japan.mp3.com

The Tokyo Music Guide

www.walkerplus.com/tokyo
Extensive coverage of the local music scene. Post your shows and events (in Japanese).

"Public radio listeners are among the best in the world. They're more often than not web-literate, so more willing to order your CD from the net; they're likely to be aware of the importance of supporting independent music; they're used to putting their money where their ears are; they've had more exposure to more diverse music; and they're more likely to be open to hearing something new and different and stellar, like, say, your music!"

Susanne Millsaps,
Thursday Breakfast Jam,
KRCL 90.9FM, Salt Lake City

Radio Promoters

Bryan Farrish Radio Promotion
airplay@radio-media.com
www.radio-media.com
Offering Signed and Unsigned-band promotion packages which obtain airplay for bands and labels on both commercial and non-commercial radio stations.

CollegeRadioPromotion.com
www.collegeradiopromotion.com
Our radio promotion program is designed to help the signed / unsigned musician achieve airtime on college radio stations in the United States. College radio DJs/stations appreciate and admire the independent artist/style. CRP's main goal is to provide college radio stations with the music they prefer to play - YOUR MUSIC!

DemoDaze
Tracy Kollker Crick tracy@demodaze.com
www.demodaze.com
The leading New Music media company. We reach an audience of approximately 25 million targeted consumers each month in person, online and through radio and television programming.

DG Systems
www.dgsystems.com
A digital distribution service operating on a private digital network to over 7500 radio stations across the US and Canada. Musicians who wish to have their music distributed to radio stations should contact a representative of DG Music at 1-800-207-7822.

Evolution Promotion
Karen Lee klee@evolutionpromotion.com
www.evolutionpromotion.com
We are committed to helping artists in the Adult Eclectic genres evolve to their full potential. As a full service company we offer all the key essentials necessary for a successful campaign - Radio Promotion, Tour Promotion, Internet Marketing, Direct Consumer Marketing, Web Design and Consulting services that capitalize on crucial opportunities that build careers.

Frequency Media
Erik Maier emaier@frequencymedia.com
www.frequencymedia.com
Provides both artists and music industry professionals with non-commercial radio airplay information. Using proprietary technology, we can tell independent artists exactly when and on which non-commercial radio stations their music is being played.

Indiego Promotions
info@indiego.com
www.indiego.com
Radio is the backbone of successful music promotion. Without radio, no artist can transcend local boundaries. Without strong ties to radio decision-makers, chances are slim an artist's CD will be promptly reviewed.

MiaMindMusic
MiMiMus@aol.com
www.miamindmusic.com
An entertainment promotion and marketing company. Within our promotion division we are concerned primarily with radio tracking and specialize in working with CMJ, as well as R&R surveyed radio stations.

Michelle Sounds
Brooke Ferris bferris@michellesounds.com
www.michellesounds.com
We promote to 500 college radio stations across the United States. College radio brings your music to over 3 million students.

Planetary Group
adam@planetarygroup.com
www.planetarygroup.com
Check out our radio team that provides full promotional services at the College, Commercial, AAA, Public and RPM; as well as targeted radio mailing services.

Protocol Entertainment
ProtocolMusic@aol.com
www.protocolentertainment.com
Focused on providing labels and artists with experienced and professional radio promotion and overall quarterbacking of a project. Our philosophy is simple - expose the most innovative music on a national level while micro-marketing a region through a high standard of consistency, follow-through and attention to detail.

Radio & Retail Promotions
Jon Flanagan promotions@radioandretail.com
www.radioandretail.com
Our goals are the building of a band's fan base, to increase CD sales, concert attendance & music industry recognition (esp. Distributors, labels & press). Jon learned the business while working at Capitol, Columbia, EMI, A&M, Tower Records & was a Radio Music Director himself.

radioDirectX
info@radiodirectx.com
www.radiodirectx.com
Over 600 Radio Stations & Media are using radioDirectX to discover new music! Sign up and start getting your music to radio programmers worldwide - today!

RAM (Realtime Airplay Metrics)
ram@cmj.com
www.cmj.com/ram
A revolutionary airplay tracking service developed by CMJ in partnership with Audible Magic Corporation, the leading provider of content-based identification technology.

RCI Music Promotion
RadioAirPlay@myrealbox.com
www.rcimusicpromotion.com
Music promotion radio airplay on a national level. Radio airplay music promotion for clients products, independent music promotion, distribution, cd marketing. Extensive website promotion and submission. Radio tracking reports.

REACH RADIO
Lou Galliani louskig@aol.com
An efficient, cost saving way to send your CD to radio without guess work or waste. Let us put your music into the hands of the music director you need to reach without wasting your CDs or time sending them to the wrong format. For more information and rates call Lou Galliani at 805-542-9999 or send an e-mail.

Research-Director.com *Canada*
Nick Andrews nandrews@research-director.com
www.research-director.com
We take advantage of our radio expertise to market independent music to stations in Canada. We use research to engage the attention of music directors and programmers.

Sheheshe Music Services
sheheshe@socket.net
www.sheheshe.com
We will mail your product; call each station on a regular basis; give you weekly email reports on each station, all included in our price! This is a one time fee, NOT a weekly or monthly fee, but we do have a monthly fee plan available.

Space 380
Matt IndieBible@Space380.com
www.space380.com
We realize that artists only need to sell a few thousand copies of a release to actually create music for a living. We offer the tools and support you NEED to be a successful independent musician. We develop name recognition for independent artists & labels of ALL genres.

Tinderbox Music
Krista Vilinskis krista@tinderboxmusic.com
www.tinderboxmusic.com
Music promotion and distribution company. Work mainly with unsigned and indie-label bands across the country. Services: Radio, Press, Distribution.

TRS Music Promotion
TRS@radiopromo.com
www.radiopromo.com
WE have helped some of today's hottest labels, artists and managers get their music releases on core college radio charts nationally, regionally and locally. With our network of regional reps, TRS can make sure that your music is getting the attention it deserves.

Stations that Play a Variety of Genres

Most stations listed in this section have weekly shows that cater to every style of music – Pop, Rock, Folk, Jazz, Various Metals, Punk, Goth, Industrial, Electronic, Hip Hop, Country, Blues etc. As one Music Director pointed out, when contacting these stations, it's very helpful to add: ATTENTION - MUSIC DIRECTOR in the subject heading of your e-mail.

North America

United States

Alabama

WBLZ *U. Alabama*
blazeradio@stupub.huc.uab.edu
138.26.166.169/blazeradio

WEGL *Auburn U.*
wegl@auburn.edu
wegl.auburn.edu

WLJS *Jacksonville State U.*
www.jsu.edu/92j

WUAL *Birmingham*
www.wual.ua.edu

WVUA *U. Alabama*
music@newrock907.com
www.newrock907.com

Alaska

KCHU *Valdez*
www.alaska.net/~kchu

KHNS *Haines*
khns@khns.org
www.khns.org

KMXT *Kodiak*
kmxt@ptialaska.net
www.kmxt.org

KSUA *U. Alaska Fairbanks*
www.uaf.edu/ksua

KTNA *Talkeetna*
ktnaprogramming@yahoo.com
www.ktna.org

Arizona

Indy Live
indylive713@yahoo.co.uk
www.indylive.gq.nu
A platform for Independent Artists, Bands, Songwriters and the companies that support them.

KAMP *U. Arizona*
kamp.arizona.edu

KASC *Arizona State U.*
www.theblaze1260.com

KXCI *Tucson*
kxcimd@kxci.org
www.kxci.org

Radio Limbo
limbo103@yahoo.com
www.radiolimbo.org
Our goal is to provide an alternative to the growing homogenization of corporate radio.

Arkansas

Blueprint Entertainment
K Shorter psalms12@yahoo.com
www.Blueprintent.com
I have a new radio show on KABF 88.3 Little Rock, AR Tuesdays from 1pm to 3pm. I am looking to play R&B and some forms of rock music. I would like to offer the opportunity for artist to send me material to the station. Support indie music!!!

KABF *Little Rock*
kabf@acorn.org
www.kabfradio.org

KCON *U. Central Arkansas*
KCON@mail.uca.edu
www.uca.edu/divisions/student/kcon

KHDX *Hendrix College*
www.hendrix.edu/Admission/scoops/khdx.htm

KSWH *Henderson State U.*
kswh@hsu.edu
stuwww.hsu.edu/kswh

KUAF *U. Arkansas*
kuafinfo@uark.edu
www.kuaf.com

KXUA *U. Arkansas - Fayetteville*
charts@uark.edu
www.uark.edu/studorg/kxua

Live at Acoustic Sounds Cafe *KUAR*
Greg Stefaniak gxstefaniak@ualr.edu
www.ualr.edu/kuar/asc.html
www.ualr.edu/kuar
Features musicians performing in a variety of styles — traditional and contemporary folk, Celtic, pop, bluegrass, jazz and blues. Concerts are presented on the second and fourth Fridays of each month.

California

DMX *Los Angeles*
www.dmxmusic.com

FreeFall
David Bassin freefall@pacbell.net
www.geocities.com/davidbassin/freefall.html
www.kusf.org
A mix of jazz, electronica, downtempo, funk and world music.

Juliette's Open Mic Radio Show
juliette@julietteriedl.com
www.julietteriedl.com
The concept for my show grew from frequenting Open Mics around town and hearing such great talent,. I wanted to create a place where independent musicians could reach their fans without asking them to sit through hours of waiting and avoid the "luck of the draw" order of most Open Mics.

KALX *U. California Berkeley*
kalx@media.berkeley.edu
kalx.berkeley.edu

KAPU *Azusa Pacific U.*
music@kapuradio.com
kapu.apu.edu

KAZU *Pacific Grove*
mail@kazu.org
www.kazu.org

KBeach *Long Beach*
md@kbeach.org
www.kbeach.org

KBHU *Black Hills State U.*
kbhufm@hotmail.com
www.kbhuthebuzz.com/

KCBL *Sacramento*
www.sacramento.org/stations/kcbl

KCIA *California Institute of the Arts*
shoko.calarts.edu/~kcia

KCPR *California Poly State U.*
kcprmd@kcpr.org
www.kcpr.org/

KCR *San Diego College*
kcr@kahuna.sdsu.edu
kahuna.sdsu.edu/kcr

KCRH *Chabot College*
kcrh@kcrhradio.com
www.kcrhradio.com

KCRW *Santa Monica*
mail@kcrw.org
www.kcrw.org

KCSB *Santa Barbara*
external.music@kcsb.org
www.kcsb.org

KCSC *California State U.*
kcsc@csuchico.edu
www.asbookstore.com/kcsc

KCSN *California State U. Northridge*
www.kcsn.org

KCSS *California State U. Stanislaus*
www.kcss.net

KCXX *San Bernadino*
www.x1039.com
Rock format!

KDNZ *U. San Francisco*
2130 Fulton St., UC402, San Francisco, CA 94117
PH: 415-422-6880

KDVS *U. California at Davis*
musicdept@kdvs.org
www.kdvs.org

KECC *El Camino College*
kecc1500@yahoo.com
www.elcamino.cc.ca.us/KECC

Kelly's Music Video Party
KellysLot@aol.com
www.MusicVideoParty.com
The place for indie artists to showcase their music videos!!!

KFJC *Los Altos Hills*
music@kfjc.org
www.kfjc.org

KFRR *Fresno*
www.newrock104.com
Rock format.

KFSR *California State U. Fresno*
kfsrfresno@hotmail.com
www.csufresno.edu/kfsr

KGFN *Grossmont College*
kgfnfm@yahoo.com
www.grossmont.net/kgfn

KHUM *Humboldt State U.*
info@khum.com
www.khum.com

KITS *Soundcheck*
www.live105.com
Independent music show.

KKUP *Cupertino*
admin@kkup.org
www.kkup.com

KMUD *Redway*
md@kmud.org
kmud.org

KNAB *Chapman U.*
MusicDirector@ChapmanRadio.com
www.ChapmanRadio.com

KOZT *Fort Bragg*
thecoast@kozt.com
www.kozt.com

KPCC *Pasadena City College*
mail@scpr.org
www.kpcc.org

KPFA *Berkeley*
postmaster@kpfa.org
www.kpfa.org

KRBS *Oroville*
krbs@cncnet.com
www.radiobirdstreet.org

KRCB *Rohnert Park*
listener@krcb.org
www.krcb.org/radio

KRFH *Humboldt College*
krfh@humboldt.edu
www.humboldt.edu/~krfh

KSAK *Mt. San Antonio College*
ksak@mtsac.edu
www.ksak.com

KSCR *Los Angeles*
kscr@usc.edu
www.kscrradio.com

KSCU *Santa Clara U.*
music@kscu.org
www.kscu.org

KSDT *U. California San Diego*
music@ksdtradio.org
ksdtradio.org

KSJS *San Jose State U.*
programdirector@ksjs.org
www.ksjs.org

KSPC *Pomona College*
www.kspc.org

KSRH *San Rafael High School*
185 Mission Ave., San Rafael, CA 94901
PH: 415-457-5314

KSSB *California State U. San Bernardino*
5500 University Pkwy, San Bernadino, CA 92407
PH: 909-880-5772

KSSU *California State U. Sacramento*
theapex@csus.edu
www.csus.edu/asi/KSSU

KSUN *Sonoma State U.*
www.sonoma.edu/ksun

KUCI *U. California*
md@kuci.org
www.kuci.org

KUCR *U. California Riverside*
kucrmusic@hotmail.com
www.kucr.org

KUSF *U. San Francisco*
kusfmusic@yahoo.com
www.kusf.org

KVMR *Nevada City*
music@kvmr.org
www.kvmr.org

KWRF *Santa Monica College*
1900 Pico Blvd, Santa Monica, CA 90405
PH: 310-434-4583

KXLU *Loyola - Marymount U.*
kxlu889fm@hotmail.com
www.kxlu.com

KYDS *El Camino H.S. - Sacramento*
www.sacramento.org/voice

KZSC *UC Santa Cruz*
kzsc.ucsc.edu

KZSU *Stanford U.*
music@kzsu.stanford.edu
kzsu.stanford.edu

KZYX *Philo*
musicdir@kzyx.org
www.kzyx.org

Morning Becomes Eclectic *KCRW*
mbe@kcrw.org
www.kcrw.org
Committed to a music experience that celebrates innovation, creativity and diversity by combining progressive pop, world beat, jazz, African, reggae, classical and new music. This three-hour show has become a very attractive whistle stop for both established and emerging artists from around the world.

Penguin Radio *Dominican U. California*
radio@dominican.edu
radio.dominican.edu

Radio Free Monterey
www.radiofreemonterey.org

Radio Goethe
radiogoethe@hotmail.com
www.goethe.de/uk/saf/radiogoethe/rgoethe2.htm
A show on KUSF San Francisco, just featuring bands from Germany, Austria and Switzerland.

Rock-it Radio *Ventura*
Rockitradio@aol.com
www.palmsradio.com/main.html
The Music we play is 1950's and early 1960's Rock and Roll including Rockabilly & Doo-wop and R&B! We also feature bands today that are out there playing the style of roots driven rock and roll, rockabilly and group harmony sound known as doo wop today.

SP Radio One
Tazy Phyllipz skaparade@aol.com
www.skaparade.com
We play 20+ different genres of music. Exclusive live in-studio performance by a variety of guests will air every week and each performance is available to listen to for the entire week following their live appearance on the website.

Stringbenders *KRCB*
Roger Bolt boltmedia@bigplanet.com
www.bolt-media.com
www.krcb.org/radio
The ONLY Northern California Radio show absolutely dedicated to the art and the artists of the GUITAR.

Titan Internet Radio *California State U.*
tir@titaninternetradio.com
tir.fullerton.edu

UCLARadio
info@uclaradio.com
www.uclaradio.com

WPMD *Cerritos College*
WPMD@Cerritos.edu
www.cerritos.edu/wpmd

Colorado

KCSU *Colorado State U.*
KCSUfm.com

KDNK *Carbondale*
www.kdnk.org

KDUR *Ft. Lewis College*
kdur_pd@fortlewis.edu
www.kdur.org

KEPC *Pikes Peak Community College*
kepc@ppcc.edu
www.ppcc.cccoes.edu/NewsEvents/KEPC

KGNU *Boulder*
music@kgnu.org
www.kgnu.org

KMSA *Mesa State College*
www.mesastate.edu/kmsa
PH: 970-248-1718

KRCC *Colorado College*
krcc@ColoradoCollege.edu
www.krcc.org

KRZA *Alamosa*
www.krza.com

KSRX *U. Northern Colorado*
ksrx@blue.unco.edu
www.unco.edu/ksrx

KTSC *U. Southern Colorado*
www.uscolo.edu/ktsc895
PH: 719-549-2822

KVCU *U. Colorado*
kvcumd@stripe.colorado.edu
www.colorado.edu/StudentGroups/KVCU

KVDU *U. Denver*
kvcumd@stripe.colorado.edu
kvdu.du.edu

KWSB *Western State College*
Taylor Hall, Room #111, Gunnison, CO 81230
PH: 970-943-3033

UNC Student Radio
ksrx@blue.unco.edu
www.unco.edu/ksrx

Connecticut

Offbeat
wpkn@wpkn.org
www.angelfire.com/music4/richk
www.wpkn.org

Radio Something
Valerie valrichardson@igc.org
wpkn.org/go/valerie
www.wpkn.org
A mixture of music and interviews.

WAPJ *U. Connecticut-Torrington*
shardan@snet.net
www.wapj.org

WCNI *Connecticut College*
www.wcniradio.org

WECS *Eastern Connecticut State U.*
WECS@hotmail.com
www.wecs.8k.com

WESU *Wesleyan U.*
www.wesleyan.edu/wesu

WFCS *Central Connecticut State U.*
WFCS1077@yahoo.com
clubs.ccsu.edu/wfcs

WHRT *Sacred Heart U.*
5151 Park Ave., Fairfield, CT 06852
PH: 203-371-7962

WHUS *U. Connecticut*
info@whus.org
whus.org

WKZE *Sharon*
info@wkze.com
www.wkze.com

WNHU *U. New Haven*
wnhu@newhaven.edu
www.newhaven.edu/wnhu

WPKN *U. Bridgeport*
wpkn@wpkn.org
www.wpkn.org
Please be sure to add: ATTENTION - MUSIC DIRECTOR, to the header of your E-Mail.

WQAQ *Quinnipiac College*
wqaq@quinnipiac.edu
go.to/wqaq

WRTC *Trinity College*
www.wrtcfm.com

WSAM *U of Hartford*
music@wsam.hartford.edu
wsam.hartford.edu

WSIN *Southern Connecticut State U.*
staff@wsinradio.org
radio.southernct.edu

WVOF *Fairfield U.*
musicdirector@wvof.org
www.ckanders.net/wvof/

WWUH *Hartford U.*
wwuh@mail.hartford.edu
www.wwuh.org

WXCI *Western Connecticut State U.*
www.wxci.org

WYBC *Yale U.*
md@wybc.com
www.am.wybc.com

Delaware

WDTS *Delaware Tech Community College*
PO Box, Georgetown, DE 19947
PH: 302-856-5400

WVUD *U. Delaware*
wvudmusic@udel.edu
www.wvud.org

Florida

M4 Radio *Sanford*
banzai@m4radio.com
www.m4radio.com
Wouldn't you love to hear you favorite local club band on the radio, or hear what other bands around the world sound like??? Well you can !!! On M4Radio.

WBRY *Barry U.*
www.barry.edu/communication/facilities/wbry.htm
PH: 305-899-3463

WBUL *U. South Florida*
www.ctr.usf.edu/wbul

WECX *Eckerd College*
4200 54th Ave. S., Box D, St. Petersburg, FL 33711
PH: 727-864-8419

WERU *Embry-Riddle Aeronautical U.*
dbweru@erau.edu
www.db.erau.edu/campus/student/weru

WFCF *Flagler College*
www.flagler.edu/news_events/wfcf.html
PH: 904-829-6940

WKNT *U. Central Florida*
music@knightcast.org
www.knightcast.org

WKPX *Piper H.S.*
www.wkpx.freeservers.com
8000 North West 44th St., Sunrise, FL 33351
PH: 954-572-1321

WMNF *Tampa Community College*
WMNF@wmnf.org
www.wmnf.org

WNSC *U. Central Florida*
WNSCmusic@yahoo.com
wnsc.ucf.edu

WNSU *Nova Southeastern U.*
musicdirector@nsuradio.com
www.nsuradio.com

WOSP *U. North Florida*
canopenersunion@hotmail.com
ospreyradio.tk
PH: 904-620-2908

WOWL *Florida Atlantic U.*
wowl.fau.edu

WPBZ *Smith College*
www.buzz103.com

WPRK *Rollins College*
wprkfm@rollins.edu
www.rollins.edu/wprk

WRGP *Florida International U.*
wrgpmusic@hotmail.com
wrgp.fiu.edu

WTFA *First Academy H.S.*
www.wtfa.org

WVFS *Florida State U.*
music@wvfs.fsu.edu
www.wvfs.fsu.edu

WVUM *U. Miami*
info@wvum.org
wvum.org

Georgia

WGHR *Southern Technical Institute College*
wghr@spsu.edu
wghr.spsu.edu

WMRE *Emory U.*
www.emory.edu/WMRE

WPLH *Abraham Baldwin College*
stallion.abac.peachnet.edu/stallion/wplh.htm

WRAS *Georgia State U.*
wrasgm@yahoo.com
www.gsu.edu/~www885

WREK *Georgia Tech*
music.director@wrek.org
www.wrek.org

WUOG *U. Georgia*
md@wuog.org
wuog.org

WVVS *Valdosta State U.*
www.valdosta.edu/wvvs

Hawaii

KKCR *Kauai*
kkcr@kkcr.org
www.kkcr.org

KTUH *U. Hawaii*
music@ktuh.org
ktuh.hawaii.edu

Idaho

KISU *Idaho State U.*
milljerr@isu.edu
www.isu.edu/kisufm

KUOI *U. Idaho*
kuoi@uidaho.edu
kuoi.asui.uidaho.edu

Illinois

UIC Radio *U. Illinois Chicago*
uicradio@uic.edu
www.uicradio.ws

WAUG *Augustana College*
waug@augustana.edu
listen.to/waug

WDBX *Carbondale*
www.wdbx.org

WDGC *Downers Grove H.S.*
wdgcfm@hotmail.com
www.csd99.k12.il.us/wdgc

WEFT *Champaign-Urbana*
weft@weftfm.org
www.weft.org

WESN *Illinois Wesleyan U.*
wesn@iwu.edu
www.iwu.edu/~wesn

WHPK *U. Chicago*
whpk@uchicago.edu
whpk.uchicago.edu

WIDB *Southern Illinois U.*
pd@widb.net
www.widb.net

WIIT *Illinois Institute of Technology*
wiit@iit.edu
radio.iit.edu

WKRP *Warrensburg*
wkrp@wkrp.fm
wkrp.fm
WKRP now sells what it plays. A new concept with Internet marketing. People listen to your song and if they like what they hear, they can buy your CD right then and there! Set-up is $25.00 US per CD.

WLFC *Lake Forest College*
wlfc@lfc.edu
www.lfc.edu/activities/wmxm

WLUW *Loyola U.*
wluwradio@wluw.org
www.wluw.org

WMCR *Monmouth College*
department.monm.edu/wmcr

WNTH *New Trier High School*
ntradio@aol.com
nths.newtrier.k12.il.us/activities/media/%7Ewnth/html/Intro

WNUR *Northwestern U.*
gm@wnur.org
www.wnur.org

WONC *North Central College*
feedback@wonc.org
www.wonc.org

WPCD *Parkland College*
wpcd@eudoramail.com
www.parkland.cc.il.us/wpcd

WQUB *Quincy U.*
www.quincy.edu/wqub

WRDP *Depaul U.*
wrdpmanagement@depaul.edu
radio.depaul.edu

WRRG *Triton College*
info@wrrg.org
www.wrrg.org

WVJC *Wabash Valley College*
www.iecc.cc.il.us/wvjc
2200 College Drive, Mount Carmel, IL 62863
PH: (618) 262-8989

WVKC *Knox College*
deptorg.knox.edu/wvkc

WZND *Illinois State U. Normal*
wznd@hotmail.com
www.wznd.com

WZRD *Northeastern Illinois U.*
www.live365.com/stations/203010
5500 North St Louis Ave Chicago, IL 60625-4699

Indiana

City of Music
Ann AMcWill882@aol.com
www.cityofmusic.com
Our sole purpose is to help independent musicians get some airplay. Every town in this country and beyond has jewels of music that will go unheard to the vast majority. We see that as a problem to solve and an opportunity to build a meaningful resource.

WCRD *Ball State U.*
wcrd@bsu.edu
web.bsu.edu/wcrd

WFCI *Franklin College*
wfci@franklincollege.edu
psj.franklincollege.edu/wfci

WFHB *Bloomington*
wfhb@wfhb.org
www.wfhb.org

WGRE *DePauw U.*
wgre@depauw.edu
www.depauw.edu/univ/wgre

WISU *Indiana State U.*
wisu.indstate.edu

WIUS *Indiana U.*
www.wiu.edu/thedog

WLAY *Purdue U.*
wlay@expert.cc.purdue.edu
expert.cc.purdue.edu/~wlay

WMHD *Rose-Hulman Institute of Technology*
5500 Wabash Avenue, Terre Haute, IN 47803
phone: 812-877-8350

WMRH *Purdue U.*
wmrh@expert.cc.purdue.edu
expert.cc.purdue.edu/~wmrh

WPUM *St. Joseph's College*
wpum@saintjoe.edu
www.saintjoe.edu/~wpum

WRFL *West Lafayette*
wrfl@expert.cc.purdue.edu
expert.cc.purdue.edu/~wrfl

WUEV *U. Evansville*
wuevfm@evansville.edu
www2.evansville.edu/wuevweb

WVFI *U. Notre Dame*
wvfi@nd.edu
www.nd.edu/~wvfi

WVUR *Valparaiso U.*
www.valpo.edu/student/wvur

Iowa

KALA *St. Ambrose U.*
kala@sau.edu
galvin.sau.edu/fm

KBVU *Buena Vista U.*
edge.bvu.edu

KDIC *Grinnell College*
kdicfm@grinnell.edu
www.grinnell.edu//groups/kdic

KICB *Iowa Central Community College*
www.iccc.cc.ia.us/kicb

KLIF *Briar Cliff College*
klif@briarcliff.edu
www.briarcliff.edu/klif

KMSC *Morningside College*
kmscfm@hotmail.com
www.morningside.edu/masscomm/KMSC

KRNL *Cornell College*
www.cornellcollege.edu/krnl

KRUI *U. Iowa*
krui@uiowa.edu
www.uiowa.edu/~krui

KSTM *Simpson College*
701 NC Street, Indianola, IA 50125
Phone: 515-961-1536

KURE *Iowa State U.*
kure@kure885.org
www.stuorg.iastate.edu/kure

KWAR *Waverly*
business@kwar.org
www.wartburg.edu/kwar

KWLC *Luther College*
students.luther.edu/~kwlc

Kansas

KFHS *Fort Hays State U.*
kfhs@fhsu.edu
www.fhsu.edu/int/kfhsradio

KJHK *U. Kansas*
kjhkmusic@ku.edu
kjhk.ukans.edu

KSDB *Kansas State U.*
radio@k-state.edu
wildcatradio.ksu.edu

Kentucky

Independent Hit Parade *WFPK*
Kim Sorise ksorise@wfpl.org
www.wfpk.org/Friday_special_features.htm
www.wfpk.org
Tune in for 60 minutes of the best in independent music.

WFPK *Louisville*
Dan Reed dreed@wfpk.org
www.wfpk.org

WMMT *Whitesburg*
wmmtfm@appalshop.org
www.appalshop.org/wmmt

WRFL *U. Kentucky*
music@wrfl.org
www.wrfl.org

WRVG *Georgetown College*
www.wrvg-fm.org

Louisiana

KLPI *Louisiana Tech*
www.latech.edu/tech/orgs/klpi

KNSU *Nicholls State U.*
knsu@nicholls.edu
www.nicholls.edu/knsu
Rock format.

KSCL *Centenary College*
kscl@centenary.edu
www.centenary.edu/students/kscl

KSLU *Southern Louisiana U.*
ksluradio@hotmail.com
www.selu.edu/kslu

KXUL *U. Louisiana*
kxul.com

WTUL *Tulane U.*
www.wtul.fm

Maine

WBOR *Bowdoin College*
WBOR@bowdoin.edu
www.bowdoin.edu/~wbor

WERU *Bangor*
info@weru.org
www.weru.org

WHSN *Husson College*
whsn@nescom.edu
www.nescom.edu/pages/whsn.htm

WMEB *U. Maine*
www.umaine.edu/wmeb

WMHB *Colby College*
wmhb@colby.edu
www.colby.edu/wmhb

WMPG *U. Southern Maine*
musicdepartment@wmpg.org
www.wmpg.org

WRBC *Bates College*
www.bates.edu/people/orgs/wrbc

WUFK *U. Maine Fort Kent*
www.umfk.maine.edu/wufk

WUMF *U. Maine*
wumf@umf.maine.edu
wumf.umf.maine.edu

WUPI *U.Maine - Presque Isle*
stationmanager@wupiradio.com
www.umpi.maine.edu/~wupi

Maryland

WFWM *Frostburg State U.*
wfwm@frostburg.edu
www.wfwm.org

WHFC *Hartford Community College*
whfc@harford.edu
www.harford.cc.md.us/Department/WHFC/main.htm

WJHU *Johns Hopkins U.*
wjhu@jhu.edu
www.hopkinsradio.com

WKHS *Kent County Highschool - Worton*
zorak@delanet.com
www.delanet.com/~zorak/wkhs.htm

WMBC *U. Maryland Baltimore County*
headmd@wmbc.umbc.edu
www.wmbc.umbc.edu

WMTB *St. Mary's College*
www.msmary.edu/wmtb

WMUC *U. Maryland*
md@wmuc.umd.edu
www.wmuc.umd.edu

WSUR *Salisbury U.*
wsurmusic@hotmail.com
orgs.salisbury.edu/wsur

Massachusetts

Radio Shanghai International *West Somerville*
shanghaii@earthlink.net
home.earthlink.net/~shanghaii

WAMH *Amherst College*
wamh.amherst.edu

WAVM *Maynard High School*
studio@wavm.org
www.wavm.org

WBIM *Bridgewater State College*
wbimmd@hotmail.com
www.bridgew.edu/wbim

WBRS *Brandeis U.*
music@wbrs.org
www.wbrs.org

WBTY *Bentley College*
www.geocities.com/wbty2000

WCCS *Wheaton College*
wccsradio@hotmail.com
wccs.wheatonma.edu

WCFM *Williams College*
wcfm.williams.edu

WCUW *Worcester*
wcuw@wcuw.com
www.wcuw.com

WDOA *Worcester*
www.wdoa.com

WERS *Emerson College*
info@wers.org
www.wers.org

WJUL *U. Massachusetts*
wjul@uml.edu
wjul.cs.uml.edu

WMBR *Massachusetts Institute of Technology*
music@wmbr.org
wmbr.mit.edu

WMFO *Tufts U.*
md@wmfo.org
www.wmfo.org

WMHC *Mt. Holyoke College*
www.mtholyoke.edu/org/wmhc

WMLN *Curry College*
www.curry.edu/WMLNWeb

WMUA *U. Massachusetts*
wmua@wmua.org
wmua.org

WMWM *Salem State College*
eboard@wmwm.org
www.wmwm.org

WOMR *Provincetown*
programming@womr.org
www.womr.org

WOZQ *Northampton*
sophia.smith.edu/org/wozq

WPAA *Phillips Academy*
WPAA@aol.com
users.aol.com/wpaa

WRBB *Northeastern U.*
wrbbradio.org

WRSI *Greenfield*
www.wrsi.com

WSFR *Suffolk U.*
radio@suffolk.edu
www.suffolk.edu/radio

WSHL *Stonehill College*
wshl@stonehill.edu
www.stonehill.edu/WSHL

WSMU *U. Mass/Dartmouth*
wsmu@umassd.edu
www.wsmu.org

WTBU *Boston U*
www.wtburadio.com

WWPI *Worcester Polytechnic Institute*
radio@wpi.edu
radio.wpi.edu

WZBC *Boston College*
www.wzbc.org

WZLY *Wellesley College*
md@wzly.net
wzly.net

Michigan

WBLD *West Bloomfield High*
wbld_fm@hotmail.com
wbld893.tripod.com

WCBN *U. Michigan*
music@wcbn.org
www.wcbn.org

WHFR *Henry Ford College*
whfr@hfcc.net
whfr.hfcc.net

WIDR *Western Michigan U.*
widr-music@groupwise.wmich.edu
www.widr.org

WLBN *Albion College*
wlbn@albion.edu
www.albion.edu/wlbn

WLSO *Lake Superior State U.*
wlso@gw.lssu.edu
www.lssu.edu/wlso

WMTU *Michigan Technological U.*
wmtu@mtu.edu
wmtu.mtu.edu

WNMC *Northwestern Michigan College*
www.wnmc.org

WPHS *Warren Cousino High School*
wphs@wphs.com
www.wphs.com

WQAC *Alma College*
wqaccharts@blazemail.com
students.alma.edu/organizations/wqac

WSDP *Salem High School*
www.wsdpradio.com

WUMD *U. Michigan Dearborn*
WUMD_GM@hotmail.com
listen.to/wumd

WUPX *Marquette U.*
wupx@nmu.edu
longyear.acs.nmu.edu/~wupx

WXOU *Oakland U.*
www.oakland.edu/org/wxou

WYCE *Grand Rapids*
comments@wyce.org
www.wyce.org

Minnesota

IJIR *St. Paul*
indiejournal@hotmail.com
www.indiejournal.com/indiejournal/IJIR

KAXE *Grand Rapids*
kaxe@kaxe.org
www.kaxe.org

KBSB *Bemidji State U.*
fm90@bemidjistate.edu
www.fm90.org

KFAI *Minneapolis*
www.kfai.org

KGSM *Gustavus Adolphus College*
www.gac.edu/oncampus/orgs/kgsm

KMSC *Minnesota State U. at Moorhead*
kmsc1500am@yahoo.com
www.dragonradio.org

KMSM *Montana Tech*
kmsm@mtech.edu
www.mtech.edu/kmsm

KMSU/SMSK *Minnesota State U.*
kmsu-radio@mnsu.edu
www.mankato.msus.edu/dept/kmsufm

KQAL *Winona*
music@kqal.org
www.kqal.org

KRLX *Carleton College*
krlxweb.carleton.edu

KSMR *St. Mary's U.*
ksmr@smumn.edu
www2.smumn.edu/studorg/~ksmr

KSTO *St. Olaf College*
ksto@stolaf.edu
www.stolaf.edu/orgs/ksto/listen.html

KUMM *U. Minnesota*
kumm@kumm.org
www.kumm.org
Hard alternative music.

KUOM *U. Minnesota*
music@radiok.org
www.radiok.org

KVSC *Saint Cloud State U.*
music@kvsc.org
www.kvsc.org

Radio Rumpus Room *KFAI*
rumpus2@bitstream.net
www.radiorumpusroom.com
Surf, Hot Rod, Rockabilly, '60s Garage, Hillbilly, Psychedelia, Back-To-The-Roots Country, Primal Pop. Radio Rumpus Room unleashes this unholy smorgasbord of sounds on an unsuspecting Minneapolis/St. Paul listenership every Friday night.

WELY *Ely*
info@wely.com
www.wely.com

WMCN *Manchester College*
wmcn@macalester.edu
www.macalester.edu/~wmcn

WTIP *Grand Marais*
wtip@boreal.org
wtip.org

Mississippi

WMSV *Mississippi State U.*
wmsv@msstate.edu
www.wmsv.msstate.edu

WUMS *U. Mississippi*
www.olemiss.edu/orgs/wums

WUSM *U. Southern Mississippi*
wusm@usm.edu
www-dept.usm.edu/~wusm/wusm2.html

Missouri

KCFV *Florissant Valley College*
www.stlcc.cc.mo.us/fv/kcfv

KCLC *Lindenwood*
FM891@lindenwood.edu
www.lindenwood.edu/studentlife/kclc.htm

KCOU *U. Missouri*
kcou@mu.org
tiger.coe.missouri.edu/~kcou

KDHX *St.Louis*
www.kdhx.org

KGLX *Webster U.*
www.kglx.org

KKFI *Kansas City*
kkfi901@aol.com
www.kkfi.org

KMNR *U. Missouri*
kmnr@umr.edu
www.umr.edu/~kmnr

KNSX *St.Louis*
x93@knsx.com
www.knsx.com
Rock format. If it's good, we'll play it!

KOPN *Columbia*
mail@kopn.org
www.kopn.org

KWJC *William Jewell College*
www.91-9.com
Modern rock format.

KWUR *Washington U.*
kwur.wustl.edu

KZLX *Northwest Missouri State U.*
kzlxradio@excite.com
www.nwmissouri.edu/~KDLX

Sonic Spectrum *KCUR*
Robert Moore moorerb@umkc.edu
www.kcur.org
*KCUR's Music Director, presents two hours of
freeform music programming, including interviews
and in-studio performances. From blues to drum n'
bass, indie rock to honky tonk...you'll hear it on The
Sonic Spectrum.*

Montana

KBGA *U. Montana*
music@kbga.org
kbga.org

KGLT *Bozeman/Helena/Livingston*
www.kglt.net

KMSM *Montana Tech*
kmsm@mtech.edu
www.mtech.edu/kmsm

Nebraska

KBUL *U. Nebraska Omaha*
maverickradio@netscape.net
maverickradio.unomaha.edu

KDNE *Doane College*
kdne@Doane.edu
webcast.doane.edu

KRNU *U. Nebraska Lincoln*
krnu@unl.edu
krnu.unl.edu

Nevada

LV Rocks
www.lvrocks.com
*Encourages everyone to take some time to visit and
enjoy the talents of the local musicians listed at our
site. Beyond that, we encourage you to go and visit
your favorites when they perform live at local venues.
There is an evening of great entertainment waiting for
you!*

New Hampshire

WDCR *Dartmouth College*
www.dartmouth.edu/~brdcast/db

WFRD *Dartmouth College*
www.wfrd.com
Mostly rock.

WKNH *Keene State College*
WKNHinfo@aol.com
www.jumblue.com/wknh

WPCR *Plymouth State College*
music@wpcr.plymouth.edu
mindwarp.plymouth.edu

WSCS *Colby-Sawyer College*
wscs@colby-sawyer.edu
www.colby-sawyer.edu/wscs

WSPS *Concord*
jt@wspsfm.com
www.wspsfm.com

WUNH *U. New Hampshire*
music@wunh.unh.edu
wunh.unh.edu

New Jersey

RLC *Rutgers U. Livingston*
thecoremusic@hotmail.com
www.thecore.rutgers.edu

WBZC *Burlington County College*
staff.bcc.edu/radio

WCCR *Rutgers U. Camden*
www.clam.rutgers.edu/~wccr

WFDU *Fairleigh Dickinson U.*
wfdu.fm

WFMU *Jersey City*
www.wfmu.org

WGLS *Rowan U. NJ*
wgls@rowan.edu
wgls.rowan.edu

WJTB *New Jersey Institute of Technology*
www.wjtb.org

WKNJ *Kean U.*
www.kean.edu/~cahss/acad_dept/comm/wknj

WMCX *Monmouth U.*
wmcxradio@monmouth.edu
hawkmail.monmouth.edu/~wmcx

WMNJ *Drew U.*
www.groups.drew.edu/wmnj

WNTI *Centenary College*
www.wnti.org

WPRB *Princeton U.*
music@wprb.com
www.wprb.com

WRLC *Livingston College/Rugers U.*
wrlc@lycoming.edu
www.lycoming.edu/orgs/wrlc

WRNU *Rutgers U. Newark*
wrnu@yahoo.com
pegasus.rutgers.edu/~wrnu

WRSU *Rutgers U. New Brunswick*
wrsu@wrsu.rutgers.edu
www.wrsu.org

WSOU *Seton Hall U.*
music@wsou.net
www.wsou.net

WTSR *College of New Jersey*
tsrmusic@tcnj.edu
www.trenton.edu/~wtsr

New Mexico

KRUX *New Mexico State U.*
info@krux.fm
www.krux.nmsu.edu

KTEK *New Mexico Tech*
ktek@nmt.edu
www.nmt.edu/~ktek

KUNM *U. New Mexico*
music@kunm.org
www.kunm.org/home

New York

106 VIC *Ithaca College*
vic@ithaca.edu
www.ithaca.edu/radio/vic

Emotional Rescue *WJFF*
www.wjffradio.org
*A weekly, 90 minute music show covering rock, pop,
R&B, Soul, Blues, Indie, Folk, Celtic, World,
Contemporary Native American and more. There are
theme shows and regular mixes from the host. All
world music, the 2nd Wednesday of every month.*

The Indie Show *WBER*
wber@monroe.edu
wber.monroe.edu
2 hours of music exclusively from Independent labels.

KSLU *Saint Lawrence U.*
it.stlawu.edu/~kslu/kslu.html

Light Show *WBAI*
www.wbai.org
*I am a DJ on 50,000 Watt WBAI-FM's Light Show in
NYC. Our station reaches 135,000 listeners in the
area plus a worldwide live Internet audience. On our
program we play unsigned and small label bands of
all musical genres. Submissions to: Evan Ginzburg,
WBAI-FM's Light Show 120 Wall St. NYC 10005.*

**The Tuesday Night Rock And Roll Dance
Party** *WUSB*
rockandroll@wusb.fm
www.wusb.fm/deadend
*If you're in or know of a band that plays in the style
that we feature around here and want to make a trip
up to our studios (in Stony Brook, New York....'bout
an hour east of NYC) and lay down a set of music, let
us know and maybe we can work something out.*

WAIH *SUNY Potsdam*
waih@potsdam.edu
www2.potsdam.edu/WAIH

WALF *Alfred U.*
WALF@alfred.edu
jobs.alfred.edu/~walf

WAMC *Albany*
www.wamc.org

WBAI *New York*
info@wbai.org
www.wbai.org

WBAR *Barnard College*
wbar@columbia.edu
www.wbar.org

WBER *Monroe College*
wber@monroe.edu
wber.monroe.edu

WBMB *Baruch College*
wbmb_radio@yahoo.com
www.geocities.com/wbmbradio

WBNY *Buffalo State U.*
www.buffalostate.edu/wbny

WBSU *SUNY Brockport*
www.acs.brockport.edu/~wbsu

WCDB *U. Albany*
wcdb@albany.edu
www.albany.edu/~wcdb

WCOT *SUNY Utica*
wcot@sunyit.edu
www.sunyit.edu/~wcot

WCVF *SUNY Fredonia*
www.fredoniaradio.org

WCWP *Long Island U.*
wcwp@cwpost.liu.edu
www.webradioWCWP.com

WDST *Woodstock*
www.wdst.com

WDVL *Fredonia State U.*
www.fredoniaradio.org

WDWN *Cayuga County Community College*
wdwn@hotmail.com
www.wdwn.fm/

WDYN *Rochester*
wdyn@wdyn.net
dynamicradio.net
*Rochester's ONLY Independent Radio Station that
plays ONLY Local and Indie Music Every Day.*

WERW *Syracuse U.*
music@werw.syr.edu
werw.syr.edu

WFNP *SUNY New Paltz*
wfnp@newpaltz.edu
www.newpaltz.edu/wfnp

WFUV *Fordham U.*
thefolks@wfuv.org
www.wfuv.org

WGCC *Genesee Community College*
www.sunygenesee.cc.ny.us/stu_act/wgcc.htm

WGFR *Adirondack Community College*
wgfr@wgfr.org
www.wgfr.org

WHCL *Hamilton College*
www.whcl.org

WHPC *Nassau Community College*
whpc@ncc.edu
www.sunynassau.edu/dptpages/whpc/whpc.htm

WHRW *SUNY Binghampton*
www.whrwfm.org

WICB *Ithaca College*
wicb@ithaca.edu
www.ithaca.edu/radio/wicb

WITR *Rochester Institute of Technology*
musicdirector@modernmusicandmore.com
www.modernmusicandmore.com

WJFF *Jeffersonville*
wjff@catskill.net
www.wjffradio.org

WKRB *Kingsborough College*
music@wkrb.org
www.wkrbfm.homestead.com

WLIR *Garden City*
www.wlir.com

WLMU *Le Moyne College*
wlmu@mail.lemoyne.edu
www.lemoyne.edu/wlmu

WNYO *SUNY Oswego*
wnyo@oswego.edu
www.oswego.edu/~wnyo

WNYU *New York U.*
Teresa Lin wnyumusic@hotmail.com
www.wnyu.org

WONY *Oneonta*
David Chait heyguy666@aol.com
www.oneonta.edu/WONY

WPOB *JFK H.S.*
www.wpob.com

WQKE *Plattsburgh State U.*
clubs.plattsburgh.edu/wqke

WRCU *Colgate U.*
wrcu@mail.colgate.edu
wrcu.colgate.edu

WRHU *Hofstra U.*
mail@wrhu.org
www.wrhu.org

WRPI *Rensselaer Polytechnic Institute*
wrpi-md@rpi.edu
www.wrpi.org

WRUB *SUNY U. at Buffalo*
www.subboard.com/wrub

WRUR *U. Rochester*
music@wrur.rochester.edu
wrur.rochester.edu

WSBU *St. John's U.*
www.wsbu.net

WSGU *SUNY at Geneseo*
wgsu@geneseo.edu
onesun.cc.geneseo.edu/~wgsu

WSPN *Skidmore College*
wspnmus@skidmore.edu
www.skidmore.edu/~wspn

WSUC *State U. New York*
wrvo@wrvo.fm
www.wrvo.com

WUSB *SUNY Stoneybrook*
music@wusb.org
www.wusb.org

WVBR *Ithica*
www.publiccom.com/web/wvbr

WVKR *Vassar College*
music@wvkr.org
www.wvkr.org

WXBA *Brentwood Public School District*
wxba-radio@88x.net
www.88x.net

North Carolina

Wake Radio *Wake Forest U.*
radio.wfu.edu

WASU *Appalachian State U.*
www.wasu.appstate.edu

WKNC *North Carolina State U.*
wknc.org

WNCW
info@wncw.org
www.wncw.org
Broadcasts over several frequencies in the Carolinas and Tennessee.

WQFS *Guilford College*
wqfs@guilford.edu
www.guilford.edu/wqfs

WSOE *Elon College*
wsoe@elon.edu
www.elon.edu/wsoe

WUAG *U. North Carolina Greensboro*
www.uncg.edu/wua

WVOD *Manteo*
99.1@wvod.com
www.wvod.com

WXDU *Duke U.*
wxdu@duke.edu
www.wxdu.duke.edu

WZMB *East Carolina U.*
wzmb.ecu.edu

Ohio

ACRN *Ohio U.*
www.acrn.com

KBUX *Ohio State U.*
www.underground.fm

Radio U *Westerville*
www.radiou.com

WAIF *Cincinnati*
WAIF@WAIF883.org
www.waif883.org

WBWC *Baldwin-Wallace College*
contact@wbwc.com
www.wbwc.com

WCBE *Columbus*
music@wcbe.org
www.wcbe.org

WCSB *Cleveland State U.*
musdirwcsb@yahoo.com
wcsb.org

WCWS *College of Wooster*
wcws@mail.wooster.edu
www.wooster.edu/wcws

WDUB *Denison U.*
cd@wdubradio.com
wdubradio.com
Indie and Modern Rock.

WGXM *U. Dayton*
flyer-radio.udayton.edu

WJCU *John Carroll U.*
www.wjcu.org

WKCO *Kenyon College*
wkco@kenyon.edu
www2.kenyon.edu/orgs/wkco

WMCO *Muskingum College*
wmco@muskingum.edu
muskingum.edu/~wmco

WMSR *Miami U.*
wmsr@muohio.edu
www.orgs.muohio.edu/wmsr

WOBC *Oberlin College*
wobc@oberlin.edu
www.wobc.org

WONB *Ohio Northern U.*
wonb@onu.edu
www.onu.edu/wonb

WOXY *Oxford*
97x@woxy.com
www.woxy97x.com

WRMU *Mount Union College*
wrmu@muc.edu
www.muc.edu/wrmu

WRUW *Case Western Reserve U.*
md@wruw.org
www.wruw.org

WSLN *Ohio Wesleyan U.*
wsln_987@owu.edu
wsln.owu.edu

WSTB *Streetsboro High School*
mail@rock889.com
www.wstbradio.com

WUSO *Wittenberg U.*
www4.wittenberg.edu/student_organizations/wuso

WWCD *Independent Playground, Indie Playground Deux*
webmastr@cd101.com
www.cd101.com

WWSU *Wright State U.*
www.wright.edu/studentorgs/wwsu

WXUT *U. Toledo*
wxut@wxut.com
www.wxut.com

WZIP *U. Akron*
wzip@uakron.edu
www.wzip.fm

Oklahoma

KRSC *Rogers State U.*
www.rsu.edu/krsc/fm

WIRE *U. Oklahoma*
wire48.ou.edu

Oregon

The Guitar Shop *KPSU*
guitarshop@pcez.com
www.pcez.com/~feech/guitarshop
www.kpsu.org
A radio program dedicated to presenting those guitarists who are considered virtuoso or well-respected in the following genres - rock, classical, jazz and blues.

KBVR *Oregon State U.*
osu.orst.edu/dept/kbvr/html/main.html

KEOL *Eastern Oregon State College*
www3.eou.edu/~keol

kittenmouse radio
web.pdx.edu/~andreay
Stay indoors with kittenmouse radio and hear the best in indiepop, emo, twee, noise and now wave from around the world. Listen on the web in real audio at kpsu.org or on the am band at 1450 am in Portland, Oregon.

KLC *Lewis and Clark College*
klc@lclark.edu
www.lclark.edu/~klc

KNRK *Portland*
www.knrk.com
Send your CD to Jaime Cooley c/o: SOMETHING COOL at 0700 SW Bancroft, Portland, OR 97201. She'll listen to it and let you know if it'll get played on SOMETHING COOL Sunday nights at 9pm.

KNRQ *Creswell*
www.nrq.com
Rock format.

KPSU *Portland State U.*
kpsumd@mail.pdx.edu
www.kpsu.org

KRVM *Eugene*
www.krvm.org

KSLC *Linfield College*
www.linfield.edu/kslc

KTEC *Klamath Falls*
www.oit.edu/d/ktec

KWVA *U. Oregon*
kwva@gladstone.uoregon.edu
gladstone.uoregon.edu/~kwva

Little Boy Crumbs *KPSU*
kpsumd@mail.pdx.edu
www.livejournal.com/users/hemlines
www.kpsu.org
Indie rock, Brit rock, pop and occasional live music.

Pennsylvania

The Pipeline Radio Show
Bullwinkle ThePipeline@comcast.net
All styles of original music are featured on the show. Unsigned original bands and musicians are urged to send their music to us for airplay consideration. Please send your original "radio edited" music, in CD format to: The Pipeline, P O Box 1242, Voorhees, NJ 08043 USA

WBUQ *Bloomsburg U.*
orgs.bloomu.edu/wbuq

WCLH *Wilkes U.*
music@wclh.net
www.wclh.net

WCYJ *Waynesburg College*
www.waynesburg.edu/%7Ewcyjfm/wcyjfmpage/index
wcyjfm.html

WDCV *Dickinson College*
omega.dickinson.edu/~wdcv

WDIY *Bethlehem*
info@wdiyfm.org
www.wdiyfm.org

WDNR *Widener U.*
wdnr895@mail.widener.edu
www.wdnr.com

WEHR *Penn State*
www.clubs.psu.edu/wehr

WERG *Gannon U.*
werg@gannon.edu
www.wergfm.com

WESS *East Stroudsburg U.*
www.esu.edu/wess

WFNM *Franklin and Marshall College*
wfnm.fandm.edu

WFSE *U. Pennsylvania*
www.edinboro.edu/cwis/wfse/index2.html

WHRC *Haverford College*
www.whrcradio.com

WIXQ *Millersville U.*
music.director@wixq.com
www.wixq.com

WJRH *Lafayette College*
wjrh@lafayette.edu
www.lafayette.edu/~wjrh

WKDU *Drexel U.*
musicdir@wkdu.org
www.wkdu.org

WKPS *Penn State U.*
www.lion-radio.com
*Check our website for the address in which to send
your particular genre of music. Improperly addressed
materials will be discarded.*

WKVR *Juniata College*
wkvr@juniata.edu
clubs.juniata.edu/wkvr

WLVR *Lehigh U.*
www.lehigh.edu/~inwlvr

WMSS *Middletown H.S.*
www.wmssfm.com

WMUH *Muhlenberg College*
wmuh@muhlenberg.edu
www.muhlenberg.edu/cultural/wmuh

WNTE *Mansfield U.*
wnte@wnte.com
www.wnte.com

WPPJ *Point Park College*
WPPJradio@hotmail.com
www.ppc.edu/~wppj

WPTC *Pennsylvania College of Technology*
wptc@pct.edu
www.pct.edu/wptc

WPTS *U. Pittsburgh*
www.wpts.pitt.edu

WQHS *U. Pennsylvania*
www.wqhs.org

WQSU *Susquehanna U.*
wqsufm@susqu.edu
www.wqsu.com

WRCT *Carnegie Mellon U.*
info@wrct.org
www.wrct.org

WRLC *Lycoming College*
www.lycoming.edu/orgs/wrlc

WRKC *Kings College*
www.kings.edu/wrkc

WRSK *Slippery Rock U.*
www.angelfire.com/music3/wrsk/index2.html

WSRN *Swarthmore College*
wsrn.swarthmore.edu

WSYC *Shippensburg U.*
wsyc@wsyc.org
www.wsyc.org

WUSR *U. Scranton*
WUSR@uofs.edu
academic.uofs.edu/organization/wusr

WVBU *Bucknell U.*
www.orgs.bucknell.edu/wvbu

WVCS *California U.*
sai.cup.edu/power92

WVYC *York College*
www.ycp.edu/wvyc

WXLV *Lehigh Carbon Community College*
wxlv@hotmail.com
www.wxlvfm.com

WXPN *U. Pennsylvania*
xpn.org

WXVU *Villanova U.*
wxvu.villanova.edu

WYBF *Cabrini College*
www.wybf.com

WYEP *Pittsburgh*
info@wyep.org
www.wyep.org

Rhode Island

WBRU *Brown U.*
wbru.com

WBSR *Brown U.*
www.bsrlive.com

WDOM *Providence U.*
studentweb.providence.edu/~wdom

WRIU *U. Rhode Island*
www.wriu.org/index2.html

WXHQ *Newport*
info@radionewport.org
www.radionewport.org

WXIN *Rhode Island College*
music@ricradio.org
www.ricradio.org

South Carolina

WPLS *Furman U.*
www-student.furman.edu/WPLS

WSBF *Clemson U.*
music@wsbf.net
wsbf.clemson.edu

WSSB *South Carolina State U.*
www.scsu.edu/Services/Radio

WUSC *U. South Carolina - Columbia*
wuscmd@gwm.sc.edu
wusc.sc.edu

South Dakota

KAOR *U. South Dakota*
kaor@usd.edu
www.usd.edu/kaor

KAUR *Augustana College*
kaurfm89@hotmail.com
inst.augie.edu/~kaur

KBHU *Black Hills State U.*
kbhufm@hotmail.com
www.kbhuthebuzz.com

KCFS *U. Sioux Falls*
kcfs@usiouxfalls.edu
www.thecoo.edu/campus/radio

KSDJ *South Dakota State U.*
geocities.com/ksdj907

KTEQ *South Dakota School of Mines and
Technology*
kteq@zoop.org
www.hpcnet.org/kteq

Tennessee

The Songwriter Sessions
www.wpln.org/songwriters
*Each week, three guests share the microphone from
WPLN's Studio C for an hour of song-swapping and
story telling. You'll hear many of Nashville's best
singer-songwriters along with a number of touring
artists. It's intimate music making at its best every
Saturday night at seven o'clock.*

WEVL *Memphis*
wevl@wevl.org
wevl.org

WFSK *Fisk U.*
wfsk@wfsk.org
www.wfsk.org

WMTS *Middle Tennessee State U.*
wmts@frank.mtsu.edu
www.mtsu.edu/~wmts

Writer's Block *WDVX*
Karen E Reynolds writersblockinfo@aol.com
www.wdvx.com/programs/WriterBlock.html
*Dedicated to the independent singer songwriter.
Created to give attention to original artists that, even
though they don't have backing from a "major label",
are quality performers that deserve listening to. The
show offers a little of everything for every listener.*

WRVU *Vanderbilt U.*
wrvu@vanderbilt.edu
wrvu.org

WRVW *Nashville*
www.1075theriver.com
Rock format.

WTPL *Tusculum College*
wtpl@tusculum.edu
wtpl.tusculum.edu

WUTK *U. Tennessee*
www.wutkradio.com

WUTM *U. Tennessee*
wutm@utm.edu
www.utm.edu/~wutm

WUTS *Sewanee U.*
wuts@sewanee.edu
angels.sewanee.edu/wuts

WVCP *Volunteer State College*
www2.volstate.edu/wvcp

Texas

KACV *Amarillo College*
kacvfm90@actx.edu
www.kacvfm.org

KANM *Texas A&M U.*
md@kanm.tamu.edu
kanm.tamu.edu

KAZI *Austin*
www.kazifm.com

KEOS *Bryan/College Station*
www.keos.org

KFAN *Fredricksburg*
www.texasrebelradio.com

KGSR *Austin*
www.kgsr.com

KNON *Dallas/Ft. Worth*
knon@acorn.org
www.knon.org

KOOP *Austin*
www.koop.org

KPFT *Houston*
music@kpft.org
www.kpft.org

KSAU *Stephen F. Austin State U.*
ksau@sfasu.edu
www.sfasu.edu/aas/comm/ksau

KSHU *Sam Houston State U.*
www.kshu.org

KSYM *San Antonio College*
ksymdj@accd.edu
www.accd.edu/sac/rtf/ksym.htm

KTCU *Texas Christian U.*
ktcu@tcu.edu
www.ktcu.tcu.edu

KTRU *Rice U.*
ktru@ktru.org
www.ktru.org

KTSW *Southwest Texas State U.*
ktswmusic@hotmail.com
www.ktsw.swt.edu

KTXT *Texas Tech*
ktxtfm@yahoo.com
www.ktxt.net

KUT/KUTX *U. Texas*
www.kut.org

KVRX *U. Texas/Austin*
kvrx@kvrx.org
www.kvrx.org

KWTS *West Texas A & M U.*
www.wtamu.edu/kwts

KXCR *El Paso*
www.kxcr.org

Utah

KRCL *Salt Lake City*
musicdirector@krcl.org
www.krcl.org

KSUU *Southern Utah U.*
ksuu@suu.edu
www.suu.edu/ksuu

KZMU *Moab*
music-director@kzmu.org
www.kzmu.org

Saturday Sagebrush Serenade
jflorenc@rochester.rr.com
www.users.qwest.net/~florencejohn
www.krcl.org
Eclectic popular music show.

Vermont

Download *WEQX*
www.weqx.com
3 Hours of the "Newest Of The New" every Sunday Night 8pm - 11pm!!

Early Warning *WBTZ*
mailbag@999thebuzz.com
www.999thebuzz.com
Every Sunday Night from 8:00pm - 10:00pm. You'll hear new music from Buzz bands, new artists and wackos you've never heard of and may never hear from again. In any case, you'll hear it on Early Warning first.

Onion River Radio
feedback@onionriverradio.com
www.neptuneradio.net
Mix of classic rock, modern rock, singer-songwriter, Americana, blue etc.

WGDR *Goddard College*
wgdrmusic@goddard.edu
www.wgdr.org

WJSC *Johnson State College*
www.wjsc.findhere.org

WRMC *Middlebury College*
wrmc@wrmc.middlebury.edu
wrmc.middlebury.edu

WRUV *U. Vermont*
wruv@zoo.uvm.edu
www.uvm.edu/~wruv

WVTC *Vermont Technical College*
music@wvtc.net
www.wvtc.net

WWPV *Saint Michael's College*
wwpv@smcvt.edu
personalweb.smcvt.edu/wwpv

Virginia

WCWM *College of William and Mary*
akacos@wm.edu
www.wcwm.org

WDCE *U. Richmond*
wdce@richmond.edu
www.student.richmond.edu/~wdce

WEBR *Fairfax*
webr@fcac.org
www.fcac.org/webr/webr.htm

WEHC *Emory & Henry College*
www.ehcweb.ehc.edu/masscomm/WEHC/WEHC_index.htm

WFFC *Ferrum College*
www.ferrum.edu/wffc

WGMU *George Mason U.*
wgmumusic@hotmail.com
www.wgmuradio.com

WMWC *Mary Washington College*
students.mwc.edu/~wmwc

WNRN *Charlottesville*
wnrn.rlc.net

WODU *Old Dominion U.*
contact@woduradio.com
www.woduradio.com

WTJU *U. Virginia*
wtju@virginia.edu
wtju.radio.virginia.edu

WUVT *Virginia Tech*
wuvtamfm@vt.edu
www.wuvt.vt.edu

WVAW *Virginia Wesleyan College*
dlbroomell@vwc.edu
facultystaff.vwc.edu/~comm/radio.htm

WVCW *Virginia Commonwealth U.*
wvcw@hotmail.com
www.wvcw.cc

WVRU *Radford U.*
wvru@radford.edu
www.runet.edu/~wvru

WXJM *James Madison U.*
www.jmu.edu/wxjm

Washington

KAEP *Seattle*
www.1057thepeak.COM

KAOS *Evergreen State College*
kaos_music@evergreen.edu
www.kaosradio.org

KCWU *Central Washington U.*
md@cwu.edu
www.881theburg.com

KEXP *U. Washington*
info@kexp.org
www.kexp.org

KGRG *Green River Community College*
Music@kgrg.com
www.kgrg.com

KNDD *Seattle*
www.1077theend.com
Rock format.

KSER *Lynnwood*
kser@aol.com
www.kser.org

KSUB *Seattle U.*
www.seattleu.edu/ksub

KSVR *Skagit Valley College*
mail@ksvr.org
www.ksvr.org

KUGS *Western Washington U.*
music@kugs.org
www.kugs.org

KUPS *U. Puget Sound*
kups.ups.edu

KWCW *Whitman College*
www.whitman.edu/student_orgs/kwcw

KWRS *Whitworth College*
www.whitworth.edu/KWRS

KZUU *Washington State U.*
md@kzuu.org
www.kzuu.org

Washington DC

WCUA *Catholic U. of America*
wcua.cua.edu
200 University Ctr. W., Washington DC 20064
PH: 202-319-5106

WGTB *Georgetown U.*
music@wgtb923.com
www.wgtb923.com

WRGW *George Washington U.*
wrgw@gwu.edu
www.gwradio.com

West Virginia

Allegheny Mountain Radio *(AMR)*
wvls@cfw.com
wvls.cfw.com
AMR's programming is eclectic ranging from country, bluegrass and gospel to rock, classical and jazz. We hope to be spinning your material soon.

WMUL *Marshall U.*
wmul@marshall.edu
www.marshall.edu/wmul

WVBC *Bethany College*
www.bethanywv.edu/wvbc

WVSC *West Virginia State College*
byersrc@mail.wvsc.edu
www.wvsc.edu/radio

WVWC *West Virginia Wesleyan*
c92@wvwc.edu
www.wvwc.edu/c92

WWVU *West Virginia U.*
www.wvu.edu/~u92

Wisconsin

Hotel Milwaukee
Dave O'Meara otom@execpc.com
www.hotelmilwaukee.com
Featuring music, poetry, comedy, interviews, author visits and more..

KUWS *U. Wisconsin*
kuws.fm

Power 100 *U. Wisconsin Stout*
www.power100.uwstout.edu

Student Radio Initiative *U. Wisconsin Eau Claire*
sri.uwec.edu

WBCR *Beloit College*
www.beloit.edu/~wbcr

WBSD *Burlington H.S.*
wbsd.basd.k12.wi.us

WCCX *Carroll College*
wccx.cc.edu

WIPZ *U. Wisconsin Parkside*
www.uwp.edu/clubs/wipz

WLFM *Appleton*
wlfm@lawrence.edu
www.lawrence.edu/sorg/wlfm

WMMM *Madison*
wmmm@1055triplem.com
www.1055triplem.com

WMSE *Milwaukee School of Engineering*
www.wmse.org

WMUR *Marquette U.*
marquetteradio.mu.edu

WORT *Madison*
wort@terracom.net
www.wort-fm.org

WRFW *U. Wisconsin River Falls*
music@pureradio887.com
www.uwrf.edu/wrfw

WRPN *Ripon College*
wrpnfm@hotmail.com
wrpnfm.homestead.com

WRST *U. Wisconsin Oshkosh*
www.wpr.org

WSRI *U. Wisconsin Eau Claire*
sri@uwec.edu
sri.uwec.edu

WSUM *U. Wisconsin Madison*
music@wsum.wisc.edu
wsum.wisc.edu

WSUP *U. Wisconsin Platteville*
wsup@uwplatt.edu
vms.www.uwplatt.edu/~wsup

WSUW *U. Wisconsin Whitewater*
wsuw@uww.edu
www.wsuw.org

WWSP *U. Wisconsin Steven's Point*
www.uwsp.edu/stuorg/wwsp

WYRE *U. Wisconsin Waukesha*
wakwyre@uwc.edu
waukesha.uwc.edu/tour/wakwyre.htm

Wyoming

Wyoming Public Radio *U. of Wyoming*
wprhelp@uwyo.edu
uwadmnweb.uwyo.edu/WPR

Canada

Alberta

Cellular Pirate Radio *Banff*
radio90.fm

CJAY *On the Verge*
ontheverge@cjay92.com
www.cjay92.com
Monday nights @ 11, Ben Jeffery and Stone Malone bring you upcoming artists.

CJSR *U. Alberta*
wormsnot@cjsr.com
www.cjsr.com

CJSW *U of Calgary*
cjswfm@ucalgary.ca
www.cjsw.com

CKUA *Edmonton*
www.ckua.org

CKRP *Falher*
ckrpfm@telusplanet.net
www.cex.gouv.qc.ca/saic/francophonie/parten/297.html
La Radio communautaire de Rivière-la-Paix.

CKUL *U. Lethbridge*
ckul.music@uleth.ca
home.uleth.ca/~ckul

British Columbia

CFBX *U. College of the Cariboo*
radio@cariboo.bc.ca
www.thex.ca

CFMI Rock 101 *Vancouver*
info@rock101.com
www.rock101.com

CFOX *Vancouver*
www.cfox.com

CFRO *Vancouver*
www.coopradio.org

CFUV *U. Victoria*
musiccfuv@yahoo.ca
cfuv.uvic.ca

CHLY *Malaspina U. College*
music@chly.fm
www.chly.fm

CIRX *Prince George*
www.94xfm.com

CITR *Vancouver*
citrmusic@club.ams.ubc.ca
www.ams.ubc.ca/citr

CJLY *Kootenay*
music@kootenaycoopradio.com
www.kics.bc.ca/kcr

CJSF *Simon Fraser U.*
cjsfmusc@sfu.ca
www.cjsf.bc.ca

CKMO *Camosun College*
www.village900.ca

just concerts
info@justconcerts.com
justconcerts.com
Interviews, audio and video coverage of the latest concerts. From Hip Hop to electronic, from Independent artists to big rock stars. If you want it, we've got it!

Radio On *CBC*
david_wisdom@cbcr3.com
www.cbc.ca/radioon
New music that is distinctive, daring and adventurous.

Radiosonic *CBC*
info@radiosonic.com
www.radiosonic.com
It is music based and will delight you with new, different, unexpected and exciting musical discoveries.

Manitoba

CKUW *U. Winnipeg*
ckuw@uwinnipeg.ca
www.ckuw.ca

CMOR *Red River College*
cmor@rrc.mb.ca
xnet.rrc.mb.ca/sa/CURRENT/Cmor/cmor_frames.htm

New Brunswick

CFMH *U. New Brunswick*
cfmh@unbsj.ca
www.unbsj.ca/cfmh

CHMA *Mount Allison U.*
chma_music@mta.ca
www.mta.ca/chma

CHSR *U. New Brunswick*
www.unb.ca/web/chsr

CJPN *Benoit Locas*
cjpn@nbnet.nb.ca
www.centre-sainte-anne.nb.ca/cjpn

Newfoundland

CHMR *Memorial U. Newfoundland*
chmr@mun.ca
www.mun.ca/munsu/chmr

Nova Scotia

CKDU *Dalhousie U.*
ckdufm@is2.dal.ca
is2.dal.ca/~ckdufm

CKNA *Natashquan*
ckna@globetrotter.qc.ca
www.arcq.qc.ca/ckna.htm

Ontario

C101.5 *Mohawk College*
www.mohawkc.on.ca/msa/cioi

CFFF *Trent U.*
trentradio@trentu.ca
www.trentu.ca/trentradio

CFMU *McMaster U.*
cfmumus@msu.mcmaster.ca
cfmu.mcmaster.ca

CFNY *Indie Hour*
www.edge102.com
If you wanna send us stuff, just send an email to our producer Barry Taylor barry@edge.ca

CFRC *Queens U.*
cfrcfm@post.queensu.ca
info.queensu.ca/cfrc

CFRU *U. Guelph*
cfru-fm@uoguelph.ca
www.uoguelph.ca/~cfru

CHRW *U. Western Ontario*
chrwmp@uwo.ca
chrw.usc.uwo.ca

CHRY *York U.*
chry@yorku.ca
www.yorku.ca/chry

CHUO *U. Ottawa*
music@chuo.fm
www.chuo.fm

CIUT *U. Toronto*
www.ciut.fm

CJAM *U. Windsor*
progcjam@uwindsor.ca
www.uwindsor.ca/cjam

CJLX *Loyalist College*
cjlx@loyalistc.on.ca
cjlx.loyalistc.on.ca

CKCU *Carleton U.*
music@ckcufm.com
www.ckcufm.com

CKDJ *Algonquin College*
ckdj_radio@hotmail.com
www.algonquinc.on.ca/ckdj

CKLN *Ryerson*
music@ckln.fm
www.ckln.fm

CKMS *U. Waterloo*
ckmsfm@web.ca
watserv1.uwaterloo.ca:80/~ckmsinfo

CKRG *Glendon College*
www.geocities.com/CollegePark/Campus/2922

CKON *Akwesasne Mohawk Nation Radio*
ckon@ckonfm.com
www.cnwl.igs.net/~ckon

CKWR *Waterloo*
www.ckwr.com

CSCR *U. Toronto at Scarborough*
cscr@utsc.utoronto.ca
www.utscradio.com

Krankit Radio *Paris*
www.krankit.com

Off the Beaten Track *CKCU*
info@ckcufm.com
www.birdmansound.com/offthebeatentrack/pagemess.htm
A host that considers musical appreciation a never ending learning process of both old & new, with a constant call for support of independent efforts that are keeping it real.

Real Audio Western *U. Western Ontario*
www.fims.uwo.ca/radio

Spirit Live Radio *Ryerson Polytechnic U.*
spiritliveradio@yahoo.com
www.spiritlive.net

Underground Radio
www.undergroundradio.ca
If anyone is interested in signing up for free online streaming of your band's music, please e-mail me and we will upload your songs. If you do decide to become and Affiliate of underground Radio, we will donate on occasion, a broadcast to only your band's music.

X-FM *Ottawa*
www.101xfm.ca

Quebec

CFAK *U of Sherbrooke*
musique@cfak.qc.ca
www.cfak.qc.ca

CFLX *Sherbrooke*
members.tripod.com/~cflx

CFOU *Trois-Rivieres*
cfou@uqtr.uquebec.ca
www.cfoufm.com

CHAA *Longueuil*
www.arcq.qc.ca/chaa.htm

CHGA *Maniwaki*
www.chga.qc.ca

CHYZ *Université Laval*
chyz-fm@public.ulaval.ca
www.chyz.qc.ca

CIBL *Montreal*
www.cibl.cam.org

CISM *Université de Montréal*
musique@cam.org
www.cismfm.qc.ca

CJMQ *Bishops U.*
cjmq@ubishops.ca
www.cjmq.uni.cc

CKIA *Québec City*
ckiafm@meduse.org
www.meduse.org/ckiafm

CKRL *Québec City*
www.ckrl.qc.ca

CKUT *McGill U.*
music@ckut.ca
www.ckut.ca

Saskatchewan

CFCR *Saskatoon*
cfcr@quadrant.net
www.cfcr.ca

_a_

ks.com

Eufonia adio

programa@eufonia.net
www.terra.com.mx
www.eufonia.net
_We have a weekly two hour radio show here in
Monterrey Mexico, where we play lots of indie rock
and other non commercial genres. It is a very
interactive concept, since we communicate with the
audience by icq, email and phone during the show._

Radio Univesidad _Universitaria en Mexico_

radiouni.uat.mx

XHUG _Radio Universidad de Guadalajara_

server.radio.udg.mx

Brazil

THE STARTRIPS SHOW _Radio Starsul FM_

Guilherme Vignini startrips@uol.com.br
www.startrips.hpg.com.br
_We are a radio station in São Paulo - Brazil and I
work in a weekly radio show called Startrips, which
have different directions, all kind of alternative
tendencies. The idea of my show is promote bands
and musicians that are unknown or almost unknown
from the audience in Brazil._

Chile

NEKKID Radio

www.nekkidradio.com
_We are proud to present over 20 DJs from around the
world and the widest mix of music anywhere on the
NET!_

Internet Radio and Syndicated Shows

2010fm

www.2010fm.com
_ATTENTION ARTISTS!!! We can: Webcast your gig
(U.K gigs). Give you valuable airtime on our radio
station. Review your new releases/live gigs! Sell your
merchandise! Stream your performances straight from
your website! Supply CD's + VHS tapes of your gig.
Showcase your promotional videos!_

2kool4radio

music@2kool4radio.com
www.2kool4radio.com
_Home to the eclectic, eccentric and electric. Hear the
best in alternative, indie, punk, hip hop, loungecore
and tons more._

3wk

3wk@3wk.com
www.3wk.com
_We love music. And we know there are fabulous artists
that belong on your speakers that aren't making their
way there because you don't know about them._

420radio.com

www.420radio.com
_Independent and unsigned music, e-commerce, MP3,
online streaming._

440MUSIC.COM

Tom Cramer 2tunes@440music.net
www.440MUSIC.COM
_My 3 hour show is not genre specific, we play only
original music form independent bands, singer
songwriters, DJ Mixes, Classical, Blues etc... We'd do
comedy if we had some.._

Access Central TV

Robin Hackett & Mykel accesscentraltv@yahoo.com
accesscentral.tv
_A show dedicated to promoting the independent artist.
And we don't limit "artist" to only music! Stay tuned
to watch other fun filled segments around computers,
cooking, travel etc._

AccuRadio

kurt@kurthanson.com
www.accuradio.com
_Listeners will discover new favorite music here — and
can click on any of the three CD covers displayed on
the player to buy any of those last three CDs played!_

AdrenalineRadio.com

info@adrenalineradio.com
www.adrenalineradio.com
_Here's the skinny...If you are an unsigned band and
want your music featured on AdrenalineRadio.com
then you need to contact us for details. But I'll tell
you right now, if ANY of your lyrics have foul
language don't even think of contacting us. We are
family friendly radio. Complete albums will be aired._

Adult Alternative Music Weekly

aamw@spotdawg.com
www.spotdawg.com/aamw
_A weekly two-hour radio show that plays the top 20
songs in Adult Alternative (AAA) music._

AEI Music

www.aeilatin.com

THE AFTER PARTY

Patty rocksolidpressure@yahoo.com
Cyberstationusa.com
expage.com/lookwhatscomin
_Those high profile net radio personalities, J-Rock and
Patty The Radio Girl, are at it again! Now accepting
all forms of Indie Music except Country, Folk and
Blues! Superstar Interviews plus the newest indie
sounds! Get involved! Sponsored by some of the
biggest names in indie and beyond! Every Wednesday
8:30pm Eastern USA time. Exclusively on
Cyberstation USA._

Airbubble

info@airbubble.com
www.airbubble.com
Free form radio covering various genres of music.

All Songs Considered

allsongs@npr.org
www.npr.org/programs/asc
_Brings to the Web full versions of the music snippets
played on NPR's afternoon news program. It's the
brainchild of All Things Considered director Bob
Boilen. Since the format is open to all musical styles,
we'll often play music that doesn't get much airplay._

The Allan Handelman Show

Ahshow@vnet.net
www.alhandelman.com
Rock And Roll and the Rock Culture.

Altavoz

altavoz@aol.com
www.altavoz.com
_Streaming some of the best independent music the
world needs to hear and heal starting with Alternative
Dance Jazz soon across about 20 genres. We will be
a place for artists and labels to call home._

Alternative BeOnAir.com

alternative.beonair.com

alternative nu

wez@nwez.net
www.alternative.nu
_Get your Music Club hosted. Stream your own 24/7
Station. Would you like to do a show here? Find out
how to do your own live show from your location.
Send in your Music Video for Play on our rerun
stream._

AMPCAST Radio

www.ampcast.com/radio
_This is the new deal in Internet Radio. Tapping into
the talent pool of our artist community, we are
introducing a fully interactive, completely live and
totally ad-hoc radio program._

The Angry Coffee Radio Show

hello@angrycoffee.com
www.angrycoffee.com
_We will compliment online marketing efforts to indie
and major record labels alike. Radio Promotion and
New Media buffs are encouraged to check it out and
contact us if interested._

Area 54 Radio

www.area54.com
_Eclectically cool music every week on your radio every
Sunday night from eight until midnight. Straight from
the Mother ship!!_

Artist Shop Radio

artshop@artist-shop.com
www.artist-shop.com/radio
_The programming at Artist Shop Radio is done by the
musicians and the independent labels and you will
definitely find it to be a breath of Fresh Air!_

ArtistFirst Internet Radio

Scott info@artistfirst.com
www.artistfirst.com
_Any Independent Artist who has a finished CD or Tape
is welcome to have a 1-hour Prime Time radio show
about their project. The programs are called "Featured
Artist Specials". The idea is to get as much publicity
and exposure for each band that requests it._

ArtistLaunch.com

submissions@artistlaunch.com
www.artistlaunch.com
_An Internet radio network which draws its material
from independent artists. It promotes these artists,
providing them with Live Showcases, internet and
real-world radio outlets, reviews and Artist Pages._

Artists Without a Label Radio _(AWAL)_

denzyl@awal.com
www.awal.com
_Our mission is to create an artist-owned environment
where a creative community of music fans can interact
with and discover great new music and artists._

AudioRealm.Com

info@audiorealm.com
www.audiorealm.com
_Just by signing up you will get FREE promotion, terra
radio airplay in a top market, online internet radio
airplay - and much more!_

AudioSurge.com Radio
info@audiosurge.com
www.AudioSurge.com
One of the fastest growing, cutting edge music communities in the world; a music community that looks and feels like a music site and not like a search engine. Its time to join a site where your presence will be felt and not just lost in a heap of no-names.

BandsRadio.com *New Internet Radio*
streammoam@prodigy.net
www.bandsradio.com
6 Channels including the best NEW artists in Funk, Boogie, Groove, New Grass, Americana and Southern Rock.

BeOnAir.com
radio.beonair.com
We currently have several bands that are looking for a break and have done very well in our rotations. We would be happy to receive music from up-and-coming artists. We prefer to receive a CD along with band bio/press packet and a contact name for the band.

BikerBar Radio
biker@bikerbar.com
www.bikerbar.com/music
We offer streaming MP3 audio of a unique nature. It offers music that you would almost never hear on "normal" radio. I want to expose you to artists that are wonderful American songwriters that get little exposure on "real" radio.

BlakeRadio
musicmassage@BlakeRadio.com
www.blakeradio.com
Music for your mind, body and soul, R&B, Jazz, Soul and Reggae slow jams.

Bohemian Radio
BohemianRadio@comcast.net
www.bohemianradio.com
A non corporate independent web radio station with an ever expanding format and playlist. Any good indie artist with all ages clean tunes are welcome to submit music.

BoomboxRadio
Lawrence Littrell info@boomboxradio.com
boomboxradio.com
Everything about independent bands and artists...CDs, band bookings, newsletters and music. Talk radio shows.

Broad and Cast Live
info@broadandcast.com
www.broadandcast.com
Attention New Artists From around the World - GET AIR PLAY!!! GET NOTICED!!! BCL's mission is to entertain and promote new independent artists. If you're one, send your CD, your Bio and a letter of permission granting us royalty free play of your music.

bumpNgrind Radio
cookieholley@tymewyse.com
bumpNgrindRecords.com
We operate and maintain our own Internet web sites, news groups and Internet radio stations.

Bumpskey.com
www.Bumpskey.com
Helping artists get exposure on the internet by broadcasting a live show featuring all independent music. They incorporate the interaction of the internet and streaming audio to get listeners to independent artist web sites. Stop in for a visit you never know what they will be up to.

Cactus Radio
www.cactusradio.com
Features a large selection of power pop, acoustic, emo and otherwise alternative tracks. At Cactus Radio, we are always interested in hearing new music. If you have suggestions, (legal) MP3s, or promotional CDs, we'd love to give them a listen. Please visit our website for submission details.

CDTV.NET
support@CDTV.NET
www.cdtv.net
We are accepting demo cds and/or music videos from solo artists, bands and singer/songwriters. All genres.

The Cindy Radio Show
www.cindyradioshow.com

Cyber Storm Radio
www.CyberStormRadio.com
The format of this station features the newest releases from known and unknown recording artists, along with live concert broadcasts and in-depth celebrity interviews. It is also a very versatile station; currently the station's format is "All Forms Rock," not just one style of rock but all forms of rock.

Cybro Radio
Larry Lowe cybroradio@juno.com
www.cybroradio.com
Internet Radio Station Broadcasting Blues, R&B, Jazz, Big Band, Swing, Cajun and Gospel music, from the USA.

Dancing on the Air
Ashokan@aol.com
dancingontheair.com
Folk, Celtic, Swing, Cajun, Zydeco, Old-Time Country, Bluegrass, Rockabilly, Blues, Jazz, Pop and more. Jay Ungar and Molly Mason are highly regarded folk musicians who consistently showcase exceptional talent in a wide variety of idioms. The music runs the gamut and it always runs deep.

DarkSide of the Radio
Jon Hensley hollywood@kih.net
www.dsotr.8m.com
Indie Section: www.dsotr.8m.com/indy.htm
We NOW offer many options to Indie Artists/Bands! Not only can you submit your music to our radio station that is one of the most popular on the entire internet, you can also view our new INDIE section to find out how we can help out your efforts.

Dreams Awake Music
attila@dreamsawake.com
www.dreamsawake.com
Our goal is to showcase independent and emerging music artists.

Dynamic Indie Radio
Dave Kaspersin drk@dynrec.com
www.dynamicindieradio.com
Playing all Independent Music 27/7.

eoRadio - Unsigned & Limited Release Artists
Ryan Smith webmaster@eoRadio.com
www.eoRadio.com
We play unsigned and limited release (meaning limited or local radio airplay) Artists. eoRadio is run like a terrestrial radio station. This means our primary goal is not to act as a promotional site for any unsigned artist, but rather to provide the best in new music to a global audience.

Evolution radio
mark@evolutionradio.org
www.evolutionradio.org
By forming our own partnerships with artists who need exposure and promotion more than anything, Evolution Radio brings the digital revolution straight to your speakers, without the fear of being shut down by a higher authority.

Excellent Radio Online
www.excellentonline.com
The home for North American fans of UK music.

Freudslipped.com
thebrain@freudslipped.com
www.freudslipped.com
We are looking for music to play on the air by Independent artists. If you have a band or know someone that has one send us your CD and we'll get it on the air for all to hear!

Future Now Radio
www.futurenowradio.com
Features the newest releases from known and unknown recording artists, along with live concert broadcasts and in-depth celebrity interviews.

Garage Radio
John Foxworthy roadrash@garageradio.com
www.garageradio.com
A site dedicated to promoting independent artists via 24/7/365 Internet radio stream.

Garage Sessions
info@garagesessions.com
www.garagesessions.com
A syndicated radio program designed to provide unsigned bands with nationwide radio exposure and music fans with the best new music.

GaydarRadio.com
studio@gaydarradio.com
www.gaydarradio.com
Featuring great music and interviews - the latest gay news - information about the stars and, of course fab competitions.

Gen X Radios
topjimmy@genxradios.com
www.genxradios.com
A big part of our broadcast is helping unsigned bands get noticed by playing their music first. We want to give musicians, from all types of musical backgrounds, the ability to get recognized on a global level.

GetSigned.com Radio
www.getindie.com/indexlowhigh.cfm

Gimme Noise
renee@gimmenoise.com
www.gimmenoise.com
Email me and tell me what your music is like, where I can find the mp3's etc. I can't promise that I'll listen to them right away, but I will. . . eventually!

Home Grown Radio
feedback@homegrownmusic.net
www.homegrownmusic.net/radio.html
The best way to discover new bands and kind music.

Homemade Music Radio

info@homemademusic.com

www.homemademusic.com/radio

If you like discovering new sounds, if you like hearing music exploring lots of different territories and learning about the perspectives of real artists, then check back here on a weekly basis and support these bands as much as you can.

I Write the Song Radio Show

www.iwritethesongs.com

The 30-minute talk show, hosted by CQK Music president, Mary Dawson and co-hosted by attorney/journalist, Sharon Braxton, is designed to appeal to "the songwriter in all of us" and offers informative and entertaining programming for more than just songwriters.

idobi.com Radio

radio@idobi.com

www.idobi.com/radio

Alternative/Rock station.

The Indie Shop

indieshop@hotmail.com

www.indieshop.org

An Internet Radio Show that features the best in Brit Pop & Rock.

indieradio.org

Danny Copacetic info@indieradio.org

www.indieradio.org

Revolutionary independent radio broadcasts containing groundbreaking music written and produced by independent artists on independent labels. indieradio.org broadcasts streaming indie rock and pop, 24/7 over the internet. All free for your listening pleasure.

InRadio

info@inradio.net

www.inradio.net

Our mission is to connect listeners with and encourage the production of, music and ideas not found on mainstream FM radio.

Jolly Roger Radio International

jr_radio@hotmail.com

listen.to/jrri

JRRI has been heard in seven continents direct from Ireland. We specialise in C&W, folk and non mainstream music. Some programmes also feature new world and ambient music.

Kill Pop Radio

urlman@killpopradio.com

www.killpopradio.com

Kilohertz Networks, Inc.

Lori Glauser lori@khz.cc

www.khz.cc

*Produces and syndicates eclectic music programs including "jungleZone", "radio*dmz presents" and "Honkytonk Hoedown".*

KnotRadio.org

hotchman@knotradio.org

www.knotradio.org

Independent artists, kick-ass college bands and crazy college kids across the country now have a completely free-form and independent voice to speak of.

Kulak's Woodshed

Paul Kulak paulkulak@earthlink.net

www.kulakswoodshed.com

We have an exciting new cutting edge Live Internet Video Web Cast Acoustic Music Showcase. Acoustic Music, Singer/Songwriter, Folk, Blues, Country, Rock, (anything goes). The Music That Music Lovers and Performers Have Taken Into Their Hearts.

Live365.com

www.live365.com

The world's largest Internet Radio network with over 3 million visitors per month and 5,000 radio stations, programmed by people who love music.

Live365 Record Pool

Betty Ray betty@live365.com

www.live365.com/community/labelservices.live

Submit your track or album to the Live365 Record Pool and reach thousands of DJs who can easily add your track to their playlists. Setup fee is $50 per track with a $25/ month maintenance fee. It's way cheaper than shipping promo copies or demos to get your music out. Not to mention the worldwide reach!

Live Club Radio

www.liveclub.co.uk

Visit our site for details on how to get your music played on Live Club Radio.

Live X Radio

Charles Leet promos@livexradio.com

www.livexradio.com

Live X Radio plays the known and unknown of Alternative music.

Lord Litter's Radio Show

LordLitter@LordLitter.de

www.LordLitter.de

www.CyberStormRadio.com - the weekly show

www.radiomarabu.de - the German on demand show

Now broad/webcasting at 6 stations ALL OVER THE WORLD! Europe's best radio program that side of John Peel Shut-Ups-Website. The show presents the variety of the true indie-scene. From Country to Experimental - from Folk to Hard Rock - the show that presents YOUR music! If you want to send releases for airplay please check www.LordLitter.de/radioshow.html

Loudeye

info@loudeye.com

www.loudeye.com

LUVeR *(Love Underground Vision Radio)*

fmoore@eroplay.com

www.luver.com

Matchbox Radio 24

matchboxradio@matchboxrecordings.co.uk

www.matchboxrecordings.co.uk/radio

We broadcast continuous new Independent music 24 hours a day, 7 days a week. Our station features the freshest new music from all over the world. The station genre ranges from Indie Rock and pop to punk, Emo, alternative, acoustic and solo artists. We only play REAL NEW music.

The Michael Anthony Show

michael@michaelanthonyshow.com

www.michaelanthonyshow.com

We play any and every genre of music by unsigned and indie artists. You may send a radio edit and the uncensored version too. My web show is totally UNCENSORED. But when I am lucky enough to have a gig on commercial radio without getting fired, I'll need that edited version.

Modern Drummer Radio

mdinfo@moderndrummer.com

www.moderndrummer.com

Our goal with MD Radio is to literally bring every monthly issue of Modern Drummer to life. You will now be able to hear the featured drummers we write about.

Monster FM

monsterfm@monsterfm.com

www.monsterfm.com

Moon Radio

info@moonradio.co.uk

www.moonradio.co.uk

Welcome all cybernauts. Our show is transmitted from the moon for your listening pleasure. Take a seat and feel free to enjoy the sounds as we take our journey through madness. But first, we ask that you buckle up. This ship's known to rock!

MUSIC CHOICE

www.musicchoice.com

44 genre specific non-stop digital quality music channels which are delivered via cable, satellite and the Internet without DJ chat or advertisements.

Music Sojourn

programs@musicsojourn.com

www.musicsojourn.com

Musicians.net

www.musicians.net

THE Indie Music Resource! Live Internet Radio and you're one stop shop to indie music! We strive to provide independent artists and musicians all of the tools, links and information they need to get their music heard. Come by and check us out!

NeverEndingWonder Radio

Lee Widener new@neverendingwonder.com

www.neverendingwonder.com/radio.htm

Eclectic internet radio station playing a wide variety of styles including: blues, jazz, alternative, folk, country, world, comedy, good-time, rock, experimental and electronic. NOT interested in rap, metal, techno, or hip-hop. We love featuring indies!

New Artist Radio

tmc@newartistradio.net

www.newartistradio.net

We will need a few things from you in order to get your music on our station. The first thing we need is your Promo Packet containing CD, Bio Photo and a letter giving N.A.R. Permission to use your material royalty free for airplay. Three songs will be placed in each artist voting booth. Artist may choose three songs or we will choose them for you. This is a free service to all N.A.R artists

NoWhere Radio

www.nowhereradio.com

We are the newest internet radio station out there and our intent is to present to you the music you've never heard from the worlds best internet artists. Not to mention the many shows we've got planned for you!

Null Set Rock Radio

Jim Egan JMFE@comcast.net

www.nullset.tv

Onthel.com
Pamella McReynolds Pam@onthei.com
www.onthei.com
We stream music on four unique channels 24 hours a day/seven days a week. If you would like airplay consideration, please send your CD and Press Kit. Please indicate which songs you would like us to air/promote and if your music is registered with ASCAP, BMI or SESAC.

Outsight Communications
outsight@usa.net
www.new-sounds.net
Outsight brings to light non-mainstream music, film, books, art, ideas and opinions. Please, keep Outsight informed with review materials, press releases etc.

PartyTown Streaming Freedom Network
Brad and Sandy partytown@charter.net
www.partytown.com
Streaming indie bands and indymedia news. Submit your bands for airplay. Submit your news for newscasts.

Pasco Radio
info@pascoradio.org
pascoradio.org
Alternative News and Music YOU WON'T hear on regular radio. Tune in if you dare! You have been warned!

Pirate Radio Network
102.1FM, P.O. box 16456, Tampa, FL 33687
pirate@ldbrewer.com
www.ldbrewer.com/pirate
We will play any indie sent to our submission address. We also sell and set up pirate radio stations.

Pirate TV
www.piratetv.net

PittRadio
pittradio@bottomlesspitt.com
pittradio.bottomlesspitt.com
Listen to music of unique structures of sounds that can possibly exist in all forms from Alternative, Rock, Metal, Jazz, Electronica, Hip Hop music and much more! Submit your song for play on PittRadio.

PlanetPopRadio
tim@planetpopradio.com
www.planetpopradio.com
We welcome music submissions.

Popbang.com
Jay Anderson jay@popbang.com
www.popbang.com
Supporting indie artists as well as deserving major label artists, Popbang Radio is also involved with many indie labels to help get the great music of the artists into the ears of the people that want it. "Popbang Radio - Lot's of newer power pop and other rock that just doesn't suck!"

PopStorm Radio
Stephanie Koles
programdirector@popstormradio.com
www.popstormradio.com
A 24/7 internet radio station that plays a unique mix of both signed and unsigned artists, that can be classified as melodic pop, powerpop, pop rock or R&B music. An artist with at least 6 tunes can submit a CD for playlist consideration.

RadioAid.com
support@radioaid.com
www.radioaid.com
Exclusive streaming for indie and unsigned artists. Streaming player that will allow you to hear new acts and travel to their sites where you will be able to download their music for free and it will benefit the artists, not the industry fat cat's bank account.

Radio CMJ
www.cmj.com/radiocmj

Radio Crystal Blue
Dan Herman
cblue@mindspring.com
www.radiocrystalblue.com
Radio with a freeform feel; old/new music plus spotlight on musicians with strong Internet presence. Live biweekly Internet radio.

Radio Destiny
playerhelp@radiodestiny.com
www.radiodestiny.com

Radio Free Exile
RadioFreeExile@aol.com
radio-exile.freeservers.com
Featuring the Best in Indie-Music, Spoken Word, Alternative Views, Commentary and Interviews - and a little bit of Humor too. Pirate Radio at its Best!

Radio Free Virgin
www.radiofreevirgin.com
Is currently creating a format for unsigned artists.

Radio Free World
webmaster@radiofreeworld.com
www.radiofreeworld.com
Broadcasts shows made up of nearly half indie music 24 hours/day via Real Audio live stream.

Radio IUMA
artisthelp@iuma.com
www.iuma.com

Radio Muse Independent Songwriter Radio
jodi@musesmuse.com
www.musesmuse.com/radiomuse.html
Every month Radio Muse invites you to join us for a wonderful excursion that leads to a place where time stops and the music begins. We hope to help spread the word about some of the truly fantastic, undiscovered talent that we know is out there.

Radio Paradise
bill@radioparadise.com
www.radioparadise.com
We welcome CD submissions from artists & record labels.

How to promote your music

Get your track some AM/FM airplay

PROS
- You become a rock star overnight
- Gets you laid

CONS
- Costs $20K for payola
- Requires signed deal with devil

Go on tour

PROS
- Meet fans!
- See the world! (or at least lots of McDonald's)

CONS
- Can only play "The Alphabet Game" so many times before madness sets in
- Deep desire to kill bandmates by end

Offer downloads from your site

PROS
- Makes record companies obsolete
- Available to the entire planet

CONS
- Makes record companies very nervous
- Tough to reach anyone who doesn't know about you

Live365 Artist & Label Services

PROS
- Reach millions of indie music fans
- Easy, affordable and a great way to promote your music!

CONS
- Not enough hours in the day to enjoy the diversity available
- More addictive than crack!!

Join the Internet Radio Revolution and get your music HEARD!
Live365 Artist and Label Services
http://www.live365.com/indiebible

Radio Storm
radiostorm.com

Radio X Chicago
Charles Leet charles@livexradio.com
www.radioxchicago.com
Independent and Alternative Internet Radio. Playing the classics to the cutting edge of Modern Rock.

RADIO!@IRIEMAN.COM
www.irieman.com/radio

RadioAid.com
Rob Vining robv@radioaid.com
www.RadioAid.com
An original, user-friendly streaming radio that allows listeners to discover new artists. The RadioAid concept originated from the realization that many unknown and/or unsigned independent artists create quality music. These artists push aside the generic sounds and production methods that consistently flood the popular music scene worldwide.

radioio
newmusic@radioio.com
www.radioio.com
Format is Adult Album Alternative ("Triple A"), playing an acoustic based, eclectic mix of alternative rock, cutting-edge pop, contemporary folk, blues and jazz.

radioKAOS
radio@radiokaos.com
radiokaos.com

RadioMOI
indie@radiomoi.com
www.radiomoi.com
We showcase your favorite hits in streaming MP3 audio and let's you be the DJ so you can create your ultimate music mix. We do accept submissions from Independent artists.

RadioMojo
feedback@radiomojo.com
radiomojo.com
We play modern and alternative rock with some rap/electronica mixed in for good measure.

RadioNonsense.com
Scott Sosna nonsense@radiononsense.com
www.radiononsense.com
Songs are played randomly without regard to mix, meaning one can hear the Sex Pistols, Miles Davis and the Klezmatics in quick succession! While the music leans heavily towards rock, jazz and Cuban music, I am open to anything and love to put new music on for others to enjoy.

Radiopositive
open@radiopositive.com
www.radiopositive.com
All of the music we play, including Adult Contemporary, Jazz, Children's, Soundtracks, Classical or Contemporary Spiritual contain messages that are positive and uplifting and promote unity and community regardless of personal beliefs.

RadioU
kahr@radiou.com
radiou.com
This is where you go in the digital domain to find out what's NEXT. It's not about the same ten songs you hear every hour on other corporate-run radio stations and video channels. The music we play is different. It's the stuff THEY don't play.

Raw Egg Radio
rawegg@lamza.net
rawegg.lamza.net
Our mission to be a refuge from the artificial constrictions of modern radio formats. How do I choose what to play? Well, you will never hear Shania Twain, Britney Spears or Death Metal here...but anything else is up for grabs.

RealNetRadio.com
info@realnetradio.com
www.realnetradio.com
A musical broadcast spanning the fastest growing music formats on the web today. Our Listening Channels cover Jazz, Rock, Independent Artists and Video Concerts.

Reel Music Online
Eric Johnson eric@reelmusiconline.net
www.reelmusiconline.net
Internet music show featuring music and interviews with bands.

Rhythm Radio
newmusic@rhythmradio.com
www.rhythmradio.com
If you're an Artist, or feel like an Artist, or look like an Artist, or believe you are really an Artist born in the body of an accountant...if you write music, record music, or know great music, or think you have a great idea about music RhythmRadio should be playing, we want to know about it!

Rock BeOnAir.com
rock.beonair.com

Rock City Radio
mark@rock-city.co.uk
www.rock-city.co.uk/radio
Bored with the boring drab pop shite currently clogging up the airwaves? Want your music played? Check back for details of how you can have your own 45 minute show!!!

Rock Solid Pressure
J-Rock and Patty The Radio Girl
RockSolidPressure@yahoo.com
rocksolidlinks.tripod.com
cyberstationusa.com
The only independent music game show on the net! Sponsored by SONY RECORDS, MAXELL, THE INDIE BIBLE, INDIE-MUSIC.COM, BANDS TO GO and many more..

Rocket Radio
support@rockete.com
www.rocketentertainment.com/rocketradio
If you believe your music is marketable and are serious about it, submit a copy of any CD that you want to sell. The CD must contain at least 25 minutes of music or 6 songs. We cannot feature your music without a sellable CD.

Seismic Radio
www.seismicradio.com
Want to have your band featured on Seismic Radio? Want us to interview your band or post a recent interview?

Shred Radio
webmaster@houseofshred.com
www.houseofshred.com

Sirius Satellite Radio
www.siriusradio.com
Dedicated to bringing you the best music you've ever heard and never heard. From what's new on the street to the classics and everything in between.

Smiling Radio
mailbox@smiling.org
www.smiling.org

SomaFM
dj@somafm.com
www.somafm.com
Listener-supported, commercial-free, underground/alternative radio broadcasting from San Francisco. Our high quality MP3 internet broadcasts reach around the world.

The Songwriters Network
Patty macromusicg@netscape.net
www.cyberstationusa.com
Live Saturdays 6-9 p.m EST. Accepts CD's & bios of original, indie label artists. Send material to: BG Enterprise, P.O.Box 1265, New Britain, CT 06050.

The Sonic Chronicles
Aaron Childs aaronchilds@ameritech.net
www.m4radio.com
A live, interactive web radio program from Jackson, Michigan and plays unsigned and independent label acts in rock, blues, jazz and electronica genres, with an emphasis on the local music scene in south central Michigan.

Soul Talk Radio
Chuck Freeman chuck@soultalkradio.com
www.soultalkradio.com
I produce a weekly interview program about people doing creative, funky, life affirming things. Looking for indie groups to interview and music to play during segues.

Sputnik7
www.sputnik7.com
Credited as the world's first real-time audio/video Internet entertainment experience, sputnik7 is a broadcast network offering a sophisticated mix of independent music, film and anime programming via interactive Video Stations, Audio Stations, Videos on Demand and Digital Downloads.

The Stepping Stone Radio Program
Rich "The Messenger" Maidment
indieradio@hotmail.com
www.thesteppingstone.cjb.net
100% Independent, everything from rock thru to blues (NO COUNTRY or DANCE)!! We are always looking to add to our listenership and playlist.

Sunnymead Internet Radio
info@sunnymead.org
www.sunnymead.org
A virtual village of independent artists, professionals, businesses and organizations, reflecting today's individuality.

Sunset Strip Radio
info@sunsetstripradio.com
www.sunsetstripradio.com
Our site's objective is to give every band an equal opportunity to be heard and discovered. Though we are growing rapidly, our philosophy and goals remain the same: to offer a totally free site, a showcase which brings the public, the clubs and the performers together.

surfingradio.com
feedback@surfingradio.com
www.surfingradio.com
Wednesday Nights 8-10 pm Eastern is the Punk Show and Thursday Nights 8-10 we play CLASSIC SURF SOUNDS. All other times we will play a wide range of music with a liberal amount of surf tunes in the blend.

thesunmachine.net Radio
aynz@thesunmachine.net
www.thesunmachine.net/radio
This station has been created to bring to you the best in music from independent artists & unsigned bands. It is our aim to help you discover a whole new world of music outside of the mainstream top 40 chart.

totallyradio
post@totallyradio.com
www.totallyradio.com
Packed with new music across the board – alt-indie, leftfield electronica, hip hop, lo-fi, Latin, jazz, country, African - anything that's worth opening your ears to.

TraceLength.com *(TLRadio)*
Rich Teslow rteslow@tracelength.com
tlradio.tracelength.com
Our format is indie music of all genres. Before you send us your new hit single make sure it fits this criteria: It must be of MP3 format and at least 128kbit/sec. Why? Because our streaming server re-encodes all MP3's at 24kbits. Because of potential quality loss, a low bit rate encoded file that is re-encoded at a low bit rate again may sound even worse. We will listen to every piece of work sent to us. If your MP3 sounds too muddy or incoherent we won't play it.

Unsigned Radio
Goopking@Unsignedmusicnetwork.com
www.unsignedmusicnetwork.com
Part of the Unsigned Music Network.

Universal Buzz Radio
info@universalbuzz.com
www.universalbuzz.com
We have a Featured Artist as well as a New Artist Spotlight.

Village Voice Radio
vvradio@villagevoice.com
radio.villagevoice.com
Musically, we do it all - from rock to jazz to blues and hip hop; from techno to trance to country; from backbeat to blue-beat to beat-box and break-beat; from garages to juke joints and stadiums - including Special Programming featuring Village Voice writers and critics.

Virtual Radio
webmaster@virtualradio.com
www.virtualradio.net
From the ghetto superstar to the backyard screamer, get yourself onto VR and promote your mp3's, post your show dates and get real feedback from the public...plus more to come!

Way Out West Radio
Bill Bruedigam williamb@thirdroad.com
www.thirdroad.com/radio
Online semi-commercial radio station playing Indie music 24/7!

WebRadioPugetSound.com
WRPS1@msn.com
www.webradiopugetsound.com
10 stations playing independent artists on The Bud and Nancy Show.

Whole Wheat Radio
Jim Kloss jim@talkeetna-alaska.com
www.talkeetna-alaska.com/radio.php
We play independent music exclusively. Interact with listeners while your music plays.

Wiccan Pagan Internet Radio
odin@witchwayisup.com
www.witchwayisup.com/wgds.htm
Artists, if you wish to have your music featured on these programs send me an email at odin@witchwayisup.com

World Café *U. Pennsylvania*
wxpndesk@pobox.upenn.edu
worldcafe.org
Want to submit music for airplay? Please send TWO compact discs (no cassettes or tapes, please) to: XPN Programming Department, 3905 Spruce Street, Philadelphia, PA 19104-6005.

WSVN Radio
WSVNRadio@yahoo.com
www.wsvnradio.net
Send your CD and additional info (press kit, bios etc.). If you plan on sending us any of your mp3s, DO NOT SEND them to our Yahoo account. We will refer you to another email address.

XM Satellite Radio
unsigned.xmradio.com
We scout the entire country for amazing new sounds that the recording industry hasn't discovered yet or won't go near. We find them playing in basements, garages and coffee bars. And their music will blow you away.

You Pick the Hits Radio
Blaque starbaze1@sbcglobal.net
pages.sbcglobal.net/starbaze1
You can purchase radio time that guarantees your CD is played on our radio show for exposure, promotion and sales.

Ytesjam Radio
webmaster@ytseradio.com
www.ytseradio.com

Europe

Austria

FM4 *Linz U.*
fm4.orf.at

Freier *Rundfunk Oberösterreich (FRO)*
fro@fro.at
www.fro.at

Orange 94.0 *Free Radio in Wien*
office@orange.or.at
www.orange.or.at

Radio 1476 *Mittelwelle Polycollege*
www.polycollege.ac.at/1476

Radio Oberösterreich *Linz*
www.fro.at

UniRadio Salzburg *U. Salzburg*
www.kowi.sbg.ac.at/multimedia/uniradio

Belgium

Belgischer Rundfunk *Eupen*
musik@brf.be
www.brf.be

Radio 1
www.radio1.be

Radio 21
www2.rtbf.be/radio21

Radio Campus *Bruxelles*
rcampus@resulb.ulb.ac.be
www.ulb.ac.be/assoc/radio-campus

Radio Canteclaer *Deinze*
info@canteclaer.be
www.canteclaer.be

Radio Hellena
radiolna@hellena.net
www.hellena.net

Radio Panik
www.radiopanik.org

Radio Scorpio
mail@radioscorpio.com
www.radioscorpio.com

RUN *Universitaires Notre-Dame de la Paix*
run@fundp.ac.be
www.run.be

URgent Radio *U. Ghent*
info@urgent.rug.ac.be
urgent.rug.ac.be

Croatia

Radio Student *Zagreb*
www.fpzg.hr/radio_student

Denmark

Dr. Demo
kogs@dr.dk
www.dr.dk/p3/demo

Station 10 *Norresundby*
www.station10.dk

Universitetsradioen *Nalle Kirkväg*
redaktionen@universitetsradioen.dk
www.uradio.ku.dk

Radio Østsjælland
fakse@lokalradio.dk
www.lokalradio.dk

XFM *Denmark Technical U.*
www.xfm.dk

Finland

Radio Extrem *Helsinki*
www.yle.fi/extrem

Radiomafia
www.yle.fi/radiomafia

Radio Robin Hood
info@radiorobinhood.fi
www.radiorobinhood.fi/rrh

France

Alternantes FM *Nantes/ Trignac*
www.naonet.fr/guest/alternantes/accueil.htm

Le Biplan
biplan@chez.com
www.chez.com/biplan

Canal B Rennes
canalb@rennet.org
www.rennet.org/canalb

Couleur 3 *Lausanne*
la.radio@couleur3.ch
www.couleur3.ch
The best radio in Europe and in French ! Indies,
house, Techno, Acid Jazz, Hip Hop, Trip Hop etc. All
the new artists are on Couleur 3!

FMR *la French independant radio libre*
fmr@radio-fmr.net
www.radio-fmr.net

Ocean Radio
cadix@wanadoo.fr
www.ocean-music.com

Radio Alpine Meilleure *Hautes-Alpes*
ram05@wanadoo.fr
perso.wanadoo.fr/jb.oury/RAM.htm

Radio Bulle *Paris*
www.multimania.com/radbulle

Radio Campus Besançon
radiocampus102.4.free.fr/fm/Index2.htm

Radio Campus Clermont-Ferrand
clermont.radio-campus.org

Radio Campus Grenoble
grenoble@radio-campus.org
www.grenoble.radio-campus.org

Radio Campus Lille
www.campuslille.com

Radio Campus Orléans
www.univ-orleans.fr/EXT/RADIO_CAMPUS

Radio Campus Paris
musique@radiocampusparis.org
www.radiocampusparis.org

Radio Canal Sud
www.canalsud.net

Radio Grenouille *Marseilles*
www.lafriche.org/grenouille

Radio Pluriel
plurielfm.free.fr

Radio Primitive *Reims Cedex*
radio.primitive@wanadoo.fr
perso.wanadoo.fr/primitive/sommaire.html

Radio Pulsar
info@radio-pulsar.org
www.radio-pulsar.org

Radio Vallée Bergerac
rvb@rvb.fr.fm
www.rvb.fr.fm

RadioceRos.com
reaction@radioceros.com
www.radioceros.com

RCT Villeurbanne
liberte@radio-rct.com
www.radio-rct.com

Germany

ALPHAbeat Radio
alphabeat@pixelhouse.de
www.ottic.de

Bayerischer Rundfunk
info@br-online.de
www.br-online.de

Campus-Welle Köln *Universität zu Köln*
musik@koelncampus.com
www.koelncampus.com

coloRadio
coloradio@freie-radios.de
www.freie-radios.de/coloradio

Doc Rock Show *Wuppertal*
www.infomusic.de

Eins live
einslive@wdr.de
www.einslive.de

elDOradio! *U. Dortmund*
musik@elDOradio.de
www.eldoradio.de

Freies Radio für Stuttgart
info@freies-radio.de
www.freies-radio.de

Frequenz B *Berlin*
www.frequenzb.net

FRITZ Radio *Potsdam*
fritz@orb.de
www.fritz.de

HSF Studentenradio *Ilmenau*
info@radio-hsf.de
www.hsf.tu-ilmenau.de

ju: N ai *Magdeburg U.*
uni-radio@uni-magdeburg.de
www.uni-magdeburg.de/uniradio

K2R Radio
www.radio-r.net

M945
m945.afk.de/m

NiceSurf
www.NiceSurf.de

Oldenburg Eins
info@oeins.de
www.oeins.de

POPSCENE with J*A*L*A*L
info@popscenewithjalal.com
www.popscenewithjalal.com
One of the leading indie radio shows in Europe from
OK Radio Bremen – Germany.

QUERFUNK *Karlsruhe*
info@querfunk.de
www.querfunk.de

Radio 101
radio101.de
Free (some people call it "pirate") radio station in
Germany and Belgium.

Radio 19/4
www.radio19-4.de

Radio Blau
musik@radioblau.de
www.radioblau.de

Radio C.T. *Ruhr-Universität*
info@radioct.de
www.radioct.de

Radio Dreyeckland
www.rdl.de

Radio Flora
postbox@radioflora.apc.de
radioflora.apc.de

Radio Internationale Stadt
orang.orang.org/ORA/ora-head.html

Radio Rheinwelle
www.radio-rheinwelle.de

Radio SIRUP Siegen
sirup.avmz.uni-siegen.de

Radio T
radiot@freie-radios.de
www.freie-radios.de/radiot

RadioActiv *Mannheim*
redaktion@radioaktiv.org
www.uni-mannheim.de/radioaktiv

recordcaster
www.recordcaster.de
Independent internet radio from Berlin.

uniRadio Berlin-Brandenburg
info@uniradio.de
www.uniradio.de

Universität *Lübingen*
uniradio@uni-tuebingen.de
www.uni-tuebingen.de/uniradio

Greece

ERA Aigaiou
www.aegean.gr/era_aegean

Hot Station
info@hotstation.gr
www.hotstation.gr
One of Greece's hottest Internet Radio stations. One
of the pioneers of internet radio.

Rhodes Radio *Rhodes U.*
www.rhodes.aegean.gr/radio.htm

Hungary

Tilos Rádió
radio@tilos.hu
tilos.hu

Italy

Kristall Radio
kristallradio@inwind.it
www.kristallradio.it
Based in Milano, we are one of very few Italian
stations that welcome all kinds of music, especially
the music of underground bands and musicians.

Megaphone
megaphone@omitech.it
www.omitech.it/megaphone

Radio Beckwith Evangelica
redazione@rbe.it
web.tiscalinet.it/rbeonline

Radio Onda Rossa
www.ondarossa.info

Luxembourg

Eldoradio *Dortmund*
eldoradio@eldoradio.lu
www.eldoradio.lu

Radio ARA
webmastARA chicken.MO@internet.lu
www.ara.lu

Radio LRB *Lëtzebuerg*
www.ara.lu/front/klecksi.htm

Malta

Radju ta *Msida*
www.vol.net.mt/unirad/front.htm

The Netherlands

3FM
3fm.omroep.nl

Amstelveen Lokaal
info@amstelveenlokaal.nl
www.amstelveenlokaal.nl

B92
helpB92.xs4all.nl

dutchsound.nl
dutchsound.nl

PopScene Radio
Nicole Blommers nicole@popscene.nl
www.popscene.nl
Dutch indie radio show. Every Tuesday between 21:00 and 23:00 hrs. You can also listen to PopScene via realaudio. BE MAD FOR IT AND LISTEN TO POPSCENE!!!!

Radio 100
radio100@desk.nl
www.radio100.nl

Radio Netherlands
www.rnw.nl

St. Radio-TV Borghende *Borne*
rtvborghende@hetnet.nl
www.rtvborghende.nl

WFM
wfmradio@hetnet.nl
www.wfmradio.nl

Zeilsteen Radio
info@bosma-multimedia.nl
www.zeilsteen.com
We bring you the latest internet news and best alternative pop music.

Norway

Radio Nova *Oslo*
www.radionova.no

Radio Tango
www.radiotango.no

Studenten Radioen i Trondheim
www.stud.ntnu.no/studorg/radion

Studentradioen i Bergen
studentradio@uib.no
studentradioen.uib.no

Studentradio'n i Trondheim
www.stud.ntnu.no/studorg/radion

Poland

Radio Akademickie *Krakow*
www.index.zgora.pl

Radio Sfera *N.Copernicus U.*
redakcja@sfera.umk.pl
www.sfera.umk.pl

Portugal

Rádio Universitária do Minho
rum@rum.pt
www.uminho.pt/xpta

Russia

Special Radio
admin@specialradio.ru
www.specialradio.ru
Broadcasting of mostly non-commercial music. It includes new releases and music of the past. Here you can listen to the music in all its diversity and multiplicity.

Serbia

ALTERNATIVES Radio Show
Predrag Strazmester sipa1@InfoSky.Net
www.INradio.co.yu
I am one of the very few people who promotes independent music here and believe me - it's a tough road! I give my best to promote the labels (promo as well) and their bands the best I can. My "quest" of bringing the best independent music here! Please send submissions to: Predrag Strazmester, Rodoljuba Colakovica, 6, 21000 Novi Sad, Serbia & Monte Negro

Slovakia

Ragtime Radio *Bratislava*
www.ragtime.sk

Slovenia

Radio Mars *Maribor*
www2.arnes.si/~mbrmars

Radio Student Ljubljana
www.radiostudent.si

Spain

Pititako Irratia *Bizkaia*
www.live365.com/stations/soniabd

Radio PICA *Barcelona*
www.gracianet.org/pica

toxicosmos.com
toxicosmos@toxicosmos.com
www.toxicosmos.com
120 minutos semanales de POP en la radio universitaria de la facultad de informática de la Universidad Politécnica de Valencia.

Sweden

Mick 102 *U. Umeå*
www.mick102.nu

Radio AF *Lund U.*
radio.af.lu.se

Rocket 95.3 FM *Stockholm*
www.rocket.fm

Stadsomroep Arnhem
radio@stadsomroeparnhem.nl
www.stadsomroeparnhem.nl

Starshine Radio
www.srs.pp.se/fr/star.html

Switzerland

Frequence Banane *Lausanne*
fbwww.epfl.ch

Radio Lora
lora@lora.ch
www.lora.ch

radio RaBe
rabe@rabe.ch
www.rabe.ch

United Kingdom

Alternative Devon
info@alternativedevon.co.uk
www.alternativedevon.co.uk
If you don't have mp3s on the net and you want to be on Alternative devon you will have to send me a cd.

BCB Radio *Yorkshire*
www.bcb.yorks.com

The Beatscene
Jim Gellatly jim@beat106.com
www.beatscene.co.uk
The home of new music in Scotland. The beatscene goes out every Sunday night on Beat106.

Clare FM *Clare*
info@clarefm.ie
www.clarefm.ie

Downtown Radio *Northern Ireland*
www.downtown.co.uk

Drive 105
www.drive105fm.com
If you would like your band to get some airplay, why not send us in your demo on CD, mini - disc or mp3 format.

Eternal Fusion
Gary Fosster garyfosster319@yahoo.co.uk
www.spydaradio.co.uk/fosster.html
A free form radio show consisting of: indie/alternative, electronica, psychedelia, folk and progressive. Currently it is webcast via SpydaRadio in the UK. For submission of music please use the e-mail address provided so we can ascertain whether material is suitable for the format of the show.

Fresh Air FM *U. Edinburgh*
music@freshairfm.co.uk
www.freshairfm.co.uk

Gravity FM *Grantham*
www.gravityfm.co.uk

Imperial College Radio
info@icradio.com
icradio.su.ic.ac.uk

interFACE Pirate Radio *London*
interface.pirate-radio.co.uk

Jimmy Possession's Radio Show *(SBN)*
rebzine@hotmail.com
www.geocities.com/sunsetstrip/backstage/1472
Band demos, unreleased tracks and (as yet) undiscovered bands from all over the world.

jockrock radio
jockrock@vacant.org.uk
www.vacant.org.uk/jockrock/jockrock.html

John Peel's Radio Show
john.peel@bbc.co.uk
www.bbc.co.uk/radio1/alt/johnpeel
John Peel has been described by his former producer and friend John Walters as "the single most important figure in popular music over the last 25 years" and it would be difficult to argue with that assessment.

Kick FM *West Berkshire*
mail@kickfm.com
www.kickfm.co.uk

Kooba Radio
Jonny Yeah contact@koobaradio.co.uk
www.KoobaRadio.co.uk
A UK based internet radio station that plays unsigned bands exclusively. We have hundreds of listeners and our site includes a viewable playlist that links to the websites of the bands we play.

LiveIreland
www.liveireland.com
Five stations that play Irish influenced music including Irish Traditional, Celtic and Folk.

Luton FM *U. Luton*
www.luton.ac.uk/lutonfm

Meantime Radio *London*
info@meantime-radio.co.uk
www.meantime-radio.co.uk

Miuzik.com
Vram Oknayan vram@blamethemusic.com
www.miuzik.com
Not your average zine. Miuzik.com also promotes the Miuzikfest gigs in London, broadcasts from its 2 radio stations in London and Edinburgh, runs an in-house label...and has been promoting music since 1885! Serious.

The Musical Mystery Tour
adam.walton@bbc.co.uk
www.themysterytour.co.uk

Phantom FM *Dublin*
www.phantomfm.com
Alternative Pirate Radio.

Phoenix FM
www.phoenixfm.com

PuLSE Radio
Azeem Ahmed a.u.ahmed@lse.ac.uk
www.pulsefm.co.uk
A London based U. radio station playing Independent music over the net.

RAD SPC
rad.spc.org

Radio Airedale
Sarah Tedder (Teddy) teddy_u2@hotmail.com
I'm a presenter on hospital radio Radio Airedale in Skipton, North Yorks and we have a very limited collection of indie records in the archives. If you would like to donate some samples/promos that I could play, that would be great (you would get recognition etc.) and would be helping out too!

Radio Telefís Éireann *(RTE)*
www.rte.ie/radio
The Irish National Public Service Broadcasting Organisation.

Radio Warwick *U. Warwick*
music@radio.warwick.ac.uk
www.raw.warwick.ac.uk

RamAir *U. Branford*
www.ramairfm.co.uk

rare FM *U. College*
info@rarefm.co.uk
www.rarefm.co.uk

Resonance104.4fm *London*
info@resonancefm.com
www.resonancefm.com

Solid Steel
solidsteel@ninjatune.net
www.ninjatune.net/solidsteel
Where else can you enjoy anything from jazz, brakes and beats, funky rock, hip hop, techno, drum and bass, soundtracks, world music, poetry, electronic oddities and even a children's story.

Split Shift Radio
splitshift@crosswinds.net.
www.idea.org.uk/splitshift

SpydaRadio
info@spydaradio.co.uk
www.spydaradio.co.uk
Our unique mix of music, interviews and live concerts embraces a wide audience profile. We believe that much of the best new music is ignored by the mainstream media and so we aim to fill the gap and give this music the promotion it deserves.

Student Broadcast Network *(SBN)*
info@sbn.co.uk
www.sbn.co.uk

SURE *Sheffield*
radio@sureradio.com
www.shef.ac.uk/sure

Today FM
dconway@todayfm.com
www.todayfm.com
Ireland's biggest Independent Radio Station. Our format is lively, Bright and Fun.

URN *Nottingham U.*
urn.su.nottingham.ac.uk

Webair *Salford U.*
hexie.memtech.salford.ac.uk/music2/webair

Wired Radio *Goldsmiths College*
wired@gold.ac.uk
www.wired.gold.ac.uk

XFM *London*
xfm.co.uk

Yugoslavia

Radio Free Belgrade
www.b92.net

Australia – New Zealand

Australia

2AAA *Wagga NSW*
fm107@2aaafmradio.org.au
www.2aaafmradio.org.au

2ARM *Armidale NSW*
2arm@northnet.com.au
users.northnet.com.au/~2arm

2BBB
2bbb@midcoast.com.au
www.2bbb.midcoast.com.au

2CCR *Baulkham Hills NSW*
mail@2ccr-fm.com
www.2ccr-fm.com

2CHY *Coffs Harbour NSW*
chyfm@midcoast.com.au
www.chyfm.midcoast.com.au

2EAR *Moruya NSW*
www.earfm.com

2MCE *Bathurst*
2mce@csu.edu.au
www.csu.edu.au/2MCE

2NCR *East Lismore*
www.2ncr.org.au

2NSB *Sydney*
www.2nsb.org.au

2NUR *Newcastle*
2nur@2nurfm.com
www.newcastle.edu.au/cwis/ra

2RDJ FM *Contact!*
contact2001@bigpond.com
www.users.bigpond.com/celt1969
International Indie/alternative/new wave pop, broadcast across Australia. Demos too.

2RRR *Sydney U.*
www.2rrr.org.au

2SER
info@2ser.com
www.2ser.com
2SER is jointly owned by Macquarie U. and U. Technology, Sydney.

2TEN *Tenterfield NSW*
twotenfm@halenet.com.au
www.halenet.com.au/~twotenfm

2UNE *U. New England/Armidale*
2une.une.edu.au

2UUU *Nowra*
www.shoalhaven.net.au/jukebox

2VOX *Illawarra NSW*
vox@1earth.net
www.vox.1earth.net

2VTR *Hawkesbury NSW*
www.hawkradio.org.au

2XX *Canberra*
www.2xxfm.org.au

3CR
home.vicnet.net.au/~threecr

3GCR *Central Gippsland / Latrobe Valley*
3gcr@gippsland.net.au
www.3gcrfm.org.au

3HOT *Mildura VIC*
www.hotfm.org.au

3MBR *Murrayville VIC*
3mbr@riverland.net.au
www.riverland.net.au/~3mbr

3MGB *Mallacoota VIC*
home.vicnet.net.au/~cootafm

3MR *Monash U.*
yoyo.cc.monash.edu.au/groups/3MU

3ONE *Shepparton VIC*
www.welcome.to/onefm

3PBS *Melbourne*
info@pbsfm.org.au
www.pbsfm.org.au

3RIM *Mowbary College, Victoria*
info@979fm.net
www.979fm.net

3RPP *Mornington VIC*
www.3rpp.asn.au

3RRR
3rrr@rrr.org.au
www.rrr.org.au

3SER *Melbourne*
www.3ser.org.au

3VYV *Yarra Valley VIC*
www.absolute-web.com.au/vyv

3WK *Undergroundradio*
www.3wk.com

3WAY *Warrnambool VIC*
3wayfm@standard.net.au
www.standard.net.au/~3wayfm

3WPR *Wangaratta VIC*
home.netc.net.au/~wprfm

4CCR *Cairns Queensland*
info@4ccr-fm.org.au
www.4ccr-fm.org.au

4CLB *Brisbane*
www.101fm.asn.au

4CRM *Mackay Queensland*
www.hotonline.com.au/fourcrm

4ZZZ *Brisbane*
info@4zzzfm.org.au
www.4zzzfm.org.au

5PBA *Adelaide*
pbafm@pbafm.org.au
www.pbafm.org.au

5 UV *U. Adelaide*
radio.adelaide.edu.au

City Park Radio *Launceston TAZ*
www.cityparkradio.com

96.5 Family FM *Milton Queensland*
www.96five.org.au

979fm *Melton VIC*
info@979fm.net
www.979fm.net

The Basement
info@thebasement.com.au
www.thebasement.com.au

Bay FM *Brisbane*
bayfm@bayfm.org.au
www.bayfm.org.au

Bondi FM
www.bondifm.com.au

ISON Live Radio
info@isonliveradio.com
www.isonliveradio.com/index.php
We're always on the look out for sample material and regular artist info/updates for our programs, which are broadcast on numerous radio stations throughout the world.

JOY Melbourne
info@joy.org.au
www.joy.org.au

KAOSFM
www.isonliveradio.com/kaosfm.php
This program is a professionally produced and announced eclectic mix of various styles of world mainstream independent and underground music.

PBA FM *U. South Australia*
www.pbafm.org.au

PBS *St. Kilda*
info@pbsfm.org.au
pbsfm.org.au

The Planet
www.abc.net.au/rn/music/planet/default.htm
The Planet searches out good, heartfelt, inspiring music from around the world.

QBN-FM *Queanbeyan, NSW*
Braidwood-FM, *Braidwood, NSW*
Rob Davidson rothshir@sci.net.au
www.braidwood.net.au/fmradio
I am seeking CD's of all genres of music to play on these two stations. Braidwood FM is due to go to air in the next 3-4 months and we need to begin compiling a CD library. A lot of airtime is (and will) be given to Independent Artists of all genres. Send your CD's to: Rob Davidson, PO Box 230, Braidwood NSW 2622, AUSTRALIA

RTR FM *Nedlands*
rtrfm@rtrfm.com.au
www.rtrfm.com.au

Southern FM *Melbourne*
www.southernfm.org.au

SRA *Melbourne*
music.library@syn.org.au
www.sra.org.au

Sub Fm
Simon Knight s.knight@latrobe.edu.au
www.subfm.org
A campus radio station based in Melbounre Australia. It streams a live broadcast 24/7 from its web site. It specializes in the support of independent music. Feel free to contact us and submit your music for broadcast.

TripleB *Barossa Valley SA*
bbbfm@mail.penalva.net
www.triplebradio.cjb.net

Three D Radio *Adelaide*
mail@threedradio.com
www.threedradio.com

Triple J
www.abc.net.au/triplej

Triple U *Shoalhaven*
manager@tripleu.org.au
www.tripleu.org.au

WYN FM *Melbourne*
wynfm@wynfm.org.au
www.wynfm.org.au

New Zealand

95b FM *Auckland*
music@95bfm.com
www.95bfm.co.nz

Radio Active
www.radioactive.co.nz

Soundwave FM *Onekawa, Napier*
soundwavefm@xtra.co.nz
listen.to/soundwavefm

Asia

Japan

beatrip.com
beatrip.com
Associated with North FM (Hokkaido), J-wave (TOKYO), FM802 (Osaka), ZIP-FM (Nagoya), CROSS FM (Fukuoka) and Music station, Space Shower TV (Satellite and Cable).

Children's Music Radio

A Place to Be *WAMC*
www.mybizz.net/~guitarhardy/ptb.html
www.wamc.org
Weekday show featuring Children's Music.

Alphabet Soup *WBRS*
info@wbrs.org
www.wbrs.org
Every weekday morning our DJs start the day with the best children's music on the airwaves, anywhere. Visit our website for submission details.

CBC 4 Kids *Music*
www.cbc4kids.cbc.ca/general/music
cbc4kids.cbc.ca/general/music/behindthebands
Hear your favourite Hot Hit from the Sound Bar Top Ten and vote for this month's KidPick. Behind the Bands features interviews and music from Canadian music stars.

Children's Corner *KUFM*
www.kufm.org
Delightful stories and music for children of all ages with local host Marcia Dunn.

The Children's Hour *KUMN*
kunmkids@unm.edu
www.kunm.org
We are on the air Saturday mornings from 9am-10am and feature music and stories for children of all ages.

The Children's Hour *KRZA*
krza@krza.org
www.krza.com
An hour of children's music.

Children's Stories & Music *KMUD*
md@kmud.org
www.kmud.org
An inspirational blend of stories and music for children of all ages. Relax in bed with the children and listen to short stories, on-going novels, or jump up to greet the day with dancing, a sure way to start your Sundays off on a happy foot.

Christian Pirate Radio *Kids Show*
Ahoy@mycpr.com
www.mycpr.com
This channel features programs for kids and kids at heart. Adventures in Odyssey, Jungle Jam, Down Gilead Lane, Paws and Tales, along with cool music from the Toonz music show, Karen and Kids and our own mix of pre-teen pop and praise sprinkled throughout the day.

HIS KIDS RADIO
mail@HisKidsRadio.net
hiskidsradio.gospelcom.net
A Christian station for the young heart.

Karen & Kids Radio Show
karen@karenandkids.com
www.karenandkids.com/radio.html
Music, stories and more!

Kids Corner *WXPN*
onlinehelp@xpn.org
kidscorner.org
xpn.org
A daily radio program produced by WXPN-FM. Its primary mission is to provide entertaining and educational programming for children.

Kids Internet Radio
www.kir.org
Committed to sharing children's music, art and stories from around the world through the Internet fostering sharing, understanding, knowledge and peace.

Kids on Fire for Jesus
mail@praiseonfire.com
www.praiseonfire.com/Kids
Saturday morning kids programming block. Drama, music, games and contests.

Kids Play *WLUW*
Sheila Donlan kidsplay@wluw.org
wluw.org
Music for kids under 11 from 2 to 3 pm on Saturday afternoons. The show features new and old releases of kids' music and stories that will entertain the entire family — including mom and dad!

KidsOwnRadio
info@kidsownradio.com
www.kidsownradio.com
Created out of our belief that there is a need to expand upon the musical interests of today's youth. In addition to their favourite teen pop stars and top-40 hits, we felt it necessary to expose today's youth to a broader scope of music and fun.

MP3.com Children Music Stations
stations.mp3s.com/stations/childrens_music
A list of MP3.com stations that are willing to listen to add your songs to their playlist.

Pea Green Boat
pgb@selway.umt.edu
www.kufm.org
Stories, songs, poetry and special guests (two- and four-legged and some with wings) for children of all ages.

PlayhouseRadio.com
indiemusic@playhouseradio.com
www.playhouseradio.com
Specifically: We want music that grabs a child's attention…gets them singing and dancing...or soothes their little souls! We are looking for "kid-friendly," wholesome songs

Radio Lollipop
info@radiolollipop.org
www.radiolollipop.org
We believe in the healing power of play - providing smiles and laughter to children at a time when they need it most. We give young patients a voice and a choice during their stay in the hospital.

Tell Us a Tale
Peter@tellusatale.com
www.tellusatale.com
Reading of tales, with music still complementing each story. Send us your CDs for radio airplay consideration or review.

We Kids Radio
Mr.Nick@WeKids.org
www.wekids.org
Pointing little people and their families to God.

Christian Radio

Promoters

HMG-Nashville Radio Promotions
ccma.cc/hmg
One of the nation's most highly respected radio promotions companies servicing both major labels as well as top indie artists within the genres of Country, Christian Country, Southern Gospel, Bluegrass & Bluegrass Gospel, Christian Contemporary and Christian Rock!

Ministry Networks
Laurie Vincent ministrynetworks@execulink.com
www.ministrynetworks.rockofages.ca
A radio servicing, distribution and tracking service to Christian radio stations around the world, with the most extensive list of Christian radio venues in Canada.

Stations

Air 1
info@air1.com
www.AIR1.com
It's pretty unusual for us to play independent music. It isn't disallowed because it is independent, but because it usually doesn't have the same quality as commercially produced pieces. If you have something with exceptional sound quality, contact us.

CCM Magazine Radio
www.ccmmagazine.com/ccmradio
Faith in the spotlight.

CHRI *Ottawa, ON*
chri@chri.ca
chri.ca

Christian Pirate Radio
Ahoy@mycpr.com
www.mycpr.com
We have a programming philosophy of playing independent artists, new artists, alternative, modern rock and contemporary Christian music.

Christian Pirate Xtreme
Josh@mycpr.com
www.cprxtreme.com
We believe in expanding the boundaries of Modern Christian Music into the realms of ska, punk, rock, loud, swing etc. We are always updating our files in spirit of keeping with the ever faster growing Christian music scene.

Christian Rock Radio
online@christianrockradio.com
www.christianrockradio.com
We also do album and concert reviews.

ChristianRock.net
mail@christianrock.net
www.christianrock.net
Do some homework and use your head. Listen to what they play on the station and only send it if it matches the style. No matter how good your music is, sending a southern-gospel CD to a rock station won't get you played (and vice-versa).

CMRadio.Net
musicmakers@CMRadio.Net
www.cmradio.net
Your favorite Christian music - Pop, Punk, Alternative, Inspirational, Metal, Rock, Celtic, Folk, Praise and Worship - is here at CMRadio.Net! Whatever your age or musical taste, we hope that CMRadio.Net will become your favorite music spot on the Internet.

Cornerstone *U. Louisiana*
kxul.com
A non-sectarian presentation of contemporary Christian music. ULM alumnus Rusty Hogue has kept his dedicated, watchful eye on this show for longer than anyone (including Rusty, himself) can remember.

Cross Rhythms Radio
radio@crossrhythms.co.uk
www.crossrhythms.co.uk/radio
We broadcast a mix of predominantly contemporary Christian music, with general and specialist programming covering all aspects of the UK CCM scene.

www.indielinkexchange.com

Effect Radio
effectradio@effectradio.com
www.effectradio.com
We DO NOT play music because others are; we play music as led by the Spirit of the living God of the Bible.

En Sound Radio
Delroy ensound@ensoundentertainment.com
www.ensoundradio.com
Provides the most comprehensive listing of gospel music anywhere on the web. From Reggae to Gospel House, this is the station for you!

The Gospel Connection *WRBB*
herosenan@aol.com
wrbbradio.org
The Longest Running Gospel Show in Boston!

Gospel Country
Les info@ccrb.org
www.gospelcountry.net

The Gospel Experience *KPFA*
Emmit Powell emmitap@aol.com
www.kpfa.org/1pro_bio/1b_gospe.htm
www.kpfa.org
One of the longest running gospel music shows in the Bay Area.

Gospel Train
wally@gospeltrain.com
www.gospeltrain.com
With a vast library from the beginning of the recording industry up to the present day, the Gospel Train will take you for a musical journey on the main line and the many branches of the soul Gospel experience.

Gospel Truth *WNCW*
info@wncw.org
www.wncw.org
Start your Sunday morning with the heartfelt sounds of Gospel Music. WNCW's Dennis Jones is your host for two hours of the finest Gospel sounds in a full range of traditions.

GospelCity.com Radio
gospelcity.com
We have re-launched the radio station this month so now you can listen to the radio station at your convenience 24hrs a day!

gospelnetwork
info@gospelnetwork.com
www.gospelnetwork.com

Grace Media Network
webmaster@gmnetwork.cc
www.gmnetwork.cc
Stay connected to the best radio play list of Black gospel music right here. GMNetwork.cc will introduce you to new connections to bring you ministry and marketplace news, features, products, resources and career opportunities.

H3O
www.h3oradio.com
Our mission is twofold 1) Take the Gospel to the streets and 2) Bring Hip Hop to the Church. It's an orientation that brings you the "The Blest in Holy Hip Hop." Radio and video shows.

HCJB World Radio
info@hcjb.org
www.hcjb.org
The world's first missionary broadcaster, has been touching lives around the globe since 1931. Together with its local partners, HCJB World Radio now has ministries in more than 100 countries and broadcasts the gospel in nearly 120 languages and dialects.

HCR *Huntington College*
www.hcradio.net

Holy Hip Hop Radio
radio@holyhiphop.com
www.holyhiphop.com/radio
Feel the Spiritual Vibe Each and Every Week in over 200 Domestic & International Markets, as well as 24/7 on the World-Wide-Web.

Intense Radio
ScottMoore@IntenseRadio.com
www.IntenseRadio.com
You won't believe the line-up we have for you on Intense Radio! Some GREAT programs, great music, interviews, WHEW....prepare to be amazed!!!

Joyful Noize *WCUW*
info@joyfulnoize.net
www.noize.net
A Christian music ministry playing Christian rap and hip-hop. We also play definitively Christian dance, reggae and R&B.

JoyUnlimited.com
www.joyunlimited.com

KCBI *Criswell College, TX*
kcbi@kcbi.org
www.kcbi.org

KCMS
www.spirit1053.com

KCWJ *Kansas City*
info@1030thelight.com
www.1030thelight.com

Kingdom Keys Network
www.kingdomkeys.org
Our desire is to equip, educate and edify through our programming of teaching, preaching, music, news, talk and commentaries.

KLRC *John Brown U. , AR*
klrc@klrc.com
www.klrc.com

KNWS *Northwestern College, MN*
www.knws.org

KOBC *Ozark Christian College, MO*
kobc@kobc.org
www.kobc.org

KTCJ *Centerville, TX*
Kenny Love, Producer kenlove@txucom.net
www.ktcj.com
The station where you neither have the time nor inclination to become bored, as a result of our diversified format of Gospel music. We are interested in receiving Blues, Gospel, Jazz, Hip Hop & RnB music. KTCJ 105.9 FM (Magic 106), 329 N. Converse, Centerville, TX 75833

KTIS *Northwestern College, MN*
www.ktis.org

KTCU *Texas Christian U.*
ktcu@tcu.edu
www.ktcu.tcu.edu/ktcu

KWAM *Memphis*
www.am990.com

Planet Light Force
jmichael@ksbj.org
www.planetlightforce.com
We play several indie bands and plan on having an "indie corner" on planetlightforce.com this year showcasing local unsigned artists.

Praise Nation Radio *UK*
sh-airplay@christworldradio.com
www.christworldradio.com/pnc
We play the music of unknown and independent bands and also give some of them a spot on our web page.

Reign Radio
md@reignradio.com
www.reignradio.com
There are some awesome Christian artists out there who don't have that much publicity. We are just one more way to help these bands out.

Rejoice Radio
www.rejoiceradio.net
We will need a promo packet and permission to play your music royalty free.

Rhema FM *Australia*
www.rhemafm.org.au
We aim to provide our listeners with a station that can change lives for good and the promotion of family values. We also aim to positively reinforce individual worth and build up the family unit based on sound moral and Biblical guidelines.

Rhythm N' Praise Internet Radio
Paul Cash pcash@rhythmandpraise.com
www.rhythmandpraise.com
We play commercial-free contemporary gospel music 24 hours a day. We will also review your music.

Solid Gospel
www.solidgospel.com

Sound of Light
billthemd@soundoflight.com
www.soundoflight.com
Yes we do play QUALITY indie music, so send it along or whatever.

Star93fm.com *Jackson, MI*
webmaster@star93fm.com
www.star93fm.com

The Sunday Night Gospel Show
www.jekererecords.com/airplay
www.texas99.com
Instead of simply airing traditional and contemporary Gospel music of both independent and top major label artists, the "Sunday Night Gospel Show" also airs Gospel music news, Bible trivia, interviews with recording artists, tour notices and contests to win free music.

talkGospel.com Radio
enquiries@talkGospel.com
www.talkgospel.com
Started to give the African and Caribbean churches air time to share their ministry with the wider community and to support the Gospel music scene, particularly British artists.

Tastyfresh Internet Radio
www.tastyfresh.com
A web community devoted to Christians who like dance music. We bring you great dj sets from some of the best djs who are professed Christians. The point of the show isn't to bring attention to Christ-friendly tunes, but instead to bring attention and publicity to the djs themselves.

Three Angels Broadcasting Network *(3AB)*
radio@3abn.org
www.3abn.org

Train to Glory *KUNM*
music@kunm.org
www.kunm.org
Black gospel music featuring traditional, contemporary and local church choirs.

trancedomain.com
trancedmn@aol.com
www.trancedomain.com
Our mission is to, through God, provide an unbiased view of our scene. It will have no boundaries. We would like to give all artists the opportunity to exchange their ideas and share a personal part of themselves through the art of music.

Uncle Samoo's Zoo
LRMinistry@aol.com
home.rochester.rr.com/heavenly/lrm/radio.htm
The very best in Contemporary Christian Music featuring Independent & Import Artists from all around the globe! Starts at Midnight on Sunday Nights Eastern Time Zone.

WAY-FM
waym@wayfm.com
waym.wayfm.com
We use radio to encourage youth and young adults in their Christian walk and to challenge them to make a difference in the world.

WBCS *Bethel College, MN*
wbcs@bethel.edu
www.bethel.edu/Majors/Communication/wbcs

WCDR *Cedarville College, OH*
cdrradio@cdrradio.com
www.cdrradio.com

WEIC *Charleston, IL*
info@weic.net
www.weic.net

WETN *Wheaton College*
wetn@wheaton.edu
www.wheaton.edu/wetn

WFCA *French Camp Academy, MS*
www.wfcafm108.com
"All Southern Gospel Radio"

WGEV *Geneva College, PA*
www.wgev.net/

WGRN *Greenville College, IL*
WGRNMusicManager@greenville.edu
wgrn.greenville.edu

WGTS *Columbia U. College, MD*
wgts@wgts.org
www.wgts.org

WMHK *Columbia International U., SC*
www.wmhk.com

WOCG *Oakwood College, AB*
wocg@wocg.org
www.wocg.org

WONU *Olivet Nazarene U., IL*
music@wonu.fm
www.wonu.org

WRCM *Columbia International U., NC*
www.wrcm.org

WRVL *Liberty U., VA*
wrvl@liberty.edu
www.liberty.edu/wrvl

WSAE *Spring Arbor College, MI*
wsae@admin.arbor.edu
www.arbor.edu/wsae

WVOE *Vision Radio*
www.icestorm.net/wvoe

Classical Music Radio

North America

United States

Classical Excursions *Texas Christian U.*
Rosemary Solomons ktcu@tcu.edu
www.ktcu.tcu.edu
On the air at KTCU since 1983. Two uninterrupted hours of music from the Baroque to the present.

Classical 89.3 WCAL *Northfield, MN*
beeby@stolaf.edu
www.wcal.org
Submissions of high quality independently produced classical music recordings are welcomed. Please send materials to: Susan Beeby, 89.3 WCAL 1520 St. Olaf Ave., Northfield, MN 55057

ClassicalMusicDetroit.com
info@classicalmusicdetroit.com
www.classicalmusicdetroit.com
Features programming hosted by three of the Detroit-area's most-recognized classical music authorities, all broadcast radio veterans of the former WQRS-FM. Local events, music and recording artists are prominent in the mix.

Colorado Public Radio
cpr.org
CPR's classical music hosts present the full range of classical music and educate listeners with stories that give the music a broader context.

The Composer's Voice
John Zech mail@mpr.org
music.mpr.org/programs/composersvoice
The public-radio program that asks current composers: Who are you? - What does your music sound like? Why does it sound the way it does?

From the Top
Christopher O'Riley
www.fromthetop.org
A weekly radio series that showcases the nation's most exceptional pre-college age classical musicians. Each one-hour program presents five young performers or ensembles whose stunning individual performances are combined with lively interviews, unique pre-produced segments, radio theatre skits and lighthearted musical games.

Harmonia
Angela Mariani harmonia@indiana.edu
www.indiana.edu/~harmonia
Produced in conjunction with Indiana University's world-renowned Early Music Institute, brings the music of these earlier periods to life for radio audiences, as performers of today cast new light on the music of the distant past.

Here of a Sunday Morning *WBAI*
Chris Whent mail@hoasm.org
www.hoasm.org
The very best in early music for more than 25 years.

In the Spotlight *Fort Wayne, IN*
price@wbni.org
www.wbni.org
Hear concerts by the Fort Wayne Philharmonic, the Heartland Chamber Chorale, the Fort Wayne Children's Choir, plus performances by local musicians and ensembles.

The Kalvos & Damian New Music Bazaar
kalvos@kalvos.org
www.kalvos.org
A radio show and website bringing composers to the wider world through their music, interviews, pictures, photos, artwork, essays, biographies, attitudes, catalogs and ideas. Forward your latest recordings directly to Kalvos & Damian's New Music Bazaar, 176 Cox Brook Road, Northfield, Vermont 05663 USA.

KANU *Lawrence, KS*
rhunter@ku.edu
kanu.ku.edu
We do play music by independent classical musicians. The contact person here for classical recordings is Rachel Hunter (Music Director). KANU FM 91.5, 1400 Hoch Auditoria Drive, U. Kansas, Lawrence KS 66045

KBIA *Columbia, MO*
Kyle Felling FellingK@missouri.edu
www.kbia.org
We love to play music from new and independent classical artists. At some point we are considering a show dedicated to new and indie artists, but for the time being we just sprinkle them in as time allows.

KBPS *Portland*
john@allclassical.org
www.allclassical.org
As Music Coordinator, I would be happy to receive any CDs by your Indie performers of standard classical (e.g., not crossover, folk, rock, jazz). You can send them to: John Pitman, Music Coordinator/Afternoon host/producer, KBPS Allclassical 89.9 FM, 515 NE 15th Avenue, Portland, OR 97232

KBYU *Brigham Young U.*
www.kbyu.org
We don't have a program at the moment specifically for new music. We do welcome new material which is reviewed and aired if deemed appropriate.

KCME *Colorado Springs*
kcmeinfo@oldcolo.com
www.kcme.org
We play independent labels both classical music - and especially jazz. We screen all music carefully for artistic and musical merit and quality.

KCSC *U. Central Oklahoma*
kcscfm@kcscfm.com
www.kcscfm.com
We program Independent music all the time!

KDFC *San Francisco*
rmalone@kdfc.com
www.kdfc.com
*We don't discriminate against struggling musicians!
Please note that our sound is very mainstream,
traditional classical. No electronic, experimental, or
atonal music. Sacred choral is the only vocal music
we play. Send your recordings to Rik Malone, c/o
KDFC, 455 Market Street
Suite 2300, San Francisco, CA 94105*

KEDM *Monroe, LA*
Mark Simmons msimmons@ulm.edu
www.kedm.org
*KEDM does play classical music by independent
musicians/composers/producers. We currently squeeze
them in during the 12:00 p.m. hour of our "Mid-day
Classics" and on Saturday afternoons.*

KFUO *St. Louis*
jconnett@classic99.com
www.classic99.com

KING *Seattle*
www.king.org
*We do air independent musician's recordings provided
they fit our format and that we have performance and
music licensing rights. Address any recordings to our
music director, Tom Olsen, KING FM, 10 Harrison
Street, Seattle, WA. 98109.*

KNAU *Northern Arizona U.*
knauradio.org

KNPR *Nevada Public Radio*
John Clare john@knpr.org
www.knpr.org
*I try to play as many independents as I can. There are
few that make it between the 3 B's and baroque music.
I would love to receive and review more Indies.*

KRPS *Pittsburg, KS*
www.krps.org
*Monday through Friday KRPS airs a total of seven
hours of locally programmed classical music. Any
music received is first reviewed by our Program
Director. They decide if it goes into the library.*

KSUI *Iowa City*
ksui@uiowa.edu
ksui.uiowa.edu
*We welcome the music of Independent Classical
musicians. We want all the best music to be out
there for people to hear!*

KUAT *Tucson*
Steve Hahn shahn@kuat.arizona.edu
www.kuat.org
*I do not distinguish between independent releases and
the small labels that may only have a few items in
their catalogue. However, I need to emphasize that we
are a "serious" classical station and I
don't want to be wading through a ton of recordings
from new-age noodlers. We are not interested in
anyone's "creative improvisations".*

KUFM *Morning Classics*
www.kufm.org
*We play a wide variety of classical music from the
Montana Public Radio library.*

KUHF *Houston*
Bob Stevenson bstevenson@kuhf.org
www.kuhf.org
*As long as your performances and recordings are of
professional quality, we'll play 'em right alongside
the New York Philharmonic and Yo-Yo Ma and
everybody else. We also have a fully digitally-
equipped performance facility at the station from
which we occasionally do live and recorded studio
sessions with classical musicians. Recordings (CD's
only) should be sent to me:
Bob Stevenson, Program Director KUHF/88.7FM,
4343 Elgin Street, Third Floor, Houston, TX 77004*

KUSC *Los Angeles*
kusc@kusc.org
www.kusc.org
*Our mission is to make classical music and the arts a
more important part of more people's lives.*

KWAX *University of Oregon*
kwax@qwest.net
www.uoregon.edu/%7Ekwax
Classical music 24-hour a day.

KWIT *West Iowa Tech Community College*
www.kwit.org

KXMS *Joplin, MO*
kxms@mail.mssc.edu
www.kxms.org
*Since the majors have cut back production and
promotion, KXMS is happy to highlight independent
classical CDs on the daily new releases program at 5
pm CT ("Southern Serenade"). Send recordings to:
Jeffrey Skibbe, General Manager, 88.7 KXMS/Fine
Arts Radio International, 3950 E
Newman Road, Joplin, MO 64801-6100*

Millennium of Music
radman@weta.com
www.classicstoday.com/mom
*An exploration into the sources and mainstreams of
European music for the thousand years before the
birth of Bach. For over 17 years, it has presented, in a
quiet and serious way, the vast scope of great music
leading up to the early Baroque. It features the
evolution of sacred music, east and west, live
performances by the best ensembles in the field of
early music and the ever growing number of new
releases in the field.*

Music Through the Night *MPR*
Jeff Esworthy mail@mpr.org
music.mpr.org/programs/mttnight
*Seven days a week, MTTN offers a choice of music
and style of presentation perfectly suited for through-
the-night listening. The program mixes standard
repertoire with the finest works by lesser-known
composers to lend perspective to major musical
figures.*

Nebraska Public Radio
wstibor2@unl.edu
net.unl.edu
*We do play a variety of classical musicians. Send your
CDs to: William Stibor, Music Director
Nebraska Public Radio, 1800 No. 33rd St., Lincoln,
NE 68583*

**If you know of a resource
that should be listed,
please contact
indiebible@rogers.com**

New Releases *WITF*
cary_burkett@witf.org
www.witf.org
*New Releases is a weekly show that often plays the
music of Independent classical musicians. We'd be
glad to receive CD's for consideration on the
program. The contact info is: New Releases/WITF-
FM, Cary Burkett, 1982 Locust Lane, Harrisburg, PA
17109*

Pipedreams
mail@mpr.org
pipedreams.mpr.org
*Host Michael Barone presents the finest organ music
from around the world in Pipedreams, brought to you
by Minnesota Public Radio.*

Saint Paul Sunday
sunday@mpr.org
www.stpaulsunday.org
*Host Bill McGlaughlin opens the studio to the world's
best classical artists—musicians of every conceivable
style and mix—for both performance and
conversation, giving listeners intimate access to how
music is created at the highest level. It's all done with
a great sense of exuberance and curiosity.*

Sound and Spirit
spirit@email.pri.org
www.wgbh.org/wgbh/pages/pri/spirit/
*Hosted by Ellen Kushner and brought to you by
Public Radio International. Sound and Spirit blends
classical, traditional and world music with myth and
history, stories, poetry and commentary, to provide
insight into the varied aspects of human experience.*

Sunday Baroque
SundayB@wshu.org
www.sundaybaroque.org
*An exploration of Baroque and early music, that is,
music written before 1750.*

WBJC *Baltimore*
info@wbjc.com
www.wbjc.com
The Baltimore region's only classical music station.

WCLV *Cleveland*
wclv@wclv.com
www.wclv.com
*We don't have a show that specifically highlights
Independent musicians. We do have a feature, called
"The Choice CD of the Day", which spotlights new
classical CDs we think would be of interest to our
audience. These CDs come from every imaginable
source: major labels, small labels and even vanity
recordings.*

WCNY *Syracuse*
wcny_online@wcny.org
www.wcny.org
*Features performances by numerous local musical
institutions. One of the stations' most popular features
is the regular broadcast of "Bravo to Youth" salutes
to outstanding young musicians from throughout the
CLASSIC FM listening area.*

WCPE *Wake Forest, NC*
music@wcpe.org
www.wcpe.org
*Our mission is to make great Classical Music
available to the public 24 hours a day.*

WDAV *Davidson, NC*
wdav@davidson.edu
www.wdav.org
We have numerous independently produced recordings as part of its regular music rotation, mostly from local and regional performers playing standard classical repertory. A few of those CDs have original orchestral or chamber compositions on them, too, from a variety of contemporary composers. Independent producers who are putting out CDs of appealing music in the classical tradition, whether old or new, are welcome to send complimentary copies to our Music Director, Ted Weiner, for audition and consideration for our music rotation.

WDIY *Bethlehem, PA*
info@wdiyfm.org
www.wdiyfm.org
We will certainly consider the efforts of independent musicians. Our classical programming is not decided by a computer months in advance!

WDPR *Dayton*
dpr@dpr.org
dpr.org
The voice for our region's performing and fine arts organizations. Many local hosts and local offerings.

WETA *Arlington, VA*
www.weta.org
If you would like to submit your music, you can send it to: WETA, Attn: Mr. Dan DeVany, 2775 South Quincy Street, Arlington, VA 22206

WFCR *U. Massachusetts*
radio@wfcr.org
www.wfcr.org

WFMR *Milwaukee*
feedback@wfmr.com
www.wfmr.com

WFMT *Chicago*
www.networkchicago.com/wfmt
We do play some self-produced CDs, usually by Chicago-area artists with whom we're acquainted.

WGMS *Washington DC*
www.wgms.com

WHRO
Dwight Davis info@whro.org
www.whro.org
We would certainly consider at least listening to any independent classical recordings for possible air play.

WILL *Urbana, IL*
www.will.uiuc.edu
Send us your classical, jazz and traditional/ethnic music.

WITF *Harrisburg, PA*
fm@witf.org
www.witf.org
Committed to offering classical music and news-and-information that educates, inspires and raises the spirit.

WKAR *Michigan State U.*
mail@wkar.org
wkar.org/radio

WKSU *Kent State U.*
letters@wksu.org
www.wksu.org
Submissions can be sent to: David Roden, Music Director, WKSU-FM, 1613 East Summit Street, Kent, OH 44240

WMNR *Monroe, CT*
info@wmnr.org
www.wmnr.org
Non-commercial classical and fine arts music for Connecticut and nearby New York.

WMRA *Harrisonburg, VA*
slottca@jmu.edu
www.jmu.edu/wmra
I would be interested in hearing contemporary composer's music. WMRA has a very mainstream format and we don't delve into electronic, experimental or dissonant music. Our mailing information is: WMRA-FM, Attn Chuck Slott, PO Box 1292, Harrisonburg, Virginia 22803.

WMUH *Allentown, PA*
wmuh@muhlenberg.edu
www.muhlenberg.edu/cultural/wmuh
We play Independent Classical music Tuesday and Wednesdays, 12 noon-2 pm Eastern.

WNPR *Hartford*
Kim Grehn kim_grehn@wedh.pbs.org
www.wnpr.org
We welcome the music of Independent classical musicians.

WQED *Pittsburgh*
Megan mtarbett@wqed.org
www.wqed.org
We don't have a show that features Independent musicians. Our focus is on local musicians. But they are more than welcome to send cds for consideration.

WQXR *New York*
listener.mail@wqxr.com
www.wqxr.com
We always welcome inquiries and submissions from independent artists.

WRTI *Philadelphia*
comments@wrti.org
www.wrti.org
We do play some independent music on both our classical and jazz programming.

WSCL *Salisbury, MD*
Pam Andrews PSANDREWS@salisbury.edu
www.wscl.org
I do listen to "all comers" who send me CLASSICAL MUSIC on CD. I evaluate each disc for three things: 1. Quality of recording as related to sound engineering. 2. Quality of performance of the music. 3. Is this music something our audience really wants to hear? Regarding No. 3, I don't air everything that is considered part of the classical music repertoire. Specifically, I don't air much in the way of "challenging" atonal, dissonant music.

WUFT *Gainesville, FL*
Henri Pensis hpensis@wuft.org
www.wuftfm.org
We do play the music of Independent Classical musicians. Many of them are featured on "Music of the 20th century" (up to the present) and this program runs from 9-11 pm Monday nights. I am the contact for that program. The music is then integrated in our regular classical music schedule.

WWFM *Trenton*
wwfm@wwfm.org
www.wwfm.org
Our mission is to provide you, the listener with the finest classical music available and to do so in a warm, friendly and professional manner.

WXPR *Rhinelander, WI*
wxpr@wxpr.org
www.wxpr.org
You can send CDs to: Walt Gander/ WXPR, 303 W. Prospect St., Rhinelander, WI 54501

WXXI *Rochester*
Julia jfigueras@wxxi.org
www.wxxi.org
We play the music of Independent artists.

Yellowstone Public Radio *Montana*
mgranger@yellowstonepublicradio.org
www.yellowstonepublicradio.org

Canada

Music Around Us
musicaroundus@cbc.ca
toronto.cbc.ca/musicaroundus
Host/Producer Keith Horner presents concerts recorded across the province of Ontario. The program features solo musicians, chamber groups, choirs and orchestras.

Northern Lights *CBC*
Andrea Ratuski northernlights@cbc.ca
radio.cbc.ca/programs/northernlights
I sometimes play indie classical artists.

Our Music
ourmusic@cbc.ca
www.calgary.cbc.ca/radio2/ourmusic.html
Host Catherine McClelland brings a wealth of musical experience of her own to the program, presenting the best of Alberta's many talented classical musicians with thoughtful insight into their backgrounds and what their music means.

Shades of Classics *CKUW*
John Iverson iversjl@ilos.net
www.ckuw.ca
We are committed to promoting the music and activities of local musicians and ensembles.

Sound Advice *CBC*
Rick Phillips soundadvice@toronto.cbc.ca
www.radio.cbc.ca/programs/advice
A weekly guide to the world of classical music and recordings. Note: The classical CDs I review on Sound Advice must be commercially available (easily accessible to listeners) across Canada (so that excludes many independents).

Symphony Hall *CBC*
Katherine Duncan symphony@calgary.cbc.ca
www.cbc.ca/symphonyhall
A showcase for Canadian orchestras and their musicians.

Two New Hours *CBC*
twonewhours@toronto.cbc.ca
cbc.ca/onair/radiobook2001/twonewhours.html
Host Larry Lake guides listeners through the world of new concert music by Canadian and international composers from Canada's main presenters of new music.

Westcoast Performance *CBC*
westcoast@vancouver.cbc.ca
vancouver.cbc.ca/wcp
Presenting the finest music being made by new and established British Columbia artists. Join host Michael Juk every Sunday at 12:06 PM for your favorite classical and world music sounds on CBC Radio Two.

Europe

Czech Republic

Cesky rozhlas 3 - Vltava
vltava@rozhlas.cz
www.rozhlas.cz/vltava
Live broadcasts opera, classical music and jazz from all over the world - feature programmes: explorations of other cultures, profiles of great personalities - jazz, ethnic music, world music and other forms of alternative music.

Denmark

P2musik
p2@dr.dk
www.dr.dk/p2musik

Germany

NDR kultur
info@ndr.de
www.ndrkultur.de
The classical station of Northern Germany.

Hungary

Bartók Radio
reklamig@radio.hu
www.radio.hu
Magyar's classical station.

Italy

Filodiffusione
isoradio@rai.it
www.radio.rai.it/isoradio
Il palinsesto del V canale "Auditorium".

The Netherlands

AVRO Klassiek
klassiek@avro.nl
klassiek.avro.nl

Classic FM
classicfm@classicfm.nl
www.classicfm.nl

The Concertzender
concert.post@concertzender.nl
www.concertzender.nl
We stand for exceptional, serious music. The Concertzender has excelled at presenting remarkable and controversial programmes with lots of genuine jazz and classical music, concert-recordings of (still) unknown musicians and non-Western music all bubbling with life.

Norway

NRK - NRK Alltid Klassisk
info@nrk.no
www.nrk.no/kanal/nrk_alltid_klassisk
The classical station of the Norwegian Public Radio.

Portugal

antena2
www.rdp.pt/antena2
Broadcasting classical music from all epochs and styles, with excursions to other kinds of music: jazz, ethnic music and soundtracks.

Switzerland

Espace 2
espace2@rsr.ch
www.rsr.ch
The classical channel of Radio Suisse Romande.

United Kingdom

BBC Radio 3
radio3.website@bbc.co.uk
www.bbc.co.uk/radio3/classical
The mother of all classical radio stations!

Hear and Now
hear.and.now@bbc.co.uk
www.bbc.co.uk/radio3/world/hearandnow.shtml
The main Contemporary music programme on Radio 3. It features live concerts, studio sessions from the best new music groups and premieres of BBC commissioned works. There are interviews with leading composers and features on who's up-and-coming. The hosts are Sarah Walker and Verity Sharp.

Lyric FM
lyric@rte.ie
www.lyricfm.ie
Irish Classical music station.

Australia

5UV Radio Adelaide
radio@adelaide.edu.au
radio.adelaide.edu.au
As a community station we particularly love independents! The most likely broadcast is on our program of classical new releases 'Coming Out' Fridays 9-11am, with alternating hosts Lisa Downie and Ewart Shaw. Our full program guide is available on our website. Please address all CDs to: Deborah Welch, Manager, 5UV Radio Adelaide, 228 North Terrace, Adelaide SA, 5000

New Music Australia
hinckley.graeme@abc.net.au
www.abc.net.au/classic/nma
A program of new Australian classical music. It ranges from computer music to traditional acoustic instruments, from new structural ideas to the improvisation which has left jazz as a heritage form. It keeps us on the edge, in what is our Golden Age; the best developments and growth in what now marks us as a contributor to the greatest music tradition of them all - classical music.

Country Radio

Includes country, bluegrass, rockabilly, alt-country, Americana, old-tyme country and fiddle music

Radio Promoters

Billy James Productions
billyjames@wnjc1360.com
www.wnjc1360.com/Shows/Billy_James/billy_james.html
We are proud to offer a promotion for artists and bands. The package includes a live 15 minute Interview "on-the-air" with Billy James. Billy will ask you about who you are, what you do and why you do it. In addition, he'll feature 2 of your songs on the show.

CounterPoint Music Group
info@americana-music.com
americana-music.com
An independent radio promotion, marketing and consulting company. The company specializes in promoting progressive, non-mainstream & roots country artists to AMERICANA® stations as well as AAA, non-commercial and college radio.

Stations and Shows

United States

A Prairie Home Companion Radio Show
phc@mpr.org
phc.mpr.org
The show is heard by nearly 2.6 million U.S. listeners each week on over 460 public radio stations and is heard abroad on America One and the Armed Forces Networks In Europe and the Far East.

AllNashvilleRadio
programdirector@allnashvilleradio.us
allnashvilleradio.us
We support Independent Artists and strive to provide the best music available in our online store.

American Routes
mail@amroutes.org
amroutes.cc.emory.edu

Americana Backroads
kglt@montana.edu
www.kglt.net

Americana Crossroads *WMKY*
wmky@moreheadstate.edu
www.morehead-st.edu/units/wmky

AmericanaRama
nprservices@npr.org
kedm.ulm.edu/americanarama/default.htm
Plays music the way we wish others did, as a rich mix of blues, Celtic, western swing, honky tonk, singer-songwriters, alternative country pick up bands and even a few string-bending jazzbos.

The Arctic Cactus Hour
stratto@alaska.net
www.alaska.net/~stratto
Covering the range of Americana/Alternative Country from Bluegrass to Cowpunk and all that rocks and honky tonks in between.

Around the World in Country Music
www.radiocountry.org/atw.htm

Bluegrass Breakdown *Antioch U.*
wyso@antioch.edu
www.wyso.org/wysopgs/blugrass.html
The show features music sets dedicated to new music, gospel music and "roots of bluegrass" music. Plus announcements of local and regional bluegrass events every Saturday night at approximately 6:30pm.

Bluegrass Breakdown *Nashville Public Radio*
talkback@wpln.org
www.wpln.org/bluegrass.html
Thematically, we're all over the bluegrassical map, boldly covering such hot topics as broken things in Bluegrassland, gospel train songs and "ain't" tunes.

Bluegrass Jam *WBJB*
comments@wbjb.org
www.wbjb.org/bluegrass
The best old-time, contemporary and gospel bluegrass.

The Bluegrass Jam Session *WYEP*
Bruce Mountjoy mtjoypgh@aol.com
www.wyep.org
Bluegrass continues to create an aura of antiquity while maintaining a freshness that carries through the generations.

Bluegrass Junction *WICN*
T.Banyai@worldnet.att.net
www.bluegrassjunction.org
That "High Lonesome Sound" floats through the air of central New England every Tuesday evening from 8-11 p.m.. Banjos ring & mandolins sing as this high energy music takes us back to days when the radio was the center of family entertainment.

Bluegrass Overnight *WAMU*
Lee Michael Demsey demsey@wamu.org
www.wamu.org
Six lively hours of bluegrass, every Sunday morning from midnight to 6:00 AM.

Bluegrass Ramble
Bill Knowlton udmacon@aol.com
www.fmhs.cnyric.org/notes/knowlton-bio.html

Bluegrass Ramble *WOSU AM*
www.wosu.org
Join Ramble hosts Rich Baker, Chet DeLong, Jessica Renwick and Don Amrine for the best bluegrass radio in the country

The Bluegrass Show *WQSU*
wendtp@susqu.edu
www.susqu.edu/wqsu-fm
Three hours of the best of bluegrass, including popular features such as "Bluegrass 101 with Professor Carl" and "Bluegrass Gospel."

Bluegrass Show *KCLC*
Larry lreighar@mail.win.org
www.bluegrassguy.com

The Bluegrass Show *KMUD*
md@kmud.org
www.kmud.org
Enjoy two hours of Bluegrass Music and keep in touch with up coming festivals and local Bluegrass shows

Bluegrass Signal *KALW*
Peter Thompson bgsignal@att.net
www.kalw.org
A weekly hour-and-a-half of bluegrass - "folkmusic in overdrive," that unique synthesis of blues and old-time country music, with elements of Celtic, jazz and a variety of folk music.

The Bluegrass Sound *SCERN*
www.scern.org
Features the best in traditional and contemporary bluegrass music each week. We do feature a good number of independent labels and artists due to the nature of our programming mission.

Bluegrass Traditions
kglt@montana.edu
www.kglt.net

bluegrasscountry.org
feedback@bluegrasscountry.org
bluegrasscountry.org
Our hosts are here to bring you the best in traditional and contemporary bluegrass.

Boot Liquor Radio
bootliquor@monkeybots.com
www.somafm.com/bootliquor
American Roots music for saddle-weary drunkards. Presented in "appropriate" AM radio quality.

Burlington County Bluegrass
Joe Wills Mrjobro@aol.com
www.wbzc.org
I do a bluegrass music program Saturdays 10:00am - 2:00pm and welcome projects by independent artists! My station covers Southern New Jersey and the Philadelphia, PA metro area. Send material to: Joe Wills, 136 Taylor Blvd., Bricktown, NJ 08724 USA.

Captain America
www.captainamericaradio.com
This critically-acclaimed show plays American Rock & Roll, Americana and alt-Country. Interviews with up and coming bands.

The Cecilian Bank Bluegrass Hour
theboman@theboman.com
www.theboman.com/cecilian.html
Bluegrass & THE BO-MAN with shows on Kentucky stations WSIP (Paintsville) and WULF (Radcliff). First Kentucky then the world!

Clinch River Breakdown *WDVX*
Barry Hodges scoby@ccdi.net
www.wdvx.com
The finest in bluegrass, old time and classic country every Sunday.

The Conman Radio Show
conmanfm@aol.com
www.countrydj.com/conman
Bar Bands & Basement Tapes is one of the latest special features on the Conman Radio Show. This 15 minute special feature will spotlight unsigned bands and give them national exposure.

Country BeOnAir.com
country.beonair.com

Country Function Bluegrass Junction
cfandbj@kdhx.org
www.kdhx.org/schedule.htm
The best Country and Bluegrass, featuring local artists and unknown artists whose music doesn't get air play at any other station; a heavy emphasis on older, classical country and lots of interviews.

Country Roads
frankbliss@30below.com
www.lssu.edu/wlso
A traditionalist country show. Most of the music is bluegrass. Other types of music often found on COUNTRY ROADS are old time, acoustic country, acoustic blues, folk and oldies country.

CountryBear.com
Stan sbc48@hotmail.com
www.countrybear.com
All material must be licensed thru one of the licensing companies and all CDs must be sent for airplay consideration to: CountryBear.com, Box 758, Lake Placid, FL 33862

CountryRadio.com
info@countryradio.com
countryradio.com
Send a full Press-Kit and CD to Country Radio. We will be considering and featuring artists for airplay and promotions on our station and site.

Cyber Country Internet Radio and Chat
tmc@cybercountrychat.com
www.cybercountrychat.com
We also feature the "Showcase Artist of the Month".

D28+5 *WOUB*
radio@woub.org
woub.org/bluegrass
A place where community volunteers continue a 20+ year tradition of (Blue) Grass roots radio for Southeastern Ohio.

Down Home
chuck@downhome.org
www.downhome.org
You'll hear regional American music from folk, roots and traditional base and beyond.

Down Home Harmonies *KASU*
Marty Scarbrough mscarbro@astate.edu
www.kasu.org
Traditional and contemporary sounds in bluegrass music.

ETC Country
radioetc@radioetc.com
www.radioetc.com
New, unsigned or independent artists can mail their promo kits (CD, brief bio and All applicable contact info - including website, e-mail and phone) to us.

The Fiddler's Grove BlueGrass Show
bluegrass@wantfm.com
www.wantfm.com/bluegrass

Freight Train Boogie Radio
frater@freighttrainboogie.com
www.freighttrainboogie.com
Features Roots music with an emphasis on Alt.Country or Americana music, including some Rock, Folk and Blues and everything in between.

Front Porch Bluegrass *KPBX*
Kevin Brown bluegrass@kpbx.org
www.kpbx.org/programs/frontporch
www.kpbx.org
"You'll hear the "classic" bluegrass sound of tight harmonies, driving rhythms and traditional bluegrass instrumentation (banjo, guitar, mandolin, fiddle, bass and dobro). But you'll also hear the more progressive offshoots—styles often referred to as "newgrass", "jazzgrass", "new acoustic" and "Dawg music".

Front Porch Fellowship
www.solidgospel.com/frontporch.html

Goin' Across The Mountain *WNCW*
info@wncw.org
www.wncw.org
Six hours of the best in traditional and contemporary Bluegrass music.

Good 'n' Country
vintagecountry@hotmail.com,
www.kfai.org/programs/goodnc.htm
One of KFAI's oldest programs.

Heartlands Hayride
mc@blast.net
www.wdvrfm.org/heartlandshayride

Hillbilly at Harvard
mail@whrb.org
www.whrb.org/hah
Hailed by critics and a devoted audience as the best country and western show in New England.

The HipBilly Jamboree
wrvu.org
If you don't like country music, it's probably because you AIN'T never heard the real thing! Every Saturday night from 10 to midnight, WRVU is a 100% Garth-Free zone!

Honky Tonk Heroes *KGNU*
music@kgnu.org
www.kgnu.org
Yodel on out with old and new country & western music!

Honky Tonk Roadhouse
www.wdvrfm.org/htroadhouse1.html

Humble Time
humble@humbletime.com
www.humbletime.com

Independent Country Universe
Mark Bee markbee@greenmountainmusic.com
www.greenmountainmusic.com
Syndicated show from Boulton Beach Studios playing independent and small label artists. Artists are also promoted on web site and there is a special 'backpage' site at artist.greenmountainmusic.com JUST for artists.

KFMM/KCUZ *Safford, AZ*
Dave Etter dave@kfmmradio.com
www.kfmmradio.com
Best mix of old country and new country.

KPIG
sty@kpig.com
www.kpig.com

Live-N-Kickin Bluegrass
Billy J. Ivers BILLYJIVERS@aol.com
www.wluw.org
A first Saturday monthly radio show on WLUW 88.7 in Chicago. We play 1 hour of recorded music by various recording artists and we feature 1 hour of "live" bluegrass music in our WLUW studio by a featured recording artist of the month.

The LoneStar JukeBox
Rick Heysquierdo rick@lonestarjukebox.com
www.lonestarjukebox.com
An independently produced radio program on Pacifica Radio that promotes Americana and Alt-Country genres as well as AAA format and world beat music.

Monday Breakfast Jam
The Iceman iceman@krcl.org
www.krcl.org/~iceman
Eclectic mix of insurgent country, contemporary singer songwriter, folk and rock.

Mountain Folk
MtnFolk@aol.com
www.mountainfolk.com
A weekly one-hour syndicated radio, web and satellite show distributed by the Mountain Laurel Network. Hosted by "East Side Dave", the show presents acoustic bluegrass, folk and mountain music. Indie artists are encouraged to send material.

M-PAK Radio
mikemikels@cox.net
www.mpakproductions.com
This website is streaming audio as a web-radio station broadcasting modern independent country, classic country, current country, Americana and oldies of all types.

Old Grass Gnu Grass *KGNU*
music@kgnu.org
www.kgnu.org
The oldest! The Gnuest! You bet your grass.

Out on a Limb *WETS*
www.wets.org
Some of the harder and/or more progressive sounds of current Americana music. Host Mike Strickland brings us not only the latest recordings, but also live recordings and an occasional live in-studio guest.

The Papa Rox Show
jbotti@jbotti.com
www.jbotti.com/LiveMusic/PRocks.htm

Progressive Torch and Twang *WDBM*
nealdoug@egr.msu.edu
www.msu.edu/~depolo
www.impact89fm.org
We're the home of roots rockin', hip-shakin', soul-swayin' music! Listen in on Tuesday nights from 8 p.m. to midnight.

Pure as Stone Country Music Jamboree
WQSU
wendtp@susqu.edu
www.susqu.edu/wqsu-fm
One of WQSU's longest-running and most popular programs. The jamboree is devoted to traditional country and western music.

The Radio Thrift Shop *WFMU*
Laura Cantrell laura@wfmu.org
www.radiothriftshop.com/radiothriftshop/index.htm
One of the city's best-known deejays among music lovers with a country-and-western bent.

radiowa
radiowa@msn.com
www.radiowa.com
You'll hear Alternative Country, Americana, Folk, Roots and much more.

La Rancherita and Friends
www.radiocountry.org/LaRanch.htm

The Ray Davis Show *WAMU*
feedback@wamu.org
www.wamu.org/raydavis
www.wamu.org
Every Sunday morning for three great hours of traditional bluegrass. Every week, Ray brings you some of the best bluegrass around, from prison songs and "plum pitiful" tunes to the great train rides - and train wrecks - of bluegrass music.

Rockabilly Radio
www.rockabillyradio.net
The voice of independent rockabilly artists.

Roots and Rhythm Mix *WYEP*
Kate Borger kateb913@hotmail.com
www.wyep.org
Devoted to the music of real people, real communities - music that exists and thrives outside of the mainstream and outside the jurisdiction of the big record companies/hype machines of the music industry.

Keep current with Bible updates www.indiebible.com/ud

Roots n' Boots *WFPK*
Michael Young myoung@wfpk.org
www.wfpk.org/programs/rootsandboots.html
www.wfpk.org
Whether it's straight-up country, rockabilly, hillbilly, western swing, alt-country, roots rock, No Depression, depression, it doesn't matter. There's room for outlaws, preachers, rockers and prophets. All you have to do is have a good story to tell, whether you tell it with a fiddle or a Fender is strictly up to you.

Roots 'n' Offshoots
www.wcbe.org
Our very own queen of the honkytonk Maggie Brennan slides on her boots and lassos the finest in American roots music and its related forms; including folk, bluegrass, rockabilly, country and more.

The Santa Fe Opry
www.dreamwater.com/blueelf/radio.htm
Showcase for hardcore, alternative, outlaw, insurgent, no depression - sometimes really depressing country (not the corporate fluff that all righteous people loath).

Sonic Detour
www.wmnf.org
A blend of many styles of music, including "roots" rock, "alternative" country, blues, swing, rockabilly, cajun/zydeco, "classic" rock, bluegrass etc.

Southbound Train *WNUR*
www.wnur.org

Southern Rail *WBRS*
www.wbrs.org
A blend of bluegrass, folk, country, western and acoustic music.

Stained Glass Bluegrass *WAMU*
Red Shipley rs@ns.gemlink.com
www.wamu.org/stainedglassbg
www.wamu.org
For over a quarter century, Bluegrass fans have awakened on Sunday mornings to the gospel sounds of Stained Glass Bluegrass. Veteran country music personality Red Shipley has hosted this WAMU program for the past seventeen years and has amassed a large and loyal audience.

String Fever *North Country Public Radio*
Barb Heller barb@ncpr.org
www.northcountrypublicradio.org/programs/local/string.html
www.northcountrypublicradio.org
There's no heavy agenda on my show — just great music for great listening. Sometimes it's instrumental fingerpicking guitar, banjo, mandolin, or dobro. I'm always looking for GREAT musicians, singly or in groups to perform LIVE on the show (it's a great way to promote a local gig).

Swingin' West
www.swinginwest.com
Specializing in vintage and contemporary Western Swing and Western Music (not Country) and its announcer, producer and historian, Mike Gross.

Third Coast Music Network *KSYM*
joe_x71@hotmail.com
www.accd.edu/tcmn

This is Bluegrass *WMNF*
wmnf@wmnf.org
www.wmnf.org

This Week in Americana
info@americana-music.com
americana-music.com/twia.html
Syndicated in 63 markets, the show combines respect for the past with a desire to say something new. Hosted by 18 year radio and television broadcast veteran, Shannon McCombs.

Topsoil *WXDU*
steve@topsoil.net
www.topsoil.net
A non-commercial free-form roots radio show on each Sunday.

Traditional Country Music Radio
Dusty Owens dusowens@hotmail.com
www.tcmradio.com
Our mission is twofold: To preserve and promote Country, Bluegrass and Gospel music in its best traditional form ... music that millions of people have enjoyed throughout the ages; and To present the most qualified work from artists past and present, in an entertaining way.

Traditional Ties *WYEP*
John Trout johntrout91@hotmail.com
www.wyep.org
New Bluegrass releases and old favorites with a down-home feel true to the roots of Bluegrass music.

Trash, Twang and Thunder
meredith@wfmu.org
www.wfmu.org/playlists/MO
Twang rock for now cowboys, gutbucket blues, front porch bluegrass, American soul of all sorts. Lots of live music too.

TwangCast Radio
Mike Hays Twang4104@cs.com
www.TwangCast.com
Dedicated to the world of Americana Music and Real Country music. We will bring you the best new releases and the classic country and independent artists you won't hear on Top 40 Country Radio!

Twangtown USA
dick@dickshuey.com
www.twangtownusa.com

WAMU *American U.*
www.wamu.org

WDVR
www.wdvrfm.org
A diversified programming station with about 40 hours of country/bluegrass/Americana per week. Quite a few of the DJ's play Indie artists, myself included.

WDVX *Clinton*
mail@wdvx.com
www.wdvx.com
WDVX plays bluegrass, Americana, classic and alternative country, western swing, blues, old time and traditional mountain music, Celtic and folk. WDVX also features area storytellers and provides local and regional musicians an outlet for their talents.

WFDU
www.fdu.edu/newspubs/wfdu

WHAY *Whitley City*
whayradio@highland.net
www.hay98.com

WHEE *Martinsville*
bill@wheeradio.com
wheeradio.com

WSM *Nashville*
mail@wsmonline.com
www.wsmonline.com

WVDR *Sergeantsville*
www.wdvrfm.org

WVLS *Monterey*
wvls.cfw.com

WWHP *Farmer City*
wwhp@farmwagon.com
www.wwhp.com
Playing the best in blues, bluegrass, alternative and traditional country, rock, gospel and American Roots music

Canada

A Bluegrass State of Mind *CKUA*
David Ward david.ward@ckua.org
www.ckua.com
I focus on straight ahead bluegrass music. I also play old timey and new acoustic music in an exploration of bluegrass' roots and branches.

The Back Forty *CKCU*
ron.moores@back40.ca
www.back40.ca
Traditional Country, Western and Bluegrass music.

Bluegrass Island
bluegrassisland@yahoo.com
members.tripod.com/~bluegrassisland/bluegrassisland.html

Spirit of the West
www.cowboylife.com
Music that's rich, listenable and seldom heard on commercial radio today along with conversations featuring spellbinding stories from pioneers, working cowboys and leading motivational experts. The music is Western in nature, different than country and features wonderfully talented Independent artists.

Wide Cut Country *CKUA*
Allison Brock Allison.Brock@ckua.org
www.ckua.com
This show, as its name implies, cuts a wide swath through the genre of country, from traditional hillbilly to pop country examples of today.

Belgium

Country Train Radio Show
Mia Heylen mia.heylen@skynet.be
listen.to/COUNTRYTRAIN

Honky Tonk Saloon & Country Western Barn Dance Music Radio Shows
cowboyradio@yahoo.com
www.cowboyradio.yucom.be/playlist_vbro
We are open for all styles of country music (TexMex, Cajun, BlueGrass, Old-Time, Yodel). If you would send me some music please mark on the green label "a gift with no commercial value" if not, we must pay import taxes on the materials and that is hard for a non commercial organisation.

Denmark

BJ the DJ
Bjarne C. Hesselbjerggaard bj-the-dj@adslhome.dk
www.dj.1go.dk
Radio DJ in Denmark, Country-Action Show since 1989, play mostly independent artists from all over the world.

Radio Oestsjaelland
country@lokalradio.dk
www.lokalradio.dk/voresprg/countrymusic

France

Country Cookin Radio Show *Radio ALFA*
radio@radioalfa.net
www.radioalfa.net
My name is Viggo Jensen. The name of my radio show at Radio ALFA is "Country Cookin'" 4 hours weekly. I also have a two hour show at Radio Hadsten Name of show is "Country time"

Country Road *Radio Arc en Ciel*
rct@radio-rct.com
www.radio-rct.com

Radio Marseillette
Dominique Costanoga melodyranch11@yahoo.fr
I would be very happy if I could receive, broadcast and promote your music during my radio shows on Radio Marseille which airs six airs of Country Music each week. Dominique Costanoga, Program Director, Radio Marseillette, 33 rue des Hts Serres, 11000 Carcassonne.

Radio Waves International
rwaves@imaginet.fr
www.rwi.ht.st
A free non commercial short wave station operating most of the time during the weekends via our own transmitters or via relay. Our format is Country music, gospel, traditional to new country.

Germany

COUNTRY - MUSIC - RADIO - SHOW!
Dieter.Trenkler@t-online.de
The show has been on air for more than 400 times - and it still goes on weekly in the new millennium. I play INDIE-Artist's music.

Hillbilly Jukebox
ashville@gmx.de
www.cashville.de

Italy

Kristall Radio Milano
info@kristallradio.it
www.kristallradio.it
The only Italian network specialized in Roots & Americana Music: country, country rock, western, Zydeco, Cajun, blues, rock blues, blues rock, bluegrass, folk, Irish and Celtic music. We give massive support to all independent artists. Get in touch to promote your music!

Luxembourg

Country Club Music Show
www.ara.lu

The Netherlands

B.R.T.O.
www.brto.nl
Plays: Bluegrass, Gospel, Cajun, Zydeco, Tex Mex, Rockabilly and Modern Country.

Country Express *Radio Rucphen*
Ries Verwijmeren verwijmerenries@zonnet.nl
www.home.zonnet.nl/verwijmerenries
I am broadcasting Country Music on my show Country Express every Monday from 9 to 11pm since August 26. 1996. Please send me material (cd's & Bio) for my show. I will always give you air play.

Country Time *Radio Noordenveld*
Joris Smits jorissmits@wxs.nl
jorissmits.freeyellow.com
I love to discover new music and I spin a lot of Independent Artists & Indie labels on my show.

PeelGrass
Rein Wortelboer Rein.Wortelboer@nld.xerox.com
www.xs4all.nl/~peelgras
If your music is in the (traditional) country, western, or bluegrass style, just send a promotional CD for review / possible airplay.

United Kingdom

Bob Harris Harris Country *BBC 2*
bobharriscountry@bbc.co.uk
www.bbc.co.uk/radio2/country/bob_harris
Every Thursday Bob Harris plays the best in country, from cowboy classics to the newest sounds coming out of Nashville.

Brand New Opry *BBC Radio Scotland*
www.bbc.co.uk/scotland/radioscotland/programmes/other/brandnewopry.shtml
Host Bryan Burnett features the best in new and old country, alt-country and Americana music.

Country Corner Radio Show *Claire FM*
info@clarefm.ie
www.clarefm.ie/progs/countrycorner.htm

Mean Country
Loretta Lupi anything@meancountry.com
www.meancountry.com
We do play the music of Independent artists. Send a cd to the address posted on our website with your contact details and we will let you know once we have heard it.

Metro Country
ray@metrocountry.co.uk
www.metrocountry.co.uk
Any artist or record company who would like their CDs reviewed on this website and played on Metro Country, please E-mail me.

Radio Caroline's European Independent Country Chart Show
country@hotdisc.net
www.hotdisc.ukgateway.net/caroline.html
In the one hour the show is on air STUART CAMERON will be counting down the Top 30 playing new entries and climbers - it is a massive boost for the independent country music scene as acts who don't have major record labels behind them, are given airplay and exposure via this prestigious programme.

Australia

Bluegrass Australia
webmaster@bluegrass.org.au
www.bluegrass.org.au

Cool Country Radio
info@coolcountry.com.au
www.coolcountry.com.au

MCR Radio *Macarthur Community Radio*
feedback@2mcr.org.au
2mcr.org.au

Music from Foggy Hollow *Hawk Radio*
foggyhollow@bluegrass.org.au
www.hawkradio.org.au/bluegrass
We welcome material from independent bands, artists etc, but we never guarantee airplay. Our show is a new releases bluegrass show, so the material must be freely available and it must be bluegrass or at least close to being bluegrass.

Saturday Night Country
backyard@your.abc.net.au
www.abc.net.au/backyard

New Zealand

The Rock 'n Country Show
j.adams.music@xtra.co.nz
www.joyadams.co.nz/radio_show.htm
If you are a Recording Artist and you think your music would suit the programme's format, please send Cd's and Bio to: Joy Adams, The Rock 'n' Country Show, C.M.B. B19, Pukemiro, R.D.1, HUNTLY NEW ZEALAND.

Dance Radio

United States

1groovE.com
music@theiceberg.com
www.1groove.com

astralwerks Radio
feedback@astralwerks.net
www.astralwerks.com
It is best to limit your demo to three (3) of the best (your favorite) tracks, hopefully showing your diversity and vision. Please, NO PHONE CALLS.

BassDrive
info@bassdrive.com
www.bassdrive.com
A 24/7 drum and bass radio station featuring live shows with guest DJs, as well as broadcasts from venues all over the world representing the best of drum and bass & jungle music. BassDrive is also a new record label promoting US drum and bass.

BeatAudio
John D. john@otis2.com
beataudio.com
I accept submissions from any beat or rhythm oriented band.

Beats in Space *WNYU*
Tim Sweeney tim@beatsinspace.net
www.beatsinspace.net
The sounds you'll hear on Beats in Space are not limited to one style. You might end up hearing down tempo/leftfield, drum and bass, afrobeat, funk, broken beat/nu jazz, 2 step, disco, post punk, electro, weird electronic, hip hop and more in one show.... space is the place.

Club Radio Network
djgyle@hotmail.com
www.clubradio.net
Our mission is to bring the very best that the dance music scene has to offer and put it at your fingertips twenty-four hours a day.

Beta Lounge Radio Show
info@betalounge.com
www.betalounge.com

Darkside Radio *(DRiP)*
stevyn@ironfeather.com
www.hyperreal.org/music/library/audio/drip
We play mixtapes, records and CDs and gossip about the underground scene. We welcome demos etc to be played on our shows. The radio show is mostly geared towards any style of dance & electronica.

DetroitMix.com
artist@detroitmix.com
www.detroitmix.com
We are looking for indie dance, trance and pop music to play on the station. We play a dance, trance & top 40 format. If you like the sounds of the station, simply submit your mp3.

Digital Club Network *(DCN)*
DCNinfo@dcn.com
www.dcn.com
Recording and webcasting performances every night from some of the best clubs and concert halls in the world. You can see thousands of those performances right here - for free. And many are also available on CD.

Digitally Imported Radio
demos@di.fm
www.digitallyimported.com
If you - artists, labels, DJs, or others - would like to submit your material to DI Radio and you think that it is good enough to be played on our channel(s), then please email us for instructions.

djmixed.com
feedback@djmixed.com
www.djmixed.com
Your one stop source for all info related to dj culture and the electronic music lifestyle. We will keep you updated with the latest news from the global scene's artists and djs, reviews of their music and features about them and topics about the culture. Visit our site to submit your bio and booking information.

dublab Radio
info@dublab.com
www.dublab.com
Positive, freeform music.

Eklektika
Kenny Kinds kennyk@blue-fortune.com
eklektika.blue-fortune.com
DJ Knock Knock and ya man Kenny K, bring you the best in Acid Jazz, Neo Soul, Spoken Word, Progressive Hip Hop, House and Drum and Bass. We are always looking for new artists, in these musical genres, to showcase and if you would like to submit music, please hit us up at eklektika@blue-fortune.com. The sound is...Eklektika.

Keep current with Bible updates
www.indiebible.com/ud

---

electroboxonline.com
timothy@electroboxonline.com
www.electroboxonline.com
Bringing Seattle the most Progressive new music from worldwide and local djs/producers. Originally it was supposed to focus only on the 'mainstream electronica' movement; however it grew out of control and now broadcasts sounds from every corner of the Seattle underground scene.

EpiphanyRadio
www.epiphanycorp.com
Broadcasting a mix of ambient/downtempo/triphop/worldbeat electronica groove. 100% Independent!

groovefactory.com
groovemasters@groovefactory.com
www.groovefactory.com
Our mission is to provide our listeners with the best house music on the web via live and pre-recorded shows from the top DJ's and clubs in the world. We will never compromise quality in order to bring you great programming.

Groovetech Radio
www.groovetech.com

Gruvsonic Dance Radio
jonathan@gruvsonic.com
www.gruvsonic.com
We have a staff of DJ's willing to spin any dance material via live mix shows. Since we are a non-profit station, we cannot afford the multiple licensing fees by large middleman corporations. That is why we are approaching artists and labels offering them 100% free promotion in a full spectrum package!

The Hitchhiker's Dance Guide *WEVL*
hdg@thinkhead.com
www.thinkhead.com/guide

Limbik Frequencies
djsam@limbikfreq.com
www.limbikfreq.com
Derives its name and logo from the human limbic system. Our gentle but powerfully emotional mix of ambient, downtempo, ethereal, industrial and intelligent techno, is an active exploration into deep and uncharted modes of existence.

m1live.com
musicone@m1live.com
m1live.com
Today's dance music. Does reviews too.

Metropolis *KCRW*
metroweb@kcrw.org
www.kcrw.org
The hypnotic pulse of modern city life. Los Angeles' flagship progressive music radio show since the early 90's.

ministryofsound radio
studio@ministryofsound.com
www.ministryofsound.com
Check our site for today's schedule and highlights, as well as complete programme details from the biggest digital dance floor on the planet.

Mix Attack
petercarli@blazenet.net
www.radiationroom.com
Your music MUST be compatible with the show's club mix format and needs to be competitive with what is currently on Billboard's Club Play chart. Mix Attack's format is open to all major label, independent and unsigned material that meets our programming requirements.

mypowermix.com
randy@mypowermix.com
www.mypowermix.com
Seattle's No. 1 non-commercial Dance-Mixshow.

N*Soul Radio
beats@nsoul.com (Canada)
ryan_richardson@nsoul.com (USA)
www.nsoul.com

PleasuredomeRadio
mail@pdomeradio.com
www.pdomeradio.com
Mix of Dance, HipHop, R&B and more!

Proton Radio
submissions@protonradio.com
www.protonradio.com
Want to hear your work on the air? Once a week, Proton Radio selects a special DJ or producer to be its Featured Artist of the Week. It can be DJ sets or tracks produced or remixed by the Artist. Or possibly both!

Radio DMZ
kryptyk@radiodmz.com
www.radiodmz.com
Our shows are produced by people who love the music!

RadioValve
e23@radiovalve.com
www.radiovalve.com

Streetbeat *WNUR*
streetbeat-md@wnur.org
server.wnur.org/streetbeat
A side of dance music that doesn't get exposure elsewhere on the dial, in the clubs, or even in the party scene.

TE! Radio
radio@tomasianent.com
www.live365.com/stations/tomasianent
We feature upcoming DJ's in our MixTape show; indie artists in our new music showcase; and much much more. We are always looking to expose new music. Please contact us or visit our website for more information.

Techno Revolution
Dj FlufferNutter djfluffernutter@yahoo.com
www.technorevolution.net
We are here to offer you a 24 hour a day online techno/trance/club and house musical experience. If you yourself are tired of all the commercials and online mumbo jumbo, stick around. Oh and YES, we do accept new submissions to our playlists.

Technotic Times Internet Radio
Times@technotica.com
www.technotica.com
Our format is Electronic Underground...great distinctive innovative well-produced tunes! Most weeks the music is brand new, occasionally we do retrospectives or artist/label/style/genre-specific shows.

Transmissions Radio Show
www.plus8.com/Audio
A weekly radio show produced by intelliNET. intelliNET selects top DJ's to produce a one hour radio program.

WMPH *Mt. Pleasant High School, Wilmington*
radio@wmph.org
www.wmph.org
Has changed their format to an all dance station. Will accept indie releases.

WOMB *Miami*
music@thewomb.com
www.thewomb.com

XTC Radio
www.xtcradio.com
This station SHOUTcasts a unique blend of Trance, Hard and Acid Trance, Underground Progressive House and Epic Trance in CD Quality for High Bandwidth Listeners.

Canada

Global Grooves Network
info@globalgroovenetworks.com
www.globalgroovenetworks.com
The first network, GGN I "The Groove", is a variety of DJs and dance genres including house, dub, drum & bass, trip hop, Latin, techno, trance, ambient, progressive, alternative electronica and international alternative.

The Groove *CKCU*
Elorius Cain music@ckcufm.com
www.ckcufm.com
Canada's longest running disco show playing every variation.

HOUSMUSIQUE
hal@netmusique.com
www.netmusique.com

In the Mix Radio Show
Andrew Duke cognition@techno.ca
techno.ca/cognition
Airing weekly since 1987. The show is syndicated internationally to radio/internet and features interviews, live PAs, guest DJs, world premieres, prereleases, new and classic tracks.

Tongue and Groove *CKUA*
Kevin Wilson kevin.wilson@ckua.org
www.ckua.com
Free your mind — and your backbone — in a sophisticated oasis of everything that grooves: funk, acid jazz, electronica, trip hop, even a little disco.

Tuned In Radio *The New Rhythm Of The Nation*
Dave tunedin@tunedinradio.com
www.tunedinradio.com
Our dance radio show is always looking for 'radio friendly' dance, r&b, reggae, soul and dance related synthpop recording artists to interview. For more information, phone, fax, email or check out our website.

Denmark

beats.dk
info@beats.dk
www.beats.dk
Our mission is to bring you the greatest, best quality and most funky LIVE and on demand musical website on the entire Internet.

France

Galaxie Radio
info@galaxiefm.com
www.galaxiefm.com

MaXXima
info@maxxima.org
www.maxxima.org
Electronic, Nujazz, Lounge, Downtemp, deepHouse, House, TekHouse...

novaplanet.com
radionova@radionova.com
www.novaplanet.com

Radio FG *Paris*
mp3.voila.fr

Germany

Klub Radio
kontakt@klubradio.de
www.klubradio.de

Magic Fly
thomas.broich@t-online.de
home.t-online.de/home/Thomas.Broich/magfly.htm

Sonix Radio
sonix.de

The Trance House Station
info@djsnoop.com
listen.to/djsnoop
Absolute new fresh Trance, Club & House Music, 24 hours a day 7 days a week with 1 hour special live mix during the week. Music for your soul and brain.

The Vinylizer
Marcus bttb@vinylizer.net
www.vinylizer.net
BTTB is a radio-show based in Hamburg / Germany. The Vinylizer presents new releases and exclusively recorded sessions by DJs from all over the world (BTTB-X-Series).

Hungary

Rádió Eger
radioeger@agria.hu
www.agria.hu/radio/r_eger

Italy

Fashion FM
fashion@fashionfm.it
www.fashionfm.it

The Netherlands

Radio X-Clusief
theo@djtheo.nl
home.wanadoo.nl/mulder.h
Listen 7 days a week to the #1 Trance-Station of The Hague.

WDISKO.net
www.wdisko.net
Disco Radio.

Switzerland

Basic.ch
basic@basic.ch
live.basic.ch
Live and archived DJ-mixes is a daily internet-only radio and music database covering quality electronic music and more.

Radio Couleur 3
www.couleur3.ch

United Kingdom

BurnitBlue.com
www.burntblue.com
We aim to capture the excitement and diversity of dance culture and provide the dance music and clubbing fraternity with an entertaining and essential resource.

CN Soho Live
studio@coppernob.net
www.cnsoholive.co.uk

| deephousenetwork |
service@deephousenetwork.com
www.deephousenetwork.com
A deep house website which contains up to date reviews & news along with users unreleased deep house tracks & more.

gaialive Radio
www.gaialive.co.uk

HappyHourRadio.com
email@happyhourradio.com
www.happyhourradio.com
Music that will put a smile on your face and a bounce in your step. Featured will be music from (or heavily influenced by) the UK's hardcore rave scene.

Interface Pirate Radio
www.pirate-radio.co.uk

Power FM
info@powerfm.org
www.powerfm.org

Radio Magnetic
studio@radiomagnetic.com
www.radiomagnetic.com
The very best of the UK and Scottish dance music scenes.

UK Rumble
www.ukrumble.com
We have been webcasting a varied style of dance music over the last three years entertaining and enlightening people all around the globe.

Vibe FM
www.vibefm.co.uk
The East of England's number 1 Dance Music radio station.

Australia

The Australian Underground Dance Station
info@isonliveradio.com
www.isonliveradio.com/index.php
The primary format is underground dance music. We play some local commercial dance and underground dance music from all around the world!

Fresh FM
music@station.freshfm.com.au
www.freshfm.com.au

Mix Up Radio Show
mixup@triplej.abc.net.au
www.abc.net.au/triplej/mixup/default.htm

Spraci Radio Shows
spraci.cia.com.au
Spraci has an extensive list of weekly dance music radio shows heard around the Sydney area.

Wild FM
www.wildfm.com.au

Experimental Radio

Experimental, Electronica, Ambient, Avant Garde and Noise.

North America

United States

Alchemical Radio
Terri~B and The Reverend Rabbit
info@archhouse9.fsnet.co.uk
www.aural-innovations.com/radio/alchemy.html
Transmitted telepathically via Aural Innovations to all like minded individuals who feel that they have been steeped in too much aural bullshit for far too long. "Alchemical Radio" seeks to break through the mainstream blocking frequencies of the prison warders of planet Earth, in order to transmit truly innovative music and lyrics into the ear canals of Earthlings.

Cyberage Radio
Tommy T tommyt@dsbp.cx
www.cyberage.cx
Specializing in all kinds of electronic music and underground sounds.

Dr. Demento On the Net
web@krellan.com
www.krellan.com/demento

EMUSIC *WDIY*
billfox@fast.net
www.wdiyfm.org/programs/emusic
An electronic, ambient and space music show. E-mail me if you wish to submit music for airplay consideration.

The Formula *WLUW*
theformulachicago@hotmail.com
www.theformulachicago.com
wluw.org
Non-Regulated, Anti-Formatted, Experiments in Sound.

KSPC *Pomona College, CA*
www.kspc.org
Any electronic, ambient, noise, industrial, experimental or strange music, as well as ANY cassettes should be sent with ATTN: Josh Weide. (Cassettes are generally rejected, but I will accept them personally).

The Latest Score *WOMR*
Canary Burton seabird@capecod.net
www.womr.org
I play new music, NonPop, high ambient, electroacoustic, total noise, synthesizer creation, sound art, anything related to the 'contemporary classical scene". Basically I play everything that comes in. I think I have trashed maybe three submissions in 6 years.

Music For Nimrods *KXLU*
Reverend Dan Buhler reverenddan@
musicfornimrods.net
www.musicfornimrods.net
A weekly radio show in Los Angeles, looking for degenerate music of all styles.

The Musical Transportation Spree *KFAI*
Chris cwaterbury@mtsradio.com
Jerry jmodjeski@mtsradio.com
www.mtsradio.com
Climb aboard the transynaptic vehicle. Come along with us on the neuron bus and ride the brain waves to the gray matter sea. We prefer home recordings.

New Dreamers *KLCC*
klcc@efn.org
www.users.qwest.net/~om14/nudreamrsm.htm
Focuses on music created with the aid of electronic devices, as well as drawing from many genres to create an eclectic mix that spotlights innovative artists who have broken the boundaries of how and why music is made.

No Pigeon Holes Radio Show
Don Campau campaudj@jps.net
lonelywhistle.tripod.com/playlists
www.RadioMarabu.de
Broadcasting to the San Francisco and Monterey Bay Areas (KKUP 91.5 FM in Cupertino CA), the internet and also throughout Europe on Radio Marabu. I accept all styles of music for airplay on my variety show of underground unknowns. Send me your music! Any style, the weirder the better!

Plastic Tales from the Marshmallow Dimention *WNYU*
wnyumusic@hotmail.com
www.wnyu.org/plastictales
BLOW YOUR MIND with a weekly 'dose' of psychedelic, garage, mod, pop-sike, freakbeat, surf-a-delic, progressive and krautrock. Tune-IN, Turn-ON and Drop-OUT! Experience it every Monday at 9:00PM on WNYU 89.1FM in New York City and the surrounding tri-state metro area. It's Far-Out man!

Press the Button
staff@pressthebutton.com
pressthebutton.com
An experimental radio show of found sound collage which interacts with unscreened phone callers.

Psych-Out *WREK*
Scott Watkins scott@angband.org
www.angband.org/~scott/psychout
A show dealing with psychedelia past and present in as many of its different forms that can fit.

Pushing The Envelope *WHUS*
Joel Krutt joelkru@aol.com
www.whus.org
We have spent the past eleven years bringing you the finest in avant ephemera, in the realms of rock, classical, electronic, jazz, world music and just about anything else that catches my ear. All this along with a healthy dollop of new and classic progressive rock.

Radio Distortion
karl@radiodistortion.com
radiodistortion.com
Bringing new music to your ears!!!

Radio Nothing
Rod Richardson TigerRod@aol.com
wpkn.org/nothing
An ongoing project with no end in sight.

Roulette Radio
info@roulette.org
www.roulette.org

Screamin' Streamin' Audio
richius@voicenet.com
www.richius.com
My own little contribution to the world of psychedelic, drone and space rock music. 60 minutes of streaming music with a new show posted each Monday and Thursday.

Some Assembly Required
Catherine Campion assembly@detritus.net
www.some-assembly-required.net
The only radio program known to focus exclusively on "tape manipulations, digital deconstructions and turntable creations." Showcasing audio work by artists who appropriate sounds from the media environment. Now nationally syndicated.

Something Else *WLUW*
somethingelse@wluw.org
www.stopgostop.com/somethingelse
Since 1995, a weekly radio program of sound art, new/experimental music and live performance in Chicago. A cassette tape submitted from an unknown artist has the same potential for airplay as a cd by a known artist.

SpaceRock Radio
jkranitz@aural-innovations.com
www.aural-innovations.com/radio/radio.html

(((Thump))) Radio
info@thump-radio.com
www.thump-radio.com
Dedicated to exposing local talent and artists from around the world.

Tommy T's Cyberage Radio Show
tommyt@dsbp.cx
www.cyberage.cx

Transfigured Night *WLCR*
newmusic@wkcr.org
www.columbia.edu/cu/wkcr
An overnight exploration of new releases of experimental music, with an emphasis on electronic works.

The Weekly World Noise *WORT*
www.wort-fm.org
A program of experimental, avant-garde and "difficult listening" music.

Weirdsville!
weird@weirdsville.com
www.weirdsville.com
A tantalizing mix of strange and obscure music. From the electronic to the organic, exotic to the narcotic, acid surf, psychedelic lounge, schizo C&W, avant-garde dub, free jazz and noise skronk.

Welcome to Weirdsville
Lee Widener weirdsville@neverendingwonder.com
www.NeverEndingWonder.com/weirdsville.htm
We play all kinds of comedy- sketch, stand-up and comedy music. We prefer to hear only from artists that are focused on making people laugh- or at least smile. So long and thanks for the fish.

Well-Rounded Radio
Charlie McEnerney charlie@wellroundedradio.net
www.wellroundedradio.net
Well-Rounded Radio is an interview program that digs deep into the creation of music-and allows songwriters and musicians to reveal what inspires and influences their work.

Canada

Brave New Waves Radio Show
bnw@cbc.ca
www.bravenewwaves.ca
Dedicated to new underground music. This could mean anything from indie rock to dance, experimental electronic and avantgardisms of every shape. We include the widest universe of genres possible every single night. We love to get mail and records (all sizes and formats).

Cranial Explosions: Sounds That Blow Minds! *CJTR*
Gil and Tony cexplosions@hotmail.com
www.cjtr.ca
A free form-odyssey of musical moments and experiences. Submit your impacting music to us and if it moves us, as per our mission statement, we will play it on our show!! Please include biographical information etc. Music can be submitted to: Cranial Explosions P.O. Box 22177, Regina, Saskatchewan, Canada S4S 7H4. Please indicate on package: Music for promotional use only. No commercial value.

Do Not Touch This Amp *CFBX*
Steve Marlow dntta@yahoo.ca
www.geocities.com/dntta
www.thex.ca
An experimental/electronic/industrial program that runs every Friday night.

Feedback Monitor Radio Show
greg@feedbackmonitor.com
www.feedbackmonitor.com
Featuring new releases in electronic and experimental music.

Le Navire Night
navire@radio-canada.ca
radio-canada.ca/radio/navire
Artistes internationaux et locaux enregistrés dans les différents festivals et événements : concerts de musique nouvelle, expérimentale électronique et acoustique, de musique improvisée et de projets inédits alliant diverses ressources technologiques.

plutonian nights
info@plutonia.org
plutonia.org
An almost completely improvised radio show that happens in the middle of the night. Musical content is predominantly electronic based, but not always.

Two New Hours
Larry_Lake@cbc.ca
www.radio.cbc.ca/programs/2newhours
Send us a CD or tape of your music. If we're impressed, we might be able to get someone to play it so that it can be on the show. We're always interested in discovering new composers and their music, but you must understand that our first duty is to Canadian artists.

Direct traffic to your website!
www.indielinkexchange.com

Europe

Finland

SPACE JUNK
Jukka Mikkola jmikkola@sci.fi
www.sci.fi/~jmikkola/english.htm
Presenting electronic and experimental music from the early electronic heroes to ambient and contemporary works. Musical visions beyond time and space, exploring the strange horizons of music and sound.

Germany

Lametta Radio
lametta@gmx.net
www.muenster.org/lametta
Our show features interviews with musicians, presentations of new albums, label and country specials. We specialize in Alternative, Electronic and Progressive Pop music.

Radio Future 2
RadioFuture2@hotmail.com
www.radiofuture2.purespace.de

Radio "Morituri te salutant"
Holger/Madrego webmaster@radio-morituri.de
www.radio-morituri.de
Almost CD-Quality using mp3pro, 4 Channels (2x mixed, electro, dark ambient/shoegazer), Interviews, CD Comments, Chat etc.

Radio Neandertal
webmaster@demo-art.de
www.transystor.de/radio/neandertal/radio_neandertal_frequenzen.htm
Mostly instrumental like Enigma, Vangelis, Kraftwerk, J.M.Jarre, Oldfield, Schulze, Mike Batt, Alan Parsons, Oliver Shanti and all around this kind of music... even the newcomer...

Latvia

Ozone
ozone.re-lab.net

The Netherlands

DFM
dfm@desk.nl(Postmaster)
desk.nl/~dfm
The offered material consists 100% of independent releases, is made or recorded by ourselves, our friends, fellow artists/musicians or is generated live using old instruments, samplers, computers, field recordings, loops, synthesizers, you name it.

Radio 100
www.radio100.nl

United Kingdom

BBC *Experimental Music*
www.bbc.co.uk/music/experimental
Electronica, post-rock & beyond.

Virtual FM
info@virtualfuturemusic.com
www.virtualfuturemusic.com

XFM Dublin
www.isis.ie/xfm

Yugoslavia

BELGRADEYARD
mail@belgradeyard.co.yu
www.belgradeyard.co.yu

Radio B2-92
xchange.re-lab.net

Australia

L'audible Net Radio
house@laudanum.net
laudible.net

Difficult Listening
difflist@westnet.com.au
westnet.com.au/mooreb
The spot on your dial for the relentless and impenetrable sound of difficult music.

Musicality *Tune FM*
tunefm.une.edu.au
Generally the albums featured are "musically" interesting, featuring experimental compositions, great improvisations, passionate playing or interesting lyrics.

Sound Quality
Tim Ritchie soundquality@your.abc.net.au
www.abc.net.au/rn/music/soundqlt
Why does everything have to fit into a genre? It doesn't. For 20 years, Tim Ritchie has been seeking out music: the interesting, the evolutionary, the inaccessible and the wonderful.

Gothic Radio

Gothic, Industrial, EBM, Synthpop.

North America

United States

13th Track Halloween Radio
mark@13thTrack.com
www.13thtrack.com

ampedOut
ampedout.net
A fledgling project that has no profitability or any personal gain for me, it's just me sharing my love of music to all who'll listen. Hopefully this can be a source for music other than the pre-fab radio stations that push bullshit posturing music into the veins of addict youth.

Arcane Asylum
webmaster@wmbc.umbc.edu
www.gl.umbc.edu/~ascott7

Audio Exotica
choneyc1@midsouth.rr.com
www.mysteryhearsay.com
www.wevl.org

Bat Country *KDVS*
www.kdvs.org
In direct response to the dangers of our advanced technology: 2 hours of dark electro-industrial, dissident music punctuated with sparkley synthpop.

The Black Cauldron *KUCI*
Matthew Brown morven@byz.org
www.kuci.org/~mbrown/cauldron.html
www.kuci.org
Goth, Industrial, Pagen, Ethereal, Electronica and Darkwave.

Black Light District *WEGL*
kustopn@mail.auburn.edu
www.auburn.edu/~kustopn/bld
Dedicated to bringing you the best in experimental, electro, gothic, ambient and industrial music.

Closed Caskets for the Living Impaired *KUCI*
Dach dach@closedcaskets.com
www.closedcaskets.com
The most popular Goth radio show of all time, broadcast locally in Irvine, California and online internationally!

cyberage *KUNM*
tommyt@dsbp.cx
www.cyberage.cx
The most listened to elektronic, industrial, experimental and diverse futuristic minded show on the map!

Dark Circles *KZSC*
victoriastar@yahoo.com
www.darkcircles.net
Hosted by myself, DJ Victoria and occasional guests, Dark Circles plays from 10:30 pm until 12:30 am on Wednesday nights. Specializing in gothic, industrial, death rock, EBM and ethereal music.*

Dark Horizons *WMNF*
Theresa Frederick info@darkhorizonsradio.com
www.darkhorizonsradio.com
A two hour radio show on WMNF 88.5FM Community Radio in Tampa, Florida featuring new releases from ethereal, gothic, industrial and synthpop bands.

Dead Sun Rising *WHUS*
info@whus.org
whus.org
Send noise, experimental and psychedelic to JAY DUNCAN, NOISETC.DIRECTOR".

Descent Radio Show
descent@descentral.net
www.descentral.net

Detroit Industrial Underground
brian@detroitindustrial.org
www.detroitindustrial.org

Digital Gunfire
shirow@digitalgunfire.com
www.digitalgunfire.com
Industrial strength aural assault. We play the music of Independent artists as they are in the industrial/ebm/synth-pop genre (or any of the sub-genres in between!)

DJ VSX
djvsx@crunchpodmedia.com
www.crunchpodmedia.com/djvsx
Industrial, electronic music, some experimental...

Eclectic Seizure *WEFT*
William@spinelessbooks.com
spinelessbooks.com/eclecticseizure/
Electrocities of the Mind with Goth, Industrial, Noise, EBM!!

Factory 911

wegl@auburn.edu
wegl.auburn.edu
An industrial and electronic show. I play everything from hard core industrial (i.e. skinny puppy) to progressive (Paul Okenfold) drum and base (ak 1200), dancy techno, to experimental and every now and then something a little on the Goth side. I basically play everything that is electronic in origin. Send CDs to: WEGL 91.1 FM Radio, 116 Foy Union, Auburn U. AL, 36849, USA.

Fear of Being Touched *WTJU*

Tas2b@virginia.edu
www.people.virginia.edu/~tas2b
wtju.radio.virginia.edu
Strange and unsettling sounds from the furthest frontiers of electronic music: IDM, dark ambient, noise, minimalism, abstract hip-hop and much more. It's two hours of shock therapy for your autistic inner child.

Generation Death *KSPC*

gendeath@excite.com
www.kspc.org
Gothic, Industrial, Ethereal, Darkwave and Shoegazer.

Im Rhythmus Bleiben Radio

www.rhythmus.net/irb
Currently, our goal is to assist record labels and musicians in alternative music, specifically the industrial, gothic and electronic music genres and pagan artists to gain exposure.

In Perpetual Motion Radio

G. R. Perye III ipm@digitalangel
www.ipmradio.com
IPM specializes in indie artists of the gothic, industrial and electronic genres & promotes the musicians and events on the weekly internet radio show as well as at live club events.

The Industrial Factory *WZBC*

industrialfactory@hotmail.com
www.geocities.com/sunsetstrip/disco/5053
Catch the best in underground cyber-electro industrial music.

Industrial Zoning *WWSP*

industrialzoning@djizmusic.com
www.djizmusic.com
Are you an industrial/darkwave band that wants to be heard? I'll review your music if you send it to: Industrial Zoning, 105 CAC - UWSP, Reserve St. Stevens Point, WI 54481

JUXTAPOSITION *KDXH*

DJ Rob Levy juxtaposition88@yahoo.com
www.crosswinds.net/~darkredhead/rl1
I play all types of music. Mostly indie rock, some industrial and ethereal music, britpop, trip hop, downtempo and some punk. It's sort of all over the place.

Liquid Gothic Radio

michael@liquidgothic.net
www.liquidgothic.net
Web Radio to Die For!

Meltdown *KCR*

amaxophobic@phreaker.net
www.subnation.com/meltdown
Specializes in dance industrial music, like the stuff you hear in the clubs. If you can dance to it, it'll be there: EBM, synthpop, a little hardcore, whatever. The main focus is on lesser-known, underground artists that don't get much exposure elsewhere.

Natasha's Batcave

natasha@meltdownmagazine.com
www.meltdownmagazine.com/show.html
www.totalrock.com
Tune in to hear the latest Goth new releases.

On the Edge

ontheedge@c895fm.com
www.ontheedgeradio.com
www.c895fm.com
I've been doing this show since December of 1990. I play mostly Industrial, some Gothic and various electronic types of music. I do live on air interviews with bands. I play mostly newer music; I also play some early industrial music, the classics.

The Shape of Things to Come

Bob Westphal TheOneBob@aol.com
www.theonebob.com
The longest running and best dark music show to air in NYC.

Sounds and Visions of Tomorrow Today

Losafa@aol.com
www.drugmusic.com

Spiderpower Sounds

spiderpower.net
I can guarantee any artist that the exposure given to them via internet radio sites like this is the only way they will gain broad listener / fan base. Send me demos, point me in the direction of download sites, mail me, talk to me.... feedback me (hmmm!) Let me promote YOU!!!

sursumcorda Radio

inquiry@sursumcorda.com
www.sursumcorda.com
New directions in electronic organic groove with underpinnings in minimalism and henry miller-ness... practically evolving daily...

Syncromesh Internet Radio

badger@badger.cx
syncromesh.net
Our mission is to spread the word about good electronic industrial and related genres of music. Please include an introductory letter if this is the first contact and some sort of BIO sheet about your band. We hate getting CDs with no idea what it's for.

Thaljana's Chartreuse Translucent

thaljana@chartrans.com
www.chartrans.com
I want to help inform fans of neo-synthpop, electro, darkwave and gothic music of what specific bands sound like. I will do my best to give objective descriptions of various bands as opposed to "reviews".

This is Corrosion

legion@thisiscorrosion.com
www.thisiscorrosion.com
Submission of music by all artists is most welcome, but please send only CDs. We receive too many requests to listen to mp3s to keep up with them in a timely manner.

The Vapour Treatment *WUSB*

vapourtreatment@yahoo.com
www.geocities.com/radiovt
www.wusb.org
Spinning the spectrum of Modern electronic music, industrial, new wave, synth pop electro and more, with your host DJ Datura.

Canada

A Shot in the Dark

www.ckut.ca
We specialize in promoting lesser known bands, basing its playlist primarily on European imports, but not only. Besides playing music, there have been a number of interviews conducted on the show.

Dark Radio

radio@gothik.zzn.com
darkradio.mybravenet.com
Gothic, NeoClassical, Medieval, NeoFolk, Dark Ambient and Industrial.

The Electric Front

DJLee@theelectricfront.com
www.theelectricfront.com
www.live365.com/stations/leereznor
Plays your favorite industrial, electronic, synth, Goth and dark-rock songs. Check our website for submission information.

Electrosynthesis

promo@electrosynthesis.cjb.net
electrosynthesis.cjb.net
We play the best in Goth, Industrial, Experimental, Ambient, Techno and more!

Les Mouches Noires *CISM*

lesmouchesnoires@videotron.ca
www.lesmouchesnoires.com
Since 1992 I have had the desire to introduce people to a new style of music and a new culture...The world of techno, Goth and industrial. Do you have a band? Do you have an album or demo? Just send your press kit and CD or demo to us.

RantRadio

info@rantradio.com
www.rantradio.com
It is a free speech and music soapbox upon which to play and vent your concerns, opinions and music. We play angry music. We play inspirational music. We make you think. RantRadio plays only the best in Industrial music.

The Real Synthetic Audio Show

todd@synthetic.org
www.synthetic.org

Ripe With Decay *CHMR*

Donald Burden ripewithdecay2000@yahoo.ca
ripewithdecay.dgraham.net
www.mun.ca/chmr
A showcase for all goodies industrial, ambient, electronic, gothic, experimental and noise related styles of music.

Europe

Belgium

Darker than the Bat Radio Show *ZRO*

www.proservcenter.be/darkerthanthebat/radio.html

De Kagen Radio Show *Radio Scorpio*

www.kagankalender.com
Wave-gothic-electro-industrial, including all the related styles. Each promo is assured to get a review (on both KaganKalender and web-site) and will be played on the radio show.

France

Dark Spirit in a Candle
frost.ds.free.fr

Doctor Avalanche Radioshow
taki666@hotmail.com
doctoravalanche.multimania.com
Since 1993 playing Industrial, Electronica, Drum and bass, EBM and Gothic.

Meiose
calyxx@wanadoo.fr
meiose.free.fr
Industriel, gothique, expérimental, électro dark, dark folk, médiéval. Si vous faites partie d'un groupe, envoyez nous vos démos sur CD ou par mail en fichiers MP3.

Radio 666 *Saint Clair Cedex*
www.radio666.com

Tormentor Radio Show
tormentor@free.fr
tormentor.free.fr
Dark, electro, industrial.

Germany

Black Channel Radio Show
info@blackchannel.org
www.blackchannel.org
Bringing you the world of Wave, Gothic, Industrial, Dark Techno, Electro, Ritual, Experimental, Ambient, Synthie and Avangarde!

Dead or Alive
www.r1live.de
Darkwave & Gothic radio.

The Underground Society
www.undergroundsociety.de

World of Decay
decay242@hotmail.com
www.radiodecay.de
The best radio show in the s/w of Germany.

Italy

Chain the Door Radio Show
radio@chaindlk.com
www.chaindlk.com
This show represents our true and sincere commitment to the scene as well as an attempt to give bands and labels as much exposure as possible. We hope that bands will appreciate having yet another way to promote their music through the Chain D.L.K. web-portal & related network and we invite anybody willing to be played to get in touch with us through the contact page.

Radio Blackout
maurito@autistici.org
www.ecn.org/blackout

The Netherlands

Gruis
martijnvangessel@yahoo.com
www.acu.nl/gruis
A dance night that takes place every two months in the former Auto Centrale Utrecht. Featured are industrial, electro, neofolk, industrial, darkwave and experimental sounds. We strive to promote talented, not well-known artists.

Spain

La Hora Muerta *(The Dead Hour)*
Rafa Cros lahoramuerta@hotmail.com
www.darksites.com/souls/goth/lahoramuerta
Dark radio show in Spanish played weekly at industrialradio.net: Goth, industrial, ebm etc...
P.O.Box 5138, 31010 Baranain, SPAIN

United Kingdom

Hidden Sanctuary Radio
darkcellmusic@cableinet.co.uk
www.darkcelldigitalmusic.net
The station provides a diversity of Gothic, Ethereal, Alternative and Electronic musicians who excel in their art. From this page you will experience the music of some of the most accomplished artists in the world.

Radio Free Abattoir
sam@slaghuis.net
www.slaghuis.net
*Featuring the best *new* Gothic, Darkwave, & Industrial music. Also a track of the week All previously featured tracks can be found in the mp3 archive.*

Australia

Blood & Black Dahlias Radio Show
dekript@hotmail.com
www.users.on.net/placebo/blackdahlias
www.threedradio.com
A diverse range of music from Gothic, Industrial, Darkwave, Dark Ambient and related genres.

Darkwings Radio Show
www.rtrfm.com.au
For all your industrial and gothic wants.

Dawntreader
www.rtrfm.com.au
Post-punk, pre-pop tack, industrial and more.

Infectious Unease Radio Show
www.infectiousunease.com
One of the things I enjoy the most about being involved in radio is my ability to promote bands and labels worldwide. There is nothing I enjoy more that seeing a relatively unknown band rise to fame as a result of my assistance with label contacts.

Sacrament *2RRR*
info@sacramentradio.org
www.sacramentradio.org
Gothic Music & Information programme.

Hip Hop Radio

Hip Hop, Rap, Soul and R&B

Radio Promoters

Mo' Better Music
mobettermusic@earthlink.net
www.mobettermusic.com
A National Marketing and Promotion company that specializes in retail, radio and video. Our company will give your product the exposure and promotional support it needs to be successful. For results that are demanded in this business, look no further.

Insomniac
insom@mindspring.com
www.insomniacmagazine.com
If you have a quality hip hop release we can help get it play on radio stations nationally.

Shocksoundpromotions.com
shocksoundpromo@yahoo.com
www.shocksoundpromotions.com
A national radio and media promotion agency focusing on urban music. We can introduce new singles and albums to over 1000 radio outlets, as well as focus on 'street' promotion, taking your music right to the buyers via clubs, concerts or other key events.

Stations and Shows

United States

African New Dawn *WRSU*
shortmary@ureach.com
newdawnradio.freeservers.com
Our musical focus on the music influenced by the African & African-American Diaspora (such as rap, soul, house, jazz, funk, hip-hop, reggae, soca, blues, r&b etc. We also extend interviews to new, unknown, un(der) exposed and established music artists.

Basmentalism.com
us@basementalism.com
www.basementalism.com
We are an independent on-line / on-air Hip Hop radio show from Colorado.

The Bassment Online Radio
spider@thebassment.com
www.thebassment.com
Send us your music!

Black Urban Contemporary *WHRB*
mail@whrb.org
www.whrb.org/buc
BUC programming is one of the best places on the radio to here the Hip-Hop, R&B, Classic Soul and Reggae that you want. A crucial component of WHRB's diverse programming BUC has been servicing the community for over twenty years.

blackmusicamerica.com
www.blackmusicamerica.com
The new online epicentre emanating music, information, culture and entertainment for the Black community and those interested in that culture.

BlakeRadio.com
Comments@BlakeRadio.com
www.blakeradio.com
Our first channel that we launched with was Music Massage that is dedicated to R&B, JAZZ, SOUL and REGGAE slow jams 24/7 streaming through Live 365. After the planets positive response to the 24-hour Slow Jam channel, BlakeRadio.com gave birth to the webcasts Mahogany Sunshine, Kids Café, Joyful Noise and Rainbow Soul.

Blue Fortune.com
Ken Kinds ettico0513@yahoo.com
www.blue-fortune.com
An artist community that promotes independent hip hop and electronic music through our website and a radio station.

Boombastic Radio
thedjs@boombasticradio.com
www.boombastic.org
An experiment to discover whether there is an audience for diverse, quality, ad-free music on the internet. Funk, soul, jazz, hip hop, Latin...

bringthenoise.com
info@bringthenoise.com
www.bringthenoise.com
Featuring live feeds, artist interviews and news.

Change up the Groove Radio Show *WCBE*
music@wcbe.org
www.wcbe.org
An hour of acid jazz, jungle, hip-hop, trip-hop, drum 'n' bass, new-school breaks and big beat. Wicked!

Chocolate City
garth.trinidad@kcrw.org
www.kcrw.org
Smooth, creamy mix of urban rhythm and soul, hosted by DJ Garth Trinidad.

CM Fam-a-Lam Show *WKCR*
american@wkcr.org
www.columbia.edu/cu/wkcr
The place to listen to hip-hop in New York City.

Dedicated *WNUR*
dj3rdrail@dj3rdrail.com
dj3rdrail.com/main.htm
www.wnur.org
A tribute to those who lost their lives; those who are dedicated in their lives and those who continue to represent HipHop.

The Fresh Connection *KPSU*
Music Director kpsumd@mail.pdx.edu
www.kpsu.org
Portland's hottest Hip Hop show!

Hip Hop BeOnAir.com
hiphop.beonair.com

Hip Hop Central *WFCS*
trees@undergroundhiphop.com
www.hiphopcentral.cjb.net
We are always looking for unsigned or underground artists to help promote. If you are interested in getting radio airplay, all you have to do is email Rob Reilly at DJTrees2000@hotmail.com with the words 'Radio Airplay' as the subject.

Hip Hop TV
hipmedia@attbi.com
hiphoptv.com
The all urban 24 hr TV network featuring all your favourite mainstream Hip Hop artist and underground Indie artist. Featuring music videos and exclusive CD listening parties.

Ill Noiz Network
info@illnoiz.com
www.illnoiz.com
Spinning the best in Reggae, Hip Hop and Soul.

Jaywhy.com
jaywhy101@aol.com
www.jaywhy.com
Hip Hop that'll knock your fuckin' teeth out!

KBXX Houston
www.kbxx.com
#1 for Hop Hop and R&B.

KFSR
kfsrfresno@hotmail.com
www.csufresno.edu/kfsr/Urbanhome.html
From underground hip-hop to r&b slow jams and special guest djs, every weekend, KFSR is the home to the best Urban music in Central California.

KJMM *Tulsa*
www.kjmm.com

KMEL *Oakland*
www.106kmel.com
Both Independent and mainstream music.

KPVU *Waller County, TX*
kpvu_fm@pvamu.edu
www.pvamu.edu/kpvu

K.T.O.P.FM
topspin@topsyte.com
www.topsyte.com
Seattle's only Hip-Hop Station in FM* Stereo!!!

KXHT *Memphis*
www.hot1071.com

Last Crate
dj3rdrail@dj3rdrail.com
dj3rdrail.com/main.htm
www.unifiedbeats.com
The longest running, radio friendly mix show in Chicago - 11 years and counting.

The Last Hip-Hop Radio Show
maxjeromeo@basically-hiphop.com
www.basically-hiphop.com/lastshow
An effort to create an alternative to the mediocrity to disposable mainstream programming that "programs you" into thinking that true hiphop is dead and fruitless.

LiquidSoulRadio.com
webmaster@liquidsoulradio.com
www.liquidsoulradio.com
We deliver an evolutionary online radio experience that crosses the vast array of musical genres of neo-soul, R&B, jazz and hip-hop. The liquid is what flows through you; the soul is what's inside of you; the radio is what you hear. Check out our "Independent Artist of the Week" feature.

Living Dangerously
djkalione@hotmail.com
djkali.50megs.com

Love Radio
tdavis@dr-love.com
www.dr-love.com
Dr. Love is a 40 year veteran of broadcasting and promotions. He has jump-started many radio stations across the country and now has his finger on the pulse of the New Millennium as a pioneer of Internet Broadcasting. Channels include Blues, R&B, Rap, Hiphop, World and Reggae.

Mic Check Radio Hip Hop Radio
djreadycee@mail.com
www.miccheckradio.com
Here you can network with other hip hop artists and entertainment related businesses, find links to audio gear, check out some past shows and pictures of the crew, or contact us to get your material played on the show.

Pleasuredome Radio
mail@pdomeradio.com
www.pdomeradio.com
There is so much good underground music out there that the masses never get to hear, due to the corporate politics of commercial radio. We are here to present the best underground music to the world.

RadioBlack.com
webmaster@blackradio.org
www.radioblack.com
A collective guide to radio stations around the world, with radio formats catering to the Black, Urban, African American market and fans there of.

Rapmusic.com
www.rapmusic.com
Check out our Underground Artist Section and submit your artist info and/or get on our Radio Show for free.

Sensimedia.net
admin@sensimedia.net
www.sensimedia.net
Reggae : Dancehall : Hiphop, Interviews, Mp3, Live Radio and more.

SimplyRadio.com
info@SimplyRadio.com
www.simplyradio.com
Home to Simply Underground Hip-Hop Radio broadcasting 24/7 around the clock.

smoothbeats.com
feedback@smoothbeats.com
www.smoothbeats.com
Streaming non-stop beats 24 hours a day.

The SOL of HIPHOP Radio
www.solofhiphop.com
Streamin' live every Friday 4-7 PM pst.

Soul 24-7.com
www.soul24-7.com
Internet radio station, aims to bridge the gap between creators and consumers of soul music.

Sunday Night Jams *KTXT*
ktxtfm@yahoo.com
www.ktxt.net
The #1 rated, longest running Urban Show in Lubbock!!

The Underground Railroad
jsmooth@hiphopmusic.com
www.hiphopmusic.com
We deliver the finest in Hip Hop music and culture every Saturday night at midnight on WBAI 99.5 FM in New York.

Vibes3000
www.vibes3000.com
We play all reggae from Old School Roots & Dub to Modern Dancehall. With Foundation Dancehall, Digital Dub & Lovers Rock being covered as well.

WFNK
wfnk@wfnk.com
wfnk.com/radio
Three high-quality audio channels covering every aspect of alternative black music, broadcasting 24-7 around the globe.

WGGO *Washington D.C.*
mailbox@dcimaging.com
www.gogolive.com

WHCR *City College of New York*
whcr903fm@yahoo.com
www.whcr.org

WJPZ *Syracuse U.*
www.z89.com
The only station in America bringing you seven "LIVE" weekend mixshows with everything u want and everything u need!!

WKXN *Greenville, AL*
wkxn@wkxn.com
www.wkxn.com
Hop Hop, Gospel and R&B.

WMOC Radio
info@mocradio.com
www.mocradio.com
You can expect nothing less than top notch quality music from all our DJ's from R&B to Hip Hop to Old School to House Music.

WNAA *North Carolina A & T State U.*
wnaalive.ncat.edu

ZJAMZ.com
programming@zjamz.com
www.zjamz.com
Record companies or artists, if you want your music played on ZJAMZ.com, E-Mail us the artist name and track title in MP3 format. Unsigned artists, just E-Mail us the song in MP3 Format with Artist Name and Track Title to unsigned@zjamz.com If you would like to send the actual CD or promotional items let us know in your E-Mail.

Canada

The Lounge
thelounge@lycos.com
listen.to/thelounge

The Wax Jungle
www.interlog.com/~bmellow/main.htm
watserv1.uwaterloo.ca/~ckmsinfo
The show focuses on hip-hop and r&b beats.

France

Skyrock
www.skyrock.com

Germany

hr XXL
xxl@hr-online.de
www.hr-xxl.de

Italy

Radio Centro Suono
centrosuono@radiocentrosuono.it
www.radiocentrosuono.it

Norway

The National Rapshow
tp@teeproductions.com
www.teeproductions.com
Send us your music/demo for possible review or airplay.

Sweden

P3 Hip-Hop
musik.p3@sr.se
www.sr.se/p3/hiphop
Timbuktu & Dj Amato bring you fat beats, rhymes & life on Swedish P3, who finally started broadcasting Live on the Internet. Yall need to peep this, because it's slammin! Nuff said!

Planet Follo
planetfollo@hawkmanimportz.com
www.hawkmanimportz.com
The show is hosted by Hawk & Bølla, giving you the latest hiphop-joints, new demos, competitions + more...

Switzerland

BoomBox.net
www.boombox.net
Send us your private mix tapes and live-shows on Cassette, MiniDisc or DAT! After listening to your material we can place it in our archive among the other crews.

United Kingdom

BBC 1Xtra
1Xtra@bbc.co.uk
www.bbc.co.uk/1xtra

Choice FM
www.choicefm.net
Welcome to the future of Urban music radio & culture.

Australia

The Mothership Connection *2SER Sydney*
Mark Pollard   editor@stealthmag.com
www.2ser.com
Sydney's longest running hip hop show. Tuesdays 2pm to 4pm.

New Zealand

The World-Famous True School Hip Hop Show
www.95bfm.co.nz
The phattest coverage of local and international hip hop. Less commercial and more underground flava.

South Africa

CBFM
info@cbfm.co.za
www.cbfm.co.za
South African community radio with online live broadcast. Has regular hiphop shows, try Sunday nights with the Mozambique-born dj Santo.

YFM
Craig@yfm.co.za
www.yfm.co.za

Jazz/Blues/Folk Radio

I have combined Jazz, Folk and Blues Radio because on most of the NPR and other community stations, there is at least one show that caters to each of the three genres.

North America

United States

Promoters

Lisa Reedy Promotions
Lisa Reedy reedylm@aol.com
www.jazzpromotion.com
A full-service radio promotions company that specializes in Jazz and related music. Solicits airplay, charting, interviews and other special promotions for artists & labels.

Internet Radio and Syndicated Shows

Acoustic Café
request@acafe.com
www.acafe.com
Each week, we air two hours of great stuff from some of the best singer-songwriters in the business, including rare acoustic cuts, classic tracks, plus exclusive, live in-studio interviews and performances each week.

Acoustic Electric Radio Show
FolkDude@aol.com
members.aol.com/folkdude/acouecle.html
A weekly radio program featuring all kinds of acoustic music, with a particular focus on contemporary singer/songwriters and acoustic instrumental music. The show features frequent in-studio performance/interviews with artists...

All that Jazz Radio
Brian Parker parker@jazz-radio.fm
www.jazz-radio.fm
On-line 24 HOURS A DAY with the Best Jazz on the Net.

Alligator Radio
info@allig.com
www.alligator.com
Internet station hosted by the blues label of the same name.

Bad Dog Blues Radio Show *WITR*
www.modernmusicandmore.com
Broadcast live from WITR 89.7 based out of the Rochester Institute of Technology in Rochester, NY.

Beale Street Caravan
info@bealestreetcaravan.com
www.bealestreetcaravan.com
The world's most popular Blues radio program. Styled in a magazine format, the Caravan is aired weekly on over 280 public, community and college radio stations nationwide. It can be heard in Europe on NPR Worldwide's 24 Hour schedule.

Big Band Jump
Don Kennedy don@bigbandjump.com
www.bigbandjump.com
A two-hour weekly radio program of Big Bands and Vocalists of yesterday and today, featuring both original and later Swing music, with background information. Now in its fifteenth year of syndication, heard on nearly 200 radio stations.

Blue Icewater Radio
smilestir@blueicewater.cjb.net
www.blueicewater.cjb.net
Plays an eclectic blend of swampy, jazzy, rock, acoustic and spiritual blues. My main goal is to present some of the hidden gems known as independent artists. I have found and continue to find, many talented artists from all around the world, just waiting to be heard.

The Blue Zone
thoeppne@aol.com
bluezone.org
A venue for Blues Bands and Musicians to promote their music.

Blues.Net Radio
jim@blues.net
www.blues.net
Send us your CDs for national airplay.

Celtic Connections

celtic@siu.edu

www.celticconnectionsradio.org

Each week you can count on hearing the finest selections from new releases as well as from Celtic classics. We also offer occasional concert performances, recorded exclusively for Celtic Connections, along with original interviews with some of the top names in the Celtic music world.

Celtic Grove Radio

crange@celticgrove.com

www.celticgrove.com

We endeavor to bring you the best Celtic radio programming on the Internet. If you have a suggestion please email us and let us know what you think!

Continental Drift *WNUR*

www.wnur.org/drift

Roots and folk music of cultures around the world.

ElectricBlues Radio

Herm@ElectricBluesRadio.com

web.tampabay.rr.com/ebradio

Sizzlin' Electric Blues Guitar.

The Electric Croude *WCVE*

www.wcve.org

Some of the best CDs I've aired come from so-called unknowns; I like to support indie music. If your music fits, I'll use it. Not concerned about who you played with or having tracks 'recommended'—90% of the time its different from what I choose. Send music to: George Maida, 88.9fm WCVE, 23 Sesame Street, Richmond, VA 23235 USA Attn: The Electric Croude

The Folk Sampler

MikeFlynn@FolkSampler.com

folksampler.com

Folk, traditional, bluegrass and blues, coming to you from the foothills of the Ozark Mountains. It is a radio program of songs that tell honest stories of the people who write and sing them.

FolkScene

folkscene@folkscene.com

www.folkscene.com

A program of traditional and contemporary music. The program features live music, interviews, remote recordings and the finest in recorded music.

GidaFOLK

multithd@hotmail.com

gida.tzo.net/RadioDB

Many artists say that just because a song is acoustic that people call it folk. A folk song is usually considered a song that has some type of moral message in it. This station is going to play whatever sounds good even if it only some-what fits the genre.

Grassy Hill Radio

radio@grassyhill.org

radio.grassyhill.org

Committed to helping listeners discover excellent new music from around North America and the rest of the planet. That means going beyond the "usual suspects" and well known artists and streaming lots of lesser known and self released songs.

Highlander Radio

webmaster@celticradio.net

www.CelticRadio.net

We broadcast a wide range of Celtic music 24 hours day! From a lone piper playing amazing grace in the Highlands of Scotland, to the latest Celtic rock bands

Hober Radio

John@hober.com

hober.com

The music should be hand played, without augmentation. A Hober band is people who could walk up to each other with their instruments in the middle of a field and just play their stuff.

Hudson River Sampler

www.wamc.org/hurisam.html

Each Saturday from 8 to 10:30 pm Wanda Fischer hosts a program of the very best folk music, bluegrass and blues.

Internet Folk Festival

feedback@internetfolkfestival.com

www.internetfolkfestival.com

If you are a performer and would like to have your music considered for airplay on the Internet Folk Festival, please send your CDs and information to us.

Jazz After Hours

jim@jazzafterhours.org

www.jazzafterhours.org

A late night jazz radio show hosted by Jim Wilke. Like the last set at a jazz club, the mood is mellow, but not without surprises. New and well-established jazz artists regularly drop in for a chat and the music ranges from latest releases to jazz classics.

Jazz with Bob Parlocha

bob@jazzwithbobparlocha.com

www.jazzwithbobparlocha.com

Our accent is on information about jazz recordings, publications, musicians and live gigs.

JAZZMUSIQUE

jeff@netmusique.com

www.netmusique.com

JazzSet

Dee Dee Bridgewater jazzset@npr.org

www.npr.org/programs/jazzset

An award-winning weekly jazz radio series presenting today's artists in exciting, recent performances from stages around the world.

Jazztrax Studio

info@jazztrax.com

www.jazztraxstudio.com

What is heard here is simply the very best songs, from the very best smooth jazz albums. Not tested, not consulted, no necessarily familiar. Just, the very best songs found in the Jazztrax Studio.

New Orleans Radio

info@neworleansradio.com

www.neworleansradio.com

Created to produce and deliver regional custom music, information and original programming to the global Internet community.

NPR Jazz

nprjazz@npr.org

www.nprjazz.org

Find a station near you that plays Jazz.

Out O' the Blue Radio Revue

Page@PageWilson.com

www.pagewilson.com

www.wcve.org

This program is a musical tapestry for styles and artists under-represented on both non-commercial and commercial airwaves. There was no existing Purebred American Mongrel radio format, so we made it up. Diversity is the key to the concept.

Quietmusic.com

nick@quietmusic.com

www.quietmusic.com

Smooth jazz.

Radio Celtic International

web2.airmail.net/samhradh

Find the station that fits your mood exactly. All you need is an Internet connection.

radiowayne

Wayne Greene radiowayne@att.net

www.radiowayne.com

Internet radio station radiowayne plays a folk and more formats on Live365.com. Currently in its 4th year of broadcasting radiowayne plays an eclectic mix of folk, singer/songwriter, acoustic, swing, blues, bluegrass, Cajun, country and whatever else seems appropriate.

Renradio

rengeek@renradio.com

renradio.com

Our goal is to capture the music and spirit of Renaissance and Celtic Festivals. If you are an artist or know some that might like to be played on Renradio you can send a CD directly to me via snail mail. Visit our site for the address. Please include a press kit if you have one or any background and contact information you feel would be helpful.

Roots and Wings

Philly Markowitz rootsandwings@toronto.cbc.ca

www.radio.cbc.ca/programs/roots

If you send music that is not appropriate for the show, I will try my best to find a good home for it within the CBC. If you've scanned the playlists and you're still not sure if your music is right for Roots & Wings, then please e-mail me first before sending your package.

SkyJazz Internet Radio

info@skyjazz.com

www.skyjazz.com

Hear great Jazz from new and undiscovered artists.

Smokestack Lightnin'

blues@worldramp.net

www.smokestacklightnin.com

Syndicated show playing Blues, Rhythm & Blues, Soul, Funk , Blues/Rock and Zydeco/Blues music.

Smoothjazz.com

music@smoothjazz.com.

www.smoothjazz.com

The Web hub for smooth jazz, an artful music format that incorporates elements of jazz, pop and r&b. For on-air consideration, record representatives may e-mail our music department.

WNJL.com

wnjl@wnjl.com

www.wnjl.com

The Home of Smooth Jazz On The Internet, live air staff broadcasting 24/7, with thousands of different artists and titles.

Woodsongs Old-Time Radio Hour

radio@woodsongs.com

www.woodsongs.com

You don't have to be famous to be on WoodSongs - you have to be good! The show is dedicated to introducing new, grassroots independent artists literally from around the world.

Alabama

Alabama Public Radio Evening Jazz
www.apr.org

WJAB *Alabama A&M U.*
ewashington@aamu.edu
www.aamu.edu/wjab

Alaska

Acoustic Accents
Bud Johnson info@acousticaccents.net
www.acousticaccents.net
Alaska's radio showcase for new acoustic music. Each week we feature some of the finest singer-songwriters and musicians on the planet. In addition to great music, our regular feature "Words and Music" provides in-depth interviews and songs from some of the best performers around.

KNIK *Anchorage*
info@knik.com
www.knik.com
Alaska's Home for Smooth Jazz.

Whole Wheat Radio
radio@talkeetna-alaska.com
www.wholewheatradio.org
We focus on independent musicians in the acoustic, folk, jazz, classical, bluegrass, singer-songwriter, swing, big-band, new-age, instrumental, blues, black-gospel, Alaskana, spoken word, humor and other adult genres. Visit our website for details on sending in your CDs or MP3s.

Arizona

KJZZ *Tempe*
mail@kjzz.org
www.kjzz.org

KYOT *Phoenix*
www.kyot.com
Smooth Jazz in Phoenix. Lots of known & unknown Jazz artists.

Arkansas

From Albion and Beyond *KUAR*
lholton@swbell.net
www.ualr.edu/kuar
home.swbell.net/lholton/fromalbionandbeyond.html
A weekly jaunt along the highways and by-ways of traditional, revival and contemporary folk music with a slight English accent.

KASU *Arkansas State U.*
kasu@astate.edu
www.kasu.org

California

The Annals of Jazz *KCSM*
www.kcsm.org
Since 1959, host Richard Hadlock has been improvising on historical themes and bringing forth worthy performers - from Armstrong to Zorn. Each Sunday, we may find annals in Europe, Asia, Latin America or Back of Town anywhere.

Capital Public Radio
npr@csus.edu
www.csus.edu/npr

Don't Get Trouble on Your Mind *KMUD*
md@kmud.org
www.kmud.org
With each show ED plays 25 or so Folk and Blues songs that he finds to be the best and most interesting that week. With commentary designed to inform, entertain and inspire.

Folk Music & Beyond
kalwfolk@eskimo.com
www.kalwfolk.org
Bringing you some of the best in contemporary folk, traditional and original music from America, England, Ireland, Scotland and other parts of the world.

FreeFall
David Bassin freefall@pacbell.net
www.geocities.com/davidbassin/freefall.html
A mix of future jazz, soul, abstract beats & world rhythms heard live on KUSF San Francisco, Tuesdays from 10pm-midnight PST.

In Your Ear *KPFA*
postmaster@kpfa.org
www.kpfa.org
Host Art Sato presents a cool fusion of jazz and Latin music, giving voice to musicians deserving wider recognition and showing that jazz and Afro-Caribbean music are separate, but "branches of the same tree".

Jazz Trax Syndicated Radio Show
jazztrax@jazztrax.com
www.jazztrax.com

KAAT *Oakhurst*
www.kaat.com
We'll keep you musically happy and bring you breaking news, frequent weather updates and specialty shows featuring local personalities.

KCBX *San Luis Obispo*
www.slonet.org/~ipkcbx
FM 90 provides news and cultural programming from National Public Radio and Public Radio International, as well as a wide selection of music and local public affairs programming.

KCLU *California Lutheran College*
www.kclu.org

KCSM *San Mateo*
info@kcsm.net
www.kcsm.org/jazz91.html

KCSN *California State U.*
www.kcsn.org

KEZL *Fresno*
www.smoothjazz967.com

KIFM *San Diego*
www.kifm.com

KJLH *Los Angeles*
www.kjlhradio.com
Los Angeles' premiere Adult Contemporary R&B station. To get your music played, call us to set up a Monday appointment (310) 330-2200. Your music must be on CD and available in record stores.

KKJZ *California State U.*
www.kkjz.org

KKSF *San Francisco*
www.kksf.com

KPFK *Los Angeles*
www.kpfk.org

KPOO *San Francisco*
info@kpoo.com
www.kpoo.com

KRVR *Modesto*
theriver@krvr.com
www.krvr.com

KSBR *Saddleback College*
www.ksbr.net

KSDS *San Diego*
www.ksds-fm.org

KTWV *Culver City*
wave@ktwv.cbs.com
www.947wave.com
You may submit your CD for review purposes to: Ralph Stewart, Assistant PD/Music Director, KTWV, 8944 Lindblade Street, Culver City, CA 90232.

KUOP *U. the Pacific*
www.csus.edu/npr/grid5.html

Music Along The Feather *KRBS*
krbs@cncnet.com
www.radiobirdstreet.org
Contemporary folk. bluegrass, country and new folk.

A Patchwork Quilt *KALW*
Kevin Vance kevin_vance@yahoo.com
www.kalw.org
A program of Celtic and other traditional music, American roots, singers and songwriters, interpreters and instrumentalists. Songs of sentiment and silliness, of things topical and timeless. We meet new friends and visit old ones.

Radio Sausalito
info@radiosausalito.org
www.radiosausalito.org
Every day we broadcast classic jazz 24 hours a day. In addition to the nonstop jazz, we feature several locally produced, jazz oriented programs every week.

Tony Palkovic's Jazz Show *KSPC*
TPJazzShow@cs.com
www.fortunecity.com/tinpan/lute/484
www.kspc.org
A mix of Jazz-Fusion, Straight Ahead and Latin. Featuring Live performances and guest interviews with Grammy Award artists as well as local LA musicians.

Wild River Radio *KMUD*
md@kmud.org
www.kmud.org
Sometimes you can hear independent new folk artists, sequenced in a string of social/political themes.

Colorado

KAJX *Aspen*
music@kajx.org
www.kajx.org

KCME
kcmeinfo@oldcolo.com
www.kcme.org

KUNC *U. Northern Colorado*
mailbag@kunc.org
www.kunc.org

KUVO *Denver*
info@kuvo.org
www.kuvo.org

Connecticut

AcousticConnections
graham@wshu.org
www.wshu.org/acoustic
*A weekly program of acoustic music, including folk,
Celtic and bluegrass, hosted by Walt Graham.*

The Blues Bus Depot *WHUS*
Dave Carpenter davecarp@cox.net
members.cox.net/bluesbus

Parlour Sessions *WKZE*
info@wkze.com
www.wkze.com/parlour.html
www.wkze.com
*Live broadcast performances held monthly at the
beautiful WKZE studios in Sharon, Connecticut.
Guests include well-known musicians and not so well-
known but emerging artists.*

Profiles in Folk
winters@wshu.org
www.wshu.org/profiles
*As the show's title conveys, the program profiles the
topic or the performers featured. At least ten shows
each year feature live, in-studio showcases by
performers, with interviews.*

Florida

WDNA *Miami*
joe@wdna.org
www.wdna.org
*Our mission: is to share the many sides of jazz music
with everyone.*

WFIT *Florida Tech*
wfit@fit.edu
www.fit.edu/CampusLife/clubs-org/wfit

WKGC *Gulf Coast Community College*
www.wkgc.org

WLOQ *Orlando*
www.wloq.com
*CD Reviews-'Smooth Jazz' shows all day, about town
tours and much more.*

WLRN *Miami*
info@wlrn.org
www.wlrn.org

WSJT *Tampa*
wsjt.com
CD Reviews, concerts, interviews.

WUCF *U. Central Florida*
wucf.ucf.edu

WUFT *U. Florida*
radio@wuft.org
www.wuft.org/fm

WUWF *Pensacola*
wuwf@wuwf.org
wuwf.org

Georgia

Appalachian Trail Vaguely Folk Music Show
WUWG
Steve sedberry3@yahoo.com
www.geocities.com/sedberrysteve/radio.html
Send us your promotional material and recordings.

The Green Island Radio Show *WSVH*
Harry O'Donoghue wsvhirish@earthlink.net.
www.wsvh.org/giarchive.htm
www.wsvh.org
Features the very best Irish and Celtic music.

The Jazz Spot *Georgia Public Radio*
Masani jazz@gpb.org
www.gpb.org/gpr/jazzspot
*A four-hour blend of mainstream and progressive
contemporary impressions of jazz music. From bop
and beyond, The Jazz Spot will the keep the vibe alive
with great music and information worthy of the true
jazz aesthetic.*

WBCX
J. Scott Fugate JAZZevangelist@aol.com
*I have been attempting to help promote and support
local musicians within the jazz continuum for the last
few years. I manage a radio station that does play,
promote and support independent artists from
throughout the Southeast - Gainesville/NE Atlanta
GA.*

WCLK *Clark Atlanta U.*
www.wclk.com

WWGC *The State U. West Georgia*
wwgc@westga.edu
www.westga.edu/~wwgc

Idaho

BSU Radio Network *Boise State U.*
radio.boisestate.edu
Radio Vision and Idaho's Jazz Station.

Iowa

KUNI's Folk Music
www.kuniradio.org/kufolk.html
*Enjoy two hours of traditional and contemporary
acoustic music, folk tunes and dance music from
around the world.*

Saturday Night Jazz
www.kwit.org
*Host Eddie Dunn plays almost entirely new or
recently re-issued material.*

Illinois

The Midnight Special
folk@midnightspecial.org
www.midnightspecial.org

WBEZ *Chicago*
www.wbez.org

WDCB *Glen Ellyn*
www.cod.edu/wdcb
*We're known for our eclectic music programming.
Lots of jazz plus other styles.*

WGLT *Illinois State U.*
wglt@ilstu.edu
www.wglt.org

WILL *U. Illinois*
www.will.uiuc.edu
*Our television and radio programs teach, entertain
and draw people into the public affairs of the places
they live and work. Send us your classical, jazz and
traditional/ethnic music.*

Indiana

The Back Porch *WVPE*
www.wvpe.org
The best of Folk and Bluegrass.

WBAA AM *Purdue U.*
www.purdue.edu/wbaa

WFIU *Indiana U.*
wfiu@indiana.edu
www.indiana.edu/~wfiu

WTPI *Indianapolis*
www.wtpi.com

WSND *U. Notre Dame*
wsnd@nd.edu
www.nd.edu/~wsnd

WVPE *Elkhart*
wvpe@wvpe.org
www.wvpe.org
*The Blues Revue is entering its 17th year on WVPE.
Hosted and produced by Harvey Stauffer. The Back
Porch is produced by Norm Mast and co-hosted by
Norm Mast and Al Kniola.*

Iowa

KALA *St.Ambrose U.*
kala@sau.edu
galvin.sau.edu/kala.html

KBSU/KBSW *Boise State U.*
radio.boisestate.edu

KCCK *Kirkwood Community College*
www.kcck.org

KHKE *U. Northern Iowa*
kuni@uni.edu
www.khke.org

KUNI *U. Northern Iowa*
kuni@uni.edu
www.kuniradio.org

WOI *Iowa State U.*
WOI@iastate.edu
www.woi.org

Kansas

Jazz in the Night *U. Kansas*
dbrogdon@ku.edu
kanu.ukans.edu

KMUW *Wichita State U.*
info@kmuw.org
www.kmuw.org

KRPS *Pittsburgh State U.*
www.krps.org

Kentucky

WKMS *Murray State U.*
wkms@murraystate.edu
www.wkms.org

WMKY *Morehead State U.*
wmky@moreheadstate.edu
www.morehead-st.edu/wmky

WNKU *Northern Kentucky U.*
wnku@nku.edu
www.wnku.org

Louisiana

KEDM *Northeast Louisiana U.*
www.kedm.org

KRVS *U. Southern Louisiana*
admin@krvs.org
www.krvs.org

Music in the Glen *WWOZ*
Sean O'Meara wwoz@wwoz.org
www.wwoz.org/volunteers/dj_sean_o_meara.html
www.wwoz.org
Irish music show.

WBRH *Baton Rouge*
www.baton-rouge.com/wbrh

WWOZ *New Orleans*
wwoz@wwoz.org
www.wwoz.org

Maine

Jigs, Hoedowns and Songs O'Tragedy *WMHB*
wmhb@colby.edu
www.colby.edu/wmhb

Us Folk *WMPG*
Chris ctdarlin@maine.rr.com
www.wmpg.org
Us as in "you and me". Roots, folk messages woven into the ballads keeping regular folk tuned in! Local, National and International folks doing the folk thing. Many live-in studio performance, live recorded material, both "vintage" and the newest of folk from independent folk artists from around the country and around the globe!

Maryland

Detour
tonysica@aol.com
www.charm.net/~dirtylin/detour.html
Detour has been on the air for over 14 years in a variety of time slots, currently 5 to 7 PM on Sunday. The show is an eclectic blend of folk and world music.

WHFC *Harford Community College*
WHFC@harford.edu
www.harford.cc.md.us/Department/WHFC/main.htm

The Folk Tradition *WKAR*
Bob Blackman blackman@wkar.org
wkar.org/folktradition
The range of music includes traditional folk songs, Celtic tunes, bluegrass, acoustic blues, gospel, Cajun and Zydeco and much more.

Friday Night Jazz *WKAR*
Doug Collar jazz@wkar.org
wkar.org/fridaynightjazz
An offering of recorded jazz, sampling old standards and new releases.

WTMD *Towson U.*
wtmd@towson.edu
www.towson.edu/wtmd

WYPR *Johns Hopkins U.*
www.wypr.org

Massachusetts

A Celtic Sojourn *WGBH*
feedback@wgbh.org
www.wgbh.org
Native Irishman Brian O'Donovan spins traditional and contemporary music from the Celtic countries and England.

The Acoustic Café *WMUA*
www.wmuacafe.com
It has been hosted by Lee Larcheveque since 1998. It features music by independent singer-songwriters, contemporary folk and acoustic pop.

Against The Grain *WICN*
david@wicn.org
www.wicn.org
The best in folk, blues, traditional and alternative country, roots, world music, traditional and good old rock n' roll!

Celtic Twilight *WUMB*
wumb@umb.edu
www.wumb.org
Contemporary and traditional music from the British Isles, including a cultural calendar and ceili segment.

Contemporary Cafe *WICN*
Nick DiBiasio nickdibiasio@yahoo.com
www.angelfire.com/nd/satnight
www.wicn.org
The best in contemporary and traditional folk, Americana, acoustic blues, interviews and live in-studio performances by local and national acoustic performers.

The Fiddle & the Harp *WOMR*
Dinah Mellin dinah164@capecod.net
www.womr.org
A hearty mix of Irish, Scottish and Canadian Maritime music with Celtic influenced American music.

The Folk Heritage *WGBH*
feedback@wgbh.org
www.wgbh.org
Each week, Dick Pleasants, host of The Folk Heritage, offers an afternoon of new and traditional folk music by local and national musicians, as well as acoustic performances and interviews with influential folk artists.

Folk Image Radio
jeff@folkimage.com
www.folkimage.com
Playing the best melodic roots music since 1977!

Jazz Safari *WFCR*
Kari Njiiri kari@wfcr.org
www.wfcr.org/jsafari.html
A journey through the international jazz world, with an emphasis on African, Afro-Latin, Afro-Caribbean and other international jazz styles.

Valley Folk *WFCR*
Susan Forbes Hansen folk@wfcr.org
www.wfcr.org/vfolk.html
We celebrate the wonderful variety found under, around and squeezing out the sides of the music labeled "folk". Listeners may hear guest performances, recorded concerts and selections from local, national and international musicians.

WBUR *Online Arts*
Bill Marx bmarx@wbur.bu.edu
www.wbur.org
www.publicbroadcasting.net/wbur/arts.artsmain
An arts show that covers the local Boston Music scene.

WFCR *Amherst*
radio@wfcr.org
www.wfcr.org

WGBH *Boston*
www.wgbh.org/wgbh/radio

WHRB *Harvard U.*
www.whrb.net

WICN *Worcester*
www.wicn.org
Many hours of jazz, cd release parties and more!

WJJW *Massachusetts College*
www.mcla.mass.edu/web/life/wjjw.html

WUMB *Umass Boston*
wumb@umb.edu
www.wumb.org

Michigan

Folk Aire *WNMC*
www.wnmc.org
We attempt to represent all quality musicians, with a very broad definition of "Folk". In other words, we don't care how famous our artists are (yet) - we just want to play good music! We can honestly say you will most often hear something here first, before any other station in our listening area has even thought about playing it.

Nightside *WCMU*
Jamie Lynn Gilbert cmuradio@cmich.edu
www.cmuradio.cmich.edu/nightside.html
www.cmuradio.cmich.edu
Your source for jazz and blues in central and northern Michigan. Artists/Labels submit your music for airplay.

WDET *Wayne State Univesity*
wdetfm@wdetfm.org
www.wdetfm.org

WEMU *Eastern Michigan U.*
wemu@wemu.org
www.wemu.org

WGVU *Grand Rapids*
wgvu@gvsu.edu
www.wgvu.org/radio

WLNZ *Lansing Community College*
www.lcc.edu/wlnz

Minnesota

Great Blend of Watercolors *KFAI*
deelin1@juno.com
www.kfai.org/programs/watercol.htm
Dee Henry Williams is on a mission to bring you the best breakfast music in the Twin Cities. Listen to Great Blend of Watercolors every Saturday morning for Jazz, Blues, Rhythm & Blues, great interviews and mo' fun.

KBEM *Minneapolis*
kbem@mpls.k12.mn.us
www.jazz88fm.com

KUMD *U. Minnesota*
KUMD@d.umn.edu
www.kumd.org

Rollin & Tumblin *KFAI*
www.kfai.org
My program focuses on the female perspective in blues and jazz. This radio show is a synthesis of the two sounds, blues and big band. Rollin and Tumblin swings, jumps and has moved listeners for the past 7 years.

Thirsty Boots *WTIP*
wtip@boreal.org
wtip.org
Three hours of the best in folk, bluegrass, Americana and Celtic music!

Urban Folk *KFAI*
johngron@hotmail.com
www.kfai.org/programs/urb_folk.htm
Bringing you the gritty edge of contemporary folk music along with plenty of forays into bluegrass, blues, traditional folk and international roots music. Urban Folk occasionally hosts musicians live in KFAI's studio.

Mississippi

WJSU *Jackson State U.*
wjsufm@jsums.edu
ccaix.jsums.edu/~edlga/wjsu

WUSM *U. Southern Mississippi*
wusm@usm.edu
www-dept.usm.edu/~wusm

Missouri

KSMU *Springfield*
ksmu@smsu.edu
www.ksmu.smsu.edu

Sunday Morning Coffeehouse *KOPN*
Steve Jerrett sjerrett@coin.org
www.geocities.com/soho/suite/3807
The best in folk and acoustic music including traditional folk, bluegrass, country, Celtic and singer-songwriter expressions of the ever-evolving folk process.

WSIE *Edwardsville*
www.siue.edu/WSIE

Montana

The Folk Show *KUFM*
www.kufm.org
A potpourri of folk music from around the world, as well as special thematic programs.

Nebraska

KIOS *Omaha*
www.kios.org

Nevada

KUNV *U. Nevada, Las Vegas*
kunv.unlv.edu

New Hampshire

NHPR Folk Show
www.nhpr.org
Three hours of traditional and contemporary acoustic and folk music.

WEVO *Concord*
www.nhpr.org

New Jersey

The Legacy Program *WTSR*
wtsrlegacy1@cs.com
www.trenton.edu/~wtsr
Supplying the area with the best and brightest in Folk and New World Music. Often guest musicians are brought down to the studio to perform on the show.

Music You Can't Hear On the Radio *WPRB*
John Weingart VerySeldom@aol.com
www.veryseldom.com
www.wprb.com
Folk music, string band music, bluegrass, blues and humor.

Tree and Root
host@wdvrfm.org
www.wdvrfm.org/treeandroot1.html
From the newest groups to the traditional styles from which they grew, Tree and Root plays a variety mix of Celtic artists from America and Canada as well as from Scotland, Ireland and England.

WBGO *Newark*
www.wbgo.org

WBJB *Brookdale Community College*
comments@wbjb.org
www.wbjb.org

New Mexico

KGLP *Gallup*
kglp@kglp.org
www.kglp.org

KRWG *New Mexico State U.*
krwgfm@nmsu.edu
www.krwgfm.org

New York

A Thousand Welcomes *WFUV*
Kathleen Biggins kathleenbiggins@wfuv.org
www.wfuv.org/wfuv/kathleen.html
www.wfuv.org
Celtic traditional music. By providing information about these concerts, inviting musicians into the studio to talk about their new releases and interviewing dance teachers and other members of the Celtic population, A Thousand Welcomes has steadily built up a reputation for providing a focus for these many different elements of the community.

Across the Tracks *WFDU*
Dave Grogan grogans@aol.com
wfdu.fm
Listen to our premier Blues formats every Monday through Friday. Our formats blend both classic Blues and Soul with new artists who perform in the traditional style.

Bound for Glory *WVBR*
www.publiccom.com/web/wvbr/bfg.html
Now, more than thirty years and a thousand concerts later, WVBR's Bound for Glory continues to provide free, live folk concerts on over thirty Sunday evenings per year.

Folk Plus *WJFF*
www.wjffradio.org/FolkPlus
The definition of folk music runs as wide as the difference in space between a living room and a stadium. Each week, I explore the music and artists that I call FOLK.

Folk, Rock & Roots
Andrew Tokash APTOKASH@AOL.COM
www.musicalmix.com
Radio show on WVKR (91.3FM) playing folk, alt.country, rock, blues, guitar instrumentals and roots rock from around the world.

The Folk Show *North Country Public Radio*
Mike Alzo folkshow@ncpr.org
www.northcountrypublicradio.org/programs/local/folk.html
www.northcountrypublicradio.org
Join host Mike Alzo each Friday afternoon from 3-5 pm for two hours of the best traditional and contemporary folk music.

Jazz on the Air
usbjazz@wusb.org
www.wusb.org/jazz
We attempt to showcase the best of the newest releases along with a firm foundation of the classic repertoire. This is usually augmented with artist interviews.

MusicAmerica *WFDU*
wfdu.fm
A blend of traditional American music forms. On the air since 1980, MusicAmerica embraces traditional and new Folk, Bluegrass, Blues, Cajun and Zydeco performances. The format is offered throughout the week with the greatest concentration found during the weekdays.

Nonesuch
nonesuch@wvbr.com
www.publiccom.com/web/wvbr/nonesuch.html
Send us a CD. We'll listen and if it fits our rather broad format, your CD will go into our music library. Occasionally, we invite musicians into the studio during the show to talk and play.

A Variety of Folk *WRUR*
wrur.rochester.edu

WAER *Syracuse*
waerfm88@mailbox.syr.edu
www.waer.org

WBFO *U. Buffalo*
mail@wbfo.org
www.wbfo.buffalo.edu

WEOS *Hobart and William Smith Colleges*
WEOS@hws.edu
www.weos.org

WGMC *Greece*
tony@yellowdog.com
wgmc.greeceny.org

WKCR *Columbia U.*
www.columbia.edu/cu/wkcr

WPBX *Long Island U.*
www.southampton.liunet.edu/stu_serv/radio/wliu

WQCD *New York City*
cd1019@cd1019.com
www.cd1019.com
CD reviews, live events and concert series.

WSKG/WSQX *Binghamton*
www.wskg.com/radiowskg.htm

North Carolina

Back Porch Music *WUNC*
WUNC@unc.edu
www.wunc.org
The longest continually running locally-produced program on WUNC. Each week, the program presents a wide range of acoustic-based folk music - from contemporary singer/songwriters to old-time musicians of the 20s and 30s and from classic Celtic to blues - and beyond.

Celtic Winds *WNCW*
info@wncw.org
www.wncw.org
It's two hours of Celtic music from around the world and around the corner. Rotating hosts Richard Beard, Tom Fellenbaum and Fox Watson also let you know of Celtic concerts and events around our listening area.

WFSS *Fayetteville*
wfss@uncfsu.edu
www.wfss.org

WSHA *Shaw College*
wsha@shawu.edu
www.wshafm.org

WZRU *Roanoke Rapids*
www.wzru.org
We're the Roanoke valley's and Southside Virginia's only commercial-free public radio station providing educational, cultural and fine-arts programming to area communities…

Ohio

Below the Salt *WOUB*
Keith Newman belowthesalt@woub.org
woub.org/belowthesalt
An eclectic mix of folk music.

Blues with Fitz *WCPN*
www.wcpn.org
Every Friday night, Michael "Fitz" Fitzpatrick hosts the best of the blues: acoustic and electricity, city and country. Fitz mixes the music he loves with his own inimitable, individual style.

Folk Music *Kent State U.*
letters@wksu.org
www.wksu.org/folk

Mama Jazz *Miami U.*
mamajazz@yahoo.com
www.wmub.org/mamajazz
A living legend of the local airwaves, Mama Jazz brings you the best in jazz from the classics to today. Mama also keeps you up to date with the latest in jazz events around the tri-state with the Jazz Calendar.

Potpourri *WYSO*
Ed Humphry ehumphrey@earthlink.net
www.wyso.org/wysopgs/potpour.html
www.wyso.org
Features a little bit of everything in the way of folk and acoustic music, focusing on contemporary acoustic music and traditional music from Appalachia to the Australian Outback.

WAPS *Akron*
www.wapsfm.com

WJZA *Columbus*
www.columbusjazz.com
Live Jazz Concerts listing, lots of jazz programming.

WKSU *Kent State U.*
www.wksu.kent.edu
Songwriters, Instrumentalists, Celtic, Bluegrass, Classics and a trip through music somewhere around the world each hour, each night, every weekend.

WMUB *Miami U.*
wmub@wmub.org
www.wmub.org

WNWV *Elyria*
thewave@wnwv.com
www.wnwv.com
Great jazz and local concert listings for the area.

WYSO *Antioch U.*
mail@wyso.org
www.wyso.org

WYSU *Youngstown State U.*
cervone@wysu.org
www.wysu.org

Oklahoma

Different Roads *KCSC*
Kent Anderson kanderson@kcscfm.com
www.kcscfm.com/programming/program_roads.asp
www.kcscfm.com
An hour-long weekly program devoted to folk-oriented acoustic music. Musical genres included in the program are traditional American and Celtic music, bluegrass, contemporary folk singer-songwriters, acoustic blues and some world music.

Folk Salad *KWGS*
kwgs.org/pgms/folksalad.html
kwgs.org
We are committed to bringing to KWGS listeners an eclectic mix of the very best of contemporary and traditional offerings in Folk, Americana and Singer-songwriter genres.

Oregon

KLCC *Eugene*
klcc@lanecc.edu
www.klcc.org

KMHD *Mt. Hood Community College*
www.kmhd.org

KMUN *Astoria*
kmun@seasurf.com
www.kmun.org

Pennsylvania

Acoustic Eclectic *WDIY*
FolkDude@aol.com
members.aol.com/folkdude/acouecle.html
All kinds of acoustic music, with a particular focus on contemporary singer/songwriters and acoustic instrumental music. The show features frequent in-studio performance/interviews with artists and is produced and hosted by Otto Bost.

An American Sampler *WYEP*
Ken Batista kbatista+@pitt.edu
www.wyep.org
Showcasing the best in new and classic folk music every Sunday morning.

The Saturday Light Brigade *WYEP*
slb@slbradio.com
www.slbradio.com
A radio program featuring acoustic music and family fun. It is one of the longest-running public radio programs in the U.S.

WDUQ *Duquesne U.*
info@wduq.org
www.wduq.org

WPSU *Pennsylvania State U.*
wpsu.psu.edu

WRTI *Temple U.*
www.wrti.net

WYEP *Pittsburgh*
info@wyep.org
www.wyep.org

Rhode Island

Traditions *WRIU*
folk@wriu.org
www.wriu.org
Since 1980, the place to hear new releases and find out what's happening in the world of folk & roots music.

South Dakota

KELO *Sioux Falls*
kelofm@midco.net
www.kelofm.com

KUSD *Vermillion*
www.sdpb.org/radio

Tennessee

WETS *East Tennessee State U.*
www.wets.org

WMOT *Murfreeboro*
wmot.org
All Jazz programming-all the time.

WUMR *U. Memphis*
www.people.memphis.edu/~wumrjazz

WUOT *U. Tennessee*
sunsite.utk.edu/wuot

WUTC *U. Tennessee*
www.wutc.org

Texas

Jazz etc. *KUT*
Jay Trachtenberg theloni760@aol.com
www.kut.org
The longest running jazz program on the Austin airwaves.

KACU *Abilene Christian U.*
www.kacu.org
A blend of easy listening, smooth jazz, new age and contemporary classics is heard every weekday from 9 a.m. to 4 p.m. and Saturday afternoons from 1-3.

KNTU *U. North Texas*
kntu@unt.edu
www.kntu.unt.edu

KPVU *Prairie View A&M U.*
www.pvamu.edu/kpvu

KTXK *Texarkana College*
www.tc.cc.tx.us/ktxk

KVLU *Lamar U.*
kvlu@hal.lamar.edu
dept.lamar.edu/kvlu

KWBU *Baylor U.*
www.kwbu.net/radio

Folkways *KUT*
David Obermann humbug@texas.net
www.kut.org
*A musical path that leads through the Blue Ridge
Mountains, Hill Country, Scottish Highlands and
beyond.*

Utah

KRCL *Salt Lake City*
musicdirector@krcl.org
www.krcl.org

KUER *U. Utah*
www.kuer.org

Sunday Sagebrush Serenade *KRCL*
www.krcl.org
*Folk and acoustic rock to ease you from your morning
cup of coffee through your Sunday afternoon.*

Thursday Breakfast Jam
Susanne Millsaps susanne365@aol.com
www.krcl.org/~susannem
www.krcl.org
*Morning drive-time show; folk, jazz, world, eclectic
mix. Signal covers most of Utah, parts of Idaho,
Wyoming & Nevada.*

Vermont

All the Traditions *Vermont Public Radio*
Robert Resnik rresnik@vpr.net
www.vpr.net/music/traditions.shtml
www.vpr.net

WNCS *Montpelier*
www.pointfm.com

The Folk Show *WWPV*
wwpv@smcvt.edu
personalweb.smcvt.edu/wwpv
*Almost 20 years on the air. Contemporary Folk,
Celtic, Blues and more.*

Virginia

Acoustic Café *WMRA*
wmra@jmu.edu
www.jmu.edu/wmra
*On any given night, the artists you hear on WMRA
can be found in coffee houses, smokey back rooms,
privately owned houses giving "house concerts",
college campuses and a few make it to the larger
places like coliseums and stadiums. However, they all
have one thing in common, a love for acoustic music
and a desire to share. WMRA has this love and desire
as well.*

Eclectic Hours *WEBR*
www.fcac.org/webr/webr.htm
Singer/Songwriter & Folk.

WJCD *Norfolk*
www.wjcd.com

WMRA *James Madison U.*
www.jmu.edu/wmra

Washington

Inland Folk *KWSU*
Dan Maher dmaher@wsu.edu
www.kpbx.org/programs/inlandfolk.htm
www.kpbx.org
*Rolling down the folk music road for two decades
with the music of local and national folk artists.*

KBCS *Bellevue Community College*
kbcs.fm
*Public radio specializing in Jazz, Folk and World
Music.*

KEWU *Eastern Washington U.*
www.kewu.ewu.edu

KPLU *Tacoma*
www.kplu.org

Sunday Brunch *KMTT*
www.kmtt.com
*Join Ruby Brown as she starts your Sunday gently
with selections from the lighter side of the music
library.*

Washington DC

Jazz Saturday Night *WAMU*
Rob Bamberger hotjazz@wamu.org
www.wamu.org/hotjazz
On the air for over 22 years.

SmoothJazz
www.smoothjazz1059.com

Traditions *WETA*
Mary Cliff traditions@weta.com
www.weta.org
*This Saturday night folk music program is known for
its breadth: a mix of traditional, revival, singer-
songwriter, ethnic, world and kitchen music, with a
strong emphasis on artists and performances in the
greater Washington area.*

WPFW
www.wpfw.org

Wisconsin

Simply Folk *Wisconsin Public Radio*
Judy Rose rosej@wpr.org
www.wpr.org/simplyfolk
*On the air since January 1979, Simply Folk brings
you concerts recorded here in Wisconsin ...songs for
the season... the music and dance of people the world
over.*

WOJB *Lac Courte Oreilles Ojibwa Community
College*
www.wojb.org

WPNE *Green Bay*
www.wpt.org

WUEC *U. Wisconsin/Eau Claire*
www.wpr.org

Canada

After Hours *CBC*
Ross Porter afterhours@winnipeg.cbc.ca
winnipeg.cbc.ca/afterhours
*We aim to speak to jazz lovers by entertaining,
informing and challenging. Jazz, Porter, Wilson and
Posen will tell you, is visceral, not intellectual. Most
importantly, it's not an elitist club with a restricted
membership.*

Café Jazz Radio Show
ted@jazzlynx.net
www.jazzlynx.net
*Artists from around the world look to Ted for his
genuine interest in their music and integrity to the
smooth jazz genre. He has always considered it a
personal privilege to expose and support new artists
from around the world.*

The Celtic Show *CKUA*
Andy Donnelly andy.donnelly@ckua.org
www.ckua.com
*Selections range from gentle traditional ballads to
hard-driving rock tunes complete with bagpipes.*

Coull Jazz *CKUA*
Bill Coull bill.coull@ckua.org
www.ckua.com
*Canada's premier jazz broadcaster Bill Coull blends
all eras of popular jazz into three hours of remarkable
radio.*

Don't Folk Around *CFBX*
radio@cariboo.bc.ca
www.thex.ca
Folk and worldbeat.

Escale Jazz *CBC*
André Vigeant escalejazz@montreal.radio-canada.ca
www.radio-canada.ca/url.asp?/radio/new_
affichage/emissions.asp?id=130
*On the menu of this supper hour jazz program are
new CD releases, musical biographies of great jazz
musicians, important anniversaries and profiles.*

Folk Oasis *CiTR*
folkoasis@canada.com
www.ams.ubc.ca/citr
*Roots music for folkies and non-folkies...bluegrass,
singer-songwriters, worldbeat, alt-country, polka and
more. Not a mirage!*

Folk Roots/Folk Branches *CKUT*
mike@ckutfolk.com
www.ckutfolk.com
*The only broadly-defined folk-oriented program on
any Montreal radio station.*

Folk Routes *CKUA*
tom.coxworth@ckua.org
www.ckua.org
*Each week, we explore both traditional and
contemporary music development, tracing folk music
from its European traditions to the blended influences
of modern North American folk styling.*

For the Folk *CHRW*
forthefolk@hotmail.com
www.geocities.com/folkie4
chrw.usc.uwo.ca
*Features the best in Folk, Roots, Traditional, Celtic
and Singer-Songwriter Programming from a pair of
Knowledgeable and Entertaining Hosts.*

In a Mellow Tone *CKCU*
www.ckcufm.com/inamellowtone.html
Jazz from every era and in every style. Each program features an artist, group, instrument, event, city or record label.

Jazz Beat *CBC*
Katie jazzbeat@montreal.cbc.ca
radio.cbc.ca/programs/JazzBeat
Host Katie Malloch presents two hours of the best in contemporary jazz. Powerful concert recordings and studio sessions, current and classic CD releases, plus exclusive interviews with top jazz performers - they're all part of the Jazz Beat package.

jazz for a sunday night *CHRW*
Barrie Woodey jazz4a@hotmail.com
chrw.usc.uwo.ca
CHRW 94.7FM, U. Western Ontario's Sunday night Jazz show.

JAZZ.FM91
info@jazz.fm
www.jazz.fm
Canada's Jazz Station! JAZZ.FM91 is dedicated to preserving the future of classic jazz and blues music. We are also dedicated to presenting the artists and music works that represent the golden era of jazz and blues and to presenting the latest jazz and blues styles, artists and their music.

The Jazz Show *CiTR*
citrmusic@club.ams.ubc.ca
www.ams.ubc.ca/citr
Vancouver's longest running prime time jazz program. Hosted by the ever-suave Gavin Walker.

Natch'l Blues *CKUA*
holger.petersen@ckua.org
www.ckua.org
Canada's longest running Blues program, now in its 33th year. Natch'l Blues is the quintessential destination for the serious blues fan or the curious newcomer.

Northern Lights Radio Hour *CKLU*
nlfbradio@hotmail.com
www3.sympatico.ca/deb.derek
Sudbury's best in folk and roots music. Tune in each week to hear your old favourites and discover new ones. We also feature interviews, special guests and in-studio concerts.

Prairie Ceilidh *CKJS*
pceilidh@shaw.ca
members.shaw.ca/pceilidh
On air for over 20 years, playing a mix of traditional and contemporary Celtic-flavoured music (Irish, Scottish, Maritime etc.), featuring musicians from Australia, Europe and North America.

Saturday Night Blues
Holger Petersen snb@edmonton.cbc.ca
edmonton.cbc.ca/snb
Each week you'll hear a mix of classic blues from the "Petersen Vaults", concerts, interviews, artist features, new releases, plus anything that boogies, jumps, or swings, plus your requests from the Bluesline.

Silence...on Jazz!
Andre Rheaume silenceonjazz@vancouver.radio-canada.ca
radio-canada.ca/regions/colombie-britannique/Radio/silenceonjazz.shtml
A smooth journey through jazz classics and more. The show focuses on historical musical events, anniversaries of great musicians and important concerts from across the country, new CD releases and anecdotes. Also featured are interviews with musicians, producers, festival organizers and other personalities who share their love and passion for jazz.

Some Experiences in Jazz
Robert Fogle robfogle@interactive.rogers.com
www.yorku.ca/chry
After 12 years still a great mix of Jazz with heavy Canadian content. Topical guests.

Europe

Belgium

In De Club
www.radio1.be

Mojo Dreams
www.srbc.8k.com

Psyche van het Folk
Gerald Van Waes Gerald.Van.Waes@pandora.be
www.radiocentraal.be/psychevanhetfolk
My radio program provides information about and for music artists (mostly with acoustic influences).

Germany

jazz-network.com
info@jazz-network.com
www.jazznradio.com
Features individual music channels - from traditional to modern, mainstream to blues and world music.

The Netherlands

Jazz & Blues Tour
Joost van Steen joost@jazzbluestourradio.com
www.jazzbluestourradio.com
A radio program with Radio Rijnwoude, a radio-station located between the city of Leiden and Alphen aan den Rijn.

The Real Roots Café
www.radiowereld.nl/realrootscafe

Norway

Jazz Scene
jazzscene.no
It's easy to get your product across, you just need the right channel. Jazz Scene welcomes good jazz music from any place on the planet and are more then happy to do interviews.

United Kingdom

BBC *Jazz Music*
www.bbc.co.uk/radio3/jazz

Ejazz.fm
www.ejazz.fm
We offer a selection of one-hour shows, compiled and presented by the UK's top jazz connoisseurs, featuring the great players and the great albums as well as specialist shows dedicated to Latin jazz, world jazz, fusion, vocalists, bebop and many more.

Jazz FM
music@jazzfm.com
www.jazzfm.com

Australia

3MBS *Melbourne*
www.3mbs.org.au

93.7 HERITAGE FM
Jayme Hanjin JaymeNatasha@aol.com
We play Rockin' Rhythms & Blues music, from across the world. Our Rhythm & Blues shows are ever-growing; and it seems we need some more music to play to our hungry listeners of Australia. One of my favorite shows is called "Cruizin' for a Bluezin"......of course; I'm the Host \ D.J, along with our own Perth Blues Club Vice-Prez: Steve Pike. Send your music to: 2 Rodgers Court, Roleystone. 6111. West Australia.

Acoustic Folkus
jim@newsouthfolk.com
www.newsouthfolk.com
Every Thursday 400pm to 600pm on Eurobodalla Live 107.5. The best is Acoustic Music with the emphasis on all the Folk Genres

Bitches' Brew
www.pbsfm.org.au
The program covers a fusion of jazz-rock and other styles including electronic, reggae, soul, funk, blues, world music and contemporary smooth jazz styles.

The Blue Room
www.users.bigpond.com/petercummins
We are dedicated to bringing you, the listener, a wide variety of blues/roots music on our programme. The genre includes electric and acoustic blues, Cajun, Zydeco and bluegrass.

The Esoteric Circle
fly.to/EsotericCircle
A main point of focus is to draw attention to the small independent labels from around the globe - music that usually stretches prevailing ideas about what jazz is and isn't.

Fiddlestix
www.southernfm.org.au
On Fiddlestix you'll hear the latest releases from the folk world, as well as interviews with and live performances by local and overseas artists.

The Late Session *RTÉ*
Áine Hensey brownep@rte.ie
www.radio1.ie/evening/latesession
Brings the best in Irish traditional and folk music to radio listeners each week. All areas of the music are catered for; from old archive recordings of the past to modern commercial releases of traditional music and song of which well over one hundred are issued every year.

Latin Radio

Alma del Barrio *KXLU*
djvicodan@hotmail.com
www.kxlu.com
A radio show dedicated to authentic and traditional Latin music since 1973.

The Aztlan Radio Network U.S.A.
www.aztlanradionetwork.com
The crossroads of Latino music from around the world!

Batanga.com
feedback@batanga.com
www.batanga.com
Plays alternative Hispanic music like rock, hip-hop, ska and techno on multiple Internet channels. Submissions: 2007 Yanceyville St., Greensboro, NC 27405, USA, attn: Programming

Cafe Brasil *WDNA*
cafebrasil@wdna.org
www.wdna.org
Brazilian music is as colorful and varied as the land and people of Brazil. Samba, bossa, jazz, MPB and more.

Canto Tropical *KPFK*
www.cantotropical.com
Celebrating over fourteen years on-air, the "Canto Tropical" show is heard every Saturday night from 8 to 10 p.m.

Chicano Radio Network
www.chicanoradionetwork.com
Chicano cyber radio around the clock!

Con Sabor *KPFA*
Luis Medina comboson@aol.com
www.kpfa.org
Afro-Caribbean dance music, a mix of salsa, Afro-Cuban and Latin jazz.

Con Salsa *WBUR*
Jose Masso jmasso@wbur.bu.edu
www.wbur.org
A bilingual music program that includes the best of Afro-Cuban music, Salsa, Latin-jazz, Merengue, Nueva Trova and World Music.

Corriente *KGNU*
music@kgnu.org
www.kgnu.org
A bilingual program featuring music, news, poetry and features.

Dimension Latina *WLUW*
wluwradio@wluw.org
wluw.org
Four hours of Latin music with occasional news.

La Esquina Latina *WPKN*
wpkn.org
A Latin program with a social conscience that entertains and educates. It's been an integral part of WPKN since 1974, celebrating a unique "Latin" style. La Esquina Latina has a strong following both behind and outside the walls. Hosted alternately by Luis or Edwin Muiz.

Horizontes *KUT*
Michael Crockett mcrockett@caravanmusic.com
www.kut.org
For nearly thirty years, KUT listeners have been traveling the musical airways of Latin America by tuning in to Horizontes.

Jazz on the Latin Side *KKJZ*
www.kkjz.org

KRZA *Alamosa, CO*
krza@krza.org
www.krza.com
We have several Latin/ Spanish shows.

Latin Beat *Georgia Public Broadcasting*
gpr@gpb.org
www.gpb.org
Features Latin music and guests from Georgia's Latin American community.

The Latin Entertainment Network *(LEN)*
www.lenradio.com
A national programmer and producer of original Hispanic programs and internet content.

Latin Lab *KJHK*
kjhkmusic@hotmail.com
kjhk.ukans.edu
From Afro-Cuban to Latin-Funk, from Bugaloo to Bossa Nova and from Cumbia to Latin Hip Hop, Latin Lab brings you a blend of styles and world fusions that lead to Latin-infused melodies and beats. "Cheo" MacGuire and "El Gringo" Centeno fuse their nationalities into one 3 hour mix of amazing music, political talk and Latin American humor. Aprieta!

Latina Del Swing *WGMC*
www.wgmc.org
Latin pop music show.

Latino America Sonando *KMUD*
md@kmud.org
www.kmud.org
The latest in salsa, songo, Latin jazz, Afro-Cuban folkloric, music from all over Latin America, plus interviews, historical features and other specials. Two hours of toe tapping Latin sounds to warm your heart with a Latin spin.

Onda Nueva *WUSB*
music@wusb.org
www.wusb.org
Everything from sun to salsa, plena, Afro-Antillean, Latin-American music, interviews, history, live in-studio jams and critique. Hosted by Felix Palacios.

Presencia Hispana *KCUR*
Silvia Ramirez kcur@umkc.edu
www.kcur.org
Chilean-born Silvia Ramirez features Latin music of all styles from Mexico, the Caribbean and South America. "We're trying to play the music that means something—music that's cultural and offers a positive message for the community."

Raices *KUNM*
music@kunm.org
www.kunm.org
Featuring Latin American news, art and culture, all genres of Hispanic music.

Raizes Radio Show *KBCS*
kbcs.fm
Roots in Portuguese, explores the music and culture of Brazil and its neighbors, with interviews and calendar.

Ritmos Latinos *KRBS*
krbs@cncnet.com
www.radiobirdstreet.org
Featuring music from North, Central and South America, Europe and the Carribbean. Traditional music as well as contemporary.

SaborSalsa.com
adriantreto@saborsalsa.com
www.SaborSalsa.com
Playing the best of Tropical music, (salsa, merengue, boleros and more), events, concerts, clubs, CD reviews & chismes...

Salsa Sabrosa *KUNM*
music@kunm.org
www.kunm.org
Friday nights are hot hot hot!

Salsumbo *WVBR*
wvbr.com/web/wvbr
Don't limit yourself to American tunes. Catch the current Latin music that's sweeping the world.

Spanish Rock 101 *WERW*
music@werw.syr.edu
werw.syr.edu

¡Tertulia! *WFCR*
Luis Meléndez tertulia@wfcr.org
www.wfcr.org/tertulia.html
The space where a dialogue takes place among Spanish speakers and all those who are interested in Latin American culture and in the music, the arts, the language and the issues of actuality for Latinos in New England. Latin Jazz, Boleros, Salsa, Merengue, Nueva Trova, Tango and Folk music.

Tiene Sabor *WWOZ*
Yolanda Estrada wwoz@wwoz.org
www.wwoz.org
I want to be the first to play a new record. If a record is played on a commercial station, I stop playing it. I want to play something new, something different.

Voz Latina *WBEZ*
Lisa Levy latina@wbez.org
www.vozlatina.info
www.wbez.org
A weekly excursion through the rich and diverse world of Latin music. The show features classic artists and rising stars, familiar styles and little-explored musical forms.

WHCR *City College of New York*
whcr903fm@yahoo.com
www.whcr.org

WKCR *Columbia U.*
Justin Padro latin@wkcr.org
www.columbia.edu/cu/wkcr
Over the years, the Latin department has developed a reputation as a leader in Latin music broadcasting and it is this tradition that is passed along to each new generation of programmers.

WRTE *Mexican Fine Arts Center*
wrte@radioarte.org
www.radioarte.org
We're a bunch of young people between the ages of 15-21 broadcasting to one of the largest Mexican communities in the Midwest (Pilsen/Little Village). As the only bilingual (Spanish/ English), youth-operated, urban, community radio station in the country we are committed to being creative and responsible broadcasters.

Metal Radio

Heavy, Thrash, Grindcore, Death, Black, Doom, Speed, Progressive, Viking metal etc.

Radio Promoters

Skateboard Marketing
Munsey excuseking@aol.com
www.skateboard-marketing.com
An independent music marketing company who focuses on street marketing & commercial specialty shows, active rock & college metal radio promotion. For eight years we have specialized in artist development for all the major labels and many Indies respectively.

North America

United States

Alaska's Tundra Trash Radio
tundratrash@hotmail.com
www.tundratrashradio.com
We play heavy metal, hardcore rock, industrial metal, numetal, stoner rock, heavier alternative rock etc. (no speed/thrash metal).

Audio Aggression
metalmark55@hotmail.com
clix.to/Metalmark
Featuring the best in the true Heavy Metal underground spectrum for over 10 years!!

Axecaliber
geno@heavyrock.com
www.heavyrock.com/radioshow.html
We pride ourselves in the promotion of the undiscovered heavyrock artist. The integrity kept is one that upholds an uncompromising attitude towards the talents of the musicians while keeping the music heavy.

Cries in the Night *KVCU*
www.colorado.edu/StudentGroups/KVCU
Terror that erupts every Thursday night in the peaceful city of Boulder, Colorado.

Death Metal Radio Online
jim@lambdatel.com
www.deathmetal.com
You certainly don't have to be a signed, or even famous group to have your music represented here. We want all types of Death Metal groups, from the biggest to the smallest, to contribute to this project.

Electric Eye Radio
requests@electriceyeradio.com
www.electriceyeradio.com
We Play A Mix Of Classic, Hard and Modern Rock, Heavy Metal, Goth and Punk.

Embrace of the Darkness & Metal *WMUA*
DJ Solveig embraceofthedarkness@yahoo.com
www.embraceofthedarkness.com
European Metal (death, black etc.) Sunday nights.

ExtremeX Radio
www.extremexradio.net
I need all of you fellow Rock Heads out there to send me promos so I can put then up on ExtremeX! We would be happy to have any Independent Artist to send their music in. We will need a few things from you in order to get your music on our stations. The first thing we need is your Promo Packet & CD and a letter giving Webzine Broadcasting Permission to use your material royalty free.

The Four Horsemen *WPSC*
Spiritfiend@yahoo.com
Gatti714@juno.com
www.angelfire.com/rock2/wpscmetal/main.html
Metal, Punk, Hardcore and Industrial music. Send in your CD!

Goat Metal *WRUW*
www.goatmetal.com
Broadcasting from Cleveland, OH. It is a metal show, playing mostly black metal, with some thrash, doom and death metal bands. Please send us your music and/or promotional materials.

HoTMetaLradio
info@hotmetalradio.com
www.hotmetalradio.com
Nobody had a satisfying answer to this. Where the HELL did all the GOOD music go? DAMN sure ain't on commercial radio stations! So, we built OUR OWN radio station and put it on the 'net. NOW we can play the music WE want to hear...and that YOU want to hear.

Into the Pit Radio Show
meng@98kupd.com
www.98KUPD.com
The shit your mama don't want you to hear.

KNAC
www.knac.com
KNAC.com Pure Rock on the Net. Have you banged you head today?

KWUR Radio *St. Louis*
kwur.wustl.edu
We play a lot of extreme music - ranging from death metal and grindcore to hardcore and industrial. Anyone interested in being played should contact us.

Last Exit for the Lost
The Mage Seriah Azkath@aol.com
wvbr.com/lastexit.html
It is a show that includes Metal (in its many forms; Progressive, Doom, Death etc), as well as many other forms of music, including Industrial, Gothic, Hard Rock and some things that just defy any kind of description. There's a little bit of everything, from National to Local and Unsigned acts.

Maddog Rock Radio
www.heavymetalradio.net
The only true heavy metal station. Broadcasting from Kailua, Hawaii on the beautiful island of Oahu, but hey, even in paradise, we need to crank up the amps to 11 once in awhile!

Megatrends in Brutality *WRBC*
megabrutal@excite.com
www.brutalradio.musicpage.com
If it is heavy and metal ... I play it.

The Metal Show
werg@gannon.edu
wergfm.com

Midnight Metal Madness *WONC*
feedback@wonc.org
www.wonc.org
The disc jockeys gear up for their own crowd from midnight until 2 am with hard-rocking heavy metal. WONC is one of the only (if not the only!) stations in the Chicago metro currently broadcasting this kind of music

Munsey Ricci Toxic Waltz
excuseking@aol.com
www.skateboard-marketing.com
www.totalrock.com
Hot metal from New York

Reality Check TV
rctv@earthlink.net
www.realitychecktv.com
Reality Check was the first TV show to take the video viewer into the real word of the wild and amazing underground world. We accept submissions!

RIFF Radio
Dan@hardrocksociety.com
www.hardrocksociety.com
New, reviews and new releases are posted as well.

Rock Hard Place Radio Show
Torch rockhardtorch@hotmail.com
www.rockhardplace.com
Rock radio show looking for new Rock, Metal, Industrial, Punk, Goth and other loud music!

The Rock & Roll Ponderosa
Charlie@rockandrollponderosa.com
www.rockandrollponderosa.com
www.totalrock.com
Biker friendly Viking Music with horns that Rocks! NO Turntables No Baseball Caps and No Rapping!!

Snakenet Metal Radio
Jerry Storch Snake@Snakenet.com
www.snakenetmetalradio.com
Bands or record labels wishing to send CDs and other promotional materials should contact me.

Sudden Death Overtime *WITR*
ron@suddendeathovertime.com
suddendeathovertime.com
If you are with a label or an unsigned band and would like to mail us info or music, just send it to us.

The Uroc Network
music@uroc.net
www.uroc.net
Provides global exposure to a gaggle of signed, unsigned, indie, punk, metal, old school rock or whatever else you want to call it. If it rocks we will play it.

Vomit Radio
vomitbag@vomitradio.com
vomitradio.com
Heavy and uncensored 24 hours a day!

WCLH *Wilkes U.*
music@wclh.net
www.wclh.net
Every Monday and Wednesday there is an entire day of loud and heavy music including gothic, death metal, hardcore, black metal, industrial, heavy metal and doom.

The X Station.com
email@thexstation.com
www.thexstation.com
Welcome to the Xtreme side of the Internet.

Canada

Bourreau Metallique *CIBL*
bourreaumetallique@hotmail.com
crash.to/bourreau

The Darkest Hours
info@thedarkesthours.com
www.thedarkesthours.com
The place where you can listen to pure metal music 24 hours a day, 7 days a week. Send us your Demos, promos & press kit!

K666 Radio
dan@stonerrock.com
www.stonerrock.com
If you're disgusted with the pathetic state of popular music, you've come to the right place.

Métal pesant *CFLX*
metalpesant@hotmail.com
iquebec.ifrance.com/metalpesant
Where the word metal finds all its meaning.

Metalurgy's "Live Evil" *CFCR*
metalurgy@shaw.ca
members.shaw.ca/metalurgy/main.htm
The most extreme & brutal radio show to be heard on the Canadian airwaves & is the only radio program that has been covering both the black & death metal genres exclusively in Canada for the past 12 years.

Midnight Metal *CHET*
mike@midnightmetal.com
www.midnightmetal.com
If you think you've got a cool band and you'd like me to review, sample or preview your album on air just send it to me.

Mind Compression *CJSR*
www.cjsr.com

Space in Your Face *CKMS*
siyf@gto.net
www.angelfire.com/on/siyf
An ever popular and always evolving metal radio show. SIYF features Metal News, Interviews, Giveaways and More!

L'Ulcère de vos nuits *CISM*
ulceredevosnuits@hotmail.com
pages.infinit.net/danko
Intense, powerful, dark metal.

Europe

Belgium

Dakka Dakka Radio Show
redant@imec.be
www.starspawn.com/foob/dakka
One of the longest running radio shows on one of Belgium's first free radio stations. We provide students and locals in the city of Leuven with their dose of guitar oriented music, be it Metal, Punk or Rock, in the widest sense.

Deafness Radio Show
deafness@wanadoo.be
www.deafness.fr.fm
We play all styles of Metal, with news, Metal agenda and interview live (sometimes by phone).

Denmark

Radio DeadBeat
brock@deadbeat.dk
www.deadbeat.dk
Coming atcha from the pleasant studios at XFM 107.4, every Tuesday from 8 PM to 9 PM, when DJs Brock and Grøn slap some sizzlin wax on the airwaves.

Finland

Meteliä Maan Alta Rado Show
radio@diypunk.net
diypunk.net/radio

France

Damase's Pirate Radio
damase@chez.com
www.pirateradio.fr.fm
The best Metal and Hard Rock Radio on the Net. Bringing you the best of Metal old and new.

Kerosene Radio
kfuel@kfuel.org
www.kfuel.fr.st
rock, noise, hard/emo core, experimental, punk, pop....

Germany

Stahlwerk-Hannover Radio Show
stahlwerk-hannover@gmx.de
www.stahlwerk-hannover.de
The best of all kinds of metal (Speed-, Thrash-, Progressive-, Death-, Black-, Gothic-, Heavy Metal, of course we celebrate classics from the 70's and 80's). In every show we support the underground. Different bands without a recent record deal are featured. If you're interested send your demotape + info, get in contact with us!

Norway

Metal Express Radio Show
mail@metalexpress.no
www.metalexpress.no
Our main focus will be straight heavy metal and closely related genres. We will try to keep a certain quality standard by avoiding all the crap that is being released all the time.

Portugal

S.O.S Heavy Metal Radio Show
dj_imperatore@hotmail.com
www.angelfire.com/mb/sosradio
Online and screaming fucking loud!

Spain

Emisión Sin Fronteras Radio Show
www.arrakis.es/~servan

Metal Age Radio Show
pica@gracianet.org
www.radiopica.net

United Kingdom

Sex to 9 with María
maria@sexto9.com
www.sexto9.com
www.totalrock.com
Rock and metal like you've never heard it before... with a touch of exotic Latin passion.

Totalrock
info@totalrock.com
www.totalrock.com
Live rock and metal radio, 24-7. The best live rock and metal news on the planet!

Zed's Psycholopedia of Rock
Zaid 'Zed' Couri zed@psycholopedia.co.uk
www.psycholopedia.co.uk
A kick-arse Rock/Heavy metal show on TotalRock.com radio. Special feature on the show is a retrospective look at particular metal/rock artist's career every week.

Australia

Critical Mass Radio Show *RTR FM*
www.rtrfm.com.au
Stay heavy metal and bang your heads.

Full Metal Racket *Triple J*
Andrew Haug fullmetalracket@your.abc.net.au
www.abc.net.au/triplej/racket
Step in to the diverse, the soulful and the aggressive realms of Heavy Metal music. It's sure to drive you to the brink of insanity in a good way. Covering a wide range of the latest and greatest heavy sounds with news updates, interviews, local and international tour announcements and tonnes more.

Metal Head Radio Show *Triple U*
metalhead@dodo.net.au
www.tripleu.org.au/metalhead.html
Four Hours of Metal with the Chief Metallurgist, thence our "auto program of Black, Death and Gothic Metal til Dawn.

New Age Radio

Alpha Rhythms *WYSO*
Lori and Jerry allank@earthlink.net
www.wyso.org/wysopgs/alpha.html
4 hours of ambient and new age music Sunday nights from 8 to Midnight.

Audioscapes
www.kcpr.org
Explores the frontiers of organized sound, where classical, electronic and progressive music merge to reveal the sounds of tomorrow.

BRAINWAVES *KXCI*
Roger brainwaves@kxci.org
www.kxci.org
New age, ambient, experimental, electro-acoustic classical, world music. There is also a spoken word segment on spiritual or uplifting topics.

Changes Radio
comments@changes.org
www.changes.org
Among other pages, we do reviews of CDs. We review folk, rock, trance, ethnic, classical and "new age", but it must have a message of hope. Examples: folk - Kirtana, rock - Yes and so on. Changes is also on the net with two radio programs and we expect to have a third soon. Check it out!

Cheeze Music *WTUL*
www.tulane.edu/~wtul
We feel the music is healthy and beautiful; wonderfully exotic, erotic, simultaneously stimulating AND calming, while containing a sense of knowing.

Common Threads *KRBS*
krbs@cncnet.com
www.radiobirdstreet.org
Spiritual music, poetry and speeches finding the common threads that run through all religions.

Echoes
echoes@echoes.org
www.echoes.org
Artists and music are, of course, the lifeblood of Echoes and we are always seeking out new material. We welcome your submissions for airplay; however, we only accept material on Compact Disc.

Gopher's Underground Music Store
gopher@gopherp.com
www.gopherp.com

The Great Awakening *WXCI*
www.wcsu.ctstateu.edu/wxci/greata.html
www.wxci.org
This Sunday morning wake to the show everyone is talking about. Join Andrea White and the Great Awakening for New Age readings, meditations and the latest in soothing sounds.

Hearts of Space Radio
radio@hos.com
www.hos.com/radio.html
National syndication to 250 non-commercial public radio stations via the NPR satellite system. If your music is already released on CD and you'd like to submit it for airing on our show, send a sample of the CD along with your one sheet and press/promo information.

Hybrid *PBS FM, Australia*
Andrew Hollo ahollo@connexus.net.au
hybrid.alphalink.com.au
The weekly atmospheric and ambient radio program from Melbourne Australia.

Innervisions *WNMC*
www.wnmc.org
From Northwestern Michigan College The ultimate forum for New Age and related music, featuring new and exciting material, much of which is exclusive to WNMC listeners. The ideal Sunday morning coffee and news companion.

KUAT *U. Arizona*
Alan Campbell alankuat@yahoo.com
www.KUAT.ORG
Classical or new age artists may submit.

Lucid Sounds *WZBC*
www.wzbc.org

Music for a New Age
Dan Bayer Dan@wkar.org
www.wkar.org/radio/mfna
A blend of smooth and introspective jazz performances and acoustic/electronic new age music.

Music From Beyond the Lakes *WDBX*
www.wdbx.org

Music Interlude *KRSC*
Cindy James CindyJ913@aol.com
www.rsu.edu/krsc/fm
A compact version of my weekly four hour show "Sunday Interlude". It is a one hour show currently airing Friday mornings at 11. The difference in the content is it is more "upbeat" and features more vocals than Sunday's show.

Musical Starstreams
info@starstreams.com
www.starstreams.com
After having aired on nearly 200 stations worldwide over the last nearly two decades, we have seen our program produce TOP RATINGS with every age group.

Mystic Music *KKUP*
Eric Mystic eameece@california.com
www.kkup.com/ericm.html
The kind of sonorous sound experience that lifts and awakens you above normal consciousness, even if only for a few moments. If you listen sensitively, it puts you in touch with your most special memories and forgotten dreams.

Mystical Moods *WLJS*
www.geocities.com/mysticalmoods92j
A program that features artists of the new age, ambient, Celtic, folk, pagan and related genres.

New Age Sampler
BEAR nasbear@bearheartltd.com
www.bearheartltd.com/nas
Lifescapes for Introspective listening through Ambient, Celtic, Instrumental, New Age, Orchestral, Smooth Jazz, Space & World Music. New Age Sampler, The radio show whose only purpose ...is to take you there.

New Frontier Magazine
info@newfrontier.com
www.newfrontier.com
Reviews of new age music and videos.

New Morning Music *WUOT*
elhigman@utk.edu
sunsite.utk.edu/wuot
An hour of contemporary/new age music, is produced and hosted by Louise Higman , WUOT's office manager

New Music Gallery *WMNR*
www.wmnr.org

New Sounds
John Schaefer newsounds@wnyc.org
www.wnyc.org/shows
A place for your left and right brain to unwind at the end of day. The program offers new ways to hear the ancient language of song. New works from the classic and operatic to folk and jazz. Tune in for the next wave or the most ancient forms of music.

Newage Collage *South Dakota Public Radio*
programming@sdpb.org
www.sdpb.org/radio
Broadcast at 10:00 Ct each Saturday and Sunday evening on South Dakota Public Radio. Jerry Cooley is your producer and host for 2 hours of modern instrumental music.

Night Music *CKUA*
Tony Dillon Davis tony.dillon-davis@ckua.org
www.ckua.org
Host Tony Dillon-Davis blends music styling covering classical, jazz, folk, pop, New Age and aboriginal. East Indian, Arabic and Asian compositions also are woven into the mix to create a soothing balm for the soul.

Night Portage *WELY*
info@wely.com
www.wely.com
Ambient and New Age Music.

Night Tides *KCUR*
Renee Blanche blanchea@umkc.edu
www.kcur.org
An eclectic blend of contemplative instrumental & electronic music that combines upbeat grooves and dubs with soothing melodies that whisper (softly) to the soul.

Nightcrossings
www.radiokansas.org/nc.cfm
A production of Radio Kansas. Based primarily on New Age music, the program also incorporates light jazz and classical crossover.

Nightstreams *KASU*
kasu@astate.edu
www.kasu.org
Relaxing, contemporary instrumental music.

Nitelite *KEDM*
kedm.ulm.edu/nitelite
Nitelite starts out with various acoustic music styles, slowly transcends into instrumental hybrids and ends with deep-space explorations.

Nocturnes *KEDM*
kedm.ulm.edu/nocturnes
One of KEDM's most popular locally produced programs. Nocturnes mixes acoustic and classical music forms in a manner that's most pleasing for late night audiences; music with little talk.

Planetary Prismatic Psonics
WKNHinfo@aol.com
www.jumblue.com/wknh

Radio Waves *Germany*
zimmert@t-online.de
home.t-online.de/home/zimmert/homepage.htm
Elektronic & New Age Music in Münster Germany. We also do CD reviews.

Sacred World Music
Richard Mauro info@sacredworldmusic.com
www.sacredworldmusic.com
A wonderful mix covering various genres. World, ethnic, new age, space, electronic, folk, classical, folk, Celtic etc. PO Box 271294, Fort Collins, CO 80527-1294

Soaring Spirit Radio
Lee Widener spirit@neverendingwonder.com
www.NeverEndingWonder.com/spirit.htm
Internet radio station featuring folk, acoustic, new age, singer/songwriter, traditional, bluegrass, country and world/international music. We support independent artists.

Solitudes *WXPR*
wxpr@wxpr.org
www.wxpr.org/program/solitudes.html
An hour of new age or "space" music to relax and unwind, from the WXPR library.

Sonic Frontiers *WFSU*
ews8748@mailer.fsu.edu
www.fsu.edu/~wfsu_fm/programs/sonic
www.fsu.edu/~wfsu_fm/wfsu/wfsufm.html
A weekly hour-long excursion featuring new releases in the field of New Age, Ambient, Native American, Celtic, World, Avant-Garde, Electronic & Acoustic Instrumental Music.

Sonic Images *WUAL*
sonicimages@apr.org
www.wual.ua.edu

Sound Sounding *The Netherlands*
webmaster@boortman.presenteert.nl
boortman.presenteert.nl
I'm trying to create a special atmosphere of smooth moods, which one can bring spiritual emotions. If you want to send promotional material, CD's, CDR's, MiniDisk, DAT-tape, or information, send it always to the studio.

Sounds of Syn *Germany*
Steffen Thieme Redaktion@Sounds-of-Syn.de
www.sounds-of-syn.de
Broadcasted at the Offener Kanal Hamburg, (Open Channel Hamburg). The word "Syn" says it all. It's a programme for syntheszier music, for Electronic Music like Klaus Schulze, Tangerine Dream, Vangelis.

Soundwaves *WUSM*
wusm@usm.edu
www-dept.usm.edu/~wusm

Star's End *Philadelphia*
info@starsend.org
www.starsend.org
The music is presented in a non-stop drifting blend, drawing from many genres including: ambient, spacemusic, chillout, avant-garde, low-intensity noise, new age, international, spoken word and classical. Please access the website for details on having your music considered for the show.

Sunday CD Showcase *WSHU*
www.wshu.org/spotlight
The latest releases in New Age and Space Music.

Sunday Interlude *KRSC*
Cindy James CindyJ913@aol.com
www.rsu.edu/krsc/fm
A foundation of relaxing instrumental music, then layered with a few harder pieces, some vocals, a bit of jazz, a bit of classical and whatever else I can add that will give it enough variety yet remain within the premise of music for a mental massage.

Sunday New Age *WSUP*
wsup@uwplatt.edu
vms.www.uwplatt.edu/~wsup
Features new age music from around the world.

Sunday Sunrise *KRVR*
theriver@krvr.com
www.krvr.com
Acoustic, new age and world music.

Tonal Vision *WICN*
Sam Watt sam@wicn.org
www.wicn.org
A unique and rare program featuring new age, acoustic, ambient and world music. Get ready for a fantastic voyage into the realms of the new age scene combined with award winning solo pianists, flamenco guitarists and the melodic sounds of rich ambient music.

Visionary Activist *KPFA*
info@ visionaryactivism.com
www.kpfa.org/1pro_bio/1b_visio.htm
www.visionaryactivism.com
The wedding of spiritual magic and compassionate social activism. Insights on the nature of magic and reality, astute political analysis, storytelling, magical ceremony, music and songs and always her brilliant humor.

WEBR *New Age Music Mix*
webr@fcac.org
www.fcac.org/webr/webr.htm

Progressive Rock Radio

Delicious Agony Progressive Rock Radio
jrgmmg@comcast.net
www.deliciousagony.com
Progressive music, interviews, news and more!

Dreams Wide Awake *WOSP*
jeller@unf.edu
www.unf.edu/~jeller/dreams.html
A music show that features progressive rock and related music, such as fusion, symphonic, RIO, electronic, Canterbury, zeuhl and other traditionally un-radio-friendly musics.

From Genesis to Revelation *Italy*
matthias@fromgenesis.net
renato@fromgenesis.net
www.fromgenesis.net
Il portale Italiano sul rock progressive.

Gagliarchives *WBZC*
gagliarchives@yahoo.com
ghostland.com/gagliarchives
A progressive and art rock program that covers neo, synth, fusion, Canterbury, metal, classic, solo, space, acid, classical, underground 70's, new and anything else somehow tied in with this mystical genre.

Groove Traffic Control *WHCL*
Sean stice@hamilton.edu
www.gtcontrol.cjb.net
Bringing listeners the best in new and up-coming jam oriented music. Listen to our program online or on the air.

Night Vision *WITR*
jluminous@hotmail.com
nightvision.musicpage.com
If you have a band looking for a new audience, get in touch with us about airplay. We'd love to hear from you.

Paperlate *The Netherlands*
radioman@paperlate.net
home.concepts.nl/~paperlte
A radio show dedicated to progressive rock. PAPERLATE also pays attention to progressive metal and melodic rock, sometimes even new age and folk-rock are coming round the edge.

progradio.com
pdirector@progradio.com
www.progradio.com
Progressive music for your mind!

The Progressive Rock Radio Network
progradio@progradio.net
www.progradio.net
We strive to provide you with access to music you might not normally hear on FM stations or at music store listening booths. We want to help you discover the joys of progressive music and show you that there is more to life than the latest AOR (Alternative or Rock) craze.

Progressive Soundscapes Radio
www.progressivesoundscapes.com
Though you will hear some of the "classic prog" from decades ago, we specialize in bringing you some of the great new offerings from contemporary bands and artists including those who are either independent or signed to small labels.

The Prog-Rock Diner *WEBR*
www.fcac.org/webr/webr.htm
The show offers a progressive rock menu spanning music from the late '60's through present day releases. You'll hear prog from all over the world.

progrock.com
www.progrock.com
Are you a new progressive rock band? Would you like ProgRock.com to play your band's music over our virtual airwaves? Please note that we can only accept Ogg Vorbis files with the quality set to 5 for playback on ProgRock.com. We cannot accept MP3 files for licensing reasons and can't convert them to Ogg Vorbis format without significant loss in quality.

The Trip
thetrip@pop.uky.edu
www.uky.edu/~wrfl/trip/trip.html
www.wrfl.org
If you're interested in having your band's music heard on the program, send us your music.

Punk Radio

Punk, Ska, Hardcore, Emo, oi

United States

BaconBitz Radio
BaconBitz@rock.com
baconbitzradio.tripod.com
We are the Heinz 57 of rock radio with an alternative focus, the way it a true alternative station should sound.

Coffee n' Smokes
coffeensmokes@earthlink.net
coffeensmokes.freeservers.com
Featuring new & vintage garage/punk, surf, psychedelic, rockabilly, pop obscurities...and a little bit o' greasy R & B here 'n' there where it fits!

Deviation Station
dollev@dollev.com
www.dollev.com
The main portion of the show is alternative or punk music. But since I have a severe dislike for formats, I also play some alt. country, electric/ambient stuff and even folk music from all over the world. Send me a few MP3's and I will play one of them in next month's show.

DIY Radio *WAPS*
diy@diyradio.net
www.diyradio.net
A punk rock radio show that has been airing since August 1993. You can listen to the show LIVE Sunday evenings from 9pm to 11pm EST.

Everything Off Beat *WLUW*
wluwradio@wluw.org
wluw.org
The world's premier ska oriented radio show, launched in 1988 by DJ Chuck Wren.

graynoise radio
info@graynoise.net
www.graynoise.net
Punk, emo and hardcore.

Hammertime *WSHL*
Nancy Hammerle nhammerle@aol.com
www.hammertimeradio.cjb.net
We have been hitting the airwaves since early 2001, throwing out heaps of punk, Oi! and rockabilly along with some Psychobilly, redneck rock and basic new school rock and roll.

idobi.com
pr@idobi.com
www.idobi.com/radio
Broadcasts alternative rock and punk music, as well as news updates and interviews with your favorite artists. We are committed to bringing you the best of the known (and not-so-well-known) artist from around the world.

In Your Ear *KRCB*
Rosa Corn rosacorn@sonic.net
www.krcb.org
*We feature new independent music of the
"alternative" flavor and traces roots back to
punk/industrial/garage rock beginnings. Airs on
KRCB 2nd and 4th Friday, 10pm - midnight. Host:
Rosa Corn. (Rosa is also the Alternative Music
Director for KRCB 91fm community radio, Sonoma
County, CA.)*

Ithaska *WVBR*
ithaska@ithaska.com
ithaska.com
*Despite our name, we play all sorts of music, including
ska, reggae, rocksteady, as well as ska-punk, punk and
emo.*

Local Is
DJ KD jetsetradiodj@aol.com
localyokels.cjb.net
*Looking to play new talents from the rock/alt/ska/punk
music scene and more, from all over th e country and
around the world.*

LOST IN THE SUPERMARKET
supermarketrock@yahoo.com
www.geocities.com/supermarkethits/
*The supermarket stocks great stuff like punk rock, new
wave, rock n roll, ska and surf tunes. This is definitely
the music to listen to while you are building your self
esteem.*

Music to Spazz By *WFMU*
spazz@wfmu.org
www.wfmu.org/~spazz
*From Hell Gate to Ho-Ho-Kus, Indiana to Istanbul,
more people get their news and entertainment from
Music To Spazz By than from any other hillbilly
chimpanzee punk rock rhythm n' blues surf garage
radio show!*

One Step Beyond *WLIR*
Jay Wolf Jay@wlir.com
www.osbradio.com
*Are you in a band that plays Ska, Punk, Reggae, Indie
Rock, Hardcore, or music? Then send us some your
stuff for possible airplay! Music on CDs only, please!*

the pAved earth
andy@thepavedearth.com
www.thepavedearth.com
*Currently offers two different streams, the original
stream and We Eat Our Young, the all-punk/ska
stream.*

Planet Ska Radio
niff007@hotmail.com
www.planetska.com
*If you want your stuff played on the Planet Ska radio
show, visit our website for contact details.*

Punk University *WSOU*
www.wsou.net
*Underground punk and ska that isn't available
anywhere on the FM dial.*

The Record Hospital *WHRB*
www.whrb.org
*For twenty years been devoted to the best in
underground rock, including punk, pop, hardcore,
emo, death-grind, new wave, no wave, indie and
crust.*

Rocket Ship Ska Trip *KFAI*
capt2much@yahoo.com
www.kfai.org/programs/rocketst.htm

Scratch
scratch@azevedo.ca
www.azevedo.ca/scratch
*The format ranges from early-1960's ska, through
rocksteady, reggae and on to modern-day dub and is
mostly Jamaican in content.*

Shredding Radio
shreddingpaper@netscape.net
www.shreddingradio.com
*A streaming MP3 webcast for faster than dial-up
connections to the net. The music played is based on
the reviews in Shredding Paper magazine and
includes, C86, Sarah Records, underground pop,
britpop, fuzzpop, twee pop, J-pop, new wave, lo-fi,
riot grrrl and shoegazer!*

Ska*Anarchy
skashow@yahoo.com
www.skashow.tsx.org
*This is your ska station! It's a Rude Boy Jamboree!
Streaming SKA 24/7.*

STARPIMP Radio
heh@starpimp.com
www.starpimp.com
*Featuring old school punk rock, post-punk, triphop,
hip hop, illbient and ambient.*

Total Punk Radio
radiogz@hotmail.com
www.totalpunkradio.com
*We are looking for small/unsigned bands to play on
the radio. If you are in a band or know a band send
us your CD/demo/press info and we'll get you on the
radio!!*

Tunnel One *WNYU*
djmush1@earthlink.net
www.wnyu.org
*During its hour and a half, Tunnel One is an even
blend of old school, rock steady and third wave Ska.
New artists in the Ska scene frequent the studios for
live performances, interviews and guest DJ spots.*

Under the Big Top *WMUA*
jerod@wmua.org
bigtop.weinman.cc
*Punk rock radio for Western Mass and beyond. Punk
to ska, emo to hardcore and more.*

The Wayback Machine *KDHX*
kopper@garagepunk.com
www.garagepunk.com
*I highly encourage bands and labels to submit
material for airplay. I will gladly play your band or
record label's music on the show, granted it fits the
format!! I will admit that my perception of "garage,"
"rock 'n' roll", or even "punk" may not be the same
as yours.*

WDOA Internet Radio
wdoa.com
*We actively encourage independent bands and artists
to send us their music. While we can't promise we
will play it, we can promise we will listen to it and if
one of our staff types like, yup, it will get played.*

Canada

Flex Your Head Radio Show *CITR*
flxyrhed@direct.ca
flexyourhead.vancouverhardcore.com
*Hardcore/punk radio program (on CITR 101.9 fm)
and website.*

On the Edge of Sanity Radio Show *CHSR*
chsrmd@unb.ca
www.unb.ca/chsr
*I play punk, hardcore and maybe an occasional dose
of ska and metal.*

Ska Party *CIUT*
skaparty@ciut.fm
www.skapages.com/skip
*Features interviews, news, reviews and some
schmooze. Don't forget, we like to dance as well!*

Skatterbrains *CFRU*
skatterbrains_radio@hotmail.com
www.sentex.net/~irm/skatterbrains
*We play ska from all waves, with an emphasis on
Traditional and Neo Traditional, without being TOO
closed minded about ska punk and other cross overs.
With previews of new ska material, local show
announcements and witty (witless) banter, you would
be a fool not to tune in.*

France

Ecrasons La Vermine *Radio Campus Lille*
chpunk@chpunk.org
chpunk.org/elv
www.campuslille.com
*Punk, hardcore, oi!, crust, ska & blabla négatif
diarrhée verbale+bouillie musicale depuis 1987
émission radio chak dimanche 18h30-20h.*

Germany

Noise Engine
webmaster@noiseengine.de
www.noiseengine.de

Norway

Lazy Punk Radio
lazypunk@datamorgana.no
lazypunk.datamorgana.no
*Send us your CD by snail mail. Contact us for our
address.*

Romania

Fun Radio
Cristian Bushuioc FunRad@yahoo.com
www.funkyradio.ro
*Located in Bucharest, Romania, Fun Radio is an
alternative radio station specialized in the
Underground Music, from noise, dub, electro to
alternative, punk, metal.*

Reggae Radio

400 Years: Radio Free Mondo *KZUM*
Carter Van Pelt cvanpelt@inebraska.com
www.kzum.org
incolor.inetnebr.com/cvanpelt/Years.html

Caribbean Linkup *CJSW*
caribbeanlinkup@shaw.ca
members.shaw.ca/caribbeanlinkup
*A weekly radio show in Calgary, Alberta dedicated to
the Caribbean - news, views and music.*

Creation Steppin' Roots Reggae Radio
John Reichle jreichle@scottsboro.org
www.creation-steppin.com
*Best of classic and modern roots reggae; some
emphasis placed on members of Reggae Ambassadors
Worldwide, many of whom are independent artists.*

Fire Corner *Austraila*
editor@firecorner.com
www.firecorner.com
Reggae broadcast from Sydney.

Freedom Sounds *Germany*
peter@freedomsounds.de
www.freedomsounds.de
Reggae show based in Germany on Radio Flora.

itsreggae.com
djdread@itsreggae.com
www.itsreggae.com

Jammin Reggae Radio
eznoh@niceup.com
niceup.com
The Gateway to Reggae Music on the Internet!

Reggae in the Fields
reggaeinthefields@canada.com
www.cyberus.ca/%7Eacdas/Reggae.html
www.ckcufm.com
The longest-running reggae program in Canada and one of the longer-running community radio shows in the country.

Reggae Evolution *KAZI*
TexasReggaeList@earthlink.net
www.texasreggae.org
www.kazifm.com
The focus of my show is positive modern roots & culture, mostly of Jamaican origin. I also mix in dancehall & reggae-related music with hip-hop & electronic influences.

Reggae Power *Israel*
www.irielion.com/israel/reggae_power.htm
The best reggae vibes from the best radio station! Since 1998.

Reggae Rhythms *WAPS*
theenergyman@cs.com
reggaerhythms.hypermart.net
Reggae music from the US and abroad, along with regional reggae news and concert information.

The Reggae Ride *WDNA*
Join Howard "Flagga" Duperly flagga@wdna.org
www.wdna.org
Authentic reggae music, encompassing the ska (60's) era up to the present.

The Reggae Train *KRBS*
krbs@cncnet.com
www.radiobirdstreet.org
Classic roots reggae music.

reggaemania.com
rnelson@reggaemania.com
www.reggaemania.com

Yard Sound *KKSM*
ihinihi@aol.com
www.yardsound.com
Spreading the Jamaican, Rasta and Reggae music vibes, representing the artists, their lifestyles, what they stand for. Our goal is to spread their message, consciousness, experience and levity.

Women in Music - Radio

United States

All Indie Women
kimberly@womeninproduction.com
www.womeninproduction.com
I don't mind if you send great music my way- zip it to me! artist-title.mp3 with your email! Broadcasting great independent women in music! We play whatever the ladies are sending me!!

Amazon Country *WXPN*
www.xpn.org
Amazon Country and Q'zine, two of the longest-running gay and lesbian/feminist radio shows in America, are celebrating a quarter-century of broadcasting in 1999.

Amazon Radio Show *WPKN*
psmith@amazonradio.com
www.wpkn.org/wpkn/amazon
Welcomes music from women everywhere, all styles.

Assorted Women *WDIY*
info@wdiyfm.org
www.wdiyfm.org
Audrey plays music that features women in key roles as composer and performer. She also reports on events of concern to women.

b-gYrL Radio
webmaster@b-gyrl.com
www.b-gyrl.com
The all female hip hop show features national and undaground b-gyrl tracks, interviews, free mp3s, deejay mixes, freestyles and spoken work, contests and more.

The Bonus Cup Radio Show
thundergrrl@rocketmail.com
listen.to/thebonuscup
wowl.fau.edu
ATTENTION MUSICIANS If you are in a punk or indie oriented band with at least one female member, drop me an email and let me know about you!!! CD's 7inches and tapes to play on my show are much appreciated as there are so many great female artists out there!

Bread & Roses *KBOO*
www.geocities.com/brroses
www.kboo.fm
Public Affairs radio produced and engineered by women interested in the world of work, current affairs, prison issues and women s physical and mental health concerns.

Chicken Rock *WEFT*
weft@weftfm.org
www.weft.org
Get your girly rock, alternative and electronic fix....

Chicks Who Rock
DJ Llu mailbag@999thebuzz.com
www.999thebuzz.com
Tune in and check out a female artist or female-fronted band. Up & coming acts, new songs from Buzz Bands, great tracks from legendary ladies. You'll hear a bit of everything, plus news, tour info and a little HERstory about each artist. Chicks Who Rock plays Indie Female artists!

Colorado Women in the Arts *KWAB – Radio For Change*
www.workingforchange.com/radio
Former Executive Director of the Womens' Art Center and Gallery, Gina Ferrari highlights women in the visual, literary and performing arts and discusses their impact on our communities.

Country Girls Only Radio
Sloane countrygirlsonly@wsld.net
www.live365.com/stations/140113
We not only get the newest song of your favorite female artist added quickly, we also look for the new 'breakout' artist that is hitting country radio across the country.

Diva Radio *KUSF*
kusf@usfca.edu
www.kusf.org
A focus on women's independently produced music, poetry and soundscape. Divas of all nationalities, religions and genders are welcome.

The Eclectic Woman *WTJU*
wtju@virginia.edu
wtju.radio.virginia.edu/eclectic
wtju.radio.virginia.edu
Showcases female singer-songwriters, musicians and composers from a variety of musical genres like folk, rock, jazz, blues, world and country.

EVE OUTLOUD *WICB*
wicb@ithaca.edu
www.ithaca.edu/radio/wicb
We're ALWAYS looking to promote new artists! Send material to: Katrina Baker and Danie Taylor, Eve Outloud (92 WICB Ithaca), Park School of Communications, 953 Danby Rd. Ithaca, NY 14850

Every Woman *WAIF*
waif@waif883.org
www.waif883.org
Women's music and issues. Send material to: EVERYWOMON, WAIF-FM, PO Box 6126, Cincinnati OH 45206

Every Woman Legacy *KKFI*
kkfi901@aol.com
www.kkfi.org

Face the Music Radio Show *WCUW*
sylly@aol.com
www.wcuw.com
Syndicated lesbian/feminist music program. Womyn's music, announcements, opinions and humor.

Female Form *KBGA*
kbga@selway.umt.edu
kbga.org
A tribute to the female form. All female artists and bands: ranging from country to punk.

Female Musician Radio
tjo@femalemusician.com
www.femalemusician.com
Dedicated to educate, promote and empower women interested in pursuing a music career. Exposing new music by artistic talented women gives this listing and learning experience an extra groovin' attraction.

Female Perspective *WAPS*
heathermoon913@yahoo.com
www.913thesummit.com
Thursday night is now "Ladies Night" here at 91.3 The Summit! Join Heather Moon for 60 minutes of nothing but female singers, songwriters and rockers from all styles of music past, present and local.

The Feminine Groove

Barb Hill brnshuga61@yahoo.com
www.cyberstationusa.com
I invite you to listen every Sunday at 11am(est) for a FULL hour of some of the best music, from today's women artists. And to top it off, I'll feature each month some local and regional artists.

Feminist Magazine

feministmagazine@yahoo.com
www.feministmagazine.org
The only feminist radio show in Southern California, heard on the only corporate-free spot on your radio dial. We do feature the work of women musicians, but we are not a music show. We are a public affairs show that eagerly spotlights the work of women in all walks of life.

La Femme Fatale *WBRS*

www.wbrs.org
Dedicated to dangerous women and their music. We bring you Pop to Folk with twists around every corner.

Femme FM *KUT*

Teresa Ferguson sanferg@austin.rr.com
www.kut.org
Intelligent, witty and wild about music describes Teresa Sansone Ferguson, producer and host of Femme FM, a program that since 1994 has placed the spotlight squarely on music performed by women artists of all musical genres.

FREEFORM *WCBN*

Kelly Szott kszott@umich.edu
www.wcbn.org
I am very interested in women in indie rock and I try to include as much of it as I can on my show. I think it's the closest thing we've got at the station to a women's music show.

Girl O'Clock *WPRB*

music@wprb.com
www.wprb.com

The Girlie Lounge *WXOU*

www.oakland.edu/org/wxou
For 90 minutes, relax in knowing that there are women out there, sending a ray of hope that men are not the only ones out there putting out music. From the earliest ladies in music to the unknown newcomers, the girls will entertain you every Monday.

The Girl's Room *KWVA*

kwva@gladstone.uoregon.edu
gladstone.uoregon.edu/~kwva
Our show is dedicated solely to female artists and airs on Thursday nights from ten to midnight.

Grrrl Action Plus *WUSB*

music@wusb.org
www.wusb.org
It's indie rock/pop/punk with post-riot grrrl sensibilities. Let your host Miss Margaret escort you through the latest releases in the world of college radio, plus a wide selection of the past decade's best in indie music.

Grrl Radio

bonnie@grrl.com
www.grrl.com

Grrrl Action Plus *WUSB*

info@wusb.org
wusb.fm/grrrlactionplus
www.wusb.org
Indie rock/pop/punk with an emphasis on riot grrrl and post-riot grrrl, plus lots of new releases.

Grrrlville *WIDR*

widr-program@groupwise.wmich.edu
www.widr.org
Estrogen-powered music of all types.

gURLradio

www.gurl.com/stop/music/radio
Radio just for you. Find some new, delicious sounds and hear some favorites!

gurlwhurls radio

www.gopha.net/whurls
We want to play as much music as possible and we don't make demands for free CDs like some other sites do. We'll even play your material if we don't like the music - because someone out there will be glad we did and that is what we're here for!

Her Infinite Variety *WORT*

www.wort-fm.org
Showcases women in all genres/styles of music. Includes feminist and lesbian music, other music made by women, interviews, comedy, poetry, community announcements.

In Other Words *KUFM*

www.kufm.org
Women's program of music, international news, interviews, local events and more. Produced locally.

Instrumental Women *KSDS*

www.ksds-fm.org
Janine Harty highlights the significant contributions women have made to the art form of Jazz.

Instrumental Women *Minnesota Public Radio*

Lauren Rico lrico@mpr.org
music.mpr.org/features/0102_instrumentalwomen
I am open to classical music performed, composed or conducted by women. I try to highlight the history of women in American orchestras and also bring attention to the current state of affairs. Submissions are most welcome: Lauren Rico, Minnesota Public Radio, 45 East Seventh Street, St. Paul, MN, 55101

It's A Girl Thang *WEVL*

wevl@wevl.org
wevl.org
Friday - 6-7 pm. New and old music from female vocalists and musicians in the blues, R&B and soul genres. Hosted by Jeanne.

Kitty Collision *KCPR*

kcprMD@kcpr.org
www.kcpr.org
Girl pop! Girl punk!

Ladies First *WKNC*

wknc.org

Ladies Lounge *WWPV*

wwpv@smcvt.edu
personalweb.smcvt.edu/wwpv
From Riot Grrl to Folk Rock.

Ladies Night *Wildcat Radio*

radio@k-state.edu
wildcatradio.ksu.edu

The Ladies of Daemon

hello@daemonrecords.com
www.daemonrecords.com/beta/radio
Webcast playing the artists of Daemon Records.

Ladies, Women, & Girls *KGLX*

www.kglx.org
Showcasing female artists.

Lesbian Power Authority *KFAI*

kfai.org/programs/l_p_a.htm
From a femmist/womanist perspective. Featuring Lesbian culture and politics, music, interviews, announcements, Dyke Chat, conversation, challenging political commentary and much more.

Luscious Voices

Paul Cattro cattrone@hotmail.com
www.live365.com/stations/103350
Created to promote the female vocalists/artists/sounds whose sound I've fallen in love with over the years. The artists featured here range over various different styles- pop, jazz, ambient, trip-hop...a lil bit of everything.

Midnight Divas *KUFM*

Andrea Imbriaco citychick59801@yahoo.com
www.kufm.org
A show featuring women jazz singers from the 1920's to the present.

MP3.com Stations for Women

stations.mp3s.com/stations/women
To date there are over 2800 online MP3.com stations that are set up exclusively for women's music.

Nette Radio

submit@netteradio.com
netteradio.com
A weekly internet radio show hosted on Musicians.Net. We feature bands/artists/singer songwriters that include at least one woman. Many of our artists are featured on GoGirlsMusic.com.

New folk Revival *WGDR*

www.wgdr.org
The show is a blend of contemporary folk, acoustic blues, bluegrass and Celtic music with an emphasis on woman artists.

Odd Man Out *WUOG*

md@wuog.org
wuog.org
From hardcore riot grrrl punk noise to the ambient and soothing melodies of the Caribbean, this show brings the voice of women straight to you. This is the show your mom wishes she'd listened to.

Open Minds *KRFC*

krfcfm.org
A weekly radio show that spotlights women's voices from music to politics. We're looking for high quality women artists in the folk, blues and jazz. Please submit cds to KRFC, 1705 Heatheridge D303, Fort Collins, CO 80525. All CDs will be reviewed and responded to.

Other Voices *WORT*

wort@terracom.net
www.wort-fm.org.
Music from world classical traditions in a wide range of styles and eras, focusing on women composers, performers and conductors. Periodically features entire shows devoted to a particular artist, composer, or theme.

Pandora's Box *KRUI*

krui@uiowa.edu
www.uiowa.edu/~krui
You can find the best variety in Female Music by listening to Pandora's Box. From Ella to Ani, Pandora's Box spans the generations and the genres of your favorite female artists.

Rocket Girl Radio
admin@rocketgirls.net
www.rocketgirls.net
We want girls that are eclectic, yet entertaining. Girls that have something to say. The few who want to break the mold and start again. Girls who can rock it.

Rock On with Yr Frock On *WBAR*
wbar@columbia.edu
www.wbar.org
Grrl rock and folk for the masses.

A Room of One's Own *WVUD*
Ann Van Den Hurk amvandenhurk@aol.com
www.wvud.org
The show's name comes from the Virginia Wolf book, A Room of One's Own. The focus of the show is to highlight female musical artists from every type of music and era of recording. Hence, the show allows female artists a room to shine in.

Satellite Sisters
sisters@satellitesisters.com
www.satellitesisters.com
The show is hosted by the five Dolan sisters consisting of in-depth and intimate conversations. Each show features 4 to 6 songs woven into the dialogue and used as transitions. Weekly, all songs, artists and labels are listed on the Web site as well as compiled on the newsletter. Because we produce in NY and LA, CD's should be sent to both: Sarah Lemanczyk, Assistant Producer, Satellite Sisters, WNYC Radio, 1 Centre Street, 24th Floor, New York, NY 10007 AND Lian Dolan, Satellite Sisters, 1083 Prospect Blvd. Pasadena, CA 91103

Sing It, Sister *KRZA*
krza@krza.org
www.krza.com
Featuring women musicians.

Sirens *KUGS*
music@kugs.org
www.kugs.org
Dedicated to women making noise.

Sirens' Muse *WEBL*
wevl.org
Sunday - 10 am-noon. Rotating hosts play a variety of genres of contemporary music by women.

Sister Sound *KAOS*
kaos@evergreen.edu
www.kaosradio.org
Music and information for, by and about women.

Sisters *KUCS*
info@kvsc.org
www.kvsc.org
We're on Sundays from 2-5pm.

SmartWomen Internet Radio
info@smartwomen.org
www.smartwomen.org
We are THE women's internet radio station!

Something About the Women *WMFO*
satwomen@aol.com
www.expage.com/somethingaboutwomen
www.wmfo.org
Boston's longest running women's program of music and commentary. Features the voices of woman artists in all genres, plus news and information of interest to women and their friends.

The Sound Job *WNCI*
oak.conncoll.edu/wcni
We are back with music by women only, but not for women only... so leave your dick at home. Oh, you are at home. Well stop thinking about it for a little while.

Southwest Women's Radio
cheryl@southwestwomen.com
www.southwestwomen.com
Singer-songwriters, performers, musical artists and groups in all genres.

Stroke the Goddess *WMHB*
Annie aandandy@somtel.com
wmhb@colby.edu
www.colby.edu/wmhb
A show devoted to music by female artists. I'm the host, Annie Earhart and I especially like to play NEW music by women. I see it as a forum for women to have their say through music. It helps the listeners keep a finger on the pulse of what's happening in our culture today.

Suffragette City *KDHX*
suffragette@kdhx.org
www.kdhx.org/programs/suffragettecity.htm
www.kdhx.org
René Saller celebrates the diverse stylistic range of women (and men) in music Mondays from 10 p.m. until Midnight. The mood and pace? Challenging but not jarring; beautiful but not sappy; fun but not mindless; sometimes catchy, sometimes cacophonous, sometimes pretty, sometimes spooky, always interesting.

Suffragette Station Online *KTUH*
www.geocities.com/Colosseum/Midfield/1244/ss
ktuh.hawaii.edu
I'm proud to roll out some of the best in contemporary folk, folk-rock and alt-folk by some incredible women singer-songwriters.

Under the Skirt *WDBX*
www.wdbx.org
Playing women vocalists (jazz, rock, indie etc.) Besides her show, Chris writes for the local entertainment weekly and is a fine singer in her own right.

The Vagina Analogues *WUAG*
www.uncg.edu/wua
Features girl driven bands.

Venus Rising *KRBS*
krbs@cncnet.com
www.radiobirdstreet.org
Music by women. Local and underplayed. Spoken word and women's issues.

Voices of Women *WRIU*
jpthabigga@aol.com
www.wriu.org

WBUST Radio
bust@aol.com
www.bust.com

WCCS *Wheaton College*
wccsradio@hotmail.com
wccs.wheatonma.edu
We have various shows which focus on woman's music but they change in format and djs from year to year because we are a free format station.

Wild Women Never Get the Blues *WNTI*
wnti@wnti.org
www.wnti.org
Features female blues artists.

Wild Women Radio
www.newhaven.edu/wnhu

Wimmin Do This Every Day *KAOS*
www.kaosradio.org
Blues, punk, folk, indigenous, spoken word and feminist rants and raves.

The Wimmin's Music Program *KKUP*
Laura rinaldi@ihwy.com
www.sans-serif.com/music.html
www.kkup.com
The show is on KKUP 91.5 from 11am to 1pm every Sunday except the third Sunday of the month, when it is hosted by someone else. I play music by, about and for women. Mostly folk-like, but I will stray sometimes. I interview authors and musicians and like to feature people that no one has heard of.

The Woman Show *KWCW*
www.whitman.edu/kwcw
Classical and modern songs by and about women. Coupled with engaging discussion concerning why women are lesser. Or more.

Woman Song *KKFI*
kkfi@kkfi.org
www.kkfi.org

Woman Voices *KUNV*
kunv.unlv.edu
Want to hear some singing women? Tune in Sundays at Noon with host Gerrie Blake.

Woman to Woman *KKFI*
kkfi901@aol.com
www.kkfi.org

Woman to Woman *WSPS*
jt@wspsfm.com
www.wspsfm.com

Woman's Voice *WUSR*
academic.uofs.edu/organization/wusr

Womanifesto *WUSC*
wuscsm@gwm.sc.edu
wusc.sc.edu
We dedicate two hours to honor women in music. We cover all genres of music from folk and pop to world and ska! Each week there's a cd showcase, showcasing a new cd/album from an artist!

Womanotes *KBCS*
kbcsdj@ctc.edu
kbcs.fm/programs.asp#folk
Enjoy Jazz music by women of the past 75 years with hosts Tracey Wickersham and Melissa Meade.

Womanrock Radio
Brenda Khan brenda@womanrock.com
womanrock.com
I think it's important for all women musicians to realize their potential as players. Although women are much more prevalent in mainstream music today, the obstacles and prejudices are still there. But to rise above the muck and really learn to play, you first have to realize that it's possible to be a girl and still rock with as much passion as any guy out there..

Womanwaves *WFPK*
www.wfpk.org
We are being developed for a nationally syndicated show, so female artists (or fronted bands) send your stuff to me at WFPK 619 S. 4th St. Louisville, KY 40202.

Women Alive *KAXE*
kaxe@kaxe.org
www.kaxe.org

Women from Mars *KWAB*
www.workingforchange.com/radio
Singer-songwriter Marca Cassity showcases the best indy label artists and digs up obscure tracks from nationally signed acts. A tough act to follow herself, Cassity promotes developing artists with live-in-studio spots. Singer-Songwriter Wendy Woo takes time off the tour to co-host.

Women Hold Up Half the Sky *KALX*
kalx@media.berkeley.edu
kalx.berkeley.edu
Talk radio and music by and about women. Featuring weekly interviews with women involved in politics, health policy, gender issues and technology, the women's events calendar and analysis of world, national and local news.

Women in the 3rd Decade *KRCL*
www.krcl.org
This is a two and a half hour program of news, information and mainly music by women.

Women in Indie
copacetic@indieradio.org
www.indieradio.org/womeninindie
www.indieradio.org
It's all girl power pop and indie rawk. Women in Indie showcases those female artists and female fronted bands, who participate in the overall indie rock and pop scene.

Women In Music
Laney Goodman WomenOnAir@aol.com
www.womenonair.com
www.broadcast.com/shows/womeninmusic
A nationally syndicated public radio show with over 70 markets throughout the States. We are always looking for exciting new female talent to add to our playlists! If you're a female musician who is looking for more exposure and airplay, send your best material (CD's only) to: Women in Music with Laney Goodman, P.O. Box 15465, Boston, MA 02215

Women in Music *WYSO*
www.wyso.org/wysopgs/women.html
www.wyso.org
Current hosts Corey Slavitt and Pam Conine's intent is to retain the strong, creative voices of women performers who may not be heard on commercial radio. Is folk and acoustic music to your liking? Women in Music features this along with bluegrass, world and alternative artists.

Women In Music *WERS*
womeninmusic@wers.org
www.wers.org

Women in Music *KRVM*
Leigh wimusic@hotmail.com
www.krvm.org
From blues to new wave to the most current to the obscure. New artists, old artists, all varieties of music played, with one thing in common, these two hours are filled with music performed by women.

Women In Music *WTIP*
wtip@boreal.org
wtip.org
A new perspective to women and their music, featured artists and interviews.

Women in Rock *WEFT*
weft@weftfm.org
www.weft.org

Women of Jazz *KEWU*
www.kewu.ewu.edu
Three hours of music from dazzling divas.

Women of Note *WRSI*
www.wrsi.com
Women's music and events.

Women of Reggae
www.vibes3000.com
Show case of the talents of female reggae artists from the past till the present.

Women on Wednesday / One of Her Voices *KMUD*
md@kmud.org
www.kmud.org
Women's voices, women's issues and women's music. From one woman's voice to the next, from issues, to dialogue, to music and spoken word.

Women on Women Music Hour *WLUW*
wowmusichour@wluw.org
wluw.org
An hour and a half focusing on female musicians from all genres of music.

Women Who Rock *KWCW*
www.whitman.edu/kwcw
A celebration of women in music.

Women's Collective *KVMR*
music@kvmr.org
www.kvmr.org

Women's Focus *KUMN*
www.kunm.org
Women's magazine on politics, art, culture, news and information.

Women's Independent Music Show *(W.I.M.S.)*
Diane Ward wimsdiane@aol.com
www.wims.ws
Our dedicated mission and labor of love continues to be that of turning hungry listeners on to great independent music that is sent to us from all over the world.

Women's Music *KLCC*
www.klcc.org
Music by, for and about women, tapping a great reservoir of overlooked artists from a feminist perspective. Songs that can make you dance, sing along, think, relax, or blush. Host Nikki Breece likes to feature local musicians whenever possible and is hoping to incorporate more interviews with local and regional artists into the show.

Women's Music *KMUN*
kmun@seasurf.com
www.kmun.org

The Women's Music Hour *WWUH*
www.wwuh.org
An eclectic mix of rock, blues, folk and feminist music performed by female artists.

Women's Music Hour *WXPN*
xpn.org
Every Friday morning from 9-10AM, XPN is the only place on the dial where you will find sixty minutes devoted to women's music — sometimes recorded, sometimes live, always different.

Women's Music Mix *KBOO*
www.kboo.fm

Women's Music Radio *WMSE*
musicwomen91_7@hotmail.com
www.geocities.com/musicwomen91_7
www.wmse.org
For 15 years Women's Music Radio has played Folk, Blues, Rock, Punk, Hip Hop, Bluegrass, Country, Latina, Jazz, international etc. EVERY WEEK, we do our best to bring you the BEST in MUSIC from a wide VARIETY of women artists!

Women's Music Show *KUMD*
KUMD@d.umn.edu
www.kumd.org
Music by women in all genres, with local interviews and information.

Women's Radio
goladies@womensradio.com
www.womensradio.com
Our passion is to bring you the music of every woman artist your heart desires. And if we don't have what you want just let us know speak up - we're listening!

The Women's Show *WMNF*
www.wmnf.org
An eclectic feminist/womanist radio magazine hosted by Mary Glenney and Arlene Engelhardt. Music is mixed with arts and multicultural features including interviews, film and book reviews, announcements, news, speeches and documentaries by and about women.

Women's Voices *KZYX*
kzyx@kzyx.org
www.kzyx.org

Women's Windows *WERU*
info@weru.org
www.weru.org

Womenfolk *KFAI*
www.kfai.org/programs/womenflk.htm
Musical genres featured on Womenfolk range from traditional folk and country music to world beat. Interviews with local and national singer/songwriters are often featured.

Womensoul *KBOO*
www.kboo.fm

Womenspace *WFHB*
www.wfhb.org
Linda Cajigas / Carolyn VandeWiele. The very best from women artists past to present, folk to funk and everything in between.

WomYn *WRCU*
wrcu@mail.colgate.edu
wrcu.colgate.edu

Womyn Making Waves *WEFT*
weft@weftfm.org
www.weft.org
This program is one of the oldest on WEFT and has evolved into one of the finest of its kind in the region. Tune in if you want to hear music by, for and about women... all types... with the emphasis on MUSIC by women of power and influence - whether they are lesbians, bisexuals, heterosexuals or anyone else.

Womyn's *KBVR*
oregonstate.edu/dept/kbvr

Womyn's Action Group Radio Show (WAG) *KRNL*
cornellcollege.edu/krnl
A radio show on behalf of the Womyn's Action Group. Anything you send has a good chance of being played.

Canada

Audible Woman *CIUT*
Sarah speeb@interlog.com
www.interlog.com/~speeb/audwoman.htm
www.ciut.fm
It's that time of the month. Explore avant-garde music & performance of the past and present in all of its enterprising forms: encompassing sound-art, electroacoustic, improvisation, classical forms and much more.

Babae(h) Mama *CIUT*
Danielle and Donna babaehmama@yahoo.ca
www.ciut.fm
Join us for an hour celebrating WOMAN! The latest news, hot discussions, poetry slams, book/film reviews, backed by energizing music. Local and global feminist perspectives, especially within in the African, Caribbean, Filipina, Guyanese and Latina communities.

Big Broad Cast *CFUV*
musiccfuv@yahoo.ca
cfuv.uvic.ca

Broadly Speaking *CHRW*
chrw.usc.uwo.ca
Discussion on a variety of women's issues from the serious to the sublime as well as musical interludes. We are a spoken word show so music is limited to intros and bridges. Once in awhile we play a full song (mostly to fill time!) and on occasion do shows on women musicians and have then played a full song or two. We welcome music and bios from independent musicians.

Dykes on Mykes *CKUT*
music@ckut.ca
www.ckut.ca

Fallopian Tunes *CHUO*
www.chuo.fm

Girl's Night *CFUV*
musiccfuv@yahoo.ca
cfuv.uvic.ca
Lesbian women of colour.

Hersay *CKUT*
music@ckut.ca
www.ckut.ca

Lois' Jazz Lane and Jazz Coach *CHRW*
chrwmp@uwo.ca
chrw.usc.uwo.ca
Lois and Andrea rotate to give you a female perspective on Jazz. Lots of vocalists and lots of swing. Wednesdays 1-3 pm

A Madwoman's Underclothes *CRFU*
www.uoguelph.ca/~crfu
An unapologetic genre hop... words and music made mostly by women.

Radio Active Femminism *CKLN*
music@ckln.fm
www.ckln.fm
A news program for and about issues that concern women and feminism. Guest interviews, call-in forums, music, newsbytes, monthly features and special programming abound. On our show, sisters support each other regardless of race, sexuality, religion, economic status or age.

Rose Petal Power Hour *CHLY*
www.chly.fm
All genres.

Spin Stir *CHRW*
chrw.usc.uwo.ca
A rotating collective of women host this show which features exclusively female voices ~ for a change. Music, features and interviews. Also community news, events and commentary on a variety of women's and lesbian issues.

Spinsters On Air *CKDU*
ckdufm@is2.dal.ca
is2.dal.ca/~ckdufm
Pro-woman, Pro change Radio..

Wench *CIUT*
www.ciut.fm
Funky feminist fury. Tough chicks who ask a lotta questions and spin a lotta sound.

Women on Air *CFUN*
cfuv.uvic.ca
Unsilencing the silences. Music, news and interviews on diverse women's voices. The women on air showcase held every third Sunday of the month features a live, local DIVA in the studio.

Women in Music *CFUV*
musiccfuv@yahoo.ca
cfuv.uvic.ca

Womenspin *CKMS*
ckmsfm@web.ca
watserv1.uwaterloo.ca/~ckmsinfo
Women's music, news and views for everyone.

Womyn's Soul *CHRY*
chry@yorku.ca
www.yorku.ca/chry
A show by women, for women, about women. International documentaries on women and feminism are used to compliment literature by women writers. Women are the producers hosts and guests.

XX *CIOI*
radiomgr@mohawkcollege.ca
www.mohawkc.on.ca/msa/cioi
Music written and performed by women either solo, as part of a collaborative effort with other women or as part of a band including members of the "other" gender. Submissions for airplay are gladly received.

France

Babes in Boyland *Clapas FM, Montpellier*
babes@babesinboyland.info
www.babesinboyland.info
Entirely dedicated to women in music, especially "rock" but it nevertheless remains open to any digression, following the mistresses of ceremony's mood or the encounters they make. Feel free to send us stuff, demos, promos of new releases and we will be happy to put them on air.

panx radio
infos@panx.net
www.panx.net
HardCore, Punk, CyberThrash, Grindcore, TechnoBruit, Crades Mélodies.

Australia

Behind the Lines, Frock Off, Women with Attitude *2XX*
www.2xxfm.org.au
As part of our commitment 2XX Women in Radio present these three weekly programs: Behind the Lines, Frock Off, Women with Attitude. 2XX's music programs endeavour to give a fair representation to performances by women. Local bands and musicians are prominently promoted through live to air performances and local recordings.

Burning Down The House *RTR FM*
rtrfm@rtrfm.com.au
www.rtrfm.com.au
Women's issues and interests plus women in music. The programme has been broadcast for more than ten years and covers everything from current events like the new prostitution legislation in WA to new works from women writers, artists and musicians, health, lifestyle, community and cultural, social issues etc.

Drastic On Plastic *RTR FM*
rtrfm@rtrfm.com.au
www.rtrfm.com.au
Featuring women in music of all genres. The programme is presented by a collective of around 6 women on a roster basis with regular special guests. It is one of the longest running programmes on RTR FM - heading towards the 20 yr mark!

Freewaves *3RPP*
rpp@peninsula.hotkey.net.au
www.3rpp.asn.au
All women's program each Thursday 3pm-4pm. The girls really like to promote the achievements of women in all walks of life and particularly promote women artists.

Girly is Good *3CR*
girlyisgood@today.com.au
www.3cr.org.au
One hour of women's multi-arts programming. Featuring women musicians, visual artists, photographers, dancers, film makers, authors, composers....basically any art form that is girly.

The Grrrly Show *2RRR Sydney*
www.2rrr.org.au

Ladies' Lounge *TripleB*
bbbfm@mail.penalva.net
www.triplebradio.cjb.net

MegaHerz *4ZZZ*
info@4zzzfm.org.au
www.4zzzfm.org.au
Women's issues and music.

Radio for the Majority *Three D Radio*
www.threedradio.com
Plays solely music composed and/or performed by women, as well as tackling a wide variety of women's issues. This program is about to enter its second decade of existence and is going as strong as ever.

Women on Waves *JOY Radio*
info@joy.org.au
www.joy.org.au

New Zealand

A Girls Own Show *95b FM*
95bfm@95bfm.com
www.95bfm.co.nz
The show airs every Sunday evening from 7 - 8pm. The show's host is Ellie Lim and material can be sent to her c/o 95 bFM c/o A.U.S.A. Private Bag 92019, Auckland.

World Music Radio

4EB *Brisbane Australia*
www.4eb.org.au

alterNATIVE Voices
www.alternativevoices.org
The alterNative Voices Program Mission - To entertain, educate and generally promote positive excellence and appropriate role models by and for, American Indian people.

The American Indian Radio
airos@unl.edu
airos.org
A national distribution system for Native programming to Tribal communities and to general audiences through Native American and other public radio stations as well as the Internet.

Bagpipe World Radio
owner@bagpipeworldradio.cjb.net
www.bagpipeworldradio.cjb.net
The first radio station of any kind dedicated to the diffusion of the Great Highland Bagpipe 24 hours a day. In this case, Bagpipe World Radio is an only-internet-broadcasting radio station.

BBC Radio 3 *World Music*
www.bbc.co.uk/radio3/world

Earthsongs
earthsongs@radiocamp.com
www.earthsongs.net
Each week, Earthsongs gives Public Radio and Net listeners the chance to explore the Native influences that help shape and define contemporary American music.

Global Village
Jowi Taylor globalvillage@radio.cbc.ca
www.radio.cbc.ca/programs/global
Reports on musical life from 305 places in 108 countries.

KBOO *Portland, OR*
manager@kboo.org
www.kboo.fm

KGOU *U. Oklahoma*
kholp@ou.edu
www.kgou.org

International Pulse!
Michel Joseph msanonjoseph@hotmail.com
www.musicalmix.org
Biweekly World Music Radio show on WVKR (91.3FM, Poughkeepsie NY): the rhythmic music of Afro-Caribbean, South/Central America and Eurasia.

Joyous Noise Radio
jmadill@joyousnoise.com
www.joyousnoise.com/radio
Didjeridu music.

New World Buzz Radio
nwbfeedback@hotmail.com
www.newworldbuzz.com
Provides a showcase to promote the composers, artists and performers of music genres from all over the world.

Other Worlds
clough.brent@abc.net.au
www.abc.net.au/rn/music/otherw/default.htm
Often described as a 'lounge' show. If 'lounge' means Incan human-sacrifice music played by a woman from Germany, a 'Jew's Harp' from the highlands of Papua New Guinea and whispers of a group of school children recorded in Helsinki, then Other Worlds is 'lounge'.

Radio 4EB
www.4eb.org.au

Radio Bilingue
www.radiobilingue.org

Radio Louisiane
Admin@RadioLouisiane.com
www.radiolouisiane.com

Radio Nunavut
north.cbc.ca/north/radionunavut.html
Across the huge Nunavut Territory and in the Nunavik region of northern Quebec, CBC North serves listeners in Inuktitut and English. From the haunting and evocative sounds of traditional throat singers, to swinging vocal jazz styling. We showcase the talents and diversity of northerners in a compelling and entertaining way.

RadioOFIndia.com
info@radioofindia.com
www.radioofindia.com
Bollywood hits along with the best of regional music.

Roots Musik Karamu *SCERN*
www.scern.org
Centers on reggae music, but, also brings you the sounds of calypso, soca, blues, jazz, gospel, drumming and other Afro-centered musical genres.

SFB4 MultiKulti *Germany*
multikulti@sfb.de
www.multikulti.de

sakapfet.com
support@sakapfet.com
www.sakapfet.com
Your cyber-highway to Haiti.

Saturday's a Party *WUSB*
reggae@wusb.org
www.wusb.org
The longest-running reggae-politics mix (RPM) in the USA. Den de Dubwise playyyyyyy, it play, it play!!! Hosted by Lister Hewan-Lowe.

Vibe FM *Ghana*
www.vibefm.com.gh

Villiage 900 *Victoria, BC*
feedback@village900.com
www.village900.ca
Our music programming is a format called Global Roots, a contemporary mix of folk, roots and worldbeat music.

WLIB
info@wlib.com
www.wlib.com

World Fusion Internet Radio
Submissions@CultureBeyondBorders.com
CultureBeyondBorders.com
Plays an eclectic mix or world-influenced music from ambient to industrial. The station streams 24/7 with a different show every day of the week. We accept submission for airplay and review, but please be aware of the specific genre we cater too - world-influenced music.

World Party *Eastern Washington U.*
www.kewu.ewu.edu
Music from around the globe: Latin, Brazilian, African, European, Hawaiian, Reggae and others.

World Music Radio
info@worldmusicwebcast.com
www.worldmusicradio.com
An independent Internet-only live-hosted radio station featuring traditional and contemporary world and folk music.

WSHL *Stonehill College*
wshl@stonehill.edu
www.stonehill.edu/WSHL
We have a great interest in World Music (Latin, Asian, Spanish music etc) and also local music from the New England area.

WTMD *Towsen U.*
wtmd@towson.edu
www.towson.edu/wtmd
A non-commercial radio station, hear our relaxing blend of New Age and Smooth Jazz music, news, features, weekend music shows.

Radio Shows that Spotlight Local Musicians

"Local" is a relative term. To some stations, "local" describes anyone within the city limits and perhaps a bit outside of them. Others consider "local" to be any artist that lives within the listening area. There are many shows that consider "local" to be musicians from anywhere within the state, province or territory, while others consider "local" to be an artist from any region of the host country. If you're not sure if you qualify for a particular show, get in touch with the station (or host) and in most cases they will happily respond and clarify what they consider to be "local" talent.

United States

Alabama

WEGL *Home Grown*
wegl@auburn.edu
wegl.auburn.edu

WVUA *The Local Show*
program@newrock907.com
www.newrock907.com
*Music from all of your favorite struggling local artists
and even some who have made it.*

Alaska

KBBI *Homer City Limits*
www.kbbi.org
*We are a community radio station which reflects the
diverse sensibilities of the Southern Kenai Peninsula.
Sometimes spotlights local acts.*

KSUP
ksup@ptialaska.net
www.ptialaska.net/~ksup
No specific show but we'll play local music.

Arizona

KASC *Underground Terminal*
md@theblaze1260.com
www.theblaze1260.com
*Showcases a lot of AZ Hip Hop and other tight shit. If
you send us local music, it will be heard!*

KEDJ *Local Frequency*
www.theedge1039.com
*Three songs from Arizona's best local bands every
week night at midnight!*

KFMA *Local Luv*
greg@kfma.com
www.kfma.com
*Get your band on kfma's local luv Sundays at
8:50PM. Post a show on our local concert calendar.*

KLPX *Live and Local*
www.klpx.com
www.liveandlocal.net
*Local bands in Tucson and the surrounding areas are
encouraged to submit music for the show.*

KXCI *Locals Only*
www.kxci.org

KZGL
www.radioflagstaff.com/kzgl/ZHome.htm
Has several shows that spotlight local talent.

Arkansas

WXFX *The Fox Consumer Guide to New Rock*
thefox@wxfx.com
www.wxfx.com/guide

California

KALX *KALX Live! (in studio performing)*
kalx.berkeley.edu
kalx.berkeley.edu

KCR *Jocelyne's Show*
www.kcrlive.com

KCXX *Local Spotlight*
www.x1039.com
Features bands in the San Bernadino area.

KFRR *Native Noise*
www.newrock104.com
*Tuesday night midnight The Reverend and Robin
Lewis host Native Noise, a showcase for local talent.
Think you've got what it takes to make it to the Big
Time? Send us a demo and you just might hear your
band on Native Noise.*

KIOZ
www.kioz.com
*If you are in a local band, this is a cool opportunity
for you! Just send us an e-mail and include
information like: band name, website address, show
dates, any audio and video. We can't promise
everything will get up but we are going to try and get
as much information up on each of you that we can!
Remember this is for ALL local music!*

KLOS *Local Licks*
klos_coxk@hotmail.com
www.955klos.com
*The longest running showcase of undiscovered local
talent in Southern California! Listen Sunday night
from 11pm - 12midnight as Kelly Cox serves up the
latest and greatest that Southern California has to
offer.*

KOZT *Local Licks*
thecoast@kozt.com
www.kozt.com
*Mendocino County musicians playing a variety of
music.*

KPFA/KFCF *Across the Great Divide (folk)*
www.kpfa.org

KPIG *Local Show*
www.kpig.com

KPOO *J.J. On The Radio*
info@kpoo.com
www.kpoo.com
Interviews with Bay area jazz artists.

KPRI
ueo.ucsd.edu/KPRI.html
*We are dedicated to playing fresh music from new
artists. Mondays we dedicate to new music by
increasing the number of newer tracks we play.*

KRFH *Local Lixx*
www.humboldt.edu/~krfh

KRXQ *Local Licks*
www.krxq.net
*Sacramento's longest running local music showcase!
The best local bands in Sacramento along with the
occasional interview and special in-studio guest.
Local Licks was the first place Northern California
heard Sacramento based National Acts such as
Oleander, Die Trying, Papa Roach and the Deftones.*

KSDS *Local Jazz Corner*
www.ksds-fm.org

KSUN *The Jungle (Hip Hop to Punk), In the
Garage (Punk), Dumpster Diving (Punk), Happy
Hour (Punk), The T@x Collection (variety)*
www.sonoma.edu/ksun

KWOD *Sound of Sacramento*
www.kwod.com
*If you're in a local band and would like to be
considered for Radio air play, please send us your cd.*

KXLU
www.kxlu.com
*Bands and musicians from all over the world submit
their homemade music on cassettes and CDRs and
Demolisten is usually their only radio outlet. We
expose the unexposable.*

KZSU *Wednesday Night Live*
kzsu.stanford.edu

On Broadway Live
www.onbroadwaylive.com
*A great showcase of San Francisco musicians that
streams live over the internet.*

West Coast Live
INFO@WCL.org
www.wcl.org
*The show entertains and informs its audience with
music, ideas and humor from a rich mix of musicians,
writers and thinkers from the Bay Area and around
the country.*

XTRA *Loudspeaker*
www.91x.com
*91X's local show featuring bands from and in San
Diego. Loudspeaker has become San Diego's
launching pad for bands, some of whom include:
Blink 182, Unwritten Law, Jewel, Inch, Buck-O-Nine
and Steve Poltz just to name a few.*

Z90
z90rico@yahoo.com
www.z90.com
*Plays the music of local artists. Mostly dance and Hip
Hop.*

Colorado

KCSU *The Local Show*
www.kcsufm.com
*The KCSU music format focuses on new college and
alternative music. The music is selected to appeal to
the 18-34 year-old audience interested in a daring,
innovative, cutting-edge sound.*

KGNU *Kabaret*
music@kgnu.org
www.kgnu.org/kabaret
*Live music/spoken word program. The weekly
program is performed absolutely live and uncensored
at KGNU.*

KSRX
ksrx@blue.unco.edu
www.univnorthco.edu/ksrx
*The mission of our student radio station is to
entertain, inform and educate members of U.
Northern Colorado community.*

KTCL *Locals Only*
www.ktcl.com
*Check out new music from some of Colorado's best
musicians.*

KVCU *Local Shakedown*
localshakedown@yahoo.com
www.colorado.edu/StudentGroups/KVCU/localshake
down.html

KVDU *The Local Hour*
kvdu.du.edu

Connecticut

UltraRadio.com
Randy RBorovsky@aol.com
UltraRadio.com
*We play lots of independent rock artists, as long as
they are from Connecticut.*

WHUS *Bluesline, One World Radio, Sunday
Night Folk Festival*
info@whus.org
whus.org
*Music programming covers everything from polka to
techno.*

WKZE *Off the Beaten Track*
info@wkze.com
www.wkze.com
The show spotlights music from unsigned and independent artists residing within the WKZE listening area.

WPKN *Live Music Special*
wpkn.org
All forms of audio performance are permitted to exist, happening completely LIVE in our WPKN megastudios, produced and hosted by the amazingly weird DAVO!!!

WPKN *Off-Beat*
wpkn.org
The patented "'Off-Beat' New Music Review" exposes and critiques the latest sounds from various genres – a euphonious (& sometimes cacophonous) array from outside the commercial purview. Frequent live performances and interviews with the best local bands are tossed into the mix. There'll be no dozing during these overnights!

WPLR *Local Bands*
Rick allison@thehotspot.com
www.wplr.com
Do YOU want to be ON Local Bands? Send your tape, CD, or DAT, to: Local Bands, P.O. Box 6508 Whitneyville CT 06517

WSHU/WSUF *Profiles in Folk*
Steve Winters winters@wshu.org
www.wshu.org
The show is an exploration of the diverse world of folk and acoustic music, with many of the weekly shows centered on a theme. As the show's title conveys, the program profiles the topic or the performers featured. At least ten shows each year feature live, in-studio showcases by performers, with interviews.

WYBC *Local Rock Lunchbox*
md@wybc.com
www.am.wybc.com
Crammed full of the latest New Haven sounds and the dates and venues for upcoming concerts around town.

Delaware

96 Rock *Local Lixx*
skipdixxon@yahoo.com
www.96rockdelmarva.com
With Skip Dixxon every Sunday 8 - 10pm (the best in regional talent).

WSTW *Hometown Heros*
wstw@wstw.com
www.wstw.com

Florida

97X *Local Motion*
largo@97xonline.com
97xonline.com
Sunday Nights from 11:00-Midnight Pat Largo plays the best and brightest of our local music scene. Check out who's been in the studio, who's playing where, submit a gig, support your local music scene.

Rock 104 *Locals Only*
Lauren O'Neil oneil104@hotmail.com
www.rock104.com
The Locals Only Concert Series and the Locals Only Radio Show on ROCK104 explores the Gainesville music scene, featuring music by local and regional bands.

WFYV
rock@rock105i.com
www.wfyv105.com
We don't specifically have a show but if something good comes down the pipe, we will definitely give it consideration for air-play!

WJBX *Local X*
99x@99xwjbx.com
www.99xwjbx.com
New Rock 99X takes you on a magical journey through Southwest Florida's local music seen. You could hear the next big thing before it becomes the next big thing.

WJRR *Native Noise*
dj@realrock1011.com
www.wjrr.com
Every Sunday from 11pm-12mid, Join DJ as he brings you the best from the local music scene.

WLRN/WXEL *Folk & Acoustic Music Show*
wlrn.org
Serving Miami-Dade, Broward, Palm Beach and The Keys.

WNMF *Live Music Showcase*
WMNF@wmnf.org
www.wmnf.org

WNSU *The Local Show*
musicdirector@nsuradio.com
www.nsuradio.com
Every Thursday from 8PM to 9PM, we play the best music Florida has to offer. Features in studio interviews with local bands and information on upcoming local concerts.

WPRK *WPRK Comes Alive*
wprkfm@rollins.edu
www.rollins.edu/wprk
The best in basement radio. The voice of Rollins College.

WTKX
www.tk101.com
We'll listen to anything that is sent to us.

WVFS *Hootenanny*
music@wvfs.fsu.edu
www.wvfs.fsu.edu
WVFS is an award winning, charting setting, void filling college radio station offering the Tallahassee community a unique and diverse mix of programming while acting as a top-notch training facility.

WVUM *Locals Only*
info@wvum.org
wvum.org

WZTA *Zeta Goes Local*
Razor@ccmiami.com
www.949zeta.com
To submit music, send your band's CD or DAT to: ZETA Goes Local c/o Razor, 7601 Riviera Blvd. Miramar, FL 33023

Georgia

SLAB Radio *(Southern Local Area Bands)*
admin@slabmusic.com
www.slabmusic.com
Playing the music of bands from the Southeast United States.

WKLS *Stage 96*
www.96rock.com
We're dedicated to bringing you the finest in local music, with band bios, concert updates and local news in the Atlanta music market.

WMRE *Local Outbreak*
www.emory.edu\WMRE
Emory U.'s student radio station.

WPUP *Local Noise*
Chris brame@rock1037.com
www.rock1037.com
Three Hours of the Best in Local Music.

WRAS *Georgia Music Show*
www.wras.org
Please note: The Georgia Music Show does NOT play bands from out of state, hence the name of the show. If you used to live in Georgia and now live elsewhere, you are no longer local.

WREK *Live at WREK*
www.wrek.org
Music you don't hear on the radio.

WUOG *Live in the Lobby*
lmd@wuog.org
wuog.org
The local music department follows the Georgia music scene (primarily Athens/Atlanta) to program local artists, as well as producing live performances of local acts at the station. We screen local music, book artists for station remotes and help out with other Athens' events involving local musicians. Twice a week (Tuesdays and Thursdays) we welcome an Athens band into the studio for Live in the Lobby.

Hawaii

Aloha Joe
alohajoe@alohajoe.com
www.alohajoe.com
Will play any music created on the Island.

KTUH *Monday Night Live*
ktuh.hawaii.edu

Illinois

ChicagoHouseRocks.com
info@chicagohouserocks.com
www.gottahavehouse.com
Every two weeks, you will find a brand new audio show featuring the DJ talents of the ChicagoHouseRocks.com crew as well as guest DJs brought over from all over the Windy City.

Goon Squad Radio
Tom Printy dj@goonsquadradio.com
www.goonsquadradio.com
Streaming Indies from Chicago. We are a Chicago based web stream that is seeking more artists from the greater Chicago/IL area. Please contact me to get your material into our playlist.

Hootenanny Saturday Night
J. Roger crimsonbeard@hotmail.com
atomicmouserecordings.com/hsn
A show on RedLine Radio 99.1FM in Chicago. We're always looking for new and interesting stuff to play on-air. CHICAGO AREA BANDS: we will be assembling the occasional local music feature.

WBEZ *Performance Space*
www.wbez.org
Devoted to the art of live performance and primarily focuses on concerts and other live productions from Chicago-based artists and events. A wide variety of styles are featured—including jazz, blues, world music, classical, folk, alternative, rock, spoken word and performance art.

WDCB *Folk Festival, Strictly Bluegrass*
www.cod.edu/wdcb
We're known for our eclectic music programming: lots of jazz, folk and classical. We also broadcast local news, features and useful information for residents of our community college district

WEFT *Local and Live*
weft@weftfm.org
www.weft.org

WESN *The Local Music Show*
wesn@sun.iwu.edu
www.iwu.edu/~wesn

Windy City Masala
www.windycitymasala.com
Dance music every Friday night.

WKQX *Local 101*
Music@Q101.com
www.q101.com
Wanna be on Local 101? Send your demo and info to: Q101's Local 101, 230 Merchandise Mart Plaza Chicago, IL 60654.

WLUW *Radio Free Chicago*
wluwradio@wluw.org
wluw.org
Interviews, music and guests explore Chicago's independent music scene.

WONC *Local Chaos*
members.tripod.com/localchaos
www.wonc.org

WIIT
wiit@iit.edu
radio.iit.edu
We have a few shows that specialize in local music!

WPGU *Innerlimits*
DrewPatterson1071@yahoo.com
www.wpgu.com
One hour of local music Sunday nights at 10pm.

WRRG *chicagocore*
info@wrrg.org
www.wrrg.org
We accept music / spoken-word submissions in the following formats: cd, vinyl, minidisc and cassette (that's listed in order of preference).

WXRT *Local Anesthetic*
Richard Milne rankenter@aol.com
www.wxrt.com
This weekly showcase of Chicago's music community features exclusive interviews and live performances, as well as artist profiles of the area's top musicians and leading cultural figures. WXRT will only accept recorded materials that are clearly labeled as such. This includes Chicago band submissions to Local Anesthetic. Any packages with hand written "send to" or "received from" information will not be accepted into the station.

Indiana

MWB Radio
Mark and Jenny Lush
mwbcontact@midwestbands.com
www.live365.com/stations/midwestbands?site=midwestbands
The Internet Radio station for MidwestBands.com, playing the music of great independent bands and artists listed at MidwestBands.com! Tune in to hear THE BEST Independent music in the Midwest on MWB Radio!

One Kind Radio
jbowles@onekindradio.com
www.onekindradio.com
An independent streamline monthly webradio bringing a worldwide audience the best in local and independent music from NW Indiana, Chicago and beyond.

WFHB *The Local Show*
www.wfhb.org

Iowa

KAZR *Local Licks*
jo@lazer1033.com
www.lazer1033.com
If your band is releasing a CD, send me an email with all of the info.

Liars Holographic Radio Theatre *KCCK*
bobs@kcck.org
www.kcck.org
A unique blend of music, stories, short plays, poetry and spurious sponsors presented by local performers.

KKEZ *Mix 94.5*
www.kkez.com
No specific show, but will play the music of local artists.

KUNI *Live from Studio One*
Karen Impola karen.impola@uni.edu
www.kuniradio.org/kustud.html
Unique weekly live broadcast featuring local and national artists.

Kansas

KJHK *Plow the Fields*
kjhk@mail.ku.edu
kjhk.ukans.edu
KJHK is the student-run radio station at U. Kansas. Our signal — 90.7 fm — spans from Topeka to KC and can also be streamed over the Internet.

KLZR *Local Lazer Music*
www.lazer.com
Wanna be on the radio? Send those cd's and concert updates to this address: Lazer Local Music, c/o Newman, 3125 W 6th Street, Lawrence, KS 66049. If you have music in the format of MP3, you can email it to me.

KSDB
wildcatradio.ksu.edu
Local show every Saturday.

Kentucky

WRFL *Local Show*
music@wrfl.org
www.wrfl.org

WTFX *Local Bandwidth*
www.foxrocks.com

Louisiana

New Orleans Radio
info@neworleansradio.com
www.neworleansradio.com
We've incorporated your user submitted information into the design of the New Orleans Radio website. So, whether you're a listener, writer, musician, record label, club owner or arts patron, you can promote it here.

Radio Free New Orleans
www.neworleansonline.com/neworleans/music/rfno.html
You can tune into the world's happiest music right here, broadcasting from the Pleasure Center of your Brain.

WRKF *The General Store (acoustic-folk)*
wrkf@aol.com
www.wrkf.org
Classical music programming throughout the day.

WTUL
www.tulane.edu/~wtul
Local Show every Saturday.

Maine

WMPG Local Motive
localmotives@yahoo.com
www.wmpg.org
Every Friday night, we bring a the sounds of a local Portland band from the tiny confines of our studio into your living room with a little help from the magic of radio. Join host Jan Wilkinson each week for a new flavor of the local music scene. Always live, always local.

WMPG *The Locals*
www.wmpg.org
Highlights local acts, singers, bands and producers who are some how, some way local. Featuring local country, folk, jazz, alternative, pop, dance, soft to medium rock; anything but a lot of noise.

WRBC *Community Forum*
www.bates.edu/people/orgs/wrbc
The student radio station of Bates College

Maryland

WWDC *Local Lix*
roche@dc101.com
dc101.com
A music show devoted to the many great local bands in the D.C. metropolitan area. Think your band is up to the challenge? Then get your CD to Roche ASAP dammit!!! The rules (and there are always rules) are simple: Your CD (and it has to be a CD...no MP3s) must be broadcast quality You MUST have a schedule playing gigs. No cuss words on the featured song.*

WRNR *Damian's Local Diner, Homegrown Music*
www.wrnr.com
Damian's Local Diner: Explore the local music scene with WRNR's legendary disc jockey, Damian, with live in-studio performances, interviews and lots of local music. Homegrown Music: WRNR continues its dedication to local music and musicians with regularly featured songs by local songwriters and performers. No other station in the region has this kind of connection to local music.

Massachusetts

BCR *The Ska of Boston*
radio@babson.edu
radio.babson.edu
BCR does not broadcast over the air waves; however, we do stream through the Web.

Exploit Boston! Radio
contact@exploitboston.com
www.exploitboston.com/radio.php
Features Boston pop and rock bands past and present. If you are a band in the Boston area, get in touch with us if you'd like to share your music with Exploit Boston!

Folk and Good Music Show
www.geocities.com/morganhuke
An experience of acoustic and electric tunes live from Studio A and also Studio Dee. Features prominent and up and coming artists.

iMassRadio
imass@timescommunications.com
www.imassradio.com
A new internet-only radio station for Massachusetts. We focus on featuring unsigned musicians of most genres on Sunday evenings from 6-11 PM with plans of expansion soon. We invite you to visit our and contact us to get your music added to our playlist.

WAAF *Bay State Rock*
Carmelita carm1073@hotmail.com
www.baystaterock.com
www.waaf.com
Playing the music of bands from the Boston area.

WAMH *Live Concert*
wamh.amherst.edu

WBCN *Boston Emissions*
www.wbcn.com
Features local artists plus a band of the month.

WBRS *The WBRS Coffeehouse, The Joint*
info@wbrs.org
www.wbrs.org

WFNX *New England Product*
fnxradio@fnxradio.com
fnxradio.com
We are your high energy down to earth show that has no musical restrictions. New England Product features special live in-studio performances and interviews and focuses on bringing you the most information to point you they way of the best club shows or the best new up-and-coming acts.

WGBH *Jazz from Studio Four*
www.wgbh.org

WICN *Jazz New England*
Joe Zupan jzupan@wicn.org
www.wicn.org
You'll hear lots of music from regional artists, conversations about the music and you'll find out where you can see this wealth of talent in performances.

WICN *The Contemporary Café*
webmaster@wicn.org
www.wicn.org
The finest acoustic performances of Folk, Blues and Americana music by the biggest names in New England and around the world.

WICN *Live From Café Fantastique*
webmaster@wicn.org
www.wicn.org
Every Saturday evening from 5 to 7:30 p.m. WICN presents some of the best local and nationally acclaimed musicians in folk, blues and country music.

WJUL *Live from the Fallout Shelter*
fallout@thechaosbakery.com
fallout.thechaosbakery.com
wjul.cs.uml.edu
The space in which live bands perform at WJUL. Started in the early 80's by Bob Weston Live From the Fallout Shelter is WJUL's most popular show.

WMBR *Pipeline Tuesdays*
music@wmbr.org
wmbr.mit.edu

WMVY *The Local Music Cafe*
wmvy.vineyard.net
This program features music from some of the best local musicians on Cape Cod and the Islands of Martha's Vineyard and Nantucket. First and third Thursday of every month at 10pm with Alison Hammond.

WMWM *Traxx of the Towns*
eboard@wmwm.org
www.wmwm.org
Underground/alternative rock, Tons O' Local Music, buttloads of rap and hip-hop, hardcore, blues, rare 50's music (Uncle Henry's Basement), hardcore, techno/rave, contemporary Christian, hardcore, country/western, psychedelic stuff....

WPXC *Homegrown*
rockbabe@pixy103.com
www.pixy103.com
Cape Cod's Original Local Artists Showcase. Includes band of the month.

WTBU *Sublimity*
www.wtburadio.com

WZBC *Mass. Avenue and Beyond*
www.wzbc.org
I play two hours of the best local rock, focusing on new music. My show includes interviews from local musicians, artists, filmmakers etc. and I update my audience on events by local talent. I have been a ZBC DJ on and off since 1991 and love to play music from old incarnations of the show along with new music.

Michigan

The Sonic Chronicles
aaronchilds@ameritech.net
www.m4radio.com
A live, interactive web radio program from Jackson, Michigan and plays unsigned and independent label acts in rock, blues, jazz and electronica genres, with an emphasis on the local music scene in south central Michigan.

WCBN *The Local Music Show*
music@wcbn.org
www.wcbn.org

WDBM *The Basement*
www.impact89fm.org

WDET *The Martin Bandyke Program*
wdetfm@wdetfm.org
www.wdetfm.org

WGRD *UltraSound*
mgrey@wgrd.com
www.wgrd.com
To submit your band's music for airplay on UltraSound, mail a studio-quality CD to Michael Grey, c/o WGRD Radio, 50 Monroe NW Ste. 500, Grand Rapids, MI 49503.

WIDR *It Came From Next Door*
www.widr.org
Hear Michigan music before everyone else.

WRIF *Motor City RIFFS*
www.wrif.com
Local rock.

Minnesota

KFAI *Local Sound Department (LSD)*
www.kfai.org

KQRS *KQ Homegrown*
www.92kqrs.com
Tune in for the most recent releases by your favorite local groups as well as classic material that you have grown to love. You can catch a live performance (from the now infamous Studio B) by a different group each week. We also feature recorded music, interviews and a roving reporter who scopes out the club scene.

KTCZ *Minnesota Music*
Jason Nagle Jason@Cities97.com
www.cities97.com
We support local artists by putting our MUSIC where our mouth is. In addition to playing their tunes throughout the playlist, we dedicate a full hour to local artists Sunday nights at 10:00 p.m. during Minnesota Music.

KVSC *Monday Night Live*
info@kvsc.org
www.kvsc.org
KVSC is proudly supporting local artists. Every Monday at 10PM, it's an hour of live music from the KVSC performance studio featuring the best in Minnesota music.

KXXR *Loud & Local*
loudnlocal@93xrocks.com
www.93x.com

Mojo Radio
info@mnmojo.com
radio.mnmojo.com
Are you an artist with Minnesota connections? Then get your music – complete songs or CDs or just samples – on Mojo Radio. Just send us an e-mail and the Minnesota Blues Association gladly will accommodate you.

KUOM *Off the Record*
music@radiok.org
www.radiok.org
Local music and a live band in Studio K.

WHMH *Minnesota Homegrown*
Tim Ryan rhino@rockin101.com
www.rockin101.com
Rockin' 101 is looking for new material from bands for Minnesota Homegrown, Sunday nights at 9:30 P.M. to 10:00 P.M. If you have a band and want some exposure send CD's and bios to us.

Mississippi

WMSV *Homegrown*
WMSV@MsState.Edu
www.wmsv.msstate.edu

Missouri

KCFV
www.stlcc.cc.mo.us/fv/kcfv
Plays local music.

KPNT *The Local Show*
Frizz jefff@stl.emmis.com
www.kpnt.com
The hottest bands from the local scene. Get in on STL's bitchin' local scene and hear the indie bands that might become tomorrow's rock superstars. Please submit songs on CD to: The Local Show on KPNT, 800 Union Station, The Powerhouse Building, St. Louis, MO 63103 Attention: Frizz.

KWUR *The Side Trip*
md@kwur.wustl.edu
kwur.wustl.edu

Pulse Radio
pulse@stl-pulse.com
www.stl-pulse.com
Providing Internet radio, MP3 downloads, a web page with photos and a concert calendar for the next generation of musicians.

WVRV *The River Home Grown*
feedback@wvrv.com
www.wvrv.com

thegrowl.smsu.edu *The Sound of Springfield*
thegrowl@smsu.edu
thegrowl.smsu.edu

Montana

KBGA *The Local Show*
programming@kbga.org
kbga.org

KUFM *Musician's Spotlight*
www.kufm.org
Montana and regional musicians performing in KUFM's studios or in area theaters or clubs.

Nebraska

KEZO *Z-92's Homegrown*
www.z92.com
We are proud to bring Omaha and the World a half hour block of local rock. This 30 minute program features the best music from local rock bands every Sunday night at 10p.m.

KZUM *Alive in Lincoln*
strawberry67@earthlink.net
www.kzum.org
Variety of local artists of all genres.

KZUM *River City Folk*
www.kzum.org
Interviews and regional folk artists.

Live From the Mill *Nebraska Public Radio*
milllive@unl.edu
www.nprn.org
Features Nebraska Artists. The series, hosted by Music Director William Stibor, broadcasts from the Mill coffee shop in Lincoln's Haymarket District and other locations throughout Nebraska. Stibor hosts discussion and performances with featured guests representing a broad range of arts topics, including writing, dance, music and theatre.

Nebraska Public Radio *Live From The Mill*
William Stibor wstibor2@unl.edu
nprn.org/nprn_live_mill
Each week presenting interviews with artists and members of arts organizations.

Nevada

KOMP *The Home Grown Show*
homegrown@komp.com
www.komp.com
Join Laurie Steele every Sunday evening from 10:00pm to Midnight, as she showcases the best local bands in Las Vegas.

KXTE *It Hurts When I Pee*
www.xtremeradio.fm
The New Music Show With a Really Goofy Name. Sunday Nights @ 10:00. Local and Indie Bands.

New Hampshire

The Studio
mojo@ncia.net
www.mojomusicstudio.com
An independent radio show featuring original Artists from the Northeastern United States, which includes most music genres.

WFRD *Homegrown*
www.wfrd.com
Upper Valley's local rock resource.

WHEB *Local Licks*
locallicks@wheb.com
www.wheb.com
Each night, WHEB takes a look at the Seacoast and New England's up-and-coming artists... Local Licks alumni include Godsmack, Jeramiah Freed and maybe your band next?

New Jersey

WBZC *Burlington County Bluegrass, World In Tune*
staff.bcc.edu/radio

WDHA *Homegrown Spotlight*
www.wdhafm.com
Weeknights at 7:30.

WFMU
www.wfmu.org
Many local acts perform live in the studio.

WNTI
www.wnti.org
We have several shows that feature local artists.

WSOU *Street Patrol*
www.wsou.net
Highlighting the area's top local hard rock acts.

WTSR *Local Noise*
hellfishw2@aol.com
www.trenton.edu/~wtsr
Highlights new and unsigned bands from the Tri-State Area. Periodically we'll be lucky enough to have a band make an appearance in the studio to perform some of their songs and discuss them with the listeners. When sending an e-mail, please put "Local Noise" in the subject line.

New Mexico

KRUX *The Local Show*
www.krux.nmsu.edu

KTAO *Acoustic Café*
ktao@newmex.com
www.ktao.com

KTEG *Local Edge*
jamie1047edgeradio@yahoo.com
www.1047edgeradio.com
Jamie plays the best music from your favorite local bands every Sunday night at 10. Support local music and listen, dammit! To contact Jamie about getting your stuff on the Local Edge, send her an email.

New York

eindie records - eindie radio
Jacob Bouchard kickitonetime@hotmail.com
www.eindie.com/NewFiles/eindieRadio.html
Playing the bands of eindie. Other local NY bands, influences of... Selection of Punk, New Wave, Classic Rock and Rap. Filling in the gaps in radio. MP3 stream.

Aural Fix
auralfix@optonline.com
www.auralfix.com
Features artists from the Long Island, New York region.

Metro Mix Radio
info@metromixradio.com
www.metromixradio.com
Your source for the best in underground dance music 24/7. Metro Mix features non stop exclusive full length, high quality streaming mp3 mixes created by some of the best known and undiscovered New York Metropolitan Area DJs.

WAIH *Local Bands*
waih@potsdam.edu
www2.potsdam.edu/WAIH
Are you a musician or belong in a band? Do you want your music to be played on the radio? Would you like to talk about or promote your music through on-air interviews and live performances? Well, now's your chance buddies and buddettes.

WBAB *The Homegrown Show*
Fingers@cox.com
www.wbab.com
For over 20 years WBAB has supported the local Long Island music scene, playing Long Island's best bands. Catch today's rising stars weeknights at 11:50pm. Past Homegrown bands include Twisted Sister, Blue Oyster Cult, Taylor Dayne, D-Generation and Zebra.

WBNY *The Local Show*
www.buffalostate.edu/wbny

WGFR *The Local Show*
www.wgfr.org

WHRW *The Big Drew Show*
www.whrwfm.org
The best in local Hip-Hop!

WICB *Home Brew*
wicb@ithaca.edu
www.ithaca.edu/radio/wicb
Check out our local music scene every Tuesday night at 9. Join Taz for local music news and in studio performances.

WLIR *Tri-State Sound*
Harlan Friedman harlan@wlir.com
www.wlir.com/shows/tss
www.wlir.com
Showcases the best up and coming musicians from Long Island, New York City, Connecticut and New Jersey.

WUSB *Local Insomniac Music*
www.wusb.org
The best in original local music from the Tri-State area, in a variety of genres, for people who like to stay up all night.

WUSB *Local Spotlight*
Bill Frey Themusicneverstops@wusb.org
www.wusb.org
The Local Spotlight show is hosted by Bill Frey on alternating weeks and various WUSB djs on the opposite weeks.

WVKR *Scene Unseen*
music@wvkr.org
www.wvkr.org
Featuring bands and music artists from the listening area. Local music news, interviews and live musical performances.

North Carolina

WSQL *Southern Exposure*
www.wsqlradio.com
Live show from the Essence of Thyme featuring local musicians.

The END 106.5 *90 Minutes*
90minutes@1065.com
www.1065.com
Since 1995 The END has supported the best local & regional music around with 90 minutes hosted by Divakar.

WKNC
wknc.org
We play one local/regional artist an hour & every Friday noon to 2 PM we have a local music show.

WXNR *Local 99*
www.wxnr.com

WZMB *Locals Only*
www.wzmb.ecu.edu

Ohio

KBUX *Tones of Home*
www.underground.fm
A selection of the best in Ohio music. We also have slots once or twice every hour where djs have to play local artists.

The Village Buzz Radio
sergio@village-buzz.com
village-buzz.coffee-black.com
All the cool with the n/e Ohio music scene.

WAIF *Kindred Sanction*
kindredsanction@hotmail.com
www.waif883.org
Local, regional music and interviews.

WAIF *Live City Licks, SpinCincinnati*
waif@waif883.org
www.waif883.org

WAPS *DIY Radio*
ron@diyradio.net
www.diyradio.net
www.913thesummit.com
Two hours of punk rock, past and present, with spotlights on the local music scene with your hosts Ron Mullens and Ed the Human Cannonball.

WBWC *Local Artist Show*
contact@wbwc.com
www.wbwc.com

WCSB *Blue Monday (blues), The True Unda Ground (truth hip hop)*
www.wcsb.org

WDUB
cd@wdubradio.com
wdubradio.com
If you're an artist or band from the Northern Ohio area, we want your music. Commercial radio gives the local artists a couple of hours late on a Sunday night. The artists of Northern Ohio deserve more recognition than that. That's where we come in.

WIOT
wiot@clearchannel.com
www.wiot.com
No specific show - but are willing to play local music.

WJCU *The Buff Mix*
www.wjcu.org
The main goal of this show is to promote both national and local modern rock acts.

WJCU *Plan 10*
www.wjcu.org
Local and modern rock with some punk, oldies and other stuff too.

WMSR *Local Band Showcase*
wmsr@muohio.edu
www.orgs.muohio.edu/wmsr

WOUB *Showdown Concerts*
radio@woub.org
woub.org/bluegrass
On the first Sunday of each month, we present local and regional bluegrass and old-time music bands in concert at the Front Room coffee shop on the Ohio University campus in Athens.

WOXY *Local Lixx, Homebrew*
Matt Sledge matt@woxy.com
www.woxy.com
97X has supported local musicians for 15 years with programs such as Local Lixx and Homebrew as well as 97Xposure, the longest running local band competition in the country.

WXEG *Joe's Garage*
Joe Winner joe@wxeg.com
www.wxeg.com
The best of the local scene on Sundays at 11:00pm.

WXUT Local Show
wxut@wxut.com
www.wxut.com
The new and improved local show featuring acts from Toledo and all over the Midwest in any vein of musical styling. More new music and always accepting anything and everything.

Oklahoma

KMOD *Local Licks at Six*
rob@KMOD.com
www.kmod.com
Tulsa's Rock Station supports Tulsa's local rock. Every weekday at 6pm Rob Hurt plays a track from a local artist. If you and your band want to be heard on Tulsa's most listened to radio station then send a tape, CD, or DAT tape to 2625 S. Memorial Dr, Tulsa, OK 74129 attention Local Licks.

KMYZ *HomeGroan*
Davit dsouders@edgetulsa.com
www.edgetulsa.com
Featuring local and regional talent.

Oregon

KBOO
rockmd@kboo.org
www.kboo.fm
We have several shows that play the music of local artists.

KEOL
www3.eou.edu/~keol
There are many locals only shows. Some encompass only the immediate local area; others reach out to all of Oregon and still others go beyond into eastern Washington and Idaho.

KINK *Local Spotlight*
Kevin Welch kwelch@kink.fm
www.kinkfm102.com
Tuesday through Friday at 9:20 p.m. we spotlight a couple of tracks from a local artist or group.

KLCC *Friends and Neighbors*
Kobi Lucas klcc@lanecc.edu
www.klcc.org
Very acoustic folk music featuring contemporary singer/songwriters, the more unique the better. A focus on new releases and local music, both recorded and live. Theme shows honoring special events and dates. Occasional live "mini-concerts" with folk artists.

KLRR *Homegrown Music Showcase*
www.klrr.com
Because good local music deserves to be heard! Sundays at 6pm we feature a full hour of music you won't hear anywhere else. If you are a musician or band from Oregon, we want to hear from you.

KMHD *Homegrown Jazz*
Mary Burlingame burlingm@mhcc.edu
www.kmhd.org

NW-Radio.com
info@nw-radio.com
www.nw-radio.com
Dedicated to bands from the Northwest United States and Lower West Canada. If you're interested in being featured on our site, as well as getting your music played on our streaming audio, fill in the form on our web site. We will contact you with further details and to verify your information.

Played in Oregon
Robert McBride robert@allclassical.org
www.allclassical.org
*Everything I play has something to do with Oregon.
Either the musicians live here, or the concert was
recorded here, or maybe it's a new CD by somebody
born in Oregon who doesn't live here anymore,
whatever. There needs to be some Oregon connection
And it needs to be "classical" music, though coming
up with a definition for that can be tough. Materials
should be sent to me: Robert McBride, Midday
Host/Producer, All Classical 89.9, 515 NE 15th
Avenue, Portland, OR 97232-2897*

Pennsylvania

WERG *The Local Show*
werg@gannon.edu
wergfm.com

WEZX
rock107@rock107.com
www.rock107.com
No specific show - but are willing to play local music.

WNWR/WWZK *Pipeline Radio Show*
www.ootweb.com
Local bands 6:30-7:30 Mondays.

W100
www.y100.com
*No one and we mean NO ONE plays more local
music than Y100! Every weeknight at 11pm Y100's
Ben Harvey lets loose the Philly File! Each night one
local band gets a chance to shine on Y100. Y100's
Dan Fein hosts an hour of local music each Sunday at
10 PM on YNOT.*

WPTS *Local Live*
www.wpts.pitt.edu

WQXA *Under the Radar*
Claudine claudine@1057thex.com
1057thex.com
*Local and regional music. To get your music to us,
write to: Under The Radar, P.O. Box 500, Hershey,
PA 17033. No phone calls please!*

WRVV *Open Mic Night*
Michael - Anthony Smith
requestsomething@yahoo.com
www.angelfire.com/biz/omn
www.river973.com
*Join us every Sunday night at 10PM for 2 hours of the
best local and regional rock and roll on.*

WXLV *The Phil Stahl Show (live music)*
wxlv@hotmail.com
www.wxlvfm.com/phil.html
www.wxlvfm.com

WZZO *Backyard Bands*
Brother Joel wzzobyb@aol.com
www.wzzo.com
*Eastern PA's #1 radio showcase for regional unsigned
bands every Sunday night at 9 p.m.*

Rhode Island

WBRU *Home BRU'd*
HomeBRUd@wbru.com
wbru.com
*It's when the best local talent from Providence and
Southern New England hits the airwaves Tuesdays at
midnight. Bands crash the BRU studios. We play stuff
hot off the local music presses, chat about gigs
happening around the area and dish out the latest in
local music news.*

WHIY *Soundcheck*
Big Jim bigjim@whjy.com
www.whjy.com
*Our local music show. Send in your stuff to
Soundcheck c/o WHJY 75 Oxford St. Providence, RI
02905*

WRIU *Vocalists & Localists*
www.wriu.org
*Offering listeners a wide spectrum of jazz vocalists
(past, present and up-and-coming) and is a showcase
for the many talented jazz artists (vocal and/or
instrumental) who call New England home. Included
is a comprehensive weekly calendar of jazz-related
events and performances.*

WXHQ
info@radionewport.org
www.radionewport.org
*The Newport Musical Arts Association and WXHQ
will assist local musicians by broadcasting original
material on selected shows. Digging it up in New
England is our showcase for regional talent. We are
currently accepting submissions for consideration.*

South Carolina

WUSC *Locals Only*
wuscmd@gwm.sc.edu
wusc.sc.edu

South Dakota

KAUR *Local Rock*
kaurfm89@hotmail.com
inst.augie.edu/~kaur
*Midnight for the coolest in Sioux Falls area rock and
way awesome regional bands too.*

KUSD *House Blend (folky - jazz)*
www.sdpb.org/radio
*The program showcases the talents of local writers,
poets, story tellers, songwriters and musicians. Their
performances are recorded live, when possible, in
smaller venues across the state. Have a taste of the
SDPR House Blend...a coffeehouse stage in cyberspace.*

Tennessee

WDVX *Local Licks At Six, Behind the Barn,
Future Tracks*
grace@wdvx.com
www.wdvx.com
*Grace hosts these three shows which help bring
exposure to local country artists.*

WDVX *Live At Laurel*
mail@wdvx.com
www.wdvx.com
*Performances recorded Live directly from the historic
Laurel Theater in Knoxville Tennessee.*

WEVL *The Memphis Beat*
wevl@wevl.org
wevl.org

WRVU *Local Music Rule*
wrvu@vanderbilt.edu
wrvu.org

WUTK *Tennessee Tracks*
www.wutkradio.com

Texas

Humble Time Texas Radio Showcase
humble@humbletime.com
www.humbletime.com

KACV *TexTunes*
kacvfm90@actx.edu
www.kacvfm.org
*Sunday mornings, it's all about Texas Music. Join
Marcie Lane for three hours of tunes from artists who
live and rock in the Lone Star State. It's not just Willie
and Waylon anymore. It's Roots Country, Americana,
Alternative Country, Modern Rock, Texas Blues and
more. TexTunes has everything that's Texan.*

KEGL *The Local Show*
localshow@kegl.com
www.kegl.com
*If you want to be considered as an act for the Local
Show send your CD or tape to: Attn: Robert Miguel,
97.1 The Eagle's Local Show, 14001 N Dallas Pkwy
Suite 1210, Dallas, TX 75240*

KFAN *Local Licks*
txradio@ktc.com
www.texasrebelradio.com
*Features unsigned local and regional Texas
Musicians.*

KGSR *The Daily Demo*
Jody Denberg jdenberg@kgsr.com
www.kgsr.com

KHYI *Texas Music Review*
www.khyi.com

KISS *Texas Tracks*
Brian Kendall brian.kendall@cox.com
www.kissrocks.com
*Local music from throughout the state of Texas.
Monday nights starting at midnight.*

KOOP *Live Bait, Around the Town Sounds*
koopradio@yahoo.com
www.koop.org

KPFT *The Lone Star Jukebox*
www.lonestarjukebox.com
*Features Americana, AAA, Alt-Country, Juke Joint
Road House and Border music.*

KPFT *Spare Change*
lcw90@juno.com
www.kpft.org

KPLX *The Front Porch*
Justin Frazell Justin@995thewolf.com
www.995thewolf.com
*Proud and Honored to live and breathe in TEXAS.
Proud and Honored to be born and raised in TEXAS.
Proud and Honored to play TEXAS MUSIC.*

KSTV *Texas Style Saturday Night*
erin@kstvfm.com
www.kstvfm.com

KSTX *Sunday Nite Session*
www.tpr.org
*Features interviews, live music and recordings of
contemporary musicians from San Antonio and
around Texas, with an occasional visiting nationally-
known artist.*

KTRU *The Local Show*
www.ktru.org

KTXT *Domestics*
domestics_88@hotmail.com
www.ktxt.net
Lubbock's only local music show. Giving you the best from all around the hub city.

KUT/KUTX *Live Set*
www.kut.org
Some of the best darned music you'll hear anywhere on the planet! Although LiveSet is hosted by a different one of our on-air producers each week, one thing remains constant (besides Walter, that is): the great live performances.

KUT/KUTX *Texas Radio*
Larry Monroe LM@larrymonroe.com
www.kut.org

KUT *Austin Music Minute*
Teresa Ferguson austinmusic@austin.rr.com
www.kut.org
Just one more way for KUT to promote live music events in Austin. If you'd like to contribute to the show, send your notices about music events to Teresa Ferguson. Remember, in order to give KUT listeners a preview of your music, we need a music sample.

KVLU
KVLU@hal.lamar.edu
dept.lamar.edu/kvlu
Texas artists are featured on all of our local programs.

KVRX *Local Live*
local_live@kvrx.org
www.kvrx.org
Since 1996, Local Live has been handmade according to an ancient Austin recipe, using only the choicest barley, hops and spring water.

KWTS
kwts@mail.wtamu.edu
www.wtamu.edu/kwts
We are beginning an initiative to promote local music. We are currently seeking submissions of original music from local bands.

LiveFromTexas.com
billward@livefromtexas.com
www.livefromtexas.com
Introducing fresh new Texas music.

TexasInternetRadio.com
ContactUs@TexasInternetRadio.com
www.texasinternetradio.com
The best independent music from Austin, Texas!

Utah

Channel 1057 *Channel Homegrown*
channelhomegrown@hotmail.com
www.channel1057.com
Utah's only show dedicated to local music. Each week we play 2 hours of local music.

Vermont

WBTZ *Buzz Homebrew*
mailbag@999thebuzz.com
www.999thebuzz.com
We scratch the surface of our ever-expanding music commonwealth. Here, the Buzz plays welcome wagon to our ambitious and talented neighborhood musicians, introducing bands from all points throughout Plattsburgh, Burlington and Montreal. Buzz HOMEBREW, a show for local acts to prove that good music comes in all forms and genres, be it punk, pop, ska, metal, screamo, electronic, instrumental, or experimental. If it's local and it won't get us into too much trouble—we'll play it!

WEQX *EQX-Posure!!*
www.weqx.com
The BEST Local/Regional music!

Virginia

i95.freesounds.net
i95@freesounds.net
i95.freesounds.net
An mp3 music stream featuring east coast experimental, alternative, punk, hard-core and independent artists.

Radio Del Ray
generalmanager@radiodelray.com
www.radiodelray.com
We play the best local and emerging artists from rock, country, folk, jazz and Americana—all of them "free agent musicians." Send us your stuff! We're building our music collection and we need to include your works.

Richmond Underground Radio
rur@freesounds.net
rva.freesounds.net

WKOC
info@thecoast.com
thecoast.com
Plays local music.

WNOR
www.fm99.com
No specific show - but are willing to play local music.

WNRN *Local Motive*
wnrn@rlc.net
wnrn.rlc.net

Washington

KMTT *Underground*
www.kmtt.com
You'll hear intriguing new artists, promising locals, international releases, imports, "B" sides, obscure nuggets and exclusive rarities. It's frightening at first, but soon you start to feel all warm and tingly and everything's okay...

KPLU *Jazz Northwest*
kplu@plu.edu
kplu.org/jandb/wilke.html
kplu.org
Hosted by Jim Wilke, the show focuses on the regional jazz scene from Portland to Vancouver. CDs by the best resident musicians from Seattle, Portland and Vancouver are featured.

KSER *The Bluegrass Express*
Sandy sandraq@compuserve.com
www.kser.org
Live performances from our studio.

KUGS *The Corner Pocket*
thecornerpocket@bust.com
www.cornerpocket.gq.nu
www.kugs.org
Fulfilling all your local music needs and desires.

West Virginia

WAMX *Loud and Local*
erikonthex@yahoo.com
www.x1063.com
The Original Local & Regional Rock Show.

WKLC *Homegrown 105*
homegrown105@wklc.com
www.wklc.com/homegrown.htm
Features West Virginia best rock bands.

WWVU *The Morgantown Sound*
Orville Weale oweale@yahoo.com
www.wvu.edu/~u92
The exclusive source of live local music in the area. Tune in every Monday night from 8-10 to hear what's new or check out the action live at 123 Pleasant Street.

Wisconsin

WBSD *The Local Show*
wbsd@hotmail.com
wbsd.basd.k12.wi.us

Wisconsin Jukebox Radio Show
Donnie Wad donniewad@wisconsinjukebox.com
www.wisconsinjukebox.com
Local music site and radio show for Wisconsin bands.

WLZR *Local Licks*
Marcus Allen mallen@lazer103.com
www.lazer103.com
If your band has a cd, you can send it to me, along with a one page bio.

WMSE *Midnight Radio*
www.wmse.org

WMUR *Wisconsin Jukebox*
www.mu.edu/stumedia/wmur

WORT *Hootenanny*
wort@terracom.net
www.wort-fm.org
Rock and Roll, live music, local bands, insurgent country, dirty blues, punk, indie. Additional comments: "Having a great time being a foot soldier for rock'n roll".

WSUW *Local Edge*
www.wsuw.org

WWSP *Club Wisconsin*
Jeff clubwi@hotmail.com
www.uwsp.edu/stuorg/wwsp
The best in Moo-town music. Jeff has local concert information and interviews of bands playing in the area. Be sure to tune in for the best in Alternative Dairy Rock.

Canada

120 Seconds
info@120seconds.com
www.120seconds.com
A showcase for the latest in Canadian bite-sized entertainment. Videos, cartoons, interactive web design, spoken word, music and film.

Back To The Sugar Camp
steve@backtothesugarcamp.com
www.backtothesugarcamp.com
Weekly radio show featuring Canadiana music.

Bandwidth
bandwidth@cbc.ca
ottawa.cbc.ca/bandwidth

CHOM *Made In Canada*
TooTall tootall@chom.com
www.chom.com
The show came about on a weekly basis 15 years ago and there are not many Canadians acts that I haven't interviewed...many for the first time ever.

CiTR *Canadian Lunch*
citrmusic@club.ams.ubc.ca
www.ams.ubc.ca/citr
From Tofino to Gander, Baffin Island to Portage La Prairie. The all-Canadian soundtrack for your midday snack!

CJAY *On The Verge*
ontheverge@cjay92.com
www.cjay92.com
For all Canadian artists.

CKCU *Canadian Spaces*
Chopper McKinnon chopper@nutshellmusic.com
www.ckcufm.com
Canada's most respected folk and roots music and interview show.

CKDU *Canadian Bacon*
ckdufm@is2.dal.ca
is2.dal.ca/~ckdufm
Canadian Rock and pop.

Definitely Not the Opera
dnto@cbc.ca
www.cbc.ca/dnto
We like to play Canadian indie bands on the show and we're always looking for new music. Visit out site to see how to get your disc on air. It's a good idea to include a one-page bio of the band and any extra information, such as tour dates.

Galaxie - The Continuous Music Network
information@galaxie.ca
www.galaxie.ca
Galaxie's mission is to offer the Canadian public a vast selection of continuous music channels. As well, Galaxie showcases the top Canadian talent alongside international artists.

Madly Off in All Directions
madlyoff@toronto.cbc.ca
radio.cbc.ca/programs/madlyoff
We travel the country to bring that unique comedy to CBC Radio. Host Lorne Elliott showcases a mix of comedy that includes everything from the lyrical story telling of the East Coast to poetry from the cowboys of the Prairies, as well as music, improvisation and satirical stand-up from all across Canada.

Out of the Blue
hemsworp@Halifax.cbc.ca
cbc.ca/outoftheblue
This weekly show presents interesting musicians, poets, writers and artists with stories to tell from across the country. Stories of people who have never been heard before on CBC Radio Two and told in new and interesting ways. Included in every show will be a profile on a music creator called 'Sounds New'.

Richardson's Roundup
roundup@vancouver.cbc.ca
radio.cbc.ca/programs/roundup
www.sadgoat.ca
Features tales from you, your next-door neighbour and from around the world. The seasoning is music and it's chosen to fit; everything from the latest smart pop melody to the songs your grandpa used to sing after his second glass of sherry!

Sounds Like Canada
soundslikecanada@cbc.ca
www.cbc.ca/soundslikecanada
A national radio show featuring a mix of in-studio and on-location production. Our goal is to drench the airwaves with voices and sound from all over the country and bring the listener what is new, surprising and thought provoking, while presenting familiar voices in different and creative ways.

SPIRITlive *Brand New Low*
brandnewlow@hotmail.com
www.spiritlive.net
puregold.cooltrap.com/brandnewlow
You've got the radio on, but you hear the same Canadian songs again and again. Why? Because to many, Canadian Content is merely a quota. A requirement. Something to get around. That's where A Brand New Low comes in. We play the best in CanCon not because we have to, but because we think it rocks on its own.

The Sunday Edition
thesundayedition@cbc.ca
radio.cbc.ca/programs/thismorning/sunday.html
Hosted by Michael Enright, has a relaxed tone and pace to suit the weekend time-slot. Interviews tend to be reflective and are allowed to expand. Here you will also find a particularly eclectic mix of music. featured.

Vinyl Cafe
vinylcafe@toronto.cbc.ca
www.cbc.ca/vinylcafe
You'll find a jukebox filled with good listening. You can also get to know some of the regulars, check for upcoming shows and specials.

Alberta

CFBR *Red, White & New*
www.TheBearRocks.com
If you wanna hear the latest, greatest Canadian rock from homegrown to our international superstars, listen to the Bear's Red, White & New... Sunday nights at 11 with host Park Warden.

CKUA *Live Sets From The Alberta Sessions*
radio@ckua.org
www.ckua.com
Features live sets from The Alberta Sessions Songwriter Series.

Key of A
keyofa@cbc.ca
calgary.cbc.ca/radio1
We go behind the scenes with musicians and performers from across Alberta to introduce listeners to the up-and-coming and as well as the famous.

British Columbia

CFOX *Sunday Blues*
www.cfox.com
Airplay/interviews with local blues artists.

CiTR *Local Kids Make Good*
citrmusic@club.ams.ubc.ca
www.ams.ubc.ca/citr
Local Mike and Local Dave bring you local music of all sorts. The program most likely to play your band!"

CJSF *Sonic Heights*
www.cjsf.bc.ca
Music and Sound Art from SFU, BC and Canada

North by Northwest
Sheryl MacKay nxnw@cbc.ca
vancouver.cbc.ca/nxnw
Presenting creative people and what they create. Artists, writers, performers and "just plain folks" talking about what they do and what others do. It's musical, theatrical, literary, artistic and delicious.

On the Island
victoria@cbc.ca
vancouver.cbc.ca/ontheisland

Radio Bandcouver
info@bandcouver.com
www.bandcouver.com
Artists & Bands send your CDs and press kits in.

Westcoast Performance
Michael Juk westcoast@vancouver.cbc.ca
vancouver.cbc.ca/wcp
Presenting the finest music being made by new and established British Columbia artists. Join host Michael Juk every Sunday at 12:06 PM for your favorite classical and world music sounds on CBC Radio Two.

The Zone FM's Band of the Month *Victoria*
www.thezone.fm
It's not a battle of the bands and it's not making of the band, it's all about promoting hard working local talent that already exists. Each month, our featured band will receive feature play of their music on The Zone @ 91.3, plus they'll be highlighted in a mini audio bio that will air on The Zone between five and seven times each a day.

Manitoba

Arts Encounters
artsenc@winnipeg.cbc.ca
winnipeg.cbc.ca/radio2/artsencounters
Your weekly window on the performing arts in Manitoba. Every show revolves around a featured performance: It could be a concert recorded live on location by our CBC Manitoba crew, it could be a brand-new CD, or it could even be a special live-to-air event that showcases Manitoba talent.

Beer for Breakfast
b2ware@hotmail.com
www.beerforbreakfast.org
A splendid feast of the best local artists, with an added dose of Bad Broose's personal Folk, Roots, Rock & Reggae faves thrown in for good measure. Send us your stuff and we'll get it out to the masses! We'll review it for Stylus Magazine, spin some tracks on CKUW, or interview you on Beer For Breakfast!

Culture Shock
cultureshock@winnipeg.cbc.ca
winnipeg.cbc.ca/radio1/cshock
Every Saturday as we showcase the rich cultural life of the province. Our mission is to discover and expose the best music on offer on the block be it rock or jazz, classical or Latin, folk or hip-hop.

Weekend AM Show
weekend@winnipeg.cbc.ca
winnipeg.cbc.ca/radio1/amshow
The weekend wake-up call for Manitobans features eclectic music, comedy, entertainment events, interesting people and special features on everything from cooking tips and vintage vinyl recordings to a weekly column on spirituality with the Reverend Karen Toole.

New Brunswick

Mainstreet New Brunswick
mainstreet@cbc.ca
www.nb.cbc.ca/mainstreet
Host Gary Mittelholtz gives the New Brunswick perspective on breaking provincial, national and international news, as well as some fun features and East Coast music.

Newfoundland

Musicraft
Francesca Swann musicraft@cbc.ca
www.stjohns.cbc.ca/musicraft
Musical talent is one of the resources found in abundance in Newfoundland and Labrador. Every Sunday, Musicraft brings you musical events from across the province and Francesca Swann talks to the people who bring the music to life.

On the Go
onthego@cbc.ca
www.stjohns.cbc.ca/onthego
A lively package of news, weather, interviews, mini-documentaries and the best in local music.

The Performance Hours
theperformancehour@cbc.ca
www.stjohns.cbc.ca/performance
Newfoundland's finest Singers and Songwriters recorded live at the LSPU Hall in St. Johns.

Nova Scotia

All The Best
Adrian ahoffman@halifax.cbc.ca
novascotia.cbc.ca/radio/allthebest
CBC Radio Two's showcase for Maritime performers. We seek out new talent and outstanding achievement in the performing arts. The show presents music ranging from classical through classic jazz to traditional.

Atlantic Airwaves
gmeisner@halifax.cbc.ca
novascotia.cbc.ca/radio/atlanticairwaves
Music and profiles of music makers from Canada's four Atlantic Provinces as well as national and international Artists appearing in festivals and live performances throughout the region. The range of music featured is a broad range of styles representing much of the popular music produced and enjoyed in the region.

CIGO *East Coast Rising*
www.1015thehawk.com/ecr.html
Tune in to get updates on the East Coast music scene!!

CKDU *Halifax*
is2.dal.ca/~ckdufm
We would like to help promote new music by local musicians by providing publicity for CD (or tape/vinyl) release performance/parties etc. If you are about to release something please contact our Promotion Committee by email and we can help with ads, on air interviews and other ways to get the word out!

CKDU *The One Inch Punch*
is2.dal.ca/~ckdufm
Punk focusing on the local scene.

CKDU *Saturday Morning Musical Box*
is2.dal.ca/~ckdufm
Classical music. Interviews with local performers.

Connections
connections@halifax.cbc.ca
novascotia.cbc.ca/radio/connections
From Halifax, host Olga Milosevich presents an uplifting mixture of music - largely Maritime and ranging from classical to folk, jazz, pop and world-beat.

Mainstream Halifax
mainstreet@halifax.cbc.ca
www.halifax.cbc.ca/radio/mainstreet

Musically Yours
Adrian Hoffman ahoffman@halifax.cbc.ca
novascotia.cbc.ca/radio/musicallyyours
A weekly program of music and "musings." The show features a mix of the host's musical favorites along with memories and images of living and working in Atlantic Canada. The music ranges from classical to Atlantic folk, with plenty of traditional, jazz and popular selections thrown in for good measure.

The Nova Scotia Kitchen Party
info@novascotiakitchenparty.com
www.novascotiakitchenparty.com
A weekly live performance show. As a performer, it is where you met your first audience, the one that really matters, the one that has known you the longest and loves you the best. No matter how far you go or how long you are gone, you are always welcome in the kitchen-a place where family and friends meet, talk and where the party always ends up, close to the warmth of the fire and your favourite dark beverage.

WEEKENDER
Peter Togni weekender@halifax.cbc.ca
www.radio.cbc.ca/programs/weekender
Peter's musical interest spans eight centuries of classical music, but he also enjoys a world of musical styles including the folk music of WEEKENDER's home turf - Canada's east coast! Listeners appreciate Peter's ability to integrate all of this music into an easy, seamless flow.

SATURDAY NIGHTS ON CBC RADIO TWO

Ontario

All in a Day
allinaday@cbc.ca
www.ottawa.cbc.ca/allinaday
CBC Ottawa local show. Music binds the program's elements together. In any given program, you're likely to hear rock, jazz, pop, world beat, classical or blues. It might be absolutely new, it might be very old, but it will always be the kind of music that engages you.

Artscape
gary_hayes@cbc.ca
ottawa.cbc.ca/artscape
A weekly program on CBC Radio Two in Ottawa focused on the local arts scene. Host/Producer Gary Hayes plays performances by Ottawa musicians ranging from the most promising of our young prodigies to our top performers.

Canadian Online Radio Experience (CORE)
info@core-online.net
www.core-online.net
CORE plays a great variety of pop rock and adult contemporary from today's best artists, as well as the best music that the great country of Canada has to offer.

CFFF *Good 'n Country*
Barb Bell allen.bell2@sympatico.ca
Stephanie Bolender allen.bell2@sympatico.ca
www.trentu.ca/trentradio
A blending of the old, the new, golden oldies, bluegrass and the unusual in country music. We bring you news, views and interviews with local and area artists. We support local and all Canadian artists. Try us, you might like us.

Keep current with Bible updates
www.indiebible.com/ud

...dio
...ard Pritchard_69@hotmail.com
...ncis illradio@hotmail.com
www....tu.ca/trentradio
Bringing listeners the hip-hop they want to hear, with a lot of Canadian hip-hop, underground hip-hop and local hip-hop. With on-air phone calls, special guests and more, this is radio entertainment at its finest.

CFFF *Smooth Operator*
trentradio@trentu.ca
www.trentu.ca/trentradio
Our public service announcement show. Listen to local music, get informed on what is going on in town and listen to interviews with interesting people from Peterborough and area.

CJAM *The Windsor Scene*
progcjam@uwindsor.ca
www.uwindsor.ca/cjam

Fresh Air
Jeff Goodes freshair@toronto.cbc.ca
toronto.cbc.ca/freshair
Every weekend, CBC Radio One's Fresh Air fills the morning air with a variety of music and stories. It's like sitting around the kitchen table with old friends.

Ottawa Morning
ottawamorning@cbc.ca
ottawa.cbc.ca/ottawamorning
Matthew Crosier is your ear on entertainment and the local music scene.

Prince Edward Island

Island Music Radio
www.gov.pe.ca/radio
Listen to the sounds of the Island... twenty-four hours a day, seven days a week, all of artists from Prince Edward Island.

Quebec

A Propos
performance@montreal.cbc.ca
montreal.cbc.ca/apropos
The most popular tunes coming out of Quebec.

artTALKS
arttalks@montreal.cbc.ca
montreal.cbc.ca/arttalks
Every Saturday afternoon at 5:05, tune into artTALKS for conversation and music with producer/host Katherine Gombay. The show brings together artists and people who love the arts from around the province.

Saskatchewan

Morning Edition
Sheila Coles amradio@regina.cbc.ca
sask.cbc.ca/radio/morningedition
News reports, weather, road reports, sports, lifestyle features, music and a good sprinkling of humour are major components of our program.

Czech Republic

Musica Bona
contact@musicabona.com
www.musicabona.com
The first on-line radio station specialising in classical music written by Czech composers or performed by Czech musicians.

United Kingdom

BBC Radio 1
www.bbc.co.uk
National Variations. `Steve Lamacq - the Evening Session'. Session tracks and new music. For listeners in Scotland only: `The Session in Scotland'. With Gill Mills and Vic Galloway. For listeners in Wales only: `The Session in Wales'. With Bethan Elfyn andHuw Stephens. For listeners in Northern Ireland only: `The Session in N Ireland'. With Colin Murray and Donna Legge.

BBC Radio Scotland
enquiries.scot@bbc.co.uk
www.bbc.co.uk/scotland/radioscotland

BURBs Radio
radio@burbs.org.uk
www.burbs.org.uk/radio
24hr Streaming Internet Radio of British Rock music.

Homegrown Cuts *BBC*
Ras Kwame homegrown@bbc.co.uk
www.bbc.co.uk/1xtra/djs/raskwame.shtml
www.bbc.co.uk
Dance, Hip Hop etc.

Impact Digital Radio
theteam@impactdigitalradio.com
www.impactdigitalradio.com
The independent Scottish radio group.

London Live and Direct
studio@londonliveanddirect.com
www.londonliveanddirect.com
Our mission is to showcase London/UK street culture in all its forms, to the world, via the web. We have the full spectrum of dance/club music, with each show dedicated to a specific genre. We currently have shows playing UK Garage, Hip Hop, Trance, Drum 'n' Bass, Tech House, Reggae, R&B/Rare Groove.techno and all new emerging art forms as they happen.

Rock3.co.uk
Ken Collinson collinsonsforever@hotmail.com
www.rock3.co.uk
We review and play new and unsigned Bands from the British isles (for free). We have five radio stations that play British rock.

White Gravy *Goldsmiths College*
wired@gold.ac.uk
www.wired.gold.ac.uk
A focus on exposure for local London bands, with alternative music as in between tunes, also including live bands, with interviews and vox pops.

Australia

2RRR *Sydney Sounds*
www.2rrr.org.au
Dedicated to featuring interviews and Recordings by Garage/Surf/Punk/Psychobilly & Power Pop Bands that regularly perform in Venues around Sydney.

2SER *Electroplastique*
info@2ser.com
www.2ser.com
www.clananalogue.org
A program presented by the electronic arts collective Clan Analogue for listeners in the Sydney region, each Wednesday on 2SER 107.3FM Wed 2:30-4:00pm. With a policy of playing 100% Australian Electronic Music, Electroplastique is the place to hear the cutting edge in released and unreleased demos.

2VOX *Australian Independent Music Show*
www.vox.1earth.net

2XX *Know Your Product*
www.2xxfm.org.au
Local and National music featuring new releases and interviews.

3CR *Local and Live*
programming@3cr.org.au
www.3cr.org.au
Featuring music and interviews with local musicians, live-to-air performances and gig guides.......

3D *Local Music, Local and Live*
www.threeradio.com
All the Best Local Music

3MR *OZ Rock, H.A.T.*
yoyo.cc.monash.edu.au/groups/3MU

3PBS *Big Mob*
info@pbsfm.org.au
www.pbsfm.org.au
Contemporary & traditional Indigenous music.

3RRR *Local and or General*
localgeneral@hotmail.com
localgeneral.tripod.com
www.rrr.org.au
An Australian music show. Each week I play not only the latest music from around the country, but also local independent and unsigned artists as well as featuring demos, a gig guide, live-to-air performances and interviews.

5PBA-FM *Max Radio*
max@pbafm.org.au
www.pbafm.org.au/max
Our 'specialist' program devoted to new and local music. We present a fresh breathe of air on Tuesday night radio with regular live bands, interviews, feature albums, giveaways, music news, gossip, laughter and more.

5UV *Adelaide Concert Hour*
Alastair Mackintosh radio@adelaide.edu.au
radio.adelaide.edu.au
Local Classical performances recorded live.

5UV *Local Noise*
Darren Leach darren.leach@mail.com
radio.adelaide.edu.au
Local bands live to air from Studio 1.

ABC Backyard *Local Radio Music*
www.abc.net.au/backyard/rinermusic.htm

ABC Radio National *Live On Stage*
Paul Petran petran.paul@abc.net.au
www.abc.net.au/rn/music/liveos
www.abc.net.au/rn
Live recordings of the best musicians touring this country. Local and overseas talent - blues, folk, world, fusion, jazz, country, R&B, cabaret and even the occasional string quartet - recorded in concert at venues around Australia.

The Australian Real Underground Music Show
info@isonliveradio.com
www.isonliveradio.com
A ground-breaking program that features great new Australian music each week. If you'd like your listeners to get a taste of what our local musicians have to offer, without having to wait the usual years for it to sift through the normal channels, this is the program to do it!

Bay FM *Australian Music*
bayfm@bayfm.org.au
www.bayfm.org.au

City Park Radio *OZ Muster*
country@cityparkradio.com
www.cityparkradio.com
All Australian Country music.

Gippsland FM *Oz Factor*
3gcr@gippsland.net.au
www.3gcrfm.org.au

Heartland FM
878fm@onthenet.com.au
www.onthenet.com.au/~878fm
Features live broadcasts of local country artists.

Music Deli
info@rn.abc.net.au
www.abc.net.au/rn/music/deli/default.htm
Folk, traditional and acoustic music and what is commonly known as world music. There's a strong emphasis on Australian performance of these musical styles - at festivals, in concerts and special recordings made for the program in ABC studios around the country.

OzIndig
www.ozworld.com.au
Featuring Aboriginal and Torres Strait Islander music.

OzRock
www.ozworld.com.au
Showcasing the best musical talent Australia has to offer.

PBS FM *No Frills*
info@pbsfm.org.au
www.pbsfm.org.au
The next phase of unsigned artists, showcasing the hard working, often under represented sector of the Australian music industry. We aim to draw together music and performances of all genres, to form one very loud voice.

RTR FM *Homegrown*
rtrfm@rtrfm.com.au
www.rtrfm.com.au
Local music scene news, reviews and interviews

Three D Radio *Local Music, Local and Live*
mail@threedradio.com
www.threedradio.com

Triple J *Home and Hosed*
Robbie Buck robbie@your.abc.net.au
www.abc.net.au/triplej/homeandhosed
Australian music from all over. Music, interviews, chat, news live sounds and much more.

New Zealand

95b FM Freak The Sheep
95bfm@95bfm.com
www.95bfm.co.nz

Radio Active *NZ Music Show*
infopimp@radioactive.co.nz
www.radioactive.co.nz

South Africa

YFM Radio
www.yfm.co.za
Local music content using a unique South African take on House Music called Kwaito. That genre was mixed with R&B, Hip Hop, Classic Jams, House and Ragga.

Section Three:
Services that Will Help You to Sell Your Music

"The public are buying!

I'd recommend getting your CD on the shelves of the top vendors, and definitely sell them through your own site to ensure the highest return!"

Richard Lynch,
Kweevak's Tracks Music Portal

Promotional Services

2 Generations SPA Music Management, Inc.
management@2generations.com
www.2generations.com
Music Management and Consulting company representing signed and unsigned bands/artists, producers and songwriters in all genres of music and providing business services for entertainment companies.

4 Wall Music
thecrew@4wallmusic.com
www.4wallmusic.com
If you need someone to shop your band to labels, book you shows, or sell your merchandise, 4 Wall Music can do it. We want what's best for you and we'll do whatever it takes to reach the goals you have.

Aarvak Marketing Communications
Christopher Buttner amcarpr@mindspring.com
www.aarvak.com
Public Relations & Marketing Services for the Professional Music, Film, Video and Audio Industries.

A.K. Music & Talent Agency
Submissions@AKMusicVideo.com
www.akmusicvideo.com
We bring artists from the entertainment industry together with those searching for new talent. We feature video clips, MP3's and profiles of each of our artists, providing a showcase for their work and offering complete booking capability.

Angry Coffee
hello@angrycoffee.com
www.angrycoffee.com
We couple our knowledge of digital audio with latest Web building tools and technologies to provide our clients with the very best in Web promotion.

Ariel Publicity Artist Relations and Cyber Promotions
info@arielpublicity.com
www.arielpublicity.com
An effective national PR firm. We know what it takes to make bands stand out in today's over-saturated world of music. We have worked with bands of all shapes, sizes and genres both signed and unsigned. We are nurturing, assertive and attentive to the minutest details. We will get your name out there.

Artist 1 Promotions
info@artist1promotions.com
www.artist1promotions.com
Whether you are in need of a full scale promo package design or a demo video, we can help. Our staff has the experience and necessary tools to help you with whatever promotional project you may need.

ArtistToolBox
info@warriorgirlmusic.com
www.artisttoolbox.net
Cool and cheap marketing and promotional tools for all artists of any field. Online FORUM: Buy/sell music gear/song leads/artists wanted / events and more Industry Newswire service -bringing the industry and artists together.

Atlantic Pacific Entertainment
david@atlanticpacificent.com
www.atlanticpacificent.com
We have expanded our services to include all types and styles of high quality performing bands. If you are interested in working Europe and regionally throughout the U.S. and Canada send a complete promotional package to our office.

bandpromote.com
Mike mgalaxy@bandpromote.com
www.bandpromote.com
You will have the opportunity to have a song placed on a reputable music sampler that will be mailed out to over 950 record industry executives, including over 240 A&R representatives and nearly 500 radio stations, top Management and Attorney firms, Press, Film and TV, Internet music sites and many more.

Bands To Go
Sarah Edwards bandstogo@thoughtsfrommyheart.com
bandstogo.com
We do the grunt work that most performers and/or managers either don't like to do or don't have time to do. We start out by sending out a mass email announcement introducing the artist and/or band. The email contains a brief bio as well as web site address and contact person and information for booking the gigs.

Canary Promotion + Design
Megan Wendell info@canarypromo.com
www.canarypromo.com
Publicity and graphic design services for web and print. Full scale publicity campaigns to press kit design for indie musicians.

Celebrity Access
webmaster@celebrityaccess.com
www.celebrityaccess.com
A state-of-the art database containing profiles of over 30,000 performers. The database provides extensive contact information on musicians, comedians, lecturers, agents, managers, record companies, talent buyers and venues.

ChewinPine Records/ HormonMelon Prod.
Lorange Blix chewinpine@chewinpine.no
www.chewinpine.no
Issues on Indie-Labels, booking, promotion and so forth.

City Lights Entertainment
Michael Wood mike@citylightsent.com
www.citylightsentertainment.com
We offer musicians a unique opportunity to consult with some of the biggest names in the music industry. CLE also offers travel discounts, catering, web hosting and design and so much more!

The Coalition of Independent Music Stores
www.cimsmusic.com
A network of stores that provide labels with a cohesive national marketing effort for their developing and established bands. So, instead of having to make 29 separate phone calls to set up promotions for 74 stores in 23 states, a label may contact the CIMS office to coordinate their efforts.

CollegeArtist.com
associates@collegeartist.com
www.collegeartist.com
Online artist gallery with free promotion for artists, actors, poets and musicians.

Cooch Music
Joseph Cuccia info@coochmusic.com
www.coochmusic.com
Full services Music Publishers! Services include: Management, Production, Songwriter services and more!

Creativity in Music
npsfunk@aol.com
www.creativityinmusic.com
Founded to assist the independent musician and singer in spreading the word about their music at an affordable price.

Digital Underdog Productions - Mainfeature Records
David Thompson info@digitalunderdogproductions.com
www.digitalunderdogproductions.com
A production zoo that feeds artists to record labels. We offer non-exclusive retainable copyright contracts thru Mainfeature Records.

Downtown Marketing
Celia Hirschman celia@downtownmarketing.com
www.downtownmarketing.com
A music business consulting firm founded by industry veteran, Celia Hirschman. The goal is to provide extensive experience in micro & macro marketing for label management and artist development, at a reasonable cost.

Ear Assault Street Promotions
admin@earassault.com
www.earassault.com
We are swamped with requests for street teams at the moment and are still accepting bands we feel have the potential to make it.

Earl R. Dingman Productions
R. John info@erdprod.com
www.erdprod.com
Thirty years in media marketing, promotion, production and consultation with ASCAP 'current performance' status and member NMPA/HFA.

Earth's Temporary Solution - The Brandon Show
birch2@frontiernet.net
www.thebrandonshow.com
We are actively involved in every component of live entertainment - from event development to clean-up, budgeting to concessions, marketing and production.

Ego Trip Entertainment
dave@egotripent.com
www.egotripent.com
An independent management, marketing and publicity firm specializing in pop, rock and heavy metal music. We handle publicity, college / specialty radio, retail and grass roots street marketing.

Electric Kingdom Distribution
info@electrickingdom.com
www.electrickingdom.com
We are a national independent distributor of recorded music and accessories. EKD's coverage includes national chains and stores.

Element Publicity
Mike Schaefer element@elementpub.tk
www.elementpub.tk E
A full-service music publicity firm rooted in providing killer publicity and promotional plans for indie artists. We help you get the music out to the masses.

Evolution Promotion
info@evolutionpromotion.com
www.evolutionpromotion.com
As a full service company we offer all the key essentials necessary for a successful campaign - Radio Promotion, Tour Promotion, Internet Marketing, Direct Consumer Marketing, Web Design and Consulting services that capitalize on crucial opportunities that build careers.

f. Boo Music
fboo@pacbell.net
www.fBoo.com
L.A.-based independent record label, recording studio and publisher; also provides career consulting, graphic design and record promotion resources for indie artists.

FourFront Media & Music
Christopher Knab info@4frontmusic.com
www.knab.com
A unique consultation and education service for independent musicians and record labels that combines advice with instructions on how to establish a music related career. Through private consultations and regularly scheduled workshops in the Northwest, Chris is adept at helping musicians help themselves with the business of music.

The Gate Media Group
info@gatemedia.com
www.gatemedia.com
We have twenty years experience developing successful independent music promotional campaigns. Call us for the keys to success.

Good-New Entertainment
Joey Howell joeyh@good-new.com
www.good-new.com
We are attempting to bring good, new entertainment to everyone who's tired of the boring, old crap out there right now.

Green Galactic
lynn@greengalactic.com
www.greengalactic.com
A marketing and production media company specializing in youth culture. In addition to general marketing services such as publicity, promotions and public relations, we are emerging as a pop culture solution provider for anyone wanting to effectively reach and deliver to hip markets.

H2R Entertainment,
Phil Wilson h2rent@h2rentertainment.com
www.h2rentertainment.com
We effectively promote talented artists, musicians, producers, DJ'S and songwriters to major and independent record labels and venues. Our website will soon allow new and upcoming talent the opportunity to promote themselves by selling their CD's online.

Hardcore Promotions
www.hardcorepromo.com
Providing promotion for mp3.com artists and entertainment for everyone else.

Impact Entertainment - Artist Management
Rob Cohen impactent@aol.com
www.impactentertainmentgrp.com
Full service artist management group specializing in management, development and promotion of signed and unsigned artists.

IMR Music and Marketing
Info@imrmusic.com
www.imrmusic.com
An Independent organisation geared entirely towards promotion and marketing of Independent Record labels and unsigned artists. We represent all styles of music in over 30 countries worldwide.

Independent Records
ddiaz@indierec.com
www.indierec.com
We give you the backing of a record label which you can use in conjunction with other indie labels for your own distribution purposes. We can legitimately generate and assign a bar code for your music.

IRL Music Group, Inc.
John Mendola jmendola@earthlink.net
www.johnnyrock.com
We specialize in the International Music Market. Licensing, Publishing, Tour management and Events worldwide. Nearly a decade of hands on experience!

Jhai Entertainment
Bo Jackson info@jhai.net
www.jhai.net
A full service entertainment company dedicated to helping independent artists gain exposure.

Kari Estrin - Customized Artist Career Consulting
kestrin@mindspring.com
www.kariestrin.com
Having trouble getting your career off the ground? Can't get your career to the next level? Kari's trademark is "thinking outside the box" and individually tailoring what she offers to her clients in the realm of consulting, artist services and special projects.

Katcall Creative Studio
Kat press@katcall.com
www.katcall.com
Provides music publicity for indie musicians and labels. Includes web/print promos, press kits, press releases, media relations.

Katscan Entertainment
kat@gottagetakatscan.com
www.gottagetakatscan.com
Our objective lies in artist development so that the artist's goals become not only marketable, but attainable. So whether you're an independent artist, record label, booking agent, or other industry professional, we can help fulfill your needs.

Klipmart
www.klipmart.com
Our services provide solutions for the integration and distribution of promotional audio and video content on the Internet. Klipmart helps websites aggregate relevant local music klips through its Management and Infrastructure tools.

KSB Management
Brian Kurtz brian@ksbmanagement.com
www.ksbmanagement.com
Indie artist management for pop, rock, alt, emo, punk.

Maelstrom Music PR
curtis@maelstrompr.com
www.maelstrompr.com
The PR firm for indie and unsigned musical talent! Our goal is to provide effective publicity while staying within your budget.

Massive Music America
Aliene questions@massivemusicamerica.com
www.massivemusicamerica.com
We are an independent promotions company that offers radio, media/print, internet and tour support. Contact us for an estimate, we can customize a plan to fit your needs and your budget.

Mazur Public Relations
Michael Mazur michael@mazurpr.com
www.mazurpr.com

The Media Room
Virginia Hunt Davis Virginia@MediaRoomPR.com
www.MediaRoomPR.com
*Specializes in gaining awareness for up-and-coming
and touring artists/bands, indie labels, venues and
music-oriented businesses. We work with our clients
to attain maximum exposure for their music via print,
radio and television media. We also assist in
organizing concert events centered around exposing
new and independent music to the public.*

MPX 2000
Jack Irona mpx@search2nite.com
www.mpx2000.com
*Music Promotion X-tra, The Record Industry's #1
NYC Public Relations Firm.*

The Music Oven Network
editor@musicoven.com
www.musicoven.com
*Provides free promotional services to independent
artists, bands and singer/songwriters by offering them
exposure in restaurants, retail stores, clubs and other
public venues.*

MusicDistribution.com
www.musicdistribution.com
*The musician's guide to the best places to promote,
sell and distribute music on the Internet. Includes our
top 10 list, music promotion tips and recommended
resources.*

Musik International Corporation
PJ Birosik pj@musikinternational.com
www.musikinternational.com
*One of the leading US full service promotion
companies since 1977. Musik International also puts
its money where its mouth is, by offering discounted
pricing to artist-owned labels and non-label affiliated
musicians.*

Nina Denny Public Relations
Nina Denny ndenny@prweb.com
www.ninadenny.com
*Music and Entertainment PR Firm that offers PR with
a personal touch, affordable rates and music
expertise.*

One-sixty Productions
Frank Mastalerz oasis160music@hotmail.com
www.oasisonesixty.com
*We are a Chicago based agency that assists indie
bands in booking, marketing, advertising,
management and direction.*

Outlaw Entertainment International
Tommy Floyd info@outlawentertainment.com
www.outlawentertainment.com
*Full service Artist Management firm with divisions in
Publicity, Promotion & Career Development. Highly
specialized for the Indie Artist!*

Powderfinger Promotions
powderspam@aol.com
www.artistdevelopment.com
*With every release comes a need for promotional
support. With over seven years of experience,
Powderfinger has the power to get your CD listened
to. We also offer customized publicity packages.*

Reason Y
Moe moe@reasonY.com
www.reasonY.com
*Online support, promotion and distribution for up and
coming independent bands of all styles and genres.*

Rainmaker Publicity
rkelley283@aol.com
www.rainmakerpublicity.com
*Founded in 1996 by ex-ABC Radio exec. Rhonda
Kelley. We are looking to add a few new bands to our
roster this year. Rainmaker works with unsigned
artists and indie labels ONLY!! For more info and
rates, visit our website.*

Rainmaker Talent Group
info@rainmaker-talent.com
www.rainmaker-talent.com
*Provides management, booking, promotional,
financial and related support services to local/
regional artists who are working towards gaining
major label and/or national recognition.*

RockStar2k
Tcouch@rockstar2k.com
www.rockstar2k.com
*We work with artists we feel have solid potential for
commercial radio airplay and help them obtain
recording deals at major labels. Selected artists have
the ability to participate in industry showcases in
efforts to secure a record or publishing deal, or to find
a booking agent and/or manager.*

ShowGigs.com
info@ShowGigs.com
www.showgigs.com
*Our artist development is based on a traditional old
school economics approach: one project at a time and
always striving to generate revenue for the artist as
early and as prudently as possible.*

Signiture Entertainment
Sterling "G" sterling@signitureproductions.com
www.signiturentertainment.com
*Entertainment Company, Artist development, Audio &
Video production.*

Songwriters Showcases of America
showstage@aol.com
www.ssa.cc
*Creates showcases for songwriters and original bands
in local community centers, concert halls, art
galleries, coffee houses, night clubs and other like
venues as well as local events such as art shows,
festivals and other community events in locations
throughout the United States.*

SonicAwareness
Zach zb@sonicawareness.com
www.sonicawareness.com
*We provide services that help you increase your
exposure, sell your CDs and other band related items
(i.e. Vinyl, T shirts etc.) and manufacture and create
products essential to all Independent Artists (Retail
Ready CD production, Merchandise Production,
Graphic Design etc.)...all at discount rates! We
actively promote and recommend your music to our
listeners from all over the world!*

Space 380
info@space380.com
www.space380.com
*A music promotion company that creates name
recognition for independent artists & labels of ALL
genres. We realize that artists only need to sell a few
thousand copies of a release to actually create music
for a living.*

Stompinground.com
Jason Donlon info@stompinground.com
www.stompinground.com
*Global Independent Promotion and World Market
Place for Local Bands. Free band and record label
listings.*

Street Teamer
info@streetteamer.net
www.streetteamer.net
*Our main goal is to increase your fan base in different
areas of the USA and the world! Some of the things
Street Teamer can do for your band is run a street
team or eteam.*

SugarMamaPR.com
Jianda Johnson indie@sugarmamapr.com
sugarmamapr.com
*Got Promo? SugarMamaPR.com makes it all better
with intimate clientele, a wealth of online content and
schmooze you can use!*

Tanglewood Management Group
WT Cox wtc62@alltel.net
www.tanglewood.8k.com
*Georgia based company. Specializing in the music
industry.*

TekSunGirl Musician & Band Promotion
LaNita teksungrl909@aol.com
www.teksungirl.web.com
*Supporting both the Local & National music scenes
with photos, reviews, news, promotional tips,
resources, local band listings and more!*

Thompson Entertainment Group
Chuck Thompson
cthompson@thompsonentertainmentgroup.com
www.thompsonentertainmentgroup.com
*An Artist Development, Media/Marketing,
Management firm that uses the over 40 years of
experience of our staff to help the independent artist
realize their dream. The Thompson Entertainment
Group, where music still has a Heart and a Soul!*

Tinderbox Music
Krista Vilinskis krista@tinderboxmusic.com
www.tinderboxmusic.com
*Music promotion and distribution company. Work
mainly with unsigned and indie-label bands across the
country. Services: Radio, Press, Distribution.*

Titan Entertainment Inc.
Jim Devericks jkdtitan@earthlink.net
www.titan-entertainment.net
*We develop, manage and publish artists within the
music and entertainment industry. We discover new
and emerging talent and then introduce that talent to
various record industry contacts in hopes of obtaining
a recording contract.*

UnderCover Records
info@undercoverrecords.com
www.undercoverrecords.com
*Bookings, Promotion, National Distribution, Online
Radio etc.*

Unite PR
Jessika Jessika@UnitePR.com
www.unitepr.com
*We are an independent Publicity and Promotional
firm offering discounts to Indies and unsigned acts.*

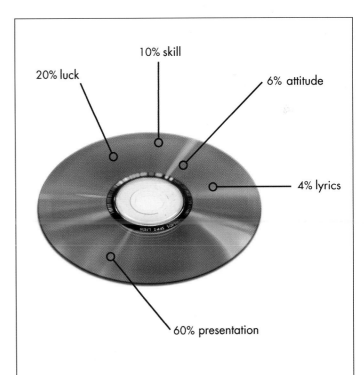

Sign up for
The Indie Contact Newsletter!

Every month you will receive a new list of places to send your music for review, radio play etc.

Sennheiser is donating an **E835** microphone and a pair of HD280Pro headphones for our monthly draw.

To sign up visit www.indiebible.com

or send an e-mail to indiebible@rogers.com

with the word "draw" in the Subject: field.

Vision Music USA

Nick Stamoulis info@visionmusicusa.com
www.visionmusicusa.com
We provide cost effective booking, management and promotions consulting services for independent musicians.

Xtreme-Zone

lorrie@xtreme-zone.com
www.xtreme-zone.com
Find all your Online Promotional Needs at one site. From Website Promotion, Full Promotional Services, Online Marketing, Search Engines, to A&R, Management and Exposure! We are dedicated to helping Indie Artists promote themselves.

YourRelease

admin@yourrelease.com
www.yourrelease.com
Combining our experience from the music, marketing and Internet industries we aim to remedy this situation by developing our own innovative solutions. YourRelease powers hundreds of websites with unique content and powerful marketing tools.

Vendors and Labels

Most of the services listed in this section offer "non-exclusive" contracts. Non exclusive means you are allowed to sign up with as many of the services as you like without violating any agreement. The fees and/or commissions vary from site to site. I suggest you visit as many as you can to find out which sites you get a good feeling from. Be weary of large setup fees!

101 Distribution

weworktogether@101distribution.com
www.101distribution.com
We can place your music into our national network of commercial music retailers; on the shelf and directly next to the major label acts. What's more, you will retain control of your publishing rights and receive up to 85% of the wholesale price for every sale that is made!

121 Music

sales@121music.com
www.121music.com
The CD store of all independent artists and labels.

25 Records

info@25records.com
www.25records.com
Our mission: To discover new and exciting bands and bring them to the world's attention.

AB?CD

shoptalk@ab-cd.com
www.ab-cd.com
We specialize in hard to find music and media, limited production special editions, small independent labels, rarities and collectables.

AmazingCDs

www.amazingcds.com
We are always looking to add new material in our Music Store. ALL CDs are accepted - ALL styles of music. We do not judge your music - we let the general public decide what they do or do not like when they choose to buy or not buy your CDs.

amazon.com *Advantage Program*

orders@amazon.com
www.amazon.com/advantage
What's the best way to sell your music, videos and DVDs at Amazon.com? Simple—join Amazon.com Advantage and make it faster and easier for our millions of customers to find, discover and buy what you're selling.

The Artist Shop

artshop@artist-shop.com
www.artist-shop.com
A music store dedicated to the independent progressive artist putting out his/her own product. The items we display we buy directly from the artist or his/her own company.

ArtistLaunch.com

submissions@artistlaunch.com
www.artistlaunch.com
For those artists who have not only the talent, but the drive and the will to succeed, ArtistLaunch is there to help in every way possible.

Atomic Records

music@atomicrecords.com
www.atomicrecords.com
We are dedicated to educating and assisting independent bands and musicians in the art of effective promotion, management and success in the music industry.

Audio Kingdom

www.audiokingdom.com
Are you an unsigned act or independent record label? If so, you'd better sit down because we think we've got something that's going to knock you off your feet. Welcome to Audio Kingdom, the world's first and finest online music retail network.

Aural Adventures

E-Mail@AuralAdventures.com
www.AuralAdventures.com
Dedicated to bringing unique and adventurous music to the ears of those who appreciate it. We're open to just about any kind of music (or non-music) as long as it's interesting, done with feeling and of good quality. About the only styles that we probably wouldn't be interested in are country or rap.

Automatic Distribution

Robert Katavic info@automaticdistribution.com
www.automaticdistribution.com
Independent music distribution and online shop.

awarestore.com

info@awarerecords.com
www.awarestore.com
Over the past few years, we have grown from carrying a handful of records to over 1000 independent artist CDs. To add your band's CDs and merchandise to Awarestore.com please contact us.

AzOz

webmaster@azoz.com
www.azoz.com
Got a CD to sell? We'll be glad to list them here and process the sales for $2 per unit sold. Interested?

BandMecca.com

bands@bandmecca.com
www.bandmecca.com
An opportunity to sell your music to an international audience at a reasonable price. It doesn't cost anything to get started. We pay you for the music and merchandise we sell and you get to set the amount per item that you want to get paid. We make money when you make money.

BenT Music

T. De La Comte bentmusic@bentmusic.ca
www.bentmusic.ca
Dedicated to helping independent artists get their music out to the public while keeping as much of the control and capital in the artists hands as possible. We provide an on line store where artists can sell their CD's, tickets to shows, T-shirts and other paraphernalia.

BIE Records

Victor Bunick bierecords@aol.com
www.bierecords.com
Independent record (music) distribution and promotion.

bumpNgrind Records

cookieholley@tymewyse.com
bumpNgrindRecords.com
Functions as a liaison between the musical artists and the music industry. We promote our artists all over the world. We sell their CDs and other products, get air play for their music, connect them with resources so they can help themselves in their own advancement.

BuyIndieMusic.com

music@blackdogpromotions.com
www.buyindiemusic.com
An online retail system that gives the independent artist a place to sell their albums and merchandise. We welcome all styles of music and merchandise from all artists.

Buzz Communications

Andrea Hubbert
andrea@buzzcommunicationsonline.com
www.buzzcommunicationsmusic.com
Beyond the noise and confusion, there is Buzz Communications. We are a full-service public relations, marketing and business development firm dedicated to providing creative and practical campaigns targeted specifically to our client's needs.

CafePress.com

Jeff Ridgeway jeff@cafepress.com
www.cafepress.com
You can sell professional quality Audio and Data CDs with no inventory or setup costs. Audio CDs include streaming audio samples in your CafePress.com store.

Canadian American/Caprice International

Joey Welz canadianamerican@webtv.net
community.webtv.net/canadianamerican
We are looking for quality radio singles for your 2004 worldwide radio release. All radio formats. We will also distribute your album, returning 75% of all sales to you.

CD Baby

cdbaby@cdbaby.com
www.cdbaby.com
We have been featured in the NY Times, MSNBC, Wired, CNET and more. 10,000 CUSTOMERS A DAY go through cdbaby.com looking for CDs like yours. Such a popular online store, you HAVE to make sure your CD is there. In addition, every album for sale at CD Baby is also for sale at Towers on the tower.com website.

CD Palace

manager@cdpalace.com
www.cdpalace.com
We will scan the album cover, digitize the audio and create the web page to sell the CD. All album sales are on consignment.

CD Quest Music

feedback@cdquest.com
www.cdquest.com
Offering over 300,000 titles from around the world allows CD Quest to reach farther into the independent world than any other site.

CD WOW! 'unsigned...AS YET!'

Jen Whitehouse unsigned@cd-wow.com
www.cd-wow.com/unsigned
All Bands and Artists deciding to sell their album on 'unsigned...AS YET!' will have their own album information page to include album cover image, track listing, album description in their own words, official band or artist website link and e-mail address and future gig listings.

CDFreedom.com

Phil Antoniades info@artistdevelopment.com
www.cdfreedom.com
Make more from on-line sales! CDfreedom takes a smaller cut than most on-line distributors!

CDPimp.com

www.cdpimp.com
If you feel like throwing your radio out the window every time you hear another boy band or pop diva, then you've come to the right place. We have music that the radio stations are afraid to play. Because it's good. It's Different. It's created by real musical artists.

CDreview.com

info@CDreview.com
www.CDreview.com
A smarter way to sell your music. We combine artist promotion with the traditional "CD Store Model". We also give the artists 100% of the sale price of there CD. Other sites simply stock your CD and wait for you to promote it. We go out and market your music to make it sell !!! If you choose to join us, make sure to type in the code "indiebible" to even waive the set up fee.

CDStreet.com

www.cdstreet.com
We enable independent music entities to add secure credit card ordering into their own website. There are no setup costs and if you do not sell anything, then there is no cost to the artist.

CDvalue

sales@cdvalue.com
cdvalue.com
We only add $1.00 to your asking price. We are here to sell CDs, not store them. Give us a look and please get your items to us so that we can begin to sell your music.

CityBoys International Management

R. Anthony Bates ABates@CityBoys-International.com
www.CityBoys-International.com
Our Mission is to increase exposure to quality independent music of various genres. We offer customers an affordable alternative to traditional music shopping.

City Lights Entertainment

Michael Wood mike@citylightsent.com
www.citylightsent.com
Regardless of what city you live in, there are great bands with great recordings. Bands trying to get ahead and get noticed. City Lights Entertainment offers online distribution of independent recordings at great prices.

Coach House Records

Amber Ray amberr@thecoachhouse.com
www.coachhouserecords.com
We provide a unique gateway for artists to successfully introduce their independent releases into the retail market. Visit our website for details. Read the requirements to make sure you can meet product, documentation, promotion and fulfillment specifications.

contactmusic.com

hello@contactmusic.com
www.contactmusic.com
We want to act as a catalyst getting the right people together and making things happen. We are passionate about music and believe that great music is still out there. We can't promise to make your music great for you, but we can promise that if it is really good we will get you noticed.

Crafty Records

dAN tREIBER designsbydan@juno.com
www.craftyrecords.net
An independent, artist friendly, record label. Our artists range from acoustic to hip-hop and all genres in between. We seek to help out the small time musician. If it rocks, we release it.

Cyber Songs

waltersargent@earthlink.net
www.cyber-songs.com
If you're on your own, or playin' in the band, if you already have a web page or need one, if you've released a CD or just a single, Cyber-Songs can help you get heard, get exposed and get paid.

Darla Records

webmaster@darlashop.com
www.darlashop.com
We offer a variety of shipping options to reach you anywhere in the world as quickly as possible

Degyshop

info@degyshop.com
www.degyshop.com
We are always trying to help music companies find the best new music for their projects and needs. degyshop.com is stocked with tons of fantastic artists in all types of music genres. Radio stations, TV shows and music zines use our music.

Delvian Records

delvian@delvianrecords.com
www.delvianrecords.com
Specializing in Electronica, Darkwave, World and New Age. Please contact us for submission guidelines.

Devil Entertainment

info@devilentertainment.net
www.devilentertainment.net
We offer a wide range of services. Sell your independent album online here for free...no contracts EVER.

DigitalCuts.com

info@digitalcuts.com
www.digitalcuts.com
We provide the convenience of buying music from independent artists, while at the same time offering our artists the opportunity to develop and promote their music. We provide consumers the ability to look for local entertainment in their cities, including listings of our artists and whey they can be seen.

Dirtbag Music

Todd Newman todd@dirtbagclothing.com
www.dirtbagmusic.com
All about helping the DIY band that just needs a break. DIRTBAGMUSIC.COM will do what we can to help out.

Disgraceland Records

paul@disgraceland.com
www.disgraceland.com
Now a full-fledged online record label with more than a dozen products available

Dollar CD

dollarcd@gajoob.com
www.dollarcd.com
If you are an artist, label or other CD publisher, your CD's can be listed on DollarCD.com for cost-free distribution to your fans, or unlisted for self-distribution

Doniryeed Records

www.doniryeed.com
A Boston, MA equal profit sharing independent record label focused on developing the careers of artists looking to pursue a major label record deal.

Dreamscape Records Ltd

W. Christian Treiber
Dreamscape_Records@earthlink.net
www.DreamscapeRecordsLtd.com
We work with the artists to help them achieve their goals. At Dreamscape we believe that the relationship between the artists and the label is a partnership with both halves working equally hard to make the artists music a success.

EarBuzz

ears@earbuzz.com
www.earbuzz.com
EarBuzz is the only site that reviews artists product, promotes artists free with a completely free web site and sells music giving 100% of the profits back to artists.

emaginemusic

info@emaginemusic.com
www.emaginemusic.com
Our Talent Pool offers new artists the prospect of a full retail presence once certain goals and sales milestones are reached. In this section we are permanently looking for new talent. Check it out, send us your music!

Energy Castle

Caleb skyinarug@juno.com
www.energycastle.com
A young indie pop record label with an international Comp Club. We are looking for indie / pop artists to become a part of the EC Comp Club. It is a great opportunity to get your music heard and also join a growing indie music community.

Everfine Records

dave@everfinerecords.com
www.everfinerecords.com
Our mission is to create an environment in which artists can flourish and further develop their natural talents.

EvO:R

evor@evor.com
www.evor.com
We work together with musicians around the world trying to keep the flames of interest alive for Indie musicians.

providing CD and DVD
replication
+
digital cassette and video
duplication

FastLane Records
Shawn C. Lane fastlanerecords1@aol.com
www.fastlanerecords.com
An indie that specializes in glam/hard rock/power pop...help in structuring bands.

FlyLip.com
webmaster@flylip.com
www.flylip.com
Free setup! When you sign up and create your artist you can create a bio, list band members, upload an artist photo, list your official website and more. On your disc pages you can list everything about the disc like producer, record label, liner notes and more.

futurepopshop.com
webmaster@futurepopshop.com
www.futurepopshop.com
CDs and vinyl.

Gadfly Records
gadfly1@aol.com
www.gadflyrecords.com
We specialize in offbeat and unique projects, whether they be singer/songwriter albums, releases from our ethnic and instrumental series, or spoken word projects. The musical styles are as varied as can be — but each project has that certain uniqueness that separates it from the run-of-the-mill, middle-of-the-pack releases in its genre.

Galaris
ariel@galaris.com
www.galaris.com
Mail us as many CD'S as you want, at least 3 please. We will send you a check for each CD that you sell. Of course - you decide how much you want to sell it for.

Galaxy CDS
Ryan Shoemaker shoe@galaxycds.com
www.galaxycds.com
We're an Independent retailer featuring unsigned artists. No up fronts, high payout consignments.

Gay Tunes Studio
Dan Schramm dschramm@glinn.com
www.gaytunes.com
The source for GLBT music. Music samples, artist bios etc. Order CDs online. Also Gay Tunes Studio record label.

GEMM
inquiry@gemm.com
www.gemm.com
We're proud of the fact that we get calls and letters every day from people who say they looked for months and even years for a hard-to-find record or CD before they found it at GEMM.

GetIndie.com
admin@getindie.com
www.getindie.com
It is our mission to devote our future, exclusively, to serve the independent artist and to insure the general public access to the wares of the independent artist.

getouthere
getoutthere@bt.com
www.getouthere.bt.com
A young vibrant online environment, set up by BT, specifically for people who have an interest in expressing creativity, or those looking for that difficult first step into a creative industry.

Goodtime Music.net
Daniel Gray info@goodtimesmusic.net
www.goodtimesmusic.net
We offer Indie Musicians a place to get their music reviewed. Musicians can showcase their works. GoodtimesMusic.net features many services for the Indie musician.

Grade 44 Records
Scott Hockenberger scott@grade44.com
www.grade44.com
Specializing in cutting edge music from genres such as rock, electronic, dance, & hip hop. We usually go the exclusive route; however we are very open to possible non-exclusive signings. We allow the artist to have a great deal of creative control if needed.

Guitar Nine Records
www.guitar9.com
Dedicated to the idea that the guitar is probably one of the most expressive instruments ever invented and has an unlimited sonic palette. New Releases and Demos Wanted! Each issue we feature twelve (12) new artists who would like the world to hear their music.

Halogen Records
Halogen Records info@halogenrecords.com
www.halogenrecords.com
Independent record label based in Vermont. Grassroots promotion, marketing, distribution and manufacture.

Harvest Media Group
info@harvest-mg.com
www.harvest-mg.com
Here you will find the very best in regional and national independent artists. If you buy or sell independent music this is the place for you.

Hearbox Recordings
info@hearbox.com
www.hearbox.com
We have many new releases plus some rare goods to satisfy your appetite for Guitar-driven rock. We pride ourselves on recommending great quality Rock that you won't hear on the Radio or see on the front page of Amazon.

Home Grown Music Network
feedback@homegrownmusic.net
www.homegrownmusic.net
Our mission: To seek out the best music being made today and spread it across the universe. Making the world a kinder, better place!

Home Made Music
info@homemademusic.com
www.homemademusic.com
Bringing you new and classic recordings which capture the unique spark of personal expression that we feel is entirely unique to home recording. All styles of music (and non-music) are welcomed and encouraged.

Hot Bands.com
webmaster@hotbands.com
www.hotbands.com
We are always on the lookout for good talent, bands and artists, but are ALSO on the lookout for people all over the world that love music and like to WRITE about it!

Immediatek, Inc.
paul.marin@immediatek.com
www.immediatek.com
We offer a software called NetBurn that allows musicians sell their music from their own websites, by downloading entire music CDs in "one click" directly to a CD burner.

iMusic
imusic.artistdirect.com
The leading online music company that connects music fans directly with their favorite artists worldwide via our online network.

Independent Musicians Marketplace
imm@secondfret.com
www.secondfret.com
Music brings the world together... don't screw it up!

IndepenDisc *Music Club*
feedback@independisc.com
www.independisc.com
We listen to every submittal for review, representation, & promotion, regardless of genre. See "Artists Submissions" on our web page.

IndiePro.com
design@indiepro.com
www.indiepro.com
There are two ways to feature your music on Indiepro.com. You can submit your CD for a review to be published on this site, or you can sell your music in our on-line catalog and be featured permanently with all sales processed by us.*

Indiespace
signup@indiespace.com
www.indiespace.com
Provides a unique way for independent musicians and performers to get their work out directly to their audience.

Insound
help@insound.com
www.insound.com
We think of Insound as being the premier site for fans of underground music and film and as representing the best of the indie spirit. We take an active role in bringing the best underground culture to the surface.

InterMixx IndieGate
CustomerService@InterMixx.com
www.IndieGate.com
The coolest place on the internet to buy indie music!

ItsAboutMusic.com
DeanSciarra@ItsAboutMusic.com
www.itsaboutmusic.com
Our goal is simple - to supply you with music that sounds like the music that changed the world - music that matters...for those who care.

JIPrecs.nu
JIPinfo@JIPrecs.nu
www.jiprecs.nu
Your alternative indie record label with mp3 and CD.

Juno Beach
slawson@junobeach.com
www.junobeach.com
A place for people who love music and for those who love to make music. It's a web site where you can hear, read about and purchase CDs from independent artists of all types. It's also a place for artists and small labels to let the world hear their music without selling their souls to the major record companies.

KlarityMusic.com
webmaster@klaritymusic.com
www.klaritymusic.com
Great music and recordings from Independent Artists around the world!

KlubKat
kba@klubkat.com
www.klubkat.com
Selling at The KlubKat Store won't cut into your profits - With KlubKat, you tell us what price you would like to receive for your CDs or goods and we make sure that's what you get!

KMB Records
Ken Wells KMBRecords@aol.com
www.kmbrecords.com
A haven for those seeking an escape from the mindless over-played music mainstream radio offers. We are always looking for more artists! KMB Records is currently involved in a major compilation project called "Sound Diversions."

Kranzke Entertaunment, Inc
Eli Swenson contact@kranzke.com
www.kranzke.com
We are committed to the incubation of emerging artists across all musical frontiers. Success will be achieved by way of positive supportive relationships encompassing: Recording, Representation, Promotion & Distribution. Dreams to Reality...

Kweevak's Tracks
mr_kweevak@yahoo.com
www.kweevak.com
Send your CDs and press kits to us at Kweevak's Tracks. When you do we'll consider it for: a Feature Listing, a CD Review, an Artist Spotlight/Interview, airplay on music webcasts and a CD of the Year nomination.

LightningCD Corporation
Nissa Madsen distribution@lightningcd.com
www.lightningcd.com
A company that supports independent artists with national distribution of their CDs via digital network. It is available as a desktop application for home users. The Lightning CD concept makes music on demand both legal and convenient for users and eliminates substantial upfront costs and hassles for artists in the form of shipping and CD replication.

Lightstage
webmaster@lightstage.com
www.lightstage.com
You don't need a UPC barcode to sell at Lightstage. Lightstage just brings independent music and unsigned bands exposure! You set your selling price at whatever you want. We keep $4 per CD sold.

Lindy-Records
webmaster@lindyrecords.com
www.lindyrecords.com
Free online promotion for independent musicians. Monthly E-Zine reviews new CD's and Demo's. Two independent music radio stations online. Online CD shop reviews CD's and sells your music at a great price.

Liquid Fusion
Liquid.fusion@verizon.net
www.liquidfusion.com
An Independent Record Label bringing you unique collections of Songs fresh from the minds of the writers / musicians that created them. Do not send CD's / Cassettes. Send email with the URL where your MP3s can be found. Do not send MP3's as this severely impacts email.

Locals Online
sales@localsonline.com
www.localsonline.com
We're not bringing the music industry to its knees. We're bringing the artist to its feet.

LOUiPiMPS
andrew@louipimps.com
www.louipimps.com
Do you have what it takes to be a LOUiPiMPS artist? Visit our website to find out how to submit a demo to LOUiPiMPS.

lowartmusic.com
Jeff Farley
info@lowartmusic.com
www.lowartmusic.com
We are an independent music label specializing in alternative rock and alternative ambient projects.

Maple Island Records
Jeff
jeff@mapleislandrecords.com
www.mapleislandrecords.com
Independent record producer & label. In search of & promoting independent songwriters.

Me No Know Records
Tim ghostofanastro@yahoo.com
www.geocities.com/menoknowrecords
A pop label collective based out of Gloucester Massachusetts and Montreal Canada. Always interested in putting out cd-r compilations and promoting the magical sounds of sweet sweet pop.

Midnight Records Network
Peter Tattlebaum
peter@midnightnet.com
www.midnightnet.com
Assisting independent musicians in album promotion. A great place for you to hear and buy great new music.

Milk Records
Dan Augustyn
dan@milkrecords.com
milkrecords.com
We provide independent recording artists the opportunity to sell their albums over the Internet.

The Minstrel Avenue Record
Paul Benshoof
tmar@zianet.com
www.zianet.com/minstrel
The Minstrel Avenue Record (TMAR) serves as a medium for musicians to advertise and market their works independent of or complementary to record distributors.

Mixonic
customercare@mixonic.com
www.mixonic.com
It's easy to sell your CDs online at Mixonic. Our unique on-line software allows you to manage the entire process from your office or home, taking the hassle out of distributing professional quality CDs.

Moozikoo
artist_services@Moozikoo.com
www.moozikoo.com
An international music Etailer that offers independent artists and record labels a platform to sell their music in the global marketplace. Our focus is more than simply building upon an artist's domestic fan base. We work to introduce American music to the emerging markets in Russia, the Commonwealth of Independent States and the Russian-speaking population within North America.

Mordam Records
ken@mordamrecords.com
www.mordamrecords.com
Mail order and MP3 distribution for more than thirty independent record labels and magazine publishers. We distribute labels. We don't work directly with artists.

mpulse
support@mPulse.com
www.mpulse.com
At mPulse we have two priorities. One is showcasing independent artists. The other is providing music fans with an honest, unbiased chart of the most popular music websites, artists and songs on the Internet.

Music Distributors.com
stemith@aol.com
www.musicdistributors.com
We cater to independent artists and Labels. We'll sell your CDs online and will pay you every week.

The Music Post
distribution@themusicpost.com
www.themusicpost.com
An alternative independent website for independent musicians to promote and sell their music online. Each musician who joins us gets their own fully featured web page. Membership is free.

MusicalRevolution.com
info@musicalrevolution.com
www.indyz.com
We are a fast growing CD store for Independent Music. We plan on expanding our site to encompass all aspects of independent music.

MusicBuilder.com
webmaster@musicbuilder.com
www.MusicBuilder.com
From the initial concept of MusicBuilder.com we want to make it easy for users to find your music with enhancements like our unique similar artist search, location search and our searchable gig calendar.

Musicfist.com
Rick Nelson musicfist@cox.net
www.musicfist.com
We can help get your name out to the public and sell some of your CDs in the meantime.

Musicheadz
support@musicheadz.com
www.musicheadz.com
We offer you your own shopping cart to sell anything from CD's and vinyl to posters and clothes. You add and update the products yourself! You send us your stock, we worry about the rest!

MusicStack
contact@musicstack.com
www.musicstack.com
A community where individuals, collectors and record stores buy and sell each others music. Selling through MusicStack is like have an extra 5000+ searches a day through all of your inventory! Your sales are practically guaranteed to go up!

MusicSteps.com
pam@musicsteps.com
www.musicsteps.com
Putting together the tools and relationships necessary for artists to reach their listeners and for listeners to find the music they are looking for in whatever format they choose. Our Vision: To provide an online music network that allows bands, labels and customers to come together for the betterment of all parties.

musictoday.com
feedback@musictoday.com
www.musictoday.com
We possess the qualities necessary to successfully develop a band's career. Our experience in sales of entertainment merchandise through mail order, telephone, fax and the web currently benefits a number of musicians.

Muze
music@muze.com
www.muze.com
We are content providers to over 250 online retailers for music, books & video as well as in-store look up systems. If you send us your CD, along with label, distributor, release date info, catalog number, barcode and genre of music, we will list it in our database, which will then be listed in the kiosk and possibly at the online retailers.

Muzi Cafe
feedback@Muzicafe.com
www.muzicafe.com
In addition to our high traffic from music fans, we actively recruit retailers, record labels, promoters and radio stations to view our artists, buy and play their music.

NETUNES.com
www.netunes.com
Regardless of style or idiom, if your CD is of professional quality, NETunes will call you PDQ and fax or mail you a Distribution Agreement.

New Artist Direct
suggestions@newartistdirect.com
www.newartistdirect.com
Each day, big business is squeezing more and more independent artists out of retail stores, radio airplay and press in general. We are helping independent artists to 'play the game' on their own terms and win. Or, at least make a living doing what they love.

The Night Cafe CD Store
Richard Hazelwood sales@nightcafe.co.uk
www.nightcafe.co.uk
Distributor of relaxing yet stimulating late night music with a high "chill out" factor. staffed by music enthusiasts! We also sell cd's by independent artists covering most genres. We offer great deals for the Unsigned artists.

Not Lame
popmusic@notlame.com
www.notlame.com
3 power pop labels and music distributor of power pop-oriented music.

The Official Soapbox Entertainment Website
Corey Corey@soapboxent.com
www.soapboxent.com
Long Island Indie Recording/Publishing label for poets and musicians. We run promotions and support for any and all indie labels and artists.

OneSource
onesource@pan.com
onesource.pan.com
A totally digital distribution system for the online sale and secure delivery of e-CD's through affiliated retail websites throughout the world.

Online Rock
info@onlinerock.com
www.onlinerock.com
A Web-based music community for bands and musicians to promote, distribute and sell their music online.

The Orange Spot
buymystuff@theorangespot.com
www.theorangespot.com
Selling your product on the Orange Spot is easy! Just fill in the registration form below and you will be contacted via email with information and instructions.

The Orchard
info@theorchard.com
www.theorchard.com
A leading supplier of independent music on the Internet, that offers worldwide non-exclusive distribution.

OurGig.com
sales@ourgig.com
ourgig.com
Designed to attract music fans looking for great new talent and music, OurGig.com with our partners Jazzpromo.com and discomat.com we provide you the opportunity to sell your music online all day, every day — all year around reaching music fans virtually anywhere around the world.

OutBoundMusic.com
info@outboundmusic.com
www.outboundmusic.com
Our mission is to provide honorable and equitable distribution and promotion services for independent recording artists and songwriters while providing listeners with a wide variety of easily attainable quality music.

Outstanding Records
Leander edgarbt_48820@yahoo.com
http//www.outstandingmusic.com
We offer a chance for musician songwriters and singers to sell their CD's off of our website.

Park Hill Music
galletta@parkhillmusic.com
www.parkhillmusic.com

PeaceWork Music
music@peacework.com
www.peaceworkmusic.net
Because we manufacture our CDs on demand, artists and labels benefit from our truly international distribution without the manufacturing, shipping and warehousing costs that would otherwise prevent them from reaching a worldwide audience.

peermusic
info@peermusic.com
www.peermusic.com
*Our approach to the creation of music is as
contemporary as the music itself. Our A & R staff
works closely with each of our writers and artists,
encouraging their creativity, directing their talent and
enabling them to achieve their career goals.*

Peppermint
mail@peppermintcds.com
www.peppermintcds.com
*We are most interested in artists who are full-time
musicians and actively touring, who have released at
least 2 professional caliber CDs and have mailing
lists of over 1500 people.*

Planet CD
contact@planetcd.com
planetcd.com
*We provide SECURE online ordering of your music,
audio samples and 2 professionally designed web
pages dedicated to your music! We provide your
customers with unsurpassed customer service, a free
newsletter, free bumper stickers and monthly prize
drawings to keep them coming back for more.*

Pop Sweatshop
Chris Barber chris@popsweatshop.com
www.popsweatshop.com
*We work furiously, in sweatshop conditions, to make
and distribute great indie releases for bands on a non-
exclusive basis.*

Prose Productions
Jason Broadwater jb@proseproductions.com
www.proseproductions.com
Label for independent musicians, artist and writers.

Rearview Music
RearviewMusic@tcpro.net
www.tcpro.net
*An online indie CD store which features some of the
best independent, underground and unsigned rock and
pop rock artists from the US and UK.*

THE REC(o)RD LINK
info@therecordlink.com
www.therecordlink.com
Let us put your recordings on the Internet...

Real Star Records
Matthew Leber mleber@realstarrecords.com
www.RealStarRecords.com
*An independent label that gives its artists respect and
creative freedom, with an agreement that the music
released does not harm the betterment of the human
race. "The golden rule" is the premise from which
Real Star Records is founded on and the music it
promotes hangs on this principle.*

RhythmNet.com
Craig Cooke craig@rhythmnet.com
www.rhythmnet.com
*A website for independent musicians. Viewers can
read about artists, listen to their music and purchase
their CDs.*

Rocket Entertainment
support@rockete.com
www.rockete.com
*We allow you to experience media from independent
artists through streaming audio and video files. We
feature music and music videos. You may also buy
products like, CD's, magazines, sheet music etc.*

Rock SexParty
seanrox@rocksexparty.com
ww.RockSexParty.com
*New Music Sex Toys and Community. Blurring the
lines of shameless promotion and retail. Hopefully,
we'll break every rule of traditional marketing.*

SCREACHEN
Al Harbison President@screachen.com
www.screachen.com
*Non profit company that reviews, manages and
produces bands. We also do the same for national
bands.*

Shut Eye Records
pete@shuteyerecords.com
www.shuteyerecords.com
*We have released music by more than 300 bands and
artists from around the world in almost every genre of
independent music. Shut Eye is best known for our
ability to facilitate musicians without sacrificing their
artistic slant or agenda.*

The Silk City Recording Company
Andy Allu silkcitycd@aol.com
www.silkcitycd.com
*An on-line retail site that offers artists and indie
labels a portal for selling their product.*

SingOnTheWeb
Delmus Jeffery filtelnetwork@sbcglobal.net
www.SingOnTheWeb.com
*Offers high exposure and promotions for music artists
as well as cd distribution, website design, cd cover
design and much much more. Offers streaming video
and music reviews. We'll also market your music to
the public and highly publicize your music act.*

Solarise Records
Paul/Lee info@solariserecords.com
www.solariserecords.com
*An online Independent resource/label. Solarise
Records help to showcase, promote and sell Talented
Original independent Artists music cds online from
any genre from all over the world. Seeking Artists
Now!*

something sacred
jon broyles bandinfo@somethingsacred.com
www.somethingsacred.com
*A collection of artists with the goal to promote, music,
art, literature and clothing. DEATH.LIFE.MUSIC.*

SongRamp
admin@songramp.com
www.songramp.com
*We offer independent artists an outlet to sell their CDs
with minimum hassle.*

songwriter.com
info@5happy.com
www.songwriter.com
*We are a floating collective of independent artists -
friends, singers, writers, strangers (new friends) etc. -
banded together to take advantage of combining our
marketing efforts and the low cost of promotions on
the web, for promoting our CDs.*

Sonic Garden
info@sonicgarden.com
www.sonicgarden.com
*ALL Programs are FREE. Web Presence and Store-
front, Artist Page with Music, Videos, Tour Info,
Album/Song Info and much more!*

Soul Surfer Records
Scott Rickett info@soulsurferrecords.com
www.soulsurferrecords.com
An independent record label by musicians for musicians about the true art of music. We have developed a network of multi-media outlets to expose and market new talent. We are looking to expand our network by working with new artist and traditional and non traditional marketing and sales outlets.

Springbound Music
www.springbound.com
The premier provider of burn-on-demand (BOD) compact disc manufacturing and music distribution services for emerging and established musicians.

starpolish
info@StarPolish.com
www.starpolish.com
We are dedicated to educating and empowering artists, with an emphasis on artist advocacy and artist development. We are also committed to supporting the arts by rewarding and highlighting the most hard-working and deserving artists. StarPolish is a collaborative effort between artists and music industry professionals.

Statue Records
Geoff Emery ge@statuerecords.com
www.StatueRecords.com
Large Indie Label in Western US. Representing over 100 recording artists.

Stinkweeds Online
kimber@stinkweeds.com
www.stinkweeds.com
Your source for independent music on the web. With reviews of new music added weekly and release lists updated weekly, you'll stay on top of everything indie.

Strange Sandwich Music
www.strangesandwich.com
This is what happens when you combine independent musicians from various genres of music and three different countries. Friends who enjoy making music. Great music!

Strange Vibes
Brian Mawhinney StrangeVibes@hotmail.com
www.strangevibes.com
A new CD distribution site for Independent Musicians to post their CDs for free.

Subterreign.com
info@subterreign.com
www.subterreign.com
We attach the sound files and bio/reviews to your page and present you to the world. Each submission is free. E-mail for more info. It pays to promote your product.

SWRECORDS.NET
info@swrecords.net
www.swrecords.net
Support Independent music and buy it online!

Thrift Store Records
Jeremy McKeen mckeen@myself.com
www.thriftstorerecords.com
We serve to create and maintain a music community based on creativity, originality, diversity and fidelity. We serve all artists interested in promoting good music and supporting others who do the same. Good music is good for you.

Twee Kitten
popmusic@tweekitten.com
www.tweekitten.com
An independent record label and an online mail-order operation. Twee Kitten primarily focuses on music possessing beauty, melody and charm. Oddly, this results in a catalog filled primarily with obscurities. But rest assured, a virtual treasure trove of tempting delights is within!

United Global Artists
Leigh Silberg uga@email.com
www.u-g-a.com
International indie music resource & promotion web site/artist collective, devoted to indie music fans & artists worldwide.

Virtual Radio
webmaster@virtualradio.com
www.virtualradio.net
It's true! Independent musicians are selling their original CD's to the globe "hassle-free" on Virtual Radio from the safety of their underground global command center studios or from their home pc, whichever is more convenient...

Wampus Multimedia
contact@wampus.com
wampus.com
The careening artistic collective. We produce CDs and wild multimedia stuff with a firm commitment to wreaking aesthetic havoc whenever possible.

Xact Records
submit@xactrecords.com
xactrecords.com
A site that promotes unsigned bands and sells their merchandise. We review all types of bands, have band contests, giveways and much more.

Canada

AllIndieMusic.com
info@allindiemusic.com
www.allindiemusic.com
Featuring the best independent artists from around the globe.

Attack Records
info@attackrecords.com
www.attackrecords.com
We listen to everything we receive but please be patient; it will take us a while to get back to you. We will probably contact you by email or phone. PLEASE, NO PHONE CALLS.

CandleView Records
www.candleview.com
We offer radio tracking for qualifying (unsigned and signed) product, non exclusive record contracts (13 titles) and have 3 exclusive artists as well (3 titles) and review product. We have multiple distribution contracts in various countries and do marketing and promotions.

Great White North Records America
Remi Cote general@gwnrecords.com
www.gwnrecords.com
Production, distribution, manufacturing, mail-order, licensing...

Last Tango Productions
lastango@pathcom.com
www.lasttangoproductions.com
Building careers and breaking artists since 1989. National Publicity & Radio Tracking. Campus Press and Radio. Tour Support. Special Events. Video/Record Pool and Internet Promotions.

TuneVault.com
steve@tenvolt.com
www.tunevault.com
Reviews, news, calendar, artist pages and more. Sell your stuff!

Mexico

I.T.D.M. (Intent to distribute Malvolio) music & merch.
Sonny Malvolio malvoliocybercafe@hotmail.com
myweb.ecomplanet.com/MALV1029
A Mexico city based indie label offering great services such as cybercafe, clothing and indie label. We internationally distribute music for artists that are hoping to get noticed and are currently accepting emo submissions.

Argentina

Rock Under Agency
Andrés Medina agencia@ru.com.ar
www.ru.com.ar/agencia
Giving bands the largest amount of services possible and offering them the best rates, taking into account the tough situation we are currently going through.

Finland

Gridrecords.com
Karie karie@gridrecords.com
www.gridrecords.com
An On-Line distributor and promoter of independent and alternative music based in Helsinki, FUNLAND!

France

Djinns Productions
FredM djprod@djprod.com
www.djprod.com
Independent Artists Collective. Artists can join our DEMOPLAYER for free during 2 months if they are selected.

Ocean-Music
cadix@wanadoo.fr
www.ocean-music.com

Sriracha Sauce
Sophie sophie@sriracha-sauce.com
www.sriracha-sauce.com
We are a French based booking and management agency.

Germany

2LOUD4U
www.2loud4u.de
Hard Alternative.

amazon.de
www.amazon.de

Glitterhouse Records
info@glitterhouse.com
www.glitterhouse.de
The ultimate Mail-order for Americana, Roots, Alternative and Folk CDs.

KLÄNG
info@klaeng.de
www.klaeng.de
"Free music". Non-profit CD compilation series. Everybody may contribute. No limitations, no censorship, no copyrights. Free author's copy for every contributor.

KVD RECORDS
Jim Allford jallford@nb.net
www.kvdrecords.com
German indie label that is looking for new unsigned artists and bands. Also, interested in merging with U.S./CANADIAN indie label. Looking for our artists and bands to be signed to either U.S./CANADIAN label. KVD RECORDS does publishing, distro and book tours of Germany. Please e-mail me, if interested in any of the above.

Pooltrax
www.pooltrax.de
Mp3 kostenlos downloaden, Charts, News, Software für Musik & Mp3, uvm. bei POOLTRAX.

RockCity Hamburg
Claudia music@rockcity.de
www.rockcity.de

ZYX Music
www.zyx.com
Music is our passion!

Italy

Alma Music
Marco Broll info@almamusic.it
www.almamusic.it a
An independent record brand of modern conception. All with the greatest respect for artists and producers choices, with proposals embracing a wide musical range. Through its site, Alma Music promotes and sells Independent music from Italy and the rest of the world.

Music & Waves
Robert Ruggeri info@omomworld.com
www.omomworld.com
Italian Independent label & great "portal" to the surf scene in both MUSIC & real life!

The Netherlands

Platenworm Recordstore / Hellworm Records
Pieter Bos pieter@platenworm.nl
www.platenworm.nl
We sell all kinds of independent / underground music. The Hellworm record label is there to release cool bands from the Netherlands and especially Groningen the place where I live.

Spain

popchild.com
popchild@popchild.com
www.popchild.com

Sweden

Fickle Fame
Torkel Skogman info@ficklefame.com
www.ficklefame.com
An independent record label and booking agency (for Europe) based in Sweden. Primarily releases music in the genres pop, alternative rock, punk, experimental, noise and electronica.

Zorch Productions
Tobba Andersson info@zorchproductions.com
www.zorchproductions.com
Label that release the best unsigned stuff from Scandinavia. We do NOT trap bands with contracts, just one release of stuff we LIKE A LOT!

United Kingdom

Promotional Services

Dead Or Alive
Nicholas Barnett n_barnett@madasafish.com
We have become one of the most respected independent music promoters in the UK. We focus on staging gigs for up and coming bands, particularly those on independent labels who have released singles / EPs and albums.

Genius Entertainment
info@genius-entertainment.com
www.genius-entertainment.com
Offers promotion to unsigned and signed bands. We accept submission from both writers and music artists seeking to further their careers. We are seeking new and exciting commercial artistes.

Maeman.Com
Martin A.Egan perfectpassion_2001@yahoo.com
www.maeman.com
An Independent Promotions Company and Agency for Independent Folk and Rock Artists. We are based in Dublin Ireland. We are agents for numerous Irish Rock, Folk and Rock Bands.

Night Café
info@nightcafe.co.uk
www.nightcafe.co.uk
A premier distributor of relaxing yet stimulating late night music with a high "chill out" factor that is not available from the average high street retailer.

Pleb Records Promotions
Graeme Sutherland plebrecords@email.com
www.plebrecords.8m.com
Independently run, non-profit making promotions and independent record company.

Prostar U.K. Talent Scouts
David Priest enquiries@prostaruk.co.uk
www.prostaruk.co.uk
International talent scouts, searching for bands musicians and artiste, singers, songwriters to promote, place your advert with pic, biography and music using streaming media technology.

RPM Records - UK music Store
Paula Machin paula@rpmrecords.uk.com
www.rpmrecords.uk.com
Well established Online Record, Cd and Memorabilia shop - Offering rock, metal, dance, pop, indie, punk, jazz, soul, blues, disco, reggae, soundtracks etc. Site features a fully searchable database and secure online ordering.

Solar Creations Independent Records & Promotions
Scott Roe scott@solarcreations.net
www.solarcreations.net
Birmingham (UK) based Independent label/promoter with non-exclusive deals working mainly with UK bands. Also involved in organizing tours, PR work etc.

Traffic Online
teams@trafficonline.net
trafficonline.net
We build, maintain and coordinate street teams in the UK for bands and record labels as well as for a whole host of other projects.

Vendors and Labels

amazon.co.uk
www.amazon.co.uk
Our mission is to provide a simple, direct and profitable way for musicians to sell their music on the UK's No. 1 online retailer.

Blue Comet Music
Anjool@mail.com
unsigned.xs3.com
By joining us you'll be an integral part of an elite directory - unlike the larger directories with thousands of unsigned bands, where being discovered is difficult due to the competition, We have just over 100 bands and artists, with something for everyone.

Blue Water Music
info@bluewatermusic.net
www.bluewatermusic.net
Primarily geared towards giving the customer a huge choice of music which will satisfy their soul (as well as some stimulating reading). We also operate as an "ethical" business and donate our profits to three charities (chosen by the customers when they place an order).

Butlermusic
submit@butlermusic.com
www.butlermusic.com
If you are a band or an artist looking for your "big break", then why not submit your music and show the world your talent!

DiscoWeb
help@discoweb.com
www.discoweb.com
International music megastore with over 350.000 CDs, LPs, DVD and Videos. Largest catalogue in U.K., Latin and other European music.

Norman Records
phil@normanrecords.com
www.normanrecords.com
The loveliest & best in new and used indie/ post-rock/ electro/ electronika/ IDM/ twee pop/ experimental alternative vinyl & cds from around the world. Delivered to your doorstep by underpaid but hopefully happy post people (that means we're mail order folks).

Opal Music
sales@opalmusic.com
www.opalmusic.com
Europe's leading specialist for indie & alternative music.

www.indielinkexchange.com

overplay.co.uk

info@overplay.co.uk
www.overplay.co.uk
*Our aim is to put unsigned bands firmly on the map.
We'll put you in touch with like-minded bands and
pass on your details to venues, record companies and
management. Whatever it takes to bring your band
the exposure you know it deserves, we'll ensure your
talents are aimed toward the right people, thereby
maximizing your chances of signing that elusive
record deal.*

Rough Trade

shop@roughtrade.com
www.roughtrade.com
*Please send us an email giving us some kind of clue
as to exactly what you do musically and we'll get
back to you and let you know if we want to sell your
beautiful product. You can always send us a sample of
your music as well and any bribes will be very
gratefully received.*

The Seventeen Music Group

Marty Hollands seventeenrecords@ntlworld.com
theseventeenmusicgroup.co.uk
*Independent Songwriting Artist and Production
Resource and Label.*

Stolenwine Records

info@stolenwine.co.uk
www.stolenwine.co.uk
*Our strategy is to get these bands onto vinyl and to
you as cheaply as possible. Please visit our site for
submission details.*

UK RockNet site

info@ukrocknet.com
www.ukrocknet.com
*Offering services that will help bands produce product
that UK RockNet can sell for them is still be the main
target of the site. It is realised that there is a ready
market place for unsigned bands and UK RockNet
intends to help those bands market themselves and
allow them and us to succeed.*

Zen Music

ar@zenmusic.co.uk
www.zenmusic.co.uk
*We aim to offer a wider selection of quality music at a
more affordable price. To do this we are putting the
artist directly in touch with the consumer. By cutting
out all the costs mentioned above we can offer our
CDs at less than half the price of similar ones found
in the shops and still pay our artists a lot more than
they'd get in a regular deal.*

Australia

Promotional Services

Australian Music Biz

mail@musicbiz.com.au
www.musicbiz.com.au
*We don't guarantee what media will pick up on your
music. We guarantee that they will hear it and we will
usually get feedback. Our history shows our successes
and a good product with good repping will usually get
good results.*

Australian Music Marketing Abroad

Norman McCourt amma@netspace.net.au
*I am the Director of Australian Music Marketing
Abroad & Australian Radio Services. We are currently
looking for material, artists, groups and albums for
publishing and licensing in various territories in
Australia. Send your product sample to: Australian
Music Marketing Abroad, PO Box 319, Fitzroy,
Victoria 3065, AUSTRALIA.*

Ausradiosearch Distribution

www.isonliveradio.com
*We can get your film clips on to Aussie TV for you!
We have the industry contacts you need to get your
video clip to the right people down under. Radio is a
great way for people to hear new music, but why
ignore the many possibilities that television also has
to offer independent music.*

PK Music

Danielle Clout manager@pkmusic.com.au
www.pkmusic.com.au
*I am an experienced and qualified music manager
that will give you an objective and insightful opinion
on your music and career direction for a fee. I
respond to all requests and provide practical steps to
get where you want to go. All styles of music
accepted. Contact us for details.*

Vendors and Labels

Astral Records

Michael A Puskas puskas@astralrecords.com
www.astralrecords.com
*We are an Australian development label of worldwide
music and we are looking for artists that want to
become part of our film and television placement
platform. Our site features artists from all around the
world.*

Groovetracks Records

Steve Cole info@groovetracksrecords.com
www.groovetracksrecords.com
*We are seeking submissions from new and existing
artists, bands or songwriters who have a finished
product for distribution. On acceptance of material,
Groovetracks ultimate goal is to boost sales through
radio airplay and the internet and to make online
samples of artists product available.*

High Beam Music

mail@highbeammusic.net
highbeammusic.net
*The on-line store aims to deliver you the best
underground rock from around the world specialising
in stoner, sludge, psychedelic, doom, high octane, true
punk, indie, metal and other forms of cutting edge
rock.*

Indie-cds.com

enquiries@indie-cds.com
www.indie-cds.com
*RealAudio and MP3 sample tracks, CDs for sale and
four web radio channels 24 hrs a day. Secure server,
world/roots/folk music specialist. Australian bands
only.*

Modern World Records

Craig Mitchell cross@castle.net.au
www.modernworld.com.au
*Australian online catalogue specializing in Australian
and overseas indie vinyl and cds.*

One World Music

Leigh Wood info@oneworldmusic.com.au
www.oneworldmusic.com.au
*We are an independent record label that focuses on
bringing together music from Australia and around
the globe blending modern and traditional styles into
a hybrid of sounds that lean towards the Chill-
out/World Beat genres.*

India

Muzik Info Inc.

Kirti Priyadarshani saptam_music@yahoo.co.in
www.ec21.com/muzikinfo
We promote Indian music and budding talent.

Japan

Influx Records

info@influxrec.com
www.influxrec.com
*Are you interested in off-line distribution in Japan?
We offer you G.P.S.(Global Promotion Support). It's
NON-EXCLUSIVE and low risk off-line distribution
project. Influx Records distributes your CDs to major
retailers (Tower Records, HMV etc) in Japan and
translates your profile and documentation to Japanese
and promotes you to media and buyers.*

Specialty

Blues

The Blue Zone

thoeppne@aol.com
bluezone.org
*Our mission is to promote blues music and the
musicians, singers and song writers that perform it.
We will contact blues organizations, festivals and
promoters, suggesting they visit the site and listen to
the talent. We have no interest in obtaining any
finders fee or commissions for the acts on the site.*

The Blues Loft

alawrence@jazzloft.com
www.jazzloft.com/bluesloft
*If you have a CD that you would like sold at The
Blues Loft, visit our site for information on how to get
your music online. We do not charge you any fees.*

DWM Music

donmadsen@DWMmusic.com
www.dwmmusic.com
*Offers top-shelf blues, blues rock, jump blues, swing,
roots rock, country rock, surf & instro and female
singer/songwriter CD's from independent musicians
around the globe.*

House of Blues

support@hob.com
www.hob.com
*We are committed to the production, capture,
promotion and digital distribution of live music
content taking place at the House of Blues
entertainment venues and other select premiere
venues worldwide.*

Stony Plain Records *Canada*

Holger Petersen holger@stonyplainrecords.com
www.stonyplainrecords.com
*Dedicated to being Canada's prominent "roots"
music label. We are passionate about our releases and
believe that the artists we represent create timeless
music from the heart.*

Children's Music

Best Childrens Music.com

tellus@bestchildrensmusic.com
www.bestchildrensmusic.com
*Our goal is to make great children's music easily
accessible to parents and teachers and to scour the
market looking for kid's music that meets our
standards for excellence. Please do not send single-
song CDs for review consideration. Do not send a
pre-release demo CD until you have established a
release date.*

The Children's Group
moreinfo@childrensgroup.com
childrensgroup.com
We are dedicated to the best in entertainment and educational value for children, parents, grandparents and teachers. We are the premier company in North America presenting classical music entertainment for children through our collection of audio CDs and cassettes, video, beautifully illustrated books, interactive CD/ROM, live concerts and educational resources.

KIDiddles.com
mail@kididdles.com
kididdles.com
We are proud to assist up-and-coming (and not-so-new) children's entertainers in getting the word out to our visitors about their products and services.

Kids' CD's and Tapes United Kingdom
info@crs-records.com
kidscdsandtapes.com
Specialist producers of children's music. A high quality range of kids music including party and dance music, nursery rhymes and children's stories.

Kidsmusic
Freya Turner freya@cypmusic.co.uk
www.cypmusic.co.uk
Specialists in the origination, marketing and distribution of quality children's audio, activity and visual products.

Music for Little People
mflp@mflp.com
www.mflp.com
Award winner producer of Children's music. Shop for music, videos, musical instruments, toys and gifts.

Music4Kids Online
webmaster@music4kidsonline.com
www.music4kidsonline.com
We will help you bring music into the lives of the children in your life. The Music4Kids Store offers wonderful musical products for children including musical instruments, musical toys, CD's and cassettes, videos, software and printed music.

Rabbit Ranch Records
info@rabbitranch.com
www.rabbitranch.com
A Christian children's music company. Our mission is to provide good, clean songs that are entertaining and have some positive message.

Youngheart Music
webmaster@younghrt.com
www.youngheartmusic.com
During the past two decades, Youngheart Music artists have sold millions of recordings to parents and educators around the globe, receiving wide critical acclaim and winning numerous awards.

Christian

Promotional Services

The BuzzPlant
Bob Hutchins Info@buzzplant.com
www.buzzplant.com
Internet marketing and Promotion for the Christian Music Industry. Largest Database of opt-in Christian Music Fans.

C&A Tracking and Promotions
Miss CJ misscj1@hotmail.com
www.gospeltrackingandpromotions.com
Distribution to radio & television stations throughout the world. Track and promote gospel music. Organize showcases and workshops.

Catholic Musicians Online
catholicmusicians@cox.net
www.catholicmusiciansonline.com
We have the sole mission of promoting Catholic artists in music. We do not discriminate against Catholic musicians in any way. Whatever race, location, musical style, or success level, all Catholic musicians that are in communion with Holy Mother Church are welcome.

Cross Movements
jd@crossmovement.com
www.crossmovement.com
A team of ministry minded individuals who primarily exist to spread the gospel of Jesus Christ throughout urban areas and assist in disciplining those who believe. We have special interest in the negative impact that secular hip-hop culture has had on urban areas and therefore place a heavy emphasis on challenging and replacing its non biblical philosophies with biblical ones.

Gideon Promotions *United Kingdom*
GideonPro@aol.com
www.gideon-promotions.co.uk
Promoters and Agents to Gospel Music.

Gospel Music Trak & Promotions
Kennya Perry kennya675@cs.com
www.gospelmusictrak.com
My mission is to build relationships with each radio director/owner by communicating, motivating and being excited about each label so we can get each music artist to the top ten Gospel Music Chart.

IDBI Recording Studio
Tim Freeman optisys@ix.netcom.com
www.freeman-enterprises.com/studio-1.html
We record and promote new/unheard Gospel Artists. Showcase your music on our website. Get a FREE MP3 download...

Independent Breakout Artists
www.ibartists.com
IBA is committed to the pursuit of independent artists and the empowerment of their artistic calling through innovative distribution, marketing and promotion. We believe in practicing business ethics according to Biblical standards.

Vendors

Agape Books and Music
office@agape-books-music.com
www.agape-books-music.com
We have thousands of music titles to choose from.

AnonymousBands.com
info@indieheaven.com
www.anonymousBands.com
Our vision is to market Independent Christian Bands/Artist to a network of Christian outlets and youth ministries with the goal of linking concert opportunities with independent artists. It is our belief that all Christian bands are not called to be famous, but all Christian bands are called to be faithful.

Bailey Records
Bryan K. Borgman bryan@baileyrecords.com
www.baileyrecords.com
Independent and Christ-centered record label in Columbus, Ohio. Featuring our own digital-platform recording studios, grassroots promotion and marketing and regional and online distribution.

blackgospelmusic.com
webminister@blackgospel.com
www.blackgospel.com
Dedicated to providing resources for supporters of and participants in the ministry of Black Gospel Music.

Blastbeats.com
staff@blastbeats.com
www.blastbeats.com
Your online headquarters for the best extreme Christian music on the net. We are proud to present some of the best independent and underground bands from all around the world.

Broken Records
info@indieheaven.com
www.brokenrecords.com
We believe that God is releasing hundreds, if not thousands of ministries.. musicians... drama teams... to go out into the world and INFILTRATE...This word is fresh... It is controversial. but it is exciting to see many groups take that step and go into the world, for the time is right to collect the Harvest.

Christian Concert Authority
Karla@ccauthority.com
www.ccauthority.com
World's Largest Christian Concert Search Engine. Also sells Christian CDs (all genres) online.

Christianbook.com
internet.marketing@christianbook.com
www.christianbook.com
Our basic goals and principles are—to offer customers the very best in Christian products at the best prices and with the best service around

ChristianDiscs.com
indierequest@christiandiscs.com
www.christiandiscs.com
We want to provide an outlet for Christians to get their favorite Christian artists at a reasonable price and hopefully find some cool new stuff along the way.

CMCentral.com
info@indieheaven.com
www.cmcentral.com
We feature some of today's hottest Christian acts offering loads of information such as biographies, tour dates, links and downloads! You can also conveniently purchase your favorite CDs through our partner.

CPR Music Group
Murphy Platero cprmusic@prodigy.net
www.nativecprmusic.com
We are native American Christian record co/dist located in Albuquerque NM. with an all Native American artist.

Crossing Music
customerservice@crossingmusic.com
www.crossingmusic.com
We specialize in import and independent music you won't find in most Christian stores.

flavoralliance.com
info@flavoralliance.com
www.flavoralliance.com
The newest national and underground releases priced LESS than your local stores. You save money and all the proceeds go directly to Crossover's hip-hop youth ministry.

GetChristianMusic.com
steve @solidwalnut.com
getchristianmusic.com
GetChristianMusic.com is an online retailer with the goal of getting your music to industry people, the consumer and other songwriters/artists. Get sales and help your career at the same time.

God's Gift Music
www.godsgift-music.com
Your independent music label with a unique difference in connecting artists to the global music industry.

Gospel Artist Network
info@gospelartistnetwork.com
www.gospelmusicmart.com
A site developed for all Gospel and Christian artists, both National and Independent. This site will provide Christian Music Lovers with a source of valuable information relating to their favorite artist and give artist an opportunity to promote themselves.

Holy Hip Hop
webmaster@holyhiphop.com
holyhiphop.com
We have diverse methods for artists to distribute, produce, market and acquire feedback regarding their music. Each artist will have their own individual web page that streams audio titles, from their CD or cassette. The tracks will be listed by name and available for digital distribution on a non-exclusive basis.

independentbands.com
caleb@independentbands.com
www.independentbands.com
We are here for the Christian independent bands that struggle to get their music out and cannot justify the expense of accepting credit cards from their own websites.

Indie Heaven
Keith Mohr info@indieheaven.com
indieheaven.gospelcom.net
Our site provides all Indie Christian artists and musicians a vehicle to fulfill their vision and mission.

indievisionmusic.com
info@indievisionmusic.com
www.indievisionmusic.com
Our goal is to provide legitimate low priced music that is creative, inspiring and fun, yet at the same time represents and encourages a profound Faith in Jesus Christ. Music that is Universal, Music that is inspiring, Music that Rocks your Mullet!

Infinity Records
Keith Pulliam info@infinityrecordsllc.com
www.infinityrecordsllc.com
Texas based cutting edge Christian music record label. Our main goal is to release cutting edge Christian music and to find new and upcoming talent from around the world.

NetMedia Xpress
info@jtshirley.com
www.jtshirley.com
A great gateway for gospel musicians to be seen and heard by music industry professionals.

PasteMusic.com
mail@pastemusic.com
www.pastemusic.com
The artists we've chosen to promote are generally independent, lesser known musicians who deserve to be heard and who we think you'll be glad to discover. The styles are as varied as alternative pop, rock and Celtic, with a concentration of modern singer/songwriter folk/rock.

RAD ROCKERS
customer.service@radrockers.com
www.radrockers.com
We stock the widest selection of CDs on small, independent, underground U.S. labels that lack broad national distribution.

Rock Solid Music
rsm777@rogers.com
www.rocksolidmusic.com
The place for Contemporary Christian Music of all styles for all ages.

The Shepherd's Nook
Tom Hypes tom@theshepherdsnook.com
www.theshepherdsnook.com
We are now carrying Christian Indie Band CDs on consignment as we strive to support these bands. If you are interested, please get in touch to receive consignment information.

Smith Gospel Music Inc.
Anthony B. Smith sgmabs@earthlink.net
www.smithgospelmusic.com
SGM Record spreads positive music, produces and distributes 3-4 new independent artists each year. Spreading the gospel by any means necessary!

Spirit Music *UK*
info@spiritmusic.co.uk
www.spiritmusic.co.uk
We are an established key supplier of contemporary Christian music to not just the U.K. Christian Music Scene but also worldwide, covering a vast range including gospel, rap/hip-hop, r&b, urban, reggae, dance, jazz/instrumental, contemporary/modern modern rock, Goth/industrial, alternative and hardcore music.

Sure Rock Records.com
support@surerockrecords.com
www.surerockrecords.com
The best Place for Independent Christian Artist and Bands. Offering free web promotion.

vineyardonline.com
info@vineyardonline.com
www.vineyardonline.com

Worship CDs from Independent Artists and Labels
Holly Simmers web@worshipcds.com
www.worshipcds.com
Buy, Hear, Sell Christian indie music. Country, Gospel, Praise & Worship, Rock, Soul.

worshipmusic.com
customerservice@worshipmusic.com
www.worshipmusic.com
If your music does not meet our standards, we will not list it on our site. I mention this so you know that we do have to say no to some projects, simply because the musicality is just not commercially presentable.

worthymusic.com
info@worthybooks.com
www.worthybooks.com
Your source for the very best Christian books, music and videos!

Classical

North America

United States

andante
info@andante.com
andante.com
A new type of classical music venture. Its aim is to document and preserve the world's recorded classical musical heritage and to become the definitive online resource for information about classical music and opera.

Centaur Records
Victor E. Sachse centrec@centaurrecords.com
www.centaurrecords.com
We are happy to accept unsolicited submissions of classical material.

Classical Discoveries
info@classicaldiscoveries.com
www.classicaldiscoveries.com
A web magazine dedicated to raising awareness for rare recordings, undiscovered pieces and underrated artists.

ClassicalPlus
classicalplus.gmn.com
Discover a wonderful group of artists, ensembles and orchestras who are an integral part of GMN ClassicalPlus and listen to their recordings.

Cliff's Classics
Tim O'Hanlon cliff@cliffsclassics.com
www.cliffsclassics.com
We plan to support independent Classical musicians by featuring their music on Cliff's program, promoting them on our site and distributing their music directly from our Website.

Composers Recordings, Inc.
John Schultz jschultz@composersrecordings.com
www.composersrecordings.com
CRI records and sells the CD's of Independent musicians.

Dorian Recordings
info@dorian.com
www.dorian.com
We are among America's largest independent classical labels. With over 350 titles in its catalog, Dorian compact discs are distributed in more than 30 countries around the world. Dorian Recordings is a no-compromise, quality-first label, dedicated to musical, technical and artistic innovation.

Eroica Classical Recordings
Larry A. Russel eroicacds@cnsp.com
www.eroica.com
Our A&R is now accepting new artists. Eroica sells and distributes classical music CDs, performed by world class independent artists on fully guaranteed recordings of the highest quality that are not available elsewhere. We started with one CD in 1993 and have grown to represent hundreds of artists on 151 CDs (and counting).

Ivory Classics
michaeldavis@ivoryclassics.com
www.IvoryClassics.com
An independent classical record label devoted to pianists. We are four years old and have 31 releases out to date. We are distributed around the world through the Naxos family of distributors.

Jeffrey James Arts Consulting
jamesarts@worldnet.att.net
www.jamesarts.com
A full service arts agency dedicated to management and public relations for today. Representing composers, ensembles, instrumentalists and special attractions since 1992, with a very special interest in the music of the 20th Century.

KOCH International
feedback@kochent.com
www.kochint.com
We have reinvented independent music distribution in America and are now America's leading independent distributor.

Marquis Classics/Marquis Records
Earl Rosen Marquis_Classics@compuserve.com
www.marquisclassics.com
We accept A&R submissions from independent musicians in several genres - classical, crossover, jazz and world. If we are interested in a title, we license it to release on Marquis. Anyone interested in submitting to marquis should first visit our website to see the range of music in our catalog.

New Albion Records
ergo@newalbion.com
www.newalbion.com
We resemble a small ship on the ocean, a small press or an art gallery; we employ the ancient art of blind navigation. With composers and performers we develop, record and release about a dozen titles a year, always looking for works that are jewel-like objects of curiosity, beauty and wonder.

New World Records
Paul Tai ptai@newworldrecords.org
newworldrecords.org
Our mission is to record the music of American composers that would not otherwise be represented in the catalogues of the commercial recording companies. The company does not issue any works that are currently available on CD.

Phoenix USA
Jeffrey Kaufman jeffkauf@ix.netcom.com
www.phoenixcd.com
A label devoted to classical music of the 20/21st century with an emphasis on American composers.

Pro Piano
ricard@propiano.com
www.propiano.com
Formed in 1993 to nourish and sustain the careers of deserving pianists.

SibeliusMusic.com
info@sibeliusmusic.com
www.sibeliusmusic.com
You can publish your music on SibeliusMusic.com, but first we need to know who you are. Please visit our website to enter your details. It's entirely free! It costs you nothing to submit scores.

Wildboar Records
Howard Kadis wildboar@musicaloffering.com
www.musicaloffering.com
An independent record label which is administered from our retail store, the Musical Offering, in Berkeley, California. We are probably the last independent classical CD store in the US. We do occasionally carry CDs from independent classical artists (if they are up to our standard of quality).

Telarc
artists@telarc.com
www.telarc.com
Our Submissions Policy requests that you submit a description of your music style as well as all touring and management information available too. Please provide as much detail as possible. If the information you provide seems like it may fit at Telarc we will request that you submit demonstration material. Unsolicited demos will not be considered.

Canada

ArtPro Artist Management
UriZur@ArtPro.co.il
Margaret@ArtPro.co.il
www.artpro.co.il
All artists are represented exclusively and worldwide. We have offices in Tel Aviv, Israel and Richmond Hill, Ontario.

Europe

Austria

VMM
Susanna Kratsch vmm@chello.at
www.xs4all.nl/~gdv/vmm
Almost all of our CDs are by independent composers and performers.

Denmark

Danacord Records
daco@danacord.dk
www.danacord.dk
The Leading Danish Record Company

France

Solstice
fy-solstice@wanadoo.fr
www.fy-solstice.com
More than ever before, we intend to remain faithful to the motto of our beginnings: "off the beaten track".

Germany

FARAO Classics
info@farao-classics.de
www.farao-classics.de
Founded by professional musicians, so that every stage of the artistic production of a recording of music, from the planning, through the recording, the editing and the audio engineering, to the release of the finished product, should be put back into the hands of musicians - which is where they really ought to be!

Pink Tontraeger
pink-tontraeger-gmbh@t-online.de
www.pink-tontraeger.de
We sell the music of Independent classical musicians if the CDs are published under our label Stieglitz".

Italy

Stradivarius
stradiva@tin.it
www.stradivarius.it
Stradivarius seleziona per la tua discoteca la produzione discografica più qualificata, fra interpreti raffinati, repertori originali e dischi più premiati ed acclamati dalla ciritica.

Spain

Malaga Music
info@malagamusic.com
www.malagamusic.com
Classical Music in Andalucia where things of note happen.

United Kingdom

Brewhouse Records
sales@brewhousemusic.co.uk
www.brewhousemusic.co.uk
We have three active labels. BREWHOUSE - includes Early Music, Traditional Music and what may best be described as Folk / Traditional based music. CALLE CLASSICS - limited edition CDs of Classical Music such as Schubert Symphonies, Great Organ Works etc. HOME BREW - records are issued for sale by the artist at concert performances or other gigs.

Chandos
enquiries@chandos.net
www.chandos.net
World's largest Independent classical record company.

Claudio Records
Colin Attwell Info@claudiorecords.com
www.ClaudioRecords.com
We are a small independent British record label. We welcome composers and musicians who wish us to produce and distribute their music.

Divine Art Record Company
Stephen Sutton sales@divine-art.com
www.divine-art.com
We are a very small independent classical label; some of our artists are "independent" though others are well-established with international reputations.

Hyperion
info@hyperion-records.co.uk
www.hyperion-records.co.uk
Founded in 1980, Hyperion is an independent British classical label devoted to presenting high-quality recordings of music of all styles and from all periods from the twelfth century to the twentieth.

METIER Records
info@metierrecords.co.uk
www.metierrecords.co.uk
We are not concerned with mass-market techniques of celebrity, hype and false promises which dominate today's record industry, but rather providing excellent composers with a top class platform through which their work can be disseminated and heard. This uncompromising approach to repertoire makes METIER unique and makes its releases necessary listening.

Music & Arts
info@musicandarts.com
www.musicandarts.com
Independent labels have quietly gone about the task of discovering and recording new talent and new musical genres. More often than not, the aim is quality— the artistry and craftsmanship of marrying true musical talent with true recording and engineering talent.

Musical Cheers
info@musicalcheers.co.uk
www.mc-uk.com
A music agency and relationship manager helping audiences find artists and artists find audiences.

tutti.co.uk
sell@tutti.co.uk
www.tutti.co.uk
"The" web shop-window for contemporary classical music in the UK. We have the latest releases from the top specialist independent classical labels. You will find a wide spectrum of work by established and up-and-coming performers and contemporary composers.

The Wire
reviews@thewire.co.uk
www.thewire.co.uk
Home of the most adventurous coverage of electronica, avant rock, breakbeat, jazz and modern classic sounds from the outer limits. All CDs, records, CD-ROMS, info etc for inclusion in The Wire MUST be sent direct to our snail mail address.

Asia

Hong Kong

Naxos.com
webmaster@hnh.com
www.naxos.com
Our intention is to add a section to our website devoted to the selling and distribution of the recordings of Independent artists. (classical and jazz artists and ensembles). Please contact us for details.

Country

Promotional Services

Honky Tonkin Music
honkytonkinmusic@aol.com
www.HonkyTonkin.com
We offer a wide variety of Independent music including Country, Texas, Western Swing, Cowboy, Bluegrass, Alternative Country, Traditional Country and Honky Tonk along with various other genres.

LC*PR/Publicity House
Laura nashvillepr@yahoo.com
www.angelfire.com/indie/lcpr
Publicity firm that works with country music artists, bands, & labels. We also do tour press. We currently work with 2 major names, several indie artists, & are promoting a major tour.

Lou Nelson Promotions
Lou LNPM@aol.com
www.LouNelsonPromotions.com
We promote artists. via various avenues to meet the world of Country Music, Gospel, Bluegrass and then some... We work to get industry executives to listen, to see and to talk with individuals to further their careers. We help individuals search and locate sponsors to help the artists, songwriters and bands continue their efforts to progress in their field of music-related projects.

Vendors

AmericanaMusicplace.com
www.AmericanaMusicplace.com
Our focus is on Americana Bluegrass, Gospel, Old-Time, Classic Country and Folk. Albums featured have Reviews, Graphics and Audio Samples prepared by its staff.

CountySales.com
info@countysales.com
www.countysales.com
The World's Largest Selection of Bluegrass and Old-Time Music.

Indie World Country Record Report
cdcenter@indieworldcountry.com
www.indieworldcountry.com
Have your most recent Indie Country CD reviewed and listed here. Call for Details and Information: (615) 683-8308

KIC – Soundtrack
info@kic-soundtrack.com
www.kic-soundtrack.com
A promotion recording label, which produces every month promotion CD's with independent artists for Radio Station all over the world.

Flat Earth Records
mark@flatearthrecords.com
www.flatearthrecords.com
If you think that you've got something going on that we would be into, by all means send it along. We are a small label with limited everything, including attention span. We tend to swing more towards things singer/ songwriter oriented and that generally have a bit of twang to them. Americana and Alt-Country are the rock we smoke.

Miles of Music
corrie@milesofmusic.com
www.milesofmusic.com
More music to the gallon!

M-PAK Productions
mmikels@voicenet.com
www.mpakproductions.com
Our heaviest concentration today is in the modern Independent Country movement which is expanding rapidly.

Music City Group
bobbylowder@musiccitygroup.com
www.musiccitygroup.com
Our Mission is to be a service orientated business that equips Independent Musicians, Artists, Songwriters etc. with everything they could possibly need to advance their Musical Careers. If you would like to be considered for one of our programs, send your video tapes, CD's along with your press kit.

The Old-Time Music Home Page
david@lynchgraphics.com
www.oldtimemusic.com
Many of these CDs are hard to find and don't find wide distribution. The best part of the deal is that the musicians themselves keep almost all the profit.

Rockabilly Hall of Fame
bob@rockabillyhall.com
www.rockabillyhall.com
Roots music. Over 12 CDs available.

USOFT Records
music@usoftrecords.com
www.usoftrecords.com
At the present time, we are primarily interested in song materials for Country, Country-Gospel and Bluegrass music productions, but will gladly review materials for other music genres.

Dance

blackmarket.co.uk *UK*
mailorder@blackmarket.co.uk
www.blackmarket.co.uk
House, Drum & Bass, Mix Tapes and Underground.

BoomBoomBap *France*
www.boomboombap.com
IDM, Ambient, House, Jungle, Techno, Electronica and more! New releases, old releases and even some out of print classics!

Clubtraxx Records *France*
Toinet David office.clubtraxx@wanadoo.fr
www.club-traxx.com
Based in France, we are making electronic music, compilations and licensing ++++ booking dj's.

Dusty Groove America
dga@dustygroove.com
www.dustygroove.com
Jazz, Soul, Funk, Hip Hop, Brazil, Latin and more on LP and CD.

e-frenchsound *France*
www.e-frenchsound.com
On e-FS you can find the ultimate tracks from the French Electronic Music Scene classified by style, label or artist.

Junkadelic Zikmu *France*
Nator nator@junkadelic.net
www.junkadelic.net
An independent label based in Paris (France). We provide beats production, artists promotion, independent distribution network over Europe, artwork etc.

Nilaihah Records
info@nilaihah.com
www.nilaihah.com
We strive to release some of the most thought-provoking dance music out there that will keep you moving and open your mind. We do not listen to MP3's. Do not email large files or ask us to listen to any music over the internet.

Sounds Unique *UK*
Lisa Hayhoe sounds@hotmail.com
www.soundsunique.co.uk
A UK based record label specializing in UK Funk/Disco House. We have many missions, one is to present otherwise unsigned exceptional artists and material to the world.

Tune Inn Records
pete@tuneinn.com
www.tuneinn.com
A lot of scrutinizing and careful listening is put into each and every record to justify stocking it - we know a record that works on a dance floor - even if it's not immediately obvious!

Web-Records.com *Germany*
info@web-records.com
www.web-records.com
World's biggest Internet shop for Club Music.

Experimental

4th Rail Productions
Rick Barnes rick@4thrail.com
www.4thrail.com
A full service music promotion and production company based in Portland, Oregon specializing in live instrument electronica.

Acids Musicks
Erik Bonner erik@acidsoxx.com
www.acidsoxx.com
Indie label specializing in bedroom-rockstar psychopop, low-budget concept albums, soundtracks for non-existent films and subliminally-enhanced electro-acoustic collage.

Bad Robot *UK*
Paul Reid info@badrobot.co.uk
www.badrobot.co.uk
Home to lo-fi, punk/pop, experimental and demo recording label. Bad Robot is a small, independent footprint in England.

BiP_HOp webzine
philippe petit ip@bip-hop.com
www.bip-hop.com
A label, a radio show and a webzine devoted to spread unconventional sound adventures, adventurous & creative electronica... sounds, based on machines, mix, modulations, modifications, sampling, glitches, clicks & cuts... blip... bleep... bip... BiP-HOp Generation.

CDeMUSIC
cde@emf.org
www.cdemusic.org
We're a group of musicians that couldn't find in stores the music that we wanted to hear. So we decided to make that music available ourselves. We hope you'll join in and share our enthusiasm.

Clamazon.com
info@clamazon.com
www.clamazon.com
We are looking for music on the edge of experimental, noise, improv, punk, metal, pop etc...whatever pushes the boundaries.

Crazy Fungus Records
contact@crazyfungus.com
www.emmultimedia.com/crazyfungus
An independent record label that focuses strictly on DIY electronic and experimental music. We feature artists that do everything on their own without the use of "fancy" big budget recording studios.

eurock.com
apatters@eurock.com
www.eurock.com
A music retailing institution that sells electronic, progressive and space music.

fencing flatworm recordings *UK*
robert.hayler@ukgateway.net
www.fencingflatworm.connectfree.co.uk
Demos are always welcomed by those interested in the label and are willing to meet our exacting demands.

Forced Exposure
mailorder@forcedexposure.com
www.forcedexposure.com
Offers a wide selection of jazz, experimental, IDM, drum and bass, techno, trip hop, hip hop and more.

Foundling Editions
R. Ketch foundling.ed@earthlink.net
home.earthlink.net/~foundling.ed
A cd/cdr label focused on releasing composed and improvised outsider music.

Frog Peak Music (a composers' collective)
fp@frogpeak.org
www.frogpeak.org
An artist-run organization devoted to publishing and producing experimental and unusual works, distributing artist-produced materials and in general providing a home for its artists.

Hello Pussy Records
Miss Miranda hellopussyrecords@hotmail.com
www.angelfire.com/super/ldr-hpr
Releases with diverse genres/styles. everything from experimental/no-wave to hardcore rock n roll. Definitely underground, definitely worth checking out.

Hypnos
mgriffin@hypnos.com
hypnos.com
Your best source for ambient/space/experimental music is the Hypnos Online Store — a wide selection of the best and latest music by a variety of artists and labels, US and import.

The Infinite Sector
klaodna@infinitesector.org
www.infinitesector.org
Dedicated to sharing and promoting experimental music. Our collective includes musicians, bands and artists from all corners of the globe. Our influences and styles include Electronica, Glitch, Noise, Ambient, IDM, Drone, Space-rock, Improvised acoustic performances and a multitude of other sounds that defy categorization.

IshtarLab Recordings
IshtarLab@aol.com
ishtar.cdemusic.org
Publisher of new music and experimental media arts.

Mathbat Records
info@mathbat.com
www.mathbat.com
We like surreal, sample-laden, drug-influenced cerebral art music that flirts with emotional gothic pretensions even as it nervously copulates with its own groovish stench.

Music Noyz.com
sales@musictoyz.com
www.musicnoyz.com
A showcase for artists and bands to have their music, pictures and bio's hosted for free on the Internet! Music Noyz.com thinks it is important to develop a community for artists to highlight "The Music". Because without the music what's its all mean...nothing?

NCC *(noise control corporation)*
krankheit_@hotmail.com
www.ncc-records.com
We support all forms of experimental, electronic and industrial/noise music. we are in no way affiliated with the band NCC (neo-cyber Christ), or star trek, wars, or anything to do with outer space.

Net Dot Music
netdotmusic@netdotmusic.com
NetDotMusic.com
Specializing in instrumental music that fuses several styles and genres, that is intentionally out of favor with mainstream music business trends. Our mission is to foster the growth and development of our roster while producing and distributing music that does not compromise our artists' or our company's visions.

Oddball Musicworks
David Thomas Peacock dtp@oddballmusicworks.com
www.oddballmusicworks.com
An independent record label that signs, produces and promotes artists that fall outside of the mainstream. We work with artists on a non-exclusive basis.

ping things *Canada*
rik@pingthings.com
www.pingthings.com
If you're interested in having your CD sold through ping things, send an email with a description of your project and a link where we can hear a little bit of what you do. Ambient, electronic, trip hop, dream pop and chill genres. We're always looking for new sounds and we'd love to hear yours, but PLEASE don't send sound files by email!

Public Eyesore
sistrum1@hotmail.com
www.sinkhole.net/pehome
Avant Garde / Experimental / Outsider Music. Featuring minor and major artists from around the world, focusing on an open-minded and expansive free music aesthetic. Non-discriminative promotion and distribution.

Sonic Arts Network *UK*
phil@sonicartsnetwork.org
www.sonicartsnetwork.org
An events, education and information resource with members worldwide. We aim to raise awareness and create new approaches to sonic art by providing information and opportunity across the UK. If you are interested in experimental approaches to sound and the ways in which new technology is transforming the nature and practice of music you might wish to join SAN.

sursumcorda.com
inquiry@sursumcorda.com
www.sursumcorda.com
An independently owned, multimedia website and venue dedicated to the growth and promotion of experimental art and music.

Tzadik
tzadik@tzadik.com
www.tzadik.com
Dedicated to releasing the best in avant garde and experimental music, presenting a worldwide community of contemporary musician-composers who find it difficult or impossible to release their music through more conventional channels.

Film and TV Music

Access Music
Ken Loomis kloomis@novato.net
www.accessmusic1.com
We are a publishing company. We primarily license our artist's music for use in feature films and nationally syndicated television shows. Our contract is non-exclusive.

All-About-the-Music
Emmit Martin emmit@all-about-music.com
www.all-about-music.com
We strive to search for quality artists and writers from around the country representing the many genres of music. We have developed a reputation that is equated with powerful relationships in the film, television and music businesses.

Broadjam
customerservice@broadjam.com
www.broadjam.com
We use innovative technology to provide efficient distribution and promotional services to musicians and provide quantifiable business solutions to music publishers serving the recording, television, film and advertising industries. In serving both the musician and the music publishers, Broadjam is in the unique position of bringing those two worlds together.

Cinecall Soundtracks

mail@cinecall.com

www.cinecall.com

Our purpose is to provide a way for the television and movie industry to be able to use fresh and original music that can be unique to their production. It is also another avenue for songwriters to be able to get their songs heard. Visit our newly revised "Artist of the Month" page.

Core Music

tom@usa-core.com

www.usa-core.com

We are a free self publishing resource for musicians. We help license and publish music. We have extensive opportunities in TV, film, video and game software. Collect 100% performance!

Countdown Entertainment

James Citkovic CountdownEnt@netzero.net

www.CountdownEntertainment.com

An International multi-faceted Artist Management & Consultant firm. We have represented Major Platinum Artists and secured: Record & Publishing deals, Int'l Licensing, TV/Film Soundtrack placement and can help connect Songwriters to Producers.

Filmtracks

tyderian@filmtracks.com

www.filmtracks.com

There are soundtracks. Then there are scores. Executive record producers of the '90s fed consumers with 'soundtracks' that consist of irrelevant song compilations. You won't find those marketing scams here. At Filmtracks, you get the score... the true, orchestral magic of film music.

degyshop.com

info@degyshop.com

www.degyshop.com

We are always trying to help music companies find the best new music for their projects and needs. degyshop.com is stocked with tons of fantastic artists in all types of music genres. Radio stations, TV shows, music zines and more have been using degyshop.com music since we've opened our site for business.

Gulp Music

Cordelia info@gulpmusic.com

www.gulpmusic.com

We licence music to Advertising, TV, Film, Computer Games companies and feel that we can help artists music be heard as well as bringing in some money at the same time.

Indie Film Composers

indifilm@earthlink.net

www.indifilm.com

IFC is a music production entity which subcontracts composition out to our worldwide affiliates. IFC acts as the executive producer of the score. This guarantees consistent production values and an optimized creative environment across a wide spectrum of projects, artists and locales.

Indy Hits

mgalaxy@indyhits.com

www.indyhits.com

Record Promoter, club promoter, music supervisor, working with the top unsigned bands helping to secure record/publishing deals and film/TV placements.

JennieWalkerCompany

info@jenniewalker.com

www.jenniewalker.com

We specialize in providing source music from regional artists for independent film as well as motivation, education and inspiration to today's music professionals via a host of unique services and events.

LicenseMusic.com

music@licensemusic.com

www.licensemusic.com

We will non-exclusively represent your tracks for synchronization, special products, compilations and other B2B licensing applications.

Living Room Theatre Productions

Shane Morris shane.morris@mailcity.com

www.livingroomtheatre.com

Independent short films, music videos and original music. LRTP is always on the lookout for film scores and soundtracks.

LoveCat Music

info@lovecatmusic.com

www.lovecatmusic.com

We offer Film & TV placements, Licensing records to record labels and Administration and collection of royalties. Once we agree to represent your music, we'll ask you for an initial number of copies of each song. We will let you know if we require additional copies of any material.

Music Without Borders

Steve Lurie smlurie@juno.com

www.MusicConsultant.net

A total solution consultancy to the Music/Entertainment industry. MWB serves a range of industry professionals, from recording artists to retailers to record labels. MWB also consults music supervisors and directors of film and television to help find the perfect music for their respective projects.

MusicForFilm.com

submissions@MusicForFilm.com

www.musicforfilm.com

Supervision, Clearance Services and Editing. If you would like to submit music for our consideration, please email me.

Must Have Music

Ken Klar musthavemusic@yahoo.com

www.musthavemusic.net

Whether you're a Film/TV Music Supervisor or an original artist looking for great songs for you next recording project, this is music you can't live without!

PolySutra Entertainment

PolySutraEnt@aol.com

www.CountdownEntertainment.com

We provide all the diverse services needed to help artists take the next step in their careers, including assisting them to secure record deals, publishing deals, International licensing, TV/Film soundtrack placement, screenplay and film distribution & placement, Artist Management and Consultant services.

Pump Audio

Ari artistsrelations@pumpaudio.com

www.pumpaudio.com

We license your music to paying customers in TV, Film and Advertising. There is no fee. You maintain ownership. Clients include MTV, Paramount, Sony, Tom Green, Sports Illustrated and more...

Realia Music Inc.

www.realiamusic.com

Our vision is to become the centre of an on-line worldwide community of musicians and 'indie-visualists' (i.e. filmmaker, producer, director, music supervisor, video game developer, on-line content provider). Using the Internet, we will provide a place for indie-visualists to come to and find any style of music needed to complete their projects.

SongCatalog Inc.

info@songcatalog.com

www.songcatalog.com

Offers a vital collection of digital tools and services that streamline music management, marketing and licensing initiatives for both online and conventional business processes.

SongLink

david@songlink.com

www.songlink.com

Providing the most up-to-date and accurate "who's looking" information to music publishers and songwriters, with hundreds of satisfied subscribers all over the world, many of whom have successfully placed songs and made valuable new industry contacts through SongLink's second-to-none leads service.

Sonic Licensing

contact@soniclicensing.com

www.soniclicensing.com

We are an agency dedicated to helping media producers find the perfect piece of music to compliment their projects. We get your music noticed and create relationships that benefit all involved.

Soundtrack Express

artists@stxpress.com

www.soundtrackexpress.com

We market music to TV and Radio Advertisers, Motion Picture Producers, Cable and TV Producers, Video Producers, Corporations, Interactive Developers & Designers, Game Developers & Producers. We catalog the music and sell individual tracks to interested parties and split the sales with you 50/50. Artist gets paid quarterly and retains all Royalties & Publishing for song used.

SoundtrackNet

webmaster@soundtrack.net

www.soundtrack.net

The art of film and television music.

TAXI

www.taxi.com

The Independent A&R vehicle connecting unsigned artists, bands and songwriters with major record labels, publishers and film & TV music supervisors.

The Warped Project

webmaster@warped-uk.com

www.warped-uk.com

Its simple really, you send us some of your music which will be tested against our A&R criteria. We will then offer you a place with us and start promoting your music for soundtracks.

Folk

Camsco Music

dick@camsco.com

www.camsco.com

Your single source for all folk recordings. If it's folk, we'll get it for you!

Dark Water Music
agent@darkwatermusic.com
www.darkwatermusic.com
A resource for musical artists, assisting with bookings and performance opportunities. Dark Water Music is NOT a Record Label. Dark Water Music is NOT a Promoter. Although Promotions coinciding with bookings is part of what we do. We work in conjunction with Promoters, but not primarily AS a Promoter.

efolk Music
www.efolkmusic.com
We started to fulfill a basic need of independent artist that need to make their music available to their audiences after they load the CD's back in the van, when the gig is over.

FolkWeb
info@folkweb.com
folkweb.com
Started in an attempt to help independent musicians financially by getting their product sold to an audience beyond their gigs.

Independent Music Source Records *(IMS)*
demo@imsrecords.com
www.independentmusicsource.org
We are looking for acoustic singer/songwriter or jazz artists that fit in with what we've been calling "Coffeehouse" genre. Include in your email a website where we can listen to your music and view a press kit online (if available). Also, be sure and tell us about yourself, your music and your objectives.

Trad&Now Music Shop *Australia*
www.tradandnow.com
Supporting Independent creativity.

tradmusic.com *UK*
enquiries@tradmusic.com
www.tradmusic.com
The aim of the site is to support and promote traditional music and traditional music artists and groups throughout the world.

Waterbug
info@waterbug.com
www.waterbug.com
We offer fine contemporary and traditional folk recordings. Welcome. Here you can discover new music from singer-songwriters and folk musicians through audio clips, artist bios and song lyrics.

Gothic

Promotional Services

Darkcell Digital Music
www.darkcelldigitalmusic.net
Contact us for information about what we can do to promote your label/band.

Nocturnal Movements
info@nocturnalmovements.net
www.NocturnalMovements.net
Full service promotions, advertising and public relations for the alternative music industry.

VersusMedia
info@versusmedia.com
www.versusmedia.com
Provider of global publicity services, Internet development solutions and film music networking opportunities. Choose one of the most original and innovative promotion companies for the music industry with a solid reputation.

Vendors and Labels

DarkLand Music
sales@darklandmusic.com
www.darklandmusic.com
If you're an emerging band or independent label, DarkLand Music is here to help you reach your listeners.

DSBP *(Ditch Sex Buy Product)*
Tommy T dsbp@dsbp.cx
www.dsbp.cx
America's most potent hard elektro / harsh industrial label. Specializing in elektro-industrial, EBM, power noise, synthpop, experimental and underground music.

Gore Galore
Kevin R. Alvey (Mr. Gore)
goregalore@worldnet.att.net
www.gore-galore.com
If you would like to submit something for review, I would be happy to give it a listen and let you know if it works for us. Just consider it should have a very dark feel that will be very suitable for Haunted Houses. We have considered some very dark industrial rock also so that is not out of the question. It can certainly be music or just sound effects. Keep GORE Alive!

Latex Records, LLC
TG Mondalf tgmondalf@latexrecords.com
latexrecords.com
Specializing in Goth/Industrial/Electronica//BDSM//Paganism and related genres.

Metropolis Records
label@metropolis-records.com
www.industrial-music.com
www.metropolis-records.com
Home to more than forty innovative industrial, gothic and electronic artists.

MIDFI RECORDS
control@midfirecords.com
midfi.com
Purveyors of Gothic, Noisecore, Industrial, Art Rock and other cruel & unusual music. Always lots of free full length mp3 files.

Planet Mu
mike@planet-mu.com
www.planet-mu.com
We strive to give exposure to new and already established musicians. DO NOT send COCK-CHEESE just cause you want to test the waters, only send material you truly believe in.

Projekt
www.projekt.com
America's premier ethereal / gothic / ambient label — has been releasing great music since 1983!

Shocklines
Matt Schwartz help@shocklines.com
www.shocklines.com
Your one-stop shop for horror. If you do horror music, we'd love to sell your music. Just let me know who I can contact to sell your CD. I buy non-returnable and as long as I can get retailer terms. We'll try just about anything horror related.

SuperGenius Records
superg@supergrecords.com
www.supergrecords.com
Our goal is to provide an online source for fans to explore all forms of Electronic and Experimental music.

Synapse Records
demos@synapse-records.com
www.synapse-records.com
We offer a platform for both established acts and innovative new artists. Our artists' material will be available directly through our label as well as through a diverse network of distributors and licensees worldwide. Remember to include bios, pics, press kits etc. along with your demos!

Van Richter Records
manager@vanrichter.net
www.vanrichter.net
Your aggro-industrial record label!

Hip Hop

Promotional Services

shocksoundpromotions.com
shocksoundpromo@yahoo.com
www.shocksoundpromotions.com
We are your multifaceted urban marketing company in the business of promoting urban recording artists, events and products/brands to: college & commercial radio stations, retail outlets, media outlets, record pools and "ready to buy" consumers on the streets in neighborhoods across the US & Canada.

Unsigned Underground
Maximum Pressure Raydiant1@hotmail.com
www.maddmuzik.org
Free unsigned Hip Hop artist promotions. CD Compilation Series.

Vendors and Labels

3A Records
hiphop3a@hiphop3a.com
www.hiphop3a.com
Our goals are establishing a friendly and professional working environment and helping artists produce their full talent.

98 Proof Recordings
M W zzmtwzz@hotmail.com
www.98proof.com
A hip hop / R&B independent record label based in Neptune, New Jersey.

A-N-B Records Inc.
Jerome Long info@anbrecords.com
www.anbrecords.com
Independent Record Label based in South Jersey specializing in but not limited to R&B and Hip Hop.

ATAK Distribution
pminus@atakworldwide.com
www.truehiphop.com
Send a copy of whatever you want ATAK to sell. If it's the dopest thing EVER, it's in the catalog; if it's doo-doo, you might not ever hear from us again. Check out our website to get the address.

basically-hiphop
maxjeromeo@basically-hiphop.com
www.basically-hiphop.com
Created For The Sole Purpose Of Playing UnderGround, MainStream and HipHop On The Net In Real Audio. We Feature Up And Coming Acts Managed By Us And We Only Play Music That Is Considered HipHop.

Battleaxe Records
deeznuts@battleaxerecords.com
www.battleaxerecords.com
A small Canadian up and coming record company, with room for more independent artists.

Beatbreaks
support@beatbreaks.com
www.beatbreaks.com
Send us a sample of your product and a follow up e-mail and we can go from there.

Big Baby Entertainment
holla@bigbabyballaz.com
www.bigbabyballaz.com
We are a fully equipped independent record label out of South Carolina. We like to describe our selves as "The Next Big Thing Coming".

Brick Records
www.brickrecords.com
An independent hip-hop record label that was established in 1996 and is based in Boston, Massachusetts. Brick is dedicated to releasing only the most innovative and highest quality underground hip-hop and has received international acclaim and respect for doing just that.

DelFuMo Records
moz@delfumo.com
www.delfumo.com
Many independent artists and song and album production.

Digable Records
digablerecords@planet-hiphop.com
www.planet-hiphop.com/records
The #1 NMA in the Rap Game.

DIYHipHop.com
en-L@vinylconnect.com
www.diyhiphop.com
Our aim is to help promote independent Hip-Hop artists. We fully support your musical endeavors. Lack of a record label or distributor doesn't mean you're left dead in the water. We will be your online distributor!

Fambam Records
Thomas Mullin tmullin@fambamrecords.com
www.fambam.com
Upbeat, Urban record label developing the new urban sound for the millennium.

Funk Squad Entertainment
Mario Marrero funksquade@aol.com
www.funksquadent.com
An Independent Hip Hop Label/productions/DJ service. Supportive of good music and talent from all styles.

HeadBOB
musician@headbob.com
www.headbob.com
We are always looking for new artists. Our agreements are non-exclusive and HeadBob artists receive 100% of the sale price for their CDs. Essentially, HeadBob provides completely free distribution with artists receiving all of the royalties.

Headquarters Records
agcee@hotmail.com
www.headquartersrecords.com
Where Rap, Reggae, R&B, Jazz, House and Gospel music rule! We are about positive vibes and do not like music that is offensive of any nature. Please DO NOT submit this type of music to us.

hiphopstore.ch *Switzerland*
info@hiphopstore.ch
www.hiphopstore.ch

JK Music
sales@jkmusiconline.com
www.jkmusiconline.com
The best in underground rap music.

Mic Fiend Records
Jymini jymini@msn.com
www.micfiend.com
Top Notch & Independent Female CEO, producer, emcee, vocalist, web designer & more!

Mumbles Underground Hip Hop Store
wmumbles@hotmail.com
www.bounce.to/mumbleshiphop
Online Store. CDS/Vinyl/Other. Mainly Underground Hip Hop, support your underground artists!

Needle Wreck
info@needlewreck.com
www.nedlwrek.com
Where vinyl lives. Funk, House, Gospel, Hip Hop and Soul.

Noc On Wood Records
noconwood@noconwood.com
www.noconwood.com
We represent a new breed of record label run by a team of smart, enterprising young executives. Listening to music is entertainment; making music is business, so why not surround yourself with businessmen?

Partners Recording Corporation
Charles Kelly ceo@partnersrecording.com
www.partnersrecording.com
Neo-Soul, Jazz, Hip-Hop/Urban Indie Record and publishing Corporation.

PhatSoul.com
email@phatsoul.com
www.phatsoul.com
If you are an independent artist looking for a way to sell your music online, then we have an avenue for you.

Rap Sheet
onlinestore@rapsheet.com
www.rapsheet.com
Due in part to its brand recognition, selling your products on the Rap Sheet website could be quite profitable. We sell cassettes, cds, vinyl and mp3 downloads. We will encode all songs to be sold as downloadable mp3s.

Rap and Soul Mail Order *UK*
MikeyMike@RapAndSoulMailOrder.com
www.rapandsoulmailorder.com
If you do not have distribution please send us a review copy. This is done on a 'don't call us, we'll call you' basis. You will be responsible for the cost of return carriage should your product not sell. This may seem harsh but it's the only way to stop people dumping a hundred mix-tapes on us that don't sell.

Rap.de *Germany*
mischa@rap.de
www.rap.de

Red Brick Records
Louis Courcy mchilds2@twcny.rr.com
www.redbrickrecords.com
A Hip Hop label. We help all independent artists in any way we can!!

Righteous But Ruthless Inc.
Power power@righteousbutruthless.com
www.righteousbutruthless.com
Independent record label who sign and release artists whose artistic skills are in hiphop/rap and r&b.

Rotation Music Entertainment
Mailbox@rotationmusic.com
www.rotationmusic.com
Developed to bring you the phattest hip hop music in the world. This label is expanding tremendously, so send in your demos.

Solid Ground Records
Jesse Morales jecjam@solidgroundrecords.com
www.solidgroundrecords.com
New hip hop indie out of central Cali. Site is a must see!!!! Phat Graphics!!

Stones Throw Records
info@stonesthrow.com
www.stonesthrow.com
Maintaining relationships is the biggest challenge because it is so time intensive. You have relationships with your artists, distributors, radio stations, video stations, stores, writers, promoters, publicists, designers, pressing plants and of course the people buying your records.

Streetjamz.com
thebigal@streetjamz.com
www.streetjamz.com
A new website showcasing local and Independent unsigned black music.

SubVerse Music
jus@subversemusic.com
www.subversemusic.com
An underground hip hop record label. We promote our culture by dropping a significant body of the musical works of our artists

Support Online Hip Hop (SOHH)
felicia@sohh.com
www.SOHH.com

Terrelonge Recordings
mt@terrelongerecordings.com
www.terrelongerecordings.com
Our goal is become one of the leading Independent labels worldwide.

UndagroundArtists
Jason Undergroundcuts@hotmail.com
www.UndagroundArtists.com
Showcasing solid Hip Hop talent that gets lost behind the industry shuffle.

UndergroundBeatOnline
Aaris Schroeder ceo@undergroundbeatonline.net
www.undergroundbeatonline.net
Comprised of people who are interested in creating literature, music and art that is individual, different and yet still stays within the parameters of uniqueness. Includes a taste into urban life with music such as rock, hip-hop, punk, R&B, dance and more.

UndergroundHipHop.com
webmaster@undergroundhiphop.com
www.undergroundhiphop.com
If you have a product that is shrink-wrapped (i.e. we do not accept CD-R's etc.): We would more then likely be interested in carrying your product in our online store on a consignment basis. If this interests you, please e-mail us.

vinylconnect.com
en-L@vinylconnect.com
www.vinylconnect.com
Include a brief description of what you are submitting along with your contact information on the product. VinylConnect is very selective with its product and if we are interested then you will be contacted.

Way 2 Real Entertainment
Ted Selu admin@way2realent.com
www.way2realent.com
Record Label Based in the San Francisco CA Bay Area bringing new emerging artist into the music industry. Rap, Urban and Jazz.

WholeTeam Entertainment
info@wholeteam.com
www.wholeteam.com
A resource for independent artists in search of online distribution, management, production, photography and web design.

Jazz

Promotional Services

Jazz Promo Services
Jim Eigo info@jazzpromoservices.com
www.jazzpromoservices.com
We are uniquely qualified to advise artists on career development, self-producing and media campaigns. Our experience enables us to work closely with record labels and Jazz organizations as well to help you plan a cost effective campaign that gets results by budgeting and assisting with production, promotion, marketing and distribution.

Vendors

All Jazzzzzz and More!
www.alljazzandmore.com
Website focusing on the promotion and CD sales of independent jazz musicians.

AppleJazz
info@applejazz.com
www.applejazz.com
Offering online sales of Jazz CDs, with unique, emotional recordings of independent jazz artists, as well as merchandise for the jazz enthusiast.

Counterpoint Music
www.counterpoint-music.com
Specialists in Jazz CDs! Mainstream, Contemporary, Big Band and much more. New Age too!

InterJazz
staff@interjazz.com
www.interjazz.com

The-Jazz-Link.com
mail@the-jazz-link.com
www.the-jazz-link.com
With our open consignment policy, just send items to us. There is no setup charge. Your music will be put on sale and listed in our catalog.

The Jazz Loft
alawrence@jazzloft.com
www.jazzloft.com
Your online resource for truly Independent Jazz! If you have a CD that you would like sold at The Jazz Loft, visit our site for information on how to get your music online. We do not charge you any fees.

Jazz Now Direct
jazzinfo@jazznow.com
www.jazznow.com/jnd
Some of the finest independently-produced music and products on this planet.

Jazz Valley France
mail@jazzvalley.com
www.jazzvalley.com
Our mission is to help jazz artists reach their fans and to provide a commercial outlet for independent jazz labels and self-produced jazz artists, to make their music easily available to fans and to build a solid and fluent distribution network.

Jazzpromo.com
info@jazzpromo.com
www.jazzpromo.com
We carry hundreds of Independent jazz CDs.

JazzSteps.com
Todd Williamson todd@jazzsteps.com
www.jazzsteps.com
We provide online distribution services for jazz & blues artists and independent labels.

Panda Digital
pandadig@pacbell.net
www.pandadigital.com
We offer some of the most eclectic sounds from all over the world.

Playscape
info@playscape-recordings.com
www.playscape-recordings.com
Conceived with the idea of releasing creative, hard hitting original music, performed by serious uncompromising musicians. Playscape will only release music performed and recorded at the highest of levels.

Latin

AudioMúsico Latino
AudioMusico@aol.com
amlatino.com
The culmination of a great many years of understanding the needs for a one-stop resource for the Latino music industry community and its providers.

Barrio Records
info@barriorecords.com
www.barriorecords.com
We are pleased to receive your submission of material for our consideration and honored by your interest in us. Your material will be treated with respect and appreciation for your talents.

Boogalu Productions
www.boogalu.com
An independent organization from the San Francisco Bay Area focused on presenting and promoting the creative work of outstanding Cuban as well as North American musicians and artists involved in Cuban culture.

DESCARGA.com
Webmaster@descarga.com
www.descarga.com
The ultimate source for hard to find tropical Latin compact discs, videos, books, instructional material and percussion instruments.

Discuba.com

ventas@discuba.com
www.discuba.com
This Havana based site has a great on-line store for Latin music, particularly Cuban CDs, videos and free downloadable MP3 files.

Esp-Music.net

info@esp-music.net
www.esp-music.net
Based on 35 years of successful music industry experience, it is our mission to assist emerging independent musical artists, producers, record labels and publishers, both new and established, by giving their products greater exposure directly to the music buying industry through our cost effective, national distribution system.

Freestylemusic.com

freestylemusic@mailcity.com
www.freestylemusic.com
The freestyle (music patronized and popularized by Latinos beginning in the early 80s) website with an upcoming distribution network for independent artists and Djs, review and chat facilities.

Gaucho Records

info@gauchorecords.com
gauchorecords.com
We are a record label specialized on all types of Hispanic and Latin music genres, all the way from rock to pop, including electronic music, tango and all the sounds we're able to find in music.

IslaMusical.com

customerservice@islamusical.com
www.islamusical.com
Provides a huge selection of Latin titles from a number of different genres. The site also allows Real Audio and Windows Media users to sample songs before they purchase an album.

Midwest Latino Entertainment and Talent

maya@sabortropical.org
www.midwestlatinoentertainment.com
Minnesota's premiere agency for Latino music and entertainment. MLET is booking local and national throughout the Midwest.

Picadillo.com

bishikawa@picadillo.com
www.picadillo.com
A solid resource for Latin musicians, Picadillo.com is a combination CD-vendor and news source, as well as the web's largest archive of articles on Latin music. Picadillo.com also provides links to Latin music education programs.

Qi Music Distributors *Argentina*

info@holimar.com.ar
www.qiartes.com.ar
We are dedicated to the distribution of independent labels and musicians, with a special accent on material quality, in order to bring together our artists selection with sensible people willing to hear new musical trends.

Tejanoclassics.com

info@tejanoclassics.com
www.tejanoclassics.com
An online music vendor which promises a large selection and reliable service. Catalogue includes both classic and current titles.

Tumi

music@tumi.co.uk
www.tumimusic.com
The leading website and record label for Latin American and Caribbean music.

USOFT Records

Alfonse Armendarez alfonse@usoftrecords.com
www.usoftrecords.com
At the present time, we are primarily interested in song materials for Country, Country-Gospel and Bluegrass music productions, but will gladly review materials for other music genres.

Metal

Promotional Services

Desert Rock Promotions

Benjamin Niebla II
desertrock@desertrockpromotions.com
www.desertrockpromotions.com
Hard Rock / Heavy metal music company based in Southern California. We deal in Band Management, Public Relations, Mexico Radio Airplay, A&R, CD Reviews.

Risestar Promotion

info@risestar.cl
www.risestar.cl
Dedicated to promote Hard Rock and Heavy Metal bands worldwide of way to diffuse in masse they music, through albums reviews and interviews in Radio Shows, Magazines, Webzines, television programs etc.

SoundCheckMusic

Danny Wu submit@soundcheckmusic.com
soundcheckmusic.com
Rock, punk, metal etc. types of music. We find all levels of bands whether they are local, breakthrough, and/or mainstream to promote them.

V.Q. Promotions

Publicity@vqpr.com
www.vqpr.com
We understand the protocol of how publications work and how writers like to be approached. V.Q. Promotions will campaign hard to get your band editorial or your CD reviewed.

Vendors and Labels

bandbitch

jon@streetteam.net
www.bandbitch.com
We are looking for bands who are ready to go to the next level. We all know the future of music is/are the unsigned bands. We are looking for bands who have decided to take their band, music and their careers seriously. If you wish for us to place your CD for sale online, check out our website for details.

BMU *Belgium*

filip.lasseel@pandora.be
bmu.lasseel.be
A simple postman who wants to do something for the underground bands in Belgium.

Carnage Inc.

Jason totalcarnage@carnageinc.com
www.carnageinc.com
A great resource for death metal, black metal and gothic artists to get there material heard and seen.

Caustic Productions

Pete Hammoura causticproductions@juno.com
www.causticproductions.com
We are a distributor of underground metal music. We sell cds, cassettes, vinyl and magazines.

deathrock.com

ghoul@deathrock.com
www.deathrock.com
Offers selected deathrock music and items for sale by mail and at special events. Interested in having your material for sale? Send us an email.

Emperor Multimedia *Canada*

info@rrca.diskery.com
rrca.diskery.com
An international rock music association dedicated to the promotion, distribution and preservation of rock music. Has large on-line resources.

Great White North Records America *Canada*

Remi Cote general@gwnrecords.com
www.gwnrecords.com
Production, distribution, manufacturing, mail-order, licensing for Metal / Hardcore and Grind Releases.

Headbanger's Delight

info@headbangersdelight.com
www.headbangersdelight.com
Our Indie Store is here to help promote independent heavy metal bands or any metal band without major distribution.

Metalmuff.net

featuredmetal@metalmuff.net
www.metalmuff.net
We give you a Featured Band Page, MP3 Hosting, Album Photo, Track Listing, Archive of Reviews, Band Contact Info. We will also review your CD for our reviews section and sell your CDs in the Muffshop, the internet's first Metal/Porn superstore. Thus, giving you even more promotion then you ever thought possible!

Nightmare Records & Distribution

Lance King Lance@nightmare-records.com
www.nightmare-records.com
A label and distributor of indie based Melodic Hard rock, Progressive and Power Metal. We sell Wholesale and Retail Internationally.

The Pure Rock Shop

music@tprs.com
www.tprs.com
Looking for additional exposure for your band? Allow The Pure Rock Shop to help you. We are now accepting promotional packages from heavy metal / pure rock style bands for review and spotlight here on the site.

Screaming Ferret Wreckords

info@screamingferret.com
www.screamingferret.com
Any band interested in submitting their music, send us your music on a tape, CD or dat tape. We accept all styles of metal. (We also accept unsolicited material).

Shoutweb.com

daniel@shoutweb.com
www.shoutweb.com

Xtreme Alt Records

Laura Evans laura@xtremealtrecords.com
www.x-rairecords.com
We let our artists be as diverse as they want with a label that will truly back their creative freedom and expression. The purpose of starting this label was to give artists in the metal and punk genre a chance to express who they are without major label prejudices.

New Age

Backroads Music
mail@backroadsmusic.com
www.backroadsmusic.com
Your premier source for over 6,000 titles of Ambient, New Age, Space, Tribal & Global sounds and other fascinating music and videos since 1981.

Blue Water Music *UK*
info@bluewatermusic.net
www.bluewatermusic.net
The best body & mind, trance dance and world music CD store on the planet!

Etherean Music
Mail@Ethereanmusic.com
www.ethereanmusic.com
Providing the highest quality music since 1985.

GROOVE Unlimited *The Netherlands*
kees@groove.nl
www.groove.nl
We have a large diversity of Electronic Music CD's and this means that you can find Rhythmic, Melodic, Ambient as well as Space and New Age music in our catalog.

Hearts of Space
radio@hos.com
www.hos.com/radio.html
If you want to submit material for the RECORD LABEL to consider, please send it to "HEARTS OF SPACE, PO BOX 31321, SAN FRANCISCO, CA 94131-0321, USA". Mark the outside of the package, ATTENTION: A&R. Please, don't call us about your package. If we are interested in your music, or we need more information, we will contact you.

Magical Blend
info@magicalblend.com
www.magicalblend.com

Music "à la Carte" *Australia*
customerservice@musicalacarte.net
www.musicalacarte.net
International indie music store for people who love relaxing, soothing sounds, chants, meditation, healing, shaman music or the uplifting energy of world fusion music from different countries and cultures. Located in Australia, ships world wide.

New Earth Records
info@newearthrecords.com
www.newearthrecords.com
Our label has become synonymous with frequencies designed to point deeper into the inner journey of meditation and celebration of the body. Aspiring to the highest quality recordings to please both the Buddha-mind and the dancing feet of Zobra within each one of us!

NewAgeMusic.com
info@newagemusic.com
www.newagemusic.com
Serving the New Age Music industry in all aspects, such as production, packaging, marketing and promotion.

paganmusic.com
earthtones@paganmusic.com
www.paganmusic.com
It is very easy to get your product into our catalogs (especially CDs!). You need to send a CD Demo copy for review and possible inclusion to: Earth Tones Studios, 61 Alafaya Woods Blvd. #324, Oviedo, FL 32765 USA. Please DO NOT write "DEMO" on the CD Artwork or CD Jewel Case.

Punk

Promotional Services

Creative Eclipse PR
mj@creative-eclipse.com
www.creative-eclipse.com/pr
We offer simple and unique solutions for any press needs you might have, striving to fulfill the specific needs of each customer to the fullest extent. This concern is driven by our musical interests as we have been involved in hardcore, punk rock and independent music for a long time.

Earshot Media
info@earshotmedia.com
www.earshotmedia.com
An independent publicity company specializing in alternative, indie, punk hardcore and metal music. Our hands-on, grass-roots, one-on-one approach to working a project from the ground up is what sets us apart from other PR Firms.

Hardcore Promotions
www.hardcorepromo.com
Promotes independent / underground artists of all genres and all calibers both online and to the real world. Also does full CD reviews.

Pop! Explosion Music
Mark Langgin popexplosionpublicity@hotmail.com
www.popexplosionmusic.com
Music publicity and promotional services for the discerning independent. Tour booking, promotion and publicity for punk, indie, emo and whatever else could trip your trigger.

Vicious promotions *UK*
viciouspromotions@talk21.com
www.viciouspromo.com
Uk Punk/Goth/Alternative promotion Agency. The whole concept of VICIOUS is to deal with our artists and clients with the utmost respect and logic.

Vendors and Labels

Big Beaver Music *Canada*
info@bigbeavermusic.com
www.bigbeavermusic.com
Your source for Maximum Rock 'N Roll - stoner, punk, garage, psychedelic, fuzz, sludge, groove, space, acid etc. Now featuring bands and labels from Canada, USA, Sweden, Australia and Scotland.

Blackened Distribution
blackened@visi.com
www.profaneexistence.com
We work on a strict consignment basis, where monthly inventories are made and payments sent. If you would like to submit your release for possible distribution consideration, please send us a sample copy and we will get back to you as soon as possible.

Double Crown Records
Sean Berry records@dblcrown.com
www.dblcrown.com
Bellingham, WA based surf and garage rock label, with an online catalog featuring 100's of releases.

EightNineThree Records
eightninethree@eightninethree.com
www.eightninethree.com
An independent label focused on hard-rockin' underground music like oi!, punk, street punk, hardcore, rockabilly and metal.

Eyeball Records
Hambone Hambone@eyeballrecords.com
www.eyeballrecords.com
Record label where bands like Thursday, H20 and the Casualties got their start.

Fall Records
Chris info@fallrecords.com
www.fallrecords.com
An Independent record label out of Michigan looking to create a unique roster featuring indie, rock, emo, punk and so on.

Interpunk
sales@interpunk.com
www.interpunk.com
A place where you can discover new bands in your own town, or in some unknown town across the country (or even around the world.) All of the bands in Interpunk Local have sent their music to us in hopes that you will like and buy their music.

Microcosm Publishing.com
joebiel@ureach.com
www.microcosmpublishing.com
We publish and distribute records, stickers, pins, zines and more. We also manufacture custom pins and stickers.

NICOTINE RECORDS *Italy*
alberto rosa31@libero.it
www.nicotinerecords.com
An Italian label specialized in punk, r'n'r, garage and psychobilly.

Pshaw Music
Johann pshawmusic@hotmail.com
pshawmusic.com
Record Label and Distribution based out of Minneapolis, Minnesota. Fueled by passion not profit.

Punk Unknown *United Kingdom*
phil@punkunknown.co.uk
www.punkunknown.co.uk
We have no quality control restrictions in place, which basically mean any band who fits into one of our accepted genres can sell their CDs through the site.

punklist.com
noi@punklist.com
www.punklist.com
Specializing in hardcore, punk, emo and other styles of underground music. Check back often for catalog updates, interviews, new listings and articles you can't find anywhere else.

Radical Records
yoon demo@radicalrecords.com
www.radicalrecords.com
NYC indie label seeks punk, hardcore bands and the like. Please NO mellow rock, alt. pop... etc. If you rock hard, drop us a demo. Band must tour... no tour, no deal.

RevHQ.com
webmaster@revhq.com
www.revhq.com
The best source for Independent music. Hardcore, Straight Edge, Punk, Indie, Online Mail-order, records, cassettes, CDs, shirts, stickers, posters and more!

Swinging Arms Productions
Aryn Aryn@swingingarmsproductions.com
www.swingingarmsproductions.com
We're a small independent record label located just outside of Cleveland Ohio who specialized in Punk and Indie Music and a whole world of other stuff too. Check us out!

truepunk.com
webmaster@truepunk.com
www.truepunk.com
If you are an unsigned band please send us a previous independent full-length or EP and a press kit. We will contact you, if we like what we hear and we'll be pouring our hearts into making your band heard.

unT3rm dUR(h$chn/tt *Germany*
andreas info@unterm-durchschnitt.com
www.unterm-durchschnitt.com
unterm durchschnitt (engl. under the average, substandard) is a non-profit d.i.y. indierock stoner grunge garage punk hc/punk label from Germany.

Vagrant Records
info@vagrant.com
www.vagrant.com
Indie and Punk Rock Record Label. MP3, streaming audio and video.

Walked in line Records *France*
Chris Pelle redac@wilrecords.com
www.wilrecords.com
The French underground label: offset Fanzine + CD audio compilation / Webzine with tons of reviews and info concerts / +1500 records Mailorder...and more!

Wolverine Records *Germany*
Sascha Wolff sascha@wolverine-records.de
www.wolverine-records.de
Germany's finest Independent Punk, Ska and Swing Label (and many more other noises...) since 1992. Over 100 Releases and still counting... Check our web page. Free Mp3s and lots of cool stuff to find!

Reggae

reggaeCD.com
info@reggaecd.com
www.reggaecd.com
Your comprehensive online Reggae CD, DVD, video, mp3, t-shirt and merchandise store.

Women In Music

Promotional Services

International Alliance of Women in Music
IAWM-info@grove.iup.edu
music.acu.edu/www/iawm/home.html
A resource on women composers and women in music topics. This community archive is developed and maintained by members of the IAWM and contains more than 3500 pages of archival resources.

Warrior Girl Music
info@warriorgirlmusic.com
www.warriorgirlmusic.com
Specializing in production and promotion of music, art and the screen arts through live events, the silver screen and cyberspace. We are a recording, publishing and promotions company that is about developing artists, songs and projects that capture the spirit of youth and personal self-empowerment.

Women In the Arts
wia@wiaonline.org
wiaonline.org
Our purpose is to produce and sponsor programs that promote and affirm the creative talents and technical skills of women in the visual, performing and fine arts. WIA strives to facilitate the growth, knowledge and empowerment of women in the other varied aspects of their lives.

Vendors and Labels

28 Days Records
www.28daysrecords.com
A small indie niche label dedicated to showcasing the best of the indie rock girl scene!

Celestial Voices
submit@loobie.com
www.loobie.com
Dedicated to promoting haunting, atmospheric and ethereal female vocals on the internet. We feature both well-known performers as well as many newly discovered artists who are leading innovators in this field of music and have yet to receive recognition.

Chainsaw Records
donna@chainsaw.com
www.chainsaw.com

chicks on speed records
chicka@gandalf.dungeon.de
www.chicksonspeed.com
Located in Germany, we are hoping to work with many electronic women in the near future.

Daemon Records
hello@daemonrecords.com
www.daemonrecords.com
Our purpose is to help break down the barriers within the music community, while providing an opportunity for musicians to create and control their own recordings within a free and nurturing environment.

essex D.I.Y collective
riotgrrrlessex@smartgroups.com
www.gurlpages.com/diyessex
We're always looking for new items to distribute - especially feminist and D.I.Y projects. If you have a zine/demo/video etc then please send us a sample copy with a little bit of info on yourself and the project.

Folkdiva Records
folkdiva@folkdiva.com
www.folkdiva.com
We are a grassroots record label committed to producing quality music, especially by women.

Goldenrod Music
music@goldenrod.com
www.goldenrod.com
An eclectic collection of alternative voices and sounds that can be hard to find among mainstream "noise." Women ... lesbians and gay men ... people of color ... peacemakers and world builders and poets. We think they'll surprise and delight you with their passion, rhythms, visions and fun! Enjoy!

Green Girl Records
mail@greengirlrecords.com
www.greengirlrecords.com
GGR means to serve as a powerful, responsive connection between the artist and local venues, radio and stores. We are accepting submissions of MUSIC, POETRY, ART and whatever else you're making.

Harmony Ridge Music
hrmusic@hrmusic.com
www.hrmusic.com
Dedicated to Female Singer Songwriters.

Kill Rock Stars
krs@killrockstars.com
www.killrockstars.com
Send us your demo tapes!! we don't have time to write back to everyone personally and we won't be able to send them back, but we do listen to them all. we love to hear new music. No mp3's please!

The Ladies Art Revival
ladiesartrevival@hotmail.com
ladiesartrevival.com
We are always accepting videos and other art for possible distribution or screening! So send your goodies in (but please include postage if you would like it returned!)

Ladyslipper.org
info@ladyslipper.org
www.ladyslipper.org
A non-profit organization whose primary purpose is to heighten public awareness of the achievements of women artists and musicians and to expand the scope and availability of recordings by women.

modmusic.com
General-Info@ModMusicRecords.com
www.modmusicrecords.com
ModMusic continues to have their artists featured on network television (Providence, Felicity, Dawson's Creek), feature films (Miramax's Serendipity, Winter Films' Ropewalk) and cable (HBO's The Sopranos, Sex & the City and Bravo's Tail Lights).

Mr. Lady Records
info@mrlady.com
www.mrlady.com
We started Mr. Lady for a number of reasons, partly because we felt like there weren't enough women &/or dyke run record labels and there are even fewer affordable and accessible means of distributing work by independent video artists and film makers.

No Concessions
nat@ncrds.freeserve.co.uk
www.geocities.com/ncrds
London based punk, HC, indie pop and underground pop record label. We do keep our eyes and ears open to all kind of punk/pop music, though we do particularly like female and queer bands.

On the Rag Records
webmistress@ontherag.net
www.ontherag.net
Site dedicated to females in the diy music scene and activist scene. Something for everyone.

panx *France*
infos@panx.net
www.panx.net
HardCore, Punk, CyberThrash, Grindcore, TechnoBruit, Crades Mélodies.

Paroxysm Records
info@paroxysmrecords.com
www.paroxysmrecords.com
D.I.Y. punk/grrrl record label.

Pink & Black Records
pinkandblackrecords@yahoo.com
www.pinkandblack.com

She's Gone Records
shesgoner@yahoo.com
geocities.com/shes_gone_records
Punk label and distro.

SisterRecords *Japan*
sister@kt.rim.or.jp
www.sister.co.jp/english
Japanese label specializing in female artists of many genres.

Sonic Cathedral
rick@soniccathedral.com
www.soniccathedral.com
Specializing in female vocal metal.

Thunderbaby Records *Germany*
info@thunderbaby.de
www.thunderbaby.de
The great girl-group-label for cool chicks! est.1991. We are not specialized in a type of music, but the spirit is punk rock, sixties and surf, screamin' guitars & noise, which is decisive to select the bands.

Twin Dragon Records
tdr@twindragonrecords.com
www.twindragonrecords.com
A small Indie label dedicated to the female fronted bands. Our mission is to identify and sign select groups and give them that boost their music career needs to be successful.

Wiiija *UK*
www.wiiija.com
From the Camden lurch scene through the fiery passions of Riot Grrl, to Cornershop's smash hit single Brimful Of Asha, the raison d'etre and the highs and lows of one of the UK's most eclectic labels.

Women In Music National Network
www.womeninmusic.com
Our goal is to help encourage and support the activities of women in all areas of music.

Women's Revolutions Per Minute *UK*
music@wrpm.net
www.wrpm.org.uk
We have supplied music performed, composed and produced by women since 1977. WRPM supports Independent Women Musicians and the catalogue presents many hard-to-find artists.

WOMANROCK Music Shop
brenda@womanrock.com
www.womanrock.com
As an Internet record store we not only sell your CDs, but we provide you with your own artist page, which you can update at any time. We help promote your music with sound clips and MP3 files online. Your CDs will be shipped though CD Baby and if you're already a member of CD Baby, you can register at WOMANROCK at a discounted rate.

World Music

Afrodicia
afrodicia@yahoo.com
www.afrodicia.com
African music, afrobeat, afropop and world music.

Atlas Music
Carmen L. Gomez clgomez@atlasmusic.biz
www.atlasmusic.biz
Our mission is to foster global musical culture awareness and understanding, by providing music that is both delightful and tasteful to the heart and the intellect. Our productions are distinguished for our special attention to detail, from state of the art graphic design to excellent sound quality.

Deep Down Productions
whitla@deepdownproductions.com
www.deepdownproductions.com
Our commitment is to promote and share traditional music from around the world.

IrieShopper.com
Christopher Hunt
chris@irieshopper.com
www.irieshopper.com
An online catalog for Jamaican and West Indian artists and artisans, where they can express their true artistic talents and to spur their creativity.

MaraRecords Brazilian Music Vinyl Record Store
mrec@bigfoot.com
www.mararecords.com
World's Best Brazilian Music Seller Since 1998, we carry Brazilian Lps, Groove, Bossa, Jazz, Soul, Funk and Rare Records

Onzou Records
www.onzou.com
Producing traditional West African music.

Putamayo World Music
info@putumayo.com
www.putumayo.com
Established in 1993 to introduce people to the music of other cultures.

Silverglobe Records
Silvanus silvergloberecords@yahoo.com
silvergloberecords.tripod.com
We are Roots Reggae Label from Montreal, Canada. We are commited to bring positive and uplifting Reggae Music to the public.

Six Degrees
info@sixdegreesrecords.com
www.sixdegreesrecords.com
An eclectic, independent music label that produces and markets genre-bending, accessible recordings that explore world music, ambient, folk, contemporary classical and intelligent pop music.

The World Loft
alawrence@jazzloft.com
www.jazzloft.com/bluesloft
If you have a CD that you would like sold at The World Loft, visit our site for information on how to get your music online. We do not charge you any fees.

World Music Store
info@worldmusicstore.com
www.worldmusicstore.com

Zook Beat
info@zookbeat.com
www.zookbeat.com
Pulsing to the Groove! Check out some wonderful up and coming artists and all time favorites!!

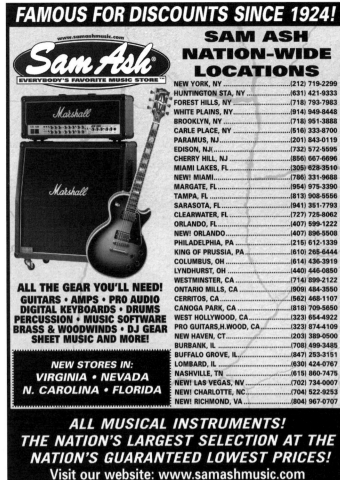

...tion Four:
...tes that Will Allow You to Upload Your Music and Video Files.

"The Internet is a powerful force, still in its infancy, that shows no sign of letting up.

If you want to get your music to where the action is, get online. This is one bus you don't want to miss."

David Nevue, author of
"How to Successfully Promote
Your Music on the Internet"

As is the case with Section Three, the sites in this section vary a great deal cost wise. Many will allow you to upload your files for free, while others charge a fee or commission.

All Styles

North America

United States

A and R Online
Chris info@aandronline.com
www.aandronline.com
The leading internet A&R source for record companies, music publishers and music supervisors worldwide

Acid Planet
www.acidplanet.com
An Artist Profile is an alter ego or image that you can create for uploading songs and writing reviews. It consists of an artist name, an optional picture and background information, all of which will be displayed on the Artist Page for that profile.

afternight
tony@afternight.com
www.afternight.com
Join up and get 2 sound clips in real audio format that will play as soon as you click on them. A picture of each band member with a bio. A gig date list which may be updated every month. A link to an existing mailbox where people could e-mail you.

agent155.com
info@agent155.com
www.agent155.com
We have crafted a site that allows you to upload your own video, pictures and text, which will instantly create your personalized page. You also become part of an ever-growing catalogue of content submitted from all over the world.

Alternative.NU
alternative.nu
Place you're Music Video for Play on our stream. Or do you want your own live show from your own location?

Amazon Digital Music Network
www.amazon.com/advantage/music
Uploading your songs is quick and simple and you can include information about your music—like song lyrics, notes and Images — to help fans learn more about you.

AMPCAST.COM
www.ampcast.com
Our mission is to provide the internet's foremost site dedicated solely to the musical artist and, in so doing, free him or her from the constraints of traditional methods of promoting music (i.e., major label record companies).

Apple's iTunes Music
indies@applemusic.com
www.applemusic.com
It's what music lovers have been waiting for: a music store with Apple's legendary ease of use, offering a hassle-free way to preview, buy and download music online quickly and easily. The iTunes Music Store has virtually every category of music to choose from.

Aquaunderground
Dave koolaid_man@msn.com
www.aquaunderground.com
We are a music promotions web site that does not charge the artist, bands, or DJs a single cent. The artists can submit material through our ftp server and can be published for free exposure on the site.

audiorocket.com
audiorocket.com
An MP3 audiozine for indie bands and artists to promote their work around the globe.

AudioSurge.com
www.AudioSurge.com
Whether or not you have joined one of the other 'artist promotion' sites, it's time that you join one of the fastest growing, cutting edge music communities in the world; a music community that looks and feels like a music site and not like a search engine

AX3.com
www.ax3.com
This site was created out from my hopes for a more exclusive community for Independent Artists.

Bandradio
suggest@bandradio.com
www.bandradio.com/botw
Each week we'll post 5 new reviews of songs in the MP3 format. This section was designed to help you with your music. You can take the advice or trash it. It is entirely up to you.

bandtattoo.com
lotus@bandtattoo.com
www.bandtattoo.com
Unsigned band and indie group database. Streaming audio, downloads.

BeSonic.com
www.besonic.com
You can only upload music, lyrics and pictures (material) to which you have the copyright or the written approval of the copyright owner.

Big Shoes and Music Online *(BSAMO)*
Darrell.Stern@bsamo.com
bsamo.com
An entertainment megaplex dedicated to promoting talented new music artist for FREE!

bowienet
support@davidbowie.com
www.davidbowie.com
Features include: A "Gallery" area showcasing members' artwork including original music, writing, photography and more.

CD Baby Digital Distribution
cdbaby@cdbaby.com
cdbaby.net/dd
We can distribute your music to all the legitimate online music services like Apple iTunes Music Store, Listen.com's Rhapsody and more. Best of all, since CD Baby has been doing sales and distribution successfully for 5 years, we've got it down to a streamlined system and can do it for only a 9% cut!

Clear Channel New Music Network
newmusicnetwork@clearchannel.com
www.clearchannelnewmusicnetwork.com
Share your music with your fans and music industry professionals who want to find new, promising acts.

CleverStreet MUSIC
contact@cleverstreet.com
music.cleverstreet.com
A website where musicians/artists can submit their music for others to hear, rate and review. If the musician gets good ratings and good reviews they will be broadcasted online 24/7 and will be sold online and in stores. This website is FREE and any musician with any type of music can join.

Club Knowledge
walt@clubknowledge.com
www.clubknowledge.com/bands
Benefits include an Artist of the Day promotion, where ALL the ClubKnowledge patrons PROMOTE the artist for 24 hours!

contactmusic.com
hello@contactmusic.com
www.contactmusic.com
100% dedicated to music. What does this mean? Well put simply, if you get a deal through our site, you'll get 100% of the royalties.

cornerband.com
webmaster@cornerband.com
www.cornerband.com
We provide an unprecedented online musical forum for both independent and record-labeled musicians. Anyone who creates a free MyCornerband Account can experience this innovative musical bazaar.

DemoDaze
webmaster@demodaze.com
www.demodaze.com
Visitors can explore and enjoy high quality New Music online, in live music venues and on the radio. DemoDaze Artists can promote themselves to Music Lovers globally in a professional and effective manner utilizing the many company resources.

Digital Club Network *(DCN)*
DCNInfo@digitalclubnetwork.com
dcn.com
Every week DCN webcasts and archives more than 50 concert performances (audio and video) from our network clubs, capturing the cutting edge of today's music scene.

Digitalphile.com

Lisa Fairbanks drezdon1@yahoo.com
www.digitalphile.com
"Don't Give Your Music Away!" You don't have to with Digitalphile.com and its innovative MP3 downloading system that empowers the indie artist to reach fans throughout the world and earn money on their downloads.

DigitalSoundboard.net

dave@opcenter.net
www.DigitalSoundboard.net
Reality: we know music fans across the country and around the world are hungry for your live recordings from both the band archives and upcoming shows. Solution: DigitalSoundboard.net can deliver *paid-for* MP3s and FLAC digital music file downloads of soundboard recordings by your band.

DMusic

www.dmusic.com
We encourage and invite artists to submit their music for airplay consideration. If you would like your music to be played on our DJs broadcasts, with the possibility of being featured on the DMusic website, please contact us.

DOWNLOADSdirect

editor@artistdirect.com
listen.artistdirect.com
The music download hub which showcases downloads from high-profile artists as well as independent bands.

DuckOnBike.com

www.duckonbike.com
Devoted to providing a home for independent music in various formats on the Internet. DuckOnBike also produces a semi-regular Internet radio show featuring live performances from Independent bands.

EMusic.com

submissions@emusic.com
www.emusic.com
We have digital distribution contracts with over 650 independent labels. Because we focus on labels, we are very busy. We do NOT offer deals with unsigned artists. If you represent a record label and are inquiring about making your catalog available on EMusic, please send an email.

epitonic.com

www.epitonic.com
Our goal is to exalt the unexalted. Utilizing the liberated mp3 format, Epitonic.com aspires to live up to our neologistic moniker, the center from which waves of disruptive purity emit.

eveo.com

info@eveo.com
www.eveo.com
My filmmaker lovelies, we will continue to accept your videos, but will only post the most delicious of the bunch. But don't be discouraged, we will hem and haw and spend sleepless nights trying to decide.

garageband.com

advertising@garageband.com
www.garageband.com
Gathering, nurturing and promoting new music using the technical assets and cost effectiveness of the Internet. We are rewriting the rules about how the music industry operates and was built from the ground up as an Internet-savvy record label.

getoutthere

biged@getoutthere.com
www.getoutthere.bt.com
We have loads of great stuff to browse and play with. You can download some of the best work from tomorrow's new young talent, or you can get creative and play with some of the easy-to-use-tools we've put online.

GetPlayed.com

Aaron Thomas
admin@getplayed.com
www.GetPlayed.com
Dedicated to providing amateur musicians with a listening audience. Visitors submit their songs into the category of their choice where they receive ratings and comments from visitors, as well as an individual Play Counter. Winners receive long-term spots on the site and the grand prize winners win a GetPlayed.com homepage for their band.

GigAmerica

info@gigamerica.net
www.gigamerica.net
Submit your music for our College Tours, Venue Showcases, Music Television Program etc. If selected, your band will gain exposure that money cannot buy. Featured Artists routinely have their songs downloaded 2,000 times in a week.

GimmeFiles

info@gimmefiles.com
www.gimmefiles.com

gracenote

musicbrowser@gracenote.com
www.gracenote.com
With over 1,000 licensees in 35 countries, 20 million unique users a month and more than 800,000 albums and 10 million songs in our database, Gracenote is the most comprehensive and widely accessible platform for delivering music related content and services in the world.

hatch 11

email@hatch11music.com
www.hatch11music.com
The site contains original music of all genres. Bands submit songs to the site and we take the ten most original and put them on. The site is updated each month with new material. The song or songs which get the most hits each month stay on the site for an extra month. The best part is that it's FREE!

iamusic.com

add-your-music@iamusic.com
www.iamusic.com/add_your_music.php
For Instrumental music only! If you are a production music library, publisher or composer of music and would like to have your music considered for inclusion on the iamusic.com, then visit our website and read the submission rules.

Imaginotion Songs

mail@imaginotionsongs.com
www.imaginotionsongs.com
A business dedicated to providing original songs to recording artists and bands in Australia and overseas.

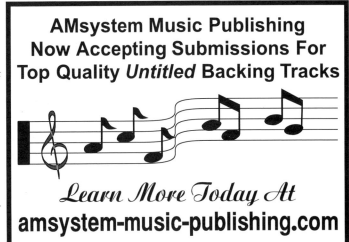
Indie Haven

webmaster@mandell.net
indiehaven.shapebyforce.com
For the artist, we offer a powerful search engine to allow potential fans to find your music. We also feature resources and news on internet music distribution and promotion.

Indie Journal

indiejournal@hotmail.com
www.indiejournal.com/indiejournal
Reviews, interviews, Internet radio, mp3 site guide, poetry, art and more.

Indulged

alex@indulged.com
www.indulged.com
We advocate open minds toward music and support all genres that are noteworthy. Our goal is to spread the word about the latest musical artists, whether they are unsigned or signed. It's the music that counts; not a fancy label or music video.

iPLUGiN

info@iplugin.com
www.iplugin.com
A unique and fun opportunity for artists to get their work in front of a larger audience. If you are an artist, we can help you promote and sell your work to buyers who get to know you through the Artist's Advantage program.

Insound

help@insound.com
www.insound.com
We think of Insound as being the premier site for fans of underground music and film and as representing the best of the indie spirit. We take an active role in bringing the best underground culture to the surface.

IUMA

www.iuma.com
For every artist with a record deal there are a thousand talented artists chasing that dream and a million new music fans who will never get to hear their music. We're changing all that - bringing these artists and fans together, getting the music out and giving new music fans a cool new way to discover new music.

The Jukebox
support@thejukebox.tv
www.thejukebox.tv
We host and promote independent artists and bands from around the world. Songs are not actually stored on the Jukebox server, instead, the Jukebox acts like a grand central switching station, storing links to songs, artists and stations as well as other music related information.

Launch.com
www.launch.com
We are always looking to add new music! For proper consideration, please include a cover letter with contact info and indicate where on the site you would like to appear along with your commercially available (NOT a demo or unreleased) CD.

Liquid Audio
musicservices @liquidaudio.com
www.liquidaudio.com
We offer an extensive catalog and flexible commerce solutions that enable hundreds of music sites in the Liquid Music Network to sell music online.

Listen.com *RHAPSODY*
www.listen.com
The celestial jukebox that gives you unlimited access to thousands of albums right from your PC. Only RHAPSODY brings together the largest legal collection of digital music in the world, the Internet's best radio, flexible CD burning and detailed music information - all in one easy-to-use service.

The Logoed CD
David Cubitt david@mmsdirect.com
www.thelogoedcd.com
We pay royalties for music used by our corporate clients for customized music CDs. we offer our clients ALL styles of music for various marketing and promotional campaigns. We would like to add your music to our catalogue It's FREE...and if used by our clients, you get credit and...WE PAY YOU ROYALTIES!

MEDIASTORM Independent Multimedia
Mark Mushkin Mark@MediaStormTV.com
www.MediaStormTV.com
We promote new artists by offering samples of their CD and music video with the option to buy the CD. We also will be offering single mp3's for 80¢ soon. Media Storm also publishes new artists music videos on a compilation DVD offered FREE on the website.

The Mod Archive
mods@modarchive.com
www.modarchive.com
Songs on this site are provided for free download by the artists.

ModernRock.com
Support@mail.ModernRock.com
www.modernrock.com
Worldwide distribution and promotion for recording artists.

MP3 charts.com
contact@mp3charts.com
www.mp3charts.com
Bands no longer have to rely on the individual and unrelated rankings produced by the sites that host their mp3s. Because our charts reflect the downloads from all sites that promote their music, we can offer bands the highest possible visibility.

MP3 College Radio Network
iwantmymp3_2002@yahoo.com
www.mp3collegeradionetwork.com
Your Source For The Best MP3 Music.

MP3 ME @ Rhythm Radio
newmusic@rhythmradio.com
www.rhythmradio.com
An "IMP" is an Interstitial Music Piece - Rhythm Radio creates hundreds of original music pieces of any length, any genre, all with one thing in common, to carry the message: "too much fun is never enough."

MP3.com
www.mp3.com
With more than 10 million visitors to our site each month, MP3.com is the best place to reach your audience and build your fan base. Get your FREE MP3.com home page and customize your favorite music links, song picks, hometown concert alerts and more!

MP4.COM
www.mp4.com
For those that like to watch. Upload your music videos!

mpulse
support@mPulse.com
www.mpulse.com
At mPulse we have two priorities. One is showcasing independent artists. The other is providing music fans with an honest, unbiased chart of the most popular music websites, artists and songs on the Internet. Our new features include video downloads from a band's Artist page.

MSSVision
info@mssvision.com
www.mssvision.com
How many sites will Webacast your Indie video? Very few! How many will make your music video or slide interactive like ours? Nobody else (at this time)!

Music Gorilla
info@MusicGorilla.com
www.musicgorilla.com
Bands, Artists, Songwriters. Receive guaranteed exposure to major labels, indie labels, film studios and publishers. Your songs appear on dedicated pages that we've built for the pros while they view your picture, profile and gigs.

MusicRebellion.com
drfisher@musicrebellion.com
www.musicrebellion.com
Interested listing your media with MusicRebellion.com? Well check out our Artist Section for more details.

MusicBroadcast.com
www.musicbroadcast.com
A world of sound, a universe in sight.

MusicianMP3.com
musicianmp3@musicianmp3.com
www.musicianmp3.com
A FREE musicians resource and band promotion website. Artists can create their own free Musicians Profile web page complete MP3 uploads, links, interviews and more. Sell your merchandise with an artist profile account.

Musician's Network
MN@MusiciansNetwork.com
www.MusiciansNetwork.com
The place musicians and music industry 'call up' when they want to access information or contacts about other people or events in the world of music.

MUSICMATCH
support@musicmatch.com
www.musicmatch.com
Our Jukebox software lets you find, record, manage and play your favorite music. You can also discover new music with the MUSICMATCH Guide and personalized MUSICMATCH Radio. Send your music submissions for possible review, interview or download offering to us.

Music Recruiters International
info@musicrecruiters.com
www.musicrecruiters.com
With contacts in the music and recording industry, we know how to take you through the steps of refining your sound, getting your band a label contract and producing a CD with finished artwork. There is a nominal charge for our service of a $50 one time sign up and $25 for each song.

Netmusician.org
support@netmusician.org
www.netmusician.org
We offer services which include creating and hosting your own website, help with selling your musical products online and the streaming of your music (and video) across the internet.

NEW Music Network
newmusicnetwork@clearchannel.com
www.clearchannelnewmusicnetwork.com
It's a free service for performers to share their music with fans and music industry professionals who want to find new and promising acts.

New Music Reporter
dave@newmusicreporter.com
www.newmusicreporter.com
We provide a space where emerging artists can connect with fans, music industry professionals and other talented, driven and passionate musicians. NMR wants to change what it means to be an emerging musical artist.

PlanetMG
admin@planetmg.com
www.planetmg.com
Enter a progressive environment and get ready for an ultimate experience in downloadable music, streaming of movies, music videos and Internet Radio

PLAYER'S SERVER
help@players-server.com
www.players-server.com
From now on artists can own their own copyrights of their music and sell music sung in their own language. It really doesn't matter if you're pro or an amateur, all you need to do is to attract the fans with your music.

PYBand.com
info@pyband.com
www.pyband.com
A service provided to musicians, to help promote their music and get the word out. Bands can upload a limited selection of their songs and provide information to potential and existing fans regarding their status.

Radiotakeover
Tom Fear tom@radiotakeover.com
www.radiotakeover.com
Promotional services including audio streaming, distro, advertisement, screen printing. We also construct web radios.

The Rain Dog Records
digital@oasisCD.com
RaindogRecords.com
We have been hand-picked by Apple to help supply independent ("Indie") music to the Apple iTunes Music Store. Your music will be encoded and submitted for consideration to the iTunes Music Store AND to Listen.com, emusic and other digital distributors.

Resort Records
Dave2@resortrecords.com
www.resortrecords.com
Pioneering Internet music delivery, the company operates a virtual organization and state-of-the-art technology to achieve zero-inventory, point-to-point music retail.

RisingMusic.com
joseph4829@yahoo.com
www.risingmusic.com
Individual band and artist websites have noticed a 10 fold increase in traffic after getting listed on Rising Music.

RockTheMic.com
www.rockthemic.com
Our mission is to create a community for independent rock artists to learn, share, market, promote and interact amongst themselves and with the rock community at large.

Search MP3
www.searchmpthree.com
If you have a song and you want thousands of international listeners to hear it, register at Search MP3 and create your own personal homepage containing your songs.

SlipstreamPresents.com
Matthew Sabatella matthew@slipstreampresents.com
www.slipstreampresents.com
An Internet-based music company that features CDs, MP3s, videos and more by a select group of independent recording artists.

The Song Site
simon@thesongsite.com
www.thesongsite.com
Whether you are an artist, a music manager, a record label or a music publisher, there's bound to be something here of interest to you. So sit back, relax and have a listen to some of the songs in our catalogue...

Songwriter Street
www.songwriterstreet.com
We provide special priority services to help you get noticed and help you get more exposure for MP3 downloads and CD sales. We also offer free artist web pages. If you are a musician, create a free artist page to point to your official web site, MP3 download page or CD sale page...

Songwriting.Org
kent@newsome.org
www.songwriting.org
Post lyrics and audio links for critique and discussion.

SonicFish.com
support@sonicfish.com
www.sonicfish.com
By musicians, for musicians. News, reviews, spotlight bands, downloads etc.

Soundbuzz.com
music@soundbuzz.com
www.soundbuzz.com
An innovative integrated music media business with a focus on the Asian markets.

soundhub.com
hello@soundhub.com
soundhub.com
A web site offering news, reviews, software and hardware information, comprehensive MP3 searching and generally aims to cover all your digital music needs.

SRSWOWcast Technologies
sales@srstechnologies.com
www.srstechnologies.com
We develop and license audio and voice enhancement technology solutions for Internet streaming, Internet radio, encoded material on demand, live events, as well as for traditional television and cable broadcasting.

The Synthesis
Bill@synthesis.net
www.thesynthesis.com
Our goal is to provide a forum for entertainment, music, community awareness, opinions, change and political involvement.

takeoutmusic.com
mori@takeoutmusic.com
www.takeoutmusic.com
We focus on all the music of our culture.

takeoutpop.com
mori@takeoutpop.com
www.takeoutpop.com
Teens will learn about marketing & promotions and qualify for rewards programs including scholarships, trips...

TVU Music Television
NIKKI@TVULIVE.COM
www.tvulive.com
The music video channel that actually plays music videos! Watch TVU here on the Internet, on the SkyAngel satellite system and even on YOUR cable system!

TwoBigToes
help@twobigtoes.com
www.twobigtoes.com
We enable music fans to download and burn music CDs in one easy step. By downloading the music directly to a CD-R, the software leaves no compressed music file on the hard drive of the fan's computer and therefore offers a secure way of legally delivering music to fans onto CDRs.

The Ultimate Band List
editor@artistdirect.com
ubl.artistdirect.com
The leading online music company that connects music fans directly with their favorite artists worldwide via our online network, "The ARTISTdirect Network."

UnionBay.com
www.unionbay.com
So, you want to be a rock star? Find inspiration right here!

unsignedartistsdemos.com
info@unsignedartistsdemos.com
www.unsignedartistsdemos.com
Welcome Musicians to the music website that promotes your songs directly to major record labels, independent record labels, recording studios and production houses.

unsignedunlimited.com
paul@unsignedunlimited.com
www.unsignedunlimited.com
A database for unsigned bands/artists of all genres. Each band/artist has up to 2 tracks for FREE listening.

ZeBox
No_spam@zebox.com
www.zebox.com
Our goal is to create a great efficient music engine that is self-driven by the artists themselves, where everything is instantaneous, all artists pages are automatically created and all updates instantly implemented. Sample and download songs. Discover new artists!

Canada

Sunnymead
info@sunnymead.org
www.sunnymead.org
A virtual village of independent artists, professionals, businesses and organizations, reflecting today's individuality.

Europe

France

MadeinMusic.com
helpmusicians@MadeinMusic.com
www.madeinmusic.com
We give you access to the largest independent online music catalog available in Europe: over 12,000 tracks, 1,200 artists and 200 music genres.

peoplesound.fr
service@peoplesound.fr
www.peoplesound.fr
La première cybervitrine musicale pour les artistes montants et pour les nouveaux talents. Les amateurs de musique peuvent ainsi avoir accès à des milliers de titres de grande qualité qui représentent tous les genres musicaux.

Germany

besonic.com
www.besonic.com
Our vision is music anytime, anywhere, tailored to the individual likes of users.

Music Center
musicstuff@gmx.de
www.musichit.de
Present your own band here! The visitors of this site can listen, judge and vote your demo.

Keep current with Indie Updates
www.indiebible.com/ud

...tuff
...@t-online.de
www.....usicstuff.de
Present your own band here! The visitors of this site can listen, judge and vote your Demo. Use this chance to get more attention!

Songs Wanted
ellie@songswanted.com
www.songswanted.com

web62.com
www.web62.com
Internet Television.

Spain

WebListen.com
david@weblisten.com
www.weblisten.com

Sweden

MP3Lizard.com
mp3lizard.com
Promote your band for free!

United Kingdom

Cube-music
Mick Hilton Mick@cube-music.com
www.cube-music.com
Video & audio programmes for retail entertainment. I can promote your video or audio tracks to UK audiences in excess of 10M each month, via our in store music programmes.

getoutthere
musiceditor@getoutthere.com
www.getoutthere.com
Our overall philosophy is about helping unsigned talent get a foothold in their chosen industry. Since launching music over a year ago, we now have over 5000 tracks uploaded and hundreds of films.

IntoMusic
support@intomusic.co.uk
www.intomusic.co.uk
One of the UK's Fastest growing Legal Downloadable Music Websites featuring independent musicians, all files are checked to ensure they are virus free and of good sound quality.

Mod Monster
andy@andysav.free-online.co.uk
www.andysav.free-online.co.uk/mod.htm
If you've got some mod files you'd like to see on this site you can email me the urls for up to 5 songs and I'll paste the links to them on this page.

MP3Songs
chrisz@addr.com
www.mp3songs.org.uk
Are you a musician? Song writer? In an unsigned band? Or do you just love music? Then MP3Songs is the site for you!

Music Choice
info@icrunch.com
www.crunch.co.uk
Dedicated to bringing you cutting edge tunes, great back catalogues, impossibly hard to find rarities, exclusive DJ mixes and specially selected live performances from clubs and venues across the globe.

OSRecords
support@osrecords.com
www.osrecords.com
Our continuing mission: to provide you with new music from great independent artists, without the usual record industry hype. If you're looking for celeb gossip or crass planet-sized ego trips, go someplace else. It's the music that matters here.

peoplesound.com
www.peoplesound.com
A revolutionary new way to get your music heard - on the Internet. Visited by over a million people each month we're the UK and Europe's No1 new music download site.

poptones.co.uk
www.poptones.co.uk

VirtualMusicStores
enquiries@vmusicstores.com
www.vmusicstores.com
A revolutionary way to sell music.

Vitaminic
info@vitaminic.com
www.vitaminic.com
The leading European platform for the promotion and distribution of digital music over the Internet and other digital networks. You'll get your own homepage and gain exposure throughout Europe and the US, building new fan bases at the same time. Best of all, it's free!!

Australia/New Zealand

Australia

Asylum TV
Susan Hedley asylumtv@hotmail.com
www.asylumtv.com
Music television program focusing on independent artists, broadcast in Melbourne, Australia on community television Channel 31. All genres. Overseas submissions welcome. For video clip submission details see www.risingstar.com.au/tv.htm

ChaosMusic
info@chaosmusic.com
www.chaosmusic.com
Indie artists WANTED!!! Sell your CDs/sound files, no up-front costs.

MP3Machine.com
mp3admin@hitsquad.com
www.mp3machine.com

Africa

Egypt

Mazika.com
help@mazika.com
www.mazika.com
Arabic music MP3s, video clips, MIDIs and more. Includes pages about Egyptian singers.

If you know of a resource that should be listed, please contact
indiebible@rogers.com

Asia

Cyprus

Orientaltunes.com
info@orientaltunes.com
www.orientaltunes.com
We shall try to cover an area as wide as possible, from Morocco to Iran and further east if we can, to Pakistan and India. We shall not emphasize traditional music alone, but will follow what is new, the modern trends in oriental music, how it is influencing the world music and how it is influenced by it.

Japan

listen.co.jp
www.listen.co.jp

MCJP
info@musiccopyright.jp
www.MusicCopyright.jp
A new gateway to Japanese music market. MCJP works for "Digital Delivery", "Internet Radio" and "Music Licensing". MCJP will digitally purchase your music compositions from the music market here in Japan as many as possible and it will help both the foreign artists who want to sell their music in Japan.

Specialty Sites

Christian

Acaza.Com
jmacleod@acaza.com
www.acaza.com
There's a ton of music out there and we want every bit of it listed here. So drop us an email and tell us who we need to add and watch with us as our database of artists grows... and grows... and grows...

CCAuthority
Karla@ccauthority.com
www.ccauthority.com

ccmp3s
webmaster@ccmp3s.com
www.ccmp3s.com
The premier Christian mp3 website featuring tons of legal Christian mp3 files!

Christianmp3.com
www.christianmp3.com
This site has served over 675,000 mp3s. Thanks to everybody who have shared music or downloaded some!

GospelHouseMusic.com
Thomas@gospelhousemusic.com
www.gospelhousemusic.com
The one and only, dedicated Gospel House and Garage music website online.

The Gospel Zone
crj_lawn@msn.com
www.thegospelzone.com
Have Your Videos Played on our site. Contact us for details.

Jamsline.com
jamsline@jamsline.com
www.jamsline.com
We make it possible for you to get your singles to radio and other industry entities at a cost that you can afford. We can offer your music the security, speed and reliability needed to cruise in the fast lane in today's competitive market.

MP3HolySpirit.com
mp3holyspirit@aol.com
www.mp3holyspirit.com
Here you will find an inspirational selection of FREE spiritual and Christian music greetings and ecards, covering a wide spectrum of events, occasions and themes.

SongScope.com
writerinfo@songscope.com
www.songscope.com
To build your online song catalog, start by sending a CD of your material to us. Also, got to our site and post your lyrics, describe your material, create your login and password.

Classical

ChoralNet
www.choralnet.org
We operate three primary mailing lists — Choralist, ChoralAcademe and ChoralTalk — and a newsgroup, rec.music.makers.choral, for choral musicians to exchange ideas, make professional connections and learn about choral music. ChoralNet's Repertoire database includes almost 50,000 titles, including both old masters and present-day composers.

The Classical Music Archives
www.classicalarchives.com
Do not submit MP3 files made from MIDI sequences. (MIDI files should be submitted as .mid files.) Submit only MP3 files of live performances or recordings to which you have the appropriate rights.

Classical.com
Heather Buettner heather@classical.com
www.classical.com
A classical music subscription offering online listening, downloads, custom CDs and a resource of entertaining information.

Early Music Network & News *UK*
info@earlymusic.org.uk
www.earlymusic.org.uk
We welcome new early music groups & performers and they are welcome to be included in our paper and on-line directory and can pay £15 to have a sample MP3 placed on our download site.

eClassical.com
info@eclassical.com
www.eclassical.com
A completely virtual record label and a secure online store open 7 days a week, 365 days a year. Customers and visitors can download great classical music in MP3 format and also find out more about classical music and its history.

LudwigVanWeb
info@classicall.net
www.ludwigvanweb.com
We provide the means to download, via the Internet, the wealth of musical resources contained in the catalogs of the Independents, any time, day or night. The site provides instant effective access, removing distribution barriers and enabling users to choose what they want when they want it.

NetNewMusic
netnewmusic.net
A portal for the world of non-pop/extreme indy/avant-whatever music. We feature the best composer/performer sites that offer complete musical works. No teasers, no excerpts. Complete musical compositions ready to be heard right now.

newmusicnow.org
www.newmusicnow.org
We give you a detailed look at several exciting works for orchestra by American composers, all written within the last thirty years. You can hear the music and explore its background. You'll also meet the composers and learn how you can hear their works on CD.

Society of Composers *Composerver*
wells.7@osu.edu
composerver.sss.arts.ohio-state.edu
A streaming audio/video archive by the Society of Composers. Members may submit excerpts, complete pieces, or any presentation they like, within the fifteen-minute maximum limit. Video submissions will be made via in QuickTime Movie Format.

Country Music

Banjo Newsletter MP3 Soundfiles
bnl@infionline.net
www.banjonews.com
Downloadable MP3 Sound Files of tabs that have appeared in Banjo Newsletter.

Bluegrass Connection
pmilano@gotech.com
www.gotech.com
Listen to a sound bite before you purchase a CD or Cassette.

Cowpie Corral
cowpie@olga.net
www.roughstock.com/cowpie
Uploading is free and a great way to get your music in front of other guitar pickers.

Inside Nashville Jukebox
wanttobeonjukebox@countrymusicplanet.com
www.countrymusicplanet.com/jukebox.htm
You will hear some of the greatest country music on Planet Earth, just click on the play buttons beside the songs of your choice to listen to complete songs being streamed to you in real audio.

Dance Music

ClubFreestyle.com
info@ClubFreestyle.com
www.clubfreestyle.com
Meet Fans, Producers, Artists on the Worlds Largest Freestyle Music community. Be the First to find out about upcoming events - shows & promo's. Download Free MP3's You get the newest tracks first! Plus More.

dancetech.com
www.dancetech.com
Feel free to add music if that is the sort of user you sign-up as.

Definition of Sound
John Frankel john@definitionofsound.com
www.definitionofsound.com
We provide space for DJ's that want to sell their music, or play it.

DJ Kuffdam's Site
trance@kuffdam.co.uk
www.Kuffdam.co.uk
This site will direct you to the most upfront Trance from the UK, Holland, Germany and Belgium.

headstrong dance music
DON headstronghq@aol.com
www.headstrong-hq.com
This is a new and fantastic site getting better daily. Also put your demo's on the website to get heard by record companies and D.J's. This site is for lovers of dance music, rave techno, club, dj, anthem, trance, house.ambient, groove. Site includes clubbers mix tunes forum, news, samples tracks etc.

InternetDJ.com
webmaster@internetdj.com
www.internetdj.com
Hosts and plays MP3s and Real Audio from Independent musicians, bands and DJs from around the world. Including instant web page creation, free email, streaming net-casts, classifieds and live chat!

Pitch Adjust
www.pitchadjust.com
Pitch Adjust is also a site where labels can find new talents, new talents can find a label and promoters can post information about their clubs. Buy music or search the base for interesting events in your city.

Technomusic.com Artist Nation
www.technomusic.com
Discover the new sounds of the techno scene!

Experimental Music

bio-d.net
mindnebula@alascom.co.uk
www.bio-d.net
Dedicated to the promotion / distribution of original music. Our aim is to enable all contributors to reach a wider audience with their work and get 'networking' with other like - minded musicians / performers with a view to collaborating on future events / promotions.

Computer Music Magazine
kevin.redding@futurenet.co.uk
www.computermusic.co.uk
Every issue, we put the best reader music we receive on our cover mounted CD ROM and now the website in both audio and (sometimes) MIDI file format. Its the ideal way for you to get some added publicity for your efforts and pass on handy computer music composition tips to our many other readers.

no type
david.t@steam.ca
www.notype.com

tapegerm
feedback@tapegerm.com
www.tapegerm.com
A new and vibrant center for music creativity. Tapegerm is an international recording artist collective of 25 prolific artists, collaborating over the Internet.

Wigged.net
submit@wigged.net
www.wigged.net
A digital magazine focused on bringing innovative short videos, animations, music and interactive works over the internet. Its mission is to be a showcase and promotion center for media artists via the World Wide Web.

Folk

Celtic MP3s Music Magazine
Marc Gunn marc@thebards.net
www.celticmp3s.com
A free weekly Celtic Music magazine featuring free mp3 downloads from Ireland, Scotland, Wales, Nova Scotia and beyond. Subscribe to win free Celtic CDs. Accept submissions. Visit the site for details.

Independent Musicians Marketplace
imm@secondfret.com
www.secondfret.com
A selection of REAL music by REAL people.

Hip Hop

Bag Lunch Tapes
Maya Maravilla baglunchtapes@hotmail.com
www.baglunchtapes.com
Street level hip-hop mixtapes. So far 3600 units distributed of most recent issue, more distributed with each issue. Each CD features 20-30 hip-hop and electro songs submitted on vinyl format. This is for hip-hop and electro only and we only include what we like in order to keep fan base happy.

freshsites.com
dolores@freshsites.com
freshsites.com
Promoting independent, underground hip hop culture. Send your content (video, flics, mp3s) via email to dolores@freshsites.com account and we'll post them as soon as we can.

Hip Hop Cheeba Style *Norway*
rleknes@broadpark.no
www.cheebadesign.com/hiphop.htm
The Phat beats of Hip Hop and Electronica.

Hip Hop Havoc
webmaster@hiphophavoc.com
www.hiphophavoc.com
ASCAP licenses hiphophavoc.com the right to perform musical works by ASCAP composer, lyricist and music publisher members and members of foreign performing rights organizations.

Hip Hop Palace.com
Rob Wright promoradiony@yahoo.com
www.hiphoppalace.com
Artists can upload their music and also be placed on our radio show.

Rapstation.com
artistsrule@rapstation.com
www.rapstation.com
Chuck D's website project. This is a great place to post up your music for the world to hear! You will also find videos and short movies and Hip Hop columnists from all around the world.

Rapworld
oze@home.se
www.rapworld.com
Get a free E-Mail or a Free Redirection URL @ The Biggest Rap, HipHop, R&B Music Archive On The Net. This site has everything a good site needs... audio, pictures, videos and a banner exchange.

Real-HipHop.com
admin@real-hiphop.com
www.real-hiphop.com
Real MC's, Real DJ's, Real Fans, Real Music, Real Videos, Real-HipHop.com!

Urban Earth
editor@urbanearth.com
www.urbanearth.com
So you think you got skills? Let the World Wide Hip-Hop World decide. Send your bangin ass tracks to us and we'll put it up for heads to listen to or download. If your shit is really dope (and I mean REALLY dope), you just might get featured in our Time Bombs section.

Ya Heard
yaheard.bet.com
This is the home of the most talented unreleased artists. Unsigned artists upload your original songs and create your own personal artist page and tell all your friends and label reps to check you out on Ya Heard?

Jazz/Folk/Blues

Any Swing Goes
doug@anyswinggoes.com
www.anyswinggoes.com
We currently focus on the revival of big band and swing music and dancing and maintain this web site to be a resource for those interested in the same.

Cjazz
michele@Cjazz.com
www.cjazz.com
Not only is this a place to explore the music but also an opportunity for anyone involved in this exciting genre of music to show the world who they are and what they do.

efolk Music
support@efolkmusic.com
www.efolkmusic.com
Your independent mp3 and CD source. The "Ben & Jerry's of Bluegrass"- where the cream rises to the top.

The Jazz Vocal Coalition
www.vocalvisions.net/jzvoc.htm
An organization dedicated to helping Jazz Singers by educating, promoting and uniting them...and giving the solo jazz artist recognition in the educational, recording and performing fields.

JazzSteps.com
suggestions@jazzsteps.com
www.jazzsteps.com
Want your music to be featured on our Digital Downloads page? Read about our Digital Download Program. This section will be continually evolving.

Metal

EarAche.com
digby@earache.com
www.earache.com
Metal MP3s and videos.

The Gauntlet
moshpit@thegauntlet.com
www.thegauntlet.com
Huge archive of metal indie musicians, bi-weekly mailing list, reviews, videos and more.

metalvideo.com
metalvideo@hotmail.com
www.metalvideo.com

MetalVideos, Inc
volkan@immortalvideos.com
www.metalvideos.tv
We are the fastest growing metallic website and is the home of the darkest and the hardest videos in this universe!

RockCandyOnline.com
RockCandyz@aol.com
www.RockCandyOnline.com
If you have an unsigned band that plays the style music that we feature, visit our RockCandy's Unsigned Bands Page for information on how to get your video aired on the show.

Punk

BlankTV.com
smitty@blanktv.com
www.blanktv.com
Your home for punk, oi, ska, hardcore, rockabilly and indie music videos. If you're in a band and you have a video, we'll put it up, as long as it's not total crap.

Enough MP3s
david@punkrawk.de
www.enoughfanzine.com
Feel free to upload your band's/label's mp3 files Make sure the MP3 file holds all information (ID3) such as Songname, Artist, Album, Year and Genre.

Epitaph
www.epitaph.com
Trying to get people to check your band but don't know how? Well here's the answer you've been looking for, post a link to it on the Epitaph website! Keep it punk! If you don't know what that is, then don't bother posting!

Guerrilla Warfare
m.conforti@gte.net
www.gwvf.net
If you have any good video footage of dancing, stage diving, your band, your friend's band, fighting, funny shit, something meaningful or creative etc. - send it in!

mp3s4punx.com
webmaster@mp3s4punx.com
www.mp3s4punx.com
Free punk mp3s and email. Also, free mp3 hosting for bands who either cannot afford to host their own mp3s or their host does not support media file hosting.

Poppunk.com
steve@poppunk.com
www.poppunk.com
I felt that a lot of pop/punk music wasn't being properly exposed on the internet. I figured it was time that someone who had a clue about pop/punk and its origin create a web site.

punkrockvideos.com
georgehewitt@punkrockvideos.com
www.punkrockvideos.com
This is a web site that has live video of punk bands. All the shows found here are for sale or trade. E-mail us about your band or send me a copy of the show on VHS or Mini DV.

Supersphere
jason@supersphere.com
www.supersphere.com
Integrating live web-casting technologies, both video and audio, Supersphere is a global experiment in bringing independently produced media to our contemporaries and peers.

Women In Music

Dyke TV
staff@dyketv.org
www.dyketv.org
The only lesbian cable access show that airs nationwide. We are now seeking video submissions for special broadcast during our "Get Your Stuff Out There!" screenings on our cable access show. We accept fiction, documentary and experimental short videos by, about and of interest to lesbians.

GoGirlsMusic.com
madalyn@gogirlsmusic.com
www.gogirlsmusic.com
The oldest online community of independent women artists, was started in 1996 to promote women in music. It's run by women musicians, for women musicians.

GuitarGirls.com
Lynn Carey Saylor Lynn@guitargirls.com
www.guitargirls.com
A resource & support site for female artists who write, sing and play guitar. The site features MIDI, MP3 & Real Audio files plus a GuitarGirls contest which showcases & promotes independent female talent.

Les Filles du Metal
metalgirls@fr.st
www.metalgirls.com
This website is here for you to discover the "Female Atmospheric Metal".

Music4Women.com
Melissa Adams
melissa@music4women.com
www.music4women.com
Women making music for women. Free music and information about M4W artists. Membership fee to join as a member artist.

World Music

Surforeggae
contato@surforeggae.com.br
www.surforeggae.com.br

www.indielinkexchange.com

Section Five:
Helpful Resources for Musicians and Songwriters!

"Every big leap that happened in my career always happened because of 'someone I knew.'

Make a point of meeting three people each week that you think could help your career.

In a shallow way, each person you meet is a lottery ticket."

Derek Sivers,
CD Baby

Resources for ALL Styles of Music

2x4Productions.net
Charlie Dubovici vaz879@aol.com
www.2x4productions.net
We are here to help bands who help themselves. We supply resources, information and marketing tools designed to help bands reach larger audiences.

48 media
J.Morrison Info@48media.com
www.48media.com
We produce mid to high end music videos for Television broadcast and Webcast.

Acidfanatic.com
Peter Prins acidfanatic@acidfanatic.com
www.acidfanatic.com
I produce sound & loops libraries and provide a music community website for over 8,000 people.

All Media Guide *(AMG)*
feedback@allmusic.com
www.allmusic.com
Massive database of CDs. Add yours!

Allied Artists
ghammond@alliedartists.net
www.alliedartists.net
A public service arena for the performing artist. We never charge for our services. Our information is always free to performing artist worldwide.

The American Federation of Musicians of the United States and Canada *(AFM)*
www.afm.org
With over 250 local unions throughout the United States and Canada, we are the largest union in the world representing the interests of the professional musician.

American Federation of Television & Radio Artists *(AFTRA)*
aftra@aftra.com
www.aftra.com
Represents actors and other professional performers and broadcasters in television, radio, sound recordings, non-broadcast/industrial programming and new technologies such as interactive programming and CD ROMs. Union rules generally require members to work only for employers who are signed to AFTRA contracts.

The American Society of Composers, Authors and Publishers *(ASCAP)*
info@ascap.com
www.ascap.com
A performing rights society that represents its members by licensing and distributing royalties for the non-dramatic public performances of their copyrighted works. These royalties are paid to members based on surveys of performances of the works in our repertory that they wrote or published.

AMOnline.net
Carl Logan clogan@amonline.net
www.amonline.net
AMOnline.net helps its members to quickly create a low cost professional web presence that includes real audio without any technical knowledge.

AMsystem Music Publishing
Michael Borges am.system@verizon.net
www.amsystem-music-publishing.com
Our primary purpose is to connect with the creators and producers of professionally produced and sounding backing tracks. On our site you will learn about this facet of the music business and how you can get involved to turn your compositional creativity and production skills into an opportunity for financial success!

The Artist Couch Exchange
Audra Coldiron audra@couchexchange.org
couchexchange.org
A network of independent artists and supporters who offer free lodging to other independent touring artists.

Artist Forum
webmaster@artistforum.com
www.ArtistForum.com
A place to post information. Registration may be required if you plan to post new topics or reply to existing topics (depending on the particular forum you are using). Registration is free and you are not required to post your real name.

ArtistManager.com
www.artistmanager.co.uk
Matching music industry artists with managers worldwide.

Artists Against Racism
aar@idirect.com
www.artistsagainstracism.org
Our mission is to build an understanding of all peoples. To speak to the youth, the future of our global community, about the basic human right of equality, so that a civilized society will, in the next millennium, finally result.

Artists In Residence
info@aarcharity.org
artists-in-residence.com
A Web hosting service that offers free personal, business and organizational Web sites exclusively to those in the Performing Arts, Visual Arts and the Humanities. As part of the free service, each resident receives up to 5 MB of Web space, e-mail forwarding and a number of other features.

artists on the net
webmaster@artistsonthenet.com
www.artistsonthenet.com
This site has been designed with technology that allows employers and casting agents to search quickly and free of charge for the talent or service they require - from a DJ to an orchestra, a production company to a lighting engineer.

Asian Music Source
info@asianmusicsource.com
www.asianmusicsource.com
Committed to being your ultimate source of information for the entire Asian American entertainment industry. We strive to bring you the latest and greatest information on talented artists who are stirring it up and breaking through the music scene.

The Band Register
www.bandreg.com
An essential website with an invaluable A-Z look-up database featuring over 330,000 bands and artists complete with contact info and music links.

BandHub
sales@bandhub.com
www.bandhub.com
Web Hosting package designed specifically for bands. Each BandHub Website has its own Web Application Software, Database, Administrative Tools and Web Hosting Resources.

Bandlink CD Intelligence
Cedric Gore cgore@bandlink.com
www.bandlink.com
The first Internet-powered music CD service. It provides the most direct, vibrant, updateable, community-driven experience available to fans and artists.

bandlink.net
webmaster@bandlink.net
www.bandlink.net
A UNIQUE resource in that each artist has their own page, clearly and comprehensively listing all known information in distinctive categories so that it is easy to find what you are looking for.

bandportals
info@bandportals.com
www.bandportals.com
With our easy to use web-based project management system you can create real-time itineraries, share important documents, track radio/sales progress and never miss a beat. It's a complete solution with calendars, contact databases, a messaging system, bulletin boards and much more!

Bandradio
www.bandradio.com/botw
Gain valuable exposure as BandRadio's "Band of the Week".

bands 411
Dana beatgrrrl@bands411.com
www.bands411.com
We offer you the tools to promote your band on the Internet. Build contacts, manage a Web site and distribute your music, all from one place. Streaming MP3 files, email sign up and your gig dates are available to a GLOBAL audience.

       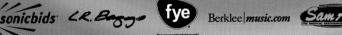 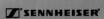
        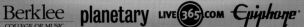

BandsBackStage
lyricbackstage@yahoo.com
bandsbackstage.com
One of the few sites that promote artists from the heart. As an artist/visitor to BandsBackStage you are welcome to use the many resources we provide to promote your music.

bandsforlabels.com
Curtis maelstrompr@earthlink.net
www.bandsforlabels.com
A free band-label matchmaking site. The site features band and label profiles, band and label reviews, a music glossary and a difference between terms sections that explains the differences between certain topics that people mess up on all the time.

Bandwear.com
makeit.bandwear.com
A full-service merchandising company specializing in creating unique branding products and advertising specialty items. We specialize in screen-printing, embroidery, vinyl stickers, custom paper printing like posters, point-of-purchase displays, glossy photos and thousands of advertising specialties. If you can put a logo on it, we can get it!

Bandwidth Discussion Group
www.onelist.com/subscribe.cgi/bandwidth
Discussion of web design as it relates to bands, labels and other music related sites. Everything from adding audio and video; format types, linking strategies, site promotion, search engine placement.

The BardsCrier.com
bardscrier.com
Guerrilla music marketing ezine promotes subscribers on MP3.com with free BardsCrier.com radio play and weekly featured artists.

The Beat Goes On
sales@thebeatgoesontoday.com
www.thebeatgoesontoday.com
We post booking and promotion companies, bands and DJs. Check it out! Free exposure!

Berkleemusic.com
feedback@berkleemusic.com
www.berkleemusic.com
Provides songwriters opportunities to take online music writing courses and explore new music career directions. Users can create a personal or band web page containing bios, MP3s, images, reviews, news and links that are useful resources to potential employers, collaborators and students.

bestmusiczines.com
bigmeteor@rogers.com
www.bestmusiczines.com
A free site that showcases the best music zines, magazines, artists and Independent music resources on the Internet. EVERY style of music is covered. Submit your site today!

The Black Rock Coalition (BRC)
info@blackrockcoalition.org
www.blackrockcoalition.org
We represent a united front of musically and politically progressive Black artists and supporters. The BRC seeks to foster cooperation among musicians and like organizations through networking and sharing resources.

Broadcast Music, Inc (BMI)
www.bmi.com
Non-profit-making company, founded in 1940, collects license fees on behalf of those American creators it represents, as well as thousands of creators from around the world who chose BMI for representation in the United States.

BuscaMusica.es.fm Spain
info@buscamusica.org
www.buscamusica.es.fm
Site that allows Independent artists to post information about themselves for free.

The Buzz Factor
Bob Baker info@thebuzzfactor.com
www.thebuzzfactor.com
Inspiration and low-cost marketing ideas for songwriters, musicians and bands on a budget.

CCNow
service@ccnow.com
www.ccnow.com
A low-risk way for small and medium sized businesses to sell their product online.

CDBaby.net
cdbaby@cdbaby.com
www.cdbaby.net
Great tips on promoting your music, touring the college market, selling more CDs, getting a UPC Barcode etc...

cdmusicpage.com
www.cdmusicpage.com
Promoting Independent music with text, images and audio. Your Artist Profile allows you to add an artist page to the site. This page provides concise information about the artist. You can add a bio, links to the artist's main site and audio files and contact information.

CDstands.com
info@CDstands.com
CDstands.com
We manufacture our own line of CD Boxes for artists to sell their music at shows or in stores. We are also the creators of that cool Trophy CD Stand. A clever alternative to framing a CD and hanging it on your wall. It's a product that lets you display your CD, along with your CD cover, like a trophy. It let's you show off your CD by displaying it on your bookcase, dresser, mantle, or desktop. It also makes for a great sales display when using it with our CD Boxes.

Circle of Songs
showcase@circleofsongs.com
www.circleofsongs.com
The "411 for songwriters and bands." Learn to build a lifetime career in music.

Coast To Coast Musicians Resource
Amy pressed_fairy@yahoo.com
www.geocities.com/pressed_fairy
Website design, web promotion, logo design and JUST IN: Independent artists review.

Copyright & Fair Use
fairuse.stanford.edu
Stanford U. information on copyright law.

Copyright Law in the United States
www.bitlaw.com/copyright
A discussion on the copyright laws.

Copyright Your Song
www.loc.gov/copyright/forms/formpai.pdf
The PDF form to file with the U.S. Copyright Office.

Copyright Your Sound Recording
www.loc.gov/copyright/forms/formsri.pdf
The PDF form to file with the U.S. Copyright Office.

Crazewire
www.crazewire.com
The affinity of passion and sound — a community where musicians, journalists, fans and wannabe-rock stars spontaneously connect, however random or constructive it may be. We are slowly empowering gifted or latent writers with the inspiration to think more articulately about music and share results with others.

Creative Musicians Coalition *(CMC)*

Ron Wallace aimcmc@aol.com

www.aimcmc.com

A fellowship of artists and labels that share and network to the betterment of its whole membership population. Since 1984.

Dayscar Connect

cf@dayscar.com

www.dayscar.com

Sooner or later, you are ready for the big time. Ready to get serious about a career creating your music. When you reach that point, it's time to call us. Dayscar Connect sends messages to your fanlist via mobile phones, pagers, or other devices using SMS or Voice.

Degyshop Monthly Shopper

info@degyshop.com

www.degyshop.com

Each month, we post tons of new companies that are looking for music and get the artists to send kits right to your door. Visit our site and sign up!

DigiCircSM

support@digicirc.com

www.digicirc.com

We allow intellectual property or "Music Rights" of recordings created by artists to be placed on the market for direct investment. Through DigiCirc, artists have several options to raise capital.

Digital Independence

digitalindependence@hotmail.com

www.digitalindependence.org

Dedicated to the promotion of independent entertainment and media such as independent record labels, independent films, radio stations and more! If you have music, movie, or publishing news that you would like to see posted on our site, then please email me with your submission!

Dirtbag Music

Todd Newman todd@dirtbagclothing.com

www.dirtbagmusic.com

The one stop marketing/merchandising site for up and coming bands!

Eat This Music!

Ian Davy iandavy@breathemail.net

www.eatthismusic.com

An interactive music management environment for unsigned bands to not only advertise their stuff but also to have venues, management companies, promoters etc. to be part of our infrastructure, allowing everyone to use the site to organize their music business. We also review Demos, EPs and gigs and soon will be reviewing companies as well.

EntertainmentDiary

info@entertainmentdiary.com

www.entertainmentdiary.com

We allow you to publicize yourself (session/dep musician) or your band and gigs on-line. Once registered you can print flyers, posters and business cards that automatically include your photo, contact details and gigs.

FanList.com

ali@fanlist.com

www.fanlist.com

The ultimate in generating exposure for artists/bands and venues. By querying our extensive databases of music lovers of all different music genres, we are able to promote your show to a targeted audience, in any city, at any time.

Festival Network Online *FNO*

info@festivalnet.com

www.festivalnet.com

There's nothing like a live performance! FNO lists more than 6,000 events throughout the U.S. (& some in Canada) seeking performers from national & international to local. Event dates, locations & basic info (including music genre & # of performance stages) are available free to all visitors.

FestivalFinder

help@festivalfinder.com

www.festivalfinder.com

Discover the latest details on more than 2,500 music festivals in North America. Click to your favorite genre, or use the search feature to locate festivals by date, location, performers or festival name.

Festivals.com

alliances@rslinteractive.com

www.festivals.com

Welcome to the online gathering place of the worldwide festival community! We invite you to delve into our festival search. Submit your festival photos, share your festival experiences, nominate an event to be featured and join our online communities.

Forever Unholy Productions

Jon Dunmore dunmore_ego@foreverunholy.com

www.foreverunholy.com

The Business Of Rock And Roll. For all your rock and roll business: CD & Video Production, Create Press kits and merchandise, Online listings for Bands and Musicians, Photography, Tutors, Graphic Arts, Live entertainment for Special Events, Web Design. Get Listed - or Get Serviced!

Freemusic.org

webmaster@freemusic.org

www.freemusic.org

This is a great place to promote your music for free! Expand your fan base now. All genres are welcome.

Freelance Musicians' Association

info@freelancemusicians.org

www.freelancemusicians.org

Comprised of instrumentalists, vocalists, musical support staff and supporters of live music. It is dedicated to furthering the respective interests of its members and to providing specific services required by musicians who perform primarily in small concert venues, night clubs, community halls and at a wide variety of public and/or private events.

Future of Music Coalition

mbracy@bracytuckerbrown.com

www.futureofmusic.org

We built this organization as an attempt both to address pressing music / technology issues and to serve as a voice for musicians and citizens in Washington, DC, where critical decisions are being made regarding intellectual property rights without a word from either citizens or creators — the only two groups mentioned in the copyright code.

Getmemusic.com

www.getmemusic.com

Getmemusic.com doubles up as a music site and CD cyberstore, where artists can either sell their existing CDs or, if they haven't got a CD, Getmemusic.com can design, manufacture and release a CD for them.

getsigned.com

www.getsigned.com

EVERYTHING you ever wanted to know about: starting a band, getting signed, getting radio airplay, playing live, booking a tour, starting a record label, building a fan base, becoming a record producer, growing an indie music career, getting FREE press and much much more! Free daily music 'biz articles and career advice from music industry legends.

GIGPAGE.com

gigs@gogirlsmusic.com

www.gogirlsgigs.com

Everyone wants to save time and money and GIGPAGE.com can help! We are musicians who understand the frustrations of keeping a gigs page up-to-date on your web site. GIGPAGE.com was developed to help bands and venues maintain their gigs quickly and easily online.

GigMasters

info@gigmasters.com

www.gigmasters.com

A complete entertainment booking agency, offering customers the ability to hire live bands and singers. Customers save time and money because they can contact an unlimited number of entertainers with just one click of the mouse, then watch as the entertainers compete with bids in order to get hired for the job.

Gigplayer.com

John sales@gigplayer.com

www.gigplayer.com

Free monthly gig tips for ALL musicians.

Global Zero International

Rob Zero pibetousan@hotmail.com

gzi.8m.com

Helping unsigned/underground bands with promotion and gig network.

Gracenote

Ross rblanchard@gracenote.com

www.gracenote.com

Providing information about music to millions of music fans around the world every day. Make sure that information about your music is in their acclaimed CDDB service: download their free application at www.gracenote.com/metacredit.

Grapevinez.com

Charles R. Mack grapevinez2@yahoo.com

www.grapevinez.com

A place for industry-shaping A&E executives and talented up-and-coming artist to meet. Our goal is to facilitate access into the entire spectrum represented by the field of music. Grapevinez.com will provide the resources you need to launch, revitalize or advance your career.

GreatMusicSites.com

music@blackdogpromotions.com

www.greatmusicsites.com

Find Great New Music at GreatMusicSites.com! Attention Artists: Promote your music FREE at GreatMusicSites.com

Ground Zero Music Network

Matt Mesnard elwood@extremezone.com
www.GroundZeroMusic.net
All styles accepted from anywhere in the world. ALWAYS free and award-winning. Also free club/chat/message boards/classifieds.

The Guild of International Songwriters and Composers

Carole Jones (General Secretary) songmag@aol.com
www.songwriters-guild.co.uk
International songwriters organisation representing songwriters, composers, lyricists, artistes, musicians, performers and publishers. Music industry consultants. Publisher of Songwriters and Composing Magazine.

HearItAgain.net

Mike Corso mike@hearitagain.net
www.hearitagain.net
We record artists who perform, on average, 60 times per year before audiences of at least 500 per show. We aim to provide artists and labels with an incremental revenue stream while, at the same time, giving fans exactly what they want.

HitQuarters

JP Sperwer jp@hitquarters.com
www.hitquarters.com
Huge, detailed database of record companies, A&Rs, music publishers, managers, producers + their contact info & track-records, free of charge. Plus music business cards, daily Q&A, music classifieds, music charts, recommended links etc.

Hitsquad.com

admin@hitsquad.com
www.hitsquad.com
Music resource and industry information.

Hostbaby

hostbaby@hostbaby.com
www.hostbaby.com
The best place to host your website/domain! Fast and reliable web hosting where you get treated like royalty. AND it has much-needed musician tools for you.

Hot Bands.com

webmaster@hotbands.com
www.hotbands.com
We're looking for some quality original bands of all genres. We offer free cross-linking, promotion, reviews, news, artists web pages and communities and much more.

hotmail

www.hotmail.com
The world's first web-based e-mail provider, which means you can send and receive messages from any computer connected to the Internet. You can use Hotmail from home, work, school, an Internet café, a friend's house or any other computer in the world with an Internet connection.

The Indie Band Manager

charlie@charliecheney.com
www.indiebandmanager.com
THE database software for independent musicians on Macintosh or PC. People compare it to ACT, QuickBooks & Outlook.... It includes a Booking Calendar, Contact Manager, To Do List, Personalized Mass Email Tool, Invoice module and Expense Tracker.

Indie-Connections.com

info@indie-connections.com
www.indie-connections.com
We look for good production and songs. We also check that the music is "up-to-date" and marketable within its genre. If your material is accepted, we give you a free web page with a photo/logo, bio, point of contact, a demo clip and a link for up to three related sites.

The Indie Contact Newsletter

indiecontactnewsletter@rogers.com
www.bigmeteor.com/newsletter/index.shtml
Each month you will receive new listings to contact, as well as several well written articles from industry experts that will help you to reach your musical goals. The newsletter is free! Simply send an e-mail to the address above with the word "newsletter" in the subject: field.

The Indie Link Exchange

indielinkexchange@rogers.com
www.indielinkexchange.com/ile
A site that lists hundreds of people who wish to exchange links with other music related sites. It's a simple one to one exchange of links. Only common courtesy is asked of you. All you have to do is contact whoever you feel like exchanging links with.

Indie Music Beat

indieonestop@gajoob.com
www.indiemusicbeat.com
A FREE indie music newsletter, published every month in PDF format by gajoob.com.

IndieDisco

Lise LePage
lepage@indiedisco.com
www.indiedisco.com
An independent music community, with users contributing reviews, articles, news, downloads and more.

IndieGroup

staff@indiegroup.com
www.indiegroup.com
We welcome you to utilize our growing list of services from Free Web Sites and E-Mail to the Advanced Marketing Tools and the ONE-UP/Short Run CD Programs!

IndieMail

mike@bandradio.com
www.indiemail.com
Bands can use this service when they are on the road to communicate with friends, family and fans. 6MB of FREE email storage.

IndieWave
Rob cs@indiewave.net
www.indiewave.net
We offer FREE web hosting for indie musicians. Each account includes form mail, mailing lists and other interactive tools. Registration is free, so there's nothing to lose.

InsideSessions
info@insidesessions.com
www.insidesessions.com
An innovative, multi-media distance-learning and mentoring program. InsideSessions offers students the fun and flexibility of interacting with leaders of the music and publishing industries on multiple media platforms including the Internet, CD-ROM, DVD and Home Video.

InterMixxGroups
InterMixxGroups@InterMixx.com
www.InterMixxGroups.com
Free Email Groups for Indies, with NO spam, NO ads...

InterMixx InterNetwork
MixxMag@InterMixx.com
www.InterMixx.com
The nation's only true internetwork for independent musicians.

International Association of African American Music
iaaam1@aol.com
www.iaaam.com
For over 12 years, IAAAM has led the cause in promoting, perpetuating and preserving America's indigenous music.

International Musician's Trading Post
admin@younameit.com.au
www.musicians-classifieds.com/usa
With 40 different Categories, you will also find other musicians looking to a join band & other bands looking for musicians. There are listings of various music industry services and resources here also (this site links to other International classified pages).

International Songwriters Association
jliddane@songwriter.iol.ie
www.songwriter.co.uk
Extensive information service for songwriters, lyric writers and music publishers.

jambase.com
webmaster@jambase.com
www.jambase.com
A provider of tour dates, links, articles and contact information for over 3,000 improvisational bands nationwide. These are rock, jazz, funk, fusion, bluegrass and jam bands that - well, that Jam!

Jägermusic.com
jagerinfo@sidneyfrankco
www.jagermusic.com
How does Jägermeister sponsor a band? Well, once we decide we dig their scene, we supply them with giveaway items where legal. Items are branded with the Jägermeister logo and the name of the band. From posters to guitar picks, t-shirts to hats, we cover our bands.

JMI Publications
comments@jmipub.com
www.jmipub.com
Free music business articles.

Just Plain Folks
jpnotes@aol.com
www.jpfolks.com
We are a free internet based music organization that networks, promotes and educates musicians, songwriters and industry folks at all career levels. We are glad to have you with us and our Motto is....We're all in this together!

The Kings of A&R
Maribeth Guinee maribethguinee@aol.com
www.kingsofar.com
An industry site that exposes unsigned acts to the music industry.

LIFEbeat
info@lifebeat.org
www.lifebeat.org
A national non-profit organization dedicated to reaching America's youth with the message of HIV/AIDS prevention. LIFEbeat mobilizes the talents and resources of the music industry to raise awareness and to provide support for the AIDS community.

Li'l Hank's Guide For Songwriters
halc@halsguide.com
www.halsguide.com
If you are a creator of lyrics or a composer of music then you'll find this an excellent place. You will find all kinds of advice and tips on lyric writing, song publishing, copyright information, performing, music law, recording, live music, venues, books and inspiration for what you do.

LiveWire Contacts
jaime@LiveWireContacts.com
www.LiveWireContacts.com
A contact manager specifically designed for musicians. Use it to keep track of communication with booking agents, gigs and your fan base. Use it to send emails, faxes and print mailing labels. Also search the Musician Community for industry contacts.

LocalSound.com
www.localsound.com
Sign up and advertise your songs, check our promoters, find a club to play at, find other bands and etc! Once you sign up you can customize your profile to maximize your exposure!

Loopwise.com
Taylor tre@loopwise.com
www.loopwise.com
If you are seeking help on a current music project of yours you may post that project here at the Loopwise site for free. Once you post your guitar lines, vocal beds, hip hop beats etc. along with your MP3 you will get bids in your email from the community of virtual studio musicians here at the Loopwise Site wishing to work with you.

The Mad Hand Arts Graphics and Design
info@themadhand.com
www.themadhand.com
We give a 25% discount to Independent artists on CD cover graphics & all music graphics needs (banners, logos etc.). Digital design & fine arts savants, a killer design, sound technical execution and painless business experience are our standard package.

M.A.T.E. *Music Around The Earth*
Fatz Lee FatzLee@cs.com
www.musicaroundtheearth.com
Our mission is to create a community network among musicians and music lovers all over the globe. Every single person in this world should have the chance to experience music and the qualities of life it teaches. Find out how you can help. Spread the word..."I Support Music Around The Earth."

Market Wire
www.marketwire.com
We post news released by small to large businesses worldwide. This Web site attracts journalists and management executives looking for news in rapidly evolving business categories. Our site provides journalists and executives an insider's look at the latest news before it becomes news.

Marketing Your Music
www.marketingyourmusic.com
An array of tips on how to call attention to your music. Sponsored by CDBABY.com.

Maverick Films
Sebastian Cluer rep@maverickfilms.com
www.maverickfilms.com
A music video production company for the Canadian Indie artist.

The MODE
brew@theMode.com
www.themode.com
Find band mates and network with other musicians, even buy and sell equipment. Anybody can place a listing as long as it's related to musicians and/or the music industry. Off topic spam will be deleted, or not listed in the first place.

mojam
webmaster@mojam.com
www.mojam.com
Promote your upcoming events, add info to your artist page, or submit the info you know about upcoming concert dates, artists or venues.

Music Biz Solutions
success@mbsolutions.com
www.mbsolutions.com
Helping musicians, songwriters and industry careerists start and grow successful music businesses through vital information and creative management strategies.

Music for People
mfp@musicforpeople.org
www.musicforpeople.org
An organization dedicated to re-vitalizing music making for individuals and groups and to promoting music as a means of self-expression. Our "Connections" newsletter offers a small selection of articles and poems and reviews of MfP member CDs.

Music Industry News Network *(mi2n)*
editor@mi2n.com
www.mi2n.com/submit_top.html
A service that allows you to submit press releases for free. It will post your full release on its site and send a brief description of it to thousands of industry folks through one of its many newsletters. It's a fast and easy way to get exposure.

The Music Tap
rick@themusictap.com
www.themusictap.com
Dedicated to helping musicians spread the word about their music.

Music Law Offices

Michael McCready McCready@music-law.com
www.music-law.com
Free articles on copyright and music publishing.

The Music Office

gregforest@musicoffice.com
musicoffice.com
Remember, every musician that got screwed, got screwed in writing! Legal library, IRS forms, Library of Congress forms.

The Music Pages

www.themusicpages.com
If your band needs a gig or if your club needs a band please visit our Gig Board. If you need a new band member or want to play in one please use our free Musician Referral Service.

Music Thoughts

www.musicthoughts.com
Read inspiring quotes by famous composers or any musician on the street. Add your own favorite quotes to the site full of great ideas here, free for the taking.

Music Thoughts Discussion Group

musicthoughts-subscribe@egroups.com
Valuable discussion group that has several hundred members. All areas of music are discussed from promotion to tips on playing live. You can subscribe by sending a blank email to the e-mail address above. If you subscribe, I recommend that you switch to "DIGEST" version immediately so that you're not swamped with emails.

The Music Biz Academy

musicbiz@rainmusic.com
www.musicbizacademy.com
At the Music Biz Academy, we have one primary focus: teaching musicians how to use the internet to their financial advantage. Whether using the internet to sell CDs, 'get the word out,' or simply to make some extra cash, we help musicians help themselves.

MusiCares

Dee Dee deedee@grammy.com
www.grammy.com/musicares
Our mission is to ensure that music people have a place to turn in times of financial, medical or personal crisis. MusiCares' primary goal is to focus the attention and resources of the music industry on human services issues that directly impact the health and welfare of music people.

MusicBootCamp.com

www.musicbootcamp.com
A valuable resource site that lists articles and information on Bar Codes, Trademark, Copyright, Soundscan etc.

MusicCareers.net

guitarnoise_feedback@hotmail.com
www.MusicCareers.net
Start or build a career in the music industry with knowledge and confidence thanks to our well informed community. Learn the keys to working on the road or in the studio; learn about writing songs, getting them published and much more.

MusicClassifieds.us

webmaster@musicclassifieds.us
www.musicclassifieds.us
Features instant posting of ads, the ability to post an image with your ad, over 80 music categories, an advanced search engine and the ability to change and renew your ad instantly.

musicgalley.com

Mary Ann Wilson
info@musicgalley.com
www.musicgalley.com
We offer independent musicians a minimum of 15 mb of streaming media space and the opportunity to sell their CDs.

MusicianHunter.com

billingdept@musicianhunter.com
www.musicianhunter.com
Whether you're looking for to join a band your need a musician for a band, MusicianHunter.com will make the connection.

Musician's Contact

info@musicianscontact.com
www.musicianscontact.com
We've been supplying musicians and singers to thousands of employers and band leaders everywhere since 1969. Located in Los Angeles, we remain under the same ownership with a full time staff.

Musician's Cyber Cooler

Dave Jackson
cybercooler@hotmail.com
www.jammindave.com
Our mission is to create a music community where musicians of all genre's can come together and exchange ideas on music, marketing, in an effort to mentor each other so we can avoid each other's mistakes. To provide tools and resources for musicians to promote their band, their music, their web site.

The Musician's Guild

Vince Smith vince@themusiciansguild.com
www.themusiciansguild.com
We are a free website that offers free services to musicians and bands to further their musical career. Get your own free web page with an mp3, photo and bio, as well as other perks.

Musicians and Injuries

eeshop.unl.edu/music.html
Instrumental musicians are a special risk group for repetitive motion injuries. Sizable percentages of them develop physical problems related to playing their instruments; and if they are also computer users, their risks are compounded and complicated. This page addresses that issue.

Musician's Network

MN@MusiciansNetwork.com
www.musiciansnetwork.com
Networking is the key to success for musicians and people in the music industry. We are here to help you make it happen (yearly fee).

Musicians On Call

info@musiciansoncall.org
www.musiciansoncall.org
Using music to complement the healing process for patients in healthcare facilities through our programs: Music Performance, Music Instruction, CD Pharmacies, Ticket Donations and Project Playback. In bringing both live and recorded music to patients' bedsides we provide a much needed outlet for the many feelings that a hospitalization engenders.

The Musician's Toolkit CD ROM

toolkit@indie-music.com
www.indie-music.com/cgi/affiliates/click.cgi?icn
Need to book gigs and advance your career? The Musician's Toolkit is packed with essential tools to save you time and money and give you a competitive advantage in the music business. The ToolKit comes with nearly 50 articles, printable copyright forms, templates for common music items like flyers, music fonts, musician papers, software and much more!

MusiciansRegistry.com

julia@musiciansregistry.com
www.MusiciansRegistry.com
We are currently selecting musicians who upload music to feature, so as soon as you register someone will be reviewing your listing as a potential feature.

Musicianzoo.com

musicianzoo@yahoo.com
www.musicianzoo.com
This site is dedicated to helping promote local bands, as well as major label artists, providing information and links to industry related businesses.

MusicJournalist.com

cj@musicjournalist.com
www.musicjournalist.com
The largest community of music writers and photographers on the planet. We personally search every media news site daily for music publishing news to bring you the only such collection of links on the web. We sift through hundreds of articles every day.

MusicPromotion.net
webdesign@tacotruffles.com
www.MusicPromotion.net
Our mission is to empower Artists with the tools and knowledge necessary to create an effective online presence that will enhance their offline success. Contact us now to find out how we can create an online presence that will work for you.

MusicRemedy.com
info@musicremedy.com
www.musicremedy.com
This is what we would like to call an interactive music resource. Visitors can react to every news item, review etc... giving their own opinion about the subject.

musicSUBMIT.com
Trevor Lyman webmaster@musicSUBMIT.com
www.musicSUBMIT.com
Promote your music! A website and press release submission service for musicians that can save you a lot of time.

Must Have Music
info@musthavemusic.com
musthavemusic.com
We are affiliated with BMI, CCLI & NARAS and other Professional Songwriter Organizations that come together in order to protect all sorts of Intellectual Property. We celebrate great songs and songwriting. We sponsor a free online Newsletter E-zine, the Must Have Music News, where we publish (and welcome) articles written by Industry Professionals.

MyMusicJob.com
hrexpress@mymusicjob.com
www.mymusicjob.com
If it's music and a job, it's here. Created to provide assistance to those who make their living in the day to day, not always glamorous but usually fulfilling, music industry. All employers are welcome to post their music related jobs here for free.

National Endowment for the Arts
webmgr@arts.endow.gov
www.arts.endow.gov
We serve the public good by nurturing the expression of human creativity, supporting the cultivation of community spirit and fostering the recognition and appreciation of the excellence and diversity of our nation's artistic accomplishments.

New Music Reporter
newmusicreporter@msn.com
www.newmusicreporter.com
NMR was founded to provide artists results. We are proactive, connected and determined to see you succeed. We create and nurture the artist- industry relationship

North American Band Name Registry
information@bandname.com
www.bandname.com
Free band name registration helps your band establish whether the name is uniquely yours and assist in consolidating its awareness. Once registered your band will be able to post press releases at Bandpress.com and advertise or find musicians in Bandclassifieds.com. You will also have access to our Databases to locate more than 7,000 venues and important contacts in the music industry.

One Stop Indie Shop
John Whiteman john@arete100.com
www.onestopindieshop.com
We provide all the resources an indie artist needs to be their own record label.

Parade of Stars
info@paradeofstars.com
www.paradeofstars.com
Our newsletter carries music news and views that you can not get in other trade publications. Parade of Stars is not a fan publication. We want to offer information that professionals can use. We carry listings of the major acts that are looking for material. We have opinions, but the opinions come from years of experience. One thing sure, Parade is never dull.

Performing Artists Network *(PAN)*
Perry Leopold pan@pan.com
www.pan.com
A free tracking system is now available for independent music sites. It automatically collects and compiles song download data from sites like yours on a daily basis and ranks the artists on a chart showing the most popular (i.e. most downloaded) artists and songs.

POLLSTAR
tour_dates@pollstar.com
www.pollstar.com
We track mostly national touring acts and can not guarantee the entry of any dates, but you, your manager or agent are always welcome to submit your itineraries to our Route Book department.

PowerGig
www.powergig.com
The power tool for finding, booking and promoting gigs. Be found when talent buyers are looking!

PR Web
prweb@dataovation.com
www.prweb.com/submit.htm
We have helped over 4,000 companies distribute their press releases. You might be surprised to know that many fortune 500 companies are even using the site. We distribute as many as 150 press releases a day.

Press Release Writing Tips
info@press-release-writing.com
www.press-release-writing.com
Contains free tips on writing good press releases. There are also some enhanced services for a fee.

promosquad
info@promosquad.com
home.promosquad.com
The world's first Internet music promotion company where the fans do the talking - and get free stuff for it!

Pubs & Bands
mron@pubsandbands.com
www.pubsandbands.co.uk
The best place to advertise your band, pub, or studio. Browse our classified ads and Advertise your shows and songs.

PutMeOnTheWeb
Melissa Esquibel melissa@putmeontheweb.com
www.putmeontheweb.com
Low cost, high-quality, fast turnaround websites for artists and musicians. Web development, hosting and maintenance.

PXSmusic.com
customerservice@pxsmusic.com
www.pxsmusic.com
We strive to be the very best band merchandise store on earth. It is our goal to bring bands and their fans together. We want every band to have a chance to get their merchandise to their fans and we want fans to have full access to the merchandise they want in a convenient and exciting online store.

QuickBanner
quickbanner.com
Using QuickBanner, you do not have to be a graphic artist to develop a successful, professional-looking advertising banner. This free tool is designed for all webmasters and web-advertisers.

RAMPANT!
sales@rampanthosting.com
www.rampanthosting.com
Our mission is to provide affordable, straightforward quality web hosting and customer support. Initially created for musicians, RAMPANT websites allow the easy upload of music and video files as well as text and images on any PC at anytime. The system is ideal for musicians, bands, clubs and any business that needs to frequently update its website.

Rate Our Band
feedback@digitalwhammy.com
www.rateourband.com
A quick way to get the general public's opinion of "your band's music and looks", on a scale of 1 to 10. Does your band have what it takes? Your fans have the power to decide!

Really Big City Festivals
Mike mike@reallybigcity.com
www.reallybigcity.com
We are a festival that reaches college students across America. We highlight indie bands with a Christian worldview at our festivals. We can provide excellent exposure for upcoming bands!

record labels on the web
contact@rlabels.com
www.rlabels.com
Here you'll find 5000+ links to record label web pages with more being added continually. This list does not include distribution-only labels or online stores.

Recording Artists Coalition
info@recordingartistscoalition.com
www.recordingartistscoalition.com
Formed to represent the interests of recording artists with regard to legislative issues in which corporate and artists' interests conflict and to address other public policy debates that come before the music industry.

The Recording Industry Association of America *(RIAA)*
www.riaa.com
The trade group that represents the U.S. recording industry. Our mission is to foster a business and legal climate that supports and promotes our members' creative and financial vitality. Our members are the record companies that comprise the most vibrant national music industry in the world. RIAA® members create, manufacture and/or distribute approximately 90% of all legitimate sound recordings produced and sold in the United States.

Rock Band Merchandise
niki@rockbandmerch.com
www.rockbandmerch.com
Bands, we would love to carry your merchandise. We even have an in-house design and production team to handle all your needs. Our goal is to make it convenient and secure for the fans to buy your goods on-line. We take care of all the hassle for you so you can concentrate on creating rock pleasure for the masses.

Rock-n-Roll Web Design and Hosting
audra@rock-n-roll-design.com
www.rock-n-roll-design.com
*Looking for a hot alternative avenue in which to
promote your music? Let Rock-n-Roll Web Design
and Hosting give you the tools you need!*

Rockbites Alternative Daily
press@rockbites.org
www.rockbites.com
*Providing daily underground music news as a thinly
veiled ploy to raise money for human rights charities.
Send in your press releases!*

RTS Promotions
Hazel O'Keefe info@rtspromotions.co.uk
www.rtspromotions.co.uk
*Not for profit promotions and event management
raises money for local charities and helps local
unsigned bands.*

Sane Society
www.sanesociety.org
*An international organization that offers an
unprecedented power of communication to artists,
musicians and writers. In Sane Society it is the
authors themselves who publish their own work, other
members who evaluate it and us who promote it.*

SelfPromotion.com
selfpromotion.com
*Here you will find all the information and automatic
submission tools you need to do the job quickly,
efficiently and most of all, properly! If you invest a
little time into reading and using this resource, you'll
not only do a much better job of promoting your site,
but save yourself a lot of time and effort in the
process. And best of all, it's FREE.*

Seriously Groovin.Org
Jason Rowley jrowley@groovin.org
www.groovin.org
*Allows independent artists the place to post
information about their band as well as gig dates and
more.*

SESAC
www.sesac.com
*SESAC is not an acronym for anything these days.
For history's sake, we can tell you the name originally
stood for Society of European Stage Authors &
Composers. With an international reach and a vast
repertory that spans virtually every genre of music,
SESAC is the fastest growing and most
technologically adept of the nation's performing rights
companies.*

SignHere Online, Inc.
Michael O'Kane mok2@msn.com
www.signhereonline.net
*Provides unsigned artists with an opportunity to
promote original material. Artist acceptance and
popularity is rated based upon survey results that site
visitors voluntarily provide. This information is shared
with interested music companies.*

Singer Song
bandbseek@hotmail.com
www.singersong.com
*Independent Singers and Songwriters are featured
prominently on our site. Aspiring songwriters, find the
information you need to start your successful career.*

Singer/Songwriter Directory
info@singer-songwriter.com
www.singer-songwriter.com
*In our directory you will find links to sites dedicated
to singer/songwriters. We also list new CD releases,
featured CDs and "Site of the Week".*

Singer Songwriter Resources
Dave Blackledge dave@dblackledge.com
www.SingerSongwriter.ws
*Aiding indie singer songwriters by guiding them to the
places to get their music heard or improve their craft.*

The Singers' Workshop
www.thesingersworkshop.com
Provides valuable articles that singers need to know.

Society of Singers
sos@singers.org
www.singers.org
*A nonprofit charity that helps professional vocalists,
worldwide, in times of crisis. SOS provides emergency
financial aid, case management, counseling and
referral services.*

Song Shark!
songshark@yahoo.com
www.geocities.com/songshark
*Your source for scams and rip-offs in the music
business.*

SongFile.com
hfalicensingsupport@songfile.com
www.songfile.com
*If you're a community group, religious organization,
school/U. or individual and not an existing Harry Fox
customer and would like to obtain a license to make
and distribute within the U.S. 2500 or less recordings,
you can now get an HFA mechanical license here at
SongFile.com!*

Songlounge.com
info@songlounge.com
www.songlounge.com
*The web's first quarterly song contest site, awarding
over $4,000 in cash and prizes every THREE months
to the best 3 songs.*

songrepair.com
bronson@songrepair.com
www.songrepair.com
*It is not a music publishing company; it is a
songwriter/song development company. The staff of
songrepair.com is comprised of long time Music
Industry Professionals, all of whom have had many
years experience working with established
Songwriters and Music Publishers.*

SongRights.com
info@songrights.com
www.songrights.com
*This site will take you through the basic concepts of
law as it pertains to the music industry. Written in
plain English and designed for easy navigation,
SongRights.com is fast becoming one of the most
popular sites for up and coming musicians and
songwriters.*

SongScope.com
info@songscope.com
www.songscope.com
*A tool for submitting song material that is directly
accessible only to proven music industry
professionals. Other songwriters will not have access
to your ideas. You will immediately begin receiving
email requests from our 300+ industry users the day
the requests come in.*

Songstuff
songs@songstuff.com
www.songstuff.com
*Written some songs and you want people to hear them
but you're not sure how? Maybe you're looking for
some technical info. Songstuff, or some of the
Songstuff site visitors, might be able to help.*

Songwriters Resource Network
info@SongwritersResourceNetwork.com
www.songwritersresourcenetwork.com
*A free online news and information resource for
songwriters and lyricists everywhere.*

The Songwriter's Tip Jar
Robert Cote robert@songwriterstipjar.com
www.songwriterstipjar.com
*FREE weekly ezine focused on helping craft a better
song. Full of juicy, creative songwriting tips and eye-
opening ideas.*

Songwriting Contests
jodi@musesmuse.com
www.musesmuse.com/contests.html
*The Muse's Muse up-to-date listing of all the best
songwriting contests.*

The Songwriting Education Resource
songU@songu.com
www.craftofsongwriting.com
*Designed to provide you with educational articles on
the craft of songwriting, as well as inform you of
upcoming songwriting courses and seminars.*

Songwriters Directory
www.songwritersdirectory.com
*Providing songwriters and musicians with a
Songwriters Listings database used by music fans,
music industry executives, A&R reps and the listening
public. It also provides access to business and career
tools through its extensive resource center.*

The Songwriters Guild of America
sganash@aol.com
www.songwriters.org
*The nation's largest and oldest songwriters
organization, serving its members with the vital
information and programs to further their careers and
understanding of the music industry.*

Sonicbids
artists@sonicbids.com
www.sonicbids.com
*The Sonicbids Electronic Press Kit (EPK) is at the
heart of Sonicbids. For musicians, it's a professional
press kit that combines a bio, photos, MP3s, reviews,
calendar and more. It can be e-mailed to anyone,
anywhere, anytime!*

Soul City Café
info@soulcitycafe.com
www.soulcitycafe.com
*The brainchild of Jewel Kilcher. We want to create
grassroots support for anything that truly rocks in its
own way, be it art, entertainment, humanitarian
projects and even politics. So if you have ideas, let us
know!*

Sound Shots

musicNews@localsrock.com
www.Ackphooey.com
Music news from around the globe and your backyard. Submit your music news.

sound@45rpm

soundat45rpm@hotmail.com
www.soundat45rpm.i12.com
Believe it or not, we do it for fun! Ok, there is just one thing...to qualify for a free website; all we ask is that you don't already have another website out there on the world wide web. That's it!

SoundExchange

info@soundexchange.com
www.soundexchange.com
We are dedicated to making the process of licensing music and collecting royalties as accurate, simple and fair as possible for all involved.

SoundScan

clientservices@soundscan.com
home.soundscan.com
Designed to provide weekly, point-of-sale data with the highest possible degree of accuracy and integrity. Functioning as a central clearinghouse for music industry data, SoundScan enables its subscribers to access comprehensive reports from a wide variety of perspectives.

STICKER GUY!

info@stickerguy.com
www.stickerguy.com
Since 1993, we have been making stickers for independent bands, zines, record labels, businesses and propagandists. If you are one of these, we would really like to help promote your endeavors and spread your message.

studiofinder.com

www.studiofinder.com
With over 5350 recording studios, StudioFinder is the most comprehensive online recording studio search engine. Search for a studio by name, location, equipment, price, and/or area of expertise.

TalentBox.com

mailbox@talentbox.com
www.talentbox.com
Our goal is to build a large interactive community of people involved in the entertainment industry and help them exchange information about various talents or services that they have to offer.

TalentMatch.com

ms@talentmatch.com
www.talentmatch.com
Designed to help artists at all levels - ranging from garage bands and hopeful models to accomplished actors and directors - gain exposure to the general public and the entertainment, publishing and advertising industries.

tinfoil.music

Joe McGuire contests@tinfoil.net
music.tinfoil.net
A free service to allow bands, musicians and the musically inclined to post information and mp3s and talk to fellow musicians.

Topica

support@get.topica.com
www.topica.com/channels/music
A free email publishing service delivering hundreds of newsletters on music related subjects such as songwriting, mp3s, music theory etc.

TourBaby

TourBaby@nogenre.com
www.tourbaby.com
A grass-roots co-operative effort by independent musical artists from around the world. Artists whose interests range from hip-hop to classical and everything in between. Each TourBaby event has been organized by the artists involved in your own community. Some artists will be coming from the previous event and others will carry the torch on to the next.

Trademark Search

www.uspto.gov/main/trademarks.htm
Valuable information on trademarks in the US, as well as a search engine that allows you to do a free search on your band's name to see if it is legally available.

TrueFire

truefire.com
A self-publishing tool and open marketplace for authors and artists wishing to promote and distribute their original poetry, guitar lessons, novels, music, reference material, photography and artwork. TrueFire membership is free and includes immediate access to all of TrueFire's content management and self-publishing tools.

Tunesmith

info@tunesmith.net
www.tunesmith.net
We want to be known as an organization that speaks honestly to our members about their commercial songwriting potential, rather than give them lip service.

Ultimate Band List

editor@artistdirect.com
ubl.artistdirect.com
Join the best and only site devoted to getting music information for ALL bands and ALL kinds of music into the hands of fans. Music fans only need one bookmark - UBL.com. Get listed here.

Uniform Code Council

info@uc-council.org
www.uc-council.org
The UCC administers the Universal Product Code (U.P.C. bar code) and provides a full range of integrated standards and business solutions.

United States Copyright Office

copyinfo@loc.gov
www.loc.gov/copyright
Here you will find all our key publications, including informational circulars; application forms for copyright registration; links to the copyright law and to the homepages of other copyright-related organizations.

United States Patent and Trademark Office

TrademarkAssistanceCenter@uspto.gov
www.uspto.gov
The official website.

Unknownstyle.com

webmaster@unknownstyle.com
www.unknownstyle.com
A site dedicated to promoting new artists on the internet.

USA Musicians Network

usamusician.com
Musicians can create a free web page to promote their music and post their gigs in their local city calendars. Find bands, musicians, events and entertainment nationwide.

Vista Prints

www.vistaprint.com
Get 250 free business cards.

Vocalist. co.uk

info@vocalist.co.uk
www.vocalist.co.uk
Our mission is to empower and inform singers of all ages, amateur and professional, at all stages of your musical journey. We give free access to resources, products and services relevant to singers and provide support and opportunities to network via the Green Room Noticeboard and advice page.

Yahoo! Music Related Groups

dir.groups.yahoo.com/dir/Music
What is a Group? One email address & website that allows you to share photos & files, plan events, send a newsletter, discuss music related topics... and more

yourDictionary.com

WordMan@yourDictionary.com
www.yourdictionary.com
The most comprehensive and authoritative portal for language & language-related products and services on the web with more than 1800 dictionaries with more than 250 languages.

Specialty Sites

Children's Music

The Canadian Children's Songwriter's Network

duncanw@geocities.com
www.geocities.com/EnchantedForest/Cottage/5207/ccsn.html
If you are a Canadian Children's Songwriter or Performer we would like you to join us as we bring the craft of songwriting for children to the world.

The Children's Entertainment Association

CEA@kidsentertainment.com
www.kidsentertainment.com/cea
The country's leading trade association for those involved in children's entertainment. CEA members come from all areas of the industry, including music, theater, performance, publishing, film, television, video and radio.

The Children's Music Network

office@cmnonline.org
www.cmnonline.org
We meet and stay in touch to share songs and ideas about children's music, to inspire each other about the empowering ways adults and young people can communicate through music and to be a positive catalyst for education and community-building through music.

Children's Music Web

pickle@well.com
www.childrensmusic.org
There is a growing body of hundreds of professional musicians and groups who specialize in creating and performing music perfect for children. We use the Internet to connect families and kids with all this great music that might otherwise go unnoticed!

Children's Music Workshop

www.childrensmusicworkshop.com
A music education resource for students, parents and teachers.

Kids Music Web

kidsmuze@kidsmusicweb.com
www.kidsmusicweb.com
If you're not listed on the site but you are a Kids Music artist with your own web site, please let us know so we can get you on here.

KidScreen

www.kidscreen.com
An international trade magazine serving the information needs and interests of all those involved in reaching children through entertainment.

The National Association for the Education of Young Children *(NAEYC)*

naeyc@naeyc.org
www.naeyc.org
The nation's largest and most influential organization of early childhood educators and others dedicated to improving the quality of programs for children from birth through third grade.

The Parents' Choice Awards

awards@parents-choice.org
www.parents-choice.org
Comprised of moms, dads, teachers, performing artists, librarians and yes, kids themselves, search out and recommend products that help kids grow - imaginatively. Products are now being accepted throughout the year. Details and entry forms are available online.

Christian

Academy of Gospel Music Arts

www.gospelmusic.org/agma
Launched in 1995 for the purpose of educating, encouraging and supporting growth and development in the next generation of gospel artists. Through various seminars, individuals receive in-depth instruction from the gospel music industry professionals-from practical concerns to improving an individual's skills.

AnonymousBands.com

info@anonymousbands.com
www.anonymousbands.com
Our vision is to market Independent Christian Bands/Artist to a network of Christian outlets and youth ministries with the goal of linking concert opportunities with independent artists.

Association of Independent Christian Artists *(AICA)*

norm@theaica.org
theaica.org
A support network for Christian Artists in their local communities. Our mission is to build chapters or "communities" in which Christian musicians, singers, songwriters and other Christian music enthusiasts can meet regularly for spiritual growth, accountability, artistic development, fellowship and exposure.

Christian Country Music Association *(CCMA)*

www.ccma.cc
Dedicated to faithfully serve its members who are interested in or involved with Christian Country Music or other forms of Christian or Positive music through their careers, ministries and businesses.

ChristianRadio.com

contactus@christianradio.com
www.christianradio.com
A list of over 1950 Christian radio stations in the United States. We are your Source for Christian Radio on the Web!

Club Praize

clubpraize@yahoo.com
clubpraise.homestead.com
The #1 site and source for Gospel Music Events on the East Coast. Highlighting Gospel Artists, DJ's, Praise Dancers, Praise Poets, Christian Comedians and Playwrights from all over the world.

ColorBlindMusic Ministries

Lynn Geyer info@colorblindmusic.com
www.ColorBlindMusic.com
We offer Christian music, programs and services as well as links to other music ministry sites and opportunities. We accept new artists who meet our standards of professionalism.

Country Gospel Music Guild

crider@network-one.com
www.countrygospelguild.com
To spread the gospel of Jesus Christ through the genre of country gospel music, promoting country gospel artists, songwriters and radio personalities to the world. We have the Top 50 Country Gospel Charts that appear in the US Gospel News.

The Cutting Edge

Dan Kennedy baptistboy_46@yahoo.com
www.geocities.com/SunsetStrip/Venue/1006
Ultimate Christian Music Discography.

festboX.net

info@festbox.com
www.festbox.net
If you are an organizer or you have a band, just insert your concert and/or festival dates in our database. And they are available for the whole world.

FindJesusFreaks.com

corey@findjesusfreaks.com
www.findjesusfreaks.com
It's a database/network of free classifieds for Christian musicians & industry professionals to get gigs, buy and sell equipment and network with one another in YOUR local area.

The Gospel Music Association *(GMA)*

www.gospelmusic.org
Supporting, encouraging and promoting the development of all forms of gospel music. The GMA provides an atmosphere in which artists, retail stores, radio stations, concert promoters and local churches can coordinate their efforts for the purpose of benefiting the industry as a whole.

The Gospel Music Workshop of America *(GMWA)*

Manager@gmwa.org
www.gmwa.org
Dedicated to the perpetuation of gospel music as an original American art form and to the promotion of gospel music to the world. GMWA is committed to utilizing gospel music as an alternative outlet for frustrations brought to our young people by peer pressure and social ills.

Heaven's Metal

webmaster@heavensmetal.com
www.heavensmetal.com
This is meant to be an informational resource for people looking for obscure and/or minor-label CD releases. Any Christian bands from AOR, to hard rock, to melodic metal, to thrash metal and death metal styles.

HeavenSound

gary@heavensound.com
www.heavensound.com
An artist-supported effort to bring up-to-date concert and artist information to the supporters of Gospel Music all over the country. Several artists have their web pages hosted on HeavenSound and others have a "Gateway" page to their official site.

Hip-HopZone.com

jelani@urbancross.com
www.hip-hopzone.com
Where Hip Hop meets its Creator. Representing God to the fullest in the urban hip-hop community. Check out the reviews, news and more.

Informazione Musica Cristiana *(Italy)*

christianmusic@fastwebnet.it
www.informusic.it
Il primo portale di musica cristiana.

monastereo.com

webguide@monastereo.com
www.monastereo.com
Home Of The Gospel Radio Locator. Find a gospel radio station near you...

The National Association of Christian Rock Radio *(NACRR)*

nacrr@nacrr.org
www.nacrr.org
Designed specifically to serve and support radio stations, shows and personnel involved in the more progressive forms of Christian Radio such as Rock, Alternative, Metal, Rhythmic etc. We are a community to help bring unity, encouragement and support to those struggling to work in this new and progressive avenue of ministry.

Ucbands.com

info@ucbands.com
www.ucbands.com
Dedicated to the promotion of Independent Christian Musicians.

The Urban People's Directory

www.urbanweblink.com
A listing of Christians, broken up by categories such as singers, DJs, webmasters etc. The next time your church is looking for a Christian rap artist or DJ, just log on here to get some referrals.

Classical

Afrocentric Voices in Classical Music

majordomo@afrovoices.com
www.afrovoices.com
Focusing on African American performers and composers and on the vocal music forms they influenced, especially opera, art songs and Negro spirituals composed for concert performance.

The American Composers Forum

mail@composersforum.org
www.composersforum.org
We are committed to supporting composers and developing new markets for their music. Through granting, commissioning and performance programs, we provide composers at all stages of their careers with valuable resources for professional and artistic development.

American Guild of Musical Artists

www.musicalartists.org

We are a labor organization that represents the men and women who create America's operatic, choral and dance heritage. Performing artists live to perform, but their talents and the beauty they create won't necessarily pay the rent or put food on the table. Without forceful advocacy and defense of their rights, artists may be vulnerable to exploitation or illegal discrimination. They need protection. They can find it by joining the AGMA.

The American Guild of Organists

jem@agohq.org

www.agohq.org

The AGO provides a wealth of benefits and opportunities under the guidance of the National Officers; Councilors for Education, Professional Development, Competitions and Conventions and Finance and Development; Regional Councilors; and working committees — all volunteer leaders of the Guild.

American Harp Society

kmoon@UCLAlumni.net

www.harpsociety.org

Our aim is to promote and foster the appreciation of the harp as a musical instrument, to encourage the composition of music for the harp and to improve the quality of performance of harpists.

The American Music Center (AMC)

center@amc.net

www.amc.net

Our goal is to foster and encourage the composition of contemporary (American) music and to promote its production, publication, distribution and performance in every way possible throughout the Western Hemisphere.

The American Pianists Association

apainfo@AmericanPianists.org

www.americanpianists.org

Dedicated to advancing the career of American classical and jazz pianists between the ages of 18 and 30. It is unique, in that it offers equal fellowships rather than traditional competition rankings and tailors caring assistance to the needs of each Fellow.

The American Viola Society (AVS)

cforbes@uta.edu

www.americanviolasociety.org

An association for the promotion of viola performance and research.

American Symphony Orchestra League

league@symphony.org

www.symphony.org

A membership organization providing leadership and service to American orchestras while communicating to the American public the value and importance of orchestras and the music they perform.

Brave New Works

www-personal.umich.edu/~cyoungk

Dedicated to the work of composers across the entire aesthetic spectrum, our mission is to foster New Music, its creation, performance and by working with and on behalf of Composers. BNW also seeks to expand the audience for new music through performances, workshops and collaborations with the arts.

Cadenza Musicians' Directory

www.cadenza.org

A collection of short biographies and contact details, designed to put performers, composers and teachers in touch with those organising concerts, those commissioning new works and those wanting music tuition. To add your name to the list, please complete our entry form.

The Center for the Promotion of Contemporary Composers (CPCC)

cpcc@under.org

www.under.org/cpcc

An Internet-based service organization for composers, dedicated to providing a single, comprehensive resource containing opportunities (competitions, faculty openings, grants etc.), as well as a platform from which members can disseminate information about their own works and activities.

Chamber Music America

info@chamber-music.org

www.chamber-music.org

Our mission is to promote artistic excellence and economic stability within the profession and to ensure that chamber music, in its broadest sense, is a vital part of American life.

Chorus America

service@chorusamerica.org

www.chorusamerica.org

More than 1,200 choruses, individuals and businesses are members of Chorus America. This powerful group of conductors, arts administrators, board members, singers and choral music lovers are at the core of the growing choral movement in North America.

Classical Composers Database

utopia.knoware.nl/users/jsmeets/frames.htm

An ever-growing list of composers. Links and contributions accepted!

Classical Notes

Gutmann, Peter PGutmann@wcsr.com

www.classicalnotes.net

Updated and expanded versions of Goldmine "Classical Notes" columns include recommended recordings of various classical works and artists; links section emphasizes non-commercial sites and resources for historical performances.

Classical Search

www.classicalsearch.com

In order to save our time and your own, please submit only those sites which are of direct relevance to the world of Classical Music.

Classicalist.com

info@classicalist.com

www.classicalist.com

A classical music artists' directory. Its aim is to provide the most comprehensive directory of professional musicians and their CVs in the world and to help individuals in the classical music industry to maximize their publicity by using the power of the Internet.

classicOL.com

info@classicol.com

www.classicol.com

Build a free, easily constructed website specifically designed for classical musicians. No programming knowledge is required. Our site, based within the United Kingdom, is designed specifically for classical musicians and classical music enthusiasts.

The College Music Society

cms@music.org

www.music.org

A consortium of college, conservatory, U. and independent musicians and scholars interested in all disciplines of music. Its mission is to promote music teaching and learning, musical creativity and expression, research and dialogue and diversity and interdisciplinary interaction.

The Composers Concordance

info@composersconcordance.org

www.composersconcordance.org

A New York-based, non-profit, composer-oriented, music presenting organization devoted to a wide spectrum of contemporary music continuously soliciting scores, primarily American, from composers via a national search effort.

The Composer-Conductor Bridge

ccbridge@music-usa.org

www.music-usa.org/ccbridge

The purpose of this site is to help conductors locate new scores that are of high quality, inexpensive and suitable for performance by their ensembles. Many such scores are unpublished, unperformed and written by composers who are not well-known.

ConcertoNet.com

useconcertonet@yahoo.com

www.concertonet.com

Providing information, analysis and alert our members to pertinent information about classical music worldwide. Our mission is to connect the people of the classical music sector by providing information, analysis and inspiration.

Copyright and Music

marbeth@marthabeth.com

www.serve.com/marbeth/music_copyright.html

This site contains generalizations based on my study of copyright law and are not meant to be construed as legal advice. If you have a question, consult a competent attorney specializing in copyrights and intellectual property law.

Early Music America

info@earlymusic.org

earlymusic.org

EMA offers members an array of benefits, resources and publications designed to save them money, assist in career development, provide scholarship and networking opportunities

Early Music Newsletter

www.priceclan.com/nyrecorderguild

We are a publication of the New York Recorder Guild. The Newsletter welcomes contributions: any length, any topic, as long as it's relevant to early music.

earlyMusic.net

www.earlymusic.net

Our mission is to support and promote early music and historical performance by providing information and services which would benefit and help early music organizations, ensembles and solo musicians (such as free web hosting, instrument exchange, help with organization of concerts, to provide info about education, master classes etc.).

The Gaudeamus Foundation

info@gaudeamus.nl

www.xs4all.nl/~gaud

Our special projects include courses on and by composers, master classes, lectures, festivals and exchange programs. We advise international organisations on new developments in contemporary music. We also facilitate the attendances of Dutch composers and ensembles at leading festivals.

hornplayer.net
www.hornplayer.net
Free classifieds and information archive.

Impulse Classical Music
impulse@impulse-music.co.uk
www.impulse-music.co.uk
Our website provides personalized pages on performers and composers together with entries for record labels and affiliated organisations and holds classical music tracks with copy-right protection in the digital domain.

The International Association of Music Information Centres
gratzl@iamic.net
www.iamic.ie
A world-wide network of organisations promoting new music. IAMIC has 43 members in 38 countries. Each Music Information Centre is responsible for documenting and promoting the music of its own country or region, as well as co-operating internationally with other centres and international organisations on issues of common concern.

International Horn Society
manager@hornsociety.org
www.hornsociety.org
We are dedicated to performance, teaching, composition, research and the preservation and promotion of the Horn as a musical instrument.

The International Society of Bassists
info@isbworldoffice.com
www.ISBworldoffice.com
Dedicated to inspiring public interest, raising performance standards and providing an organization for those who teach, study, play, repair, build, research and enjoy the double bass.

International Trumpet Guild
editor@trumpetguild.org
www.trumpetguild.org
A non-profit organization, founded in 1974 to promote communications among trumpet players around the world and to improve the artistic level of performance, teaching and literature associated with the trumpet.

The International Tuba and Euphonium Association (ITEA)
www.iteaonline.org
An international organization comprised of performers, teachers, students and other interested parties who desire to promote the literature, pedagogy and performance of the euphonium and tuba.

The Internet Bass Clarinet Society
md@new-music.org
www.new-music.org
Provides a free and accessible resource for information about bass clarinet performance.

The Internet Cello Society
editor@cello.org
www.cello.org
An international cyber-community of cellists, seeks to advance the knowledge and joy of cello playing around the world. We welcome cello enthusiasts of all ages and skill levels. We currently have over 6770 members representing 84 different countries of the world. Contact us about our "Featured Artist" section.

Meet the Composer
Sharon Levy slevy@meetthecomposer.org
www.meetthecomposer.org
Our mission is to increase opportunities for composers by fostering the creation, performance, dissemination and appreciation of their music.

Musical Chairs
links@musicalchairs.info
www.musicalchairs.info
World-wide orchestral jobs and competitions. If YOUR orchestra is NOT listed in our database, please tell us.

MUSIClassical
www.musiclassical.com
A website devoted to classical music education and information about composers, performers, news and historical information.

National Association of Composers
nacusa@music-usa.org
www.music-usa.org/nacusa
One of the oldest organizations devoted to the promotion and performance of American music. Many of the most distinguished composers of the 20th Century have been among its members. NACUSA sponsors several concerts each year that feature music by its members.

New Directions Cello Association
ndca@clarityconnect.com
www.newdirectionscello.com
The goals of the NDCA are to encourage interaction and awareness among cellists and the musically oriented public about the contributions that cellists are making in many styles of contemporary music. This encompasses styles that are not commonly taught to cellists at music schools (jazz, blues, rock, ethnic, new age, folk, experimental etc.) especially those styles involving improvisation.

New Music Links
tmoore@umbc.edu
research.umbc.edu/~tmoore/musiclinks.html
This site, which contains more than 9,500 links to other new music sites, is provided by Thomas Moore at UMBC and serves the contemporary classical music community. Contact us If you would like your site listed here.

Operissimo
opera@operissimo.com
www.operissimo.com
Performers and composers, add your information to our database.

Society of Composers
secretary@societyofcomposers.org
www.societyofcomposers.org
A professional society dedicated to the promotion of composition, performance, understanding and dissemination of new and contemporary music. Members include composers and performers both in and outside of academia interested in addressing concerns for national and regional support of compositional activities.

SongTrellis
davidlu@songtrellis.com
www.songtrellis.com
If you compose music, you can submit one of your compositions to obtain a listing here automatically, no charge. If you don't yet compose, the SongTrellis Music Editor can help you learn how to compose incredibly quickly.

soundcell.net
in@soundcell.net
www.soundcell.net
This site provides a space to gather and find information about composers, musicians, sound designers. For people with musical interests this is a place to quickly find creative individuals.

The Stradivari Society
mail@stradivarisociety.com
www.stradivarisociety.com
Dedicated to identifying the world's most promising young artists and uniting them with the superb Italian instruments they need to help launch and sustain their professional careers.

The Viola Web Site
tasks@viola.com
www.viola.com
Viola Events and Competitions, articles, resources and publishers.

World Intellectual Property Organization
wipo.mail@wipo.int
www.wipo.org
Site of the international organization dedicated to promoting the use and protection of works of the human spirit, through patents and copyright

Young Artists International
info@youngartists.org
www.youngartists.org
A non-profit organization formed to support, promote and develop the careers of exceptionally gifted young musicians, thus securing a future generation of artists who will pass on traditions of the great musicians of all time and carry classical music into the next century.

Young Concert Artists
yca@yca.org
www.yca.org
Dedicated to discovering and launching the careers of extraordinary young musicians. The artists are chosen through the Young Concert Artists International Auditions, which are unique in that there are no rankings and any number of winners, or none, can be selected. The sole criteria are musicianship, virtuosity, communicative power and readiness for a concert career.

Germany

The Male Soprano Page
kopp@linmpi.mpg.de
www.linmpi.mpg.de/~kopp/disc
Database of male sopranos past and present.

France

IRCAM
webmaster@ircam.fr
www.ircam.fr
Open to the international music community, each year the Institute welcomes young talent and established composers. It offers composers a framework for efficient technical production.

La Lettre du Musicien
info@lettre-musicien.fr
www.lettre-musicien.fr
A magazine dedicated to bringing you the latest news and information from the classical music scene, not only in France but also the rest of Europe.

United Kingdom

OrchestraNET

editor@orchestranet.co.uk
www.orchestranet.com
www.orchestranet.co.uk
We are the worldwide orchestra directory updated by visitors.

Japan

The Classical Music Information Center

music@musicinfo.com
www.musicinfo.com
We can assist you in promoting your artist or upcoming concerts. Using our internet homepage, the largest and most well-known among all Japanese concert agencies, you can greatly increase your access to the Japanese concert market.

Country

The Americana Music Association

info@americanamusic.org
www.americanamusic.org
The mission of the AMA is to provide a forum for the advocacy of Americana music, to promote public awareness of this genre and to support the creative and economic viability of professionals in this field.

The Association of North Country Fiddlers

n2xbw@northnet.org
www.fiddlers.org
International Event Listings For Fiddlers and All Acoustic Musicians. Get Your Event Listed Here Free!

Country Music Showcase International

haroldl@cmshowcase.org
www.cmshowcase.org
Our purpose and goals are to preserve, protect, promote, perpetuate and educate, the general public about 14 art forms of COUNTRY MUSIC!

FiddleFork

info@fiddlefork.com
fiddlefork.com
Created and maintained by fiddle players from around the world, FiddleFork's mission is to provide a one stop platform for exchanging fiddle tunes, fiddle information and anything fiddle related. FiddleFork allows members to post links to midi files, mp3 files, wav files, sheet music and fiddler related resources as well as promote exchange between its members.

iBluegrass

iblue@ibluegrass.com
www.ibluegrass.com
Our mission is to further advance the cause of acoustic-related music by educating the unknowing, enlightening the informed and entertaining the readership while remaining perched on the leading edge of Internet technology.

International Bluegrass Music Association

ibma@ibma.org
www.ibma.org
A professional trade association dedicated to promoting and expanding the success of bluegrass music. The organization has over 2500 members in all 50 of the United States and in over 30 foreign countries.

The North American Fiddlers Association

bshull@iland2.internetland.net
www.internetland.net/~bshull/NAFA
The preservation and development of the various traditions of fiddle playing. Develop and implement a strategy for supporting fiddling at all levels and in all styles.

ProgressiveCountry.com

info@progressivecountry.com
www.progressivecountry.com
A comprehensive, easy to use database designed to provide credible and accurate information to radio professionals, record labels and recording artists.

The Western Music Association

www.westernmusic.org
Our purpose is the preservation and promotion of the traditional and contemporary music of the Great American West.

Dance

KindKidz

roundz@optonline.net
www.kindkidz.com
We are a collective of old-skool kidz and new-skool kidz who together hold a passion and desire to continue the positive growth of our culture. We are always looking for fresh new talent, if you have a demo and would like us to hear it, please contact us.

partypeople.nl

www.partypeople.nl
Add your link, music and press releases.

The Record Pool

Support@therecordpool.com
www.therecordpool.com
Through this medium everybody gets what they want. Djs get great affordable music, independent labels no longer have to waste their precious time, money and energy in industry scams. The labels music is heard and played by all the best DJs on the planet and they get the Information and Data they need to make moves. The world of music now has a communal voice.

RIOTRECORDINGS

RiotSound@RiotSound.com
www.riotsound.com
Our goal is to bring together art, music and information from all corners of the globe in seamless harmony creating an orifice through which our message will resonate louder and clearer than the voices of politicians for whom we do not vote and corrupt business leaders that consistently exploit our very existence.

SPRACI

Michael MD mdagn@spraci.com
www.spraci.com
A worldwide resource site for parties/clubs/festivals... events listings (listings are free), news, directory of artists/djs/promoters/services, forums and more. Mostly (but not exclusively) electronica.

Experimental

Ambient.us

Cameron Akhunaton info@ambient.us
www.ambient.us
A positive energy ambient music guide featuring related articles and artist listings from around the world.

clan analogue

clan@clananalogue.org
clananalogue.org
We allow artists to produce work free of the constraints of the commercial music industry by developing self funded, artist initiated, recording and publishing projects. This 'do it yourself' philosophy encourages the direct transmission of the artist's works to the listener without filtering it via label mediation.

Computerized Music Association

orpipop@surfree.net.il
lightning.prohosting.com/~orpipop
If you're a talented musician, yet unknown and would like to get published somehow, join our new organization and we'll provide you the necessary publicity and distribution, free of charge.

Electronic Music Foundation *(EMF)*

emf@emf.org
www.emf.org
A not-for-profit organization dedicated to increasing public understanding of the role that electronic music, in its myriad forms and technologies, plays in our world.

The Gas Station

nick@sonicstate.com
www.the-gas-station.com
The electronic musicians knowledgebase and number one discussion site. We have over 30,000 postings with 'pumps' serving a wide variety of topics. (see left-hand list) You may read, but must register to post.

The International Computer Music Association

icma@umich.edu
www.computermusic.org
An international affiliation of individuals and institutions involved in the technical, creative and performance aspects of computer music. It serves composers, computer software and hardware developers, researchers and musicians who are interested in the integration of music and technology.

Society for Electro-Acoustic Music *(SEAMUS)*

seamus.lsu.edu
A non-profit national organization of composers, performers and teachers of electro-acoustic music representing every part of the country and virtually every musical style. Electro-acoustic music is a term used to describe musics which is dependent on electronic technology for their creation and/or performance.

Film and TV

Film Music Directory

www.filmmusicdirectory.com/pages

Film Music Magazine

info@filmmusicmag.com
www.filmmusicmag.com
www.filmmusicchannel.com
A monthly trade publication for professionals in the film and television music business; includes news, feature articles, investigative reporting and an event calendar.

The Film Music Network

info@filmmusic.net
www.filmmusic.net
We exist for only one purpose - to facilitate communications and networking among professionals in all aspects of the film music business. We are not an advocacy group, union, guild, or society - we are simply an organization created to improve communications and networking among film music professionals.

Film Score Monthly

lukas@filmscoremonthly.com
www.filmscoremonthly.com
America's leading magazine about motion picture and television music. Although song-oriented soundtrack albums are today bigger than ever, we are primarily interested in the background music; the instrumental underscores which play such an important part of the film going experience.

Filmmusik 2000

filmmusik2000@gmx.de
www.filmmusik2000.de
German online magazine for soundtracks.

MusicForYourFilm.com

www.musicforyourfilm.com
Download free sample film and television contracts, deal memos and music licenses.

Sonic Licensing

Cameron@soniclicensing.com
www.SonicLicensing.com
We are an agency dedicated to helping media producers find the perfect piece of music to compliment their projects. Our staff of industry professionals is ready to handle every aspect of the licensing procedure, from selection of material, to negotiations with the artist or label, to delivery of master copies and drafting of contracts.

Goth

C8

stevvi@c8.com to
c8.com
Resource which posts articles, interviews, reviews etc.

Carpe Mortem

staff@carpemortem.com
www.carpemortem.com
Does your Gothic, Industrial or Ambient band need a home on the World Wide Web? We can provide qualifying bands with FREE web space! For more information, send email with a brief description of your band and your requirements to free-web-offer@carpemortem.com.

darksites.com

sire@darksites.com
www.darksites.com
Various boards where you can post information - views, articles, interviews, reviews etc.

goth.net

webmistress@goth.net
www.goth.net
We provide free web space and email to gothic users worldwide and we try to be a common resource point that people may turn to for any gothic needs they may have.

The Kids Are Bored *Live Electronic Music Listings*

Corey H Maass mail@thekidsarebored.com
www.thekidsarebored.com
Electronic music artists and promoters create a basic profile and list their live events.

Music Database

Ed Klein eklein@kzsu.stanford.edu
KZSU.stanford.edu/eklein
The web's largest Industrial/Gothic music index. More than 4000 artist listings and still growing!

unspunrecords.com

info@unspunrecords.com
www.unspunrecords.com
Send us an email info@unspunrecords.com if you'd like to be added to our monthly newsletter list detailing new releases and concert announcements.

Hip Hop

The Connex List

ConnexList@wondertwinz.com
wondertwinz.com/connexlist.htm
A resource reference for the Hip-Hop industry.

En Sound Entertainment

Delroy Souden ensound@ensoundentertainment.com
www.ensoundentertainment.com
Dedicated to the exposure of independent gospel music of all genres. Taking gospel music to another level.

The G Funk.Era

webmaster@gfunk.de
www.gfunk.de
Here you will find reviews of hot releases submitted by fans. Send us your review!

HipHop-Directory.com

www.hiphop-directory.com
Your guide to Hip Hop resources world-wide.

HipHop-Network.Com

info@hiphop-network.com
www.hiphop-network.com
The main goal of the Network is to represent the 4 main elements of hip-hop equally and everyday life in the hip-hop community.

hiphopbiz.com

info@hiphopbiz.com
www.hiphopentrepreneur.com
www.hiphopbiz.com
This unique publishing company provides music industry success tools, job listings as well as business advice, an online calendar and books and videos strictly for the Hip Hop Entrepreneur.

The HipHopClassifieds

Shizzy shizzy@HipHopClassifieds.com
www.hiphopclassifieds.com
An outlet for independent artists and small businesses to make the connections they need to further their careers.

HipHopHotSpot.Com

Remi Blais support@hiphophotspot.com
www.hiphophotspot.com
HipHopHotSpot.Com supports the growth of hip hop artists world wide through exhausting a network of all free resources designed to give artists more promotion, exposure and positive press on a global scale.

Jackin4Beats.com

pressreleases@jackin4beats.com
jackin4beats.com
Send in your press release! We also have various message boards to help get the word out. If you're submitting to Unsigned Artists, don't forget to add your link in the 'Listen To It' field.

Rap Coalition

rapcoalition@aol.com
www.rapcoalition.org
Dedicated to the support, education, protection and unification of Rap artists, producers and DJs. We believe it's time for Hip Hop artists to take control of their own art form. Rap Coalition protects rappers, producers and DJs, from this hostile environment and provides artists with a place to turn when they need help or support, at no cost to them.

Rappers Resource

Sales@rappersresource.com
www.rappersresource.com
The purpose of this site is to help everyone associated with the hip-hop industry find the tools, people and resources necessary to thrive in the rap music business.

rapsearch.com

staff@rapsearch.com
www.rapsearch.com
The biggest HipHop search engine online. Every Rap artists, record label, promotion company, news source. Everything Rap & HipHop related.

Urban Tip *The Urban Music Information Network*

al_urbantip@msn.com
www.urbantip.com
A good source for Urban Music and an extensive network of Record Pools for Discs for DJs.

webjhn.com

johng@webjhn.com
webjhn.com
Daily Hip hop and R&B Music News and information. Including a JHN Exclusive: television listings of your favorite artists.

Jazz/Blues/Folk

The American Federation of Jazz Societies

don@americanrag.com
www.jazzfederation.com
Our mission is to build an inter-national jazz community by being a proactive advocate for jazz music of all styles, jazz organizations, jazz musicians, jazz educators and students, jazz venues and other entities which present, promote or support jazz, America's national treasure and only true original art form.

Blues Bank Collective

www.bluesbankcollective.org
Our mission is to further awareness of Blues music and its African American heritage.

The Blues Foundation

bluesinfo@blues.org
www.blues.org
Continuously encourages and recognizes the highest achievements of artists, writers, promoters and other supporters of the Blues.

The Blues Highway

thebluehighway.com
Listings of Blues radio shows from all over the world.

Blues Music Association

info@bluesmusicassociation.com
www.BluesMusicAssociation.org
Blues needs the same kind of professional push that rock, country and smooth jazz have gotten. None of us has the resources — neither time nor money — to make that goal happen by ourselves. By working together to market the blues, we can increase our audience and so increase our income.

Christer's and Vanja's P.A.W.S.

christer@fridhammar.com
www.fridhammar.com

Jazz Festivals Nationwide

www.festivalfinder.com/jazz
Find out information on Jazz Festivals nationwide.

JAZZCORNER.com

info@jazzcorner.com
www.jazzcorner.com
News, reviews, interviews, web hosting.

JazzWeek

info@jazzweek.com
www.jazzweek.com
The definitive Jazz and Smooth Jazz national radio airplay chart—a weekly report of the top fifty Jazz and Smooth Jazz recordings played on radio stations across the United States and Canada.

Warta Jazz Online *Indonesia*

info@wartajazz.net
www.wartajazz.com
The ultimate source for Indonesian Jazz Lovers with music, musicians, festivals, workshops, records labels etc.

World Folk Music Association

webmaster@wfma.net
wfma.net
To keep its members informed about its activities, WFMA publishes a newsletter, FOLK NEWS. In addition to WFMA activities, it features stories about and interviews with artists and songwriters, CD and tape reviews and information on where to buy the music you love.

Latin

AfroCubaWeb

main@afrocubaweb.com
www.afrocubaweb.com
A great source for information about current Cuban music events happening all across the country.

AudioMusico Latino

AudioMusico@aol.com
www.amlatino.com
Completely bilingual site which provides a roster of unsigned Latin artists, classifieds, net groups and a helpful "industry guru" question and answer section.

DJ Marquee

contact@djmarquee.com
www.djmarquee.com
Support Latino Hip Hop. We've got everything from the latest Beats in Real Audio & MP3s, the hottest Hip Hop and Latin Linx, DJ Mixtapes, Blazin' Photos, Real Videos and Lyrical Battle Boards.

Justsalsa.com

home@justsalsa.com
www.justsalsa.com
A vast and far-reaching site for Salsa enthusiasts with club dates, an events calendar, photos and more. Numerous fan pages feature photographs, news and concert and concert information.

LAMC *(Latin Alternative Music Conference)*

lamc@cookman.com
www.latinalternative.com
An annual gathering of industry and artistic players. The conference showcases international, Latin American and North American Latin rock acts.

The Latin American Music Center

lamc@indiana.edu
www.music.indiana.edu/som/lamc
Fosters the research and performance of Latin American art music.

Puro Mariachi

WebJefa@mariachi.org
www.mariachi.org
A comprehensive site for mariachi performers and enthusiasts, featuring current news on national mariachi events. Includes links to mariachi group websites all over the United States and other cultural and industry resources.

Salsa Planet

salsaplanet@hotmail.com
www.salsaplanet.net
This Italian based site covers Salsa events, music, dance workshops and concerts in Europe. There is space available for ALL Latin music bands, singers etc. Send your material and I'll be happy to include it.

SalsaArtists.com

info@salsaartists.com
www.salsaartists.com
We endeavor to connect record companies, famous artists, up-and-coming stars, DJs, dancers, unsigned artists and fans to create a new level of excitement around this passionate Latin sound. Site features online connections, tours, festivals, digital downloads and more.

Metal

deathmetal.com

jim@lambdatel.com
www.deathmetal.com
We offer COMPLETELY FREE (permanently) Web pages (both design and serving) to ANY Death Metal Band, anywhere in the world. In addition, we also offer various E-mail services to these bands.

Hard Radio

metaltim@hardradio.com
www.hardradio.com
The metal radio with no alternative aftertaste.

Heavycore.org

contact@lowtwelve.com
www.heavycore.org
Our vision is to provide a centralized organization that offers service to, recognition to and promotion to heavy bands and musicians. Heavycore is engineered strictly on a voluntary basis. Any proceeds "given to" or "generated" by Heavycore is invested back into the organization for the better wealth of its members.

International Longhairs United

robin@namastepromotions.com
www.internationallonghairs.com
This is a free submissions website. Submitting on this site requires an active email & an active telephone number in which a member of your band can be contacted.

Internet@Metal *Germany*

Juergen jgarus@nbnet.nb.ca
www.internet-metal.de
We offer a "free of charge" commercial website for all bands who like to join us. If you would like to display your band on our site, please contact Juergen and he will translate it to German. He's our metalmaster for the USA and Canada. All other countries are welcome too!

The Metal Index

Jason webmaster@metalindex.com
www.metalindex.com
Link archive and huge metal search engine for unsigned metal bands.

Metalshop.com *Australia*

www.Metalshop.com
The Beast is a section at Metalshop where you can build a free website for your band, or interest. You can also post wanted ads and sell Cds, Records, or anything you desire!

True Metal

universe@truemetal.org
www.truemetal.org
Here's a list of the services you'll receive: your own unique url, web space, guestbook and message board on request, ftp-access to your web space. The service we're offering is completely free.

New Age

The Harp Column

hbrock@harpcolumn.com
www.harpcolumn.com
A place for people interested in the harp to share information and ideas through interactive discussion groups, a calendar of events and news announcements.

Punk

Book Your Own Fucking Life

byofl@byofl.org
www.byofl.org
A resource guide for the punk/hardcore DIY community primarily used for booking tours. Take a gander at the listings.

Capitol Board Room

dave@capitolboardroom.com
www.capitolboardroom.com
Check out our online radio, shows, punk news, bands database and much more. Want to add your band to our database? You can edit your bands info at any time.

graynoise.net
info@graynoise.net
www.graynoise.net
To have a page on the Band Index all you have to do is send us your music for review. We will then, most likely, put your band's information on the database and that's that.

Grunnen Rocks scene *The Netherlands*
grunnenrocks@hetnet.nl
www.grunnenrocks.nl
Best thing to do is to send me some promos, preferably vinyl naturally. If I like the music and it's more or less connected to the "Grunnen Rocks scene" the band will be included a.s.a.p. I have to state the fact that specially sending me 7" singles makes my knees weak and gets your band included easily.

PunkRockShows.com
punkrockshows.com
Bands, Labels, Clubs - inform your fans of your upcoming shows by adding your dates to our extensive database of shows.

Ska, Mod and Punk Search Engine & Fanzine
(SKAHOO)
www.skahoo.com
Skahoo is a project brought to you by volunteers around the world and sponsored by Adelaide Ska band The Seen.

skapages.com
webmaster@skapages.com
www.skapages.com
This site has been set up to bring together different parts of our fragmented ska community, ie bands, ska Radio hosts, Record labels, Promoters, Zines etc... We'll all be able to help bring the music we love to larger and larger audiences.

SkaPonk.com
blax@SkaPonk.com
www.skaponk.com
Mainly a punk & ska lyrics search engine. It is a nice way to promote your band by adding your own lyrics and show them to the world.

Reggae

IREGGAE
www.ireggae.com
A web site livicated to change through the WORD, SOUND and POWER of Reggae Music.

The Official Israeli Reggae Site
www.irielion.com/israel
Reggae Concerts, Festivals, Shows and Radio in Israel.

One Love Reggae
onelove@humboldt.net
www.onelovereggae.com
A Reggae public service featuring band listings, calendar guide, festivals and much more!

Reggae Festival Guide Online
kaati@reggaefestivalguide.com
www.reggaefestivalguide.com
Online version of the popular, Reggae Festival Guide magazine. Find reggae festivals around the world!

USABB Reggae
info@ReggaeMusic.us
reggaemusic.us
USABB is provided as a free service website to all USA based reggae bands. Send us your band profile!

Women in Music

Ask Nancy!
Nancy Falkow   asknancynow@hotmail.com
stations.mp3s.com/stations/0/the_women_of_mp3com.html
A Q&A format that addresses a wide spectrum of music related issues. E-mail Nancy with any music related questions you may have.

Bad Ass Bitch Bands
brookemh@isoc.net
www.angelfire.com/punk2/femalebands
This site is dedicated to punk/metal/grunge/Goth female musicians everywhere.

Banner Women
bannerwomen.com
A banner network designed to help women-oriented websites with limited or no advertising budget earn free advertising/promotion for their website to a target audience of women online!

Beauty in Music
info@beautyinmusic.com
www.beautyinmusic.com
The ultimate guide to the hottest women in classical music.

beer for grrls
wonthecat_fight@hotmail.com
www.dork.com/bfg
I promote bands that play the kind of music I am into. (Hardcore punk, 77 style punk, oi, punk rock...) However; if you're sure I'll be blown away by your band go ahead and email me anyway.

BGIRLSTYLE.com
bgirl@bgirlstyle.com
bgirlstyle.com
Hip hop website dedicated to promotion and providing an alternative means of exposure for female hip hop artists. Got what it takes to be our featured B-GIRL of the month? We are looking for the dopest female DJ's, the loveliest lyricists and the most butteriest break girls to feature each month.

Billy Caldwell Photography
billcaldwell@bcphotos.com
www.bcphotos.com
I shoot subjects that I am passionate about and nothing else. You will never find any pop stars or "supermodels" here.

blackgirl international
staff@blackgirl.org
www.blackgirl.org
The sites we host are now being ranked with one, two, or three stars. One star represents a good solid web site. Two stars represent an outstanding, well-designed professional Web site. Three stars represent Web sites that absolutely must not be missed — and our reviewing staff is reluctant to hand out three stars.

Blood Sisters
hannah@ravenousplankton.com
kzsu.stanford.edu/~hannah
We're attempting to collect info on every woman who's ever been a permanent member of a heavy band - but we also have individual listings for women who've done large amounts of session work for heavy bands and women who've done other things to advance the cause.

BunnyBass
bunnies@bunnybass.com
www.bunnybass.com
Looking at our girl's gallery, some people may say 'so where are the guys?' well, I figure it's okay to have an all-girl archive since pretty much the whole net is already an all-guy bass players picture archive.

Chick Bands that Rock
ju924@hotmail.com
geocities.com/grrlbands
This page is dedicated to all the female musicians. Power of music is the Power of life. This page consists of punk, crust, metal, Riot grrl and other types of music, however NO BRITTNEY SPEARS shit here. Want To plug your band/ or other cool band you know of? Then e-mail me!!!!

Chick Singer Night
la@chicksingernight.com
www.chicksingernight.com
The nation's original and longest-running songfest for female artists. The format is a simple one. All singers are welcome; all styles of music, all levels of experience, all walks of life.

DiVAstation.com
yiannis@divastation.com
www.divastation.com
This site will focus on a panorama of female singers - from those who have proven themselves worthy to those who are just starting out on the road to the divine. You will find pictures, bios, news and reviews of some of your favorite female singers.

Donne in Musica *(Women in Music)*
controcanto@donneinmusica.org
www.donneinmusica.org
Holds many concerts and events promoting women's music in Italy, especially championing women composers. Organizes an annual Symposium in Fiuggi, Italy: women from around the world come together for music and discussion.

European Tourdates
www.sphosting.com/grlbndzring/rge/tourdates.html
Tour- and gig dates of European Grrrlbands, or grrrlbands visiting Europe. If you know of any dates you think should be put up on our site, send them in!

FEMALE PRESSURE
indigo@indigo-inc.at
www.indigo-inc.at
International database for female djs and/or producers, mostly in the electronic scene. Everybody represented on the list is able to update and modify her personal data independently. If you want to be part of it or you know somebody who should appear, don't hesitate to send me an e-mail. You never walk alone!

Feminine Pressure
info@femininepressure.co.uk
www.femininepressure.co.uk
www.femininepressure.co.uk/femininepressure.htm
London's Hottest Female DJ's. During the early years DJ Touch successfully promoted female DJ'ing at its best. Working with various female DJ's under her Feminine Pressure umbrella, DJ Touch laid the foundations for many females to follow suit.

FemMuse
rynata@shredmistress.com
www.femmuse.com
Female musicians and artists network. FemMuse is dedicated to furthering the cause and development of female performers everywhere.

Fiddlechicks

webmaster@fiddlechicks.com
www.fiddlechicks.com

The website was a result of my journey of getting started with electric violin. There wasn't a lot of information for beginners, or role models. I have since discovered that there are LOTS of little-known and unknown FiddleChicks.

FIRE Feminist International Radio Endeavour

fuegocr@racsa.co.cr
www.fire.or.cr

Our objective is to promote the presence of women in the media. To contribute to strengthen local, national, regional and global communications networks of women, participating in their activities and organizations. To promote the human rights of women. To produce FIRE — Feminist International Radio Endeavor — in English and Spanish for radio and Internet.

Girlband.org

dave@girlband.org
girlband.org

Database of girl bands and female artists of all genres.

Grrrl Band Network

hazelokeefe1@hotmail.com
tribe8industry.tripod.com

Our aim is to help unsigned grrrl bands in the UK.

Grrrl Bands Classified

Dautobrody@aol.com
members.aol.com/dautobrody/gbc/f2.html

A free ad space for grrrls all around the world to help them find other grrrls nearby with similar musical interests.

Guerrilla Girls

gg@guerrillagirls.com
www.guerrillagirls.com

We are available to speak at schools, museums and organizations of all types. We've appeared in almost every state in the U.S. and on almost every continent. We tailor our performances and lectures to each audience; we can also do gigs coupled with workshops or informal meetings with smaller groups

gURLpages

gURLpages@gurl.com
www.gurl.com

The homepages here on gURLpages are FREE. There is no cost to you to make a page and later edit it. You must be at least 13 years old to set up a homepage on gURLpages.

Heartless Bitches International

nataliep@heartless-bitches.com
www.heartless-bitches.com

Join up and be proud to use phrases like: "Keep it in your pants, asshole", "Oh why don't you just masturbate and get over it!?", "No, you can't watch.", "Wah, fuckin', Wah." List information about you or your band on our music page.

Herland Sister Resources

HerlandSisters@cox.net
members.cox.net/herlandsisters/main.html

We are a womanist organization with a strong lesbian focus. However, Herland is not restricted to just lesbians. All women are welcome. We are located at 2312 N.W. 39, OKC, OK 73112.

Indiegrrl

hsfigueroa@indiegrrl.com
www.indiegrrl.com

A forum for information, networking and conversation about independent music from a female perspective. Indiegrrl has evolved into several entities, including Indiegrrl Records (a not for profit label, releasing 4 compilations per year) Indiegrrl Inc. (a non profit organization supporting women in the industry) ITA and Indiegrrl Events. There is also a popular discussion list that you can subscribe to.

International Women in Jazz

zenzalai@aol.com
www.internationalwomeninjazz.com

Our goal is to create equal opportunity for women in the jazz community by undertaking advocacy efforts and by providing programs and activities that offer information, assistance, support and opportunity for professional development to our membership.

Ladyfest

www.ladyfest.org

Each Ladyfest is dedicated to showcasing, promoting and encouraging the artistic talents, organizational abilities and political goals of women. Ladyfest is an all-inclusive, women-run event and all are welcome to attend. Ladyfests are now world-wide. Check out website for an event taking place near you.

Lawgirl.com

jodisax@earthlink.net
www.lawgirl.com

A free, interactive legal resource for those in the arts and entertainment, with an emphasis on music issues. Learn about copyright and trademark issues for your band, what it takes to get signed and more.

Les Filles du Metal

webmaster@metalgirls.com
www.metalgirls.fr.st

Pictures gallery, multimedia pages, links, directories and a forum.

Lesbian and Gay Bands of America

LGBAinfo@aol.com
www.gaybands.org

The national musical organization comprised of concert and marching bands from cities across America and the world. Bringing Pride and Understanding through music.

National Association of Black Female Executives in Music and Entertainment (NABFEME)

NABFEME@aol.com
www.womenet.org

A professional referral, networking, empowerment and support group for African American women in radio, recorded music, film, television, print media and related entertainment industry fields.

The National Women's Music Festival

wia@wiaonline.org
wiaonline.org/nwmf

The Festival is a three-day musical and cultural extravaganza that tries to incorporate all facets of women's lives. It's a jam-packed weekend where you can choose from workshops, concerts, theatre presentations, dances, a shopping mall, newly released films and videos and much, much more!

ONLINE COMPENDIUM OF CHICK ROCKERS

dahlia@rockerchick.com
www.rockerchick.com

Select women and/or bands which have been influenced by, or have been influential in, the punk and alternative music scenes.

The Other Side

Laura Lasley babydoclaz@aol.com
www.guitarnoise.com/otherside

Have you ever noticed that most of the people playing and talking about playing guitar are guys? Many of the artists talked about are guys. What about the Other Side??? Don't think of guitar as a male sport; it's for anyone with a love of music.

Pan Pipes

Marcia Williams pipesSAI@aol.com
www.sai-national.org/pubs/panpipes.html

A fraternity journal that goes to all college chapter members, alumnae in good standing, patronesses, , public libraries and leaders in musical circles. It carries news of chapter activities, achievements of individual members, reviews of books and recordings and articles by well known leaders in the music field.

Punk Girl

infos@panx.net
www.panx.net/punkgirl

A cool punk rock girl art gallery, made for you to enjoy! Do not hesitate to send your punk rock girl pics to us (in bands, at gigs...) so that we include them in our art gallery.

Riot Grrrl Tabs & Lyrics

carrotsandcelery@yahoo.com.
www15.brinkster.com/grrrltabs

Yr struggles won't go unnoticed. Send a rad picture of yourself rocking out and I'll put it here!

rockabillygirls.com

kelly@rockabillygirls.com
www.rockabillygirls.com

We are dedicated to compiling the largest Internet database hopelessly devoted to rockabilly, psychobilly, western swing and swing female-led bands.

Rocket Girl

admin@rocketgirls.net
www.rocketgirls.net

The one stop source for all things grrrl. Aren't you tired of being looked down on just because of your gender? People who think you're a novelty just because you can play and write music?

Sigma Alpha Iota International Music Fraternity

nh@sai-national.org
www.sai-national.org

Our mission is to encourage, nurture and support the art of music. Our vision is to be recognized throughout the world as the foremost fraternity that supports and encourages women musicians of all ages, races and nationalities. Supports and promotes successful and innovative educational programs in music for all stages of life and cultivates excellence in musical performance.

Sirens of Song

brian@sirensofsong.com
www.sirensofsong.com

A web page dedicated to some of my favorite female singers. I've decided to shine the spotlight on some great singers who aren't household names or multi-platinum selling artists, but deserve to be.

Sirens Wild Ride
Athena Reich info@sirenswildride.com
www.sirenswildride.com
*A national touring collective of female
singer/songwriters. The tour will be pairing up with
women's rights organizations, women and LGBT
organizations in local markets to create more than
just a show. Rather, each show will become a
gathering where local women's groups can publicize
upcoming events, meet and greet and learn about
other national companies reaching out to women's
communities.*

SISTA Factory *(Soulful Inspirational Sounds To
Admire)*
sistafact@aol.com
www.sistafactory.com
*A leading performance series, which promotes and
showcases diverse performing artists. These
performers were selected for their ability to move
audiences with the soulful essence of their music
whether they are performing classic R&B, alternative,
rock, jazz and gospel.*

Skirt Magazine
editor@skirtmag.com
www.skirtmag.com
*We try to feature CDs by women each month. No
reviews — they go in what we call Skirt! Soundtrack
— basically what we are listening to each month.
Send your CD in. I can't promise to use it but I will
definitely consider it.*

Women at the Piano
PianoWomenEditor@aol.com
www.pianowomen.com
*This site lists the names of over 200 women who
concertized on a national/ international level from
1750 to the present.*

Women in Jazz
jazzmaster@jazzusa.com
jazzusa.com
*We have attempted to collect and present information
here about Women in Jazz, both past and present. This
collection covers the full spectrum of years and
genres, but is by no means all-encompassing. This is a
work in progress. If you know of someone that should
be included here, please let us know.*

Women in Metal
metalkeir@yahoo.com
www.geocities.com/svipdaag/grrls
*This page focuses on permanent female members of
heavy metal bands.*

Women in Music, Inc
wim@womeninmusic.org
www.womeninmusic.org
*Through educational seminars, networking events,
showcases, jams, publications, our annual Touchstone
Awards and other gala events, we provide
camaraderie and tools for advancement to hundreds
of members at all stages of their careers. We also
publish Women in Music Magazine (WIM). You'll find
interviews, profiles, opinion pieces, explanations of
important legal issues and more.*

Women In Music Ministry
WomeninMusicTalk@aol.com
www.womeninmusicministry.com
*Our goal is to connect Music Ministry Wives across
the nation for the purpose of encouragement and
support. Through this web site and through the
Women In Music Ministry newsletter, you will be able
to share your thoughts and perspectives with hundreds
of other Women in Music Ministry.*

Women in Production
kimberly@womeninproduction.com
www.womeninproduction.com
*Reviews, features, links, on and offline resources for
Independent women in music.*

Women in Rock Concert Series
WomenNRok@aol.com
www.womennrock.com
*We help bands of various rock genres, band formats
and professionalism all for a good cause. Network
with bands from different regions as well as different
levels of experience...from the new local artists to the
more professional and established regional acts, to
International & National Recording Artists.*

The Women of Metal
discowabbit@aol.com
drink.to/thewomenofmetal
*If you think I left any great artists out please mail me
and I would be more than glad to add them. Be sure
to put "Woman of Metal" in the subject area.*

Women of Rock Pic Collection
ric@women-of-rock.com
www.women-of-rock.com
*You'll find over 500 photos here from more than 100
women of rock. The selection is subjective and there is
a lot more to come! I prefer pictures with an erotic
aura, but there's not too much naked skin here.*

Women Rockin' 4 Women Festival
webmaster@womenrockin4women.org
www.womenrockin4women.org
*Founded in late 1998 by Tiffany Poinsett of the band
Baby Jane Hudson. Tiffany's vision was to combine
her talent, friends, contacts and knowledge of the
music business to help victims of domestic violence.
With the support of her former band and several other
local artists, Tiffany was able to make this dream an
annual event featuring female performers.*

Women's Festival
editor@womensfestival.com
www.womensfestival.com
*Women all over the world are creating festive
environments where we celebrate women's talents,
accomplishments, ideas, humor and friendships. We
hope that Women's Festival - A Global Listing helps
provide you the contact information you're looking
for.*

Women's Radio Fund
Abbott4Art@aol.com
www.womensradiofund.org
*Our mission is to build a support network for women
radio producers and broadcasters worldwide.*

wOMENinRocK
Jeff Harlan womeninrock@aol.com
www.womenrock.org
*Dedicated to providing music industry resources and
performance opportunities for new and emerging
independent women in music. We are accepting
material solicitations.*

World

Buenos Aires Tango Jazz
Andrea Bo tangojazz@argentina.com
tangojazz.sitio.net
*Data, music, videos online about tango, jazz, world
music, ballet, flamenco, artists from Argentina.*

Section Six:
Articles that will Help you to Succeed in the Music Business

"Remember that each time you sing, play, write, perform, discuss, pitch, etc. you are creating a reality that supports your dream.

Don't forget to applaud the little steps, as well as the big."

Janet Fisher,
Goodnight Kiss Music

While creating The Indie Bible I have been fortunate enough to have met many of the most knowledgeable people in the Independent music industry. Successful authors, publicists, music reviewers, entertainment lawyers etc. I thought it would be a perfect fit if I presented several of their articles to help you gain insight on how to deal with the many twists and turns of this complicated industry. The articles in this section are sure to be helpful to musicians and songwriters, and especially to those that are just starting out. Every author I asked was kind enough to submit an article that will help you to move forward with your music career. Do yourself a favor, and put their experience to work for you!

r a d i o   a i r p l a y

GETTING RADIO AIRPLAY
by Lord Litter, host of Lord Litter's Radio Show
© 2004, Lord Litter. All Rights Reserved. Used By Permission

It was the late 80's and I was doing freelance work for a commercial radio station. The first thing I discovered was an enormous heap of releases in the hallway. I asked "what's this all about?" - "these are releases that didn't reach a *fitting* DJ" - "what will happen to these?" - "they will be thrown away, we get piles every day". This made me realize that there is something definitely wrong with the commercial music world. I wanted to DJ 'cause I love the music ... so I left this *music scene*.

Ever since I started to keep my radio work on a *controlled and personal* level, I never again sought mass appeal. Here are some hints how to approach DJs on what I like to call *our level*. Small real indie bands/companies with a professional attitude. Practical advice based on my experience. Not very structured because I have to listen to another 78468264 releases by tomorrow... yes it's that *bad*!

An important aspect of a release surely is that it can be used to promote the band/musician. If you don't take care of certain areas, your music MIGHT be on air but no one will get to know who you are and where they can buy your music...so the whole promotional effect is lost.

Here are things that give me trouble and that I think may cause other DJs to NOT play the release.

1. EVERY item you send should have a clearly marked address. Info material will be separated from the release. So if there is no address on the cover for example, then you'll get no playlist, your address will be not spread etc...

2. Since the CD became THE medium, some bands should send magnifying glasses with their releases. Some covers look great but the writing is either much too small or the use of colors make it impossible to read. Make it as easy as possible to identity the name of your band, the song order and a contact address. You wouldn't believe how many releases I get that are a real pain concerning the before mentioned aspects.

The more *well known* a DJ is the *better* the *promotional effect*. It also means that a *known* DJ gets piles of releases every day. Therefore, the time to care about the individual release shrinks to almost *seconds* - leaving no time left to care about questions like "what is the name of the band and what is the title of the release?"... even that is unclear with some releases.

3. Info/pix/etc.: Don't send heaps. It is impossible to read ten pages to get the basic info about a band. Send a reduced informative version of your material with the offer to send more if interested. A link to your website is what I appreciate.

4. Give all of your material a professional approach. I'm not talking about spending more money. Copied sheets are ok. Copied on a bad machine causes making it very difficult to read is not ok. Just a little hint to go by.

5. DJs are human beings - yes they are! Treat them like you want to be treated. *My rule* is if a band/label never answers to any of my comments, I lose interest in them completely. No need to send endless letters, but a short "Hey, thanks - airplay really appreciated!" proves that you *care* about your music and about the one that *cares* about your music - the DJ.

6. The best way to get in touch is to check in before you send your music and say something like "We heard about your show from ... would you be interested in our music? We play some ... our website is ...". That's a perfect way to start. If the DJ doesn't answer you can forget him/her anyway. You might not even get playlist later. The basic idea here is to keep it somehow personal. You'll discover that it creates a very positive effect - in some cases you might even find a friend!

7. If you send CDRs (I do broadcast these!) make sure they really work! I have one CD player that doesn't take badly burned CDs. So, if your CD (in the running order of the show) must be played on that player and it doesn't work, it will not be played... nor on the next show on another player 'cause in-between I received another zillion CDs. Your CD will be lost *forever*.

I could go on forever talking about this... the basic idea is: make it as easy as possible to *handle* your material. Before you finish your material, take it to the printing etc. and give it to someone who doesn't know anything about it, and ask if the required aspects are clear. If not - change it!

And on *our* level: never forget *the personal aspect*!

I know it's a lot of work ... the alternative would be: become rich, hire a professional promoter and watch how your release will be thrown away with the others...

The answer is always *somewhere in the middle* as we say in Germany. Be professional but never forget the personal aspect - that indicates the difference to the *music only as commercial value* scene...

Lord Litter has earned the reputation for producing and delivering what is arguably one of the world's best independent music programs. Since the early 1990s, Lord Litter has known the pulse of independent music, and today, indie musicians from all over the planet know that his program is one of the ultimate destinations for their music. website: http://www.LordLitter.de

♦

RADIO AIRPLAY - TIPS FOR SUCCESS
by Geneva World, GirlMedea

As a former DJ and Music Director of the college station KCRH, I have experienced a variety of self-promotion (dare I say guerrilla?) tactics of indie musicians trying to get airplay. I have wept as indie musicians have hounded me and other times politeness has resulted in high rotation for an artist on my show.

There are tricks to submitting your music to radio stations. Don't assume that your talent alone will get you airplay, nor believe that your great selling techniques will get you on the playlist. You can save a lot of money, time and self-respect by following the below guidelines.

1. **Make sure your music is ready to be heard on the radio.**

    This is the most important rule I can give you. Unless the radio station says that it accepts demos or indie recordings, don't send material that has not been properly recorded and mastered.

2. **Just because you "give" the station your CD, it doesn't mean they owe you.**

    I get bands that call me every week, telling me that they sent in their album and are telling their friends about my radio show. They continue to tell me who else is playing them, where they are appearing, how many times they have called and ask why am I not jumping all over them. I expect this from PR and record labels. That's their job, and in most cases they are offering a product that is suitable, popular and have a relationship developed with me. But, if you're going it alone, do not make yourself a nuisance. Do not make me feel like I OWE you for the CD you sent in. It's the quickest way to becoming a coaster.

3. **Do not go through DJs (unless otherwise noted).**

    Little known fact: DJs are at the bottom of the barrel. Unless they produce their own show (normally only college stations) the playlist is made by the Music Director. You want to send your material to the Music Director. Not the DJ.

4. **Do not make more then one follow-up phone call.**

    You have two choices. Call once and make contact with the Music Director to tell them the CD is on their way, or call about 3 weeks after sending the CD to check on its status. Unless you are told to make contact again, don't. You will be considered a pest (and Music Directors talk to one another). When you make the follow-up phone call, inform the Music Director of who you are, the band name, what type of music you play and when you sent the CD. Give them your phone number (it probably won't be written down) and say you are free to talk anytime.

    If the Music Director says s/he has listened to the CD and does not think it is suitable, don't continue to sell yourself. They have made up their mind, and rarely do they reverse it. What you should do is ask for *why* the CD was not chosen (you may get tips for improvement next time) and if they know anyone who may be interested. Thank them for listening to it.

    If you are told that you are going to be on the playlist, do not go overboard with questions. Ask when you may expect to see yourself in rotation, what songs will be used and if the station would be interested in having you appear live on one of the shows. If the answers are not available, ask when it would be a better time.

    * I've been seeing bands include a postcard SAS (self addressed stamped) prompting me to pop it in the mail when I receive the CD and if I plan on playing any songs. Expensive, but wonderfully effective.

5. **Research before you send your CDs out.**

    CDs cost money - don't waste yours. Only send your CD to radio stations that play your style. As simple as it sounds, too many bands don't research where they send their music. At a rap station, I still know of folk CDs that get sent in. At a classical station, I've heard of classic rock appearing. This does not get you airplay. So, call the station or check out their website and find out the station's format.

6. **List which songs could be singles.**

    Labels tend to pick which songs will be singles and radio will follow those guidelines (most of the time). Don't make the Music Director search your entire CD for a hit. I will normally try three tracks and listen for 30 seconds. If nothing moves me, to the pile it goes. What if I hit the wrong three tracks? I don't add you to the playlist. Invest in buying stickers to place on your CD with tracks listed that you think make good singles.

7. **Don't send a book for your press release.**

    Personally, I like bulky press releases. I like knowing about the bands that I like. But that's because I do interviews and reviews. With the rare exception of myself, sending in big press releases just destroys trees. In a cover letter, try to cover the most important information about yourself. Keep it simple and include contact info. Including a photo of the band signed.

    Make good use of The Indie Bible. This will help you with your research and get those CDs of yours out the door. Also, don't neglect internet radio stations. They are a perfect training ground for new bands.

Geneva World is a former DJ and Music Director of the college station KCRH in Los Angeles, and also produced the highly popular Internet radio show, Girl Power Flower Hour.

♦

RADIO AIRPLAY 101 - COMMERCIAL AIRPLAY MYTHS
by Bryan Farrish, Bryan Farrish Radio Promotion

When talking to people who are launching their first couple of projects, invariably the same misunderstood points come up concerning commercial regular-rotation airplay. Here they are:

DJs PLAY THE RECORDS: This only applies to non-commercial radio, and specialty/mixshow radio. The majority of people in the U.S. listen to commercial regular-rotation radio, and on these stations, the DJs have no say at all in what is going to be played (unless, in the case of a smaller station, the DJ is also the PD). So, the biggest pitfall to avoid is asking a DJ at a commercial station "Can I give you my CD for possible rotation?" The DJ is not allowed to say "No", and he/she is probably not going to explain that only the PD can approve regular rotation. The DJ is just going to say "OK".

GOOD SONGS SPREAD TO OTHER STATIONS: Good songs (or for that matter, good programs) do not mystically spread to other stations. Every single song you hear (or every syndicated program you hear) on commercial regular-rotation radio is on that station because of layers of promotion and marketing. The song you hear was the one that made it... it beat out the other 300 songs that were going for adds that week. What you don't hear are the endless phone calls, faxes, trade ads, personal meetings, consultant recommendations, call-out research, and other things which went into getting the station to add the record. All you heard was the record itself. The station owners make it a requirement that DJs make it sound like they picked the music themselves.

COLLEGE OR SPECIALTY/MIXSHOW WILL EXPAND TO COMMERCIAL: Just because you do well on non-commercial or specialty/mixshow radio, it does not mean anything will happen on commercial regular-rotation radio. Nothing at all will happen at commercial unless a separate, higher-level campaign is put into place to take the record into regular rotation. The pitfall here is that a listener will hear something on college, and then a month later hear it on commercial, and conclude that the college caused the commercial to happen. The listener did not know that both campaigns were in place simultaneously, and the college simply went for adds a month earlier.

YOU HAVE TO BE SIGNED: Untrue. Being signed is only a signal to the stations that the basic marketing practices are going to be done right. If you have the budget, you can duplicate the marketing practices of larger labels, provided you know how. The band Creed set a good example of putting their $5 million marketing dollars into the right place.

REQUEST CALLS WILL HELP: Not really. They won't hurt, but your time is better spent doing other things, like inviting people to your gigs. Stations know which calls are real, and which are bands and their friends. Stations have consultants and seminars which cover this *one* topic.

I CAN'T GET AIRPLAY WITHOUT DISTRIBUTION: It depends on the size of radio that you are going after. Smaller commercial regular-rotation stations in smaller markets won't make this too much of a sticking point, especially if you have a powerful radio campaign going, or if you are doing great gigs in their city, or if you have great college or specialty/mixshow results. But the larger stations... which you can't work anyway until you do the smaller ones... won't touch a project that has no distribution.

I CAN'T GET AIRPLAY WITHOUT GIGS: Again, it depends on the size of radio that you are going after. Not being able to gig is a serious handicap at any station, but you can overcome it in smaller markets with intense radio promo, press, sales, and non-comm results.

NON-MONITORED STATIONS ARE OF NO USE: Non-monitored stations are of no use only on the Billboard, R&R, and the seven Album Network mag charts. But FMQB, CMJ and all specialty/mixshow charts are compiled manually. Since you need to start off on these smaller charts first, this works out just fine.

Bryan Farrish is an independent radio airplay promoter. He can be reached at 818-905-8038 or airplay@radio-media.com. Information and other articles can be found at http://www.radio-media.com

◆

HOW RETAIL AND RADIO WORK TOGETHER
by Bryan Farrish, Bryan Farrish Radio Promotion
© 2004 All Rights Reserved. Used By Permission

We recommend that a new label get their radio and gigs going first (so they can sell their CDs at the gigs). If the label gets to where it has at least four or five acts, and EACH one is charting in their respective airplay chart, and is doing 100+ gigs per year, and is getting 50+ articles/reviews per year, then it MIGHT be time to consider real retail promotion and distribution. No sooner than this, and not with less than four acts. And when we say retail, we're not talking about consignment.

The first thing you'll want to do once your distro is set up (real distro, not web) is set up a retail promotion. This will cost you $3,000 to $15,000 with particular chains; and will probably include ads in the chain's house publication, and a buy-in of 500 to 3000 units from the chain. You will also want to tag the fact that you are doing radio. If the promotion is big enough ($35,000+) you'll get POP in addition to the listening stations and ads. You can also go beyond this by trying to get talkers on your bin or listening stations, on which you would print something like "As Heard On WXWY"... provided of course you are spinning on that station.

Next up on the cost ladder are co-op ad (or underwriting) buys on the pertinent stations. In the case of music, "co-op" is you paying 100% of the bill. You run the spots for your release(s), which include tagging of the local retailer. And, if you can afford it, a remote at the retailer would make everyone happy. Remotes start at about $300 in small/unrated markets, $3,000 in medium markets, and $30,000 in major markets. Your releases are not the focus of a remote, but then they don't need to be... everyone at the station will know who paid the bill.

You'll also want to coordinate drop-bys (or "meet-and-greets" or

full performances) with the stores, while the artist is in-town visiting stations. While at the stores, ask the GM if he/she would like to post the playlist of the station somewhere in the store (hopefully you are on it) if it's not already there. While it's true that the first thing a station does is try to get its playlist into stores, extra help from smiling folks like you won't hurt.

Don't forget to ask the stations (or have your radio promoter ask the stations) for their recommended stores that your product should be placed in, and further, what is the name of the buyer is that you or your retail promoter should speak with there. When you do speak to that buyer, you have a greater chance of them caring what you have to say if you preface it with "Bob at WXYZ is playing our record and said you might be interested in it... can I send you a copy?"

One last area of available exposure would be the community events announcements that stations make. Many stations (even college stations) have someone whose job it is to collect and announce what interesting things are occurring in their town that week. When you have a confirmed appearance/performance at a store, make sure the station hears about it. If your announcement is aired, try to get a tape or transcription of it, and give it to the store GM or buyer to impress them.

Lastly, there is the need to inform the distro's reps about your project. Even with real distro, you (being a new indie) are just a single page in their book of 1000 other releases that they take with them when they meet with buyers. In their twenty minute meetings, maybe they get around to talking about ten releases; yours will not be one of them, unless it has more "apparent activity" than all the other 990 releases (most of which are major labels.) So you have to make it appear to the rep that you have a lot of things going on, and you do this by informing them, once a week, of everything that is happening with your project.

Bryan Farrish Radio Promotion is an independent radio airplay promotion company. 818-905-8038 www.radio-media.com. If you live in Los Angeles and want to be informed of any events, seminars or parties we do, email meet@radio-media.com and tell us what town you are in.

◆

INDEPENDENT RADIO PROMOTER CHECKLIST
by Bryan Farrish, Bryan Farrish Radio Promotion
© 2004 All Rights Reserved. Used By Permission

If you are hiring a promoter to push your artist to radio, here are a few things you can consider which will help you have the greatest chance of success (and when I say promoter, I mean an airplay promoter, not a club or booking promoter). The big concern with this process is, if you choose the wrong person(s) to promote your artist... and end up with bad results... you can't just go back and do it over again. That's it for that CD (at those stations). That CD is now "an old project" at those stations, and you can't go back to them until you have a new release.

USING A FRIEND: Non-experienced friends sometimes offer to work artists to radio for free or "for a few dollars". This is fine as long as you use them for the right tasks... like helping with the mailing, etc. If you are working college radio... say, no more than 20-30 stations... then they could make some calls too. But if they try to call any more stations than this, or if they try to call commercial radio, they will probably stumble after just a couple of weeks. And forget about any capacity of doing reports or trade charts.

SOMEONE FROM THE MAJORS: Staff promoters at major labels sometimes offer to "help you out on the side" for a fee. On their days off, or on the weekend, they say they will "make some calls for you". What happens is that their company finds out and disallows it, or, the person gets tied up on their days off and can't do it. You are then stuck. Either way, it is a conflict of interest for them.

PR PEOPLE: Public Relations (or "publicity") people sometimes offer to work an artist to radio for airplay. But don't, however, confuse PR with airplay. A real radio campaign has nothing to do with publicity. They are two separate techniques, with different contacts, lead times, terminology, call frequency, and so on. A person who is good at one is usually terrible at the other. This is why they are always separate departments at labels.

STATION PEOPLE: Station employees are sometimes recruited to work an artist, and will tell you that "they know what stations want." This sounds convincing, but in reality, taking the calls (which they do/did at the station), and making the calls, are very different animals. Until station people are trained (at a label or indie), they make poor promoters.

OWN CHART: When you do hire a real promoter, make sure he/she is not affiliated with the chart that they say they are going to promote you to. Some promoters actually publish their own chart, and they can put you on it wherever they want to. And they can take you off just as quick. Also, any advertising money you place with the publication actually just goes straight to them. They won't make any of this clear to you... you'll have to ask around.

BIG CLIENTS: The most-often used sales technique of promoters is to tell you they have worked "some big artist", and that this would benefit you. Ask them what they mean by "worked". Were they solely responsible for charting that artist? Probably not (you will have to ask the artist to verify this... the promoter is just not going to tell you the truth.) More than likely, the promoter was probably just partnered with a label or another promoter, or worse, was just an assistant or sidekick. Again, they WILL NOT tell you they were not the only promoter. You will HAVE to ask the artist or the artist's management directly. Promoters who really do work major label projects just do not like to work with entry-level projects. With major label projects, the indie promoter ALWAYS has staff promoters at the label doing a ton of the work - in addition to heavy retail (the CD is on the shelf at most bookstores), touring (20-200 cities in major venues), and press (10-100 articles in major publications like Spin or Billboard, along with 50-500 articles in small publications.) And all this is on top of TV appearances. So, if you think that the indie promoter is the one person who made the artist chart, think again. He will not be able to do the same for you.

The following are the more subtle things you should look for when hiring one...

CONTACTABILITY: This is probably going to be the one thing that you end up really liking or disliking about the way your indie operates. Some Indies are always there when you call, others are never there. The ones who never answer will invariably tell you, "I spend all my time on the phone talking with the stations... Isn't that what you want me to do with your project?" Good try. What these non-contactable Indies are actually doing is spending "some" time on the phone with "some" stations, and spending a lot more time dining at restaurants and seeing friends. And if you thought it was difficult reaching them before you hire them, just wait until AFTER they get your money. I see this again and again and again. If you think about it, an Indies' sole job is to talk on the phone. Why then, since they are by the phone, would they not pick up when you call? What if a station calls?

And that is the problem - they are NOT there when a station calls... because they REALLY DON'T spend that much time talking to stations on the phone. They only want you to think that they do. And worse, if they say they give clients (and potential clients) a different phone number to call than the one they give the stations, then you can guarantee that you (the paying client) will never get that person on the phone when you need them.

A true indie promoter is a non-stop call center, who gives TOP priority to incoming calls. They should have several people available to answer calls. If everyone is on another line when the phone rings, someone should HANG UP and answer that incoming call. Remember, incoming calls are top priority... it could be a station, and stations normally only call when they have good news.

REPORTS: Reports are a requirement that well-organized promoters provide to you. Without a report, there is no other way you are going to be able to understand what is going on with your airplay each week... much less someone else such as stores, papers, clubs etc.

OFFICE: If the promoter does not have an office (even a small one), then you will be competing with things like the promoter's sleep, TV, neighbors, dinner, etc.

ASSISTANTS: If a promoter handles more than one genre of music at the same time, or if the promoter does college radio at all, then assistants are mandatory. The phone calls have to be made, and no one person can call more than 150 stations a week AND do reports AND do faxes AND do emails AND talk to you when you call. Impossible!

COLLEGE RADIO: College should be considered for every campaign, even if you are doing high-level commercial radio. College radio is relatively inexpensive, and will allow you to create some good looking charts and reports to show retail, press and clubs.

FAXES: Serious promoters use faxes. Faxing is simply the fastest way to get a one-page synopsis of info to the stations... with pictures if needed. They are not cheap, but a good promoter should still include these faxes.

EMAILS: While you may get excited about email, remember that since email is free, stations get them from every artist on the planet. And all the emails look the same. So, in order to build a solid project, you must use faxes and phone calls, because most artists can't afford them (and that is why you will stand out.)

REFERENCES: Any promoter worth consideration will have a list of past clients. What you are looking for is a promoter with projects that are on your (independent) level. A list of "big" clients, however, means the promoter is used to having massive help from major label staff promoters, national tours, retail promotions, advertising, not to mention hundreds of newspaper, magazine, and TV appearances. Since that promoter will not have these with your project, your music will be very difficult for them to work. You need a promoter who is set up to work with indie projects like yours. Besides, real "major label" promoters DO NOT take indie projects.

The "major label" promoter was actually not the promoter that worked the major projects in the first place. They were probably just assistants in the office, or were mail people, or more often than not, they were just outright lying. It happens all the time. Ask the artist directly to find out.

Bryan Farrish is an independent radio airplay promoter. He can be reached at 818-905-8038 or http://www.radio-media.com. Want to be informed of any events, seminars or parties we do in Los Angeles?... send an email to meet@radio-media.com

getting your music reviewed

HOW TO SUBMIT MUSIC FOR REVIEW
by Jodi Krangle, The Muse's Muse

Getting the attention of music reviewers can be almost as difficult as breaking into a bank - and let's face it - sometimes far less profitable. But a good review is worth its weight in gold. So how does one go about getting reviewers to give your particular package the time of day? I receive quite a few of these packages myself, so while I'm no expert, I do have a few suggestions:

This may sound like it's too obvious to mention, but trust me - if you contact a potential reviewer by demanding their submissions address because you are simply the best thing that has happened to music since the microphone and the reviewer would be out of their mind to pass you up, you're likely to be disappointed at the response you receive. Sure, every artist deserves a chance. But you're biasing a reviewer against you right from the start if you use that tactic. Reviewers despise being taken for granted. Never assume you *deserve* a review - ASK for one.

Your initial contact should be polite and brief. A simple, "Hello, my name is (so and so) and I'm interested in a possible review in your (publication/web site). Would you be able to supply me with the proper contact information so that I can send you my CD?" will be kindly received. Even if it takes the reviewer a little while to get back to you - whether it's by regular mail, e-mail or through the feedback form of a web site - their reply will usually be helpful.

One last word on the subject of "first contact": PLEASE don't send an e-mail with your web site address and only a "Check this out!" line for clarification. You don't want to know how much spam e-mail I receive in a day and messages like that simply make me feel as if I'm being asked to check out the latest in cheesy porn. I delete such messages on sight and I honestly don't know many reviewers who pay them any attention either.

LEAVE THE KITCHEN SINK AT HOME

Your package should include an intro letter that addresses the reviewer by name whenever possible, a bio that's hopefully no longer than a page, a CD (CDs are the preferred medium these days. I'm afraid you're kidding yourself if you think otherwise), no more than three reviews in other publications and/or web sites, and that's about IT. Pictures are nice but they don't really matter as far as most publications are concerned. If a publication requires further material, you'll be contacted for it. Frankly, for myself, I'd rather give other reviews a complete miss. I rarely pay attention to them. I prefer to make up my own mind rather than read others' opinions before I've even had a chance to listen to the music myself. But I think that's really dependent on the type of publication you're sending your package to. Some publications and/or web sites might feel that favorable reviews elsewhere lend more credibility to the artist - which is one of the reasons you'd be asking for another review in the first place, right? Just because I disagree with that sentiment, doesn't mean that all reviewers will feel as I do. However, keep in mind that if you include too much, you run the risk of it all being ignored. After all, it's the MUSIC that really counts.

PRESENTATION

That said, the presentation of the CD itself is probably the most important element of your package. It's that CD that will give the reviewer their initial impression of your music - and (unfortunately or fortunately, depending on how you look at it) your professionalism. That doesn't mean you have to have spent thousands of dollars on your presentation, a huge CD insert, a gorgeous color cover, etc. That just means that your "look" should be consistent. Some of the packages that impress me the most are the ones that have an actual design in mind carried through from the CD to the stationary the cover letter is printed on and further. If you're not getting a professional printing of anything, a color inkjet printer creating your own letterhead along with a similarly designed CD covering sticker, will work quite nicely. Simplicity is often the best way to go. Above all, avoid sending in a blank recordable CD with black marker written on it. Your contact information should be on both the CD and the insert and/or cover. No matter *what* you do, make sure your contact information is easy to find. The insert certainly doesn't need to be in color but there should *be* one if at all possible. The insert is the perfect place to put contact information, credits (the reviewer is often fascinated by who did and wrote what. I know *I* am!), anecdotal information, etc - the things that make you special and different from the other folks the reviewer will be listening to.

I know what you're thinking. "Why not just include that stuff on a separate sheet of paper inside the package?" Well, for the same reason that your contact information NEEDS to be on the disc itself: the reviewer may not actually be taking the entirety of your package around with him/her (in fact, it's pretty unlikely!). The CD might become separated from the rest of your package and for that reason, you want it to be able to stand on its own as a professional piece of work, whether it retains its case or not. You want the reviewer to be able to contact you from that CD alone.

AS A RECAP:

Things to send in your package:

- A brief cover letter addressing the reviewer by name (a MUST)
- A bio (1 page!)
- A CD (tapes are a thing of the past folks!) - preferably with an insert of some kind.
- Up to 3 reviews if you really feel you need them (try to keep this on one or two pages)
- Keep the "look" simple and professional. You don't have to spend a lot of money to accomplish this!
- Make sure your contact information is on EVERYTHING.

Keep in mind that if your CD itself is a nice little package all on its own including inserts, you may not need the bio or the reviews and could probably get away with just sending in the CD and a cover letter. If you have a web site and include the URL to that site in your cover letter, the reviewer can find out tons more information on you should they wish to. As mentioned earlier, sometimes simple is best.

BE PATIENT

I don't mean to say that you shouldn't ever re-contact the reviewer. Not at all. Remind the reviewer you're around! Just don't do it every day. Wait a couple of weeks between contacts. Reviewers have a lot of demands upon their time and are frequently several weeks - or even *months*! - behind in their reviews depending on the publication(s) they write for.

BE POLITE

I mentioned that once before, didn't I? Probably because I consider it to be very important. The way in which you treat people will reflect upon your professionalism even more so than the look of your CD. It takes years to build up a good reputation and only a few minutes to completely destroy it. As with anything in the music business, you never know when someone you were kind to will be in a position to return that kindness. It's all about relationships. Make sure you're the sort of person who fosters good ones and it'll all come back to you.

How does this relate to tips about getting reviews? Above all, try to be pleasant. It may not seem like much, but believe me - the reviewer appreciates it a great deal. Don't demand to know why your CD wasn't chosen for a review and/or spotlight if you are told that it wasn't - not unless you actually want to hear what the reviewer has to say. And if that reviewer *does* let you know why, don't bad mouth him/her for telling you. You asked! I prefer not to review CDs that haven't impressed me, for whatever reason. I don't like the idea of putting up a lukewarm (or even BAD) review on a web site where people can be referring to it forever. I don't feel that's fair to the artist. In other words, if I'm not giving you a review, don't consider it a rejection. Consider it a kindness. Move on and keep in contact with the reviewer. It might be that a future release of yours will be better received.

I hope these hints have helped. Meanwhile, good luck with your music!

Jodi Krangle is Proprietress of The Muse's Muse Songwriting Resource http://www.musesmuse.com Visit http://www.musesmuse.com/musenews to find out more about our free monthly e-zine.

♦

WHAT A REVIEWER WANTS FROM AN ARTIST

by Keith Hannaleck, Independent Music Reviewer
© 2004 All Rights Reserved. Used By Permission

If you're an artist looking for reviews for your press kit, website, or quotes for your new album, how do you find the right people to review your music?

I am a music reviewer. When I started, I had to do something to build my reputation. I focused on acquiring music I enjoyed and sought out labels and artists that represented my interests. A lot of research and testing of the waters was involved. The same applies for the independent artist that does not have representation, nor can afford it. As an independent, you must do everything from promoting your music, running a website, and one of the most important pieces of the puzzle, getting some good reviews to attract attention to your product.

Whenever I would contact an artist or label, they requested a sample of my work. I would tell them that my website was my resume, and asked them to check it out. I designed, maintained, and uploaded all the content for my site, and that included all the reviews and interviews I had done. It was an effective combination that brought me to where I am today. I am all over the Internet. Do a search on Goggle under MuzikMan, you will get hundreds of hits.

As an artist, similar success is obtainable if you target your market. Find reviewers that cover your genre. Read their reviews and become familiar with their style of writing to see if you are comfortable with it.

The one thing that artists do all the time, that has me shaking my head, is that they will send me e-mails such as "Where do I send a CD for review?" or "Check out this song". Okay, first of all you are not telling me who you are, what kind of music you have created, where you are from, and if you have read any of my previous reviews. You are basically telling me you did zilch for research and are just sending out as many e-mails as you can to see what kind of response you will get. That's a crap shoot, and a huge waste of my time and yours. Once again, target your market. In a broader sense, target your audience, the potential reviewers, and the publications that they write for. Do your homework. Such an e-mail is liable to get no response, or something like "I'm sorry, I am not accepting reviews at this time."

The same thing goes when you send off your CD without contacting the reviewer. Don't do it! I don't have time to ask all of these questions to someone that wants me to do all the work; and then I have to pamper them to give them some direction and information that they should already have before approaching me for my free services.

You are asking for a professional review for no charge - something that is going to help you to promote your product and make money? Where else is this done? Think about that for a moment. It's a sweet deal for the artists. Just send your CD out and a review comes back no strings attached. Not a bad deal. I have piles upon piles of CDs in front of me at all times. What I have to do is eventually sit down and go through them all track by track to initiate a process of elimination. Can I afford to be selective? Your damned right I can. And once that's done, I discard at least 50% of what was sent to me, because it's something I simply do not like or it just isn't that good.

Most reviewers are just like you, they work day jobs, have families to support and they do all of their work at night while everyone else is winding down. Respect and treat others as you would like to be treated yourself. Do you think if you "make it" and hit it big you will have time to answer e-mails and promote yourself? I doubt it. There will be somebody else doing that for you. Respect the time it takes the media to get back to you.

I am in the position I always wanted to be in, which is to have access to the music I want to hear and enjoy. It took me a few years to get to that point, but I paid my dues like everyone else to position myself. Keep in mind, with success you will have a busy and tight schedule, and you only can do so much in a day.

There are tons of sites out their designed specifically for the Indie artist. There is also a lot of free information to educate yourself on the right way to market your music. You spend time and money to send out all those CDs and press kits - don't you want your music to end up in the right hands? Don't you want people that are into your kind of music to hear it and write about it? It makes sense.

Most artists do not have clue how to market themselves. I can you how many CDs I get that fall into genres I won't, and never have covered. I have received blank CDs with no tracks listed on them, no information to follow up with an artist, burned CDs with atrocious artwork and quality, CDs that skip all the way through. You name it and I have got it one time or another. On the flip side I have people that send me binders of information, and the music is just not my cup of tea. Online press kits are the way to go. If a reviewer accepts your invitation to listen to your music send back a link to your press kit. If they want more information on you they will get online and read it. Save yourself some time and money!

This is the life of a reviewer. This is reality. All of this is only my personal viewpoint and opinion...other reviewers may not agree. For a popular reviewer that is in demand, time is critical. If you are a good reviewer, you take your time and really listen to the music, and give it your best with every review. I do, and that's why the process is longer for me, and the CDs continue to pile up. A lot of reviewers just flip through a few tracks and write a paragraph. Anyone can do that. Believe me, it's always an honor to hear someone's work. The reward is the response you get from the artist after sending them a glowing review. For me the words that make it all worth it are "Thanks for the great review, I think you really got it." This means I understood their message and their music. For me that's what it's all about. So an "atta boy" never hurts. We have egos to you know. Just a quick e-mail to say thanks and acknowledge the work on your behalf is a nice gesture. To not acknowledge someone is rude and unacceptable. As hard as you work at putting that music together, a reviewer is out there that knows that, and expects nothing less from themselves. They will give back to the artists and their fans the same kind of effort with a fair, and well thought out review.

I do 30 to 40 reviews a month, including interviews and the occasional article when requested (like this one). I do it because I love it, period. I don't expect a pat on the back or kudos, I expect professionalism and respect from the person that wants my attention and a write-up.

Make sure you know who you are sending your requests to. What publications do they write for? Are they accepting submissions? If they are, how long before a review would be forthcoming? Do not bug the reviewer with e-mails asking if they have listened to the music yet; they will contact you when a review is ready. If you don't hear back in a reasonable amount of time, then contact them to ask if they plan on reviewing your music. You will get a yes or no, at least you would from me.

So, that's my viewpoint as the guy at the keyboard pounding out all the words. Don't forget now, I started reviewing my own music from my own personal collection before I wrote for all the publications I do now. I also had no formal journalism experience or education. When I look back at the reviews I wrote in 1998, I cringe. They were awful. I could look at any review I ever wrote and make changes to improve it, just as musicians do with their music.

What's my point with all of this? Some kind folks with experience helped me, and gave me a chance to get to where I am today. I know how that feels. That is why I support Indie artists. In a sense I am one too.

I will never forget from whence I came, but I refuse to deal with arrogance, laziness and unmotivated people. Those are my choices as an individual that insists upon high standards. That's what it's all about for me today as a reviewer and music lover. I want to give my best because I know each and every artist out there does the same when they record their music, whether I like it or not. We are all in the same boat traveling on the same sea. I hope all of this helps you before you decide to start promoting your music without thinking about how you are going to do it.

Keith "MuzikMan" Hannaleck is an independent music reviewer. Keith writes reviews for over a dozen music sites on the Internet, including Music Dish and ProgressiveWorld.net.

♦

GOOD REVIEWS BUT NO SALES? – 5 POSSIBLE REASONS WHY

by Marco Mahler, Recording Artist

© 2004 All Rights Reserved. Used By Permission

Wrong timing:

Coordinate your marketing/promotion program. Usually people need to hear or read more than once how great your music is until they buy it.

Do everything at once for each local market. For example: Locals read about you in the paper (pick the right paper(s) for your music) and in the article it also says that you are playing a gig next week in their town (pick the right place for your music). They hear your music played on the local station(s) (pick the right station(s) for your music). While they are walking down the street the next day they see your flyers, posters etc.

The night before the show arrange a live interview on the local station and mention again that you are playing tomorrow night (mention the time, place and how to get there). If there are some popular local bands playing on the same card, make sure you mention that. If you do all these things, you can expect more people to show up, which creates better sales.

Wrong time:

Some places/towns are just plain dead in certain seasons.

Lack of information on where to check your CD out:

Always give the best and most professional service, in the easiest and most comfortable way, and tell people that if they order your CD they will get it within X days (as fast as possible - they love it right now and they want to be able to listen to it right now (or within the next few days) "You can get the CD from the store around the corner / order it by phone / on the web / mail order / you can check us out next week at the venue in your neighborhood / we have samples on the web, as well and all other information / etc.

Get back to everyone right away / if possible personally / always let everybody know what's going on with your band.

Lack of mentioning your selling points / qualities (obvious ones and hidden ones) and qualities that differentiate you from the competition:

How many times have you read an article about a musician/band and it sounds great but it also sounds like any other review you've read - Tell them very specifically why you're great and why you're not just a copy/like every other band that does the same kind of music (a great, creative, unusual story always helps big time). Try to get all this into the material you send to the media.

Wrong audience/readers/listeners etc. :

"It doesn't make sense trying to sell meat to vegetarians". If you get the greatest review in a paper that's read by people who are not into the kind of music you create, you won't get any sales (unless you have a very smart marketing strategy, meaning one that builds a bridge between them and your music, giving them a reason why they would want to buy your music).

My music received airplay on WQXR (The station of the New York Times). This station has listeners who are mostly into classical music. My music is not classical and I didn't detect any results from the airplay even though the DJ said some very nice things about it.

Marco Mahler is an independent musician based in Brooklyn, NY. He has worked for several music marketing companies. Marco also creates visual art. Visit his site at http://www.marcomahler.com

♦

CREATING REAL AUDIO FILES

by Lynn Carey Saylor, GuitarGirls.com

© 2004, Lynn Carey Saylor. All Rights Reserved. Used By Permission

Often I have been asked how I create streaming Real Audio files for my GuitarGirls.com Web site. In this article I will share my knowledge about what programs I use to create these files and give a tutorial of the programs.

The software programs I use to make streaming Real Audio files are readily available for free download on the Internet. There are two basic programs I use to create the files from either an audio CD or an MP3 file - CDex file converter software (I got my copy at download.com) and RealSystem Producer basic (downloadable at RealNetworks.com). There is a MAC and a PC version of the RealSystem Producer available for free download at the site. When you go there, you will see a "plus" version which is fairly expensive to purchase, but you do not need that version to create Real Audio files. Downloading the free basic version of the software will get the job done.

The CDex file converter (available for PC only) is what I work with first when I want to make a Real Audio file of a song that is on CD or is in MP3 file form on my computer. File conversion software is critical to the making of Real Audio files because the RealSystem Producer, which is what you use to make the actual file, will only accept previously recorded audio files recorded in the following file formats: WAV, PCM and AU (on a PC) and AU, AIFF and System 7 SND (on a MAC).

For the record, another popular choice for file conversion on the PC is CoolEdit. The drawback though, is that unlike CDex, CoolEdit is shareware rather than freeware. In the demo version, there is a time limit of 30 minutes per session, and the save and clipboard functions are apparently disabled. The full version will set you back about $69. For the MAC, I have heard that Macromedia's SoundEdit 16 is very good, but as with CoolEdit, you'll be dipping into your pocket for this software.

With CDex, I don't spend a dime, and I turn my audio CD tracks and MP3 files into RealSystem Producer acceptable WAV files in a matter of seconds. It is extremely user friendly software.

1. First, if you are working with a CD, put it in your CD ROM drive and then open CDex. Automatically, all the tracks on your CD will appear in the main window.

2. You select (highlight) the track you want, pull down the "convert" menu and select "Extract CD track(s) to WAV file."

That's it! The rest is done for you. CDex will process your request and put the newly created WAV file in an output folder on your desktop.

Besides its ease of use, another nice feature of CDex is that you can set start and end points for your WAV file by selecting "extract partial CD track" (also located on the "convert" pull down menu). Using this feature, you can have total control over how much of your song you would like people to be able to stream - 30 seconds, 1 minute or any other length that you want to set. Are you starting with an MP3 file instead of a CD track? No problem. Use the very same "convert" pull down menu and select "MPEG to WAV." A "locate file" box pops up, you find the MP3, click on it and CDex is off and running creating your WAV file.

Once you have your WAV file, it's time to open up the RealSystem Producer software.

1. A box will pop up asking you to select a Recording Wizard for the media clip that you want to create.

2. Select the option "Record from File" and then click "O.K."

3. When the Recording Wizard box comes up, it will ask you to input or browse to find your file, which in the case of our discussion, is the WAV file we just created with CDex. Since I know that the file was sent by CDex to my desktop in a folder called "Output files," I know right where to go to find it.

4. Once the file is located and opened, it will appear back in the Recording Wizard box. Click "next."

5. The box that comes up will ask you to input the title, author and copyright information.

(Worth noting here is that the Recording Wizard will refer to the clip you are making as RealMedia rather than Real Audio. This is because the software makes both audio and video clips, so they refer to the output of either as RealMedia. This also explains why the Real Audio clip you are about to make will have the extension ".rm" after the song title).

6. When you are finished with the song information box, click "next" to select the file type. Always select the option "Single rate for Web Servers."

7. Click "next" once again to select your target audience. Since (generally speaking) most people now have at least a 56k modem, that is what I always select for my target audience.

8. The next page up will be the Audio Format page. The option to select here for a song with vocals is "Music" or "Stereo Music" depending on whether you want a higher quality mono output or a slightly less quality output in stereo. Now you are almost there.

9. The next page will be the Output File page. Since I want to keep my audio files organized in a certain directory on my computer, I always select "save as," and select where I want to store them. Then, I type in the title of my song with the extension .rm attached (songtitle.rm) and hit "save."

10. Now you are back to the Output File page. Again, you click "next" and then "finish" on the following pop up window.

11. Finally, you are at the last window where you will see all the settings that you just put in place for your new RealMedia file. All you do on this page is select the start button under the heading "Recording Controls." You're finished! The software does the rest and you now have successfully made your new streaming Real Audio file.

I sincerely hope this article is helpful to those of you interested in the subject of streaming Real Audio, but without the know-how to make the files yourselves.

♦

POSTING REAL AUDIO FILES ON YOUR WEBSITE
by Lynn Carey Saylor, GuitarGirls.com

For all of you who followed the previous instructions and were successful in making your files, congratulations, you're almost there! Posting them correctly so that they stream flawlessly is your final step and the subject this of discussion.

The first thing you'll want to do is to upload one of your newly created .rm files to your Web server. For the purposes of this tutorial, we will call this file "hitsong.rm." You'll want to put all of your .rm files in one place to keep them organized. I always send mine to the audio folder of my server. Using our file "hitsong.rm" and the Web site "anysite.com" as examples, the URL of the uploaded file into the audio folder would be the following: http://www.anysite.com/audio/hitsong.rm. Knowing the URL where you have sent your .rm file is very important to the next step in the process, so you'll need to make a mental note of it.

The big misconception about Real Audio is that people often think that all they have to do is upload the song file, link to it and it will stream. That would be the procedure for other music files such as MIDI files or MP3's, but Real Audio works in a different, slightly more complicated way, because there is a second file in addition to the .rm that you need to make and upload to your sever. This is a pointing file (often called a metafile) which will have the extension .ram. What is a "pointing file," you may ask? It is just a simple text file that contains the actual URL of where your Real Audio file is located on your server. This file is the means by which your Real Audio file is directed to

"stream." Your Web page will therefore contain a link to the .ram file, instead of to the actual .rm song file.

To make the pointing file, follow these steps:
1. Open your text editor. I use what is probably the most widely known text editor, "Notepad."
2. Type in the URL where the file is located. For our example, that would be the URL: http://anysite.com/audio/hitsong.rm
3. Next, save it to your desktop (or wherever you can easily locate it for uploading) as the name of your song with the extension .ram (hitsong.ram).
4. Upload the newly created hitsong.ram pointing file to the audio folder of your server (or wherever you uploaded your .rm file to). Remember that it is an ASCII text file and not binary, so be sure to send it up as such.

Now you should have two files uploaded to your server - "hitsong.rm" and "hitsong.ram". You must have both of these files correctly made and uploaded before completing the final step of how to set up the link on your Web page.

Recall that I mentioned above that you must link to the .ram file and not to .rm file? This is critical. Your song will only stream if you link to the pointing file. That file (hitsong.ram) will direct your real audio file (hitsong.rm) to begin to stream when you click on the link. So type out what ever you want on your Web page ("Listen to Real Audio of hitsong here" for example) and then link the text to the following URL: http://www.yoursite.com/audio/hitsong.ram

Viola! You've done it! You now have streaming Real Audio on your Web site.

Lynn Carey Saylor is a singer/songwriter/guitarist and co-owner of the Los Angeles area recording studio, Skip Saylor Recording. In early 2000, Lynn founded GuitarGirls.com which seeks to promote up and coming female singer/songwriter/ guitarists. You can reach Lynn at www.guitargirls.com

♦

STREAMING YOUR MP3 FILES
by Luke Sales, GlassWing Media

So you want to stream your mp3s? No problem! What follows is a brief tutorial about streaming your mp3s online.

There are two major parts to play in streaming mp3 files: serving up the files correctly and configuring your computer to receive them. If you are running your own website, you only need to worry about serving the files, but you should know how to receive them too. How else will you be able to test that the streaming works?

Serving up the Mp3s:
There are several different ways to serve up streaming mp3s. This technique is the most straightforward and simple. First, you must encode your mp3s at a low bit rate, so that listeners will be able to hear the music without having to stop and download. A good compression setting for most listeners is 32kbps Mono. The audio quality at this setting is fairly low, since we are trying to accommodate listeners with slow Internet connections. You may wish to make two different versions of your music - one at 32kbps mono (for modem users) and another at 128kbps for broadband.

Name the mp3 files appropriately (ending with '.mp3') and upload the files to your web server. Figure out what the address of the files is. For example, http://yourserver.com/mymusic.mp3, where 'yourserver.com' is the name of your server and 'mymusic.mp3' is the name of the mp3 file.

Now create a plain text ".m3u" playlist file containing the address of the mp3 file you wish to stream. This file should be a plain text document that contains only one line. (Use a program like Notepad to create this file). Using the example above, the file would only say http://yourserver.com/mymusic.mp3

this text file as 'mymusic.m3u', where 'mymusic' is the name ...g. Upload this file to your server. Now just create a link to ... rom somewhere on your web site. This sample HTML link would display 'click here to stream' and would link directly to the .m3u file above:

`<a href = "/mymusic.m3u">click here to stream</a>` If the listener's computer is configured correctly, all they need to do is click on this link and their mp3 player should pop up and begin to stream. How does a person set themselves up to hear streaming mp3s?

Receiving and listening to an mp3 stream:

If your computer is not set up for mp3 streaming, it will not know what to do with the .m3u playlist file. To solve this problem, install a streaming-capable Mp3 player. Here are some good ones:
Windows: Winamp, Kjofol, Sonique, Windows Media Player, or Real Player. Mac: Soundjam, Macamp, or Audion.

To sum things up: Create an .m3u playlist that contains the address of the mp3 you want to stream. Create a link to this file. That's it - Have fun streaming!

Oh yes - keep in mind that there are many online resources to help you. Lycos' Webmonkey website <webmonkey.com> contains many great tutorials about all aspects of web development (including streaming). Into Internet radio? Check out shoutcast.com, a free technology that makes it easy to run an Mp3 radio station. If you just want something easy, go to live365.com - you have to pay, but they do all the work.

Luke Sales is a trumpet player/programmer/web dude who works for GlassWing Media in Portland, OR. His advice to anyone getting set up doing web sites or Internet? "I feel your pain. The learning curve never stops; just keep going." GlassWing Media is available to help you get established as a musician, no matter how big or small your project. CD-ROMs, DVDs, web sites, guitar tuning - you name it, they do it. Check out the GlassWing web site at www.glasswing.com

legal

HOW TO COPYRIGHT YOUR MUSIC
by Nancy Falkow , Ask Nancy
© 2004 All Rights Reserved. Used By Permission

Sometimes musicians think every song written needs to be immediately copywritten, but this isn't always true! Copyrighting, registers your music so that if a situation arises that someone is stealing your music, your registration of copyright is on file, which protects you. So, if you're singing these songs in your living room for your family, you don't need to run to Washington, DC!

What can be copy written? Literary works; musical works, including any accompanying words, dramatic works, including any accompanying music, pantomimes and choreographic works, pictorial, graphic, and sculptural works, motion pictures and other audiovisual works, sound recordings and architectural works. Phew, thank god for the arts!

If you are a songwriter and you plan on distributing your music through the web you should copyright your songs. Go to US COPYRIGHT REGISTRATION (http://www.loc.gov/copyright) site and download the forms you need. Each situation is different, read all of the information, and figure out which best applies to you.

Basically you need to put your music and lyrics on tape or cd, fill out the appropriate forms and write the check. In approximately 6 weeks you receive the paperwork and a number of registrations.

Use this as a Checklist:
*   A properly completed application form.
*   A nonrefundable filing fee of $30+ for each application.
*   A non returnable deposit of the work being registered. (tape, cd, poem, lyrics etc)

Mail to:
Library of Congress
Copyright Office
Register of Copyrights
101 Independence Avenue, S.E.
Washington, D.C. 20559-6000

You can copyright more than one song on one tape or cd by sending it in as an anthology. In short, you put your songs on one format, give it a name like "Greatest Hits" and send it in. This is the best way to save money! You aren't copyrighting each song for $30, you're copyrighting an entire batch for $30.

It's always important to protect yourself and your songs. Good luck!

Nancy Falkow is known throughout the Philadelphia area for writing catchy and melodic pop-folk songs with dynamics and soul. Nancy also writes a weekly online music advice column at The Women of MP3.com called Ask Nancy! She still finds time to play bass and sing background vocals in an all girl rock band called The Dirty Triplets! http://www.nancyfalkow.com NanceNet@aol.com

♦

ENTERTAINMENT INDUSTRY LAWYERS: WHO, WHAT, WHEN, WHERE AND HOW MUCH?!
by Wallace Collins, Entertainment Lawyer
© 2004 All Rights Reserved. Used By Permission.

As a creative artist in the entertainment industry you do not need to know everything about the business in order to succeed, but you should hire people who do. When I was a teenage recording artist back in the late 70's, I can remember being intimidated by the "suits". Now that I am on the other side of the desk, I have a broader perspective. I am here to tell you that those "suits" can help you; provided, however, that like any other aspect of your life, you use your instincts in making your selection.

The best place for you to start building your "team" of representatives is with a competent lawyer who specializes in entertainment law, which is a combination of contract, intellectual property (copyright, trademark and patent) and licensing law. Eventually, your team could possibly include a personal manager, a booking agent and a business manager/accountant. Your lawyer can assist you in assembling your team. He may then function as the linchpin in coordinating the activities of your team and insuring that these people are acting in your best interests.

A good lawyer will navigate you safely through the minefield that is the entertainment industry. Record contracts, publishing agreements and licensing arrangements can be extremely complicated. Proper negotiating and drafting requires superior legal skills as well as knowledge of entertainment business and intellectual property practice. Your lawyer can explain the concepts of copyrights, trademark and patents to you and assist you in securing proper protection for your work. In addition to structuring and documenting a deal to maximize the benefits to you, some lawyers also actively solicit deals for their clients. Moreover, if you are not properly compensated in accordance with your contract, you will look to your lawyer to commence a lawsuit for you.

When looking for a lawyer, you should not be afraid to interview a few before retaining one. Some lawyers are with large firms but many are solo practitioners. Lawyers have various personalities and legal skills and you should seek out a situation where the "vibe" is right. Although your first contact may be on the telephone, most likely you will have an initial interview for which, if you so request in advance, there is usually no charge. Remember, your lawyer's time is money, so be prepared and be on time for your appointment.

It is not necessary that your lawyer like or even understand your creation. It is more important that you feel he or she is a trustworthy and competent advisor. The lawyer/client relationship is known as a "fiduciary" relationship which means that a lawyer must always act in your best interest and not his own or that of anyone else. Your lawyer is also under a duty to keep your conversations with him confidential. It is often in your best interest that it stays that way.

Keep in mind that a lawyer with other big name clients is not necessarily the best lawyer for you; if it comes down to taking your calls or those of a superstar, which do you think will get preference?

You are probably wondering, "How much will this cost?" Well, remember that the only thing a lawyer has to sell is his time.

A lawyer, much like a doctor, is selling services, so if you go to him for advice you should expect to pay. With the odds of success in this business being what they are, very few lawyers will agree to work for you and wait for payment until you are successful and can pay your bills.

A lawyer specializing in the entertainment field usually charges an hourly fee or a percentage of the money value of your deal. Hourly rates generally run from $200 and up. Percentages are based on the "reasonable value of services rendered" and generally run around 5% of the deal. A few lawyers may charge a set fee, such as $1,000 or $1,500, to review and negotiate certain documents. Check around to see if the fee arrangement proposed is competitive.

Most lawyers will require a payment of money in advance or "retainer", which can range anywhere from $1,000 to $10,000. Even those who take a percentage of the deal as a fee may require that you pay a retainer. In addition to the hourly fee or percentage, you are usually required to reimburse your lawyer for his out-of-pocket costs, including long distance telephone calls, photocopies, postage, fax, etc.

You should realize that in retaining a lawyer you are making a contract even if your agreement is not written. In return for a fee, the lawyer promises to render legal services on your behalf. However, some lawyers may want a fee arrangement in writing (specifically in connection with a percentage deal) and/or a payment direction letter. A cautious lawyer will advise you that you have the right to seek the advice of another lawyer as to the propriety of a percentage fee arrangement.

As a general rule, you need a lawyer if you are asked to sign anything other than an autograph. Too many aspiring creative artists want to get a deal so badly they will sign almost anything that promises them a chance to do it. Even successful careers have a relatively short life span, especially in the music, movie and television business. Therefore, it is important for you to get maximum returns in the good years and not sign away rights to valuable income.

As a general proposition, never sign anything without having your own lawyer review it first. Do not rely on anyone else (or even their lawyer) to tell you what your contract says. Your lawyer will "translate" the deal for you and explain to you exactly what you are getting into. Do not let anyone rush you or pressure you into signing any agreement. There is really no such thing as a standard "form" contract. Any such contract was drafted by that party's attorney to protect that party's interests; your lawyer can help negotiate more favorable terms for you.

Everyone needs someone to look out for his or her interests. That is why you need a lawyer. If you believe in yourself and your talent, give yourself the benefit of the doubt, invest in legal representation and do not sign anything without consulting your lawyer.

Wallace Collins is an entertainment lawyer with the New York law firm of Serling Rooks & Ferrara, LLP. He was a recording artist for Epic Records before attending Fordham Law School. Contact: (212) 245-7300 http://wallacecollins.com

♦

ROYALTIES IN THE MUSIC BUSINESS
by Joyce Sydnee Dollinger, Entertainment Lawyer

What is a royalty? In the real world, the word royalty is synonymous with the power or rank of a king and queen. In the music world, the word royalty is synonymous with MONEY. Royalties are the most important entitlements of the musician. These entitlements warrant them to receive money from their craft - the craft of MAKING MUSIC.

TYPES OF ROYALTIES
There are many types of royalties. The list is constantly growing because of the new technology, but here are some to name a few: Artist Royalties, Mechanical (Publishing) Royalties, US Performance Royalties Synchronization Royalties, Grand Rights Royalties, Foreign Royalties for record sells and performances, Lyric Reprint Royalties.

Let's look at the topic of Artist Royalties.

GENERAL DEFINITION
Artist Royalties, in a nutshell, are monies paid to the recording artist from the record company. They are the share of the proceeds from the sale of the artist's records paid directly to the artist after the artist records material for the record company. This, in turn, gives the record company permission to exploit the musical work in the marketplace.

RECORDING CONTRACTS
In artist recording contracts, artist royalties are usually negotiated in points. When record label business affairs attorneys use that terminology, they are referring to the percentage points the record company will pay an artist on each album sold. For example, if an artist gets 10 points, it usually means that the artist receives 10% of the retail cost of each record sold.

Royalty rates in a recording contract are usually negotiable; however, it really depends upon the leverage of the artist.

1. **Superstar Deals**
   Royalties usually are:
   16%-20% of retail of top-line records plus escalations
   18-20% is quite high and the artist must sell a lot of records - usually more than 5 million
   100% CD rate and can receive new configuration royalties
   12-14% of singles + escalations receive increased royalties when contract options are exercised

2. **Mid-Level Deals**
   Royalties usually are:
   14%-16% of retail top-line records plus escalations (escalations usually based on genre)
   16% is high and the artist must sell a lot of records
   85-90% CD rate and new configurations
   12-13% of singles or 3/4 of LP rate receives increased royalties when contract options are exercised

3. **New Artist Deals**
   Royalties usually are:
   11%-13% of retail top-line records
   75-85% CD rate and new configurations
   10-11% of singles

ALL-IN
More likely than not, the record royalty section of the artist recording contract will have a phrase in it called "all-in". It will state something like the following: "The royalty rate for the artist will be 'all in'." This means that if anyone else is receiving points on the record, like a third party producer or engineer, that person will be paid out of the artist's personal own royalty share. The artist is responsible to pay the third party receiving those points. However, usually the artist will sign a *Letter of Direction* with the record label. This document gives permission to the record label to pay the third party directly. For example, if an artist who has a 15 point deal in the recording contract has an agreement with a producer to give the producer 3 points, those 2 points are subtracted from the artist's personal own royalty share, leaving the artist with only 12 points.

RECORD ROYALTY RE-NEGOTIATION
If the artist sells a ton of records, the artist can usually re-negotiate with the record label and try to receive increased royalty rates. Here are

some topics to try to re-negotiate:
- increase net royalty rates on remaining LPs in the contract increase rate for each successive LP include escalations for attaining sales plateaus
- receive the increase royalty rate on future sales of past LPs improve the royalty computations increase foreign rates, the CD rate, the new technology rate, licensing fees and free goods
- reduce the recoupment percentages

RECORD ROYALTY FORMULA

The record royalty formula is usually based upon a percentage of records that are sold. In using the formula, the record company looks to the retail price of the commercial top-line records and standard deductions that every record company takes from the gross income from the sales of those records. Some of the deductions are: recording costs of the records, packaging, returns and reserves, discounted military sales, video costs, tour support, promotional records and free goods. Please note, records on which royalties are paid are quite different from deductions from gross royalties.

Joyce Sydnee Dollinger is an attorney admitted in New York and Florida. She is also the Vice President of 2 Generations SPA Music Management, Inc. http://www.2generations.com and SPA Records, Inc. http://www.sparecords.com

♦

ARTIST-MANAGEMENT CONTRACTS

by Richard P. Dieguez, Entertainment Lawyer
© 2004 All Rights Reserved. Used By Permission.

HOW LONG IS LONG?

Next to a record label deal, the artist management contract is the most exciting agreement an artist will sign. As with any legal document, a contract shouldn't be signed without the advice of a music attorney. In addition to being your legal counselor, your attorney is also your advocate because his is especially needed to play the role of the "bad guy." What I mean is that there are many aspects of the contract that will have to be negotiated. It can be somewhat awkward if you and the manager were to try negotiating these points on your own because you may end up putting a strain on the close working relationship you're supposed to have with each other. The attorneys for each side, however, are disinterested third parties who have the objectivity and professional training to vigorously fight for their client's interest without (hopefully!) coming to blows or shouting matches. So let your lawyer take the blame for "asking too much" or for being such a "tough negotiator" — that's what he is being paid to do.

There are at least three big questions in artist management contracts that you and your lawyer have to ask: how long will the agreement be in effect; how much will the manager get paid during the agreement; and how much will the manager get paid after the agreement has ended. How you ultimately answer these questions is the result of what can be some heavy negotiation. Why? Because these questions cover areas where your interests are not going to coincide with those of your manager. The goal of the negotiating process is to produce a deal that will be fair to both sides.

Consider the first big question. You and your manager are each likely to have a legitimate difference of opinion as to the amount of time for which the contract will be binding. From your point of view, you would generally want a short-term contract. If it turns out, for any number of reasons, that you're not happy with your manager, you want the assurance of being freed from the contract within a short period of time. After the initial excitement wears off, for example, you may come to feel that you and your manager don't really get along well. Or perhaps it turns out that he or she isn't as experienced or doesn't have all the contacts and "pull" that he said he did. Maybe he's simply not doing his job effectively. Whatever the reason, you don't want to get locked in with a loser for the next seven years.

But now put yourself in the manager's shoes. Generally, he will want the contract to be as long as possible because his compensation is based on a percentage of whatever money you make. Not every artist out there is going to be an overnight success. Chances are that your manager's early efforts will not result in financial success for you until much later. So that manager will want a contract that will last long enough for her to enjoy the rewards she toiled for in the beginning. Nothing can be more frustrating for a manager than to have her budding artists go to another manager, where they then make it to the big time.

So depending on the particular circumstances of the parties, the negotiation will center on a contract term ranging from as short as six months to as long as several years. What length of time is fair really depends on what you and your manager are each bringing to the relationship you wish to form. For example, let's say that neither of you has too much experience in the music business. In this situation, you're both probably better off with a short-term contract, like six months or one year, so that you can check each other out without getting locked in to a big commitment. You can always enter into another agreement if it turns out, at the end of the contract, that you have a future together.

MORE ABOUT TIME AND MONEY

Now let's take the other extreme and assume that both you and your manager are established veterans of the music business. Under these facts, it may be more practical to enter into a long-term contract, since you will each presumably have some track record of success. In this situation, the risks involved are not as great as they are when you're both newcomers to the business.

Perhaps you and your manager will fall somewhere between these two extremes. What happens if you can't agree to a fixed amount of time? Well, to satisfy both parties, the attorneys can always try to hammer out a compromise: a short-term contract with the potential of being converted into a long-term contract. For example, the parties could agree to a one-year contract. Part of the agreement, however, would be that the manager must meet certain conditions during this one-year period — such as getting you a record deal, a publishing deal or even guaranteeing that you earn a minimum amount of income. If the manager fails to meet the conditions, then the contract ends when the year is up. If, however, the manager is successful in meeting the conditions, then he has the right to automatically extend the contract for an additional period of time, say for another year. Under this kind of an arrangement, the best interests of both you and your manager are met.

Guess what the next subject of negotiation will be? That's right. Money. The custom is for the manager to work on a commission. In other words, the manager gets compensated for his efforts by taking a percentage of whatever income you earn as an artist. Obviously, your attorney is going to try to negotiate for as small a percentage as possible. Your position will be that ultimately it's your guitar virtuosity that will make you a success. You'll argue that the manager simply manages, and without your talent, there is nothing to sell to the labels or to the publishers. Therefore, you'll confidently conclude, the manager's commission should be negotiated toward the low side since you are entitled to keep as much of the money your talents have earned as possible.

But, as you should soon be appreciating, there are two sides to every coin. The manager's attorney is going to negotiate for as high a commission as possible. Their position will be that there is a lot of talent out there — especially in the major music centers like California and New York — and that the difference between those who make it and those who don't is the quality of their management. Without the manager, your career development may slow down to a crawl. Why? Because instead of honing your talents, you'll be too busy running around doing all the things that a manager is supposed to be doing. Talent is important, but without a manager exposing you to the people who can make a difference, you're just another unknown basement band.

MONEY

The custom is for the manager to work on a commission. In other words, the manager gets compensated for his efforts by taking a percentage of whatever income you earn as an artist.

Obviously, your attorney is going to try to negotiate for as small a percentage as possible. Your position will be that ultimately it's your musical virtuosity that will make you a success. You'll argue that the manager simply manages, and without your talent, there is nothing to sell to the labels or to the publishers. Therefore, you'll confidently conclude, the manager's commission should be negotiated toward the low side since you are entitled to keep as much of the money your talents have earned as possible.

But, as you should soon be appreciating, there are two sides to every coin. The manager's attorney is going to negotiate for as high a commission as possible. Their position will be that there is a lot of talent out there — especially in the major music centers like New York, Los Angeles, Nashville and London — and that the difference between those who make it and those who don't is the quality of their management.

They will also point out that without the manager, your career will slow down to a crawl. Why? Because instead of honing your performance, songwriting and recording skills, you'll be too busy running around doing all the things that a manager is supposed to be doing. Talent is important, but without a manager exposing you to the people who can make a difference, you're just another unknown artist.

So what's the range of the amount of the commission? It can generally be anywhere from 10% to 25% of your gross income. But as I have stressed before, the amount that is settled on may very well depend on the circumstances. Again, the art of compromise may bring new life to a negotiation that is at a deadlock on the issue of the commission amount.

MONEY...NEGOTIATION IDEAS

In the last section, I discussed how the amount of the commission can be anywhere from 10% to 25% of your gross income. But as I have stressed before, the amount that is settled on may very well depend on the circumstances. Again, the art of compromise may bring new life to a negotiation that is at a deadlock on the issue of the commission amount. The attorneys can suggest that the commission percentage be staggered. In other words, your attorney can suggest, for example, that the first $25,000.00 of gross income will be commissioned at 10% and the next $25,000.00 of gross income will be commissioned at 15%. The manager's attorney may rearrange these numbers and offer a counterproposal. Some further give and take may be necessary before something is finally agreed upon.

Regardless of the particulars, the concept here is that the lower percentage rate should be satisfactory to you, while the manager is also given an incentive to make a bigger percentage if he can get you to earn in excess of a certain amount of gross income. And, of course, getting you over that amount, whether it's $25,000.00 or whatever, will be to your benefit as well. As you can see, the concept of staggered commissions is an alternative compensation plan that can be suggested during negotiation, but, even so, the actual percentage rates and the income levels when these rates kick in must still be negotiated.

Another factor in this negotiation is determining which of your income-earning activities will be subject to the commission. The manager will try to have his commission apply to every conceivable entertainment-related activity from which you could possibly earn an income. Examples of such money-making activities would be live performances, record sales and the sale of promotional merchandise such as T-shirts, posters, buttons, programs and pictures. So if you feel that the commission rate the manager is asking for is too high, you can try to compromise by proposing that you'll accept the commission rate, but only if certain activities are excluded from the commission.

Your attorney may want to suggest, for example, that the commission not apply to any publishing income you earn from your songwriting activities. If you are multi-talented and occasionally earn extra money as a model or actor, your attorney may argue that these activities be excluded from the manager's commission as well. However, if the manager insists that all your activities be commissionable, then you may want to agree, but only if the commission rate is lowered.

MONEY... AFTER THE CONTRACT ENDS

So far we've discussed the issues involved in negotiating the manager's compensation during the life of the contract. Another touchy subject that is especially close to the manager's heart, is whether he will continue to get a commission on gross income earned by the artist after the contract has ended. Your response will probably be "of course not!" After all, once the contract is over, neither party has any further obligation to the other. The manager shouldn't continue to get paid when his isn't even the manager anymore. He got paid enough when he was the manager. Besides, you may feel that despite the manager's efforts, there comes a point when the band becomes somewhat established enough to sell itself with little help from the manager. So once the contract is over, there should be a clean break. No more ties.

Well, maybe not. During the course of the contract, and through the manager's efforts, you may be fortunate enough to have signed some money-making deals. For the life of the contract, you earn money from these deals. As agreed, the manager gets his percentage and you keep the rest. But it may be that your money-making contracts will still be in effect for quite some time after your management contract has ended. Since you will continue to profit from a deal he helped you obtain, the manager may feel that he should also continue to profit even after the artist-manager relationship legally ends.

Consider another scenario. During the course of the contract, and through the manager's efforts, you are fortunate enough to take part in negations for some money-making deals. But the final handshake on these deals may not take place until after the contract with your manager has ended. As a result, the money earned from these deals doesn't start pouring in until after the contract has ended. Again, the manager will want to enjoy his percentage of the profits you are earning from a deal that had its genesis with the artist-manager relationship — even after the relationship has legally ended.

But before you agree to compensating your manager after the contract ends (after all, you've learned by now that there are two sides to every coin), consider yet another twist. If you enter into a contract with a new manager, that new manager will probably be no different from your former manager on the question of compensation. The new manager's attorney will probably demand that the commission apply to every conceivable entertainment- related activity from which you could possibly earn an income. And this would include the money pouring in from deals your former manager obtained! You don't need me to tell you that you wouldn't want to be stuck paying two commissions on the same money.

Well, skillful lawyering can help straighten out this mess too. Remember the staggered commissions we discussed? A special schedule can be set up whereby the manager continues to get compensated after the contract has ended, but with the commission rates adjusting downward as certain income levels are reached. You may even want to try something like limiting this compensation to say three years after the contract has ended. If you can get your new manager to accept a staggered commission schedule on the money-making deals of your former manager, you can greatly alleviate the financial drain of paying two full commissions on the same income.

CONCLUSION

If you've read this entire article, you'll begin to appreciate how the negotiations can go around and around until everyone settles on a deal they can live with. Of course, there are many other aspects of the artist management contract that will be subject to negotiation. An issue may be made of as to who collects the income: the manager, you or maybe a third party like a business manager or accountant. Another traditional sticky point is the extent of the manager's authority to sign contracts on your behalf.

There may even be some negotiating points that to you and the manager don't seem crucial, but to the attorneys seem to mean everything. For instance, the attorneys may wrangle over whether all or some breaches of contract must be brought to arbitration rather than litigated in court. You may even find the attorneys considering which law applies to disputes arising from the contract. Will California law, New York law or some other state's law apply? Perhaps it's even a question of whether the contract is governed by American law or English law.

In fact, the personal circumstances surrounding any given artist management contract can be so unique, that I suppose the three big questions covered by this article may actually end up being among the easier things to negotiate for some artists and managers. A point that can be agreed upon in five minutes between an artist and a manager on one deal, may bring about a deadlock for another artist and manager in a different deal.

The point is that, unlike your musical instrument, studio or promotional plans, a contract is not something you should try playing solo or doing on your own. But with the professional help of an attorney, there is much room for creativity in the negotiation process to try protecting everyone's best interests, especially on the difficult points like the time, the money or whatever it happens to be in your case. As you can see, the art of compromise expands the parameters of the so-called "standard" contract.

An NYU Law graduate, Richard P. Dieguez has over 16 years experience in entertainment law. He has represented hundreds of clients across the U.S. and several nations in music, film, television, publishing and other legal matters. Mr. Dieguez is also the founder of The Circle, a monthly music industry seminar held in New York City. More info on Mr. Dieguez and The Circle is available at www.RPDieguez.com

◆

HOW TO TRADEMARK YOUR BAND NAME
by Derek Sivers, CEO CD Baby
© 2004 All Rights Reserved. Used By Permission

Anytime you're promoting, you're promoting your NAME - so make sure it's yours!

I'm giving you some unofficial advice here from my own experience. There are attorneys and specialists that can help you much more. Most of all, you should REALLY go get a book called "TRADEMARK - Legal Care for Your Business & Product Name" by Stephen Elias - from Nolo Press. It covers *everything* and even includes the forms you'll need to register. FOR BASIC TRADEMARK ADVICE, go to my web page of reprints from NOLO Press: http://www.hitme.net/useful/c.html

Anyway - here's some introductory advice from a fellow bandleader:

RESEARCH TO MAKE SURE NO ONE ELSE IS USING A SIMILAR NAME
• check the PhonoLog at your nearest record store.
• if you can, check Billboard's Talent Directory. (it's expensive to buy).
• if you've got $$, hire a search firm (attorneys) - this is the most reliable but it'll cost you between $300-$500.
• I also heard CompuServe has a trademark research center.

Call the nearest largest Public Library and ask if they have a Federal Trademark Register CD-Rom. Between 1-3 libraries in each state have it. You can go in and they'll show you how to do a search. Search for your full band name, then each word individually.

Example: my band HIT ME: search "HIT ME" then search "HIT" then search "ME") The reason is - there may be a band called "KICK ME" or "HIT US" that could be a conflict. If you can think of other similar words to search, try those, too. You can get a printout of all this.

If there's nothing even remotely similar, you're doing OK. If someone, even a clothing company, is using your name, then you should consult an attorney.

Make sure you search the *Federal* Register, then the *Pending* Register. These are for the names that have been applied for, but not completed yet.

Call Washington, DC: (703)308-HELP and ask for the book "BASIC FACTS ABOUT REGISTERING A TRADEMARK"

Trademark covers a product. Servicemark covers a service.

As a musical act, we are a service. If ALL you do is make CDs and tapes, but never play live, maybe your name only applies to a

product. But for most of us, it's a service first, then a product second. It's all the same form, just a technicality. You'll still use the ® [little (R) in a circle] when you are registered.

On that note, you can start using "TM" or "SM" after your name now. It means you have intent to register, or are claiming legal ownership of that name. You can use the ® *after* and only after the whole registration is complete.

Each registration class costs $245. If you want to register a Servicemark, and a trademark, that's $490. That's the *complete* way to do it. But when I called the Patent & Trademark office help line, they said if you register your servicemark, that's plenty of protection for now. (Until you start selling loads of T-shirts, hats, action figures...)

You may get a form that says it's only a $200 fee, but those are old forms. It's $245. Save this information for when you are filling out the form: (because they don't really tell you this anywhere)
For a servicemark for a musical act, you want to file a "CLASS 41" description of product/services is: "Entertainment Services in the nature of Musical Performance." Everything else will be explained when you get the book.

Don't forget - do this NOW, or ALL the work you're doing to promote your act will be wasted.

© 2004 Derek Sivers - all rights reserved - if you like this article check out my websites: cdbaby.com | hostbaby.com | agentbaby.com | marketingyourmusic.com | musicthoughts.com | hitmedia.com

◆

TRADEMARKING YOUR LOGO
by Vivek J. Tiwary and Gary L. Kaplan, StarPolish.com
© 2004 All Rights Reserved. Used By Permission

A good logo is an invaluable tool in the imaging and marketing of a developing artist— so it's worthwhile to design a logo immediately after you have settled on your name. But unlike your name, it's more acceptable to change your logo over the years without losing or confusing fans. 311 and The Rolling Stones are great examples of bands that have either changed or modified their logos to adapt with changing times or the themes of certain albums or tours.

Of course, not every artist has a logo. But a logo can only help. Remember that your name simply and consistently printed in a certain standard font can be a fine logo (e.g. Cheap Trick).

Good logos, simply put, are logos that look cool. I personally like logos that are minimal, easy to remember, tied into the artist's name, and easily reproduced— i.e. anybody could scribble the logo on the cover of their notebook, it doesn't take a great artist to reproduce it. Like your name, your logo should somehow also be in line with the vibe of your act— it should gel with the sound of your music and the attitude of your band members. My favorite logo belongs to Nine Inch Nails.

I would recommend that a band member or friend design the logo, so that there is a genuine and intimate connection between the logo and the band. On the other hand, if no one you know is talented in the visual arts, or you are unhappy with the drafts of potential logos you've come up with, you can seek help from local design companies, but be careful, as some of these companies can be expensive. Alternately, you can solicit help from local design schools, whose students may be willing to design a logo for free in order to gain working experience and build up their own design portfolios. Try putting flyers/posters up in the schools or posts on school bulletin boards announcing that you are a local band/songwriter looking for a logo designer.

Once you have a logo that you are satisfied with (if only temporarily), put it on everything— all over your website, your merchandise, your CD and CD cover, your letterhead, etc. Make stickers of the logo and stick them everywhere you can; always keep a small stack of your logo stickers in your pocket for this purpose. Consistency and repetition are critical marketing keys. The more times people see the same logo, the more they will remember it and your act.

Once you've settled on a logo, you should consider registering your logo as a trademark with the U.S. Patent and Trademark Office (or comparable body if you are based in another country). Much like with your name, you acquire rights to your logo when it is publicly used in commerce. This means that when you sell your merchandise, or play a show where your logo is displayed, you automatically obtain some common law rights in that logo. Registering your logo as a trademark, however, will provide you with important additional rights:

Assuming that you are the first to use this logo, registering your logo will help secure both your right to use the logo, and your right to prevent others from using the same or a similar logo in any manner likely to confuse consumers anywhere in the country. Before reading any further, review the StarPolish section on Registering and Keeping a Name. The advice and instructions that you need here are parallel to the advice and instructions from that section, so I'm not going to repeat all of the information. There are, however, some subtle differences, so read on.

The problem is that unlike your name, it is an incredibly tricky process trying to figure out whether someone else's logo is similar enough to yours that it is likely to cause confusion among consumers. The following illustration should highlight the difference: If you call your band The Dave Matthews Band, and Dave Matthews is not a part of the band, I can guarantee that there will be a lot of fans who are confused (and really pissed)— and, if it comes to Matthew's attention, you will be enjoined (i.e. stopped) from further use of that name. Now, however, if you were to choose as your logo some variation of a lips theme, it becomes incredibly subjective whether your logo is so close to that of the Rolling Stones that it will create confusion among consumers. The point is that while trademark law is not an exact science with respect to names, it is even less of an exact science when dealing with logos.

Because of the extremely subjective nature of the trademark analysis for logos, it might not be worthwhile to perform a search, as you'll probably only have some certainty if you discover the exact or nearly exact logo being used by another band. If you choose to perform a search, you can try Thomson & Thomson , or you might want to try the folks at www.tradename.com, but you'd be best served to have a lawyer take care of the whole thing. The analysis is so touchy that only an experienced trademark attorney will be able to offer sound advice.

The good news is that, as you may have guessed, it is not quite as disastrous if you are forced to change your logo. It might not be what you'd ideally like to do, but it pales comparison to having to change your name. Moreover, you may wind up going through a couple of different logos anyway. But if you've got a kick-ass logo, and can afford to hire an attorney to assist you, go ahead and trademark your logo. If your problem is that you're strapped for cash, try to register your trademark yourself by using the website of the U.S. Patent and Trademark Office . Like registering your name, registering your logo is not the easiest thing to do, but there are directions to help you through the process, and you'll save yourself a few hundred dollars in attorney's fees.

Vivek J. Tiwary is the founder and President/CEO of both StarPolish and The Tiwary Entertainment Group, a multi-faceted entertainment venture focusing on artist management, marketing consultation, and project production. Vivek has 10 years experience in the arts and entertainment industries, primarily working in music and theatre. http://www.starpolish.com Prior to joining StarPolish.com, Gary L. Kaplan spent three years at Skadden, Arps, Slate, Meagher & Flom, one of the world's preeminent law firms. Gary was a member of Skadden's Intellectual Property Department, focusing on patent litigation, and also working on copyright, trademark, trade secret, and new media law matters.

♦

THE WRITTEN AGREEMENT AMONGST BAND MEMBERS
by John Tormey III, Entertainment Lawyer

I have seen references to the above-mentioned document as both "Inter-Band Agreement", and "Intra-Band Agreement". Rather than initiate any argument with grammarians as to which term is correct - although "intra" is probably technically closer to the mark - let's simply call this all-important document the "Agreement Amongst Band Members"; or, "AABM", for short. (As for the grammarians who want to debate the use of "amongst" versus "among", well... you can discuss this amongst yourselves!) Now, on to the issues of interest to musicians who might be reading this article.

If one is a musician playing in a multi-member band, is an AABM needed? Absolutely, yes.

There are some parallels to an agreement amongst band members, on the one hand; and a pre-nuptial agreement between prospective spouses, on the other hand. But I actually find the case for having an AABM more compelling than a pre-nup. A marriage should be a function of love. A band formation, on the other hand, is often a commercial exercise - with perhaps some attendant art and love themes to it, playing in the background.

Written agreements should be considered required for any collaborative commercial endeavor between 2 or more people. One should use one's discretion as to whether or not to skip the pre-nup - after all, the prospective spouse could get insulted, if he/she originally thought the other spouse was in it for love only. But no band member should skip the AABM if the band member takes his or her band or career seriously. And no one band member should ask another to leap into a state of blind trust, in default of a good operative document.

If the band formation is not viewed as a commercial exercise, then I suppose the band members can simply agree on a handshake, and then gig for free in the subways. However, the majority of bands that I hear from, are concerned about their financial, as well as their artistic, futures. Many are trying to find a way to become economically self-sufficient on music alone, while preparing to quit their "day jobs". This result is not easy to achieve. And, this result is even harder to achieve without careful planning. An AABM is one planning tool which is essential - and which can also become virtually worthless if "left to a later day".

No one wants to be required to negotiate and close the AABM once the band is already successful, or once the band has already been furnished with a proposed recording agreement. The optimal time to close the AABM is while the band is just being formed or while it is still struggling. Period.

When business partners or stockholders agree amongst themselves in connection with a business formation, they do so in one or more signed writings. So, too, should it be with band members. A good AABM should be firm enough to recite the substance of the agreement at the moment, but should also be flexible enough to contemplate future changes, such as changes in personnel and in artistic direction.

If every marriage were a true 50/50 proposition, I suppose that one could say that no pre-nuptial agreements would ever be needed. Similarly, if every business partnership were truly 50/50, maybe a written partnership agreement could be viewed by some as a waste of time. But the fact of the matter is, the percentages of investment and return are seldom exactly identical amongst all co-venturers.

In the average 4-person band, each member may play a different instrument. Some may have been in the band longer than others. Some may be older and more experienced in the business of music. Some may have "connections" to clubs and labels, where other band members don't. Some may have more free time to invest in the running of the band's business, while others may be working 2 day jobs.

And finally, perhaps most importantly, some may have more of a hand in the writing of the words or the music of the band's original songs, than other members. This potential disparity is probably the best reason for creating the AABM as early as possible.

od AABM takes into account all of these types of factors, and conversely, if none of these questions came up while one was ...gether one's AABM, then the resulting document is probably not worth very much today. An AABM is a forward-looking document that asks "What if...?"

The real value of a contract - any contract, including the AABM - is as a dispute-resolution and dispute-avoidance tool. In other words, tackle the likely-occurring and even possibly-occurring long-range events that might come up in the band's lifetime; fight over and resolve them now; and put the results on paper. Better to do it now, than pay litigators thousands upon thousands of dollars to do it in the courts later.

Oftentimes, band members just "don't want to think about" what would happen, for example, if the bass player departs to raise kids in Maui, or if the singer-songwriter front-man just up and leaves to join the Air Force. But if the other band members at all value their investment of time, sweat and money in the band, then they should know and have fully thought through - in advance - the answers to these types of questions. Who owns and administrates the copyrights in the songs? Who is responsible for storing the masters? Who has final say in the hiring and firing of a manager? If the band breaks up, which member or members, if any, may keep using the band's name? And these are just some of the questions that should come up.

Every band's situation is different, and the lists of questions to contemplate will therefore be as different as there are different band personalities and different band members. It is true that the band should be better off, if a lawyer prepares the AABM. In a perfect world, all band members would be separately represented by a different attorney, and the resulting document would therefore have more presumptive fairness than if but one band member had counsel. It is also true that a non-lawyer lay-person cannot practice law without a license in the United States.

But should all these considerations prevent a band from taking their first shot at creating a good AABM? Absolutely not. The band should at least try to resolve amongst its own members, the answers to all of the "what if" questions that will likely come up in the life-cycle of any band. The band can try to resolve these questions on paper. Thereafter when affordable, one of the band members may decide to consult with an attorney to review and revise the band's starting-point document - (typically, this turns out in practice to be the band member with the most at stake in the outcome).

Conversely, be aware that one attorney may well not be able or be allowed to represent all band members simultaneously, due to concerns regarding possible conflicts of interest, especially if different band members have different percentage investments at stake in the band's commercial endeavors.

There should be plenty of time in the future for the band to consider the technicalities regarding rules of attorney-client representation, and "who represents who". And when the time for representation is right, these are serious threshold questions that should be taken seriously. Besides, no lawyer would take on a client without first carefully evaluating these types of issues, as well as asking a lot of additional questions himself or herself on his or her own.

In the meantime, all bands should carefully deliberate upon the question of what written agreement should be drafted and negotiated amongst the band members. Doing so now, in the present tense, could save a lot of heartache and expense down the road in the future.

John Tormey III is a New York lawyer who handles general commercial, transactional, and corporate matters. John is also admitted to practice law in California, and in Washington, D.C. John's focus is in the area of entertainment, arts, and media, including endeavors to market artistic material to professional entertainment industry recipients. Please feel free to contact John for his current law practice statement and submission guidelines. http://www.tormey.org

THE 10 RULES OF SUCCESSFUL INDEPENDENT MUSICIANS

by Nyree Belleville, author of "Booking, Promoting & Marketing Your Music"

Rule One: Be determined and dedicated

On your path you will, inevitably, collide with people who don't understand or like your music. When this happens try to remember that even the most successful musicians have been in your shoes. Every famous artist started out as an unknown musician struggling to get a gig in his or her hometown. Sarah McLachlin and the Counting Crows were playing twenty seat cafes in Canada and Berkeley for tips in their early years. No doubt many bookers told them, "Sorry, we can't fit you in the schedule." Or, "We don't book your kind of music here." Or, "Your band plays too loud for my room." Clearly, they continued with dedication to their plan, determined to keep booking and playing shows.

When you are truly determined to book a show for Friday and your first call doesn't turn up a gig, you will have no problem making another call to a different venue. When you are truly dedicated to "making it" as a musician, you will stay on your planned course of action. You will take the time to figure out, "What do I want to achieve? What is my mission? What are my goals?" True determination and dedication means that you will commit time and energy to your plan and take vigorous action in the pursuit of your dreams.

Rule Two: Believe in yourself.

You must believe that every song you write, every recording you make, and every gig you play is the absolute best that you can make it be. However, don't despair if right at this moment you aren't thrilled with every aspect of what you are doing as a musician. Musical development, progress, and pride will come from experience. After ten shows, you will know how to present yourself effectively on stage. After 100 shows, you will find that you are becoming a truly great musician and performer. After 200 shows, fans will approach you saying, "Wow! You're even better than [fill in the blanks with your most revered musical influence]."

Each show you play will help you to believe in yourself a little more. Each album you make will teach you that you are, indeed, a talented artist. And the more you believe in your talent, the more the audience will believe in you!

Rule Three: Maintain a dual-focus. Be a great musician and a street-smart entrepreneur.

First and foremost, to succeed as a musician you must possess great musical talent. You can work towards this by practicing and performing, by working with a great teacher and mentor, and by writing song after song. However, you must also be a wise and wily entrepreneur. Since your ultimate goal is to fund your future artistic exploration (and car and house payments!) through the income you earn from writing and playing music, you must master the full array of entrepreneurial skills. Among them, budgeting (your money and time), marketing (reaching your target audience), setting prices (for CDs, tapes, T-shirts), and selling (your services and your merchandise).

Understand that once you have made the commitment to be a working, professional musician, you have also made the commitment to be a street-smart entrepreneur. You won't sit around waiting to be discovered. Instead, you will put "luck" into your own hands and be responsible for your own lucky breaks. The truth is I've only seen people "be discovered" after working for years with dedication, determination, creativity, and smarts; they are inevitably seen and heard by special people that help advance their career.

Rule Four: Educate yourself. Know your genre inside-out!

It is imperative that you know the ins and outs of your own genre. Fortunately, the information you are looking for can be easily found in books, magazine articles, on the Internet, or in album liner notes. Look closely at the careers of artists whose paths you would like to emulate. Find out, do they release their albums independently or with help from a label? At what point did they start to work with a manager or booking agent? What type of venues do they most often play?

Read magazines in your genre such as "Jazz World" or "Performing Songwriter," which are loaded with useful articles. And watch for newsstand publications such as "The Musician's Guide to Touring & Promotion" and the "Musician's Atlas," which are good starting points for venues, contact numbers, and the type of music each venue books. Use the Internet to search for resources, venues, and fellow musicians. For example, if you are an acoustic singer-songwriter, type "Acoustic Music" and "Folk Music Venues" in a search engine. You can also search for online chat-groups and discussion lists of musicians, DJs, venue operators, house-concert operators, etc.

Take the time to get to know musicians that are currently performing in and around your area. Join a local songwriter's group and get involved with the local scene. And don't forget to read your local weekly entertainment papers to become familiar with the names of clubs, bands, and concert promoters in your area.

Rule Five: Let go of the "starving artist."

Are you wooed by the vision of the "starving artist?" Don't be! Too many musicians, painters, and writers unthinkingly worship at the altar of the starving artist, believing that selling their art is "selling out." Bah! Think of the thrill you'll get from selling your first CD or depositing a $1,000 check for a one-hour performance.

Utopia, for me, is every musician making enough money from music to play full-time. As artists, we must take full responsibility for making this utopia a reality. We need to accept the responsibility for our own finances. Just as bills are a reality, payment for services rendered is also a reality.

If you need to ease into selling your music, have a friend sell your merchandise for you. But always stand next to your sales table ready to talk to fans, sign CDs, and shake hands. Believe me, your fans are thrilled that you have recorded an album they can listen to over and over again, and they have no regrets about paying you $15 for it.

Rule Six: Create a plan and then follow up on it.

One neat thing about making a plan for your career is that it forces you to examine the driving force behind your will to play music for a living. What do you want from a career in music? Do you want to play for 40,000 screaming fans, or will you be perfectly happy playing piano at the local hotel bar for twenty appreciative listeners? Working on a Business and Marketing Plan will help you define your vision and the steps you need to take to succeed. Working on an Artist's Plan will help you set up rituals for preserving and growing yourself as a musician and artist.

You will find that following up on your actions is the difference between attaining or not attaining goals. In fact, the dictionary definition of 'follow up' is "To increase the effectiveness of by further action." Exactly right. Be sure to increase the effectiveness of each package you send out by following up.

Rule Seven: Take action despite your fears.

As an independent musician you will wear many different hats each day. Some of the duties and roles you assume may feel natural and easy. If you love to talk on the phone and meeting new people feels like an adventure, then booking shows will be a piece of cake. However, while other roles might not come as easily, don't let fear prevent you from sending out packages or making follow-up calls. In the grand master plan, one person does not have the power to make or break your career. And in order to spread the word about your music, you have to take the steps to let people know about it. Likewise, the more contacts you make, the more often you will be told, "Yes. We would love to book your band. Let's pick a date."

The first ten calls you make might not feel so great. Don't wo your next ten calls will be easier. By call thirty, you will sound calm, collected, and professional. Learning to deal with people over the phone, in cover letters, and at shows is a learned skill. The more you do it, the better you will be at it.

Rule Eight: Appreciate and respect your fans.

Fans of your music are your greatest supporters in the present and they have the greatest power to propel your career forward in the future. Loreena McKennitt, a hugely successful independent musician, says that her dedicated fans along with word-of-mouth helped her sell more than four million albums.

Your fans keep you going. They come to hear you play time and time again. They pay you money for your albums. They play your music for friends and word-of-mouth takes off with a life of its own. They bring friends to see you play, making it possible for you to book gigs at bigger venues. They write you letters and send you e-mails that perk you up on down days and inspire you to keep going. They shake your hand and hug you at shows, letting you know in the most personal way how much your music means to them.

So, be sure to respect your fans. After a show, always go stand by your merchandise table. Offer to sign CDs. Be ready and willing to chat with fans. And, make the effort to appreciate your fans. Mail them gig postcards that are easy to read, visually stimulating, and arrive early enough for them to plan an evening around your performance. Take the time and spend some extra money every few months in putting together a newsletter that lets your fans know what your band has been doing and what is planned for the future. Reply to every letter and e-mail that fans send to you with, at least, a thank you and always offer them the highest quality merchandise.

Rule Nine: Build a supportive team.

Regardless what stage your career is at, having a great team behind you will make a huge difference. At the beginning, your team might be your best friend who says, "You can do it!" Or, you may team up with another local musician and give each other a helping hand and a shoulder to cry on. At some point, your team may take care of everything from press releases to booking shows.

In building your team, first consider close friends and ardent fans. Thankfully, during the course of your career many fans will offer you help. One fan might know the owner of a club you've been trying to break into and will gladly make the introductions. Another may offer to help put up posters around town for upcoming gigs. Yet another may offer you money to record a new album. Take your fans seriously by, perhaps, meeting the following week for coffee and asking them what they would like to help you with. Find out if they can volunteer their time and expertise until you are making enough money to pay them. Other options are setting up an internship program with the local high school or college for class credit or placing an ad in the local paper asking for calls from folks who want to gain hands-on experience in the music industry.

However you build your team, make sure to surround yourself with people you can trust implicitly. Anyone doing work for you, no matter how insignificant it may seem, is representing you as both an artist and business owner. If you are comfortable with the person and what they want to do, I urge you to give them a try.

Rule Ten: Work harder after every success.

Every time you have a great success-a big show or a great review in a major paper-you should get working even harder than you did before. One great review can be transformed into a dozen reviews across the country. A big show with a national act can create relationships with a series of national acts.

Inform the world of your success, using phone, fax, and e-mail after each coup. Call several venues that you want to play at and let them know your last show was a sell-out. Call the booking agent you've had your eye on and introduce yourself. Make copies of the great review and include it in your press kit. Mail off five more copies of your album to publications with the new review

ur press kit.
ven harder after good news comes is part of the process
nomentum. If all goes well, each success will lead to
more success. And then eventually you will be so
great opportunities that you will have to hire a team to
help out!

Nyree Belleville, the author of "Booking, Promoting & Marketing Your Music" (Hal Leonard/Mix Books) is an independent musician with four independent CD releases. She has taught many musicians how to succeed on their own in the music industry through hew music business seminars and private consultations. For more information about Nyree's seminars, consultations, and music please visit her website at http://www.nyree.com or call 1-877-42NYREE.

♦

ALERT THE MEDIA! - PUBLICIZING YOUR CAREER
by Publicist Teresa Conboy
© 2004, All Rights Reserved. Used By Permission

Major or independent record labels have several avenues in which to promote an artist's career with the aid of in-house publicity, independent publicist (hired by the label or artist), marketing department, tour support, distribution, videos and radio promotion. Though this does not guarantee an artist the cover of Rolling Stone or Spin (or coverage within its pages), it (hopefully) enables him or her easier access to the media. The independent or unsigned artist (without the aid of a label or publicist) can also achieve a fair amount of publicity through various media avenues and even more so now, of course, with the Internet.

If you're releasing a CD, touring, landed a song in TV or film, received an award, or any other significant news item you need to "alert the media." But, before you do there are a few things to understand about the unpredictable nature of publicity.

- In the world of entertainment nothing is impossible but rest assured there are some things that are highly unlikely. Concentrate your efforts where they'll be most effective. Look at your career realistically and start from there. We live in a celebrity culture, however, you are most likely not yet a celebrity. Given that, unless you are a Billboard Top 10 artist you most likely will not be booked on Jay Leno or David Letterman. You'd have a better chance of figuring out where Jay might be hanging out interviewing people on the street, giving odd answers and then being selected to provide commentary from the Grammys or the Olympics. Though, I did hear there was an opening for an intern...
- You most likely will not get reviewed in Rolling Stone or Spin magazine. Read Rolling Stone or Spin magazine and notice for yourself who is reviewed or featured in either publication. If you have read about one or two unsigned acts they were most likely winners of a corporate sponsored contest such as VH1's "Bands On The Run" or yes, on a rare occasion, there is enough of a buzz about an artist that the magazines will feel it warrants coverage.
- You may not land a single interview your first time around promoting a CD. The mere fact you've recorded a CD doesn't guarantee an interview. If you can start out getting mentions of your CD and/or reviews – this is a part of the building process that starts familiarizing your name with the media and the public.
- Publicity is a process that involves researching the media, writing press releases and bios, mailings, communicating with the media, and then...waiting. The first few months require a fair amount of patience because unless you have a breaking news story, it could take just that long before any coverage or reviews appears in print. Interviews and reviews don't happen overnight. The web, of course, has proven to be a quicker source for reviews being posted and email is, I think, the best way to communicate with any number of writers. Persons in all areas of the media receive enormous amounts of mail and it takes at least two weeks or more

(a very generous estimate) before a CD makes it to the listening pile. Major label releases as well as news concerning popular recording artists usually receive priority coverage. And there are times, when reviews and/or interviews, even if already written never see the light of day. A story or review could be "bumped" if say, some bluegrass movie soundtrack CD wins a Grammy or the new- much-anticipated CD by said artist of the moment arrives on the Music Editor's desk. Unlike advertising, which secures your place in a magazine, the number one rule of publicity is that nothing is guaranteed.

Basic Publicity Tools
Keep your mailings simple which will help keep postage costs down. You need only send the CD, a few press clips, press release, bio and cover letter. Artist photos are not always necessary to include when sending out your CDs for reviews as the publication or website will usually use your CD cover to accompany the review.

WEBSITE
Have your bio, press release, photos, music samples, video clips (if any) and CD ordering information on your website. Be sure to include in your press release and bio where the CD is available (Amazon.com, your website, or if it has distribution). Have your photos available on your website and the CD cover so that any interested party can access them to accompany reviews or interviews. However, not any old photo will do.

PHOTOS
When it comes to photos I have seen artists waste more money on trying to save money. Poor quality photos are difficult to reproduce in print. In this day and age with digital cameras you should be able to produce a decent photo. But the best case scenario is to hire a photographer. An experienced photographer understands lighting and composition and good, quality photos make all the difference when submitting to newspapers and magazines. Before hiring a photographer, ask to see their "book" or portfolio. Make sure their style suits what you are trying to portray. If your funds are low seek out student photographers at local universities or new photographers who want to enhance their portfolio. Sometimes they will shoot for free, charging only for the rolls of film and developing.

If you are mailing your photos - whereas 8x10 is the standard size for black & white photos, color slides or transparencies are the preferred "color" format for newspapers and magazines, though sometimes the former will accept color prints. Again some will just grab them directly off your website.

BIOS
The bio is an essential item for any press kit or mailing and should let the reader know the following - who is the artist, style of music, influences, instruments played, experience (tours, music training, studio), awards, releases, radio airplay etc. Pull a positive quote from your reviews (or add quotes later as you gather reviews) and note credit i.e., "brilliant musicianship, and beautiful songs make up this artist's CD" (Los Angeles Times). Discuss past musical endeavors and if it relates to your current project. If inspiration fails you - call a publicist, journalist, fellow college student, bio writers, etc. Professional fees for composing bios may range anywhere from $50 up to $300 or more. Once written a bio should be periodically updated, keeping current with each project.

THE PRESS RELEASE
One of the most effective publicity tools for generating press (aside from pure word of mouth) is a well-written press release. If you are not sure how to write the information, read the industry news columns in various music magazines to get a feel for how it is presented to the reader. Keep it basic and to the point, without too much editorializing i.e., "it is the greatest song ever written," unless it is a quote from an outside source (review or producer of recording). If your press release is announcing a forthcoming show - tie it in with any significant news. Stay away from throwaway lines such as "come see

what everybody is talking about...the buzz on this band is huge...major label interest" - if there is a buzz your press release will be filled with quotes from positive reviews or news about which labels are vying for your attention. As with bios, keep it to no more than two pages in length. One page if possible. The writer who decides to run your press release may alter whatever is written.

To get your show listed, forward the information by email, snail mail or fax (depending on type of publication the lead time is anywhere from two to six weeks in advance) to your local daily and weekly newspapers. Necessary contact information is sometimes provided in the entertainment listings section in the paper or on their website.

Writing the press release - Using the "who, what, where, why" format let's write a press release for the following group.

Here is what we know about the alternative-sans-grunge-psychedelic-jazz styled w/a Salsa feel-group - Rosarita & The Refried Beans.

- Rosarita & The Refried Beans will play the Coconut Teaszer in Hollywood.
- Rosarita is being sued by the Bean Company for use of the name without permission
- R&TRB's shows are usually zany and often feature guest musicians
- R&TRB haven't played much in town lately because they are touring in support of their recently released debut CD

Current Date

For Immediate Release

Contact Name
Phone Number/Email

ROSARITA & THE REFRIED BEANS TO PLAY COCONUT TEASZER , FRIDAY, JANUARY 14

ROSARITA & BEANS SLAPPED WITH LAWSUIT UPON RETURN FROM COAST TOUR
Fresh from their California coastal tour in promotion of their recently released "Too Many Beans, Not Enough Tacos" CD - Rosarita & The Refried Beans will play the Coconut Teaszer, Friday, January 14, 11:30 p.m. As can be expected the band will serve up its alternative-sans-grunge- with-a -Salsa-flavor brand of music. A recent gig was described by the Los Angeles Times as "their show reminds me of eating chili peppers with my grandma." R&TRB will feature the usual round of antics and special guest musicians.

In other matters, Rosarita & The Refried Beans, were recently slapped with a lawsuit by the company of the same name in a "cease and desist" order. A portion of the proceeds from the gig will be donated to the band for its impending legal fees. Commenting on the lawsuit, lead singer Wendy Pragmatic nee Rosarita, stated, "it's very disheartening to all of us because we grew up eating those damn beans."

Rosarita & The Refried Beans' CD is available through UGOTTABKIDIN' Records.

Researching & Communicating with the Media

Researching media avenues you plan to target will result in more effective placement as you supply the appropriate news to the appropriate writers and columns. If you have access to the publication, notice the format, editorial style, music genres covered, if they use black & white or color photos, review CDs, and how often is it published (daily, weekly, bi-weekly, monthly, quarterly)?

If contacting a writer by phone, find out which days they are on deadline and the best times to call. It will help establish a good relationship. E-mail is a great way to communicate with busy writers. Keep your conversation and emails brief and to the point. If you submit a CD for review always follow up (by phone or email). As in any area of the business, don't berate the person if they "pass" on reviewing it or

have to give priority to other releases. Thank them for their time and get over it. You can always send them the next CD.

Such useful guides as The Indie Bible (www.indiebible.com) published annually or the Musician's Guide To Touring And Promotion provide media lists with contact and content info. Magazines and websites do come and go and writers move from publication to publication, so be sure and double check the contact name by email or accessing its website before sending out your materials. For a listing of newspapers and magazines city by city in the U.S. some local libraries carry the Bacon's Media Guide.

Cover Stories - I wish I had $1.00 for every time I've been asked "so do you think we can get on the cover of ....?" The best way to figure out who or what ends up as a cover story of a magazine is to notice with each issue, who or what is on the cover. Covers are generally to sell the magazine. So notice the following … Are the subjects are high-profile celebrities? High profile stories? Legendary artists? New Artists? Buzz Artists?

Again the Internet comes to the rescue with its plethora of music websites catering to independent releases. And many times, if your CD is a featured pick, the cover or review will often be posted on the home page with a link to your website.

Tour Press

Press coverage from out-of-town publications is a great addition to any press kit. After you have booked the shows, ask the club owners for a list of local media. Many times they will also include radio stations open to playing independent releases and/or who also announce a weekly calendar of gigs. Or do a search on the Internet for that particular city. In many cases you can find information about their local media that may have their own web pages. Send emails to the editors and ask who handles music listings, concert previews or CD reviews. If you have a local angle with a particular city include it in your press release and it may result in an article or a preview, both which usually run with a photo and information, of course, about the show. Always ask how far in advance they need the material and which days are their deadlines. If they need it the next day or within two days to ensure delivery, spend the extra money and send it by overnight delivery.

Sometimes you may find it easier to achieve a photo and mention of your gig on tour (in less saturated markets) than in your own hometown. You may not "score" the first time but as the various media become more familiar with your name - you will stand a better chance of receiving advance press and hopefully a writer assigned to review your show.

Hiring a Publicist

Maybe at this point you're thinking "hey I don't have the time to do all of this - why don't I just hire someone to do it for me!?" If you have the funds to hire a publicist, there are some things you should know. Independent publicists or PR firms charge anywhere from $500 to $6000 per month and that may not include expenses. Some may negotiate their fees or accept a flat rate for the whole project. Some require a 2 -3 month non-refundable deposit up front (so you don't "bail" because you haven't landed on Leno). Most publicists or firms do not work out payment plans because of the nature of publicity. Clients often expect publicists to wave the PR wand and magically they will find themselves in every magazine on the racks. It is a common misconception stemming from the belief that if a publicist has contacts with high profile publications and TV shows that the client is automatically guaranteed such coverage. If any publicist ever gives you such a guarantee - run! Granted they may have an easier time (than you would) convincing their contacts to listen to your music but that doesn't mean you are a "shoe in." It takes time for even a major public relations firm to generate press. Also, for a variety of reasons, such higher profile publicity firms prefer to work with artists signed to a major record label or a well-known independent label because - they are extremely busy with high profile clients; may feel there is really nothing to publicize or feel it would be too much work to try and land the coverage they are used to securing for celebrities (magazine covers, TV interviews, etc.).

And unless you are out on tour and/or there is daily newsworthy

bout your project – try to refrain from calling or emailing your
every day. Remember that everything takes time and for a
the job is as much about writing the press releases, bios (if
necessary), letters, phone calls, emails, mailings, thinking about,
focusing on the material and researching possible media avenues, as it
is about securing reviews and interviews. Again, nobody can really
guarantee the coverage. But if after a three or four months you don't
have any idea of where its going then perhaps a different publicist can
provide a different perspective to take it another direction. There's not
much we can do if few writers are interested in covering a particular
artist. I personally have never worked on a project that nobody wanted
to cover, but again, I have also turned down some that I knew would
stand little chance of getting what I thought would be a fair amount of
coverage. And many times after wrapping up a project I've had reviews
appear six months to a year later due to various writers and magazines'
backlog of reviews and publication schedules.

Whatever road you decide to take, the time to start is now. Don't
expect results overnight or underestimate the amount of coverage you
receive. As your career builds so will the publicity.

*Since 1992 Teresa has worked as an independent publicist through her
company Teresa Conboy PR. Prior to starting her own business she
worked at a major entertainment public relations firm and with
numerous independent artists. Teresa's clients have included major and
independent record labels, films, entertainment industry support
services, music & cultural festivals, authors, music equipment
manufacturers, radio & film personalities and theatre projects.
http://home.earthlink.net/~tcpr tcpr@earthlink.net*

♦

HOW TO BE YOUR OWN PUBLICIST
by Ariel Hyatt, Ariel Publicity
© 2004 All Rights Reserved. Used By Permission

For this article, I interviewed several entertainment writers from
across the country. Their comments and advice are included throughout.
Writers who will come up throughout are: Mike Roberts (The Denver
Westword), Jae Kim (The Chicago Sun Times), Silke Tudor (The SF
Weekly).

MYTH: A Big Fat Press Kit Will Impress a Writer.

TRUTH: Writers will only become exasperated by a press kit that is not
succinct and to the point. A bio, a photo and 6-8 articles double-sided
on white paper is a good sized kit. If a writer wants to read more than
that he will contact you for further information. If you don't have any
articles, don't worry, this will soon change.

The first step in your journey is to create a press kit, which consists of
four parts — the Bio, the Photo, the Articles and the CD.

Jae Kim: "The ultimate press kit is a very basic press kit which
includes: a CD, a photo with band members' names labeled on it — not
a fuzzy, arty photo — a clear black and white, a bio, and press clips —
10 at most, one or two at least. 40 is way too much."

PART 1: The Bio
Write a one page band bio that is succinct and interesting to read. I
strongly advise avoiding vague cliches such as: melodic, brilliant
harmonies, masterful guitar playing, tight rhythm section, etc. These are
terms that can be used to describe any type of music. Try to make your
description stand out. Create an introduction that sums up your sound,
style and attitude in a few brief sentences. This way if a writer is
pressed for time, she can simply take a sentence or two from your bio
and place it directly in the newspaper. If you try to make a writer dig
deeply for the gist, that writer will most likely put your press kit aside
and look to one of the other 30 press kits that arrived that week.

TIP: Try to create a bio with the assumption that a vast majority of
music writers may never get around to listening to your CD (500 new
releases come out in the United States each week). Also, writers are
usually under tight deadlines to produce copy — so many CD's fall by
the wayside.

Q.   Whose press materials stand out in your memory ?
A.   Jae Kim: "Action shots of bands. Blur has had a few great photos,
and Mariah's are always very pretty. Also, Mary Cutrufello on Mercury
has a great photo — enigmatic with a mysterious quality. Her picture
was honest and intelligent, just like her music."
A.   Silke Tudor: "The Slow Poisoners — a local SF band who are very
devoted to their presentation. They have a distinct style and everything
leads in to something else. Photos are dangerous. If the band looks
young and they're mugging you have a pretty safe idea of what they're
going to sound like."

PART 2: The Photo
It is very tough to create a great band photo. In the thousands that I
have encountered only a few have had creativity and depth. I know it
can seem cheesy to arrange a photo shoot but if you take this part
seriously you will deeply benefit from it in the long run.

Create a photo that is clear, light, and attention grabbing. Five
musicians sitting on a couch is not interesting. If you have a friend who
knows how to use PhotoShop, I highly recommend you enroll him or
her to help you do some funky editing. Mike Roberts tends to gravitate
towards: "Any photos that are not four guys standing against a wall.
Also, a jazz musician doesn't always have to be holding a horn."

MYTH: Photos Cost a Fortune to Process in 8 x10 Format.

TRUTH: Photos do not have to be expensive. There a few places to
have photos printed for a great price. My personal favorite is ABC
Pictures in Springfield, MO. They will print 500 photos (with layout
and all shipping) for $80. Click the link to check out their web site or
telephone 888.526.5336. Another great resource is a company called 1-
800-POSTCARD, which will print 5000 full-color, double-sided
postcards for $250. Extra postcards not used in press kits can be sent to
people on your mailing list, or you can sell them or give them away at
gigs

PART 3: The Articles
Getting that first article written about you can be quite a challenge.
Two great places to start are your local town papers (barring you don't
live in Manhattan or Los Angeles) and any local fanzine (available at
your favorite indie record store). In addition, a few hours of net surfing
will reveal the hundreds of sites that review CD's. Look for reviews of
music that is similar to your band's type of music and then send your
CD's to those reviewers. As your touring and effort swell, so will the
amount of articles written about your band.

PART 4: The CD
I assume that if you are reading this you probably already have
your CD printed and ready to go. If this is not the case, CD's are easy
to print up and lots of manufacturers can guide you in the process. My
favorite CD manufacturing house is AMG CD's. They do a great job,
have a quick turn-around time, and their prices are great. Mention that
you found out about them through us and you will get a discount!!

The CD artwork, like the press kit, must be well thought out. You
should customize your press kits so that they look in sync with your
CD. This way when a writer opens up a package the press kit and the
CD look like they go together. Also, put your phone number and
contact info in the CD so if it gets separated from the press kit, the
writer knows how to contact you. I asked Eric Rosen, the VP of
Radical Records, how he oversees the development of product. He had
a few things to say about stickering CD's (placing an extra sticker on
the cover to spark the interest of a writer).

"If you are going to sticker your product, be unique in the way you
present it — try to be clever about it — plain white stickers are
boring." He went on to say that "Recommended Tracks" stickers are

great for the press (suggesting no more than two or three selections). Eric does not think that stickers are too advantageous in CD stores, because then "You are just covering up your artwork."

Don't waste precious CD's! Keep in mind that 500 new CD's come out every week in the United States. Unless you are sure a writer actually writes CD reviews (many are not given the space to run them) don't waste your hard-earned dollars sending that writer a CD. Again, ask the promoter which writers like to receive CD's for review and which ones don't need them.

Q. What do writers like ?
A. Silke Tudor: "When people personalize things and use casual words. If an envelope is hand-addressed, I will notice it right away and I always open things that people put together themselves. Hand-written stuff gets read first. . .The bands that do PR for themselves are the ones that stand out for me"
A. Mike Roberts: "Include the name, show date, time, ticket price, place, and who you are playing with. If I don't see the contact number I have 69 other kits to get to."

Q. What do writers hate ?
A. Jae Kim: "I hate those padded envelopes that get gray flaky stuff all over you — I feel like it's asbestos." She also dislikes "When I get a package with glitter or confetti in it — it gets all over my desk." "I [also] don't like Q & A sheets" — She prefers to come up with questions herself rather than receive answers pre-fabricated for her and spoon-fed.
A. Silke Tudor similarly reports: "I never open anything over my computer."
A. Mike Roberts: "I don't have much interest in gimmicks like hard candy. If I tried to eat it, it might kill me. Also you can't expect a writer to shove something in the paper at the last minute. Please give as much lead time as possible."
Q. What do writers throw in the garbage immediately?
A. Mike Roberts: "Anything past deadline."
A. Jae Kim: "Pictures of women's butts or profanity that is degrading to women."
A. Silke Tudor: "If I already know the band and I know that I don't like it."

GETTING YOUR PRESS MATERIALS OUT THERE

So, you have a press kit together, now what? Try to start planning PR for any tour 6-8 weeks before you hit the road. As soon as a gig is booked, ask the promoter for the club's press list (most clubs have one). This is a list of all of the publications in the area that write about music. Promoters are dependent on this local press to help sell tickets. Have the list faxed or e-mailed to you. Don't be shy — you are working with the promoter to make the show happen and promoters love it when the show is well publicized. Also be sure to ask the promoter who his or her favorite writers are and which ones will like your style of music. Then, when you call those writers, don't be afraid to say which promoter recommended them and invite them to the show. I was the PR director for The Fox Theatre in Boulder, Colorado for five years and the bands who get the biggest push from me were the ones who cared about their PR and who kept in touch with me before they were coming to town.

If the local promoter has a publicist, let that publicist do his job. This person lives where you only visit a few times a year. He will pay for the postage and send the press kits.
Pack everything up and mail it to the promoters. Make sure you ask the promoters how many posters they would like and send them along with the press kits. After a few days, call to verify that the material was received.

If you can't afford to send kits to everyone, ask the promoters in each area which three or four writers would most likely cover a band that plays your style of music. Also, ask the promoters where the clubs run strip ads — these ads will be in the papers that cover music and inform people in the area about club happenings.

If you are servicing press yourself, and the club does not have a

press list, pick up The Musician's Atlas, or The Musician's Guide To Touring. Both of these guides are packed with a wealth of information on publicity outlets across the country, as well as venues, record stores, labels, etc. I recommend sending materials 4-6 weeks prior to the gig. Beware of monthly publications — if you are not at least six weeks out, don't bother sending to them.

CALL THE WRITERS

Most of the time you will be leaving messages on voice mail. Be polite, get right to the point, and be brief!! 9 times out of 10 writers will not call you back.

PERSEVERE

If you are a totally new band and you are worried because a paper did not cover you the first time around, keep sending that paper information every time you play in the area. I have never met a writer that ignores several press kits from the same band sent over and over again. It may take a few passes through in each market, but the more a writer sees over time, the more likely he will be to write about you.

DON'T LET ALL THAT VOICEMAIL DISCOURAGE YOU

I have placed hundreds of articles, mentions, and photos without ever speaking to the writer.

WRITERS USUALLY RESPOND MUCH BETTER TO E-MAIL

It's free for them and does not take too long to respond to. If you are sending e-mail follow-ups, put a link to your site, or the club's site if you don't have one. You can also send a sound clip if you have the capability. IMPORTANT NOTE: Don't bother sending out materials a few days before the gig. Writers are usually way past their deadlines by then and they won't be able to place your band.

POSTERS

Posters are a great form of PR and they don't have to cost you a fortune. The most cost-effective way to make posters is to buy 11x17 colored paper from your local paper store (approx. $7 per ream of 500) and run off copies at the copy shop (approx. 7 cents each). Make several white copies and include these with your colored posters — this way the promoter can make extras, if needed. For higher quality posters, I recommend a copy process called docutech. These cost a penny or so more apiece, but they are computer-generated and look better than regular copies. Have whoever designed your poster also design small lay-ups to send out as fliers and ad-mats. Make sure your logo is included on them so the promoter can use them for strip or display advertising.

HAVE PATIENCE

The first few times you play a market, you may not get any press. PR is a slow moving vehicle that can take time to get results. I have worked with some bands that have needed to go through a market 3-4 times before any results started showing up in the press. When sending materials on repeated occasions, include a refresher blurb to remind the writer of your style. ALWAYS include the following information: date, show time, ages, ticket price, club name and address, time, and who is on the bill. Don't make writers hunt around for the event info. Make their job as easy as possible by providing as much information as possible. Also keep in mind that some writers will probably not write about you over and over again. If you hit the same markets continually, try to lay off the press who have already written about you — a great tactic is to change your photo every few months and write "New Band Photo" on the outside of the envelope so writers know they have something new to work with.

FIELD STAFF

Try to enroll a fan to be on your field staff in each market you visit. In exchange for a few tickets to your show, have this person put up posters, hand out fliers, and talk to the college newspaper about writing a feature or the local radio station about spinning your CD. To get a field staff started, include a sign up column on your mailing list and on your web site. If they sign up, they are the people for you! With a bit of planning and focus, you can spin your own publicity wheel. All it takes is foresight and organization. A band that plans well is a band that receives the most PR.

YOUR WEBSITE

If you don't already have one — get on it!! Websites can be easy and inexpensive to design — you can buy software that can take you through it step by step. Better yet, have a friend or a fan help you design a site. Your site should include your upcoming tour dates, as most people will visit it to find out when you are coming through town. Another great place to post all of your dates is tourdates.com — it is FREE and you can also put your bio and photo up as well. More advanced sites include merch as well as CD sales. This is a great idea if you are at the point where you're selling a lot of merch. If you are not there yet, at least link your site to a place where fans can order your CD.

Happy Publicizing and Good Luck!! If you are playing in New York City, please let us know.

Ariel Hyatt is the President of Ariel Publicity, Artist Relations, and Cyber Promotions, in NYC. For the past five years she has worked closely publicizing a diverse family of touring and developing indie bands including Sally Taylor, Leftover Salmon, K-Floor, The Stone Coyotes, Soulhat, Fathead, and devon. http://www.arielpublicity.com

◆

PREPARING FOR DISTRIBUTION

by Daylle Deanna Schwartz, author of "The Real Deal"
© Copyright, 2004, Revenge Productions. Reprinted with permission.

People who want to press up their music in order to sell it are most concerned about getting distribution. But, that shouldn't be your focus in the beginning. If you want to make money from your music, first take yourself seriously as a business. Whether you like it or not, outside of your circle of fans, you and your music are looked upon as products. If you prefer being idealistic, create and perform music for fun. But, if earning a living from your music is an eventual goal, developing a *business attitude* is critical.

What's necessary? Read books on the biz and attend seminars if you can. Get a good picture of how the music industry operates. Network as much as possible to create a support system of folks you can call on for resources, advice and encouragement. While you shouldn't negotiate your own contracts, you should know enough to discuss the terms of one with your lawyer. Don't be one of those musicians who tell their lawyer, publisher, manager, etc., "Whatever you say." Gather enough knowledge so you can make informed decisions based on input from your representatives. Think of yourself as a professional. Even if you're only pressing up your own music, you're a record label. Act like one! Being responsible will max your chances of others wanting to work with you.

Getting distribution isn't the end-all, cure-all. You can ship 500 pieces and get them all back if you haven't been able to promote your product to a target audience. Distributors get records into stores. Most don't promote them. Stores tell me that records sell because people know the artist. Before taking in your product, distributors need to see that you have a market already interested in buying it. Creating a demand is what sells records. Distributors want you to have a handle on promotion before they work with your label. Once you have that, they'll want your product.

Do the groundwork before trying to get distribution. Be patient until you have a foundation to sell from. Until you identify your potential market and develop strategies for letting them know about your music, having distribution won't sell CDs. The most important thing you can do first is to target the group who might buy your product and figure out how to reach them. Distributors want product that will sell. They want to work with labels that have artists with a buzz going. They don't care how good the music is if nobody knows about it.

It still amazes me how many folks come to me for consultations and aren't sure who is most likely to buy their music. They tell me since it's good music, everyone will buy. That usually means they have no clue and don't want to bother to figure it out. That's not good business! If you can't target your audience, play your music for people who work in record stores or other music related folks and ask for their honest feedback. Ask a bunch so that you have a well-rounded picture.

Of course there may be people outside of your identified market who will buy your product. But promote it to the group more likely to appreciate it. Is it college students? Young adults? Teens? Baby boomers? Once you know that, what kinds of promotion will you do to make them want to buy your record? Figuring this out sounds simple at first but if it was, there would be a lot more records making big money independently. Many people think if the music is great, people will buy it. Not true! They need to hear it and be enticed to buy it. How will you reach their ears? What will make them buy it? Figuring out a marketing plan can be the hardest part of putting out your music. Distribution is easy once you get this in place.

The best way to get your product into stores is to develop a story around your act first. Focus your energy on getting reviews, getting radio play (college and public radio are best to start with), selling product on your own, and increasing your fan base by touring. Create a demand. Then put together a one-page synopsis of the artist's story, known as a one-sheet. This has the artist's story - reviews and stories in the media (include quotes), radio play, gigs, direct sales, internet presence, etc, as well as details about the record itself. Include anything that shows the act is marketable, concisely on one sheet of paper. A small photo of the act and/or the album cover should be on the sheet too.

Send your one-sheet to potential distributors. Don't send a sample of the music until they request it. The story is more important than the music. Some distributors take calls if you want to try that first. But if their interest is piqued, they'll ask you to fax them a one-sheet. Be prepared. Don't approach distributors until you have a good foundation. Make them take you seriously the first time! Distributors are in the business of selling records. If they think yours will sell, they'll carry it. It's that simple. Start with a local distributor until your buzz gets stronger and you prove you can sell product on a wider scale. Then work your way up to larger ones.

Daylle Deanna Schwartz is the author of Start & Run Your Own Record Label and The Real Deal: How to Get Signed to a Record Label from A to Z, both on Billboard Books. She also teaches full day seminars and does consulting on these topics. http://www.outersound.com/revenge   revenge@erols.com

◆

MUSIC MARKETING STRATEGIES

by Derek Sivers, CEO CD Baby
© Copyright, 2004, Derek Sivers. Reprinted with permission.

CALL THE DESTINATION, AND ASK FOR DIRECTIONS

Work backwards. Define your goal (your final destination) - then contact someone who's there, and ask how to get there? If you want to be in Rolling Stone magazine, pick up the phone, call their main office in New York City, and when the receptionist answers, say "Editorial, please." Ask someone in the editorial department which publicists they recommend. Then call each publicist, and try to get their attention. (Hint: Don't waste Rolling Stone's time asking for the publicist's phone number. You can find it elsewhere. Get off the phone as soon as possible.)

If you want to play at the biggest club in town, bring a nice box of fancy German cookies to the club booker, and ask for just 5 minutes of their advice. Ask them what criteria must be met in order for them to take a chance on an act. Ask what booking agents they recommend, or if they recommend using one at all. Again, keep your meeting as short as possible. Get the crucial info, then leave them alone. (Until you're back, headlining their club one day!)

I know an artist manager of a small unsigned act, who over the course of a year, met with the managers of U2, REM, and other top acts. She asked them for their advice, coming from the top, and got great suggestions that she's used with big results.

In other words: Call the destination, and ask for directions. You'll get there much faster than just blindly walking out your front door, hoping you arrive someday.

PUT YOUR FANS TO WORK

You know those loyal few people who are in the front row every time you perform? You know those people that sat down to write you an Email to say how much they love your music? You know that guy that said, "Hey if you ever need anything - just ask!" Put them to work!

Often, people who reach out like that are looking for a connection in this world. Looking for a higher cause. They want to feel they have some other purpose than their stupid accounting job. You may be the best thing in their life. You can break someone out of their drab life as an assistant sales rep for a manufacturing company. You might be the coolest thing that ever happened to a teenager going through an unpopular phase. You can give them a mission!

If they're a fan of your music, invite them over for pizza to spend a night doing a mailing to colleges. Go hit the town together, putting concert flyers on telephone poles. Have them drive a van full of friends to your gig an hour away. Have the guts to ask that "email fan" if she'd be into going through the Indie Contact Bible and sending your press kit to 20 magazines a week. Soon you can send them out on their own, to spread the gospel message of your amazing music, one promo project at a time. Eventually, as you grow, these people can be the head of "street teams" of 20 people in a city that go promote you like mad each time you have a concert or a new CD.

Those of us busy busy people may think, "How could ANYone do this slave work?" But there are plenty of people out there with time on their hands that want to spend it on something besides TV.

Don't forget that to most people, the music business is pure magic. It's Hollywood. It's glitter and fame and fantastically romantic. Working with you might be the closest the get to that magical world of music. Give someone the chance to be on the inside circle. Put 'em to work.

GO WHERE THE FILTERS ARE

Have you been filtered? If not, you should start now. (Huh?) With the Internet, there are more "media outlets" than anyone can digest. A site like MP3.COM has 100,000 artists on there. Many of them are crap. People in the music biz get piles of CDs in the mail everyday from amateurs. Many of them are crap. But you're not crap, are you? No! So prove it! Don't sit in the bin with the rest.

You need to go through filters. Places that reject many, only letting the best of the best pass through. As long as you're good (really good) - what you want are MORE filters! More obstacles... More hurdles... Because these things weed out the "bad" music. Or the music that isn't ready. Or the people that weren't dedicated.

I worked at Warner Brothers for 3 years. I learned why they never accept unsolicited demos: It helps weed out the people that didn't do enough research to know they have to go meet managers or lawyers or David Geffen's chauffeur FIRST in order to get to the "big boys." (Deal with the 'gatekeepers' to get to the mansion.) If you REALLY REALLY BELIEVE in your music, have the confidence to put yourself into those places where MOST people get rejected. (radio, magazines, big venues, agents, managers, record labels, promoters...) Because each gate you get through puts you in finer company. ("the best of the best") And you'll find many more opportunities open to you once you've earned your way through a few gates.

HAVE SOMEONE WORK THE INSIDE OF THE INDUSTRY

I prefer to ignore the music industry. Maybe that's why you don't see me on the cover of Rolling Stone. One of my only regrets about my own band was that we toured and got great reviews, toured and got lots of air play, toured and booked some great-paying gigs. BUT... nobody was working the inside of the music business. Nobody was connecting with the "gatekeepers" to bring us to the next level. We just kept doing the same gigs. Maybe you're happy on the outside of the biz. (I know I am.) But if you want to tour with major-label artists, be on the cover of

national magazines, be in good rotation on the biggest radio stations in town, or get onto MTV, you're going to have to have someone working the inside of the biz. Someone who loves it. Someone who is loved by it. Someone persuasive who gets things done 10 times faster than you ever could. Someone who's excited enough about it, that they would never be discouraged. Like your love of making music. You wouldn't just "stop" making music because you didn't get a record deal would you? Then you need to find someone who's equally passionate about the business side of music, and particularly the business side of YOUR music.

BE A NOVICE MARKETER, NOT AN EXPERT

Get to the point of being a novice marketer/promoter/agent. Then hand it to an expert.

Moby, the famous techno artist, says the main reason for his success was that he found experts to do what they're best at, instead of trying to do it himself. (Paraphrased:) "Instead of trying to be a booking agent, publicist, label, and manager, I put my initial energy into finding and impressing the best agent, publicist, label, and manager. And I just kept making lots of the best music I could."

If you sense you are becoming an expert, figure out what your real passions in life are and act accordingly. Maybe you're a better publicist than bassist. Maybe you're a better bassist than publicist. Maybe it's time to admit your weakness as a booking agent, and hand it off to someone else. Maybe it's time to admit your genius as a booking agent, and commit to it full- time.

REACH THEM LIKE YOU WOULD WANT TO BE REACHED

Reach people like you would want to be reached. Would you rather have someone call you up in a dry business monotone, and start speaking a script like a telemarketer? Or would you rather have someone be a cool person, a real person?

When you contact people, no matter how it's done (phone, email, mail, face-to-face) - show a little spunk. Stand apart from the crowd. If it sounds like they have a moment and aren't in a major rush, entertain them a bit. Ask about their day and expect a real answer. Talk about something non-business for a minute or two. Or - if they sound hectic, skip the "how are you", skip the long introduction, ask your damn question and move out of the way. This means you must know your exact question before you contact them, just in case that ultra-quick situation is needed.

Reach them like you would want to be reached. Imagine what kind of phone call or Email YOU would like to get. If you're contacting fans, imagine what kind of flyer they would like to get in their mailbox. Something dull and "just the facts" - or something a little twisted, creative, funny, entertaining and unique? Something corporate, or something artistic?

This is a creative decision on your part. Every contact with the people around your music (fans and industry) is an extension of your art. If you make depressing, morose, acoustic music, maybe you should send your fans a dark brown-and-black little understated flyer that's depressing just to look at. Set the tone. Pull in those people who love that kind of thing. Proudly alienate those that don't.

If you're an in-your-face, tattooed, country-metal-speedpunk band, have the guts to call a potential booking agent and scream, "Listen you fucking motherfucker! I'm going to explode! Ah! Aaaaaaah!!!" If they like that introduction, you've found a good match. Be different. (Even if it's just in your remarkable efficiency.) Everyone wants a little change in their day.

WHAT HAS WORKED ON YOU?

Any time you're trying to influence people to do something, think what has worked on YOU in the past. Are you trying to get people to buy your CD? Write down the last 20 CDs you bought, then for each one, write down what made you buy it. Did you ever buy a CD because of a matchbook, postcard, or 30-second web soundclip? What DID work? (Reviews, word-of-mouth, live show?) Write down your top 10 favorite artists of all time, and a list of what made you discover each one and become a fan.

This goes beyond music. Which TV ads made you buy something?

What anonymous Emails made you click a link and check out a website? Which flyers or radio ads made you go see a live show by someone you had never heard?

HAVE THE CONFIDENCE TO TARGET

Bad Target Example: Progressive Rocker Targeting Teeny Bopper

On CD Baby, there is a great musician who made an amazing heavy-progressive-metal record. When we had a "search keywords" section, asking for three artists he sounds like, he wrote, "britney spears, ricky martin, jennifer lopez, backstreet boys, mp3, sex, free" What the hell was he thinking? He just wanted to turn up in people's search engines, at any cost.

But for what? And who? Did he really want a Britney Spears fan to get "tricked" into finding his dark-progressive-metal record? Would that 13-year-old girl actually spend the 25 minutes to download his 10 minute epic, "Confusing Mysteries of Hell"? If she did, would she buy his CD? I suggested he instead have the confidence to target the REAL fans of his music. He put three semi-obscure progressive artists into the search engine, and guess what? He's selling more CDs than ever! He found his true fans.

IF YOU DON'T SAY WHAT YOU SOUND LIKE, YOU WON'T MAKE ANY FANS.

A person asks you, "What kind of music do you do?" Musicians say, "All styles. Everything." That person then asks, "So who do you sound like?" Musicians say, "Nobody. We're totally unique. Like nothing you've ever heard before." What does that person do? Nothing. They might make a vague promise to check you out sometime. Then they walk on, and forget about you! Why??? You didn't arouse their curiosity! You violated a HUGE rule of self-promotion! Bad bad bad!

What if you had said, "It's 70's porno-funk music being played by men from Mars." Or... "This CD is a delicate little kiss on your earlobe from a pink-winged pixie. Or... "We sound like a cross between AC/DC and Tom Jones." Or... "It's deep-dancing reggae that magically places palm trees and sand wherever it is played, and grooves so deep it makes all non-dancers get drunk on imaginary island air, and dance in the sand." Any one of these, and you've got their interest.

Get yourself a magic key phrase that describes what you sound like. Try out a few different ones, until you see which one always gets the best reaction from strangers. Use it. Have it ready at a moment's notice. It doesn't have to narrow what you do at all. Any of those three examples I use above could sound like anything. And that's just the point - if you have a magic phrase that describes your music in curious but vague terms, you can make total strangers start wondering about you. But whatever you do, stay away from the words "everything", "nothing", "all styles", and "totally unique". Say something!

TOUCH AS MANY OF THEIR SENSES AS YOU CAN

The more senses you touch in someone, the more they'll remember you. BEST: a live show, with you sweating right on top of someone, the PA system pounding their chest, the smell of the smoky club, the flashing lights and live-in-person performance. WORST: an email. a single web page. a review in a magazine with no photo.

Whenever possible, try to reach as many senses as possible. Have an amazing photo of yourself or your band, and convince every reviewer to put that photo next to the review of your album. Send videos with your press kit. Play live shows often. Understand the power of radio to make people hear your music instead of just hearing about it. Get onto any TV shows you can. Scent your album with patchouli oil. Make your songs and productions truly emotional instead of merely catchy. (Touching their emotions is like touching their body. If you do it, you'll be remembered.)

BE AN EXTREME VERSION OF YOURSELF

Define yourself. Show your weirdness. Bring out all your quirks. Your public persona, the image you show to the world, should be an extreme version of yourself.

A GOOD BIZ PLAN WINS NO MATTER WHAT HAPPENS

In doing this test marketing you should make a plan that will make you a success even if nobody comes along with their magic wand. Start now. Don't wait for a "deal". Don't just record a "demo" that is meant only for record companies.

You have all the resources you need to make a finished CD that thousands of people would want to buy. If you need more money, get it from anyone except a record company. And if, as you're following your great business plan, selling hundreds, then thousands of CDs, selling out small, then larger venues, getting on the cover of magazines... you'll be doing so well that you won't need a record deal. And if a record deal IS offered to you, you'll be in the fine position of taking it or leaving it. There's nothing more attractive to an investor than someone who doesn't need their money. Someone who's going to be successful whether they're involved or not.

Make the kind of business plan that will get you to a good sustainable level of success, even without a big record deal. That way you'll win no matter what happens.

DON'T BE AFRAID TO ASK FOR FAVORS

Don't be afraid to ask for favors. Some people LIKE doing favors. It's like asking for directions in New York City. People's egos get stroked when they know the answer to something you're asking. They'll gladly answer to show off their knowledge.

One bold musician I know called me up one day and said, "I'm coming to New York in 2 months. Can you give me a list of all the important contacts you think I should meet?" What guts! But I laughed, and did a search in my database, E-mailing him a list of 40 people he should call, and mention my name.

Sometimes you need to find something specific: a video director for cheap, a PA system you can borrow for a month, a free rehearsal studio. Call up everyone you know and ask! This network of friends you are creating will have everything you want in life. Some rare and lucky folks (perhaps on your "band mailing list") have time on their hands and would rather help you do something, than sit at home in front of the TV another night. Need help doing flyers? Help getting equipment to a show? Go ahead and ask!

KEEP IN TOUCH!

Sometimes the difference between success and failure is just a matter of keeping in touch! There are some AMAZING musicians who have sent a CD to CD Baby, and when I heard it, I flipped. In a few cases, I've stopped what I was doing at that moment, picked up the phone and called them wherever they were to tell them I thought they were a total genius. (Believe me - this is rare. Maybe 1 in 500 CDs that I hear.) Often I get an answering machine, and guess what... they don't call back!! What masochistic anti-social success-sabotaging kind of thing is that to do? Then 2 weeks later I've forgotten about their CD as new ones came in.

The lesson: If they would have just called back, and kept in touch, they may have a fan like no other at the head of one of the largest distributors of independent music on the web. A fan that would go out on a limb to help their career in ways others just dream of. But they never kept in touch and now I can't remember their names. Some others whose CDs didn't really catch my attention the first time around, just keep in touch so well that I often find myself helping them more as a friend than a fan.

Keep in touch, keep in touch, keep in touch! People forget you very fast.

A SHORT DESCRIPTION - 10 SECONDS OR LESS

Most of the world has never heard your music. Most of the world WON'T hear your music, unless you do a good job describing it. It's like a Hollywood screenplay. You not only have to write a great screenplay, but you have to have a great description of it that you can say in 10 seconds or less, in order to catch people's attention. Find a way to describe your music that would catch anyone's attention, AND describe it accurately. No use coming up with a funny description of your music if it doesn't actually describe what you really sound like!

READ ABOUT NEW MUSIC. USE THE TRICKS THAT WORKED ON YOU

Go get a magazine like CMJ, or Magnet, or Alternative Press. You'll read about (and see pictures of) dozens of artists who you've never heard of before. Out of that whole magazine, only one or two will really catch your attention. WHY?

I don't have the answer. Only you do. Ask yourself why a certain headline or photo or article caught your attention. (Was it something about the opening sentence? Was it a curious tidbit about the background of the singer? What was it exactly that intrigued you?)

Analyze that. Use that. Adapt those techniques to try writing a headline or article about your music.

WHO'S WRITING THIS? Derek Sivers. Musician. Founder of CD Baby. I've been a full-time musician for about 8 years. Toured the world as a guitarist sideman with some famous folks, (played to sold-out 15,000 seat stadiums.) Toured the country in a circus, too. Ran a recording studio. Worked inside the industry at Warner/Chappell Music for 3 years. Had some really great teachers that taught me a lot about the music business. Cracked the college market and got hired by 400 colleges in 3 years. Sold a few thousand of my own CD.

◆

HOW TO GET INTO THE COLLEGE MARKET IN 4 STEPS
by Derek Sivers, CEO CD Baby
© 2004 All Rights Reserved. Used By Permission

I've made a good living playing colleges for the last 4 years. I've been hired by over 350 colleges around the Northeast. I made good money doing it, but also wasted TONS of money sometimes, doing things wrong. Here's my best advice, from experience, on what works and what doesn't...

1. Get the database of colleges and complete contact info for the current person that does the hiring of entertainment at each college. There are about 2800 colleges in the U.S. that constantly hire entertainment. You better have a good database or contact management program. I recommend Indie Band Manager. Though other popular ones are Filemaker, ACT, MS Access, Claris Works, MS Works, MS Outlook, Goldmine, etc.

   I still constantly maintain an updated list of 2880 colleges and the full contact info for the exact person at each school that is doing the hiring of entertainment. I sell it for $75, which includes free updates for as long as I have them. You can buy it at https://www.cdbaby.com/artists

2. Send a one-page flyer to every school. A GOOD one-page flyer with picture, price, testimonial quotes, contact info. Fun, colorful, exciting. Describe things in their terms. Don't talk about the drummer's background or the member names. Prove in 6 seconds why you will be a reliable good time for an evening at their college.

   Name your price clearly! (I recommend $950 for a band, and $450 for a solo act. If they like you, charge a little more next time. But for a new, unknown act even in their circles, don't expect more than this.) My advice on how to make a good college flyer is here: http://cdbaby.org/collegeflyer

3. Tell them, on the flyer, to call for free CD and video. Send it ASAP when they DO call. Follow-up until they say no thanks. Once they say "No" do NOT call them back. They hate that.

4. When one school books you, call ALL the other schools in the area. Send them great promo material. Have colorful posters, table tents, postcards. And do not be depressed when you play to 4 people on a Tuesday afternoon in a fluorescent lit cafeteria. Be nice, take the money, go home, thank them, and keep in touch...

Voila. That's it. The best bang for the buck in the college market. (And believe me I tried MANY other ways of doing it. Don't waste your money. Do it this way.)

COLLEGE FYI:
1. Sending 500 flyers will usually get you 4 phone calls. 2 of those will hopefully turn into bookings. But it only costs $150 to mail 500 flyers, and you'll make that back with one gig.

2. They often book a semester in advance. In October they book their February - May entertainment. In March they book their September-December calendar.

3. Don't email. Don't call unless it's crucial. Just send a short flyer that can be read in 10 seconds. Send more than that and they won't read it. Trust me. (I once spent $3000 sending every college the ultimate kit with video, CD, 10 pages of info, etc. I didn't get one single phone call!!! A few months later I sent a single effortless one-page flyer. I got 20 calls and 10 gigs. Go figure...)

4. Student activities people that hire you are the squeaky clean girls than run for class treasurer. College radio people are the rebels with pierced faces. The two camps do NOT communicate. If you want college radio play, it's a whole different world. Don't think that they'll just fall into place for you.

5. Don't bother joining NACA and going to the conferences and all that mess unless you're totally committed to it. Yes it may get you some more gigs, but you'll spend $3000 to find out. Those conferences are way too expensive. My band HIT ME got the big main stage showcase one year and yes we booked 30 gigs that weekend. BUT - it took me three years, 12 conferences, and about $20,000 to get it. My best advice to start, is to save the $, go with my plan #1-4 at the top of this page.

© 2004 Derek Sivers - all rights reserved - if you like this article check out my websites:
cdbaby.com | hostbaby.com | agentbaby.com | marketingyourmusic.com | musicthoughts.com | hitmedia.com

◆

THE IMPORTANCE OF TEST MARKETING
by Derek Sivers, CEO CD Baby
© 2004 All Rights Reserved. Used By Permission

In this indie music world, the best thing you can do is think in terms of "Test Marketing." This is what food companies do before they release a new product. They release it just in Denver (for example), and see what people think of it there. They get feedback. They try a different name. They try an improved flavor, based on complaints or compliments. They try a different ad campaign. They see what works. Constantly improving. When it's a huge success in Denver, they know they're on to something good. They can now release it in Portland, Dallas, and Pittsburgh. Do the same thing.

When everyone seems to like it, they get the financial backing to "roll it out" and confidently spend a ton of money to distribute it around the whole country, or the whole world. The people investing money into it are confident, because it was a huge success in all the test markets.

Think of what you're doing with your music as test marketing.
When you're a huge success on a lower level, or in a small area, THEN you can go to the big companies and ask for financial or resource help to "roll it out" to the country or world. Then they'll feel confident that their big money is being well invested.

© 2004 Derek Sivers - all rights reserved - if you like this article check out my websites:
cdbaby.com | hostbaby.com | agentbaby.com | marketingyourmusic.com | musicthoughts.com | hitmedia.com

◆

CAREER AWARENESS BY INCREASING INTERNET PRESENCE

by Borg, author of "The Musician's Handbook".

Most of you are already up to speed on the vast opportunities the Internet provides, but in case you've missed out on something, let's take a quick look at some of the ways you can be more proactive about your career by promoting yourself over the World Wide Web.

Online Stores

Digital recording equipment and home studio gear has made it far easier for artists to record their musical compositions. The cost of CD duplication and packaging is also more affordable. But, if the thought of selling 1,000 or more CDs seems like a daunting undertaking, then you should know that there are a number of "online stores" that can provide you with some help. Highly traveled websites such as Amazon.com and CD Baby will advertise your CD on their sites and process orders. You'll receive a percentage of sales, and in some cases, you'll even receive detail tracking information about the fans that purchase your music.

Surely you can also sell your music on your own website, but keep in mind that you'll not only have to design an interesting website that people frequent, but you'll have to set up a system that accepts credit card payments, and/or you'll have to deal with the lengthy process of accepting personal checks in the mail.

Digital Downloads

Taking your music online, Web sites, such as MP3.com, allow you to upload MP3 music files, as well as biographical information and photographs. People surfing the web can both listen to your music and download files for a small fee for which you'll be compensated! This is a great way to get both your name and music out over the world wide web, make new fans, and essentially get immediate feedback from the "net community". You will be happy to know that A & R scouts at record labels also keep their eyes glued to the Internet for new talent. MP3.com also provides a number of special services such as the "payback for playback" program where you can earn money every time someone visits your home page and listens to your music. There's also a music "licensing program" where your music is made available to producers and directors who may be interested using your music in television commercials and movies. If that weren't enough, MP3.com also has an "on demand" CD manufacturing program where they'll manufacture CDs as people request them and send them out for a reasonable price. Of course you'll be compensated for every CD sold. Some of MP3.com's services are free, while others require a small monthly fee. Visit MP3.com's website, at http://www.MP3.com. Other websites worth checking out are Ampcast.com at http://www.ampcast.com, and Vitaminic at http://www.vitaminic.com.

Net Radio

Another interesting way to get your music exposed on the Internet is to get it played on net radio stations. Net radio stations are just that; radio stations that broadcast over the Internet. With nothing more than your computer, a modem, and speakers, you can tune into radio shows around the world. Sites such as Virtual radio (http://www.virtualradio.com), and Live365.com (http://www.live365.com) are just a few of the many net radio stations that exist. By sending out your music to net radio stations like these, you may find that you get some exposure. However, to take even a more proactive approach, you can actually create your own net radio station and broadcast your own music. That's right! It's not entirely difficult to do. In fact, SHOUTcast radio (www.shoutcast.com) is one site that can help make it possible. From what I'm told, SHOUTcast allows anyone to broadcast their MP3 collection. Be sure to check this site out.

Chat Rooms, Web Rings, Newsgroups, Mailing Lists, and Webzines

Getting on the web and just hanging out with the music online community is another good way to spread the word about your music. By getting on sites such as iMusic (www.imusic.com), you can find over 1.5 million fans of all shapes and sizes, and begin spreading the word 24/7 via message boards and live "chat rooms" (chat rooms are places where you can talk with other people over the web in real time).

The Internet also allows you to join and/or create what's known as "web rings." Web rings are groups of websites all linked together by people who share similar interests. For instance, there's a U2 web ring. A huge directory of existing web rings can be found by logging on to webring (www.webring.com).

"Newsgroups" are also a great way to make new contacts and increase your fan base. Newsgroups are places on the web that allow you to post messages and converse with other readers about specific topics. A list of all types of newsgroups can be found by logging on to Google Groups at (www.groups.google.com).

Another great way to connect with particular interest groups is to become part of e-mail based discussion groups called "mailing lists." Mailing lists are similar to newsgroups but only more private. Messages on niche topics are sent directly to your computer from other people who have chosen to subscribe. You can find a variety of existing mailing lists by connecting to Liszt (www.liszt.com/select/music).

And finally, there are a number of online magazines known as "fanzines" or "webzines" in which you can get your music reviewed, post pictures, and list your concert events.

Needless to say, the Internet provides endless opportunities to spread the word about your music. The key to becoming part of the net community is to get involved a little bit at a time. You'll be surprised at how fast you get a hang of it.

Personal Websites

Even if you make your presence known on a variety of other web sites, creating your own web site is still a good idea - it's your place to shine! Your personal website becomes your headquarters - a place in which you can provide links to other sites on the web where your information and music can be found. You can get listed in search engines and directories such as Excite, Lycos, and Alta Vista to help people find you. However, once someone logs on to your site, the key is to a give them a reason to keep on coming back.

Keep your web design simple and easy to navigate. Keep your site fresh and up-to-date so that visitors can always expect something new. Create your own newsletter. Provide message boards where people can post messages for other fans visiting your sites. Give people an opportunity to converse with other fans in chat rooms. Provide your e-mail address so that fans can contact you personally and so that you can respond to as many people as possible. You can also include MP3 files of your music for people to download, and give people an opportunity to purchase your CD. You can include streaming video clips of concert footage, live interviews, or even your own home-made music video. Try posting pictures and posters that fans can download. You can provide concert and tour information. You can also create opportunities for people to join and form "street teams" to help you promote your music in their home town. The opportunities are limitless. Be sure to surf the web and see what your favorite bands are including on their websites. You can be sure to find some really impressive sites. Check out Radiohead's site at www.radiohead.com, and Prince's site at www.npgonlineltd.com as a start.

Okay, that's about all on Internet promotion for now. For more ideas, or to brush up on some terms you may be unfamiliar with, check out author Peter Spellman's book, The Musician's Internet (Berklee Press, 2000), or David Kushner's Music Online for Dummies (IDG Books Worldwide, Inc, 2001).

Bobby Borg is the author of "The Musician's Handbook". He has performed extensively throughout the United States, Japan and Europe with a variety of artists ranging from pop to R & B to rock. As a signed artist with both Atlantic Records, BMG, and several other labels, Borg has worked alongside some of the world's best personal managers, attorneys, producers, and agents. For more information please visit his website http://www.bobbyborg.com or e-mail him at bborg@earthlink.net

◆

25 THINGS TO REMEMBER ABOUT RECORD DISTRIBUTION
by Christopher Knab, author of "Music Is Your Business".

1. Distributors will usually only work with labels that have been in business for at least 3 years or have at least 3 previous releases that have sold several thousand copies each.

2. Distributors get records into retail stores, and record labels get customers into retail stores through promotion and marketing tactics.

3. Make sure there is a market for your style of music. Prove it to distributors by showing them how many records you have sold through live sales, internet sales, and any other alternative methods.

4. Be prepared to sign a written contract with your distributor because there are no 'handshake deals' anymore.

5. Distributors want 'exclusive' agreements with the labels they choose to work with. They usually want to represent you exclusively.

6. You will sell your product to a label for close to 50% of the retail list price.

7. When searching for a distributor find out what labels they represent, and talk to some of those labels to find out how well the distributor did getting records into retailers.

8. Investigate the distributor's financial status. Many labels have closed down in recent years, and you cannot afford to get attached to a distributor that may not be able to pay its invoices.

9. Find out if the distributor has a sales staff , and how large it is. Then get to know the sales reps.

10. What commitment will the distributor make to help get your records into stores.

11. s the distributor truly a national distributor, or only a regional distributor with ambitions to be a national distributor. Many large chain stores will only work with national distributors.

12. Expect the distributor to request that you remove any product you have on consignment in stores so that they can be the one to service retailers.

13. Make sure that your distributor has the ability to help you setup various retail promotions such as: coop advertising (where you must be prepared to pay the costs of media ads for select retailers), in-store artist appearances, in-store listening station programs, and furnishing POP's (point of purchase posters and other graphics).

14. Be aware that as a new label you will have to offer a distributor 100% on returns of your product.

15. You must bear all the costs of any distribution and retail promotions.

16. Furnish the distributor with hundreds of 'Distributor One Sheets' (Attractively designed summary sheets describing your promotion and marketing commitments. Include barcodes, list price, picture of the album cover, and catalog numbers of your product too..

17. Distributors may ask for hundreds of free promotional copies of your release to give to the buyers at the retail stores.

18. Make sure all promotional copies have a hole punched in the barcode, and that they are not shrink-wrapped. This will prevent any unnecessary returns of your product.

19. Don't expect a distributor to pay your invoices in full or on time. You will always be owed something by the distributor because of the delay between orders sent, invoices received, time payment schedules (50-120 days per invoice) and whether or not your product has sold through, or returns are pending.

20. Create a relationship that is a true partnership between your label and the distributor.

21. Keep the distributor updated on any and all promotion and marketing plans and results, as they develop.

22. Be well financed. Trying to work with distributors without a realistic budget to participate in promotional opportunities would be a big mistake.

23. Your distributor will only be as good as your marketing plans to sell the record. Don't expect them to do your work for you, remember all they do is get records into the stores.

24. Read the trades, especially Billboard for weekly news on the health of the industry, and/or the status of your distributor.

25. Work your product relentlessly on as many fronts as possible… commercial and non commercial airplay, internet airplay and sales campaigns, on and offline publicity ideas, and touring...eternally touring!

Christopher Knab is a music business Consultant, Author and Lecturer. He was recently honored by Seattle's Rocket magazine as "One of the Most Influential People in the Northwest Music Industry." You can visit Christopher's website at: http://www.4frontmusic.com or contact him personally at: Chris@Knab.com

◆

DESIGNING YOUR CD COVER
by Valerie Michele Hoskins, President of The Pursuit Studio

The images described in this article can be viewed online at: http://www.indiebible.com/valh

Visual (graphic and web) design in the music industry is about identity. Who you are, and your product or service must be well represented. What your audience, potential customer or client can expect to hear, feel, experience, or achieve must also be successfully communicated.

A talented visual communications professional understands the power of typography and images, and knows how to use them creatively to meet these expectations. The best creative professional for your project is well-trained, familiar with your industry and your target market, and makes design decisions based on accomplishing specific objectives you have identified. One of the most primary objectives is selling your music to consumers, or music industry professionals (e.g., securing a producer, record label or distributor through a demo).

Have you ever purchased a CD solely based on the cover design, or been attracted to an artist, band, producer or record label based on their logo, poster or web site? If so, the designer has succeeded.

Design plays a part in purchase decisions. When browsing for CDs, choices are made. People usually pick up what visually attracts them and then look at the listed songs, unless they are looking for a specific artist or title. This process is the way a person gets a feel for the CD artist, mood, and messages; and ultimately, hopes to be satisfied that the CD delivers what the design and the title suggests.

The first time I purchased music based on the design was in 1977 by the group Caldera. The album cover had a colorful picture of a volcano (caldera) erupting, and I got the feeling the music by this group would erupt as potently as that volcano. As it turned out, the Latin-jazz fusion album did. It was their debut album and the cover design got me to buy it.

More recently, I bought two CDs: Count Basic (www.countbasic.com), "Trust Your Instincts" (see figure 1), and Marilyn Scott, "Avenues of Love" (see figure 2). On the Count Basic cover, what grabbed me was the woman's face bolstered by the low cut dress she wore showcasing her significant cleavage, and a man behind her giving two major thumbs up! I wanted to be that woman. As for Marilyn Scott, she is standing alone on a rocky shore, looking pensively at the ground, barefooted, wearing what looks like a full-length camel hair coat. The image paired with the title created an appealing pensive and serene mood, and I was stirred to buy it.

I'm totally pleased with both purchases though they're quite different. Chalk up two more sales due to an art director, photographer, and graphic designer working as a team to successfully well-reflect an energy, style, essence, tone, and message to me about the artist and the music.

Let the Music Take Your Mind

Music is not defined as visual art, but sound does create mental imagery. One of the reasons I'm not glued to MTV, VH1 or other music video networks, is that I prefer to give my mind complete freedom to conjure its own images in response to music. Music package design (CD, VHS, DVD) is an hors d'oeuvre, an invitation, and a precursor to a total sound experience - perhaps a journey. When you work with a designer, it's important to share the imagery in your mind to help the art direction along. It's also good for the art director and/or designer to listen to the music, so there's a healthy amount of imagery to feed the creative process.

Between the two, a wealth of visual ideas will emerge. Music videos have multiple images to help sell an artist and the music. A CD, poster, logo, or Web site doesn't have as many visual chances, so it's important to get it right with less visual opportunities.

Count the Ways

Music professionals use graphic design in specific ways and have definite ideas about what they want the designs to accomplish. Neil Alexander is primarily a performer/composer, but is also active in engineering, production and programming, and has P-Dog Records, a small independent record label he uses to release his own discs.

Neil has a logo, stationery, CD packaging for his releases, packaging for a CD business card, posters to launch new releases (see figure 3), press releases, and a web site from which people can purchase directly. "I have always found that how CD packaging looks is a big part of its impact, its connection with the listener. Logos and other symbols can become part of the performer's identity. It is in my case. As with any business, consistent graphics help define the company's image and products for the consumer," Neil stated.

As for a strong web site presence, Neil had this to say: "A solid web presence is very important these days. Information (text, audio and visual) must be well organized and clearly presented. I found it desirable to hire a professional designer to put together a simple and easily navigated Web site (www.pdogrecords.com).

Sweet Sight of Success

When working with a designer, there are definite criteria to use for assessing quality and success. There are well-established design industry factors for every product: logos, posters, CDs, business cards and stationery, advertising, and Web sites. To cover each one

specifically in this article would take too long, so these are some of the main criteria to help judge a design's success: 1) It must be unified with the product or service's content or identity. This creates a sense of family, of belonging, and it's immediately apparent; 2) There's an information and visual hierarchy. This means there's a focal point or image that grabs your attention first, and then your eye is led around the design in the order of what's important sequentially; 3) The design has graphic impact and is distinctive and/or memorable. There are many designs competing with yours for attention (lots of demos are sent out to producers, record labels and distributors), so yours must be a major contender; and 4) It must be appropriate for who you want to attract and the environment in which it will be presented. A poster or CD for a country audience will not have the same look and feel presentation as for a heavy metal one.

Who can forget the strong identity between the Stones and that bright, red tongue sticking out logo? It's a very powerful example of a highly successful pictorial visual logo. The logo formats are logotype, initials, pictorial visual, abstract visual, and combination, and a well-trained designer is knowledgeable about them all. The Stones logo has graphic impact, is distinctive and memorable, and is appropriate for its rock audience.

For a web site, success is measured by whether your goals for establishing it are being met. Does it reflect your identity? Are you making sales? Is your visibility increasing? Is it easy for users to navigate and locate what they want? Are there lively and beneficial discussions or information being shared? Are people returning multiple times to your site?

Once you and the designer decide on the success criteria for your project, the real fun begins: designing it.

The Design Process: What You Can Expect

Professional art directors and designers will have processes to assist them creatively. In terms of process, there will be an initial consultation during which lots of questions are asked. Some design studios may use a creative brief form. The questions on the form are designed to crystallize and solidify your identity and vision, so you and the designer are clear about it. Both get a copy, and sometimes you'll be asked to sign it to approve the accuracy before concept development production begins. You'll be asked to sign a contract and to return it with a retainer (a retainer is a portion of the total cost for the project that must be paid up front before any work begins).

The first thing you'll see is thumbnails: anywhere from 4-10 tiny creative ideas sketched out. You'll review them and choose one or two on which the designer will focus and create more detailed drawings called rough compositions. Sometimes, if a designer feels very secure about the creative direction of your project, the thumbnail stage will be bypassed, and you'll first see about three roughs. The roughs may be hand-drawn as closely as possible to what a final version would be (see figure 4), or they might be created on the computer.

You review the roughs, and choose one to be developed further (see figure 5). You may receive up to three versions and you choose your favorite: it will be your final design. The designer will work with you to fine-tune it. Once you approve it, it is ready to be printed. If it's a web design, it will be implemented and programmed. You pay the balance due, and the process is complete.

Budget, Low Budget, No Budget

Pricing for different types of projects can range vastly depending upon the business structure and the length of time the business has been operating. The business can be a design studio, freelance or consultant, or a print shop franchise like Kinko's and have years of experience or be newly established in the industry.

If you're interested in reviewing industry standard fees for graphic design, web design, or illustration, take a hike to Barnes and Noble bookstore and glance through the "Handbook of Pricing and Ethical Guidelines," published by The Graphic Artist's Guild of America. It's the creative professional's bible, and includes everything you always wanted to know about fees, contracts, copyright, and other professional issues. The fees quoted are based on nationwide surveys distributed to creative professionals. Standard fees are not cheap. The visual communications creative field is a highly valued, for-profit industry, so fees reflect our need to make a living at what we do. When someone gives you an estimate, make sure it details every service being provided to justify the cost.

When the estimate is too rich for your blood, there are other options to consider. A few include:
1) Supply your own photos and/or illustrations (see figure 6). Photography and illustration are specialties requiring additional compensation
2) Personally coordinate printing and CD or other types of duplication. Our time is money so coordinating printing for your project and getting your CD duplicated will cost you more
3) Barter for pro bono service. We may reduce the fee or work for free if you'll do some things for us in return
4) Contact your local college or university and request a referral to a recent graduate or current senior student. There are some extremely talented young people who are eager to get client experience and build their portfolio
5) Explore a business-education partnership project relationship www.portfolios.com/pursuitgallery

Where there is a will, there is a way.
Who are you? Whom you want to attract? What do you want to accomplish? A marriage between sight and sound can only have a positive impact on your career. Successful visual design is the key.

Valerie Michele Hoskins is a songwriter, soon-to-be music publisher, educator, and president of The Pursuit Studio, a visual communications creative service for art and entertainment industry professionals and businesses. Contact Valerie at: val.hoskins@thepursuitstudio.biz

♦

SUCCEEDING WITHOUT A LABEL
by Bernard Baur, Music Connection Magazine

Is a label deal the only real measure of success? According to many artists, the answer is a resounding "NO!" In fact, more than a few with label experience would rather do it themselves. It's not easy, for sure, but neither is getting a record deal and making it work.

The truth is, except for what a label theoretically offers (worldwide distribution and exposure), artists can do it alone. In fact, if they want a great record deal or demand creative control, they should do it themselves.

With that in mind, Music Connection set out to see how realistic the independent route is, and if artists can find success on their own. We found that independent artists are very popular with music fans; and, that acts like The Dave Matthews Band, Godsmack, Nickelback and The White Stripes didn't depend on a record company to break them. They did it themselves and sold thousands of records, which naturally attracted hundreds of labels. Moreover, those who enjoyed independent success negotiated deals that were superior to the average deal most artists are offered. Overall, going it alone looks like a win-win situation.

To find out what it takes, MC contacted a variety of artists who took the "Do It Yourself" approach and are making it work. They are self-sufficient artists who found that they didn't need a label to live their dream. They prove that the DIY option is not only viable; it may also be the best course of action. After all, who wouldn't like to call their own shots in a market that's up for grabs?

CHOOSING THE ROAD LESS TRAVELED
Sitting in a label president's office suite can be surreal, especially when he's explaining what an artist needs to do to get signed. The list is so long (covering a variety of areas) that after he finishes, you can't

help but ask, " If an artist did all of that, why the hell would they need you?"

Well, some artists don't think they need an established label at all. Award winning artist, Aimee Mann, has had three major record deals but now says, "I can't recommend signing a label deal. Why should you give them all the power? Really, it's frustrating. You think labels are supposed to sell records, but they don't always do what they're supposed to. So, why deal with them?"

In response, Mann formed her own company, Super Ego Records, and became a poster girl for DIY success thanks to her Oscar-nominated song from the film "Magnolia" and the 200,000 units sold of her "Bachelor No. 2" album. Today, she claims to be happier than she ever was at a major. "Now, I have the freedom to do what I want, when I want. And, if any mistakes are made, I get to make them myself rather than have someone make them for me." One other thing Mann is absolutely certain about: She won't miss the suits reviewing her work. "You know," she laughs, "no one ever said, 'We're really excited about this! It's obviously the single!'"

Other artists choose the independent way because their music doesn't fit the usual formats or marketing schemes. Industry may love the music, but they don't know what to do with it. When he started out, Bob Malone thought he was just a day away from a deal. "Everyone seemed to love my music, but they didn't know how to market it. After a few years, I concluded that quality can be a liability. They actually told me, 'You're too good,' and I thought they were nuts."

These artists, and many others like them, decided they didn't need a record deal to do what they wanted. Instead, they struck out on their own and established their own companies and careers. They're a tough breed who work hard, but every one of the artists interviewed is happy with their decision and satisfied with their career. Because the bottom line is: they're not chasing the dream anymore – they're living it.

THE INDEPENDENT MINDSET
It seems simple. You don't have to be signed to release a record. In fact, if you wait to be signed it could be a very long time according to Tim Sweeney, a consultant who specializes in independent artists. He not only presents workshops on DIY, but has also written books about it. Sweeney maintains, "Less acts are being signed nowadays, and of those that do get a deal only 1-3% will make it beyond a record or two before they get dumped."

DIY avoids that scenario, but artists need to be a special breed to do it right. According to Pat McKeon, former owner of Dr. Dream Records and general manager at Ranell Records, states, "An independent artist will have to wear more than one hat. When they first start out, they'll probably be doing everything themselves, and not every artist can handle that."

An additional prerequisite is a strong belief system. Gilli Moon, who left an indie label to start her own (Warrior Girl Music), wrote a book based on the lessons she learned titled, "I Am a Professional Artist. " She explains, "You need to be optimistic. You have to believe in yourself and your art. Belief and dedication are the keys to making it work."

Last but not least, you need to understand how much work DIY truly is. "Everything about it is hard," relates K.K. Martin, an independent artist who survived several label deals. "If you do it right, it's a real job and some musicians are horrified by that idea. You have to learn about the business and pay attention to it. If you can't do that, find someone you trust, or you'll never progress."

KEEP IT REAL
If you want DIY success, you have to have realistic expectations. Nearly every artist dreams of playing The Forum or appearing on MTV. Unfortunately, that doesn't even happen to major label acts unless they have a hit and are extremely successful. Most independent artists have to set their sights a little lower. That's not to say it could never happen, because it does. But, the fact is you'd have to have fantastic connections or enjoy phenomenal success to reach that level.

"Keeping your goals realistic is essential for all independents," Moon points out. "If you don't do that, you're going to be disappointed." Moon suggests keeping it real and at a level you can achieve. "Set up small goals on a monthly, quarterly and yearly basis. Then, evaluate the results. If you reached your goals, move on – if not, figure out why."

Perhaps the greatest state of mind independent artists need is patience. Angus Richardson, of the band BROTHER, has known phenomenal success, selling over 150,000 records and playing almost 250 dates a year. Nevertheless, even BROTHER had to suck it up. " When we didn't get a quick record deal, it would have been easy to get discouraged," Richardson reveals. "But, we believed in our music, our fans and ourselves. And, the fact is," he stresses, "if you get hurt every time you're rejected in this business, you're going to have a lot of scars. Just look around at all the bands that have disappeared. You have to realize that you can't please everybody, and if you want to make it, you have to have patience and determination."

TOURING IS KEY

Now that you're in the right frame of mind, it's time to form "The Master Plan" for world domination. Everyone agrees that the most important part of the plan is playing live. Everything, including radio, promotions, distribution and marketing, should revolve around that because it's the way you sell records. Of course, you're going to need a recording, but according to Moon, it need not be up to industry standards. "Even a live recording will do," she says. "Your fans want to hear your songs, not the production."

Most artists have booked themselves before, so this area should be familiar. The difference, however, is that you have to book gigs beyond your backyard. Sweeney suggests that artists should start by looking 2-3 hours in each direction. "That will only cost $30-40 in gas, and you should be able to make that in sales," he says. "If an act is based in Los Angeles, they can look as far as San Diego and Santa Barbara. Eventually, they can increase the drive time and even look at neighboring states. But," he warns, "don't try to do it all at once."

Naturally, when it comes to touring solo artists have it the easiest. Moon, Malone and Martin only occasionally bring a full band along. "It's a matter of economics as well as personal dynamics," Martin maintains. "Traveling in a van with five other guys can challenge your patience." To cut costs, Malone, who toured eight times across the country in three years, established a network of musicians he hires in each city. "That way," he says, "I only have to pay them for the gig."

But, if you're a real band, expenses become a concern. Tina Broad, BROTHER'S manager, relates that their merchandise table is a critical part of their financial success. "If we didn't have product to sell we couldn't do it. Our merchandise sales (CDs and goods) have a dramatic impact on our ability to tour. Traditionally, we make 2 to 3 times more from our merchandise than we do from tour guarantees or ticket sales." Broad also advises bands to take a serious look at their hospitality riders. "Include things that you need (towels, water, food, backline, etc) so that you have fewer things to deal with. And, when you can," she recommends, "insist on a 50% deposit so that you're not shouldering all the cash flow until the performance check clears."

YOUR BANK

Touring, recordings, and merchandise obviously require money, and artists should be ready to dip into their own pockets. Sweeney contends that if artists aren't willing to invest in themselves, he questions how serious they are about a career. "However, if resources are severely limited, you just have to start smaller and think smarter," he says. "Find a sponsor to help with costs. Play free shows for them and put their name on your CD. " Moon suggests doing your own artwork or finding a friend who's talented. In fact, every independent artist who is successful uses a network of resources to help them defray costs.

Some, such as Skywind, a Minneapolis band who tours over 100 days a year and plays before 1000 or more fans, got their family and friends to loan them seed money. Bill Berry, their manager, indicates, "Everyone got paid back in just over a year. And since then," he relates, "we've been able to pick up sponsorships and lines of credit." Each band member contributes to pay off loans and, by doing this, Skywind has been able buy a van and tour three states.

The bottom line is that you're going to need a budget, so that you

know what you can do. Indeed, BROTHER'S manager, Broad advises artists to be realistic about costs. "If you don't know what your real expenses are," she informs, " you're going to be operating in a vacuum."

ART MEETS COMMERCE

If you want to be an independent artist who's self-sufficient, don't deceive yourself: you are in business, and there are two parts to business – the legal side and the practical side. Legally, you must protect your interests and follow the law. Everyone agrees that you should consult with counsel when setting things up. You may need a band contract, a business license, and an assortment of other things that make you a legal entity.

On the practical side, you need to keep accurate records of all your sales and income. Get a unique Bar Code and register it with SoundScan. Online sites, such as CDBaby offer a discount on unique Bar Codes with savings of several hundred dollars. SoundScan offers several programs for independent artists, including a Venue Verification Form that allows club owners and promoters to vouch for your gig sales.

Sweeney informs us that you can simply pay the tax on your sales to obtain a verifiable record. These figures are all important if you hope to convince anyone – including a label, a distributor or a lender – to work with you. Indeed, Broad says it still makes her guts churn to think that BROTHER neglected to register the sales from their 2001 Summer Tour. "That was 15,000 unverifiable sales," she sighs. "We've got manufacturing records, but it's not the same."

Finally, protect yourself when you're on the road and prepare for the worst. Broad reports that BROTHER was involved in an accident while on tour. There were serious injuries and catastrophic damage. "It was every band's worst nightmare," she recalls. "It derailed us for months and ran up debts that we're still paying off. It was almost the end of BROTHER."

MARKETING & PROMOTIONS

Mann contends that marketing and promotion is always a challenge, whether you're on a label or not. "It was my biggest cause for concern with every deal I had," she reports. "At least, now, I have the freedom and control to do it the way I want." But, when you're independent, you have to think outside the box. You cannot compete with the majors, so you have to do things differently.

For starters, McKeon points out, "All independent promotions must revolve around live performances. That has to be your focus because it's your moneymaker. After booking gigs, you can contact press, radio and retail." Of all of them, radio is usually the most difficult, but persistence pays off.

Skywind's Berry relates that they maintained a two-year relationship with a local station before their songs were played. "We bought advertising time late at night because it's cheaper and played radio events for free. After they got to know us, they put our songs in rotation." Sweeney suggests attending station concerts and handing out free CDs. "It gets your music to their audience," he says.

Artists should also learn to cooperate with each other. Sweeney advises, "Instead of competing, artists should work towards a common goal. They should book shows together, share expenses and even buy commercial time on cable TV. Cable companies will sell 30-60 seconds for less than $100 and you can promote your act on MTV. If you run a few commercials about a week before your show, you'll see tremendous results."

The ultimate goal, however, is to put on a "Great Show." "That's where it's at," K.K. Martin explains. "You can set up all the promotion in the world, but if you don't deliver live, you won't sell any records."

THE DISTRIBUTION MONSTER

Distribution is one of the biggest issues facing all independent artists. You need to stock your CDs wherever you play, but getting distribution isn't easy. For some artists, consignments may be the way to go. Many record stores will accept your CDs on spec and if they sell, will order more. "You might start with only 10-20 in a store, but if they move the orders will increase," Martin explains. "The only problem with consignment is that you have to keep on top of it on a regular basis."

Other artists, like Nashville songwriter, Hal Bynum, have found alternative markets. He reveals, "I've been a songwriter for 50 years, and it's still not easy to get distribution." So, Bynum created a unique package – a book and CD – that Barnes & Noble will carry. "I agreed to make in-store appearances and they agreed to promote me."

Some artists set up their own organization. With the help of her New York manager, Michael Hausman, Aimee Mann founded "United Musicians," a sort of cooperative for artists. Hausman explains, "We found that distributors don't like to work with a single artist. They want product every few months, so we set up United Musicians for other artists who may be in the same boat. R.E.D. agreed to distribute our records and we're sharing our contacts with artists who bring something to the table."

Hausman continues, "We're not looking to build a big company, but we believe there are artists like us, who may have limited resources. Our idea is to combine and share resources so that we all benefit. We'll simply license a record and put it into distribution." Of course, Hausman points out, that they're only interested in artists who can sell records, by either touring or getting press.

If you're not quite to that stage yet, there are services to meet your needs. The independent network is full of companies that cater to independent artists, and one of the newest and most intriguing is 101 Distribution. Damon Evans, 101's executive director, describes his company as an alternative solution to traditional distribution. "We service over 2100 retail stores across the country and into Europe." Essentially, 101 takes the work out of consignments. They give stores product on consignment, collect revenue and pay artists every 30 days. Their split with artists is generous (70-80% of wholesale) and they will handle promotions and marketing, unlike other distributors. "Our deals are non-exclusive for one year," Evans continues, " and we will help develop the market for artists who are willing to work at it."

THE ULTIMATE REWARD

Of course, for some, whose music may not be mainstream, independence is their only choice; while for others it's by design. But, regardless of whether you're a maverick or an act still seeking a deal, the same rules apply. If you want success, you have to work for it.

While DIY may be a lot of work, it can be very rewarding. "It is time consuming and takes a lot of patience but," Gilli Moon concludes, " there's nothing quite like having control over your own destiny. You can be as big or as small as you want and go at your own pace."

The independent route is empowering as long as you're up to it. K. K. Martin reflects, "Everything is a challenge that must be met. But, if you believe in yourself and take care of business, you can make it work. And, there is one thing you can be sure about - at least, it's not boring."

SIDEBAR - TEN STEPS TO SUCCESS FOR THE INDEPENDENT ARTIST

(All the artists profiled are self-sufficient. They make a living "solely" with their music. This list was compiled from their interviews.)

1. BELIEVE IN YOURSELF

You must believe in yourself. Realize that you don't need a label to be a success. Don't be egotistical, but be confident. Be optimistic – believe you are good enough and can get what you want. If you don't have faith in yourself – no one else will.

2. BE REALISTIC

Do research – Get objective opinions - Identify your market. Know that you're going to have to tour. Know when to ask for help. Accept the fact that you probably won't become a star or get on MTV, but that you can make a living playing music.

3. MAKE A WISH LIST

Create a Wish List – What do you ultimately want and how do you plan to get it? What are the things you need to do and how long will it take? Set reasonable goals and break your Plan into phases: 3 months –

6 months – 1 year – 3 years, etc…

4. KNOW YOUR BUDGET

If you're serious about a career, you're going to have to invest in yourself. Itemize your expenses and add 20%. Approach Sponsors with a detailed plan. Negotiate deals that take care of the basics: travel, food, lodging, backline, etc... And, don't forget manufacturing and promotional costs.

5. TAKE CARE OF BUSINESS

Remember – it is the music "business." Network as much as possible. Organize a team, as soon as you can, with each person responsible for a specific area. If you're solo, manage your time wisely. Get your own Bar Code. Seek professional advice to set up your business entities. Pay attention to licenses and tax implications. When you tour, get insurance.

6. MARKET YOURSELF

Think creatively. Make time for "personal appearances" before your gigs. Set up cross-promotions with radio stations, sponsors, venues, and retail stores. Make sure you have enough products to sell – both CDs and merchandise. Offer promotional contests. Play Special Events. Work your mailing list and keep in touch with your fans at least once a month.

7. KEEP RECORDS

Keep books that reflect income and expenses. Accurately account for sales. Register and report to SoundScan. Maintain tax records. Record your draw – note the venue/locale that draws best. Keep updating your mailing list.

8. ADAPT & ADJUST

Evaluate results: What works – What doesn't? Revise your plan and adjust your approach accordingly. Find ways to increase your fan base and make a profit. What can be done better?

9. KEEP THE FAITH

No matter how hard you work, there will be frustrating times. Keep the faith and don't let it deter you. Everyone experiences setbacks. Those that persevere will prevail.

10. MAKE IT FUN

If it's not fun anymore – don't do it. Reward yourself (and your team) whenever possible. Acknowledge a job well done. Take a break – enjoy life – then, get back to work.

Bernard Baur is the Review Editor & Feature Writer for Music Connection Magazine http://www.musicconnection.com Tel: 818-755-0101 Ext.519 EqxManLtd@aol.com

♦

INDIE POWER: A BUSINESS-BUILDING GUIDE FOR RECORD LABELS, MUSIC PRODUCTION HOUSES AND MERCHANT MUSICIANS
by Peter Spellman, author of "The Self-Promoting Musician"
© 2004 All Rights Reserved. Used By Permission

The Power's In Your Corner

"The real social revolution of the last 30 years, one we are still living through, is the switch from a life that is largely organized for us to a world in which we are all forced to be in charge of our own destiny." - Charles Handy

What is happening today in the world of business affects us all. A global revolution is changing business, and business is changing the world. With unsettling speed, two forces are converging: a new generation of business leaders is rewriting the rules of business, and a new breed of fast companies is challenging the corporate status quo.

What are some of the manifestations of these forces?

The rapid growth of networked business - Internet and intranets are allowing for a greater flow of information and quicker decision-making. The Internet alone is responsible for enabling thousands of companies to affordably transact commerce on a global scale, no matter what their size.

A rapidly segmenting marketplace - Mass markets are giving way to micro markets as customers demand to have it their way. Companies that can meet this market's demands most effectively will be the winners.

The use of technology in the workplace - Affordable desktop computers, fax machines, copiers, scanners, and wireless technology have brought the look and efficiencies of larger companies to the fingertips of micro business owners worldwide. Digital recording technology has literally revolutionized the music business and sparked the emergence of whole new genres of music, most notably hip-hop, dance/electronica and new age.

. The marked rise of entrepreneurship - A new U.S. business starts every 14 seconds. The SOHO (small office, home office) movement has spawned an entire industry that serves this market. It includes retail chains like Staples and Office Depot, magazines like Entrepreneur and Home Office Computing, and book publishers specializing in "do-it-yourself" literature like Allworth Press and the "Dummies" series - all in the service of the micro business owner.

These enormous developments overturn 50 years of received wisdom on the fundamentals of work, markets and competition. No part of business is immune. The structure of the company is changing; relationships between companies are changing; the nature of work is changing; the definition of success is changing. The result is a revolution as far-reaching as the Industrial Revolution was in its day.

We are just beginning to comprehend this new world even as we create it. This much we know: we live and work in a time of unparalleled opportunity and unprecedented uncertainty. An economy driven by technology and innovation makes old borders obsolete.

Because of corporate downsizing, decentralizing authority structures, relaxing regulations, affordable technology, and a revolution in consciousness, people around the world are gravitating to small business in record numbers.

We are at a turning point in the history of business practice and its accelerant is the Internet. Because the internet is so new and dynamic, there are few set rules about how to use it to market. Non-conventional, small business tactics are capturing market share from large established corporations. And this trend will continue in most industries, especially those that trade in "information" (read, "music").

The industry needs independent record companies and music production houses to both find and nurture artists, and to do it right! This book is written for those who want to start and run these kinds of independent music companies.

The Times Are Bright For Indie Efforts. Indies show us how a combination of intuition and good management can allow a small business to boldly go where the big multinationals have failed: discovering, promoting and distributing authentic styles of music.

I'm sure you have your own story of why you would like to start your own label or production company. No matter what it is, you can be certain that the times are currently favorable for indie start-ups. Here are some reasons why:

A rapidly segmenting marketplace means more opportunity for independents whose releases detail the richness of particular or "niche" musical forms: the blues of Black Top and Alligator, the hip-hop of Roc-a-Fella, the industrial dance meshes of Nettwerk and Radikal, the world folk of Green Linnet, the rock'n'roll of Tone Cool; the list goes on and on. All began out of a love for a certain style of music - a style the majors didn't want anything to do with initially.

Accessible telecommunication and desktop technologies like cable, the personal computer, digital radio, full-featured phone services, e-mail and others are giving small companies the look, efficiencies and reach of larger companies.

The ongoing failure of larger companies to provide what people want are making people look elsewhere to quench their musical thirst. Major record labels are too large and ponderous to be in a position to

discover and nurture great music and talent. Independents world- wide have been, and will continue to be, the life blood of the music industry. As a result, most significant musical trends have their origins in independent companies.

Consolidation of retail and distribution is allowing Indies to penetrate traditional record retail like never before. By linking up with key national distributors independents can now potentially reach about 90% of the U.S. record-buying public! Online placements in stores like Amazon, extend that reach to the entire planet!

Indie music is charting like never before. Beginning around 1992, people began noticing a substantial increase in the presence of indie albums on the Billboard Top 200 chart (the music industry's key barometer of music sales). By 1996 indie product began dominating the chart. While this trends ebbs and flows, it does indicate a large and growing appetite for independently-produced music. All in all, indie market share has grown from 9% in 1990 to about 25% today.

New transmission technologies are leveling the playing field. Probably the greatest threat to the traditional music industry has arrived through computers. Digital transmission of music via power line and satellite is transforming the recording industry as we know it. On-line opportunities for independent labels are multiplying rapidly and leveling a playing field that was decidedly tilted in favor of larger companies.

The above is an excerpt from "Indie Power: A Business-Building Guide for Record Labels, Music Production Houses, and Merchant Musicians" by Peter Spellman, http://www.mbsolutions.com Available in both print and .pdf formats.

◆

WHY AND WHEN IS CONSIGNMENT BETTER THAN DISTRIBUTION?

by Tim Sweeney, author of "Tim Sweeney's Guide To Releasing Independent Records"
© 2004 All Rights Reserved. Used By Permission

Almost every time I pick up the phone or do a free workshop these days, the inevitable question is, "how do I get national distribution ?" My first response is, "why do you need it?"

With that glassy look in their eyes, most artists respond, "because I want to get my CDs in all the stores across the country." Then I frustrate them by saying, "what if I could do that for you, what are you going to do to make them sell?"

Again inevitably the response is, "I'm going to play shows and tell my mailing list and then probably mail out to college radio across the country." I respond, "so if you are only going to do that, why do you need your CDs in various record stores across the country ?" The usual response is, "because once they are in the store, people will buy them."

Guess what, as much as you would like him to, God doesn't watch over people shopping for CDs and spiritually guide them or smack them on the head, to your CD in the rack out of thousands of choices. People buy CDs they have heard of. Most importantly, they are more likely to buy them on impulse.

What does this have to do with you? Everything! Especially the fourth quarter of the year. The quarter when most CDs are sold and the stores have no credit available with distributors. Why is this important? Because when the stores have little or no credit available, they only want to order what will sell fast. Not CDs that will hopefully sell 2 or 3 copies per month.

So with the stores coming into the time of the year when they ignore independent CDs, what do you do? Consignment!

The simplest, oldest and fastest way to get paid, form of distribution in our industry. How does it work? Simple. A store takes 5 of your CDs and places them on the shelves. When they sell, they pay you your percentage. If they don't sell, the store doesn't have to pay you. In a distribution relationship, the store has to pay the distributor in 60 days for the CD they have ordered. In most cases, they are paying for the CD before it sells!

With consignment, there's no waiting for 6 months for your distributor to send you a check for 20% of what they owe you. You stop by the store, check how many they have in the bins and most stores will pay you cash right then and there for what you have sold.

In a time when the stores are betting their money or credit on already successful "boy bands" and not on you, use consignment to yours (and the store's) advantage.

By the way. You don't need your CDs in all stores across the country. Live shows and the word of mouth generated by the promotion of the shows are 75% of all your sales (and aren't you going to sell your CDs at your shows?). Commercial radio airplay for an independent artist is only 9% and college radio airplay is less than 1% of your sales.

The big question is, are you really going to tour the country every month to play shows for 20 people in clubs 3,000 miles away, just because a college station in a corn field is playing it? Especially for no money?

Then use consignment first and become successful in your home market, home state, and the neighboring markets you can reach on a monthly basis. After you have sold 10,000 copies in each market, consider expanding outward.

You can learn more about Tim Sweeney, TSA and his International Best Selling books, Tim Sweeney's Guide To Releasing Independent Records, Tim Sweeney's Guide To Successfully Playing Live and Tim Sweeney's Guide To Succeeding At Music Conventions by visiting his web site at, http://www.tsamusic.com

GETTING YOUR MUSIC INTO FILM
by Scooter Johnson, Musician/Actor
© 2004 All Rights Reserved. Used By Permission.

As more and more music is being made available online for different uses it is natural for production people to turn to the internet to find music. Why? Because you can buy anything on the internet! Savvy bands are spending time on film bulletin boards offering up their music for soundtrack use, indie labels are offering licensing options on their websites and composers are banding together and starting their own online write-for-hire agencies. If you or your bandmates don't have the time, effort or expertise to find soundtrack opportunities and successfully pitch your music there are avenues for you.

WHO TO TRUST?
I'm on movie sets a lot and I can tell you how hard it is to approach the music supervisor or the producer with CD. They may love it or I might lose my job. Not wanting to jeopardize my finances I've found a few online companies that specialize in indie music licensing and are non-exclusive (which means you can join as many as you want - no exclusive memberships). Before signing with any company remember you are entering into a business relationship that involves your work and payment for use of that work.

CONTRACTS?
The licensing company should have a legal contract that requires the signatures of the owners or the authors/composers of the music sent in. If the company is legit they will want to protect themselves from fraud artists that will send in other peoples music and profit from it. Also there is the final license contract with the filmmakers or whomever to peruse - is it for a Master/Sync license? or just a Sync license? (www.ascap.com, www.bmi.com or www.socan.com can define these terms if you are not familiar with the industry jargon).

FEES?
The contract should also state very clearly the fees (monthly? yearly? by the byte?) involved and how future licensing income will be split between you and them and how often you will be paid.

PRE-CLEARED OR RESTRICTED?
Also, ask about whether the tracks are required to be pre-cleared or if you can request restrictions. Some companies have a standard restriction that reads something like 'this track cannot be used on scenes depicting racism, pornography, use of tobacco, alcohol or drugs'. Requesting a restriction will obviously limit the amount of interest your music garners and ultimately the pay-out. Personally I don't care if a European sausage company wants to use my music on a television commercial - I'm an indie musician who can barely pay the rent, who is going to blame me for taking the money? I'll take that money and invest it in my bands future.

WHERE TO START?
Start where you begin all your other research - on your favorite search engine (www.google.com is huge). If you want to go the total DIY personal route based on your location, use your city name and keywords like 'film production', 'indie movies', 'production companies', 'music wanted', etc. Most cities and provinces have film associations and unions that keep track of local shoots and list them on their websites with contact information. Be prepared to be your own sales agent - you will have to send each of the interested parties a pitch package (some require two - one for the director and one for the music supervisor), diligently follow-up, negotiate your terms and if needed, hire a lawyer to proof your contract.

If you are willing to let go of a lot of control, a full-service online licensing agency like Realia Music Inc. (www.realiamusic.com) may be worth looking into. One of the larger agencies online, their online catalogue consists of indie music from around the world and it's pre-cleared and priced by a sliding scale that caps at $5,000/world-wide usage. They have restrictions available but only a special case basis (pre-existing contracts between musicians and other parties - I asked) and provide a one-stop service for people who have limited budgets, tight schedules and credit cards. They have a one-time $5 membership fee and a $1/song submission fee, 50/50 license split and a $2/song shipping fee for songs licensed. Your songs are represented for as long as you wish and if you get an exclusive deal with a publishing company or label, they promise they will remove your songs within 24 hours.

If you have a good idea of what your music is worth and prefer to wrangle your deals yourself try SongCatalog Inc. (www.songcatalog.com). Their system provides a virtual middleman for your negotiations. You submit as many tracks as you wish for placement in their online 'Active List' or in the 'Vault' and pay per track. Fees are billed monthly and start at $4.95 for up to 25 audio files stored in the 'Vault' and $9.95 for up to 25 songs featured on the 'Exchange' (site search engine) and increase by smaller increments every 50/100/200 songs registered. There are different levels of search capabilities that have a separate fee rate but you can check out there website for more details. People who wish to license music register at no cost, browse the catalogue and when a suitable track is located, they send an email - through the website - to the owner who then responds. Dialogue and negotiations ensue and you are ultimately responsible for finalizing your deal.

I would advise to check out the smaller companies, they appear to have more staying power than the large online music companies (licensemusic.com - one of the first and definitely the largest - shut down business abruptly months ago and is currently being auctioned off on the internet through a bankruptcy trustee). Many have forayed into licensing but the complicated traditional licensing system (long protracted negotiations, complicated territorial and usage structures, clearances, exorbitant fees, favored nations, and script/scene approval) has not translated well online. There was no immediacy, no click through satisfaction that everyone has come to expect from the web. Once the costs of software development, technical support, hosting fees and high-priced management were factored in the license fees were unaffordable and potential buyers were back in the nightclubs chatting up bands after their sets.

Online there is a market for indie music even if the band has broken up, doesn't tour, is brand new or not commercially friendly, and it requires hardly any work on behalf of the band. You fill in an

ion, get the appropriate signatures, mail it in and wait for the
to arrive. It is the agency's business to market their catalogue,
ner services and bring the buyers in.

With record labels setting their standards higher and higher for
new signings, showing up with a portfolio of licensed tracks in your
package just might be the wedge you need to get in the door. It really
doesn't matter where the track was used or for what product, the fact
that your music can be sold for hard cash is the attractive quality they
are looking for.

Always remember to be realistic with your expectations and tell
everybody that you have a 'licensing agency' (it does sound impressive
and looks even better on your bio). There are hundreds of thousands of
bands in the world with at least one album under their belts. That's a lot
of competition for the same dollar. It's also unlikely that directors
Steven Spielberg or Kevin Smith are cruising these sites for music for
their next big project - they have budgets that afford them just about
any song they want. As an indie musician with an indie agency, your
music will be marketed to projects without a great deal of exposure
attached to them. Focus will usually be on the catalogue not the
individual bands, there are fees and it is a relatively new industry - it
may take years for it to take off and compete with traditional process.

But don't despair, it only takes one new digital filmmaker with a
vision and a few thousand dollars to help pay off the band van or press
those extra 500 CDs. It's a cheap and viable new way to get your music
heard by a larger and potentially lucrative audience - and that's what
you want. Isn't it?

*Scooter Johnson spent 5 years touring Canada with his Hillbilly band
The Hard Rock Miners and has created 5 internationally distributed
albums. His search for fame and immortality has almost been
concluded and it is time to pass on his knowledge to the next
generation of seekers after the flame. deadcat@shaw.ca*

tools

WHAT ARE PERFORMANCE RIGHTS
ORGANIZATIONS? (ASCAP, BMI, SESAC…)
by Jer Olsen, CEO MusicBootCamp.com
© 2004 All Rights Reserved. Used By Permission.

Performance rights organizations like BMI, ASCAP and SESAC all
perform a similar task but in slightly different ways. Essentially, they
all perform the duty of collecting royalties for non-dramatic
performances of intellectual property. In simpler terms, they collect the
income from radio stations, TV stations, programming companies,
Internet marketers and any other entity where music and
related intellectual property is used. These royalties are then, in turn,
paid to the various publishers and authors associated with a particular
recording or performance.

The fundamental reason behind the birth of these organizations is
the simple fact that individual artists and song writers can't possibly
devote the time, attention and research required to collect royalties
from the plethora of companies that use their music, even though by
law they are entitled to those royalties. Artists depend on these
performance rights organizations to do the hunting and collecting for
them—a small price to pay for a piece of a much, much bigger pie!
There's a saying, "50% of everything is a whole lot better than 100% of
nothing!" Well, we don't know exactly how much money these
organizations charge for their services, but we can be certain it covers
their time an energy (similar to how music publishers earn money for
getting music played in movies, TV shows, or recorded by other artists,
etc.). The moral of the story is that performance rights organizations are
a necessary and helpful tool for musicians and publishers. The toughest
decision is choosing which one you want to align yourself with.

Please visit the page of each organization to find on-line information
about joining as well as a ton of other terrific resources. Compare and
make a decision on which one best suits you. If you don't, you can
practically assure yourself of never being paid for airplay—OOPS!

United States
BMI - Broadcast Music, Inc http://www.bmi.com
ASCAP - The American Society of Composers, Authors and
Publishers http://www.ascap.com
SESAC (SESAC is no longer an acronym, it's the actual name of the
service) http://www.sesac.com
Canada
SOCAN - The Society of Composers, Authors and Music Publishers
of Canada http://www.socan.ca
The UK
PAMRA - Performing Arts Media Rights Association
http://www.pamra.org.uk
PRS - The Performing Right Society http://www.prs.co.uk
MCPS - The British Mechanical Copyright Protection Society Limited
http://www.mcps.co.uk
France
SACEM - Societe Des Auteurs Compositeurs Et Editeurs De Musique
http://www.sacem.fr
CISAC - Confédération Internationale des Sociétés d'Auteurs et
Compositeurs http://www.cisac.org
Germany
GEMA - The German Society For Musical Performing Rights And
Mechanical Reproduction Rights http://www.gema.de
Italy
SIAE - Societa Italiana Degli Autori ed Editori http://www.siae.it
Spain
SGAE - Sociedad General de Autores y Editores http://www.sgae.es
Sweden
STIM - Svenska Tonsattares Internationella Musikbyra
http://www.stim.se
Australia
APRA - The Australasian Performing Right Association Limited
http://www.apra.com.au

Note: If you are looking for information on how to start your own
publishing company, inquire on each site or call each company on how
to obtain membership as a publisher. Becoming a publisher is not as
nearly as difficult as performing the duties of a publishing company
since a publisher's principal task is exposing compositions and
recordings to as many profitable opportunities as possible. Many of the
duties of publishing companies can be effectively performed through a
membership with the Harry Fox Agency http://www.harryfox.com by
the publisher.

*Jer Olsen is the founder and CEO of MusicBootCamp.com, home of
"Dirt-Cheap CD Replication and FREE Music Business Training!"
This article is a sample of the many free resources available on the Web
site. Visitors can find stock piles of helpful, hard-to-find information
that can otherwise take years to collect. Jer is also an accomplished
musician and producer. As half of the team known as Outstanding
Productions, he has several top 20 Billboard hit remixes to his credit.
http://www.MusicBootCamp.com*

♦

BAND AND PRESS KIT ESSENTIALS
by Richard V. Tuttell, author of "Good Press: An Insider's Guide to
Publicizing Business and Community News"
© 2004 All Rights Reserved. Used By Permission

Destiny's Mother-in-Law may not be the best local band in town
— or even the loudest — but they know how to attract attention. The
heavy metal group's marketing plan included an obvious first contact
for any promotion — their hometown newspaper. Many bands overlook
this option when promoting their CDs and gigs. What may seem stuffy
and low-tech, however, is a golden opportunity for getting publicity and
building a local following.

In the case of Destiny, a power trio based in eastern North
Carolina, the first move involved a phone call to the editor to introduce
the band, gauge interest and find out the preferred method of

submitting information. That was followed by a press kit containing a few simple essentials — a press release, photo and CD. Let's look at each item.

Press Release

This is the most important piece of the promotion program. It should answer six questions: who (the name of the band and its members), what (the style of music, gigs, or recording being promoted), where (the location of the performance or where the recordings are available, when (the time and date of the show), why and how (is the show a benefit, then for whom, why should people want to hear the band and how can people get advance tickets or find the club or other venue?) Leave the detailed back-story — how the lead singer while working at the Citgo station met the guitarist when he drove in with a flat — for a later full-blown feature.

Format is just as important as content. A sloppy presentation reflects a lack of professionalism and reduces the chances the release will run as written, or at all. Type the release on standard letter-size sheets or submit it as a digital text file on diskette or by email. Use plain text, which is compatible with most computer programs and operating systems used by newspapers. Not everybody has a copy of Microsoft Word around. If you email your release, paste the text of the release into the body of the message because editors are wary of opening attachments from strangers. Write in narrative form with complete sentences (use both lowercase and uppercase letters) rather than sending a flyer, because it gives the band a better shot at controlling how the information will be printed. Be sure to include contact information (names, phone numbers and email addresses) in case additional information is needed.

Photos.

Destiny's Mother-In-Law sent a standard 8x10 black and white print, which was fine for our paper, but I would suggest sending color prints. It leaves open the opportunity of it being used on a feature front. If the image is to go on an inside page a color photo can still be scanned as grayscale.

Many papers are using digital cameras and will accept digital images with a resolution of at least 2 megapixels. Submit a jpeg or tiff file on a diskette or by email. It's helpful to provide a paper printout to show what the digital image looks like. You can also refer to a Web site from which the photo can be downloaded.

Don't print a digital image on your inkjet, submit it on a sheet of copy paper and expect it to be published. The quality just won't be acceptable. Also avoid Polaroids that usually have poor production quality. Spend a few bucks for a professional portrait or get a friend with a decent camera and an eye for composition to help you out. Keep the shot tight with members grouped closely together to avoid dead space. Filling the viewfinder to the max allows you to decide how the photo should be cropped rather than a photo editor.

Always attach caption information to the photo on a piece of paper taped the back or bottom of the print. Name everyone in the photo, identifying each person. Even if that information is already on the accompanying press release put in the caption. Photos and releases are often separated.

Recordings

Including a CD showcasing your talent is a nice touch with a press release, but is more important when requesting a music review or feature story. Some newspapers prefer to experience the band live and others may accept MP3 files. Do not send your only master copy of your sure-fire hit, because there's often no guarantee that it will be returned.

Don't be discouraged if the big metro paper rejects your submission. For every daily paper there are about nine weeklies or other non- daily publications, and they depend on local content — news about area folks just like Destiny's Mother-in-Law and you.

Daily newspaper editor Richard Tuttell is the author of Good Press: An Insider's Guide to Publicizing Business and Community News, available from Barnesandnoble.com, Amazon.com and other on-line

booksellers. This article originally appeared in Disc Makers Fast Forward newsletter. For a free one-year subscription, call 1-800-468-9353, or visit www.discmakers.com.

♦

SO, WHAT'S THE SCOOP WITH ELECTRONIC PRESS KITS?
by Panos Panay, CEO Sonic Bids
© 2004 All Rights Reserved. Used By Permission

It seems that the big buzz out there in the music word today is all about Electronic Press Kits (EPK(). Should independent musicians use an EPK™or a traditional press kit when approaching club promoters, festival organizers, radio programmers or record label A&R representatives? Do they work as well as regular press kits or should one stick with the tried and true method of snail mail kits? Are industry insiders even using them?

The answer is simple: like every other major innovation over the years ranging from the Compact Disc to the MP3, the industry was slow to initially accept it but it's fast becoming the ubiquitous standard that everyone from up-and-coming independent artists to word-renown festival directors is using to send and receive information about groups and artists from around the globe.

An EPK™ is like a virtual passport that you can use again and again to gain entry into hundreds of conferences, festivals, clubs, music competitions, colleges, or to even get your songs played on radio or reviewed by record companies or music producers. It contains everything your regular press kit contains and more: music samples, downloadable photos, bio, pres reviews, and even an up-to-date gig calendar (try that with a regular press kit). What's great about an EPK™ is that it takes literally 20 minutes to create one online and you can put it to use and start saving money almost immediately. For the cost of a little more than sending out two regular press kits, you can sign up for an account, create an EPK™ and email it out to anyone, anywhere, at anytime. An EPK™ not only communicates all the information that is found in your average press kit or web site, but it does so more quickly, more efficiently and far more effectively. Think how mind-blowing it is to be able to email someone everything they need to know about you or your band as soon as you get off the phone with them (or better yet, while you are even still talking with them).

Think of the implications of this innovation for the average up-and-coming artist. For the first time in history, there is no direct correlation between how many people you can reach and the cost of reaching them. For example, with a traditional press kit there is a vast cost difference between sending out 10, 100, or 1,000 of them. This means that even though today an independent artist has access to an unprecedented amount of information (think of the wealth of information contained in this very book you just bought), the ability to take full advantage of this access had, until now, been limited to all but the richest of us (consider the vast cost involved in sending a regular press kit to every single possible contact contained this book).

The Electronic Press Kit has changed all this. Every day there are artists that are sending out their EPK™ to say, 100, or 200 college buyers at practically zero cost and frequently get two or three offers from people that they would normally have to spend way too much money in their attempt to reach them (and often paying way more in reaching them than the actual fee they receive). The cost and effort of emailing an EPK™ to all these buyers is a small fraction of the corresponding investment in regular press kits – not to mention the benefits of the fact that communication is practically immediate (versus waiting for a week or so to get a press kit in the mail).

Does all this mean that you will never have to send another press kit in the mail? What about the promoters who want to listen to a full CD blasting through the speakers of their car stereo? The answer is simple: traditional press kits and CDs still have their place but, save your money and send them to the few people that specifically ask for them after they review your EPK™. Then you at least know that these are high prospects that are worth spending an extra $20 in trying to communicate with them.

So, who is using EPK™ today? Musicians, agents, managers, music conference directors, festival organizers, radio programmers and record companies ranging from the scruffy up-and-comers to the world-renown — as well as the band right next door to you.

Panos Panay is the founder and CEO of Sonicbids, the online pioneer of the EPK™ platform Prior to founding Sonicbids, he was VP of the International Division of the Ted Kurland Associates Agency, where he was responsible for the international tours of over 50world-renown artists.

♦

WHY MAILING LISTS ARE SO IMPORTANT
by Vivek J. Tiwary, CEO StarPolish.com

The very first piece of business you should attend to is starting and maintaining a mailing list. Your mailing list will be your most direct and personal link to your fans and entertainment industry contacts— in many ways, the mailing list can be considered the "business lifeblood" of a developing artist.

Keep your mailing list on computer, using any good database program. I have found Microsoft Access to be very versatile and easy to use, but any good database software should suffice. Remember to back up your mailing list by keeping identical copies on both your hard drive and a removable disk.

You will want to keep the following information about each member of your mailing list: name, snail-mail (i.e. regular postal) address, email address, and perhaps telephone number. Other fields you may want to consider including are company affiliation and job title (if applicable) or school address (if applicable and if your act does/will appeal to a college fanbase).

Building Your Mailing List

Start your mailing list by personally adding all the folks you think would support your act, and all your entertainment industry contacts you want to keep posted on any new developments. As a test, in addition to your industry contacts, your list should include everyone who would come to a show or would buy/download your music. In other words, if your grandmother who lives in another state would buy a CD, she very much belongs on the mailing list. You will find that apart from industry contacts, these early members are mostly friends and family— that's both normal and acceptable. Don't think that because they're close to you or your band they somehow "don't count." In your early days, where else do you expect to get your support? Remember this important piece of advice: every single name on the mailing list makes a difference.

If you are a band, I suggest that one band member maintain the mailing list and that once a week, every band member must submit 10 new names to the mailing list until you exhaust your collective resources of appropriate friends, family, contacts, etc. Be aggressive about your mailing list. Whenever you bump into an old friend or acquaintance on the street and they ask you what's new, tell them about your act and ask them for their information to include on your mailing list. You'll find that as you grow busier with your musical career, your mailing list becomes a good way to keep in touch with people, especially those folks you don't see often.

You must also solicit new names for your mailing list after shows. Prepare one or more clipboards, each loaded with several signup sheets. Each signup sheet should have sections clearly marked for name, address, and email. Space permitting, it may be useful to include a section on "comments" to see what new fans thought of your act. Remember that people may be filling out these sheets in a dark bar or venue and will therefore need to write in big letters, so don't put too many signup boxes on each sheet, and make sure there is plenty of space for each entry— I recommend no more than four new signups per sheet. Make each signup sheet look professional and presentable— have them designed on computer, or if they're hand-made, be

extremely neat. Adding artwork or some other creative presentation can never hurt, but remember that the most important thing with the signup sheets is that they are easy to use.

Building Your Mailing List

Provide potential fans with thick, dark-colored pens, again keeping in mind that they may be writing in a dark bar or venue. If possible, go the extra step and bring a penlight with you to make it even easier for them to fill out the form.

At the risk of sounding like a sexist asshole, I'm going to offer the following piece of advice because no one else may tell it to you, and it can quite literally be the difference between 100 and 600 names on your mailing list in the early days of your career. So forgive me, and here goes: I recommend that an attractive and friendly/personable woman walk around with each clipboard and solicit additions to your mailing list. It is actually a statistically-proven fact that audience members— both male and female— are more likely to fill out a mailing list signup form when asked by an attractive and friendly/personable woman. I'm not exactly sure why that is, but it's definitely a truth I have observed through years of experience. Try it and see for yourself.

You or any band member who is not selling merchandise after the show can also assist with soliciting names for the mailing list, because potential fans may want to say hello and that can be a good opportunity to solicit signup. However, your friends and your bandmates' friends who are already on the list will also want to say hello— so what was supposed to be an excursion into the crowd to collect names can easily turn into a series of lengthy conversations with friends. It is more ideal to have a friend or several friends of the band deal with the mailing list and have band members selling merchandise behind a booth or table where they can still say hello to their friends while generating and controlling customer traffic.

Using Your Mailing List

Your mailing list is your lifeline to your fans, supporters, and industry contacts. You should use it regularly to keep in touch with list members and let them know what you've been up to. Even if it has been a fairly inactive period for your act, let the list members know that you're still around but taking some time off from the public eye. One common mistake many developing artists make is using their mailing list only to promote an upcoming show. Your mailing list should be an informational source, like a regular newsletter, informing list members not only about your shows, but new CD releases, new additions to your website, new career developments, funny stories from the road (if you're on tour), etc. On average, you should send a mailing to your list about once a month.

Of course, sending snail-mail or regular postal mailings to a large mailing list can be very expensive— the cost of producing mass flyers and newsletters in addition to the costs of mass postage can add up to depleting your budget. Don't be surprised if in your early days, the money you make from your shows barely covers the cost of mailing announcements about those same shows to your list. Depending on the size of your mailing list, it may be cost-effective to sign up for U.S. Bulk Mail Service, which gives you a per-letter/postcard discount on very large mailings. But there are several restrictions to Bulk Mail Service; call your local post office for more details.

And remember that email is free. There is no reason why you can't send at least one email a month to your entire list in newsletter format. But keep these emails on the shorter side, noting the most pertinent details up front— most folks don't like to receive and wade through lengthy emails.

Using Your Mailing List

If you can afford it, also send monthly postal mailings to bolster your emails (the regular mail pieces can be more lengthy and informative than the emails). But if you can't afford it, focus on the emails and only use the regular post to announce very special events or developments, like a particularly important upcoming show or the release of a new record. Remember that if you are promoting a concert, you need to mail your postal mailings 10-14 days in advance so they arrive well before the upcoming show date. Finally, remember to draw a balance between keeping in touch and being a pain in the ass— regular mailings/emails are important, but several messages a week are annoying.

Apart from being a lifeline to your fans and contacts, your mailing list is one of your most valuable "calling cards" to the entertainment industry: People who work in the industry— from A & R talent scouts to club owners— are always impressed with large mailing lists. In the same way they are impressed with a large number of CDs sold, your mailing list is a quantifiable way of noting how popular you are. Once you've built a large mailing list, mention its existence and the total number of people on it in appropriate business cover letters.

Never remove a name from your mailing list unless you are confident that the address(es) attached to that name are outdated. However, if someone asks to be removed from the mailing list, be professional and remove him or her immediately. But remember that every name counts.

Never forget that a large mailing list is both an important tool and an impressive asset.

Vivek J. Tiwary is the founder and President/CEO of both StarPolish and The Tiwary Entertainment Group, a multi-faceted entertainment venture focusing on artist management, marketing consultation, and project production http://www.starpolish.com

♦

DATABASE TIPS
by Derek Sivers, CEO CD Baby
© 2004 All Rights Reserved. Used By Permission

Best programs, in order:
(1) Filemaker Pro. www.filemaker.com Sells for $299 but you can find it used on EBay.com for $40.
Both Mac and Windows. Totally flexible.
(2) MS Works or Claris Works comes with a database section. These programs are usually free and included on your computer.
(3) ACT. www.symantec.com Also sells for $299. ACT is meant more as a "salesman's tool" and so it's more corporate, and less flexible. But it is already set up to do exactly what you want. On the Mac, I've heard that "Now Contact Manager" is very similar to Act.
(4) MS Access. It's like using an army tank to go do your groceries. It's so powerful and complicated that it might take you a long time to learn. But like Filemaker, it can do everything you need if you harness it.
(5) MS Outlook. Blech. One of the worst Microsoft programs in my opinion. Inflexible. But if you have it already and you can't afford something new, go with it.
(6) Do NOT use a spreadsheet like MS Excel, or a word processor, or a notebook of paper. These just won't do the job. Choose from #1-#5.

Keywords!
Multiple keywords are the most important thing in your database. Every person in your address book should have a few words attached to their record like "drums, webdesign, percussion" or "agent, clubowner, songwriter". Some folks will only have one word there, some will have a list of the 25 instruments they can play. This comes in the most handy when you need to find "drums" in Texas, or you're trying to remember the full name of that webdesigner named "Dave". If your address book program doesn't have keywords already, put it in there! Find out how! It'll save your life many times.

Collect all the information you can.
Have areas in your database program for first name, last name, two phone numbers, fax, email, website (know their website!), two address lines, country, keywords (see above), mailing list tags (who gets your mailings and who doesn't want them), date last contacted, and very important: NOTES. Other ideas would be birthday, interests, and referred by (or "met through").

NOTES:
There should be a big giant text area underneath their contact info, where you're free to type type type anything you want. Type notes from your conversations. Cut-and-paste Emails they've sent you. In ACT and Filemaker you can set it up to make an "event" for every single conversation or contact you have, each with its own notes. Very handy. Set this up if you can. But even if you do, keep the big giant Notes field for all permanent notes you want to remember about this person

Learn how to mail-merge:
Mail merge these people, so you can send them all a personalized Email or letter. Using a person's name in the letter instead of "Dear Music Industry Professional".

© 2004 Derek Sivers - all rights reserved - if you like this article check out my websites:
cdbaby.com | hostbaby.com | agentbaby.com | marketingyourmusic.com | musicthoughts.com | hitmedia.com

♦

LEARN THE IMPORTANT SKILLS
by Derek Sivers, CEO CD Baby
© 2004 All Rights Reserved. Used By Permission

Like proper manners, or knowing how to drive, here are some things in the online world you just need to know:

1. EMAIL
- Have a good signature file that tells who you are, how to find you, and entices people to click through to your web address. All in 4 lines or less.
- Learn how to make good subject headers, so when your Email is one of 500 in an "IN" box, it will say exactly what is contained inside, from the other person's point of view.
- Learn how to quote someone's email message back to them. Or not.
- Learn how to subscribe to, post messages to, and unsubscribe from to a mailing list.
- Learn Manners. Spelling. Punctuation. How to turn off your caps lock key, and not use 25 exclamation points in a row.
- Learn how to how to communicate personality through these typewriter keys.
- Separate sentences into paragraphs. Reading a computer screen is different from reading a book. There's no paper to waste - leave plenty of space.

2. DATABASE SKILLS
- Know how to work your "address book" program. How to find people, sort, print, add, remove, change, and do bigger find commands (how to find all guitarists in the 818 area code)
- Keep it nice and clean and updated. Keep street address separated from the city, state, zip, country. Don't be sloppy in these early stages.
- Assume you ARE going to get more popular and soon your little address book will need to sort thousands of people.
- If you get really fancy, track each contact you have with someone: each call, email, visit. It comes in handy when someone from a year ago calls you up saying, "It's George! Remember?"

3 . WEB SKILLS
- Get comfortable uploading an Mp3 file. (Practice at mp3.com, iuma.com…)
- Sort your bookmarks/favorites into categories/folders so you can find things later.
- The more senses you touch in someone, the more they'll remember you.

BEST: a live show, with you sweating right on top of someone, the PA system pounding their chest, the smell of the smoky club, the flashing lights and live-in-person performance. WORST: an email. a single web page. a review in a magazine with no photo. (Let's say that "emotions" are one of the senses.)

Whenever possible, try to reach as many senses as possible. Have an amazing photo of yourself or your band, and convince every reviewer to put that photo next to the review of your album.

(Touching their emotions is like touching their body. If you do it, you'll be remembered.)

© 2004 Derek Sivers - all rights reserved - if you like this article check out my websites:

cdbaby.com | hostbaby.com | agentbaby.com | marketingyourmusic.com | musicthoughts.com | hitmedia.com

♦

HOW TO MAKE THE MOST OUT OF A MUSIC CONFERENCE
by Valerie DeLaCruz, Musician/Songwriter
© 2004 All Rights Reserved. Used By Permission.

OK, so you've decided to take a positive step toward your goal as a songwriter or artist; you want to check out that music conference you keep getting brochures or email blasts about. It's time to take the plunge, whether you are a seasoned veteran and have attended them before, or a "newbie" hoping nobody at the conference notices! Here are some steps to take to make sure you get the most out of the reinvigorating and inspirational experience that they always are:

1. Review the promotional materials to determine what the main focus of the conference is; i.e.: songwriting, legal issues, performance, and make sure that this is an area you are interested in.
2. Define your goals. Are you going to strengthen some qualities you already have? Gain more knowledge about something technical or legal? To network with others at your level and hopefully move up a notch in your field of expertise? Write them down and refer to them as you determine your schedule. Often, panels or workshops are taking place at the same time and you have to choose between them. If you go with a friend, you can split up and compare notes and resources later.
3. Figure out the overall cost including travel, accommodations, conference fees, etc. Start saving up and realize this is an investment in your profession. You may be able to interest a friend to go and share the expenses of a room.
4. There is almost always the opportunity to showcase at these events, and usually, if you are selected to showcase, you can attend the conference at a reduced fee or for FREE. This is certainly worth doing as you will get to show the industry professionals and potential collaborators what you can do. Be realistic about the costs involved in bringing your band to the conference. You may elect to do a solo or duo acoustic set to cut costs if that presents your material well. If not, again it may be a worthwhile investment to perform a showcase, always more fun than a bar gig and in a concert setting where people actually listen. We'll touch on the showcase preparation further on.
5. Send in the application. Many times there is a reduced "early bird" registration fee and this is great if you can take advantage of it. If you are also applying for a showcase slot, tailor your presentation materials to the theme of the conference to better your chances of being selected. Remember that professional presentations, or something that stands out, will cut through the many, many packages that the organizers will be receiving. Perhaps your press materials are printed on black and you make the edges ragged if you are a hard metal band; perhaps you spray paint the outside of your envelope a bright color to have it rise to the top of the pile.
6. Reserve your room and travel arrangements. Often the conference will have blocks of rooms reserved for the conference at a reduced rate. It is always better to spend a little more and stay right at the

hotel where the conference is taking place. A great deal of the networking and connections that take place are during casual times between seminars, and you don't want to waste time in a taxi getting back and forth. You may need to run back up to your room to get another package or CD to give out. They usually have special airfare rates, too. I use www.expedia.com for the best rates and schedules.

7. Now that you are set to go, you need to prepare the materials you will need. Make a checklist and give yourself a few weeks to gather them. Once I left printing out lyric sheets and bios 'til the last minute, and of course, the cartridge on my printer started to act up on a Sunday evening when there were no stores open! I also email things like the bio file and one-sheets to myself so that in a pinch, I can download them at Kinko's or forward them to someone I meet. They are up there in my virtual file cabinet wherever I go.

Bring 5-10 full packages that include:
1. bios
2. photos
3. one-sheet of several of your reviews and critics' quotations
4. photocopies of great press if you had a photo in print or if it is from a major publication like Billboard. Use the magazine's actual heading on your press sheet to get attention and gain credibility.
5. business card and CONTACT INFORMATION (the most important thing, seemingly obvious, right?)

The packages should be set up so that your name (or band name) and photo are on the front. If you have a CD, using the CD cover on the front of your folder looks very professional too. You want them to quickly identify you when they are digging through a huge pile of packages. Inside, have something visually compelling like a color copy or photo on one side and your bio immediately available on the other. Insert a CD or demo into one of the pockets. I hate to say this, but it's time to bite the bullet if you are

a. still using cassettes and get a CD burner so you can make CD demos tailored to the audience you are trying to reach.
b. Loose extras of all of the above materials in case you need to throw together more packages or don't want the expense of handing out an entire package when selected materials will do.
c. Flyers of your performance time and venue if you are showcasing to hand out and leave all over the place.
d. A stack of business cards. It is worth it to spend a little extra on these, as they are truly your calling card, and will remind someone of whom you are. I always like to have a photo on it, and color stands out. An unusual layout is important, and if you are a band, have a graphic designer (not your cousin's girlfriend) design a logo that will identify you. The most important thing here is to make it legible! A card that you need a magnifying glass to read already makes your contact frustrated. Business card basics 101: NAME, ADDRESS, PHONE NUMBER, EMAIL, WEBSITE.
e. Plaster your website on all of your materials. Everything you hand out should have all your contact information. This seems obvious, but how many CDs have ended up in the trash can because no one could find the envelope or cover it came in? A website is the most important business tool you can have. Busy industry people are inundated with wanna-be and would-be artists. They love to peruse your site in the privacy of their own office/home and get the important info at their own pace. Please do not have frustrating extra plug-ins, etc. that slow down your site viewing, just to say you have the latest whiz-bang technology. A slow-loading site is one that will not be viewed as they go on to the next one.

8. Take advantage of early check-in, arrive the night before so you are rested and don't have to fight a crowd. I always plan to stay one more day if possible too so that I can really enjoy the last day and night, which is when you are really feeling connected to the other participants and start making plans to get together for follow

ups or collaborations.

9. Get the materials upon registration and go back to your room and plot out your schedule. Leave time for regrouping; non-stop seminars can be exhausting.

10. Networking is the name of the game. You will meet so many people that you won't remember them all when you leave, and the same of them remembering you. The single most important thing you can do is exchange and collect business cards. Write a note to yourself about what you talked about, or if you told the person you would like to follow up. I refrain sometimes from giving packages out with the throng that accosts the panelists after their presentation, and instead collect their card and ask if I can send it along in a week or two. This again separates out your stuff from the crowd. But use your judgment; seize the moment. If you have the opportunity to hand deliver a package to the producer you never thought you'd be lucky enough to meet, take it!

11. Practice remembering names; it will go a long way to be able to address someone you met by their name. Everyone wants to feel valued.

12. Find out where everyone is hanging out after the sessions. Definitely go to the "mixers" to talk to people in a more casual atmosphere. Sometimes there are informal "jams" or guitar-pulls late into the night where you hear some of the most compelling music. I ended up booking someone to share a bill with me after being astonished at her beautiful song during one of these sessions.

13. In the question-and-answer session that normally follows a presentation, be conscious of not wasting the time of the panelists or other attendees with your personal request. (I heard recently and saw many eyes roll when a participant used his chance at the microphone to go into microscopic detail about the steps he had taken to get his demo played on radio, naming deejays, etc.!). Ask yourself if the question you have would benefit everyone, such as clarifying a point, or if it would be better to get to the speaker later privately.

14. Take advantage of signing up for one-on-one critique sessions. These are invaluable and educational, not to mention making a personal connection with someone in the industry that may be able to help you. Even if there is an extra charge for this, sign up for at least one. Here is where you can pick the brains of the experts. And if you ask for a critique, take it graciously; don't challenge the reviewer's advice or become defensive. This is how we learn and progress. You may not agree entirely with them (it is, after all, one person's opinion), but there is probably a grain of truth in there.

15. If you showcase, prepare a great and tight set list that shows what you have that is different than everyone else. I always prefer to do a fantastic five-song set than two hours in a bar where no one pays attention. If they can't get a flavor of your style, performance and sound in five songs, then you have not focused on a genre, and you will have a lot of problems anyway. It's good to start with a strong, driving, up tempo song. Plan your segues for a smooth transition. Don't stand around onstage while you and the band are trying to decide the next song; this looks unprofessional. However, if you judge the crowd and think a different song would maintain your momentum, say that…speaking candidly to the audience makes them feel involved. Just be well-rehearsed and prepared for this possibility if you do it. Plan your appearance to maximize your shot at getting noticed or having a style identification. No more than one ballad, which should be a pleasant change of pace, then close with another fantastic up tempo song.

16. Have your cards and demo CDs at the stage readily available for people to take. You never know when Miles Copeland will be in the audience!

17. OK, it's over and you are overwhelmed, but in a good way. When you get home, the real work begins, unless you were signed to a recording contract right on the spot.
    a. follow up with thank you notes to the organizers and panelists of the conference.
    b. Organize the business cards you collected and assign action steps to them.
    c. Put the packages together and send them to the people you

said that you would (within a week or ten days while it is still fresh). Tailor them now that you know what they are looking for.
    d. Keep a log of your contacts, what you did to follow up, and then call in about two weeks to follow up on the packages you sent out.
    e. Schedule those co-writing or demo sessions you connected with.
    f. Order the publications and/or resources that you discovered.

Good luck and enjoy the experience!

Valerie is one of the 60 original Just Plain Folks members and her passionate career pursuit and professionalism has been a model for other grassroots artists. Through hard work and persistence (and talent!) she's continued to make headway in the rough and tumble music industry. To learn more about her, visit her website at www.valeriedelacruz.com. This article originally appeared in the Just Plain Notes! newsletter July 3, 2002

♦

WHAT IS A BUSINESS PLAN AND WHY DO YOU NEED ONE

by John Stiernberg author of "Succeeding In Music: A Business Handbook for Performers, Songwriters, Agents, Managers, and Promoters".

© 2004 All Rights Reserved. Used By Permission

Frequently, indie music people plunge into the music business with strong musical chops and a lot of ambition, but without a business plan. Too often the results are disappointment and burnout rather than artistic and financial success.

Can business problems be anticipated and prevented? Can you learn from the business world and apply lessons without "selling out"? The answer to both questions is yes! Whether you are already making all or part of your living from music, or just thinking about the possibilities, this article provides fundamental concepts and encouragement for constructing or updating your business plan.

Why have a business plan?

You may have heard the expression "Fail to plan, plan to fail". Most businesses (music or otherwise) do not have written business plans. They may have revenue, checkbooks, and even budgets. If they do not have a complete business plan, they are at risk, and many fail as a result. Here are seven positive reasons to construct a written plan:

1. Road Map. The plan shows you the best route to your goals and objectives.
2. Measuring Stick. The plan includes financial and non-financial objectives and measurement criteria so you can track your progress along the way.
3. Opportunity Management Tool. The plan describes what business you are in and how you conduct business. This allows you to identify viable business opportunities, and avoid or manage the opportunities that do not make sense for you.
4. Lower Stress. When you have a plan, you spend less time and energy worrying about whether you are doing the right thing. Your plan helps keep you grounded and calm.
5. Catalyst for Your Best Work. A business plan is like a song arrangement, set list, or lesson plan. It assures that everyone is playing in the same key and performing the material in the right order
6. Competitive Weapon. Relatively few music people have written plans. When you do, you have an automatic edge on your competition. This helps boost your confidence as you build your competitive position in the market.
7. Essential for Securing Financing. At some point in your music career, you are likely to need cash for operations or business development and beyond your revenue from your regular business.

Your business plan helps you anticipate cash needs. A solid business plan is a requirement of any worthy financial institution

What's in a business plan?

A business plan is a written system of documents that puts your business and its market environment in context over the course of the next several years. It describes 1) what you are going to do, 2) how you are going to do it, and 3) what the consequences are.

The main text is 15 to 20 pages long. In addition, the plan document includes financial schedules and supplemental material that are included in the reference section or appendix. The reason for the brevity is simple. If it is too long, few people will actually read and use the document.

Here is a brief description of the contents of each of five main sections or "chapters".

Chapter 1: Description of your company, business, and industry. This is where you talk about the music industry and your role in it.

Chapter 2: Description of products and services. This is where you describe what you do in detail, plus the features, benefits, and advantages of your product vs. the competition. "Products" are what you get paid for. Examples of products include:
- Songwriter: original compositions, songbooks, records
- Performer: repertoire, stage show, records, merchandise
- Agent or manager: business services, sales (bookings), advice, support
- Music Teacher: lessons, original teaching materials

Chapter 3: Market overview and marketing strategy. This is where you describe the size and growth of target segments, the competitive environment, your promotional strategy, product distribution channels, types of performance venues, your sales force, and target audience. The marketing section is a "plan within a plan", and is the most important section of the whole document.

Chapter 4: Management and organizational overview. This section describes your business experience, history, and personnel needs. This is the place to identify key people, their job functions, and credentials. In addition to yourself, comment here on agents, managers, accountants, lawyers, or other service providers who round out your team. Future needs refers to people who will be added to the business as it grows.

Chapter 5: Financial summary. This section includes $ projections for sales revenue, expenses, sources and uses of working capital (cash) over a three year period. These are summarized briefly in the text of the plan, and shown in full detail in the appendix.

Good business plans also include an Executive Summary. This is a one or two page document that includes the essence of the whole business plan. Executive summaries are helpful when seeking financing, especially when many people are reviewing the plan.

What If This All Seems a Little Scary?

You may be a great performer, songwriter, teacher, salesperson, recording engineer, promoter, networker, or fan businessperson. You may find that aspects of running your business are tedious or even scary. That's OK, but it does not take away the need for a business plan.
Here are three key points:

1. Double the planning time and cut the implementation time in half. This is a tried-and-true rule of time management. It's easier and less costly to do the planning on paper than to learn by trial and error. This points to the value of constructing your business plan early in the game.
2. The biggest challenge is competing for attention. We are continually bombarded with information today, and things are unlikely to change. This points to the value of the marketing

section of your business plan in the overall scheme of things.
3. Someone has to handle the business. If not you, find someone who will your strengths and weaknesses and building your team as your business grows.

The Payoff

Are you (or your friend, spouse, or partner) already in the music business? Are you thinking about "turning pro"? Constructing a business plan is essential for long term success. Your business plan will guide you and help you prevent mistakes and disappointment.

Once you are implementing your business plan, you'll find that you are spending more time making great music, bringing entertainment to new audiences, and making a good living doing something you love. From my standpoint, it's worth the effort!

John Stiernberg is principal consultant with Stiernberg Consulting, the Sherman Oaks, CA-based business development firm. John has over 25 years of music industry experience including eight years as musician and agent, twelve years working for sound equipment manufacturers, and nine years as business analyst and consultant. John's book "Succeeding In Music: A Business Handbook for Performers, Songwriters, Agents, Managers, and Promoters" is published by Backbeat Books. For details, visit http://www.succeedinginmusic.net or e-mail John at askjohn@succeedinginmusic.net

♦

WEBSITE BASICS FOR THE SINGER/SONGWRITER
by Valerie DeLaCruz, Recording Artist
© 2004 All Rights Reserved. Used By Permission

You can't market yourself properly anymore without a website. People want instant information, and they like to save time by searching a website when they feel like it. Here are some basics that should be part of a musician's website for maximum value.

First, if you haven't already, you should register your website. This is called registering your domain name. Even if you don't put anything up on your website, you should register so that you will be guaranteed the name you want once you are ready to add content.

Here are a few good sites to register inexpensively:
http://www.domainofmyown.com
http://www.domainsnext.com
http://www.actnowdomains.com

It is a good idea to use the name you are best known as for your domain/website name. This is how people search for you. "Free" websites on things like Angelfire, etc. are not that great because the long URL is nearly impossible for someone to remember.

Remember, the simpler the better. How would someone who heard about you look you up? And I also would not recommend putting a dash between your first and last name because if someone doesn't think of that, they will not get you in a search. By the way, the best and least cluttered search engine is http://www.google.com

Unless you are great with computers and have hours and hours of time to build your own website, I'd suggest hiring a professional. Finding a "webmaster" should be fairly easy; ask other friends, and check out other websites that you like and the name is usually listed on the homepage with an email link. I had someone build my site and then teach me how to write simple HTML (or use HTML for Dummies) and an FTP (file transfer program) so that I could update it weekly with gig dates and news. The best rule of thumb with html is to copy and paste from a page that has the format you want, and then modify the text. But I'm not going to get all technical here…this is just a primer to make sure you cover the pieces you need on a site.

The opening page is your Home Page and should open up fairly quickly (avoid FLASH and other fancy huge files that will daunt some users' machines). The quickest way to turn someone off is to have them

STOP the download of your site because it was taking too long.

The Home Page should have a synopsis of what viewers will find on your website. I think it should always include a picture (still worth 1000 words), READABLE typeface (some are so small from trying to cram in so much information, that it's uncomfortable to read and again may be skipped), and "buttons" that lead to the other pages on the site. Something I am also a stickler about is having contact information right on the Home Page. I don't make people dig around for it in several layers; again they may give up or be frustrated. I have an email link to me on EACH page of my website. I also have links to my manager, publicist and booking agent, as well as telephone numbers. Try to have 800 numbers if possible. I can't tell you how many times I have been frustrated trying to contact someone right away and there was only an email link, like "info@xxxx.com."

Buttons should be VERY simple and understandable; again ease and convenience should be your first concern. Buttons you will need are:

Bio: this gives background information on you and can be used by a reporter for reviews, concert listings, etc.

News: this is the most recent stuff that has happened and new stuff about to happen. This keeps people coming back to your site to see what is new.

Music: DUH, you are a musician! There must be a place for them to hear clips of songs, either Real Audio or MP3 format. Here is where your albums are shown, track listings, anything to do with your actual music.

Order: This is how people will buy your CDs and merchandise, either by mailorder, credit card (there is a service called PayPal (http://www.paypal.com) that you can use to take credit cards if you don't have a merchant account or a connection to other sites that sell your music like CDBaby, CDStreet and Amazon.com.

Schedule: You can use TOUR DATES, or GIGS, anything to indicate that this is where people will find out your schedule.

Reviews: This is where you will place links to sites that have reviews of your music, and you will have actual quotes from media that can be used in a press kit.

Awards: If you have enough, this can warrant its own page; if not, add this information to the Reviews page.

Mailing List: Here is where you will entice people to join your email list so you can send mass emailings when you have something newsworthy (nomination for an award; new CD release) or gig dates.

Links: Some people make a separate links page. I have sprinkled links throughout the text and logos on my site. Hypertext (underlined names or outlined pictures) again create convenience for the viewer.

Then you can add as many other buttons that are unique to your situation as you'd like. I have a button for my music video, a Journal page, and one that I've found really helpful with A&R people and publishers: Song Pitch. On this page, I have information for licensing songs and links to hear them.

Use a lot of pictures! People enjoy that more than anything. Caption them to add information and that reduces the need for a lot of superfluous text.

So go out there and build a great website that will be your calling card….you can simply tell people you meet to check out whatever they want to know on your website. Print your URL on all materials you distribute including press releases, flyers and business cards. Include it on your CDs prominently, not buried in the liner notes, and at the end of your music video.

Valerie DeLaCruz's passionate career pursuit and professionalism has been a model for other grassroots artists. Through hard work and persistence (and talent!) she's continued to make headway in the rough and tumble music industry. To learn more about Valerie, visit her website at http://www.valeriedelacruz.com.

♦

BUILDING A MUSIC WEBSITE THAT SELLS: PROMOTE YOUR CD, NOT YOURSELF

by Mihkel Raud, author of "How to Build a Music Website that Sells"
© 2004 All Rights Reserved. Used By Permission.

Marketing your CD on the Internet isn't really that different from marketing any other product on the Net – be it some fancy million dollar mansion in the Hollywood Hills, a how-to-get-divorced-in-less-than-ten-days consulting service, a super-cheap South Korean DVD player, or a subscription to a "Mature Golden Babes" kind of website…whatever….it's the same game. To play any game, you have to know the rules.

When it comes to music, I encourage people to get as crazy as they can. Break all the rules you've ever heard of. Try new! Don't think just of radio! Forget about what anyone else may or may not think of your music! Be yourself! Do what you want to do! And do it now! You have to dare to do!

Still, marketing your music – be it on the Internet or offline – is a totally different ballgame. You need to use some rational sense if you want to see results.

I know that it's pretty uncomfortable to think of your CD as a piece of merchandise. After all, music is supposed to be art, right? It is. Tell the opposite and I'd be the first to protest.

Nevertheless, your CD is just as much of a product as a bottle of beer. Your CD is a product that everybody should "need."

This concept of "need" is exactly what sooooo many musicians fail to understand. Almost every band or singer/songwriter website that I have seen concentrates on the artist. A typical performer website advertises the following information about the artist:

- Biography
- Photo gallery
- News
- Gigs
- Sound samples

Of course, there are many other possibilities. Some bands post lyrics on their websites. Some websites have discussion boards and chat rooms. Nevertheless, the most commonly used concept in the music business is still to build the website around the artist.

So what's wrong with that approach? Nothing really…. except that it's so common. And the artist approach will not sell your CDs. You ask… how is that true? Let's look at an example.

Let's say you're planning to buy a Mesa Boogie amp. You want to get yourself the best full stack in the world. Go to http://www.mesaboogie.com and take a close look at what's on that site.

Are you being bombarded by raves about just how great a guy Randall Smith is? He's the mastermind behind Mesa amplifiers. Do you see any Smith family snapshots on the front page? Or "better" yet, is there a guest book form asking you to leave Randall an "I love you" message? Nope. None of that "person" stuff is on the Mesa Boogie amp website. Why? Because it's the product you're after, not touchy feely with its inventor.

So I ask why on earth should your website be any different? It shouldn't.

If you really want to succeed in this huge jungle called the Internet, you need to stand out from the competition. In order to beat that competition, you will have to use The Billion Dollar Baby Website Concept, as I have ironically titled the concept (if you know the Alice Cooper song, you know what I mean!) In other words, create a website that is solely focused on your product – the CD.

That's right. The only hero of your movie should be your cool-sounding-grammy-winning-absolutely-fabulous CD. Every other detail of your website has to serve the same master - your CD. Nothing is more important than that music that you want to sell. If you use The Billion Dollar Baby Website Concept, you can turn the whole internet music game upside down. And you will win. It's as simple as that!

OK, this may hurt your ego a little bit. I understand perfectly. After all, you wrote the songs. You spent hours singing them in perfect tune. Heck, you may even have produced the CD all by yourself and that's no easy task. But now I'm asking you to spotlight the CD instead of yourself?

Remember this important point. I'm NOT telling you to shut down your existing artist website. On the contrary, it's smart to have one. In fact, you can have a bunch of them…. the more, the merrier. You can have your loyal fans create them for you. However, on your Billion Dollar Baby Concept Website you are going to play a supporting role. Your CD will be the main player.

It is absolutely essential to have a separate website for your CD only. Let me spell it out one more time: IT IS ABSOLUTELY ESSENTIAL TO HAVE A SEPARATE WEBSITE FOR YOUR CD!!!

And when the time comes, for your next CD…. plan a separate website for it too. And also for your third. Every time you put out a new CD, you will build a new website designed just for it.. Yes, my concept demands a lot of time and dedication. And of course loads of work. And yes, it will cost you some money BUT……. the good news is – your effort will pay off. If you play by the website rules of "show your product", you'll be a success. Trust me. I am speaking from my own experience.

I found a medieval music band from Estonia and produced a record of Black Sabbath songs in the 14th Century style of music. "War Pigs" sung in Latin. "The Wizard" played on Gothic harp and a fiddle http://www.sabbatum.com

I sold well over 1000 copies in the first few months. I sold 1000 copies entirely on the Internet with no marketing funds whatsoever. I did it all from my small apartment in Tallinn, Estonia.

Now, if I could do it, so will you. Period.

Mihkel Raud is the author of "How To Build A Music Website That Sells". To order your copy, please go to:http://www.musicpromotiontips.com

♦

CLARIFYING YOUR MUSICAL MISSION STATEMENT
by John Stiernberg, Stiernberg Consulting
© 2004 All Rights Reserved. Used By Permission

Each indie music person has a unique set of education, experience, aspirations, and motivations—different from anyone else. Consequently, each of us is likely to answer the "why" question a little differently from the next person. What makes us tick? What motivates us? How does the answer to the question "Why am I in the music business?" relate to my career and business plan? This article explores the topic and offers suggestions for clarifying your music business mission, vision, and values.

The Five Motivations
Whether you are full time or part time in music, your motivation is likely to fall into one or more of the following categories:
1. Make a living. This ranges from "pay the bills" to "get rich". Some people are motivated primarily by money or financial need. Everyone needs some source of income. For those of us who are not already independently wealthy, the prospect of making a living doing something we love (like working in music) is attractive—a positive motivator.
2. Fulfill a dream. "I've always wanted to do something in music", or "If only I could be in the industry doing music full time". Some of us want to see our name on the marquee, on records, or in the Billboard charts. Others aspire to business or technical support roles, but still be involved in music as a career.
3. Create a legacy. "When I'm gone I want people to remember my music (or influence on the music industry)." Looking a little further into the future, some of us are motivated by the idea of creating a company or a body of work that takes on an identity or a life of its own.
4. Benefit other people. "Take care of my family", or "Inspire others". Some of us focus on our immediate family and friends while others are driven to benefit the broader music community or society as a whole.
5. Adrenaline rush. "There is no other feeling like the energy coming from a crowd during a show". This applies whether you are on stage, backstage, or in the audience, and it can also be a positive motivator.

A possible sixth category is "all of the above". See how this sounds to you.

"I've always wanted to do something with music that will benefit mankind—the big audience out there. If I'm successful, I'll make a good living along the way and be remembered as a positive influence on the world. When I hear the applause after one of my shows, I remember what it's all about—the music."

Sound idealistic? Maybe so, but a whole lot better than, "Oh well, I might as well get a job in the music factory because it's better than working the counter at McDonald's for minimum wage all my life."

The Profit Motive: A Fundamental Issue for Music People
Here's a simple formula which drives all businesses—music or otherwise.

Revenue minus Expenses = Profit

Profit is simply the money left over after a business pays the costs of doing business. If you are a one person music business, profit also represents the money that is available to pay for your life: food, housing, clothing, recreation, education, etc.

Some music people are put off by the concept of profit, feeling that the idea of having something left over after "working hard for the money" is evil, tacky, lowlife, non-artistic, anti-art, or whatever pejorative word comes to mind. Here are my observations on this situation, gathered over a 30-year period.
- Unless you are independently wealthy (some are, but relatively few), the need to make money is a motivator for music people.
- The general public buys concert tickets, records, merchandise, and related material created by musicians and promoted by the industry. Fans "vote with their pocketbooks", meaning they buy what they like and come back to the music that they enjoy on a repeated basis.
- To judge whether a specific song, record, or performance is "good or bad" from an artistic standpoint is largely subjective. What appeals to me may or may not appeal to you, and that's OK. Diversity keeps things interesting.

What is the business point? Here it is:
Musical integrity, business integrity, and commercial success go hand in hand. You don't need to compromise musical or artistic values to make money in music. Also, simply being commercially successful does not assure positive reviews by the critics, or any other measure of artistic success. Top selling records don?t necessarily win Grammy awards. Remember, I'm talking about the majority of us music folks, not the exceptions publicized by the media.

How To Write a Mission Statement
A mission statement answers the question "Why are you in business?" Whether you are a self-employed performing songwriter, band member, owner of a small music business, or in a management position in a larger firm, the answer to this question is the foundation for your strategic planning. This applies whether you are full time or part time in music. Here are some guidelines for writing your mission statement.
1. Strong mission statements are usually one or two sentences long. I've seen mission statements that have gone on to two or three pages of cryptic single spaced text. Longer ones are flawed, in that you and the people around you will not remember them and may not put emphasis in the right areas when it comes to planning and taking action.
2. Short mission statements are often supplemented by clarifying comments. These most frequently take the form of "vision statements" and "values statements". This is a good way to deal

with the temptation to make your mission statement too long.
3. Vision statements describe your view of the future of the industry or market. Vision statements are part predictions, part trend analysis, part context information.
4. Values statements are your code of ethics, or the operating principles that are 1) fundamental to your business and 2) unlikely to change over a long period of time.

If you work alone or own the company, you can assert your own values in your music business. If you work for someone else, it is important to make sure that your personal values are reasonably aligned problems, but more importantly drives the business in a positive way.

Writing It Down Is Liberating

A rule of thumb in strategic planning is "if it's not written down, it's not a plan". Sure, you have to think through the issues, and yes, you may have a good memory. Yet, there is something about the act of writing that is both clarifying and liberating.

If you are a songwriter or composer, you know what I mean. You write down titles, sketches, notes, or fragments and put them together later. The words or notes jump off the page and make more sense the second or third time around. It's the same idea with your mission statement, and the rest of your business plan for that matter.

The other real benefit of writing everything down is that the material can then be shared with others: your band members, co-workers, employees, family, investors, vendors, or other stakeholders. For now, I suggest that you take a stab at drafting your mission statement, or revising the one you currently have. Start by completing the following sentence:
We are in business to

Congratulations! You've taken the first step in understanding the fundamentals of business and in taking your music business to the next level. Good luck, keep making music, and don't forget to write it down!

John Stiernberg is principal consultant with Stiernberg Consulting, the Sherman Oaks, CA-based business development firm. John has over 25 years of music industry experience including eight years as performer, recording artist, and agent, twelve years working for sound equipment manufacturers, and ten years as business analyst and consultant. John's book "Succeeding In Music: A Business Handbook for Performers, Songwriters, Agents, Managers, and Promoters" is published by Backbeat Books. For details, visit www.succeedinginmusic.net or e-mail John at askjohn@succeedinginmusic.net.

the music business

MAKE $$$$ FROM YOUR MUSIC!
by Daylle Deanna Schwartz, author of "The Real Deal".
© 2004 All Rights Reserved. Used By Permission

A record deal is not the answer to most dreams. Most signed recording artists don't make a dime in royalties. That's why in the new edition of my book, The Real Deal: How to Get Signed to a Record Label (Billboard Books) I take the position that the BEST way to get a record deal is to not go looking for it. The happiest signed artists are those who got their deals by building a big enough foundation to get a label's attention and have more say in the terms of the deal. I encourage you to focus on making money on the road to a record deal. Wouldn't you rather be passionately earning a living from your music than be a poor, bitter artist signed to a label that ignores them?

Why jumpstart your own career? A record label is more likely to sign an artist who's gotten exposure and a fan base. Artist development is history. And, labels don't know what to do with music that doesn't fit molds. Why be at the mercy of folks at a label when you can prove your music can sell your way? Show them by getting gigs, press, radio play, placement in film and TV, and CD sales! The more you do yourself, the better chance of attracting a deal on your terms. Don't

settle for any deal! Columbia recording artist Shawn Mullins told me that because he developed his career first, he got a deal that made him happy. If your engine is already running, a record label can add fuel to it with radio and retail promotion, distribution, tour support, and publicity. But it won't start a cold engine.

If you want to do music for a living, go after a career! A record deal can be short lived. Develop a business attitude. In your eyes, your music is special. But, in the larger scheme of the music industry, you're a product. If that offends your ideals, consider doing music as a hobby. If you want an income from it, start seeing it as a business, like marketing shoes or fruit. It sucks to think of your music as a product but that's the bottom line. Work with that or bitch and don't make money. I interviewed bands that are earning a living from music and they all take business seriously. If you think like a business now, you'll have the best opportunity to quit your day job.

One common ground between most musicians who are making money is talent. Too many musicians get jaded and think that if people come to their shows and buy CDs, they're good enough. NOT! This is where so many musicians fall short. Stop chasing record deals and hone your craft! I believe that IF you have tremendous talent, you can make a living from it and attract a record deal. Do everything you can to get so good that people want you. Practice ? Practice - Practice! Find ways to get critiqued by pros. Use a good producer. Improve your songwriting by going to crafting classes. Study with a reputable vocal coach or master musician to sharpen your skills and develop your talent fully. Do whatever you can to polish your music to a level that works in the big leagues, if you want to be in them. It takes patience to wait until you're developed enough to go after a career. But it will put you ahead of the pack.

Once your music is honed to an awesome level, develop a marketing/press package. Do as many live performances as possible. Be prepared for whatever opportunities come your way. Labels want you to have your act together. Don't approach them too soon and risk blowing an opportunity or settling for a bad deal. Wait until you have as many pieces as possible together. Create a foundation that shows you're serious. Develop your product to the max for the best chance of attracting a GOOD deal. Meanwhile, go make money!

How can an unsigned artist make real money? If you have songwriting talent, use it! Unknown songwriters can make a lot more money than signed artists. There's a much greater potential to earn money from songs than from record sales. Learn what makes a song extremely marketable. Great commercial songs sell. Study songwriting markets. Gather information at workshops and panels. Get advice from pros at organizations and from other songwriters. Keep thinking W.I.N. <<Write your ass off! Improve your skills! Network your ass off!>>

There's much opportunity to get songs placed in film and TV. Once your foot is in the door and you have credits, you can place songs regularly if they're good. According to artists I've spoken to, it's great money. Network to get contacts for smaller publishers or Music Supervisors who use indie music. They want you! Using an unsigned artist's music is faster because you own the master and can license it immediately, and it's cheaper because you're happy to take less money. It's very possible to reach the right people, IF you have the goods.

Many artists are also developing careers by touring. You have to get VERY GOOD. Practice by doing as many gigs as possible. Touring artists say that you can't worry about money at first. Begin by developing a following where you live. If you're good, people will eventually come see you. Or, try another town. Cities like NY and LA can be discouraging. Play elsewhere if it's not working where you live! Breaking out of your hometown is do-able. I interviewed enough artists to believe that. And I interviewed enough media people to believe that if you do consistent PR tour support, you can develop a lucrative touring career. You may not make money at first (or second or third!) Many musicians consider a tour that breaks even successful. But if you persevere, you can make money, especially if you have CDs and other merch to sell.

There are many alternative routes that can keep you out of a day job. I interviewed musicians who are doing well by playing fairs and festivals, frat parties, house parties, cruise ships, and more. If you check who's coming to your region in Pollstar (pollstar.com), you can approach their management, agent, tour promoter, etc. to talk yourself on as the opening act. Many tours use local acts so they don't have to pay travel expenses. Musicians who've made it to Europe swear by it. There are many avenues for touring abroad. It helps if you approach a local label for a licensing deal so they can support your tour. Many will sign you if they know you'll tour in their region. Research can also help your music get into TV commercials and product promotions. Once you're making a living from music, it's easier to attract a record deal that will enhance the career you already have. At that point, you may not want one!

This article was condensed from several chapters of the newest edition of Daylle Deanna Schwartz's best-selling book "The Real Deal: How to Get Signed to a Record Label" (Billboard Books). The Real Deal elaborates on the various ways that musicians can make money along the road to making a deal. Daylle is also author of Start & Run Your Own Record Label (Billboard Books). Through Revenge Productions, she does private consulting and teaches seminars based on her books. To order one of Daylle's books, or find out when her next seminar takes place, visit http://www.revengeproductions.net

♦

LOOKING FOR AN AGENT
by Jeri Goldstein, author of "How to Be Your Own Booking Agent and Save Thousands of Dollars"
© 2004 All Rights Reserved. Used By Permission

You have reached that point in your career development when adding an agent to your team would be a logical next step. Before you pick up the phone and start calling around, I suggest you do the following three steps.

1. Take inventory and create an overview of your career position to date. This process and information will help you present a clear picture of your career for yourself and assist you in making a more powerful pitch to any agent you are considering.

Taking inventory includes re-evaluating your past two year's growth. I would include a list of all your past performance venues, the fees you actually received, the capacity of the venue and the number of seats you sold. If you haven't been keeping track of this information, it is not too soon to begin. Along with these details, I would also list the merchandise sales you had for each venue. All of this information helps assess your growth from year to year and venue to venue especially when you play a specific venue a number of times during the year. If your numbers increase each time, there is good indication you are building a following. This is exactly the type of information a booking agent wants to know when determining whether they will invest their time and money to add you to their roster. When you present an organized evaluation of your career development to an agent along with your promotional package, you immediately set yourself above most scouting for an agent. This presentation tells the agent that you are mindful of your growth and are organized in the manner in which you conduct your business. These are attractive aspects of an artist's livelihood to any agent.

2. Create a set of career goals, timelines and projections. Most artists are looking for an agent to relieve them of work they dislike doing for themselves-making calls to book gigs. Look for an agent to help you raise the level of your performance dates and increase the number of dates and the performance fees. Set career goals for the types of venues you would like to play and present this to prospective agents. Determine a specific time line in which you would like to have these goals accomplished. Then based on the kind of concrete information you've gathered from your evaluation (step 1 above), you can make some realistic projections about what percentage of increase you foresee in the next two years. For example, based on last year's information, you are able to determine that your bookings, fees and merchandise will increase by 20% during the next year and 20% the year after. When you present an agent with hard numbers they can more effectively

evaluate whether or not it is worth their involvement.

3. The final step before making phone calls is to do some research. It doesn't matter how well organized you are or how talented you are, if you are calling the wrong type of agent, you are wasting your time. There are many different databases or agency listing one can review. You may need to purchase some of these directories, but it will be well worth the expense when you begin calling appropriate agencies for the type of performance you present. Some resources with agency listings are: Pollstar (www.pollstar.com), The Musician's Atlas (www.MusiciansAtlas.com) and Music Review (www.musreview.com).

Some agents book specific genres music or styles of performance. When researching agencies, determine if the genre of music or the type of performance is compatible with your own. Check their roster of artists to see if you recognize anyone. There may be some acts for which you might open-when finally speaking with someone at the agency, mention that. Create a list of appropriate agencies and make sure you get the names of one or two or the head of the agency if it is a small company. If you know any acts who are working with a specific agent with whom you might be compatible, ask that act if they would mind sharing some information about their agent. You may get some insider information regarding whether or not it is a good time to make your pitch based on who the agent just signed or if they are looking for new acts to add.

Another method of researching agents is to attend booking and showcasing conferences. Agents often use these conferences to scout for new talent. Seeing acts in live performance help agents get a sense of audience reaction as well as getting a better picture of what they might potentially be selling. The other great benefit to attending booking conferences is that you can walk around the exhibit hall and meet all the agents who are representing their acts. View their booths to see who is on their roster as well as examining how the agency presents their artists with their booth display. You can get a sense of the agent's organization and creativity by the manner in which they represent the talent. Stand by and listen to the way they pitch their artists to prospective buyers.

In conclusion, with these three tasks under your belt, you can confidently present yourself to appropriate agencies when you feel you are ready to make a pitch. You will present a much more professional overview of your act with a clear evaluation of your past performance and a realistic projection of your future.

Jeri Goldstein is the author of, How To Be Your Own Booking Agent - A Performing Artist's Guide to a Successful Touring Career. She had been an agent and artist's manager for 20 years. Currently she consults with artists, agents, managers through her consultation program Manager-In-A-Box and presents The Performing Biz, seminars and workshops at conferences, universities, arts councils and to organizations. Her book and information about her other programs is available at http://www.nmtinc.com or phone 1-888-550-6827 toll free.

♦

10 KEY BUSINESS PRINCIPLES
by Diane Rappaport, author of "A Music Business Primer"
© Copyright, 2004, Reprinted with permission.

Given two bands (or two businesses) that have equal talent, the one that incorporates the business principles below will often have a competitive edge.

1. Get to know the people you work with personally. Go out of your way to meet them.
2. Make it easy to for people to associate with your business
   * Show up for gigs and appointments on time
   * Keep promises you make
   * Phone people back in a timely manner
   * Have a positive attitude
   * Pay your bills on time. If you cannot, call people up and explain your situation.

- Be nice to secretaries and receptionists. Often they are the "gatekeepers" for access to their bosses.
- Develop long-term relationships with service vendors.
- Don't waste people's time. Often, key business people have only a few minutes to listen. This means stating what you want succinctly and politely.
- Say thank you. Forgive easily. Anyone can make a mistake.

3. Treat your employees courteously, pay them a fair wage, be appreciative of their good work, and when you can afford it, reward them with bonuses and other benefits. They'll repay you with loyalty and good work. Retraining a new employee costs time and money.

4. Listen to the needs of the people and businesses you work with. Find out what is important to them.

5. Do every job and every gig as though it mattered.

6. Provide value added to people you do business with. This can mean everything from playing an extra encore, having special prices for CDs for fans who buy them at gigs; sending out a free newsletter once a month; providing one free CD for every ten a customer buys; and sending favored vendors free goods.

7. Keep track of your money. Negotiate for better rates. Keep business debt to a minimum. Pay your loans on time

8. Cultivate a good reputation. Be principled in your dealings. Leadership in ethics and good conduct will be rewarded many times over in loyalty, in people speaking well of your business, and, perhaps most importantly, of people you do business with dealing fairly and ethically with you. If you examine the histories of people who are constantly being taken advantage of or stolen from, you will almost invariably find that their business conduct invited it.

9. Good advice is invaluable, and, often freely given. Learn to invite advice. Feedback it important, even when it is negative. Receive criticism with neutrality and graciousness.

10. When you are successful, give something back to the industry that has served you. Share information with other bands. Donate time or profits to a nonprofit organization.

This article is from Diane Rappaport's book, "A Music Business Primer" published by Prentice Hall (Pearson Education). Diane Rappaport is also the author of How to Make and Sell Your Own Recording. Her company, Jerome Headlands Press, designs and produces The Musician's Business and Legal Guide; and The Acoustic Musician's Guide to Sound Reinforcement and Live Recording by Mike Sokol. the books are published by Prentice Hall (Pearson Education). jhpress@sedona.net

♦

WHEN TO QUIT YOUR DAY JOB - YOUR RISK ANALYSIS AS A BUSINESS PLANNING TOOL
by John Stiernberg, Stiernberg Consulting
© 2004 All Rights Reserved. Used By Permission

Many indie music people aspire to full time jobs as performers, songwriters, agents, managers, or promoters. What's at risk in business? How do you feel about risk? Are you ready to pursue your music full time from a business standpoint? Whether you are already doing music full time or not, read on to understand "when to quit your day job".

How Do You Feel About Risk?
Any business involves risk. Risk is the possibility of danger, loss, or some other negative consequence. In any business—whether you work for yourself or someone else—your time, money, reputation, and self esteem are at risk. Let's look at each of these briefly.
- **Time.** You may spend a lot of time learning new skills (musical chops, business chops), establishing relationships, and working at the music business before you achieve your financial or creative goals. How much time do you have? Can you afford to take time away from other things? Are you patient or impatient by nature?

- **Money.** Starting and operating a business requires working capital—cash. Do you have enough? Are you willing to put your own money at risk? If yes, how much? If no, where are you going to get the money?
- **Reputation.** Your reputation is what others say about you, your character, and your accomplishments. When you operate a business, whatever you do both in your business and in your personal life is subject to public scrutiny. How do you feel about that? Are you open to praise and criticism on a regular basis, or are you more private?
- **Self esteem.** Your confidence is an asset which needs to be protected. I'm not referring to vanity, arrogance, or exaggerated self-importance. I am referring to the need to have a positive feeling about yourself and what you do. In any business—especially a subjective and creative field like music—your self esteem is always at risk. Some people are "thick skinned" or more resilient than others.

Some people are very comfortable taking risks. Others are "risk averse"; that is, they consciously avoid risk and are willing to accept lower returns (like less money or notoriety) as a result. Ask yourself where do you fall on the risk spectrum. If you tend to be risk averse, that's OK, but indicates that you should look for work in the music business on someone else's payroll.

When To Quit Your Day Job
If you are working a straight job to make a living and would like to focus on music full time, this is the important question. If you already doing music full time, the conditions below are still valuable to review and put in perspective.

Here are three conditions to be met before you can "quit your day job" with confidence.
- You have a business plan—written down and ready to share with others. (Editor's note: Planning is a primary subject of "Succeeding In Music: A Business Handbook for Performers, Songwriters, Agents, Managers, and Promoters" by John Stiernberg) . You have funding to cover both business and personal expenses for at least one year. Once you have drafted your business plan and budget, you'll know how much money you need.
- You are comfortable taking the risk. Some people handle risk easily, others don't. There is no rule on how much risk to take, so don't feel that one or the other is the best way.
- It helps a lot to have family and friends who are comfortable with your music career too. Having that emotional support is likely to make things go a lot easier, especially on the home front.

A Final Thought
Don't quit your day job pre-maturely. Once again, the three conditions for full time focus in the music business are 1) you have a written business plan, 2) you have enough cash on hand to cover business and personal expenses for a minimum of one year, and 3) you are comfortable taking the risk involved in being in the business. If one of the three elements is missing, you are probably not ready to do music full time.

Why did you read this article? How did you get to this point? It is probably because you want to get ahead by some means other than trial and error. Just like practicing your musical chops, developing your "business chops" helps you deal with the important decisions, and keeps you focused on your path to success in music. Good luck!

John Stiernberg is principal consultant with Stiernberg Consulting, the Sherman Oaks, CA-based business development firm. John has over 25 years of music industry experience including eight years as performer, recording artist, and agent, twelve years working for sound equipment manufacturers, and nine years as business analyst and consultant. John's book "Succeeding In Music: A Business Handbook for Performers, Songwriters, Agents, Managers, and Promoters" is published by Backbeat Books. For details, visit www.succeedinginmusic.net or e-mail John at askjohn@succeedinginmusic.net.

CHOOSING A PRODUCER (an interview with Producer Arty Skye)

by Daylle Deanna Schwartz, author of "The Real Deal"

DDS: What are some things that should be considered in choosing a good studio?

Arty Skye: All of these are factors to consider, but the weight you attach to each depends on your level of experience.

For an artist with little experience in the studio, the first thing to look at is are you comfortable in the environment and did you meet the engineer you'd be working with and do you like him? If you feel nervous, uncomfortable or intimidated, chances are you will not achieve your goals in the studio and end up wasting money.

If you're more experienced, the equipment becomes the number one priority. Do they have what you need? Will you be compatible with other studios or is their format so out of date or unique that no one else is using it? This could put you in a bind if you decide to remix or continue your project at another studio.

Who is their regular clientele? Are they primarily a midi studio doing lots of hip hop and R&B, but you have a live rock band? Or vice versa? Either way, it's a mismatch. Look at their client list and ask to hear some examples of work that was done the in the style of music that you're doing. The equipment necessary for one style of music may be totally irrelevant for another style. Make sure that you have a match.

DDS: Describe the role of a producer. What should one be careful about in choosing one?

Arty Skye: The role of a producer is different depending on the style of music and the point of view. I've seen producers do nothing more than hire the right people to do all the work, to writing the song, playing the instruments, engineering and doing background vocals and ad-libs.

From a record company's point of view, they are interested in hiring a producer that they know will give them a consistently great product. Where they do it and with whom mean nothing to them. I know one Grammy award winning producer who used to go away on weekends and leave us kids in the studio to produce the track. As long as the final product meets their high standard of quality, they will continue to hire him.

From an artist point of view in most styles of music, a producer's role is to understand the artists vision and have the technical and musical ability to not only make it a reality, but to make it shine. A producer should keep the sessions running smoothly, anticipate any problems beforehand, and get the best out of everyone from the artist to the engineer. The producer is responsible for everything while in the studio and their experience in the studio can save massive amounts of trial and error, thus saving time and money. A great producer should be able to take something ordinary and make it extraordinary, or to take something terrible and make it acceptable. But don't expect a producer to be able to turn a turd into gold!

In pop music, many producers are songwriters as well as musicians, so often an artist's role might be regulated to singing. This allows the artist to concentrate on what they do best. In rap and hip hop, often a producer will just be the guy that comes up with the track and has little involvement beyond that. Of course there are exceptions to all of this and as time changes, so does the role of the producer.

In choosing a producer, there are several things to consider because anyone can call themselves a producer, just like anyone can call themselves a singer. It doesn't mean they are. First, do you like them and do you trust their judgment? If not, walk away. If you don't like them, you won't enjoy being in the studio working on your music, and if you don't trust them, you're not letting them do the job you're paying them for. Next, what is the level of experience they have? Ask to see a discography of records they've worked on, as well as asking to hear some of their work. Do they produce part time and have regular day jobs, or are they pros with countless years in the industry? Will you be working in a real studio or in someone's apartment? Will they be hiring an experienced engineer or doing it themselves? Basically, you're looking for producers with credentials and experience or you might as well do it yourself.

DDS: Describe the role of an engineer.

Arty Skye: Engineers are the ones responsible for the sonic quality of a recording. They record and mix the music and handle all the equipment and technical aspects within the studio. While being a technical wizard is a pre requisite for the job, a strong musical background and a creative mind are necessary as well.

A potential hit song with a lousy mix will not have much success, while a simple song with a great exciting mix might have more of a shot.

A bad engineer can wipe your master tape (or disks) run up the time in the studio, erase stuff they shouldn't, create tension and basically destroy your session!!

Since the engineer is driving the session while recording, an engineer who is fast will save time and money. A good engineer becomes the co-pilot to the producer and often has a say in the artistic quality of the music. A great engineer will keep everything running smoothly and make your music sound better than you dreamed possible.

DDS: How can a person tell if it's okay to use the same person in both roles or should they be separate most of the time?

Arty Skye: Many producers used to engineer and it's not at all uncommon to find them still sitting behind the console engineering while they're producing. The engineering aspect almost becomes second nature when you've worked on hundreds or thousands of records. However, I do sometimes find a problem when I see some producers with no engineering background trying to engineer. They may be wonderful arrangers, but the creative technical tools and tricks are only learned from years and years of hard work with countless producers.

Most big time producers have engineers they work with, and most producer/engineers used to be only engineers so they have that background.

DDS: What is mastering and why is it important?

Arty Skye: Mastering is the process of taking the completed mix or mixes and sculpting it with compression, limiting, EQ and more so that it has the best possible sound quality for the specific style of music. A rock record and a rap record are mastered much differently. The levels will be pushed to their limit so that the music comes screaming off of the CD at a much louder volume. EQ and levels will be matched between the various songs and put in the order required, with the proper spacing between the tracks.

Great mastering can do wonders for an okay mix. Nothing sounds quite finished until it's mastered.

Arty Skye has been engineering and producing around the New York City area for 15 years. After his band got dropped from RCA in the early 80's, Skye pursued a career as a recording engineer and producer. He has since worked with artists such as Madonna, Brandy, Will Smith, Third World, Public Enemy, Wu-Tang, Santana and more. http://www.skyelab.com Daylle Deanna Schwartz is the author of Start & Run Your Own Record Label and The Real Deal: How to Get Signed to a Record Label from A to Z, both on Billboard Books. She also teaches full day seminars and does consulting on these topics. http://www.outersound.com/revenge revenge@erols.com

STAGE FRIGHT? ME?

by Anne Minnery, Recording Artist
©2004 Anne Minnery. Used by Permission

I am one of those people who suffer dreadfully from stage fright. I find that I am fine until about 2 minutes before going on stage and then my stomach starts to churn. Then, as soon as I hear my name called, my mouth suddenly goes completely dry. Worse than that, when I start to sing I find that my stomach is fluttering and my chin quivers. Once the first song is over, I seem to settle down, and by the second and third songs I am in full control again.

I have tried everything I can think of to get over stage fright. I have attended lectures, read books, looked on the internet for ideas and talked to singing coaches. The only thing that really seems to work for me is 'comfort'. If I am comfortable in a setting or a club and know members of the audience that seems to help. I used to sing at happy hour in a piano bar in Greenwich Village in New York called "Rose's Turn". At the beginning I had all the prior problems that I mentioned, but the more I sang there the more comfortable I became and I found that the symptoms seemed to disappear - all except the dry mouth - that I still had. My singing teacher told me to bite the inside of my cheek or bite down on the inside my mouth to try to get a bit of moisture going, but nothing seems to work.

Then I discovered another horrible tendency I have - and that is to allow my mind to wander while singing. I have had to really talk to myself about this and force myself to stay focused on the song from beginning to end. I have read that people are so worried about forgetting the first few lines of a song that once they get past that part they let their guard down and then they run the risk of forgetting the middle part. That describes me to a tee.

What I have found works in helping me get over my stage fright is "control". If I have done all the rehearsal necessary and know all my patter and moves, then my nerves don't seem as bad. And, as I mentioned earlier, if I know the place and feel comfortable in the surroundings it helps too. However, how many times are we going to have the occasion to get used to a place before we have to play it? Mostly, we just get a gig and have to show up and perform. So, I have to use other tools at my disposal.

My sister is an entertainer with tons of confidence and is completely at ease speaking with the audience. She can work an audience better than anyone else I know. I asked her once why she never has stage fright and she told me "Because I know when I get up there that I am the best singer in the room and that I am the best person to entertain them". This coming from a person who is quiet and unassuming off stage. But, she is right....she KNOWS that she is the best when she gets on stage - and she is. She takes command of the stage and is totally at ease with her performance. Why? Because she rehearses her material so well off stage that it is second nature to her when on stage. She knows her lines so well that if something unexpected happens (and when doesn't it in a live show?) she is able to handle it and move on. She told me that the audience deserves the very best from a performer and that comes from the performer providing the very best she or he can.

I had a wonderful singing coach who once told me that I had to be so well rehearsed before a performance that I knew each song as well as I knew "Happy Birthday". We all know that song so well, by heart, that if the walls started crumbling around us while we were singing it, we could still carry on while moving out of harm's way. She told me that I had to know each and every song as well as "Happy Birthday" - to OWN each song, make it mine. And that I had to own not just the first few songs but the entire repertoire of songs.

Another trick she told me was to always 'eye' the parameters of the room or stage, not only what was in front or at the side of me but at the back as well. She said this could be done quickly while entering the stage area and while saying hello to the audience. Her reasoning for this was so that the singer would own her space and give her a sense of control or comfort..

I am getting better at focusing, I have noticed. I have learned the hard way that I must stay completely focused on the words and meaning of each and every song and to sing it from the heart, not just mouth the words. If I am in touch with the meaning of the song, I don't lose focus - not as much.. A good trick I learned was to actually say the words of the song out loud during rehearsal. Each song has a story or message to convey and by speaking them we commit them better to memory and to heart.

I hope by sharing my story of stage fright I have helped some of you who suffer from the same thing. There are probably many of you who have never suffered the fear of being on stage like I have but this article is for those who have, and who may have an even worse case of it than I.

There are many books on dealing with stage fright and I can recommend a great internet site run by Art Nefsky that has online help available at http://www.nefsky.com Give it a try. It is fun and has some great ideas. Hope it helps.

Anne Minnery is a Country singer/songwriter with 3 CDs to her credit. Anne has been featured and has enjoyed #1 status for her songs at MP3.com, Amp3.com, FranceMp3.com and presently has 5 of the top 10 country songs at Besonic.com in Europe. Check her out at www.minnery.com

♦

DRUNKEN MELODIES

by Kate Hart, Recording Artist
© 2004. All Rights Reserved. Used By Permission

The other night there was a special on television about the amazing Roy Orbison. Memories of opening for him in 1985 came flooding back........or rather faint recollections came seeping through. The day I stood in the Coliseum in front of eleven thousand people I was horribly hung over. Bonnie Raitt stood at the side of the stage, Roy and his band waited backstage as I numbly went through the "schtick" of being a blues mama. Walking off stage Bonnie grabbed my hand and said, "You can sing the blues!"

So what's really wrong with that picture? It took me a while to have the answer revealed to me. I was there in body, but I wasn't there in spirit. Here was this golden moment and I couldn't grab a hold of it. It was as if it had happened to someone else. Even as I sit here, years later writing this article with eleven years of sobriety under my belt, I wish I could remember the details of that evening. What was I wearing? How did it feel to sing in front of all those people? What did the roar of the crowd sound and feel like? That's what it really boils down to, isn't it? All we have is the moment, as human beings and especially as artists. When you get done singing in front of a band humping so hard you think you are going to die, singing notes that just fall out of the front of your face to an audience that is hanging on every note, you realize if you are lucky, that it only lasts as long as the song. And then, it's over. And that is how it is supposed to be. But the booze and the drugs keep you out of the center of things and feed the rockets on your back, keeping you from re-entry. But of course you have to stop sometime and when you do, honey, re-entry ain't no pretty picture. Because all you want to do is just put those rockets back on and chase the magical moment all around, just sure that you can recreate it.

I had gone to bed 5 or 6 A.M. The rhythm the night before had been intense and frantic coming off of a great gig in Pioneer Square. The show had moved too fast, it was hard for me to stay in the center of it. I was trying to make it all manageable. At that point in my life I was still trying to control the flow of things, but that evening I just couldn't get drunk right away and I was so tired that I had no choice but to let go and feel the madness. The crowd in the bar was a part of the beat change, making it impossible to separate any of the moving parts.

When I did finally wake up from my drunken stupor years later, I realized that I had gathered pieces from the past, the present, and worries about the future and created my own monster. My head belonged to someone else, because when I looked in the mirror I didn't elf anymore. If I could just undo those two bolts on the ck and find a new head, one that had a familiar look to it; le stop screaming inside. Just like Dr. Frankenstein's monster had taken on a life of its own and was out e countryside. But I was in the bars and the little girl I almost drowned was me.

I have spent over thirty years in the music business and today I won't touch caffeine, sugar, cigarettes, drugs, alcohol and starch. I walk and meditate and incorporate Tai Chi in my life. I have come to believe that if I am going to be an artist with any true vision that I have to be clean and connected to someplace above my hair. I have become so sensitive to that connection that even a cup of coffee disrupts the place where the truth comes from. Being "plugged in" or "connected" or whatever the hell you want to call it, I wouldn't trade for any amount of whiskey in the world.

But there was a time when it was necessary. I had to play it out until it didn't work anymore. Play it out like you do a bad poker hand…..just sure this time you are going to win, only to lose over and over again. Not only do you not care if you are going to lose that hand but you begin to look forward to it. And then one morning, if you are lucky, like I was, you will wake up and know you can't do it anymore. That none of it works and there must be something else out there. Another life that is part of the dreams you originally had before the booze and drugs stole them from you. When that happens that is when your life truly begins. Allowing the music to finally begin to play.

Kate Hart has been in the music business for over thirty-years. Kate has been nominated for a Grammy, as well as the recipient of numerous awards. In 1996, Kate was honored with the prestigious Women's Leadership Award. She has produced major festivals and recording projects. In the last year, she has produced and performed on her own CD "Queen of the Night" and Seattle Women's "Backporch Gossip" and "We Are Not Good Girls" which have all been supported by national tours.

♦

DEALING WITH REJECTION IN THE MUSIC BUSINESS
By Suzanne Glass, CEO Indie-Music.com

Being a musician, by and large, is a rewarding thing. We get to indulge our muse, spend time with other artistic types, and hear a lot of great sounds. When it comes to jobs, being a musician is great work if you can get it.

Unfortunately, it's not all roses. The tremendous amount of competition makes it likely that we will sometimes lose a gig, get fired from a band, or be turned down for a songwriting award.

And most of us handle the rejections pretty well most of the time. However, problems can start to occur if you have a run of too many rejections in too short a time. Musicians may begin to doubt their talent, commitment, and even sanity when repeatedly slapped with "no's".

Here's a few tips to help you through the hard times.
1. Believe in your music and yourself. People tell you this all the time, and you need to take it seriously. Many mega-hit songs were repeatedly rejected before someone decided to release them to become #1 hits. Believe that your talent is unique, and continue to pursue your own musical path.
2. If you hear the same type of rejection often, ("You need to pick up your choruses" or "Work on your pitch"), you may want to look into the criticism. Having an open mind may help you improve your craft.
3. If you get down on music, take some time out. Go to the beach, the mountains, or your backyard, and do something enjoyable that has nothing to do with music.
4. Give yourself the freedom to quit. This may sound contradictory, but giving yourself a mental "out" can help diffuse the pressure

when nothing is going right. Chances are you won't quit, but you'll know you COULD.
5. Go jam with some musician friends who do it just for fun, and forget the business. People who strictly do music as a hobby sometimes have a positive energy that will help your jaded, negative energy slip away, and bring you back to the joy of playing music.
6. If you are in a situation where you can't find a band to jam with, and have excess creative energy, consider another type of art or craft. Doing something creative, even though it's not music, will keep your creative juices flowing. Painting, carving, candle making - activities like these may also open your creative flow and inspire you musically.
7. If the problem is due to a conflict in your band, talk it out honestly with the people involved instead of keeping it to yourself and becoming cynical. Conflicts are common in bands (and every other kind of group), and surviving them means the difference between success and failure, since most bands will break up if the unresolved conflicts are not addressed. It will NOT be a pleasant experience.
8. Write a song about it. Who knows, it might be a masterpiece.
9. Think back on all your successes and good times in music, and focus on that energy. Try to balance the current bad times by realizing it's all part of the flow.
10. If you can't kick the down feelings in a few weeks, don't hesitate to talk to your doctor. Artists are known to have high rates of depression and stress-related illnesses, and today there are many new treatments. Make sure you follow a healthy diet and get some exercise.

Getting through those periods when "music sucks" is an experience all musicians have been through at one time or another. Those that master the down times go on to have productive musical careers. Those that get bogged down in the problems and become bitter are doomed to less happy - and maybe less musical - futures.

Suzanne Glass is the founder of Indie-Music.com, one of the internet's premier musician websites. The company offers thousands of resources and contacts to achieve success in the music industry, including venues, labels, radio, media, studios, and band listings, plus articles, interviews, and reviews of indie music. http://www.indie-music.com

♦

THE PROCESS AND POWER OF PERSISTENCE
by Brian Austin Whitney, Founder of the Just Plain Folks Music Organization

If you speak with successful people in nearly any business, especially those with an artistic bent, one common factor you'll find among nearly all of them is that they were persistent. Whether it was in the face of competition, lack of understanding or acceptance among their peers and their industry or their family asking when they were going to get a day job, those who persist through the ups and downs, and do it with hope and a positive spirit seem to last the longest and do the best. But there is more than just relentlessness to that formula. While being persistent, you need to evolve. You need to develop. You need to remain cognizant of change and focused on goals you have. This isn't simply a matter of moving forward like a drone. You still need a plan and you need to progress. Here are a few suggestions and guide markers to help you along the way:

1. Keep Learning.
One of the things that persistence offers is an ongoing education. You learn by doing and you learn by trial and error. You also learn by reading books and taking advantage of various resources surrounding the music community. But you have to keep doing it. It never stops and you never know everything there is, and even if you did, it changes.

2. Keep making friends.

It really is about whom you know and how well they like you. Sure talent matters, but there is a lot of talent out there. Being friends with the right people is always the tiebreaker, and in a business filled with so many worthy talents, you need the tiebreaker on your side. But that doesn't just mean the well-known stars and the already successful industry figures. In fact, the most important friends you can make are those who are also on their way up or are developing their own network of connections. One of my most important music industry allies is someone I met when I was 22 and he was 15 and we played in a band together in a small town in the middle of nowhere Indiana. Now I run the one of the world's largest music organizations and he is a key player with Virgin's Internet Radio Division. You can never have too many friends and one enemy often turns out to be one too many.

3. Be sincere and honest.

Don't exaggerate your skills. Don't falsely praise other's either. Find your real strengths and emphasize those. Admit those things you need help with and do the same for your peers. It's an old cliché, but if you always tell the truth, you never have to remember your lies. If you are always sincere, people will support you even when you make a mistake or are wrong. And if you DO make a mistake, the quicker you admit it and take full responsibility for it, the quicker others will forgive and forget and in some cases rally to your side to help. Denial of the truth is the biggest downfall of politicians and one of the biggest weaknesses an artist can possess. The best artists are those who are the most honest in both their business and their art.

4. Reinvent yourself.

Few, if any, of us get it right the first time. As we mature as artists or performers, we need to take that new knowledge and allow it to adjust the way we write or perform. Being persistent doesn't mean being rigid and unchanging. It means constant motion forward. Traveling to a destination is never a completely straight line. Your style, technique, presentation and approach shouldn't try to be a straight line either.

5. Create your art for yourself, market it for everyone else.

A lot of self important (and usually obscure) artists will insist that your art should only concern yourself and no one else. This is partially true. But it is also partially deadly to your long-term career. You SHOULD create the art that is true to yourself, true to your vision and true to your heart. But once you bring it to life, you must shift gears and concern yourself with everyone else. Find out who your audience is, what they want and how you can market your art to them. Are you mainstream? Are you part of a small niche? Learn who you are through the eyes of your potential audience and plan your marketing accordingly. This means lose the attitude about being in a genre or sounding like another artist. Being able to categorize yourself and your music makes it easier for your audience to buy your music, see your show, and become your fan. And that is what it needs to be about. Your job is to remove any barrier between you and the music consuming public at large on their terms, not yours.

6. Help others along the way.

Small-minded people think they can succeed by the failures of their peers. Good business people understand that a strong peer makes for a larger and more vigorous market for your work as well. Retailers often build near similar rivals so that customers get used to going to a particular shopping area to buy that product. They use the marketing efforts of their competitors to bring people within their grasp. The same holds true with musicians. If there are bands with similar fan bases and niches as you, it is always in your best interest to work with them and share the limelight and double the spotlight that your combined efforts will bring on the music you all make. Help your fellow bands get gigs. Not only will they return the favor but the music fan base will begin to expect more live music and will start associating all the cooperative bands with the others, and will begin to support all of you instead of just one of you.

7. Get out of your basement and into your community.

Even if you are a solo writer who doesn't perform, get out into your community and participate. See other bands. Attend area songwriter and music organization meetings. Spend a few hours at the local music store and get to know the people working there (they are usually the most in touch with who is active in your community musically). Get to know the people at the local recording studios and ask if you can watch some recording sessions now and then. Being out in your community not only networks you with others but it will keep you up on the area industry gossip and goings on. It will also keep you hip to trends and styles and what is working for some and not working for others.

8. Seize the day.

Make positive progress every single day. Even if that progress is tiny. If you are performing, ALWAYS give it your best, even if you are performing for 3 people at an open stage at 1 AM. If you are a performer, then treat every performance as if it is THE pivotal one. Treat every audience member as if THEY hold the key to the rest of your career. If you do that, one day they WILL. A performer giving her all when it matters least is a sure thing to give it her all when it matters most. Industry people and those they know come in all shapes and sizes. Never underestimate the impact a great performance by you will have on any audience. Also, never assume that a small opportunity isn't worthy of your best effort. You are creating music because you love it. Show it every single chance you have and the word will be out about you. Your enthusiasm will be contagious and your zest for making the most of any situation will not go unnoticed.

9. Perform every chance you get. Co-Write every chance you get.

If you are a writer or performer, you probably feel the need and desire to do it at every chance. If you don't feel this desire, it might not be the right career path after all. If you do, it's possible that you can never get your fill of it and struggle to find opportunities, especially if you don't have a band, don't know other writers and so on. I suggest performing every single chance you get. That means sitting in with others at open stages, singing back up or playing harmonica, guitar, keys, tambourine or anything else for other bands during their shows (or if they are opening for you or vice versa.) The same goes for writing. If you hear something interesting by a local writer, suggest co-writing. Challenge yourself to write with folks who write differently or within another genre completely. Stretch your artistic perspective. Writing talent is always evolving over time. Performing with different artists doing different types of music will only expand your repertoire and improve your chops, not to mention expose you to more audience members and gain you a reputation as a musician's musician.

And most importantly:

10. Always remember, the persistent journey IS the thing. Not the destination.

Your life isn't about the destination. After all, that final destination is death. Your life is about what happens in between birth and death. The same is true for your musical life. It is all about your development, your trials and tribulations, your successes and failures and all the things you do along the way. It is about the people you meet, the songs you write, the people you perform for and pure joy of the creative effort. Persistence IS life. Enjoy it. Learn from it. Succeed on your terms. Thrive on the experience. As artists, we're all in this together. This crazy journey that begins with our first creative step forward and keeps going until we stop persisting is what it is all about. As long as you keep going, the life, the dream and the art keeps growing and going right along with the effort.

I will leave you with a final thought about persistence and never giving up on your dream that seems appropriate to this topic.

Sometimes reaching a goal earlier than planned is a great achievement. It shows you have worked hard, pushed ahead and made it happen. However, sometimes reaching a goal far past your original deadline, long after you wanted to complete it, and after the accolades you might once have gotten for the achievement are over, it is an even greater achievement. This shows you persisted and never gave up, due to adversity, deficit, criticism and those little life detours that end many dreams and goals. In many ways, this is a reason for even more pride!

Brian Austin Whitney is the Founder of the Just Plain Folks Music Organization, which is one of the largest groups of artists, writers and industry professionals in the world. To become a member, or learn more about all the organization has to offer, visit their website at http://www.jpfolks.com

◆

MAKING A GOOD LIVING AS AN INDEPENDENT ARTIST
by Daylle Deanna Schwartz, author of "How to Start and Run Your Own Record Label"

© 2004 All Rights Reserved. Used By Permission

Rich Hardesty earns a 6-figure income by working his original music in the college market. He was finishing his 8th CD when I spoke to him. While studying business at college in Indiana, he'd get his guitar out and entertain. Hardesty wrote a song called "Never Wanna to F'n See You Again." Everybody in the dorm requested it and he played that trademark song at open mic nights.

He decided to try making money from his music, and began by performing acoustically in bars. Hardesty says, "It seemed too good to be true. I thought I was supposed to go out into the real world. I didn't know how long it would last but I had to do it. I had no idea that 10 years later I'd still be doing it."

Fraternities called Hardesty to do parties. He used his college education to structure his business and recorded live shows to pass around. People made copies. He learned when they heard a live show on tape, they'd want more and come see him. Word about him spread. People lined up to hear Hardesty play his trademark song. That song was a vehicle to invite people to shows and to sell his first CD. Hardesty realized what a large profit margin he had from selling CDs direct and his business education took over.

He's sold over well 50,000 CDs with NO distribution. He runs his business in-house. I sat down with Rich to find out why he finds his independent career so satisfying.

DDS: *Why do you spend so much time marketing?*

RH: I want to make money - this is my business. I do everything now. There's so much involved it drains me. You have to be business oriented to succeed in selling albums. I don't want to just be an artist sitting under a tree writing songs. If you want this to be your full time job, then you have to do business. People ask why I'm not with a record label, as if that would be the greatest thing. They don't understand - I am my own record label.

DDS: *How did you get the buzz going in the beginning?*

RH: My gigs were mostly word of mouth. It turned into a business. I'd record live. I'd pass around tapes. People would record them. When they heard a live show they'd want to come to one. In college markets people love live music. I'd say people's names into the mic throughout the show. They'd have their name on the live recording and think that was a big deal. People would make copies for friends. They ask me if they could. Live shows is what helped sell me. My live show is way different than a recorded one.

DDS: Why did you press a CD?

RH: Having a CD was all I wanted. I had no idea I'd keep recording and make money from them. I wanted to have my name on a CD – MY CD. For the first CD, half the songs I'd originally written in high school. I wanted to get them documented and have something tangible. I never dreamed I'd be the singer/songwriter/recording artist. I was going to be the business dude. All of a sudden I had a CD. I was so proud of that before I learned I could make money from it. That was

more of a success to me in my heart.

DDS: *How much free music do you give out?*

RH: In my office I have about 38 live CDs recorded at shows with a label on them. I mostly give them away for free because it's a fan that will keep coming to shows. Fans pass them around. They end up on the internet. It's live and I'm not worried about it being passed around because it creates new fans. That's the bottom line.

DDS: *Why do you like putting out your own CDs?*

RH: After the third year I realized you sell CDs that cost about $1.25 to make for $10 or $15 at a show. I realized the profit margin and positive cash flow and decided I'd do a CD every year. The songwriting and passion were all there. A CD was a product of that which could be sold for a profit. Most are sold at gigs but I sell a lot nationally and internationally over the internet. College kids are from all over the U.S. They go home on breaks and show their friends my CD. When they get older they graduate and move elsewhere.

DDS: *Do the college kids stay fans when they graduate?*

RH: I did a show in LA for the Rosebowl. The alumni from Purdue asked me to come there and play in a bar because Purdue was playing. We got emails out. Alumni remembered me. Because of networking on the internet, we packed the bar silly with my alumni following - people coming into for the Rosebowl. The bar owner said he'd never seen anything like it. It was cool how the alumni support kicked in.

DDS: *How do Europeans find out about you?*

RH: I post a song on an MP3 file and share it. If you type my name into a search engine, there's thousands of things that come up. All my songs are on the temporary steal sites. Radio DJs around the world are playing my songs. The songs get bootlegged live and end up on the internet. If someone is going to an extreme to get a live copy, it's an honor to me. They're a true fan and will spread the word.

DDS: *How do you feel about being independent?*

RH: Sometimes you feel like you don't fit into society – about 15-20%. The rest of the time it's a very large buzz. Being independent, I do what the hell I want whenever I want. It seems like everyone is trapped in a mold.

DDS: *What makes you appealing to college market?*

RH: I like to talk to the crowd on the microphone. They feel comfortable because I talk to them. Some of my songs are off the wall. I also have an ability to capture an audience with certain ballads. Some of the girls like what I write about relationships because they can relate. Most of my songs come from an experience in my life.

DDS: *How did you become a Jagermeister artist?*

RH: I heard that Jagermeister needed a band from Indiana because the other band wasn't doing their job. The business side of me was thinking that I'm in the college market, and all I drank in college was Jager. I videotaped myself performing for frat parties and had someone following me around with a camera, filming some of the crazy things I do in my lifestyle. I sent Jagermeister a VHS of me. They hired me right away. It was because of the numbers I performed in front of. I sent them photos of the fans drinking Jager. They give t-shirts with your logo on them, bumper stickers, matchboxes, lighters. I won an award with them selling 100 bottles of Jager in one night. They put me on a national tour with my own tour bus. I was the emcee with a guitar. They paid me well. I played my songs in between the band and got my bottle out. Everybody was drinking Jager. Jagermeister sponsors me so I promote Jager.

DDS: *What other promotions have you created?*

RH: I've taken my act to Jamaica for spring break 6 years in a row. I got the spring break companies to pay for me. I called the president of a big spring company and said "I can do this for you." I told them I'd bring my fans and play. When I played my first gig in Jamaica, there were kids from all over the country. So I stacked my suitcase full of

CDs and bumper stickers. I had a marketing plan to get as many CDs out with the website on it to all these diversified kids from different parts of the country. I hired Jamaicans to promote and give them out. They put me at the most popular bar. There were probably about 2,500 – 3,000 people without shoes on in the sand. I've taken my band and done solo acoustic shows.

DDS: Why do you do private parties?

RH: They charge $10 or 15 a head. I can make anywhere from $800-3,000. They have it in private houses, especially at college campuses. I always sell CDs. And you entertain a market of under-age kids who will support you on the college or club scene as they turn 21. At those in-house things you're more of a rocker in that atmosphere – the kids sign up for your email, they want your autograph, and you're creating a fan for life. I see under-age kids as an untapped market.

DDS: How do you stay on top of things?

RH: I try to follow the motto- "There is no substitute for daily preparation." I maintain a healthy lifestyle-swimming daily and don't abuse substances. I have learned from some of my icons - Garcia,Crosby, Clapton, Marley - that moderation is the route to go.

This interview was done for the new edition of Daylle Deanna Schwartz's best-selling book, Start and Run Your Own Record Label (Billboard Books). Excerpts from it appeared in Daylle's News & Resources, her free newsletter. http://www.daylle.com revenge@erols.com Rich Hardesty earns a 6-figure income by working his original music in the college market. He started off playing solo acoustic shows for about 7 years. During that time he gained a lot of experience and recognition doing three to four shows a week on college campuses and clubs. Rich has a list of 400 songs that have accumulated over the years. http://www.richhardesty.com

♦

SO HOW DO WE MAKE OUR DREAM BECOME REALITY?

by Janet Fisher, Director of Goodnight Kiss Music
© 2004, All Rights Reserved. Used By Permission

Define the dream.

What is it you are actually trying to do? Be the world's best writer? Become a megastar performer? Lead the church choir? Own a record label that records other acts?

You would not believe how many writer/artists come to me, saying they just want to do "something" in the Music Industry. Sorry, you have to specialize a bit more than that!

Sit down with paper and pen. Define EXACTLY what it is in your heart that you dream of. (Hint, the bigger the dream, the harder to achieve... but as long as you are prepared to give what it takes, you'll find a place in the scheme of things.)

By the way, I have to do this, because I get sidetracked by wanting to do too many things. I constantly have to reassess projects and schedules... just part of business in a busy, busy world.

Research the dream.

Let's say you decided that you want to be a great writer, who is successfully cut on the charts, and makes a lot of money. Do you know what the real charts are? Who's on them currently? What labels are consistently charted? The styles of the top ten successes in the last two years?

Do you know what the actual elements of a great standard song are? Can you name the top sellers of all time in your genre? The top sellers of the current year? And do you know why they attained success? Do you hone your skills and knowledge whenever you have a chance?

Can you make the presentation of your art a commercial reality? Not just WILL you, CAN you?

Practice the dream.

Go do 150 sit ups without practice. Go write a great song without practice. You have to practice (i.e., actually write) everyday, just like you would with any improvement program.

If the newest song you are showing is old, you are not competing as a writer.

Rewrite the dream.

If something doesn't go the exact direction you thought it should have, rewrite the situation. If it's the song that has flaws, rewrite it until they are gone. If it's the voice, get some training.

If it's the gig, create one that works for you (when I was playing gigs in KCMO, I went to the Plaza, to nice places that DIDN'T have entertainment. I'd offer the owner a free evening of music, if he liked it, I'd work X amount of weekends for X amount per night. I almost always got the gig, partly because I was prepared, partly because few can resist something for nothing and not sense some obligatory return. (Most wanted entertainment, but had no idea they could afford it. For me, it was a way to go).

If you find that you thought you wanted the big dream, but then you realize that your dream didn't include all the nonsense that goes along with one of those in exchange for your "other dream(s)", (perhaps your family or job?), it is TOTALLY alright to adapt your dreams to accommodate each other. Unfortunately, some dreams require 24 hour dedication to maintain (ask any professional who is a megastar in their field.)

Pursue the dream.

Don't give up. That's the first thing ANYONE successful who is giving advice says, so it MUST be true.

(Ok, it's pretty logical that if you DO give up, your odds will go way down...) What I'm really saying is leave no stone unturned. Take advantage of all opportunities, work, work, work at it!

Live the dream.

Remember that each time you sing, play, write, perform, discuss, pitch, etc., you are creating a reality that supports your dream. Don't forget to applaud the little steps, as well as the big. You write a birthday song for your sister-in-law, and it makes her cry with your kindness. Your song is used in a campaign for adoption, and though it didn't earn a dime, it was perfect, and said so much to so many. A peer complimented your writing at a recent song pitch. You were the hit of the community musical. GOOD FOR YOU! It all matters.

All these things make us more professional, and give us the reasons for doing the work. They are as important as the royalties, and enrich our life of music. Don't overlook them.

Appreciate your dream.

Did you know that most of your little steps are someone else's big dream? Some people would give a great deal to have the opportunity to perform ONE karaoke song in front of an audience... or have anyone use a song for any reason.... or play a great guitar lick... or own a computer... or you name it. Appreciate the skills and opportunities God has blessed you with that you might even have a dream.

Just my opinion.

Janet Fisher is Managing Director of Goodnight Kiss Music (BMI) http://www.goodnightkiss.com along with its sister company, Scene Stealer Music (ASCAP). Both are Music Publishers dedicated to supplying the Entertainment Industries with perfect material for any musical need. Janet is also an author in, and the editor of "MUSIC HORROR STORIES", a collection of gruesome, true tales as told by innocent victims seeking a career in the music business". janet@goodnightkiss.com

Can you really die from exposure?

Not if you're a musician!

Introducing TOP—Oasis CD's
Tools of Promotion™ Services

Yes, Oasis makes CDs. Those lovely round discs. And—ask anyone—we do the best job of it in the biz: The most interesting packaging. The friendliest customer service. CDs that sound great, play reliably, and look like a million bucks.

But we don't stop there. Because if we did, you'd have an apartment full of beautiful coasters. Cute but no fun. If your music is going to grow, your new discs need exposure. Oasis CD's Tools of Promotion shine a spotlight on your music.

The following Oasis Tools of Promotion™ are FREE when Oasis makes your CDs:

- XM Satellite Radio Show featuring only Oasis clients
- OasisSampler™ Radio promotion to up to 550 radio stations
- Electronic Presskit (EPK) service from Sonicbids®
- Submission opportunites with Newport Folk Festival, JVC Music Festival, and more
- National distribution at amazon.com, borders.com, cdnow, target.com, waldenbooks.com, virginmega.com AND at Indie favorites cdstreet.com and CD Baby
- Priority consideration by Soundtrack Express
- Direct upload into the SoundScan® database, display boxes, bar code and more

Find out more at **(888)296-2747** or **oasisCD.com/top**.
We'll not only make your CDs. We'll get them the exposure they need to shine.

[:OASIS:]®
CD MANUFACTURING
oasisCD.com

*The trusted name in
disc manufacturing.*

toll-free: (888) 296-2747

tel: (540) 987-8810

fax: (540) 987-8812

email: info@oasisCD.com

web: oasisCD.com

12625 Lee Hwy. (P.O. Box 214)
Sperryville, VA 22740

 BBB Member — Oasis reviews received masters using RepliCheck™ to protect against piracy.

96% customer approval rating as of 11/1/02